Winter Park Library

The Diary of a Writer

THE
DIARY OF
A WRITER

F. M. DOSTOIEVSKY

TRANSLATED AND ANNOTATED
BY
BORIS BRASOL

New York
GEORGE BRAZILLER
1954

Authors - Cre

PREFACE

FEODOR M. DOSTOIEVSKY was born on October 30, 1821, in Moscow, where his father, a physician at the Mary Hospital for the Poor, and a man of modest means himself, was then residing. Young Dostoievsky's education began rather early, when he was only five. His parents were very religious and imparted their simple, but fervent, faith to their son. In the evenings the father used to read aloud to all the members of his family Karamzin's (q.v.) *History of the Russian State,* or some other classical literary work. When Feodor reached the age of ten, his father bought a small estate in the Province of Tula, not far from Moscow. There the boy came into contact with rural Russia. At the age of fourteen, Feodor entered a high school in Moscow, in which Michael, his elder brother, was also studying at the time. This was a model school, where even University professors gave courses for pupils in the higher grades. In 1837 Dostoievsky lost his mother, to whom he was tenderly devoted. Shortly after her death he matriculated at the Engineering School in St. Petersburg. This, too, was an excellently appointed educational institution which was then under the patronage of Grand Duke Michael, the brother of Emperor Nicholas I. Even during that early period Dostoievsky began to evince gloomy and hypochondriac traits of character. He took no interest in his schoolmates, keeping aloof from their entertainments and distractions. The six years which he spent in the Engineering School contributed much to his mental development, particularly because he spent a great deal of his time in reading and in self-education. In 1839 Dostoievsky's father died, and this was the second severe shock in Feodor's young life.

After graduation, Dostoievsky entered Government service, but all his leanings lay in the field of literary work. In 1845 he completed his first novel, *Poor Folk,* which, a few months later, was published in *The St. Petersburg Collection,* a magazine edited

v

by N. A. Nekrasov (q.v.), a famous Russian poet. This first
work of Dostoievsky was enthusiastically greeted by the Russian
literary world, and won the approval of Bielinsky (q.v.), whose
fame as a critic was then at its zenith. The success which accompanied Dostoievsky's literary début brought him into personal
contact with Bielinsky and that radical circle of which he was the
recognized leader. Dostoievsky began associating with these men,
with whose views he had no sympathy whatsoever. It was then that
he made the acquaintance of one Petrashevsky, a revolutionary,
whose activities came to the notice of the police under Nicholas I.
On April 23, 1849, Petrashevsky and all his associates, including
Dostoievsky, were arrested. Dostoievsky was accused of having read
aloud at one of Petrashevsky's meetings, Bielinsky's notorious letter
to Gogol (q.v.) of July 15, 1847, apropos the latter's *Correspondence
with Friends,* in which he expounded conservative views. After seven
months of confinement in the SS. Peter and Paul Fortress the
Petrashevsky trial came to an end. All the defendants were sentenced to death, and on December 22, 1849, they were brought for
execution to the Semenovsky Square in St. Petersburg. However,
the death penalty was commuted by the Emperor, and Dostoievsky
was sentenced to four years of hard labor in Siberia. On March 2,
1854, he was released from prison, after which, for several years,
he served as a private in the Seventh Siberian Battalion. He returned to European Russia in 1859. Two years later he published
his *Memoirs from the House of Death,* an ingenious résumé of his
prison experiences. In 1864 appeared his *Letters from the Under-
world,* which revealed the full power of his analytical genius. This
novel may be regarded as the nucleus of many profound ideas which
were subsequently developed in *Crime and Punishment* (1866), *The
Insulted and Injured* (1867), *The Idiot* (1868), *The Possessed*
(1871–1872), and in *The Brothers Karamazov* (1879–1880).

Dostoievsky expounded his political philosophy in *The Diary
of a Writer* (1873, 1876, 1877 and one issue each in 1880 and
1881). The last is, in a way, a unique literary production, having
no counterpart in world literature. Evading every established belletristic pattern (novel, satire, drama, reminiscences, essay, fable,
etc.), it is a bold attempt on the part of a man of genius to enter
into an informal colloquy with his readers, critics and correspondents
—at times, on most intimate topics. In some of the sketches appearing in the *Diary* Dostoievsky touches upon many of the burning problems with which Russia had to contend after the liberation
of the peasants in 1861. The people became confused and the country was in a state of both natural and stimulated unrest. These
conditions, of necessity, found their reflection in literature, which,

in Russia, has always been an accurate barometer of public moods and aspirations. As Nekrasov aptly put it:

> A writer, if he be a wave,
> And Russia be a stormy ocean,
> Cannot but be in great commotion
> When elements in fury rave.

While much space is devoted in the *Diary* to political questions, especially to Russia's part in the ultimate settlement of the future destinies of Slavdom, Dostoievsky's Slavophile ideas are hardly the most appealing or important portion of the book. What is of genuine and lasting interest is—to use Pushkin's phrase—

> His mind's dispassioned observations
> And doleful records of his heart.

Where human psychology is assayed, where man's sufferings, perplexities and mental agonies are dwelt upon, Dostoievsky, the unrivalled, perspicacious reader of the mind and heart, emerges as a great friend of humanity, as a good Samaritan, ever ready and eager to lend his helping hand to him who stands helpless and hopeless, battered by the storms and tragedies of life. In this sense the *Diary* is a noble human document. Rousseau's and Tolstoy's somewhat pretentious "confessions," Goethe's *Dichtung und Wahrheit,* Musset's *La Confession d'un Enfant du Siècle,* and similar public avowals, are either more or less entertaining memoirs, or autobiographical discourses, essentially egocentric and, despite their self-denunciation, obviously intended either to diagnose the author's "moral malady" or to justify it by reason of the morbid influences of a vicious "milieu" or other circumstances beyond one's control. The *Diary,* on the other hand, contains little autobiographical material. The author's "I" is bashfully hidden behind the coulisses of the impetuous narrative; only now and then does it appear as a mere casual allusion to something having a general significance in the treatment of a vital subject. The emphasis here is not on "I" but on "you," on the things that are common to all men, to every stratum of modern society. If some of Dostoievsky's views may well be challenged, their sincerity cannot—and never has been—questioned. At any rate, they are the product of a deep and keenly analytical mind which was fascinated by the invisible "chemical" and "thermal" spectra of *other* people's consciousness and emotions. Precisely in these fields, carefully concealed from idlers' curiosity, Dostoievsky discovered all the clandestine longings, morbid states and temperamental crises secretly dwelling, or merely subconsciously slumbering, in man's ego.

Even today the prolific literary heritage of Dostoievsky is not fully appraised and evaluated. If Pushkin can be called the Raphael of Russian literature, Dostoievsky should be recognized as its Michelangelo. His fame reached its climax in 1880, after his brilliant speech at the unveiling of the Pushkin monument in Moscow. This famous address is recorded in the *Diary* for the year 1880.

Dostoievsky died in St. Petersburg, on January 28, 1881. Enormous crowds attended his funeral: men and women from all walks of life—statesmen of high rank and downtrodden prostitutes; illiterate peasants and distinguished men of letters; army officers and learned scientists; credulous priests and incredulous students—they were all there.

Whom did Russia bury with so great a reverence? Was it only one of her famous men of letters? Indeed not: in that coffin lay a noble and lofty *man,* a prudent teacher, an inspired prophet whose thoughts, like mountain peaks, were always pointed toward heaven, and who had measured the depths of man's quivering heart with all its struggles, sins and tempests; its riddles, pains and sorrows; its unseen tears and burning passions. For he did teach men to live and love and suffer. And to the meekest he would offer his brotherly compassion—to all who labor and are heavy laden. He would come to them as an equal, laying before them the wisdom of his soul, his tender understanding of all that, in modern man, is human and even inhuman. He would counsel the doubting and soothe the wounds of those afflicted with distress. And many a hope would thus be restored, many a soul resurrected by the grand visions and magic of his genius.

Now he was no longer. The cold blast of Death had extinguished a luminous torch of Truth.

The news of Dostoievsky's passing spread instantly, like an electric current, to the remotest parts of Russia, and a wave of mourning swept through the hearts of her saddened people. Millions humbly prayed that he, to whom happiness was so cruelly denied on earth, be granted eternal bliss in the smiling Garden of Heaven.

BORIS BRASOL

CONTENTS

1873

1876

January

CHAPTER I: In Lieu of a Preface on the Great and Little Bears, on the Prayers of the Great Goethe and, Generally, on Bad Habits. . . . The Future Novel. Again, an "Accidental Family." . . . Christmas Tree at the Artists' Club. Reasoning Children and Relieved Children. "Gluttonous Youth." "Yes-Girls." Jostling Raw Youths. The Hurrying Moscow Captain. . . . The Golden Age in the Pocket

CHAPTER II: A Boy with His Hand Stretched out for Alms. . . . A Little Boy at Christ's Christmas Tree. . . . A Colony of

February

March

April

CONTENTS

1877

January

February

March

1880

1881

The
Diary
of a
Writer

1873

INTRODUCTION

ON THE TWENTIETH OF DECEMBER I learned that everything has been decided, and that I am the editor of *The Citizen*. This extraordinary event, that is, extraordinary to me—(I have no desire to offend anyone)—occurred in a rather simple manner.

On the twentieth of December I had just been reading in the *Moscow Gazette* of the nuptials of the Chinese Emperor. This magnificent, and apparently most complicated, event is also remarkably simple: the whole affair had been anticipated and decreed, in every detail, as far back as one thousand years ago in a ceremonial book comprising close to two hundred volumes. On comparing the enormity of the Chinese event with my appointment as editor, I suddenly began to feel an ingratitude toward my domestic institutions, despite the ease with which I was appointed, and it occurred to me that it would have been far more profitable to us, meaning Prince Meschersky and myself, to publish *The Citizen* in China. There, everything is clear. . . . On a designated day we would both be reporting at the local office in charge of the press. Having knocked our foreheads against the floor, and after licking the floor with our tongues, we would rise and lift our forefingers in front of our noses, respectfully inclining our heads. Of course, the director-in-chief of the bureau supervising the press would pretend that he was paying as little attention to us as to so many flies flying in and out of the room. However, the third assistant to his third secretary would stand up, and, holding in his hands the diploma of my appointment to the office of editor, would utter in an impressive, yet kind, voice a behest required by the ceremonial etiquette. It would be so clear and intelligible that we both would be immensely pleased to listen to it.

If, in China, I were to become so stupid and so pure in heart that, when assuming my editorial duties and realizing the limitations of my ability, I should grow fearful and should start experiencing rackings of conscience, it would be promptly proved to my satisfaction that I was doubly stupid because of entertaining such feelings; that precisely, beginning with this moment, I would need no mind whatsoever, even granting I had one, and that it would be far safer not to possess any intellect at all.

Surely it would be most pleasant to listen to this. And concluding his oration with the beautiful words: "Go, editor; henceforth

I

thou mayest eat thy rice and drink thy tea with a new peace in thy conscience," the third assistant to the third secretary would hand me a pretty diploma printed on red satin in gold letters; Prince Meschersky would give a substantial bribe, and we both, returning home, would forthwith publish a most gorgeous issue of *The Citizen*, such as we shall never publish here.—In China we would be publishing splendidly.

I suspect, however, that in China Prince Meschersky would certainly try to dupe me by offering me the post of editor primarily for the purpose that I act as his substitute at the chief bureau for the supervision of the press every time he might be summoned thither to be cudgelled on his heels with bamboo sticks. But I would outwit him: I would immediately cease printing *Bismarck*, while I myself would be quietly writing articles, so that I would be invited to the bamboo ceremony only after every other issue. In exchange, I would learn to write.

In China I should be writing very well. Here, this is much more difficult. There, everything is anticipated and calculated one thousand years in advance; here, everything is topsy-turvy for the next thousand years. There, willy-nilly, I would be writing intelligibly, so that I do not even know who would be reading me. Here, in order to compel people to read me, it is even better to write unintelligibly. Only in the *Moscow Gazette* editorials are one and a half columns long and, surprisingly, they are being written plainly. In *The Voice* such articles extend to eight, ten, twelve and even thirteen columns. So this is how many columns have to be wasted in order to make people respect you.

Here, merely speaking to anyone is a science, *i.e.*, at the first glance, perhaps, much in the same way as in China: as there, there are several rather simplified and strictly scientific devices. In days gone by, for instance, the words "I understand nothing" meant merely ignorance on the part of him who uttered them; yet, at present they bring great honor. One has only to declare with an open air and uppishly: "I do not understand religion; I understand nothing in Russia; I understand nothing in art"—and at once one is lifted to lofty heights. And this is all the more advantageous if one, in fact, understands nothing.

However, this simplified device proves nothing. Essentially, everybody here, without giving further thought, suspects everybody else of being stupid, without asking himself the question: "Is it not I, indeed, who am stupid?"—The situation is altogether pleasing, but nevertheless no one is pleased, and everybody is angry. Besides, in our day, thoughtfulness is next to impossible: it is too expensive a luxury. True enough, ready ideas are being bought. They are being sold everywhere, even gratis, but gratuitously, in the long run, they prove more expensive, and people begin to forbode this fact. As a result, there is neither profit nor advantage, but a state of upheaval, as heretofore.

Perhaps, we are but a replica of China, only without her orderliness. We are scarcely beginning that which is coming to an end in China. No doubt, we shall come to the same terminus—but when? In order to accept one thousand volumes of *Ceremonies,* so as finally to win the right to think about nothing, we have to live at least a millennium of meditation. And yet, nobody wants to accelerate this term, since no one is prepared to cogitate.

True: if no one wishes to reflect, it would seem, things are made easier for the Russian writer. In fact, they are easier; and woe to that writer and editor who, in our day, do meditate. Still worse off is he who, of his own accord, seeks to study and to understand things. Even harder is the lot of him who candidly divulges such an intention. But if he ventures to declare that he has succeeded a bit in grasping something, and that he intends to express his thoughts, he is promptly deserted by everybody. Nothing is left to him but to find some one suitable fellow, or even hire him, in order to converse with him alone; perhaps to publish the magazine for him alone. It is a despicable situation, since it is as if one were speaking to oneself and publishing a periodical for one's own amusement.

I strongly suspect that for a long time *The Citizen* will be talking to himself and for his own pleasure. To begin with, according to medical science, soliloquy signifies a predisposition to insanity. *The Citizen,* of necessity, must speak to citizens, and therein lies its whole trouble!

So, then, this is the publication with which I have affiliated myself. My situation is extremely indeterminate. But I, too, propose to speak to myself and for my own pleasure, in the form of this diary, and let things be as they may.

What shall I speak about?—About everything that might impress me or make me think. And if, perchance, I should find a reader—and one who, God forbid, should turn out to be an opponent—I realize that I must understand how to speak, and must know whom to address and in what manner. I will try to master this task, since for us this is the most difficult thing—I mean, in literature. Besides, there are different opponents: it is not with every opponent that one can start a conversation.

I shall recite a fable which I heard the other day. It is said that this fable is of ancient, almost Hindu, origin, which is very encouraging.

Once upon a time a pig quarreled with a lion and summoned him to a duel. Having returned home, the pig changed his mind and got frightened. The entire herd assembled, deliberated awhile and decided thus:—Now, pig, here in the vicinity there is a ditch; go and take a good roll in its mud, and in this garb proceed to the place of the duel. You will see.

The pig acted accordingly. Presently the lion appeared on the scene, sniffed, frowned and walked away. For a long time afterward the pig kept boasting that the lion turned coward and ran away from the battlefield.

Such is the fable. Of course, in Russia there are no lions: the climate does not suit them, and, besides, this would be too grand a setting. But substitute for the lion a decent man—and every man has to be decent—and the moral will be identical.

By the way, I will add this flourish.

On one occasion, conversing with the late Hertzen, I gave high praise to one of his books—*From the Other Shore*. Much to my delight, Mikhail Petrovich Pogodin also lauded this work in his excellent and curious article on meeting Hertzen abroad. The book is written in the form of a dialogue between Hertzen and his opponent.

"And what I like most," I remarked *inter alia*, "is the fact that your opponent is also very clever. You must concede that many a time he has pinned you to the wall."

"Why, that is the whole trick," said Hertzen, laughing. "I will give you an anecdote. When I was once in Petersburg, Bielinsky dragged me into his apartment and made me sit down and listen to his article, *A Conversation Between Mr. A. and Mr. B.*, which was written in a fervent vein. (It is included in his collected works.)

"Mr. A.—of course, Bielinsky himself—is portrayed there as being very clever, while Mr. B., his opponent, is mentally inferior. When Bielinsky had finished reading, he asked me, with feverish expectancy, 'Now, what do you think?'

"Oh, it's good, quite good, and one can see that you are quite smart, but why should you be wasting your time on such a fool?"

"Bielinsky threw himself upon a sofa and, burying his face in a cushion and laughing heartily, exclaimed:

" 'You're killing me! You're killing me!' "

OLD PEOPLE

This anecdote about Bielinsky reminds me now of my first steps in the field of literary pursuit, God knows how many years ago: this was a sad and fatal time for me.

I recall precisely Bielinsky himself, as I met him then and the way in which he met me. I frequently think of people of the past, of course, because at present I am meeting new ones.

Bielinsky was the most ardent person of all those whom I have met throughout my life. Hertzen was quite different. He was a product of our noble class—a *gentilhomme russe et citoyen du monde* above all—a type which developed in Russia, and which could have sprung up nowhere but in Russia. Hertzen did not emigrate; he did not begin Russian emigration;—no, he was already born an emigrant. They all, akin to him, were ready-born emigrants, even though the majority of them never left Russia. During the hundred and fifty years of the preceding life of the Russian nobility, with very few exceptions, the last roots had rotted, the last ties with Russian soil and Russian truth had disintegrated. History itself, as it were, predestined Hertzen to embody, in a most vivid type, this rupture of the overwhelming majority of our educated class with the people. In this sense it is an historical type.

Having detached themselves from the people, they naturally also lost God. The restless among them became atheists; the apathetic and placid ones waxed indifferent. For the Russian people they felt nothing but contempt, believing, however, that they loved the people and wished them the best of everything. But they loved the people negatively, conceiving in their stead some ideal people, such as, according to their notions, the Russian people ought to be.

This ideal people, in the minds of certain progressive representatives of the majority, involuntarily incarnated themselves in the Paris rabble of '93. In those days this was the most captivating ideal of a people.

It goes without saying that Hertzen had to become a socialist, and precisely after the fashion of a nobleman's son, that is, with neither need nor aim, but merely as a result of "the logical flux of ideas" and the heart-emptiness at home. He renounced the foundations of the former society; he denied family, and, it seems, was a good father and husband. He denied property, but at the same time he managed to arrange his affairs, and abroad he experienced with pleasure his financial independence. He engineered revolutions and incited other people to participate in them, and at the same time he loved comfort and family peace. He was an artist, a thinker, a brilliant writer, an extraordinarily well-read man, a wit, a wonderful conversationalist (he spoke even better than he wrote), and an excellent reflector. The reflex—the faculty of turning a most profound personal sentiment into an object which he set before himself, which he would worship and which, a minute later, he would ridicule—that faculty was highly developed in him.

Unquestionably, this was an unusual man, but whatever he

may have been—whether he wrote his memoirs or published a magazine in collaboration with Proudhon; whether, in Paris, he mounted
a barricade (which he so comically described in his reminiscences);
whether he suffered, or felt happy, or was afflicted with doubts;
whether, as in 1863, to please the Poles, he sent his proclamation
to Russian revolutionists in Russia, even though he did not trust
the Poles, and realized that they had deceived him, and knew that
his appeal doomed hundreds of these unfortunate young men;
whether, with astounding naïveté he confessed to these things in
one of his subsequent articles, failing to perceive in what light he
had placed himself by such an avowal—invariably, everywhere and
all his life, he was above all a *gentilhomme russe et citoyen du
monde*, a mere product of former servitude which he hated and
from which he descended, not only from his father, but precisely
as a result of the severance with his native land and its ideals.

Bielinsky—he, on the contrary, was not a *gentilhomme* at all;
oh no! (God knows from whom he descended! His father, it seems,
was a military surgeon.)

Substantially, Bielinsky was not a reflective person, but all
his life he was always a boundlessly enthusiastic individual. My
first novel, *Poor People,* delighted him (subsequently, appproxi-
mately one year later, we parted for various reasons which, however, were most insignificant in every respect); yet, at the time,
during the first days of our acquaintance, having attached himself
to me with all his heart, he hastened, with a most naïve precipitancy,
to convert me to his creed.

I do not at all exaggerate his ardent attraction to me, at
least during the first months of our acquaintance. I found him a
passionate socialist, and, straight off the bat, he embarked upon
atheism. This, namely, his wonderful insight and his unusual faculty
for becoming profoundly imbued with an idea, is to me very significant. Some two years ago, the International prefaced one of its
proclamations with this straightforward, meaningful statement:
"Above all, we are an atheistic society"—that is, they started with
the very essence of the matter Such was also Bielinsky's prelude.

Treasuring above everything reason, science and realism, at
the same time he comprehended more keenly than anyone that reason,
science and realism alone can merely produce an ant's nest, and
not social "harmony" within which man can organize his life. He
knew that moral principles are the basis of all things. He believed,
to the degree of delusion and without any reflex, in the new moral
foundations of socialism (which, however, up to the present revealed none but abominable perversions of nature and common
sense). Here was nothing but rapture. Still, as a socialist, he had

to destroy Christianity in the first place. He knew that the revolution must necessarily begin with atheism. He had to dethrone that religion whence the moral foundations of the society rejected by him had sprung up. Family, property, personal moral responsibility —these he denied radically. (I may observe that, even as Hertzen, he was also a good husband and father.) Doubtless, he understood that by denying moral responsibility of man, he thereby denied also his freedom; yet, he believed with all his being (much more blindly than Hertzen, who at the end, it seems, began to doubt) that socialism not only does not destroy the freedom of man, but, on the contrary, restores it in a form of unheard-of majesty, only on a new and adamantine foundation.

At this juncture, however, there remained the radiant personality of Christ himself to contend with, which was the most difficult problem. As a socialist, he was duty bound to destroy the teaching of Christ, to call it fallacious and ignorant philanthropy, doomed by modern science and economic tenets. Even so, there remained the beatific image of God-man, its moral inaccessibility, its wonderful and miraculous beauty. But in his incessant, unquenchable transport, Bielinsky did not stop even before this insurmountable obstacle, as did Renan, who proclaimed in his *Vie de Jésus*—a book permeated with incredulity—that Christ nevertheless is the ideal of human beauty, an inaccessible type which cannot be repeated even in the future.

"But do you know," he screamed one evening (sometimes in a state of great excitement he used to scream), "do you know it is impossible to charge man with sins, to burden him with debts and turning the other cheek, when society is organized so meanly that man cannot help but perpetrate villainies; when, economically, he has been brought to villainy, and that it is silly and cruel to demand from man that which, by the very laws of nature, he is impotent to perform even if he wished to . . . ?"

That evening we were not alone: there was present one of Bielinsky's friends whom he respected very much and obeyed in many ways. Also present was an author, quite young, who later gained prominence in literature.

"I am even touched to look at him," said Bielinsky, suddenly interrupting his furious exclamations, turning to his friend and pointing at me. "Every time I mention Christ his face changes its expression, as if he were ready to start weeping. . . . But, believe me, naïve man," he jumped at me again, "believe me that your Christ, if He were born in our time, would be a most imperceptible and ordinary man; in the presence of contemporary science and contemporary propellers of mankind, he would be effaced!"

"Oh, no!" interposed Bielinsky's friend. (I remember that we were sitting and he was pacing up and down the room.) "Oh, no! If Christ were to appear in our day, He would join the movement and would head it. . . ."

"Yes, of course; yes," conceded Bielinsky in remarkable haste. "Precisely, He would join the socialists and follow them."

These propellers of mankind, whom Christ was designed to join, were then the French: George Sand, the now altogether forgotten Cabet, Pierre Leroux and Proudhon who was then only beginning his activities. As far as I remember, at that time Bielinsky respected these four most.—Fourier had already lost much of his prestige.—They were being discussed through whole evenings.

There was also a German before whom Bielinsky bowed with great deference, namely, Feuerbach. (Bielinsky, who all his life was unable to master any foreign language, pronounced the name of Feuerbach as Fierbach.) Strauss was spoken of with reverence.

With this warm faith in his idea, Bielinsky was, of course, the happiest of all human beings. Oh, in vain it was said later that had Bielinsky lived longer, he would have joined the Slavophile doctrine. He would never have ended with that. Perhaps, he would have ended by emigrating, that is, if he had lived longer and if he could have managed to emigrate; if so, now, he, a tiny and enraptured little old fellow, with his original warm faith precluding any slightest doubt, would be hanging around somewhere at conventions in Germany and Switzerland, or he might have enlisted as adjutant to some German Madame Hegg, rendering petty services in connection with some feminine problem.

Even so, this most blessed human being, endowed with such a remarkably serene conscience, would sometimes become very sad; but this melancholy was of a special kind—resulting not from doubts, not from disillusions—oh, no—but from the query: why, indeed, not today, but tomorrow?—In the whole of Russia he was the most hurried man. I met him once, about three o'clock in the afternoon, near the Znamensky church. He told me that he had been out for a walk and was going home.

"I come here often to watch the progress of the construction (of the terminal of the Nikolaievsky railroad, which was then being built). My heart is appeased somewhat when I stand here observing the work: at last, we, too, are going to have a railroad. You wouldn't believe how this thought at times comforts my heart."

This was said well and enthusiastically; Bielinsky never showed off. We proceeded together. On our way, I recall, he said to me:

"And when they will bury me in a grave (he knew that he

had consumption), only then will they discover whom they have lost."

During the last year of his life I did not visit him. He took a dislike to me, but then I had passionately embraced his teaching. One year later, in Tobolsk, when we, awaiting our further lot, were assembled in a prison courtyard, the wives of the Decembrists prevailed upon the superintendent to arrange a secret meeting with us in his apartment. We saw these great sufferers who had voluntarily followed their husbands into Siberia. They had renounced everything: eminence, wealth, connections and relatives; they sacrificed everything for the sublime moral duty, the freest duty that can ever exist. Guilty of nothing, they endured over a long period of twenty-five years everything which their convicted husbands were forced to endure.

The interview lasted one hour. They blessed us who were about to start on a new journey; they crossed us and gave us copies of the New Testament—the only book permitted in prison. It lay for four years under my pillow in penal servitude. Sometimes I read it to my self and sometimes—to others. I used it to teach a convict how to read.

Around me were precisely those men who, according to Bielinsky's belief, *could not* have failed to commit their crimes, and, therefore, were right and merely less fortunate than the rest. I know that the whole Russian people called us "sufferers"; I have heard this term uttered many a time by many a mouth. Yet, here there was something different, not at all that about which Bielinsky used to speak, but that which sounds in some of our jurors' verdicts. In this term "sufferers," in this people's verdict, there sounds a different thought. Four years of forced labor was a long school; I had the time to convince myself. . . . And this is exactly the thing which I should like to discuss now.

The Citizen, 1873, No. 1.

THE MILIEU

It seems that the one feeling common to all jurors throughout the world, and to our jurors in particular (aside, of course, from other emotions), must be the feeling of authority, or, to express it better, absolute power. This is a miserable feeling, that is, when it prevails over all others. But though in imperceptible form, though suppressed by a whole maze of other nobler feelings, it must nevertheless nestle in every juror's soul, even in the face of the highest realization of one's civic duty. I believe that this somehow emerges from the very laws of nature, and, therefore, I recall that when

our new (upright) courts of law had recently been instituted, this feeling, in one sense, aroused in me intense curiosity.

In my fancies I was dreaming of court sessions made up, for instance, almost exclusively of peasants, serfs of yesterday. The district attorney and the lawyers would address them, seeking their favors, while our good peasants would be sitting and silently pondering in their heads: "See how things have shaped themselves: now if it pleases me, I'll acquit; if it pleases me, I'll send him away to Siberia!"

And, nevertheless, the remarkable thing is that now they do not punish but keep acquitting by the wholesale. Of course, this is also exercise, and even abuse, of power, but only in some peculiar direction—is it the sentimental direction?—difficult to say. Yet, everywhere it is a common, almost a preconceived tendency, as if people had come to a general agreement. The sweeping character of this "tendency" cannot be doubted. And the problem is that the acquittal mania *quand-même* affects not only the peasants, the humiliated and insulted of yesterday; it has captured all Russian jurors without distinction, even those of the highest grades—noblemen and university professors. Such a universality, in itself, presents a most curious theme for deliberation, suggesting manifold, and at times, perhaps, strange, conjectures.

Not long ago in one of our very influential newspapers, in a rather modest and certainly well-intentioned little article, in passing, the following conjecture was set forth: is it not conceivable that our jurors, as people who, without any apparent reason, having suddenly grasped their great power (as if it fell from the sky), especially after ages of humiliation and oppression, are inclined on every opportune occasion to vex the "authorities"—the district attorney, for example—merely as a matter of waggery, or, so to speak, by way of contrast with the past? The conjecture is not a bad one, and one which is also not devoid of some jocularity, but, of course, it does not explain everything.

"Simply, it is a pity to ruin somebody else's fate: they are human beings too. The Russian people are compassionate."—Such is the opinion of others, as this has sometimes been expressed.

However, I was always under the impression that in England, too, the people are compassionate, and that even if they do not possess such a kindheartedness, so to speak, as our Russian people, at least they are not devoid of humaneness; that they do have a realization and vivid feeling of the Christian duty toward their neighbor—a feeling which, perhaps to a high degree, to a firm and independent conviction, is one which may be more unflinching than

ours, bearing in mind their culture and secular independence. For truly, over there that much power did not fall on them "suddenly from the sky." Besides, they themselves have invented the jury trial without borrowing it from anyone; they themselves have sanctioned it through ages, carving it out of life itself and not merely receiving it as a gift.

And yet, over there a juror comprehends that the moment he ascends his bench in a courtroom, he is not only a sensitive man with a tender heart, but above all—a citizen. He thinks—whether rightly or erroneously—that compliance with civic duty is, perhaps, even more important than the performance of a wholehearted private exploit. Only recently there was general rumbling throughout their Kingdom when the jurors acquitted a notorious thief. The general commotion all over the country proved the fact that if there, too, as in Russia, such verdicts are possible, they do occur only rarely, as exceptional cases which promptly arouse public opinion. Over there the juror, first of all, understands that he holds in his hands the banner of England as a whole; that he ceases to be a private person, but that he must represent the opinion of his land.

The ability to be a citizen is exactly the ability to lift oneself to the level of the common opinion of the country. Certainly, there too, there is "compassion" in the verdict; there also, "the degrading mileu"—this seems to be our present-day pet doctrine—is being taken into account, but only to a certain limit, as far as this is tolerated by the sane opinion of the country and the level of its civilization based upon Christian morality (and this level appears to be pretty high).

As against this, the juror over there reluctantly renders a "yes, guilty" verdict, realizing above all that his duty preeminently consists in that he, by his pronouncement, certifies before all his countrymen that in old England, for which every one of them would shed his blood, vice, as heretofore, is called vice, and villainy—villainy; and that the moral foundations of the country are still the same—firm, intact, and standing as they stood before.

"Even though it be presumed"—I can hear a voice—"that your solid (that is, Christian) foundations are the same and that, in truth, one has to be, above all, a citizen, and, well, that one must hold the banner, etc., as you retailed—even if this be presumed for the time being, without challenge—think, where shall we find citizens? Consider only what we had yesterday! Now, you know that civil rights (and what rights!) rolled down upon him as from a hill. They crushed him and, as yet, they are to him but a burden—indeed, a burden!"

"Of course, there is truth in your observation," I answer the voice, slightly downcast—"nevertheless, the Russian people . . ."

"The Russian people?—Let me tell you!"—I hear another voice—"Here, we are told that the gifts rolled down from a hill and crushed the people. But, perhaps, they feel that that much they have received as a gift; and, on top of this, they realize that they have received these gifts gratis; and that as yet they, the people, are not worthy of them. Please observe that this does not mean at all that the people in reality are unworthy of the gifts, and that it was *not necessary* or it was *too early* to bestow them upon the people; quite the contrary is true: the people themselves, in their humble conscience, realize the fact that they are unworthy of such gifts and this humble, but lofty, popular avowal of their unworthiness is precisely a pledge that they are worthy. Meanwhile, however, the people are confused in their humility. Who penetrated the innermost recesses of their hearts? Is there anyone among us who can maintain that he is fully familiar with the Russian people? —No, here we have not merely compassion and kindheartedness, as you deign to prattle. Here, the power itself is dreadful! We got frightened by this terrible power over human fate, over the lot of our own brethren; and until we grow up to your citizenship— we forgive. We sit as jurors, and, perhaps, cogitate: 'Are we ourselves better than the defendant?—We are rich, provided with means; but should we happen to be in a situation such as his, we might be acting even worse than he—and so we forgive.' Maybe, this is a good thing—I mean, the heart's compassion. This is, perhaps, a pledge of something sublime, Christian, in the future—something that is as yet unknown to the world!"

"This, in a way, is a Slavophile voice"—I say to myself. "The thought is, indeed, encouraging, while my conjecture concerning popular humility before the power received gratuitously, and bestowed upon the still 'unworthy,' is certainly smarter than the suggestion of a desire 'to tease the district attorney,' notwithstanding the fact that this suggestion continues to appeal to me by reason of its realism (of course, accepting it rather as a special case, as, indeed, it is being set forth by its author himself). However . . . this is what disturbs me most: that our people suddenly began to fear their compassion. It is very hard, we mean, to convict a man." What of it? Depart with your pain. Truth is higher than your pain.

In fact, if we believe that, at times, we ourselves are worse than the criminal, we thereby also admit that we are half-guilty of his crime. If he broke the law which the country prescribed for him, we ourselves are at fault that he stands now before us. For

if we all were better, he, too, would be better, and he would not be standing facing us. . . .

So, then, we should be acquitting at this juncture?

No, on the contrary, at this juncture it is necessary to state the truth, and to call evil—evil. As against this, however, we should assume half the burden of the verdict. This distress of the heart which nowadays everybody fears so much, and with which we shall leave the courtroom, will be our punishment. If the pain is genuine and sharp, it will purify us and make us better. In fact, having ourselves become better, we will improve our environment and will make it better. This alone can rectify it. Because escapism from one's own compassion for the sake of evading personal suffering and wholesale acquittals is easy. In this way, by-and-by, we may reach the conclusion that there are no crimes at all, and that "environment is guilty" of everything. We will come to the point, following the thread of a ball, that crime is even a duty, a noble protest against "environment." "Since society is wickedly organized, it is impossible to struggle out of it without a knife in hand."

Indeed, this is what the doctrine of environment contends in opposition to Christianity which, fully recognizing the pressure of the milieu, and which, having proclaimed mercy for him who has sinned, nevertheless makes it a moral duty for man to struggle against environment, and draws a line of demarcation between where environment ends and duty begins. Making man responsible, Christianity *eo ipso* also recognizes his freedom. However, making man dependent on any error in the social organization, the environmental doctrine reduces man to absolute impersonality, to a total emancipation from all personal moral duty, from all independence; reduces him to a state of the most miserable slavery that can be conceived.

For in this way a man may wish for tobacco, but because he has no money be at liberty to kill another man to get tobacco. Think: "An educated man, who suffers more than an uneducated one from the failure to satisfy his wants, requires money for their satisfaction; so, then, why shouldn't he kill the uneducated, if there is no other way of obtaining money?"—Is it possible that you have not listened to lawyers' voices: "Truly," they say, "the law has been violated; it stands to reason that this is a crime; that he has killed the uneducated, but, gentlemen of the jury, please take into account that . . . etc." Such opinions were almost ready to be voiced, and not only "almost . . ."

"However," I can hear a sarcastic voice—"it seems that it is you who are pressing on the people the latest environmental philosophy, for whence did it come to them? Since these twelve jurors

—at times, all of them peasants—sit there, and each one of them considers it a mortal sin to eat forbidden food in Lent you should have accused them point-blank of social tendencies."

"Of course, of course, why should they be worrying about the 'milieu,' I mean, they as a body—I began to ponder—yet, the ideas are soaring in the air; there is something penetrating in an idea. . . ."

"There you are!"—laughs the caustic voice.

"And what if our people are particularly inclined toward the environmental doctrine—by their very nature, by their, let us say, Slav propensities? What if they—our people—are the best material in Europe for certain propagandists?"

The sarcastic voice laughs still louder, but somewhat artificially.

No, as far as the people are concerned, as yet we have here merely a trick and not an "environmental philosophy." Here, there is one error, one deceit, and in this deceit there is a great seduction.

This fraud may be explained, by way of an example at least, in the following manner:

Granted that the people call convicts "sufferers" and give them pennies and white loaves. What, in the course, possibly, of ages, do they mean to express thereby?—Christian truth, or "environmental" truth? Precisely here is the stumbling block; precisely here is that lever which could be successfully seized by the "environmental" propagandist.

There are unexpressed, unconscious ideas which are merely strongly felt. There are many such ideas and they are, as it were, fused with the soul of man. They also exist in a nation at large, and in mankind taken as a whole. So long as these ideas dwell unconsciously in the people's life, and are but strongly and truthfully felt—up to that time only can the people pursue a vigorous and animated life. In the endeavors to interpret these concealed ideas consists the whole energy of the existence of the people. The more firmly the people cling to these ideas, the less they are capable of betraying the original feeling; the less they are inclined to submit to different misinterpretations of these ideas, the more powerful, solid and happy they are. Among these ideas concealed in the Russian people—ideas of the Russian people—is the denomination of crime as a misfortune, and of criminals—as sufferers.

This is a purely Russian idea. In no other European people has it been recorded. In the West it is now being expounded only by philosophers and commentators. However, our people proclaimed it long before those philosophers and commentators. But from this it does not follow that the people cannot be misled, at least temporarily and superficially, by the false interpretation of this idea by some glossator. The ultimate meaning and the last word, no doubt, will always belong to the people; yet, *temporarily*—this may be different.

Briefly, by this word "sufferers" the people, as it were, say to the "sufferers": "You have sinned, and you are suffering; but we, too, are sinful. If we had been in your place, possibly, we should have done even worse. If we ourselves had been better, perhaps, you would not be kept in jails. Together with the retaliation for your crimes you have also assumed the burden for general lawlessness. Pray for us, and we shall pray for you. Meanwhile, accept, you 'sufferers,' our pennies; we give them to you so that you may know that we remember you and that we did not sever our brotherly bonds with you."

You must agree that there is nothing easier than to apply to this view the doctrine of "environment": "Society is wicked, and, therefore, we, too, are wicked; but we are rich, well provided; we missed by mere accident that with which you have collided. Had we done so, we should have done the same thing which you have done. Who is guilty? The environment is guilty. Thus, there is but a vile setup of the environment, and there are no crimes at all."

Now, the trick, which I have mentioned, lies in this sophistical inference.

No, the people do not deny crime, and they know that the criminal is guilty. It is only that the people are aware of the fact that they themselves are guilty in common with every criminal. Still, blaming themselves, the people do not prove thereby that they believe in "environment"; on the contrary, they believe that environment is wholly dependent on them, on their uninterrupted repentance and self-betterment. Energy, work, and struggle—these are the things which reform environment. By work and struggle alone, independence and the sentiment of self-respect are being achieved. "Let us become better, and environment will improve." This is what the Russian people, by a strong feeling, are tacitly conceiving in their concealed idea of the misfortune of the criminal.

Now, imagine: what if the criminal himself, on hearing from the people that he is a "sufferer," were to consider himself only a sufferer, and not a criminal?—In this case the people would turn away from such a misinterpretation and would call it a betrayal of the popular truth and faith.

I could cite examples in support of my contention, but let us postpone this for the time being, and let us say this.

A criminal and a person contemplating the commission of a

crime are two different beings, belonging, however, to one and the
same category. What if, deliberately planning a crime, the criminal
should say to himself: "There is no crime!"—Would the people call
him a "sufferer"?

Possibly, even for certain, they would so label him. The people
are compassionate; besides, there is no criminal more unfortunate
than he who no longer even considers himself a criminal: he is an
animal, a beast. What is there in the fact that he does not understand that he is an animal, and that he has killed conscience in
himself? He is but doubly unfortunate—doubly unfortunate, but
also twice as criminal. The people will pity him, but they will not
renounce their truth. Never did the people, when calling a criminal
a "sufferer," cease to regard him as a criminal! And there would
be no greater misfortune for us should the people agree with the
criminal and answer him: "No, thou art not guilty, since there
is no 'crime'!"

Such is our faith—our common faith—I should like to say;
the faith of all who trust and hope. Let me add two more words.

I was in penal servitude, and I saw "desperate" criminals.
I repeat, this was a hard school. Not one of them ceased to consider
himself a criminal. To look at, they were a dreadful and cruel
lot. However, only the simpletons and newcomers were "braggarts,"
and these used to be ridiculed. Mostly, they were gloomy, pensive
people. No one spoke about his crimes. I never heard any grumbling.
It was even impossible to speak aloud about one's crimes. Now
and then someone would utter a word with a challenge and a twist
—and all the inmates, as one man, would "put a check on" the pert
fellow. It was a rule not to speak about *this*. Nevertheless, I believe,
probably not one among them evaded long psychic suffering within
himself—that suffering which is the most purifying and invigorating.
I saw them solitarily pensive; I beheld them in the church, praying before confession; I listened to their single, spontaneous words
and exclamations; I remember their faces—and, believe me, not
one of them, in his innermost, considered himself right!

I would not wish my words to be deemed cruel. Nevertheless,
I shall venture to speak frankly. I will say plainly: by harsh
punishment, by prison and penal servitude, perhaps, you would have
saved half of them. You would have assuaged, and not burdened,
them. Self-purification through suffering is easier, I tell you: easier
—than that destiny which you are paving for many of them by
wholesale acquittals in court. You are merely planting cynicism
in their souls; you are leaving in them a seductive question and
a contempt for yourselves. You do not believe?—A contempt for
yourselves, for your judgment, for the judgment of the whole

country! You infuse into their souls incredulity in the popular truth, in the truth of God; you are leaving them confused. . . . They will walk away and think: "Oh, that's the way things are now; there is no strictness. Well, they have grown wiser. Perhaps, they are afraid. Therefore, one can do it again. It stands to reason: if I was in such a need, why should I not have stolen!"

And do you really believe that by acquitting them all, or by declaring them "deserving every consideration," you are giving them a chance to reform?—What's his worry! "Possibly, I am not guilty at all!"—this is what, *in the long run,* he will say. You yourselves will suggest to him such an inference. And—most important of all—faith in the law and in popular truth is being undermined.

Only recently, for several years in succession, I have been living abroad. When I left Russia, the new courts were merely beginning to function. How avidly I used to read there in our newspapers everything concerning the Russian courts. Abroad I was observing our émigrés with sorrow, their children ignorant of their native tongue, or forgetting it. It was clear to me that half of them, by the very nature of things, will finally turn into expatriates. I always suffer when thinking about this: so much vigor, so many of the best people, perhaps, and in Russia people are so needed! Yet, gentlemen, by God! sometimes leaving the reading room, involuntarily I felt reconciled to absenteeism and with the absentees. I experienced real pain in my heart. I would be reading: a wife, who murdered her husband, was acquitted. The crime was an obvious and proved one; she confessed to it. And yet: "No, not guilty." Then, again, a young man breaks open a strong box and steals the cash: "He was very much in love, you see; he had to get money to please his sweetheart.—No, not guilty." And if at least all these cases could be explained by compassion or pity! But the thing that I could not understand was the reason for the acquittals—and I got confused. The impression which I gathered was a vague one, almost insulting. In these angry moments at times I would be picturing Russia as a marsh or a swamp on which someone started building a palace. On the surface the ground appears solid and even, whereas this is something akin to the surface of pea soup: just step upon it and you will slip down, into the very abyss. I reproached myself for my pusillanimity; I was encouraged by the thought that, from afar, perhaps I am mistaking things; that, temporarily, be that as it may, I myself am an absentee; and, so, I do not see things at close range, I do not hear clearly. . . .

And here I am—for a long time—again in my native land.

"Let's be frank! Are they really sorry?"—That's the question!

Don't laugh because I am attaching so much importance to this. "Compassion" at least tends to explain something and somehow; it at least leads one out of darkness, whereas, without such explanation, there is nothing but obscurity in which there dwells some lunatic.

A peasant beats up his wife, mutilates her over a period of long years; insults her more than a dog. In despair and in an almost senseless state, having made up her mind to commit suicide, she goes to the village court. There, they dismiss her and, with an apathetic mumble, she is told: "You should live on more amicable terms." Is this compassion? These are the dull words of a drunkard waking up after a spell of hard drinking; he scarcely discerns that you are standing in front of him; stupidly and aimlessly he waves his hand at you, so that you shouldn't be in his way; he can scarcely move his tongue—fumes and madness invading his brain.

By the way, the story of this woman is known; it is quite recent. It has been read in all the papers, and, perhaps, it is still remembered: briefly and simply, as a result of her husband's beating, the wife hanged herself. The husband was tried and was found deserving clemency. But for a long time I kept dreaming about the whole situation; I am also dreaming now. . . .

I kept picturing to myself his figure: it was stated that he was tall, stout, strong, light-haired; I would have added—scanty-haired. The body—white, bloated; movements—slow and grave; his glance—concentrated; he speaks little and rarely; he drops words as if they were precious pearls which he himself values most. Witnesses testified that he was of a cruel disposition: he would catch a chicken and hang it by its legs, head down—for mere pleasure; this amused him—a splendid, characteristic trait!

He beat his wife over a period of several years with whatever happened to be around—with ropes, sticks. He would pull out a floor board, thrust her feet into the opening, pressing upon the board, and would flog and flog. I believe that he himself did not know why he beat her: just so, prompted by the same motives which made him hang the chicken. He also used to starve her, leaving her without bread for three days. He would put the bread on a shelf, would call her and tell her: "Don't dare to touch that bread; it's *my* bread"—which is also a very characteristic trait! With her ten-year-old child she used to go begging among neighbors: if they gave her some bread, they—mother and child—would eat; if not—they would stay hungry.

He demanded that she work; she attended to everything steadfastly, speechlessly, in dismay, and at last—as if in a state of delirium.

THE DIARY OF A WRITER

I can also visualize her appearance: probably, she must have been a very little woman—emaciated, lean as a rake. It happens sometimes that very big and stout men, white and puffed-up of body, marry tiny and skinny women (I have noticed that they are inclined to such a choice); and it is so strange to observe them when they stand or walk side by side. It seems to me that if she had become pregnant by him during the very last stage, this would have been the most characteristic and most essential trait to complete the picture; otherwise, something would seem to be missing.

Did you ever see how a peasant whips his wife?—I did. He begins with a rope or a strap. Peasant life is devoid of æsthetic delights—music, theatres, magazines; naturally it has to be enlarged somehow. Tying up his wife, or thrusting her legs into the opening of a floor board, our good little peasant would probably begin—methodically, phlegmatically, even sleepily—with measured blows, not listening to the screams and entreaties! to be more correct—precisely listening to them, listening with delight, for otherwise what pleasure would he be deriving from the whipping?—Do you know, gentlemen, that people are born in different surroundings? Would you not believe that this woman, in other surroundings, might have been a Juliet or a Beatrice from Shakespeare, a Gretchen from *Faust?* I do not say that she would be—it would be very silly to make such an assertion—but there might have been in her soul, in embryo form, something noble, possibly something not inferior to what one finds among the noble class, namely, a loving and even lofty heart, a character full of most original beauty.

The fact itself that she tarried so long to commit suicide puts her in such a quiet, benign, patient, affectionate light. And this very Beatrice or Gretchen is being whipped, whipped like a cat! Countless blows are being showered more and more frequently, more sharply; he is getting excited; he begins to savor the thing. Presently he becomes wild, and this he realizes with pleasure. The animal shrieks of the tortured woman go to his head as liquor. "I'll wash your feet and drink that water," shouts Beatrice in an inhuman voice. At length she grows quiet; she shrieks no longer; now she merely groans wildly; her breath comes in gasps every minute; but right then the blows come down more frequently, more violently. . . . Suddenly, he throws away the strap; like a madman, he seizes a stick, a bough, anything, and breaks it over her back with three last, terrific blows.—No more! He quits, plants himself by the table, sighs, and sets himself to his kvass.

The little girl, their daughter—they did have a daughter!—trembling on the oven in the corner, tries to hide: she hears her mother shrieking. He walks out. At dawn, mother will come to her

senses; she will get up and, heaving sighs and crying out at every
movement, she will go to milk the cow; she goes to work.

And he, when departing, admonishes her, in his methodical,
grave voice: "Don't you dare to eat this bread; it's *my* bread."

Lastly, he also became fond of hanging her by her legs, just
like that chicken. Probably he would hang her, then he would step
aside, sit down, set himself to his porridge, eat, and, suddenly grasping the strap, he would again start beating the hanged creature. . . .
And the little girl keeps shivering, shrinking on the oven; stealthily
she throws a wild glance at her mother hanging by her legs, and
she hides again. . . .

The mother hanged herself in May, early in the morning;
probably on a bright spring day. She was seen on the eve, beaten
up, in a state of complete madness. Before her death she went to
the village court, and it was there that she was mumblingly advised:
"You should live on more amicable terms."

When she hanged herself and the throat rattle started, the
girl cried out from her corner: "Mama, why do you choke?" After
that, timidly she approached her, called to the hanged woman,
gazed at her wildly, and several times that morning she came out
of the corner to take a look at her mother, until father returned.

And here he is before the court—grave, puffed up, concentrated. He denies everything: "We lived in perfect harmony"—drops
the rare words like some precious pearls. The jurors, "after brief
deliberation," come out and render their verdict:

"Guilty *but deserves clemency.*"

Bear in mind that the little girl testified against her father.
She told everything, and it is said that she made those present
weep. Had it not been for the jurors' "clemency," he would have
been exiled to Siberia. But, with the "clemency," he is to spend
only eight months in jail; after which he will return home, and
will summon the little girl who testified against him on behalf of
her mother. Again there will be someone to hang by the legs.

"Deserves clemency!" And this verdict was deliberately rendered. They knew what would be awaiting the child. Clemency—
to whom, to what?—One feels as if in some whirl: one is seized
and turned and twisted around.

Wait. I will relate another anecdote.

Some time ago, before the inauguration of the new courts
(true, not long before), I read in our papers about this little
incident: a mother carried in her arms a baby of twelve or fourteen
months. At this age children are cutting their teeth; they are sick,
they cry and they suffer much. Maybe the mother got tired of the
baby, and there was much work to be done; and here she had

to carry the baby in her arms and to listen to its shrill wailing. She grew angry. Yet, is so tiny a child to be beaten for this? It is such a pity to beat it, and, besides, what can it understand?— It is so helpless, so dependent upon everything around. . . . Nor will it stop crying if one beats it: it will burst into tears, and will clasp you with its little hands; or else, it will start kissing you, and will weep and weep. So she did not beat it. But there stood in the room a samovar with water boiling in it. She placed the baby's little hand right under the faucet and turned it open. She kept that little hand under boiling water for some ten seconds.

This is a fact; I read about it. But imagine if this were to happen in our day, and the woman were summoned to court. The jurors would retire, and "after brief deliberation," they would render the verdict: "Deserves *clemency*."

Only imagine such a thing. I urge mothers at least to picture this. How a lawyer would be wheedling on such an occasion:

"Gentlemen of the jury, of course this is not what you would call a humane incident; but look at the case *in toto ;* please visualize the environment, the surroundings. This is a poor woman; she is the only worker in the household; she suffers disappointments. She cannot even afford to hire a nurse. It stands to reason that in a moment when anger against the all-devouring milieu, so to speak, penetrates one, then, gentlemen, it is only natural that she should have drawn the little hand under the faucet of the samovar . . ., and then . . ."

Oh, of course, I realize the whole usefulness of the lawyer's profession, which is respected by everybody. Still, at times, it is impossible not to view the problem from this—I concede—light-minded, but nevertheless forced, point of view: indeed, on occasions, what a beastly job is his—one ponders: he spins around, and tries—oh, how hard!—to extricate himself; he lies against his conscience, against his conviction, against all morality, against everything human!. No, he is not being paid for nothing.

"Look here!"—suddenly exclaims the familiar caustic voice— "This is all nonsense, and nothing but your fantasy: jurors never have rendered such a verdict. The lawyer never did go a round-about way. It's you who invented the whole thing!"

But the wife hung head over heels, as a chicken! And "this is *my* bread: don't you dare to touch it!" And the little girl shivering on that oven, listening for a half hour to her mother's shrieks! And, "Mama, why do you choke?"—Isn't all this identical with the little hand under boiling water?—Indeed—*almost* identical!

"Ignorance — dullness — have pity — environment," insists the peasant's lawyer. But millions of them are living—and not all of them indulge in hanging their wives by the legs!—All the same, there must be here a demarcation line. . . . Oh, gentlemen of the bar, stop spinning around with your "environment"!

The Citizen, 1873, No. 2.

SOMETHING PERSONAL

Several times I have been urged to write my literary reminiscences. I don't know whether I shall write them, and, besides, my memory is weak. Furthermore, it is sad to recollect; I don't like to recollect. However, some episodes of my literary career stick in my mind with extraordinary lucidity, notwithstanding my weak memory.

Here, for instance, is an anecdote.

One morning, during spring, I called on the late Egor Petrovich Kovalevsky. He was very much pleased with my novel *Crime and Punishment*, which just then had appeared in *The Russian Messenger*. He ardently praised it, and he conveyed to me a precious comment by a certain person whose name I cannot reveal. Meanwhile, two magazine publishers entered the room, one after the other. One of these magazines subsequently acquired a very large number of subscribers—indeed, unheard-of in the annals of our monthly perodicals—but at that time it was only beginning. The other journal, on the contrary, was about to terminate its existence which had exercised a remarkable and potent influence upon both literature and the public. But then, that morning, its publisher did not know that his magazine was so near to its close. It was with the latter publisher that we went into another room, and we found ourselves alone.

Without mentioning his name, I will merely say that my first meeting with him was an extremely warm one—one that I shall always remember. Perhaps, he also recalls it. In those days he was not yet editor. Later, there developed many misunderstandings. Upon my return from Siberia, we met only on rare occasions, but once, in passing, he spoke to me very sympathetically and, in connection with a certain matter, he called my attention to a poem —the best he had ever written. I may add that in his appearance and habits no one less than he resembled a poet, especially of the category of "suffering" poets. Yet, he is one of the most passionate, most gloomy and "suffering" among our bards.

"Well now, we have scolded you," he told me (that is, in his magazine, for *Crime and Punishment*).

"I know," said I.

"And do you know why?"

"Probably, as a matter of principle."

"For Chernyshevsky."

I stood dumbfounded in surprise.

"N. N., who wrote the critical review"—continued the publisher—"told me: 'The novel is good; but since in one of his stories, two years ago, he was not ashamed to insult a poor exile, and caricatured him, I shall denounce his novel.'"

"So this is the same stupid tattle about *The Crocodile*," I exclaimed, grasping what it was about. "Is it possible that you, too, believe it? Have you yourself read this story of mine—*The Crocodile?*"

"No, I haven't read it."

"But all this is gossip, the most trivial gossip that one can imagine. Indeed, one has to have the mind and the poetic instinct of a Bulgarin, to perceive between the lines in this bagatelle, in this comic story, a 'civic' allegory, and, in addition, one directed against Chernyshevsky! If you only knew how silly this strained explanation is! By the way, I shall never forgive myself that two years ago I did not protest against this mean calumny, when it had just been launched!"

This conversation with the editor of a now long defunct magazine took place some seven years ago, and up to the present time I have not protested against the "calumny"—through neglect, and because of "lack of time." And yet, this meanness, ascribed to me, continues to dwell in the memories of certain persons as an unquestionable fact; it has been propagated in literary circles; it has spread among the public, and on more than one occasion it has already caused me annoyance. It is time to say at least a few words about all this, all the more so as this is an opportune occasion to refute, even without proof, a calumny which, by the way, is also absolutely proofless. By my protracted silence and neglect up to the present, I countenanced it, as it were.

I first met Nikolai Gavrilovich Chernyshevsky in 1859, during the year of my return from Siberia—I don't remember where and how. Later, we would meet sometimes, but very rarely; we would converse, but very little. Yet, invariably we used to shake hands. Hertzen told me that Chernyshevsky gave him a disagreeable impression, that is, by his appearance and manners. For my part, I liked Chernyshevsky's appearance and manners.

One morning I found at the door of my apartment, on the handle of the lock, one of the most remarkable proclamations of those which had been appearing at the time, and there had been a good many of them. It was entitled: *To the Young Generation*. One could not have imagined anything more nonsensical and stupid.

Its content was most shocking and expressed in a most ludicrous form, that could have been conceived only by a villain. I was very much annoyed, and all day I felt sad. All this was then still novel, and so close that it was difficult to gain a clear view of these men. Precisely, it was difficult because somehow one refused to believe that such a trifle was concealed under the whole upheaval. I am not referring to the movement, as a whole, which was then on foot, but merely to the people involved in it. As to the movement, it was a distressing, pathological phenomenon, yet one that was inevitable by reason of its historical logic; it will constitute a grave page in the Petersburg period of our history. And it seems that this page is far from being fully written.

And here, I, who heart and soul disagreed with these people and with the meaning of their movement—I became suddenly vexed and almost ashamed, as it were, of their incompetency: "Why is everything so stupid and ignorant about them? And what do I care about this matter?" But I regretted—not their failure. Strictly speaking, I did not know the disseminators of the proclamations; I do not know them even to this day; but the thing that was precisely sad was the fact that this phenomenon was not just a single one, nor was it merely a silly trick of these particular men who meant nothing to me. But I was oppressed by this fact: by the educational, mental level and the absence of any comprehension. of reality—this, to me, was terribly oppressive.

Even though I had lived in Petersburg some three years and had observed certain events, this proclamation that morning stupe- fied me, as it were, and came as an altogether new and unexpected revelation: never before that day had I experienced such nullity! Precisely the degree of that nullity was frightening.

Towards evening I suddenly decided to go to Chernyshevsky. Prior to that time I had never visited him, nor had he visited me.

I recall, it was about five in the afternoon. I found Nikolai Gavrilovich all alone: even the servants were not at home, and he himself opened the door. He greeted me with extreme cordiality and led me into his living room.

"Nikolai Gavrilovich, what is this?"—I handed him the proc- lamation.

He took it as something quite unknown to him and read it. There were only about ten lines.

"Now, what?"—he asked me, with a slight smile.

"Is it possible that they are so stupid and ridiculous? Is it possible that they can't be stopped and that an end can't be put to this abomination?"

He answered very weightily and impressively:

"Do you really suppose that I am in sympathy with them and that I could have taken part in the compilation of this scrap of paper?"

"Indeed, I do not suppose,"—I answered—"and I even deem it unnecessary to assure you of this. But at any rate they should be stopped by all means. Your word carries weight with them, and they certainly are afraid of your opinion."

"I know no one among them."

"I am also convinced of this. However, one doesn't have to know them at all or to speak personally to them. It would suffice if you would express aloud somewhere your reproof. This will reach them."

"Maybe it will have no effect. Besides, these, as side facts, are inevitable."

"And yet they are damaging to everybody and everything."

Presently another guest rang the bell—I don't recall who. I left. I deem it my duty to remark that I spoke to Chernyshevsky sincerely, and I believed, as I also believe now, that he was not "in sympathy" with these disseminators. I was under the impression that Nikolai Gavrilovich was displeased with my visit. Several days later he confirmed this, having personally called on me. He stayed with me for an hour or so, and I confess that I have rarely met a more kindhearted, cordial man, so that even then I felt puzzled over certain comments on his alleged harsh, uncongenial character.

It was clear to me that he wanted to become acquainted with me, and I recall that this pleased me. Once more after that I went to see him, and he also visited me again. Soon, owing to personal circumstances, I went to live in Moscow, and I stayed there about nine months. The acquaintance which had begun, thus came to an end. After that Chernyshevsky's arrest took place and his exile. I was never able to find out anything about his case; nor do I know anything at present.

About eighteen months ago it occurred to me to write a fantastic tale—something along the lines of Gogol's story *The Nose*. Never before did I attempt to write in a fantastic vein. This was a purely literary prank, solely for the sake of humor. In fact, I had come across several comical situations which I sought to unfold. Though the subject is not worth it, I shall relate it so that what has later been made out of it will be understood.

A Petersburg government official, before leaving for abroad, goes with his young wife and his inseparable friend to the Passage, and, among other things, they all stop to look at a crocodile. This clerk belongs to the middle class, but he is one of those who possess an independent fortune; he is still young but devoured by ambition; above all, he is a fool—just as the unforgettable Major Kovalev who had lost his nose. Comically, he is convinced of his great merits, he is half-educated, but considers himself almost a genius; in his department he is looked upon as a man full of emptiness, and he is always offended by the general neglect of him. As if in revenge therefor, he bosses and tyrannizes over his pusillanimous friend, pluming himself over him by his intellect. The friend hates him but endures everything because secretly he is fond of the wife.

In the Passage, while this little young and good-looking dame, of a purely Petersburg pattern, a brainless and coquettish petty creature of the middle class, forgets herself in gazing at monkeys whch are being shown along with the crocodile, her ingenious husband manages somehow to exasperate the hitherto sleepy creature which has been lying still as a log. Suddenly, the beast opens wide its jaws and swallows him up, leaving no trace of him. It develops soon that the great man had suffered not even the slightest injury from this episode; contrarywise, with his peculiar obstinacy, he declares from the insides of the crocodile that he feels quite comfortable sitting there. Presently, friend and wife depart to solicit the aid of the authorities for the liberation of the prisoner. In order to do so, it appears quite inevitable to kill the animal, to cut it up and thus release the great man. But, of course, the German, owner of the crocodile, and his inseparable *Mutter* must be compensated for the loss of their crocodile. At first, the German is indignant and he fears that the creature which has swallowed a "whole government official" may die; but shortly he guesses that the swallowed member of the Petersburg administration, and one who, in addition, has happily survived, henceforth may bring him in Europe an extraordinary harvest. He demands an enormous sum for the crocodile, and—on top of that—the rank of a Russian colonel.

On the other hand, the authorities feel quite embarrassed, since this, in the annals of their Ministry, is too novel a case, for which, up to then, there had been no precedent. "If only we could dig up an analogous example, no matter how trifling, we could start acting, but as things stand—it is difficult." The authorities also suspect that the bureaucrat thrust himself into the crocodile, prompted by some forbidden liberal tendencies. Meanwhile, the spouse begins to feel that her status, "akin to that of a widow," is not devoid of piquancy. At the same time, the swallowed husband definitely declares to his friend that it is far better for him to remain inside the crocodile than in government service, inasmuch as now at least, willy-nilly, he is going to be noticed—something which he had never been able to achieve. He insists that his wife start giving evening parties, and that he be brought to these parties in a chest, together with the crocodile. He is sure that the whole of Petersburg and state dignitaries will rush to these parties, to behold the new phenomenon. At this point he is resolved to score a victory: "I shall utter the truth and teach; I shall give advice to the statesman, and I shall prove my ability to the Minister," says he, already considering himself, as it were, not of this world and, therefore, entitled to give advice and pronounce judgments. In answer to the cautious, yet venomous, question of the friend: "And what if, as a result of some unexpected process, which, however, must be expected, he should be digested into something which he does not expect?"—the great man states that he has already given thought to this, but that he will indignantly resist this phenomenon though it be conforming to the laws of nature.

However, the wife refuses to give parties for the specified purpose, notwithstanding the fact that the idea itself appeals to her. "How could it be that my husband should be brought to me in a chest?"—she argues. Besides, the status of a widow pleases her more and more. She acquires a taste for it; people sympathize with her. Her husband's chief comes to visit her and he plays cards with her. . . .

Such, then, is the first part of this burlesque story—it is not finished. Some day, by all means, I will finish it, even though I have forgotten it and have to read it over to recall it.

And yet, here is what people managed to make out of this bagatelle. No sooner had the story appeared in the magazine *Epoch* (in 1865), than *The Voice*, unexpectedly, printed a strange notice. I do not literally recall its contents and, besides, it would take too much trouble to check it, but its meaning was somewhat along these lines: "In vain, it would seem, does the author of *The Crocodile* choose this path; it will bring him neither honor nor anticipated advantage," etc., etc., followed by a few most nebulous and inimical stings. I read it in passing, understood nothing, but perceived much venom without comprehending why. This vague feuilletonistic comment, in itself, of course, could cause me no damage: all the same no one among the readers could have understood it—even as myself. Yet, a week later, N. N. S. said to me: "Do you know what they are thinking there?—There they are convinced that your *Crocodile* is an allegory, the story of Chernyshevsky's exile, and that it was your intention to portray and ridicule him." Although surprised, I wasn't much worried—what kind of conjectures can't be set forth? This opinion seemed to me too isolated and far-fetched to produce any effect, and I deemed

it altogether unnecessary to protest. This I will never forgive myself, since the opinion took root and did spread. *Calomniez, il en
restera toujours quelque chose.*

However, even now I am certain that here there was no
calumny at all—and what would be the purpose?—In literary circles
I had quarrelled with almost no one—at least, seriously. At present,
this very moment, I am talking about myself for the second time
only during the period of the twenty-seven years of my literary
career. Here, there was simply dullness—gloomy, suspicious dullness
planted in some head "with a tendency." I am convinced that this
wise head is quite certain—even up to the present day—that it has
not erred, and that, of course, I must have ridiculed ill-starred
Chernyshevsky. Furthermore, I am convinced that even today I
should be unable, despite any explanations and apologies, to sway
this head to my side. Not in vain is this a wise head. (It goes
without saying that I am speaking here not about Andrei Alexandrovich: as editor and publisher of his paper, in this matter,
as usual, he had no part.)

Wherein is the allegry?—Why, certainly—the crocodile signifies Siberia; the self-conceited and light-minded bureaucrat is
Chernyshevsky. He got into the crocodile, but still hopes to teach
the whole world. The pusillanimous friend of his typifies all the
local friends of Chernyshevsky. The good-looking but stupid little
wife of the bureaucrat, enjoying her status "as that of a widow"
—this is . . . But this is dirty to such an extent that I decline
to soil myself and to continue the explanation of the allegory.
(And yet it did take root; and it did so, perhaps, precisely because
of this last insinuation. I have irrefutable proof thereof.)

So that the presumption was made that I, myself a former
exile and a convict, rejoiced in the exile of another "unfortunate";
even more—I wrote on this occasion a diatribe. Yet, where is the
proof of that? In the allegory? But give me whatever you please:
The Memoirs of a Lunatic, the ode *God, Uri Miloslavsky,* the verses
of Fet—anything—and I undertake to prove to you by the very
first ten lines, designated by you, that therein is precisely an
allegory on the Franco-Prussian war or a pasquinade on the actor
Gorbunov—in a word, on anyone you please, on anyone you may
insist upon.

Please recall how, in olden days, at the end of the Forties,
for instance, censors used to examine manuscripts: there wasn't
a line, there wasn't a dot in which something, some allegory,
wouldn't have been suspected. Let them produce anything at all
from the record of my whole life in support of the fact that I

resemble a malicious, heartless lampooner, and that one may expect from me allegories of this kind.

On the contrary, the very haste and promptitude of such inferences prove a certain vileness of spirit in the accusers, the coarseness and inhumanity of their views. Here, the simplemindedness of the conjecture itself is no excuse. Why not?—One can be simplemindedly vile—and that's all.

Perhaps, I had a personal hatred of Chernyshevsky?—To forestall this accusation I gave above an account of our brief and cordial acquaintance. It may be said: this is not enough, for I may have nourished a concealed hate. Then, let them set forth pretexts for such animosity, if they have anything to produce. But there were no such pretexts. On the other hand, I am certain that Chernyshevsky himself would corroborate the veracity of my account of our meeting, if some day he should read it. And I pray God that he be given an opportunity to do so. I am longing for this as warmly, as ardently as I sincerely regretted, and do regret, his misfortune.

But, perhaps, this was hate generated by convictions?

Why?—Chernyshevsky never offended me by his convictions. One can very much respect a man, even though radically disagreeing with his ideas. On this point, however, I can speak not altogether without foundation, and I even have a little proof. In one of the last issues of the magazine *Epoch*, which at about that time terminated its existence (it may even have been in the very last issue), there appeared a long critical review of the "famous" novel by Chernyshevsky, *What to Do?* This is a remarkable article, coming from a renowned pen. And what?—In it just tribute is paid to Chernyshevsky's intellect and talent. In fact, his novel is being warmly praised. And no one has ever doubted his outstanding intellect. The article merely mentions the peculiarities and deviations of his mind; yet, the very seriousness of the review is proof of the due respect of our critic for the merits of the author discussed by him. Now, please concede: if there was in me hatred arising from convictions, of course, I would not have permitted an article in the magazine in which Chernyshevsky was spoken of with due respect; for I, not anyone else, was editor of the *Epoch*.

Maybe, by publishing a venomous allegory, I was hoping to gain somewhere *en haut lieu?*—But when and who can say that I have ever sought favors or have gained anything in this sense in some *lieu*—in other words, that I have sold my pen? I believe that the author of the conjecture himself had no such thought, notwithstanding his simplemindedness. Nor, under any circumstances, would it have been given credence in literary circles, had the accusation been confined to this alone.

As to the possibility of a vile allegory concerning some domestic facts in the life of Nikolai Gavrilovich, I repeat, I do not even wish to touch on this point lest I become soiled.

I am very sorry that on this occasion I started speaking about myself. This is what it means to write literary memoirs. I never will write them. I regret very much that I have undoubtedly bored the reader, but I am writing a diary, a diary of my personal impressions, and only recently have I acquired a "literary" impression, which all of a sudden indirectly reminded me also of the forgotten anecdote about my forgotten *Crocodile*.

The other day one of the men whom I respect most, and whose opinions I treasure highly, said to me:

"I have just read your article on *The Milieu* and on the verdicts of our jurors (*The Citizen*, No. 2). I am quite in accord with you, but your article may produce an unpleasant misunderstanding. It may be thought that you are advocating the abolition of jury trials and that you favor renewed interference by way of administrative tutelage. . . ."

I was sorrowfully surprised. This was the voice of a most impartial man, standing outside of any literary parties and "allegories."

Is it possible that my article may be interpreted in such a sense! If so, there is nothing one can speak about. The economic and moral condition of the people after the abolition of serfdom is awful. Irrefutable and most disturbing facts attest to this every minute. Decline of morality, cheapness, shyster-innkeepers, theft and daylight banditry—all these are undeniable facts; and the thing keeps growing and growing. And what?—If anyone, being spiritually and in his heart alarmed, should grasp the pen and write about all this—why, is it really possible that people would start shouting that the man favors serfdom and would have it restored among the peasants?

"At any rate, it is desirable that the people possess full freedom to get out of their sad situation without any tutelage and any turns backward."

Quite so, and this is precisely my thought! And even if as a result of national decadence (sometimes, here and there, looking upon themselves they admit: "Yes, we've weakened, weakened!")—even, I say, if a real, indubitably popular calamity should occur—some colossal collapse, some big misfortune—even then the people would save themselves, and us, too, as it has happened to them many a time—a fact which is confirmed by their whole history. Such

is my idea. Precisely—no more meddling! . . . Still, how words may
be understood and misinterpreted! Possibly, I may run into another
allegory!

The Citizen, 1873, No. 3.

VLAS

Do you remember Vlas? For some reason I am reminded of him.

> In a ragged coat—open collar—
> With his old head white and bare,
> Through the cities full of squalor,
> Paces Vlas with anxious stare.
> On his chest—a copper ikon:
> He collects for God's own church . . .

As is known, in days gone by, this same Vlas "had no God."

> . . . . flogging
> Sent his wife into her grave,
> And to bandits, skilled in robbing,
> To horse-thieves, he shelter gave.

Even to horse-stealers!—the poet scares us, adopting the tone
of a pious old woman. My, what sins! And he had been struck
with lightning. Vlas fell sick, and he saw a vision, after which he
took an oath to become a beggar and to engage in collections for
the church.

> He did see the world's damnation,
> Sinners did he see in hell:
> Devils torture them and tingle,
> Restless witch stings them with cries,
> And with her Ethiopians mingle—
> Ugly, black, with glowing eyes
>
> . . . .
>
> Some hang strung on long wood rods,
> Others lick the red-hot floor . . .

Briefly, unimaginable horrors—so that one is even scared to
read. "But," the poet continues, "it is impossible to describe everything."

> Pilgrim-women, humbly clever,
> Even better stories tell.

Oh, poet!—(Unfortunately, you are our genuine poet)—if you would only cease approaching the people with ecstasies, about which

> Pilgrim-women, humbly clever,
> Even better stories tell—

you would not offend us by the deduction that, after all, in consequence of such trifles, women's trifles

> Churches rise—God's holy churches—
> On the face of our land.

And even though Vlas is wandering with his sack, out of mere "foolishness," still you did grasp the gravity of his suffering; still, you did become impressed with his stately figure. (Of course, you are a poet; it could not have been otherwise.)

> His whole soul's enormous power
> On a godly task was spent.

—you say beautifully. However, I wish to believe that you have inserted your sarcasm unwittingly, for fear of the liberals, since this awful, even intimidating, power of Vlas's humility; this craving for self-salvation; this burning thirst for suffering—have also struck you, a cosmopolitan and a Russian *gentilhomme,* and the stately popular image wrought enthusiasm and respect from your highly liberal soul!

> All that Vlas had owned and treasured
> He forsook, and barefoot, bare,
> He went forth, in footfall measured,
> To collect God's churches' share.
> Ever since he roams and wanders—
> Soon it will be thirty years—
> And he lives on alms, and ponders
> O'er his vow which he endears.
>
> .   .   .   .
>
> Full of deep, despairing sorrow,
> *Swarthy-faced, erect and tall,*

(This is wonderfully beautiful!)

> Paces he from day to morrow
> In the heat and rainy fall.
>
> .   .   .   .

With his book for church collection
Paces Vlas through woods and plains,
And he bears for soul's perfection
On his body iron chains.

Wonderful, wonderful! So wonderful that it seems it was not you who wrote this; it seems that not you but somebody else in your stead has later been playing antics "on the Volga"—also, in superb verses—about the haulers' songs. Perhaps, you did not play antics "on the Volga," maybe just a little; on the Volga, too, you loved in the hauler the universal man, and you suffered for him, that is, strictly speaking, not for the hauler but, so to speak, for the universal hauler. You see, to love the universal man necessarily means to despise, and, at times, to hate the real man standing at your side.

Intentionally I emphasized the immeasurably beautiful verses in this burlesque poem (taking it as a whole—if you will pardon me).

The reason why I recalled this poetical Vlas is that a few days ago I heard a most fantastic story about another Vlas, even about two hitherto unheard-of Vlases. The episode is a real one, and is certainly remarkable by reason of its strangeness.

There are in monasteries in Russia, it is said, ascetics, monks-confessors and light-bearers. Whether this is good or bad; whether such monks are or are not needed, I shall not discuss at this moment; nor did I take up my pen for this purpose.

However, since we are living in a given reality, it is impossible to eject from the story even a monk, if the story itself is based on him. These monks, light-bearers, are at times, it would seem, endowed with great intellect and erudition. At least, so they are described, although I know nothing about it. It is recounted that among them there are such as possess a wonderful gift for penetrating the human soul and mastering it. Several such men, it is said, are known to the whole of Russia, that is, substantially, to those whom this concerns. Let us suppose that such an elder lives in the Kherson province, and yet the people journey to him, sometimes even on foot, from Petersburg or Archangel, from Siberia or the Caucasus. Of course, they go with souls crushed by despair, souls which no longer hope for recovery, or with such a terrible burden at heart that the sinner refrains from speaking about it to his priest-confessor—not from fear or distrust, but simply because he absolutely despairs of his salvation. But if he happens to hear about any such monk, light-bearer, he will go to him.

"You know"—said one of these elders, in a friendly, face-to-face conversation with a certain listener—"I have been listening to people for twenty years and, believe me, I have learned—oh, how much—about the most hidden and complex ailments of the human soul; but even after twenty years sometimes I begin to shiver with indignation when listening to certain secrets. I lose the calmness of the spirit which is needed for giving consolation and, instead, I feel compelled to fortify myself in humility and serenity."

At this point he told me the strange story taken from popular life, which I mentioned above.

"I see there, creeping into my room, a peasant on his knees. I had seen him before out of my window, creeping on the ground. His first words to me were:

" 'There's no salvation for me. I'm damned! And whatever you may say—all the same, I'm damned.'

"Somehow I managed to calm him. I could see that the man had crawled from afar, after suffering.

" 'Several of us lads got together in the village'—thus he started —'and we began to bet: which one of us would outdo the others in some temerarious deed? Because of pride, I challenged the rest. A lad took me aside, and said to me, face-to-face:

" ' "It is impossible for you to do what you are telling. You're boasting."

" 'I began to swear to him.

" ' "No, wait, swear"—says he—"by your salvation in the other world that you will do exactly as I tell you."

" 'I swore.

" ' "Soon we'll have Lent,"—he says—"start fasting. When you go to Holy Communion—accept the Eucharist, but do not swallow it. Step aside—take it out with your hand and preserve it. And later I will tell you what to do."

" 'I did as he told me. Straight from the church he led me into a kitchen garden. He took a rod, thrust it into the earth and said: "Put it!" I put the Eucharist on the rod.

" ' "Now"—says he—"bring a gun."

" 'I brought it.

" ' "Load it."

" 'I loaded it.

" ' "Lift it and shoot."

" 'I lifted my hand and started aiming. And just as I was about to fire the shot, suddenly there appeared before me a cross, and on the cross—our Savior. I fell down with the gun and became unconscious.' "

This had occurred several years before he came to the old monk. Who this Vlas was, whence was he, and what his name was

—the elder, of course, did not disclose; nor did he divulge what penitence he had conferred upon him. Probably, he had burdened the soul with some dreadful load, which human strength could not have borne, on the theory that the heavier—the better: "He himself had crept after suffering."

Isn't this a rather characteristic episode, hinting at many things, so that, perhaps, it is worthy of special—though, two or three minutes'—scrutiny. I am still of the opinion that theirs will be the last word—I mean, these different "Vlases," the repenting and non-repenting ones; they will show us the new path and the new solution to all our seemingly insoluble difficulties. Certainly, it will not be Petersburg that will finally settle the Russian destiny. For this reason, every slightest *new* trait characterizing these "new people" may be worthy of our attention.

To begin with, I am puzzled—indeed, this is the most surprising point—over the very inception of the affair, that is, over the very possibility of such an argument and contention in a Russian village: "Who will outdo the others in some temerarious deed?" This is a fact hinting at a good many things and, to me, it is almost wholly surprising—even though I have met many and most queer people. I may add that the seeming singularity of this fact is, however, proof of its authenticity: when people lie they will invent something much more common and conforming to conventional things, so that everybody might believe it.

Further, the strictly medical aspect of the facts is remarkable. Hallucination is pre-eminently a pathological phenomenon; it is a very rare malady. The possibility of sudden hallucination, even in a very excited, yet fully normal, individual, is perhaps an unheard-of case. But this is a medical problem, and I am not much versed in it.

The psychological aspect of the facts is a different matter. Here we have two popular types, in the highest degree characteristic of the Russian people as a whole. First of all—the oblivion of every measure in everything (and note, almost always, a temporary and passing oblivion constituting, as it were, a hypnotic phenomenon).

This is an urge for the extreme, for the fainting sensation of approaching an abyss, and half-leaning over it—to peep into the bottomless pit, and, in some very rare cases, to throw oneself into it head-forward as in a frenzy.

This is an urge for negation in a man, sometimes, most believing and venerating—negation of everything, of the most sacred thing in one's heart, of one's loftiest ideal in its totality, which only a moment before one had worshipped, but which, all of a sudden, had seemingly become an almost unbearable burden.

Particularly remarkable is that haste, that impetuosity, with which the Russian hurries to reveal himself in certain significant moments of his own or the nation's life—to reveal himself whether it be in good or in evil. Sometimes here there is simply no restraint. Be it love, or liquor, debauch, egotism, envy—in all these some Russians will give themselves away, heart and soul; they are ready to sever with everything, to forswear everything—family, customs, God.

The kindest man, suddenly, may somehow turn into a most wicked debauchee and criminal—simply because he is caught into this whirl, into the fatal tornado of convulsive and momentary self-negation and self-annihilation, which is so typical of the Russian national character in certain crucial moments of his life.

As against this, the individual Russian, as well as the people as a whole, with equal force and impetuosity, with equal thirst for self-preservation and repentance, save themselves, usually, when they have reached the utmost limit, that is, when there is already nowhere to go. But it is most significant that the back-stroke, the shock of restoration and self-salvation, is invariably more serious than the former impulse of negation and self-destruction. This means that the latter impulse is to be credited to petty pusillanimity, whereas the Russian invests in his restoration an enormous and solemn effort, regarding the former negative motion with contempt for himself.

I believe that the main and most fundamental spiritual quest of the Russian people is their craving for suffering—perpetual and unquenchable suffering—everywhere and in everything. It seems that they have been affected by this thirst for martyrdom from time immemorial. The suffering stream flows through their whole history —not merely because of external calamities and misfortunes: it gushes from the people's very heart.

Even in happiness there is in the Russian people an element of suffering; otherwise, felicity to them is incomplete. Never, not even in the most solemn hours of their history, do they assume an uppish and pompous air; there is an air of tenderness bordering on suffering; they are heaving sighs attributing their glory to God's mercy. The Russian people, as it were, delight in their afflictions. And that which is true of the people as a whole is also characteristic of individual types—of course, generally speaking.

For example, look at the manifold patterns of the Russian debauchee: here we have not merely excessive debauch, sometimes astounding us by the boldness of its scale and the abomination of corruption of the human soul. That debauchee, to begin with, is a sufferer himself. In the Russian, even if he be a fool, there is no trace of naïve and pompous self-sufficiency.

Take a Russian drunkard and compare him, let us say, with a German drunkard: the Russian is more abominable than the German; still, the German drunkard is unmistakably more stupid and ridiculous than the Russian. The Germans are pre-eminently a self-conceited people; they are proud of themselves. In a drunken German these fundamental national traits increase with the measure of beer consumed. He gets home drunk as a fiddler, and yet proud of himself. The Russian toper likes to drink from grief, and to weep. And even while he assumes bold airs, he does not triumph, but is merely turbulent. Invariably, he will recall some offense and will start reproaching the offender, whether or not he be present. Insolently, he will, perhaps, argue that he is something next to a general; he swears bitterly and, if people refuse to believe him, he will finally sound an alarm and cry out for help. Still, the reason why he is so ugly and why he cries out for help is that, in the innermost part of his tipsy soul, he is unquestionably convinced that he is no "general" at all, but merely a nasty sot, and that he has become filthier than a beast.

The thing which we perceive from a microscopic example is also true in larger instances. The biggest debauchee, one who is even attractive by his temerity and elegant vices, so that fools seek to imitate him, nevertheless scents through some instinct—in the innermost of his perverted soul—that, in the last analysis, he is nothing but a scoundrel. He is not pleased with himself; there grows a reproof in his heart, and so he takes vengeance on those around him; he rages and assails everybody, and at this juncture he reaches his limit, struggling against his affliction which steadily accumulates in his heart and, at the same time, delightedly slakes his thirst with that suffering. If he is capable of rising from his degradation, he cruelly avenges himself for his past wickedness, even more harshly than he had been avenging others in the turmoil of the debauch, for his secret torment resulting from his dissatisfaction with himself.

Who provoked both lads to the argument: "which one of us will outdo the others in some temerarious act?"—and what has caused the possibility itself of such a rivalry remains unknown; but it is certain that both were suffering: one—by accepting the challenge, and the other—by proffering it. No doubt, here there were some preliminaries: either a hidden hatred between them, or a hate dating back to childhood, which they themselves had never suspected and which burst forth in the course of the argument or at the moment of the challenge. The latter seems more likely: probably, they had been friends up to that minute, living in accord which, the longer it lasted, was becoming more and more unbearable. However, by the time of the challenge the tension of mutual hate and envy of the victim toward his Mephistopheles had become quite extraordinary.

"I will be afraid of nothing; I shall do whatever you may suggest. Let the soul perish, but I will disgrace you!"

"You're boasting! You'll run as a mouse into a cellar. I'll humble you. Let the soul perish."

For the contest something different might have been chosen, something very bold—robbery, murder, open rebellion against a man of power. Didn't the lad swear that he would dare anything, and his seducer knew that this time it was meant seriously, and that he would, indeed, go to the limit?

No. The most dreadful "boldness" seems to the seducer too commonplace. He invents an unheard-of challenge, one that had never been known before, incredible, while its selection reflects the people's whole philosophy.

Incredible? Yet, the fact itself that he had selected it shows that, perhaps, he had already pondered over it. Long ago, maybe in childhood, the fancy had crept into his soul, shook it by its horror and, at the same time, by its torturous delight. That everything had been invented long ago—the gun, the vegetable garden— and that he had kept it in solemn secrecy, can hardly be doubted. Of course, he had invented this not for the purpose of perpetrating it; besides, alone, he would probably not have dared to perpetrate the thing. Simply, he liked this vision; now and then it pierced his soul; it lured him, and he would be timidly retreating, growing cold from horror. But one single moment of such unheard-of audacity —and after that let everything perish! And most certainly, he believed that he would be punished for this by eternal perdition. But— "Anyhow, I did reach such a height!"

Much may be not conceived, but merely felt. Much may be grasped unconsciously. But, truly, isn't this a curious soul—especially, in such a milieu? Herein lies the whole matter. It would be nice to find out whether or not he felt more guilty than his victim.— Judging by his apparent mental development, one is inclined to think that he considered himself more, or, at least, equally guilty, that when challenging his victim to a "bold act," he was also challenging himself.

It is said that the Russian people know the Gospel poorly, that they are ignorant of the fundamental principles of faith. Of course, this is true, but they do know Christ, and they have been carrying Him in their hearts from time immemorial. Of this there can be no doubt. How is the true conception of Christ possible without religious teaching?—This is a different question. But the heart-knowledge of Christ, a true conception of Him, does fully exist. It is being passed from generation to generation, and it has merged with the heart of the people. Perhaps, Christ is the only love of the Russian people, and they love His image in their own way, to the limit of sufferance.

And,, more than on anything else, the people pride themselves on the name "orthodox," that is, as confessing Christ more genuinely than all others. I repeat, much may be known unconsciously.

Now, to scoff at such a popular sanctity; thereby to tear oneself from the whole land; to destroy oneself forever and ever by negation and pride, for the sake of one brief moment of triumph—this is the most daring thing a Russian Mephistopheles could have possibly conceived! The possibility of such a tension of passion, of such sinister and complex sentiments in the soul of a commoner, is really astounding! And note—all this reached the stage of an almost conscious idea.

However, the victim does not shrink, is not humbled and is not intimidated. At least, he pretends that he is not scared. The lad accepts the challenge. Days pass by, but he clings to his position. Presently, it is not the vision but the deed itself that comes true; he goes to church; he hears daily the words of Christ, but he insists on his own.

There are horrible murderers who do not shrink even at the sight of the victim slain by them. One such murderer, an obvious murderer, caught on the spot, refused to confess and, to the very end, continued to lie to the examining magistrate. When the latter got up and ordered the man to be conducted to prison, the culprit, with an imploring air, asked as a favor to be permitted to bid farewell to the murdered who lay right there (his former sweetheart whom he had slain from jealousy). He stooped down, kissed her tenderly; broke into tears and, without rising from his knees, stretching his hand over her, again reiterated that he was not guilty. I only wish to note the bestial degree which insensibility may reach in man.

Here, however, it is not insensibility at all. We have here, in addition, something altogether peculiar—a mystical horror which exercises an enormous power over the human soul. Unquestionably it was present, at least judging by the denouement of the affair. The lad's vigorous soul was able to enter into a contest with this horror; he proved it. But is it strength or the ultimate degree of cowardice?—Possibly, this and that combined in the contiguity of the extremes. Nevertheless, this mystical awe not only did not put an end to the struggle but it even prolonged it; and, no doubt, that feeling of awe helped to bring the contest to an end precisely

by the fact that it took out of the sinner's heart every sentiment
of touching emotion; the more strongly the latter had been suppressed, the more impossible it became. The sensation of horror
is a harsh sentiment; it dries and hardens the heart, rendering it
inaccessible to any kindness and lofty emotion. This is why the
sinner did endure the moment before the cup, even though, perhaps,
benumbed and overpowered by fear.

I believe that mutual hate between the victim and his torturer
must have disappeared altogether. In fits the tortured may have
hated with pathological anger, himself, those around him, worshippers
in the church, but least of all his Mephistopheles. Both felt that
they mutually needed each other in order to finish the undertaking
jointly. Each of them, no doubt, felt impotent to terminate it alone.
Why, then, did they pursue the venture? Why did they assume so
much torture?—Strictly speaking, they could not have broken the
alliance. Had their agreement been breached, mutual hate—ten times
more intense than heretofore—would have immediately flared up,
and would have unfailingly resulted in murder: the tortured would
have killed his torturer.

Be this as it may. Even this would have been nothing compared with the terror endured by the victim. The main point is
that here there must have been in both of them, in the depth of
their souls, some diabolical delight in their own perdition, the
fascinating urge to bend over the abyss and to peep into it, the
heart-thrilling ecstasy over their own daring. It is virtually impossible that the matter could have been brought to an end without
these exciting and passionate emotions. Certainly, these were not
merely mischief-makers, or dull and stupid rogues—with that whole
range of events, beginning with the "boldness contest" and cul-
minating in the despair before the elder-monk.

And note also that the seducer did not reveal his whole secret
to his victim: when leaving the church, he knew not what he was
to do with the Sacrament, up to the very moment when he was
ordered to bring the gun. So many days of mystical incertitude,
again, goes to prove the terrible obstinacy of the sinner. On the
other hand, the village Mephisto, too, appears as a great psychologist.

But, perhaps, when they arrived in the kitchen-garden, they
were already insensible?—Still, the lad did remember how he had
loaded the gun and pointed it. Maybe, even though retaining full
memory, he acted automatically, as, indeed, happens sometimes in
a state of horror?—I don't think so: if he were reduced to a plain
machine, continuing its functioning by mere inertia, certainly, later,
he would not have beheld the vision; he would simply have fallen

down unconscious after having exhausted the whole supply of energy —and not *prior* to but after the shot.

No, most probably, consciousness had been retained all the time with extraordinary lucidity, notwithstanding the deadly horror progressively growing every second. And the mere fact that the victim had endured such a pressure of progressively increasing terror, I repeat, shows that he was unquestionably endowed with an enormous spiritual power.

Let us note that the loading of the gun is an operation requiring at any rate certain attention. In a moment such as this, the most difficult and unbearable thing is to detach oneself from one's own horror, from the oppressive idea. Usually, individuals stricken by terror are no longer capable of abstaining from its contemplation, from the object or idea which dumbfounded them: they stand facing it straight in the eyes, as if bewitched. But the lad had attentively loaded the gun; this he remembers. He also remembered how, after that, he began pointing it; he remembered everything, up to the last moment.

It may have been that the process of loading proved to him a relief, a way out, to his agonizing soul, and he was glad to concentrate—if only for a second—his attention on some external object. This happens on the guillotine to him whose head is being chopped off. Dubarry cried to the executioner: *"Encore un moment, monsieur le bourreau, encore un moment!"* She would have endured twenty times more during that minute of grace, had it been granted her, but, even so, she did cry out and entreat for this minute. But if it be supposed that, to our sinner, the loading of the gun was something akin to Dubarry's *"encore un moment,"* certainly, after that, he could not have again turned to his horror, from which he had detached himself, and continued the business by pointing and firing the shot. At this juncture his hands would have grown numb and would have refused to obey him, notwithstanding even the retained consciousness and will power.

And now, at the very last moment, the whole deceit, the whole abomination of the deed, the whole cowardice taken as a sign of strength, the whole shame of the debacle—all this suddenly, in a moment, burst forth from his heart, and rose before him as a menacing indictment. The incredible vision appeared to him . . . everything was finished.

Of course, the judgment thundered out of his heart. Why did it thunder not consciously, not in the form of a momentary clearing of reason and conscience? Why did it reveal itself in a vision, as if in an altogether external fact, independent of the spirit?—Therein

lies the immense psychological problem and the act of God. Vlas
became a beggar and demanded suffering.

And what about the other Vlas?—The remaining one, the
seducer?—The legend does not tell us that he had crept after repentance; it makes no mention of him. Maybe, he, too, had crept;
and, maybe, he stayed on in the village and lives there up to the
present day, keeps on drinking and tittering on holidays: indeed,
it was not he who had beheld the vision. Is this so, however?—It
would be most desirable to learn about his story—just for the sake
of information, for the record.

Here is why this also would be desirable: what if he is a
genuine village nihilist, a home-baked negator and thinker, an un-
believer, who had selected the object of the contest with a haughty
smirk; one who did not suffer, who did not quiver along with his
victim, as we have suggested in our sketch, but who had been
observing with cold curiosity its palpitations and convulsions, out
of mere craving for another man's suffering, human humiliation—
devil knows, perhaps—as a matter of scientific survey?

Even if such traits be present in the character of the people—
(in our day everything may be presumed)—and, on top of that,
in our villages—this would be a new and, moreover, unexpected
revelation. Somehow, such traits were never heard of before. The
seducer in Mr. Ostrovsky's excellent comedy *Don't Live as Thou
Willst* is portrayed pretty poorly.—It is a pity that nothing can be
positively ascertained.

It goes without saying that the interest of the story told here
—if there be an interest in it—lies in the fact that it is a true story.
It is not unnecessary to peep, from time to time, into the soul of
the contemporary Vlas. He changes quickly. There, below, he has
the same vision as we have it on the top, ever since February 19.
The giant woke from his sleep and is stretching out his limbs:
perhaps he will wish to start revelling, to transgress all limits. It
is rumored that he did already go merry-making. Dreadful things
are being told and published: drunkenness, banditry, intoxicated
children, drunken mothers, cynicism, destitution, dishonesty, god-
lessness. Some serious-minded, but somewhat too hasty, people contend, basing themselves on facts, that should such "merry-making"
last even another ten years, the consequences, from the economic
standpoint alone, would be inconceivable. But let us recall "Vlas"
and be appeased: the whole conceit, if there be conceit, will spring
out of the people's heart and rise before it with an incredible power
of indictment. Vlas will come to his senses and will take up God's
labours. At any rate he will save himself, should things really turn
into a calamity. He will save himself and us, since—I repeat once

more—light and salvation will come from below (in a form, perhaps, altogether surprising to our liberals, and in this there will be a great deal of comedy). There are hints as to this surprise, and even now we have some facts to this effect. . . . However, this may be discussed at some future time. Be that as it may, our insolvency as "fledgelings of Peter's nest" is at present beyond doubt. Besides, after February 19, strictly speaking, the Peter period of Russian history came to an end, so that long ago we commenced to dwell in total obscurity.

The Citizen, 1873, No. 4.

BOBOK: NOTES OF A CERTAIN MAN

This time I am publishing "Notes of a Certain Man." It is not me; it is an altogether different person. I believe that no further introduction is needed.

The day before yesterday Semen Ardalionovich asked me:
"Ivan Ivanovich, tell me, for God's mercy, will you ever be sober?"

What a strange demand! I am taking no offence; I am a timid man; even so, I was declared insane. An artist, by mere accident, painted my portrait: "Anyhow," said he, "you are a writer." I gave my consent, and he exhibited the portrait. I read: "Go and look at this ailing face which borders on insanity."

Let it be so; nevertheless, why should it be heralded in the press? The press should print nothing but noble things; it should be propagating ideals, and, yet, look. . . .

At least, they should have stated it indirectly; style exists just for this purpose. But no; they don't want to put it indirectly. Nowadays humor and elegant style are disappearing, while abuse is accepted for witticism. I'm taking no offence: God knows, I'm not too prominent a writer to go mad. I wrote a novel—they refused to print it. I wrote a feuilleton—it was turned down. I peddled a lot of these feuilletons from one editorial office to another; but, everywhere, they shook their heads: "You're lacking salt"—they say.

"What kind of salt do you expect?"—I asked them sarcastically—"Attic salt, perchance?"

They don't even understand. Mostly I'm translating from the French for bookdealers. I'm also penning ads for merchants: "Rarity! Red tea, so to speak, coming from our plantations." . . . I got a big wad for a panegyric of his excellency, the late Pëtr

Matveievich. For a book-dealer I composed *The Art of Pleasing the Ladies*. Of such books, I wrote about half a dozen during my life. I'm planning to compile Voltaire's *bons mots,* but I'm afraid our folks will find them stale. What's Voltaire today?—Nowadays it's a cudgel, and not Voltaire! They knock each other out to the last tooth!

Such, briefly, is my literary record. In addition, over my full signature, I am gratuitously mailing letters to editorial offices. I keep sending admonitions and advices. I am criticizing and pointing out the right way. Last week I sent the fortieth letter, over a period of two years, to one of the editorial offices: on postage alone I have spent four rubles. I have a bad disposition—that's the thing.

I believe that the artist painted my portrait not because of my literature, but on account of my two warts growing symmetrically on my forehead: it's a phenomenon, so to speak. Lacking an idea, they try to make phenomena work for them. But how beautifully the warts came out on the portrait—they are alive! They call it realism.

As to madness, last year many were recorded as lunatics. And what a style was used: "Notwithstanding such a, so to speak, original talent . . . what an end. . . . However, this was to be anticipated long ago. . . ." This is rather smart; so that, from the point of view of pure art, perhaps, it deserves commendation. But, unexpectedly, they came back even more clever. Now, that's the point: we drive people mad, but as yet no one has ever been made more clever.

He, I take it, is the most intelligent who at least once a month calls himself a fool—in our day this is an unheard-of faculty! In the past, the fool, at least once a year, would recognize the fact that he is a fool; but today—nothing doing. And they mixed things up to such a degree that it is impossible to distinguish a fool from a clever man. This they did on purpose.

I recall a Spanish witticism about the French who, two and a half centuries ago, had constructed in France the first insane asylum: "They locked up their fools in a special building to convince people that they themselves were wise men." Indeed: by locking up the other fellow in a madhouse one can't prove one's own intelligence. "K. went mad, so it means that now we are clever." No, it means nothing of the kind. . . .

But, what the deuce! . . . Why am I fussing about my mind: I'm grumbling and grumbling. Even my maid-servant is tired of me. Yesterday a friend dropped in. "Your style," he said, "is changing; it's choppy. You're chopping and chopping—then you squeeze in an incidental proposition, and you add to it another incidental proposition; after that you will insert something in brackets, and again you start chopping and chopping. . . ."

My friend is right. Something strange is transpiring in me. My disposition is changing, and I have headaches. I begin to see and hear some strange things—not exactly voices, but as if someone beside me keeps whispering: "bobok, bobok, bobok."

Who, the deuce, is bobok?—I should divert myself.

I went out to divert myself, and ran into a funeral. A distant relative. However, a collegiate councilor. A widow, five daughters—all maidens. Think, what shoes alone must cost! The deceased had been earning, but now there is only a miserable pension. They'll have to cut down. They always received me inhospitably. Even now I would not have gone, were it not for an emergency case. Among others, I accompanied the procession to the cemetery. They shunned me and behaved haughtily. True, my uniform is a bit shabby. I believe I haven't been to a cemetery for almost twenty-five years. What a spot!

To begin with—the atmosphere! Some fifteen corpses arrived together. Palls differently priced. There were even two catafalques—one for a general, and the other one—for some lady. Many sad faces and much simulated grief; also much candid joy. The clergy shouldn't be complaining: income. But the atmosphere! The atmosphere!—I wouldn't like to be a clergyman there.

I peeped cautiously at the faces of the dead, not relying on my nerves. Some expressions are tender, but some are disagreeable. Speaking generally, the smiles are unpleasant—on some faces, very much so. I don't like them. I'm dreaming of them.

After the Mass I went out of the church into the open air. The day was grayish but dry. It was cold, too. Well, of course, it's October. I roamed around the graves. Different grades. The third grade costs thirty rubles: it's fitting and not so expensive. The first two grades are given space in the church under the porch. But this is too dear. On that occasion some six persons, including the general and the lady, were buried in the third grade.

I peeped into the graves—horrible! Water—and what water! Quite green and . . . Well, what is there to say? Every minute the grave-digger bailed it out with a scoop. While the service was being officiated, I went to roam outside the gate. There, in the immediate vicinity, is an almshouse, and a little further—a restaurant. Not a bad little restaurant: one can take a bite, and so forth. It was crowded; among others, there were quite a few of those attending the funerals. I noticed much hilarity and genuine animation. I ate and had a drink.

Thereupon, I participated in carrying, with my own hands, the coffin from the church to the grave. Why do the dead grow so heavy in the coffin?—It is said that this is due to some inertia, that the body somehow does not control itself . . . or some such nonsense: this contradicts mechanics and common sense. I don't like it when people with merely a general education venture to pass judgment on special problems and, with us, it is a common habit. Civilians are eager to deliberate on military, and even field-marshal, subjects, while men with engineering education pass judgment mostly on philosophy and political economy.

I didn't go to the requiem. I have my pride, and if I am being received merely because of urgent necessity, why should I drag myself to their dinners, even though these be funeral dinners?—I seated myself on a tombstone and started musing respectfully.

I began with the Moscow exhibition, and finished with the subject of surprise—generally speaking, of surprise as a topic. This is what I reasoned about "surprise."

"To be surprised at everything is foolish, of course. But to be surprised at nothing is much prettier and is, for some reason, considered bon ton. I doubt, however, that this is so. In my opinion, to be surprised at nothing is far more foolish than to be surprised at everything. Besides, to be surprised at nothing is almost the same as to respect nothing. And a stupid man is incapable of respect."

Yes, above all, I wish to respect. "I'm *thirsting* for respect" —an acquaintance of mine told me the other day.

He thirsts for respect! By God—I thought—what would happen to you if, at present, you only dared to put this in print.

At this point I forgot myself. I don't like to read epitaphs. On a slab near me lay a half-eaten sandwich—stupid and out of place. I threw it off onto the ground, since this is not bread but merely a sandwich. However, it seems that there's no sin in letting crumbs fall on the ground; it is a sin, though, to let them fall on the floor. I must check it in Suvorin's almanac.

I presume that I'd been sitting for a long while, much too long. I even laid myself down on an elongated stone in the shape of a marble sepulcher. And how did it happen that I started hearing all sorts of things? At first, I paid no attention, assuming a contemptuous attitude. Still, the conversations continued. I hear—the sounds are dull, as if the mouths are covered up with pillows; and at that—they are audible and seem quite close. I woke up and began listening intently.

"Your excellency, this is absolutely impossible. You declared hearts; I led hearts, and all of a sudden—you have a slam in diamonds. You should have declared diamonds in the first place."

"What of it—should one be playing by heart? Where would be the attraction?"

"Your excellency, it's impossible wthout a guaranty. One has to play with a dummy, and the deal must be blind."

"Why, a dummy can't be gotten here."

Indeed, what arrogant words! It's strange and even unexpected. One—such a weighty and solid voice; and the other one—as if softly sweetened. I shouldn't have believed it had I not heard it myself. It seems, I have not attended the requiem. And still, how does it happen that there is a game of preference, and also a general? That the sounds came from down under, in the graves, there couldn't be a shadow of doubt. I bent down and read the inscription on the tomb.

"Here lies the body of Major-general Pervoiedov . . . knight of such and such orders." Hm! "Died in the month of August of this year. . . . Lie in rest, dear body, till the glad morn!"

Hm! devil, a general indeed! On the other grave, whence the adulating voice sounded, as yet there stood no monument; there was but a cut stone. Probably one of the novices. Judging by the voice—a court-councilor.

"Oh, oh, oh!" sounded a wholly new voice, some five sajen from the general's place, from under a quite fresh little grave—a masculine, plebeian voice, but an enfeebled and reverently tender one.

"Oh, oh, oh!"

"Ah, he is hiccoughing again!"—came suddenly the squeamish and haughty voice of an irritated lady, seemingly of the *beau monde*. —"It's a curse to be near the shopkeeper!"

"I didn't hiccough at all, nor did I taste food: this is merely my nature. Lady, you still can't get over those local caprices of yours."

"Then why did you lie down here?"

"I was laid down, laid by my spouse and little children—I did not lie down of my own accord. Mystery of death! Nor would I have lain down next to you—not for any amount of gold—but I repose here according to my means—that is, judging by the price. This we can always afford to pay for our burial place, of the third grade."

"He hoarded money! He cheated the people!"

"Not easy to cheat you: since January, I gather, we've never received payment. The bill debiting you is available in the shop."

"Now, this is stupid! It is quite silly, in my judgment, to collect debts down here! Go upstairs. Sue my niece. She's the heiress."

"Where can one go? And what's the use of suing now?—We both have reached the limit, and before God's judgment we are equal in our sins!"

"In our sins"—contemptuously mocked the deceased lady.—"And don't you dare speak to me!"

"Oh, oh, oh!"

"The shopkeeper, however, obeys the lady, your excellency."

"Why shouldn't he obey?"

"Of course, your excellency, because here it is a new order."

"What's that new order?"

"But, your excellency, we've died, so to speak."

"Oh, yes! Still, as to the order . . ."

What is one to say?—I'm obliged and cheered! If, down there, things have reached this point, what can we expect on the upper floor? But what tricks! Yet, I continued to listen, even though with utmost indignation.

"No, I'd be willing to live a little longer! Yes, indeed, I would"—unexpectedly sounded somebody's voice—a new one, somewhere in the space between the general and the waspish lady.

"Do you hear, your excellency?—Our man is at it again. He keeps silent for three long days and suddenly: 'I'd be willing to live a little longer!' And so relishingly, hee-hee!"

"And light-mindedly."

"He's thrilled, your excellency. And you know, he's falling asleep, he's almost asleep. He's been here ever since April, and all of a sudden—'I'd be willing to live!'"

"It's a bit boring, however"—remarked his excellency.

"It is a bit boring, your excellency. Why not start teasing Avdotia Ignatievna again?"

"No, I beg to be relieved. I just hate this snarlish female."

"And I, on the contrary, hate both of you," squeamishly declared the female. "You two are most boring, and you are unable to relate anything idealistic. About you, your excellency—pray, don't be conceited—I know a little story: how the lackey swept you out with his broom from under one conjugal bed."

"A bad woman!"—muttered the general through his teeth.

"Avdotia Ignatievna, dear"—again suddenly shouted the shopkeeper—"dear little lady, tell me, forgetting your grudge, why do I have to pass through all sorts of trials, or is something else . . .?"

"Ah, he's at it again. I had a presentiment, because I scented his spirit—yes, his spirit: it is he who tosses around!"

"I'm not tossing, dear lady; nor do I exhale any particular smell, since I have fully conserved my body; but you, little lady, you're beginning to taint—since your odor is unbearable, even as far as this place goes. I keep silent out of mere politeness."

"Oh, wicked insulter! He himself smells dreadfully, and yet he accuses me!"

"Oh, oh, oh! But that our fortieth day might come sooner: I can hear above me their tearful voices—my wife's shrieks and my children's gentle lamentation."

"Pooh! What's he wailing about?—They'll stuff their stomachs with boiled rice and raisins, and off they'll go. Oh, if only anyone should wake up!"

"Avdotia Ignatievna"—suggested the flattering bureaucrat—"wait a little while, and the newcomers will start speaking."

"Are there any young men among them?"

"There are young ones, too, Avdotia Ignatievna. There are even youths."

"Oh, that wouldn't be bad at all!"

"Haven't they started yet?" inquired his excellency.

"No, even those of the day before yesterday haven't come to their senses: you yourself know that sometimes they remain mute during a whole week. It's good that yesterday, the day before that and today, somehow, they were brought in all together; because around here, some ten sajen around, they're almost all of the past year."

"Yes, that's interesting."

"Today, your excellency, Privy Councilor Tarasevich was buried. I found this out through the voices. I am acquainted with his nephew; recently he helped me to take down the casket."

"Hm—where is he?"

"Some five steps from you, your excellency—to the left. Almost at your feet. Why not strike up an acquaintance with him, your excellency?"

"Hm, no—why should I take the initiative?"

"No, that's right, your excellency. He'll take the lead. He'll even be flattered. Leave it to me, your excellency, and I . . ."

"Oh! . . . Oh! What has come to me?"—suddenly groaned some new frightened thin voice.

"A new one, your excellency—a new one, praised be the Lord; and how soon! At times, they stay mute for a week!"

"Ah! Seems to be a young man!"—shrieked Avdotia Ignatievna.

"I . . . I . . . I . . . because of a complication, and so suddenly"—the youth started lisping again. "Only yesterday Schultz warned me: 'You have a complication,' he said. And, suddenly, before morning I passed away. Ah! . . . Ah!"

"Well, there's nothing to be done, young man"—graciously remarked the general, obviously welcoming the novice. "One must get over it. You are welcome to our valley of Josabad. We're kind folks. You'll get to know and value us.—Major General Vasily Vasiliev Pervoiedov—at your service."

"Oh, no! No!—Is it me? I am at Schultz's. I had, you know, a complication: first, the chest became affected and a cough set in; and then I contracted a cold; the chest and a grippe . . . and then, quite suddenly . . . the main thing—quite unexpectedly."

"You say: first, the chest"—mildly intervened the bureaucrat, as if seeking to enhearten the novice.

"Yes, the chest—and mucus. And then, suddenly—no more mucus . . . the chest, and I can't breathe . . . you know . . ."

"I know. I know. But if it's the chest, you should have seen Eck, and not Schultz."

"And, you know, I was thinking of going to Botkin . . . and suddenly . . ."

"But Botkin bites"—observed the general.

"Not in the least—he never bites: I was told: he is so attentive, and tells you everything in advance."

"His excellency referred to the fee"—corrected the bureaucrat.

"What do you mean?—Only three rubles, and he examines so thoroughly, and the prescription . . . why, I meant to go by all means, because I was told . . . Now, gentlemen, should I try Eck or Botkin?"

"What? Whom?"—the general's corpse, pleasantly laughing, began to rock. The bureaucrat seconded him in falsetto.

"Sweet boy, sweet, joyous boy, how I love you!"—enthusiastically screamed Avdotia Ignatievna. "If only such a one were laid beside me!"

No, I will not tolerate a thing of this sort! And this is a contemporary dead person! However, I shall listen a little more without jumping to conclusions. This snotty novice—I remember him in the coffin—with the expression of a scared chick, the most disgusting expression in the world! However, what's next?

But after that there ensued such a jumble that I did not retain everything in my mind, since quite a lot of them woke up all together: a bureaucrat, a state councilor, woke up, and forthwith he began to converse with the general on the project of a new subcommittee in the Ministry of ———— affairs, and on the probable shifts of the functionaries, as a result of the appointment of the subcommittee. To the general this was quite a diversion. I confess, I, too, gathered much information, and I even started pondering over the ways through which one may be tipped off to administrative news in this capital of ours. Then, a certain engineer —he was but half-awake—mumbled protractedly all sorts of nonsense, so that our folks did not press him, leaving him to rest awhile. Finally, the prominent lady who, in the morning, had been given a burial under the catafalque, began to reveal symptoms of sepulchral animation. Lebeziatnikov (for such proved to be the name of the hated flattering court-councilor quartered next to General Pervoiedov) grew restless and kept wondering why this time everyone is waking up so soon. I confess—I, too, was puzzled. True: some of those who woke up had been buried the day before yesterday: for instance, quite a young girl, say, of sixteen, who kept giggling . . . giggling abominably and carnivorously.

"Your excellency, Privy Councilor Tarasevich is about to wake up!"—suddenly announced Lebeziatnikov with extraordinary haste.

"Eh? What?"—squeamishly and in a hissing voice mumbled the suddenly awaking privy councilor. In the sound of his voice there was something capriciously commanding. I was listening with curiosity because lately I had heard something about this Tarasevich —something seductive and extremely disturbing.

"It's me, your excellency; as yet, it's only me."

"What are you soliciting and what do you want?"

"Solely to inquire about your excellency's health. For lack of habit, everyone here feels cooped up at first, as it were. . . . General Pervoiedov would like to be granted the honor of being introduced to your excellency, and he hopes . . ."

"I haven't heard of him."

"But, your excellency, General Pervoiedov, Vasily Vasilie-vich. . . ."

"Are you General Pervoiedov?"

"No, your excellency, I'm only court-councilor Lebeziatnikov —at your service. But, General Pervoiedov . . ."

"Nonsense. And please, do leave me alone."

"Stop it"—General Pervoiedov finally, with dignity, checked the hideous impetuosity of his sepulchral client.

"They are not yet awake, your excellency—this has to be taken into account. It's due to lack of habit. When they wake up, they will receive you; otherwse . . ."

"Stop it"—repeated the general.

"Vasily Vasilievich! Hey, you, your excellency!"—suddenly sounded loudly and daringly an altogether new voice, right next to Avdotia Ignatievna—an aristocratic and defiant voice, with a fashionable, fatigued accent and insolent tone. "I've been observing all of you for two hours. You see, I've been lying here for three days. Do you remember me, Vasily Vasilievich? I'm Klinevich; we met at the Volokonskys, where—I don't know why—you also were received."

"Is it possible, Count Piotr Petrovich. . . . Is it possible that it's you . . . and so young. . . . I'm awfully sorry!"

"Well, I'm sorry, too, but it makes no difference to me, and I want to derive every possible advantage from everything. Nor am I a count. I'm a baron, nothing but a baron. We're scabby, petty barons, descending from lackeys—I don't know why. But I don't give a hang. I'm merely a scoundrel of the pseudo-*beau monde*, and I'm considered an '*aimable polisson.*' My father is an insignificant general of some kind, while my mother, in days gone by, used to be received *en haut lieu.* With that Jew Zifel, I smuggled some fifty thousand counterfeit bills, and on top of that I denounced him, while Julia Charpentier carried away all the money to Bordeaux. And imagine, I was already formally betrothed to Schevalskaia—in three months she will be sixteen; she's still in a girls' college; her dower would come to some ninety thousand. Avdotia Ignatievna, do you remember how you seduced me, some fifteen years ago, when I was a fourteen-year-old cadet in the Corps of Pages?"

"Oh, it's you, scoundrel; at least, God sent you, for otherwise here . . ."

"You suspected in vain your neighbor, the shopkeeper, of bad odor . . . I kept silent, and only laughed. It comes from me: it is simply that I was buried in a nailed-up casket."

"Oh, you rascal! And yet I'm glad. You wouldn't believe, Klinevich, what an absence of life and wit prevails 'round here."

"Quite so, quite! And I intend to start something original here. Your excellency—not you, Pervoiedov—your excellency, the other, Mr. Tarasevich, privy councilor! Please respond!—Klinevich, who, during Lent, took you over to Mademoiselle Furcy? Do you hear?"

"I can hear you—it's Klinevich; I'm very glad, to be sure. . . ."

"I don't believe you that much, and I don't give a hoot. Dear old man, I'd like to kiss you but, praised be the Lord, I can't. Do you know, folks, what this grand-père did?—He died three or four days ago and, can you imagine, he left a deficiency in government accounts of fully four hundred thousand?—Widows' and orphans' money, and for some reason he had been managing the business alone, so that, at length, he hadn't been audited for eight years or so. I can imagine what long faces they are all displaying there and how they are cursing him. Don't you think it's a seductive thought! Last year I kept wondering—how could such a seventy-year-old little fellow—a gouty and chiragric fellow, too—preserve so much strength for debauch? And here's the solution to the riddle! These widows and orphans—why, the very thought of them must have inflamed his imagination! . . . I knew about this long ago, and I was the only one who knew it—Charpentier told me about it. No sooner did I find it out than I started pressing him in a friendly way—this was during Easter week: 'Come across with twenty-five thousand—otherwise, tomorrow you'll be audited.' And, imagine, he had then only thirteen thousand left, so, it seems, now that he died in good time. Grand-père! Grand-père! Do you hear?"

"Cher Klinevich, I'm in full accord with you, but it was to no purpose for you to embark upon these details. In life there is so much suffering, torment, and so little reward. . . . Finally, I made up my mind to repose myself and, as far as I can see, I hope to derive everything from this place here."

"I bet he scented out Katish Berestova!"

"Whom? What Katish?"—voluptuously quivered the old man's voice.

"Aha, what Katish?—Right here, to my left, five steps from me; from you—ten. She's already here her fifth day. And if you only knew, grand-père, what a nasty little woman she is . . . of good birth, educated—and a monster, a monster in the highest degree! Over there I showed her to no one. Only I did know her. . . . Katish, respond!"

"Tee-hee-hee!"—responded a half-broken girlish, thin voice; but in it one felt something akin to a needle's prick. "Tee-hee-hee!"

"And a li'l-blon-die?" lisped grand-père abruptly in three syllables.

"Tee-hee-hee!"

"I . . . I . . ."—lisped the old man, losing his breath—"I've been entertaining with pleasure the vision of a little blonde . . . of fifteen or so . . . and precisely in a setting such as this one. . . ."

"Oh, monster!"—cried Avdotia Ignatievna.

"Enough!"—decided Klinevich—"I see that the material is excellent. Forthwith we shall arrange everything here for the best. The main thing is to spend the remaining time pleasantly. But what time? Hey, you, functionary of some sort; Lebeziatnikov—is that your name?—I heard you called so!"

"Lebeziatnikov—court councilor, Semën Evseich, at your service, and I'm very, very glad."

"I don't give a hang if you're glad. But only you seem to know everything about this place. Tell me, first of all—(I've been wondering since yesterday)—how is it that we're conversing here? Well, didn't we die—and yet we're conversing: we seem to move and, yet, we neither move nor speak? What's the trick?"

"This, baron, if you wish, Platon Nikolaievich can explain better than I could myself."

"Who's Platon Nikolaievich?—Don't mumble; get down to business."

"Platon Nikolaievich, our home-baked, local philosopher, naturalist and magister. He has published several philosophy books, but for three months he has been falling asleep, so that here it's difficult to shake him to his senses. Once a week he starts murmuring a few irrelevant words."

"Get down to business!—To business!"

"He explains it all by a most simple fact, namely, that when we'd been living upstairs we mistook the yonder death for death. Down here the body, as it were, is revived once more, but only in consciousness. This means—I don't know how to put it—that life continues, as it were, by inertia. Everything is concentrated, according to him, somewhere in consciousness, and persists another two or three months—sometimes, even as long as six months. For example, we have here one fellow; he's almost completely decomposed, but once every six weeks or so he suddenly will murmur one little word—senseless, of course—about some bobok: 'Bobok, bobok'; this means that in him, too, life continues to glimmer as an imperceptble spark. . . ."

"Pretty stupid. And how is it that I have no sense of smell, and still I can scent a stench?"

"As to that . . . hee-hee. . . . Well, at this juncture our philosopher is in a fog. Precisely about the sense of smell, he remarked, that stink we scent is, so to speak, moral stink—hee-hee!— Offensive odor emanating from the soul, so as to give us a chance during these two or three months to come to our senses, and this is, as it were, the ultimate mercy. . . . Only it seems to me, baron, that this mystical delirium is, indeed, quite excusable in his situation."

"Enough. Besides, I'm sure all this is fiddlesticks. The main thing: two or three months of life, and, finally—bobok. I suggest that we all spend these two months as pleasantly as possible, and —with this in mind—try to settle on a new basis. Gentlemen! I suggest that we be ashamed of nothing!"

"Oh, let's, let's be ashamed of nothing!"—sounded many voices and, strangely, among them there were quite new voices— that is, of those who had in the meanwhile awakened. With particular readiness the engineer thundered his consent in basso—he was fully awake. The little girl, Katish, started giggling joyfully.

"Oh, how eager I am to be ashamed of nothing!"—exclaimed Avdotia Ignatievna with delight.

"Do you hear: now, if Avdota Ignatievna wants to be ashamed of nothing . . ."

"No, no, no, Klinevich, over there I still used to feel shame, but here I'm awfully, awfully anxious to be ashamed of nothing!"

"I understand, Klinevich"—said the engineer in a bass voice —"that you suggest organizing our local life, so to speak, on a new and rational basis."

"Oh, I don't give a hoot! On this score let's wait for Kudeiarov —he was brought in yesterday. He'll wake up, and then he'll explain everything to you. He's such a person, such a gigantic person! Tomorrow, I believe, they'll drag in one more naturalist—an officer, for sure; and, if I'm not mistaken, in three or four days—a columnist, perhaps, together with the editor. However, let them go to the devil! Only we'll have a little company of our own, and everything will shape itself of its own accord. Meanwhile, however, I hope that there will be no lying. I want this only because this is the main thing. To live on earth without lying is impossible, since life and lies are synonyms. But down here let's not be telling lies—just for fun. What the deuce!—The grave must, indeed, mean something! We all shall tell our stories aloud without any shame. First, I'll give an account of myself. You know, I'm one of the carnivorous. Up there, all this was tied with rotten strings. Down with the strings! And let's live these two months in a most shameless truth! Let's uncover ourselves and be nude!"

"Let's be nude! Let's be nude!"—voices shouted everywhere.

"I'm awfully anxious to uncover myself!"—screamed Avdotia Ignatievna.

"Oh! . . . Oh! I see we'll have fun here! I don't want to go to Eck!"

"No—you know, I'd like to live a little longer!"

"Tee-hee-hee!"—giggled Katish.

"The principal thing is that no one can forbid us; and even though, I see, Pervoiedov is angry today, nevertheless he can't reach me with his hand. Do you agree, grand-père?"

"I quite agree! Quite—and with utmost pleasure—on condition, however, that Katish give her bi-o-graphy first."

"I protest! I protest most strongly!"—uttered General Pervoiedov firmly.

"Your excellency!"—lisped and argued, with hurried agitation and lowering his voice, the scoundrel Lebeziatnikov. "Your excellency, it's even to our advantage to agree. Here, you know, is this little girl . . . and, finally, all these various jests . . ."

"Well, of course, a little girl, but . . ."

"It's to our advantage, your excellency, by God, it is! Oh, let's try it—just for the sake of a little experiment. . . ."

"They won't let you rest even in the grave!"

"To begin with, general, you're playing a game of preference in the grave; and, secondly, we have contempt for you!"—intoned Klinevich.

"Dear sir! I wish you would not forget yourself."

"What? You can't reach me, whereas I can tease you from here, as Julia's lap-dog! And, first of all, what kind of general is he here? It's up there that he was a general, but here—he's a plain civilian!"

"No, not a civilian . . . even here I'm . . ."

"Here you'll rot in the casket, and nothing but six brass buttons will remain of you."

"Bravo, Klinevich! Ha-ha-ha!"—roared the voices.

"I served my emperor . . . I have a sword."

"Your sword is only good to stab mice with and, besides, you never drew it out!"

"All the same: I formed a part of the whole."

"There are many different parts of a whole!"

"Bravo, Klinevich, bravo! Ha-ha-ha!"

"I don't understand what a sword is"—exclaimed the engineer.

"We'll run from the Prussians like mice! They'll scatter us like down!"—shouted a distant, unfamiliar voice, literally choking with delight.

"The sword, sir, means honor!"—the general was about to shout. But this was the last I heard of him. There ensued a protracted and fierce uproar, a riot and hubbub, and one could only hear impatient, hysterical screams from Avdotia Ignatievna:

"Oh, let's hurry, let's! Oh, when will we begin to be ashamed of nothing!"

"Oh, verily, the soul is being dragged through sufferings!"—faintly sounded the commoner's voice, and . . .

At this point I sneezed. This happened suddenly and unavoidably, but it had an amazing effect: everything became silent, as in any cemetery, and disappeared as a dream. Verily, sepulchral silence ensued. I don't think they became ashamed because of my presence: in fact, hadn't they decided to be ashamed of nothing! Nor is it likely to suppose that they were scared by the possibility of a denunciation to the police: for what could the police do in a matter such as this?—Willy-nilly, I came to the conclusion that, in spite of all, they must hold some secret, unknown to a mortal—one which they carefully conceal from any mortal.

"Well, dearest"—I said to myself—"I'll pay you another visit." And with these words I left the cemetery.

No, I can't concede it: verily, I can't. Bobok does not confuse me. (Here, then, he did prove a bobok!)

Depravity in such a place; debauch of ultimate hopes, debauch of flabby and rotting corpses—even without sparing the last moments of consciousness! They're given—given gratuitously—these moments, and . . . But the main, the cardinal, point is—in a place such as this! No, this, I can't concede . . .

I'll try other graves. I'll listen everywhere. That's really the thing to do: I must listen everywhere, and not merely in some one spot, in order to form a judgment. Mayhap, I'll also strike something comforting.

But, to these fellows I shall return by all means. Disgusting! Yet, I will by all means come back: this is a matter of conscience!

I'll take this over to *The Citizen:* there, the portrait of an editor has also been placed on exhibition. I do hope he'll print this.

The Citizen, 1873, No. 6.

"PERPLEXED AIR"

I have been reading a few things in current literature, and I feel that *The Citizen* should make mention of them in its columns. But what kind of a critic am I? In truth, I did intend to write a critical article, but it seems that I can merely say something "apropos." I have read Mr. Leskov's *Ensealed Angel;* a poem by Nekrasov, and an article by Mr. Schedrin. Also, I have perused the articles by Messrs. Skabichevsky and N. M. in *The Domestic Records.* The latter two articles are, in a sense, as it were, a new revelation to me. Sometime, I want to discuss them by all means. But, for the present, I shall begin with the beginning, that is, in the order I have read—with *The Ensealed Angel.*

This is a story by Mr. Leskov in *The Russian Messenger.* It is known that here, in Petersburg, it was widely read and many people liked it. Indeed, it is worth it: it is characteristic and entertaining. This is a novel recounted by a certain dissenter at a station on Christmas night, about how some one hundred and fifty men, all of them dissenters, as a workers' artel, embraced the Orthodox faith as the result of a miracle.

That workers' artel had been engaged in the construction of a bridge in a big Russian city—living for three years in special barracks on the shore of the river. They had a chapel, and in it they kept many ancient holy images which had been consecrated prior to the times of Patriarch Nikon. The story of a certain man —not an altogether unimportant bureaucrat—who sought to exact from the artel a bribe of some fifteen thousand, is told quite entertainingly. Having arrived suddenly in the chapel with members of the administration, he demanded a ransom of one hundred rubles for every ikon. The artel was unable to comply with this demand. Thereupon he sequestrated the images; holes were bored through them, they were strung, like so many cracknels, on an iron rod, and were carried away to some cellar. But among the ikons was an ancient one of an Angel, particularly revered by the artel; it was believed to be a miraculous image. In order to deal a blow which would avenge and insult the workers, the bureaucrat, irritated by the refusal of the dissenters to pay the graft, took a piece of sealing wax and, in the presence of the whole assembly, poured drops of the wax on the face of the Angel and affixed to it an official seal. The local archbishop, after having looked upon the ensealed face of the sanctity, said: "Perplexed air!" and ordered the desecrated ikon to be placed on a window in the cathedral. Mr. Leskov maintains that the archbishop's words and his order to have the defiled image placed in the cathedral, instead of in the cellar, pleased the dissenters.

This is followed by an involved and entertaining story of how that "Angel" was stolen from the cathedral. An Englishman of noble birth, seemingly the contractor of the bridge under construction, got mixed up with the dissenters; he took a liking for them and, since they were outspoken with him, he undertook to help them.

Particularly noteworthy in the novel are the conversations of the dissenters with the Englishman about ikon painting. This is a serious portion and the best one in the whole novel. The story winds up with an account of the theft of the image from the cathedral, during the evening service. The seal was removed from the Angel's face; the ikon was replaced by a new one—not yet consecrated—which the Englishman's wife agreed to "seal" in the manner of the former. And at this critical moment a miracle occurred: light was seen (true, by only one man) emanating from the newly sealed image, and after it had been brought to the cathedral, it had been found unsealed—that is, without the sealing wax over the face. This made such an impression on the dissenter who had brought it that, then and there, he went to the archbishop in the cathedral and made a full confession to him. The archbishop granted absolution and uttered these words:

"This must convince you, whose faith is more effective: you" —said he—"have removed the seal from your Angel by fraud, whereas our Angel removed it himself, and brought you here."

The miracle created such a sensation among the dissenters that the whole artel—the hundred and fifty men, or so—were converted to Orthodoxy.

At this point, however, the author made a slip and finished the story rather awkwardly. (Mr. Leskov is apt to make such blunders: let us recall only the end of the deacon Akhilla in his *Cathedral Folk*.) It seems that he grew scared lest he might be accused of being inclined toward prejudices, and he hastened to explain the miracle. The narrator himself, meaning the little peasant, the former dissenter, "mirthfully" confessed that one day after their conversion to Orthodoxy, it was discovered why the Angel had unsealed himself. The Englishwoman did not dare to pour the wax over the face on an ikon even though it had not yet been consecrated; instead, she affixed the seal on a slip of paper which she inserted under the edge of the trimming. Naturally, on the way the slip had slid down, and the Angel had thus been unsealed. Consequently, it is somewhat incomprehensible that the dissenters would continue to adhere to Orthodoxy, despite the elucidation of the miracle.—Of course, it was because they were moved by the kindness of the archbishop, who had granted forgiveness. However, taking into account the firmness and purity of their former beliefs; bearing in mind the desecration of their sacred object and the humiliation of their own reverent feelings; and, finally, if one considers the general character of our schismatic movement—it is hardly possible to explain the conversion of the dissenters by mere emotional sensibility, and to what—to whom?—As a mere matter of gratitude to the *archbishop's absolution?* Indeed, didn't they comprehend—and even more clearly than the rest—what precisely the archbishop's ecclesiastical authority must have meant in a case where he, an archbishop, after such an unheard-of, publicly shameless and violent sacrilege on the part of the grafter-bureaucrat—a sacrilege that concerned both the dissenters and *all Orthodox believers*—confined himself to the sighing remark: "Perplexed air!"; an archbishop who was impotent to prevent even a second-rate functionary from perpetrating acts so bestial and invective to religion!

And, generally speaking, in this respect Mr. Leskov's novel left in me a sickly impression and a certain distrust of the truth of the story. Of course, it is excellently told and deserves much praise. But the question is: indeed, is everything in it true? Is it possible that all this could have happened in our midst?—But the point is that it is said that the story is based upon an actual fact.

Let us only imagine such a case: let us say that there is somewhere, in our day, in some Orthodox church, a thaumaturgical ikon generally revered by Orthodox people. Let us suppose that some dissenters' artel, as a united group, steals that image from the cathedral—strictly speaking, in order to keep that ancient sanctity in their own chapel. Of course, all this could have happened. Let us further presume that a decade later some government official finds that ikon, and bargains with the dissenters in the hope of a fat bribe. They are unable to raise any such sum. Then he takes sealing wax, pours drops of it on the face of the image and affixes the official seal. Now, can it be maintained that because of the mere fact that the ikon had remained a certain time in the possession of dissenters, it has lost its saintliness?—In fact, the ikon of the "Angel," about which Mr. Leskov tells us, was an Orthodox ikon, consecrated in ancient times, and one which, prior to the schism, had been generally revered by the Orthodox world.

And is it conceivable that on this occasion the local archbishop would have been unable, and would not have had the right, to raise at least one finger in defense of the sacred object, and would have merely uttered with a sigh: "Perplexed air"?—My *disturbing* queries may seem to our educated people trifling and prejudicial. But I am of the opinion that an insult to a popular sentiment, to everything the people hold sacred, is a terrible outrage and an extraordinary inhumanity.

Can it be that the thought did not occur to the dissenters: "How would this Orthodox dignitary have protected the church, should the offender have been a still more prominent person?" Could they have felt respect for a church in which the ecclesiastical authority, as the novel describes it, possesses so little power?—Since how, otherwise, can the archbishop's action be explained than by the fact of the meagreness of his authority? Can it really be explained by indifference and indolence, or by the incredible supposition that, having forgotten the duties of his office, he turned into a mere functionary of the government? For if such nonsense were to penetrate the heads of his spiritual children, it would signify the worst calamity: his Orthodox children would gradually lose all zeal in the matter of faith, their love and devotion to the church, while the dissenters would be looking upon the Orthodox church with contempt. The spiritual overseer must mean something —mustn't he? Don't the dissenters understand this?

Now, these are the thoughts which are evoked in one's mind after reading Mr. Leskov's admirable story. Thus—let us repeat— we are inclined to regard it, in certain details, as almost implausible.

Meanwhile, I read in one of the recent issues of *The Voice* the following news:

"One of the village priests in the province of Orel writes to the newspaper *Present Time:* 'Having taught the children of my parishioners how to read and write almost ever since the time of the abolition of serfdom, I relinquished this duty only when our

D-sky zemstvo assumed the cost of teaching and expressed the desire to have teachers who were free of other occupations. However, in the beginning of the current academic year 1872–1873, it was ascertained that there was a deficiency of schoolteachers in our county. Being opposed to the closing of the school in my village, I decided to declare my desire to assume the office of teacher, and I sent to the school board an application for my confirmation in the said office. The board replied that I would be confirmed in the office of schoolteacher if and when the peasants' community expresses its consent thereto. The peasants' community did express its willingness and drew up a respectful resolution. Then—abiding by the instructions of the school board—I applied to the volost administration for certification of the resolution. The volost administration, headed by the ignorant clerk M. S. and the chief, obedient to him in all matters, refused to certify the resolution, giving as a pretext the alleged fact that I have no time to teach—but, in reality, prompted by other motives. I applied to the mediator. Straight to my face he uttered these remarkable words: *"The government, generally, is not disposed to have popular education in the hands of the clergy."* "Why so?"—I asked him. "Because"—replied the mediator—"the clergy propagates superstition." ' "

How do you like this bit of news, gentlemen? Of course, in an indirect sense, it almost restores the verisimilitude of Mr. Leskov's story, which we have so strongly called in question and which we stubbornly continue to doubt. Here, it is not important that such a mediator happened to turn up: what is there in the fact that some fool utters, in idle talk, a foolish word? And what do we care about his convictions?—The important point here is that the matter was put so candidly and authoritatively, with such deliberate authority, with such untroubled unceremoniousness. He expresses his profoundly wise conviction without hesitation, straight to one's face, and, in addition, he has the impudence to ascribe his convictions to the government and to speak *in the name* of the government.

Now, would any sort of mediator, even a person vested with ten times greater authority, dare to tell this, for instance, to a Baltic pastor?—God! What a row such a pastor would have started, and what turmoil, in fact, would have ensued! In our midst the priest modestly accuses the arrogant fellow by resorting to publicity.

But this thought occurs: had this person been more prominent than a mediator (which would be quite possible since in our country everything may happen), perhaps, our good shepherd would have altogether refrained from accusing him, knowing that this would merely result in a "perplexed air," and in nothing else. Besides, we cannot expect from him the zeal of the first centuries of Christianity, much as we may long for it. We are, generally, inclined to accuse our clergy of indifference toward the sacred task. However, under given circumstances, what else is to be expected? And yet, at no time has the clergy's help to the people been so urgently needed as in our day. We are living in a transitory, and, perhaps, the most fatal, moment in the whole history of the Russian people.

A very strange phenomenon has recently occurred in one section of Russia: German Protestantism in the midst of Orthodoxy, a new sect—the Stundists. At the proper time *The Citizen* has given notice of it. It is an ugly phenomenon, but there sounds in it, as it were, something prophetic.

In the province of Kherson a certain pastor Boneketberg, seeing the local Russian people unenlightened and spiritually backward, kindheartedly felt sorry for them; so he began preaching the Christian Gospel to them, adhering, however, to Orthodoxy and urging them not to deviate from it. But things took a different turn: though the preaching met with full success, yet the new Christians promptly started with the desertion of Orthodoxy, making this their first and binding condition; they turned away from the rituals, the ikons, and began to congregate according to the Lutheran fashion and sing psalms and use prayer books. Some of them even learned the German language. The sect spread wth fanatical swiftness, extending to other counties and provinces. The sectarians changed their mode of living and gave up carousing. They argued, for instance, along these lines:

"They (that is, the German Lutheran Stundists) live well, honestly and decently because they have no Lenten seasons. . . ."

This is miserable logic; yet, whatever one may say, there is some sense in it, particularly if Lent be regarded as a mere ritual. And where would the poor man learn about the salutary and profound meaning of Lent?—In fact, he used to conceive his former religion as a mere ritual.

It means that he protested against a ritual.

Well, this, let us say, is comprehensible. But why did he so suddenly and hastily start protesting? What was the prompting cause?

Perhaps, the cause is a very general one, namely, that ever since February 19, the light of a new life has begun to gleam on him. With his first steps on the new path he may have stumbled, and fallen down; but he had to recover by all means and, having done so, he realized all of a sudden how "pitiful and poor and blind and miserable and bare" he was. The main thing is: he started craving for the truth, even sacrificing everything that hitherto had been held sacred by him. In fact, no degree of depravity, no pressure, no kind of humiliation can kill or eradicate in the hearts of our people the thirst for truth, since this thirst is dearest of all to them. They may terribly decay, but even at the moment of their most unbridled debauch they will remember that they are but debauchees, and nothing but that, and that somewhere there is sublime truth which stands above everything else.

Such is the phenomenon. Perhaps, as yet, it may be a single and superficial one, but, hardly, is it accidental. It may abate and harden at its very inception and transform itself into some ritualism, as in most Russian sects, especially if they be left alone. But say what you please, there may be in this phenomenon—I repeat—something prophetic, as it were. In our day, when the future is so mysterious, it is permissible to believe even in prophecies.

What if something simlar should spread all over Russia? Not exactly Stundists (particularly, as it is rumored that proper measures have already been adopted), but something similar? What if the whole people, having reached the limit of their debauch and perceived their misery, should say to themselves: "We do not want debauch. We don't want any liquor. But we do want truth and fear of God—but, most important, truth, truth above all."

That they will thirst for truth is, of course, an encouraging phenomenon. And yet, instead of truth, the greatest deceit may develop, as in the case of the Stundists.

In fact, what kind of Protestants and Germans are our people? And what is the use of their learning German in order to sing psalms? And does not Orthodoxy comprise everything, indeed everything, which they are seeking? Isn't there in Orthodoxy alone both the truth and the salvation of the Russian people, and—in the forthcoming centuries—of mankind as a whole? Hasn't there been preserved in Orthodoxy alone, in all its purity, the Divine image of Christ? And, perhaps, the most momentous preordained destiny of the Russian people, within the destinies of mankind at large, consists in the preservation in their midst of the Divine image of Christ, in all its purity, and, when the time comes, in the revelation of this image to the world which has lost its way!

Yes, but before all this would come to pass, the pastor would wake up earlier, with the first birds, and would go to the people in order to reveal to them the truth—the Orthodox truth, since he would be very scrupulous. However, the people would follow him, and not Orthodoxy—not out of mere gratitude, but for the reason that it was from him that they first learned the truth. And it would develop that "his life is good because there are no Lenten seasons." —Quite an intelligible inference once the personal element has become involved.

But, by the way, what about our priests? What is heard about them?

Our priests, too—it is rumored—begin to awake. It is said that our clergy began long ago to reveal signs of life. We read with humble gratification the admonitions of the ecclesiastical masters in churches, regarding the virtues of preaching and of the moral way of living. According to all reports, our spiritual leaders are resolutely beginning to compose sermons and are getting ready to deliver them.

Only, will they arrive in time? Will they manage to wake up with the first birds?—The pastor is a bird of passage, a bird of different feathers, differently constituted. Besides, his is a different kind of service, his superiors are different, and so forth. Be that as it may, our priest, too, indeed, is no functionary! Isn't he the preacher of the sole great Truth, destined to revive the whole world?

The pastor did arrive earlier than he—this is so. However, what was the priest to do, for instance, in the case of those Stundists? We are inclined to accuse our priests; but let us consider: is it possible that they were to confine themselves to a mere denunciation to the authorities? Oh, of course, not: we have many good shepherds—perhaps, more than we may hope for, or more than we ourselves deserve. Even so, what would he start preaching here?—(I, as a laic person, unfamiliar with the problem, sometimes question it myself.)—On the advantages of Orthodoxy over Lutheranism?—But our peasants are ignorant people: perhaps, they would understand nothing and would not be convinced. Speaking generally, without going into details, would they preach good behavior and decency in the mode of living?—But how is "decency" to be expected when the people are drunk all day?—Abstinence from liquor, perhaps, to exterminate the very root of evil?—No doubt, that would be the thing, although—without entering into details— one has to take into account the greatness of Russia, as a great power, which is so expensive a proposition. . . . Well, this, in a sense, is almost equivalent to the "perplexed air." So that there is nothing else left except to preach that the people *drink a little less*.

And what does the pastor care about Russia's greatness, as a great European power? Nor is he afraid of any "perplexed air," and his is a different kind of service. This is why he won.

The Citizen, 1873, No. 8.

"A CERTAIN PERSON'S" HALF-LETTER

Below I am printing a letter—to be more exact, half of a letter of a "certain person," addressed to the editorial office of *The Citizen*. It would be quite impossible to publish the whole letter. It is the same "person," the one who has already distinguished himself in *The Citizen* in the matter of "little graves." I confess, I am printing this solely to get rid of him. The editor's desk is literally clogged with his articles. First, this "person" resolutely comes forth as my defender against my literary "enemies." He has already written in my defense, and on my behalf, three "anti-criticisms," two "notes," three "casual notes," one "apropos," and, finally, an "instruction on how to behave." In the latter polemic composition of his, under the guise of an instruction to my "enemies," he attacks me, and he attacks me in a tone more energetic and furious than I have ever encountered even in my "enemies." He hopes that I shall print it all! I told him quite definitely that, to begin with, I have no "enemies" whatsoever and that these are but phantoms. Secondly, that it is already too late, since all that journalistic tumult which had broken out after the appearance of the first issue of *The Citizen* in the current year of 1873, with such unheard-of rage, lack of indulgence, and naïveté of methods of attack, has now —since two or even three weeks ago—suddenly ceased for some unknown reason in the same way as, for some unknown reason, it had started. Finally, that were I to make up my mind to answer anyone, I should manage to do so myself, without his assistance.

He grew angry with me and, after quarrelling with me, he departed. Of this I was even glad. He is an ailing man. . . . In his article, which we have previously printed in our journal, he gave in part certain facts pertaining to his biography: an aggrieved man and one who is daily "vexing" himself. But the main thing is that I am afraid of the excessive strength, of the "civic energy," of this contributor. Can you imagine that at the very outset he declared that he required no honorarium whatsoever, and that he was writing solely as a matter of "civic duty"? He admitted even with proud candor, in no way damaging to his reputation, that he had written not at all with a view to defending me, but—taking advantage of the occasion—for the sole purpose of revealing his ideas, since no other periodical would print his writings. Simply, he entertained the sweet hope that he might secure for himself— even though without pay—a permanent little corner in our magazine, so as to be able continually to reveal his thoughts.

Now, what are these thoughts?—He writes about everything; he reacts to everything with bitterness, with rage, with venom and

with a "tender tear." "Ninety percent dedicated to venom and one
percent to the tender tear"—he declares himself in one of his
manuscripts. A new magazine or newspaper comes into existence,
and he is right there on the spot—teaching and dispensing instructions. It is quite true that he had sent to one of the newspapers
some forty letters, with instructions as to how they should be
publishing; how they should be behaving; what they should be
writing about, and what they should be paying attention to. In our
editorial office, in the course of two and a half months, there accumulated twenty-eight of his letters. Invariably he writes over his
full signature, so that he is already known everywhere. Moreover,
he spends his last kopecks on postage and, on top of that, he keeps
enclosing return stamps on the supposition that at length he will
succeed in starting a civic correspondence with the editorial offices.

The thing that puzzles me most is the fact that, in spite of
his twenty-eight letters, I have been utterly unable to discover
what his convictions are and what he is trying to accomplish.—It's
all trash and nonsense. . . . Along with the coarseness of his
methods, the cynicism of the red nose and "offensive odor"; along
with the ecstatic style and torn boots, there gleams some hidden
craving for tenderness, for something ideal—a faith in beauty, a
Sehnsucht for something lost. And all this takes, in him, an
abominable form. Generally, I am sick and tired of him. True, he
is candidly rude and demands no money for it, so that in a way
he is an honorable man, but God be with him and his honor!
Only three days after our quarrel he appeared again with "the last
attempt," bringing with him this "Letter of a Certain Person." There
was nothing to be done but to take it, and now I am obliged to
publish it.

It is absolutely impossible to print the first half of the letter.
It is nothing but personalities and cursing at virtually all Petersburg and Moscow periodicals, a cursing exceeding all limits. None
of the incriminated magazines has ever reached such a cynicism
in invectives. And the main point is that he himself curses them
solely for their cynicism and for the vulgar tone of their polemics.
I simply clipped off with scissors the entire first part of the letter,
returning it to him. I am printing the concluding part because here,
as it were, the theme is a general one: this is a certain admonition
addressed to some imaginary columnist—an admonition suitable to
columnists of all ages and nations because it is so general. The
style is exalted, and the impetuosity of the style can only match
the naïveté of the ideas set forth. Addressing the admonition to
the columnist, he calls him *thou,* as in odes of ancient times. He
emphatically objected to my starting after a period or full stop,

and insisted that the printing of the half-letter begin in the middle
of a sentence, precisely as it had been cut by the scissors: "Let
them see how I was mutilated!" It was also he who insisted on
the title. I meant to entitle it, "Letter of a Certain Person"; but
he categorically demanded that it be designated: "A Certain Person's
Half-Letter."

And so, this is the half-letter:

"A CERTAIN PERSON'S HALF-LETTER

. . . and is it possible that the word 'swine' has such a magic and
attractive meaning that it is forthwith and unfailingly credited to
one's own account? I observed long ago that in Russian literature
this little word invariably carries a certain peculiar, and even, as
it were, mystical, meaning. Realizing this, even grandpa Krylov
used 'swine' in his fables with special affection. An author who is
silently reading in solitude, coming across this word, immediately
shudders and forthwith begins pondering: 'Is it not me? Isn't this
written about me?'

"I admit, this is an energetic little word, but why should one
presume that it applies to him and to him alone? There are others
besides thine own self. Perhaps, thou hast secret reasons therefor?
For how is one to explain otherwise thy suspiciousness?[1]

"The second thing I shall remark to thee, O my columnist
friend, is the fact that thou art intemperate in the planning of
thy feuilletons. Thou stuffest thy columns with such a multitude
of generals, stockholders, princes, relying on thee and on thy witticisms, that, when reading, I conclude willy-nilly that despite the
abundance of the many thou hast not a single one. Now thou art
present at an important board meeting and thou utterest *bons
mots*, haughtily and carelessly, but thereby thou throwest a ray
of light, and the board immediately and hastily changes for the

[1]Unquestionably this is an exaggeration, and yet, partly, it is true.
Strictly speaking, this is a hint to the fact that in the first issue of *The
Citizen* I had the misfortune of citing a very ancient Hindu fable about
the duel between a lion and a pig, and adroitly I obviated the very possibility of the supposition that the word "lion" immodestly referred to myself. And what? As a matter of fact, many people have expressed extraordinary and hasty suspiciousness. There even occurred something akin to
a phenomenon. A letter had been received by the editorial office from one
of the subscribers in a remote border region of Russia. That subscriber
impudently and haphazardly accused the editors of the alleged fact that
by the word "swine" they unquestionably meant their subscribers—a presumption so absurd that even some of the Petersburg columnists did not
dare to make use of it in their attacks . . . and this, of course, is a measure
of everything.—Ed.

better. Now thou hast ridiculed a wealthy prince straight to his face, in reward for which he invites thee to dinner, but thou passest him by and uppishly—yet in a liberal fashion—thou refusest the dinner invitation. Now again, jestingly, thou revealest, in intimate salon talk with a foreign lord, the whole secret underlayers of Russia. He is appalled and delighted; then and there he wires to London, and the very next day Victoria's cabinet is overthrown. On another occasion, on the Nevsky, during a walk from two to four, thou solvest a state problem to three ex-ministers running after thee. Then thou runnest into a guard captain, who has lost everything at play, and thou throwest him a loan of two hundred rubles; thou goest with him to Fifina to spill noble (presumably) indignation.

"Briefly, thou art here, thou art there, thou art everywhere; thou art dispersed in society; thou art torn asunder; thou swallowest truffles, eatest candies; thou art being driven by cabmen; thou maintainest friendship with waiters at Palkin—in a word, nothing transpires without thee. Such a high position as thine, in the long run, creates suspicion. A modest provincial reader, in truth, might take thee for one unjustly deprived of a reward, or, at least, for a retired minister seeking anew to regain his office with the aid of a free, but opposition, press.

"However, the seasoned dweller of both capitals knows differently, since he is aware of the fact that thou art nothing but a scribbler hired by a contractor-editor; thou hast been hired and art obliged to defend. It is also he (and no other) who instigates thee against anyone he chooses.

"So that, all this anger and irritation in thee, all this barking of thine—all this is but a hired proposition, directed by somebody else's hand. And it would be something to thy credit if thou shouldst defend thine own independent stand! Contrarywise, the thing that surprises me most in thee is the fact that thou actually growest excited, that thou takest things to thy heart as if they were thine own; thou quarrellest with a rival columnist as though about some cherished idea, some conviction dear to thee. However, thou knowest thyself that thou hast no ideas of thine own—not to speak of convictions. Or, perhaps, as a result of many years of agitation and enthusiasm over thy fetid success, thou hast finally fancied that thou hast an idea, and that thou art capable of having a conviction? —If so, how canst thou, after that, count upon my respect?

"In times gone by thou wert an honest and decent youth. . . . Oh, do recall Pushkin—if I am not mistaken, it's a version from the Persian language: a venerable old man says to a youth eager to throw himself into a battle:

'Yes, I fear, amidst hard fighting
Thou shalt lose thy movements tame:
With their modesty inviting
And the lovely sense of shame.'

"Alas! Thou hast lost all these long ago and forever! Look, thyself, at the way thou polemizest with thy rival columnist, and realize to what limit ye both have carried your abuses! Since ye both are not as vile as ye are picturing one another. Recall that in early years children come to blows mainly because they have not yet learned to express their thoughts. But thou, a gray-haired child, because of the absence of thoughts, thou cursest, employing all words at once—this is a bad device!

"Precisely, owing to lack of convictions and genuine erudition, thou seekest to peep into the private life of thy rival; avidly dost thou learn his trespasses, distortest them and deliverest him unto salutary publicity. Thou sparest not his wife and children. Presuming each other dead, ye write mutually one to the other obituaries in the form of pasquinades.

"Well, tell me, who in the long run shall believe thee? Reading thy feuilleton, bespattered with saliva and ink, I am compelled to think that thou art not right; that in thy article there is a peculiar and secret meaning; that ye must have come to blows at some country resort and ye are unable to forget it. Willy-nilly, I favor thy rival, and thy arrow has gone astray. Is this what thou hast sought?

"And what a childish incompetency in thee! Having scolded thy rival, thou windest up thy feuilleton with the words: 'I can see you, Mr. N. N.—how, after having read these lines, you are running about your room in a rage, tearing your hair, shouting at your wife who, in a state of fright, came running to you; how you are driving away your children and, grinding your teeth, you are hammering the wall with your fists in a fit of impotent frenzy. . . .'

"Oh, my friend, thou simple-minded but enraged sufferer from thy fictitious rage, assumed for the benefit of thy manager. Oh, my columnist-friend! Tell me: upon reading in thy article such lines, as it were, about thy rival, is it conceivable that I shall not guess that thou—thou thyself, and not thy rival—art running around thy room, tearing thy hair; that thou beatest the frightened lackey —if thou hast one, and if after February 19 he hath not lost his primitive innocence; with screams and grinding of thy teeth, thou rushest against the wall, smashing thine own fists till they begin to bleed? This is how thou betrayest thyself.

"Do come to thy senses and do acquire some shame. Having acquired it, thou shalt also learn to write feuilletons—this is the advantage.

"I shall give thee an allegory. All of a sudden thou advertisest on a poster that next week, on Thursday or Friday (in a word, imagine a day on which thou writest thy feuilletons), in the Berg Theatre, or on premises specially adapted therefor, thou shalt exhibit thyself naked, even in all minute details. I am sure, amateurs will be forthcoming: shows of this sort carry a particular appeal to contemporary society. I really believe that people—a multitude of them—will come. But will they come to pay thee respect?—And where, then, and what is thy triumph?

"Now, consider, if thou canst: do not thy feuilletons portray the same thing? Dost thou not appear every week, on a certain day, nude even in all details, before the public? And what for—for whom dost thou exert thyself?

"The funniest part of it all is that the entire public is cognizant of the secret of your warfare; it knows and yet does not care to know; it passes you by indifferently. But ye are exerting yourselves, imagining that everybody is sympathizing with you.

"Oh, simpleminded man! The public knows only too well that the manager of a newspaper in the capital, when, following his own example, another newspaper had been founded, seized himself by his pocket and exclaimed: 'This newly-founded, good-for-nothing wretch may deprive me of two thousand or twenty-five hundred subscribers. All right. I'll hire a barking dog and will set it at my rival.' Thou art the barking dog!

"The manager is pleased with thee, he strokes his whiskers and, after luncheon, he smilingly cogitates: 'How well I instigated him!'

"Dost thou recall Turgenev's *Antropka?* This piece by an author beloved by the public is, indeed, ingenious. Antropka is a provincial urchin, or—more correctly—the brother of another provincial urchin; Antropka (let us call the former—Nefed) disappeared from the hut on one dark summer night because of some mischief perpetrated by him. Their austere father sent the elder boy to bring back his mischievous little brother. And presently, over the bank, shrill cries begin to sound:

"'Antropka! Antropka!'

"The guilty scamp remains silent for a long while but, finally, 'as if from the other world,' comes his trembling and timid, thin little voice from the other side of the bank:

"'Wha-a-t?'

"'Daddy wants to spa-a-nk you!'—with bitter but hasty joy, echoes the elder brother. . . .

"The voice 'from the other world,' of course, is heard no more. But the strained, impotent screams, full of exasperated anger, continue to resound endlessly in the dark night:

"'Antropka! Antropka-a-a!'

"This ingenious exclamation—and most important: its impotent, yet angry; strain—may be re-echoed not only among provincial urchins but equally among grown-up people having attained a venerable gray-haired age, among members of our contemporary society disturbed by the reforms. And doesn't something at least remind thee of those Antropkas in the capital? Since between these two managers of periodicals in the capital, dost thou not observe something of the Antropka pattern? Thou and thy rival—haven't ye both been sent out by your masters for the purpose of finding Antropkas? The Antropkas—aren't they those new subscribers conceived by you who might give credence to your innocence? Ye are both aware of the fact that your rage, the whole strain and all your efforts will be in vain; that Antropka will give no answer; that neither of you will take away a single subscriber from the other; that each of you will have enough subscribers anyway. However, ye have gnawed yourselves into this game, and ye are so fond of this heart-scratching journalistic strain of yours that ye can no longer desist! And thus, weekly, on specified days, there sounds the strained and raging exclamation: 'Antropka! Antropka-a!' And we are listening to it.

"I'll indulge in another allegory.

"Imagine that thou hast been invited by decent people, since I presume that thou art also visiting respectable strata of society. Thou goest to a formal evening party of a person as high in rank as that of a state-councilor, on his saint's day. Guests have been informed in advance about thy wit. Thou enterest politely, well dressed; thou bowest courteously to thy hostess and tellest her amiable things. Thou sensest with pleasure that everybody is looking at thee and thou art ready to distinguish thyself. And suddenly —oh, horror!—thou observest in a corner of the hall thy literary rival who has arrived earlier and whom, till the last minute, thou hast not even suspected of being acquainted with these people. Thy face hath changed, but thine host, attributing this to thy momentary indisposition, hastens naïvely to introduce thee to thy literary foe. Ye bow and then immediately turn your backs on each other. The host is embarrassed, but regains his composure, believing that it is merely a new literary device of which he is not aware, owing to the pressure of his official business. Meanwhile, a game of cards is being hastily arranged, and the hostess, with her usual amiability, invites thee to take part in a game of whist. In order to rid thyself of thy rival, thou pickest joyously a card.— A new affront! It develops that thou art to be seated with him at one and the same table! It is too late to refuse because thou hast, as thy partners, two cheerful, well-meaning and socially prominent ladies. They hurriedly take their seats. Gathered around them are several relatives and acquaintances, and all are eager to listen to two *littérateurs;* all of them are staring into your mouths, catching every word of yours, intently looking at you.

"Thy rival turneth to the lady and calmly saith to her: 'I believe, it's your deal, madam.' Everybody smiles, looking at one another. The witticism meets with success; and thy heart begins to quiver from envy. Cards are being dealt. Thou openest thine: threes, twos, sixes and the highest card is a jack. Thou grindest thy teeth, while thy rival smiles. He has all the cards, and proudly bids a slam. Thine eyes grow dim. Thou seizest a heavy bronze family candlestick, of which thy host is proud; all year long it is kept in the hostess's cupboard and it is being exhibited only on some saint's day. Thou seizest the candlestick and violently flingest it into thy rival's forehead. Screams and perplexity! People leap to their feet, but ye have already sprung upon each other and ye are clawing each other's hair in a foam of rage.[1] Because of thine impatience in literature and thine inability to restrain thyself, I also have the right to infer thine impatience in private company. Thy partner, the young lady who had been expecting from thee so much wit, with a scream, seeks shelter under the wing of her husband— an important engineer and lieutenant-colonel. Pointing at both of you, clawing each other's hair, he says to her: 'I have warned you, my dearest—what can one expect from modern belles-lettres!'

"However, both of you, having been dragged down the staircase, are kicked out into the street. The host, celebrating his saint's day and realizing his guilt before his guests, makes his apologies to all present, urging them to forget about Russian literature and bidding them to continue their whist. But thou hast deprived thyself of a social evening party, of some pleasant, though innocent, moments with a Petersburg lady, and of a supper.

"Yet, ye both are not concerned about all this: ye hire cabmen and dash through the stinking Petersburg streets, each heading for his apartment, in order to start immediately composing his feuilleton. Thou art spurring on thy coachman, inadvertently envying his innocence, but thou art already pondering over thine article.

[1] The editors consider this picture slightly exaggerated.

Presently, thou hast arrived; thou graspest thy pen, and thou recountest, to the last dot, every minute detail of the things that happened to thee at the councilor's home!

"Thou indictest the host celebrating his saint's day, his wife, their refreshments; thou protestest against the custom of celebrating saints' days, against the engineer lieutenant-colonel, against thy lady partner—and, finally, thou reachest thy rival.

"Oh, at this juncture—everything is being set forth in the most minute details, fully in accord with thy present-day fashion to reveal all the ins and outs. Thou tellest how he beat thee, how thou didst beat him; thou promisest that thou shalt beat him and thou also tellest that he had promised to beat thee. Thou wishest to append to thine article a patch of hair torn from his head.

"But it is already morning. . . . Thou runnest around thy room, waiting for the office hour to strike. Thou goest to the editor and, suddenly, with a calm air, he declares to thee that already, only yesterday, he had made peace with his rival manager who hath discontinued his periodical, transferring his subscribers to him, thy manager; he also telleth thee that the peace pact hath been celebrated at Dussot's with a bottle of champagne. Thereupon, he thanketh thee for thy services and declareth that thou art no longer needed by him. Now, tell me, what is thy situation?

"Least of all, do I like the last days of butter-week, when the common people are getting drunk in a most obnoxious fashion. Dulled ugly faces of topers, in torn dressing gowns and dirty old coats, assemble in crowds in front of saloons. Here are two fellows who have stopped in the street: one of them claims he is a general; the other shouts in reply: 'Liar!' The former rages and curses, and the latter keeps on shouting, 'Liar!' The first one exerts himself ever more strenuously; but the other persists in his—'Liar!' And so on and so forth, maybe two hundred times! Both precisely perceive beauty in the impotent and endless repetition of one and the same word, sinking, so to speak, into delight in the importance of their degradation.

"When reading thy feuilletons, somehow I visualize an endless, drunken and senseless, butter-week that hath been persisting too long in our literature. Since, is not thy case identical with that of those two insipid, drunken dressing-gown peddlers? Doth not thy rival claim in each one of his articles that he is a general, and dost thou not, even as that peddler at the crossroads, reply to him in each one of thine: 'Liar!' And all this, a countless number of times without even the slightest suspicion on thy part of how all this, in the long run, maketh me weary and tired. I visualize you, crazed and intoxicated, precisely on the last (forgiveness!) day

of butter-week. I see each of you lying in front of the windows of
your editorial offices, and wallowing in the dirty brown snow of
the capital and shouting at the top of your hoarse voices at each
other: 'Help! He-e-lp! H-e-elp!'
        "But I remain silent, hurrying by. . . .
                                            Silent Observer."

   N. B. "Silent Observer" is the pseudonym of "A Certain Person." I forgot to note this beforehand.
                                        The Citizen, 1873, No. 10.

APROPOS OF THE EXHIBITION

   I went to see the exhibition. A good many pictures by our
Russian artists are being dispatched to the Vienna international
exhibition. This is not the first time, and modern Russian painters
are getting to be known in Europe. Even so, I wonder: is it possible
over there to understand our artists, and from what angle are they
going to be evaluated there? In my opinion, if Ostrovsky's comedy
—say, *We're No Strangers—We'll Settle It,* or, in fact, any of them
—were translated, and translated as well as possible, into German
or French, and if it were produced on some European stage—I don't
know what would come of it. Of course, something would be understood and—who knows?—some pleasure might be derived from it,
but at least three-quarters of the comedy would remain inaccessible
to European understanding.
   I recall, in my youthful days, I became greatly interested in
the fact that Mr. Viardot, a Frenchman (the husband of the famous
singer who, at the time, had been singing in our Italian opera),
not knowing a word of Russian, had been translating our Gogol
under the guidance of Mr. Turgenev. True, Viardot was endowed
with an artistic and critical faculty and, in addition, with a sensitiveness to the understanding of poetry of alien nationalities—this
he had proved by his admirable French version of *Don Quixote.*
At the same time, it goes without saying that Mr. Turgenev understood Gogol in every minute detail, enthusiastically loved him,
I take it—much as everybody else in those days—and, on top of
that, was himself a poet, although then he had hardly begun his
poetic pursuits. (N. B. He had only written several poems, I forget
which ones, and also a novel, *Three Portraits*—already a noteworthy
piece.) Thus, something could have come of it. I may note that
Mr. Turgenev, probably, knows the French language to perfection.
   But what was the result?—Such a strange thing was produced

by this translation that, even though I had anticipated that Gogol cannot be rendered into French, nevertheless I had not expected such an outcome. This translation is available at present—look what it amounts to. Gogol has literally vanished. All the humor; all that is comical; all individual details and the principal phases of the denouements which if suddenly recalled in solitude (and oftentimes in the least literary moments of one's life) will set one breaking into irresistible laughter to one's self—all this has vanished, as if it had never been there.

I cannot imagine what opinion the French could have formed at the time about Gogol, judging by that translation. For the rest, it seems, they have formed no opinion whatever. No doubt, *The Queen of Spades* and *The Captain's Daughter*, which had also been translated into French, must likewise have half-vanished, notwithstanding the fact that in these much more could have been understood than in Gogol.

Briefly, in my opinion, everything characteristic—everything that is ours, preeminently national (and therefore, everything genuinely artistic)—is unintelligible to Europe. Translate Turgenev's novel *Rudin*—(I speak of Mr. Turgenev because he has been translated more than other Russian authors, and of the novel *Rudin*, for the reason that among all of Mr. Turgenev's works it conforms the most to something German)—into any European language, and even then it will not be understood. The real gist of the matter will even remain unsuspected. *A Hunter's Sketches* will be as little understood as Pushkin and Gogol. So that—it would seem to me —all our outstanding talents are, perhaps, destined, for many years to come, to remain utterly unknown to Europe; and even: the greater, the more original, the talent—the more unintelligible he will be.

We, however, understand Dickens, when rendered into Russian, almost as well as the English—perhaps, even all nuances. Moreover, we love him—perhaps, not less than his own countrymen. And yet, how typical, original and national is Dickens! What can be derived from this?—Is such an understanding of alien nationalities a special gift of the Russians, as compared with Europeans?—Perhaps, such a special gift actually exists; and if it exists (as well as the gift of speaking foreign languages which, indeed, is more pronounced among us than among other Europeans), it is a very significant gift, carrying a great promise for the future— one that predestines the Russians to many a thing, although I do not know whether this is a good gift or whether there is something bad in it. . . .

More correctly—many will maintain—Europeans know little

about Russia and Russian life simply because, as yet, they have
had no particular need of being informed about them in any detail.
It is true that Europe, up to this time, has had no special need
of being informed about us in any detail. Nevertheless, it seems
certain that for a European, regardless of his nationality, it is always easier to learn some other European language and penetrate
the soul of any other European nationality than to master the
Russian and to grasp our Russian essence. Even those Europeans
who have deliberately studied us for some specific purposes—and
there have been such—and who have spent much labor on this,
have been leaving us, though with much knowledge, yet without
a complete understanding of certain facts; it may even be said that
they will long fail to comprehend these facts, at least in contemporary, and in the closest, generations.

All this suggests our long, and perhaps sad, solitude amidst
the family of European peoples; mistakes of Europeans in their
judgments about Russia even in the remote future; and their apparent inclination to judge us unfavorably. All this, possibly, explains also that permanent, general animosity of Europe toward us,
which is based on some powerful, immediate and squeamish feeling; a disgust for us as for something repugnant; partly even, her
superstitious fear of us—and the eternal, familiar verdict of long
standing that we are not Europeans at all. . . . Of course, we feel
offended and exert every effort to prove that we are Europeans.

Of course, I do not maintain that, in Europe, our landscape
painters, for instance, will not be understood: the scenes of the
Crimea, the Caucasus, even of our steppes, will naturally be found
interesting. However, I do believe that our Russian, preeminently
national, landscape, that is, of the northern and central regions of
our European Russia, will produce in Vienna no great impression.
And yet, to us, this "weary nature," whose whole characteristic
resides, so to speak, in its lack of characteristic, is dear and charming. Take, for instance, those two little birches in Mr. Kuindgi's
landscape *A Scene in Valaam:* in the foreground—a marsh and
swampy sedge; in the background—a forest; over it—not exactly
a cloud, but mist, dampness—one is, as it were, penetrated by it;
you almost feel it; and in the middle, between the forest and yourselves, two little white birches, bright, hard—the strongest point
in the picture. Now, what is there peculiar about this? What is
there characteristic here?—And yet, how beautiful this is! . . . I
may be mistaken, but this will not please the German as much.

It isn't even worth while speaking about historical painting.
In the strictly historical painting we have long been failing to
glitter, so that we will cause no surprise in Europe; nor in battle

painting. Even the transmigration of the Circassians (an enormous, many-colored canvass, perhaps with great merits—I cannot judge) —in my opinion, will create no strong impression abroad. But genre, our genre—what will they comprehend in it? And yet, in Russia it has been reigning almost supreme over a period of many years; and if we can pride ourselves on something—if we have something to show—certainly, it is our genre.

Here, for example, is a small picture by Makovsky—I believe, *Amateurs of Nightingales' Singing;* I don't know just what it is called. Look: a small room of a commoner or some discharged soldier, a dealer in singing-birds, perhaps, and, besides, a fowler. Several bird cages may be seen; benches, a table and, on it, a samovar, around which guests are seated—two merchants or shopkeepers, amateurs of nightingales' singing. The nightingale is in a cage hung beside the window, and probably he is whistling, trilling, chattering, while the guests are listening. Both of them are, apparently, serious-minded people—close-fisted shopkeepers and jobbers, advanced in age, and, perhaps, debauchees in family life (somehow, it is a custom that this "dark kingdom" is necessarily composed of debauchees behaving themselves indecently in their family life); and yet, it seems that they have already grown soft from delight—the most innocent and almost touching delight. Here, something moving, to the point of foolishness, is taking place. The one sitting by the window slightly lowers his head and lifts one hand, holding it in suspense; he is hearkening, melting, with a blissful smile on his face; he is listening to the last sounds of the trill. He wants to grasp at something—he is afraid of losing something.

The other one sits at the table, with his tea; his back is almost turned, but you are aware of the fact that he is "suffering" not less than his companion. In front of them is the host who had invited them to listen to the nightingale and, it goes without saying, to sell them the bird. He is a somewhat lean, tall fellow, of about forty or more, dressed in his domestic, rather unceremonious suit (and why should he indulge in ceremonies!); he is telling something to the merchants, and one feels that he talks with authority. Compared with these shopkeepers, from the standpoint of his social position—his pocket—he is, of course, an insignificant person; but now he has a nightingale—a good one, too—and so he looks haughtily (as if he himself were singing); he speaks to the merchants even with a sort of insolence, sternly (there's no other way!) . . .

It is noteworthy that the shopkeepers sit and unquestionably think it should be thus—that he should slightly scold them, because "the nightingale is darned good!" Tea will soon be finished and the bargaining will then ensue. . . .

Now, I ask you, what will a German or a Viennese Jew (Vienna, even as Odessa, they say, is full of Jews) understand in this picture? Perhaps, somebody will explain the gist of the matter, and they will learn that a Russian merchant of average standing has two passions—the race horse and the nightingale—and that on this account the picture is awfully amusing. But what will this come to? This is some abstract knowledge, and it will be hard for the German to comprehend why this is amusing. But we look at the little picture and we smile; later, we recall it and, for some reason, we feel amused and pleased.

In truth—and let the people laugh at me—in these little pictures, in my opinion, there is love of humanity, not merely and particularly Russian, but humanity in general. I have referred to this small canvas merely as an example. But the thing which is most annoying is the fact that we should understand a similar German picture, portraying German genre, just as well as they would, and we should even be delighted as much as they, experiencing almost their German sentiments, whereas, in Russian painting, they will understand nothing at all. But then, maybe, in a sense, this is to our advantage.

Now here, a game of cards is portrayed in an Esthonian or Livonian cabin: of course, this is intelligible, especially the figure of a boy taking part in the game; everybody is playing cards and guessing, so that *The Ten of Spades* (such is the name of the picture) would also be fully comprehensible. But I doubt if, for example, Perov's *Hunters* would be understood. I am intentionally referring to one of the most intelligible pictures of our national genre. It is a well-known one—*Hunters at a Halting-Place*: one of them is enthusiastically and deliberately telling lies; the other one is listening and believing with all his heart, while the third hunter believes nothing; he lays himself down right there and laughs. . . . How delightful! Of course, with proper explanation the picture would be understood by the Germans, too; still they would not comprehend, as we do, the fact that this is a Russian liar, and that he lies in a Russian fashion. For we almost hear him and we know what he is talking about, the whole trend of his prevarications, his style and his emotions. I am sure that if Mr. Perov were to portray (and, no doubt, he would be capable of doing it) French or German hunters—of course, in a different manner and picturing different characters—we Russians would understand both German and French taradiddle, in all the minute details and all the national variations, the style and the theme of the fib; we would guess all these things merely by looking at the picture. But the German, no matter how much he may be exerting himself, would not grasp our Russian lies. Certainly, thereby he wouldn't be losing much; and, again, this might be to our advantage. However, he would not fully understand the picture, and, consequently, he would not properly appreciate it. And this is a pity because we are making the journey in order to be praised.

I don't know what attitude will be taken in Vienna toward Makovsky's *Psalm-Readers*. In my judgment this is no longer genre, but an historical painting. I am joking, of course, but do look attentively: nothing but choristers—in a sense, an official choir —singing a concerto at a liturgy. They are all in formal habit with clean-shaven chins. Look attentively at this gentleman with whiskers, for example: it is clear that he, so to speak, is disguised in a garment which is altogether out of harmony with himself; he is wearing it as a matter of official duty. True, all choristers wear similar habits on official occasions only; this has been the custom since patriarchal times, but here this disguise somehow is particularly noticeable. One is accustomed to behold such a decorous functionary in uniform only in a government office: this is a little fellow belonging to the middle class, modest and solid, with appropriately cut hair. He is dragging out something like the notorious "I am stung!," but, looking at him, even the "I am stung!" is converted into something official. There is nothing funnier than to imagine that this well-intentioned man, basking in his official position, could have been "stung!" If one doesn't look at them, turning away from them and merely listening to them, something charming would emerge from it. But if one looks at these figures, it will seem that the psalm is being chanted merely for some pretense . . . and that there is something altogether different about the whole scene.

I am terribly afraid of "tendency" when it takes its hold on a young artist, especially at an early stage of his career. And what do you think I am specifically afraid of?—Specifically, that the aim of the tendency is not going to be attained. Will a certain dear critic whom I have been reading of late and whom I do not wish to name at present—will he believe that every artistic creation, without a preconceived tendency, produced solely because of the artistic urge, dealing with a strictly neutral subject hinting at nothing "tendentious"—will this critic believe that such a creation will prove much more useful *for his own purposes* than, for instance, all songs of the shirt (not by Hood, but by our writers), even though it may on the surface resemble that which is denoted as "satisfaction of idle curiosity?" If even men of learning, apparently, have not yet guessed this, what may sometimes occur in the hearts and minds of our young authors and artists? What a jumble of conceptions and preconceived feelings! For the gratification of public pressure a young poet suppresses in himself the natural urge to reveal himself in images that are peculiarly his own; he is afraid that he might be condemned for "idle curiosity"; he crushes and effaces images which, of their own accord, are evoked from his soul; he leaves them undeveloped, and, with painful convulsions, he draws out of himself a theme conforming to the general, "uniformed," liberal and social opinion. Still, what an awfully simple, naïve and coarse blunder this is! One of the coarsest blunders consists in that the indictment of vice (or that which liberalism is wont to conceive as vice) and the instigation to hate and vengeance are considered the only road to the achievement of an aim! True, even on this narrow path a forceful talent might extricate himself and save himself from being smothered at the beginning of his career. One should only recall more frequently the golden rule that an uttered word is silver, and the unuttered one is gold. There are quite a few considerable talents who were so promising, but who were so chewed up by tendency that the latter clothed them in some sort of uniform.

I have read the last two poems by Nekrasov: decidedly, this eminent poet of ours is at present wearing a uniform. And still in these poems, too, there is something good, reminding one of Mr. Nekrasov's former talent. But what is to be done? the "uniformed" contents of the theme; the "uniformed" character of the technique; the "uniformed" substance of thought, style and naturalness . . . yes, indeed, even the "uniformed" approach to naturalness itself. For example, does our respected poet know that no woman, even replete with the loftiest sentiments, one who has conferred upon herself so many labors in order to come and see her ill-starred husband; one who has journeyed six thousand versts in a cart and who has "learned the delights" of a cart; who has fallen, as you claim yourself, "from a high ridge of the Altai" (which, by the way, is quite impossible); do you know, poet, that this woman, under no circumstances, would first kiss the chains of her beloved, but would most certainly kiss him first, and only after that—his chains, should there awake in her so impetuously and so suddenly the magnanimous impulse of civic duty. Most decidedly, every woman would act thus.

Of course, mine is a trifling observation, and it wouldn't be worth mentioning, since the poem itself has been written for no important purpose: just so—perhaps, as to get out something in anticipation of the first of January. . . . However, Mr. Nekrasov has a prominent literary name, which is almost fixed and complete, and he has many admirable verses to his credit. He is a poet of suffering, and he almost deserves this name. But still one pities the little novices: not every one of them possesses so forceful a talent as to manage not to submit to the "uniformed" thought at the inception of his career, and, consequently, to protect himself against literary consumption and death. What is to be done? the uniform is so pretty—indeed, embroidered and shining. . . . And also how profitable! That is, it is particularly profitable in our day.

The moment I had read in the papers about Mr. Repin's haulers, I got frightened. The theme itself is horrible: somehow we take it for granted that haulers are particularly fit to symbolize the familiar idea of the insolvent debt of the upper classes to the people. And I was ready to meet them all in uniforms with well-known labels on their foreheads. And what? Much to my joy all my fears proved unfounded: haulers, genuine haulers, and nothing more. Not one of them is shouting from the canvas to the spectator: "Look, how unfortunate I am, and what indebtedness you have incurred to the people!" This alone must be credited to the artist as a great merit. Nice, familiar figures: the two fore-haulers are almost laughing; at least, they are not weeping at all and, certainly, they are not pondering over their social status. The little soldier uses cunning and deceit; he is trying to fill his pipe. The urchin pretends to be serious; he is shouting and even quarrelling— a wonderful figure, practically the best in the picture, and it is analogous in its conception to that of the posterior hauler, a miserable, drooping little peasant, creeping along separately from the rest, his face not even visible. It is quite inconceivable that the idea of politico-economic and social debts of the upper classes to the people could at any time have penetrated the poor drooping head of that miserable little peasant cast down by perpetual grief. . . . And do you know, dear critic, that precisely this humble innocence of thought in that peasant achieves the purpose—your tendentious, liberal purpose—much more effectively than you suspect! Some spectators will walk away with a sore spot in their heart and with love—and what love!—for this miserable little peasant or for that urchin, or for that rogue and scoundrel—the little soldier! Indeed, it is impossible not to take a liking to them, these defenseless ones; it is impossible to walk away without having grown fond of them. It is impossible not to start reflecting that one is indebted, actually indebted, to the people. . . . For this haulers' "gang" later will recur in one's dreams; it will be recalled some fifteen years hence! And had they not been so natural, innocent and simple, they would not have produced such an impression and they would not have presented such a picture.

But here we have almost a picture!—Besides, the collars of
uniforms are disgusting, no matter how they be embroidered with
gold! However, what is there to discourse about? Besides, there is
no need of recounting a picture; pictures are much too difficult to
be expressed in words. I will simply say: Gogolesque figures. This
is a big word, but I am not saying that Repin is Gogol in his line
of art. Our genre has not yet grown up to Gogol and Dickens.

However, a certain over-emphasis may be discerned even in
Repin: precisely in the dresses, and this—only in two figures. Such
tatters are even inconceivable. That shirt, for example, must have
accidentally fallen into a trough in which cutlets had been chopped
with a chaff-cutter. No doubt, haulers make no display of their
clothing. Everybody knows whence these people have come: at
home, as has been at least frequently reported, by the end of
winter they subsist on bark; in the spring they go to a master to
be hired to haul barges—some of them for nothing but porridge,
almost without any agreement. There have been instances when the
hauler, during his first days, would die right at his gruel, falling
on it from hunger; he would choke to death and "burst." It is said
that medical men performing the autopsy upon these men would
find nothing but porridge sticking up to their throats. Such sometimes are these subjects. Still, an unuttered word is gold, more so
as a shirt such as this cannot even be put on if once it has been
taken off: it will not fit. But, compared with the merits and independence of the conception of the picture, this trifling over-emphasis
on the clothing seems negligible.

It is a pity that I know nothing about Mr. Repin. It would
be curious to know whether he is or is not a young man. How I
would wish that he might be a very young man, and a beginner
artist. Several lines above, I hastened to make the reservation that
he is still not a Gogol. Yes, Mr. Repin, it is a mighty long stretch
to Gogol: don't let your deserved success go to your head. Our
genre is following a good road, and there are also talents; yet,
something is lacking in it, something that prevents it from expanding and broadening. Indeed, Dickens is genre, too, nothing but genre.
But Dickens created Pickwick, Oliver Twist, and grandfather and
grand-daughter in the novel *The Old Curiosity Shop*. No, our genre
is still a long way off: it still stands on its "hunters" and "nightingales." Dickens has them, too, in secondary places. Judging by
certain indications, I am inclined to think that at the present juncture of our art Pickwick and the grand-daughter would seem something ideal to our genre. And, as far as I could observe from conversations with some of our most prominent painters, they are as afraid

of the ideal as of an evil spirit. No doubt, it is a noble apprehension, but a prejudicial and unjust one. Our artists need more boldness, more independence of thought, and, perhaps, more education. This is why, I take it, our historical painting is ailing and has somehow slowed down. Apparently, our contemporary artists are afraid of historical painting and have launched into genre as the only genuine and legitimate escape for every gifted person. It seems to me that they have a presentiment, as it were, that in historical painting, according to them, they would have to "idealize" by all means and, consequently, to lie. "Reality should be represented as it is," they say, whereas there is no such reality, never has been because, to man, the substance of things is inaccessible, while he apperceives nature as it reflects itself in his idea after having passed through his senses. This is why one should give more leeway to the idea without fearing the ideal.

A portraitist, for instance, seats his subject, in order to paint his portrait; he is getting ready; he stares. Why is he doing this? —Because he knows from experience that a man does not always resemble himself and, for this reason, he tries to discover "the fundamental idea of his physiognomy"—to arrest that moment in which the subject resembles himself most. In the ability to find and arrest this moment lies the gift of the portraitist.

Now, what else is the artist doing here than trusting his idea (the ideal) more than the projected reality? The ideal, indeed, is also a reality as legitimate as current reality. Take, for example, Bronnikov's *Hymn of the Pythagoreans:* some genre-painter (even a very talented one) will start wondering how it is possible for a modern artist to indulge in such themes. And yet, these themes (almost fantastic) are as real and as neecssary to art and man as current reality.

What is genre, in substance? Genre is an art of portraying contemporaneous, current reality which the artist has personally felt and seen with his own eyes, as distinguished, for instance, from historical reality which cannot be beheld with one's own eyes, and which is being portrayed not in a fluent but completed state. (I will make a *nota bene:* we say: "beheld with one's own eyes." But Dickens had never seen Pickwick with his own eyes, merely perceiving him in the diversity of the reality observed by him; he created a character and presented him as a result of his observations. Thus, this character is as real as an actually existing one, even though Dickens had merely taken an ideal of the reality.)

Meanwhile, we precisely confuse the conceptions of reality. For example, historical reality in art, of course, is not identical with contemporaneous reality (genre), precisely because it is a structuralized and not a fluent one. Ask any psychologist you please, and he will explain to you that if one visualizes a past event (and to live without visualizing the past is impossible), and particularly an event of the remote past, a structuralized, historical event—such an occurrence *necessarily* will appear in its completed state, that is, with the supplement of the whole subsequent development which has not been taking place at that particular historical moment at which the artist seeks to visualize a character or an event. For this reason, the essence of an historical event cannot be represented by the artist exactly as it probably has been occurring in reality. Thus, the artist is seized by a sort of superstitious fear that willy-nilly he would have to "idealize," which, according to his understanding, means to lie. In order to avoid the imaginary error he endeavors to fuse (cases of this kind do happen) both realities—the historical and current ones. As a result of such an unnatural blending, the worst kind of lying ensues. In my opinion, this pernicious error may be observed in several of Mr. Gué's pictures. For instance, out of his *Lord's Supper,* which has caused so much comment, he produced a perfect genre. Look attentively: this is an ordinary quarrel among most ordinary men. Here Christ is sitting, but is it really Christ? This may be though a very kind young man, quite grieved by the altercation with Judas, who is standing right there and putting on his garb, ready to go and make his denunciation, but it is not the Christ whom we know. The Master is surrounded by His friends who hasten to comfort Him, but the question is: where are the succeeding eighteen centuries of Christianity and what have these to do with the matter? How is it conceivable that out of the commonplace dispute of such ordinary men who had come together for supper, as this is portrayed by Mr. Gué, something so colossal could have emerged?

Here, nothing has been explained; here, there is no historical truth; nor is there even the truth of genre here; here everything is spurious.

From whatever angle one might be judging, that event could not have occurred in this way: here everything transpires altogether incommensurately and disproportionately to the future. At least Titian would have given to the Master that countenance with which he portrayed Him in his well-known picture *Caesar's Unto Caesar;* then much would have been intelligible forthwith. Whereas in Mr. Gué's picture some nice people have simply quarrelled among themselves. As a result, we have deceit and a preconceived idea; and every kind of deceit is a lie, and no realism at all. Mr. Gué was after realism.

However, I seem to have forgotten about the exhibition. By the way . . . what kind of a reporter am I?—I merely meant to jot down several remarks "apropos." Nevertheless the editorial office promises to give a detailed survey of the pictures of our artists which are to be sent to the Vienna exhibition. Or, better perhaps, it will try to make mention of them from the exhibition, with a ready account of the impression which these canvases, in turn, will produce upon the foreigners attending the exhibition.

The Citizen, 1873, No. 13.

MUMMER

Who prompted thee!

In *The Russian World* (No. 103) there appeared a notice scolding me. I am not answering any upbraiding articles; I shall answer this one because of certain considerations, which will become clear in the course of my reply.

And, to begin with, the point is that my reviler is an ecclesiastic: I least expected an attack from this side. The "notice" is signed: "Pr. P. Kastorsky." What is "Pr."? Priest? What can this abbreviation mean other than "priest"? All the more so as the subject deals with a church matter. In issue No. 15–16 of *The Citizen* there was published a novel *Sexton* by Mr. Nedolin. Well, it is to this that the "notice" refers. Here it is.

"UNMARRIED CONCEPTIONS OF A MARRIED MONK"

"In our day clergymen and churchmen are quite frequently being chosen by our authors and novelists as heroes of their stories. Even oftener, they appear there in the quality of interpolated, so to speak, accessory characters. And it is very good that they are being portrayed: in the clerical world there are a good many typical characters, so why shouldn't they be portrayed with both their good and their bad traits? The recent success of 'Sketches by a Churchman' in *The Domestic Review,* and, also, the still greater success of 'The Cathedral Folk' in *The Russian Messenger* demonstrate the fact that much interest may be aroused among the public by artistic descriptions of the ways of life of our clergy. Both works mentioned portray members of our clergy from different angles, and both have been read with attention and pleasure. And why?—Because they were written well, artistically, and with a knowledge of the subject. But something altogether different emerges when, prompted by imitativeness or by something else—for example, by self-confidence or lightmindedness, the task is being undertaken by people who have no conception of it. They merely humiliate themselves and harm the cause by setting forth false views, and for this reason to leave these injurious attempts—to caricature the ways of life of our clergy—without notice is impossible, and, following the example of the *psalm-reader* who has recently, in *The Russian World,* pointed out the ignorance of the writer Dostoievsky regarding choristers, I feel it impossible to keep silent on a still coarser, more ludicrous and unpardonable ignorance again manifested in the same magazine, *The Citizen,* which has been signed by the same Mr. Dostoievsky as editor."

Let us, for the time being, stop here. What is meant by "following the example of the *psalm-reader* who revealed in *The Russian World* the ignorance of the writer Dostoievsky"? I have not read it. (And again *The Russian World!*) I find (No. 87) that there is, in fact, an accusation signed "Psalm-Reader." Let us see what this is:

"ON THE CHORISTERS' LIVERY"

(A Letter to the Editor)

"In issue No. 13 of the magazine *The Citizen* (March 26) I happened to read an article by Mr. F. Dostoievsky apropos of the academic exhibition of paintings. Mr. Dostoievsky, treating in that article of psalm-readers, portrayed by the artist Makovsky, wrote the following lines: 'They are all gentlemen in *formal gowns* with clean-shaven chins. True, all choristers, too, wear similar gowns on official occasions only, and *from time immemorial they have been wearing such gowns, and so it has been the custom from time immemorial ever since patriarchal times . . .'* "

Let us interrupt this for a moment: to begin with, I have no such stupid sentence at all. I wrote: "True, all choristers, too, wear similar gowns on official occasions only, and, from time immemorial, this has been the custom—since patriarchal times . . ." which is quite different.

We continue the quotation:

"This is incorrect: neither *from time immemorial* nor since *patriarchal* times have church choristers in the Russian Church ever donned such gowns as those in which we see them at present and in which they are portrayed on Mr. Makovsky's canvas. This livery is a more recent borrowing from the West or, more correctly speaking, from Poland, and among the eminent dignitaries of our Church there are—and have been—not a few who regard this liveried masquerade as inappropriate, while the choristers of the choirs, assigned to them, sing in ordinary black frock-coats, which, of course, are more modest and more dignified than the Polish uniform. And 'from time immemorial,' in 'patriarchal times' choristers have sung standing up in long black caftans, and unfailingly with music-sheets in their hands. In the same manner also do choristers stand in our day in the churches of the dissidents and in the chapels of the dissenters."

It would appear, perhaps, that in our present-day Orthodox churches choristers sing seated. It is always useful to listen to an expert.

"Fearing [much is there to fear!] that through Mr. Dostoievsky's incompetent word the erroneous opinion on these liveries may be consolidated [will an earthquake result from this—or what?], which liveries should long ago have been remodelled to the Russian fashion, I have the honor to beg the editorial office of *The Russian World* to give space to these brief lines of mine.

Psalm-Reader."

Such is the notice of the psalm-reader, to which Priest Kastorsky makes reference. Before continuing with Kastorsky, let us finish with the "psalm-reader."

Mr. Psalm-Reader, why did you get angry? You say: "It is incorrect: neither *from time immemorial* nor since *patriarchal* times have church choristers in the Russian Church ever donned such gowns . . ." How is this? Why is this "incorrect"? Why can't one say: *from time immemorial* and since *patriarchal* times? Well, did they start wearing these clothes yesterday?—Why, they have been doing so since great-great-grandfather's times! Knitting your brows, with the air of a profound historian, you come to correct us, and you yourself make no precise statement! One is expecting that the profound historian is going to determine with precision the epoch, the year and, perhaps, even the day when clerics put on this garb for the first time; but after all the things you have heralded, you confine yourself to the withered conjecture: "This came to us from Poland"—nothing but that! But how much tolling and bell-ringing!

Please answer only, Mr. Psalm-Reader, what is your opinion: did Polish influence which, in Russia, has simultaneously reflected itself in many fields—and even, you see, in clerical matters—start, according to you, long ago or merely the day before yesterday? Why, then, is it not permissible, for the sake of mere intelligibility, to use the expression that this custom has been in existence *from time immemorial*, since *patriarchal* times?—Not only from *patriarchal* times, but it dates back almost to the times of the *Patriarchs*.

These costumes (or ones similar to them) appeared at the time of Peter the Great; consequently, they almost coincide with the times of the Patriarchs, or nearly so. Is this—recently? Why isn't it permissible to say—*from time immemorial?* Or—*since patriarchal times?* And if, in my article, I myself have not determined with historical precision since what time specifically our choristers have been wearing these clothes, the reason for this was that I had no such purpose or aim in mind, and that I merely meant to say that this dates back to the remote past—so remote that the expression *from time immemorial* could well have been used, and everyone would understand it. I was not referring to the epoch of Dmitry Donskoi, nor to that of Yaroslav. I meant to intimate "very long ago," and nothing but that.

But let's leave the learned psalm-reader. He jumped to the forefront, did a lot of hand-waving—and nothing came of it. At least, he spoke politely: "Fearing (so to speak) that through Mr. Dostoievsky's incompetent word," etc. However, priest Kastorsky promptly exceeded the limits set by the "psalm-reader." A sportive man! . . . "The ignorance of the writer Dostoievsky regarding the choristers . . ." "I feel it impossible to keep silent on a still coarser, more ludicrous and unpardonable ignorance again manifested in the same magazine *The Citizen,* which has been signed by the same Mr. Dostoievsky as editor."

What horrible crimes—one might think—have been perpetrated by that Dostoievsky: it is even *impossible* to forgive them! A clergyman who, it would seem, ought to be love incarnate—even he cannot forgive!

However, what is this "ignorance"? What is the matter?— Well, there is nothing to be done: let us transcribe the whole of Kastorsky; let us give a treat to the readers. Why should one have only "a little bit of the good"? The more—the better. Such is my idea.

"In issue No. 15–16 of *The Citizen,* which appeared on the 16th day of the current April, there was published 'The Sexton. A Story told among Friends,' by Mr. Nedolin. The story is built upon a most erroneous and impossible foundation: in it there is portrayed a sexton with a high-sounding voice, who is *being beaten* by his wife so assiduously and cruelly that he escapes from her into a monastery, where he consecrates himself to God and must no longer think about any earthly matters. He stays behind the monastery wall, while his wife, who has long been beating him, is standing outside the gates. He is sonorously singing there an adaptation of the psalm:

Oh, holy is Thy chosen, blessed Lord;
And when, as envoy of Thy sacred will,
His arm will draw the mighty vengeful sword
The wicked giant shall be crushed and still.

"And the deserted wife is again standing at the monastery gate, and pressing her burning head against the monastery wall, she is weeping; she is begging that her husband, who has been admitted to the monastery, be beckoned out, and she promises to become his 'slave and dog.' The husband, however, never did come out, and died in the monastery.

"What a pitiful, inconceivable and ludicrously idle story! Who this Mr. Nedolin is—we don't know, but most certainly he is a man absolutely ignorant of Russian legislation and of Russian life—ignorant to such an extent that he supposes that in Russia a married man could be admitted to a monastery and that he would be permitted to stay there. Yet, how is it possible that these things are unknown to the editor, Mr. Dostoievsky, who has recently so protractedly announced that he is an ardent Christian, and, in addition, one of Orthodox faith, orthodoxly believing in the most amazing miracles? Does he, perchance, class among miracles this admission to a monastery of a married man?—Then it's a different thing; but anyone even slightly familiar with the law and the regulations of one's church could convince Mr. Dostoievsky that in Russia such a miracle is even impossible because it is strictly forbidden and is prosecuted by our substantive laws which no monastic authority can violate, and that a married man may not be admitted to a monastery.

"Nevertheless, the most miserable and inexpertly knit-together plot of the story *The Sexton* could have gained to some extent if its denouement were verisimilar, and it could easily have been made such by an author or an editor familiar, though superficially, with the customs of the depicted milieu. For instance, the story could have led up to a rather familiar dramatic situation in which the sexton, in order to steal away from his snarlish wife, runs from one monastery to another; but here, he is being driven out by the authorities because he is married; there, he is called for by the wife herself, and, perhaps, again she starts beating him. . . . Thereupon, seeing no escape from his wife in his own country and, at the same time, longing for a monastic life, the ill-starred sexton could run away, say, to Athos where, under the Mohammedan administration of the Turkish Sultan, the Orthodox Church in many respects is functioning more independently than in Russia. There, as is known, monasteries sometimes do not hesitate to admit married men seeking monkhood. There, the Russian sexton, who was being mercilessly smitten by his wife, could have found refuge; he could be praying and singing, but under no circumstances that metrical adaptation which *The Citizen's* sexton sings. This on the ground that: *first*, as is well known, it enjoys no popularity among the clergy; *second*, it is not adapted to singing and is not being sung, and, *third*, no laic metrical adaptations are permitted to be sung within the walls of Orthodox monasteries, and no one living there may disregard this interdiction lest the tranquillity appropriate to such a place be disturbed.

Pr. P. Kastorsky."

Now, let us answer point after point. And, to begin with, let us reassure the aroused priest Kastorsky on the main point, by explaining to him that the novel *The Sexton* is not a genre novel at all. Its esteemed author, Mr. Nedolin (not a pseudonym), who had spent part of his life in very active government service, was in this particular instance in no way concerned about church life. His hero the *"sexton,"* with no disadvantage to either himself or the story, might have been, for example, a post-office clerk, and if in the story he had remained a sexton, it is solely because this is a true event. This poem is an exceptional, almost fantastic, one.

Do you know, priest Kastorsky, that true events, depicted with all the exclusiveness of their occurrence, nearly always assume a fantastic, almost incredible, character? The aim of art is not to portray these or those incidents in the ways of life but their general idea, sharp-sightedly divined and correctly removed from the whole multiplicity of analogous living phenomena. In Mr. Nedolin's story, a quite different phenomenon of the human spirit has been synthesized. On the contrary, had he aspired to a genre delineation, from this point of view and with this one anecdote of his, he would of necessity have run into an exceptionality.

It is said that recently, *i.e.*, several months ago, in one of our most renowned monasteries a cruel monk had beaten to death in the school a ten-year-old boy—and this, in the presence of witnesses. Now, at first glance, isn't this a fantastic happening? And yet, it seems, it is quite true. Well, were someone to describe it, people would at once start shouting that it is incredible, exceptional; that it has been depicted with a preconceived aim.—And they would be right if one were to judge that event from the standpoint of the mere genre authenticity of the description of our monasteries. In the light of this one story alone there would have been no authenticity: even to this day there is to be found in our monasteries angelic life for the glory of God and the Church, while the occurrence involving the cruel monk will forever remain exceptional.

However, the novelist, the poet, may have other problems, aside from the genre aspect: there are general, eternal and—it would seem—forever unexplorable depths of human character and spirit. But you think that once the word "sexton" has been written, it must necessarily signify a special genre description. And if it be that, we must have by all means segregated and patented authors for such descriptions, and then others wouldn't dare to poke into our field. This is our corner, our exploitation, our source of income. Isn't it true, priest Kastorsky, that it is precisely this which has disturbed you? But, for goodness' sake, the word "sexton" may be penned with no aim of taking anything away from Mr. Leskov. And so, do calm down.

Having appeased you, I will ask you to pay attention to the title of your polemic article:

"Unmarried Conceptions of a Married Monk."

In passing I shall ask: what is the meaning of "unmarried" here? To what extent would the conceptions be changed if they were married persons? And are there unmarried and married conceptions?—Well, of course, you are not a littérateur, and all this is but a trifle; you are a disturbed priest, Kastorsky, and one shouldn't be expecting any style from you, particularly in such a state. The principal point here is this: who told you that our sexton had joined the monastic order? Where—in Mr. Nedolin's whole novel—did you find any mention of the fact that the sexton had taken the veil? Yet, this is very important: having given it this title, you are simply misleading a reader unfamiliar with Mr. Nedolin's novel. "Yes, indeed," he will reflect, "a married sexton could not have become a monk! How can it be that *The Citizen* does not know this?" Therefore, having turned the reader's eyes away by the word "monk," you exclaim triumphantly in the middle of your article:

"What a pitiful, inconceivable and ludicrously idle story! . . . How can the editor, Mr. Dostoievsky, be ignorant of this, he who, etc. . . ."

And yet you have simply fraudulently shuffled the matter, and I am very quietly catching you at your cheat. But, dear little Father, you made a slight slip without giving the matter due thought. A married man will not be *consecrated* into monkhood—this is so; but why will "no monastic authority admit to a monastery one who has a living wife," as you are haphazardly asserting?

Whence did you derive such information? For example, someone might wish to take abode in a monastery (where, let's say, there are convenient quarters); but he is married. Suppose his wife is somewhere in the capital or abroad; and now, only because he is married will he be driven out of the monastery? Is that so? Father, you do not know the business—and yet you are a clergyman. I could even point out certain persons, well known in Petersburg society and still remembered by it, who, at the end of their lives, finished up by taking abode in monasteries, and they have been living there for some time since, and are still there. All this transpired with mutual consent. Exactly in the same way Mr. Nedolin's sexton *took abode* in the monastery. Eliminate the fraudulent shuffling regarding the consecration into monkhood—deliberately invented by yourself, and a thing which does not appear at all in Mr. Nedolin's whole novel—and everything will at once be explained to you. Here it occurred even better than "with mutual consent"; here, the thing took place with the permission of the authorities. I have, Father, a very effective device with which to pacify you on this score. Just suppose that I have made inquiries and have received the following information:

First, the artist-sexton, as long as six months prior to his *admission* to the monastery—when bidding farewell to the landowner—revealed to him for the first time that he was planning to *take abode* in a monastery, and even then he knew what he was talking about—precisely because he had already told the superior of the monastery about his plans. The latter was very fond of him —rather, he liked his singing, he himself being an ardent admirer of music and patronizing Sofron to the best of his ability. It even seems that the superior had been urging him to come and *live* in the monastery. The sexton hesitated to accept the landowner's offer to go abroad, and this is the reason why he had tarried another six months or so; however, when his patience came to an end, he departed to the monastery. And this was very easy to arrange: Father John was on friendly terms with the superior of the diocese, and when two such persons come to an agreement, no pretexts are needed. No doubt, however, a pretext was nevertheless found, under which the sexton was, so to speak, "deputed" to the monastery. The vow taken by him to "consecrate himself to God" (which makes you particularly angry) was an altogether free, inner, unofficial one—a matter of his conscience—and the promise was given to himself.

Moreover, in Mr. Nedolin's story there is a very clear hint of the fact that the sexton merely *resided* in the monastery, and that by no means had he been made to take the veil, as you, Father, have so unceremoniously lied. Specifically: the landowner, who had come back, still continues to urge Sofran to leave the monastery and go abroad, while the sexton, on the first day of the negotiations, even feels undecided. Now, could this have happened if Sofron had already taken the veil? Finally, do not conceal the fact that the sexton is a most remarkable artist—at least, extraordinarily gifted —and, as such, he appears in the novel from its very beginning. And, this being so, the fondness for him by Father John, an ardent admirer of music, is intelligible. . . .

"But this has not been explained in the novel!" you will exclaim, in a fit of violent anger.—No, it has partly been explained; much should be surmised in the story, though it is swift and brief. But supposing that not everything has been explained--why should it be? So long as it be plausible. And if you eliminate the fraudulent shuffling regarding the veil, everything becomes plausible.

Yes, Mr. Nedolin's story is somewhat condensed; but do you know, Father, you are not a literary man; you proved it, too—I will tell you frankly that a great many contemporaneous stories and novels would gain if they were condensed. What is gained by an author's dragging you through four hundred and eighty-odd pages, and then, for no reason whatsoever, abandoning his narrative in Petersburg or Moscow, dragging you somewhere to Moldavo-Wallachia with the sole intent of recounting to you how a flock of crows and owls took wing from some Moldavo-Wallachian roof; and, having given this account, suddenly he deserts the crows, leaves Moldavo-Wallachia, as if they had never existed, and in the remaining portion of the story not once does he return to them. Why, the reader is finally left in a state of utter confusion. People write for money, and the more pages—the better! Mr. Nedolin wrote dfferently and, perhaps, he was right.

"But the wife, the wife!"—I can hear you exclaiming and rolling your eyes—"how could the wife permit it? Why didn't she 'claim' the husband legally, by force!"—And precisely here, Father, on this feminine point, you have failed most emphatically. In your article you became so playful that you even started composing a romance yourself: namely, how the wife has finally repatriated her sexton; how she began beating him again; how he "escaped" to another monastery; how she had him sent back, and how he finally escaped to Athos, where he found peace under "Mohammedan" administration of the Sultan (imagine: up to the present time I have been thinking that the Sultan is a Christian!).

Leaving all jokes aside: remember, Father, that because of your office alone, you should know, though slightly, the human heart; yet you don't know it at all. Despite the fact that you are a mean author, you might, nevertheless, if you should take up your pen, depict the genre aspect of the clergy more correctly than did Mr. Nedolin; but as far as the human heart goes, Mr. Nedolin knows more than you. A woman who spends entire days standing at a monastery wall and wailing, will not go serving petitions, nor will she resort to force. Enough of force! You keep coming back to beating all the time: in a trance of an author's enthusiasm you continue the romance, and again you inject the beating. No, enough of beating! Recall, Father, in Gogol's *Wedding*—in the last scene, after Podkolesin had jumped out of the window—Kochkarev shouts: "Make him come back! Make him come back!"—imagining that a fiancé, after he had jumped out of the window, is still in a mood for a wedding. Now, you are arguing exactly in the same manner. Kochkarev is restrained by the matchmaker's words: "Eh, thou dost not understand the wedding business; it might have been all right if he had walked through the door, but once he flew through the window, there's nothing further to be done!"

Ennoble the case of Podkolesin and it will exactly fit the situation of the poor sexton's wife, deserted by her husband. No, Father, the beatings had come to an end! That woman is an exceptional character, a passionate and strong creature—by her spiritual powers far superior, by the way, to the artist, her husband. Under the influence of her environment, habits, lack of education, this woman, indeed, could have started with the beating. A reasonable, understanding man would certainly appreciate the realism of the event, and Mr. Nedolin has acted masterfully when he did not mollify the reality. Women with excessive spiritual force and character, particularly if they are passionate, cannot love otherwise than despotically, and they even have a special predilection for such weak and childish characters as that of the artist-sexton. Why did she take a liking for him? Does she know it? He weeps and she cannot but despise his tears; but carnivorously, suffering herself, she is delighted with his tears. She is jealous: "don't you dare sing before gentlemen!" It seems, she could swallow him alive from love.

But he escaped from her—she would never have believed it! She is proud and self-confident; she knows that she is beautiful and —this is a strange psychological problem—would you believe that all the time she is convinced that he is as much in love with her as she with him; that he cannot live without her in spite of the beatings! For this was her whole faith. More than that: on this point she had no doubts. And, suddenly, everything comes to light: that child, the artist, does not love her at all; had ceased to love her long ago; perhaps, too, in the past he had never loved her!

At once she feels humbled; she hangs her head; she feels crushed. Even so, she has no strength to renounce him; she loves him madly, even more madly than before. Still, because she is endowed with a strong, noble and unusual character, she rises way above her former way of life and her former environment. No, now she is not going to claim him by force. If force has to be resorted to, she will not have him—even for nothing. She is still immensely proud, but now her pride is of a different kind—it has already been ennobled: she would die right there on the grass beside the wall rather than resort to force, write petitions and start proving her rights. Oh, Father, therein is the whole novel, and not at all in the genre aspect of the church folks. No, Father, this minute little story is far more significant than it may seem to you—far deeper.

I reiterate: you could not have written so, nor would you have understood the gist of the matter. You have, in a certain measure, Kochkarev's soul (in a literary sense, of course; I don't go any further), as I had the honor to report to you.

As for your authorship and your artistic understanding, Pushkin's well-known epigram is fully applicable to you in this connection:

Subjecting once an artist's sketch to close inspection,
A cobbler in the boots discovered some defect;
The artist with his brush forthwith made the correction.
"There's something more"—the cobbler said—"I can detect:
"That face looks slightly curved—such is my estimation;
"Besides, that breast, to me, seems much too nude and bare!"
Impatiently Apelles stopped the cobbler's dissertation:
"Judge not above the boots—this is your only care!"

You, Father, resemble to the dot that cobbler, with the only difference that you have failed to teach Mr. Nedolin, even with respect to boots, a fact which, I hope, I have amply proved to you. And fraudulent shuffling in no way helps. Here, you see, to be able to understand something in a human soul and "to judge above the boots," one has to be more developed in a different direction; one has to have less of that cynicism, of that "spiritual materialism," less of that contempt of people, less disrespect for and indifference towards them; less of that carnivorous covetousness, and more faith, hope and love! Look, for example, with what coarse cynicism you are dealing with me personally; with what want of decency, quite improper to your office, you are talking about miracles. When I read to myself these lines of yours, I refused to believe them:

"Yet, how is it possible that these things are unknown to the editor, Mr. Dostoievsky, who has recently so protractedly announced that he is an ardent Christian, and, in addition, one of Orthodox faith, orthodoxly believing in the most amazing miracles? Does he, perchance, class among miracles this admission to a monastery of a married man?—Then it's a different thing . . ."

To begin with, Father, this, too, is an invention (what a passion for inventions you have!).—Never did I declare myself *personally* as regards my faith in miracles. All this is your invention, and I challenge you to state where you have found it. Permit me one more word: had I, F. Dostoievsky, anywhere declared this about myself (which I never had), believe me, I would not have renounced my words for some liberal fear, or for some *Kastorsky* fear. The simple matter is that nothing of the kind had taken place, and this I am stating as a fact. But even if it were so— what is your concern about my faith in miracles? What relation has this to the matter? And what are amazing and not amazing miracles? How do you, yourself, manage to reconcile such divisions? Generally speaking, I wish you to leave me alone in this respect— if only for the reason that, despite all your modern education, it does not become you to annoy me with all this. You, a clergyman, and so irritable! Shame on you, Mr. Kastorsky!

And do you know that you are not Mr. Kastorsky at all— still less: priest Kastorsky? All this is counterfeit and humbug. You are a *mummer*—exactly like one performing during Christmas season. And do you know what else? I haven't been deceived by you—not even for a brief little moment: I at once recognized you as a mummer, and this gives me pleasure because I can see from here your long nose. You were fully convinced that I would mistake the jester's mask of crude workmanship for a genuine face. You should know that I have answered you somewhat too unceremoniously, solely because I at once recognized a mummer. Had you, in fact, been a clergyman, I would have—notwithstanding all your rudeness, which in the concluding part of your article reaches the level of some triumphant seminary neighing—answered you "with observance"; not because of personal respect for you, but because of respect for your high office, for the lofty idea contained in it. Since, however, you are only a mummer, you must suffer the penalty. I shall begin the castigation with a detailed explanation of why I have recognized you—(*entre nous,* I had even guessed beforehand who precisely is hiding behind the mask, but for the time being I shall not announce the name aloud)—and, of course, this will be very vexing to you.

And, if you have guessed beforehand—you may ask me—why

did you frame your reply as if it were addressed to a clergyman? Why did you, in the first place, write superfluous things?

Because one meets a man in accordance with his dress—I answer you. And if I wrote something disagreeable to Mr. "Priest," let this weigh upon the conscience of the fellow who has resorted to the unworthy device of disguising himself as a priest. Yes, this is an unworthy device, and he felt it himself. Moreover, he sought, as much as he could, to protect himself. He did not sign his name: "Priest P. Kastorsky"; but he signed abbreviatedly: "Pr. P. Kastorsky." "Pr."—if it comes to close reasoning—is still not equivalent to "Priest," since it could always be maintained that the abbreviation stood for "priest-like," or something of the kind.

I recognized you, Mr. Mummer, by the style. You see, here is the main trick: contemporaneous critics will sometimes praise present-day belles-lettrists, and the public is even pleased (since, after all, what will it be reading?). However, criticism, too, has long been on the decline, while most of our drawers of pictures resemble poster-painters more than artists. Of course, not all of them. There are a few endowed with talent, but the majority are impostors.

In the first place, Mr. Mummer, you have it over-salted. Do you know what it means to speak in terms of essences or patterns? You don't? Well, I will explain it to you. A contemporary "belles-lettrist" who delineates certain types and who segregates for himself some special field in literature (depicting, for example, merchants, peasants, and so forth) usually walks about all his life equipped with a pencil and a copybook; he keeps eavesdropping and recording characteristic little words; at length, he manages to collect several hundreds of such words. After that he embarks upon a novel, and the moment a merchant or a clergyman starts speaking, he begins to concoct his speech from the expressions recorded in the copybook. Readers laugh and praise it: it seems so authentic—copied directly from nature. Yet it proves to be worse than a lie precisely because the merchant or the soldier in the novel speaks in terms of *essences*, that is, as no merchant and no soldier ever speaks in real life. For instance, in reality he may utter a certain sentence—one that has been recorded as spoken by him—but it will be one phrase out of eleven; the eleventh little word is characteristic and ugly, but the ten preceding words are all right, akin to those of all other people. But in the case of the specialized author he will utter characteristic sentences all along, exactly according to the record, and the result is—falsehood. The delineated character converses as though he were *reading from a book*. The public gives its praise, but you cannot deceive an old experienced writer.

Mostly this is signboard and house painters' work. Yet, in the long run, the "artist" comes to consider himself a Raphael and it is impossible to dissuade him! It is good and useful to record these little words, and one cannot do without them; however, one should certainly not employ them quite mechanically.

True, there are nuances even among "artists-recorders": one is still more talented than the other and, therefore, he uses these expressions with resignation, taking into account the epoch, the locality, the man's mental level, and abiding by a certain proportion. Even so, he cannot avoid the essence-standard. The precious rule that an uttered word is silver and the unuttered one is gold has long ago ceased to be the fashion among our artists. There is little faith. The sense of measure is fast disappearing.

Finally, one should also consider that our artists (as any group of commonplace people) are beginning to take sharp notice of the phenomena of reality, paying attention to typicalness and treating a given character in art when, in most cases, it has already passed out of existence or is vanishing, degenerating into some other pattern in accordance with the character of the epoch. Thus, almost invariably we are being served at our table old food under the guise of fresh fare. And they themselves believe that it is fresh and new, and not something obsolescent.

However, to our author-artist, this observation is, perhaps, a little too sophisticated; perhaps he will not understand it. Nevertheless, I will state that only an ingenious writer or one endowed with a great talent divines and produces a type *on time;* whereas triviality merely follows his path more or less slavishly, laboring in accordance with ready patterns.

For instance, in all my life, never did I meet a single clergyman—even among the most enlightened ones—in whose manner of speech there would not be some characteristic peculiarities pertaining to his professional milieu. There is at least a drop of something. Meanwhile, if one were to record his conversation stenographically, and later have it printed, perhaps no peculiar characteristics would be discernible—at least in the case of some highly educated priest who had long been frequenting society. In the opinion of the majority of the readers, plebeians in Pushkin's stories speak worse than those in the writings of Grigorovich, who, all his life, has been depicting peasants. I believe this also is the opinion of many artists. Grigorovich will not tolerate having a priest, for instance, speak almost without any typicalness peculiar to his calling, his environment; therefore, he will not have him in his novel, but will introduce a most typical one. Thus, he will sometimes compel a present-day priest, living in given circumstances and in a given environment, to converse as a priest of the beginning of the century who had also been living in specific circumstances and in a given milieu.

Priest Kastorsky begins as any other—for a while scarcely reminding one of his environment. So long as he keeps praising the artistic merits of the writer Leskov, he speaks, *as any other,* without employing typical little idioms and thoughts peculiar to the profession. But this was the author's intent; the profession had to be set aside in order that the literary praise sound more serious —and the censure of Mr. Nedolin, more rigid, since a funny and typical phrase would have toned down the rigidity. But suddenly the author, having grasped the fact that the reader, perhaps, might not believe that it is a priest who is writing, got scared and threw himself headlong into typicalities, and of these we have a whole cartload: every single word is a typical word! And, naturally, in this haste and bustle, typicality becomes false and disproportionate.

The principal trait of an uneducated man—but one who for some reason is compelled to resort to a language and conceptions not of his own environment—is a certain inaccuracy in the employment of words, the meaning of which, let's suppose, he even knows, but he is unfamiliar with all the nuances of their usage in the sphere of conceptions of some other profession. "And, therefore, to *leave without notice* such *injurious* attempts . . ."; "ignorance again *manifested* in the same magazine . . ."; "in it is portrayed a sexton with a *high-sounding* voice," etc. The latter word *"high-sounding"* is much too coarse, specifically because Pr. Kastorsky, seeking to express the conception of a person endowed with a beautiful voice, believes that the word "high-sounding" conveys the meaning. The author-specialist forgot that although, of course, even in our day there are among the clergy poorly educated people, only very few of them would be ignorant to the extent of not comprehending the meaning of words. This, Mr. Mummer, would do in fiction, but it does not stand the test of reality. Such an erroneous expression might be expected from some vestry-keeper, but certainly not from a priest.

I do not list all idioms and expressions, yet—I repeat—of these there is a whole cartload roughly piled up from the copybook. But, worst of all, is the fact that the author-pattern-drudge (if one may speak of an author-*artist,* one may equally entertain the idea of an author-*artisan,* while the word *pattern-drudge* denotes manual work or handicraft) portrayed his character in a light which was morally so unattractive. Be that as it may, but Pr. Kastorsky should have been depicted as a dignified and virtuous man, and typicality would have been no impediment. But the pattern-drudge, on his own part, was placed in a difficult position, out of which he was unable to extricate himself: willy-nilly, he had to give a scolding to his *confrère*—the author—to ridicule him, and so he, the mummer, of necessity was obliged to impose his lofty impulses upon his priest.

And, as regards miracles, the pattern-drudger utterly failed to restrain himself. As a result—an awful absurdity: a clergyman ridiculing miracles and dividing them into amazing and unamazing ones! Bad, Mr. Pattern-drudge!

I believe that the "Psalm-Reader," too, is the product of the same pen: the incompetent artisan at the end displayed too much naïveté, in the part dealing with the psalm-reader's "fears," which certainly do not sparkle with intelligence.

Briefly, gentlemen, this whole signboard job may somehow be all right in novels, but, I repeat, it will not survive in a collision with reality; it will promptly betray itself. Not even you, gentlemen-artists, can deceive an old littérateur.

What, then?—Are these jests on their part? Oh no, by no means jests. This is Darwinism, as it were, a struggle for existence. Don't you dare to enter our field. But in what way—how, gentlemen, can Mr. Nedolin injure you?—I assure you that he has no intention whatsoever to portray the genre aspect of the clergy; you can rest at peace. True, for a moment I was confused by one strange circumstance: indeed, if the mummer-pattern-drudge attacked Mr. Nedolin, then, by scolding him, in contradistinction he would have praised himself. (In this connection, these people have absolutely no self-respect: with utter impudence they are ready to write in their own handwriting, and publish, praises to themselves.) And yet, much to my surprise, the pattern-drudge puts forward and commends the talented Mr. Leskov, and not himself. Here there must be something different, and certainly it will be clarified. Yet that he is a *mummer* is beyond a shadow of doubt.

And what is the part of *The Russian World* in this matter?— I haven't the slightest idea. I have had no relations whatever with *The Russian World,* nor do I intend to have any. God only knows why people will jump at one.

The Citizen, 1873, No. 18.

VISIONS AND REVERIES

In the preceding issue of *The Citizen* we again raised the question of drunkenness—or rather, of the possibility of curing the ulcer of general popular drunkenness—of our hopes, of our faith in the immediate better future. However, involuntarily the heart feels afflicted with sorrow and doubts. Of course, owing to current important affairs (and we all look like such important business-men), there is no time—and it seems foolish—to speculate as to what is going to happen in ten years or by the end of the century, that is, when we shall no longer be living. The motto of the genuine businessman of our times is—*après moi le déluge*. But idle, not practical, people—those who have no business—truly may be excused for meditating, if they be inclined to meditate, now and then about the future. Didn't Poprischin (in Gogol's *Memoirs of a Lunatic*) meditate about Spanish affairs?—"All these events killed me, shook me so, that I . . .," etc., wrote he forty years ago. I confess: many things make me, too, quiver sometimes and, in truth, I feel de-spondent over my reveries. The other day, for instance, I was pondering over the status of Russia as a great European power, and what thoughts did not occur to me on this sad theme!

To begin with, consider that at all cost we must become a great European power as soon as possible. True, we are a great power, but what I mean to say is only that this costs us much too much—greatly in excess of what it costs other great powers, and this is a very bad symptom. So that whole thing becomes unnatural, as it were.

However, I hasten to make this reservation: I am judging solely from the Westerners' standpoint; and from this angle I am, indeed, drawing my conclusion. The case appears different from the national—and, so to speak, a bit Slavophile—point of view: here, as is known, there is faith in some inner independent forces of the people—in some popular, altogether individual and original powers inherent in our people, which are supporting and saving them.

But having read Mr. Pypin's articles, I became sober. It stands to reason that, much as hitherto, I continue to wish with all my heart that the precious, solid and independent principles, inherent in the Russian people, be actually existing. Nevertheless, you will also concede this: what are these principles which Mr. Pypin himself does not perceive, hear and discern; which are hid-den, have hidden themselves, and have no intention of being re-vealed at all? And consequently, willy-nilly, I have to do without these principles consoling one's soul.

Thus, I come to the thought that, as yet, we are clumsily clinging to our summit of a great power, exerting all our efforts to prevent our neighbors, as long as possible, from taking notice of this. In this we can be greatly assisted by the general European ignorance of everything concerning Russia. At least, thus far this ignorance could not have been doubted—a fact over which we should not be lamenting. On the contrary, it would be to our great disadvantage if our neighbors were to perceive us more minutely and from a shorter distance. In the fact that, so far, they have understood nothing about us—lay our great strength. But the point is that at present it seems, alas, that they are beginning to comprehend us better than heretofore: this is very dangerous.

Our colossal neighbor is relentlessly scrutinizing us and, it seems, he sees through many things. Without going into details, let us take the most obvious things striking one's eyes. Take the area occupied by us and our borders (inhabited by foreigners and aliens who, from year to year, have been consolidatng the individuality of their own alien, and partly foreign, neighboring elements). Take these things and consider: in how many points are we strategically vulnerable? To protect all these we have to maintain a far greater armed force than those of our neighbors (at least, in my opinion as a civilian). Also, consider that in our day wars are conducted not so much with ammunition as with brains, and you will agree that the latter circumstance is particularly disadvantageous to us.

At present weapons are being changed every ten years, and even more frequently. In another fifteen years or so, people will use for shooting not rifles but some kind of lightning, some sort of a machine emitting a holocaustal electrical stream. Tell me: what can we invent in this line so as to surprise our neighbors? What if in fifteen years every great power will have secretly stored away one such surprise for any kind of eventuality? Alas, we are merely capable of imitating and purchasing ammunition from others, and—at best—of repairing it at home. To invent such machines we should have to have our own independent, and not purchased, science, not an imported but a free one—one that has taken root in our soil. As yet we do not possess such a science, nor do we even have a purchased one.

Again, take our railroads: consider our distances and our poverty. Compare our capitals with those of the other great powers and try to understand: what would be the cost of the road network needed by us as a great power? And please bear in mind that they have built their networks long ago, and gradually, while we have to hurry and catch up. Their distances are short, while all of ours are on a Pacific-like scale. Even now we feel painfully the burden of the cost of nothing but the beginning of our network, and what a heavy, one-sided diversion of capital it has meant to the detriment, let us say, of our poor agriculture and any other industry. And the point here is not so much in the monetary sum as in the extent of the nation's effort.

Why, we should never come to the end if we were to enumerate, one by one, our needs compared with our poverty. Finally, consider education, that is, science: and think only how much we have to expend to catch up with the others in this respect. According to my humble way of thinking, we should be expending annually for education at least as much as for the army, if we were to attempt to catch up with any of the great powers. And we should also take into account that much time has already been lost; that we do not possess commensurate monetary resources, and that, in the long run, all this would merely constitute a spurt and not a normal undertaking—as it were, a concussion, and not education.

Of course, all these are but dreams; but . . . I reiterate, one begins to dream along these lines despite one's self, and so I will continue to meditate. Please note that I am evaluating everything in terms of money. Yet is this the correct way to reckon?—Under no circumstance can money purchase everything: only an ignorant shopkeeper from Mr. Ostrovsky's comedy would argue to the contrary. With money, for example, you may build schools, but you would be unable forthwith to produce teachers. A teacher is a delicate proposition; a popular, national teacher is the product of centuries; he is maintained by tradition, by endless experience.

But let us suppose that with money you would produce not only teachers but, eventually, even scientists. Even so, you would not produce men. What is there in the fact that a man is a scientist if he does not understand business? For instance, he will master pedagogy, and from his chair he will teach pedagogy quite efficiently, but nevertheless he will not become a pedagogue. Men, men—this is the most essential need. Men are dearer even than money. In no market, and no matter for what amount of money, can men be purchased, because they are neither salable nor purchaseable, but, again, they are evolved by centuries; well, and centuries require time—some twenty-five, or say, thirty years, even in our midst when centuries have long lost any value.

A man of ideas and of independent learning, a man independently versed in business, is capable of being moulded only by the long independent life of a nation, its century-long labors full of suffering; in short, he is produced by the country's historical life in its totality.

Now, our historical existence during the last two centuries, after all, has not been independent. It is absolutely impossible to accelerate artificially the necessary and continual historical phases

of national life. We see this in our own example: two centuries
ago it was sought to hurry and speed up everything, and instead,
we got stuck, since, notwithstanding all triumphant exclamations
of our Westerners, we undeniably did get stuck.

Our Westerners are people with extraordinary malignancy and
triumph, who are trumpeting today through all the trumpets that
we have no science, no common sense, no patience, no skill; that
we are destined to creep along behind Europe, to imitate her
slavishly in everything; and that, in view of European tutelage,
it is even a crime to think of our own independence. Yet, tomorrow,
if you should only dare to hint at your doubt as to the unquestionably salutary effect of the revolution which two centuries ago
occurred in our midst, they would start shouting in a chorus that
all your dreams about popular independence are nothing but kvas,
kvas and kvas; that two centuries ago we had been converted
from a mob of barbarians into the most enlightened and happiest
Europeans, and that we should be gratefully remembering this to
the end of our days.

But let us leave the Westerners alone, and let us suppose
that with money everything may be accomplished; that time itself
may be purchased, and that even independence of life may somehow be steamed up and re-enacted. The question is: where is such
money to be found?—Almost half of our present budget is paid
for by vodka; in other words, this means that, judging by the
present, the whole future of the people is dependent upon national
drunkenness and popular depravity. We are paying, so to speak,
with our future for our stately budget of a great European power.
We are cutting the tree at its very root, in order to get the fruit
as quickly as possible. And who sought this?—It happened involuntarily, of its own accord, as a result of the strict logic of historical
events. Our people, liberated by the great word of the Monarch,
are inexperienced in the new ways of life; as yet, they have not
lived independently, and they are merely taking their first strides
along the new road: this is an enormous and extraordinary break;
it is almost wholly unexpected, almost unheard of in history by
reason of its completeness and character. These first, and now independent, steps of the liberated giant along the new path, fraught
with great peril, require extraordinary caution. And yet, what did
our people encounter at these first steps?—Vacillation among the
upper strata of society; the alienation from the people of our intelligentsia which, for centuries, has been in existence (this is the
principal thing), and on top of these—trash and the Jew. The people
began revelling and drinking—first, from joy; and later, from force
of habit. Were they shown anything better than trashiness? Were

they diverted, were they taught anything?—At present in some, even in many, localities, pot-houses are so numerous that they exist in the proportion of not only one to hundreds but even to dozens of inhabitants—moreover, to only a few dozens. There are localities with some fifty dwellers, or less, and yet they have a pot-house of their own.

The Citizen has already reported once in a special article the detailed budget of our present-day saloon: it is impossible to suppose that these inns could be existing only on liquor. How, then, do they manage to be self-supporting?—By popular depravity—theft, receiving stolen goods, usury, banditry, destruction of the family and by popular disgrace—this is how they manage to thrive!

Mothers drink; children drink; churches are being deserted; fathers are engaged in banditry: the bronze arm of Ivan Susanin has been sawed off and brought to a pot-house, and there it was received! Do but consult medical science: what kind of generation can be begotten by such drunkards! But let—(and I pray God it may be so!)—let this be a mere dream of a pessimist, exaggerating the calamity ten times! We believe and wish to believe, yet . . . if in the forthcoming ten or fifteen years the people's addiction to drunkenness (which is still undeniable) does not diminish, but persists, and, therefore, expands—in this case wouldn't the vision itself be vindicated?—Here we have to have the budget of a great power and, therefore, we need money ever so badly. The question may be asked: who, then, is going to provide the money during these fifteen years, should this state of affairs persist? Labor, industry?—Since a sound budget is based only upon labor and industry?—Yet what kind of labor is to be expected in the face of such pot-houses?

Genuine, sound capital accumulates in a country in no other way than by being based upon a general labor prosperity; otherwise only capital owned by kulaks and Jews can come into existence. And thus it shall be if the people will not come to their senses and the intelligentsia will not help them. If the people should fail to come to their senses, they, as a whole, will find themselves in a very short time in the hands of all sorts of Jews, and in such an event no commune is going to save them: there will be merely uniformly equal paupers, mortgaged and enslaved as a whole commune, while, in their stead, Jews and kulaks will be providing the money for the budget. There will emerge petty, depraved and mean little bourgeois, and a countless number of paupers enslaved by them—such will be the picture! Yiddishers will be soaking up the blood of the people and subsisting on their debauch and humiliation; inasmuch, however, as they—these Yiddishers—will provide money for the budget, they will have to be supported. This is a bad, horrible dream and, praised be the Lord, it is merely a fancy! —titular councilor Poprischin's dream—I concede. But it will not come true! Not only once have the people saved themselves! They will find within themselves a protective force which they have invariably been finding; they will discover within themselves protective and salutary principles, those very principles which our intelligentsia stubbornly refuses to perceive in the people. They themselves will reject the pot-houses; they will start longing for work and order and honor—and not for the saloon!

And, thank God, all this—it seems—is being corroborated; at least, there are indications to this effect: we have already mentioned temperance societies. True, these are in only an embryonic state; these are but weak, scarcely noticeable, endeavors—but let them only not be impeded in their development, under some special pretexts! On the contrary, how desirable it is to support them! What if, on their own part, they be supported by all our progressive minds—our littérateurs and socialists, by the clergy and by all those in the press who, from month to month, are succumbing under the burden of their indebtedness to the people. What if they be supported also by the schoolteachers who are now coming into being! I know that I am not a practical man (at present, after the recent notorious speech of Mr. Spasovich, it is even gratifying to make this confession), but—can you imagine?—I am convinced that even the poorest schoolteacher of some sort may accomplish a great deal by his initiative, if only he should wish to! Herein is the real point: that in this matter the personality and character are important; the businessman is of moment, one who is really capable of exercising his will.

At present, teachers' positions are mostly occupied by our young men who, even when intending to do some good, do not know the people; they are suspicious and distrustful; after the first, at times most ardent and noble, endeavors they quickly become tired; they look sombre and they begin to regard their positions merely as transitory to something better; and then they either become accomplished topers or, for the sake of ten extra rubles, they quit everything and run away, no matter whither, even without being paid anything, even to America, in order "to experience free labor in a free state." This used to happen and continues to take place even now, it is said. There, in America, some vile contractor starves the schoolteacher on some manual job, cheats him and even beats him with his fists, and after every blow our schoolteacher fondly exclaims to himself: "God! How reactionary and dishonorable are these blows in my native land and, on the contrary, how noble, tasty and liberal they are here!" And so it will seem to him for a long time; but why should he renounce his convictions because of such trifles!

However, let us leave him alone in America. I will continue my thought. My thought—let me remind you—is that even a most insignificant rural schoolteacher could, if he only would, assume the whole initiative of the liberation of the people from the barbarous passion for drunkenness. On this subject I even have a plot for a novel and, perhaps, I shall risk revealing it to the reader prior to the writing of the story.

The Citizen, 1873, No. 21.

APROPOS OF A NEW DRAMA

This new drama is one by Mr. Kishensky: *Drinking to the Last Drop Will Yield No Good Crop,* the last three acts of which we ventured to print *in toto* in this 25th issue of *The Citizen,* notwithstanding the fact that it has consumed nearly half of our space. But we sought not to break the impression, and maybe the readers will agree that the drama deserves their special attention. It is conceived for the popular stage and it is written with knowledge, precision and talent—and this is the main thing, especially nowadays when virtually no new talents are to be found.

These are all characters of the factory pattern, of a "factory hamlet"; they are most heterogeneous and sharply delineated. The plot is here, and we shall not dwell upon it in detail. The idea is serious and profound. This is essentially a tragedy whose *fatum* is vodka; vodka has bound, filled and directed everything, and has brought about ruin.

True, the author, being a genuine artist, could not have failed to perceive the world depicted by him from a broader point of view, even though in the title of his drama he had proclaimed that *Drinking to the Last Drop Will Yield No Good Crop.* Here, in addition, we find a reverberation of the enormous economic and moral percussion resulting from the all-embracing reforms of the present reign. The former world, the old order, bad as it was, nevertheless constituted an order which has vanished forever.

Strangely, the dark moral aspects of the old order—egotism, cynicism, slavery, disunity and venality—not only have not disappeared with the abolition of serfdom but, as it were, they have grown stronger, more developed and more numerous; whereas from the good moral aspects of the old order—which actually did exist —there remains virtually nothing. All this is also reflected in Mr. Kishensky's picture, at least as we understand it. Here everything is in a state of transition and vacillation, and, alas, there is nothing even hinting at a better future.

The author energetically points to education as the salvation and the only solution; meanwhile, however, vodka has captured and poisoned everything and, having invaded and enslaved the people, has made things worse. And Mr. Kishensky draws a somber, dreadful picture of this new slavery which befell the Russian peasant after he had been freed from the former one.

Here we have two different sorts of types—of vanishing people and of those belonging to the new young generation.

The author is familiar with the young generation. His favorite types, whom he conceives as the hope for the future and who represent the halo in the dark picture, are portrayed fairly well (this is strange, since "positive" types are hardly ever successfully conceived by our poets). At least, Maria is perfect. Ivan, her fiancé, is drawn less successfully, notwithstanding the truth with which he is depicted. He is a young fellow, handsome, bold, literate—one who has seen much and learned new things, a kind and honest fellow. His whole defect consists in that the author has taken too much liking for him and has depicted him in too favorable a light. Had the author taken a more negative attitude toward him, the reader's impression would have been more favorable to his beloved hero.

Still, as an artist of refinement, the author did not overlook even the most disadvantageous traits in his Ivan's character. He is endowed with vigorous energy and a good mind, but he is young and presumptuous. He believes, magnanimously, in truth and in the right way, yet he confuses truth with men and unjustly demands from them the impossible. For instance, he is familiar with certain laws, so that the scribe "Levanid Ignatiich" is somewhat afraid of attacking him directly; but Ivan believes too naïvely in his knowledge; for this reason, he stands defenseless before evil, and not only does he not understand danger but he does not even suspect it. All this is so natural, and it could have come out perfectly because thus it must have been. Moreover, the author did not fail to take heed of a multitude of sympathetic details: Vania, even comprehending the whole abomination of the scoundrels (who, in addition, are hostile to him), as a young, fresh and strong man, to whom everything in life is still so attractive, does not sufficiently loathe them, keeps company with them, and *sings songs* with them. This youthful trait greatly attracts the reader to him.

Still—we repeat—the author took too much liking to him, and not even once does he look upon Ivan from above. It would seem to us that it is insufficient to set forth correctly all given qualities of a person: one has resolutely to illume him with one's own artistic vision. A genuine artist, under no circumstances, should remain on one level with the person portrayed by him, confining himself to mere realistic truth; the impression will carry no truth. Had there been, on the part of the author at least, a little drop of irony for the self-confidence and youthful arrogance of the hero, he would have become dearer to the reader. Otherwise one may think that the author actually meant to make him appear altogether guiltless in the face of the calamity wrought upon him.

Other persons of the younger generation—people lost almost since childhood, a "sacrificed generation"—are portrayed even more truthfully than the "positive types." There are two categories of them: the innocent ones and the guilty ones. Here, for instance, we have a little girl (Matriosha)—a sacrificed and unhappy creature; and what is most horrible is that one feels that of such "unhappy" ones there are in Russia as many as you please, multitudes—all villages are full of them. The truthfulness of the description is apt to terrify a kindhearted man who intelligently envisages our future. This is a generation which grew up after the reform. In early childhood it came face to face with a family already in a state of decomposition and cynical with wholesale drunkenness; and, later, it landed in the factory. Poor little girl! She has indulged in debauch, perhaps ever since the age of twelve, and she is almost unaware of the fact that she is depraved. On Christmas she went from the factory to her hamlet for a short stay, and she is sincerely surprised that her former companion, the peasant girl Masha, holds honor in greater esteem than fineries: "Now, Stepan Zakharych, ignorance sticks out"—says she.—"What's the harm in a shopkeeper, or a gentleman, playing around with a girl?" This she utters fully convinced of the truth and justice of her words, and—even more —pitying Masha and the villagers. When Masha spurns a dirty little merchant, a despicable scoundrel, Matriosha says frankly: "What's the use of talking to these people! They're groggy! Another, in her place, would have been only too glad! She would have bewitched and attracted him, and she would have made something for herself and would have humored her brother!" And, finally, when this unfortunate, in collusion with the miserable merchant, administers to Masha some sleeping powder, so that he may rape the poor, honest girl while she is lying unconscious, and when after that she climbs up onto the oven to ascertain whether the victim has fallen asleep, she commits this villainy not only without any conception of wrong, but earnestly convinced that she is doing Masha, her former companion, a favor—a benefaction for which she, Masha, will later thank her.

In the fifth act, in the ultimate horrible catastrophe, neither the despair of Masha, her father or her fiancé, nor the murder which is about to be committed—nothing perplexes Matriosha; of course, she is absolutely heartless, for how could she have acquired a heart? She shrugs her shoulders and utters her pet word: "Ignorance!" The author did not forget this exclamation, thus adding the artistic finishing touch to this character. Tragic fate!—A human being is converted into some rotten worm, fully content with itself and its pitiful horizon.

Here we have environment, the *fatum:* this unfortunate one is not guilty, and one understands it. But here is a different type —the most accomplished in the drama: the type of the depraved, tipsy, detestable factory lad, Masha's brother, selling his sister out to the miserable little merchant for three hundred rubles and a velvet jacket; this one is surely a type belonging to the guilty ones of the "sacrificed" generation. Here we have not only environment; true, the setting and the milieu are identical—drunkenness, family in a state of decomposition, and the factory. But this one does not naïvely, as Masha, embrace faith in debauch. He is not naïvely vile, as she, but lovingly; he adds to meanness something of his own. He does understand that debauch is debauch; he knows what is not debauch; but he takes a conscious liking for perversity and he despises honor. Consciously does he reject the old order of family and tradition; he is stupid and dull—this is true—but there is in him a sort of enthusiasm for sensuality and for the meanest, most cynical materialism. He is no longer a mere little worm, as is Matriosha, in whom everything is petty and withered. He stands there at a meeting of the village community, and one realizes that he no longer comprehends, or is capable of comprehending, anything in it; that he is no longer "of this world" with which he has completely severed all relations. He sells his sister with no rackings of conscience, and next morning he comes to his father's hut, to the scene of despair, in his velvet jacket and with a new harmonica in his hands. There is one thing in which he believes, as in omnipotence; this is vodka. With the dullest, yet most appropriate gesture, before every one of his undertakings, he offers vodka—bitter to the peasants, and sweet to their women—convinced that everything will transpire according to his desires and that vodka can accomplish anything. To make irony complete in him, as he is portrayed, side by side with unrestricted cynicism, there dwells a longing for the polite manners of days gone by—for traditional peasant "civility." Having arrived in his village, and not yet having seen his mother, he plants himself in the inn and politely sends her vodka. When he and Matriosha drag their mother into the pot-

house, in order to be at liberty to screw out of her the permission
to sell her own daughter to the merchant for rape, he civilly offers
her, before anything else, sweet vodka and, beckoning her to be
seated, he says: "If you please, mother dear"; and she is quite
pleased with his "civility."

Our author has been reproached by people who have read
the first act, for the too *natural* speech of the peasants, maintaining
that it could have been more literary. We ourselves feel displeased
with this *naturalness of the speech;* everything should be artistic.
However, after attentively reading and then re-reading the drama,
one is forced to concede that, in certain places at least, it would
have been impossible to change the language without weakening
the characteristic flavor of the play. This: "if you please, mother
dear"—could not have been modified; it would have sounded so
mean. And please note that sonny respects his "mother dear," this
miserable, stupid, tipsy old hag, as little as his own soul.

Here are the tragic words of the father of that family—an
old man addicted to liquor—about the "sacrificed generation":

Zakhar (swallowing a glass of vodka): "Drunkards! Just think,
friends: a factory workman keeps sitting all week long at his
lathe; his feet and hands will grow numb, and that head of his
will be filled, as it were, with fog! They're all crazy, so to speak!
They've lost human countenance! The premises are stuffy—the
walls bare; disgusting to look at! The sun never peeps into
the place! One sees it only on holidays! Well, friends, that
holiday's coming: thou, grandfather, canst start reading the
Scriptures; another fellow will go to the field to look at the
crop, or to the woods, maybe, to the bees, or else to neighbors
for a chat about zemstvo, let's say, or some meeting or corn
prices—now, I ask you, where's the factory hand to go? What's
he going to talk about?—To him, all things are measured and
weighed! Only fines, maybe, are exacted—who knows for what?
And rotten food is provided, or a ruble's worth of tea is being
sold for two-fifty; he's not to leave the gate so that provisions
be bought from him[1] and there be more debauch. Isn't this so?
—Well, there's but one road—to the pot-house! It's nothing but
idle talk about vodka and lewdness!"

Vasily: "That's right!"

Zakhar: "Think, friends, one also wants to have recreation!
Well, it's youth! People gather for a round dance, songs, laughter
—and a policeman disperses them! So the whole pack go to the
saloon and the tavern! Then they'll start babbling about girls

[1] The factory owner. (B. B.)

and who's going to out-drink the other! Girls of twelve are looking for sweethearts! Spool-workers lap up vodka like water!
In the mill—obscenities, shamelessness; the air is permeated with
groans of cursing, regular hell! Children are grownups! We send
our children there for ruin! Is there a single girl without lewdness, a single lad not a toper—in factories, I mean?"

But the most characteristic scene of all in this popular drama
is the third act—the peasants' community meeting. A strong thought
is invested in this episode of the play. This meeting is *all* that is
left of the firm, cornerstone foundations of Russian life; its main
traditional link and its future hope. And now this meeting already
bears the element of decomposition; it is already ailing in its inner
content. One can perceive that in many respects it is merely a
form, but its inner spirit and its inner secular truth are tottering—
they started tottering with the tottering people.

At this meeting a most revolting injustice takes place: contrary to custom and law, the only son of a widow—Ivan, the hero
of the drama—is being drafted into the army in place of a lad
from a well-to-do family with three sons. And the worst thing
is that this is being done knowingly, with deliberate disrespect for
truth and custom: this is being done for liquor and money. Here
it is not even a bribe—a bribe, after all, would not be so bad: it
may be a solitary and corrigible crime. No, here everything arises
out of conscious disrespect for oneself, for one's own court, and,
thus, for one's own traditional ways of life. Cynicism is already
revealed in the fact that, in violation of the custom and ancient
rule, the community permits a drinking bout at the beginning of
the meeting: "Better will be the judgment with some fumes in the
head"—sneeringly declare the leaders of the gathering.

Half of the assembled citizens have long ago lost faith in
the authority of the communal decision and, consequently, in its
necessity; they almost consider it a futile form which may always
be eluded—may be and must be, contrary to the truth and for the
sake of an immediate advantage. In a short time, one feels, cheap
wits of a more modern pattern will start regarding this whole
ceremony as mere foolishness, a futile burden, since the communal
decision, no matter what happens, will be such as is sought by
the rich and powerful bloodsucker who is directing the meeting.
So that, instead of the empty formalities, it is better to go straight
into subjugation of this bloodsucker. And, in addition, he will
be serving vodka. Do you see that the majority of these autonomous
members have lost the very thought that their decision could be
rendered contrary to the will of the strong man? They have all

"grown flabby" and their hearts have grown fat; everybody is craving for sweets, for material gain. Essentially, they are all slaves, and they can't even conceive that a matter may be decided for the sake of truth and not for personal benefit.

The young generation is present there, and they look at their fathers' business not only without respect, not only scoffingly, but as some obsolete nonsense—precisely as a foolish, futile form which manages to persist exclusively through the obstinacy of two or three stupid old men who, besides, may always be bought. Thus does Stepan stand and behave there—that tipsy, detestable lad who later sells his sister.

All these episodes of the communal meeting are successfully portrayed by the author. And the main thing is that Stepan is almost right about the fact that not only does he understand nothing transpiring in that communal meeting, but that he does not even deem it necessary to comprehend it. Of course, he could not have helped but notice that an external element was permitted to influence the meeting, namely, the merchant who had made up his mind to ruin Vanka and wrest from him his girl-fiancée. The commune, having consumed the merchant's liquor, permitted his clerk to utter aloud to himself that, without him, the merchant-factory owner—who, through factory work provides them with their daily bread—"your whole volost would have been begging on church porches, but should they render a decision in accord with his dictate, 'his sedateness,'[1] the merchant, would waive many a fine imposed upon the people." Of course, the matter is decided in favor of the merchant, and Vanka is drafted into the army.

At this meeting (attended by most diverse personages and characters) there are two almost tragic persons: one is Naum Egorov, an old man, who for twenty years has been occupying the front seat at the meeting and directing it, and the other is Stepanida, Ivan's mother. Naum Egorych is a reasonable, firm and honest old man with a lofty soul. He views communal decisions from an elevated standpoint. To him this is not a mere gathering of house-owners of such and such a hamlet—no, spiritually, he has lifted himself to the broadest conception: in his view, a decision of a meeting even of his own hamlet is, as it were, a part of the judgment of all of peasant Russia, which persists and stands solidly only because of the peasants' commune and its judgment.

But, alas, he rationalizes too much: he is unable to perceive the communal vacillation and the orientation whither the commune has been swayed for some time. Untruth and villainy, of

[1]A title applied to Russian merchants of olden times—something akin to "his honor." (B. B.)

course, used to exist at meetings in days gone by—twenty years ago; nevertheless, disrespect for the meeting on the part of its members, disrespect for their own business, was unknown or, at least, it was not raised to the level of a principle. People used to commit villainy but they knew that they were perpetrating a disgraceful thing, and that there was good; at present, however, they do not believe in good, nor in its necessity.

Still, Naum is a sort of a last Mohican; he continues to believe in communal truth *quand-même,* almost *forcibly,* and therein is his tragicalness. He is a formalist; sensing that the content is slipping away, he clings all the more tenaciously to the form. Seeing that the commune is drunk, he is ready to make the request that the meeting be postponed, but when people begin to shout: "Better will be the judgment with some fumes in the head!"—he yields: "The commune has decided, and one shouldn't oppose the commune." In his heart he knows only too well that, strictly speaking, their hired despicable scribe, Levanid Ignatiich, has the last say, and that the meeting is going to render such a decision as it will be ordered to render by the merchant's clerk. But the old man still continues, for the time being, though against his will, to deceive himself: he dismisses Levanid from his front seat and, as chairman of the meeting, reprimands the clerk for his discourteous words directed against the commune.

Several truthful voices are raised in favor of Vanka; they praise him; they say that he is a good, sensible lad who is useful to the commune; that a lad, such as he, should be spared. But, at this juncture, the voice of an old tipsy head, among others, exclaims: "Why, if he's better than the rest—let's make him a recruit!" This means deliberate scoffing at truth, a flagrant display of untruth, sport. . . . The judge jokes about himself, and this in a matter involving the fate of a man!

Naum hears and, of course, realizes that his "commune" is coming to an end. Ivan's mother stands there. She is a proud, strong and not yet old woman. Long ago she became a young widow. As a widow, she has been persecuted and wronged by the commune. But she has endured everything: she has repaired her humble little cottage; she has raised her only beloved Vania for her joy and consolation, and now she is listening to the commune taking away from her her best hope, her last joy, her own son. Naum Egorych, foreboding the tipsy, unruly decision of the commune, hastily says to Stepanida: "Ekh, what's to be done! The commune is a power! Beg, Stepanida, beg the commune!" But she does not want to beg; instead, she haughtily accuses the commune of untruth, of bribery, of tipsy judgment, of envy toward her Vania.

"Stepanida, thou shalt embitter the commune still more!"—exclaims Naum with alarm. "Dost thou not think, Naum Egorych"—replies Stepanida—"that if I saw law and conscience here—here's only vodka! . . . —If I knew that here it were possible to gain their compassion, I'd rub the skin off my knees against the bare ground; I'd wash the floor in a hut clean with my tears; I'd smash my head bowing to the commune! But here they'll not listen to entreaties! They'll have no pity! Dost thou not see that here everything is concocted and prearranged? They, the crows, will ruin my bright falcon, they'll peck him to death! Ye sell your souls for vodka! What are ye worshipping?—Vodka! He who hath treated ye more —he hath bought ye! See, Vania, thou hast offended the fat merchant! Don't ye know that the drunken fat merchant sought to cover with shame Vania's bride! Ye don't know this!—Why, the merchant's vodka tastes good! Ye ribalds—bloodsuckers! Ye even reproached me for having adopted a homeless orphan! But it's not going to be your way! It's just not going to be! The mediator knows my Vaniusha—he's not going to let ye offend him!" (She walks away hastily.)

This proud woman is one of the characters which our poet has portrayed very successfully. Be that as it may, gentlemen, but this is a potent scene. Of course, this is a Russian village— and the person, a simple peasant woman who even cannot talk literately—but, by God, this monologue about skin-rubbed-off-knees, "if it were possible to gain their compassion," is worth many a pathetic scene in some tragedies of this kind. Here there are no classical phrases; there is no beautiful language, no white curtain; there are no glowing black eyes of a Rachel; yet, I assure you, if we had our Rachel, you would have shivered in the theatre at this maternal malediction upon the communal court, at all its unembellished truth. The scene winds up with a most significant movement—with the flight after truth to "the mediator," to complain to him against the communal decision. This is a distressing prophecy.

It is almost superfluous to point further to all the best scenes in this work. But I cannot refrain from conveying my impression, and I will say frankly: rarely have I read anything more potent and more tragic than the finale of the fourth act.

The victim—sold out by her mother and brother to the merchant, drugged with a philter into a state of unconsciousness—falls asleep on the oven. Matriosha, that innocent delinquent, climbs upon the oven to take a look, and, almost with joy, virtually convinced that now she has made Masha happy, announces to the miserable merchant: "Ready! She won't move even if she be cut up into pieces!" The scribe Levanid, the merchant's companion, gets up and walks out: "What a life is given to you merchants"—he utters enviously. And now, the merchant, before climbing onto his victim, is seized with a sort of exalted pathos: " 'Cause we're a power now!" —he exclaims voluptuously and prophetically. "We can do anything we please. If a merchant fancies something nowadays, he can have it—'cause we're a power!"—"Power—there's no argument!"— confirms the victim's brother. Thereupon, those not needed leave the hut; the scoundrel creeps toward Masha, while the drunken mother, who had sold her innocent daughter, the promised bride of unfortunate Vania, in a state of intoxicated unconsciousness, falls asleep right there on the floor at the feet of the hopelessly drunken father of this happy family. . . . *Drinking to the Last Drop Will Yield No Good Crop.*

I do not enumerate all these traits of the dreadful picture which impress one with their truth; I do not point to these criminals who almost fail to comprehend their crime—fail to comprehend and yet are already deprived of the right to curse their crime—such as the tipsy father of the family, upon whom the daughter tragically, straight to his face, invokes her daughterly malediction.

There are some most keenly observed traits: Masha, during the first moments after she comes to her senses, is about to commit suicide; but then she puts on the silk sarafan which the merchant had left for her with her mother; however, she puts it on out of malevolence, *for the sake of torture,* in order to inflict more torment upon herself: "Now, look, I have become a harlot myself!" Here is the conversation between the "innocent" mother and the "innocent" Matriosha on the day after the calamity:

Matriosha (walking in): "Good morning, Aunt Arina! What's doing here? Yesterday—I confess—I was even scared to call on you!"

Arina: "Oh, oh, girlie, what fears we've endured! Awful! When at morn the girl found it out, she grabbed a knife and was ready to kill us—and after that, herself! With very great difficulty did we succeed in subduing her! Now she'll not admit Stiopka to her eyes!"

Matriosha: "So he told me."

Arina: "Well, towards evening, you know, she calmed down— now she has become like a stone! 'God,' says she, 'punished me for Matriosha; now,' says she, 'I am as she'! Presently, girlie, I gave her the sarafan, the one Silanty Savelych had bought from you. She put it on: 'I,' says she, 'turned into Matriosha, so I'll be wearing the sarafan'! That's the way things are!"

Matriosha: "Where is she now?"

Arina: "Oh, oh, girlie, she'll go to the shed, bury herself in the straw, and she'll be lying there face-down."

Matriosha: "She's likely to take her life into her own hands—in a passion, I mean."

But the victim does not take her life into her own hands. "I got scared," she herself tells us later. Our poet possesses much psychological knowledge concerning the people. Here is Vania unexpectedly returning from the mediator after an absence of twenty-four hours. The poet did not spare his hero for the sake of realistic truth: in the first moments Ivan is in a state of bestial rage; he blames Masha alone; he is unjust and disgusting. However, having at last grasped how the thing had happened, he involuntarily, as it were, proposes to Masha that she marry him even *so*. But the author knows only too well that according to the customs of our people this is almost inconceivable, if the love affair is an honorable one. A girl dishonored, even though by deceit, even without any guilt on her part, is nevertheless regarded as unclean—if not altogether dishonest. Besides, Masha, too, is prideful: "Don't soil yourself against me, Vania!"—she shouts—"Go away! Farewell, Vania!" And then in the last monologue, she hurriedly approaches the table, pours a glass of vodka, and with a glowing glance at everybody she looks around and shouts with a desperate, malevolent twist:

"Well, why have ye become sad?—Rejoice, it's your job! Mother dear! Father dear! Let's all drink and be merry! Not alone shalt thou prowl about pot-houses!— With your daughter! It's weary, mother dear, to drink in solitude; now, it's the two of us—with your daughter! Overflow, thou wine! Drown my woe, my conscience!"

And she lifts the glass to her lips. Such is the end of the drama.

I don't mean to say that it is altogether faultless; but there are so many genuine merits in this work that any mistakes seem almost insignificant. For example, Masha's tone in the monologue of the fourth act, which she winds up with a delightful and lofty psychic impulse: "Now, it has become so easy!"—That tone is a bit too sweet. True, this is almost not a monologue at all, but a meditation, a sentiment—those very meditations and sentiments under whose influence, among Russian men with heart and poesy, all the songs of the Russian people have been conceived. For this reason also, Masha's meditation, essentially truthful in a high degree and natural, could have assumed a somewhat lyrical form, as it were. Yet art has its limitations and rules, and the monologue could have been made shorter.

Nor, perhaps, is Masha's tone quite correct at the end of the drama, after the catastrophe: it would have been better if she had talked a wee bit less. Her horrible words, addressed to her father, would have been far more forceful if they had been briefer and not so melodious.

Still, all this is corrigible; the author may well correct these things in the second edition, and—we repeat—compared with the undeniable merits of his work, these are almost trifles. It would also be good if the author should altogether delete from his drama the appearance at the end (wholly unnecessary) of the virtuous old factory-owner, who is practically preaching about our "debt to the people." His appearance is all the more absurd as this is the very manufacturer who has enslaved all the neighboring population, exhausted them with wanton fines, and who is feeding his workers with rotten food.

Finally, the master of the house, Zahar, is portrayed somewhat indeterminately. In his own explanation as to why he took to drinking, there is something false, something unexplained and strained, whereas the matter could have been presented much more simply and naturally.

However, this is only my opinion, and I may be mistaken; but I am certain that I am not mistaken about the solid merits of this serious work. I am only too glad to share my impressions with the reader. Of late, and perhaps for some considerable time, there has appeared in our literature nothing more serious.

The Citizen, 1873, No. 25.

LITTLE PICTURES

1

Summer, vacation-time and heat—heat and dust. It is painful to stay in town. Everybody is away. The other day I was about to start reading the manuscripts which have accumulated at the editorial office. . . . However, let us postpone discussing manuscripts, although there is something to be said about them.

One longs for air, ease, freedom, and instead of air and freedom, one roams alone through streets covered with sand and lime, and one feels as though offended by someone—truly, a feeling akin to it! It is a fact that half of one's affliction vanishes if only someone can be found to share the guilt of it, and it is all the more disappointing if absolutely no one can be found.

A few days ago I was crossing Nevsky Prospect from the sunny to the shady side. It is known that one crosses Nevsky Prospect with caution—otherwise one may be promptly crushed; one manœuvres, watchfully looks around, trustingly seizes a favorable moment before embarking upon the perilous journey; one waits for a time when traffic will be clear, though only a little bit, of carriages rushing one after the other in two or three rows.

In winter, for instance, two or three days before Christmas, it is particularly interesting to cross: one takes great chances, especially if a frosty fog has been blanketing the town since the morning dawn, when at a distance of some three steps one hardly recognizes a passer-by. Somehow one manages to slip by the first rows of coaches and cabmen rushing in the direction of the Police Bridge, glad that one no longer has to fear them: the trampling and rattling and coachmen's hoarse halloos are left behind one, and yet there is no time to rejoice; one has only reached the middle of the dangerous crossing, while further on—it's risk and incertitude. Hastily and anxiously one looks around, and hurriedly one conjectures how to slip through the second row of carriages speeding in the direction of the Anichkov bridge. But one feels that there is even no time to think—and, besides, this infernal fog; one merely hears trampling and cries, but one can see only a sajen around. And suddenly, out of the fog, one discerns swift, accelerated, hard, rapidly approaching sounds, dreadful and ominous at this minute —very similar to the sounds of six or seven men with a chaff-cutter chopping cabbage in a vat. "Where's one to escape? Forward or backward? Will one have time or not?" And one is lucky to have stood still: suddenly out of the fog, at a distance of only one step, there emerges the gray snout of a heavily breathing trotter, madly rushing at the speed of a railroad express train: foam on the bit, the bow slanting sideways, reins are strained, while the beautiful, strong legs, with every stroke, even and firm, measure off a sajen. One brief moment, a desperate halloo of the coachman —and everything flashes and flies out of the fog into the fog— trampling and chopping and cries—everything vanishes again, like a vision. Verily, a Petersburg vision! One crosses one's self, and almost disregarding the second row of carriages, which only a minute ago seemed so frightening, one quickly reaches the welcome sidewalk, still trembling from the sensation just experienced, and, strangely, at the same time feeling for some unknown reason a feeling of pleasure—and not because one had escaped danger, but precisely because one had been subjected to it. A retrograde pleasure, no doubt, and, in addition, one that is useless in our age—all the more so as, contrariwise, one had to protest and seem not to have been experiencing pleasure, since the trotter is not liberal in the highest degree; he reminds one of a hussar, or a reveling shop-keeper. Consequently—inequality, impudence, *la tyrannie*, etc.

This I know, and I am not arguing, but now I merely wish to finish. And so, the other day, with the customary winter caution, I started crossing Nevsky Prospect and, suddenly, awaking from musing, I stopped with astonishment in the very middle of the passage: there's no one—not a single carriage, not even some jarring cabman's droshky! The place is empty some fifty sajen on either side: one could stop and start discussing Russian literature with a friend—it is safe to that extent! It's even insulting. When was such a thing ever known?

Dust and heat, strange odors, raked-up pavement, and houses in a state of reconstruction. Mostly, it is façades that are being remodeled; old ones are being modernized—just for flaunt, for the sake of typicality. To me, this present-day architecture of ours seems astonishing. And, generally, the architecture of the whole of Petersburg is extremely characteristic and original; it has always struck me precisely by the fact that it expresses its whole lack of character and its impersonality throughout the entire period of its existence. Of typicalness, in a positive sense, of its own, there are, perhaps, only these wooden, rotten little houses still surviving, even in the most fashionable streets, side by side with enormous houses, and suddenly striking one's eye as a heap of firewood near a marble palazzo.

As regards palazzi, it is precisely in them that the character-less idea is reflected, the whole negatory substance of the Petersburg period, from its beginning to the end. In this sense there is no such city as Petersburg: from an architectural standpoint it is a reflection of all architectures in the world, of all periods and fashions: everything has been gradually borrowed and distorted in its own way. In these buildings one may read, as from a book, the tides of all ideas, and petty ideas, which, justifiably or at random, have flown to us from Europe and which have gradually subdued and enslaved us.

Here is the characterless architecture of the past century; there, a pitiful copy, in Roman style, of the beginning of our century; and still further—we come to the epoch of the Renaissance and a building in old Byzantine style, said to have been discovered during the preceding reign by the architect Thon.

And then we see several edifices—hospitals, institutes and even palaces of the first decade of our century—these in the style of Napoleon I: colossal, pseudo-majestic and incredibly weary; something strained and deliberately invented at the time, together with those bees on Napoleon's mantle, intended for the expression of the grandeur of the epoch, which just then had begun, and of the unheard-of dynasty claiming everlastingness.

Next, we behold mansions—almost palaces—of some of our noble families, but of very recent times: these are in the fashion of certain Italian palazzi, or in a not quite pure French style of the pre-revolutionary epoch. But there, entire generations, one after the other, throughout centuries have died out or are dying out in those Venetian and Roman palazzi, whereas we have planted our palazzi only during the past reign but, it seems also with a claim to everlastingness: the order of things which had then come into existence seemed all too solid and encouraging, and in the appearance of these palazzi the faith in that order, as it were, was reflected: they, too, meant to live for centuries. All this, however, has occurred almost on the eve of the Crimean War and, afterwards, came the liberation of the peasants. . . .

I shall feel very sad if some day, on such a palazzo, I should read a signboard of a tavern with an amusement garden, or of a French hotel for travelers.

And, finally, here we have the architecture of a modern, enormous hotel: this is a businesslike trend—Americanism, hundreds of rooms, a formidable industrial enterprise. One sees at once that we, too, have built railroads, and that all of a sudden we have become businessmen.

And now, now . . . in truth, one does not know how to define our present architecture: here we have something nondescript which, however, is in full accord with all the nondescript things of the present moment. Here we see a lot of very high (height being their main characteristic) houses for tenants, with extremely thin walls, it is rumored, and stingily constructed, displaying an amazing number of architectural styles of façades: here we have Rastrelli, and late rococo; doge balconies and windows, by all means *œils-de-bœuf*, and also by all means five stories—and all these in one and the same façade. "Now, brother, at all cost stick in a doge window, because in what way am I inferior to some of their belly-pinched doges? well, and as regards the five stories, these must nevertheless be erected—for tenants; window-to-window, and stories should be stories, since I can't be losing our capital for playthings only!"

However, I am not a Petersburg feuilletonist, and I started to talk about altogether different matters: I began with editorial manuscripts and wound up with a matter that is of no concern to me.

2

Dust and heat. It is said that for those who have remained in Petersburg several parks and amusement establishments have been opened, where one can "breathe" fresh air. I don't know if there is any air to breathe there, because as yet I have been nowhere. In Petersburg, it is better, more stifling, more melancholy. One roams, meditates in full solitude—this is better than the fresh air of the Petersburg amusement parks. Besides, in the city itself many parks have been opened, unexpectedly, in places where they would never have been suspected. Virtually in every street, at some gate-entrances, at times piled up with lime and bricks, one finds a sign: "Entrance to the tavern's garden." There, in the courtyard, in front of a little old shanty, some forty years ago, a minute grass plot—ten steps long and five steps wide—had been fenced off. Well, then, this is now the "tavern's garden."

Tell me: why is it that on Sundays in Petersburg one feels far sadder than on weekdays? Is it because of vodka? Because of drunkenness? Because drunken peasants lie and sleep on Nevsky Prospect amidst bright . . . evening, as I have witnessed myself? —I don't think so. Revellers from among the working people do not disturb me and, having now stayed on in Petersburg, I got quite used to them, although formerly I could not stand the sight of them, even to the point of hate. On holidays they sometimes roam around drunk, in crowds, crushing and running into people—not because of unruliness, but just because a drunken person cannot help running into and pushing people, cannot but curse aloud despite the presence of whole crowds of children and women whom they encounter; and it is not due to impudence, but just because a toper can use no other language than an obscene one. Precisely, this is a language, a whole language—of this I recently became convinced—a most convenient and original language, adapted to the drunken or only slightly intoxicated state, so that it was likely to come into being, and, if it were altogether nonexistent, *il faudrait l'inventer*. I am not joking at all. Consider: it is known that, to begin with, in a state of intoxication the tongue becomes tied and moves tightly, whereas the influx of thoughts and sensations in an intoxicated person, or in anyone who is not as drunk as a fiddler, increases nearly ten times. For this reason, naturally it becomes necessary that a medium be found which should satisfy the two conflicting states. Such a language, from time immemorial, has been found and adopted throughout the whole of Russia. This simply takes the form of one unprintable noun, so that this whole language consists of only one word, which is extraordinarily easy to pronounce.

Once, late in the evening on a Sunday, I chanced to take some fifteen steps side by side with a group of six drunken workmen; and suddenly I became convinced that it is possible to express all thoughts, feelings, and even profound arguments, by the mere utterance of that one noun which, besides, is composed of very few syllables, indeed. First, one of the lads sharply and energetically pronounces this noun to express his contemptuous negation of something that had been the general topic of their conversation. Another lad, answering him, repeats the same noun, but in an altogether different tone and sense—namely, in the sense of complete doubt as to the veracity of the former's negation. The third fellow suddenly blows up with indignation against the first lad, bitterly and excitedly bursting into the conversation, and he shouts to him the same noun, but this time in the sense of invective and abuse. At this juncture the second lad again butts in, incensed against the third one, the offender, and stops him, as if inferring: "Now why did you, young fellow, break in? We've been talking calmly, and whence did you come?—Why do you start scolding Filka?" And he expresses this whole thought by uttering the same forbidden word, the same strictly monosyllabic appellation of a certain object, and was ready to lift his hand and grasp the third lad by his shoulder. But, unexpectedly, a fourth little chap—the youngest in the whole group—who until that moment had kept silent, but probably has suddenly discovered the solution to the initial difficulty which had caused the altercation, raises his arm and shouts with delight . . . Eureka, you would think? Found it? Found it? No, not Eureka at all; nor did he find anything: he merely keeps repeating the same unprintable noun, only one word—nothing but one word, but with delight, with screams of rapture, perhaps a bit too enthusiastic; but to the sixth morose lad, the oldest one, it did not "seem" so, and he promptly takes down the youngster's enthusiasm, turning towards him and repeating in a morose, didactic bass . . . the same noun that shouldn't be mentioned in the presence of ladies, and which this time clearly and precisely meant: "What art thou straining thy throat and brawling about?"

Thus, not once having uttered any other single word, they repeated six times this one pet little word of theirs, in strict succession, and they fully understood each other. This is a fact which I have witnessed.

"Have pity!"—I shouted at them, suddenly, for no reason. (I was in the very middle of the crowd.) "You took only ten steps and you have uttered (I mentioned the word) six times! This is a shame! Aren't you ashamed of yourselves?"

All of them suddenly began to stare at me, as one stares at

something wholly unexpected, and for a moment they kept silent.
I thought they would start abusing me, but they did not; only the
youngster, having walked off some ten steps, turned toward me
and, as he continued on his way, he shouted:

"And why dost thou thyself mention *him* the seventh time if
thou counted six times to our credit?"

There sounded a burst of laughter, and the group walked off
without taking further notice of me.

3

No, I am not speaking about these revellers, and it is not
because of them that I feel particularly sad on Sundays. Recently,
I have discovered with great astonishment that in Petersburg there
are peasants, commoners and workers who are quite temperate and
who do not "use" liquor even on Sundays. And it was not this that
astonished me, but the fact that of such people there are, it seems,
infinitely more than I had hitherto supposed.

Now, to me it is even sadder to behold these than the tipsy
revellers, and this is not from compassion for the former. Nor is
there any reason to feel compassion for them; but even so—a
strange thought keeps coming to my mind. . . .

On Sundays, toward evening (on weekdays they are not seen
at all) a great many of these absolutely sober people, engaged all
week in work, go out into the streets. Precisely, they come out for
a walk. I have noticed that they never go on the Nevsky: mostly
they stroll near their homes, or they walk along "leisurely," returning with their families after visiting some people. (It seems
that there are also a great many married workers in Petersburg.)
They walk along sedately and with awfully serious faces, as if it
were not just a walk, conversing very little with each other, especially husbands with their wives—almost silently, but invariably in
their holiday clothes.

Their clothing is old and bad—on women, it is many-colored;
but everything is cleaned and washed for the holiday, intentionally
—perhaps, for this hour. There are some in Russian dresses, but
many are in German clothes, with shaved beards.

The most annoying part is that they really and seriously
imagine, it seems, that by strolling in this manner they are providing themselves with genuine Sunday recreation. Now—one may
ask—what pleasure is there on this wide, bare, dusty street—still
dusty after sunset?—That's exactly the point: to them this seems
paradise. So, everybody to his own.

Quite frequently they are accompanied by children; there
are also a lot of children in Petersburg, and yet it is said that here

a great number of them die. As far as I could observe, they are mostly very young children, of the earliest age; they can barely walk, or they have not yet learned to walk. Is the reason why there are so few children of an older age that they do not survive, but die? Here I see in the crowd a solitary worker, but with a child, a little boy; they are both lonely, and they both look so lonely. The worker is about thirty; his is a lean, unhealthy face. He is in his holiday clothes: a German suit, worn out at the seams; the buttons are rubbed off and the collar of the coat is quite greasy; his breeches are "accidental"—they are third-hand pants from a rag fair; yet everything has been cleaned up as well as possible. A calico shirt-front, a necktie, a top hat—quite rumpled. He has shaved his beard. Probably he is working in a locksmith shop or is employed in some capacity in a printing office. The expression of his face is gloomy, morose, pensive, hard, almost spiteful. He holds the child by its hand, and it wobbles, behind him, swinging some-how from side to side. It is a little boy, slightly over two years, very weak, very pale, but he is dressed in a tiny kaftan; he wears little boots with a red edging, and a hat with a little peacock feather. He is tired; father said something to him—probably nothing much, but it seemed as if he had scolded the child. The boy grew still. But after having taken another five steps or so, the father stooped down, cautiously lifted the child, took him into his arms and car-ried him. The boy, in an accustomed manner and trustfully, clung to him, clasped his neck with his little right hand and, with childish astonishment, began to gaze at me: why do I follow them and look at them in this way? I was about to nod and smile, but he frowned his little brows and still more tightly clutched at his father's neck. Probably, the two are great friends.

I like, when roaming through the streets, to look attentively at certain wholly strange passers-by, to study their faces and to conjecture: who are they, how do they live, what is their occupation and what, at this particular moment, attracts their particular in-terest?

As regards the worker with the little boy, it occurred to me at the time that only some two months before his wife must have died, and necessarily—I don't know why—of consumption. Tem-porarily, the little motherless boy is being cared for by some little old wench (father is working all week in the shop) in a basement where they are renting a tiny room or, perhaps, a corner-space. Now, however, on a Sunday, the widower and his son have been somewhere far away, to the Viborgskaia, for a visit to a sole sur-viving relative—most probably, to a sister of the deceased—on whom, in the past, they did not call so very frequently; she is married to some non-commissioned officer with a stripe who must be living in some huge governmental building, and also in a basement, but in a separate apartment. The woman, perhaps, had heaved a few sighs about the deceased, but not much; the widower, I am sure, also did not sigh much during the visit, but was morose, spoke rarely and little, and suddenly turned to a special business topic, but shortly he stopped talking even about that. Probably a samovar was brought and tea was drunk with little nibbles of sugar. The little boy was sitting shyly all the time on a bench in the corner, kept knitting his brows and, finally, fell asleep. The aunt and her husband paid little attention to him, but still, after a while, they did give him some milk with bread, and the host—the non-commissioned officer, who up to that time had quite ignored the boy —made, by way of endearment, some witty remark about the child; but it was a salty and inopportune remark which made him (but him only) laugh, while the widower, on the contrary, at just that moment sternly—no one knows what for—started scolding the little fellow, in consequence of which he immediately began to feel a need to use the toilet; at this juncture father, now refraining from chiding and with a serious air for a minute, carried the child out of the room. . . .

They parted as gloomily and ceremoniously as they had carried on their conversation, abiding by all conventions and decorum. Father took the boy into his arms, carrying him home from the Viborgskaia to Liteinaia. Tomorrow, he is going back to his shop, and the little boy—back to the old woman.

And thus, I am roaming and roaming around and keep inventing for my own diversion such trifling little pictures. There is no sense in this and "nothing instructive can be derived therefrom." This is the reason why on Sundays, while on vacation, I am experiencing spleen in the dusty and gloomy Petersburg streets. Did it never occur to you that streets in Petersburg are gloomy?—To my way of thinking, this is the gloomiest city in the world!

True, on weekdays, too, a great number of children are being taken out, but on Sundays, toward evening, there are almost ten times more of them in the streets. What lean, pale, emaciated, anæmic, gloomy little faces they all have—particularly those still carried in the arms. And those who already can walk all have crooked little legs and all of them, when walking, keep rocking from side to side. Still, almost all are dressed with great care. But, good Lord, a child is like a flower, like a tiny leaf set on a tree in spring: it needs light, air, ease, fresh food—and, instead of all these, a sultry basement with some kvas or cabbage odor, with a disgusting stink at night, unhealthy food, cockroaches and fleas, humidity, dampness dropping from the walls, and outside—dust, bricks and lime.

But these people are fond of their pale and emaciated children. Here, a little three-year-old girl, good-looking in a fresh little frock, hastens toward mother, who is sitting at the gate in a big group assembled from the whole house for a one- or two-hour chat. Mother prattles but keeps an eye on the child, who is playing ten steps away from her. The little girl bows down to pick up something, some little pebble, and incautiously she steps with her little feet on her skirt, and now she is unable to get up; she tries it twice, falls down and starts crying. Mother was about to get up to help the child, but I lifted it first. The girl stood up; she looked at me quickly and curiously, still with little tears in her eyes, and suddenly, slightly frightened and confused, she leaped to her mother. I approached and politely inquired about the age of the girl; mother replied cordially but with great reserve. I told her that I, too, have such a girl, but to this there came no reply. "Perhaps, you are a good man"—silently the mother looked at me—"but what business is it of yours to stand here? You'd better get going." All the people, who had been conversing, likewise became silent, as though struck by the same thought. I touched my hat and walked away.

Here, at a busy street crossing, another little girl became separated from her mother, who up to then was leading her by her hand. True, some fifteen steps away, the little peasant woman saw a girl-friend who was coming to visit her, and, hoping that the child would know its way, she dropped its hand and ran to meet her guest; but the child, suddenly finding itself alone, became frightened, started crying and, in tears, tried to catch up with its mother.

A grey-haired passer-by—a total stranger, a bearded commoner —unexpectedly stopped the running woman whom he did not know, and seized her by the hand:

"What's the use of racing! Can't you see the child behind is crying; this won't do! It may get frightened!"

The little peasant woman started to make a lively rebuttal, but she did not make it; she changed her mind: without any hurt feelings or impatience, she picked the girl up in her arms, who had by then run up to her, and now with decorum she walked up to her guest. The commoner sternly waited for the denouement and then proceeded on his way.

Trivial—most trivial—little scenes, which are even not worth being recorded in the diary. Henceforth, I shall try to be much more serious.

The Citizen, 1873, No. 29.

TO A TEACHER

A Moscow columnist—it seems, from chastity—has scolded me in our Petersburg *Voice* (No. 210) for my recent "three little pictures" (*The Citizen*, No. 29) on the ground that in picture No. 2, having referred to the obscene language of our tipsy folks, I mentioned, of course without naming directly, a certain indecent object. . . . "It could never even have occurred to me what limits can be reached by a feuilletonist in his writings when he has no appropriate material at his disposal"—says my Moscow accuser about me. Thus, it appears that I have resorted to an unbecoming subject solely for the purpose of adding animation to my feuilleton, for the sake of Cayenne pepper. . . .

This makes me sad, since I even thought that people would draw an opposite deduction from my article, *i.e.*, that I have derived little from a vast amount of material. I thought that the title might save me: little pictures, and not large pictures; from little ones—less is to be expected. And thus I jotted down but a few sad thoughts about the holiday pastime of our Petersburg manual workers. The scarcity of their joys and recreations; the paucity of their spiritual life; the basements where their pallid, scrofulous children are growing up; the weary, wide Petersburg streets—stretching out straight as a cord—as places for their walks; that young widower-workman with a child by the hand (a true little picture)—all these seemed to me sufficient material for a feuilleton, so that—I repeat —I could have been reproached in an altogether contrary sense, namely, that I have derived little from such abundant material.

I felt consoled by the fact that I at least hinted at my principal inference: that in the overwhelming portion of our people, even in Petersburg basements, even within a most pitiful spiritual setting, there is nevertheless a longing for dignity, for a certain decency, for genuine self-respect; that love for family and children is preserved. I was particularly impressed with the fact that they love their sickly children genuinely and even tenderly. Precisely, I was gladdened by the thought that disorder and debauch in the family life of the people, even in the face of a setting such as in Petersburg, are still exceptions—although, perhaps, numerous—and I sought to share this fresh impression with the readers.

Just at that time I had recently read in a feuilleton a very candid admission on the part of a certain unquestionably intelligent man apropos of the publication of an official book, viz.: that, essentially, it is an idle occupation to dwell upon the question as to whether or not the reform proved beneficial to the people; that even had the reform not been useful to the people—let everything go on the rocks, for it had to take place (and in this, perhaps, there is much truth in accordance with the principle *pereat mundus*, despite the approach to the question). And, finally, as far as the people—the peasants—are concerned, the feuilletonist admitted very frankly—"in truth, strictly speaking, our people were not worthy of the reform . . . and that if, prior to the reform, in literature and criticism we—together with Messrs. Marko-Vovchok and Grigorovich—have been crowning the peasants with laurel and roses, we know very well that we have merely been crowning lousy heads. . . . But, at the time, this was necessary for the purpose of pushing the matter," and so on and so forth.

Such is the gist of the idea (I am not expressing it verbatim) set forth in the article with such candor and no longer with the slightest suggestion of the former ceremony. I confess, this is all too candid a thought; its very bareness which, for the first time, had revealed itself with such gratification, threw me into a rather curious mood. I recall that I concluded then that we, for instance, in *The Citizen,* even though being in accord with the first part of the proposition, *i.e.,* the reform regardless of any consequences— nevertheless, under no circumstance, do we share the latter part of that fatal contention, and we are firmly convinced that the lousy heads were still worthy of the reform and in no sense inferior to it. I believe that such a conviction may constitute precisely one of the characteristic aspects of our own orientation. This is why I am mentioning it now.

As to my feuilleton. . . . In passing, my Moscow literary confrère believes—I don't know why—that I am ashamed of the name feuilletonist, and he asserts in French that I am *"plus feuilletoniste que Jules Janin, plus catholique que le pape."*

Of course, this French language from Moscow is there to make people believe that the author is of *bon ton;* still I don't understand—what is the sense of the avowal of Catholic religion attributed to me, and why was it necessary to drag into the matter the poor Pope?

Now, as regards myself, I have merely stated that I am not a "Petersburg" feuilletonist, and by this I meant to say, for any eventuality in the future, that in my *Diary,* strictly speaking, I am writing and intend to write not only about Petersburg life, and consequently, there is no point in expecting from me very detailed reports on Petersburg life whenever I should find it necessary to allude to it. If, however, my Moscow teacher chooses *quand-même* to call my *Diary* a feuilleton, let him do so; I am quite satisfied.

My Moscow teacher assures me that my feuilleton created a

sensation in Moscow "among shopkeepers and in Zariadie,"[1] and
he calls it a bazaar feuilleton. I am very glad that I gave so much
pleasure to the readers from those quarters of our ancient capital.
But the venom of it is that I, as it were, purposely sought to be
sensational: because of the lack of more intellectual readers, I was
looking for readers in Zariadie, and it was with this aim in mind
that I started speaking about *"him,"* and, thus, I am "the shrewdest
among all feuilletonists. . . ."

"Now, I can't grasp it [writes the teacher describing the effect
of my feuilleton in Moscow]—I can't grasp it: 'What's the wonder
that there's such a demand for *The Citizen?*' a newsboy said to
me with surprise, in answer to my question as to the demand for
The Citizen. When I explained to him what the reason was, he
ran to Mecklenburg and Jivarev—our wholesale newspaper dealers
—to pick up the remaining copies, but they were all sold out: 'The
point is that the shopkeepers' district learned that an article about
him has been printed in *The Citizen,* and so the shopkeepers, instead of buying *Diversion,* rushed for *The Citizen.* . . .'"

Well now, this is not bad at all—I mean, this news—and you
are vainly shaming me about shopkeeper-readers. On the contrary,
I should be very anxious to enlist their support, since my opinion
of them is far more favorable than yours. You see, they have been
buying for fun, of course, and also because there developed a
scandal. Everybody is eager for a scandal; such is the nature of
every man, especially in Russia (you, for instance, pounced on me),
so that the shopkeepers should not be particularly despised for
this. As for diversion and fun, there are different diversions and
a different kind of laughter even in most seductive cases. However,
my teacher makes a reservation; he adds: "I am convinced that
the pen of the author of 'the little picture about him' was inspired
by the best intentions when he was writing this shopkeepers'
feuilleton"; in other words, the teacher honors me by admitting
that, when mentioning *him,* I was not primarily and directly
prompted by the aim of corrupting the people. We are grateful
at least for that. Since the author also writes for *The Voice,* this
magnanimous reservation is, perhaps, useful—knowing that Andrei
Alexandrovich would not hesitate to accuse me of whatever it be,
even of perversive intentions with regard to the people and Russian
society. (For didn't he accuse me of favoring serfdom!) Under your
pen, Andrei Alexandrovich also revealed himself in a remarkable
reverse conjecture: "And if such 'little pictures' of yours should
contribute nothing toward the reform of the revellers from among

[1]A section in Moscow, in the rear of a row of shops, running parallel
to Varvarka. (B. B.)

the working people . . ."—you say. Such a conjecture emanates straight from the head of Andrei Alexandrovich! So it did occur to him that I was writing with the direct and immediate purpose of curing (of ribaldry) our cursing working people! But they have never heard not only about us, but even about Andrei Alexandrovich —I mean, these workers whom I have depicted in my feuilleton!

No, I was writing with a different intention about that "noun" —"unmentionable before the ladies . . . but most generally used among drunkards," and I insist that I had a rather serious and excusable aim—and this I shall prove.

My idea was to point out the chastity of the Russian people, the fact that even if, in a state of intoxication, our people are resorting to invectives, in a sober state they are using obscene language far rarer, they are doing so not from love for profane words, not from pleasure in cursing, but simply because of a bad habit which has almost grown into a necessity, so that they even express thoughts and feelings ever so remote from ribaldry in obscene words.

Furthermore, I have stated that the main cause of this cursing habit is to be sought in drunkenness. You may think whatever you please about my conjecture that in a tipsy state—when the tongue moves tightly, and yet there is a strong desire to talk—there arises a necessity to use brief, conventional and expressive words. But it was worth while to point out that our people are chaste, even when they are using obscene language.

I even venture to assert that the æsthetically and mentally developed strata of our society are infinitely more depraved in this sense than our coarse, and most backward, common people. Among men—even those belonging to the highest society, and even among gray, star-covered, elderly fellows—it sometimes happens that after supper, when all important matters, occasionally state matters, have been settled, they gradually veer over to touch æsthetically upon themes. These themes, in turn, are promptly converted into such depravity, such ribaldry, such lewd thinking, that popular imagination would never conceive anything of the kind. That happens very often among all subdivisions of that circle of men who stand so far above the people. Men reputed to possess the loftiest and most ideal virtues—even churchgoers and most romantic poets—eagerly participate in these conversations. Here the really important point is that some of these men are unquestionably respectable and, also, are doing many good deeds. They are attracted, precisely, by filthiness and the refinement of filthiness— not so much by the obscene word itself as by the idea expressed in it; they are attracted by the depth of corruption—precisely, by the stink, much as Limburger (unknown to the people) is relished by a refined gastronome. Here there is essentially a craving for smearing, for the odor, for relishing the odor.

Of course, they laugh, they speak haughtily about their filth, but one can see that they are attracted to it and that they no longer can remain without it, though it be only in conversation. The people's laughter, even at the same themes, is different. I am sure that in your Zariadie they have been laughing not for filth's sake, not from love *for it* and not for art's sake, but with extremely naïve, not depraved, healthy, though slightly coarse, laughter—altogether different from that of some of the smudgers in our society or in our literature. The people use obscene language without reflection, and often without meaning what they utter. Our people are not depraved, and they are *even very chaste,* notwithstanding the fact that they are the most ribald people in the whole world. Now, in truth, it is worth while giving at least a little thought to this contrast.

My Moscow teacher winds up his feuilleton about me with excessive, almost satanic, haughtiness:

"I shall avail myself of the example of my esteemed colleague [meaning me]"—says he—"when I should happen to be writing a feuilleton, and I should have no material at all [what contempt!], but just now there is no need for me to take advantage of the example set forth before me [in other words: a clever man, even without '*him,*' is always full of thoughts], since even in Moscow we also have 'dust and heat,' 'heat and dust' [those are the opening words in my feuilleton—this is to put me to shame once more], but through this dust [ah-ah, now we come to the vital point: now he is going to show us forthwith what a clever Moscow head may deduce from this 'dust,' compared with Petersburg heads], through this dust and from beneath this heat [what does 'from beneath this heat' mean?] it is possible, with a certain attentiveness, to perceive [hear! hear!] that the living pulse of our Whitestone capital, beating much weaker in the summer, begins, so to speak, to grow more lively and, throbbing more and more energetically, it reaches in winter months that intensity which the pulse of Moscow life no longer can exceed."

What a thought! That's how things are in our Moscow! And what a lesson to me! And do you know what, teacher?—It does seem to me that you have intentionally pilfered from me the thought about *him,* in order to make your feuilleton more entertaining (otherwise, what is that intensity!); perhaps you became envious of my success in Zariadie! This may well be so. You would not be rummaging and smearing so much, and referring to it so many times; not only did you mention it and smudge, but you were even smelling . . .

". . . even so, we have grown up to the point where, at least, we can smell when we are offered something that shoots up into our noses, and we are capable of evaluating it regardless of the author's intentions. . . ."

Now, what does it smell like?

The Citizen, 1873, No. 32.

SOMETHING ABOUT LYING

Why is everybody here lying—every single man? I am convinced that I will be immediately stopped and that people will start shouting: "Oh, what nonsense, by no means everybody! You have no topic, and so you are inventing things in order to begin in a more imposing fashion." I have already been upbraided for the lack of themes. But the point is that now I am earnestly convinced of the universality of our lying. One lives fifty years with an idea, one perceives and feels it, and all of a sudden it appears in such an aspect as to make it seem that one had hitherto not known it at all.

Lately, I was suddenly struck by the thought that in Russia, among our educated classes, there cannot be even one man who wouldn't be addicted to lying. This is precisely because among us even quite honest people may be lying. I am certain that in other nations, in the overwhelming majority of them, only scoundrels are lying; they are lying for the sake of material gain, that is, with directly criminal intent.

Well, in our case, even the most esteemed people may be lying for no reason at all, and with most honorable aims. We are lying almost invariably for the sake of hospitality. One wishes to create in the listener an æsthetical impression, to give him pleasure, and so one lies even, so to speak, sacrificing oneself to the listener.

Let anyone recall: has it not happened to anyone to add twenty times, let us say, the number of versts which, in one hour, horses have driven him, if only this be needed to strengthen a pleasurable impression on the listener. And, indeed, wasn't the listener pleased to such an extent that he would start at once to assure you that a certain troika, which he had known, on a bet outran a railroad train, and so on, and so forth.

Well, what about hunting dogs? Or how, in Paris, teeth were replaced in one's mouth? Or how, here, you were cured by Botkin? Regarding your illness, haven't you related such wonders that you started believing them yourself by the time you had reached the middle of your story (since by the middle of a story one always begins to believe it), but, when going to bed at night and recollecting with pleasure how agreeably your listener had been impressed, you would suddenly stop and involuntarily utter: "Eh, how I lied!"

However, this is not a convincing example, since there is nothing more agreeable than to talk about one's illness, if only a listener can be found; and once you start talking, it is no longer possible to refrain from lying; this will even cure a patient. But, returning from abroad, didn't you speak about a thousand things which you beheld "with your own eyes . . ."? No, I shall withdraw this example: for a Russian returning home it is impossible not to exaggerate things about "abroad," for otherwise why should he have been journeyng thither?

But take, for instance, natural sciences! Did you not discuss natural sciences or bankruptcy cases and escapes over the border by different Petersburg, and other, Jews, understanding nothing about them and not knowing the A B C of natural sciences?

Excuse me—did you not relate some anecdote, as if it happened to you, to the very person who had told it to you as if it had happened to him? Did you possibly forget how, by the time you reached the middle of the story, suddenly you recalled and guessed this fact, which was clearly confirmed in the suffering look of your listener, who was intently staring at you (since in such cases people, I don't know why, stare at each other with an intensity magnified ten times)? Do you remember how, despite the loss of all your humor, nevertheless, with a courage worthy of the great cause, you continued to lisp your story? And then, when hurriedly you did get through with it, you both, with nervously hasty civilities, shook hands, smiled and ran in opposite directions from each other?—So that when, for no reason, in an ultimate convulsion, some demon drove you to cry to the listener, running down the staircase, a question about his auntie's health, he did not turn to you and made no reply—which fact stuck in your recollection as the most painful thing in the sum total of the incident that happened to you?

Briefly, if to all this anyone should answer me with a *nay*, namely, that he did not relate the anecdotes, did not touch upon Botkin, did not lie about Jews, did not shout on the staircase about auntie's health, and that nothing of the kind ever happened to him —I would simply not believe it. I know that the Russian liar, time and again, lies without even noticing it himself, so that one may not perceive the fact that he is lying. See what happens: no sooner will a man tell a successful lie, than he will include the anecdote among the unquestioned facts of his personal life, and then he acts quite conscientiously because he fully believes it; besides, it is unnatural sometimes not to believe it.

"Eh, rubbish!"—I will be told—"These are innocent lies; there is nothing universal about them." Be this as it may, I agree that all this is quite innocent, and merely hints at noble traits in one's character—for example, at a feeling of gratitude. Because if you were listened to when you were lying, it is impossible not to let the listener lie, if only from mere gratitude.

Courteous reciprocity in lying is virtually the prime condition of Russian society—of all Russian meetings, evening entertainments, clubs, scientific bodies, etc. Indeed, it is only a dull blockhead who, in cases of this kind, will suddenly begin to doubt the number of versts driven by you, or the miracles which Botkin performed when treating you. But these are heartless and hemorrhoidal creatures who themselves are forthwith punished, wondering thereafter why they have to suffer punishment. Men without talent.

Still all this lying, despite its innocence, hints at some very momentous fundamental traits of ours to such an extent that here the element of universality almost begins to reveal itself. For example: *first*, that we Russians are primarily afraid of truth—*i.e.*, we are not really afraid, if you please, but we always regard truth as something too weary in our intercourse, something prosaic, insufficiently poetic, too banal; and thereby, always evading truth, we, finally, made it something most extraordinary and rare in our Russian world (I am not referring to the newspaper by this name). Thus we have totally forgotten the axiom that truth is the most poetic thing in the world, especially in its pure state. More than that: it is even more fantastic than the ordinary human mind is capable of fabricating and conceiving.

In Russia, truth almost invariably assumes a fantastic character. In fact, men have finally succeeded in converting all that the human mind may lie about and belie into something more comprehensible than truth, and this prevails all over the world. For centuries truth will lie right on the table before people but they will not take it: they will chase after a fabrication precisely because they look upon it as something fantastic and utopian.

Second, this is a hint at the fact that our wholesale Russian lying suggests that we are all ashamed of ourselves. Indeed, every one of us carries in him an almost innate shame of himself and of his own face; and the moment Russians find themselves in company, they hasten to appear at all cost something different from what they in reality are; everyone hastens to assume a different face.

Already Hertzen has remarked about Russians abroad that they don't know how to behave in public; they speak in a loud manner, when everybody else is silent, and they cannot utter a single word politely and naturally when it is necessary to speak. And this is true: at once we observe a twist, a lie, a painful cramp; at once there arises the urge for being ashamed of everything that is actual, of concealing and effacing one's own face, given by God to the Russian, and of assuming a different, an alien, as un-Russian a face as possible. All this comes from the firm inner conviction in every Russian that one's own face is necessarily trivial and shamefully comic, and that if he should assume a French, an English—in brief, somebody else's—face, something more respectable would come of it, and that in this guise he would not be recognized.

In this connection I will note something very characteristic: this miserable petty shame of one's self and this vile self-negation are, in most cases, unconscious; this is something convulsive and unconquerable; yet, consciously, the Russians—even the most ardent self-negators among them—do not readily admit their triviality, and by all means demand respect for themselves: "I am, indeed, quite like an Englishman"—the Russian argues—"therefore, I should be respected, since everybody respects the English."

This fundamental type of our society has been moulding itself over a period of two hundred years, in accordance with the express principle formulated two centuries ago: "Never, under any circumstance, should one be himself; one should assume a different face, bespitting one's own face once and forever; one should always be ashamed of one's self and one should never resemble one's self." The results proved most complete. There is no German, no Frenchman, there is no Englishman in the whole world, who, when meeting other people, would be ashamed of his own face, provided he be honestly convinced that he had perpetrated nothing bad. A Russian is perfectly aware of the fact that there is no such Englishman, while an educated Russian also knows that the essential point of self-respect is not to be ashamed of one's own face, wherever it be. This is the reason why he hastens to assume the appearance of a Frenchman or of an Englishman, precisely so as to be taken as quickly as possible for a person who never, and nowhere, is ashamed of his face.

"Innocent things; old stuff; it has been told a thousand times already," people will say again. Be that as it may, but here is something even more typical. There is one point on which any Russian of the educated pattern, appearing in society or in public, is extremely exacting, and which he will yield under no circumstance. This point is intellect—the desire to appear more clever than he is, and—this is remarkable—this is in no sense a desire to seem more clever than the rest or even more clever than anyone in particular, but merely—*not more stupid than anyone*. "Concede," he means, "that I am not more stupid than anyone, and I will concede that you are not more stupid than anyone."

Here, again, we have something on the order of reciprocal gratitude. As is known, for instance, a Russian bows before European authority with happiness and haste, even without permitting himself to analyze: in such cases he is particularly opposed to analysis. Oh, it's different if a man of genius should descend from his pedestal, or merely cease to be in vogue: then, and with regard to such a person, there is no one harsher than the Russian intelligentsia; then there is no limit to its haughtiness, contempt and scoffing. Later, very naïvely we wonder if somehow we happen to learn that in Europe people still continue to look with respect upon the person who descended from his pedestal and to value him according to his merit. Yet that same Russian who had bowed before a genius in vogue, even without any analysis, nevertheless, under no circumstance and never, will admit that he is more stupid than this genius before whom he had just bowed, no matter how ultra-European he may be. "Well, Goethe—all right, Liebig—now then, Bismarck; why, all right; nevertheless, I too, am a somebody,"—so it necessarily seems to every Russian, even from among the most miserable and rascally, if it should come to that. And not that he may be pretending, because here there is hardly anything conscious, but only that he is pulled in that direction. There is an incessant feeling of idle ambition, knocking about the world, an ambition in no way justifiable. In a word, a Russian of the upper classes will never, and under no circumstance, reach that level—perhaps, the highest level—of the manifestation of human dignity, where a man admits that he is more stupid than another, when the latter is, in fact, more intelligent. I even do not know whether there are exceptions in this respect.

Let people refrain from laughing at my "paradox." Liebig's rival may not have terminated his high-school term, and, of course, he will not start arguing about his supremacy over Liebig should he be told and shown that this is Liebig. He will keep his mouth shut but, even so, he will be tempted even in Liebig's presence. . . . It would be different if, let us suppose, he should meet Liebig, without knowing it, somewhere in a railroad car. And should there ensue a conversation about chemistry, and should our fellow succeed in getting into the conversation, he would keep up the most learned dispute, knowing but one word in chemistry: chemistry. Of course he may surprise Liebig, but—who knows?—in the opinion of the listeners he might turn out the victor. Since in the Russian there is virtually no limit to the arrogance of his scientific language.

At this juncture there develops a phenomenon encountered in the soul only of the Russian educated classes: in that soul, the moment it feels itself in public, not only is there no doubt about its intellect, but even about its supreme learnedness, if only it comes to erudition. One may, perhaps, understand such an attitude toward intellect, but it would seem that as regards one's erudition every man must possess the most accurate information on the subject. . . .

Of course, all this transpires only in public, when strangers are around. But at home, in one's mind . . . Why, at home, inwardly, no Russian ever troubles himself about his education and erudition; he never even raises a question regarding them. But even if he should raise it, most probably at home, too, he would decide it in his favor, notwithstanding the fact that he would have most accurate knowledge about his erudition.

Not long ago I personally, while sitting in a railroad car, chanced to listen during two hours of the journey to a whole treatise on classical languages. One man was speaking and all the others were listening. The speaker, unknown to the other passengers, was a middle-aged man, of an imposing, reserved and seigniorial appearance, who dropped his words weightily and slowly. He aroused everybody's interest. It was obvious from his very first words that not only did he speak but probably, had thought about this theme for the first time. So this was merely a brilliant improvisation.

He emphatically rejected classical education, and its introduction into our schools he termed "historical and fatal folly"; but this was the only sharp word which he had permitted himself. He had adopted too lofty a tone which restrained him from flying into passion, from contempt itself for the subject. The grounds on which he stood were most primitive, permissible, perhaps, to a thirteen-year-old schoolboy—practically the same ones which up to the present are being adhered to by some of our newspapers campaigning against classical languages, to wit: "Since all Latin works have been translated, Latin is not needed," and so forth and so on, along these lines.

In our car he produced an extraordinary effect; many people, when parting with him, thanked him for the treat he had given them—especially, the ladies. I am convinced that he departed with the greatest respect for himself.

Nowadays in public (be it in railroad cars or elsewhere) conversations differ very much in comparison with olden times; now people are eager to listen and are craving for instructors in political and social subjects. True, our conversations ensue with but great effort; all keep back for a long time before making

up their minds to start talking, but, once they have started, they
will be seized sometimes with such a pathos that one almost
has to hold their hands. More reserved and solid, so to speak,
more elevated and isolated conversations pivot on stock exchange
and governmental topics, but from a secret, travestied point of view,
claiming knowledge of the highest mysteries unknown to the
uninitiated public. The latter listen meekly and respectfully, while
babblers gain in their demeanor. It stands to reason that few of
them believe each other but, as a rule, they part quite content with
each other and even in a somewhat grateful mood.

The problem of making a pleasant and joyous trip on our
railroads consists in the skill of letting others lie and of believing
as much as possible; then you, too, will be given a chance to tell
a lie impressively if you, also, be tempted to do so. Thus it is a
reciprocal advantage.

However, as I have stated, there are general, burning, pressing topics of conversation in which the whole public takes part,
and not only for the purpose of enjoying their time. I repeat: they
are thirsting for knowledge, for explanation of contemporary difficulties; they are craving for teachers, particularly women and
especially mothers of families.

It is noteworthy that despite all this extraordinarily curious
and most significant thirst for social advisers and guides—notwithstanding all these noble impulses, people are too easily satisfied,
sometimes in a most unexpected manner; they believe everything;
they are very poorly prepared and armed—much more weakly than
one's most flaming fantasy could have imagined several years ago
when it was more difficult to form a precise judgment on our
Russian society than at present when more facts and information
are available.

It can be positively asserted that every chatterbox with but
moderately decent manners (our public, alas, up to the present
has a prejudicial weakness for good manners, despite the ever-ex-
panding education disseminated through feuilletons) may win out
and convince his listeners of anything he pleases, receiving thanks
and departing with deep respect for himself. It goes without saying
—one doesn't even have to mention it—that he has got to be liberal:
this is a condition *sine qua non.*

Another time, also in a railroad car, and also recently, I
happened to hear a whole treatise on atheism. The orator—a man
of a socialite and engineering, though gloomy, appearance, and with
a pathological thirst for an audience—began with monasteries. About
the monastery problem he understood nothing at all, not even the
A B C of it. He regarded the existence of monasteries as something

inseparable from the dogmas of faith, imagining that monasteries
are maintained by the state, and cost much to the crown. Forgetting the fact that monks constitute an altogether voluntary association of persons, just like any other association, he insisted—in the
name of liberalism—that they be abolished as a sort of tyrannical
institution. He wound up with absolute and unlimited atheism on
the basis of natural sciences and mathematics; to these he made
abundant references without, however, citing in the course of his
whole dissertation a single fact from these disciplines.

Again, this man alone talked, while all the others were merely
listening. "I shall teach my son to be an honest man—that's all,"—
he uttered in conclusion, with the full and obvious conviction that
good deeds, morality and honesty are something given and absolute, depending upon nothing whatsoever; something that can always be found in one's pocket, whenever it be needed, without
labor, doubts and misunderstandings.

This gentleman, too, scored an extraordinary success. Here
there were officers, old men, ladies and grown-up children. When
parting with him, the people thanked him warmly for the pleasure
he had given them, and one lady—a mother of a family, smartly
dressed and quite good-looking, with a charming giggle—declared
that now she was fully convinced that in her soul "there was nothing but vapor." This gentleman must have gone away with a feeling
of unusual self-respect.

Now, this self-respect is the thing that confuses me. That
there are fools and chatterers is, of course, not surprising; but
this gentleman was obviously no fool and certainly, also, neither
a villain nor a swindler; it may even be that he was an honest
man and a good father. Only, he understood nothing about the
problems which he ventured to solve. Is it possible that an hour,
a day, or a month later the thought would not occur to him: "My
friend, Ivan Vasilievich (or whatever his name is)—now, you have
argued, but you understand nothing about the things you discussed.
You know this better than anyone. You referred to natural sciences
and mathematics, but you know better than anyone else that you
long ago forgot the scanty mathematics which you learned in your
technical school and which, even then, you did not know thoroughly,
while about natural sciences you never did have any conception.
How, then, did you venture to talk? How could you teach?—
Indeed, you must realize that you were only lying, and you feel
proud about yourself.—Aren't you ashamed of yourself?"

I am sure that he could have asked himself all these questions, notwithstanding the fact that, perhaps, he is engaged in
"business" and that he has no time to spare on idle questions. I

am quite certain that these questions, though in passing and mincingly, have visited his brain. *But he was not ashamed! He did not blush!*

Now, this dishonesty of a certain kind in the educated Russian is, to me, a decisive phenomenon. What is there in the fact that with us it is so common and that all of us got used to it and it seems so familiar? Even so, it remains an astonishing and extraordinary fact. It bears witness to such an indifference for one's judgment of one's own conscience, or—which is the same thing—such extraordinary disrespect for one's self, that one is seized with despair, one loses all hope for something independent and salutary for the nation—even in the future—from such people and such a society.

The public—that is, the exterior—European appearance, the law once and forever enacted by Europe—this public produces in every Russian a crushing effect: in public he is a European, a citizen, a knight, a republican, with conscience and with his own firmly established opinion. At home, to himself: "Eh, what the devil do I care about opinions! Let them even whip me!" Lieutenant Pirogov, who forty years ago, on the Bolshaia Meschanskaia, was whipped by the locksmith Schiller, was a dreadful prophecy—a prophecy of a genius who had divined so terribly, since of the Pirogovs there is an immense quantity, so many that it is even impossible to whip them all. Please recall that after the incident the lieutenant forthwith ate a puff-paste patty, and that same evening, at a saint's day party of an important government official, he distinguished himself while dancing the mazurka. What would you think: when he capered that mazurka and exhibited, while performing the steps, his so recently offended limbs—did he think about the fact that only two hours earlier he had been whipped?—Unquestionably, he did. But was he ashamed?—Unquestionably, he was not!

Waking up next morning, he no doubt said to himself: "Eh, what the devil! Is it worth starting something if no one is going to find out! . . ." This "is it worth starting"—of course, on the one hand, suggests such a predisposition to accommodation to anything whatsoever, and at the same time, such a breadth of our Russian nature that, in the face of these qualities, even the unlimited is dimmed. The two-hundred-year disuse of the slightest independence of character and the two-hundred-year spitting upon our own Russian face have expanded Russian conscience to such a fatal boundlessness, from which may be expected . . . well, what would you think?

I am convinced that the lieutenant was, perhaps, capable of

reaching such limits, or such an unlimitedness, as to avow his love that same evening and make a formal proposal to his partner in the mazurka—the host's elder daughter. Infinitely tragic is the image of that young miss fluttering with the fellow in a lovely dance and ignorant of the fact that only two hours before her cavalier had been whipped and that he does not mind it a bit. Well, and what would you think if she were to learn this fact, and the proposal, nevertheless, had been made anyway? Would she marry him (of course, on condition that no one would find out)?—Alas, unfailingly, she would marry him!

Even so, from among the Pirogovs and, generally, "the boundless ones," it seems, the overwhelming number of our women should be excluded. In our women one observes more and more sincerity, perseverance, seriousness and honor, sacrifice and search for truth, and in Russian women all these qualities have always been more pronounced than among the men. This cannot be doubted, notwithstanding all present-day deviations. The woman lies less, some of the women do not lie at all, whereas of the men who do not lie there are hardly any. I am speaking of the present moment in the life of our society.

The woman is more persistent and patient in work; she seeks, more *seriously* than the man, work for work's sake, and not merely for the sake of *pretending*. Perhaps it is from her that we must expect great help!

The Citizen, 1873, No. 35.

ONE OF THE CONTEMPORANEOUS FALSEHOODS

Some of our critics have observed that in my last novel *The Possessed* I have made use of the plot of the notorious Nechaiev case; but they hastened to add that, strictly speaking, there are no portraits in my novel and there is no literal reproduction of that story; that I took a phenomenon and merely sought to explain the possibility of its occurrence in our society as a social phenomenon and not in an anecdotal sense of a mere depiction of a particular Moscow episode.

On my own part, I may say that all this is quite correct. I have not discussed in my novel the notorious Nechaiev and his victim Ivanov. The face of *my* Nechaiev, of course, does not resemble that of the real Nechaiev. I meant to put this question and to answer it as clearly as possible in the form of a novel: how, in our contemporaneous, transitional and peculiar society, are the Nechaievs, not Nechaiev himself, made possible? And how does it happen that these *Nechaievs* eventually manage to enlist followers —the Nechaievtzi.

And recently—true, already about a month ago—I have read in *The Russian World* the following curious lines: ". . . it seems to us that the Nechaiev case could have demonstrated the fact that our student youth does not participate in such follies. An idiotic fanatic of the Nechaiev pattern manages to recruit proselytes only among idlers, defectives—and not at all among the youths attending to their studies."

And further:

". . . all the more so as only a few days ago the Minister of Public Education had declared (in Kiev) that after the inspection of the educational institutions in seven districts he could state that *'in recent years the youth has adopted an infinitely more serious attitude toward the problem of learning, and has been studying far more diligently.'*"

These lines, taken by themselves, and judged abstractly, are rather trivial (the author, I hope, will excuse me). But in them there is a twist—an old habitual lie. Their fully developed and fundamental idea is that if, at times, the Nechaievs appear in our midst, they are all necessarily idiots and fanatics, and even if they succeed in recruiting proselytes, these are necessarily found *"only* among the idle defectives and *not at all* among youths attending to their studies."

I do not know exactly what the author of the article in *The Russian World* sought to prove by this twist: did he mean to flatter the college youth? Or did he, on the contrary, by this crafty manœuvre, so to speak, under the guise of flattery, try to cheat them a little, but only with the most honorable motive and for their own benefit? And, to achieve this, did he resort to the well-known device which governesses and nurses apply in the case of little children: "Here, dear children, see how *those* bad, unruly kids are screaming and fighting: they'll surely be spanked because they're so 'undeveloped'; but you are such nice, commendable, sweet little things; here, at your table you sit up straight; you do not swing your little feet under the table, and for this you will surely be given candies."

Or, finally, did the author simply attempt to "shield" our college youth from the government, resorting for this purpose to a device which he, perhaps, considers extraordinary, crafty and refined?

I will say candidly: even though I did raise all these questions, yet the personal motives of the author of the article in *The Russian World* do not interest me in the least. And, in order to make myself fully understood, I will even add that the lie and the old worn-out twist expressed in that thought by *The Russian World*, I am inclined to regard as unintentional and accidental, *i.e.*, that the author of the article fully believed his own words and took them for the truth with that sublime naiveté which, in any other case, would be so laudable—and even touching, by reason of its defenselessness.

However, aside from the fact that a lie mistaken for the truth always assumes a most dangerous appearance (even though it be printed in *The Russian World*), one is struck by the thought that never before had this lie been revealed in so naked, precise and artless a form as in this little article. Verily, make some man pray God —he will smash his forehead. Now, it is interesting to analyze this lie in this particular guise—exposing it, if possible, to the light— because one may be waiting long for another instance of candidness as unskillful as this one.

From time immemorial in our pseudo-liberalism, in our newspaper press it has become a rule to "shield the youth"—from whom? from what?—Often this remains concealed in the gloom of uncertainty, and, therefore, assumes a most absurd and even comic aspect, especially in attacks directed against other periodicals in the sense that "we are more liberal, whereas you are upbraiding the youth and, consequently, you are more retrograde."

I may parenthetically remark that in the same article in *The Russian World* there is an accusation directly pointed against *The Citizen* to the effect that in it there are wholesale charges against our college youth in Petersburg, Moscow and Kharkov. Even leaving aside the fact that the author of the article himself *knows perfectly well* that in *The Citizen* there is nothing, and never has been anything, akin to wholesale and incessant accusations, I shall ask our prosecutor to explain: what does it mean to accuse youth by the wholesale? This I do not understand at all! Of course, this means that, for some reason, one dislikes the youth as a whole—and even not so much the youth, as our young men of a certain age. What twaddle! Who would believe such a charge?—It is clear that both the accusation and the defense were made haphazardly, without giving the matter much thought. Indeed, is it worth while to deliberate upon this: "I have shown that I am liberal; that I praise the youth; that I am scolding those who do not eulogize them—and this suffices as far as subscriptions are concerned, and that's all there is to it!" Precisely, "that's all there is to it," since only the bitterest enemy of our young people would venture to defend them *in this manner* and to bump into such a strange twist as that into which the naïve author of the article in *The Russian World* has bumped (accidentally —of this I am now convinced more than ever).

The real importance of the matter is that this device is the invention not only of *The Russian World*—it is a device common to many periodicals of our pseudo-liberal press, and there, perhaps, it is being used not quite so naïvely. Its essence is: *first*—in wholesale eulogies of the youth, in everything and *quand-même,* and in coarse attacks on all those who occasionally venture to take a critical attitude toward the young people. This device is based upon the ridiculous assumption that they are still so immature and so fond of flattery that they will not understand and will accept everything at its face value. And, in truth, we have reached the point where quite a few among our young men (we are firmly convinced that by no means all of them) actually do grow fond of coarse praise, and do seek to be flattered, and are ready to accuse recklessly all those who do not applaud everything they do, particularly in certain respects. However, here we have as yet a temporary damage: with experience and age the views of our youth are likely to change. But there is another side to the lie which entails direct and material harm.

This other aspect of the device of "shielding our youth from society and from the government" consists of simple *denial of the fact,* at times most impudent and coarse: "There is no fact, there never has been, never could have been; he who says that the fact did take place, calumniates our youth and, therefore, is their enemy!"

Such is the device. I repeat: the bitterest enemy of our young people could not have invented anything more injurious to their direct interests. This I want to prove by all means.

By the denial of a fact quand-même one may achieve amazing results.

Well, gentlemen, what will you prove and in what manner are you going to facilitate the problem, if you start asserting (and God only knows for what purpose) that the "led-astray" youth— that is, those who are capable of being "led astray" (even though by Nechaiev)—must necessarily be composed of none but "idle defectives"—those individuals who do not study at all—in a word, good-for-nothings with the worst propensities?—In this way, by isolating the matter, by withdrawing it from the sphere of those who attend to their studies and by focusing it *quand-même* on none but "idle, defective" individuals, you are thereby condemning in advance these unfortunate young men and definitely forsaking them: "it's their own guilt—they are unruly fellows, idlers, who would not sit still at the table."

By isolating the case and by depriving it of the right to be examined in conjunction with the generic whole (and therein consists the only possible defense of the unfortunate "delusioned" ones), you thereby, as it were, not only seal the final verdict against them, but you even alienate from them mercy itself, because you are directly asserting that their very errors were caused solely by their repulsive qualities and that these youths, who even are guilty of no crime, must arouse contempt and disgust.

On the other hand, what if it should happen that some *case* were to involve by no means "defectives"—not the unruly ones swinging their feet under the table, and not merely idlers—but, on the contrary, diligent, enthusiastic youths precisely attending to their studies, even endowed with good, but only misdirected, hearts? (Please grasp the word: *misdirected*. Where in Europe will you find more vacillation in all sorts of tendencies than in Russia in our day!) And now, according to your theory of "idlers and defectives," these new "unfortunate" ones would prove three times more guilty: "they were well provided; they completed their education; they worked diligently—they have no justifications! They are worthy of mercy three times less than the idle defectives!"—Such is the result directly derived from your theory.

Please, gentlemen (I am speaking generally and not merely to the contributor of *The Russian World*), you are asserting on the strength of "the denial of the fact" that the "Nechaievs" must necessarily be idiots—"idiotic fanatics." Well, is this really so? Is it correct? In this case I am setting aside Nechaiev, and I am referring to the "Nechaievs," in the plural.

Yes, among the Nechaievs there may be very gloomy creatures—disconsolate and distorted ones—with a thirst for intrigue of a most complex origin and for power, with a passionate and pathologically premature urge to reveal their personalities, but why should they be "idiots"?—On the contrary, even real monsters among them may be highly developed, most crafty and even educated people. Or you may think, perhaps, that knowledge, "training," little bits of school information (picked up even in universities) finally mould a youth's soul to the extent that, upon the receipt of his diploma, he immediately acquires an irrevocable talisman enabling him once and forever to learn the truth, to avoid temptations, passions and vices? Thus, according to you, all these graduating youths will at once become something on the order of so many little infallible Popes.

And why do you believe that the Nechaievs must necessarily be fanatics?—Very often they are simply swindlers. "I am a swindler and not a socialist"—says one Nechaiev; true, in my novel *The Possessed*, but, I assure you, he could have said it in real life. There are swindlers who are very crafty and who have studied precisely the magnanimous phase of the human, usually youthful, soul so as to be able to play on it as on a musical instrument.

And do you really and truthfully believe that proselytes whom some Nechaiev in our midst could manage to recruit are necessarily good-for-nothings? I do not believe it: not all of them. I am an old "Nechaievetz" myself; I also stood on the scaffold, condemned to death; and I assure you that I stood there in the company of educated people. That whole group had graduated from the highest institutions of learning. Some of them, subsequently, *when everything had passed,* have distinguished themselves by remarkable works in special fields. No, Nechaievtzi are not always recruited from among mere idlers who had learned nothing.

I know that you, no doubt, will say in rebuttal that I am not one of the Nechaievtzi at all, and that I am only a "Petrashevetz." All right—a Petrashevetz. (Although, in my opinion, this is an incorrect name, since a much larger number—compared with those who stood on the scaffold, but quite as we Petrashevtzi—have been left intact and undisturbed. True, they have never known Petrashevsky, but it was not he who was the crux of that long-past story. This is merely what I meant to observe.)

But all right—a Petrashevetz. How do you know that the Petrashevtzi could not have become the Nechaievtzi, *i.e.,* to have chosen the "Nechaiev" path, *would things have turned that way?* Of course, in those days this could not even have been imagined— meaning *that things could have taken such a turn.* Times were altogether different. But permit me to speak about myself only: probably I could never have become a *Nechaiev,* but a Nechaievetz —for this I wouldn't vouch, but maybe I could have become one . . . in the days of my youth.

Now, I have started speaking about myself in order to be entitled to speak about others. Nevertheless, I shall continue to speak only about myself, and if I should mention others it will be only in a general and impersonal sense, quite abstractly.

The Petrashevtzi's *case* is such an old one, belonging to such ancient history that, perhaps, it will be of no harm if I should remind people of it, particularly in such a slippery and abstract sense.

Among us Petrashevtzis (among both those who stood on the scaffold and those who had been left intact—it is the same) there were neither "monsters" nor "swindlers." I do not think anyone would contradict this statement of mine. That among us there were educated people—this, too, as I have remarked, is probably not going to be contradicted. However, undoubtedly, among us there were but few who could have managed to struggle against

a certain cycle of ideas and conceptions which had a strong grip
upon youthful society. We were contaminated with the ideas of the
then prevailing theoretical socialism. In those days political socialism was nonexistent in Europe, and the European ringleaders
of the socialists even used to reject it.

Louis Blanc was vainly slapped on his cheeks and pulled by
his hair (as if on purpose—his was very thick, long black hair!)
by his colleagues—members of the National Assembly, Rightist
deputies, from whose hands he was then, on that ill-starred morning
in May, 1848, torn by Arago (the astronomer and a member of
the government—now dead), when the Chamber was invaded by
a mob of impatient and starving workers. Poor Louis Blanc, for
a while a member of the provisional government, had in no way
incited them: he had merely been reading at the Luxembourg Palace
to these pitiful and hungry people about their "right to work"—to
people who had lost their jobs, owing to the revolution and the
republic.—True, since he was still a member of the government,
his lectures on this subject were awfully tactless and, of course,
ridiculous.

Considérant's journal, as well as Proudhon's articles and
pamphlets, were seeking *inter alia* to propagate among these same
starving and penniless workers profound disgust for the right of
hereditary property. Unquestionably, from all this (*i.e.*, the impatience of hungry people inflamed with theories of future felicity)
subsequently there arose political socialism, the substance of which,
notwithstanding all aims proclaimed by it, thus far, consists of the
desire for universal robbery of all property-owners by the destitute
classes, and thereafter "be that as it may." (Since, properly speaking, so far nothing has been decided as to how future society is
going to be shaped—and up to date such is the whole formula of
political socialism.)

But at that time the affair was conceived in a most rosy and
paradisiacally moral light. Verily, socialism in its embryo used to
be compared by some of its ringleaders with Christianity and was
regarded as a mere corrective to, and improvement of, the latter, in
conformity with the tendencies of the age and civilization. All these
new ideas of those days carried to us, in Petersburg, a great appeal;
they seemed holy in the highest degree and moral, and—most important of all—cosmopolitan, the future law of all mankind in its
totality. Even long before the Paris revolution of '48 we fell under
the fascinating influence of these ideas. Already in '46 I had been
initiated by Bielinsky into the whole *truth* of that future "regenerated world" and into the whole *holiness* of the forthcoming
communistic society. All these convictions about the immorality

of the very foundations (Christian) of modern society, the immorality of religion, family, right of property; all these ideas about the elimination of nationalities in the name of universal brotherhood of men, about the contempt for one's native country, as an obstacle to universal progress, and so on, and so forth—all these constituted such influences as we were unable to overcome and which, contrarywise, swayed our hearts and minds in the name of some magnanimity. At any rate, the theme seemed lofty and far above the level of the then prevailing conceptions, and precisely this was tempting.

Those among us—that is, not only the Petrashevtzi, but generally all *contaminated* in those days, but who later emphatically renounced this chimerical frenzy, all this gloom and horror which is being prepared for humankind under the guise of regeneration and resurrection—those among us were then ignorant of the causes of their malady and, therefore, they were still unable to struggle against it. And so, why do you think that even murder *à la* Nechaiev would have stopped—of course, not all, but at least, some of us— in those fervid times, in the midst of doctrines fascinating one's soul and the terrible European events which, forgetting altogether our fatherland, we have been watching with feverish tension?

Unquestionably, the monstrous and disgusting Moscow murder of Ivanov was represented by the murderer Nechaiev to his victims —the "Nechaievtzi"—as a political affair, useful to the future "universal and *great* cause." Otherwise, it is impossible to understand how several youths (whoever they may have been) could agree to commit such a saturnine crime.

And in my novel *The Possessed* I made the attempt to depict the manifold and heterogeneous motives which may prompt even the purest of heart and the most naïve people to take part in the perpetration of so monstrous a villainy. The horror lies precisely in the fact that in our midst the filthiest and most villainous act may be committed by one who is not a villain at all! This, however, happens not only in our midst but throughout the world; it has been so from time immemorial, during transitional epochs, at times of violent commotion in people's lives—doubts, negations, scepticism and vacillation regarding the fundamental social convictions. But in our midst this is more possible than anywhere else, and precisely in our day; this is the most pathological and saddest trait of our present time—the possibility of considering oneself not as a villain, and sometimes almost not being one, while perpetrating a patent and incontestable villainy—therein is our present-day calamity!

By what in particular is our youth protected in comparison with other ages which makes you, gentlemen-defenders of youth, unhesitatingly demand from them—just as soon as they have studied diilgently and learned—such firmness and maturity of convictions as have not been possessed by their fathers and which nowadays are scarcer than ever. Our young men belonging to the educated classes, brought up in the fold of their families where, as a rule, one encounters dissatisfaction, impatience, coarse ignorance (despite the fact that these are educated classes), and in which, almost everywhere, for genuine education is substituted impudent negation of other people's opinions; where material motives prevail over the loftiest idea; where children are brought up without foundation, without natural truth, with disrespect for, and indifference to, their native land and with a scoffing contempt for the people, which has been spreading so fast, particularly in recent times—is it from here, from this wellspring, that our young men will draw the truth and faultlessness of their convictions during the initial stage of their lives?

Herein is the root of evil: in tradition; in the succession of ideas; in the century-old national self-suppression of any independence of thought; in the conception of the rank of a European subject to the express condition of disrespect for one's self as a Russian!

But, probably, you will give no credence to these all too general statements. "Education"—you keep repeating—"diligence"; "idle defectives"—you keep saying. Please note, gentlemen, that all these high European teachers, our light and our hope—all those Mills, Darwins and Strausses—sometimes consider the moral obligations of modern man in a most astonishing manner. And yet these are by no means sluggards who have learned nothing, nor unruly fellows swinging their feet under the table.

You will start laughing and you will ask: why did it occur to you to start talking precisely about these names?—For the reason that it is even difficult to conceive—speaking of our intelligent, enthusiastic and studious youth—that these names, for instance, would escape them during the initial stages of their lives. Is it possible to conceive that a Russian youth would remain indifferent to the influence of these and similar leaders of European progressive thought, and especially to the Russian aspect of their doctrines?— This is a funny expression: "Russian aspect of their doctrines"; let people excuse it; I am using it solely because this Russian aspect does actually exist in these doctrines. It consists of those inferences from these doctrines which, in the form of unshakable axioms, are drawn only in Russia, whereas in Europe, it is said, the possibility of such deductions is not even being suspected.

Perhaps I may be told that these gentlemen do not in any

manner teach villainy; that if Strauss, for example, hates Christ and made it the business of his whole life to spit upon and scoff at Christianity, he nevertheless adores humankind as a whole, and his teaching is as lofty and as noble as it can be. It is very possible that all this is true, and that the aims of all modern leaders of European progressive thought are philanthropic and grand. Still I firmly believe that if all these modern, sublime teachers be given ample opportunity to destroy the old society and to build it up anew, there would result such a darkness, such chaos, something so coarse, so blind, so inhuman, that the entire edifice would crumble away to the accompaniment of the maledictions of mankind, even before it would finally have been constructed. The human mind, once having rejected Christ, may attain extraordinary results. This is an axiom. Europe, in the persons of her highest intellectual representatives, renounces Christ, while we, as is known, are obligated to imitate Europe.

There are historical moments in the life of men when flagrant, impudent and the coarsest villainy may be deemed a grandeur of the soul which breaks out of its fetters only through the noble courage of mankind. Are examples really needed—are there not thousands, tens and hundreds of thousands of examples? . . . Of course, the theme is a complex and boundless one; it is very difficult to touch upon it in a feuilleton article; nevertheless, in the long run, my conjecture may also be entertained: that even an honest and naïve boy, even one who had studied diligently, may, at times, turn out a Nechaievetz. . . . Of course, I repeat, if he should run into a Nechaiev; this, naturally, *sine qua non*.

We, Petrashevtzis, stood on the scaffold and listened to our verdict without the slightest repentance. It stands to reason that I cannot testify for all of us, yet I believe that I shall not err if I state that then, that minute, the majority of us, if not every single one, would have considered it an ignominy to renounce his convictions. This is an old story and, for this reason, perhaps, the question may be asked: is it possible that obstinacy and non-repentance were merely the result of the ill nature of defectives and unruly persons?

No, we were not unruly and, perhaps, we were even not bad young men. The verdict of capital punishment, by facing a firing squad, preliminarily read to all of us, had been read by no means jestingly: almost all the condemned were convinced that it would be carried out, and they endured at least ten dreadful, boundlessly horrible minutes awaiting death. During these last minutes several among us—this I know positively—instinctively wrapped ourselves deep in our thoughts and momentarily glanced over our whole, still so youthful, lives, even perhaps repenting some of our bad deeds (those which in every man lie secretly buried in his conscience). But the deed for which we were convicted; those ideas and conceptions which ruled our spirit, were regarded by us not only as not requiring repentance but even as something purifying—as martyrdom, for which we would be forgiven much! And thus it has lasted long. Not the years of exile—not suffering—have subdued us. On the contrary, nothing has subdued us, and our convictions merely tended to support our spirit by the realization of a fulfilled duty. No, something different has changed our outlook, our convictions and our hearts (of course, I venture to speak only of those among us whose changed convictions have become known and who, in one way or another, have themselves attested to them). This something different was the direct contact with the people, the brotherly merger with them in a common misfortune, the realization of the fact that one has become even as they, that one has been made equal to them, and even to their lowest stratum.

I repeat: this did not occur so quickly, but gradually—and after a long, long time. Not pride, not self-love, prevented confession. And yet I was, perhaps, one of those (again, I am speaking only about myself) to whom the return to the popular root, to the understanding of the Russian soul, to the recognition of the people's spirit, has been made particularly easy. I descended from a pious Russian family. As far as I can remember myself, I recall my parents' affection for me. We, in our family, have known the Gospel almost ever since our earliest childhood. I was only ten when I already knew virtually all the principal episodes in Russian history —from Karamzin whom, in the evenings, father used to read aloud to us. Every visit to the Kremlin and the Moscow cathedrals was, to me, something solemn. Others may not have had recollections such as I had. Very often I stop to think, and I am now asking myself: what kind of impressions do our contemporaneous youth mostly derive from their childhood? And now, even if I, who naturally could not have haughtily and indifferently passed by that new and fatal environment into which misfortune had cast me; if I, who could not have taken a superficial and haughty attitude toward the manifestation of the spirit of the people; if I—I say— had so much difficulty in finally convincing myself of the deceit and falsehood of practically everything which hitherto we used to regard as light and truth, what must others have experienced—those who had severed more radically their bonds with the people, those in whom the rupture was a successional and hereditary one, acquired from their fathers and grandfathers?

It is very difficult for me to tell the story of the regeneration of my convictions, all the more so as, perhaps, it is not so interesting and somehow it does not fit a feuilleton article. . . .

Gentlemen-defenders of our youth, please consider the milieu, the society in which they are growing up, and ask yourselves: is there anything in our day that is less protected against *certain influences?*

First, please pose this question: if the fathers themselves of these youths are not better, not firmer and not healthier in their convictions; if, from their earliest childhood these children have encountered in their families nothing but mere cynicism, haughty and indifferent (mostly) negation; if the word "fatherland" has been uttered in their presence not otherwise than with a scoffing expression; if for the cause of Russia all those who have been bringing them up have maintained contempt or indifference; if the most magnanimous among the fathers and the educators have kept talking about "cosmopolitan" ideas; if, even in their childhood, their nurses have been dismissed because, over their cradles, they— those nurses—said the prayer "Mother of God"—tell me: what may one demand from these children, and is it humane, when defending them, if defense be needed, to get off by a mere negation of the fact?

Recently in the newspapers I came across the following *entrefilet:*

"*The Kama-Volga Gazette* reports that a few days ago three high-school pupils of the Second Kazan High School, in their third year, were charged with some crime connected with their contemplated flight to America." (*St. Petersburg Messenger,* November 13.)

Twenty years ago the news of high-school boys of the third grade fleeing to America would have seemed an absurdity. But the fact itself that *in our day* this does not seem to me absurd, but a thing which I *comprehend*—this fact in itself appears to me its justification.

Justification! Good Lord, is it possible to say so?

I know that these are not the first schoolboys to embark upon such a venture; that, before them, others have fled and those because their elder brothers and their fathers had fled. Do you recall Kelsiev's story about a poor army officer who fled *on foot,* via Torneo and Stockholm, to Hertzen in London, where the latter gave him employment as a compositor in his printing plant?

Do you recall Hertzen's own story about that *cadet* who proceeded, I believe, to the Philippine Islands for the purpose of establishing a commune, bequeathing 20,000 francs for the future emigrants?—And yet all these are already ancient history! Since then, old people, fathers, brothers, maidens, guard-officers . . . have fled to America to have a taste of "free labor" in a free country. . . .

Perhaps only pupils of theological seminaries were not included among these fugitives. Should we be blaming such little children —these three high-school boys—if they have mastered with their weak little heads *the grand ideas* about "free labor in a free country" and the commune and the inter-European man; should we blame them if all this rubbish is conceived by them as religion, while absenteeism and treason to the fatherland is conceived as a virtue? And if one should be blaming them—to what extent?— That's the question.

In support of his idea that in our midst only idlers and good-for-nothing defectives participate in "such follies," the author of the article in *The Russian World* quotes the well-known and encouraging words of the Minister of Public Education, recently spoken by him in Kiev, to the effect that as a result of the inspection of educational institutions in seven school districts, he had been convinced that *"in recent years the youth has adopted an infinitely more serious attitude toward the problem of learning and has been studying far more diligently."*

Of course, these are encouraging words in which, perhaps, our *sole* hope resides. In the educational reform of the present reign— lies almost *all* our future, and this we know. However, if I correctly recall, the Minister of Education himself stated in that same speech of his that the results of the reform would have to be awaited for a long time. We have always believed that our youth is quite capable of adopting a more serious attitude towards learning. Still, thus far, we have been enveloped in such a fog of false ideas; so many mirages and prejudices surround us and our youth, while our social life, the life of the fathers and mothers of that youth, is assuming ever so strange an aspect that, willy-nilly, one begins to look for all sorts of means to overcome the perplexity. One of such means is for us to be less insensible, not to be ashamed if, even only occasionally, someone should call us a citizen, and sometimes to speak the truth, even though to your mind it be not liberal enough.

The Citizen, 1873, No. 50.

1876

January

CHAPTER I

1

In lieu of a preface on the Great and Little Bears, on the prayer of the great Goethe and, generally, on bad habits.

... KHLESTAKOV, at least, lied—lied at the bailiff's house —even so, he was a bit afraid that presently he might be thrown out of the drawing room. Modern Khlestakovs are afraid of nothing and they lie with a perfect peace of mind.

Nowadays all people have perfect peace of mind: they are calm and, perhaps, even happy. It is doubtful if anyone renders an account to oneself; everybody is acting "simply," and this already is complete happiness. Nowadays, much as heretofore, everybody is corroded with egoism, but heretofore egoism used to enter timidly, feverishly looking around, staring at faces. "Did I enter as I should have? Did I speak as I should have?"—But nowadays everyone, entering anywhere, is convinced from the start that everything belongs to him alone. And, if not to him, he does not even grow angry, but instantly settles the problem. Haven't you heard about little epistles such as:

"Dear papa, I am twenty-three, and as yet I have accomplished nothing; being convinced that nothing will come of me, I have decided to commit suicide. . . ."

And he shoots himself. Still, here at least something may be comprehended: "What, if not pride, is the point of living?" But another fellow will look around, will roam awhile and will silently shoot himself, solely because he has no money to hire a mistress. This is already utter swinishness.

It is being maintained in the press that theirs is a case of too much thinking. "He thinks and thinks and then he emerges

exactly at the contemplated spot." On the contrary, I am convinced
that he does not think at all; that he is wholly incapable of forming a judgment; that he is savagely undeveloped, and if he should
long for anything, he could be longing not consciously but in an
animal-like fashion—simply perfect swinishness—and there is nothing liberal about it.

And in this connection—not a single Hamletian question:

But that the dread of something after death . . .

And in this there is much that is strange. Is it possible that
it is thoughtlessness in Russian nature?—I say: thoughtlessness, and
not absurdity. All right: do not believe, but at least give thought.
In our felo-de-se there is even no shadow of doubt, no shadow of
suspicion that he is called "*I*" and that he is an immortal creature.
It seems as if he had even never heard anything about this. And
yet neither is he an atheist. Do recall former atheists: having lost
faith in one thing they would promptly start passionately believing
something else. Do recall the fervent faith of Diderot, Voltaire.
. . . In our case—a perfect *tabula rasa,* and where does Voltaire
come in here?—Simply, there's no money to hire a mistress; nothing more.

The self-destroyer Werther, when committing suicide, in the
last lines left by him, expresses regret that he would nevermore
behold "the beautiful constellation of the Great Bear" and he bids
it farewell. Oh, how was the then still youthful Goethe revealed in
this little trait! Why were these constellations so dear to young
Werther?—Because, whenever contemplating them, he realized that
he was by no means an atom and a nonentity compared with them;
that all these numberless mysterious, divine miracles were in no
sense higher than his thought and consciousness; not higher than
the ideal of beauty confined in his soul, and, therefore, they were
equal to him and made him akin to the infinity of being. . . . And
for the happiness to perceive this great thought which reveals to
him who he is, he is indebted exclusively to *his human image.*

"Great Spirit, I thank Thee for the human image bestowed
on me by Thee."

Such must have been the lifelong prayer of the great Goethe.
In our midst this image bestowed upon man is being smashed quite
simply and with no German tricks, while no one would think of
bidding farewell not only to the Great, but even to the Little, Bear,
and even if one should think of it, he would not do it: he would
feel too much ashamed.

What in the world did you start talking about?—an astonished
reader will ask me.

I was about to write a preface, since it would be violating the rule to have no preface at all.

In this case you had better explain your orientation, your convictions. Explain what kind of a man you are and how you did venture to announce *A Writer's Diary.*

This, however, is very difficult, and I can see that I am not an expert in writing introductions. A preface is, perhaps, as difficult to pen as a letter. As for liberalism (instead of the word "orientation," I shall simply use the term "liberalism,") as regards liberalism, the Stranger, well known to everybody, in one of his recent feuilletons—when speaking about the way in which our press has greeted the new 1876th year, *inter alia*—remarked, not without sarcasm, that everything came off fairly liberally. I am glad that in this connection he displayed sarcasm. Verily, our liberalism, of late, has been converted everywhere into a profession or into a bad habit. That is, in itself this wouldn't be a bad habit at all, but among us it has somehow turned out to be one. And it is even strange: our liberalism, it would seem, belongs to the category of pacified liberalisms—pacified and pacific—which, to my way of thinking, is bad, since quietism, it would seem, is least capable of getting along with liberalism. And yet, despite such a quietude, everywhere we see unmistakable signs to the effect that in our society the conception of what is, and what is not, liberal is gradually disappearing altogether, and in this respect we begin to be very much confused. There are even examples of utter confusion.

In brief, our liberals, instead of becoming freer, have bound themselves with liberalism as with ropes and, therefore, I, too, taking advantage of this curious situation, shall keep silent on the details of my liberalism. But, generally speaking, I might say that I consider myself more liberal than the rest, if only because I have no desire whatever to be pacified. And now, enough of this. And as regards the question of what kind of a man I am, I may say about myself: *"Je suis un homme heureux qui n'a pas l'air content,"*—meaning in Russian: "I am a happy man but one displeased with something."

With this I am bringing my preface to a close. Besides, I wrote it only for the sake of form.

2

THE FUTURE NOVEL. AGAIN AN "ACCIDENTAL FAMILY"

At the artists' club there was a Christmas tree and a children's dancing party, and I went to see the children. Even formerly,

I always used to observe children, but now I am especially observing them. Long ago I set myself the ideal of writing a novel about contemporaneous Russian children and, of course, about their present-day fathers, in their actual mutual interrelation. The poem is ready; it was conceived before anything else—and so it must always be in the case of a novelist. I shall take fathers and children, if possible, from all strata of society and I shall trace the children from their earliest childhood.

When some eighteen months ago Nikolai Alexeevich Nekrasov asked me to write a novel for *The Domestic Records,* I was about to start on my *Fathers and Sons,* but, thank God, I refrained from doing so; I was not ready. In the meantime I have written merely *A Raw Youth*—this first proof of my thought. But there the child has already outlived his childhood and appears merely as an unready man, timidly and yet boldly seeking to take the first steps on the path of his life. I took an innocent soul, but one already polluted with the dreadful possibility of depravity, early hate, because of his nothingness and "accidentalness," and that breadth with which a still chaste soul already admits vice to his thoughts, fondles it in his still bashful but already daring and tempestuous visions—all this left solely to his own forces, his own reasoning and, perhaps, in truth, to the will of God. They are all cast-offs of society, "accidental" members of "accidental" families.

Everybody has recently read in the papers about the murder of the common woman Perova and the suicide of her murderer. She had cohabited with him; he was a worker in a printing plant, but he had lost his job. She rented an apartment and took in roomers. Discord ensued. Perova asked him to leave her. The murderer's character was on the ultra-modern pattern: "if it's denied to me, no one shall have it." He gave her his word that he would "leave her," and then barbarously butchered her at night, deliberately and with premeditation, and after that he cut his own throat. Perova left two children, boys of twelve and nine—illicitly begotten by her, not by the murderer, however, but before she had become acquainted with him. She loved them. They had witnessed how, in the evening, during a terrible scene, he tortured her with reproaches till she fainted; they asked her not to go to his room, but she did go.

The Voice appeals to the public for help for the "unfortunate orphans," of whom the elder attended the Fifth High School, while the other one was still living at home. Here, again, is an "accidental family"—again, children with gloomy impressions in their adolescent souls. The dark picture will remain there forever, and it may pathologically cripple their youthful pride from those days—

When all impressions of existence
To us are still so strangely new.

And, hence, problems beyond one's powers: the early suffering of vanity; the blush of false shame for the past; and the dull, inwardly concealed hatred of people—and thus it may persist during one's whole life. Let God bless the future of these innocent children, and let them continue to love throughout their whole lives their poor mother, without reproach and without shame for their love. But help them we must by all means. In this respect our society is responsive and noble. Is it conceivable that they ought to be leaving high school once they have started there? The elder one, it is rumored, is not going to leave it, and his fate seems to have been assured. But the younger one? Is it possible that people will collect seventy or a hundred rubles, and will then forget all about them? And thanks are due to *The Voice* for reminding us about these unfortunate ones.

3

CHRISTMAS TREE AT THE ARTISTS' CLUB. REASONING CHILDREN AND RELIEVED CHILDREN. "GLUTTONOUS YOUTH." "YES-GIRLS." JOSTLING RAW YOUTHS. THE HURRYING MOSCOW CAPTAIN.

Naturally, I am not going to depict in detail the Christmas-tree party and the dance at the Artists' Club; all this has long ago been described and I myself have read about it with pleasure in other feuilletons. I will merely say that prior to that I had been nowhere for quite a long time—at no meeting—and I have long led a solitary life.

First, the children danced—all of them in charming dresses. It is curious to trace how the most complete conceptions are being quite imperceptibly inoculated into the child who, being still incapable of connecting two thoughts, sometimes grasps the deepest phenomena of life. A learned German once stated that every child, upon completing the first three years of his life, has already acquired a full third of the ideas and knowledge with which, as an elder, he will be laid in his grave.

Here there were even six-year-old children, but I know for sure that they understood perfectly why and for what purpose they had been brought here all dressed up in such expensive little dresses, while at home they are accustomed to wear slovenly clothes (with the present-day means of the middle class, unfailingly they must be wearing slovenly clothes). Even more: they certainly comprehended that this must be precisely so—that is, in no way a deviation from, but a normal law of, nature. Of course, they could not express this in words, but inwardly they knew—and yet this is an extremely complicated thought.

Among the children I liked most the smallest ones: these are very charming and unrestrained. Those a little older also are unrestrained, but with a certain boldness. It stands to reason that the most unrestrained and cheerful are those who in the future will belong to mediocrity and be without talent: this is a general rule; mediocrity is always unrestrained, be it among children or among parents. More gifted and segregated children are always more reserved, and if they are joyous, it is invariably with a knack at leadership and bossing.

It is also a pity that nowadays everything is being made easy for children, not merely study, acquisition of all knowledge, but even plays and toys. Just as soon as a child begins to lisp its first words, forthwith people begin to relieve it. At present pedagogy is altogether dedicated to the task of relieving. At times easement does not signify progress but, on the contrary, constitutes a deviation. Two or three thoughts, two or three impressions, deeply felt in childhood as a result of one's own effort (or, if you please, also as a result of suffering), will enable a child to penetrate life much more deeply than the easiest school which frequently produces something that is neither this nor that, neither good nor bad—something that even in depravity is not depraved, and in virtue not virtuous.

> Have oysters come?—They have! Oh, grand!
> Youth gluttonous is quick at hand
> To swallow them . . .

Now this "gluttonous youth" (the only one bad verse in Pushkin because it is written with no irony but almost with praise)— now this gluttonous youth must be the product of something. Nasty and undesirable youth; and I am convinced that too easy education is very instrumental in its production, while products of this kind we have galore!

Little girls somehow are more comprehensible than boys. Why is it that girls, almost up to the time of full age (but not later) are always more developed, or seem to be more developed, than boys of the same age? Girls are particularly comprehensible in the dance: one promptly discerns in some of them a future "yes-girl" who will never succeed in getting married, notwithstanding all her longing for it. I call "yes-girls" those maidens who almost up to the age of thirty answer one: "yes" and "no." However, there are

others who—it may be seen even now—will soon marry, just as soon
as they make up their minds.

It is quite cynical, in my opinion, to dress a virtually grownup
girl in a childish frock: it is really bad. When, at midnight, the
children's ball came to an end and parents began to dance, some
of these girls in short dresses and with bare legs, stayed on—dancing
with the grownups.

However, I was quite pleased with everything, and if only
raw youths had not pushed around, everything would have been
fully satisfactory. In fact, adults were elegantly, and in a holiday-
like manner, polite, but the youngsters in their teens (not children,
but youngsters—future young men in all sorts of uniforms, who
were quite numerous) kept jostling intolerably without apologizing
and passing by as if fully entitled to this kind of behavior. I was
shoved some fifty times; maybe they are being taught to do so
in order to develop in them a sense of unrestraint. Nevertheless,
after long want of habit, everything pleased me despite suffocating
heat, electric "suns," and the frantic, commander's cries of the
dance master.

The other day I picked up a copy of *The Petersburg Gazette,*
and there I read a correspondence from Moscow about holiday
scandals at the nobility club, in the artistic circle, at a masquerade,
etc. If one should believe the correspondent (who, when reporting
vice, may have deliberately kept silent on virtue), our society never
has been closer to scandal than at present. And strangely: why is
it that all my life, ever since childhood, the moment I would find
myself at a large holiday assembly of Russian people, I would at
once begin to feel that they were merely pretending, and suddenly
they would get up and start a row just as at home. The thought
is a nonsensical and fantastic one—and how ashamed I felt of
myself, how I reproached myself for this thought—even in childhood!—A thought that will not stand the test of even the mildest
criticism. Oh, of course, storekeepers and captains about whom our
truthful correspondent (I fully believe him) tells his story—these
have been known in days gone by; they have always existed—they
are an undying type; even so, they used to be more afraid and they
used to conceal their feelings; at present, however, at intervals,
such a fellow will suddenly burst forth to the very foreground, and
he seems convinced that this is his newly acquired right.

And it cannot be denied that in the last twenty years a very
great number of Russians suddenly, for some unknown reason, began to imagine that they have received full right to infamy; that
nowadays this is quite all right, and that they will be praised therefor, instead of being thrown out. On the other hand, I also under-

stand that it is very pleasing (oh, to quite a few, quite a few!) to stand up in the midst of a gathering—with ladies, cavaliers and even authorities all around, where everybody is so sweet-tongued, so polite and so equal one to another, as if it were really in Europe —to stand up amidst those Europeans and to bawl in the purest national dialect, to deliver a cuff to somebody, to pour forth some filth to a maiden and, generally, to perform some obscenity right there in the hall: "See, this is to reward you for the two centuries of Europeanism; and I am just as they, just as we all used to be; we disappeared nowhither." This is pleasing. But even so, the savage will be mistaken: he is not going to be recognized and he will be ejected. Who will eject him?—The police force?—No, not in the least the police force, but, precisely, those same savages as he—that savage! Herein is the force. I will explain it.

Do you know to whom this European and holiday appearance of Russian society, convening in a European fashion, is most pleasing and precious?—Precisely to the Skvoznik-Dmukhanovskis, the Tchitchikovs and, perhaps, even to Derjimorda, that is, to those very people who at home, in their private lives, are nationalistic in the highest degree. Oh, they have gatherings and dances of their own, there at their homes; but they do not appreciate and respect them; they do, however, treasure the governor's ball, the ball of the beau monde, about which they have heard from Khlestakov. And why?—Exactly because they themselves do not resemble good society. This is the reason why European forms are dear to them, although they are firmly aware of the fact that they will return home from a European ball the same fistfighters as before; yet they are consoled because they had paid homage to virtue even though in an ideal. Why, they know well that all this is a mirage; still, having attended the ball, they ascertained the fact that the mirage continues to persist; it persists through something, through some invisible but extraordinary force, and they did not have the nerve to come forward and plant themselves in the middle of the gathering and to bawl something in a national dialect. And the thought that they have not been, and henceforth will not be, permitted to do so, is immensely pleasing to them.

You will not believe how strongly a barbarian may become fond of Europe: thereby he participates, as it were, in the cult. No doubt, oftentimes, he is unable to determine of what this cult consists. Khlestakov, for example, maintained that this cult was expressed in a hundred-ruble watermelon which was served at the balls of the beau monde. Perhaps Skvoznik-Dmukhanovsky to the end clung to the belief in the watermelon, notwithstanding the fact that eventually he did learn who Khlestakov was and did despise

him; and yet the bailiff is glad to pay homage to virtue even in
the form of a watermelon. And this is by no means hypocrisy, but
perfect sincerity; more so—a necessity. Besides, here hypocrisy fits
the situation well, since what is hypocrisy?—It is a ransom which
vice is compelled to pay to virtue—which is an extremely comforting thought to him who wishes to remain vicious in practice but
at the same time not to sever, in his soul at least, with virtue. Oh,
vice is very fond of paying ransom to virtue, and this is good:
temporarily we should be satisfied with even that much—isn't this
so?—And, therefore, the captain who started bawling in the middle
of the hall continues to be a mere exception and a hurrying man
—I mean, temporarily at least; still even "temporarily" is consoling
in our unsteady times.

Thus the ball is decidely a conservative affair in the best
sense of the term and, when I say so, I am not joking at all.

4

THE GOLDEN AGE IN THE POCKET

And yet I also felt weary—that is, not weary but a little
annoyed. The children's dancing party came to an end, and the
father's ball began.—Oh, Lord, what incompetence!—Everybody
wearing new clothes, and no one knows how to wear them; everybody makes merry and no one is merry; everybody is ambitious
and no one knows how to make the most of himself; everybody
is envious; everybody keeps silent and everybody shuns everyone
else. They even do not know how to dance. Look at this whirling,
very short officer (such a brutishly whirling, very short officer one
is sure to encounter at every middle-class ball). His whole dance,
his whole technique boils down to this: almost brutishly, as if by
saccades, he turns his lady-partner around, and he is capable of
turning her thirty or forty times in succession, and he feels proud
of it. But what is there graceful about it! A dance is almost an
avowal of love (do recall the minuet!), whereas he fights. And the
most fantastic, the wildest, thought occurred to me: "What if"—I
started conjecturing—"all these nice and respectable guests should
make up their minds to become sincere and naïve, even for a moment? What would become of this stuffy hall? What if each one
of them should suddenly learn the whole secret? What if each one
of them should suddenly learn how much straightforwardness,
honesty, most sincere, heartfelt cheerfulness, purity, magnanimous
feelings, good will, intellect—nay, what's intellect?—wit, most refined
and communicative wit, there is in him—in each one, decidedly—in

each one of them! Yes, gentlemen, in each one of you all these
are present and contained, and not one—even not one—of you knows
anything about it! Oh, dear guests, I swear that each one of you
—whether lady or gentleman—is cleverer than Voltaire, more sensitive than Rousseau, infinitely more seductive than Alcibiades,
Don Juan, the Lucreces, the Juliets and the Beatrices! You do
not believe that you are so beautiful?—But I give you my word
of honor that in neither Shakespeare nor Schiller, nor in Homer,
if they all be put together, could there be found anything more
charming than could be found among you this very moment in
this very ballroom. What is Shakespeare!—Here we should behold
such things as are not dreamed of by our sages.

But the trouble is that you do not know yourselves, how
beautiful you are! Do you know that each one of you, if only
he would so desire, could at once make everybody in this hall happy
and captivate everybody? And this power is within each one of
you, but it is so deeply hidden that long ago it began to appear
incredible. And is it really possible that the golden age exists only
on porcelain cups?

Don't frown, your excellency, at the words *golden age:* I give
my word of honor that you will not be compelled to wear golden
age attire with a fig leaf; your whole general's uniform will be left
with you. I assure you that even people with the rank of a general
may be admitted to the golden age. Why, you have only to try
it, your excellency, right now; you are highest in rank, the initiative
is yours—and you will see for yourself what a, so to speak, Piron
wit you could reveal quite unexpectedly to yourself. You laugh;
this seems incredible to you? I am glad I made you laugh, and yet
all the things I have just been exclaiming are not a paradox but
a perfect truth. . . . Your trouble is that, to you, they seem incredible.

CHAPTER II

1

A Boy with his Hand Stretched out for Alms

CHILDREN ARE strange people; I dream about them—they
appear in my visions. Right along, before Christmas, and on the
very day of Christmas Eve, I have been meeting on a street, at
a certain corner, an urchin—certainly not older than seven. In a
terrible frost he was clad almost in summer clothes, but he had
around his neck some kind of old rags, which would mean that

somebody had been equipping him before sending him out on his mission. He was wandering "with a little hand"; this is a technical expression meaning—begging alms; it has been invented by the boys themselves.

There are a multitude of children such as this one; you keep meeting them along your way; they howl something learned by heart, but this one did not howl; he was uttering words innocently somehow, and he looked into my eyes unwontedly and confidently; thus, he was only beginning his profession. In answer to my inquiries, he told me that he had an ailing sister who was out of a job; this may have been true, but later I learned that there are a whole lot of such urchins; they are being sent out "with a little hand" even during the severest frost, and if they fail to collect anything a beating is unfailingly awaiting them.

Having collected a few kopecks, the boy, with red, numb hands, returns to some basement where a gang of peddlers are fuddling—those very fellows who "having quit their work on a Sunday eve, return to work not before evening on Wednesday." There, in those basements, the hungry, beaten wives of these fellows take part in the drinking bout; and there too, their hungry sucklings are squeaking. Vodka and filth and depravity, but principally—vodka. The urchin with the collected kopecks is at once being sent to the pot-house, and he brings some more liquor. Sometimes, for fun, they will pour a glass of vodka into his mouth, and they will laugh merrily when, with breath cut short and almost fainting, he drops on the floor.

> . . . and pitilessly horrid vodka
> He poured and poured into my mouth.

When he grows older they promptly get rid of him; he is being sent to some factory; yet whatever he manages to earn, he has to bring to those peddlers, and they, in turn, spend it all on drinks. However, even before these children reach the stage of the factory, they become accomplished criminals. They prowl about the town, and they know spots in different basements through which one may climb and spend the night without being detected. One of them spent several nights unnoticed in some basket at the quarters of a house-porter.

Of course, they become petty thieves. Pilfering grows into a passion even among eight-year-old children, at times, without their realizing the criminal character of their deeds. At length, they will endure anything—hunger, cold, beatings—for but one thing: freedom; they will run away from their peddlers to embark upon vagabondage, now for their personal benefit. Sometimes these savage

creatures understand nothing at all, not even where they are living;
they do not know to what nation they belong, whether there is a
God or a Czar. Such things are even told about them as seem quite
incredible, and yet they are all actual facts.

2

A LITTLE BOY AT CHRIST'S CHRISTMAS TREE

But I am a novelist, and it seems that one "story" I did
invent myself. Why did I say "it seems," since I know for certain
that I did actually invent it; yet I keep fancying that this happened somewhere, once upon a time, precisely on Christmas Eve,
in *some* huge city during a bitter frost.

I dreamed of a little boy—very little—about six, or even
younger. This little boy woke up one morning in a damp, cold
basement. He was clad in a shabby dressing gown of some kind,
and he was shivering. Sitting in the corner on a chest, wearily
he kept blowing out his breath, letting it escape from his mouth,
and it amused him to watch the vapor flow through the air. But
he was very hungry.

Several times that morning he came up to the bedstead, where
his sick mother lay on bedding thin as a pancake, with a bundle
of some sort under her head for a pillow.

How did she happen to be here?—She may have come with
her little boy from some faraway town, and then suddenly she had
fallen ill.

Two days ago the landlady of this wretched hovel had been
seized by the police; most of the tenants had scattered in all directions—it was the holiday season—and now there remained only two.
The peddler was still there, but he had been lying in a drunken
stupor for more than twenty-four hours, not even having waited
for the holiday to come. In another corner of the lodging an eighty-
year-old woman was moaning with rheumatism. In days past she
had been a children's nurse somewhere. Now she was dying in
solitude, moaning and sighing continuously and grumbling at the
boy so that he grew too frightened to come near her. Somehow he
had managed to find water in the entrance hall, with which to
appease his thirst; but nowhere was he able to discover as much
as a crust of bread. Time after time he came up to his mother,
trying in vain to awaken her. As it grew dark, dread fell upon him.
Though it was late evening, the candle was not yet lit. Fumbling
over his mother's face he began to wonder why she lay so quiet,
and why she felt as cold as the wall. "It's rather chilly in here,"

he said to himself. . . . For a moment he stood still, unconsciously resting his hand on the shoulder of the dead woman. Then he began to breathe on his tiny fingers in an attempt to warm them, and, suddenly, coming upon his little cap that lay on the bedstead, he groped along cautiously and quietly made his way out of the basement. This he would have done earlier had he not been so afraid of the big dog upstairs on the staircase, which kept howling all day long in front of a neighbor's door. Now the dog was gone, and in a moment he was out in the street.

"My God, what a city!"—Never before had he seen anything like this. There, in the place from which he had come, at night, everything was plunged into dark gloom—just a single lamp-post in the whole street! Humble wooden houses were closed in by shutters; no sooner did dusk descend than there was no one in sight; people locked themselves up in their homes, and only big packs of dogs—hundreds and thousands of them—howled and barked all night. Ah, but out there it was so warm, and there he had been given something to eat, while here . . . "Dear God, I do wish I had something to eat!"—And here—what a thundering noise! What dazzling light! What crowds of people and horses and carriages! And what biting frost! What frost! Vapor, which at once turned cold, burst forth in thick clouds from the horses' hot-breathing muzzles. Horseshoes tinkle as they strike the stones through the fluffy snow. And men pushing each other about. . . . "But, good heavens, how hungry I am! I wish I had just a tiny bit of something to eat!" And suddenly he felt a sharp pain in his little fingers.

A policeman passed by and turned his head away, so as not to take notice of the boy.

"And here is another street.—Oh, how wide it is! Here I'll surely be run over! And how people shout and run and drive along! And what floods of light! Light everywhere! Look, what's this?— Oh, what a huge window and, beyond it, a hall with a tree reaching up to the ceiling. It's a Christmas tree covered with gleaming lights, with sparkling bits of gold paper and apples, and all around are little dolls, toy-horses. Lots of beautifully dressed, neat children running about the hall; they laugh and play, and they eat and drink something. And see, over there, that little girl—now she starts to dance with a boy! What a pretty little girl she is! And just listen to the music! You can hear it from inside, coming through the window!"

The little boy gazes and gazes and wonders; he even starts laughing, but . . . his toes begin to hurt, while the little fingers on his hand have grown quite red—they won't bend any longer, and it hurts to move them. And when at last he became fully aware of the sharp pain in his fingers, he burst into tears and set off running.

Presently, through another window, he catches sight of a room, with trees standing in it, and tables loaded with cakes, all sorts of cakes—almond cakes, red cakes, yellow cakes! . . . Four beautifully dressed ladies are sitting in the room; whoever enters it is given a cake. . . . Every minute the door opens, and many gentlemen come in from the outside to visit these ladies.

The boy stole up, quickly pushed the door open, and sidled in. Oh, how they started shouting at him and motioning him out! One of the ladies hurried toward him, thrust a small copper coin into his hand, but she opened the door into the street. How frightened he was! The coin rolled from his hand, bouncing down the steps he was just unable to bend his little red fingers to hold on to it.

Very fast, the little boy ran away, and quickly he started going, but he himself did not know whither to go. Once more he was ready to cry, but he was so frightened that he just kept on running and running, and blowing on his cold little hands. How dreadfully lonesome he felt, and suddenly despair clutched at his heart.

But lo!—What's going on here?—In front of a window people are standing crowded together, lost in admiration. . . . Inside they see three tiny dolls, all dressed up in little red and green frocks, so real that they seem alive! A kindly-looking old man is sitting there, as if playing on a big violin; and next to him—two other men are playing small violins, swinging their heads to the rhythm of the music; they look at each other, their lips move, and they talk —they really do, but one simply can't hear them through the window pane.

At first the little boy thought that these moving figures were alive, but when at last he realized that they were only small puppets, he burst into laughter. He had never seen such figurines, and he didn't even know that such existed! He felt like crying, and yet the dolls looked so funny to him—oh, how funny!

Suddenly he felt as if somebody grabbed him by his dressing gown: a big bully of a boy, standing close by, without warning, struck him on the head, tore off his cap and kicked him violently. The little fellow fell down, and the people around began shouting. Scared to death, he jumped quickly to his feet and scampered off. All of a sudden he found himself in a strange courtyard under the vault of a gateway, and leaped behind a pile of kindling wood: "Here they won't find me! Besides, it's dark here!"

He sank down and huddled himself up in a small heap, but he could hardly catch his breath for fright. But presently a sen-

sation of happiness crept over his whole being: his little hands and
feet suddenly stopped aching, and once more he felt as comfortable
and warm as on a hearth. But hardly a moment later a shudder
convulsed him: "Ah, I almost fell asleep. Well, I'll stay here awhile,
and then I'll get back to look at the puppets"—the little boy said
to himself, and the memory of the pretty dolls made him smile:
"They seem just as though they're alive!" And all of a sudden he
seemed to hear the voice of his mother, leaning over him and
singing a song. "Mother dear, I'm just dozing. Oh, how wonderful
it is to sleep here!"

Then a gentle voice whispered above him: "Come, little boy,
come along with me! Come to see a Christmas tree!"

His first thought was that it might be his mama still speaking
to him, but no—this wasn't she. Who, then, could it be? He saw
no one, and yet, in the darkness, someone was hovering over him
and tenderly clasping him in his arms. . . . The little boy stretched
out his arms and . . . an instant later—"Oh, what dazzling light!
Oh, what a Christmas tree! Why, it can't be a Christmas tree,"—
for he had never seen such trees.

Where is he now?—Everything sparkles and glitters and shines,
and scattered all over are tiny dolls—no, they are little boys and
girls, only they are so luminous, and they all fly around him; they
embrace him and lift him up; they carry him along, and now he
flies, too. And he sees: yonder is his mother; she looks at him,
smiling at him so happily. "Oh, Mother! Mother! How beautiful
it is here!"—exclaimed the little boy, and again he begins to kiss
the children; he can hardly wait to tell them about those wee
puppets behind the glass of the window.

"Who are you, little boys? Who are you, little girls?"—he
asks them, smilingly, and he feels that he loves them all.

"This is Christ's Christmas Tree,"—they tell him. "On this
day of the year Christ always has a Christmas Tree for those little
children who have no Christmas tree of their own."

And then he learned that these little boys and girls were all
once children like himself, but some of them have frozen to death
in those baskets in which they had been left at the doors of Petersburg officials; others had perished in miserable hospital wards; still
others had died at the dried-up breasts of their famine-stricken
mothers (during the Samara famine); these, again, had choked to
death from stench in third-class railroad cars. Now they are all
here, all like little angels, and they are all with Christ, and He
is in their midst, holding out His hands to them and to their sinful
mothers. . . . And the mothers of these babes, they all stand there,
a short distance off, and weep: each one recognizes her darling—

her little boy, or her little girl—and they fly over to their mothers and kiss them and brush away their tears with their little hands, begging them not to cry, for they feel so happy here. . . .

Next morning, down in the courtyard, porters found the tiny body of a little boy who had hidden behind the piles of kindling wood, and there had frozen to death. They also found his mother. She died even before he had passed away.

Now they are again united in God's Heaven.

And why did I invent such a story, one that conforms so little to an ordinary, reasonable diary—especially a writer's diary? And that, after having promised to write stories pre-eminently about actual events! But the point is that I keep fancying that all this could actually have happened—I mean, the things which happened in the basement and behind the piles of kindling wood. Well, and as regards Christ's Christmas Tree—I really don't know what to tell you, and I don't know whether or not this could have happened. Being a novelist, I have to invent things.

3

A COLONY OF JUVENILE DELINQUENTS. GLOOMY CREA-
TURES. CONVERSION OF VICIOUS SOULS INTO INNOCENT
ONES. MEASURES RECOGNIZED AS MOST EXPEDIENT THERE-
FOR. LITTLE AND BOLD FRIENDS OF MANKIND.

On the third day of the holiday season I saw all these "fallen" angels—a whole group of fifty of them. Please do not think that I am jesting when calling them "fallen" angels: that they are "insulted" children there can be no doubt. Insulted by whom? How? In what way? And who is to be blamed?—As yet, these are idle questions, to which there is nothing in reply. Better that we get down to business.

I was at the colony of juvenile delinquents, which is located beyond the Powder Plant. I have long sought to go there, but somehow I could not manage it, and here, unexpectedly, I happened to have some spare time, and kind people came forward and volunteered to show me everything.

We went there on a warm, somewhat overcast day; having passed the Powder Plant, we came directly to a forest in which the colony is situated.

How beautiful is a forest in winter, covered with snow; how fresh; how pure the air, and how isolated. Here, some five hundred dessiatins have been donated to the colony, which consists of several handsomely constructed, wooden houses, standing a certain distance apart. Everything has been built with donated money; each house cost about three thousand rubles, and in each one of them there lives a "family." The family is a group of twelve to seventeen boys, and each family has its instructor.

It is planned to house eventually up to seventy boys, in accordance with the colony's size, but at present, for some reason, there are but fifty pupils. It has to be admitted that money has been provided on a liberal scale, and each juvenile delinquent costs annually a considerable sum. Also, it seems strange that sanitary conditions in the colony, as has recently been reported in the papers, are not quite satisfactory: of late, there has been considerable sickness, despite the fact that the air and the upkeep of the children are so excellent!

We spent several hours at the colony—from eleven in the morning till dusk. But I came to the conclusion that one visit is insufficient to provide time for looking into everything and for grasping everything. The director invited me to come and stay with them two days, or so. This is very tempting.

The director, P. A—ch R—sky, is known in literature. From time to time his articles appear in *The Messenger of Europe*. He gave me a most cordial reception and exhibited much complaisance. At the office there is a book in which visitors, if they wish, may inscribe their names. Among those who have signed their names I observed many prominent persons: this means that the colony is known and that people take an interest in it. However, in spite of all his complaisance, the esteemed director, it would seem, is a very reserved man, although he emphasized to us, almost with delight, the encouraging aspects of the colony—at the same time, however, soft-pedalling everything disagreeable and unorganized. I hasten to add that this reserve—so it seemed to me—is caused by a most ardent affection for the colony and for the project undertaken.

All four instructors (I believe there are four of them, in accordance with the number of the families) are not old men; they are almost young; each receives a salary of three hundred rubles, and almost all of them are graduates of theological seminaries. They live quite in common with their pupils, and they even wear practically the same clothes as the latter—something akin to blouses girded with leather belts.

When we inspected the wards, they were empty: it was a holiday and the children were playing somewhere; this made the inspection of the premises all the easier. There is no superfluous luxury, nothing too profuse, inspired by excessive kindness or humaneness of the donors and founders of the institution; this could easily have been the case, and this would have been a grave error.

For instance, the iron folding cots are most simple; the bed linen is of rather rough cloth; nor is there anything fancy about the blankets, but they are warm. The pupils get up early and, all together, they get dressed; then they clean the wards and, whenever necessary, wash the floors. Near some cots I could discern a certain smell, and I learned an almost incredible thing: that some pupils (not many, but still eight or nine of them), not too young either, of the age of twelve or even thirteen, urinate during their sleep, without getting up from their cots. In answer to my question as to whether this was due to some ailment, I was told that such was not the case at all, but that this was due to the fact that they were savage—savage to such an extent that they even could not comprehend that one could and should behave differently. But in this case, where—in what wretched haunts—could they have been growing up and whom did they see! There is no peasant family so destitute which, on an occasion such as this, would not teach a child how to behave, and where even the tiniest little boy would not know it. Thus, it may be asked, what sort of people did the young inmate encounter? And what a bestially indifferent attitude did they take toward his existence!

However, this is a true fact and I consider it very important. Let people refrain from laughing at me because I am "inflating" this dirty little fact to such an extent; it is more serious than it may seem. It signifies that thus there are, indeed, human specimens so gloomy and dreadful that all signs of humanity and civility are obliterated in them. One can also comprehend into what such a savage little soul may be converted in the face of such forsakenness and isolation from social intercourse.

Yes, these children's souls did see sombre pictures and they are used to strong impressions which, of course, will forever be retained by them and which will come back to them all through their lives in dreadful dreams. Thus, reformers and instructors of such children should seek to overcome these horrible impressions; to eradicate them and to plant new ones. This is a momentous problem.

"You would not believe in what a savage state some of them are when admitted here"—P. A—ch said to me.—"Some of them know nothing either about themselves or about their social status. They have been prowling about almost unconsciously, and the only thing they know in this world—the only thing they were able to conceive—was their liberty, the freedom of vagrancy. We have a little boy here, not older than ten; up to this day he is wholly unable to refrain from stealing things. He pilfers with no aim or profit—solely for the sake of stealing, mechanically."

"How, then, do you expect to reform such children?"

"Work; an altogether different way of living, and fairness in our dealings with them. Finally—the hope that after three years their old predilections and habits will be forgotten of their own accord, by the mere lapse of time."

I inquired whether among the boys there were certain other notorious and vicious children's habits. In passing, I may state that here there are boys between the ages of ten and as old as seventeen, even though only children not older than fourteen are admissible.

"Oh, no; no such bad habits can exist," promptly replied P. A—ch. "Their instructors are undeviatingly and incessantly keeping their eye on them in this respect."

However, to me, this seemed incredible. In the colony there are several boys who formerly had been inmates in the now abolished division of juvenile delinquents at the Lithuanian Castle. I have visited that prison, some three years ago, and I have seen these boys. Later I positively ascertained that extraordinary perversion has been prevalent among those inmates in the Castle; and also that those vagabonds kept at the Castle, who, at the time of their admission there, had not yet been contaminated with lewdness and, at first, loathed it, subsequently submitted to it almost against their will, because their comrades scoffed at their chastity.

"Were there many recidivists?"—I inquired.

"Not so many: out of the total number of those who had been discharged from the colony, there were only about eight." (Still, this is not a small figure.)

I may observe that the pupils are discharged mostly in the capacity of artisans, and "preliminary" lodging quarters are secured for them. Formerly, passports issued to them by the colony constituted a great handicap in their existence. However, at present ways have been found to issue passports from which, at least at first glance, it cannot be perceived that its bearer comes from the delinquents' colony.

"But," P. A—ch hastened to add, "we have among our discharged men some who even now cannot forget the colony, and just as soon as there is a holiday, unfailingly they come to visit us and stay with us for a while."

Thus, the strongest means of re-education, of converting a stunted and vilified soul into a serene and honest one is work. The day begins with work in the ward, and after that the pupils go to workshops. In the locksmith and carpentry shops their wares were shown to me. The products are good, within the limits of possibility, but, of course, they will be greatly improved as the business is better organized. These wares are being sold for the pupil's benefit, so that by the time of his discharge from the colony each one has accumulated a certain sum of money. The children are engaged in work in both the morning and afternoon, but without suffering fatigue. And it does seem that work, in fact, exercises a rather potent influence upon their moral being: they compete with each other to do a better job and they are proud of their success.

Another means toward their spiritual development is, of course, autonomous justice instituted among them. Everyone guilty of something is tried by his respective "family" court: the boys either acquit him or convict him. The only punishment is the exclusion from games. Comrades who refuse to submit to their fellows' judgments are punished with total excommunication from the colony. For this end they have their "Petropavlovka": thus the boys have labelled a special remote hut, equipped with cells, for those temporarily expelled. However, it seems that confinement in the "Petropavlovka" depends solely upon the director's decision.

We visited that "Petropavlovka"; at that time there were only two inmates there. And I may note that boys are incarcerated there with the exercise of due caution and discretion—for something really important and inveterate. These two inmates were kept under lock and key, in separate cells, but they were not shown to us.

Essentially, this autonomous court is, of course, a good thing, but it smacks of something bookish. There are many proud children —proud in a good sense—who may feel insulted by this self-governing authority of boys and delinquents such as themselves; and thus they may misunderstand this authority. There may happen to be some individuals much more talented and clever than the rest of the "family," and the judgment of their milieu may thwart their ambition and instill hate into them. And the milieu is practically always the average, the mediocre. Besides, do the boys themselves, when passing judgment, properly understand their business? On the contrary, is it not possible that among them, too, there might develop children's groups of some rivalling boys, stronger, more alert than the others, who always and unfailingly appear among children in all schools, and who give tone to the rest and lead the others as by a rope?—After all, these are only children—not adults.

Finally, will the convicted, and those who have suffered punishment, later treat their former judges as simply and as brotherly as heretofore, and does not this autonomous justice impair the spirit of comradeship?—Of course, this formative pedagogic device has been conceived and founded upon the idea that these hitherto delinquent children, by means of such right to autonomous justice, get used, as it were, to lawfulness, self-restraint and truth, about which they formerly have known nothing, and that they will develop within themselves a sense of duty. All these are beautiful and lofty thoughts, but somehow they are also double-edged. As for punishment, of course, the most effective and restraining one has been selected—that is, deprivation of one's freedom.

In passing, I may here interject a strange *nota bene*. The other day, by accident, I happened to hear a rather unexpected comment on corporal punishment, which has been abolished in all our schools: "Well, in schools everywhere, they have abolished corporal punishment, and it is a good thing they did, but what, *inter alia*, was achieved thereby?—Only that among our youth there are more cowards than in days past. They are afraid of even the slightest physical pain, of any suffering, privation, or even offense, of any sting to their ambition, to such a degree that some of them— as examples illustrate—hang or shoot themselves when they are called upon to face even some paltry threat—some difficult lesson or examination."

Indeed, it is most appropriate to explain several of these actual cases by nothing but the cowardice of lads when confronted by something disagreeable or threatening. Yet this is a strange point of view on the subject, and this *observation* is, to say the least, original. I record it for memory.

I have seen all the boys at dinner. Meals are most simple, but healthful, abundant and excellently cooked. We tasted the food with pleasure before the pupils had arrived. Yet, the cost of food for each boy per day is only fifteen kopecks. Porridge or sour cabbage soup with meat was served; for the second course—gruel or potatoes. In the morning, when the boys get up, they are given tea with bread, and between dinner and supper—bread with kvas. They are quite satiated. At the table they were being waited on in turn by pupils on duty. Before taking their seats at the table all the boys sang excellently the prayer: "Thy Nativity, O Christ, Our Lord." They are taught to sing prayers by one of the instructors.

Here, at dinner, when all the pupils were assembled, the thing that interested me most was to study their faces. These are not too bold or arrogant, but simply the faces of boys who are abashed by nothing. There was hardly a single stupid face (although I was told that there are stupid ones among the pupils, particularly among the former inmates of the foundling hospital). On the contrary, there are even quite intelligent faces. There are plenty of bad faces, but not physically bad; the features of virtually all the faces are almost handsome, yet in some of them there seems something too deeply hidden. Also, there are few smiling faces, despite the fact that the pupils behave in an easy manner in the presence of both their superiors and strangers, although not quite in the same way as more open-hearted children. And probably quite a number of them are longing to steal away from the colony. Many of them are anxious not to betray themselves in speaking: this is apparent from the expression of their faces.

The humane and obliging—to the point of refinement—treatment of the boys by their instructors (however, when necessary, they know how to be severe), in some cases, it seems to me, does not reach their hearts—and certainly not their consciousness. *You* is used in addressing them, even the youngest ones. This *you* sounded to me somewhat strained and, perhaps, a little superfluous. Maybe the boys admitted here will consider this a gentleman's fancy. Briefly, this *you* is, probably, a mistake, and even a somewhat serious one. To my way of thinking, it alienates, as it were, the children from their instructors: in that *you* there is something formal, bureaucratic, and it would be a pity if some boy should take it as something contemptuous toward him. Indeed, he will not believe that he who had witnessed most extraordinary scenes and who had listened to most unnatural obscene cursing; he who had been engaged in unbridled thieving, for some reason, deserves this kind of gentleman's treatment. In a word, in my opinion, *thou*, in these circumstances, would resemble more real truth, whereas here everybody seems to be pretending a little. Certainly it would be far better if the children would at length realize that their instructors are not tutors, but fathers, and that they themselves are but naughty children who must be reformed.

On the other hand, perhaps, this *you* will not spoil the boy and when, later, the *thou*, or the cursing which he will inevitably hear again on the very same day of his discharge from the institution, will shock him, he might, with so much more affection, heave a sigh for his colony.

Among the lagging things is reading. I was told that the children are very fond of reading, that is, to listen when they are being read to on holidays or at spare moments, and that among them there are skilled readers. I heard but one of them: he read well, and it is said that he likes very much to read aloud to all of them and to be listened to. However, there are among them some who can hardly read and also some quite illiterate ones. But what do they read?—After dinner, I saw on the table of one of the "families" a volume by some author; and there they are reading about Vladimir and how he conversed with some Olga on different profound and strange subjects, and how subsequently the inescapable milieu "shattered their existence."

I have seen their "library": it is a bookcase containing Turgenev, Ostrovsky, Lermontov, Pushkin, and others; there are also several useful travel stories, etc. The whole collection is a scattered and accidental one, which also has been donated.

Of course, once reading has been permitted, it must be conceived as a very formative influence; yet I know that if all our educational agencies in Russia, headed by pedagogical boards, sought to determine and outline exactly what should be read by these children and under these particular circumstances, they would certainly adjourn without having decided upon anything, because this is a very difficult problem—one which will never be finally settled at some meeting. On the other hand, in our literature there are no books whatsoever which would be comprehensible to the people. Neither Pushkin nor *The Sebastopol Stories;* neither *Evenings on a Farm* nor the tale about Kalashnikov, nor Koltzov (Koltzov in particular) are at all intelligible to the people. Of course, these boys are not the people, but, so to speak, God knows who—such specimens of human beings as can hardly be classified and assigned to any division or type. However, even were they to understand something, they would not have treasured it because all this wealth, as it were, would have fallen from heaven; but for this, owing to their past record, they would not be prepared.

As for accusatory writers and satirists—do these poor children, who have seen so much filth, need such spiritual impressions anyway? Perhaps these little folks have no desire at all to laugh at people. Maybe these souls, plunged into gloom, would gladly and affectionately lay themselves open to the most naïve, most elementary and simple-minded impressions, quite childish and plain, which would be disdainfully scoffed at by a contemporary high school or lyceum pupil of the same age as these delinquent children.

The school is also in its infancy, but it is being planned to have it organized in the very near future. Drawing and painting are virtually not being taught. There is no religious instruction at all. There is no priest on the premises. But they will have one after the church is built. It is to be a wooden church which is now under construction. The superiors and architects are proud of it. In fact, the architecture is not bad, though in a somewhat official, conspicuously Russian style, of which one is tired.

I might observe in passing that unquestionably religious instruction in schools—whether for criminals or our other elementary schools—should not be entrusted to anyone but priests. But why

couldn't even schoolteachers relate simple episodes from the history
of the Church?—No doubt, among the great multitudes of village
schoolteachers there may be some really bad persons. However,
if such a bad person should seek to teach a boy atheism, he could
do so without teaching the history of the Church—by merely speaking of a duck and "what it is covered with."

On the other hand, what do we hear about our clergy?—Oh,
I have no intention of offending anyone, and I am convinced that
in the schools for criminals there will be a most deserving "batiushka." Still, of late, what were practically all of our papers reporting with special zeal? Most disturbing facts were reported to
the effect that there were religious teachers who, by the dozens
and wholesale, deserted the schools and refused to teach in them
without an increase in their salaries. No doubt, "he who works has
got to be paid," but this everlasting howling about a raise in compensation hurts one's ear and tortures one's heart. Our papers side
with those who are howling, and, of course, I, too, am favoring
them. Even so, in this connection I always dream of those ancient
ascetics and preachers of the Gospel who went around, naked and
barefooted, enduring blows and suffering, preaching Christ without
any increase in their salaries.

Why, I am not an idealist, and I fully realize that nowadays
times are different. But would it not be nice to hear that even a
tiny drop of good will had been acquired by our spiritual enlight-
eners before their salaries had been raised? I repeat: let them take
no offense: everybody knows perfectly well that among our clergy
the spirit is not exhausted and that there are zealous workers in their
midst. And I am convinced in advance that such will be the priest
in the colony. But it would be best if the pupils were simply told
episodes from the history of the Church without any special bureaucratic moral, temporarily confining the religious instruction to
this alone. A series of pure, holy, beautiful pictures would exercise
a potent influence upon their souls craving beautiful impressions.

However, I bade farewell to the colony with a comforting
feeling in my heart. If there are things which are not yet "fixed,"
there are, on the other hand, facts of great achievement with respect
to the aims of the institution. I will recount two of them—thus
bringing my story to an end.

At the time when I visited the colony there was incarcerated
in the "Petropavlovka" a pupil of the age of about fifteen. Before
that he had been kept for a while in the prison of the Lithuanian
Castle when it still maintained a division of juvenile delinquents.
Having been ordered to join the colony, he escaped from it—twice,
I believe. Both times he had been caught—once already outside the

boundaries of the institution. Finally, he frankly declared that he would not obey, and for this he had been subjected to solitary confinement. On Christmas relatives brought him some presents which, however, were not permitted to be delivered to him, since he was kept imprisoned, and the instructor confiscated them. This greatly impressed and offended the boy, and, during the director's inspection of the "Petropavlovka," he began to complain bitterly, harshly accusing the instructor of having confiscated the package with the gifts for his own benefit. At the same time, angrily and scoffingly, he spoke about the colony and about his companions. He blamed everybody. "I sat down at his side and spoke to him earnestly."—P. A—ch told me.—"All the time he remained gloomily silent. About two hours later he sent for me, imploring me to come and see him. And what would you think?—He rushed to me with eyes full of tears, in a state of violent commotion, quite transformed. He began to repent, accusing himself, and he started telling me things which heretofore he had been concealing—things that hap- pened to him in the past. He also divulged the secret that for a long time he has been addicted to a shameful habit, of which he could not rid himself, and that this tormented him. Briefly, this was a full confession. I spent about two hours with him," added P. A—ch. "We conversed. I suggested certain remedies to overcome his habit, and so forth."

Recounting all this, P. A—ch refrained from telling what they had been conversing about. But one has to admit that it is a gift to know how to penetrate the ailing soul of a profoundly embittered young criminal, who had heretofore never known what truth meant. I confess, I wish I knew the details of that conversation.

Here is another fact. Every instructor in each "family" not only sees to it that the pupils set their wards in order, washing and cleaning them, but he also takes part in the work. There, floors are washed on Saturdays. The instructor not only shows how the wash- ing should be done, but he proceeds along with them to wash the floor. This is a most perfect understanding of one's vocation and of one's human dignity. Where, for example, will you find in bureau- cratic circles such an attitude toward business? And if in reality, in truth, these men make up their minds to tie the aims of the colony to their whole lives, of course, matters will be "fixed," despite any theoretical errors, even should such occur in the beginning. "Heroes!—You, gentlemen-novelists, keep looking for heroes!" a man of vast experience said to me the other day: "And not finding heroes in our midst, you feel angry; you grumble against all of Russia. But I will tell you an anecdote. Once upon a time, long ago, during the reign of the late Emperor, there lived a certain government official. First, he served in Petersburg, and later, I believe, in Kiev, and there he died. This, apparently, is his whole biography. And yet, what would you think?—This little fellow, modest and taciturn all his life, was so grieved, inwardly, over serfdom, over the fact that, in Russia, man—God's own image—so slavishly depended upon a man just like himself that he began to accumulate savings out of his negligible salary, denying to himself, his wife and children almost the bare necessities; as he would manage to save enough money, he would redeem from a landowner one of the latter's serfs and would set him free—of course, only one man every ten years. Thus, during his lifetime he had redeemed three or four men, and, when he died, he left nothing to his family. All this occurred without any notoriety—quietly, obscurely. Of course, what kind of a hero is he!—Merely 'an idealist of the Forties,' perhaps even a funny and incompetent one, since he sought to cure the whole calamity with a microscopical, isolated instance. And yet it would seem that our Potugins should take a kindlier view of Russia and not throw mud at her for everything, at random."

I am recording here this anecdote (which, perhaps, is quite irrelevant) only because I have no grounds for doubting its authenticity.

However, those are the men we need! I am awfully fond of this comic type of little fellow, earnestly imagining that with his microscopical effort and perseverance he will be able to help the general cause without awaiting a general upswing and a common initiative. A little chap of this kind, perhaps, would also come in handy in the colony of juvenile delinquents . . . Oh, it goes without saying—under the guidance of more enlightened and, so to speak, higher supervisors. . . .

However, I have spent only a few hours in the colony, and I could have falsely conceived, skipped and mistaken many things. At any rate, I find that the means for converting vicious souls into innocent ones are as yet inadequate.

CHAPTER III

1

Russian Society for the Protection of Animals. Courier.
Green Liquor. Itch for Debauch and Vorobiev. From the
End or from the Beginning?

IN ISSUE No. 359 of *The Voice* I happened to read about the solemn celebration of the tenth-year anniversary of the Russian

Society for the Protection of Animals. What a nice and humane Society! As far as I could understand, its basic aim is almost fully expressed in the words taken from the address of Prince A. A. Suvorov, the President of the Society.

"In fact, the aim of our new charitable institution seemed all the more difficult of achievement as the majority was not prepared to perceive in the protection of animals those moral and material advantages to men which result from a humane and rational treatment of domestic animals."

Indeed, not only little dogs and shabby jades are dear to the Society but, equally, man—the Russian, in whom the human image must be restored[1] and who has to be humanized—a task in which the Society for the Protection of Animals, no doubt, can assist. Having once learned to pity the animals, the peasant will also begin to pity his wife. And, therefore, even though I am very fond of animals, I am only too glad that not only animals but also callous, inhuman men, half-barbarians awaiting enlightenment, are dear to our esteemed Society.

Every educational means is precious, and it is to be hoped that the aim of the Society, in reality, will become a means of enlightenment. Our children are being brought up and grow up beholding many a repulsive picture. They see a peasant who, having excessively loaded a cart, whips across its eyes his jade, his bene-factrix, that is sinking in the mud; or, for instance—this I recently witnessed myself—a peasant who, having loaded a big cart with ten or more calves which he was to drive to a slaughterhouse, got into the cart and unhesitatingly seated himself on one of the calves. It felt soft to sit on the animal, as if on a springy couch, but the calf, with its tongue sticking out of its mouth and with its protrud-ing eyes, may have heaved its last even before it had reached the slaughterhouse. This little scene, I am sure, incensed no one in the street: "All the same, they are being driven to be slaughtered." Yet scenes of this kind make man bestial and have a demoralizing effect, especially upon children.

True, the esteemed Society has been attacked; not only once have I heard jibes about it. For instance, it has been said that some five years ago the Society brought charges against a cabman, ac-cusing him of cruel treatment of his horse, and that a fine of fif-teen rubles was imposed on him. Of course, this was a *faux pas* because after such a verdict had been rendered many people did not know whom they should pity: the cabman or his horse. At

---

[1] *Obrazit* is a popular word, meaning to restore in man the human image. People say to a man who has been drinking hard for a long time: "Thou shouldst *obrazit* thyself." I have heard this expression among convicts.

present, however, on the strength of the new law, it is provided that
a fine should not exceed ten rubles.

Also, I have heard that the Society busies itself too much
about the problem that stray and, therefore, harmful dogs which
have lost their masters be put away under chloroform. In this connection it has been observed that so long as human beings in our
famine-stricken provinces are dying from starvation, such tender
care with respect to little dogs hurts, as it were, one's ear.

However, all these objections cannot stand the test of criticism.
The aim of the Society is more enduring than any temporary accidentals. The aim is a fair and just one; sooner or later it will strike
root and triumph. Nevertheless, considering the question from another viewpoint, it is very desirable that the activities of the Society
and "the temporary accidentals," mentioned above, should, so to
speak, arrive at a state of mutual equilibrium. Of course, then the
salutary and beneficial path along which the Society may achieve
abundant and—what is more important—practical results in the
actual realization of its aims, would be more clearly revealed. Perhaps, I do not make myself fully understood. I shall relate an anecdote—a true event—and I hope that by its perspicuous account I
shall convey my thought more graphically.

This incident happened long ago in my, so to speak, pre-
historical times—in 1837—when I was about fifteen years old and
was en route from Moscow to Petersburg. My elder brother and
I were going with our late father to Petersburg for matriculation
in the Chief Engineering School. It was in May and it was hot.
We drove with hired horses almost at a footpace, halting at stations
for as long as two or three hours. I remember how, at length, we
had grown weary of this journey which had lasted almost a whole
week. My brother and I were then longing for a new life; we were
meditating intensely about something, about everything "beautiful
and lofty": in those days these were still novel words and they
used to be uttered without irony. And, at the time, how many beautiful little words were in use! We passionately believed in something, and although we knew well everything that was required for
the examination in mathematics, we dreamed only about poetry and
poets. My brother wrote verses, three poems every day, even during
our journey, while I kept busy planning in my mind a novel dealing
with Venetian life. Only two months[1] before, Pushkin had died,
and en route brother and I agreed to visit without delay the place
of the duel and to try to make our way into the former apartment

[1]Dostoievsky made a mistake: Pushkin died on January 29, 1837, *i.e.*,
over *three* months prior to the event described here ("it was in *May* and
it was hot"). B. B.

of Pushkin, in order to behold the room in which he had passed away. One evening we were stopping at a station, an inn, in some village—the name of which I have forgotten—in the province of Tver, if I correctly recall. It was a large and well-to-do village. In half an hour we were to resume our journey and, meanwhile, I was looking through the window, and I saw the following:

Across the street, directly opposite the inn, was the station building. Suddenly a courier's troika speedily drove up to the station's platform; a courier jumped out of the carriage; he was in full uniform, with narrow little flaps on the back, as was the fashion in those days, and he wore a large three-cornered hat with white, yellow and, I think, green plumes. (I have forgotten this detail, which I could check; but I seem to recall the glimpse of green plumes too.) The courier was a tall, very stout and strong chap, with a livid face. He ran into the station house and there, surely, must have "swallowed" a glass of vodka. I recall that our coachman then told me that such couriers always drink a glass of vodka at every station, for without it they would be unable to endure "such a torment."

Meanwhile, a fresh, spirited, substitute troika drove up to the postal station, and the yamschik, a young lad of about twenty, in a red shirt and holding an overcoat in his hands, jumped into the coachman's seat. Forthwith, the courier came running down the staircase and seated himself in the carriage. The yamschik stirred on, but hardly had he started to move than the courier rose up and silently raised his hardy right fist and, from above, painfully brought it down on the back of the yamschik's head. He jolted forward, lifted his whip and, with all his strength, lashed the wheel horse. The horses dashed forward but this in no way appeased the courier. Here there was method and not mere irritation—something preconceived and tested by long years of experience—and the dreadful fist soared again and again and struck blows on the back of the head. And then, again and again, and thus it continued until the troika disappeared out of sight. Of course, the yamschik, who could hardly keep his balance, incessantly, every second, like a madman, lashed the horses and, finally, he had whipped them up to the point where they started dashing at top speed, as if possessed.

Our coachman explained to me that virtually all couriers are riding in approximately the same manner, but that this one is particularly notorious and everybody knows him; that after jumping into the carriage, he begins with the beating and he beats "always in one and the same fashion," for no reason, regularly, swinging his fist up and down, "holding the yamschik at his mercy under the blows of his fist, for a verst or so, and then he stops beating.

Should he grow weary, he might renew the ordeal in the middle of the journey, but God may prevent it. But on approaching a station, he invariably gets up on his feet: he starts at a distance of approximately one verst and he keeps swinging his fist up and down, in the same manner, until he reaches the station, so that everybody in the village should gaze at him with amazement. Well, after that one's neck hurts for a whole month." Upon the return of the lad, people laugh at him: "See, the courier cudgelled your neck!" And that same day he may beat his wife: "At least, you'll pay for it!" Maybe also because "she looked and saw . . ."

No doubt, it is inhuman on the part of the yamschik to lash the horses so ferociously: of course, they reach the station all out of breath and quite exhausted. Still, who among the personnel of the Society for the Protection of Animals would venture to bring a charge against the peasant lad for his inhuman treatment of his little horses? Am I right?

This disgusting scene has remained in my memory all my life. Never was I able to forget it, or that courier, and many an infamous and cruel thing observed in the Russian people, willy-nilly, I was inclined for a long time thereafter to explain obviously in a too one-sided sense.—You will realize that I am speaking of times long past. This little scene appeared to me, so to speak, as an emblem, as something which very graphically demonstrated the link between cause and effect. Here every blow dealt at the animal leaped out of each blow dealt at the man. In the late Forties, during the period of my most unrestrained and fervent dreams, it suddenly occurred to me that should I ever happen to found a philanthropic society, I would by all means engrave this courier's troika on the seal of the society, as an emblem and warning sign.

Oh, no doubt, today the situation is not as it used to be forty years ago: couriers no longer beat the people, but the people beat themselves, having retained the rods in their own court. And the point is not in this, but in the causes which produce effects. There is no courier but there is poison liquor. Well, in what way is "green liquor" comparable with the courier?—It certainly is in that it also may make man bestial and cattle-like; it makes him cruel and detracts him from serene thoughts; it makes him dull and unreceptive to any constructive propaganda. A drunken man has no compassion toward animals; he deserts his wife and his children. A drunken husband came to his wife, whom he had deserted and whom, along with her children, he had failed to support for many months, and demanded vodka from her; he began to beat her so as to extort more vodka from her; then she, that galley-slave working-woman (please think of how, thus far, woman's labor has been rated!), who did not know how she could manage to feed her children, seized a knife and thrust it into him. This happened recently and she is going to be tried. But there is no point in my speaking about her; such cases may be counted by the hundreds and the thousands—one has merely to open the papers.

However, the main point of similarity between liquor and the courier is in the fact that it dominates the human will as inescapably and as fatally as the courier.

The esteemed Society for the Protection of Animals has seven hundred and fifty members who may be potentially influential. What if it should make up its mind to assist in the reduction—at least a little—of drunkenness among the people and of the poisoning with liquor of a whole generation! In fact, the strength of the people is being drained, the source of future wealth is becoming exhausted, intelligence and development have become poor. And what will present-day children of the people, brought up on the filth of their fathers, carry off in their minds and hearts?—A fire broke out in the village and it spread to the church. Presently, the innkeeper appeared on the scene and cried out to the people that if they would cease putting out the fire in the church, but would save his pot-house, he would give them a barrel of liquor. The church burned down, but the pot-house was saved. These are but insignificant incidents compared with the innumerable horrors of the future.

Should the esteemed Society desire to assist in the elimination of the prime causes, it would thereby unquestionably facilitate its most worthy propaganda. Because how is one to make people compassionate if things have precisely shaped themselves so as to eliminate in man every sign of humaneness?

And is it only liquor that plays havoc with, and debauches, the people in our amazing times?—Everywhere there seems to be soaring some sort of a drug, as it were, jimson, some itch for debauch. The people have become affected with an unheard-of distortion of ideas and a wholesale worship of materialism. By materialism, in this case, I mean the worship of money by the people, their adoration of the power inherent in a bag of gold. The idea seems to have burst forth to the people that the bag contains all the power, and that everything he has been told and taught up to the present by his fathers—is all nonsense. It would be a calamity should the people become confirmed in such a belief. And yet, how can they be reasoning differently? Do you think, for instance, that the recent wreck on the Odessa railroad, of the train which transported the Czar's recruits, in which more than one hundred of them were killed—do you think that such neglect on the part of the authorities would not have a demoralizing effect upon the people? The people see and wonder at such power: "they do what they please"—and, willy-nilly, they begin to doubt: "here, then, is where the real power lies; here is where it has always resided; get rich, and everything is yours, and you may do as you please." No more demoralizing an idea can exist. And yet it soars everywhere and gradually penetrates everything. The people, however, are in no way protected from such ideas—by no enlightenment, by no propaganda whatsoever of opposing ideas.

All through Russia we see railroads stretching out—almost twenty thousand versts of them—and everywhere along them even the lowest functionary appears as a propagandist of this idea; he poses as a man invested with unlimited power over you and your fate, over your family and your honor—just only dare to be caught by him on a railroad. Not long ago a station-master, by his own authority and with his own hands, dragged out of a car a lady passenger, in order to turn her over to some man who had complained to that station-master that this was his wife who had deserted him. And this—without any court proceedings, without any suspicion even that he, the station-master, had no right to act in this way. It is obvious that if he had not been in a state of delirium, still he must have gone crazy over his own authority.

Now, all such incidents and examples burst forth over the people as a stream of uninterrupted temptations; day after day, they are beholding them, and are drawing the inevitable conclusions. Formerly, I almost used to condemn Mr. Suvorin for his incident with Mr. Golubev. It seemed to me that one should not drag an altogether innocent man into disgrace, especially with a full description of his psychic emotions. But, at present, I am viewing even this incident in a somewhat different light. What is it to me that Mr. Golubev is not guilty! Mr. Golubev may be as clear as a crystal, yet Vorobiev is guilty. Who is Vorobiev?—I have no idea; I am convinced that there is no such man; but he is the very Vorobiev who rages on all lines; who imposes arbitrary taxes; who forcibly drags passengers out of the car; who wrecks the trains; who, over a period of many long months, keeps merchandise rotting at stations; who, with immunity, causes damages to entire cities, provinces, to the whole Empire, and who, in a savage voice, shouts: "Get out of my way! I am coming along!"

However, the principal guilt of this newcomer is that he has placed himself over the people as a demoralizing idea. However, why do I attack Vorobiev so bitterly? Is he alone domineering, as a seductive idea?—I repeat: something permeated with materialism and scepticism is soaring through the air: an adoration of gratuitous gain, of enjoyment without labor, has ensued; every fraud, every villainy, is perpetrated in cold blood; people are being murdered for the mere purpose of stealing, be it only one ruble, out of a man's pocket.

Of course, I know that in days past there has also been much evil; but at present it has unquestionably increased ten times. Some three weeks ago, in Petersburg, a cabman—a young lad, hardly of age—was driving an old man and an old woman; having noticed that the old man was drunk and in a state of complete unconsciousness, the cabman drew out a *penknife* and began to slash the old woman. He was arrested, and the little fool confessed then and there: "I don't know how this happened, and how I came to have the little knife in my hands." And, verily, he did not know it. Indeed, we are dealing precisely with environment: he was caught and dragged, as into a machine, into the contemporaneous itch for debauch, into the present-day popular tendency—gratuitous gain. Why shouldn't one try, even with a little penknife?

"No, this is no time for propaganda for the protection of animals: this is a gentleman's fancy."—This is the very phrase I have heard, but I reject it emphatically. Not being a member of the Society, nevertheless I am ready to serve it, and, it seems, I am already serving it. I do not know if I have made clear, though partly, my desire about "the equilibrium of the activities of the Society with the temporary accidentals," which I have mentioned above; but, realizing the humane and humanizing aims of the Society, I am profoundly devoted to it. I was never able to understand the thought that only one-tenth of the people should have the benefits of higher education, while the remaining nine-tenths should merely serve as material and means therefor, continuing to dwell in darkness. I do not wish to think, or even to live, otherwise than with the faith that all of the ninety millions of us, Russians (or whatever number of them may eventually be born), will some day all be educated; humanized and happy. I know that universal education can harm none of us. I even believe that the reign of reason and light may be inaugurated in our Russia, perhaps even sooner than elsewhere, since even now, in Russia, no one would favor the idea of the necessity of bestializing one part of the people for the well-being of another part representing civilization, as we find it all over Europe. In Russia, serfdom was abolished voluntarily by the upper class, headed by the Czar's will! And, for this reason, once more I welcome most warmly and with all my heart, the Society for the Protection of Animals; I merely meant to express the thought that it would be desirable to act not always from the end but, at least partly, from the beginning.

2

Spiritism. Something about Devils. Extraordinary Craftiness of the Devils, if only These are Devils.

Now, however, I have written all over the paper, and there is no room any more, and yet I was about to discuss the war and our border regions; I meant to dwell on literature, the Decembrists and, at least, on some fifteen topics or more. I can see that I must write more compactly and that I ought to compress myself: this is something to be remembered in the future.

In passing—a few words about the Decembrists, so as not to forget. One of our journals, when announcing the recent death of one of them, stated that he was among the very last survivors of the Decembrists. This is not quite correct. Among the surviving Decembrists are: Ivan Alexandrovich Annenkov—the same one whose original story has been distorted by the late Dumas-père in his well-known novel *Les Mémoires d'un Maître d'Armes;* Matvei Ivanovich Muraviev-Apostol, the brother of the executed one; Svistunov and Nazimov. Perhaps there are other survivors also.

Briefly—many things have to be postponed until the February issue. Still, I should like to bring my January diary to a close with something more jolly. There is a humorous theme and—this is important—it is in vogue; namely, the topic of devils, of spiritism. Indeed, something strange is taking place. For instance, they write me that a young man seated himself in an armchair, crossing his legs in a Turkish fashion, and the armchair started jumping all over the room.—Mind you, this happened in Petersburg, in the capital! Why, indeed, in days gone by, no one ever jumped, with crossed legs, in armchairs, and everyone was serving and modestly earning their ranks.

People assert that in some province, in the house of a certain lady, there are so many devils that there aren't even half as many of them in the cabin of Uncle Eddy. Indeed, why shouldn't there be devils in our midst?—Gogol, writing to Moscow from the world beyond, positively asserted that these are devils. I have read the letter: the style is his. He urges us not to evoke the devils, not to turn tables, not to have anything to do with them. "Don't tease the devils; don't traffic with them. It is a sin to tease the devils. . . . If at night you should begin to suffer from nervous insomnia, don't get angry, but pray: those are devils. Cross your breast and say a prayer."

Clergymen are raising their voices; they are counselling science itself not to traffic with magic, not to investigate "that witchery." And if the clergy have raised their voices, this means that the thing is assuming momentous proportions. But the trouble is: are they devils? Now, this question should be settled by the committee formed in Petersurg for the investigation of the whole subject of spiritism. Because, should it be finally determined that those are not devils, but some kind of electricity, some new modality of universal energy, then, at once complete disenchantment would ensue. "What a prodigy!"—they would say; "What a tedium!" And, promptly, everybody would forsake and forget spiritism, and they would start, as heretofore, attending to business. However, in order to determine whether or not these are devils, it would be necessary that at least one of the scientists, on the formed committee, be capable and be given the possibility to admit the existence of devils—even as a mere hypothesis. But there will be hardly one found among them who would believe in the devil, notwithstanding the fact that among those people who do not believe in God there are very many who, with pleasure and readiness, believe in the devil. For this reason, the committee is incompetent in this matter.

My whole trouble is that I, too, cannot believe in devils; this is really a pity, since I have conceived a very clear and most remarkable theory of spiritism, but one exclusively based upon the existence of devils: without them, my whole theory comes to nought of its own accord. Now, it is this theory which, in conclusion, I intend to expound to my readers. The point is that I am defending the devils: for once, they are being attacked without any guilt on their part, and they are considered fools. Don't worry: they know their business; and this is what I intend to prove.

To begin with, people write that the spirits are stupid (that is devils, the evil spirits, for what spirits other than devils can there be?); that when they are being evoked and questioned (by means of table-turning), they respond with mere trivialities; that they do not know the grammar; that they have conveyed not one new thought, not a single invention. To judge thus is a grave error. What would have been the result, for instance, should the devils at once reveal their might and overwhelm men with inventions? If, let us say, all of a sudden they were to invent electrical telegraphy (that is, if it had not already been invented), or to divulge to man various secrets: "Dig over there, and you will find a treasure, or deposits of coal" (by the way, firewood is so expensive!)—well, all this is but a mere trifle! Of course, you understand that human science is still in its infancy—actually, it is only beginning its work; that if it did achieve anything solid, it is only that, for the time being, it stands firmly on its feet. And, unexpectedly, a series of inventions would come showering down, such as the fact that the sun remains motionless while the earth revolves around it (because surely there are many identical inventions, in magnitude, which have not yet been discovered, and of which our sages have not even dreamed). All of a sudden all knowledge would descend upon human-kind, and—what is most important—altogether gratis, in the form of a gift! I ask you: what, in such an event, would happen to men? —Oh, it goes without saying that, at first, they all would be seized with rapture. People would be ecstatically embracing one another; they would rush to study the discoveries (and this would take time); they would feel, so to speak, bestrewn with happiness, interred in material blessings; perhaps, they would be walking or flying in the air; they would be flying over immense distances, ten times more quickly than they are now travelling on railroads; they would be extracting out of the earth fabulous harvests; maybe they would be chemically creating organisms, and there would be three pounds of meat for every person, as our Russian socialists are wont to dream. Briefly: eat, drink and be merry. "Well," all philanthropists would exclaim in unison, "now that man is provided for, only now is he going to reveal himself! There are no more material privations, there is no more of that degrading 'milieu' which used to be the cause of all vices, and now man is going to become beautiful and righteous! There is no more incessant work for one's subsistence, and now all men will occupy themselves with lofty and profound thoughts, and with universal phenomena. Only now has sublime life begun!" And what clever and good people, perhaps, would shout all this in unison and, possibly, in the beginning they would sway all others, and they would all start vociferating in one common hymn: "Who is equal to this beast? Praise to him who has brought us fire from heaven!"

But it is doubtful if these raptures would suffice even for one generation! People would suddenly realize that there is no more life for them; that there is no freedom of spirit, no will, no per-sonality; that someone has stolen everything from them; that the human image has vanished and the bestial image of a slave, the cattle image, has come into being, with that difference, however, that the cattle do not know that they are cattle, whereas men would discover that they had become cattle. And mankind would begin rotting; people would become covered with sores and ulcers; they would start biting their tongues with pain, seeing that their lives had been taken away from them in exchange for bread, for "stones turned into bread." Men would grasp the fact that there is no happiness in inaction; that idling thought must die; that it is not possible to love one's neighbor by sacrificing to him one's labor; that it is a nasty thing to be living gratuitously, and that *happiness is not in happiness but in its pursuit.* Tedium and anguish would ensue: everything has been accomplished—there is nothing more to accomplish; everything is known—there is nothing more to know. There would be crowds of felos-de-se, and not as at present—merely in miserable tenement houses; people would be gathering in multitudes, seizing each other by the hand, and spontaneously annihilating themselves by the thousands by means of some new device revealed to them along with other inventions. And, then, maybe, the remaining ones would cry out to God: "Thou art right, oh Lord: Man shall not live by bread alone!" Then they would rise against the devils and would forsake witchery. . . . Oh, never would God inflict such a torture upon mankind! And the devils' kingdom will be destroyed! No, the devils will not commit a political error as momentous as this. They are shrewd politicians, and they pursue their goal by the most subtle and sanest means (that is, if devils actually exist).

The principle of their kingdom is discord—or rather it is upon discord that they seek to found it. Why do they need discord precisely here?—Certainly: think only that discord, in itself, is a terrible power; discord, after a protracted strife, leads men to folly, to blindness and to distortion of reason and feelings. In discord the affronter, having realized that he was the one who gave the offense, does not go to make peace with the offended, but he says: "I offended him, and so I must avenge myself on him." But the main point is that the devils know world history perfectly well, and they especially remember everything that was based upon discord. For example, they know that if sects persist in Europe—those which detached themselves from Catholicism—if they continue to adhere to their beliefs as to a religious creed, this is solely due to the fact that in days past blood was shed on their account. Were, let us say, Catholicism to come to an end, the Protestant sects would of necessity be destroyed: in this event what would there be left to protest against? Even now, virtually all of them are inclined to embrace some sort of "humanity," or even outright atheism— this, by the way, has long been observed in their midst—and if they continue to vegetate as religions, this is due to the fact that they are still protesting. Even last year they were protesting, and how? They aimed at the Pope himself.

Why, of course, in the long run the devils will have it their own way, and they will crush man, like some fly, with "stones turned into bread": this is their fundamental aim, but they will embark upon this venture not otherwise than by securing in advance their future kingdom against man's rebellion, and thereby they will assure longevity of their reign. But how is man to be tamed? Naturally, by *"divide et impera"* (split the enemy and you will triumph). For this, discord is needed. On the other hand, people will grow weary of stones turned into bread, and, therefore, it is necessary to find occupation for them so that they will not grow weary. And isn't discord an occupation for men!

Now, please observe how the devils sow discord among us, and, so to speak, they start our spiritism with discord. Our disturbed time in this respect comes to their assistance. How many people, among those believing in spiritism, have already been offended! They are shouted at; they are being ridiculed because they believe in "tables," as though they had committed, or were contemplating, some dishonest deed; but they stubbornly continue to investigate their problem in spite of the discord. Indeed, how can they give up their inquiries: the devils begin from the far end, they arouse curiosity, but they are causing confusion instead of explaining the thing; they perplex people and laugh at them straight before their eyes. An intelligent man worthy of every respect stands and knits his brow; he keeps asking himself: "What is this?" Finally, he is ready to give up the problem, to leave it alone, but laughter among the public grows merrier, and the affair expands to the point where the adept, willy-nilly, must stay on out of mere amour-propre.

We have before us the committee for the investigation of the subject of spiritism, fully armed with science. There is expectancy among the public. And what?—The devils do not even pretend to offer any resistance; on the contrary, most humiliatingly, they "pass": séances are unsuccessful; deceit and trickery are disclosed. Angry laughter sounds on all sides; the committee leaves with contemptuous glances; adepts in spiritism are plunged into shame; a spiteful feeling creeps into the hearts on both sides. Now, it would seem that there is nothing left to the devils but to perish. But no! —The moment scientists and serious-minded people turn their heads, the devils promptly perform some even more supernatural trick to their former adepts, and they are again convinced—even more firmly than before. Again temptation! Again discord!

Last summer, in Paris, a photographer was tried for spiritistic frauds: he had been evoking deceased persons and photographing them. He had been getting heaps of orders. But he was "pinched," and made a full confession at the trial; he even produced the lady who had helped him by representing the evoked shadows. What would you think? did those who had been deceived by the photographer believe it?—Not in the least. One of them was reported to have said: "Three of my children have died; no pictures of them were left; now, the photographer has taken their pictures for me; they all resemble them—I recognized them all. What is it to me that he has confessed his frauds to you?—This is up to him, but I hold in my hand a fact; and do, please, leave me in peace." This appeared in the newspapers. I don't know if I have correctly stated the details, but the gist of the matter is correct.

Now what, for instance, if an incident such as this should happen here?—The moment the Committee, after finishing its business and exposing the pitiful tricks, would turn away, the devils would seize one of its most obdurate members—say, Mr. Mendeleev himself, who has exposed spiritism at public lectures—and would catch him in their net, as they have, in the past, caught Crookes and Olcott; what if, after that they would take him aside, would lift him in the air for five minutes, and would materialize for him some deceased person with whom he used to be acquainted, and all this in a manner precluding any doubt—well, what would happen then? As a genuine scientist, he would have to recognize the *fait accompli*—he who has been delivering lectures! What a tableau, what a shame, what a scandal; what cries and what indignant vociferation!—Of course, this is merely a jest, and I am convinced that nothing of the kind will happen to Mr. Mendeleev, although in England and in America the devils, it would seem, acted exactly in accordance with this plan.

And what if the devils, having prepared the ground and having sufficiently sown discord, should suddenly decide to expand unlimitedly their activities and turn to real, serious business? They are sarcastic and unpredictable folks, fully capable of such a thing. What, for instance, if they should unexpectedly, together with literacy, burst into the common people's midst? And our people are so defenseless, so addicted to darkness and debauch, and in this respect they have, it would seem, so few leaders! The people might take passionate credence in these new phenomena (don't they believe in the "Ivans Filippovichs"?)—then, what a delay in their spiritual development, what damage, and for how long! What an idolatrous worship of materialism, and what discord! What discord!—A hundred, a thousand times more than before, and this is precisely what the devils are after. And discord would unquestionably ensue, especially should spiritism succeed in invoking restrictions and perse-

cution (these would inevitably follow on the part of the rest of the
people who would not take credence in spiritism) ;—in this case it
would instantly diffuse itself, as burning petroleum, and everything
would be set afire. Mystical ideas enjoy persecution; they are
created by it. Every persecuted idea is similar to that petroleum
which was poured over the floors and walls of The Tuileries by the
incendiaries before the conflagration in the building which they
were supposed to guard. Oh, yes, the devils know the power of an
interdicted belief, and maybe they have been waiting many a century for mankind to stumble against tables. Of course they are
ruled by some immense evil spirit, some dreadful force—one far
smarter than Mephistopheles who, according to the assertion of
Yakov Petrovich Polonsky, has made Goethe famous.

Naturally, I have been jesting and laughing from the first
word to the last; yet this is what I wish to express in conclusion:
if one were to regard spiritism as something carrying within itself
a new creed (and virtually all spiritists, even the sanest among
them, are a bit inclined toward such a view), certain of the above
statements could be accepted—even not in a jesting sense. And,
for this reason, may God speedily bring success to a free investigation by both sides; this alone will help to eradicate, as quickly as
possible, the spreading stench, and this might enrich science with
a new discovery. But to shout at each other, to defame and expel
each other from society on account of spiritism—this, to my way
of thinking, means nothing but consolidating and propagating the
idea of spiritism in its worst sense. This is the beginning of intolerance and persecution.

And this is precisely what the devils are after!

3

A Word Apropos of My Biography

The other day I was shown my biography printed in *The
Russian Encyclopedic Dictionary,* published by Professor I. N.
Berezin of the St. Petersburg University (Second Year, Issue V,
2nd Book, 1875) and compiled by Mr. V. Z. It is difficult to imagine
that so many errors could have been crowded into half a page.
I was born not in 1818, but in 1822.[1] My late brother, Mikhail
Mikhailovich, the editor of the magazines *Time* and *Epoch,* was
my elder brother, and not my junior by four years. After the expiration of my term at hard labor, to which I was sent in 1849 as

[1]Dostoievsky himself made a mistake: he was born not in 1822, but on
October 30, 1821. (B. B.)

a *state criminal* (not a word is mentioned by Mr. V. Z. on the nature
of my crime, it being merely stated that I was "mixed up with the
Petrashevsky case," *i.e.,* God knows what the crime was, since no
one is obliged to know and remember the Petrashevsky case, while
an Encyclopedic Dictionary is designed for general information, and
people might think that I was exiled for robbery)—after the term
of my conviction, by the will of the Emperor, I was immediately
inducted as a private, and three years later I was promoted to the
rank of officer. But I was never deported [settled] to Siberia, as
Mr. V. Z. states. The order of my literary works is mixed up: stories
belonging to the earliest period of my literary career are attributed
in the biography to the latest period. There are many such errors,
and I am not enumerating them in order not to bore the reader;
however, if I should be challenged, I will indicate them. But there
are pure fabrications. Mr. V. Z. asserts that I was editor of *The
Russian World*. In answer to this, I declare that I was never editor
of the newspaper *The Russian World;* moreover, never did I have
a single line printed in that esteemed publication.

No doubt, Mr. V. Z. [Mr. Vladimir Zotov?] may adopt his
own point of view; he may regard as the least important matter
the presentation, in a biographical sketch of a writer, of correct
information on the year of his birth, the adventures he has experienced, where, when and in what order his works have been published; which of them should be considered as the initial ones, and
which the concluding ones; which publications he has edited, and
to which ones he has contributed. Nevertheless, for the sake of
mere accuracy, one would wish more sense. Otherwise, perhaps,
readers may think that all the other sketches in Mr. Berezin's dictionary are compiled as slovenly as the one relating to my biography.

4

A TURKISH PROVERB

In passing, and at all events, I will interject here a Turkish
proverb (a real Turkish one and not an invented one):

"If thou hast started out to reach a certain goal, and if
thou shouldst be stopping en route to throw stones at every dog
barking at thee, thou shalt never reach thy goal."

As far as possible, I shall in my *Diary* try to abide by this
wise proverb, even though I should not wish to bind myself beforehand with promises.

FEBRUARY

CHAPTER I

1

On the Subject that We All are Good Fellows. Resemblance between Russian Society and Marshal MacMahon.

THE FIRST issue of *A Writer's Diary* has been received cordially: almost no one has scolded it—I mean, in literature; as for the rest, I don't know. If there has been literary abuse, it has been unnoticeable. *The Petersburg Gazette* hastened to remind the public that I do not like children, youngsters in their teens and the young generation; and in the same issue, in its feuilleton at the bottom, it reprinted from my *Diary* a whole story, *A Little Boy at Christ's Christmas Tree,* which, at least, goes to prove that I do not hate children wholeheartedly. Of course, these are mere trifles, and I am interested only in the question: is it, or is it not, good that I have pleased everybody? Is it a good or a bad sign? For it may be a bad sign. But no: why should it be?—Better accept it as a good and not a bad sign. I shall stop at that.

Indeed, we are all good fellows—except the bad ones, of course. Yet, I shall observe in passing that among us, perhaps, there are no bad people at all—maybe, only wretched ones. But we have not grown up to be bad. Don't scoff at me, but consider: we have reached the point in the past where, because of the absence of bad people of our own (I repeat: despite the abundance of all sorts of wretches), we used to be ready, for instance, to value very highly various bad little fellows appearing among our literary characters, mostly borrowed from foreign sources. Not only did we value them, but we slavishly sought to imitate them in real life; we used to copy them, and in this respect we were ready to jump out of our skins. Do please recall: didn't we have a number of Pechorins who, in fact and in reality, committed many villainies after having read *A Hero of Our Days?* The forefather of these bad men in our literature was one Silvio in the story *The Shot,* which was borrowed by the naïve and beautiful Pushkin from Byron. Besides, Pechorin himself killed Grushnitzky only because he was not showy enough in his uniform, and at balls in the Petersburg beau monde he little resembled, at least in the opinion of the fair sex, a real dashing fellow.

And if, in those days, we used to value and respect these evil people, it was solely due to the fact that they appeared as men of *solid* hate in contradistinction to us, Russians, who, as is well known, are people of very fragile hate, and this trait of ours we have always particularly despised. Russians are unable to hate long and seriously, and not only men but even vices—the darkness of ignorance, despotism, obscurantism and all the rest of these retrograde things. At the very first opportunity we are quick and eager to make peace. Isn't this so?—In point of fact, please consider: why should we be hating each other? For evil deeds?—But this is a very slippery, most ticklish and most unjust theme—in a word, a double-edged one; at least, in our day one should not be touching upon it. There remains, then, the hatred arising out of convictions, but in this respect I disbelieve altogether the seriousness of our hatreds. For instance, in the past we had our Slavophiles and Westerners, and they used to fight bitterly with each other. But at present, with the abolition of serfdom, Peter's reform has been terminated, and there has ensued a general *sauve qui peut*. And now Slavophiles and Westerners are agreed on one and the same thought: that at present one has to expect everything from the people, that they have arisen and they are marching, and that they—and they alone—will utter the last word. It might have seemed that on this basis peace between Slavophiles and Westerners could be brought about, but things have happened differently: Slavophiles believe in the people because they admit in them the existence of their own principles, peculiar to them; whereas Westerners are ready to believe in the people, on the express condition, however, that the people be devoid of their own principles. So the fight continues. Now, what would you make of this?—I even refuse to believe that there is a fight; fighting is fighting, but love is love. And why couldn't fighters at the same time love each other?—On the contrary, in our midst this happens quite often in cases where really good people come to blows. And why aren't we good fellows (again: except the wretched ones)?—The point is that we are fighting primarily and solely because now it is no longer a time for theories, for journalistic skirmishes, but the time for work and practical decisions. All of a sudden it became necessary to pronounce positive judgments—on education, pedagogy, railroads, zemstvos, medical matters, etc., on hundreds of topics—and, what is most important, it has got to be done right away, as quickly as possible, in order not to delay the work. And since we all, due to two centuries of lack of habit of work, have proved altogether incapable of any, even of the most trifling, work, naturally people are clutching each other's hair, and even the more incompetent one feels, the more eager he is to fight. What, I may ask you, is there bad about it?—Only, that this is touching—and nothing more. Look at children: they fight precisely at the age when they have not yet learned to express their thoughts—exactly as we. Well, in this there is absolutely nothing discouraging; on the contrary, this merely proves to a certain extent our freshness and, so to speak, our virginity. True, in literature, because of the absence of ideas, people scold each other, using all invectives at once: this is an impossible and naïve method observed only among primitive peoples; but, God knows, even in this there is something almost touching: exactly that inexperience, that childish incompetence even in scolding in a proper manner. I am by no means jesting; I am not jeering: among us there is a widespread, honest and serene expectation of good (this is so, no matter what one might say to the contrary); a longing for common work and common good, and this—ahead of any egoism; this is a most naïve longing, full of faith devoid of any exclusive or caste tinge, and even if it does appear in paltry and rare manifestations, it comes as something unnoticeable, which is despised by everybody. This is very important—and do you know why?—In that this is not only little but, indeed, ever so much.

Well, this would seem plenty for us, and why should we be looking for "solid hate"?—The honesty and sincerity of our society not only cannot be doubted, but they even spring up into one's eyes. Look attentively and you will see that, in our case, first comes faith in an idea, in an ideal, while earthly goods come after. Yes, nasty folks in our midst, too, manage to arrange their affairs in a very different sense; and this seems to be true in our day even infinitely more than ever before; yet these wretches never command public opinion, they do not lead; on the contrary, even when enjoying top honors, time and again, they have felt compelled to adapt themselves to the tone of idealistically inclined, young, abstract, poor people, who seem funny to them. In this respect our society is akin to the people, who also treasure their faith and their ideals above anything mundane and transient, and herein is the main point of contact between society and the people. This idealism is pleasing both here and there: should it be lost, it couldn't be retrieved with any amount of money.

Even though our people are addicted to debauch—now more strongly than at any time in the past—as yet, in them, there has never been a sense of lawlessness, and even the basest scoundrel among the people didn't say: "One has to act as I do,"—but, contrariwise, he always lamentingly believed that he was doing wrong; that there exists something far superior to him and his doings.

And our people do have ideals—lofty ones, too—and this is the main thing: circumstances will change; matters will improve, and perhaps debauch will spring away from the people, while the noble principles will be held still steadier, with even greater reverence than ever before. Our youth is longing for glorious exploits and sacrifices. The lad of our days, about whom so many controversial things are said, often adores a most naïve paradox, sacrificing for it everything—the world, his fate, his very life; but this is due only to the fact that he regards his paradox as the truth. Here we are merely confronted with lack of enlightenment. When light appears, different viewpoints will arise of their own accord; paradoxes will vanish, but the purity of heart, the thirst for sacrifice and exploits, which gleam in him so brightly, will not fade. And this is what really counts.

Of course, this is another matter and an altogether different question: wherein do all of us, longing for the general welfare and hoping in full accord for the success of the common cause—precisely wherein do we perceive the means therefor? One has to admit that in this respect we have as yet by no means reached any agreement, so that our present-day society closely resembles Marshal Mac-Mahon. During one of his most recent journeys through France the esteemed Marshal, in one of his solemn addresses in response to the mayor's greetings (and the French are so enthusiastic about all sorts of greetings and speeches in reply!), declared that, in his opinion, the whole policy may be expressed in the motto: "Love of fatherland." This opinion has been uttered at a time when the whole of France, so to speak, strained herself in expectation of what he would say. This is a strange, unquestionably laudable, and yet remarkably indeterminate, opinion, since that mayor could have answered in rebuttal that some love may drown the fatherland. But the mayor said nothing—no doubt, because he was afraid of receiving the reply: *"J'y suis, et j'y reste!"*—a phrase beyond which, it seems, the honored Marshal will not go.

Even so: this is exactly as in our society: we all agree on our love, if not of our native land, then—of the common cause (words mean nothing), but wherein we perceive the means—not only the means, but the common cause itself—on this point there prevails in our midst the same confusion as in Marshal MacMahon's mind.

For this reason, even though I have pleased everybody, and despite the fact that I am, indeed, very grateful that a hand has been extended to me, nevertheless I anticipate that in further details there may arise very substantial differences, since I am unable to be in accord with everybody no matter how accommodating a man I may be.

2

ON THE LOVE OF THE PEOPLE. THE NECESSARY CONTRACT WITH THE PEOPLE.

For instance I have written in the January issue of my *Diary* that our people are coarse and ignorant, addicted to darkenss and debauch; that they are "barbarians awaiting the light." Since then, I have just read in *Brotherly Help* (a volume published by the Slavic Committee for the benefit of the Slavs fighting for their freedom), in an article of the unforgettable late Konstantin Aksakov, so dear to all Russians, that the Russian people have been enlightened and "educated." What then? Was I taken aback by such an apparent difference of opinion between myself and Konstantin Aksakov?—Not in the least: I share his opinion, and I have long and ardently sympathized with it. How do I reconcile the contradiction? —The point is that, to my way of thinking, it is very easy to reconcile it, whereas, according to others, much to my surprise, the two propositions are irreconcilable.

One has to be able to differentiate in a Russian belonging to the common people between his beauty and his alluvial barbarism. Owing to circumstances, almost throughout the whole history of Russia, the people have been so addicted to debauch, they have been subjected to so much depravity and seduction, to so much torture, that it is really surprising how they have managed to succeed in preserving their human image, not to speak of its beauty. Yet they did preserve also the beauty of their image. A true friend of mankind whose heart has but once quivered in compassion over the sufferings of the people, will understand and forgive all the impassable alluvial filth in which they are submerged, and will be able to discover diamonds in this filth.

I repeat: judge the Russian people not by those villainies which they frequently perpetrate, but by those great and holy things for which they long amidst the very villainy. Besides, the people are not composed of scoundrels only; there are also genuine saints —and what saints! They themselves are radiant and they illuminate the path for all of us! Somehow, I am blindly convinced that there is no such villain or scoundrel among the Russian people who wouldn't admit that he is villainous and abominable, whereas, among others, it does happen sometimes that a person commits a villainy and praises himself for it, elevating his villainy to the level of a principle, and claiming that *l'ordre* and the light of civilization are precisely expressed in that abomination; the unfortunate one ends by believing this sincerely, blindly and even honestly. No, judge our people not by what they are, but by what they strive to become.

And their ideals are vigorous and sacred; they have saved the people during the ages of their martyrdom. These ideals have grown into their very soul, rewarding it with candor and honesty, with sincerity and a broad, all-receptive mind—and all these, in an attractive harmonious blending. If, despite this, there is so much filth, the Russian himself suffers from it most and believes that it is something alluvial and transient, a diabolical suggestion; that darkness will disappear and perpetual light will beam.

I will not recall the people's historical ideals, their Serges, Theodosiuses Pechersky and even Tikhon Zadonsky. By the way, do many people know about Tikhon Zadonsky? Why should one be so blankly ignorant; why should one promise oneself not to read? Is it for lack of time? Believe me, gentlemen, much to your astonishment, you would be learning beautiful things. But I had better turn to our literature: all that is genuinely beautiful in it has been borrowed from the people, starting with the humble, ingenious type of Belkin conceived by Pushkin. Indeed, in Russia everything emanates from Pushkin. His turning to the people at so early a period of his work is so unprecedented and amazing; in those days it was such an unexpectedly new idea that it may be explained, if not by a miracle, then by the extraordinary greatness of his genius which, I will add in passing, we are as yet unable to evaluate. I shall not mention the purely national types which have appeared in our time, but do recall *Oblomov* and Turgenev's *Gentlefolk's Nest*. Of course, here we are not dealing with the people; yet all that is lasting and beautiful in these types of Goncharov and Turgenev—all this is due to the fact that, through them, they established contact with the people. This contact with the people has conveyed to them extraordinary potency. They have borrowed the people's candor, purity, gentleness, breadth of mind and benignancy, in contradistinction to everything that is distorted, false, alluvial and slavishly imitative.

Don't be surprised that unexpectedly I have started to speak about Russian literature. Our literature precisely has the merit that, almost without any exception, its best representatives, ahead of our intelligentsia—please note this point—bowed before the popular truth, and recognized the people's ideals as genuinely beautiful. In fact, literature was compelled to adopt them as standards, almost involuntarily. Verily, in this respect, it was prompted by artistic instinct rather than by free will. However, for the time being, enough has been said about literature; besides, I started speaking about it only apropos of the people.

The question concerning the people and one's opinion of them

—of understanding them—is at present the most momentous question from the standpoint of our whole future; moreover, in our day, it is, so to speak, our most practical question. And yet, to all of us, the people are still a theory and they continue to loom as an enigma. We all, lovers of the people, regard them as a theory, and it seems that none of us like them as they really are, but as each one has represented them to himself. Even more: should the Russian people, at some future time, turn out to be different from our conception of them, we all, despite our love of them, would possibly renounce them without any regret. I am speaking about everybody, not excepting Slavophiles; these would, perhaps, renounce the people more bitterly than the rest.

As for myself I shall not conceal my convictions, precisely in order to give a clearer outline of the future orientation which my *Diary* is going to assume—just to avoid misunderstandings—so that everybody should know in advance whether or not it is worth while extending to me his literary hand.

I think this way: hardly are we so good and beautiful as to set ourselves up as an ideal to the people and to demand from them that they should become as we *quand-même*. Please don't be surprised at the nonsensical way in which the question has been put. However, we never did put this question differently: "Who is better —we or the people? Do the people have to follow us, or do we have to follow the people?"—This is what everybody says—among those who are at least not devoid of a shadow of thought in their heads and a drop of concern in their hearts for the common cause. For this reason I shall candidly reply: it is we who have to bow before the people and await from them everything—both thought and expression; it is we who must bow before the people's truth and recognize it as such—even in that dreadful event if it has partly emerged out of the *Acta Martyrum*. In a word: we must bow like prodigal children who, for two hundred years, have been absent from home, but who nevertheless have returned Russians—which, by the way, is our great merit.

On the other hand, however, we must bow on one condition only, and this—*sine qua non:* that the people accept from us those numerous things which we have brought with us. Indeed, we cannot completely exterminate ourselves in the face of the people, or even —before any truth of theirs, whatever it may be. Let our own remain with us, and for nothing in the world shall we part with it, not even—if it should come to this—for the happiness of the fusion with the people. In the reverse case, let us separate and let us both perish, apart. But there will never be a "contrary case." And I am firmly convinced that this *something* which we have brought with us really does exist; it is not a mirage, but it possesses both form and weight. Nevertheless, I repeat, there is much ahead of us that is an enigma—so much, in fact, that one dreads to keep on waiting.

For instance, it is being predicted that civilization will spoil the people: supposedly, it might assume a course in which, along with salvation and enlightenment, there will burst in so much that is false and deceitful, so many nasty habits and so much agitation that, perhaps, only in some future generations—in two hundred years maybe—will healthy seeds grow up, while we and our children must probably anticipate something dreadful. Is this your opinion, gentlemen? Are our people predestined to pass through an additional phase of debauch and deceit, similar to that through which we have passed when we have been inoculated by civilization? (I believe that no one will deny that we have started our civilization directly with debauch!)—In this connection I should like to hear something more encouraging. I am strongly inclined to believe that our people constitute such an immensity that in it all the new muddy currents, should they happen to spring up from somewhere, will be eliminated of their own accord.

To this end—let me have your hand; let us jointly help to carry out the task—each one by his own "microscopical" action—in a straighter and less erroneous manner. True, in this respect we ourselves are devoid of any skill; we merely "love our fatherland"; we shall find no common language on the questions of means; we shall quarrel many a time. Still, if it has been decided that we are good fellows, then, no matter what the outcome may be, in the long run things will adjust themselves.

Such is my creed. I reiterate: here we have a two-hundred-year-old want of habit of work—nothing more. Owing to this lack of habit, we have terminated our "cultured period" with the fact that all of us have ceased to understand one another. Of course, I am speaking only about serious and sincere people: only, these do not understand each other; speculators—well, that's a different affair: they have always understood each other. . . .

3

PEASANT MARÉI

However, all these *professions de foi*, I believe, must make weary reading. Therefore, I will relate an anecdote; why, even not an anecdote: just a remote reminiscence which, for some reason, I am quite eager to recount precisely here and now, in conclusion of

our treatise on the people. I was then only nine years old. . . . No,
I had better start with the time when I was twenty-nine.

It was the second day of Easter Week. The air was warm,
the sky was blue; the sun stood high—a "warm," bright sun—but in
my soul it was very dark. I was roaming in the rear of the barracks;
I was looking at and counting the planks of the solid prison fence;
but still I had no desire to count them, although this became a
habit with me. It was on the second day that, in the prison, "merriment was in full swing": convicts were not taken out for work;
there were many drunken people; revilements and quarrels ensued
every minute in every corner. Hideous, nasty songs; card-playing
beneath the sleeping-boards; several convicts, already beaten almost to death for exceptional turbulence, by verdict of their companions, were lying on the boards and covered up with sheepskin
coats till such time as they might revive and come to their senses;
knives, already drawn several times;—all this in the course of the
two-day holiday had exhausted me to the point of sickness. Never
could I stand without disgust drunken popular rakishness, and
particularly in this place. On these days even the authorities avoided
the prison; no searches were conducted; nor was liquor looked for;
they understood that, after all, once a year it was necessary to
permit even these outcasts to indulge in merriment, thereby preventing worse happenings.

Finally, anger arose in my heart: I met a Pole, M—tzki, a
political criminal. He looked at me gloomily, his eyes flashing; his
lips began to tremble: *"Je hais ces brigands!"*—he told me in a low
voice, grinding his teeth, and passed by. I returned to the barracks,
notwithstanding the fact that only a quarter of an hour before I
had run out of it, like a madman, when six robust peasants, all
together, threw themselves upon the drunken Tartar Gazin, in order
to subdue him, and started beating him; they beat him foolishly—
a camel could be killed with such blows, but they knew that it was
difficult to kill this Hercules, and so they beat him without fear.
As I came back I noticed in the far end of the barracks, on sleeping-
boards in the corner, the now unconscious Gazin, with almost no
signs of life. He lay there, covered with a sheepskin coat, and everybody passed around him in silence: they firmly believed that by
the next morning Gazin would come to his senses, "but of such
blows the man—God forbid—might, perhaps, die." I made my way
to my place opposite a window barred with an iron grating and
lay down on my back, throwing my arms behind my neck and closing my eyes. I was fond of lying in that position: people will not
annoy a sleeping person, and yet one may be meditating and thinking. But somehow I could not meditate: my heart was beating

irregularly, and in my ears I could hear M—tzki's words sounding: *"Je hais ces brigands!"* However, what is the use of describing my impressions: even now, at times, I have dreams about this at night, and none of my dreams are ever more poignant than this one. Perhaps I will be reminded that up to the present day almost never have I spoken in print about my life in prison, whereas I wrote my *Letters from a Dead House* fifteen years ago under the name of a fictitious person, a criminal who supposedly had murdered his wife. In passing, I may add, by way of detail, that since that time many people have been under the impression, and are even now asserting, that I was exiled for the murder of my wife.

By-and-by, I really forgot myself and became absorbed in reminiscences. Uninterruptedly, I was recalling all of the four years of my forced labor and, it seems, once more I was living my whole life over again in these recollections. They invaded my mind of their own accord, and only on rare occasions did I evoke them by a deliberate effort of my will. It used to begin with some speck, some trait—at times almost imperceptible—and then, gradually, it would grow into a complete picture—some strong and solid impression. I used to analyze these impressions, adding new touches to things long ago outlived, and—what is more important—I used to correct, continually correct, them. Therein lay my whole diversion. On this occasion I suddenly realized one imperceptible moment in my early childhood, when I was only nine years old—a moment which, so it seemed, was altogether forgotten by me; but in those days I used to be particularly fond of reminiscences about my earliest infancy. I recalled the month of August in our village: a dry and clear day, though somewhat chilly and windy; the summer was coming to an end, and soon I should have to go to Moscow, again to be wearied all winter over French lessons; and I was so sad over the fact that I would have to leave the country. I went beyond the barns and, having descended to a ravine, I climbed up to the "Losk"—thus was called a thick shrubbery on yonder side of the ravine, which extended as far as the grove. Presently I plunged deeper into the bushes, and then I heard not far off—some thirty steps away—in a field, a solitary peasant plowing. I knew that he was plowing steeply uphill, that it was difficult for the horse to get along, and, from time to time, I heard the man's halloos: "Giddap—giddap!" I knew virtually all of our peasants, but I didn't recognize the one now plowing; but this was of no concern to me, since I was absorbed in my task—I also was busy: I was trying to break a walnut whip for myself, to hit frogs; walnut whips are so pretty, though not solid—no comparison with birch ones! I was also interested in insects and beetles; I was collecting them—among them there are very neat ones. I was also fond of little agile lizards with tiny black dots; but I was afraid of little snakes; these, however, were found far more rarely than lizards. Here, there were few mushrooms—to find mushrooms one had to go to the birch grove, and I intended to proceed thither. And in all my life nothing have I loved as much as the forest, with its mushrooms and wild berries, its insects and birds and little hedgehogs and squirrels; its damp odor of dead leaves, which I so adored. Even now, as I am writing these lines, it seems that I can smell the odor of our country birch grove: these impressions remain intact throughout one's whole life. Suddenly, amidst the profound silence, clearly and distinctly, I heard the cry: "A wolf's running!" I let out a scream and, beside myself with fright, and vociferating, I ran out into the field, straight up to the plowing peasant.

This was our peasant Maréï. I don't know if there is such a name, but everybody called him Maréï; he was almost fifty years old, stocky, pretty tall, with much gray hair in his bushy flaxen beard. I knew him, but up to that time I had never had occasion to talk to him. When he heard my cries, he stopped his little filly, and when I, in the heat of running, seized the plow with one hand, and with the other—his sleeve, he sensed my dread.

"A wolf's running!"—I shouted, quite out of breath.

He raised his head and impulsively looked around, for an instant almost believing my words.

"Where's the wolf?"

"Shouted . . . someone had just shouted: 'a wolf's running!'" —I lisped.

"What's the matter with you?—What wolf?—This appeared to you in a dream! Look! How can a wolf be here!"—he muttered, trying to enhearten me. But my whole body was trembling and I was clinging ever so fast to his coat. I must have looked very pale. He looked at me with an uneasy smile, apparently alarmed on my account.

"See, how thou art frightened! Oh, oh!"—he said, shaking his head. "Never mind, dear. See, little kid! Oh!"

He extended his hand and stroked me on my cheek. "Do stop fearing! Christ be with thee. Cross thyself."

But I did not cross myself; the corners of my lips quivered and, I believe, this was what impressed him most. Slowly he stretched out his thick finger, with the black nail soiled with earth, and gently touched my trembling lips.

"See! Oh!"—And he looked at me with a long motherly smile.—"Good Lord! What's this? Oh, oh!"

Finally, I grasped the fact that there was no wolf, and that

the cry "a wolf's running" must have been falsely heard by me.
Still, there was a clear and distinct cry, but pseudo cries of this
kind had been heard by me two or three times before, and I was
aware of this. (Later, with childhood, these hallucinations disappeared.)

"Why, I'll go!"—I said, questioningly and timidly looking at
the peasant.

"All right, go! And I shall be keeping thee in sight! Be sure,
I shall not surrender thee to the wolf!"—he added with the same
motherly smile.—"Well, Christ be with thee. Now, go!"—And he
crossed me with his hand and then crossed himself. I started, but
every ten steps I kept looking back. To be frank, I was a little
ashamed that I got so frightened in his presence. Yet, on my way
I was still quite afraid of the wolf till I had reached the slope of
the ravine, and then the first barn. There, fright left me altogether.
Presently, as if from nowhere, our house dog Volchok rushed to
me. Well, of course, with Volchok I felt quite safe, and so, for the
last time, I turned back toward Maréi. No longer was I able to
discern him distinctly, but I felt that he still kept tenderly smiling
at me and nodding. I waved my hand to him; he waved his hand,
too, and stirred his filly.

"Giddap! Giddap!"—sounded his distant halloo, and the filly
again started pulling the plow.

All this I recalled at once—I don't know why—but with remarkable precision in the details. All of a sudden I awoke, seated
myself on the sleeping boards and, I remember, I still felt on my
face the calm smile of reminiscence. For a minute or so, I still kept
on recollecting.

Upon my return home from Maréi, I told no one about my
"adventure." Besides, what kind of an adventure was this! And
very soon I also forgot about Maréi. Subsequently, when meeting
him on rare occasions, I never even spoke to him—not only about
the wolf, but about anything. And suddenly now—twenty years
later, in Siberia—I was recalling that meeting, so distinctly, in every
minute detail. This means that it had hidden in my soul imperceptibly, of its own accord, without any effort of my will, and
then it came to my mind at the needed time: that tender, motherly
smile of a poor peasant serf, his crosses, the shaking of his head:
"See, how thou art frightened, little kid!" I remembered particularly that thick finger of his, soiled with earth, with which he so
calmly, with such timid tenderness, touched my trembling lips. No
doubt, anyone would have cheered up a child—but here, at this
solitary meeting, something, as it were, altogether different had
happened; and if I had been his own son, he could not have be-

stowed upon me a glance gleaming with more serene love. And yet, who had prompted him?—He was our own peasant serf, while I was a nobleman's son anyway. No one would find out how he had caressed me and no one would reward him. Was he, perhaps, extremely fond of little children?—There are such people. The meeting was a solitary one, in a vacant field, and only God, maybe, perceived from above what a profound and enlightened human sentiment, what delicate, almost womanly, tenderness, may fill the heart of some coarse, bestially ignorant Russian peasant serf, who, in those days, had even had no forebodings about his freedom.

Tell me: was it not this that Konstantin Aksakov had in mind when he spoke about the high educational level of our people?

And when I climbed down off the boards and gazed around, I suddenly felt that I could behold these unfortunate men with a wholly different outlook, and, suddenly, by some miracle, all the hatred and anger completely vanished from my heart. I went along, gazing attentively at the faces which I encountered. This intoxicated, shaven and branded peasant with marks on his face, bawling his hoarse drunken song—why, he may be the very same Maréï; for I have no way of peering into his heart.

That same evening I met M—tzki once more. Unfortunate!—Perhaps he could not have had reminiscences about any Maréïs, and he could not have viewed these men differently than: *"Je hais ces brigands!"* Yes, the Poles in those days had endured more than we!

CHAPTER II

1

Apropos the Kroneberg Case

I BELIEVE THAT everybody knows about the Kroneberg case, which was tried a month ago in the St. Petersburg Circuit Court; everybody has been reading reports, as well as newspaper comments, on this case. It was a very noteworthy one and the reports thereon were quite heated. Being a month old, I shall not dwell upon it in detail, but I feel an urge to utter my apropos, too. I am in no sense a jurist; yet here there was revealed so much deceit on all sides that it appears clear even to a non-jurist. Such cases spring up, as if by chance, and they merely tend to confuse society—and even, perhaps, the judges themselves. But, inasmuch as at the same time they involve general and most precious interest, it is clear that they sting to the quick, so that, at times, it is impossible to refrain from discussing them, even after a month's delay, which seems an eternity.

I will remind the reader about the case: a father flogged a child, his seven-year-old daughter, too cruelly—according to the indictment—and he had treated her cruelly previously. A stranger —a woman of low birth—could not stand the screams of the tortured daughter who, again according to the indictment, had been crying for a quarter of an hour under the rod: "Papa! Papa!" And in the opinion of one of the experts, the rods proved not to be rods, but "Spitzruten," *i.e.*, absolutely inappropriate to the age of seven. Besides, they lay there in court, among the other exhibits, so that everybody—including Mr. Spasovich himself—could see them. The prosecutor has mentioned the fact, among others, that when the father, prior to the flogging, was told by someone that at least a certain twig should be broken off, he replied: "No, this will add zest." It is also known that the father, following the punishment, almost fainted himself.

I remember the impression produced upon me by the issue of *The Voice* in which I read about the beginning of the trial, the first account of the case. This occurred after nine o'clock in the evening, altogether accidentally. I had spent all of that day at the printing office, and I had no chance to see *The Voice* earlier, and so I knew nothing about the case. After having read it, I made up my mind to find out that same evening, notwithstanding the late hour, about subsequent developments in the case—in the supposition that, perhaps, the trial might have been finished that same day, which was a Saturday—knowing that reports invariably appear in newspapers with delays. I decided to proceed forthwith to a very well-known man with whom, however, I was but slightly acquainted, on the theory that, for certain reasons, at that particular moment he was more likely than any other of my acquaintances to know about the outcome of the case, and that he must surely have been personally present in court. I was not mistaken: he had been in court and had just returned from there. I found him shortly after ten in the evening and he told me about the acquittal of the defendant. I was indignant against the court, the jurors and the defense lawyer. This all happened three weeks ago, and in many respects I have changed my opinion after having personally perused the newspaper accounts and having listened to several weighty outside opinions. I am very glad that at present I can regard the father-defendant no longer as a villain, as a man taking delight in the torture of his children (such types do exist), and that here we are confronted with "nerves" only, and that—to use his lawyer's expression—he is but a "bad pedagogue." Essentially, I wish to dwell in some detail upon the speech of the defense lawyer, so as to make it clear in what a false and absurd position a noted, talented and honest man may be placed—solely because of the false foundation upon which the case itself had initially been built.

Wherein lies the falsehood? First of all—here is a little girl, a child; she was "tortured, racked"; the judges wish to protect her. Indeed, what a noble case, it would seem! Yet, what does it come to?—They were on the verge of making her unhappy forever. Maybe they already have made her unhappy! In point of fact, what would have happened had the father been convicted? The prosecution presented the case in such a way that in the event of a "yes, guilty" verdict, the father could have been exiled to Siberia. The question may well be asked: what then would have been left to that daughter, now a child devoid of all understanding—to her soul in the future, for all her life, even if she were later forever after rich and "happy"? Would not the family have been destroyed by the court itself, which, as is known, is supposed to protect the sanctity of the family?

Further, take into account another feature: the girl is seven years old—and what impression is created at this age?—Her father was not sent into exile—he was acquitted; this is good (although, in my opinion, the jurors' verdict should not have been applauded; yet, it is said, there has been applause). Even so, the little girl had been dragged into the courtroom; she did make her appearance; she did see and hear everything; she did make the self-confession: *"Je suis voleuse, menteuse."* The secret vices of this little child (of seven years only!) were revealed aloud before the whole public by grown-up, serious and even humane people.—What a monstrosity! *Mais il en reste toujours quelque chose,* for one's whole life—do comprehend this! And this will remain not only in her soul but, perhaps, will project itself in her fate. Something foul and bad has touched her in that courtroom, leaving an ineradicable trace. And, who knows?—Maybe twenty years hence someone will tell her: "Even as a child you appeared in a criminal court."

However, once more I see that, not being a jurist, I do not know how to express it and, therefore, I had better turn directly to the defense lawyer's speech: in it all these misunderstandings were graphically revealed of their own accord. The lawyer for the defendant was Mr. Spasovich. He is a man of talent. Wherever people begin to speak about Mr. Spasovich he is mentioned as being a "man of talent." I am very glad of this. I may note that Mr. Spasovich was appointed as defense-attorney by the court and, consequently, he conducted the defense, so to speak, under certain coercion. . . .

Again, on this point I feel incompetent, and I shall keep silent. However, before turning to the above-mentioned remarkable speech, I wish to say a few words about lawyers in general, and talented ones in particular—I wish to convey to the reader several impressions and doubts of mine, which, of course, may seem in no way serious to competent people. But I am writing my *Diary* for myself, and these thoughts have stuck firmly in my head. I should confess, perhaps, that these are hardly thoughts—rather, some kind of sensations.

2

SOMETHING ABOUT LAWYERS IN GENERAL. MY NAÏVE AND
INCOMPETENT PRESUMPTIONS. SOMETHING ABOUT TALENTS
IN GENERAL AND IN PARTICULAR.

However—only two words specifically about lawyers. The moment I took up the pen, I began to be afraid. I am blushing in advance because of the naïveté of my questions and presumptions. It would be too naïve and innocent on my part to be dwelling, for instance, on the question of how useful and pleasant an institution the bar is. A man, let us say, has committed a crime; he does not know the law; he is ready to confess, but then the advocate appears and proves to him that not only is he, the criminal, innocent, but that he is a saint. The lawyer finds the applicable laws and leading decisions of the Cassation Department of the Senate which, unexpectedly, convey to the case an altogether different aspect, and he finishes up by pulling the unfortunate fellow out of the hole. What a pleasant thing!

True, it may be argued and contended that this, to a certain extent, is immoral. Yet here stands before you an innocent, altogether innocent, simpleton, but the evidence has been set forth by the district attorney in a manner which would seem to doom the man for somebody else's guilt. Besides, the man is ignorant—he hasn't the faintest idea about the law—and he merely keeps mumbling: "I know nothing. I'm guilty of nothing!"—which, at length, begins to irritate the jurors and the judges. But presently the advocate appears; his knowledge of the law is perfect; he cites a certain section, a leading decision of the Cassation Department of the Senate; he manages to confuse the district attorney, and the innocent is acquitted.—No, this is useful. What would the innocent be doing in Russia without an advocate?

All these—I repeat—are naïve and commonly known considerations. I have experienced this feeling myself when, once upon a time, while editing a certain newspaper, by mere oversight (which may happen to anyone), I unintentionally endorsed for publication a news item which should not have been printed without the express permission of the Minister of the Imperial Court. And thus I was notified that I must appear in court as a defendant. I had no intention of defending myself; my "guilt" was obvious, even to myself; I did violate a clearly expressed law', and *legally* there could be no argument. But the court appointed a lawyer for my defense (a man whom I had known slightly and who was a member of a certain Society of which I, too, was a member). Much to my surprise, he told me that not only was I not guilty but that I was absolutely right, and that he was firmly determined to defend me by all means. Of course, I listened to this with pleasure. However, when it came to the trial, I confess, I gained a wholly unexpected impression. I saw, and listened to, my lawyer, I heard him speak, and the thought that I, an undeniably guilty man, was quite innocent, was so amusing and, at the same time, somehow so attractive, that I confess that I consider this half hour in court the jolliest in my life. But, of course, not being a jurist, I did not comprehend that I could be quite innocent. Naturally, I was convicted—writers are judged sternly: I paid a fine of twenty-five rubles and, in addition, I spent two days in jail at the Sennaia; there I spent the time very pleasantly, even with some profit—striking up acquaintance with certain people and certain things. However, I feel that I have gone far afield, and I shall return once more to serious matters.

It is moral and touching in a high degree when an advocate employs his time and talents for the defense of the unfortunate ones: he is a friend of humanity. But then the thought occurs to you that he is deliberately defending and acquitting a guilty one; even more—that he is unable to act differently, even if he desired to do so. I shall be told that the court cannot deprive any criminal of a lawyer's assistance, and that an honest defense attorney will invariably remain honest, since he will always seek and determine the true measure of his client's guilt, and will merely prevent the court from punishing him in excess of his guilt, etc. This is so, although this supposition is akin to the most boundless idealism. It seems to me that, generally speaking, it is as difficult for an advocate to avoid falsehood and to preserve honesty and conscience as for any man to attain a paradisiacal state. Indeed, have we not had occasion to hear lawyers in court almost swearing—addressing themselves to the jurors—that they undertook the defense of their clients because they had convinced themselves of their clients' innocence. And when one hears these oaths, the nastiest suspicion at

once inevitably creeps into one's mind: "Well, what if he's lying
and is merely doing this for money?" And, in fact, subsequently
it often developed that the clients, defended so ardently, proved to
be fully and undeniably guilty. I do not know if in our annals there
have been cases recorded where lawyers, seeking to maintain consistently the appearance of men fully convinced of the innocence
of their clients, would have fainted when jurors rendered a "guilty"
verdict. But that they did shed tears, this seems to have already
happened in our still youthful courts. Whatever you may say, there
is in this institution, in addition to that which is undeniably beautiful, something sad. Truly, one can hear: "Plotters! Ticks!"—
and also the popular saying: "Advocate—hired conscience." But
the principal point is that one seems to be haunted with the
most nonsensical paradox that a lawyer is never able even to act
in accord with his conscience; that he cannot but play with it,
even if he wished not to do so; that he is a man doomed to dishonesty, and, finally, that—and this is the most important and most
serious point in the whole matter—this sad state of affairs has been,
as it were, legalized by somebody and something, so that it is
regarded not as a deviation at all but, on the contrary, as a most
normal condition. . . .

However, let us leave this; I fully realize that I began to
speak on a theme which is not mine. And I am even convinced that
in jurisprudence all these misunderstandings have long ago been
settled to everybody's satisfaction, and that it is only I, among all
people, who know nothing about it. Better let us speak about talent:
on this point I am at least a bit more competent.

What is talent? To begin with, talent is a most useful thing.
Literary talent, for example, is the ability to say or express well
that which a nullity will say and express badly. You might say
that, above all, orientation is needed, and only after that—talent.
All right. I agree: I meant to speak not about the artistic quality,
but merely about certain properties of talent in general. The properties of talent, speaking generally, are extremely diversified and
somtimes really unbearable. First, *talent oblige*, "talent obliges"—
to what, for instance? At times, to very bad things. There arises
an insoluble question: does talent possess man, or man possess his
talent?—As far as I am able to observe men of talent, both living
and dead, it does seem to me that in the rarest cases only is a man
capable of mastering his gift; and that, contrariwise, talent almost
always enslaves its owner—grabbing him, so to speak, by his neck
(quite so—oftentimes in this humiliating manner), carrying him far
away from the right road. In Gogol (I have forgotten where) a liar
started relating something, and, perhaps, he would have told the

truth, "but, of their own accord, there developed in the story such details" as made it impossible to tell the truth. This I am mentioning merely for the sake of comparison, although there do exist liars' talents or talents of lying. The novelist Thackeray, depicting a certain socialite liar and wit belonging to good society, who used to saunter from one lord's house to another, tells us that this chap, when departing from somewhere, was wont to save his funniest sally or witticism for his exit. Do you know: it seems to me difficult to remain and, so to speak, preserve oneself as an honest man, when one is anxious to save the wittiest word for the finale in order to leave behind one's self a burst of laughter. Besides, if a witty word for the exit has not been saved, one has to invent one, and for a witty word and a fad—

One spares neither mother nor dad.

I might be told that if such be the requirements, it wouldn't be worth living. However—you must admit—in every man of talent there is nearly always a certain ignoble and excessive "responsiveness" which tends to lead the soberest man astray.

Whether 'tis beast that roars in gloomy woods,

or whatever else may happen, the man is ready and eager to be carried away; he leaps for joy, he swells, he is allured. Bielinsky, in one of his conversations with me, has compared this excessive "responsiveness" with "prostitution of talent" and strongly despised it. In its antithesis, of course, he perceived a certain fortitude of the soul capable of resisting responsiveness even in the presence of a most ardent poetic mood. Bielinsky said this about poets, but all men of talent are poets, though in slight degree—even carpenters, provided they are talented. Poesy is, so to speak, the inner fire of every talent. And if even a carpenter may be a poet, then certainly a lawyer, if he is endowed with talent. I am by no means denying that with rigidly honest principles and spiritual firmness even a lawyer may succeed in mastering his "responsiveness"; yet there are cases and circumstances where a man will be unable to resist: "of their own accord there will develop such details"—and the man will be carried away.

Gentlemen, everything I am saying here about this responsiveness is really not nonsense; much as it may seem simple, yet it is an extremely important matter in everybody's life—even in yours and mine. Please investigate carefully; render an account to yourselves, and you will see that at times it is most difficult to remain honest, precisely because of this excessive "responsiveness," spoiled with overindulgence and compelling us to lie uninterruptedly.

However, the words "honest man" I am using here only in the "loftiest sense," so that we may remain calm without growing alarmed. Besides, I am sure that on account of my words no one will grow alarmed.

I continue. Does anyone among you, gentlemen, remember Alphonse Lamartine, the former ringleader, so to speak, of the Provisional Government during the February revolution of '48? It is said that, to him, there was nothing more pleasing and more delightful than to deliver endless speeches to the people and to the various deputations, which in those days used to come from all over France, from all the cities and small towns, to introduce themselves to the Provisional Government, during the first two months following the proclamation of the Republic. Of such addresses he has delivered, perhaps, several thousand. He was a poet and a man of talent. His whole life was innocent, and full of innocence; all this—coupled with a handsome and most impressive appearance, created, so to speak, for keepsakes. I do not at all compare this historical personage with those types of responsively poetic men who, as it were, are born of mucus in the nose, even though he did write *Harmonies Poétiques et Religieuses*—an unusual tome of endlessly protracted verses, over which three generations of college-graduate demoiselles got hopelessly stuck. As against this, he later wrote an extremely talented book *A History of the Girondists*, which won for him popularity and, finally, the position, as it were, of chief of the Provisional Revolutionary Government. That's when he delivered so many endless speeches, in the first place feasting on them himself and floating in some everlasting rapture. A certain talented wit, pointing at him, exclaimed: *"Ce n'est pas l'homme; c'est une lyre!"* (It is not a man; it is a lyre!)

This was a commendation but it was uttered with profound cunning, since, please concede, what can be more comic than to compare a man with a lyre? Just touch it—and forthwith it will begin to tinkle! It goes without saying that it is impossible to compare Lamartine, the man who has ever been speaking in verse, that orator-lyre, with some of our dexterous advocates, roguish even in their innocence, always self-possessed, always resourceful, always managing to grow rich. Would they be the ones who wouldn't know how to make use of their lyres? Yes, is this so? Is this true, gentlemen? Men are yielding to praise, and even a rogue is "responsive." To some of our talented advocates, instead of a "lyre," there may happen—in an allegorical sense—something on the order of the thing that happened to a certain Moscow merchant. His papa died leaving him some capital ("capital" should be read with an accent on the *i*). But his mama was also engaged, in her own name, in some commercial pursuit, and she got in a hole financially. It was necessary to come to mama's assistance, that is, to put up a large sum of money. The little merchant loved his mama dearly; yet he began to hesitate: "Why, we can't think of being without the capital. To lose the capital does not suit us at all, 'cause it's impossible for us to remain without the capital." So he gave nothing to his mama, and she was dragged into the insolvent debtors' jail. Please take this allegorically and substitute talent for capital, and you would have the following speech: "Why, we can't think of being without glitter and display." And this may happen even to a most serious, most honest talented advocate, at the very minute when he starts his defense, even though the case be repulsive to his conscience. I was reading once that in France, long ago, a certain lawyer, having convinced himself in the course of the trial of the guilt of his client, bowed to the court when the time came for him to make his defense speech, and silently took his seat. In our midst, I believe, this could not have happened.

"How is it possible for me not to win if I am a man of talent? And is it conceivable that I myself should be ruining my reputation?" Thus, *not money alone is to be feared* by a lawyer as a temptation (all the more so as he is never afraid of money), but his own power of talent.

However, I repent for having written all this, since it is a matter of general knowledge that Mr. Spasovich, too, is a remarkably gifted lawyer. To my way of thinking, his speech in this case is a climax in art. Nevertheless it produced in me an almost disgusting impression. You see that I am starting with most sincere avowals. Yet the blame should be laid at the door of the falsehood of all circumstances which, in this case, grouped themselves around Mr. Spasovich; from this falsehood he was unable to extricate himself, owing to the very force of things. Such is my opinion. Therefore, all that was strained and extorted in his status as defense lawyer, *ipso facto,* also reflected itself in his speech. The case was so framed that in the event his client were found guilty, he could have suffered a very heavy, incommensurate punishment. This would have been a calamity: a disintegrated family; no one would have been protected and all would have been left unhappy. His client was charged with "torture"—and it was precisely this premise that was dreadful. Mr. Spasovich opened his defense with an emphatic rejection of the very idea of torture. "There was no torture, there was no offense inflicted upon the child!" He denied everything: "spitzrutens," bruises, blows, blood, integrity of witnesses of the opposing side, everything, everything—an extraordinarily bold device, an onslaught, so to speak, against the jurors' conscience;

but Mr. Spasovich knows his strength. He has even rejected the child, its infancy; he extracted out of the hearts of his listeners pity itself, its very root. The cries to the accompaniment of the flogging, which lasted a quarter of an hour (even if it were five minutes): "Papa! Papa!"—all this has disappeared, and, instead, there appeared in the foreground "a mischievous little girl with a rosy face, laughing, artful, spoiled and with secret vices." Listeners almost forgot that she is seven years old. Mr. Spasovich has adroitly confiscated the age as a thing most dangerous to him. Having destroyed all this, he, naturally, scored a verdict of acquittal. Yet what could he have done? "What if the jurors should find my client guilty?"—So that, by inertia, he was unable to hesitate before any device, or to use kid-glove methods. "All means are good if they lead to a lofty goal." But let us examine this remarkable speech in detail; it is well worth it. You will see.

3

MR. SPASOVICH'S SPEECH. ADROIT METHODS.

Even beginning with the first words of the speech you feel that you are dealing with an extraordinary talent, with a power. Mr. Spasovich at once fully reveals himself; and he is the first to point out to the jurors the weak element of the defense which he undertook; he reveals its weakest spot, the thing which he himself dreads most. (By the way, I am citing this speech from *The Voice*. It is such a wealthy periodical that, probably, it is in a position to employ a good stenographer.)

"I am afraid, gentlemen of the jury"—says Mr. Spasovich— "not of the verdict of the Court of Appeal; not of the charges brought forth by the district attorney. . . . I am afraid of an abstract idea, of a phantom; I am afraid of the fact that the crime —as it is being called—has as its object a weak, defenseless creature. The very words 'torture of a child,' first of all, arouses a feeling of great compassion for the child and, secondly, a sensation of strong indignation against him who was its torturer."

This is very clever. Extraordinary sincerity. The listener who had bristled himself up; who had in advance prepared himself to hear something by all means crafty, devious, deceitful, and who had just said to himself: "Now, brother, let's see if you can deceive me"—is suddenly struck with the virtual defenselessness of the man. The supposed trickster himself is seeking protection—and precisely from you, from those whom he sought to deceive! By this device Mr. Spasovich at once breaks the ice of suspicion and, through this one little drop he infiltrates into your heart. True, he speaks about the *phantom;* he says that he is afraid merely of a "phantom," that is, almost of a prejudice. As yet you have listened to nothing further; but already you feel ashamed that you may be held to be a man with prejudices. Isn't this so?—Very clever.

"Gentlemen of the jury"—continues Mr. Spasovich—"I am not a partisan of the rod. I can quite understand that *a system of education may be introduced* [but don't you worry, all these are such novel expressions, and they are borrowed in toto from various pedagogical treatises], from which the rod will be eliminated; nevertheless I have as little hope for a complete and absolute eradication of corporal punishment as for the condition where you would cease functioning in court because of the discontinuance of criminal deeds and the violation of that truth which must prevail in both the family and the state."

So, then, the whole affair is confined to a rod, and not to a bundle of rods, not to "spitzrutens." You begin to look attentively, you are listening—no, the man speaks seriously; he is not jesting. So the whole turmoil was started only over a little rod in connection with childish age, and the question as to whether or not the rod should be used. Was it worth our while to assemble? True, he himself is not a partisan of the rod: he declares himself that, but, on the other hand . . .

"In a normal state of affairs normal measures are employed. In the case at bar an obviously abnormal measure has been resorted to. Yet, if you should scrutinize the circumstances which have called forth this measure; if you should consider the nature of the child, the temperament of the father, those aims which prompted him at the time of the punishment, you would comprehend many a thing, because a *profound* understanding of the case inevitably leads to a condition where much becomes intelligible and will appear natural and not necessitating a penal reaction. My task is to explain the case."

So you see, it's "punishment," not "torture"; so he says himself. Thus, it is only a case of a father who is being tried because he has beaten the child a little too hard. Think of the times we have come to! However, if one should scrutinize more deeply . . . Now, that's really the point: neither the Court of Appeal nor the district attorney knew how to scrutinize. And once we, the jury, manage to scrutinize, we will acquit, since "*profound* understanding leads to acquittal"—so he says himself, while this means that only on our bench is there *profound understanding.* "The darling must have been waiting and waiting for us! He got weary of dealing

with courts and district attorneys." In a word: "flatter, flatter!"
This is an old routine method, and yet how very reliable!

Next, Mr. Spasovich turns directly to the exposé of the historical part of the case, and he begins *ab ovo*. Of course, we shall
not quote him verbatim. He recounts the whole life history of
his client. Mr. Kroneberg, you see, had gone through a full cur-
riculum: first, he had studied in the University at Warsaw, then
in Brussels, where he became fond of the French; after that—again
in Warsaw, where, in 1867, he graduated from the Superior School
with the degree of master of laws. At Warsaw he struck up an
acquaintance with a certain lady, his senior, and had a liaison with
her; he parted with her because he could not marry her, but when
parting he was even unaware of the fact that he was leaving her
pregnant by himself. Mr. Kroneberg was grieved and started looking for distraction. During the Franco-Prussian War he joined the
French Army and took part in twenty-three battles; he received the
Order of the Legion of Honor and retired with the rank of second
lieutenant. In those days, we Russians, all of us, had been wishing
every success to the French; somehow we heartily dislike the Germans although, intellectually, we are prepared to respect them.
Upon his return to Warsaw, he again met that lady whom he had
loved so much; she had already married and she told him, for the
first time, that he had a child who was then in Geneva. The mother,
at the time, had made a special trip to Geneva to deliver the child,
who had been placed in the care of some farmers for monetary
remuneration. Having learned about the child, Mr. Kroneberg at
once expressed the desire to provide for it. At this juncture Mr.
Spasovich uttered several stern and liberal words about our legislation for its severity toward illegitimate children, but he promptly
consoles us with the statement that "within the boundaries of the
Empire there is a country, the Kingdom of Poland, which has its
own special laws." Briefly, in that country it is easier and more
convenient to adopt an illegitimate child. Mr. Kronberg "wished to
do for the child the maximum of what could be done according
to the law, even though at that time he did not have an independent
fortune. But he was sure that his relatives, in case of his death,
would take care of the little girl bearing the name of Kroneberg,
and that if worse should come to worse, she could be placed in
some governmental educational institution in France, as a daughter
of a Knight of the Legion of Honor." After that Mr. Kroneberg
took the little girl from the Geneva farmers and placed her in
the home of pastor de Comb, also in Geneva, for upbringing; the
pastor's wife was the girl's godmother. Thus passed the years 1872,

1873 and 1874 till the beginning of 1875, when, because of some change in circumstances, Mr. Kroneberg again went to Geneva and took the little girl to Petersburg—this time into his own home.

Mr. Spasovich states, among other things, that his client is a man craving for family life. Once he was about to marry but the wedding was called off, and one of the main obstacles in this connection was precisely the fact that he did not conceal that he had a "natural daughter." This is the first little drop; Mr. Spasovich adds nothing, but you comprehend that Mr. Kroneberg has partly suffered for his good deed, for the fact that he had recognized his daughter, whom he could have abandoned forever with the farmers. Thus, he had the right, so to speak, to repine at this innocent creature: at least one feels so. However, in these little, delicate, as it were, fleeting, but incessant, innuendoes, Mr. Spasovich is the greatest master, and an unrivalled one, of which you will become convinced further.

After that, unexpectedly, Mr. Spasovich begins to speak about Miss Jesing. You see, Mr. Kroneberg has met in Paris a Miss Jesing, and, in 1874, he brought her with him to Petersburg.

"You could appreciate"—suddenly announces Mr. Spasovich—"to what extent Miss Jesing does or does not resemble those women of the demi-monde with whom fleeting liaisons are being formed. Of course, she is not Mr. Kroneberg's wife, yet their relations preclude neither love nor respect."

Well, this is their own personal, subjective business, and to us it makes no difference. However, Mr. Spasovich seeks to solicit respect by all means.

"You could see whether this woman is heartless and whether or not the child loves her. She tried to do all possible good to the child. . . ."

The whole point is that the child called this lady "maman," and that the girl took out of "maman's" chest a prune, for which she had been flogged. Now, you must not think that Jesing is hostile to the child, that she falsely derogates the girl and thereby incites Kroneberg against her. Well, we do not think it; we believe that this lady has no reason for hating the child: the child is inured to kiss her hand and to call her *"maman."* It even appears from the case that the lady, having become afraid of the "spitzrutens," begged (although with no result) just before the flogging had started, to be permitted to break off a certain dangerous twig. According to Mr. Spasovich's statement, Jesing was the one who suggested to Kroneberg the idea of removing the child from de Comb in Geneva. "At that time Kroneberg had no definite intention of taking the child, but he made up his mind to go to Geneva to see for himself. . . ."

This is important news; let us bear it in mind. It appears that at that time Mr. Kroneberg was not yet much concerned about the child, and he had no heartfelt urge at all to have her live with him.

"In Geneva he was astounded: the child whom he had visited by surprise, not at a fixed time, was found in a sullen state; *she did not recognize the father.*"

Take special notice of the phrase: "she did not recognize the father." I have mentioned before that Mr. Spasovich is a great master of casting such little words: it might seem that he had merely dropped the phrase accidentally; yet, toward the end of the speech, it will bear its result and fruit. If the child "had not recognized the father," this means that it is not only sullen but also depraved. All this will be needed further on; we shall see later that Mr. Spasovich, by casting his little phrases here and there, will at length utterly disillusion you about the child. Instead of a seven-year-old infant, instead of an angel, there will appear before you a "mischievous" girl, an artful, obstreperous girl with a bad disposition, who cries when she is ordered into the corner; who is "great at screaming" (what Russicism!); a liar, a pilferer, untidy and with a filthy secret vice. The whole trick comes to this: your sympathy for the child must somehow be destroyed. Such is human nature: one does not pity him to whom one takes a dislike or to whom one feels an aversion, and, more than anything else, Mr. Spasovich fears your compassion: otherwise, if you should start pitying the child, you might find the father guilty. Herein is the falsehood of the situation. Of course, the whole grouping, all these facts clustered by him over the child's head, taken separately, are not worth an empty egg-shell, and later you will, no doubt, notice this yourselves. For instance, no man is ignorant of the fact that a three- or, even, four-year-old child, relinquished by someone, will necessarily forget the face of that person, will forget even the most minute circumstances connected with that person, as well as everything pertaining to the time; and that a child's memory, at this age, does not extend to more than one year or even nine months back. The blame here lies with those who have abandoned the child for so many years, rather than in the depraved nature of the child. And it stands to reason that a juror, too, would understand this, had he the time and desire to think and reason; but he has no time for reasoning: he is under the sway of the irresistible pressure of talent; he is dominated by the grouping;

the case does not revolve around any individual fact but, so to speak, a cluster of facts. And say what you wish, these insignificant facts, grouped together in a bunch, at length create, as it were, a hostile feeling toward the child. *Il en reste toujours quelque chose:* this is an old and notorious device, particularly if it be a skillful and studied grouping.

Looking forward, I shall refer to another, similar, example of Mr. Spasovich's art. By resorting to this device, at the end of his speech he absolutely annihilates with one stroke Agrafena Titova— the most damaging witness from the standpoint of his client. Here there is even no grouping: he merely caught one little word and, of course, pounced on it to his advantage. Agrafena Titova is Kroneberg's former housemaid. She, together with the porter's wife, Ouliana Bibina, at the summer cottage in Lesnoie which Mr. Kroneberg was then renting, was the first to bring charges of torturing the child. As for me, I may remark in passing that, in my opinion, Titova and, particularly, Bibina, are nearly the most attractive personalities in the whole case. They love the child. The child was weary. Having just been brought from Switzerland, the girl almost never saw her father, who was occupied with the affairs of some railroad; he used to leave the house in the morning and return late in the evening. When, upon his return at night, he would learn of some childish prank of the girl, he would flog her and beat her on her face (these facts have been corroborated and Mr. Spasovich himself did not deny them). The poor little girl, as a result of such a cheerless life, had grown sullen, feeling more and more melancholy. "At present the girl always sits alone and will speak to no one"—these are the exact words which Titova used, when making her complaint. They have the sound not only of profound sympathy, but one may perceive in them the delicate glance of an observer—a glance permeated with inner compassion for the sufferings of an insulted tiny creature of God. It is only natural that the little girl grew fond of the servants in whom alone she sensed love and tenderness, and at times she used to run down to visit the porter's wife. For this Mr. Spasovich blames the child, attributing her vices "to the corrupting influence of the servants." Please note that the girl spoke nothing but French, and that Ouliana Bibina, the porter's wife, could not understand her well; therefore, she must have grown fond of her from mere pity, mere sympathy for the child, which is so typical of our common people.

"One evening in July (so it is stated in the indictment) Kroneberg again started flogging the little girl, and this time he flogged her so long and she cried so dreadfully that Bibina became frightened, fearing that the girl might be beaten to death; therefore, jumping out of her bed, just as she had been lying there, in her nightgown, she ran to Kroneberg's window and shouted that the flogging of the child must be stopped, threatening to summon the police; *then the flogging and the cries ceased.*"

Can you visualize that hen—that brood-hen—shielding her chicks, spreading out her wings to protect them? These pitiful hens, when protecting their chicklings, sometimes become most dreadful. During my childhood, in the country, I used to know an urchin, from among the house servants, who was terribly fond of torturing animals and particularly of killing chickens with his own hands, whenever they had to be cooked for the master's dinner. I remember he used to climb on the straw roof of the barn in search of sparrows' nests: upon finding one, he would immediately begin wringing off their heads. Now, imagine this same torturer being awfully afraid of a hen when, in a fury, with its wings spread out, it stood in front of him, shielding its chicklings. On such occasions he used to hide behind me.

So, then, about three days later, having lost all patience, this pitiful hen, after all, did go to the authorities to make her complaint, taking along with her that bundle of rods with which the girl had been flogged, as well as her blood-stained underwear. In this connection, please consider the aversion of our common folk to courts and their fear of getting mixed up with them, when one himself is not dragged into court. Yet she did go to plead and complain on behalf of a stranger—a child—knowing that, in any event, she would receive no other reward than bother and disappointments.

Now, it is when referring to these two women that Mr. Spasovich speaks of "the corrupting influence of servants upon the child." Moreover, he snatches at the following little fact: the child, as will be seen further on, had been charged with theft. (Later you will see how adroitly Mr. Spasovich twisted the taking of a prune without permission into a theft of banknotes.) However, at first, the girl did not confess to *theft,* and even stated that she "had taken nothing from them."

"The girl [says Mr. Spasovich] answered with stubborn silence; thereafter, several months later, she recounted that *she meant to take the money for Agrafena.* If he [*i.e.,* the girl's father] had investigated more carefully the circumstances of the theft, he might have come to the conclusion that the corruption which had sneaked into the girl should be   tributed to the influence of the people close to her. The girl's very silence was proof of the fact that the child did not wish to betray those with whom she was on good terms."

"She meant to take the money for Agrafena"—that's the little phrase! "Several months later," of course, she *invented* the story that she sought to take the money for Agrafena; she fabricated this as a mere fantasy, or because this had been suggested to her. Indeed, didn't she say in court: "*Je suis voleuse, menteuse*," whereas she had stolen nothing but a berry, a prune, while during these months the irresponsible child was made to believe that she had been stealing; they made her believe it even without persuasion, but solely because of the fact that incessantly, day in and day out, everybody around her had been saying that she was a thief.

However, even if it were true that the girl meant to take the money for Agrafena Titova, yet from this it would not follow that Titova herself taught her this and that Titova herself had urged her to steal the money for her. Mr. Spasovich is skillful: under no circumstance would he state this in express terms; in the absence of direct and solid evidence, he would not inflict such an offense upon Titova; as against this, however, forthwith after the girl's words that "she meant to take the money for Agrafena," he dropped his little insinuation that "the corruption which has sneaked into the girl should be attributed to the influence of the people close to her." And, of course, this is enough. Naturally, the thought seeps into the juror's mind: "Ah, such are these two principal witnesses; it is for them that she has been thieving; they themselves have taught the child to steal; considering that, what is their testimony worth?"

True: this thought cannot be avoided by one's own mind, once it has been suggested under circumstances such as these. And thus, dangerous testimony is crushed and destroyed, and precisely at the moment when it is convenient to Mr. Spasovich—at the end of his speech, as a last resort, as a winding-up effect. Yes, this is skillful. Burdensome, indeed, is the task of an advocate placed in such a difficult situation. What else can he do?—He has got to save his client. Still, all these are but little flowers; the berries come later.

4

Little Berries

I have already stated that Mr. Spasovich denies all cruelty, all torture, inflicted upon the little girl; he even scoffs at such a supposition. Turning to "the July 25th catastrophe," straightway, he begins to count the scars, the bruises—each gash, each little scab; tiny bits of fallen-off skin; then he puts all these on the scales: "So many zolotniks—there was no torture!" Such is his opinion; such is his device. The press has already called Mr. Spasovich's attention to the fact that these calculations as to scars and gashes are irrelevant and even ridiculous. However, to my way of thinking, all this bookkeeping must have created a weighty impression on the public and on the jurors: "See! What precision! What conscientiousness!" I am convinced that among the listeners there must have been men who were especially pleased to learn that inquiries concerning some tiny particular scar had been made in Geneva, and information had been sought from de Comb. Mr. Spasovich triumphantly points out that there were no gashes of the skin:

"Despite all the unfavorableness to Kroneberg of the opinion of Mr. Lansberg (the doctor who, on July 29th, examined the punished girl and whose opinion Mr. Spasovich very caustically derides)—I am using for the defense many data set forth in his findings of July 29th. Mr. Lansberg had positively certified that on the posterior parts of the little girl's body there were no gashes of the skin, but *only* dark purple subcutaneous stains and identical red streaks. . . ."

Only! Please note this little word. And—this is most important —five days after the torture! I could prove to Mr. Spasovich the fact that these dark purple subcutaneous stains disappear very quickly, with not the slightest danger to one's life. Still, don't they constitute torment, suffering and torture?

"The majority of these stains appeared in the left ischial region, spreading also to the left hip. Having found no traumatic marks, nor even scratches, Mr. Lansberg certified that the streaks and stains constitute *no danger whatsoever* to life. Six days later, on August 5th, when the girl had been examined by Professor Florinsky, he had observed not stains but merely streaks—some short, others longer; yet he did not at all find that those streaks constituted an important injury of any kind, even though he did acknowledge that the punishment was a harsh one—particularly in view of the instrument with which the child had been chastised."

I will state to Mr. Spasovich that in Siberia, in the convicts' wards in the hospital, I chanced to see the backs of prison inmates immediately after they had been subjected to flogging with spitzrutens (driven through the ranks) after five hundred, one thousand and two thousand blows inflicted at a time. This I saw several dozens of times. Would you believe me, Mr. Spasovich, that some backs swelled one vershok thick, and yet think how little flesh there is on one's back! These backs were precisely of a dark purple color, with a few gashes from which blood would be oozing. Be sure, no one among our present-day medical experts has ever observed anything like this; (besides, what chance do we have, in our times, to observe things!). These chastised men, provided they had received not more than one thousand blows, used to come in maintaining a vigorous air although, apparently, in a highly nervous state, and that—only during the first two hours. As far as I can remember, not one of those inmates would lie down, or sit down, during these first two hours; they merely kept pacing back and forth in the ward, their whole bodies shuddering at times, with a wet bed sheet over their shoulders. The whole treatment consisted of this: a bucketful of water was brought to the inmate, and from time to time he soaked that bed sheet in it, when it would dry on his back. To the best of my recollection, they were all quite eager to be discharged from the ward as quickly as possible (because prior to that, they had been kept locked up for a long time awaiting trial), while others simply sought again to escape at the earliest possible opportunity. And here is a fact: such chastised men got discharged from the hospital on the sixth—at most, on the seventh—day after the punishment, because during that period *the back would almost completely heal up,* save for some slight—comparatively speaking—remnants; however, after ten days, for example, everything would have disappeared without leaving any traces.

The punishment with spitzrutens (*i.e.,* in fact, with sticks), if inflicted not too excessively—that is, not more than two thousand blows at a time—constituted not the slightest danger to one's life. On the contrary all those sentenced to hard labor and military inmates (and they see sights!) many a time and always told in my presence that rods are more painful, more "shrinky" and far more dangerous, since one can endure even more than two thousand blows with sticks, whereas after only four hundred blows with rods one may die; five or six hundred blows with rods *at a time* results in imminent death; this can be endured by no one.

Now, I will ask you, Mr. Defense-Lawyer, I will ask you this question: even though these sticks did not threaten one's life and had caused no injury whatever, isn't such a punishment cruel and doesn't it constitute torture? Indeed, didn't the little girl suffer during a quarter of an hour under the dreadful rods, which lay on the table in court as an exhibit, crying: "Papa! Papa!"? Why, then, are you denying her suffering, her torture?

However, I have stated above why there is such confusion here. I repeat: the point is that in our *Code of Punishments,* according to Mr. Spasovich, in the conception and definition of torture, there is "an ambiguity, a deficiency, an omission."

". . . On this ground the Ruling Senate has held, in those very decisions upon which the prosecution is relying, that, on the other hand, by torture and racking should be meant such infringements upon the person and personal inviolability of man as are

THE DIARY OF A WRITER

accompanied by torment and cruelty. In the opinion of the Senate, physical pain caused by torture and racking must necessarily represent the highest degree of suffering and one more lasting than in ordinary, though severe, beating. If beating cannot be called severe —and torture must be more severe than severe beating—if no one of the experts qualified it as severe, except Mr. Lansberg, who himself has disclaimed his findings, then *it may be asked how is it possible to apply to this deed the definition of torture and racking? I believe this to be impossible.*"

Herein, then, is the point. In the *Code of Punishments* there is an ambiguity, and to Mr. Spasovich's client, charged with torture, one of the most rigid sections of the law could have been applied, which, in any event, should have been inapplicable to the measure of his violation of the provisions of the law; and the latter entail a punishment altogether incommensurate with his "deed." It would seem that one should simply explain to us this misunderstanding— "true, there was torture, yet not such as is being defined by the law, that is, *not more severe than severe beating,* and, for this reason, my client cannot be charged with torture." But Mr. Spasovich does not wish to yield anything; he seeks to prove that there has been no torture at all, neither lawful nor unlawful, and also no suffering —not a bit of it! But, for goodness' sake, what is it to us that the torture and racking of this girl do not comply with the letter of the legal definition of torture?—You have stated yourself—have you not?—that there is an omission in the law. All the same the child did suffer: indeed, didn't she suffer? In truth, hadn't she been subjected to torture? Is it permissible to deceive us to such an extent? Yes, Mr. Spasovich has specifically undertaken this very task; he makes a determined attempt to lead us astray: the child—says he —next day "had been playing" and "attending to a lesson." I do not think that the child had been playing. On the contrary, Bibina testified that when she had examined the girl—before she had gone to lodge her complaint—"the girl bitterly wept and kept uttering: 'Papa! Papa!'"

Good heavens! Such little children are so impressionable, so receptive!—What does it matter if, next day, she did, perhaps, play a little—with those dark purple stains still on her body? I have seen a five-year-old boy, almost dying of scarlet fever—in a state of complete impotence and exhaustion—and yet he was lisping about a doggie which some people had promised to give him, and he begged that all his toys be brought and placed around his tiny bed: "at least I can look at them!"

But the climax of skill is reached by Mr. Spasovich when he manages to "confiscate" altogether the age of the child! He keeps talking about some girl, corrupted and vicious, caught several times at thieving, with a secret, lewd vice in her soul; and he completely forgets, as it were (and we—with him), that we are dealing here only with a seven-year-old infant, and that this very *flogging*—for a whole quarter of an hour—with those nine sorb-tree "spitzrutens" would certainly have been ten times lighter not only to an adult but even to a fourteen-year-old youth than to this wee bit of a creature! Willy-nilly, one asks onself: why does Mr. Spasovich require all this? What is his purpose in denying so stubbornly the suffering of the little girl? Why should he be wasting virtually his whole skill and resourcefulness on an attempt to lead us astray? Is it only because of mere advocate's vanity: "I'll not only save my client's skin, but I'll manage to prove that the whole case is nothing but ridiculous nonsense, and a father is being tried because on one occasion he beat a bad girl with a rod"? But I have already stated that he has got to destroy in you all sympathy for the girl. And, although to this end he has abundant supplies in store, to be used in the future, nevertheless he fears that the child's suffering might—who can tell?—evoke in you humane feelings. And it is precisely such feelings that are dangerous to him: maybe you will become angry at his client; he must crush these feelings in advance; he must distort and ridicule them; briefly, it would seem, he must embark upon some impossible venture—impossible because of the fact alone that we have before us the very clear, precise and most outspoken testimony of the father who has firmly and truthfully admitted the torture of the child:

"On July 25th, irritated by his daughter (testified the father), he beat her with this bundle; he beat her severely and, on this occasion, he *beat her long, frantically, unconsciously, at random.* Whether, during this last beating, the rods broke, he does not know; but he does remember that when he began to flog the little girl, they were longer."

True, despite this testimony, at the trial the father did not plead guilty to having tortured his daughter, and stated that prior to July 25th he had always punished her lightly. I may observe in passing that the opinion on lightness and severity, in a case such as this, is an individual matter: blows on the face of a seven-year-old infant, with blood trickling from the nose, which is denied by neither Kroneberg nor his lawyer, are obviously regarded by both of them as light punishment. In connection with this, Mr. Spasovich has other precious pranks—many of them. For example:

"You have heard that the marks on the elbows almost unquestionably appeared only because during the punishment *she was held by her arms.*"

Do you hear: *only because!* They must have been held pretty hard if bruises had been caused thereby! Oh, Mr. Spasovich does not assert—in so many words—that all this is just fine and sweet-scented. Here, for instance, we have another little argument:

"They say that this punishment exceeds the scope of ordinary ones. This definition might have been excellent if we could determine what an ordinary punishment is; *but so long as there is no such definition,* anyone would be at a loss to state whether it exceeded the scope of ordinary punishments [and this—after the father's testimony that he beat *long, unconsciously* and *frantically!*].

"Let us admit that this is true. Well, what does this mean?—That this punishment is one that, in the majority of cases, should not be administered to children. However, there may be exceptional cases even among children. Don't you admit that parental authority, in exceptional cases, may be placed in a position where a father must resort to a severer measure than ordinarily—one which does not resemble ordinary measures employed habitually."

However, this is all that Mr. Spasovich is willing to concede. He reduces, then, the whole torture to "a measure severer than ordinarily." Yet he repents even for this concession. At the end of his defense speech he retracts all this and says:

"A father is being tried; for what? For abuse of authority. The question may be asked: where is the limit of this authority? Who can determine how many blows, and in what circumstances, a father may administer without injuring, at the same time, the child's organism?"

Does it mean: without fracturing the child's leg? And so long as he does not fracture the child's limbs—everything is permissible? Are you speaking seriously, Mr. Spasovich? Do you seriously claim that you do not know where the limit of this authority is, and "how many blows, and in what circumstances, a father may administer"? If you do not know, I will tell you where this limit is! The limit of this authority is that one should not *flog* with nine sorb-tree "spitzrutens," flog for a quarter of an hour a seven-year-old, altogether defenseless, wee bit of a creature, despite all its "vices" (which must be corrected in a wholly different manner)— a creature in the image of an angel, incomparably purer and more sinless than you, Mr. Spasovich, and me, than all those in the court-room who have been judging and condemning this little girl—one shouldn't be flogging this child and listening to her cries: "Papa! Papa!" which almost drove mad and made frantic a simple peasant woman, that porter's wife! Finally—according to the man's own confession he "beat long, frantically, unconsciously, at random"— one should not be beating *frantically* because there is a limit to all rage, even against a seven-year-old irresponsible infant over a little berry, a prune, and a broken knitting needle!

Yes, skillful defense lawyer, there is a limit to everything, and if only I had not known that you are saying all this purposively, that you are pretending to the best of your ability to save your client, I should have added, specifically for your own benefit, that there is even a limit to all sorts of "lyres" and advocates' "responsiveness," and that the limit consists in that one should not be giving vent to the verbosity which has led you, Mr. Defense Lawyer, as far afield as the pillars of Hercules. But—alas!—you were sacrificing yourself on behalf of your client, and I have no right to speak to you about limits, and I am merely wondering at the greatness of your sacrifice.

5

HERCULES' PILLARS

But the pillars, the real pillars of Hercules, earnestly begin where Mr. Spasovich comes to "the just wrath of the father."

"When this bad habit in the girl had been revealed"—says Mr. Spasovich—(that is, the habit of lying)—"added to all her other defects; when the father learned that she had been *stealing,* he was really seized with great wrath. I believe that *each one of you would have been seized with a similar wrath,* and I believe that to prosecute a father because of the fact that he has severely, but *deservedly,* punished his child, is poor service to the family, poor service to the state, because the state is solid only when it can rely for its support upon a solid family. . . . If the father grew indignant, he was fully within his rights. . . ."

Now, wait, Mr. Defense-Lawyer! For the moment I am not interrupting you at the word "stealing," which you have used. But let us talk briefly about that "just wrath of the father." And the upbringing—since the age of three in Switzerland at de Comb's, where you testify yourself that she had been corrupted and had acquired bad habits?—At such an age, in what way could she personally have been guilty of any bad habits, and, if so, where is the justness of the father's wrath? I insist upon the total irresponsibility of the girl in this case, even if it be admitted that she did have bad habits. And no matter what you may say, you cannot refute this irresponsibility of a seven-year-old child. She does not, and cannot, possess sufficient intelligence to observe evil in herself. Look: we all—perhaps, even you, Mr. Spasovich—we all are no saints, notwithstanding the fact that we possess more intelligence than a seven-year-old child. How, then, can you cast upon this wee bit of a creature the burden of responsibility which you yourself have no strength to bear? The words: "for they bind them heavy burdens and grievous to be borne" come to one's mind. You may say that we must improve the children. Listen: we should not be taking pride in ourselves over children—we are worse than they. And if we teach them anything so that they be better, they, on their part, are teaching us many a thing, and they, too, are making us better merely by our contact with them. They humanize our souls by their mere presence in our midst. This is why we must respect them and approach their angels' images (assuming that we have something to teach them); their innocence, notwithstanding some vicious habit contracted by them; their irresponsibility, and their touching defenselessness. But you, on the contrary, are asserting that beating on the face, till blood begins to trickle, by a father—is just and inoffensive. The child had some scales in its nose, and you say:

"Perhaps, blows on the face have accelerated the discharge of that blood from the scrofulous scurf in the nostril, but this is in no sense an injury: *blood would have run a little later even without a wound or injury.* Therefore, this blood constitutes nothing prejudicial to Kroneberg. At the time when he had delivered the blow, *he may not have remembered, he may even not have known that the child was subject to nosebleeding.*"

"He may not have remembered, he may even not have known!"—For goodness' sake, can you suppose that Mr. Kroneberg had knowingly struck on a sore spot?—Certainly, he did not know. Thus, you yourself testify that the father did not know about his child's malady and, yet, you insist upon his right to beat the child. You claim that the father's blows on the face are inoffensive. Yes, for a seven-year-old infant they may, perhaps, be inoffensive, but the insult? In the course of your whole speech, Mr. Defense Lawyer, you have mentioned nothing about the moral, heartfelt insult; you kept talking about physical pain merely. And for what has she been beaten on her face? Where are the pretexts for such horrible wrath? Is she an important criminal? This little girl, this criminal, will presently run to play "robbers" with little boys. Here we are dealing with the age of seven—only seven—years; this has to be constantly remembered in this case. Indeed, all that you are saying is a mirage! And do you know what it means to insult a child? Children's hearts are full of innocent, almost unconscious, love, and such blows evoke in them a sorrowful astonishment and tears which God beholds and will count. For their intellect is never capable of grasping their full guilt. Have you ever seen, or heard about, tortured little children—say, little orphans in some strange, cruel

families? Have you ever seen a child hiding in a corner, so that
he may not be seen, and weeping there, twisting his little hands
(yes, twisting the hands—I have seen it myself) and *striking his
chest with his tiny fist*, not comprehending what he was doing, not
fully grasping his guilt and the reason why he was being tortured,
but realizing only too clearly that he was not loved? Personally,
I know nothing about Mr. Kroneberg; I do not wish to, nor am
I in a position, to invade the souls and hearts of himself and of
his family, since, not knowing him at all, I may commit a grave
injustice. Therefore, I am judging him solely by your words and
statements, Mr. Defense Lawyer. You said about him in your speech
that he was "an inept pedagogue." In my opinion, this is the same
as an inexperienced—or better, let us say, unaccustomed—father. I
will explain it: only then do these creatures penetrate our souls and
take hold of our hearts when we, having begotten them, are watching *over* them ever since their childhood, never parting with them
from the time of their first smile, and thereafter continuing spiritually to be mutually drawn closer to each other, day after day,
hour after hour, throughout our whole lives. This is family; this
is sanctity! For the family, too, is *created,* and is not given to us
ready-made; and here no obligations are made to order, but they
all result one from the other. Only then is this unit solid; only
then—holy. And the family is created by the incessant labor of love.
However, Mr. Advocate, you admit that your client committed two
logical errors (are they only logical?), and that one of these, *inter
alia*, consists of the fact that he "has acted too rashly: he has supposed that it is possible to eradicate at once, by one stroke, the evil
which has been sown and which reared up in the child's soul over
a period of years. But this can't be done; one has to act slowly
and with patience."

I swear that not much patience would have been required,
since the little creature is only a seven-year-old girl. Again and
again—this "seven years" which vanishes everywhere in your speech
and in your speculations, Mr. Defense Lawyer. "She was stealing!"
—you exclaim—"She was thieving!"

"On the 25th of July the father came to his summer cottage
and learned with surprise that the child had been rummaging in
Jesing's chest, breaking the hook (that is, a knitting needle, and
not any kind of lock), and was reaching out for the money. I don't
know, gentlemen, if one may be indifferent to such acts of a
daughter? It is said: 'For what?' Is it permissible to punish so
severely for a few prunes and sugar? I believe from prunes to
sugar, from sugar to the money, from the money to the banknotes
—is a straight path, an open road."

I will tell you a little anecdote, Mr. Defense Lawyer. A father, earning his livelihood by hard work, is sitting at his desk. He is a writer, just as myself; he is writing. Presently, he puts down his pen, and his little girl, six years old, comes up to him and begins to tell him that he should buy her a new doll, and then—a calèche, a real one, with horses; she will seat herself in the carriage with the little doll and her nurse, and she will drive to Sasha, the nurse's granddaughter. "Then, papa, you must also buy me . . ." etc., etc. —there's no end to the purchases. All these she has just invented and fabricated in her little corner, while playing with the doll. In these six-year-old infants imagination is boundless, and this is excellent; therein is their development. The father is listening smilingly:

"Ah, Lilia, Lilia"—suddenly says he half-jestingly, half-sadly —"I would buy you everything, but where shall I get the money? You don't know how difficult it is to earn money!"

"Then, papa, do this"—exclaims Lilia, with a very serious and confidential expression. "Take a small pot, take a small shovel and go to the woods; there, dig under the bush, and you'll dig up money; put it into the pot and bring it home."

I assure you that that little girl is by no means stupid; yet this is the idea she has conceived as to how money is procured. Do you really think that the seven-year-old girl outdistanced greatly the six-year-old one in her conception of money?—Of course, perhaps, she may already have learned that money can't be dug up from under a bush; but whence, in fact, it is derived; subject to what laws; what are banknotes, stock certificates, concessions—this she can hardly know. For goodness' sake, Mr. Spasovich, can one say about such a one that she has been reaching out for the money? This expression, and the meaning implied in it, are applicable only to an adult thief who understands what money is and how it is being used. Even if such a one had taken the money, it would not have been a theft at all, but merely a childish prank—the same as if taking a prune, because she has no idea what money is. But you have made up the story that she is not far removed from banknotes, and you are shouting that "this threatens the state!" If that be true, is it possible, is it permissible to conceive the thought that for such a prank the kind of flogging to which this girl had been subjected is *just* and *justifiable?* However, she does not need money; heavens!—is she going to run away to America with it, or, maybe, she is going to obtain a railroad concession. As a matter of fact, you do say: "from sugar, it is not far to banknotes." Why, then, should you recoil from concessions?

Aren't these pillars, Mr. Defense Lawyer?

"She has a vice, a secret, filthy vice . . ."

Now, wait—halt, gentlemen-prosecutors! Is it possible that there was no one to grasp the whole impossibility, the whole monstrosity of this picture. A tiny little girl is brought before people —serious-minded and humane people, too—a child is being disgraced, and they speak aloud about its "secret vices"! And what is there in the fact that she does not yet understand her ignominy and says: *"Je suis voleuse, je suis menteuse"*? Say what you please, but this is impossible and intolerable; this is an insufferable falsehood. And who has ventured, who has dared to utter about her that she has been "stealing," that she has been "reaching out for the money"? Is it possible to utter such words about an infant! Why is she befouled with "secret vices"?—so loudly that the whole courtroom may hear? Why was so much mud splashed on her—to leave its stain forever?—Oh, do acquit your client as quickly as possible, Mr. Advocate, if only to drop the curtain at the earliest opportunity and to rid us of this spectacle. But, at least, leave us our pity for this infant: do not judge her with such a serious air, as if you were convinced of her guilt. This pity is our treasure, and it is dangerous to exterminate it in society. If society should stop pitying the weak and persecuted, it would be painfully affected itself; it would grow hard and wither; it would become lewd and sterile. . . .

"Why, if I should leave you your pity—what if, out of great pity, you should convict my client?"

Such, indeed, is the situation!

6

The Family and Our Sanctities. A Concluding Word about a Certain Young School.

In conclusion, Mr. Spasovich utters a pithy word:

"In conclusion, I take the liberty of stating that, in my opinion, the entire prosecution of Kroneberg has been framed altogether incorrectly—namely, that the questions which are going to be propounded to you cannot be decided upon at all."

Now, this is clever; therein is the whole gist of the case, and from this follows its whole falsehood. However, Mr. Spasovich adds a few rather solemn words on the subject: "I take it, you will all concede that there is family and parental authority. . . ." Earlier he has been exclaiming that "only then is the state solid, when it is founded upon solid family."

In this connection, I shall take the liberty of interjecting one little word only—and this merely in passing.

We Russians are a young people; we are just beginning to live, even though we have already lived one thousand years, but a big vessel is designed for sailing on a long journey. We are a fresh people, and we do not possess sanctities *quand-même*. We love our sanctities but only because they are, in fact, holy. We support them not only to defend *l'ordre* by using them. Our sanctities are founded not upon their utility but upon our faith in them. We shall even refuse to defend those sanctities should we ever cease to believe in them—unlike those ancient priests who, at the end of paganism, continued to defend their idols which they had long since ceased to regard as gods. Not even one of our sanctities need ever fear a free scrutiny, but this is only because it is in reality solid. We love the sanctity of the family when it is in reality holy, and not because the state is solidly founded upon it. And, believing in the solidity of our family, we should not become afraid even if the abuse of parental authority should be brought to light and prosecuted. We shall not defend this authority *quand-même*. The sanctity of a genuinely sacred family is so solid that it would never topple as a result of this, but would grow even more sacred. However, at any rate, there is a limit, there is a measure—this we too are ready to realize. I am not a jurist; still, in the case of Kroneberg, I cannot help but admit some deeply rooted falsehood. Here there is something wrong; something must have been different, despite the actual guilt. Mr. Spasovich is profoundly right where he speaks of the framing of the question. Still, this settles nothing. Perhaps we need a penetrating and *impartial* revision of our laws in this connection, in order to fill the gaps and to measure up to the character of our society.' I cannot make up my mind as to what is needed here; I am not a jurist. . . .

However, willy-nilly, I exclaim: yes, the bar is an excellent institution but, somehow, also a sad one. This I have stated in the beginning, and I repeat it again. So it does seem to me, and unquestionably only because I am not a lawyer—therein is my whole trouble. I keep visualizing a certain young school turning out shrewd minds and dry hearts—a school distorting every sane feeling whenever occasion calls for such distortion; a school of all sorts of challenges, fearless and irresponsible; a continual and incessant training, based on need and demand, raised to the level of some principle—and because of our want of habit—to the level of prowess, which is applauded by everybody.

Well, do I encroach upon the bar, upon the new courts?— God forbid me this: the only thing I desire is that we all should become a little better. This is a modest desire, but—alas—a most idealistic one. I am an incorrigible idealist; I am seeking sanctities; I love them; my heart thirsts for them, because I have been so created that I cannot live without sanctities; still I should like to see sanctities just a bit more holy; otherwise, there is no point in worshipping them!

One way or the other, I have spoiled my February *Diary* by excessively enlarging upon a sad theme—but only because it had so astounded me. But, *il faut avoir le courage de son opinion*, and this wise French saying, it seems, could serve as a guide to those many who are looking for answers to their queries in our confused time.

MARCH

CHAPTER I

1

Is the Proposition Correct: "Better Let's Have Bad Ideals as Long as Reality is Good"?

I HAVE READ the following comment in Mr. Gamma's "Leaflet" (*The Voice*, No. 67) on my words concerning the people, in the February issue of *The Diary:* "Be that as it may, we have from one and the same writer, within the stretch of only one month, two opposite views concerning the people. And yet, this is not vaudeville, not a painting at a traveling exhibition; this is a verdict on a living organism; it is the same as if one were manipulating a knife in human flesh. Mr. Dostoievsky extricates himself from the real or imaginary contradiction by suggesting that we judge the people 'not by what they are but by what they strive to become.' The people, you see, are actually awful rascals but their ideals, on the contrary, are good. These ideals are 'vigorous and sacred,' and 'they have saved them during the ages of their martyrdom.' One wouldn't be apt to feel too well as a result of exculpations of this kind! Indeed, hell itself is paved with good intentions, and Mr. Dostoievsky knows that 'faith without works is dead.' Besides, whence have these ideals become known? What prophet or heart-reader is able to penetrate and unscramble them, if the total reality contradicts them and is unworthy of them? Mr. Dostoievsky exonerates the people in the sense that 'they may be overcharging some, yet they don't drink—be it vodka or rum.'

However, from here it is not far to the moral: 'better let's have bad ideals as long as reality is good.'"

The most important point in this excerpt is Mr. Gamma's question: "Whence have these ideals (*i.e.*, ideals of the people) become known?" I positively refuse to answer such a question, since no matter how long we might be debating this theme with Mr. Gamma, we should never come to any agreement. This is a most protracted controversy and, to us, it is most momentous. Have the people ideals, or haven't they?—This is a question of our life or death. This controversy has lasted all too long, and it has reached the point where to some of the contestants the ideals have been revealed as clearly as sunlight, while the others do not notice them at all and definitely refuse to take heed of them. Who is right?— This question will be decided not by us, but it will be settled, perhaps, rather soon. Lately, several opinions have been expressed to the effect that in Russia there can be nothing conservative, since here "there is nothing to conserve." Indeed, if we have no ideals of our own, is it worth while to take care of anything or to conserve anything? Well, if this idea brings about so much peace— all the better.

"The people, you see, are actually awful rascals, but their ideals, on the contrary, are good." This phrase, or this thought, I have never expressed. Solely with a view to clarifying this point, I am answering Mr. Gamma. It is quite the reverse: precisely, I have observed among the people, too, that "there are genuine saints, and what saints!—They are radiant themselves and they illuminate the path to all of us!" They exist, my esteemed publicist, they do actually exist, and happy is he who can discern them. I believe that, in this connection, specifically in my wording there isn't the slightest ambiguity. Besides, ambiguity is not always the result of the fact that a writer is ambiguous, but at times it is produced by altogether different causes.

As for the moral—"better let's have bad ideals as long as reality is good"—with which you wind up your article, I will tell you that this is a desire wholly impossible of achievement: without ideals, that is, without even vaguely specified longings for the better, no good reality can ever ensue. It may even be positively asserted that there would ensue nothing but still more obnoxious abomination. I, at least, am leaving a loophole: if things look unbecoming at present, but with a clearly conceived desire to become better (that is, with ideals of a better future), some day we may make up our minds and really become better. In any event, this is not at all impossible; it is more conceivable than your proposition to become better with "bad" ideals, *i.e.*, with evil aspirations.

I hope, Mr. Gamma, you will not grow angry with me for these few words of mine. Let each one of us adhere to his own opinion and wait for the denouement. I assure you that the denouement is, perhaps, not too remote.

2

A CENTENARIAN

"That morning I was much too late"—a lady was telling me the other day—"and I left home almost at noon, and, as if on purpose, there was a heap of things I had to attend to. On Nikolaievskaia Street I had to make two calls, one not far from the other. First—at an office; and at the very gate of the building I met that little old woman; she seemed to me so very old and stooping, with a walking cane. Still I could not guess her age. She came up to the gate and, right there in a corner, she sat down on the porter's bench—just for a little rest. However, I walked by, merely glancing at her.

"Some ten minutes later I left the office, and only two houses farther down there is a store, where last week I had ordered a pair of shoes for Sonia, and, taking this opportunity, I went to fetch them. Now, the little old woman was sitting on the bench at the gate of this house, and she was looking at me. I smiled at her, walked into the store and took the shoes. Well, this took three or four minutes, and I proceeded farther, in the direction of the Nevsky.—Lo! there, again, is my old woman, at a third building, also near the gate, but not on a bench—there was none at this gate —but seated snugly on a projection. Willy-nilly, I suddenly stopped in front of her: why—the thought came to me—does she seat herself at every house?

" 'Are you tired, little old woman?'—I asked her.

" 'I'm getting tired, dearie; I feel tired all the time. It's warm —I ponder—sun is shining; why shouldn't I go for dinner to my granddaughter's?'

" 'So you're going to have dinner, good woman?'

" 'To have dinner, dear, to have dinner.'

" 'But this way you'll not get there.'

" 'No, I'll get there; see, I walk a few steps, and then I rest myself; afterwards I get up and again start going.'

"I looked at her and became very curious. The woman—a tiny, neat, old little creature, wearing old clothes—probably one of the commonalty—with a small cane; her face pale, yellow, the skin drying on the bones; colorless lips—a regular mummy; but she sits and keeps smiling, and the friendly sun is shining straight on her.

" 'Probably, you are very old, little grandmother?' I asked her, jestingly, of course.

" 'Hundred and four, darling; I'm *only* (she said jokingly) a hundred and four years old. . . . And where are you going?'

"And she looked at me and laughed. Probably, she was glad that there was someone to talk to; but that curiosity as to where I was going seemed, to me, strange in a centenarian.

" 'See, grandmother'—said I, laughing too—'I called at the store for these shoes for my girl, and now I am taking them home.'

" 'Look, what tiny bits of shoes they are; yours is a little girl? That's good. Any other children?'

"And she kept on laughing and looking at me. Her eyes were dim, almost lifeless eyes, and yet a warm ray, as it were, radiated from them.

" 'Grandmother, won't you please take five kopecks; buy yourself a loaf of white bread'—said I, handing her the coin.

" 'Why should you be offering me five kopecks?—Well, thanks, I'll take your money!'

" 'Take it, grandmother, don't mind it.'—She took it. One could see that she was not begging, that she had not been reduced to that state, and she accepted my money so gracefully—not at all as if it were charity, but somehow as from mere politeness or because of kindheartedness. However, this may have pleased her, since who would start conversing with an old woman? Whereas now someone is not only talking to her but taking tender care of her.

" 'Well, good-bye, grandmother'—I said. 'Reach your destination in good health.'

" 'I shall, dearie—I shall. And you go along to your granddaughter!'—said the old woman, losing the thread of our conversation and forgetting that I had a daughter and not a granddaughter. Apparently she must have been thinking that everybody had granddaughters.

"I started going, and turned to look at her for the last time. I saw her getting up slowly, with difficulty; she tapped her cane and crawled along the street. Perhaps, ten times more would she repose herself before she finally reached her folks 'for dinner.' And whither does she go to dine? Such a strange little old woman!"

That morning I had listened to this story—why, not even a story, but some sort of an impression of meeting a centenarian (in truth, when does one meet a woman centenarian, especially a woman so full of spiritual life?)—and I forgot all about it. Only, late at night; having read a magazine article and having put aside that periodical, I suddenly recalled that old woman, and promptly put the finishing touches to the picture of how she had reached her folks for dinner. And there emerged another, maybe quite plausible, little picture.

Her granddaughters—perhaps even great-granddaughters, but all the same she called them "granddaughters"—are probably some artisans and, naturally, married women; otherwise, she would not be calling on them for dinner; they are living in a basement, or maybe renting some barber shop; they are poor people—this stands to reason—and yet they are subsisting and keeping their home in good order. She dragged herself up to them, possibly sometime after one o'clock. She wasn't expected; even so, they greeted her rather cordially.

"There she is, Maria Maximovna; come in, come in; be welcome, God's servant!"

The old woman walks in, with a little laugh; the doorbell continues to ring—long, sharply, in a thin tinkle. Her granddaughter is, most probably, the wife of that barber, while he is not yet an old man—a man of thirty-five or thereabouts, as steady as his trade, even though that trade is a frivolous one; of course, he is wearing a suit as greasy as a pancake—is it because of the pomade? —I can't tell, but I have never seen "barber-surgeons" looking otherwise; and also the collars of their coats invariably look as if they had been rolled in flour. Three youngsters—a boy and two little girls—came running in a jiffy to their great-grandmother. Usually, such all too old little women are somehow on intimate terms with children; they themselves become spiritually akin to children—sometimes to the very dot. The old woman seated herself. Maybe a guest or someone calling on business—a man of about forty, an acquaintance—was about to leave the host. Besides, a nephew—the sister's son, a lad of seventeen—is staying with them for a while; he hopes to find a job in some printer's shop. The old woman crosses herself, and sits down, looking at the guest.

"Oh, I'm tired! Who's this with you?"

"You mean me?"—says the guest, laughing. "Now, Maria Maximovna, is it possible you didn't recognize me? Only two years ago—don't you remember?—we'd been planning—you and I—to go to the woods after golden-brown mushrooms?"

"Oh, yes, now I know who you are, you teaser! I remember you; only I forgot your name; but I remember. Oh, how tired I am!"

"Now, Maria Maximovna, esteemed old woman, I meant to ask you, why don't you grow at all?"—the guest continues to joke.

"Go on!"—laughs the grandmother, apparently pleased, however.

"Maria Maximovna, I'm a good fellow."

"And it's nice to speak to a good fellow. Oh, mother, I'm always out of breath. I see you've already sewn Serejenka's overcoat."—She points at the nephew.

The nephew, a chubby and healthy young urchin, gives a broad smile and comes up closer; he is wearing a brand-new, gray overcoat and, as yet, he is unable to put it on with an indifferent air. Indifference will come only in a week maybe, but now every minute he keeps looking at the cuffs, the facing and, generally, at himself, in the mirror, and he feels a special respect for himself.

"Now, come and turn"—chatters the barber's wife. "Just look, Maximovna, what an overcoat we've tailored! Six roubles to the kopeck! Prokhorych says that nowadays 'tisn't worth starting the job for less; you'd be shedding tears yourself, while this one—there will be no end to its wear. See, what cloth!—Do turn, you! What a lining! And how solid!—Turn, I'm telling you! Thus money flows away, Maximovna! That's the last we saw of our kopecks!"

"Yes, dear, living has grown so expensive nowadays—simply impossible! Better you didn't talk about this: it just upsets me" —spiritedly remarks Maximovna, who is still out of breath.

"Now, that's enough!" observed the host. "It's time to have a bite! What's that, Maria Maximovna, I can see you must be quite tired out!"

"Why, good man, indeed I am tired—d'you see, it's a warm day; sunny. Now—I ponder—I'll call on them. . . . What's the use of lying all the time! Oh! . . . On my way here I met a little lady, a young one; she bought shoes for her children. 'You're tired, old dear'—she says. 'Here, take five kopecks and buy yourself a loaf of white bread!' And, d'you know, I did take the five kopecks. . . ."

"Now, grandmother, first you better rest a while. See, how you're losing breath today!"—suddenly observed the host, with emphasized solicitude.

Everybody is looking at her: indeed, suddenly she has grown so pale; her lips have turned quite white. She also is staring at everybody, but somehow dimly.

"Here"—I ponder—"gingerbreads for little children . . . see, the five kopecks. . . ."

And again she stops, to catch her breath. Everybody becomes silent, just for about five seconds.

"What's the matter, grandmother?" asks the host, bending over her.

But grandmother made no reply. Again there was silence for about five seconds. The old woman, as it were, had become even whiter, while her whole face had shrunk. Her eyes became motionless and a smile froze on her lips.

"A priest should be sent for! . . ."—the guest suddenly, half aloud, speaks from behind them.

"Yes . . . but . . . isn't it too late?" . . . mumbles the host.

"Grandmother! Hear! Grandmother!"—cries the barber's wife, turning to the old woman and suddenly seized with alarm. But grandmother is immobile, only her head begins to incline sideways. In her right hand, which rests on the table, she is holding that five-kopeck coin, while her left hand remains on the shoulder of her great-grandson Misha—a boy of six. He stands motionless and, with his eyes wide open, stares at his great-grandmother.

"She has passed away!"—measuredly and solemnly pronounces the host, stooping and crossing himself lightly.

"That's it! I could see her all sinking down"—warmly and abruptly says the guest. He is quite astounded and looks around at everybody.

"Oh, God! What a thing! How are we going to manage it, Makarych? Shall we put her there?" the hostess hastily twitters, quite upset.

"Hither—thither"—sedately retorts the host. "We'll manage it ourselves. Isn't she a relative of yours? But I must go and report it."

"A hundred and four years! Just think!"—the guest keeps repeating in a state of ever-increasing affection. Somehow, he even turns red all over.

"Yes, in recent years she began to forget life itself"—still more solemnly and more soberly remarks the host, looking for his hat and taking his cloak.

"And only a minute ago she was laughing, and how cheerful she was! See, the five-kopeck coin in her hand! 'Gingerbreads'—she said. Oh, oh! Such is our life!"

"Well, let's go, Petr Stepanych!"—the host cuts short his guest, and they both depart.

Of course, over such a one no tears are shed. A hundred and four years—"and she passed away painlessly and unashamed." The hostess sent to the neighbors for help. The neighbor women came running in haste, listening almost with pleasure to the news, sighing and screaming.

It goes without saying that, to begin with, a samovar was brought in. Children with an astonished air, hiding in a corner, stare at the dead grandmother. No matter how long Misha may live, he will remember the little old woman—how she died, pressing her hand upon his shoulder. Well, and when he dies, no one on earth will learn that once upon a time there lived such an old woman, and that she had lived one hundred and four years—how and what for, God only knows. Thus, millions of people pass away: they live unnoticed and they die unnoticed. Only, perhaps, in the instant of death itself of these centenarians—both men and women—there is something touching, as it were, and calm, even solemn and pacifying: even in our time, one hundred years strangely affect men. God bless the lives and deaths of simple, kind folks!

However, this is but a light and themeless little scene. Truly, one intends to recount, from among the things heard in the course of the month, something more entertaining, but when one starts writing, it develops that the thing either cannot be recorded or that it is irrelevant, or else that "one shouldn't tell everything one knows," and, in the long run, there remain only the most pointless subjects. . . .

3

"SEGREGATION"

And yet, I am writing about "things which I have seen, heard and read." It is fortunate that I did not bind myself with the promise to write *about everything* which "I have seen, heard and read." And, in truth, I hear strange things mostly. How is one to recount them if everything, of its own accord, drifts asunder and stubbornly refuses to shape itself into one bundle! Verily, I keep thinking that we have reached an epoch of some universal "segregation." Everybody segregates himself, keeps aloof from others; everybody seeks to invent something of his own, something new—never before heard of. Everybody sets aside all that which formerly used to be shared in common—in ideas and sentiments—and begins with his own thoughts and feelings. Everybody strives to start from the beginning. Former ties are being severed without regret and everybody acts by himself, and in this alone does he find consolation. If he doesn't act, he wishes he could act. True, a great many people are not starting anything and never will start; even so, they are detached; they stand apart, staring at the empty spot and idly waiting for something. We all are awaiting something. Meanwhile, in almost nothing is there moral accord: everything has been, or is being, broken up, and not even into groups but into units, and—what is more important—sometimes with the easiest and most satisfied air.

Take our contemporaneous belles-lettrist—I mean, one of the new ones. He embarks upon his profession and refuses to know anything of the past; he acts on his own behalf and all by himself. He preaches new things, unhesitatingly setting forth the ideal of the new word and of the new man. He is unfamiliar with either European literature or with that of his own country. Not only has he not read Pushkin and Turgenev but, truly, he has hardly read his own writers, *i.e.*, Bielinsky and Dobroliubov. He depicts new heroes and new women, and their whole novelty boils down to the fact that they take their tenth step, forgetting the first nine —thus, suddenly, finding themselves in a situation as false as can be conceived—and they perish for the edification and seduction of the reader. The whole edification is limited to this falsehood of the situation. In all this there is very little that is new; on the contrary, there is a great deal of shabby, old rubbish. But this is not the entire point: the point is that the author is firmly convinced that he has uttered a new word; that he stands by himself; that he has segregated himself—and, of course, he is very pleased. True, this is a trifling and old example, but only the other day I heard a story about a new word. There was a certain "nihilist": he denied and suffered, and after many troubles, and even exile, he suddenly discovered a religious feeling in his heart. Now, what do you think he did forthwith? In a jiffy "he went into retirement and segregated himself"; promptly and carefully, he shoved away our Christian faith; he set aside all former things and, without delay, invented his own religion—also a Christian religion, but "his own." He has a wife and children. He does not live with his wife, while the children have been placed with strangers. The other day he ran away to America, most probably with a view to propagating there his new religion.

In a word—everybody by himself, everybody in his own way. Is it possible that they all seek merely to appear original, that they are only pretending?—Not in the least. Now we are living through a truthful, rather than reflective, period. Many people— perhaps a great many of them—actually languish and suffer; they did in truth—and most seriously—sever all their former ties and are *compelled* to begin anew, since no one is offering them any light. And the sages and ringleaders merely cater to them—some of them for fear of the Jews (why not, they argue, let him go to America?—isn't it liberal to run away to America?); others— simply to make money on them. And thus fresh energies perish. I may be told that these are but two or three facts which mean nothing, and that, on the contrary, everything is consolidating itself and uniting even closer than hitherto; that banks, companies and associations are being formed. But, would you really, and in truth, point at this mob of triumphant Jews and Yiddishers who have sprung upon Russia?—Triumphant and enraptured—for in our day there have appeared even enraptured Jews of Hebrew and Orthodox faiths. And imagine, even about them, it is stated in our newspapers that they go into retirement and that, for instance, the foreign press is making great fun of the conventions of representatives of our Russian agricultural banks, on account of "the secret meetings of the first two conventions, asking not without irony: how and by what right have the Russian agricultural credit institutions the nerve to expect to gain public confidence if they, at secret meetings held behind the Chinese wall which carefully protects them, are concealing everything from the public, thereby hinting to it that, in fact, something suspicious is taking place. . . ."

So that even these gentlemen segregate and closet themselves, devising something all their own, in their own fashion and not as things are being transacted all over the world. However, I interjected my remark about the banks jestingly: this, as yet, is none of my business; I am merely speaking about segregation. How best should I explain my thought? In passing, I may state a few considerations about our corporations and associations, borrowing them from a manuscript—not my own, but one that has been sent to me and which has been published nowhere. The author addresses his provincial opponents:

"You say that the arteli, associations, corporations, co-operatives, commercial, and all other, companies are founded upon the gregarious instinct in man. Defending the Russian artel which, thus far, has been studied too little to make any positive statements about it, we believe that all these corporations, associations, etc.— all these are but unions of certain groups against others, unions founded upon the instinct of self-preservation and generated by the struggle for existence. This opinion of ours is corroborated by the history of the origination of these unions, which were first formed by the poor and the weak against the rich and the strong; subsequently, the latter began to utilize this weapon of their adversaries. Indeed, history undeniably shows that all these unions came into being because of fraternal strife, and they are based not upon the need of intercourse, as you maintain, but upon a feeling of fear for one's existence, or upon the desire for gain, profit, or interest —even at the expense of one's neighbor. And, analyzing the organization of all these offshoots of utilitarianism, we perceive that their principal concern is to establish firm control of everyone over everybody and of everybody over everyone—simply wholesale espionage, from fear that one fellow may cheat the other fellow. All these associations, with their internal control and their external activities envious of everything extraneous, present a perfect parallel with things taking place in the political world, where the mutual relations of the nations are characterized by armed peace, interrupted by bloody conflicts, and their internal life—by an endless strife of the factions. In this connection, how can one speak of communion and love? Is it not because of this fact that all these institutions are so slowly domesticated by us, since we are still living spaciously; that there is still no reason for us to arm ourselves against each other; that we still possess a good deal of affection for, and faith in, each other, and that these feelings prevent us from organizing such a control—such an espionage—against each other as is required when all these associations, commercial co-operatives and similar companies are organized, while, in the case of insufficiency of control, they cannot function and inevitably go on the rocks?

"Shall we lament over these defects of ours compared with our better educated Western neighbors? No, we, at least, perceive in these defects our wealth; we see that in us there still lives, with certain vigor, that feeling of unity without which human societies cannot exist, notwithstanding the fact that this feeling, dwelling in people unconsciously, leads them both to great exploits and, quite often, great vices. Yet he in whom this feeling has not yet been killed, is capable of everything, on condition that it be converted from an unconscious one, from an instinct, into a conscious power which should not toss one hither and thither, by the blind caprice of accident, but be directed by us toward the realization of sensible aims. However, without this feeling of unity, of mutual affection, of intercourse between men, nothing great is conceivable, since society itself is inconceivable."

In other words, you see, the author, perhaps, does not quite damn the associations and corporations, but he merely asserts that their *present-day* fundamental principle is confined to nothing but utilitarianism plus espionage, and that is in no sense the *communion of men*. All this is youthful, fresh, theoretical, impractical, but, in principle, it is quite correct, and is expressed not only sincerely but with suffering and compassion. And, note a general trait: our whole problem resolves itself into the first step—to practice—whereas everybody, to the last man, is shouting and busying himself about principles; and practice, willy-nilly, has slipped into the hands of Jews alone.

The history of the manuscript from which I took the above excerpt is as follows: its distinguished author (only I don't know if he is a young man or one of those young old men) published a short sketch in some provincial periodical, the editor of which—having given space to that sketch—also printed a note of reservation, partly disagreeing with the author. Thereupon, when the latter, in refutation of the editor's note, wrote a whole article—not too long, however—the editorial office refused to print it, under the pretext that "it is more a sermon than an article." The author then wrote me a letter, and mailed the manuscript and asked me to read it, think it over and express my opinion of it in my *Diary*. First, I wish to thank him for his confidence in my opinion, and, second—for the article, since it gave me great pleasure: rarely have I read anything more *logical*. And even though I am unable to print the article *in toto*, nevertheless I made the above excerpt with an intent which I shall not conceal: the point is that in the author, who advocates genuine communion of men, I also perceived an extraordinarily "segregated" diapason in a certain sense—specifically, in those portions of the manuscript which I do not risk quoting; it is so segregated that one seldom finds anything like it. Thus, not only the article but the author himself, as it were, corroborates my idea about the "segregation" of units and the extreme, so to speak, chemical decomposition of our society into its component parts, which has occurred suddenly in our time.

I may add, however, that if nowadays everybody is "on his own and by himself," still one is not without a link with the past. On the contrary, such a link must exist, even though everything would seem scattered and out of tune with everything else, and it is most interesting to trace this link. In a word, I admit: this is an old simile—our Russian educated society reminds one of that antiquated bundle of twigs which is solid only on condition that the twigs are tied together, but just as soon as they are disjoined, the whole bundle falls apart into so many tiny blades which will be scattered by the first gust of wind. Now, it is this bundle that has fallen apart in Russia. Is it not true, however, that our government, throughout the twenty-year period of its reforms, has failed to receive full support on the part of our educated strata?—Isn't it true that the overwhelming majority of our young, fresh and precious elements have gone in some queer direction—into scoffing and threatening segregation—and precisely in order to take all at once the tenth step, forgetting that the tenth step without the preceding nine, *in any event*, must be reduced to a fancy, even if it meant something by itself. The point most to be regretted is that perhaps only one out of a thousand of these apostates has some comprehension of the meaning of this tenth step, while the rest have merely heard the sound of the bells without knowing whence it comes. The result is that a hen has hatched a chatterbox. Have you seen a forest fire during hot summer? How pitiful it is to observe it! What a sad sight! What a mass of precious material perishes in vain! How much energy, fire and warmth is absorbed to no purpose, uselessly, without leaving any trace.

4

Meditations about Europe

"And in Europe—why, everywhere—isn't it the same? Haven't all these cohesive forces, which we had so trusted, been converted into a sad mirage? Isn't their decomposition and segregation even worse than ours?" These are questions which cannot be evaded by a Russian. Besides, what true Russian doesn't think first about Europe?

Quite so, judging by appearances, there, perhaps, things are worse than at home; only the historical causality of the segregations is more obvious; but, maybe, this is all the more cheerless. Precisely in the fact that at home it is most difficult to trace any reasonable cause and to pick up all the loose ends of our torn threads—precisely in this fact there is some consolation for us: at length it will be ascertained that the dissipation of energy is immature, altogether insensate, half-artificial, and, maybe, an accord will be agreed upon. So there still is hope that the bundle will again be rejoined. But over there, in Europe, no bundle will ever be tied together; there, everything has become segregated in a manner different from ours—maturely, clearly and with precision; there, groups and units are living their last days, and they themselves are aware of it; yet they refuse to cede anything, one to the other; they would rather die than yield.

By the way, at home everybody is talking peace. Everybody predicts lasting peace; everywhere, clear horizons, alliances and new energies are being discerned. Even in the fact that in Paris a republic has been established, people perceive peace; moreover, even in the fact that that republic has been established by Bismarck—even in this, people perceive peace. In the accord of the great Oriental powers people unhesitatingly see great pledges for peace, while some of our newspapers begin to observe even in the present Herzegovina disturbance unmistakable symptoms of the stability of European peace, instead of their former apprehension. By the way, is it not because the key to the Herzegovina problem also turned up in Berlin, and also in Prince Bismarck's casket? But at home it is the French Republic that cheers us most. In passing, why does France continue to occupy the front place in Europe despite victorious Berlin? To this day, the most insignificant happening in France arouses in Europe more sympathy and attention than any important Berlin event. It is unquestionably because that country has been invariably the land of the first step, the first test, the first ideational initiative. This is why thence everybody also firmly expects "the beginning of the end." Who, but France—before anyone else—will take this fatal and ultimate stride?

This is, perhaps, the reason why yonder, in that "progressive" country, there has appeared the maximum number of the most irreconcilable "segregations." Peace "to the very finish" is altogether impossible there. Acclaiming the republic, everybody in Europe has been asserting that it is needed by both France and Europe by the fact alone that only its existence will render the "revanche" war with Germany impossible, and that the republic alone—among all the governments that have been only recently claiming power in France—will neither risk nor desire it. And yet all this is a mirage: the republic has been proclaimed precisely for the purpose of war, if not with Germany, then with a still more dangerous adversary, an adversary and enemy of the whole of Europe—communism. And now, with the republic, this adversary will rise sooner than under any other form of government! Every other government would have compromised with it, and would thereby have postponed the denouement, whereas the republic will make no concession to it and will even provoke the combat, and will be first to compel the enemy to engage in it. Thus, let people not maintain that "the republic is peace."

Indeed, who was it this time that proclaimed the republic? —All bourgeois and small proprietors. Since when have they become such staunch republicans? And didn't they fear the republic more than anything, perceiving in it nothing but chaos and the one step toward communism dreaded by them?—The Convention, at the time of the first Revolution, split up the large estates of the emigrants and of the Church into small lots and started selling them because of the continual financial crisis of those days. This measure had enriched the overwhelming majority of the French and it enabled them, eighty years later, to pay the five-billion contribution, almost without a frown. But, having enhanced temporary prosperity, this measure for many long years paralyzed democratic aspirations by excessively increasing the army of proprietors and by surrendering France to the boundless sovereign power of the bourgeoisie—the outstanding foe of the demos. Without this measure the bourgeoisie, having replaced her former masters, the nobility, would under no circumstances have retained power in France. But as a result of this, the demos became irreconcilably enraged: the bourgeoisie itself distorted the natural course of democratic tendencies, converting it into a thirst for vengeance and hate. The segregation of the parties has assumed such proportions that the state organism has been utterly demolished, beyond any possibility of repair. If France continues to stand, as if it were intact, this is solely due to that law of nature on the strength of which even a handful of snow cannot thaw prior to a determined time. It is this phantom of wholeness that the unhappy bourgeois—and with them a multitude of naïve people in Europe—continue to treat as a living force of the organism, deceiving themselves with hope and at the same time trembling from fear and hatred. But, essentially, communion has vanished completely. Oligarchs are thinking only about the interests of the rich; democracy is thinking only about the interests of the poor—but the commonweal, the good of all people and the future of France as a whole—is at present nobody's concern there, save that of socialistic and positivistic dreamers boosting science and expecting everything from it, that is, a new communion of men and new principles on which the social organism should be founded—for once, mathematically secure and immovable principles. However, science, from which so much is expected, is hardly in a position to tackle this task forthwith. It is difficult to conceive that it should possess such a thorough knowledge of human nature as to devise unmistakably new laws for the social organism. Since, however, this problem cannot be held in suspense and in a state of oscillation, there naturally arises the question: is science ready for this particular task *forthwith*, even if in its future development this task be not exceeding the efficacy of science? (For the present we shall refrain from asserting that this problem unquestionably surpasses the efficacy of human science, even in its combined future development.) Inasmuch as science undoubtedly will refuse to heed such an appeal, it is clear that the whole movement of the demos is now ruled in France (and also in the whole world) by mere dreamers, and the dreamers—by all sorts of speculators. Besides, aren't there dreamers in science itself? True, the dreamers have captured the movement with full right since they alone in all France concern themselves with the communion of all people and with the future; for this reason, succession in France, as it were, on moral grounds passes unto them, notwithstanding their apparent weakness and fantasticality. This is being felt by everybody. But the most dreadful thing in this connection is the fact that, aside from everything fantastic, there developed a most cruel and inhuman tendency which is by no means fantastic, but, indeed, quite real and historically inevitable. It is fully expressed in the saying: *"Ôte-toi de là, que je m'y mette!"* ("Get out of there, so that I may place myself in your stead.") To the millions of the demos—save for all too rare exceptions—the plunder of property-owners is the principal object, the crown of all desires. Yet one cannot blame the paupers: the oligarchs themselves have kept them in ignorance to such an extent that, save for insignificant exceptions, all these millions of wretched and blind people, no doubt, actually and most naïvely believe that they will enrich themselves precisely as a result of this robbery, and that the whole social idea, which their ringleaders preach to them, consists exactly of this. Besides, how can they understand their ringleader-dreamers or any of their prophecies about science? Nevertheless, they will unquestionably be victorious and, if the rich do not yield in good time, dreadful things will ensue. But nobody is going to yield in good time—maybe, because the time for concessions is over. Nor will the paupers themselves desire them; they would reject any accord even if they were given everything; they would keep thinking that they were being misled and cheated. They wish to take the law into their own hands.

The Bonapartes held their ground only because they held out the promise of a possible compromise with the paupers; they even made microscopical efforts—however, invariably treacherous and insincere—to this end. But the oligarchs lost their faith in these efforts; nor does the demos believe them even a bit.

As for the government of the kings (the senior line), essentially, these can offer the proletarians, as a means of salvation, nothing but the Roman Catholic faith, which not only the demos, but likewise the overwhelming majority in France, has long forgotten and does not wish to know. It is rumored that, of late, among proletarians—at least, in Paris—spiritism has been spreading with extraordinary vehemence. The junior Orleans line of the kings is hated by the bourgeoisie itself, even though for a time that dynasty was considered, as it were, the natural leader of the French property-owners. But their ineptness became obvious to everybody. Nevertheless, the proprietors had to save themselves; they were faced with the necessity, by all means and as quickly as possible, to pick a leader for the great and last battle with the dreadful future enemy. This time, reason and instinct whispered to them the right solution, and they chose the republic.

There is a political—perhaps even natural—law which consists in that two powerful and adjacent neighbors, no matter how friendly, always in the long run seek to annihilate each other and, sooner or later, they do succeed in their scheme. (We, Russians, should be giving more thought to this law of strong neighborship.) "It is a direct transition from the red republic to communism." This is the thought which, so far, has been intimidating the French property-owners. And so much time was designed to elapse until suddenly they—the overwhelming majority of them—grasped the fact that the nearest neighbors, by virtue of the mere principle of self-preservation, would become their bitterest enemies. In point of fact, despite the close neighborship of the red republic with communism, what can be more hostile, more radically opposed to communism than a republic, even the bloody republic of '93?—In a republic the republican form of government stands above everything else: *"La république avant tout, avant la France."* The form is the whole hope of the republic: let there be "MacMahonia," instead of France, but let it be called a republic—such is the characteristic of the present "victory" of the republicans in France. Thus, salvation is sought in the form. On the other hand, what does communism care about the republican form if, in substance, it rejects not only every form of government, but the state itself and modern society?

This outright contrast and mutual antithesis of the two opposing forces should have been conceived by the French masses eighty years ago. Finally they did grasp it, and inaugurated the republic: and, at length, they confronted the enemy with the most dangerous and most natural adversary. The republic, after making its transition to communism, under no circumstance will agree to annihilate itself. Essentially, a republic is the most natural expression and form of the bourgeois idea; besides, the French bourgeoisie *in toto* is a child of the republic; it was begotten and organized exclusively by the republic, at the time of the first Revolution. Thus, ultimate segregation was achieved.

It might be said that war is still remote. Hardly is it so remote. Perhaps it is better not to seek postponement of the denouement. Even now, socialism has corroded Europe, while by that time it will finally have undermined her. Prince Bismarck is aware of this, but in a too German-like fashion he relies on blood and iron. But what can one accomplish with blood and iron in a situation such as this? . . .

5

DEAD FORCE AND FUTURE FORCES

It might be argued: still, at present, there isn't the slightest ground for alarm; everything is clear; everything looks bright: in France—"MacMahonia"; in the East—the concord of the powers; military budgets are swelling excessively everywhere—isn't this peace?

But the Pope? Today or tomorrow he will die—then what? Is it conceivable that Roman Catholicism will consent to die with him for company's sake?—Oh, never did it thirst to live so intensely as at present! However, can our prophets do otherwise than scoff at the Pope? We haven't even raised the question of the Pope; it has simply been reduced to naught. And yet this is an all too enormous "segregation," replete with boundless and incongruent aspirations to agree to renounce it for the sake of universal peace. And for what, for whose gratification should it be renounced?— For the sake of humankind? Why, it has long considered itself above mankind as a whole. So far, it has been plotting only with those possessing mundane power and has been relying upon them to the last moment. But that time is over, it seems, forever, and Roman Catholicism will unquestionably forsake the earthly potentates who, in truth, have long ago betrayed it and instigated in Europe a universal baiting campaign whose organization is at present fully completed. Why, Roman Catholicism is known to have made even sharper turns: once upon a time, when this was necessary, it did not hesitate to sell Christ in exchange for mundane power. Having proclaimed the dogma that "Christianity cannot survive on earth without the earthly power of the Pope," it thereby has proclaimed a new Christ, not like the former one, but one who has been seduced by the third temptation of the devil—the temptation of the kingdoms of the world: "All these things will I give thee if thou wilt fall down and worship me!"

Oh, I have heard ardent refutations of this thought: I have been told that faith and the image of Christ up to the present continue to dwell in the hearts of many Catholics in all their original truth and purity. This is unquestionably true, but the main wellspring has been made muddy and has been befouled forever. Besides, Rome has only too recently proclaimed its assent to the third temptation of the devil in the form of a solid dogma, and for this reason, as yet, we have had no time to discern all the direct consequences of this momentous decision. It is noteworthy that the promulgation of this dogma, this revelation of "the whole secret," took place precisely at that moment when united Italy was already knocking at the gates of Rome. In Russia, in those days, many people used to joke: "angry, but weak . . ." Only hardly is he weak. No, such men, capable of such decisions and turns, cannot die without fighting. There might be the objection that thus it has always been in Catholicism, at least that it was implied, so that, essentially, no revolution has occurred. Quite; but there always has been a secret: during many centuries the Popes have been pretending that they were satisfied with their tiny dominion—the Papal State; but all this was for the sake of mere allegory; still, the important point is that in this allegory there was always hidden the kernel of the main idea, coupled with the indubitable and per-

petual hope of papacy that in the future the kernel would grow
into a grand tree which would shade the whole world. And now,
at the very final moment, when the last acre of his earthly dominion
was to be taken away from him, the lord of Catholicism, seeing
his approaching death, suddenly arose and proclaimed *urbi et orbi*
the whole truth about himself: "So you thought that I was satisfied
with the mere title of King of the Papal State? Know that I have
ever considered myself potentate of the whole world and over all
earthly kings, and not only their spiritual, but their mundane,
genuine master, sovereign and emperor. It is I who am king over
all kings and sovereign over all sovereigns, and to me alone on
earth belong the destinies, the ages and the bounds of time. And
now I am proclaiming this in the dogma of my infallibility."—Nay,
in this there is power; this is solemn and not funny; this is the
resurrection of the ancient Roman idea of world dominion and
unity, which never did die in Roman Catholicism; this is the
Rome of Julian the Apostate, but not of him who had been conquered, but, as it were, of Christ triumphant in the new and final
battle. Thus, the sale of the true Christ in exchange for the kingdoms of the world has been consummated.

And in Roman Catholicism it will be actually consummated
and brought to an end. I repeat: this dreadful army is equipped
with too sharp eyes not to discern, finally, where at present lies
the real power upon which it may lean. Having lost its allies—
the kings—Catholicism, no doubt, will rush to the demos. It has
at its disposal tens of thousands of tempters, profoundly wise and
adroit heart-readers and psychologists, dialecticians and confessors
of faith, while the people everywhere are straightforward and kind.
Besides, in France—and nowadays also in many other parts of
Europe—even though the people hate religion and despise it, nevertheless they have no knowledge whatever of the Gospel—at least in
France. All these heart-readers and psychologists will rush to the
people and will bring to them their new Christ, the one who has
acceded to everything and who has been proclaimed at the last
impious *sobor* in Rome. "Why, friends and brethren"—they will
say—"everything you are busying yourselves about—all this we have
had in store for you in this book for a long time—all this has been
stolen from us by your ringleaders. If, thus far, we have talked
to you a little differently, it is only because up to the present you
were like little children, and it was too early for you to learn
the truth; but now the time has come for your truth, too. Know
that the Pope holds the keys of Saint Peter, and that faith in God
is but faith in the Pope who has been instituted on earth for you
by God Himself in His stead. He is infallible, and Divine power

has been conferred upon him, and he is the sovereign of ages and bounds of time. He has decided that your term, too, is now due. In days past the main force of faith consisted of humility, but now humility must come to an end, and the Pope has the authority to abrogate it, since he possesses the full power. Yes, you are all brethren, and Christ Himself has ordained that all be brethren; if, however, your elder brothers refuse to accept you as brethren, arm yourselves with sticks and enter their houses and compel them to become your brethren by force. Christ has long waited for your corrupt elder brothers to repent, and now He grants you His own permission to proclaim: *'Fraternité ou la mort!'* ('Be my brother or else death to you!') Should your brother refuse to share with you his property, half and half, take it all away from him, since Christ has long waited for his repentance, but now the time for wrath and vengeance has come. You should also know that you are innocent of all your former and future sins because all your sins have been caused merely by your poverty. And if this has already been announced to you by your former ringleaders and teachers, you should know that even though they spoke the truth to you, they had no authority to announce it prematurely, since this authority is possessed only by the Pope from God Himself. And the proof of it is in the fact that your teachers have led you to nothing sensible—merely to executions and the worst calamities, and each one of their undertakings collapsed of its own accord. Besides, they have all been cheating, in order to appear stronger, relying upon you, and afterwards selling themselves at a higher price to your enemies. But the Pope will not sell you because there is no one stronger than he, and he is the foremost among the first. You must believe only—not in God—but only in the Pope and that he alone is the earthly king, while all others shall perish because their time has come. So rejoice now and be exceeding glad, since the earthly paradise has now been established: you shall all become rich and, through wealth, righteous because all your desires shall be satisfied, and every cause of evil will be thus eliminated."

These are flattering words but the demos, no doubt, will accept the offer: they will discern in the unexpected ally a great consolidating force acceding to everything and hindering nothing, a real and historical force in lieu of ringleaders, dreamers and speculators in whose practical ability—and, at times, honesty—they often do not believe even in our day. Here the point of the application of force is suddenly provided, and the lever is put into their hands; it suffices that the whole mass press upon it and turn it. And aren't the people capable of turning it? Aren't they the mass? Besides, on top of it, once more they are provided with faith and thereby

many a heart will be assuaged, since many among them have long
felt anguish without God. . . .

On one occasion I have already discussed all these things,
but merely in passing, in a novel. Let people excuse my self-reliance, but I am convinced that, in this or that form, all this will
come to pass in Western Europe, *i.e.*, that Catholicism will thrust
itself into democracy, into the people, and will forsake the earthly
kings because they, on their part, forsook it. All public authorities
in Europe despise it, since now it seems so destitute and crushed;
still they do not picture it to themselves in so comic an appearance
and state as it is being naïvely conceived by our political publicists.
However, Bismarck, for example, would not have persecuted Catholicism so strongly if he had not sensed in it a dreadful, proximate
enemy in no distant future. Prince Bismarck is too proud a man
to waste in vain so much energy on a comically impotent foe. Yet
the Pope is stronger than he. I repeat: in our day papacy is, perhaps, the most dreadful among all "segregations" threatening universal peace. And the world is threatened by many a thing: at no
time in the past has Europe been loaded with such elements of
ill-will as at present. It seems that everything is undermined and
loaded with powder, and is just waiting for the first spark. . . .

"And what's this to us? All this is there, in Europe, and
not at home!"—Well, it is our concern because Europe will be
knocking at our door, crying for help and urging us to save her
when the last hour of her "present order of things" strikes. And
she will demand our help, as it were, by right; she will demand
it with a challenge, commandingly. She is going to tell us that we
too are Europe; that, consequently, we have exactly the same "order
of things" as she; that not in vain have we imitated her during two
hundred years, boasting that we were Europeans, and that by saving her, we are thereby saving ourselves. Of course, perhaps we
might not be disposed to settle the matter exclusively in favor
of one party; but should we be equal to such a task, and haven't
we long ago lost the habit of all reasoning on the question as to
what is our real "segregation" as a nation and what is our genuine
role in Europe? Nowadays, not only do we fail to comprehend
such things, but we even do not admit such questions and we consider it folly and backwardness to listen to them. And should Europe
actually knock at our door, urging us to get up and march to save
her *l'Ordre,* then, perhaps, for the first time, all of us would grasp
at once to what extent all the while we did not resemble Europe,
despite our two-hundred-year craving for, and dreams about, becoming Europe—dreams which used to reach the proportions of

passionate fits. But even then, perhaps, we would not grasp it, since it would be too late. And, if so, we should naturally fail to understand what Europe would be expecting and soliciting from us, and how, actually, we could help her. And, on the contrary, should we not, maybe, march to subdue the enemy of Europe and of her order with the same iron and blood as even Prince Bismarck did? Oh, well, in the event of such an exploit, we could boldly congratulate ourselves upon being *thorough Europeans.*

But all this is the future! All these are such fancies! But the present is so bright, so bright!

CHAPTER II

1

Don Carlos and Sir Watkin. Again, Symptoms of "the Beginning of the End."

I HAVE READ with great interest about Don Carlos' entry into England. People are wont to say that reality is weary and monotonous; to distract themselves they resort to art, to imagination and to the reading of romances. To me, on the contrary, what can be more fantastic, more unpredictable than reality? Even, at times, what can be more incredible than reality? Never can a novelist conceive such impossibilities as reality offers us daily by the thousands in the guise of most ordinary things. Sometimes even no imagination is capable of inventing them. And what an advantage compared with fiction! Try to *invent* in a novel an episode such as, for instance, happened to attorney-at-law Kupernik; fabricate it yourself, and next Sunday a critic, in his feuilleton, will prove to you clearly and irrefutably that you are in a state of delirium; that in reality this never did take place, and—this is the main point—that it never could occur on this and that ground. In the long run you will agree, with shame. However, an issue of *The Voice* is brought to you. Unexpectedly, you read in it a full account about our sharpshooter—and what?—At first, you read with surprise, with the greatest astonishment—so great that while you are reading you refuse to believe anyone. But just as soon as you have read to the last dot, you put the paper aside and, suddenly, without knowing the reason why, you boldly say to yourself: "Yes, all this must have happened exactly this way." And some people may even add: "I forboded it!" Why such a difference in the impressions one derives from a newspaper and from fiction? I don't know, but such is the privilege of reality.

Don Carlos quietly and solemnly enters into England as her guest, after the blood and slaughter in the name of "King, Faith and the Madonna"; here is another figure, one more "segregation"! Now, is it possible for one to invent such a thing! Apropos, do you remember the episode—two years ago—of Count Chambord (Henry V)? He is also a King, a legitimist, and he was also claiming his throne in France, at the very same time when Don Carlos was claiming his—in Spain. They may even be considered relatives: they belong to one and the same family, to the same branch—but what a contrast! One—firmly wrapped up in his convictions—a melancholic, elegant and humane figure. At the most fatal moment, when he could have actually become king (of course, for an instant only!), Count Chambord was tempted by nothing; he did not surrender his "white banner," thereby proving that he was a magnanimous and true knight, almost a Don Quixote, an ancient chevalier with the vow of chastity and poverty, a figure worthy of bringing to a close his ancient lineage of kings. (It seems solemn, and only, maybe, a little funny, but without comicality there is no life.) He renounced power and the throne solely because he sought to become King of France, not merely for his personal benefit, but for the salvation of France; and inasmuch as her salvation, in his opinion, was incompatible with the concessions which were demanded from him (quite feasible concessions), he refused to assume power. What a contrast with the recent Napoleon, the swindler and proletarian, promising everything, surrendering everything and cheating everybody only to attain power!

I have just paralleled Count Chambord with Don Quixote, but I know not any greater praise. Who was it—Heine, was it not? —who recounted how, as a boy, he had burst into tears when, reading *Don Quixote,* he had reached the place where the hero was conquered by the despicable and common-sense barber-surgeon Samson Carasco. In the whole world there is no deeper, no mightier literary work. This is, so far, the last and greatest expression of human thought; this is the bitterest irony which man was capable of conceiving. And if the world were to come to an end, and people were asked there, somewhere: "Did you understand your life on earth, and what conclusion have you drawn from it?"—man could silently hand over *Don Quixote:* "Such is my inference from life.— Can you condemn me for it?" I am not asserting that man would be right in stating so, but . . .

Don Carlos is a relative of Count Chambord; he is also a

knight, but in that knight the Great Inquisitor may be perceived. He has shed rivers of blood *ad majorem gloriam Dei* and in the name of the Mother of God, the benign supplicant on man's behalf, "the ardent intercessor and assistant," as our people call Her. To him, much as to Count Chambord, proposals were made and he, too, had rejected them. This, if I am not mistaken, took place shortly after Bilbao and immediately after his great victory, when, during the battle, the commander-in-chief of the Madrid army lost his life. At that time emissaries were sent to him from Madrid: "What would he say if he were let into Madrid? And would he not outline some little program with a view to opening negotiations?" But he haughtily declined the very thought of negotiations —and, of course, not from mere pride, but also because of the principle deeply rooted in his soul: he could not recognize those who had sent emissaries as belligerents, and he, the "King," could not enter into any agreements with "the revolution"! Tersely, by a mere inkling, but clearly, he let it be known that "the King himself knows what he shall have to do when he reaches his capital," and to this he added nothing. Of course, people promptly turned their backs on him, and shortly after that they summoned King Alfonso. The favorable moment was lost, but he continued to wage the war; he kept writing manifestoes in a stately and high-flown style; and he was the first fully to believe in them; haughtily and majestically he kept shooting his generals for "treason" and subduing the rebellions of his tired-out soldiers. And in all justice to him as a warrior it should be said that he had fought to the very last inch of his soil. At present, when departing from France to England, he announced to his French friends, in a gloomy and haughty epistle, "that he was pleased with their services and support; that by serving him, they have been serving themselves, and that he was ever ready to draw his sword in answer to an appeal of his unhappy country." Don't you worry: he will appear again. Apropos, this letter to "friends" throws a little light on the riddle: with what means and with whose money did this horrible man (they say he's young and handsome) wage the war so long and so relentlessly?—Apparently these friends are both numerous and strong. Who could they be?—Most likely he got the greatest support from the Catholic Church because he was its last hope in kings. Otherwise, no friends could have raised so many millions for him.

Please note that this man who had so haughtily and sharply rejected any compromise with "the revolution," went to England, and he knew perfectly well that he should go to seek hospitality in that free-minded and liberal country—revolutionary according to

his way of thinking. Indeed, what a compatability of conceptions!
And at the time of his arrival in England an insignificant but characteristic episode occurred to him. He took a boat in Boulogne, to
disembark at Folkestone. However, on the same boat there were
sailing to England, also as guests, members of the Boulogne mu-
nicipality, who had been invited by the English for the peaceful
celebration of the inauguration of a new railroad station at Folkestone. On the English shore a crowd of English people—authorities,
smartly dressed ladies, guilds and delegations of various societies,
with banners and bands—were assembled to greet these guests,
among whom there was also a deputy from the department of Pas
de Calais. There happened to be there a member of Parliament,
Sir Edward Watkin, accompanied by two other members of Parliament. Having learned that among the landing passengers was Don
Carlos, he promptly went to him to introduce himself and to pay
him homage. With the utmost politeness he led him to the station
and placed him in a private compartment of a car. But the rest
of the public was not as polite: as Don Carlos was proceeding to
the station and boarding the train, sounds of whistling and hissing
broke out. Such behavior on the part of his compatriots greatly
shocked Sir Edward. However, he personally described the incident
in a newspaper, toning down as much as possible the rude reception
of the "guest." He stated that a mere accident was responsible
for the whole episode; otherwise, it would have turned out differently. "At the time"—he tells us—"when we were approaching
the platform and Don Carlos lifted his hat in acknowledgment of
the acclamations of several persons greeting him, the wind unfurled
the banner of the Odd Fellows association, and on the banner there
appeared the picture of Mercy protecting children with the motto:
'Do not forget widows and orphans!' The effect was spontaneous
and extraordinary: grumbling broke out in the crowd, but it signified sorrow rather than outbursts of anger. Even though I regret
the incident, nevertheless I must say that no people, assembled for
a jolly celebration and suddenly being placed face to face with the
leading actor in a bloody, fratricidal war, could have shown greater
politeness than that which was exhibited by the overwhelming majority of the Folkestone public."

What a peculiar viewpoint, what a firmness of one's personal
opinion, and what a jealous pride in one's own people! Perhaps
many of our liberals would regard the conduct of Sir Edward Watkin almost as infamy; as a manifestation of base feelings in ingratiating himself with a famous man; as a trivial, pert show-off.
However, Sir Edward's reasoning differs from ours. Of course, he
himself knew that the newly arrived guest was the leading actor

in a bloody and fratricidal war; but by meeting him he thereby satisfied his patriotic pride and served England to the utmost of his ability. Extending his hand to a blood-stained tyrant, in the name of England, and as a member of Parliament, he told him, as it were: "You are a despot, a tyrant, and yet you came to the land of freedom to seek refuge in it. This could have been expected: England receives everybody and is not afraid to give refuge to anyone: *entreé et sortie libres*. Be welcome." And it was not the mere rudeness of "a small portion of the assembled public" that grieved him, but also the fact that in the unrestraint of the sentiment, in the whistling and hissing, he discerned a *faux pas* against personal dignity which every true Englishman must irrevocably possess. "Let it be considered excellent, there on the Continent, and among mankind at large, when the people do not restrain their insulted feelings and publicly brand the villain with contempt and whistle, even though he be their guest. But all this will do very well for some Parisians and Germans: an Englishman must behave differently. In such moments he must be cool-headed, as a gentleman, and he should not express his opinion. It is far better if the guest learns nothing about what those meeting him think of him. It would have been best if everyone had been standing motionless, crossing his arms behind his back, as befits an Englishman, and staring at the newcomer with a glance full of chilly dignity. Several polite exclamations, but hushed and moderate, would have been of no consequence: the guest would promptly have understood that these were but mere custom and etiquette, and that, essentially, he could have evoked no emotion in anyone, even if he were a genius. And now, since they did start shouting and whistling, the guest may think that this was a senseless street mob, just as on the Continent." Apropos, I recall a rather amusing anecdote, which I have recently read—where and by whom I don't remember—about Marshal Sebastiani and a certain Englishman; this happened in the beginning of the century under Napoleon I. Marshal Sebastiani, then an important personage, wishing to pay his respects to an Englishman—and in those days the English were treated as underdogs because they were waging a continuous and relentless war against Napoleon—after lavishing eulogies upon his nation, said to him with a polite air: "If I were not a Frenchman, I should like to become an Englishman." The Englishman listened but was in no way moved by the compliment, and promptly replied: "And if I were not an Englishman, I should still like to become an Englishman."

Thus, in England all Englishmen equally respect themselves, perhaps solely because they are Englishmen. This alone, it would seem, should prove sufficient for a close bond and the people's communion in that country. And yet, as a matter of fact, even there we see the same as everywhere else in Europe: a passionate craving for living and the loss of the sublime sense of life. Here, I shall cite—as an example of originality—the view of an Englishman on his religion, Protestantism. We must recall that, in their overwhelming majority, the English are extremely religious people: they are thirsting for faith and are continually seeking it. However, instead of religion—notwithstanding the state "Anglican" religion—they are divided into hundreds of sects. Here is what Sydney Dobell says in his recent article, *Thoughts on Art, Philosophy and Religion:*

"Catholicism is (potentially) great, beautiful, wise, powerful, one of the most consistent and congruous constructions man has made; but it is not *educational* and will, therefore, die; nay, must be killed as pernicious in proportion to its excellence.

"Protestantism is narrow, ugly, impudent, unreasonable, inconsistent, incompatible: a babel of logomachy and literalism: a wrangling club of half-thinking pedants, half-taught geniuses, and untaught egotists of every type: the nursery of conceit and fanaticism: the holiday of all the 'fools that rush in.'

"But it is *educational* and therefore it will live; nay, must be fed and housed, cared for and fought for, as the *sine quâ non* of the spiritual life of Man."[1]

What impossible reasoning! And yet, thousands of Europeans are seeking their salvation in similar inferences. In fact, is a society wholesome, in which, seriously and with so great ardor, such inferences as to the spiritual quests of man are being propounded? "Protestantism—you see—is vulgar, ugly, narrow and stupid, but it is *educational,* and therefore it should be conserved and protected!" To begin with—what utilitarianism in a matter such as this and in such a question! The matter to which everything must be subordinate (if Sydney Dobell is actually concerned about *faith*)— this matter is, on the contrary, considered solely from the point of its utility to the Englishman. And, of course, such utilitarianism

---

[1] *Thoughts on Art, Philosophy and Religion* was not an "article," as Dostoievsky calls it, but a posthumous anthology "selected from the unpublished papers of Sidney Dobell with an introductory note by John Nichol, M.A. Oxon, etc." . . . published by Smith, Elder & Co., London, 1876. The paragraphs quoted are an isolated note, "gathered from a chaos of Memoranda—thrown together with no attempt at method and of various date—and arranged under heads," *i.e.,* by Dobell's literary executrix. The above lines appear under the "head" RELIGION, sub-head "Theoretic." It is possible that Dostoievsky found them quoted in some "article" about the book or extracted from the book.

is worthy of that non-educational seclusiveness and finality of Catholicism for which this Protestant damns it so resolutely. And aren't these words akin to those statements of "the profound thinkers among politicians and statesmen" in all countries and nations who, sometimes, utter wise apothegms such as this: "Of course, there is no God, and religion is humbug, but it is needed for the plebs, because without it they could not be restrained." The difference, perhaps, comes down to the fact that this dictum of the wise statesman is, essentially, based upon cold and cruel depravity, whereas Sydney Dobell is a friend of humanity and busies himself merely about its immediate interest. However, his view on utility is precious: the whole utility—don't you see?—consists in the fact that the gate is thrown wide open to every judgment and every inference; to and from one's mind and heart—*entrée et sortie libres;* nothing is kept under lock, nothing is protected; nothing brought to an end. Swim in a boundless sea and save thyself as thou pleasest. Besides, the judgment is a broad one, very broad like that boundless sea, and, of course, "in its waves there's nothing one can see"; as against this—it is a national judgment. Oh, here we are met with profound sincerity; yet, isn't it true that this sincerity borders, as it were, on despair? Here also the method of reasoning is characteristic; the things people over there are thinking and writing about are characteristic. Now, would our publicists, for instance, write and concern themselves about these fantastic subjects and, besides, place them on so high a plane? So that it may even be said that we, Russians, are people possessing a far more realistic, profound and prudent view than all those Englishmen. But the English are not ashamed of their convictions or of our opinion of them: in their extraordinary sincerity one perceives, at times, even something pathetically touching.

Here, for instance, is what an observer who keeps a keen eye on these things in Europe, told me about the character of certain altogether atheistic doctrines and sects in England: "You enter into a church: the service is magnificent, the vestments are expensive; censers; solemnity; silence; reverence among those praying. The Bible is read; everybody comes forth and kisses the Holy Book with tears in his eyes, and with affection. And what do you think this is? This is the church of atheists. Why, then, do they kiss the Bible, reverently listening to the reading from it and shedding tears over it?—This is because, having rejected God, they began to worship 'Humanity.' Now they believe in Humanity; they deify and adore it. And what, over long centuries, has been more sacred to mankind than this Holy Book?—Now they worship it because of its love of mankind and for the love of it on the

part of mankind; it has benefited mankind during so many centuries—just like the sun, it has illuminated it; it has poured out on
mankind its force, its life. And 'even though its sense is now lost,'
yet loving and adoring mankind, they deem it impossible to be
ungrateful and to forget the favors bestowed by it upon humanity. . . ."

In this there is much that is touching and also much enthusiasm. Here there is actual deification of humankind and a
passionate urge to reveal their love. Still, what a thirst for prayer,
for worship; what a craving for God and faith among these atheists,
and how much despair and sorrow; what a funeral procession in lieu
of a live, serene life, with its gushing spring of youth, force and
hope! But whether it is a funeral or a new and coming force—to
many people this is a question.

I take the liberty of quoting here a passage from my recent
novel *A Raw Youth*. Only recently have I learned about this
"Church of Atheists"—a long time after I had finished and published
my novel. I am also speaking of atheism; but this is but a dream
of a Russian of our times—the Forties—a former landowner, a
progressive, a passionate and noble dreamer, side by side with our
Great Russian breadth of life in practice. This landowner also has
no faith and he, too, adores humanity "as it befits a Russian progressive individual." He reveals his dream about future mankind
when there will vanish from it every conception of God, which, in
his judgment, will inevitably happen on earth.

"I picture to myself, my dear"—he began, with a pensive
smile—"that the battle is over and that the strife has calmed down.
After maledictions, lumps of mud and whistles, lull has descended
and men have found themselves *alone*, as they wished it; the former
great idea has abandoned them; the great wellspring of energy,
that has thus far nourished them, has begun to recede as a lofty,
inviting Sun, but this, as it were, was mankind's last day. And
suddenly men grasped that they had been left all alone, and forthwith they were seized with a feeling of great orphanhood. My dear
boy, never was I able to picture people as having grown ungrateful
and stupid. Orphaned men would at once begin to draw themselves
together closer and with more affection; they would grasp each
other's hands, realizing that now they alone constituted everything
to one another. The grand idea of immortality would also vanish,
and it would become necessary to replace it, and all the immense
over-abundance of love for Him who, indeed, had been Immortality,
would in every man be focussed on nature, on the universe, on
men, on every particle of matter. They would start loving the earth
and life irresistibly, in the measure of the gradual realization of

their transiency and finality, and theirs would now be a different love—not like the one in days gone by. They would discern and discover in nature such phenomena and mysteries as had never heretofore been suspected, since they would behold nature with new eyes, with the look of a lover gazing upon his inamorata. They would be waking up and hastening to embrace one another, hastening to love, comprehending that days are short and that this is all that is left to them. They would be laboring one for another, and every man would be surrendering to all men all he possessed, and this alone would make him happy. Every child would know and feel that everyone on earth is his father and his mother. 'Let tomorrow be my last day'—everyone would think, looking at the setting sun—'but all the same, I shall die, yet they all will remain, and after them, their children'—and this thought that they will remain, as ever loving and palpitating, would replace the thought of the reunion beyond the grave. Oh, they would be losing no time to love, so as to quench the great sorrow in their hearts. They would be proud and bold on their own behalf, but they would be timid on each other's behalf; everyone would be trembling for the life and happiness of every man. They would grow tender toward one another and would not be ashamed of this, as at present, and they would fondle each other, even as children. Meeting one another they would be beholding each other with a deep and meaningful look, and in that look there would be love and sorrow. . . ."

Isn't there here, in this fantasy, something akin to that actually existent "Atheists' Church"?

2

LORD REDSTOCK

By the way—speaking of these sects. It is rumored that just at this moment Lord Redstock is in Petersburg—the same one who some three years ago had been preaching here all winter and also had founded something on the order of a new sect. At that time I happened to hear him preaching in a certain "hall," and, as I recall, I found nothing startling; he spoke neither particularly cleverly nor in a particularly dull manner. And yet he performs miracles over human hearts; people are flocking around him; many of them are astounded: they are looking for the poor, in order, as quickly as possible, to bestow benefits upon them; they are almost ready to give away their fortunes. However, maybe, this is only here in Russia; abroad, it would seem, he is not as prominent. On the other hand, it is difficult to assert that the full strength of his charm can be attributed to the fact that he is a lord, an independent man, and that he preaches, so to speak, a "pure," seigniorial religion. True, all these sectarian preachers always destroy, even against their will, the image of faith given by the Church, substituting for it their own image. The present success of Lord Redstock is based, essentially, solely on "our segregation" —our detachment from our own soil, from the nation. It appears that at present we—*i.e.*, the educated strata of our society—are an altogether alien little people, very little, quite insignificant, but a people who have their own customs and their own prejudices, which are taken for originality, and—as it now develops—with a desire for a religion of their own.

Strictly speaking, it is difficult to state of what the teaching of the lord consists. He is an Englishman, but it is rumored that he does not belong to the Anglican Church and that he is severed from it; instead, he is preaching something independent. This is so easy in England: there, as well as in America, there are, perhaps, even more sects than among our "common people." The sects of jumpers, Shakers, convulsionaries, Quakers, awaiting the millennium, and, finally, the Khlysti (a universal and very ancient sect)— why, it's impossible to enumerate all of them. Of course, I am not speaking scoffingly of these sects side by side with Lord Redstock; he who has detached himself from the true Church and contemplates establishing his own, even to all appearances a most respectable one, will of necessity wind up in the same way as these sects. And let the lord's admirers refrain from frowning: in the philosophical essence of these very sects—these tremblers and Khlysti—sometimes there lie concealed very profound and vigorous ideas. It is said that around the Twenties, at the home of Tatarinova, in the Mikhailovsky Castle, alongside with herself and her guests—among them, for example, a Minister of those days—her serf domestics also used to whirl and prophesy. This means that there must have been an impetus of thought and emotion if such an "unnatural" communion of the believers could have arisen; and it would seem that Tatarinova's sect belonged to the Khlysti or to one of their innumerable ramifications. Among the accounts about Lord Redstock I have not heard any suggesting that people attending his meetings were whirling and prophesying (whirling and prophesying is a most essential and most ancient attribute of virtually all these Western sects, and also of our sects—at least, of their overwhelming majority. The Templars, too, used to whirl and prophesy, and for this they were burned at the stake, and subsequently eulogized and praised in song by French thinkers and poets prior to the first Revolution). I have merely heard that Lord Redstock teaches rather peculiarly about the "descent of the blessing," and that, according to one of the informants, "Christ is" in the lord's "pocket" —in other words, that he treats Christ and the felicity quite triflingly. I must confess, however, that I did not understand what was reported about people throwing themselves upon cushions and awaiting some sort of inspiration from above.

Is it true that Lord Redstock is contemplating a trip to Moscow?—It would be desirable that on this occasion no one among our clergy vouch for his sermons. Nevertheless, he does produce extraordinary transformations and inspires in the hearts of his followers magnanimous sentiments. True, this is as it should be: if he is genuinely sincere and preaches a new religion, he must, of course, be inspired with the spirit and zeal of a founder of a sect. I repeat: here we are faced with our lamentable segregation, with the ignorance of the people and our detachment from our nationality, but principally with our poor and negligible knowledge of Orthodoxy. It is remarkable that, with a few exceptions, our press keeps almost silent on Lord Redstock.

3

A Little Word on the Report of the Scientific Committee on Spiritistic Phenomena

Are the spiritists a "segregation"?—I think—yes. Our embryonic spiritism, to my way of thinking, threatens to become in the future an exceedingly dangerous and nasty "segregation." "Segregation," indeed, signifies disunion. It is in this sense that I am saying that in our youthful spiritism one may discern strong elements tending to amplify disunion among the Russians, which is assuming ever more impetuous and progressive proportions. To me, it seems foolish and vexing to read now and then in the writings of our thinkers that our society is asleep, or slumbers idly and apathetically. On the contrary: never in the past has there been noticeable as much restlessness, as much tossing hither and thither, as strong a quest after something upon which one might morally lean, as in our day. Even the most insensible little idea, if it presages the slightest hope for solving something, is sure to meet with undeniable success. And its success is invariably confined to the "segregation" of some new handful of people. This is also true of spiritism. And what a disappoinment it was to read at last in *The Voice* the report of the well-known Committee, about which there has been so much clamor and notoriety, on spiritistic phenomena which have been observed throughout the winter, in the

house of Mr. Aksakov. And I was so anxious and hopeful that
this report would crush and annihilate this profligate (in its mystical meaning), novel doctrine. True, it would seem that in Russia
there are no *doctrines* and that we are still conducting mere "observations." However, is this actually so? It is a pity that just
now I have neither time nor space to expound my thought in more
detail; but in my next, April, *Diary,* I shall, perhaps, venture to
raise again the question concerning the spiritists. Still, maybe, I
am condemning the committee's report unjustifiably: it cannot
be blamed for the fact that I have trusted it so much and that
I have been expecting something impossible from it—something
which, perhaps, it never could have achieved. At any rate, the
Report is faulty in the method of its exposition, in its wording.
The exposition is such as will surely enable the opponents of the
Report to find a "preconceived" attitude toward the matter (and,
consequently, a most unscientific one), even though, perhaps, there
wasn't so much of this "prejudice" as to justify such charges. (Well,
there was a little prejudice; but we cannot really avoid that.)
However, the wording is undoubtedly faulty. For instance, the
Committee ventures to draw conclusions on some spiritistic phenomena (on the materialization of the spirits, for example) which,
according to its own admission, it had not observed at all. True:
it did so, as it were, in the form of a moral, in a moralizing and
admonishing sense, anticipating things in the interest of society,
in order to save light-minded people from seduction. The intent
is a noble one but hardly an opportune one in this particular case.
Well, what of it: is it possible that the committee, composed of
so many learned men, was seriously hoping to quash the silly idea
in its very inception? Alas, had the Committee produced even the
most obvious and direct proofs of "forgeries" and had it caught
and descried the "cheats" in action, so to speak, seizing them by
their arms—which, however, did not happen—even then no person
among those carried away by spiritism, or those who are merely
desirous of being captivated by it, would believe it, owing to that
primordial law of human nature, on the strength of which in mystical ideas even the most precise mathematical proofs mean absolutely nothing. And here, in this embryonic spiritism of ours, I
swear, the mystical idea is the focal point. Well, what are you
going to do about it? Faith and mathematical proofs are two incompatible things. He who makes up his mind to believe in something, can't be stopped. And besides, here, the proofs are far from
being mathematical.

Even so, the *Report* might have been useful. It might unquestionably have been useful to all those not yet corrupted and still

indifferent to spiritism. But now, with the "desire to believe," the desire might be equipped with a new weapon. Besides, the much too contemptible and presumptuous tone of the *Report* should have been soft-pedaled. Verily, when reading it, it may be supposed that the two esteemed parties, for some reason, had engaged in a personal quarrel. On the rank and file, this will bear a reaction unfavorable to the *Report*.

4

Isolated Phenomena

But there comes into existence another class of phenomena, a rather peculiar one, especially among young people. True, as yet, these are but isolated phenomena. Side by side with accounts about several unfortunate young men "going into the thick of the people," stories about an altogether different kind of youth are beginning to circulate. These new young men are also restless; they keep writing letters to you or they come to you in person, with their articles, quests and unexpected ideas; yet they are in no way akin to those whom up to now we have been used to encountering. So that there is definite ground to suppose that among our youth there is originating a movement diametrically opposed to the former one. Well, perhaps, this should have been expected. In point of fact: whose children are they?—They are, precisely, the children of those "liberal" fathers who, at the beginning of Russia's renaissance during the present reign, detached themselves *en masse* from the general cause, imagining that therein lay progress and liberalism. And yet—since all of this is more or less a matter of the past— were there then many true liberals, many who had been really suffering, pure and simple people—like, for instance, Bielinsky, who had then recently died (not to speak of his intellect)? On the contrary, the majority was still made up of a mass of coarse, petty atheists and great scoundrels—in substance, mere extortioners and "petty tyrants," but braggarts of liberalism in which they managed to perceive nothing but a right to infamy. And just think what hasn't been said and asserted; what abominations haven't been set forth under the guise of honor and prowess! In substance, that was a vulgar stream into which an honest idea had been launched. And just then the liberation of the peasants had come, and along with it—the decomposition and "segregation" of our educated society in every conceivable sense. People did not recognize each other, and liberals failed to recognize their kindred liberals. And after that—how many sad misunderstandings and painful disillusions!

The most shameless reactionaries would sometimes suddenly come to the forefront as progressives and leaders, and they met with success. What, then, could children of those days have beheld in their fathers? What reminiscences could they have retained about their childhood and their youth?—Cynicism, scoffing, pitiless assaults on the earliest, tender, holy beliefs of the children; and thereupon— not infrequently—the open debauch of fathers and mothers, with assurances and "instruction" that thus it should be and that these are genuinely "sane relations." To this should be added a great many disintegrated fortunes, and, as a consequence, impatient dis- content, high-strung words screening mere egotistical, petty anger against material reverses. Well, at length, our youth managed to decipher and rationalize all this! And since youth is pure, serene and magnanimous, it may, of course, have happened that some of them refused to follow such fathers and rejected their "sane" in- structions. In this way such a "liberal" upbringing could have caused altogether reverse consequences, at least in certain instances. These, perhaps, are the young men and the raw youths who are now seeking new paths; and they begin with a direct repudiation of that cycle of hateful ideas with which they had been faced in childhood, in the nests of their pitiful parents.

5

ABOUT URIJ SAMARIN

And firm people—men of conviction—are passing away: Urij Samarin died—a most gifted man with unyielding convictions, a most useful worker. There are people who command everybody's respect, even the respect of those who disagree with their ideas. *The New Times* gave a very characteristic story about him. So recently—in the latter part of February—on his way through Peters- burg, Samarin read in the February issue of *The Domestic Records* an article "Black Earth and its Future," by Prince Vasilchikov. It created such an impression upon Samarin that he could not sleep all night. "This is a very good and sound article"—Samarin said to a friend of his in the morning. "I read it last evening, and it produced such an impression upon me that I couldn't sleep: all night I kept visualizing the picture of an arid, woodless desert into which our central black-earth region of Russia was being converted, as a result of a continuous, almost unhampered deforestation."

"Are there many people among us who would lose sleep over worries about their native land?"—adds *The New Times*. I think that such people can still be found, and—who knows?—at present, judging by our alarming situation, more than ever before. We always did have enough worrying people in every conceivable sense —nor are we sleeping as soundly as is being maintained about us. But the point is not that worrying people are plentiful among us, but in the way they reason; and in the person of Urij Samarin we have lost a firm and vigorous thinker—therein is our loss. Elderly men are passing away, while our eyes are being dazzled when we look at the future ones.

APRIL

CHAPTER I

1

Ideals of Vegetative Still Life. Kulaks and Bloodsuckers of Peasants. Higher-Ups Whipping Russia Forward.

IN THE MARCH issue of *The Russian Messenger* of this year there appeared a "criticism" of me by Mr. A., *i.e.*, Mr. Avseenko. There is no advantage in my answering Mr. Avseenko: it is difficult to imagine a writer giving less thought to the things he is putting down on paper. However, even if he had given thought, the result would have been identical. Everything in his article that concerns me is written on the subject that not we, cultured men, should be bowing to the people—since "popular ideals are pre-eminently ideals of vegetative still life"—but, on the contrary, the people should seek enlightenment from us, cultured men, and adopt our ideas and our guise. In a word, Mr. Avseenko was very much displeased with my statements about the people in the February issue of the *Diary*. I believe that this is a mere misunderstanding, for which I myself am to be blamed. This misunderstanding should be cleared up, but it is literally impossible to answer Mr. Avseenko. What can one have in common with a man who suddenly utters the following words about the people: "On their shoulders [*i.e.*, on the people's shoulders], on their patience and self-sacrifice, on their viable strength, ardent faith and magnanimous contempt for their personal interests—Russia's independence has been founded, her strength and fitness for an historical mission. They have preserved the purity of the Christian ideal, a lofty heroism, humble in its grandeur, and those beautiful traits of the Slavic nature which, having been reflected in the vigorous sounds of Pushkin's poetry,

continually thereafter kept feeding the living stream of our litera-
ture. . . ." And no sooner had this been written, that is, rewritten
from the Slavophiles, than Mr. Avseenko states on the very next
page exactly the reverse about the same Russian people: "The
point of the matter is that our people have failed to give us the
ideal of an active personality. All that is beautiful, in our observation of them, and which our literature, to its great honor, accustomed us to love in them, appears merely on the plane of elemental
existence, of a secluded, idyllic [?] mode of living, or of a passive
life. Just as soon as *an active, energetic* personality emerges from
the midst of the people, its fascination usually vanishes, and more
often than not the individuality assumes the unattractive features
of a peasants' bloodsucker, a kulak, a stupidly-willful person. As
yet, there are among the people no active ideals, and to rely upon
them would be equivalent to starting from an unknown, perhaps
an imaginary, quantity." And just think of uttering all this immediately after having declared on the preceding page that "on the
shoulders of the people, on their patience and self-sacrifice, on their
viable strength, ardent faith and magnanimous contempt for their
personal interests Russia's independence has been founded"! But
in order to reveal a viable energy one cannot be *merely* passive!
And in order to build Russia it was impossible not to reveal
strength! In order to reveal *magnanimous* contempt for personal
interests, it was absolutely necessary to reveal magnanimous and
active *vigor* in the interest of others—that is, in common, fraternal
interest. In order to "carry through on one's shoulders" Russia's
independence, one could not have been *passively* sitting in one
place, but it was absolutely essential to get up from one's seat
and to take at least one step—at least, to do something. And yet,
it is promptly added that no sooner do the people begin to do
something than they assume the "unattractive features of a peasants'
bloodsucker, a kulak or a stupidly-willful person." It means, then,
that kulaks, bloodsuckers and stupidly-willful people have carried
Russia through on their shoulders. This means that all these saintly
metropolitans (the people's protectors and the builders of the
Russian state), all our pious princes, all boyards and rural people
who have worked for, and served, Russia to the point of sacrificing
their lives, whose names history has reverently preserved—they all
are mere bloodsuckers, kulaks and stupidly-willful persons! Perhaps, it might be said, Mr. Avseenko speaks not of the former but
of the contemporary ones, and that history is but history, and
that all this has happened under Czar Gorókh. But in this case
would it mean that our people have undergone a radical transformation? And about what contemporary people does Mr. Avseenko

speak? Where does he trace their beginnings?—In Peter's reforms? In the cultural period? In the final establishment of serfdom? But if it be so, the cultured Mr. Avseenko betrays himself: everybody will ask him: what was the use of making you cultured in exchange for corrupting the people and converting them into mere kulaks and swindlers? Is it possible, Mr. Avseenko, that you possess to such an extent "the gift of seeing nothing but evil"? Is it possible that our people who had been made serfs precisely for the sake of your culture (at least, according to General Fadeev's theory), after two centuries of serfdom have earned from you—a man who has become cultured—instead of gratitude or even pity, nothing but a presumptuous spittle in connection with kulaks and swindlers?! (The fact that you have praised them formerly I discard altogether because you have annulled your commendations on the very next page.) It was for you that they were bound—arms and feet—so that you might be given a chance to improve your intellectual faculties, borrowing them from Europe. And now that you have improved your intellectual faculties (?), borrowing them from Europe, you—setting your arms akimbo and standing before the bound one and looking down upon him from your cultured height—you suddenly come to the conclusion that the people "are bad and passive and that they have manifested but little activity [this—in a bound state!], revealing only certain passive virtues, which, though they kept feeding literature with living sap, essentially aren't worth a penny, since just as soon as the people begin to be active, they forthwith turn out to be kulaks and swindlers." No, Mr. Avseenko does not deserve to be answered, and if I do answer, it is only because I admit my mistake, which I am explaining below. Nevertheless —inasmuch as we started speaking on the subject—I deem it opportune to give the reader a certain idea about Mr. Avseenko: as a writer, he represents a petty cultural type *sui generis* which is most interesting to observe and which has a certain meaning; this, indeed, is very bad.

2

Cultured Little Types. Corrupted People

Mr. Avseenko has been writing criticisms for a long time, for several years now; and I confess that I have been entertaining hopes of him: "Well"—I used to say to myself—"he'll keep writing and writing, and in the long run, he may utter something." I persisted in this error until the October issue of *The Russian Messenger* for the year 1874, in which, apropos of Pisemsky's comedies and dramas, he stated the following: ". . . . Gogol has led our writers to take too careless an attitude toward the inner content of their works and to rely too much on the artistic element only. This view of the aim of belles-lettres was shared by many in our literature of the Forties, and one has to seek in it the reason why *that literature was deficient from the standpoint of its inner content*[!]"

Now, think of literature of the Forties being deficient from the standpoint of inner content! Never in my life did I expect so strange a bit of news. This is the very literature whch gave us the complete collection of Gogol's works, his comedy *The Wedding* (deficient in inner content—good heavens!); which thereupon gave us his *Dead Souls* (deficient in inner content—why, that man should have said something different, any word occurring to him first! It would still have been more opportune!); which produced Turgenev, with his *Sportsman's Sketches* (are these, too, deficient in their inner content?); and then Goncharov who, as early as the Forties, had written *Oblomov*, and who at that same time had published *Oblomov's Dream*—the best episode in the novel—which the whole of Russia has read with delight! This is that very literature which, finally, has given us Ostrovsky—but it is precisely upon Ostrovsky's types that Mr. Avseenko, in the same article, spits most contemptuously.

"The milieu of government officials, for external reasons, is not fully accessible to the theatrical satire; owing to this, our comedy burst forth with all the more zeal and predilection into the world of the Zamoskvorechie and Apraksin shopkeepers, into the midst of women pilgrims and matchmakers, drunken merchants' clerks, village bailiffs, churchmen and 'piterschiks.' The aim of the comedy has been incredibly narrowed down to the mirroring of the drunken or illiterate jargon, to the reproduction of the vulgar manners of coarse types and characters offensive to human sentiments. On the stage, genre enthroned itself undividedly—not that warm, jolly, bourgeois[?] genre which, at times, is so fascinating on the French stage [is that petty vaudeville meant here, where a fellow crawls under the table and another one drags him out by his legs?] —but a vulgar, slovenly and repulsive genre. Some writers—for example, Mr. Ostrovsky—have contributed to this literature much talent, heartfelt sentiment and humor; on the whole, however, our theatre has reached the lowest intrinsic level, and soon it became apparent that it had *nothing to say* to the educated stratum of society and that it had nothing in common with this portion of society."

Thus, Ostrovsky has lowered the level of the stage! Ostrovsky has said nothing to the "educated" stratum of society! Thus, it was uneducated society that has been admiring Ostrovsky on the stage and has been reading and reading him over again! Oh, of course, educated society, you see, has been frequenting the Mikháilovsky Theatre where it could behold that "warm, jolly, bourgeois genre which, at times, is so fascinating on the French stage." But Lubim Tortzóv is "vulgar and slovenly." It would be curious to ascertain what kind of educated society Mr. Avseenko does speak about. — Filth is not in Lubim Tortzóv: "he is pure in heart"; but filth is, perhaps, precisely where that "warm, bourgeois genre, which at times is so fascinating on the French stage," reigns supreme. And what's the idea about the artistic element precluding "the *inner content*"? — On the contrary, the former, in the highest degree, contributes to the latter: Gogol in his *Correspondence* is weak, although typical. Gogol, in those sections of the *Dead Souls* where he ceases to be an artist and begins merely to reason, is simply weak and even not typical; and yet his *Wedding*, his *Dead Souls*, are the most profound creations, richest from the standpoint of their inner content, precisely because of the artistic characters portrayed in them. These delineations, so to speak, burden one's mind with the deepest, the most unbearable, problems; they evoke in the Russian mind disturbing thoughts which, one feels, can be mastered only in the distant future; moreover, it is a question whether they can ever be mastered. And Mr. Avseenko vociferates that in the *Dead Souls* there is no intrinsic meaning! But take *Woe from Wit*: it is potent only because of its brilliant artistic types and characters; and it is artistic labor only that conveys to the work its entire inner content. However, the moment that Griboyedov abandons his role as an artist and starts reasoning on his own, on behalf of his individual intellect (through the mouth of Tchatzky, the weakest character in the comedy), he immediately sinks to a rather unenviable level, even incomparably lower than that of his contemporaneous representatives of our intelligentsia. Tchatzky's didacticisms are on an infinitely lower level than the comedy itself and, partly, consist of sheer nonsense. The whole depth, the whole content of an artistic work, is thus encompassed merely in types and characters. And this is almost invariably the case.

So the reader can judge for himself with what kind of a critic he is dealing. And already I hear the question: why, then, do you mix with him? — I reiterate: I am merely endeavoring to correct my own error, while, as stated above, I am dealing here specifically with Mr. Avseenko not as a critic but as a separate and curious literary phenomenon. Here we have a type *sui generis* which is useful to my purpose. For a long time I could not understand Mr. Avseenko—*i.e.*, I don't mean his articles: I never could understand

them, and, besides, there is nothing to understand or not to understand in them. But ever since his article in the October 1874 issue
of *The Russian Messenger,* I have given him up for lost; however,
I kept wondering all the while why articles of so muddled a writer
should be appearing in such a serious journal as the *Russian Messenger.* But presently there happened a comic episode, and at once
I grasped who Mr. Avseenko was: in the beginning of the winter
he began, unexpectedly, to publish his novel *The Milky Way.* (And
why did they cease printing it?) All of a sudden this romance explained to me the whole character of Avseenko as a writer. Strictly
speaking, it is not fitting for me to discuss the novel: I am a belles-
lettrist myself and I shouldn't be criticizing a *confrère* of mine. For
this reason I shall in no way criticize it, especially as it gave me a
few genuinely jolly moments. For example, the young hero of the
novel—a prince—sitting in a box at the opera and having grown
sentimental under the influence of the music, is publicly sobbing,
while a lady of the *beau monde* fondly keeps pestering him: "You're
crying? You're crying?" However, this is not the point at all;
the matter of the fact is that I had grasped the essence of the writer:
as such, Mr. Avseenko represents a man who had lost his wits in his
adoration of the *beau monde.* Briefly—he lies prostrate and adores
gloves, coaches, perfumes, pomade, silk gowns (especially at the
moment when a lady is about to sink into an armchair and the gown
rustles around her feet and body), and, finally, lackeys going out
to meet their mistresses as they return home from the Italian opera.
He writes about all these things continually, reverently, imploringly
and worshipfully—in a word, he is celebrating, as it were, a Mass.
I heard (I don't know, maybe this was said jeeringly) that this
romance had been undertaken with the object of correcting Leo
Tolstoy, who in his *Anna Karenina* had adopted too objective an
attitude toward the beau monde, whereas he should have treated it
more worshipfully, more kneelingly. And, of course, it wouldn't
have been worth bringing up all these things at all, were it not for the
fact—I repeat—that they interpret an altogether novel cultural type.
It appears that in coaches, in pomade, and particularly in the fact
that footmen are waiting on their mistresses, Mr. Avseenko, the critic,
perceives the whole object of culture—all its achievements, the culmination point of the two centuries of our debauch and suffering—
and he beholds all this not mockingly but admiringly. The seriousness and sincerity of this admiration constitute one of the most
curious phenomena.

The principal thing is that, as a writer, Mr. Avseenko does
not stand alone: even prior to him there have been "merciless Juvenals of calico shirts-fronts," but never of such an intensely reverent

pattern. True, not all of us are fashioned in this way, but it is my misfortune that, even gradually, I did finally become convinced that there are a great many similar representatives of culture—both in literature and in life—although not of so pure a pattern. I admit that I was enlightened, as it were: of course, after that, one can understand the pasquinades against Ostrovsky and that "warm, jolly, bourgeois genre which, at times, is so fascinating on the French stage." Why, neither Ostrovsky nor Gogol is really the crux of the matter! Nor the Forties (who cares about them!). Here it is simply a case of the St. Petersburg Mikháilovsky Theatre, patronized by the *beau monde,* to which people come driving up in coaches. That's all. This is what has lured and captivated a writer with merciless force; this is what has seduced him, confusing his mind forever.

I repeat, one should not be viewing this exclusively in a comical light: all this is much more curious. Briefly, in this respect we are dealing with a situation which is largely caused by a sort of mania—almost pathologic—by an infirmity, so to speak, for which one should have consideration. A *beau-monde* coach, let's imagine, is driven to a theatre: do, please, behold how it is being driven; how the lights of the lanterns, gleaming through the windows of the coach, glamorize the lady sitting inside! This is no longer the province of the pen: this is a prayer, and one must commiserate with this! No doubt, many among them are bragging to the people about things ostensibly even loftier than gloves: among them there are a great many extremely liberal folks, almost republicans, and yet, unexpectedly, one is apt to run into a "glover." This weakness, this mania, for *beau-monde* pulchritudes, with their oysters and hundred-ruble watermelons; this mania—innocent though it be —has generated in our midst, for example, even advocates of serfdom of a peculiar kind, *i.e.,* among persons who never even did own serfs. But having once decided that coaches and the Mikháilovsky Theatre are the ultimate achievement of the cultured period of the Russian Empire, they suddenly became convinced advocates of serfdom. And, notwithstanding the fact that they haven't the slightest intention of restoring serfdom, at least they spit upon the people with utter candidness and with an air of the fullest cultural right. They are precisely the ones who shower upon the people the most astonishing accusations: they are teasing a people who have been bound two hundred years in succession with passiveness; a pauper, from whom quit-rent tax has been mercilessly exacted, is being charged with slovenliness; a man who has been taught nothing is reproached for lack of education, and one who has been flogged with sticks—for the coarseness of his habits; at times, they are even ready to accuse him of the fact that he has not been pomaded and that his hair hasn't been dressed at a hairdresser's on the Bolsháia Morskáia. This by no means is an exaggeration; this is literally so, and the whole point is that it is not a hyperbole. They have a furious disgust for the people, and even if, at times, they praise them—well, as a matter of politics—they do so merely by resorting, for the sake of politeness, to high-strung phrases, in which they themselves do not understand a single word, because a few lines further on they contradict themselves.

By the way, I recall an incident which occurred to me two and a half years ago. I was going to Moscow by train, and at night I started a conversation with a landowner who was sitting next to me. As well as I could see in the darkness, he was a lean little fellow of about fifty, with a red, slightly swollen nose and, I believe, with ailing feet. He was a man of a very respectable type—in manners, in the way he talked, in his judgments—and he even spoke quite sensibly. He talked about the difficult and indeterminate situation of the nobility, the extraordinary economic disorganization throughout Russia; he spoke almost without bitterness, maintaining, however, a stern view on the subject, and I became intensely interested in him. And what would you think? Unexpectedly, in passing, without paying the least attention, he said that in the physical respect too he considered himself superior by far to the peasant, and that this, of course, was an undeniable fact.

"In other words, you mean to infer—as a specimen of a morally developed and educated man?"—said I, in an attempt to elucidate his thought.

"No, not at all: not only my moral, but likewise my physical nature is superior to that of a peasant: my *body* is superior to, and better than, that of a peasant, and this is so because throughout many generations we have evolved into a superior type."

There was nothing to argue about: this weak little man, with a scrofulous nose and ailing feet (gout, perhaps—the noblemen's disease), quite honestly considered himself physically, *bodily,* superior to, and more perfect than, a peasant! I repeat: there was no bitterness in him, but you must admit that this kind man, even in his kindness, may unexpectedly and occasionally perpetrate a gross injustice against the people—quite innocently, calmly and honestly, precisely because of a contemptuous opinion of the people, an opinion which is almost unconscious and independent of one's self.

Nevertheless, I must correct my own error. I was then writing about the ideals of the people and suggested that we, "like prodigal children, returning to their home, must bow before the people's truth, awaiting from it alone both thought and expression. But that, on the other hand, the people, on their own part, must accept from us something which we have brought with us; that this *something* exists in reality; it is not a mirage, but possesses an image, a form and weight, and that, in the reverse case, should we fail to agree, it would be better to separate and to perish apart." It is precisely this—as I see now—that seemed misleading to everybody. First, people started asking: what are those ideals of the people before which we should bow? And, secondly, what do I mean by that treasure which we have brought with us, and which the people must accept from us *sine qua non?* And, finally, would it not be simpler if not we but the people should bow before us, solely because we are Europe and cultured men—whereas the people are Russia, and they are passive? Mr. Avseenko answers this question in the affirmative; but I intend to give my reply not to Mr. Avseenko alone, but to all "cultured" people who have failed to understand me, beginning with "the merciless Juvenals of calico shirt-fronts" and including those gentlemen who have proclaimed that *we have nothing to conserve.* Now, let's get down to business. If, at the time, I had not sought to be brief and had been more explicit, of course, people might have disagreed with me, but, at least, my thoughts would not have been distorted and called misleading.

3

CONFUSEDNESS AND INACCURACY OF THE CONTESTED POINTS

It is boldly declared that the people possess no truth whatsoever—truth is only in culture—and that it is being preserved only by the upper stratum of cultured men. To be quite honest, I shall accept our dear European culture in its loftiest sense, and not merely in the sense of coaches and footmen—namely, in the sense that, compared with the people, we have developed spiritually and morally, we have become humane and, thereby, to our honor, we radically differ from the people. Having made such an unbiased statement, I shall ask myself this direct question: "Is it true that we are really so good, and that we have become so faultlessly culturized that popular culture should be brushed aside, and the people should bow before our own? And, in the last analysis, what did we bring to the people from Europe?"

However, before answering these questions, let us for the sake of orderly discussion discard all arguments—for instance, about science, industry, and so forth, on which Europe may justly pride herself over our country. Such an elimination would be quite correct, since *at present* we are dealing with a different matter, all the

more so as science is over there—in Europe—while we, the upper
strata of cultured men in Russia, do not glitter with science, despite the two hundred years of schooling, so that to bow before the
cultured stratum because of science—at any rate, it is too early.
Thus, science in no way constitutes an essential and irreconcilable
differentiation between the two classes of the Russians—*i.e.*, the
common people and the upper cultured stratum—and, I repeat, it
would not be at all correct, in fact, it would be an error, to set forth
science as an essential distinguishing mark between us and the
people. This distinction is to be sought in something wholly different. Besides, science is a universal thing: it was invented not by
some one people in Europe but by all peoples, beginning with the
ancient world; thus, science is a successional proposition. The
Russian people, on the other hand, never have been hostile toward
science; moreover, it began to penetrate into Russia even prior to
Peter. Czar Ivan Vassilievich exerted all efforts to conquer the
Baltic Coast, one hundred and thirty years before Peter. Had he
.conquered it and seized its harbors and ports, unavoidably he
would have started building his ships, even as Peter; and since
ships cannot be built without science, the latter would inevitably
have come from Europe, as under Peter. Our Potugins calumniate
our people with railleries to the effect that Russians have invented
nothing but the samovar; it is doubtful, however, if the Europeans
would join in on the chorus of the Potugins. It is only too clear and
comprehensible that everything transpires in accordance with certain
laws of nature and history, and neither imbecility, nor the low level
of the faculties of the Russian people, nor shameful indolence can
account for the fact that we have contributed so little to science and
industry. A certain tree grows up in so many years, while another
one—in twice as long a time. In this connection, everything depends
upon how a people has been settled by nature and circumstances,
and what they had to accomplish first. Here we are dealing with
geographic, ethnographic and political causes—thousands of causes
—all of them clear and precise. No one with common sense would
start blaming and shaming a boy of thirteen because he is not
twenty-five years old. "Europe"—they claim—"is more active and
wittier than the passive Russians; that's why she—and not they—
has developed science." Yet the passive Russians, while Europe
has been developing science, have been displaying a no less amazing
activity: they have been engaged in building up a Czardom and have
deliberately created its unity. Throughout the entire period of one
thousand years they have been repelling cruel enemies who, in the
absence of the Russians, would have thrown themselves upon Europe. The Russians have colonized the remotest regions of their

boundless motherland; the Russians were engaged in the defense and consolidation of their borderlands; and they have succeeded in consolidating them so powerfully that we, the present-day cultured people, would hardly be able to measure up to them—and, contrariwise, we might even shake them loose. At length, after a thousand years, we have established a Czardom and a political unity which are unprecedented in world history, even to the extent that in this respect England and the United States—the only two remaining states in which political unity is solid and original—would have to give way to us. Well, instead of this, in Europe, under different political and geographic conditions, science has grown up. As against this, alongside with its growth and consolidation, the moral and political condition of Europe has been undermined virtually everywhere.

Thus, everyone to his own, and it is still to be seen who's going to envy whom. In any event, we shall acquire science, but the question is: what is going to become of the political unity of Europe? Perhaps, only fifteen years ago, the Germans would gladly have agreed to exchange half of their scientific fame for that political unity which we possessed long ago. And the Germans—at least to their way of thinking—have now attained solid political unity; but in those days they still did not have their German Empire, and—of course, in silence—they have been envying us, notwithstanding all their contempt for us.

Thus, the question should be posed not about science or industry, but, essentially, about the fact that we, the cultured people, having returned from Europe, have become *morally and substantially* superior to the people; and also—about that priceless treasure which we brought to them in the form of our European culture. Why are we *polished* men, whereas the people are still vulgar? Why are we everything, and the people—nothing? I assert that on this point there is among us, cultured people, extraordinary confusion, and that few among the "cultured" would be able to answer these questions correctly. On the contrary, here there reigns utter discord, while railleries as to why a pine tree does not grow up in seven years but requires eight times more time to reach its full growth—are still so common and ordinary that not seldom is one apt to hear them, not only from the Potugins but even from persons intellectually far superior to them. I am not even mentioning Mr. Avseenko.

Now, I am turning directly to the question appearing in the beginning of the chapter: are we, indeed, so good, and have we become so faultlessly culturized that popular culture should be brushed aside, and the people should bow before our own? And if we are bringing something along, what precisely is it?—I will directly answer that we are much worse than the people, in nearly every respect.

We are being told that just as soon as an active man appears among the people, he turns out to be a kulak and a swindler. (This is being asserted by others besides Mr. Avseenko; anyway, never will he utter anything new.) First, this is a lie; and, secondly, among the would-be Russians, aren't there swarms of kulaks and swindlers? Maybe even a greater number than among the common people; and the former should be more ashamed of themselves because they have acquired culture, while the latter haven't. But the principal thing is that it is not possible to maintain about the people that, just as soon as an active person appears in their midst, he almost invariably turns out to be a kulak and a swindler. I do not know where those asserting this have grown up, but I, since my childhood and all my life, have seen altogether different things. I was only nine years old, I recall, when once, on the third day of Easter week, after five in the evening, all our family—father and mother, brothers and sisters—were sitting at a round table, at a family tea, and it so happened that the conversation revolved around our estate and how we all should go there for the summer. Suddenly the door opened and at the threshold appeared our house-servant, Grigory Vasiliev, who just before had arrived from the estate. In the absence of the masters, he used to be entrusted even with the management of the estate. And now, instead of the "super-intendent" who always wore a German suit and displayed a solid appearance, there appeared a man in an old shabby peasant's coat, with bast shoes on his feet. He had come from the estate on foot; he stepped into the room and stood without uttering a word.

"What is it?"—cried father, frightened.—"Look, what is it?"

"The estate has burned down!"—said Grigory Vasiliev, in a bass voice.

I shall not describe what ensued: father and mother were working, not rich, people—and such was their Easter present! It developed that everything had been destroyed by fire—everything: huts, granary, cattle-shed and even spring seeds, some of the cattle, and even our peasant Arkhip was burned to death. Owing to the sudden scare, we thought that it meant utter ruin. We threw ourselves on our knees and began to pray; mother was crying. Presently our nurse, Aliona Frolovna, went up to her; Aliona was a hired servant, not a serf, and belonged to the Moscow commoners' class. She had nursed and brought up all of us children. She was then about forty-five years old; she was a woman of serene and cheerful disposition, and she used to tell us such wonderful tales! For a number of years she had refused to draw her salary: "I don't need it." It had accumulated to the amount of some five hundred rubles, which were kept on deposit at a loan office: "It will come in handy in my old age." Suddenly, she whispered to mother: "If you should need money, take mine; I have no use for it; I don't need it. . . ."

We did not take her money; we managed to get along without it. But here is the question: to what type belonged that humble woman who died long ago in an almshouse, where her money did come in handy? For I believe that a woman like her cannot be classed among kulaks and swindlers; and, if so, how is one to interpret her action? Did she reveal it "on the mere level of elemental existence, on the level of a secluded and idyllic mode of passive ways of life," or did she manifest something more energetic than passiveness?—It would be very curious to hear how Mr. Avseenko would answer this question. It may be disdainfully argued that is an isolated case. However, during my lifetime, I personally have managed to observe many hundreds of similar cases among our common people; and yet, I am well aware of the fact that there are other observers who are able to behold the people without spitting on them. Don't you remember how in Aksakov's *Family Chronicle* the mother, with tears in her eyes, had persuaded the peasants to drive her over thin ice across the wide Volga to Kazan to her sick child? this was in the spring when, for several days already, no one had risked stepping on the ice which was just then beginning to break up and which, only several hours later, was swept downstream, after she had been taken across. Do you remember the delightful description of that crossing and how later, when it had been accomplished, the peasants refused to accept any money, realizing that they had done all this because of a mother's tears and for Christ, our Lord? And this occurred during the darkest period of serfdom! Well, are all these isolated facts? And if they be laudable— are they still merely "on a level of elemental existence, on the level of a secluded and idyllic mode of passive ways of life?" But is this so? Are these merely isolated, accidental facts?—Is it possible to conceive an active risk of one's life out of compassion for a mother's affliction as mere passiveness? Was it not, on the contrary, due to truth—to the people's truth? Was it not because of *mercy, all-forgiveness and breadth of the popular view* that this had occurred during the most barbaric—let's note—period of serfdom? Well—you might say—the people do not even know religion; they are unable to say a prayer; they worship a wooden board, mumbling some sort of nonsense about Holy Friday and about Frol and Lavr. To this I will answer that these particular thoughts have occurred to you as a result of your continued contempt for the Russian people, which stubbbornly persists in Russians of the cultured pattern. About the faith of the people and about Orthodoxy we possess merely a couple of dozens of liberal and obscene anecdotes, and we delight in scoffing stories about how an old woman confesses her sins to the priest and how a peasant prays to Friday. Had Mr. Avseenko really understood what he has written about the people's religion—and not copied something from the Slavophiles—he would not have directly insulted the people, calling virtually all of them "kulaks and bloodsuckers." But the point is that these men understand nothing about Orthodoxy, and for this reason they will never comprehend anything concerning our people. And yet our people know their Christ God—perhaps even better than we, although they did not attend school. They know, because throughout many a century they have endured much suffering, and in their sorrow, from the earliest days to our time, they have been accustomed to hear about this Christ God of theirs, from their saints who labored for the people and who defended the Russian soil— sacrificing their lives; from those very saints whom they have revered up to the present day, remembering their names and praying at their graves. Believe me, in this sense even the most backward strata of our people are much better educated than you, in your cultured ignorance, suppose them to be, and, perhaps, even much better educated than you yourselves despite the fact that you have learned the catechism.

4

The Beneficent Doorman Liberating the Russian Peasant

Here is what Mr. Avseenko writes in his March article. I want to be quite unbiased and, therefore, I take the liberty of making this very long quotation lest I be accused of having drawn out of the text scattered sentences. Besides, I regard specifically these words of Mr. Avseenko as the general opinion of the Westerners about the Russian people.

"It is important to us to determine under what circumstances our educated minority has for the first time looked attentively across the wall which separated it from the people. No doubt, the things which appeared to its eyes must have amazed it and, in many respects, satisfied the intimate needs which had been revealed in that minority. Men, dissatisfied with the role of adopted children of Western civilization, found there ideals altogether different from European ones, and yet beautiful. Disillusioned people and, to use the then prevailing expression, people torn asunder by the adopted culture, found there simple, whole characters, zealous faith reminding one of the first centuries of Christianity, stern vigor of patriarchal ways of living. The contrast between the two modes of life, as stated, must have produced an extraordinary, irresistible effect. There arose a desire to refresh oneself in the unperturbed waves of this elemental existence, to breathe the fragrant air of field and forest. The best men were astonished by the fact that in that stale manner of life—alien not only to intellectual refinement but even to elementary literacy—there appeared traits of spiritual grandeur, before which the enlightened minority must bow. All these impressions have created a tremendous longing for a rapprochement with the people. But what was specifically meant by this rapprochement with the people? The ideals of the people were clear only because the life of the people streamed infinitely far away from the life of the educated class; because the conditions and contents of these two modes of life were quite different. Let us recall that poorly educated men, who have been living in very close proximity to the people and who had long ago, in a practical and material manner, satisfied their longing for the rapprochement, did not at all notice the beautiful ideals of the people, and were firmly convinced that the peasant was a dog and a rascal. This is very important because it goes to show to what extent, as a practical matter, the educational influence of the people's ideals is weak, and that it is hardly possible to expect salvation from them. To grasp these ideals and to raise them to the level of a pearl of creation, a certain cultural degree is required. For this reason we deem it our right to state that our very worship of the people's ideals was the product of the adopted European culture, and that without the latter the peasant, in our view, would have remained up to this day a dog and a rascal. Thus, the evil—the principal, the common evil—to both us and the people, lay not in 'culture' but in the weakness of cultural foundations, in the deficiency of our 'culture.' "

What a surprising and unexpected deduction!

In this crafty little assortment of words the most important point is the deduction that the popular foundations (and along with them Orthodoxy, since, essentially, all our popular foundations are wholly derived from Orthodoxy) constitute no cultural force whatever, not the slightest educational significance, so that in order to acquire all these things we had to journey to Europe. "Poorly educated men living in very close proximity to the people," don't you see, have still not been noticing "the beautiful ideals of the people" and were still firmly convinced that the peasant was "a

dog and a rascal"—not because they had been already corrupted to
the marrow of their bones by culture, despite their poor education;
not because they had detached themselves from the people, in spite
of the fact that they lived in close proximity to them, but because
there was still not enough culture. Here the main point is the evil-
minded insinuation as to the weakness of educational meaning of
the people's principles, coupled with the deduction that, on this
ground, they lead to nothing, and that culture is everything. On
my own part, I have long ago stated that we have started our
European culture with debauch. But the following should be specially emphasized: it is precisely these poorly educated men who,
however, have managed to culturize themselves, though feebly and
externally—mostly in some acquired habits, in new prejudices, in new
clothes—these men always begin with a contempt—at times to the
point of hatred—for their former milieu, for their people and even
for the latter's faith. Such is the case of certain superior "counts'
lackeys"—petty government employees who have succeeded in acquiring the rank of nobility, etc., etc. They despise the people more
intensely than the "big guns" who are more soundly culturized,
and this—contrary to Mr. Avseenko's attitude—should cause no
surprise.

In the first, January, issue of my *Diary* I have recalled one
of my childish impressions: that little scene of a courier, a former
peasant, who, no doubt, had been close to the people; he had spent
all his life on the highway, and yet he despised and beat the people.
Why?—Because he was terribly remote from the people despite
the fact that he had been living in close proximity to them. Undoubtedly, he had acquired no culture but, as against this, he had
received the courier's uniform with flaps which entitled him to
beat uncontrollably, "to his heart's desire." And he was proud of
his uniform and considered himself infinitely superior to the peasant.
Approximately similar also was the status of the landowner whose
country house was situated at a distance of only some hundred
steps from the peasants' huts; but it was not a question of a hundred
steps: the point was that he had already partaken of the corruption
of civilization. He was in close proximity to the people—only a hundred steps distant from them—nevertheless within this space there
was room for a whole gulf. Perhaps that landowner had in him
merely a tiny drop of culture but that drop had completely corrupted him. Such must be the average case at the beginning of a
reform period. But I shall positively state that in this respect,
too, Mr. Avseenko is as ignorant as an infant: not all poorly educated men have been corrupted, nor did they despise the people
even in those days. On the contrary, there were others upon whom

popular principles did not cease to exercise a potent educational influence. Such a stratum has survived from the very epoch of Peter's reforms up to our time. There were many, even a great many, of those who had partaken of culture and who had returned to the people and to their ideals without losing their culture. Subsequently, from this stratum of the "faithful," there emerged the stratum of Slavophiles, men highly culturized by European civilization. However, it was not the high European civilization of the Slavophiles that was the cause of their remaining faithful to the people and their principles—not in the least, but, on the contrary, the inexhaustible, continual educational influence of the popular principles upon the minds and the development of a layer of genuinely Russian people who, by reason of their natural faculties, proved able to withstand the impact of civilization without reducing themselves to a zero. This layer, I repeat, dates back to the very inception of the reform. I believe that to quite a few our Slavophiles seem to have fallen from the sky, and they will fail to trace their origin to the time of Peter's reform, as a protest against everything that was erroneous and fanatically exclusive in it. Still, I repeat, there have been sparsely culturized men who have never regarded the people as dogs and rascals.

However, our cultured people are hardly aware of this, and even if they are, they despise these facts and do not, and never will, take them into consideration because these sparsely culturized men who have not lost their Christianity would be standing in direct contradiction to their fundamental and victorious thesis concerning the paltry educational value of the popular principles. They would then have to concede that it is not the latter who have been so weak and uneducational, but that, contrariwise, culture has been too corrupted, even though it was only in its embryonic state, and, therefore, it succeeded in ruining so many *unsteady* men. (And unsteady ones are always in the majority.) It is for this reason that Mr. Avseenko draws the bold conclusion that "the evil—the principal, the common evil—to both us and the people lay not in culture but in the weakness of cultural foundations"; it was, therefore, necessary to run to Europe as quickly as possible to become fully cultivated, to the extent that one would no longer be looking upon the peasant as a dog and a rascal.

And we have acted exactly in this manner: we used to journey to Europe ourselves and to import teachers from there. Prior to the French Revolution, in the days of Rousseau and the correspondence of the Empress with Voltaire, Swiss teachers were in vogue in Russia——

And Swiss disseminating learning everywhere.[1]

"Come, take the money—only humanize us!"—such, indeed was the vogue in those days. In Turgenev's *Gentlefolk's Nest,* in passing, is excellently depicted the portrait of a certain nobleman's son who, after having been culturized in Europe, returned to his father's estate. He boasted of his humaneness and intellectual refinement. The father started reproaching him for having seduced and dishonored an innocent maidservant, to which the son remarked: "What of it?—I'll marry her." You remember that little scene when the father seized a stick and started after his son, and the latter, in an English blue dress-coat, in boots adorned with tufts, and in tightly fitting elk-skin trousers, scampered off through the garden and the barn, running at top speed! And then, although he did make his escape, several days later he married the girl because of the then rampant ideas of Rousseau, but principally—because of caprice, unsteadiness of convictions, of will and of feelings, as well as of piqued ambition: "Now, look at me, all of you! See, what a fellow I am!" He did not respect his wife, treated her with boundless contempt, wearied her out by separations, and finally deserted her; he lived to old age and died in a state of complete cynicism—a wicked, trivial, vile, contemptible old man, cursing in his last moments and crying to his sister: "Glashka, Glashka—some broth, bring some broth!"

How delightful is this story of Turgenev's, and how true! And yet, this is one who has been considerably culturized. But Mr. Avseenko has a different thing in mind: he insists on genuine culture, that is, contemporaneous culture, the kind which has made our Petersburg landowners cultured to such an extent that they have been shedding tears while reading *Antón—The Poor Wretch,* and after that they made up their minds and liberated the peasants with land and decided to address the former dogs and rascals with a *"you."* Indeed, what progress! Still, later, after careful scrutiny, it was ascertained that these landowners who had been sobbing over *Antón—The Poor Wretch* proved ignorant of the people—of their life, of their principles—to such an extent that they almost mistook Russian peasants for French villagers or for shepherdesses on porcelain cups. And when the long and difficult work of the

[1] I think this is Count Khvostov's verse. I even remember the four lines in which the poet enumerates all the people of Europe:

Turks, Persians, Prussians, French, revengeful sons of Spain,
Italians and children of the German scientific brain;
Sons of mercantile pursuits vigilantly watching o'er their ware,
[that is, Englishmen]
And Swiss disseminating learning everywhere.

government in connection with the liberation of the peasants had begun, some of the opinions of these, even prominent, landowners amazed people by the virtually anecdotal ignorance on the subject of the village, of the people's life and of everything else pertaining to the popular principles. And yet, Mr. Avseenko specifically asserts that European culture has helped us to understand the people's ideals, although these are devoid of any educational significance. It could be presumed that for a comprehension of the people's ideals one had to go to Paris or, at least, to little vaudeville shows at the Mikháilovsky Theatre, to which coaches keep driving up. However, let it be said that progress and the understanding of the Russian ways of life have been conveyed to us solely from Europe. Be it so —and praised be culture! "Can't you see what genuine culture can make of men!"—exclaims the throng of Messrs. Avseenkis! "And, compared with it, what are all those petty popular principles with Orthodoxy at their head—they have no instructive effect! Down with them!"

So be it! However, gentlemen, please answer only one question: why didn't these teachers of ours, Europeans, these beneficent Swiss, these doormen,[1] who have taught us to liberate the peasants with land—why didn't they, in Europe, liberate anyone not only with land but even bare and naked as mother bore them? And thus it has happened everywhere. Why did liberation proceed in Europe not from the owners, barons and country squires, but from uprisings and rebellions, from fire and sword and rivers of blood? And if, here and there, liberation was accomplished without rivers of blood, everywhere, without exception, it was carried out on proletarian principles; a people was set free as perfect slaves. Even so, we are vociferating that we have learned from Europeans how to liberate. "We became culturized"—they say—"and we ceased to regard the peasant as a dog and a rascal." Well, why then, in France, and everywhere in Europe, is every proletarian, every penniless worker, looked upon as a dog and a rascal?—and this, of course, you will not deny. It stands to reason that on strict legal grounds he cannot be told that he is a dog and a rascal; yet everything can be done to him exactly as to a dog and a rascal, while the crafty law merely requires that in this connection politeness be complied with. "I'll be polite, but I'll not give you bread—even though you starve to death as a dog"—that's how things stand nowadays in Europe. How's that? What a contradiction! How is it that they taught us something directly opposite? Nay, gentlemen, here, at home, something altogether different has happened, and also not in the manner

[1]This is an untranslatable *jeu de mots: schveitzár* means "doorman"; *Shveitzár* is the archaic form of "Swiss." (B. B.)

you claim. Think only: had we ceased to regard the peasant as a dog and a rascal only through culture, we should certainly have liberated him according to the cultural scheme, that is, on proletarian principles, even as our teachers in Europe: "Go"—we should have said—"dear brother of ours, and have your freedom, bare and naked, as your mother had borne you, and consider this as an honor." Indeed, in the Baltic Provinces the people were liberated exactly in this manner. And why? Because the Balts are Europeans, while we are only Russians. And thus it appears that we have accomplished this task like Russians and not at all like cultured Europeans, and we did liberate the people with land—to the astonishment and horror of our European instructors and of all beneficent "doormen." Yes, to their horror: in Europe, there sounded alarmed voices—don't you remember it? They even started shouting about communism. Do you recall that little word of the now deceased Guizot concerning the liberation of our people: "How do you expect us, after that, not to be afraid of you?"—said he to a certain Russian.

Nay, we have liberated the people with land not because we have become cultured Europeans, but because we have sensed in ourselves Russians led by the Czar, exactly in the manner that forty years prior to that the landowner Pushkin had been dreaming; specifically, during that epoch he had damned his European upbringing and had turned toward the principles of the people. *It was precisely in the name of these popular principles* that the Russian people have been liberated with land, and not because Europe has taught us to do so: on the contrary—because, suddenly, for the first time, we decided to bow before the people's truth. This was not only a great moment in Russian life, when cultured men, for the first time, ventured to act in an original manner, but also a prophetic moment in our history. And, very soon, perhaps, the prophecy will begin to come true. . . .

But . . . at this point I shall break off. I see that my article would absorb the entire space in the *Diary*. Thus—till the next, May, issue of my *Diary*. And, of course, I am leaving for the May issue the most essential part of my explanations. As a matter of record, I shall enumerate here the things that will be included in it. I wish to point out the utter bankruptcy and even the triviality specifically of that *aspect* of our culture which, contrariwise, some of our gentlemen regard as our light, as our sole salvation and our fame before the people, and from the height of which they spit upon the people and consider themselves fully justified in doing so. Since, to eulogize "the people's principles," to delight in them, and in the same breath to be asserting that they are devoid of all force, of all educational meaning and that all this is mere "passiveness," and thus—let's spit upon these principles. For example, to assert, as Mr. Avseenko does, that the people are nothing but pilgrims who have not yet chosen their path, and that "to expect thought and expression, from this enigma, this sphinx, which has not yet found for itself either thought or expression—is irony"—to assert this, I say, is merely the equivalent of not knowing that subject of which one is treating, *i.e.*, of not knowing the people at all. Specifically, I wish to point out that the people are by no means as hopeless, in no sense as susceptible to unsteadiness and vagueness, as is, on the contrary, our Russian cultural stratum in which all these gentlemen take pride as the most precious, two-hundred-year-old acquisition of Russia. Finally, I should like to state that in our people is fully preserved that solid core which will save them from the excesses and deviations of our culture, and which will withstand the education coming to the people without damage to their image and self-expression. And even though I did say that "the people are an enigma," it was in a sense quite different from that which was understood by these gentlemen. At the very end, I wish to explain fully, as I conceive it myself, the confusing question which arises of its own accord after all this wrangling: "Well, if we, the culturized Russian stratum, are so weak and unsteady, compared with the people, what, then, can we bring to them of so precious a value that they should bow before it and should accept that treasure *sine qua non?*"—as I have stated myself in the February issue of my *Diary*. Now, this aspect of our culture, which should be conceived as a treasure and to which, however, all these gentlemen, *thus far,* have not paid the slightest attention, I wish to point out and explain. Thus—till the May issue. As for myself, I cannot imagine anything more entertaining and *pressing* than these questions; I don't know how the reader feels about them. But I promise—to the best of my ability—to be more brief, while I shall try to make no more mention of Mr. Avseenko.

CHAPTER II

1

Something About Political Questions

EVERYBODY SPEAKS about current political questions and everybody takes great interest in them. In fact, how is it possible not to be interested? Unexpectedly, *en passant,* a very seri-

ous man very seriously asked me: "Well, is there going to be a war
or not?" I was surprised: although I am following events very
closely—like everybody else—nevertheless I haven't even raised
the question of the inevitability of war. And, I believe, I was right:
newspapers announce the forthcoming meeting—in the nearest future
—at Berlin of three chancellors; and, no doubt, that the endless
Herzegovina problem will be settled and, most probably, in a sense
satisfactory to the Russian sentiment. I confess, I was also not very
much disturbed by those words of Baron Rodič, spoken a month
ago; truly, when I first read them, I was merely amused. Meanwhile, it has seemed to me that Baron Rodič not only did not intend to pique anyone, but that in his utterance there was no "politics" at all: simply, it was a lapsus, a slip, an inconsiderate bit of
nonsense about Russia's impotence. I even think that before he had
made his statement about our impotence, he said to himself; "Now,
if we are stonger than Russia, this would mean that Russia is
absolutely impotent. And in reality we are stronger because Berlin
will never surrender us to Russia. Oh, Berlin might, perhaps, permit
us to come to grips with Russia, but exclusively for its own amusement and for the purpose of determining more accurately who's going
to beat whom, and what means both parties have at their disposal.
However, should Russia conquer us and briskly pin us to the wall,
Berlin would say: 'Halt, Russia!'—nor would Berlin permit that
great—that is, very great—harm be inflicted upon us, well, perhaps,
just trifling harm. And since Russia will not venture to challenge
us and Berlin together, the matter may be brought to an end without great injury to us. As against that, we have this chance: should
we beat Russia, we could be gaining a lot. Thus, we have a chance,
on the one hand, to gain a lot, and, in the event that Russia should
beat us, to lose very little—this is very good, very politic! And Berlin
is our friend: she loves us greatly because she wants to annex our
German dominions and will annex them in any event, and, perhaps,
in the rather near future. However, because Berlin greatly loves us
for this, she will, without fail, compensate us for our German
dominions seized by her from us, and in exchange for these she will
grant us jurisdiction over the Turkish Slavs. This she will do without fail since this would be to her great advantage, because even
if we were compensated with the Slavs, nevertheless we should in
no way become stronger than Berlin, whereas should Russia compensate herself with the Slavs, then she would grow stronger even
than Berlin. This is why we—and not Russia—are going to get the
Slavs. This is why I could not refrain from mentioning it in my
address to the Slavic leaders. Indeed, it is necessary to prepare them
little by little for the right ideas. . . ."

Such ideas may be prevailing not only in Rodič's mind but among Austrians in general. And, of course, here there is much choas. . . . Imagine only that the Slavs might come under Austria's domination, and that, in the first instance, she would start Germanizing them, even after having lost her German dominions! However, it is true that in Europe, not Austria alone is inclined to believe in Russia's impotence, and, furthermore—in Russia's ardent desire to bring the Slavs as quickly as possible under her rule. The fullest metamorphosis in Russia's political life will take place exactly when Europe becomes convinced that Russia has no intention of annexing anything. When that time comes a new era will come into existence for us and for the whole of Europe. The belief in Russia's disinterestedness, if it should ever be held, would at once renovate and change the whole countenance of Europe. In the long run this conviction will arise without fail, but not as a result of any assurance of ours: Europe, to the very end, will refuse to give credence to any of our assurances, and will continue to look at us with hostility. It is difficult to conceive to what extent she is afraid of us. And if she is afraid of us, she must be hating us. Europe has always extraordinarily disliked us; she never did like us; she never regarded us as one of her own—as Europeans—but always has viewed us as disagreeable strangers. This is why, at times, she is so fond of consoling herself with the thought that Russia supposedly is "as yet impotent."

And it is good that she is inclined to think so. I am convinced that the greatest calamity would have befallen Russia should she have won, for instance, the Crimean campaign and should she then have conquered the Allies! Having perceived how powerful we are, everybody in Europe would then forthwith have risen against us with fanatical hatred. Of course, had they been crushed, they would have signed a peace treaty disadvantageous to them, but never could any peace have been achieved in reality. They would immediately begin to prepare themselves for a new war aiming at the annihilation of Russia, and the principal point is that they would have had the support of the whole world. For example, in this event the year 1864 would not have cost us merely an exchange of caustic diplomatic notes: on the contrary, a wholesale crusade against Russia would have ensued. Moreover, by means of this crusade several European governments, at the time, would have improved their internal situation so that it would have been profitable to them in every respect. For instance, the revolutionary parties and all those who were dissatisfied with the contemporaneous French government, would immediately have come to its support in view of "the most sacred aim" of expelling Russia from Europe. And such a war would have been popular However, at the time fate had saved us by providing preponderance in strength to the Allies, and at the same time preserving and even exalting our military honor so that the defeat could be endured by us! Briefly, we have endured the debacle, but under no circumstance could we have endured the burden of our victory over Europe, notwithstanding our viability and strength. In the same way, another time fate saved us in the beginning of the century, when we threw off Napoleon's yoke in Europe; it saved us specifically by the fact that it gave us Prussia and Austria as allies. Had we then conquered alone, Europe, the moment it would have recovered after Napoleon I, would have again—even without Napoleon—thrown herself upon us. But, thank God, things happened differently: Prussia and Austria, which we had liberated, forthwith attributed to themselves the honor of the victories, and subsequently—at the present time—they assert that in those days they won the war alone, and that Russia merely impeded their efforts.

And, generally speaking, we have been placed in such a position by our European fate that under no circumstances should we be conquering in Europe, even if we could: it is disadvantageous and dangerous in the highest degree. Well, perhaps, some private, as it were, domestic, victories they might "forgive" us—for instance, the conquest of the Caucasus. Whereas war with Turkey, under the late Emperor, and the suppression of Poland, which took place shortly thereafter, almost caused a general explosion in Europe. At present, apparently, they "have forgiven" us our recent acquisitions in Central Asia, but even so how they keep croaking at home! They can't calm down.

Nevertheless, the course of events—so it seems—must change the attitude of the European nations toward Russia in the rather near future. In the March issue of my *Diary* I have recorded some of my meditations concerning the immediate future of Europe. However, no longer meditatingly but almost with certainty, it may be stated that very soon—perhaps, in the immediate future—Russia will prove stronger than any nation in Europe. This will come to pass because all great powers in Europe will be destroyed for the simple reason that they will be worn out and undermined by the unsatisfied democratic tendencies of an enormous portion of their lower-class subjects—their proletarians and paupers. In Russia, this cannot happen: our demos is content and, as time goes on, it will grow even more content because everything tends toward this condition, as a result of the general mood, or—more correctly—by general consensus. And therefore there will remain on the continent but one colossus—Russia. This will come to pass, perhaps even much sooner than people think. The future of Europe belongs to Russia. But the question is: what will Russia then be doing in Europe? What role will she be playing? Is she ready for that role?

2

THE PARADOXICALIST

By the way, apropos of the war and the war rumors. I have among my acquaintances a paradoxicalist. I have known him for quite a long time. He is a man whom no one knows—a strange character: he is a *dreamer*. Without fail I shall speak about him later in more detail. But just now I recall how once—true, several years ago—he started arguing with me about war. He was defending it on general principles and, perhaps, solely as a matter of sportive love for paradox. I may remark that he is a "civilian," and one of the most peaceful and good-natured men on earth and in Petersburg.

"It is a wild idea"—he said *inter alia*—"that war is the scourge of mankind. On the contrary, it is a most useful thing. There is but one kind of war which is hateful and really disastrous: this is civil, fratricidal war. It deadens and disintegrates the state; invariably it lasts too long, and it brutalizes a people for whole centuries. But political, international war is useful in every respect, and, therefore, it is absolutely necessary."

"But look here: one people rises against another one; men go to kill each other. What is there necessary in this?"

"Everything, and in the highest degree. But—to begin with —it is a lie that men go to kill each other: this is never the case as a matter of prime design. On the contrary, they go to sacrifice their own lives; this must stand in the foreground. And this is altogether different. There is no loftier idea than to sacrifice one's own life, or even simply to defend the cause of one's fatherland. Mankind cannot live without magnanimous ideas, and I am even inclined to suspect that mankind loves war precisely because it seeks to participate in a magnanimous idea. This is an urge."

"But does mankind really love war?"

"Why, of course. Who feels depressed during the war?—Quite the contrary: everybody is enheartened, everybody's spirit rises, and one does not hear about the usual apathy and boredom as in times of peace. And afterwards, when the war is over, how people like to reminisce about it even in the case of defeat! And don't believe people who, when meeting during a war, shake their heads and say to each other: 'What a calamity! What things have come to pass!'—This is mere politeness. On the contrary, in everybody's soul there dwells a holiday spirit. You know, it is awfully difficult to admit certain ideas: people will say: 'brute,' 'reactionary'; they will censure, and one is afraid of this. No one will dare to praise war."

"But you are speaking about magnanimous ideas, about humanizing. Can't there be found magnanimous ideas without war? On the contrary, in times of peace, it is easier to make oneself better."

"Not at all; the contrary is true. Magnanimity perishes during long periods of peace and, in its stead, there develop cynicism, apathy, weariness, and, at most, spiteful raillery, and this—almost for the sake of idle pastime, and not for any important purpose. It may be positively asserted that protracted peace obdurates people. When peace lasts long social preponderance invariably swings to the side of everything that is bad and vulgar in humankind—principally, to wealth and capital. Honor, humaneness, self-sacrifice are still being respected, valued and rated highly immediately after the war, but the longer peace lasts—the dimmer, the more withered, the more torpid all these beautiful magnanimous things grow, while wealth and the spirit of acquisition take possession of everything. At length, there is nothing left but hypocrisy —hypocrisy of honor, of self-sacrifice, of duty, so that these will still be respected, despite all the cynicism, but merely in boastful phrases and as a matter of form. There will be no genuine honor, and nothing but formulas will be left. Formulas of honor mean the death of honor. Lasting peace produces apathy, baseness of thought, corruption, and it dulls the feelings. Coarse wealth is incapable of cherishing magnanimity, but it requires more unassuming delights, that is, those directly gratifying the carnal instincts. Delectations grow carnivorous. Sensuality generates lechery, and lewdness always produces cruelty. You cannot deny all these things because you cannot deny the principal fact that social superiority in times of lasting peace, in the long run, always passes over to vulgar wealth."

"But science, the arts—can they flourish in times of war?— And yet, these are great and magnanimous ideas."

"I catch you right at this point. Science and the arts progress precisely during the period immediately following a war. War regenerates, refreshes them; generates the thought and gives it an impetus. On the contrary, during periods of long-lasting peace science withers. No doubt, scientific pursuit requires magnanimity, even self-sacrifice. But how many scientists can remain immune to the plague of peace? False honor, self-love, sensuality will get them, too. For instance, try to master a passion such as envy: it is vulgar and trivial, and yet it penetrates the noblest soul of a scientist. He, too, will be tempted to partake of general opulence and glamor. Compared with the triumph of wealth, what is the triumph of some scientific invention, unless it be as ostentatious as, for example, the discovery of the planet Neptune? Do you think that there will be many genuine workers left?—On the contrary, there will be craving for fame, and thus charlatanism, galloping after effect, and especially utilitarianism, will invade science since there will arise a thirst for wealth. The same is true of art: the same galloping after effect, after some subtility. The simple, clear, magnanimous and vigorous ideas will no longer be in vogue: something more unassuming will be required; artificiality of passions will be in demand. Little by little, the sense of measure and harmony will be lost; there will appear distortions of feelings and passions, so-called subtilities of sentiment which, in substance, are merely its vulgarization. Art invariably yields to this at the end of a long period of peace. Had there never been such a thing as war in this world, art would completely wither. All the loftiest ideas in art have been contributed by war and struggle. Turn to tragedy, behold the statues: here is Corneille's *Horace;* there—Apollo of the Belvedere, dealing a blow to a monster. . . ."

"And the Madonnas! And Christianity!"

"Christianity itself admits the fact of war and prophesies that the sword shall prevail till the end of the world: this is very remarkable and astounding. Oh, no doubt, in the loftiest, moral sense, it rejects war and prescribes brotherly love. I shall be the first to rejoice when swords are forged into plows. But the question is: when can this happen? And is it worth while, at this time, to reforge swords into plows? Present-day peace is always and everywhere worse than war—worse to such an extent that, at length, it becomes immoral to support it: there is nothing to treasure, nothing to censure; it is shameful and trivial to conserve. Wealth, vulgarity of delights generate indolence, and indolence gives birth to slaves. To keep slaves in a servile state it is necessary to deprive them of free will and of the opportunity of enlightenment. For you cannot help but feel the need for a slave, no matter who you are, even though you be the most tenderhearted person! I may also remark that during periods of peace cowardice and dishonesty become firmly planted. Man, by virtue of his nature, is terribly inclined toward cowardice and shamelessness, and he is fully aware of it. This is the reason why he is so strongly craving for war and why he loves it so: he senses a medicine in it. War promotes brotherly love and unites the nations."

"What do you mean by 'unites the nations'?"

"By compelling them mutually to respect each other. War refreshes men. Humaneness develops most strongly on a battlefield. It is even a strange fact that war embitters people less than peace. In fact, some political offense in times of peace, some insolent treaty, some political pressure, some arrogant interpellation—akin to the one Europe addressed to us in 1863—tends to cause more bitterness than a straightforward battle. Please recall: did we hate the French and the English during the Crimean campaign?—On the contrary, we became, as it were, intimate with them, or even related to them. We used to take an interest in their opinion of our bravery; we showed signs of kindness to their captives; in periods of truce our soldiers and officers used to proceed to the outposts; they almost embraced their enemies and drank vodka with them. Russia has been reading in the papers about all this with delight, which, however, did not prevent us from putting up a superb fight. There developed a knightly spirit. And I shall even refrain from speaking about the material calamities of war: who does not know the law according to which everything, as it were, acquires new, regenerated force? The economic forces of the country are stimulated and decupled as if a storm cloud had poured out abundant rain upon parched soil. War sufferers are being speedily given aid by everybody, whereas in times of peace whole regions are left to die from famine before we deign to scratch our necks or to send a three-ruble contribution."

"But don't the people, more than anyone else, suffer during the war? Don't they endure ruin and unavoidable burdens infinitely more onerous than the upper strata of society?"

"Perhaps, but only temporarily, whereas they gain much more than they lose. It is precisely for the people that war bears its best and most blissful consequences. Just as you please, you may be the most human person, but even so you consider yourself superior to a plebeian. Who, in our day, measures souls with the Christian measure—soul by soul? Pocketbook, power, strength—these are the yardsticks with which everything is measured, and plebeians en masse are well aware of it.

"This is not exactly envy: there arises here some kind of an unbearable feeling of moral inequality which is too vexing to the common people. No matter how much you may be liberating them, no matter what laws you may be enacting, inequality cannot be eliminated in present-day society. The only medicine is war; it is a palliative, a momentary medicine, but one welcomed by the people. War arouses the people's spirit and their feeling of self-respect. War equalizes everybody during the battle and reconciles master and slave in the supreme manifestation of human dignity—in the sacrifice of life for a common cause, for everybody, for the fatherland. Do you really believe the mass, even the ignorant mass, of peasants and paupers, does not experience the need of an *active* manifestation of magnanimous feelings? And in times of peace, in what can the mass reveal its magnanimity and human dignity? We view—scarcely deigning to take notice of them—even the isolated manifestations of magnanimity among the common people, now with a smile of distrust, now simply refusing to believe them, and now—with suspicion. And when we happen to give credence to the heroism of some individual, we immediately herald this as something extraordinary. And what is the result?—Our astonishment and eulogies are akin to contempt. During the war this disappears of its own accord and there arises a complete equality in heroism. Blood which has been shed is an important thing. The common exploit of heroism creates the firmest bond between inequalities and classes. The landowner and the peasant, fighting side by side in 1812, were closer one to the other than in the country at home, on a peaceful estate. To the masses war is a pretext for self-respect, and this is the reason why the people love war: they compose songs about it, and later, during long years, they listen with delight to war legends and stories. . . . Blood which has been shed is an important thing! Yes, war, *in our day,* is necessary; without it the world would have perished or, at least, it would have been converted into some sort of slime, into some wretched mire infected with putrid wounds. . . ."

Of course, I stopped arguing. It is impossible to argue with dreamers. However, there is a very strange fact: at present people begin to argue about, and debate, such subjects as—so it seemed—had long ago been settled and sent to the archives. Now all this is being dug up. And the important point is that this is being done everywhere.

3

AGAIN BUT ONE WORD ABOUT SPIRITISM

Again I have no room for an "article" on spiritism; again I defer it to some future issue. And yet, it was as far back as February that I attended that spiritist séance with a "real" medium, which left on me a rather strong impression. Others who were present at this séance have given printed accounts of it, so that there remained nothing for me except to record my personal impression. But up to the present, during these two whole months, I had no desire to write anything about the matter, and *concealed* my impression from the readers. I may state in advance that the séance was one of a most peculiar kind and that it virtually did not pertain to spiritism. This was an impression of something dfferent, but which merely revealed itself apropos of spiritism. I am very sorry that I must be postponing it again, all the more so as now I have acquired a desire to discuss the matter, whereas up to the present time I have felt a sort of disgust for it. Aversion was the result of suspiciousness. Even at that time I spoke to several of my friends about the séance; one person whose opinion I profoundly treasure, having listened to me, asked me if I intended to describe it in the *Diary*. I said that I didn't know. And, unexpectedly, he remarked: "Don't write." To this he added nothing, and I did not insist, but I did grasp the meaning of the remark: obviously it would have displeased him if, in any manner whatever, I might have helped to promote spiritism. At the time I was all the more surprised as, in giving my account about the February séance, I repudiated spiritism with sincere conviction. Yet this man, hating spiritism, must have discerned in my account *something,* as it were, favorable to spiritism, despite all my denials. This is why, up to the present, I have refrained from discussing the matter in print—precisely because of suspiciousness and mistrust of myself. But now, it seems, I fully trust myself and I have found an explanation of my suspiciousness. Besides, I became convinced that no articles of mine could help either to promote or to exterminate spiritism. Mr. Mendeleev, who at this very moment—as I am writing these lines—is delivering his lecture at the Solianoi Gorodok, probably views the matter from a different angle, and he is lecturing with the noble aim of "crushing spiritism." It is always pleasing to listen to lectures with such excellent tendencies, but I believe that he who *wishes* to embrace faith in spiritism cannot be prevented from doing so by either lectures or entire committees, while the incredulous one, who *does not wish* to believe, will be swayed by nothing. It is exactly this conviction that I acquired at the February séance at A. N. Aksakov's house—then, at least, as a first strong impression. Until then I had *simply* denied spiritism, *i.e.,* essentially, I was incensed with the mystical meaning of this doctrine (but I was never able to deny *completely,* nor am I able to do so now, especially now that I have read the report of the learned committee for the investigation of spiritism—spiritistic phenomena with which I had been somewhat familiar even before the séance with the medium). However, after that remarkable séance, suddenly I guessed—or rather, learned— that not only do I not believe in spiritism, but, even more, that I categorically *do not wish* to believe in it, so that no proofs will *ever*

shake me. This is what I derived from the séance and what I came
to understand. And—I confess—the impression was almost a soothing
one because I was a little afraid when I was about to go to that
séance. I may add that this is not merely a personal impression:
it seems to me that in this observation of mine there is also something general. I vaguely sense some peculiar law of human nature,
a law common to everyone, specifically pertaining to faith and incredulity in general. Somehow I perceived then, precisely through
experiment—as a result of that very séance—what force incredulity
may find and develop in one, at a given moment, altogether against
one's will, although in accord with one's secret desire. . . . This is
also probably true of faith. This is what I meant to discuss.

Thus—till the next issue. However, I will add a few words in
amplification of what I have stated in the March issue, specifically
about that same *Report* of the now so widely-known "Committee."

I said, then, a few words regarding the unsatisfactoriness of
that *Report* and in what respect it may even be harmful to its own
purpose. But I have not stated the principal thing. I shall now
attempt briefly to amplify my statement, all the more so as this is
quite a simple matter. The Committee did not wish to condescend
to the most important need in this connection—to the need of society
which has been awaiting its judgment. The Committee, it would
seem, was so little concerned about the social need (otherwise one
would have to presume that it simply was unable to understand that
need) that it failed to comprehend that some "crinoline springlets
glimpsing in the darkness" will dissuade no one and will prove nothing, once people have already been harmfully affected. When reading
the *Report* it positively begins to seem that these scientists of ours
have labored under the presumption that spiritism existed in Petersburg only in A. N. Aksakov's apartment, and that they knew nothing about the thirst for spiritism which has risen in society, nor
concerning the grounds on which spiritism began to spread specifically among us, Russians. However, they did know all this
but merely neglected it. It is quite apparent that they have adopted
toward all these matters an attitude exactly identical with that
of private persons who, when listening to the accounts of the disastrous passion of our society for spiritism, merely scoff at and
giggle about it—and this only *en passant*, hardly condescending to
give thought to the matter. But having formed a committee, these
scientists have become social workers—they are no longer lay persons.
They were entrusted with a mission, and this precisely—so it would
seem—is what they refused to take into consideration: they seated
themselves beside the spiritistic table still, as hitherto, merely as

lay persons, *i.e.*, scoffing and giggling and, in addition, perhaps, vexed by the fact that they had been compelled to take up seriously so nonsensical a thing.

However, let us admit that this entire house and A. N. Aksakov's apartment are covered with springs and wires, and that the medium, besides, has some sort of a little mechanism which produces a cracking sound between his knees (this ingenious conjecture of the committee has been subsequently reported in print by N. P. Wagner). But every "serious" spiritist (pray, do not laugh at this word; in truth—this is quite serious), upon reading the *Report,* will ask: "Well, at my house where I intimately know everyone—my children, my wife, my relatives and acquaintances—well, how is it that at my house identical phenomena are taking place: the table swings and lifts itself, sounds are heard, intelligent answers are being received? Now, I know for sure and I am quite convinced that in my house there are neither mechanisms nor wires, and that my wife and my children are not going to deceive me!" And the main point is that in Petersburg, in Moscow, and in all of Russia, there have appeared all too many of those who will talk or think along these lines. This should have been taken into account even at the risk of descending from the scientific height, for this is an epidemic and people have to be helped. But the presumptuousness of the committee prevents it from such reasoning: "These are simply light-minded and poorly educated people, and this is the reason why they believe." "All right, be it so"—continues to insist a serious and disturbingly convinced spiritist (since they are all in a state of prime astonishment and first alarm, the matter being so new and so extraordinary).—"All right. Let's take it for granted that I am light-minded and poorly educated; still in my house there is no mechanism which produces the cracking sound; this I know for sure. Besides, I have no means for buying such queer instruments; and where can these be bought? Who is selling them? I swear to God, we know nothing about these things. So, then, why do we hear cracks in our house? How are these sounds produced? You are telling us that we ourselves are unconsciously pressing upon the table. I assure you that we are not childish to such an extent, and that we are watching ourselves—exactly, watching: whether we press ourselves. We are conducting experiments with curiosity and impartially. . . ."

"There is nothing to answer you"—concludes the Committee, but already angrily. "You are also being deceived, and in the very same manner as all others. Everybody is being deceived; all are simpletons. Thus it must be. Thus speaks science. We are—Science."

Well, this is no explanation. "No, apparently here there's something different"—concludes the "seriously" convinced spiritist.

"It cannot be that these are mere tricks. It's all right in the case of Madam Clire; but I know my family: there's no one to pull tricks in my house."

And spiritism persists.

I have just read in *The New Times* an account of Mr. Mendeleev's first lecture at the Solianoi Gorodok. Mr. Mendeleev makes the following positive assertion in the form of a solid fact:

"At spiritistic séances tables move and produce sounds both when hands are laid upon them and when they are not. Of these sounds, in accordance with a given alphabet, whole words, phrases and dicta are formed, which invariably bear the impress of the mentality of that medium with whose aid the séance is being conducted. This is a fact. Now, it must be explained: who does the rapping and how is it done? For the elucidation of these questions there are the following six hypotheses."

This is the main thing: "Who does the rapping and how is it done?" Thereupon, six—as many as six—hypotheses already conceived in Europe are being set forth. It would seem that even the most "serious" spiritist could be dissuaded. But to a conscientious spiritist *seeking* to elucidate the matter, the most curious point is not that there are six hypotheses, but which of these does Mr. Mendeleev himself embrace, what does he specifically maintain, and what precisely were the findings of the Committee? Our own domestic problems are closer to us, more authoritative, while those in Europe and in the United States—why, they are an obscure matter. And from the further exposé of the lecture it appears that the Committee has still adopted the hypothesis of legerdemain, and not of simple tricks but precisely based on preconceived roguery and mechanisms producing cracking sounds between the knees (I repeat —according to N. P. Wagner's statement). But this scientific "presumptuousness" is insufficient, quite insufficient, to our spiritists; it would have been insufficient *even if the Committee* were right, and here is the whole trouble. Besides—who knows?—perhaps the "seriously" convinced spiritist is right when he concludes that even if spiritism were nonsense, nevertheless here we are dealing with something different than mere coarse roguery—something which should be dealt with more cautiously, so to speak, more delicately, since "his wife, his children, his acquaintances are not going to deceive him," etc., etc. Believe me, he stands on his road from which you are not going to lead him astray. He firmly knows that here "not everything is roguery." Of this he has already convinced himself.

In fact, all the other contentions of the Committee are almost equally presumptuous: "They are light-minded, you see, unconsciously they press upon the table, and this is the reason why it swings; they seek to deceive themselves—and the table produces rapping sounds; nerves are upset; they sit in darkness; the accordion is playing; tiny hooks are inserted into shirt-sleeves (this, however, is Mr. Rachinsky's conjecture); they are lifting the table with the toes of their feet," and so on, and so forth. And still all this is not going to disillusion anyone *who wishes to be seduced.* "For goodness sake, I have a table that weighs two poods; under no circumstance can I move it by merely extending my foot and, of course, there is no way I can lift it *up into the air.* Besides, this cannot be done at all except, perhaps, by some fakir or juggler, or by that Mrs. Clire of yours with her crinoline device; but there are no such jugglers or equilibrists in my family."

Briefly, spiritism is undoubtedly a great, extraordinary and most foolish fallacy, a lecherous doctrine and ignorance; but the trouble is that all this, perhaps, does not transpire around the table as the Committee orders us to believe, and, indeed, it is also impossible to call all spiritists humbugs and fools. This method merely tends to insult everybody, but thereby nothing can be achieved. It seems that this fallacy should be specifically dealt with in some correlation with our current social conditions, and for this reason both the tone and the method of the *Report* should have been different. The mystical meaning of spiritism—this most harmful thing—should have been taken into particular consideration. Yet, the Committee has not given thought to this particular significance. Of course, under no circumstance, would it have been in a position to crush the evil; but, at least, by different—not so naïve and haughty—methods the Committee could have inculcated in spiritists even respect for its findings, while it could have exercised a strong influence on the wavering followers of spiritism. However, the Committee obviously deemed any approach to the matter other than legerdemain—and not a simple one but one fraught with roguery—degrading to its scientific dignity. Every presumption that spiritism is *something* besides a vulgar fraud or trick was inconceivable to the Committee. Besides, what would have been said in Europe about our scientists? Thus, deliberately assuming the conviction that the whole task in this respect comes down to the necessity of exposing a fraud and to nothing else, the scientists thereby have conveyed to their judgment a preconceived character. Believe me, some clever spiritist—I assure you that there are also clever people who ponder over spiritism, and not only fools—some clever spiritist, upon reading newspaper accounts of Mr. Mendeleev's public lecture, and in that lecture the following sentence: "Of these sounds, subject to a given alphabet, whole words, phrases and dicta are formed *which invariably bear the impress of the mentality of the medium* with whose aid the séance is being conducted; this is a fact . . ."—having read this sentence, he may, perhaps, all of a sudden say to himself: "Why, this invariable intellectual impress of the medium . . . perhaps, this is the most essential point in the inquiry into spiritism, and the inference has been arrived at on the strength of the most exhaustive experiments, and now our Committee, having hardly seated itself by the table (indeed, long had they been engaged in the work!), has forthwith determined that this was *a fact*. Come, come —a fact! Maybe the Committee, in this case, was guided by some German or French opinion, but, if so, where is its own experience? This is merely an opinion, and not an inference drawn from its own experience. By Mrs. Clire alone they could not have drawn the conclusion as to the answers of the tables 'corresponding to the mentality of the mediums,' as a general fact. Besides, it is doubtful whether they have investigated even Mrs. Clire from the standpoint of her intellectual, upper, cerebral characteristics, but they merely found a cracking mechanism—and this in an altogether different place. Mr. Mendeleev was a member of the Committee, and when delivering his lecture he spoke, as it were, on behalf of the Committee. No, such a hasty and cursory judgment of the Committee, *on so momentous a point of the inquiry*, and in the face of such scanty experiments—is much too presumptuous and, besides, hardly scientific. . . ."

Verily, people may reason this way. Now, such a presumptuous shallowness of *certain* deductions will furnish society, and more particularly all these already convinced spiritists, with a pretext for becoming even more confirmed in their fallacies: "Presumptuousness"—they will say—"haughtiness, prejudice, premeditation! They are much too petulant! . . ." And spiritism will persist.

P.S. I have just read the account about Mr. Mendeleev's second lecture on spiritism. Mr. Mendeleev already attributes to the Committee's report a remedial effect upon writers: "Souvorin no longer believes in spiritism as strongly as before; Boborykin has also apparently been cured or, at least, he is on the way to recovery. Finally, Dostoievsky, too, has recovered in his *Diary:* in January he was inclined toward spiritism, and in March he is already scolding it." This, then, must be due to the *Report*. Thus, it would seem that the esteemed Mr. Mendeleev thought that in January I was commending spiritism! Well, was it for the devils?

Mr. Mendeleev must be an extraordinarily kindhearted man. Imagine, having crushed spiritism by his two lectures, at the close of his second lecture he has paid tribute to it. And for what, would

you think?—"Honor and glory to spiritists" (look, we have come
to honor and glory—why so suddenly?) "Honor and glory to
spiritists"—said he—"for the fact that they have emerged honest
and bold champions of what, to them, seemed to be truth, unafraid
of prejudices!" It is obvious that this has been uttered out of
pity and, so to speak, delicacy caused by over-satiation with his
personal success. Only, I don't know if it was delicate. This is
identical with the attestations which proprietors of boarding schools
sometimes give about pupils to their parents: "Now, while this one,
unlike his elder brother, cannot boast of his mental faculties and
will achieve little, nevertheless he is openhearted and his behavior
is dependable." Think, only, how the younger brother must feel
when hearing such a commendation! Mr. Mendeleev has praised
spiritists (and again with "honor and glory") because in our materialistic age they are taking an interest in the soul: thus, if not
exactly firm in sciences, says he, they are firm in faith—they believe
in God. The esteemed professor must be a great quiz. Well, if
this was meant in a spirit of naïveté, then he must be the opposite:
a man utterly devoid of a sense of humor.

4

On Behalf of a Deceased Person

With a painful feeling have I read in *The New Times* an
anecdote, reprinted by this paper from the magazine *The Cause,*
which is injurious to the memory of my brother Mikhail Mikhailovich, the founder and editor of the magazines *Time* and *The
Epoch,* who died twelve years ago. I am quoting the anecdote
verbatim.

"In the year 1862, when Schapov decided to have no further
dealings with the contemporaneous *Domestic Records* and while
other magazines had been temporarily suspended, he sent his
Runners to *Time.* In the autumn he was badly pressed financially,
but the late editor of the magazine *Time,* Mikhail Dostoievsky, had
been greatly delaying the payment of money due to Schapov. Cold
weather set in, and Schapov did not even have warm clothes.
Finally, he lost all patience. He asked Dostoievsky to come and
see him, and on that occasion the following scene took place. 'Please
wait, Afanasij Prokopievich, dear; in a week I will bring you all
your money'—said Dostoievsky. 'But do apprehend, at length, that
I need the money forthwith!'—'Why forthwith?'—'Look, I have no
warm clothes.'—'I have an idea: I happen to know a tailor; you
can buy from him everything you need on a credit basis; later I

will pay him out of your money.' And Dostoievsky drove Schapov
to the tailor, a Jew, who fitted out the historian with some sort
of an overcoat, a suit, a vest and a pair of trousers, of very dubious
quality, for which he billed him exorbitantly, about which subsequently even the impractical Schapov used to complain."

This is quoted from an obituary of Schapov in *The Cause*.
I do not know who wrote it; as yet, I have made no inquiries at
the office of *The Cause*, and I have not read the obituary itself.
As stated, I am reprinting the above from *The New Times*.

My brother died long ago, so that it is an obscure matter;
it is difficult to defend him, and there are no witnesses to the
described episode. Thus, the accusation is devoid of proof. But I
positively assert that this anecdote is mere humbug, and if some
of the circumstances in it are not fabrications—at least, all the
facts are distorted so that truth has been greatly impaired. This
I will prove—as far as possible.

To begin with, I wish to state that I never participated in the
financial affairs of my brother, either pertaining to the magazine
or any of his former commercial transactions. While collaborating
in the editorship of my brother's *Time*, I had no connection with
any monetary matters. Nevertheless, I am fully aware of the fact
that, considering the times, that magazine was a brilliant success.
I also know that not only were no debts to writers incurred, but,
on the contrary, time and again contributors used to receive substantial advance payments. This I know positively, and many a
time have I witnessed it. Nor was the journal in need of contributors: they used to come of their own accord, and ever since
the first year of its publication articles used to be sent in great
quantities: one has only to glance through the issues of *Time* covering the whole two and one-half year period of its publication to
become convinced that the overwhelming majority of the contemporaneous men of letters had been among its contributors. This
could not have been the case had my brother failed to pay them,
or, more correctly, had he in any way disgracefully treated them.
However, even at present many persons can attest to the fact that
substantial advances had been paid. All this did not transpire in
some dark corner. Many of the former, and quite active, contributors are still living and, of course, they will not refuse to
state how, in their opinion and to their recollection, my brother
had been conducting the affairs of the magazine. Briefly, my brother
could not have been "delaying payment to Schapov," especially if
he had no clothes. However, if Schapov had asked my brother to
come and see him, it was not because "he had lost all patience,"
but precisely with the object of *soliciting an advance,* just as many

others had done. Many letters and communications from contributors addressed to the editorial office were preserved after my
late brother's death, and I have not lost hope of finding some of
Schapov's notes. In this event their mutual relations would be
brought to light. But, aside from this, the fact that at that time
Schapov had probably asked for an advance payment, is no doubt
more in conformity with the truth and to all recollections, to all
witness accounts, available even now, as to the manner in which
Time was managed and published—witness accounts of which, I
repeat, a considerable number could be obtained even at present
despite the lapse of fourteen years. Notwithstanding his "business-
like ways," my brother used to be weak to solicitations and did
not know how to refuse: he had paid out advances sometimes even
without assurance of receiving an article of a writer for his magazine. Of this I was a witness, and I would be in a position to name
certain persons. But he also had experiences of a different kind.
One of the *steady* contributors, having received from my brother,
after insistent solicitations, six hundred rubles in advance, the very
next morning set out to the Western Provinces, where, at the time,
people were needed for governmental positions. There he remained,
and my brother received from him neither article nor money. But
it is most remarkable that my brother never made any move to
recover the money, notwithstanding the fact that he had a document
in his hands. Only, much later, my brother's family, through a
court action, recovered that sum from that man (a man of means).
The case was tried publicly, and most accurate information concerning this matter may be had. I merely mean to point out how
easily and readily did my brother advance money, and that a man
of his type would not have been delaying payment to a needy
writer. Schapov's necrologist, listening to Schapov's account of his
conversation with my brother, simply could not have known what
money was then in question: money due from my brother, or an
advance payment. It is quite possible that my brother had suggested to Schapov that clothes be ordered for him on a credit basis
from a tailor whom he happened to know. This is easily understandable: not wishing to refuse to come to Schapov's assistance,
he could, for some reason, have preferred this form of assistance
to a direct payment of money to Schapov. . . .

Finally, in the quoted anecdote I do not recognize my brother's
conversation: he never did converse in *such a tone*. This is an
altogether different person, an altogether different man. My brother
never curried anyone's favor; he could not bustle around a man
with sugar-coated phrases besprinkled with subservient little idioms.
And, of course, he would never have permitted anyone to say to

him: "But do apprehend, at length, that I need the money forth-with!" After fourteen years, all these phrases have somehow got recoined and refabricated by the author of the anecdote into "remi-niscences." Let all those who remember my brother—and of these there are many—recall whether he ever conversed in such a style. My brother was a scrupulously decent man; he behaved and acted as a gentleman, which he was indeed. He was a highly educated man, a gifted writer, a connoisseur of European literature, a poet and a noted translator of Schiller and Goethe. I cannot imagine how such a man could have been standing on his hind legs before Schapov, as the anecdote implies.

I shall refer to one more fact concerning my brother which, I believe, is little known. In 1849, he was arrested in connection with the Petrashevsky case, and he was sent to the fortress where he was then kept two months. After the lapse of two months several persons (quite a few) were released as guiltless and in no way involved in the affair. And, in truth, my brother did take no part in either the secret organizational association of Petrashevsky or in Durov's group. Nevertheless, he did attend Petrashevsky's eve-ning parties and used to borrow books from the secret, common library which was kept in the house of Petrashevsky. He was then a Fourierist and passionately studied Fourier. Thus, during these two months in the fortress by no means could he have considered himself safe and expect, with any measure of assurance, that he would be released. The fact that he was a Fourierist and that he had used the library had been discovered, and, of course, he could have anticipated exile—if not to Siberia, then to some remote locality —on the grounds that he was a suspicious individual. And many among those released after two months would have been exiled— this I positively assert—had they all not been freed in accordance with the will of the late Emperor; this I learned at that time from Prince Gagarin who conducted the investigation of the Petrashevsky case. At least, I then learned the fact which concerned the release of my brother—a fact which was announced to me, just to gladden me, by Prince Gagarin, who had expressly summoned me for this purpose from the casemate to the commandant's house, where the case was being prosecuted. But I was single, unmarried, and I had no children. My brother, however, at the time of being taken to the fortress, had left in his apartment his wife and three children, of whom the eldest was then only seven years old; and, on top of that, he had left them penniless. My brother loved his children tenderly and ardently, and I can imagine what he must have en-dured during those two months! And yet, he made *no depositions* which could have compromised other people, in order to alleviate his own lot; this he could have done since, although he took no part in anything, *he did know many things*.

Now I will ask you: would many in his place have acted this way? I am boldly propounding this question because I know what I am talking about. I know and I have seen what men prove to be in calamities such as these; I am not judging abstractly. Let people evaluate this act of my brother as they please, nevertheless, even for his own salvation, he did refuse to do something contrary to his convictions. I may remark that this is not merely a groundless statement on my part: at present I am in a position to corroborate all these contentions by most accurate data. And yet, during those two months, every day and every hour, my brother was tormented with the thought that he had ruined his family, and he suffered when calling to his mind those three dear little creatures and pondering over their future. . . . And this is the man whom people now seek to represent in collusion with some Jew tailor in order, by defrauding Schapov, to divide the profits with the tailor and to pocket a few rubles. Poh! What fiddlesticks!

MAY

CHAPTER I

1

From a Private Letter

PEOPLE ASK me if I intend to write about the Kairova case. I have already received several letters containing the same question. One of the letters is particularly characteristic and it was obviously not intended for print. But I take the liberty of quoting several lines from it, naturally preserving strict anonymity. I hope that my esteemed correspondent will not object to this. Besides, I am quoting him because I am convinced of his absolute sincerity, which I fully appreciate.

". . . It is with the most profound disgust that we have read about the Kairova case. As a focus in an object glass, it reflects the picture of carnal instincts for which the leading dramatis persona (Kairova) has been moulded by means of cultural preparation: her mother, during her pregnancy, took to drinking; her father was a drunkard; her own brother lost his mind as a result of dipsomania and shot himself; a cousin of hers murdered his wife;

her father's mother was insane; it was from this cultural milieu that a despotic person with uncontrollable carnal propensities had sprung. Even the prosecutors stood perplexed before the question: wasn't she insane? Some experts positively denied it, while others admitted the possibility of insanity—not in her personally, but in her actions. Yet, throughout this whole trial one perceived not a lunatic but a woman who had reached the utmost limits of negation of everything sacred: to her there exist neither family nor the rights of any other woman—not only to her own husband but to life itself; all these are for her alone and for her carnal gratification.

"She was acquitted, perhaps, on the ground of insanity—for this God be praised! At least her moral depravity was attributed not to the progress of the mind but to the category of psychic maladies. 'However, in the lower section of the hall, which was occupied *exclusively by ladies,* applause burst out.' (*Stock-Exchange News*) Applause to what? To the acquittal of an insane woman or to the triumph of an unbridled passionate nature, to cynicism incarnated in the person of a woman?

"Ladies applaud!—Wives and mothers applaud! Why, they should be weeping and not applauding in the face of such a desecration of the feminine ideal . . ."

(N.B. Here I am omitting several too harsh lines.)

"Is it possible that you will remain silent?"

2

A New Regional Word

To stir up Kairova's story (which, I believe, is generally known, is now too late. Besides, I attach no significance whatsoever to my words as to such characteristic phenomena of our current life and amidst such typical moods of our public. But *apropos* of this "case," it would seem worth while to say a few, though belated, words. Since nothing ceases, therefore, nothing is too late: on the contrary, everything continues, assuming new forms, even though it has outlived its initial stage. And what is most important: let my correspondent forgive me for having quoted his letter. Judging by the letters which I am personally receiving, one could draw a conclusion as to an extremely remarkable phenomenon in our Russian life, at which recently I have already indirectly hinted, namely: everybody is restless; everybody seems to be concerned about everything; everybody seeks to record his opinion and to express himself. And there is only one point on which I

am not clear: are they more anxious to segregate themselves in their
individual opinions than to reach a general harmonious accord?

This is a provincial letter, a private one, but, in passing,
I may remark that our provincial districts are decidedly seeking
to establish a peculiar life of their own, almost completely eman-
cipated from the capitals. This is not merely my personal observation: a long time before, this has been recorded in the press. There
has been lying on my desk—already for two months—a solid literary
collection *The First Step,* published in Kazan; some mention should
have been made of it long ago, precisely because it came forth
with a determined intention to utter a new word—one not echoing
the capital, but a regional and "pressingly-needed" word. Well,
all these are but new voices in the old Russian chorus; therefore,
they are useful and, at any rate, interesting. This new orientation
must have its underlying cause. True, of all these projected new
words, essentially, not one has yet been uttered; but, perhaps,
something as yet unheard-of may actually come from our provincial
and border regions. Judging abstractly and theoretically, thus it
should come to pass: till now, ever since Peter, Russia has been
led by Petersburg and Moscow. But at present, when the role
of Petersburg and of "the window cut through to Europe" has
come to an end—at present . . . but that's the question: can it be
that the role of Petersburg and Moscow has come to an end? To
my way of thinking, if it has changed, it has changed very little.
Besides, in days past, during the entire period of one hundred and
fifty years, did Petersburg and Moscow actually lead Russia? Was
this an actual fact? And, on the contrary, was it not Russia, as
a whole, that has been flowing to Petersburg and Moscow and
crowding there—during that entire period—and, in fact, has she
not been guiding herself, uninterruptedly restoring herself through
the afflux of fresh forces from her provinces and border regions,
in which—I may mention in passing—the problems were identical
with those of all Russians, be it in Moscow or in Petersburg, in
Riga or in the Caucasus, or anywhere else. Now, speaking theoretically and in principle, what can be more opposed, one to the
other, than Petersburg and Moscow?—In fact, Petersburg was
originally founded, as it were, in opposition to Moscow and *her
whole idea.* And yet, these *two centers* of Russian life, substantially,
had formed one center—and this happened forthwith, from the
very beginning, at the time of the reform itself, and quite regardless
of certain characteristics which separated them. Things that took
birth and developed in Petersburg immediately, and precisely as
independently, used to take birth, consolidate themselves and develop in Moscow, and *vice versa*—to the dot. The soul was one, and

not only in these two cities, but in any two cities and in the whole of Russia, *so that everywhere throughout Russia, in every place, there was the entire Russia*. Oh, of course, we understand that every corner of Russia may, and must, have its local peculiarities and its full right to develop them. But are these peculiarities such as to threaten disunity or even some misunderstanding? Speaking generally, our future is "deep water," but concerning this point it is clearer than anywhere. In any event, let us pray God that everything capable of development, be developing—good things of course; this is first; and the second and principal point: let us pray God that we shall not lose our unity—under no circumstance, despite any blessings, promises and treasures: better, together than apart —and this, *quand même*. The new word will be uttered—this cannot be doubted; still I do not believe that anything altogether too new or too particular will be said by our provincial and border regions —at least not now, not forthwith, and nothing unheard-of or difficult to bear. The Great Russian only now begins to live; he is just arising to utter his new word—and, perhaps, to the whole world. In my judgment, Moscow—this center of the Great Russians —is designed to live long, and let's pray God that it be so. Moscow, thus far, has not been the third Rome; and the prophecy that "there shall be no fourth Rome" must be fulfilled. Nor can the world do without a Rome. However, Petersburg, more than ever, is now in accord with Moscow. And I confess that by Moscow, in the present sense, I mean not so much the city itself as a certain allegory, so that no Kazan or Astrakhan should take any offense. But we are glad of their collections, and should even *The Second Step* make its appearance, so much the better, so much the better.

3

THE COURT AND MRS. KAIROVA

However, we have drifted far afield from the Kairova case. I only meant to point out to my esteemed correspondent that even though I agree with his view on "the depravity of the instincts and the despotic unrestraint of carnal propensities," nevertheless I find in his opinion too much severity, even aimless severity (since he himself virtually considers the criminal an insane person), too much exaggeration—all the more so as he winds up with the admission of *environment which has exercised its influence* to the point where the struggle against it had become almost impossible. As for myself, I am frankly glad that Kairova has been released; I am merely not glad that she was acquitted. I am glad that she was released, although I do not believe a twopence in her insanity, notwithstanding the opinions of some of the experts; let this be a personal view which I keep to myself. Besides, without insanity one somehow feels more pity for this ill-fated woman. In a state of lunacy "she knew not what she did . . ." whereas without insanity—just try to shoulder so much torment! Murder—if it is not committed by a confirmed rascal—is a painful and complicated proposition. These several days of irresolution on the part of Kairova when the legitimate wife comes to the former's lover; this seething insult swelling by degrees, this offense growing more intense every hour (oh, Kairova is the transgressor—I have not yet gone mad—but she is all the more pitiful as in her decay she was unable even to understand that she was the offender, whereas she believed and felt the reverse); and, finally, this last hour before the "exploit," at night, on the steps of the staircase, with the razor she had bought on the eve, in her hand—nay, all this is rather painful especially to such a disorderly and oscillating soul as that of Kairova! This is an unbearable burden, and one hears the groans of a crushed woman. And, after that, ten months of trials, insane asylums, experts—she has been dragged and dragged, and yet, this poor, grave criminal woman, who is fully guilty, essentially represents something so trifling, so absurd, so devoid of understanding, so abortive, so vain and emotional, so incapable of self-control, so trivial, to the very last minute of the verdict—that somehow one felt relieved when they let her go. It is only to be regretted that this could not have been done without acquitting her because, say what you please, this created a scandal. Attorney-at-law Mr. Outin, it seems, could without fail have anticipated an acquittal and, for this reason, he should have confined himself to a mere exposé of the facts, instead of embarking upon eulogies of the crime, since *he almost did commend the crime.* . . . That's exactly the point: we know no limit in whatever it be. In the West, Darwin's theory is an ingenious hypothesis, while in Russia it has long been an axiom. In the West, the idea that crime is often but a disease, has a profound meaning because it is being dealt with with great *discrimination*, whereas to us this idea is absolutely meaningless, since we do not discriminate at all—and everything, every villainy perpetrated even by a confirmed rascal, is treated as a malady, and —alas!—is looked upon as something liberal! Of course, I am not speaking of serious people (but, in this sense, do we have many serious people?)—I am speaking of the street, of the inept mediocrity on the one hand, and the knaves trafficking in liberalism on the other, and these don't care a rap about anything so long as something be or appear liberal.

As regards attorney-at-law Outin, he "commended the crime" because, probably, he imagined that, as an attorney-at-law, he could not have acted differently. Thus, unquestionably clever men are being led astray, and the results are by no means clever. I believe that had the jurors been in a different position, *i.e.*, could they have rendered a different verdict, they would have grown indignant over such an exaggeration on Mr. Outin's part, and thus he could have harmed his client. But, as a matter of fact, literally they could not have rendered a different verdict. In the press, some people have commended them for this verdict, while others—it is rumored—have censured them. I believe that here there is no place for either praise or censure: they rendered this verdict because of the absolute impossibility of uttering anything different. Please judge for yourselves. Here is what we read in a newspaper account:

"To the question propounded by the court, pursuant to the request of the prosecution: 'Did Kairova, *having beforehand deliberated upon her action,* inflict upon Alexandra Velikanova, *with the aim of murdering her,* several wounds with a razor on her neck, head and chest, *but was prevented from the final consummation of her aim* to kill Velikanova by Velikanova herself and by her husband?'—the jurors replied in the negative." Let us stop here. This is the answer to the first question. Now, can one answer a question framed *in such terms?* Who, whose conscience, would venture to answer such a question in the affirmative? (True, here a negative answer is equally impossible, but we are merely speaking of the affirmative decision of the jurors.) Here, a question thus framed could have been answered in the affirmative only by one possessing Divine omniscience. And Kairova herself could not have known at all: 'would she slash her to death or not?' and yet the jurors were positively asked: 'Would she or would she not have slashed her to death if she had not been stopped?' But even when, a day before, she had bought the razor, though she knew for what purpose she had bought it, nevertheless she still could not have known: 'whether she would embark upon the slashing, not to speak of whether or not she would have slashed to death.' More probable still that she knew nothing about it even when she had been sitting on the steps of the staircase, already holding the razor in her hand, while her lover and her rival were lying on her bed in the rear, behind her. No one—no one in the world—could have known anything about it. Moreover—even though this may sound absurd—I assert that even when she had started cutting, *she still may not have known* whether or not she wished to murder her victim, and whether she had been inflicting the wounds *with this* specific purpose. Please note that by this I do not at all mean that she was in a state of

unconsciousness; I even do not admit the slightest degree of insanity. On the contrary, unquestionably, at the moment when she
had been wielding the razor, *she knew that she was slashing,* but
did she wish to murder her rival—was this her deliberate purpose?
—this she could well not have known at all, and for God's sake,
don't consider this an absurdity: she could have been striking,
incensed with wrath and hatred, without in the least thinking about
the consequences. Judging by the character of this disorderly and
jaded woman, this must probably have been the case. And please
note that upon the answer—let us say, an affirmative answer to the
effect that she would have killed, and what is most important, that
she has been slashing with the express intent to kill—the fate of
the ill-starred woman was dependent. This would have meant ruin,
forced labor. How could the jurors have cast such a burden upon
their conscience? And they did give a negative answer because
they were unable to modify their verdict. You may say that
Kairova's crime was not a fabricated or reflective or bookish one;
that it was simply a 'female affair,' a very uncomplicated and
simple one, and that, moreover, her rival lay on her bed. But is
it as simple as that? And what if, after having slashed Velikanova's
throat with the razor a single time, she would have shuddered,
screamed and started running? How do you know that this could
not have happened? And had it happened, most probably the case
would never have been brought to trial. But now they have pinned
you to the wall and they are quizzing you, insisting that you positively answer the question: 'would she or would she not have
slashed to death?'—and, of course, with a view to sentencing or
not sentencing her in accordance with your verdict. The slightest
variation in it is equivalent to long years of imprisonment or forced
labor! And, again, what would have happened if after slashing
Velikanova a single time and having then become frightened, she
should have started slashing herself and possibly have killed herself
on the spot? Finally, what if she not only would not have been
frightened, but, on the contrary, having sensed the first splashes
of hot blood, she would have sprung and, after slashing Velikanova
to death, would have abused the corpse, chopping off the head,
cutting off the nose and lips, and only later, suddenly, when that
head would have been wrested from her, she would have grasped
what she had done? I am asking these questions because all these
things could have taken place and could have emanated from one
and the same woman, from one and the same soul, in one and the
same mood and in one and the same setting. I am stating so because I feel that I am not mistaken.

Thus, in view of the above, how could such an amazing question of the court have been answered? Indeed, this was not a domestic conversation at the tea table; this was the determination of one's fate. By propounding such questions one runs the risk of not receiving any answer.

But—it might be argued—in this case it would never be possible to prosecute or to try a case of murder or attempted murder provided the crime had not been consummated, or the victim had recovered.—No, it would seem to me that there is no ground for such fears since there are all too obvious cases of murder where, though the crime had not been consummated (even by the individual volition of the criminal), nevertheless it is too obvious that it had been undertaken *with the intention to kill,* and that it could have had no other aim. And what is most important—to this end, we have the jurors' conscience; this is the principal and great thing. Therein is the beneficence of the reformed courts. If in a moment as grave as this a man will sense in him the resolution firmly to answer: "Yes, guilty"—in all probability he will not err as to the guilt of the criminal. At least, it is proverbially seldom that errors are committed. Only one thing is desirable: that the jurors' conscience be genuinely enlightened, genuinely firm and made steady by the civic sense of duty, and that it should avoid predilections on either side—that is, in the way of cruelty or disastrous sentimentality. True, the latter desideratum—I mean, concerning the avoidance of sentimentality—is rather difficult of fulfillment. Sentimentality fits everybody so well; it is such a facile thing; it requires so little effort; it is so profitable: nowadays, sentimentality with orientation conveys even to an ass the appearance of a respectable man. . . .

Much in the same way also, the second question propounded by the court to the jurors: "Did she inflict these wounds, and *with the same intention,* in a state of wrath and irritation?"—the jurors, again, could not have answered otherwise than in the negative—*i.e.,* "no, she did not inflict,"—since here, too, the formula "with the same intention" meant "with a premeditated aim of murdering Velikanova." And it was particularly difficult to frame an answer to the question because "wrath and irritation," in an overwhelming majority of cases, preclude "premeditated aim," so that this second question of the court contains, as it were, a certain absurdity.

However, in the third question of the court: "Did Kairova act in a state of firmly ascertained insanity?"—there is a rather obvious absurdity, since in the presence of the first two questions, these two and the third one positively exclude each other: in case of negative answers to the first two questions, or even if they had been left unanswered, it wouldn't have been clear what the question was, or even what the word "act" meant, *i.e.*, concerning which particular act the question was propounded and how it is being defined. But the jurors were in no position to modify their answer, because they were in duty bound to answer *yes* or *no*, without any variations.

Finally, the *fourth* question of the court: "If she had acted not under the influence of insanity, is she guilty of the crime described in the first and second questions?"—the jurors also left unanswered, of course, because it was a mere repetition of the first two questions.

Thus, the court *let* Kairova *off*. It goes without saying that in the jurors' answer: "No, she did not inflict . . .," there was an absurdity since the fact itself of the infliction of wounds was rejected—a fact which was contested by no one and which was obvious to everybody. Yet it was difficult for the jurors to give a different answer in the face of the questions as they had been framed. But, at least, it cannot be said that the court, by releasing Kairova, or even, so to speak, by pardoning her, had *acquitted* the defendant, whereas Mr. Outin precisely justified the act of the criminal woman, considering it almost righteous and good. Of course, this is incredible, and yet this was actually the case.

4

MR. DEFENSE LAWYER AND KAIROVA

I shall not analyze Mr. Outin's speech; after all, it was not even a talented speech: there was an awful lot of lofty style, of various "sentiments" and of that pseudo-liberal humaneness to which nowadays almost everybody—at times even utter ninnies (so that it did not suit Mr. Outin at all)—are resorting in "speeches" and in literature, in order to convey to their productions a respectable appearance and, in that way, have them "passed." In Russia, as time goes on, this pseudo-liberal humaneness reveals itself ever more strongly. And everybody is aware of the fact that all this is merely a handy tool. I am even under the impression that at present this is no longer popular—not as it used to be ten years ago—whereas, lo, there is still so much simple-mindedness in people, especially in our Petersburg! And simple-mindedness is precisely the thing for which the "schemer" is craving. For instance, he has no time to look into a "case," to give it thought. Besides, virtually all of them, as the years roll by and successes accumulate, in a measure have grown hard, and they have sufficiently served the cause of humaneness; they have earned, so to speak, the badge of humaneness so that they really can't be bothered with the misfortunes of some suffering and rattlebrained little soul of a foolish, obtruding client; while in the breasts of many of them, in lieu of a heart, there beats a morsel of something bureaucratic. And thus, once and forever, they "rent"—for all future emergency occasions—a limited supply of conventional phrases, little words, petty sentiments, microscopic thoughts, gestures and conceptions—of course, in strict accord with the latest liberal vogue—and thereupon they sink for a long time, for all their lives, into repose and felicity. And almost always they get away with it. I repeat, this definition of the modern "schemer" I am in no way applying to Mr. Outin: he is a man of talent and, probably, his sentiments are genuine, natural. Even so, he did infuse into his speech much too many crackling phrases, and this leads one to suspect—not exactly a lack of taste, but, indeed, a certain neglectful, and even, perhaps, not quite humane attitude toward a case, in this specific instance. It should be ad-mitted that our lawyers, the more talented they are, the busier they are, and, therefore, they have no time to spare. Had Mr. Outin had more leisure, he would, in my opinion, have adopted a more hearty attitude toward his case; and had he adopted a more hearty attitude, he would have given it more thought and he would not have started singing dithyrambs in honor of an essentially vulgar intrigue; he would have refrained from infusing lofty style about "aroused lionesses from which their young ones are being taken away"; he would not, with so naïve a fury, have attacked Mrs. Velikanova, the victim of the crime; he would not have re-proached her for the fact that she had not been slashed to death (indeed, virtually so!), and, finally, he would not have uttered that most unexpected calembour of his, paraphrasing Christ's words in the Gospel about the woman taken in adultery. However, per-haps, in reality all this transpired differently, and Mr. Outin ac-tually delivered his speech with a quite serious air. I was not in the courtroom; but, judging from accounts, it appears that there was a certain, so to speak, contemptuous looseness. . . . In a word, something utterly devoid of reflection and, on top of that, there was a great deal that was comical.

Almost from the very beginning of the speech, I was non-plussed and was at a loss to understand if Mr. Outin was jesting when he expressed his thanks to the prosecutor for the fact that his accusatorial speech against Kairova, in addition to being "brilliant and talented, eloquent and humane," was more an apologetic than an inculpatory one. That the prosecutor's speech was eloquent and humane, there isn't a shadow of doubt—nor can it be denied that it was an extremely liberal speech. And, generally speaking, these

gentlemen praise each other quite a lot, and the jurors are listening to this. But having eulogized the *prosecutor* district attorney
for his *defense* speech, Mr. Outin refused to be original to the end,
and to start accusing his client, Mrs. Kairova, instead of defending
her. This is a pity because it would have been amusing and, maybe,
it would have fitted the case. Nor do I think that the jurors would
have been much surprised because it is difficult to astonish our
jurors. This innocent remark of mine, of course, is nothing but a
jest: Mr. Outin did not accuse; he defended, and, if there were
defects in his speech, these were precisely due to the fact that he
conducted his defense too passionately, so to speak, he "over-salted"
it, which, as I have mentioned before, I attribute to a preliminary
neglectful attitude toward the "case." "When the time comes, I'll
brazen it out with exalted style. . . . That's all the 'gallery' deserves. . . ." Thus, probably, argue some of our busiest advocates.
For instance, Mr. Outin labors in the attempt to portray his client
in a most idealistic, romantic and fantastic guise, whereas this is
not at all necessary: without adornment, Mrs. Kairova is even
more intelligible. However, the defense lawyer aims, of course, at
the bad taste of the jurors. Everything in her is ideal; every step
of hers is remarkable, magnanimous, graceful, while her love is
something seething—it is a poem! Kairova—just to mention one
example—never having been on the stage, suddenly signs a contract
for a job as an actress and departs to a remote Russian province,
Orenburg. Mr. Outin does not set forth or insist upon the contention that in this act of Kairova "her usual gentleness and self-
sacrifice is revealed," but "there is here"—Mr. Outin continues—
"some ideality, some sort of extravagance, and, mainly—self-renunciation. She had to look for a position to help her mother; and
so, she accepts a job which is not at all suited to her; she leaves
Petersburg and goes alone to Orenburg"—and so on, and so forth.
Now, what's there in this?—It seems that here there is nothing
unusual or amazing: are there only a few people journeying hither
and thither? Are there only a few girls—poor, beautiful, ill-fated,
talented—who accept out-of-town positions far inferior to that which
Mrs. Kairova got? But in the interpretation of the defense lawyer,
as you see, this act signifies a sacrifice of self-renunciation, while
the theatrical contract almost reaches the level of an heroic deed.
And thus it goes on, along the same lines.

Very soon Kairova "becomes intimate with Velikanov, the
manager of the troupe. His business is bad: she busies herself trying to help him; she solicits and obtains a subsidy; she arranges
for his release." Again, what's there in all this?—Nothing extraordinary; besides, many women, especially those with a lively, mo-

bile temperament, such as Kairova's, would start "stirring" for the sake of a man dear to them, once they had contracted a little love affair with him. Then there ensued scenes with Velikanov's wife, and, having depicted one of them, Mr. Outin remarks that from that very moment his woman client began to regard Velikanov as "her own," her creation, her "darling child." In passing, it is reported that this "darling child" is a tall, stocky fellow of grenadier stature, with curling hair on the nape of his neck. Mr. Outin asserts in his speech that Kairova looked upon Velikanov as upon "her child," her "creation"; that she sought to "elevate him and ennoble" him. Mr. Outin apparently rejects the thought that she could have attached herself to Velikanov without this specific aim; meanwhile, this "darling child," this "creation," does not become a bit nobler, but, on the contrary, as time goes on, grows worse and worse.

In brief, in Mr. Outin's speech there always sounds too high a pitch—altogether incompatible with these individuals and this particular mise-en-scène. And, at times, one is left nonplussed. Then begins the adventure. The "darling child" and Kairova go to Petersburg; shortly thereafter he leaves for Moscow to look for a position. Kairova writes him hearty, cordial letters; she is full of passion, of sentiments, while he is decidedly a poor epistolarian, and, from this point of view, he is awfully "ignoble." "In these letters"—says Mr. Outin—"one begins to discern that tiny cloud which later spread all over the sky and produced the thunderstorm." And Mr. Outin does not know how to express himself in a plainer style; this style he uses everywhere. Finally, Velikanov returns, and again they live in Petersburg—*maritalement,* of course —and then suddenly the principal episode of the romance takes place: Velikanov's wife arrives, and Kairova is "aroused as a lioness from which her young one is being taken away." At this juncture there ensues, indeed, a lot of eloquence. Had there been no such eloquence, one naturally would feel sorrier for this poor, foolish woman, tossing between the husband and the wife, not knowing what to undertake. Velikanov turns out a "treacherous"—more correctly, a weak—man. Now he deceives his wife, protesting his love for her; now he journeys from his summer cottage to Petersburg, to Kairova, assuring her that his wife will soon go abroad. Mr. Outin presents the amour of his woman client not only in attractive hues but even in a didactic and, so to speak, sublimely moral aspect. You see, she has even made up her mind to make an offer to Velikanova to cede to the latter her own husband for good (so that, obviously, she must have been convinced that she was fully entitled to him). "If you wish to take him—take him.

If you wish to live with him—go ahead and live with him; but either you depart from here, or I will. But do decide upon something." This she meant to say; only I don't know if she did say it. However, no one has decided upon anything, while Kairova, instead of departing (if she was so anxious to bring the matter to a solution of some kind), continued to toss and boil, raising no questions and awaiting no miraculous solutions. "To surrender him without a struggle—she wouldn't be a woman!"—suddenly exclaims Mr. Outin. Well, if so, what was the use of talking so much about desires, questions and "offers"? "She was in the throes of passion" —Mr. Outin explains to the court.—"Jealousy has absorbed, annihilated, her mind and compelled her to play a perilous game." And, again: "Jealousy has pulverized her mind—no trace of it was left. How, then, could she have controlled herself?"—Thus it lasted for ten days: "She languished; she was in burning fits of fever; she wouldn't eat or sleep; she escaped now to Petersburg, now to Oranienbaum, and when thus she had been wearied down, the ill-fated Monday of the 7th of July had come." On that ill-fated Monday the jaded woman came to her summer cottage, and she was told that Velikanov's wife was there; she approached the bedroom, and . . .

"Gentlemen of the jury, is it possible for a woman to remain calm?—For then she would have to be a stone—she would have to be devoid of a heart. The man passionately loved by her is in her bedroom, on her own bed, with another woman! This was beyond her strength. Her feelings were like a stormy torrent which tears down everything encountered in its path: she tossed in a rage. She could have *annihilated everything around her.*(!!!) If we should ask that torrent what it is doing, why it is causing harm, could it give an answer? No, it would remain silent."

See! What a multitude of phrases! What an array of "feelings"! "The main thing is that it be hot, and some taste or other will be derived from it!" But let us examine these phrases: they are very bad—worse yet, they are the cornerstone in Mr. Outin's defense.

I readily agree with you, Mr. Defense Lawyer, that Kairova could not have remained composed in the scene which you have depicted, but only because she is Kairova, that is, a weak, sympathetic woman, if you please, easily becoming attached (however, about these qualities of Kairova, up to the present, I have learned only from your speech), but at the same time—a loose woman, isn't this so? I do not mean the lewd looseness of her nature: she is an unfortunate woman, and I shall not insult her—all the more so as I would not venture to pass judgment concerning this point.

I mean merely looseness of her mind and heart which, to me, is incontestable. It was due to that looseness that at this fatal moment she could not have decided the matter otherwise than she had decided it, and not because "she would have to be a stone and that she would be devoid of a heart," as you have defined it, Mr. Defense Lawyer. Think only: by asserting this, you, as it were, do not admit at all the possibility of a different outcome—a nobler and more magnanimous one. And if there had appeared a woman capable, at that moment, of throwing the razor away and of adopting a different course, you would thus have called her a "stone" and a "heartless" woman. In this way, as stated above, you would have virtually commended the crime. Of course, on your part this was but an impulsion, and, no doubt, a noble one; but it is to be regretted that such heedless words are uttered from our still young public tribunes. Please excuse me, Mr. Defense Lawyer, for taking your words so seriously. And, further, please consider: there are higher types of, and higher *ideals* in, woman. And there is no question that such ideals actually have existed, and do exist, in reality. And what if Kairova herself, at the very last moment, when holding the razor in her hand, suddenly, with a clear eye, would have looked at her fate (don't worry, this may very well happen, and precisely at the last moment), and would have apperceived her misfortune—for to love such a man is a misfortune—her whole shame and dishonor, her degradation (since, indeed, in these women "taken in adultery" there is not only "magnanimity," not only "self-renunciation," but also much deceit, much shame, vice and degradation); if she suddenly would have sensed in herself a new woman, resurrected to a new life, one realizing that it was she who was the "offender," and, in addition, that by leaving this man she would have, to a greater extent and more surely, ennobled him—and having realized all this, she would have gotten up and departed in tears, saying to herself: "How low have I fallen!"—now, were all this to have happened to Mrs. Kairova herself, is it possible that you would feel no pity for her, that you would find no responsive feeling in your unquestionably kind heart, but you would have called this woman suddenly resurrected in her spirit and in her heart—a "stone," a "heartless creature" and would have publicly branded her with your contempt from our young tribune to which everybody is so eagerly and attentively listening?

However, I hear voices: "Don't demand this from every woman—it is inhuman!" I know it, and I do not demand it. I shuddered when reading that portion where she had been eavesdropping beside the bed. I can understand all too well what she must have endured during that last hour, with the razor in her

hand. And I was very, very glad when they let Kairova go. And
I am whispering to myself: "For they bind heavy burdens and
grievous to be borne!" But He who uttered these words, when
forgiving the guilty woman, had added, "Go and sin no more."
Thus, he had still called the sin a sin; He forgave but did not
condone it, while Mr. Outin says that "she would not have been
a woman, but a stone, a heartless creature," and he even fails to
understand how she could have acted differently. I merely venture
to remark humbly that evil nevertheless should be called evil, and
that it should not be extolled almost as a heroic deed, notwithstanding any humaneness.

5

Mr. Defense Lawyer and Velikanova

And if one does proclaim humaneness, one should also show
pity for Mrs. Velikanova. He who has too much compassion for
the offender, probably has no pity for the offended. Meanwhile,
Mr. Outin deprives Mrs. Velikanova even of her role of "the victim
of the crime." It seems to me that I am positively right in my
conclusion that in the course of his whole speech Mr. Outin, time
and again, has been tempted to say something bad about Mrs.
Velikanova. I confess, this is too naïve a device and, it seems, it
is a most maladroit one; it is too primitive and too hasty. For,
perhaps, Mr. Defense Lawyer, it might be argued that you are
humane only as far as your clients are concerned—as a matter of
professional duty; yet is this true? For instance, you seized and
dwelt upon "the wild, horrible" scene when Velikanova, in a state
of irritation, said aloud that she would "kiss the hands and feet
of him who would rid her of such a husband," and that Kairova,
who had been there at the time, promptly answered to this: "I'll
take him,"—to which Velikanova, in turn, retorted: "Go ahead and
take him." Having recounted this *fact,* you even remarked that
from that time on Kairova began to consider this gentleman *her
own*—to conceive him as her own creation, as her "darling child."
All this is very naïve. And, to begin with, what is there "wild and
horrible" in this? The scene and the words are unquestionably
bad; but you admit even the possibility of excusing the razor in
Kairova's hands and of contending that Kairova could not have
remained composed. Why, then, don't you excuse an impatient,
though nonsensical, exclamation of the unfortunate wife? You admit yourself that Velikanov is an impossible man, to the point that
the fact itself of Kairova's love for him may constitute ample proof
of her madness. Why, then, do Velikanova's words about "hands

and feet" surprise you? With an impossible man, relations sometimes assume an impossible character, and, at times, impossible
phrases are being uttered. But this—only *at times,* and this is but
a phrase. And I must say that had Mrs. Kairova taken it seriously
—that the wife surrenders her husband to her, and that beginning
with that moment she had acquired the right to consider him "her
own"—she would have been a very good banterer. All this, I take
it, must have happened somehow differently. And one shouldn't be
considering so haughtily some phrase of some poor, afflicted person.
In these families (not in them alone—you wouldn't believe in what
families!) not only such phrases are being uttered. Sometimes there
is poverty, there are burdens of life, and under their influence
family relations, at times, begin to be vulgar, so that certain words
are being exchanged, which Lord Byron, for instance, would not
have said to his Lady Byron, even at the time of their final rupture, or—to cite another example—Arbenin to Nina in Lermontov's
Masquerade. Of course, this kind of slovenliness cannot be excused,
even though this is merely untidiness, a bad, impatient tone, while
the *heart,* perhaps, remains better than ours, so that if one should
consider the matter in a simpler way, the result, I assure you,
would be more merciful. And, if you please, Kairova's sally "I'll
take him"—to my way of thinking—is much more detestable: here
there is a terrible insult to the wife, torture, outspoken scoffing of
a triumphant mistress, who had wrested a husband from his wife.
Regretting, for instance, the fact that Velikanova did not appear
in court, but sent a doctor's certificate about her illness, you said
to the jurors that had she appeared, that certificate would have
lost all significance because the jurors would have beheld a healthy
and pretty woman. But what is your concern in this connection
about her beauty, vigor and health? Further, you state: "Gentlemen of the jury! What kind of a woman is it who comes to her
husband, who is cohabiting with another woman—who comes to
the house of the mistress of her husband, knowing that Kairova
is residing there; who decides to spend the night there and who lies
down on the bed, in the bedroom? . . . This is beyond my comprehension!" Let it be beyond your comprehension—even so, you
are too aristocratic and unjust. And do you know, Mr. Defense-
Lawyer, that maybe your client has gained much owing to the
fact that Velikanova did not appear in court? In the course of
the trial many bad things have been said about Velikanova—for
example, concerning her character. I do not know what her character is but, for some reason, I am pleased that she did not appear.
. . . Perhaps she did not appear because of the pride of an insulted woman; maybe even out of pity for her husband. For no
one can tell anything about why she failed to appear. . . . At any

rate, it is clear that she does not belong to the category of those persons who are fond of telling in public about their passions and depicting *urbi et orbi* their feminine sentiments. And who knows, had she appeared, it might have been an easy matter to explain why she had stopped in the apartment of her husband's mistress—a fact which puzzles you so much and which you impute to her as a special shame. It seems to me that she was staying not in Kairova's, but in the apartment of her repentant husband who had summoned her. And there is nothing to show that she had been expecting that Kairova would continue to pay the rent of the apartment. Perhaps, immediately upon her arrival it was difficult to ascertain who was paying the rent and who was the host. The husband had asked her to come to him, so he must have taken the lease in his own name; and it is very probable that he had so stated to her, since at that time he was deceiving both women. The same is applicable to your finesses concerning the bedroom and the bed. Here, some hairbreadth, some infinitessimal detail could forthwith have explained everything.

Generally speaking, it seems to me that everybody has been unjust to this poor woman, and I am inclined to think that had Velikanova surprised Kairova in the bedroom with her husband and had she killed her with a razor, in her awful capacity of a legitimate wife, she would have been rewarded with nothing but filth and forced labor. Now, is it possible, Mr. Defense Lawyer, to say, as you have, that in this "case" Velikanova has sustained no damage, since several days after the event she had already appeared upon the theatrical boards and had subsequently played all winter, whereas Kairova had been confined for ten months in prison. We pity your poor client in no lesser measure than you, but you must admit that Velikanova, too, had endured a good deal. Not speaking of what she had endured as a wife and a self-respecting woman (the latter I decidedly can't take away from her), please recall, Mr. Advocate—you, such a fine jurist and a man who revealed himself as so humane in his speech—please recall how much she must have endured that dreadful night! She endured several (much too many) minutes of *deadly fear*. Do you know what *deadly fear* is?—He who has never faced death at close range can hardly comprehend it. She had been awakened at night by the razor of her murderess who slashed her on her throat; she saw bending over herself an infuriated face; she defended herself while the other kept slashing her. Of course, during those first, unbearable minutes she was sure that she would be killed and that death was inevitable. Indeed, this is unbearable; this is a delirious nightmare experienced while awake, and thus a hundred times more torturous. This is almost akin to a death sentence to a man tied to a post

to be shot and when a hood is already pulled over his head. . . .
For heaven's sake, Mr. Advocate, you consider this kind of torture
a trifle! And is it possible that no one among the jurors even
smiled when listening to this sort of thing?—And what is there in
the fact that two weeks later Velikanova was already able to act
on the stage: does this lessen the horror of what she had endured
two weeks before, or the guilt of your client?—Recently, a stepmother threw out from the fourth floor her six-year-old stepdaughter,
but the child stood up on her feet wholly unharmed. Now, does
this in any way change the cruelty of the crime, and is it possible
to maintain that the child had endured no suffering?

By the way, I imagine how advocates will be defending that
stepmother: we shall hear about the helplessness of her situation,
and about the fact that she is a recent bride of a widower whom
she married under the compulsion of force, or by mistake. We shall
have pictures drawn portraying the miserable existence of destitute
people, their never-ending work. She, the naïve, the innocent, when
marrying, was believing, as an inexperienced little girl (particularly
under our system of upbringing!), that married life brings nothing
but joys—and here, instead of them—washing of dirty linen, cook-
ing, bathing the child: "Gentlemen of the jury, it is only natural
that she started hating that child (who knows, maybe there will
appear a 'defense lawyer' who will begin to smear the child and
will find in a six-year-old girl some bad and hideous qualities!)—
in a moment of despair, in a state of madness, almost without remembering herself, she seized that girl, and . . . Gentlemen of the
jury, who among you wouldn't have done the same thing? Who
among you wouldn't have thrown the child out of the window?"

Of course, my words are but a caricature, but if one should
undertake to *compose* this speech, something similar could be
really said, that is, something along the lines of a caricature. Precisely, it is abominable that it is akin to this caricature, whereas
the act of this monster stepmother is, indeed, too queer, and perhaps it warrants a subtle and profound analysis which might even
tend to alleviate the lot of the delinquent woman. For this reason
one is, at times, vexed by the naïveté and standardization of the
methods which, owing to various causes, are beginning to be used
by our most talented lawyers. On the other hand, I reason this way:
the tribunes of our new courts are unquestionably an ethical school
for our society and our people. Indeed, the people learn in this
school truth and morality; how, then, shall we remain indifferent
to things which once in a while are uttered from those tribunes?
However, sometimes, most innocent and jovial things are being
uttered. Mr. Advocate, at the end of his speech, applied to his
client the words from the Gospel: "She loved much, and much is

forgiven her." Of course, this is very nice—all the more so as the advocate is fully aware of the fact that Christ forgave the woman "taken in adultery" not for *this kind of love*. I consider it a sacrilege to refer in this connection to this great and touching passage in the Gospel. At the same time I cannot resist the temptation to quote an old remark of mine, very trivial, yet rather characteristic. This remark, naturally, does not concern Mr. Outin in the least. Since childhood, more correctly, since my military college years, I have observed that among a great many raw youths—high school pupils (some), military college boys (more), and most of all among former cadets—there is implanted since their school days, for some reason or other, the belief that Christ forgave the sinning woman precisely for amours, or, to be more accurate, for the abuse of amours; that He, so to speak, had pity for this attractive infirmity. This conviction was also widely prevalent in our day. I recall that now and then I would ask myself the question: why is it that these boys are so prone to interpret in this sense this passage in the Gospel? Is it because their religious instruction is so neglected?— Yet the other portions of the Gospel are understood by them more or less correctly. Finally, I came to the conclusion that principally here, so to speak, physiological causes are at work: in the face of the undeniable kindheartedness of the Russian boy, there must probably operate in him, in some manner or other, that peculiar overabundance of forces stored up in military college youths, which is set in action whenever he looks at any woman.

However, I feel that is just humbug, which should not have been mentioned at all. I repeat, Mr. Outin knows perfectly well how this text is to be interpreted, and I do not doubt that at the end of his speech he simply cracked a joke—what for, I do not know.

CHAPTER II

1

Something About a Certain Building. Respective Thoughts.
Deceit and Falsehood on Every Side! This Is What Is
Sometimes Unbearable!

JUST AT the time when the Kairova case was being tried, I chanced to visit the Foundling Institution, in which I had never been before but which, for a long time, I had been eager to visit. Thanks to a doctor, an acquaintance of mine, we inspected everything. However, I shall leave for the future the details about my impressions: I have not even jotted down anything, nor have I recorded years and figures. From the very first step it became clear that in the course of one visit it would be impossible to make a thorough inspection, and that it would be well worth while to go there several times more. And thus it was agreed by my esteemed guide, the doctor, and myself. I even intend to take a trip to the villages, to the Finnish women in whose care infants have been placed. Consequently, I am leaving my descriptions for the future; meanwhile, I am merely recording glimpses of reminiscences: Betzky's monument; a range of gorgeous halls in which the infants are kept; the remarkable cleanness (which hampers nothing); the kitchens; the nursery where calves are "made ready" for vaccination; the dining rooms; groups of little children sitting at the table; a group of five- and six-year-old girls playing "horses"; a group of older girls, perhaps of the ages of sixteen and seventeen, former pupils of the Institution, training to become nurses and trying to improve their education—they do already possess some knowledge: they have read Turgenev; their views are clear, and they converse with you very nicely. But I was more pleased with the stewardesses: they have such a kindly air (certainly they were not feigning kindness because of our visit); they have such good, composed and intelligent faces. Some of them apparently are educated. I was most interested in the fact that the mortality rate of infants brought up in that Institution (that is, in this building) is incomparably lower than that among outside infants, in families. But this is not so in the case of infants placed in villages. Finally, downstairs I saw that room into which mothers bring their infants to leave them there forever. . . . But all this is for the future.

I recall only that I gazed at these nurslings with a peculiar and, probably, strange look. Much as it may sound absurd, they seemed to me awfully arrogant, so that—this I remember—innerly I smiled at my thought. In fact, he was born somewhere; he was brought here—but look, how he cries, how he vociferates, announcing that his wee chest is healthy and that he wants to live; he bustles with his tiny red hands and legs, and screams as if he had the right to disturb you; he looks for the breast as if he is entitled to it, as if he has the right to be cared for; he demands care as if he has absolutely the same right as those other children, in the fold of families: as if everyone is going to leap and run unto him—arrogance, arrogance! And truly, I am saying this without any humor. One looks around and, willy-nilly, the thought comes: what, in fact, if he should offend somebody? And what if someone should suddenly rebuke him: "Look here, youngster, are you a prince's

son? Are you?" And aren't they being rebuked?—This is not a
fancy: they are even being thrown out of windows. Once upon a
time—some ten years ago—a certain stepmother, I believe (I have
forgotten already, but it would be better if it were a stepmother),
having become tired of dragging along a child who was left to her
by the former wife, and who kept crying and crying because of
some pain, went to a boiling and bubbling samovar, set the hand
of the disagreeable child under the faucet and turned the peg. At
the time this was reported in all the newspapers. This was certainly
a rebuke on the part of the dear woman! I don't know what kind
of a sentence she received. In fact, has she ever been tried? Don't
you think that "she deserves every consideration"?—At times
these kids keep crying and crying; this affects one's nerves, and,
besides—poverty, washing; isn't this so? On the other hand, some
mothers, even when they "rebuke" a bawling little fellow, do it
in a much more humane manner: a pretty, sympathetic girl will
sneak into some comfortable, secluded corner—and, suddenly, she
will faint there. She remembers nothing more, and all of a sudden
a little child, an arrogant bawling little fellow, appears on the scene
—whence, no one knows; well, by accident, he falls into that water
and chokes. To choke, nevertheless, is pleasanter than that faucet.
Isn't that so? Such a one shouldn't even be tried!—Poor, deceived,
sympathetic girl: she should be eating nothing but candies, and
instead—a sudden fainting fit, and, besides, if one recalls Faust's
Marguerite (among jurors sometimes there are very literary-minded
men)—well, how can such a creature be tried? Impossible!—Instead,
a collection should be taken up!

So that one is really glad for all these babies, because they
happen to be housed in this building. And I have to confess that
perfectly idle thoughts and funny questions then kept popping up
in my mind. For instance, I asked myself, and I was terribly anxious
to ascertain: just when do these children begin to learn that they
are worse than the rest—i.e., that they are not such children as
"those others," but much inferior, and that they are living not
because they have the right to live but solely, so to speak, as a
matter of humaneness? This cannot be ascertained without great
experience, without much observation of the children, but nevertheless, a priori, I have decided and I am convinced that they
learn about this "humaneness" at a very early age—so early that
it might not be believed. In fact, were the child to develop only
with the aid of scientific devices and scientific games, and were
he to gain knowledge about the world through the "duck"—I think
he would never reach such an incredible depth of understanding,
through which he manages to master—in what manner no one knows

—certain ideas seem ngly altogether inaccessible to him. A child of five or six, at times, knows such remarkable things, and so unexpectedly profound, about God, about good and evil, that one, willy-nilly, has to conclude that nature has provided an infant with some different means of acquiring knowledge which, however, are not only unknown to us but which, on the basis of pedagogy, would be virtually repudiated. Oh, it stands to reason that a child does not know facts about God, and were a clever jurist to test a six-year-old child's conceptions of good and evil, he would merely burst into laughter. But you should be a bit more patient and more attentive (for it is worth it) ; forgive the child, for instance, for certain facts; admit certain absurdities and try to get to the *essence of the understanding,* and suddenly you will perceive that he knows about God perhaps, as much as you know, while, about good and evil, what is shameful and what is laudable—perhaps even much more than you, subtlest lawyer, but one who is sometimes swayed by haste.

Among such terribly difficult ideas, so unexpectedly and in so mysterious a way acquired by children, I class, as stated above, this initial but firm conception—one that remains unshaken throughout his whole life—that "they are worse than the rest." And I am convinced that the child does not learn about this from governesses and wet nurses. Moreover, he lives in such a manner that he does not see "those other" children, and, therefore, he is not in a position to make comparisons—and yet when you begin to look attentively, you see that he already knows an awful lot, that he has already penetrated many a thing with most unnecessary haste.

Of course, I am philosophizing—but just then I was utterly unable to control the stream of my thoughts. For instance, unexpectedly, the following aphorism occurred to me: If fate has deprived these children of family and of the happiness of being brought up by their parents—since, indeed, not all parents throw their children out of windows or scald them with boiling water—will it not reward them in some other manner?—For example, with the fact that they will have the advantage of being brought up in this magnificent building; that a name will be given to them, and after that—education, the highest possible education; that they will be seen through universities; that thereupon—positions will be found for them, and they will be started on a given road; briefly—that as long as possible they will not be forsaken, and all this, so to speak, by the entire state adopting them as common, state children. Verily, if one forgives, one should be granting a full pardon. At that time another thought came to my mind: maybe, some people would say that this would tend to encourage debauch, and that people would become incensed. But what a funny thought this is: imagine only that all these charming girls might purposely and intensively start conceiving children just as soon as they would learn that their babies eventually would be sent to universities. . . .

"No,"—I kept pondering—"they should be forgiven, and forgiven completely; if it is forgiveness, let it be a full pardon!" It is true that a great many people would begin to envy—the most honest and industrious people would begin to envy: "How is it that I, for instance,"—someone might say to himself—"who have worked like an ox all my life; I who have not committed a single dishonest act; I who have loved my children; I who have struggled all my life in order to give them an education, to make citizens of them, and who have failed; I who have failed even to see them through all the grades of high school . . . now, I have started coughing—I have contracted asthma; maybe, I will die next week—and farewell, my dear children, the whole eight of you! . . . You all will stop learning and will set off wandering hither and thither through the streets or you will start off to cigarette factories—and this, at the best . . . while those outcasts will be graduating from universities and will be obtaining positions. . . . And, on top of all this, it was I who annually, directly or indirectly, have contributed to their subsistence!"

This monologue will be uttered without fail. And, yet, what contradictions! In fact, why is everything so organized that nothing can be brought into accord? Think only: what—it would seem —can be more legitimate and more just than this monologue? And yet, at the same time, it is illegitimate and unjust in the highest degree. So that it is at once legitimate and illegitimate. What a mess!

Nor can I refrain from completing my account of certain things which had then occurred to me. For example: if they should be forgiven, will they, in turn, forgive? This is certainly a question. There are beings of a sublime type; these will forgive. Others, maybe, will avenge themselves on their own behalf—on whom, on what, they will never determine or comprehend; even so, they will avenge themselves. However, as regards "vengeance upon society" on the part of the "outcasts," should such be taking place, I might state this: I am convinced that this vengeance would always be of a negative, rather than a positive, nature. Directly and deliberately, no one is going to avenge himself; besides, he himself would not surmise that he even wished to avenge himself. On the contrary, only give them education and very many among those emerging from this "building" will come out with a thirst for respectability, parentage and family life. It will be their ideal to build their own nest, to initiate a name and to acquire prestige, to bring up children and love them, and in their upbringing—under no condition to be resorting to the "building" or to state subsidies. And, generally, their first resolution will be to forget the way to this building, its very name. Contrariwise, this new progenitor will feel happy if, at his own expense, he sees his children through a university. Why, this is a thirst for the *established* bourgeois order, which will persist throughout his whole life. What is it: servility or supreme independence? In my view—the latter; however, all his life his soul' will nevertheless remain not quite independent, not quite a *master's* soul, and, for this reason, much will be quite unbecoming, although it will be absolutely honest. Complete spiritual independence is given through something different. . . . But this comes later and this, too, is a long story.

2

A Certain Inappropriate Thought

However, just now I mentioned the word "independence." But do we love independence?—That's the question. And what is our independence? Are there any two persons who would understand it in one and the same sense? Nor do I know if there is among us even a single idea which would be seriously believed. Our rank and file—whether rich or poor—love to think about nothing and, without giving much thought, simply to indulge in debauch as long as strength permits and one does not become bored with it. Men standing away from the routine "segregate" themselves into groups and pretend that they believe in something, but it would seem that they are straining themselves, merely as a matter of diversion. There is also a special kind of people who have adopted, and are exploring, the formula "the worse—the better." Finally, there are paradoxicalists—sometimes even very honest, but usually rather inept; among these, especially the honest ones, countless suicides are being committed. And in truth, of late, suicides in Russia have become so frequent that nobody even speaks of them. The Russian soil seems to have lost the strength to hold people on it. And how many unquestionably honest men, particularly, honest women! Our women are beginning to arise and, maybe, they will manage to save much. I shall discuss this later on. Women are our great hope; perhaps, at the fatal moment, they will render a service to all Russia, but here is the trouble: we have many—a great many—honest ones; that is, you see, good rather than honest ones, but none of them knows what honor is; none of them believes in any formula for honor, and they even deny the clearest formulas

of earlier times, and this is true almost everywhere and among everybody. What's the wonder? Whereas the so-called "living force"—
the live feeling of being—without which no society can exist and
the state is liable tc totter—vanishes, God only knows whither.
And why did I start pondering over suicides in that building, looking at that nursery and those infants? Indeed, a most inappropriate
thought!

We have many inappropriate ideas, and that is what oppresses
one. In Russia an idea crashes upon a man as an enormous stone
and half crushes him. And so he shrivels under it, knowing not
how to extricate himself. One fellow is willing to live, though in
a half-crushed state; but another one is unwilling and kills himself.
. . . Very typical is a letter of a girl who took her life into her
own hands; it has appeared in *The New Times;* it is a long letter.
She was twenty-five years old. Her name was Pisareva; she was the
daughter of formerly well-to-do landowners. But she came to Petersburg and paid her tribute to progress by becoming a midwife. She
succeeded in passing the examinations and found a position as a
zemstvo midwife. She herself admitted that she was not in need,
and was able to earn a decent living; but she grew *tired,* very tired
—so tired that she decided to take a rest. "And where can one rest
better than in a grave?" As a matter of fact, she did become exceedingly tired. Even the letter of this unfortunate girl is permeated
with fatigue. This is a snarling, impatient letter: "Do but leave
me alone! I am tired, tired! . . . Don't forget to pull off me the
new shirt and stockings: on my night table you will find an old
shirt and a pair of old stockings. These should be put on me."
She did not use the words *"take off,"* but she wrote—"pull off";
and so it is in everything: terrible impatience. All these harsh
words are caused by impatience, and impatience—by fatigue. She
even uses abusive language: "Did you really believe that I was
going home? What the devil would I go there for?" Or: "Now,
Lipareva, forgive me, and let Petrova forgive me [it was in the
latter's apartment that Pisareva took poison]—particularly Petrova.
I am committing a swinish act, a filthy thing. . . ." Apparently
she was fond of her relatives, but she wrote: "Don't let Lizanka
know, because she will inform sister, and she will come here and
will start howling. I don't wish that people should be howling over
me, but all relatives without exception howl over their relations."
—*"Howl"* and not *"weep"*—all this is, apparently, the result of
grumbling, impatient fatigue: "Let's hurry, let's get it over as
quickly as possible—and let me rest!" Of grumbling and cynical
incredulity there was much, painfully much, in her; she did not
believe even in Lipareva and Petrova, for whom she had so much

affection. Here are the opening words of the letter: "Don't lose your head! Don't start crying 'ah!' and 'oh!.' Make an effort and read to the end, and then decide what's the best course. Don't frighten Petrova. Maybe nothing will come of it, anyway, except laughter. My passport is in the cover of the trunk."

"Except laughter!" This thought that she, her wretched body, will be laughed at, and who would be the ones to laugh?—Lipareva and Petrova? This thought flashed through her mind in a moment such as this! That's awful!

The financial instructions concerning the paltry sum which she had left preoccupied her to the point of queerness: "Such and such monies should not be taken by the relatives; this sum should be given to Petrova; twenty-five rubles which the Chechotkins loaned me for the journey should be returned to them." The importance attributed to money was, perhaps, the last echo of the main prejudice of her whole life—"that these stones be made bread." In a word, there may be discerned the guiding conviction of her whole life, *i.e.*, "if everyone were provided for, everybody would be happy; there would be no poor and no crimes. There are no crimes at all. Crime is a pathological condition resulting from poverty and unhappy environment," etc., etc. It is precisely of this that consists that petty, conventional and most typical finite catechism of convictions to which they dedicate themselves during their lives with such ardent faith (despite the fact that very soon they grow tired of both their convictions and of life), and for which they substitute everything: the *élan* of life, the ties with the soil, faith in truth—everything, everything. Obviously, she had grown tired because of the tedium of life, having lost all faith in truth, all faith in any kind of duty. In a word—a total loss of the sublime of existence.

And thus, a good girl has died. I am not howling over you, poor girl, but at least let me pity you; do permit me this. Let me hope for your soul a resurrection to a life in which you would no longer grow weary. You, nice, good, honest girls—(all these qualities you possess!)—whither do you depart? Why is that dark, dull grave so dear to you? Look: a bright spring sun shines in the sky; trees are budding, but you feel tired even without having lived! How, then, can your mothers help but *howl* over you—those mothers who have brought you up and who have so admired you when you were still infants! Here, I look at all these "outcasts": how they long to live, how boldly they declare their right to exist! You, too, were an infant and you also desired to live; and your mother remembers this; and she compares your dead face with that laughter, with that joy which she beheld and which she remembers in your pretty little baby face—how can she refrain from "howling," how can she be reproached for doing so? Just now they showed me a little girl, Dunia; she was born with a crooked leg, that is, altogether without a leg; instead of it, there hung something resembling a string. She is only eighteen months old; she is healthy and remarkably good-looking. Everybody babies her; she nods her little head to everyone, she smiles at everyone, and she greets everybody with a smack of her lips. As yet, she knows nothing about her leg; she does not know that she is a deformed being and a cripple. But is this one, too, designed to contract hatred toward life? "We will make her an artificial leg; we will give her crutches; we will teach her to walk, and she even will not notice it," said the doctor, fondling her. And let's pray God that she *shouldn't notice it.* Nay, to grow tired, to contract hatred toward life, which means hate for everybody. . . . Nay, this pitiful, ugly, abortive generation of human beings, shriveling under stones that have fallen upon them, will pass out of existence; a new great idea will begin to shine like that bright sun and will strengthen the vacillating mind, and all people will say: "Life is good, but we have been bad." It is no indictment when I say that we are bad. Here, I see that peasant woman, that vulgar wet-nurse, that "hired milk"—I see her suddenly kissing that baby, that "outcast"! I could not even imagine that, here, wet-nurses would be kissing these children. Why, to behold this—for this alone—it would have been worth the trouble to visit this place! And she had kissed the child without seeing or suspecting that I was observing her. Is it for money that they grow fond of the babies? They are being hired to feed the children and nobody demands that they be kissing them. I was told that children placed in villages in the care of Finnish women are treated worse; even so, some of these women grow so accustomed to their nurslings that they weep when surrendering them to the Institution; and, later, they come from afar expressly to look at them, and they bring from the villages little presents for them, and "howl over them." No, here it is not a question of money, "all relatives who are howling," as Pisareva expressed herself in her suicide note; but these women, too, come to howl and to kiss and to bring along with them those humble peasant presents. These are not merely hired breasts, which have replaced mothers' breasts; this is *motherhood,* that "*élan* of life" of which Pisareva had grown so tired. After all, is it true that Russian soil is ceasing to hold Russian people on it? Why, then, right alongside, does life spout as a hot spring?

And, it stands to reason that here there are many infants born of those pretty mothers who are sitting there, on the steps of the villas, and are grinding razors to use on their female rivals. I will state in conclusion: in a sense, these razors may be very nice things, but I did very much regret the fact that I chanced to come here, to this building, at the time when I had been following the Kairova trial. I know nothing about Kairova's biography and, most decidedly, I am in no position, and have no right, to connect her in any way with this building; but her whole love affair, that eloquent description at the trial of her passions, somehow lost all significance for me and killed in me all sympathy as soon as I left this building. This I candidly confess, and it is, perhaps, for this reason that I have written so insensibly about the Kairova "case."

3

UNQUESTIONABLE DEMOCRACY. WOMEN

I feel that I must answer one more letter of a certain correspondent. In the preceding, April, issue of the *Diary*, referring to political matters, among other things I interjected, let us say, a fantasy.

"Russia will prove stronger than any nation in Europe. This will come to pass because all great powers in Europe will be destroyed, for the simple reason that they will be worn out and undermined by the unsatisfied democratic tendencies of an enormous portion of their lower-class subjects—proletarians and paupers. In Russia this cannot happen: our demos is content and, as time goes on, it will grow ever more content because everything tends toward this condition, as the result of a general mood—or, more correctly, by general consensus—and, therefore, there will remain on the Continent but one colossus—Russia."

In answer to this opinion my correspondent cites a most curious and instructive fact, given as his reason for doubting that "our demos is content" and satisfied. My esteemed correspondent will fully understand—if he should happen to read these lines—why just now I am unable to take up the fact referred to by him and to answer it, although I am not losing hope for an opportunity to discuss specifically the fact in the nearest future. Now, however, I wish to say a word in explanation about the demos—all the more so as I have been informed about other opinions disagreeing with my conviction as to the contentment of our "demos." I merely wish to call my opponents' attention to one line in the above passage quoted from the April issue: "because everything tends toward this condition, as a result of the general mood—or, more correctly, by

general consensus." In fact, if in my opponents themselves this
"common *mood* or *consensus*" had been missing, they would have
left my words without raising any objections. And, therefore, this
mood unquestionably exists: it is unquestionably a democratic and
disinterested mood. Moreover, it is a universal mood. True, in
present-day democratic pronouncements there is much deceit, much
journalistic roguery, much ecstasy—for instance, in exaggerated attacks against the opponents of democracy, of whom—it may be
stated in passing—nowadays there are very few in Russia. Nevertheless, the honesty, disinterestedness, straightforwardness and candor of democracy of the overwhelming majority of Russian society
can no longer be subjected to any doubt. In this respect, perhaps,
we have revealed, or are beginning to reveal, a phenomenon which,
thus far, has not been encountered in Europe where democracy,
even to our day, has been commonly revealing itself from below;
there, it is still struggling while the (supposedly) vanquished upper
strata are still offering fierce resistance. Our upper strata have not
been vanquished; they became democratic—or rather, popular—of
their own accord. Who can deny this?—And if this be so, our demos
can expect a happy future. If at present there is still much that
is unbecoming, it is permissible at least to entertain great hopes
that the temporary misfortunes of the demos will unfailingly be
mitigated under the unceasing and uninterrupted influence of such
enormous *principles* (for otherwise they cannot be denoted) as the
universal democratic mood and general consensus in this respect
of all Russians, starting from the very top. It was in this sense
that I said that our demos was satisfied, and that "as time goes
on they will be satisfied more and more." Well, in this it is not
difficult to believe.

And, in conclusion, I wish to add one more word about the
Russian woman. I have already stated that in her resides our only
great hope, one of the pledges of our revival. The regeneration of
the Russian woman during the last twenty years has proved unmistakable. The rise in her quests has been lofty, candid and fearless. From the very start it has commanded respect or, at least,
made people think of it, despite several parasitic anomalies which
have revealed themselves in this movement. At present, however,
it is already possible to render an accounting and to draw an
undaunted conclusion. The Russian woman chastely ignored all obstacles and all scoffs. She resolutely announced her desire to participate in the common cause and proceeded in this direction, not
only disinterestedly but even self-denyingly. During these last
decades the Russian man has become terribly addicted to the de-

bauch of acquisition, cynicism and materialism. But the woman has remained much more faithful to the pure worship of the idea, to the duty of serving the idea. In her thirst for higher education she has revealed earnestness, patience, and has set an example of the greatest courage. The *Writer's Diary* has given me an opportunity of beholding the Russian woman at closer range. I have received several remarkable letters. They ask me, the incompetent, "what to do?" I value these questions, and I make up for any lack of competency in my answers with sincerity. I regret that I am unable, and have no right, to recount here many a thing. However, I also perceive certain faults in the contemporary woman, and her principal fault—her extraordinary dependency upon several essentially masculine ideas; her inclination to accept them credulously and to believe in them without scrutiny. I am by no means speaking of all women; but this defect is also proof of excellent qualities of the heart: women value most a fresh feeling, a live word; but what they treasure even more is sincerity, and once they believe in sincerity, even if it be a false one, they are inspired by certain opinions—and this, at times, excessively. In the future, higher education could be of great help in this respect. By admitting, sincerely and fully, higher education for women, with all the rights granted by it, Russia once more would take a great and original stride in advance of all Europe in the great cause of the renaissance of mankind. Let us also pray that God will help the Russian woman to experience fewer disillusions, to grow less "tired," than, for example, Pisareva. Let her rather, like Schapov's wife, assuage her sorrow by self-sacrifice and love. But both women are painful and unforgettable phenomena; one—by the so poorly-rewarded, lofty feminine energy; the other—as a poor, tired, retiring, succumbed and vanquished woman. . . .

JUNE

CHAPTER I

1

The Death of George Sand

THE PRECEDING, May, issue of the *Diary* was already set in print and on the press when I read in the newspapers about the death of George Sand (she died on May 27/June 8). And so,

I had no time to say even a word about this death. And yet, only
having read about it, I understood what that name has meant in
my life; how many delights, how much veneration this poetess has
evoked in me at the time, and how many joys, how much happiness
she has given me! I am putting down every one of these words
unhesitatingly because this was literally the case. She was un-
reservedly one of our (*i.e., our*) contemporaries—an idealist of the
Thirties and Forties. Hers is one of those names of our mighty,
self-confident, and at the same time sick, century, replete with
most obscure ideals and unattainable desires—those names which,
having arisen over there, in "the land of sacred miracles," have
enticed from us, out of our Russia, which is eternally in a state
of creation, all too many thoughts, all too much love, holy and
noble enthusiasm, *élan vital,* all too many dear convictions. But
we shouldn't be complaining about this: by exalting such names
and worshipping them, Russians have been, and are, serving their
direct designation. Let these words of mine cause no surprise—
especially as applied to George Sand, about whom even in our days
there may be arguments, and whom half of the people in Russia,
if not nine-tenths of them, have forgotten. But, nevertheless, in
the past she did accomplish in Russia her task, and who if not we
—her contemporaries of the whole world—should gather at her grave
to say a word in her memory? We, Russians, have two mother-
lands—Russia and Europe—even in cases when we call ourselves
Slavophiles: let them not be angry at me for this remark. This
should not be disputed. The greatest among their great future
designations, already apperceived by the Russians, is the designation common to the whole human race—service rendered to mankind
as a whole, not only to Russia, not only to Slavs in general, but to humankind *in toto.* Think of it, and you will agree that the Slavophiles
held an identical view, and this is why they urged us to be more
rigid, firmer and more responsible Russians, specifically realizing
the fact that the conception of universality of man is the principal
personal characteristic and designation of a Russian. However, all
this requires much explanation: the fact itself that service to the
universal idea of humankind and the light-minded roving from
place to place, all over Europe, voluntarily and grumblingly forsaking the fatherland—are two things diametrically opposed one
to the other, whereas they are still being confused. On the contrary, much indeed, very much of what we have taken from Europe
and transplanted to Russia, we did not copy like slaves from their
masters, as the Potugins invariably insist, but we have inoculated
it into our organism, into our flesh and blood; some things we
have lived through and even *independently* suffered through, ex-

actly as they, over there, in the West, to whom all these were germane. Europeans emphatically refuse to believe it: they do not know us, and for the time being this is all the better; all the more imperceptibly and quietly will the necessary process take place—a process which will subsequently astound the whole world. This very process may be best and most concretely traced to a certain extent in our attitude toward the literary productions of other nations. Their poets are to us—at least, to the majority of our educated men—as germane as to them over there—in the West. I assert and repeat that every European poet, thinker, humanitarian is, among all countries of the world, with the exception of his native land, always most intimately understood and accepted in Russia. Shakespeare, Byron, Walter Scott, Dickens are more akin and intelligible to Russians than, for instance, to Germans—of course, notwithstanding the fact that compared with Germany, with her abundance of books, in Russia not even one-tenth of the number of copies of these authors, in translation, are being sold. Even though the French Convention of 1793, when sending the certificate of citizenship *Au poète allemand Schiller, l'ami de l'humanité*,[1] did perpetrate a beautiful, stately and prophetic act, nevertheless it did not suspect that at the other end of Europe, in barbarous Russia, that same Schiller was much more national and much more akin to the barbarian Russians than to France—not only in those days but even later, throughout our whole century—where Schiller, the French citizen and *l'ami de l'humanité,* was known, and then but slightly, only by professors of literature, and not even by all of them. Yet, in Russia, together with Jukovsky, he soaked into the Russian soul, left an impress upon it, and almost marked an epoch in the history of our development. This measure of Russian attitude toward world literature is an almost unprecedented phenomenon among other nations and all through world history; and if it really be our national, Russian, peculiarity, what chauvinism would have the right to object to this phenomenon and to refuse to discern in it a very promising and most prophetic fact in any conjectures as to our future. Oh, of course, many will smile maybe when reading what significance I attribute to George Sand; but those who might be amused would not be right: much time has now elapsed since all these past events, and George Sand herself has died—an old woman of seventy—having, perhaps, long ago outlived her fame. But everything in the being of this poetess that constituted a "new word," all that was "universally human" in her —all this, at the time, was promptly reflected in our Russia as a strong and profound impression; it did not escape us, thereby

[1] To the German poet Schiller, the friend of humanity.

proving the fact that every poet-innovator in Europe, everyone who
appeared there with a novel thought and with fresh vigor, cannot
help but become forthwith a Russian poet, cannot avoid Russian
thought, and almost becomes a Russian force. However, I do not
intend to write a critical article on George Sand: I meant merely
to say a few farewell words to the deceased at her fresh grave.

2

A Few Words About George Sand

George Sand's debut in literature coincided with the years
of my early youth, and now I am very glad this happened so long
ago because at present—over thirty years since—I can speak almost
quite candidly. It should be observed that in those days this—that
is, fiction—was the only thing permitted, whereas the rest, virtually
every thought, especially coming from France, was strictly forbidden. Oh, it stands to reason that very often we did not know
how to behold things, and, indeed, where could we have learned
this?—Even Metternich did not know how to behold things, not
to speak of our imitators. Therefore, "dreadful things" used to
slip through (for example, all Bielinsky slipped through). To
avoid any possible mistake, especially at the very end of that
period, almost everything began to be interdicted, so that, as is
known, it came to the point that one had to read between the
lines. Nevertheless, novels were permitted—in the beginning, in the
middle and at the very end of that period. And right here, specifically
in the case of George Sand, the guardians committed a grave error.
Do you remember the verses:

> Tomes by Thiers and by Rabeau—
> Those he memorizes,
> And, like raging Mirabeau,
> Liberty he eulogizes.

These are exceptionally talented verses; they will survive forever, because they are historical verses; but they are all the more
precious as they were written by Denys Davydov, a poet, a littérateur and a most honest Russian. And even if Denys Davydov,
in those days, considered—whom of all men?—Thiers (of course,
for his *History of the Revolution*) dangerous and placed him in
that verse side by side with some fellow Rabeau (there must have
been, then, such a man, too; however, I know nothing about him)
—officially, then, too little could have been permitted. And what

was the result?—That which in those days burst into Russia in the form of novels not only did in like manner serve the cause, but even so, perhaps, proved the most "dangerous" form, as things stood in those days, since there would have been but few lovers of Rabeau, whereas there came forth thousands of lovers of George Sand. At this point it may be remarked that notwithstanding all the Magnitzkys and Liprandis, ever since the Eighteenth Century, every intellectual movement in Europe invariably became promptly known in Russia, and it used to be forthwith transmitted from the upper strata of our intellectuals to the rank and file of the thinking, or even slightly interested, people. Exactly the same took place in the case of the European movement of the Thirties. Very soon, at the very beginning of the Thirties, we took cognizance of that immense European literary movement. The names of many newly appearing orators, historians, tribunes and professors were already known. Though partly and only superficially, it became known whither this movement tended. And most passionately it has revealed itself in art, in fiction, and principally—in George Sand. True, Senkovsky and Bulgarin had warned the public against George Sand even before Russian translations of her novels had appeared. They scared the Russian ladies particularly by the fact that she wore trousers; it was sought to frighten them with the idea of depravity and to ridicule her. Senkovsky himself, who had been planning to translate George Sand in his magazine *Library for Reading,* began to call her in print Mrs. Egor[1] Sand, and it seems that he was earnestly pleased with his wit. Later, in 1848, Bulgarin, in his *Northern Bee,* printed accounts to the effect that day after day she had been attending drinking bouts in company with Pierre Leroux somewhere near the town gates, and that she took part in "Athenian parties" at the Ministry of the Interior, sponsored by the robber and Minister of the Interior Ledru-Rollin. This I have read myself, and I remember it well. But then, in 1848, George Sand was known by virtually all the reading public in Russia, and no one gave credence to Bulgarin. For the first time, she appeared in Russian translation about the middle of the Thirties. It is a pity that I do not remember and do not know when and which of her works were translated in Russia. But all the more startling must have been the impression. I imagine that much as I, then a young lad, everybody in those days was impressed with the chaste, sublime purity of the characters and of the ideals, and the modest charm of the austere, reserved tone of the narrative— and such a woman wears trousers and engages in debauch! I must have been about sixteen years old when I first read her novel

[1]Egor is a Russian masculine name. (B. B.)

Uskok, one of the most delightful of her early works. I recall that I was in a state of fever all night.

I believe I do not err when I say that George Sand—judging at least by my personal recollections—promptly assumed in Russia virtually the first place among a whole Pleiad of new writers who at that period suddenly rose to fame and won renown all over Europe. Even Dickens, who appeared in Russia about the same time as she, was, perhaps, less popular with our public. I am not even speaking of Balzac who came earlier than she and who, however, in the Thirties, produced such works as *Eugénie Grandet* and *Père Goriot* (to whom Bielinsky was so unjust, having completely missed his significance in French literature). However, I am telling all this not from the standpoint of any critical evaluation, but I am simply recalling the tastes of the rank and file of the Russian readers and of the impression directly produced on them. The main thing is that the reader managed to extract even from novels everything against which he was being guarded. At least, in the middle of the Forties, the rank and file Russian reader knew, even though partly, that George Sand was one of the most brilliant, stern and just representatives of that category of the contemporaneous Western new men who, when they appeared, started with a direct negation of those "positive" acquisitions which brought to a close the activities of the bloody French—more correctly, European—revolution of the end of the past century. After it had come to an end, after Napoleon I, it was sought to express the new longings and the new ideals. Progressive minds had only too well grasped the fact that despotism had merely assumed a new guise; that nothing but *"ôte-toi de là, que je m'y mette"* had taken place; that the new world conquerors (the bourgeois) proved, perhaps, even worse than the former despots (the nobility); that *"Liberté, Egalité, Fraternité"* is but a high-sounding phrase, and nothing but a phrase. Moreover, there came into being certain doctrines, in which such lofty phrases had been converted into impossible phrases. The conquerors would be scoffingly uttering—rather recalling—these three sacramental words. Even science, in the persons of its brilliant representatives (economists), then came, as it were, with its new word, to the assistance of mockery and in condemnation of the Utopian meaning of these three words for which so much blood had been shed. Thus, side by side with the triumphant conquerors, despondent and sad faces, frightening the triumphers, began to appear. It was precisely at that epoch that suddenly a new word had been uttered and new hopes had arisen: men came who boldly proclaimed that the cause had been interrupted in vain and unjustly; that nothing had been accomplished by the political shift of the conquerors; that the cause had still to be pursued; that the renovation of humanity must be radical and social. Why, of course, along with these mottoes, a great many of the ugliest and most noxious inferences were drawn; yet, the cardinal point was that once more hope began to gleam and faith began to be regenerated. The history of this movement is known; it still continues, and it would seem that it does not intend to come to a stop at all. I do not wish to speak here either for or against the movement: I merely meant to indicate George Sand's true place in it. Her place must be sought at its very inception. At that time people in Europe were saying that she preached a new status for woman and she prophesied "the rights of free wifehood" (this is Senkovsky's expression about her). But this was not quite so, since her sermons were by no means confined to woman alone; nor did she ever invent the term "free wifehood." George Sand belonged to the whole movement, and not to the mere sermons on women's rights. True, being a woman herself, she naturally preferred to portray *heroines* rather than heroes, and, of course, women of the whole world should now don mourning garb in her memory, because one of their loftiest and most beautiful representatives has passed away, and, in addition, an almost unprecedented woman by reason of the power of her mind and talent—a name which has become historical and which is destined not to be forgotten by, or to disappear from, European humanity.

As for her heroines, I reiterate, I was astonished from the very start—ever since the age of sixteen—by the strangeness of the contradiction between what people had been writing and saying about her, and what in reality I personally perceived. In fact, many —at least, several—of her heroines represented a type of such elevated moral purity that it could not have been conceived without an immense ethical quest in the soul of the poetess herself; without the confession of most complete duty; without the comprehension and admission of most sublime beauty and mercy, patience and justice. True, side by side with mercy, patience and the acknowledgment of the obligations of duty, there was the extraordinary pride of the quest and of the protest; yet it was precisely that pride which was so precious because it sprang from the most sublime truth, without which mankind could never have retained its place on so lofty a moral height. This pride is not rancour *quand même*, based upon the idea that I am better than you, and you are worse than me; nay, this is merely a feeling of the most chaste impossibility of compromise with untruth and vice, although—I repeat—this feeling precludes neither all-forgiveness nor mercy. Moreover, commensurately with this pride, an enormous duty was to be assumed. These heroines of hers thirsted for sacrifices and heroic deeds. I was then particularly fond of several girl characters in her early works, which were portrayed, for example, in the then so-called Venetian novels (to which *Uskok* and *Aldini* belonged also)—types which culminated in the romance *Jeanne,* an altogether ingenious work setting forth a serene and, perhaps, an incontestable solution of the historical question of Joan of Arc. In a contemporary peasant girl she suddenly resurrects before the reader the image of the historical Joan of Arc, and graphically justifies the actual possibility of that majestic and miraculous event. This is a typically Georgesandesque task, since no one but she among contemporary poets bore in the soul so pure an ideal of an innocent girl—pure and so potent by reason of its innocence. These girl characters, to which I am referring, reiterate in several successive works one and the same problem, one and the same theme (not only girls, however: this theme was later reiterated in the magnificent novel *La Marquise,* also one of her early works). A straightforward, honest, but inexperienced, character of a young feminine creature is pictured, one possessing that proud chastity which is neither afraid of, nor can even be contaminated by, contact with vice—even if that creature should accidentally find herself in the very den of vice. The want of magnanimous sacrifice (supposedly specifically expected from her) startles the youthful girl's heart, and unhesitatingly, without sparing herself, disinterestedly, self-sacrificingly and fearlessly, she suddenly takes the most perilous and fatal step. That which she sees and encounters does not in the least confuse or intimidate her; on the contrary, it forthwith increases courage in the youthful heart which, at this juncture, for the first time, realizes the full measure of its strength—the strength of innocence, honesty and purity; it doubles the energy, reveals new paths and new horizons to a mind which up to that time had not known itself, a vigorous and fresh mind not yet soiled with the compromise of life. Added to this is the most perfect and delightful form of the poem. George Sand was particularly fond of winding up her poems *happily*—with the triumph of innocence, sincerity and youthful, fearless naïveté. Could these images disturb society or arouse doubts and fear?—On the contrary, the severest fathers and mothers began to permit in their families the reading of George Sand, and they merely kept wondering: "Why did everybody say such things about her?" But right here, at this point, warning voices began to sound: "Precisely in this pride of woman's quest; in this irreconcilability of chastity with vice; in this rejection of any compromises with evil; in this fearlessness with which innocence rises to the struggle and looks brightly into the eyes of the offense—therein precisely is the venom, the future poison of woman's protest, of woman's emancipation."

Well, perhaps, they were correct about that poison; poison did actually come into being. But what was it seeking to destroy, what was to perish and what was to survive as a result of its action?—Such were the questions which immediately arose and which for a long time remained unsolved.

In our day all these questions have long been settled (so it seems). In passing, it may be remarked that by the middle of the Forties George Sand's fame, and the faith in the power of her genius, stood so high that we all, her contemporaries, had been expecting from her something incomparably greater in the future —some new, yet unheard-of word, even something finitively decisive. These hopes did not materialize: it developed that by that time —by the end of the Forties—she had already said everything which she was destined and predestined to express, and now over her fresh grave the last word about her can be said.

George Sand was not a thinker but she was one of the most clairvoyant foreseers (if this flourishing term be permitted) of a happy future awaiting mankind, in the realization of whose ideals she had confidently and magnanimously believed all her life—this because she herself was able to conceive this ideal in her soul. The preservation of this faith to the end is usually the lot of all lofty souls, of all genuine friends of humanity. George Sand died a *déiste*, with a staunch belief in God and in her immortal life. But this does not fully cover the ground: in addition, she was, perhaps, the most Christian among all persons of her age—French writers—even though she did not confess Christ (as does a Roman Catholic). Of course, being a Frenchwoman, in accord with the conceptions of her compatriots, George Sand could not consciously adhere to the idea "that in the whole universe there is no name other than His through which one may be saved"—the fundamental idea of Orthodoxy—yet, despite this seeming and formal contradiction, George Sand, I repeat, was perhaps, without knowing it herself, one of the staunchest confessors of Christ. She based her socialism, her convictions, her hopes and her ideals upon the moral feeling of man, upon the spiritual thirst of mankind and its longing for perfection and purity, and not upon "ant-necessity." All her life she believed absolutely in human personality (to the point of its immortality), elevating and broadening this concept in each one of her works; and thereby she concurred in thought and feeling with one of the basic ideas of Christianity, *i.e.*, the recognition of human personality and its freedom (consequently, also of its responsibility). Hence, the recognition of duty and the austere moral quests, and the complete acknowledgment of man's responsibility. And, perhaps, in the France of her time there was no thinker and no writer who understood as clearly as she that "man shall not live by bread alone." As to the pride of her quests and of her protest —I repeat—this pride never precluded mercy, forgiveness of offense, or even boundless patience based upon compassion for the offender himself. On the contrary, time and again, in her works George Sand has been captivated by the beauty of these truths and on more than one occasion she has portrayed characters of the most sincere forgiveness and love. It is said that she died an excellent mother, working to the last days of her life as a friend of neighboring peasants, boundlessly beloved by her friends. It seems that she was partly inclined to value the aristocracy of her extraction (on her mother's side she descended from the Royal House of Saxony), but, of course, it may be positively asserted that if she did value aristocracy in people, she must have based it on the perfection of the human soul: she could not help but love the great, she could not reconcile herself with the base or cede an idea—and in this particular sense she may have been excessively haughty. True, she did not like to depict in her novels humble people, righteous but yielding, religious fanatics and downtrodden folks, such as appear in almost every novel of the great Christian—Dickens. She, on the contrary, haughtily placed her heroines on a pedestal as true queens. This she loved to do, and this peculiarity should be noted, since it is rather typical.

CHAPTER II

1

My Paradox

AGAIN THERE is a skirmish with Europe (oh, not yet war: they say that we, *i.e.*, Russia, are still far from war). Again the interminable Eastern question has appeared on the scene. Again Russians are distrustfully looked upon in Europe. . . . However, why should we be chasing after Europe's confidence? Has Europe ever looked upon Russians confidently? Can she ever look upon us with trust and without animosity? Oh, of course, *some day* this attitude will change; some day Europe will better discern and comprehend us. And *some day* it will be well worth while to discuss this topic, but in the meantime, meanwhile, an extraneous, as it were, a side question, has occurred to me, and recently I have been much preoccupied with its solution. No one needs to agree with me, but it seems to me that I am at least partly right.

I have said that Russians are disliked in Europe. That they are disliked, I believe, this no one will dispute. *Inter alia* we, all Russians without exception, are being accused in Europe of being awful liberals—moreover, revolutionists—and of the fact that we are always inclined to join the destructive, rather than the conservative, elements of Europe. For this reason many Europeans look upon us scoffingly and with haughty hatred: they cannot understand why we should be negators in an *alien cause.* They positively deny our right to European negation, on the ground that they do not regard us as belonging to "civilization." They rather perceive in us barbarians knocking about Europe and rejoicing over the thought that something somewhere may be destroyed—destroyed for the sake of destruction, from the pleasure of beholding how all this will fall apart, much as Huns ready to invade ancient Rome and to tear down a sanctity, even without any conception of what a precious thing they were destroying. That the majority of Russians have presented themselves as liberals in Europe is true; and this is even strange. Has anyone raised the question in his mind: why is this so? Why, practically nine-tenths of the Russians, all through this century, culturalizing themselves in Europe, invariably have joined that stratum of the Europeans which was liberal, the "left camp," *i.e.,* that camp which itself denied its own culture, its own civilization—of course, more or less (that which Thiers denies in civilization and that which the Paris Commune of 1871 denied in it—are altogether different things). In the same way "more or less" and equally in many different ways are Russians also liberal in Europe; nevertheless, I repeat, they are more inclined than Europeans to side, directly and from the very start, with the extreme left than to hover first in the lower grades of liberalism. Briefly, among Russians one finds a lesser number of Thierses than of Communards. And please note that these are by no means some empty-stomached fellows, but even people having a solid and civilized appearance—sometimes almost in the category of Ministers. This precisely is why Europeans distrust us: *"Grattez le Russe et vous verrez le Tartare"* [Scratch a Russian and you will find a Tartar]—they say. All this may be correct, but this is what has occurred to me: do the majority of Russians, in their intercourse with Europe, side with the extreme left because they are Tartars and are fond of destruction, as barbarians, or are they prompted by other motives?—That's the question! And you must admit that it is a rather curious one. Our skirmishes with Europe are coming to an end: the role of a window cut through to Europe is finished and there ensues—or, at least, must ensue—something different, and this is being realized by everyone who is in the least capable of reasoning. In a word, we begin to feel more and more that we must get ready for something, for some new, and now much more original, encounter with Europe than heretofore. Whether this will take place in connection with the Eastern question or in some other connection—who can tell? . . . And for this reason all such queries, analyses, conjectures and even paradoxes are curious because of the fact alone that they may be suggestive of some answer. And is it not a curious phenomenon that it is precisely those Russians who most consider themselves Europeans, who are known in Russia as "Westerners," who are vainglorious and pride themselves on this nickname, and who, even up to this day, taunt the other half of the Russians by labelling them "kvasniks"[1] and "zipynniks,"[2]—is it not curious, I ask, that they are precisely the ones who join the negators of civilization, its destroyers; who side with the "extreme left"; and that in Russia this causes no surprise whatsoever and this was never even questioned?—Certainly, this is curious!

I will say at once: I have framed an answer, but I shall not try to prove my idea; instead, I will merely expound it slightly, seeking only to develop the fact. Besides, it cannot be proved, because not everything is capable of proof.

This is what I think: is there not revealed in this fact (that is, in the siding with the extreme left—essentially, with the negators of Europe—even by our most ardent Westerners)—is there not revealed in this the protesting Russian soul, to which European culture in many of its manifestations has always, ever since Peter, been hateful and has always been felt alien to the Russian soul? —I do think so. Of course, it stands to reason that this protest has nearly always been an unconscious one; but the thing that is precious is the fact that the Russian instinct has not died: the Russian soul, though unconsciously, has been protesting precisely in the name of its Russism, in the name of its Russian own, and against its suppression. Of course, even if this be so, it might be said that there is no ground for rejoicing: "Nevertheless he is a negator—a Hun, a barbarian, a Tartar; he denied not in the name of something sublime, but because he was so mean that even, in the course of two centuries, he has been unable to discern European loftiness."

This, unquestionably, is what will be said. I agree that this

---

[1]Kvas drinkers.

[2]"Zipun" is a peasant coat; hence, "zipynnik"—one who wears a peasant coat. (B. B.)

is a question, but precisely this question I will not answer; without producing any proof I merely declare that I emphatically deny the Tartar hypothesis. Of course, who, among all Russians—especially now when everything is over (because, in fact, that period has come to an end)—who would challenge the Peter cause, the window cut through; who would rebel against it and who would be dreaming about the Moscow Czardom? Nor is this the point at all, and never was this the subject of my discussion, but the fact that no matter how good and useful all this has been—I mean, everything which we beheld through the window—nevertheless in that there was so much that was bad and detrimental that the Russian instinct never ceased to revolt against it, never ceased to protest (although that instinct got so absolutely lost that, in an overwhelming majority of cases, it did not comprehend what it was actually doing). It protested not because of its Tartarism but, in fact, perhaps, because it conserved in itself something loftier and better than that which it perceived through the window. . . . (Well, of course, it protested not against everything; we did receive a great many beautiful things, and we do not wish to be ungrateful; but, at least, against half of the things it had the right to protest.)

I repeat that all this took place in an extremely original manner: precisely, our most ardent Westerners, the champions of the reform, became at the same time the negators of Europe and joined the ranks of the extreme left. . . . And thus it happened that *eo ipso* they revealed themselves as most fervent Russians—as champions of Russia and of the Russian spirit. Of course, if, at the time, this had been explained to them, they would either have burst into laughter or have been terrified. There is no doubt that they themselves did not conceive any loftiness in this protest. On the contrary, all along, throughout the two centuries, they have been denying their loftiness, and not only their loftiness but their very self-respect (there existed even such amateurs!), and to such an extent that they have set Europe to wondering. And yet, it develops that, precisely, they have proved to be genuine Russians. Now, it is this conjecture of mine that I call a paradox.

Bielinsky, for example, who by nature was a passionately enthusiastic man, was one of the first Russians straightway to join European socialists, who denied the whole order of European civilization. At the same time, in our Russian literature it was he who fought the Slavophiles to the very end, apparently for an altogether opposite cause. How surprised he would have been had those very Slavophiles then told him that precisely he was the utmost champion of the Russian truth, of the Russian individuality,

of the Russian principle—specifically of everything which he denied
in Russia for the sake of Europe, which he considered mere fiction;
moreover, if it were proved to him that, in a certain sense and
essentially, precisely he was a conservative for the very reason
that in Europe he was a socialist and a revolutionary. And, in
truth, this was nearly so.

Here, there occurred one great mistake on the part of both
camps; above all, in the fact that Westerners of those days had
confused Russia with Europe, taking the former seriously for the
latter, and, by denying Europe and her order of things, they believed the same negation was applicable to Russia, whereas Russia
was by no means Europe, but merely wore the European uniform;
however, under that uniform there was an altogether different
being. And Slavophiles did urge people to grasp the fact that she
was not Europe, but a different being. They directly pointed out
that Westerners equalize things dissimilar and incommensurate, and
that the inference which holds good in the case of Europe is in
no way applicable to Russia, partly because all that which they
seek in Europe has already been long existent in Russia—at least
in embryo form and as a potentiality—and that it even constitutes
her substance, only not in a revolutionary guise but exactly in that
form which the ideas of universal revival of mankind must assume
—in the form of God's truth, of Christ's truth, which some day
must be realized on earth and which is fully preserved in Orthodoxy. Slavophiles insisted that Russia be studied first and that
only after that should inferences be drawn. However, at the time,
it was impossible to study, and, besides, in truth, no means therefor
were available. Furthermore, who, in those days, could have known
anything about Russia?—Of course, Slavophiles knew a hundred
times more than Westerners (and that's the minimum); yet even
they were virtually groping, reasoning metaphysically and abstractly, rather than relying upon their extraordinary instinct. It
is only during the last twenty years that it has become possible
to gain any knowledge. But even in our day, who knows anything
about Russia?—At best, a foundation for the acquisition of knowledge has been laid; but just as soon as an important question
arises, forthwith there ensues general discordance among us. For
example, at present the Eastern question is again being raised:
well, please confess, are there many of us—and who are they?—
who are capable of reaching a common decision relative to it?
And yet, for us, this is such a momentous, fatal and national question! But why should one speak of the Eastern question? Why
should one be taking up such big questions? Look at hundreds and
thousands of our domestic, everyday, current problems: what a

universal unsteadiness; what a lack of crystallized opinion; what want of habit of work! Here Russia is being deforested; landowners and peasants alike are destroying the forests as if in a state of rage. It may be positively asserted that our forests are being sold at one-tenth of their real value, since how long can supply continue? Our children will not yet have grown up when there will be only one-tenth of the present timber in the market. What will happen then?—Perhaps, ruin! And yet, go and talk to any one about the curtailment of the right to deforestation! And what will you hear?—On the one hand, state and national necessity; and on the other, violation of the right of private property—two opposite ideas. Forthwith two camps will be formed, and it is uncertain with which of them the liberal, all-decisive opinion will side. In truth, will there be two camps?—And the matter will be delayed for a long time. Who is it who dropped the witty remark—liberal in our present-day fashion—to the effect that there's no evil without good, and should all Russian forests be destroyed, there would be the advantage that corporal punishment with rods would be definitely obliterated since the peasant volost courts would have nothing with which to flog the delinquent peasants and peasant women. Of course, this is a consolation but, somehow, one doesn't believe it: even though no forests be left, there will always be enough left for flogging—rods would be imported from abroad. Now Jews are becoming landowners—and everywhere people write and shout that Jews are draining the soil of Russia; that a Jew, after having invested a certain amount of capital in the purchase of an estate, in order to retrieve the capital plus interest, promptly exhausts all productive forces of the purchased land. Yet try to say something against this and people will immediately start vociferating about the violation of the principle of economic freedom and civil equality. But what kind of equality is this if we have here an obvious and Talmudic *status in statu*—above all and in the first place; if this is not only the exhaustion of the soil but also the future exhaustion of our peasant, who, having been liberated from the landowners, unquestionably and very soon will be driven —as a commune *in corpore*—into a much worse slavery of far more pernicious landowners—those same new landowners who have already drained the sap out of the peasant in Western Russia; those who are now purchasing not only estates and peasants, but who have begun to buy liberal opinion, and who continue to do so quite successfully. Why do we have all these things? Why such indecision and disagreement with regard to every decision, even to any decision? Please note, isn't this true? To my way of thinking, this is by no means due to our ineptitude or our incapacity for work,

but to our continued ignorance of Russia—her essence and individuality, her significance and spirit—despite the fact that, compared with the times of Bielinsky and the Slavophiles, we have
already had twenty years of schooling. Even more: during these
twenty years of schooling the study of Russia, as a matter of fact,
has advanced very considerably, while the Russian instinct, so it
would seem, has diminished compared with the past. What is the
reason? But if Slavophiles in those days used to be saved by
their Russian instinct, this instinct was also present in Bielinsky
to such a degree that Slavophiles could have regarded him as their
best friend. I repeat: here there was a great misunderstanding on
the part of both camps. Not in vain did Apollon Grigoriev, who
also sometimes spoke rather sensitive things, say that "were Bielinsky to have lived longer, he would no doubt have joined the Slavophiles." In this phrase there is thought.

2

DEDUCTION FROM THE PARADOX

Thus, I may be told: "You assert that every Russian, turning
into a European Communard, thereby forthwith becomes a Russian
conservative."—No, it would be too risky to draw such a conclusion. I merely meant to observe that in this idea, even if it be
taken literally, there is a little drop of truth. Here, there is much
that is unconscious, while on my own part there may be too strong
a faith in the unceasing Russian instinct and in the viability
of the Russian spirit. But let it be so: let us admit that I myself
know that this is a paradox. However, this is what I should like
to set forth in conclusion: this too is a fact and a deduction therefrom. I have said before that the Russians in Europe distinguish
themselves by liberalism, and that at least nine-tenths of them side
with the left—and the extreme left—the moment they come in
contact with Europe. I am not insisting on the figure: perhaps they
do not constitute nine-tenths; but I do merely insist upon the
fact that the liberal Russians are incomparably more numerous
than the non-liberals. Yet there are non-liberal Russians. Yes, indeed, there are—there always have been—Russians (the names of
many of them are known) who not only did not deny European
civilization but who, on the contrary, have worshipped it so ardently
that they lost the last traces of their Russian instinct, their Russian individuality, their language; who forsook their native land
and, if they did not become foreign subjects, at least they did stay

in Europe, generation after generation. But it is a fact that, as opposed to liberal Russians with their atheism and communism, the former forthwith joined the right—and the extreme right—and became awful European conservatives.

Many of them changed their religion and embraced Roman Catholicism. Aren't these conservatives? Isn't this the extreme right?—But, if you will permit: conservatives in Europe and, on the contrary, utter negators of Russia. They became destroyers of Russia, enemies of Russia! This is what it meant to be ground from a Russian into a genuine European, to become at last a true son of civilization.—This is a remarkable fact derived from two hundred years of experience. The deduction is that a Russian who has become a genuine European, cannot help but become at the same time a natural enemy of Russia. Was this what those who had cut through the window desired? Did they have this in mind? And so there developed two types of civilized Russians: the European Bielinsky who, in those days, denied Europe, proved a Russian in the strictest sense, notwithstanding all errors which he had uttered about Russia; whereas the full-blooded, ancient Prince Gagarin, having become a European, deemed it necessary not only to embrace Catholicism but straightway to leap over to the Jesuits. Which, then, of the two—tell me now—is a greater friend of Russia? Which of the two remained more Russian? And does not this second example (of the extreme right) corroborate my initial paradox to the effect that, to begin with, Russian European socialists and Communards are not Europeans, and that, in the long run, when the misunderstanding shall have been dispelled and they know Russia, they will again become full-blooded and good Russians? And, secondly, that under no circumstance can a Russian be converted into a real European as long as he remains the least bit Russian. And, if this be so, it means that Russia is something independent and peculiar, not resembling Europe at all, but important by itself. Besides, Europe herself is, perhaps, not in the least unjust when condemning Russians and scoffing at their revolutionary theories: it means that we are revolutionists not merely for the sake of destruction where we did not build—like the Huns and the Tartars—but for the sake of something different, something which, in truth, we do not know ourselves (and those who know, keep silent). In a word, we are revolutionists, so to speak, because of some personal necessity—if you please, by reason of conservatism. . . . But all this is transitory, as I have already stated, extraneous, a side issue—at present we have on the stage the interminably insoluble Eastern question.

3

THE EASTERN QUESTION

The Eastern question! Who among us, this month, did not live through rather extraordinary sensations? And what a lot of newspaper comment! What confusion in our minds! What cynicism in some opinions! What honest trepidation in some hearts! What hubbub in some veins! But one thing is certain: there is nothing to fear, although there were many who kept frightening us. Besides, it is difficult to imagine that there could be many cowards in Russia. She has *deliberate* cowards—this is true—but, it seems, they made a mistake in the matter of time and, even for them, it is now too late to lose courage, and, besides, it does not pay: they would score no success. But deliberate cowards, too, know their limit and they would demand no dishonor from Russia, such as when, in ancient times, Czar Ivan Vasilievich, the Terrible, sent envoys to King Stephen Bathory and demanded from them that, if necessary, they endure even flogging if only peace be granted. Briefly public opinion, so it would seem, has manifested itself, and will submit to no flogging for the sake of any kind of peace.

Prince Milan of Serbia and Prince Nicholas of Montenegro, trusting in God and in their right, have taken the field against the Sultan, and, perhaps, when these lines are being read, we shall have news about some important encounter, or even a decisive battle. Now things will develop quickly. Irresolution and procrastination on the part of the great powers; the diplomatic twist of England which refused to ratify the findings of the Berlin conferences; thereupon, the sudden revolution which broke out in Constantinople and the outburst of Mohammedan fanaticism, and finally, the dreadful slaughter by the bashibazouks and the Circassians of sixty thousand peaceful Bulgarians—old men, women and children—all these simultaneously caused the conflagration and led to war. The Slavs have many hopes. If all their forces are added up, they possess up to one hundred and fifty thousand fighting men, of whom more than three-quarters belong to the fairly well-trained regular army. But the main thing is the spirit: they are taking the field, believing in their right and in victory, whereas among the Turks, despite their fanaticism, there is a serious lack of discipline, as well as confusion. It would not be surprising if even after the first encounters confusion turned into panic. I believe that it may already be predicted that if Europe does not intervene, the Slavs will without fail be victorious. Apparently, non-intervention on the part of Europe has been decided upon, yet it is difficult to assert that there is, at the present moment, anything firm and finite in European politics. In the face of the suddenly arisen immense problem, tacitly—as it were—everybody has decided to wait, postponing the final decision. However, it is rumored that the triple alliance of the great Eastern powers continues and personal meetings of the three Monarchs are still taking place, so that non-intervention in the struggle of the Slavs, from this side, *for the time being,* may be considered certain. England, which isolated herself, is looking for allies; whether she will find them— is a question. If she should find them, it will probably not be in France. Briefly, all Europe will be watching the struggle of the Christians against the Sultan, without intervening, but . . . only for the time being . . . till the division of the heritage. But is this heritage conceivable? It is a question whether there is going to be any heritage at all. If God crowns the Slavs' efforts with success, what limit shall Europe set to their success? Will she permit the sick man to be dragged from his bed for good? This is hard to suppose. On the contrary, after a new and solemn concilium, will she not decide to minister unto him again? . . . So that the Slavs' efforts, even in the case of huge success, may be rewarded with rather weak palliatives only. Serbia took the field, relying upon her strength; but, of course, she is aware of the fact that her ultimate destiny fully depends upon Russia. She knows that only Russia will save her from ruin—in case of a big calamity; and that also Russia, through her potent influence, will in the event of success help her to retain a maximum gain. She knows this and relies upon Russia, but she is also cognizant of the fact that all Europe is looking upon Russia with concealed distrust, and that Russia is in a troubled situation. In a word, everything rests in the future. But what action will Russia take?

Is it a question? To every Russian this should not, and must not, constitute a question. Russia will act *honestly;* such is the full answer to the question. Let the Prime Minister in England, because of political reasons, distort the truth before Parliament and report to it that the massacre of sixty thousand Bulgarians was the work not of the Turks, not of the bashibazouks, but of the Slav emigrants. And let the whole Parliament, also because of political reasons, believe him and tacitly approve his lie. In Russia nothing of the kind can or will take place. Some people might say that Russia, in any event, should not act to her own direct detriment. However, wherein is Russia's benefit? Her benefit is precisely in that, if necessary, she must act to her direct detriment, she must make a sacrifice, lest justice be violated. Russia cannot afford to betray a great idea, bequeathed to her over a whole range of centuries, to which, thus far, she has been undeviatingly adhering. This idea—among other things—is the general Slavic communion; but this general communion is not seizure, not violence, but supreme service to mankind. Besides, when—how often—has Russia acted in politics for the sake of her direct benefit? Contrariwise, hasn't she, during her entire Petersburg period, served mostly alien interests with a disinterestedness which might have surprised Europe, could she but have been seeing clearly, and not viewing us distrustfully—with suspicion and hate? In Europe no one, and in no respect, would believe in Russian disinterestedness; they would rather believe in roguery and stupidity. But we do not have to be afraid of their verdicts: in the self-denying disinterestedness of Russia is her whole power, so to speak, her whole individuality and the whole future of Russian destiny. Only, it is to be regretted that this power, at times, has been misdirected.

4

The Utopian Conception of History

Throughout these hundred and fifty years after Peter we have done nothing but live through a communion with all human civilization, affiliating ourselves with their history and their ideals. We have learned, and trained ourselves, to love the French, the Germans and everybody, as if they were our brethren—notwithstanding the fact that they never liked us and made up their minds never to like us. However, this was the essence of our reform—the whole Peter cause; we have derived from it, during that century and a half, an *expansion* of our view, which, perhaps, was unprecedented, and cannot be traced in any other nation, whether in the ancient or in the new world. The pre-Peter Russia was active and solid, although politically she was slow to form herself; she had evolved unity within herself and she had been ready to consolidate her border regions. And she had tacitly comprehended that she bore within herself a treasure which was no longer existent anywhere else—Orthodoxy; that she was the conservatrix of Christ's truth, genuine truth—the true image of Christ which had been dimmed in all other religions and in all other nations. This treasure, this eternal truth inherent in Russia and of which she had become the custodian, according to the view of the best Russians of those days, as it were, relieved their conscience of the duty of any other enlightenment. Moreover, in Moscow the conception had been formed that any closer intercourse with Europe might even exercise a harmful and corrupt influence upon the Russian mind and the

Russian *idea;* that it might distort Orthodoxy itself and lead Russia along the path to perdition "much in the same way as all other peoples." Thus ancient Russia, in her isolation, *was getting ready to be unjust*—unjust to mankind, having taken the resolution to preserve passively her treasure, her Orthodoxy, for herself, to seclude herself from Europe—that is, mankind—much as our schismatics who refuse to eat with you from the same dish and who believe it to be a holy practice that everyone should have his own cup and spoon. This is a correct simile because prior to Peter's advent, there had developed in Russia almost precisely this kind of political and spiritual relation with Europe. With Peter's reform there ensued an unparalleled broadening of the view, and herein— I repeat—is Peter's whole exploit. This is also that very treasure about which I spoke in one of the preceding issues of the *Diary*— a treasure which we, the upper cultured Russian stratum, are bringing to the people after our century-and-a-half absence from Russia, and which the people, after we ourselves shall have bowed before their truth, must accept from us *sine qua non*, "without which the fusion of both strata would prove impossible and everything would come to ruin." Now, what is this "expansion of the view," what does it consist of, and what does it signify?—Properly speaking, this is not enlightenment, nor is it science; nor is it a betrayal of the popular Russian moral principles for the sake of European civilization. No, this is precisely something inherent only in the Russian people, since nowhere and at no time has there ever been such a reform. This is actually, and in truth, almost our brotherly love of other peoples, which was the result of the hundred-and-fifty-year-long living experience of our intercourse with them. This is our urge to render universal service to humanity, sometimes even to the detriment of our own momentous and immediate interests. This is our reconciliation with their civilizations; cognition and *excuse* of their ideals even though these be in discord with ours; this is our acquired faculty of discovering and revealing in each one of the European civilizations—or, more correctly, in each of the European individualities—the truth contained in it, even though there be much with which it be impossible to agree. Finally, this is the longing; above all, to be just and to seek nothing but truth. Briefly, this is, perhaps, the beginning of that active application of our treasure—of Orthodoxy—to the universal service of mankind to which Orthodoxy is designated and which, in fact, constitutes its essence. Thus, through Peter's reform our former idea—the Russian Moscow idea—was broadened and its conception was magnified and strengthened. Thereby we got to understand our universal mission, our individuality and our role in humankind;

at the same time we could not help but comprehend that this mission and this role do not resemble those of other nations since, there, every national individuality lives solely for, and within, itself. We, on the other hand, will begin—now that the hour has come—precisely with becoming servants to all nations, for the sake of general pacification. And in this there is nothing disgraceful; on the contrary, therein is our grandeur because this leads to the ultimate unity of mankind. He who wishes to be first in the Kingdom of God must become a servant to everybody. This is how I understand the Russian mission *in its ideal*. After Peter the first step of our new policy was revealed of its own accord: it had to consist in the unification of the whole Slavdom, so to speak, under Russia's wing. And this communion is to be effected not for the sake of usurpation, not for the sake of violence, not for the purpose of the annihilation of Slavic individualities in the face of the Russian colossus—but with the object of their own regeneration, so that they may be placed in a proper relation to Europe and to mankind, and that they may finally be given an opportunity to compose and repose themselves after their never-ending secular plight, to restore their spirit, so that when they shall have perceived their new strength—they be given a chance to contribute their own mite to the treasury of the human spirit and to utter their word to civilization.

Oh, of course, you might laugh at all these "fancies" about the Russian mission; however, tell me: do not all Russians desire the resurrection of the Slavs precisely on this basis—precisely for the sake of their full individual liberty and the resurrection of their spirit—and not at all for the purpose that Russia may politically acquire them and, through them, increase her political power? Yet it is exactly of this that Europe suspects us. Indeed, isn't this so? —And thus, at least partly, are my "fancies" substantiated. Of course, it is for the same purpose that, sooner or later, Constantinople must be ours. . . .

God, what a sceptical smile would appear on the face of some Austrian or Englishman, were he to peruse all the above *fancies,* and suddenly read the passage concerning the *positive* deduction: "Constantinople, the Golden Horn, this most important political spot in the whole world . . . isn't this seizure?"

Yes, the Golden Horn and Constantinople—they will be ours, but not for the purpose of seizure, not for the sake of violence—I would reply. To begin with, this will come to pass of its own accord, precisely because the hour has come, and even if it has not yet arrived, indeed it will come in the near future; all symptoms point to this. This is a natural solution—so to speak, the word of nature herself. If this has not occurred before, it has been precisely because the time has not yet been ripe. In Europe, people believe in some "Testament of Peter the Great." It is nothing but a forged document, written by the Poles. However, even had the thought then occurred to Peter to seize Constantinople, instead of founding Petersburg, I believe that, after some deliberation, he would have abandoned this idea—granted that he was powerful enough to crush the Sultan—since in those days the time was inopportune and the project could even have brought ruin to Russia.

If in Finnish Petersburg we did not elude the influence of the neighboring Germans who, though useful, had paralyzed Russian progress before its genuine path had been ascertained, how then in Constantinople—so enormous and original, with her remnants of a most powerful and ancient civilization—could we have managed to elude the influence of the Greeks, men far more subtle than the coarse Germans, men who have infinitely more points in common with us than the Germans who do not resemble us at all—numerous courtiers who would promptly have surrounded the Throne and who, ahead of the Russians, would have become educated and learned, who would have captivated Peter himself, not to speak of his immediate successors, taking advantage of his weak spot by their skill in seamanship.

Briefly, they would have captured Russia politically; they would forthwith have dragged her along some new Asiatic path—again into a seclusion of some sort—and the Russia of those days, of course, could not have endured this. Her Russian strength and nationality would have been arrested in their development. The mighty Great Russian would have remained in estrangement in his grim, snowy North, serving merely as material for the regenerated Constantinople, and, perhaps, in the long run, he would have made up his mind not to follow her at all. At the same time the Russian South would have been captured by the Greeks. Moreover, there might have occurred a schism in Orthodoxy itself which would have been divided into two worlds—the regenerated world of Constantinople and the old Russian. . . . In a word, this would have been a most untimely event. At present things are quite different.

Today, Russia has already visited Europe and is herself educated. More important still: she has become conscious of her strength—and is, indeed, strong. She has also learned wherein she is strongest. Now Russia understands that Constantinople may be ours not at all as her capital, whereas had Peter, two centuries ago, captured Constantinople, he could not have helped but transfer thither his capital—and this would have spelt ruin, since Constan-

tinople is not Russia and *could not* have become Russia. Even if
Peter might have avoided this error, his immediate successors would
not have eschewed it. However, if Constantinople may be ours, not
as the capital of Russia, it may be ours not as a capital of Slavdom
as a whole—as some people are dreaming. Slavdom without Russia
would exhaust itself there in its struggle with the Greeks, even in
the event that it might succeed in forming from its parts some
political whole. But, for the Greeks alone to inherit Constantinople
is at present altogether impossible: it is impossible to surrender
to them so important a spot on the globe; this would be something
altogether out of proportion. Slavdom with Russia at its head is a
wholly different proposition, but whether or not it is a good proposition is again a question. Would it not resemble a political seizure
of the Slavs—a thing we do not need at all? Thus, in the name
of what, by virtue of what *moral* right could Russia claim Constantinople? Relying upon what sublime aims could Russia demand
Constantinople from Europe?—Precisely as a leader of Orthodoxy,
as its protectress and guardian—a role designated to her ever since
Ivan III, who placed her symbol and the Byzantine double-headed
eagle above the ancient coat of arms of Russia, a role which unquestionably revealed itself only after Peter the Great when Russia
perceived in herself the strength to fulfill her mission and factually
became the real and sole protectress of Orthodoxy and of the people
adhering to it. Such is the ground, such is the right to ancient
Constantinople, which would be intelligible and not offensive even
to the Slavs most sensitive to their independence, even to the Greeks
themselves. Besides, thereby would be revealed the true essence of
those political relations which inevitably must develop between
Russia and all other Orthodox peoples—whether Slavs or Greeks
makes no difference. Russia is their guardian, or even their leader,
perhaps, but not their sovereign; their mother, but not their mistress. Even if she were to become their sovereign some time in the
future, it would be only by their own election and subject to the
preservation of everything by which they themselves would define
their independence and individuality. So that eventually, and in
the long run, such a union could even be joined by non-Orthodox
European Slavs who would see for themselves that common unity
under the protection of Russia is merely the assurance to each of
his independent personality, whereas in the absence of this immense
unifying force, they would, perhaps, again exhaust themselves in
mutual strife and discord, even if they should some day become
politically independent of the Mohammedans and Europeans to
whom they now belong.

What's the use—it may be said—of juggling with words: what

is this "Orthodoxy"? And wherein, here, is there a peculiar idea
—a special right to the unification of the peoples? And would it
not be a purely political union like all other similar ones, founded
upon the broadest principles, akin to the United States of America
—or even broader? Such may be the questions propounded to me.
And these I will answer.—No, this would not be the same, and
this is not verbal jugglery: here there is *in reality* something peculiar, something unheard-of. This would not be merely a political
union and, of course, not one for the sake of political usurpation
and violence—this seems to be the only way Europe can conceive
the proposition. And it would be a union not for mercantile pursuit,
personal gain—those invariable and eternal deified vices, under the
guise of official Christianity which is believed by no one but the
plebs. No, this would be a genuine exaltation of Christ's truth,
preserved in the East, a new exaltation of Christ's Cross and the
final word of Orthodoxy, which is headed by Russia. This would
precisely constitute a temptation to the mighty of this world, to
those who thus far have been triumphant in it and who have
always looked upon such "expectations" with disdain and derision;
to those who are even unable to understand that one may seriously
believe in the brotherhood of men, in the general reconciliation of
the nations, in a union founded upon the principles of common
service to mankind, and, finally, in man's regeneration based on
the true principles of Christ. And if the belief in this "new word"
which may be uttered by Russia, heading united Orthodoxy, is a
"Utopia" worthy of nothing but ridicule, let people class me, too,
among these Utopians, while the ridicule—leave that to me.

"But"—it may perhaps be argued—"that Russia will ever be
permitted to head the Slavs and to enter Constantinople, is in itself
a Utopia. One may be dreaming about it, and yet these are but
dreams!"

In truth, is this so? But, aside from the fact that Russia
is strong and, maybe, much stronger than she herself realizes—
aside from this, have there not arisen before our eyes, during recent
decades, immense powers which have reigned in Europe, one of
which has been reduced to dust, swept away by God's tempest in
a day, and in its place a new Empire has come into being—an
Empire which, seemingly, has never before been surpassed in
strength? And who, in good time, could have predicted this? And
if such sweeping changes, which have already occurred before our
eyes in our day, are possible, can the human mind unmistakably
predict the fate of the Eastern question? Where are the real grounds
for despair in the resurrection and unity of the Slavs? Who knows
the ways of Providence?

5

Again About Women

All the newspapers have already become sympathetic with the cause of the Serbs and the Montenegrins who have arisen for the liberation of their brethren, while society and even the people are enthusiastically watching the successes of their armed forces. But the Slavs need help. Information—what seems to be accurate information—has been received that the Turks are being helped, though "anonymously" yet very actively, by the Austrians and the English. At that—almost not "anonymously." Help is given in the form of money, ammunition, shells—and also with men. There are many foreign officers in the Turkish army. An enormous British fleet is anchored off Constantinople . . . because of political considerations—more correctly, for any eventuality. In Austria, an enormous army is kept ready—also for any eventuality. The Austrian press maintains an irritable attitude toward the Serbs and Russia. It should be noted that if Europe at present looks upon the Slavs *insensibly,* this of course is due to the fact that Russians are also Slavs. Otherwise, the Austrian newspapers would not be so fearful of the Serbs—too negligible an armed force compared with the Austrian might, and they would not be comparing them with Piedmont. . . .

Therefore, Russian society must again come to the assistance of the Slavs—of course, even though it be only with money and some equipment. General Cherniaiev has already sent word to Petersburg that the sanitary facilities throughout the whole Serbian army are extremely poor: no doctors, no medicaments, insufficient care of the wounded. The Slavic Committee in Moscow has launched an energetic appeal throughout Russia for help to our insurgent brethren, and its members attended *in corpore,* in the presence of a huge crowd, a solemn Te Deum at the Church of the Serbian Hospice, held for the granting of victory to Serbian and Montenegrin armies. In Petersburg there begin to appear in the newspapers letters from the public, accompanied by donations. Obviously, the movement is expanding, even despite the so-called "dead summer season." But it is dead in Petersburg only.

I was about to finish my *Diary* and I was already reading the proof when, unexpectedly, a young girl called on me. She had met me during the winter, after I had started the publication of my *Diary*. She is planning to take a rather difficult examination for which she is studying energetically, and, of course, she will pass it. She comes from a well-to-do family and does not need money, but she is quite concerned about her education, and she used to call on me for advice as to what to read and to what she should be paying particular attention. She visited me not oftener than once a month, staying not longer than ten minutes; she spoke exclusively about her problems, but not loquaciously—modestly, almost shyly, and with remarkable confidence in me. However, it was impossible not to discern in her a very resolute character, and I have not been mistaken. This time she came in and directly stated:

"In Serbia the sick lack care. I have made up my mind to postpone for the time being my examination, and I want to go to take care of the sick. What would you say?"

And almost timidly she looked at me, but meanwhile I distinctly read in her glance that she had already decided upon the matter and that her decision was unalterable. But she also needed my approbation. I am not in a position to recount our conversation in detail lest I betray her anonymity by some most minute trait, and I am merely recording its general contents.

Suddenly I felt pity for her—she is so young. To scare her with pictures of hardships, war, typhus in hospitals, would have been absolutely superfluous; this would have meant pouring oil on fire. Here there was solely a thirst for sacrifice, for heroism, for a good deed, and—most important, most precious—was the fact that there was no vainglory, no self-infatuation, but merely the desire "to care for the wounded," to render service.

"But you don't know how to care for the wounded!"

"Quite, but I will manage it, and I have called on the Committee. Those enlisting are given two weeks' training and, of course, I will get prepared."

And, no doubt, she will get prepared; here the word is not in discord with the deed.

"Look here"—I told her—"I do not wish to scare or dissuade you, but consider my words and weigh them honestly. You grew up in totally different surroundings; you have seen only good society, and you have never seen people otherwise than in a calm state, in which they would not transgress the *bon ton*. But these same men during a war, under crowded conditions, amidst hardships and labours, sometimes become quite different. Suppose you cared for the sick, served them, got exhausted; you might be hardly able to stand on your feet, and, suddenly, a doctor—possibly a very good man *in se,* but tired, overstrained—who had just amputated several arms and legs, turns to you in a state of irritation and says: 'You are only spoiling things; you are doing nothing! Once you have decided to shoulder the task, you've got to serve!' etc.,

etc. Wouldn't it be difficult for you to endure this? And yet, this must necessarily be anticipated, and I am revealing to you only the tiniest glimpse. Reality is sometimes unpredictable. And, finally, are you sure that you would be able, despite the firmness of your resolution, to undertake that very nursing? Wouldn't you faint at the sight of some death or wound or operation? This occurs unconsciously, without one's will . . ."

"If I should be told that I am spoiling things, and not serving, I would quite understand that the doctor himself is irritated and tired out, and to me it would suffice to be inwardly convinced that I am not guilty and that I did everything as it should have been done."

"But you are so young! How can you vouch for yourself?"

"Why do you think I am so young? *I am already eighteen:* I am not at all so young. . . ."

"Well, God be with you!" I said. "Go—but as soon as the thing is over, do return promptly."

"Oh, of course, I have to pass the examination. But you wouldn't believe how you have gladdened me."

She left with a beaming face, and, of course, in a week she will be *there*.

In the opening part of my *Diary,* in the article on George Sand, I wrote a few words concerning her girl characters which particularly pleased me, in her novels of the first, earliest, period. Now, this one is precisely in the genre of those girls. Here we have precisely the same straightforward, honest but inexperienced young feminine character—with that proud chastity which does not fear and cannot be soiled even by contact with vice. Here is an urge for sacrifice, for work supposedly expected from her, and the conviction that it is necessary and that she must start herself, first, without any excuses, all the good which she expects and demands from other people—a conviction which is sound and moral in the highest degree, but one which, alas, is inherent mostly in youthful purity and innocence. But the main point is—I repeat—that here there is only work and not the slightest vainglory; not the slightest self-conceit and self-infatuation with one's personal exploit, which—contrariwise—we often perceive in our contemporaneous young men, even among mere raw youths.

After she had left, the thought again involuntarily occurred to me about the necessity in Russia of higher education for women—a most urgent necessity, particularly now in view of the serious quest of work in the present-day woman, quest of education, of participation in the common cause. I believe that the fathers and mothers of these daughters should be insisting on this themselves and for themselves, if they love their children. In fact, only the highest science possesses sufficient seriousness, fascination and power to pacify this virtual agitation which has ensued among our women. Only science is capable of answering their questions, of strengthening their minds and, so to speak, of placing under its tutelage their seething thought. As for this girl, though I pity her youth, still, aside from the fact that I could not have stopped her, I believe that in a way this journey may, perhaps, even prove useful to her: all the same, this is not a bookish world, not an abstract conviction, but an enormous forthcoming experience which God, Himself, in His infinite goodness, has sent her to save her. Here is a forthcoming lesson for her active life—an ensuing broadening of her thought and views; here is a future reminiscence, for her whole life, of something dear and beautiful, in which she had taken part and which will make her treasure life and not get tired of it without actually having lived—like that unfortunate suicide Pisareva, about whom I spoke in the preceding, May, issue of my *Diary*.

JULY—AUGUST

CHAPTER I

1

Departure Abroad. Something about Russians in Railroad Cars.

TWO MONTHS have elapsed since I have conversed with the reader. Having brought out the June issue (which completed the first half-year of my publication), forthwith I took a train and proceeded to Ems—oh, not for a rest, but for that purpose for which people journey to Ems. And, of course, this is an altogether too personal and private matter; yet the point is that sometimes I am writing my *Diary* not only for the public but also for myself. —(Possibly, this is the reason why there are some asperities and surprises in it, *i.e.*, thoughts quite familiar to me which have long been moulding themselves within me, but which, to the reader, may seem to be something that has suddenly leaped out of somewhere without any connection with preceding thoughts.) And hence, why should I also be omitting from my *Diary* my departure abroad? Of course, had I my own choice, I should have gone somewhere to the south of Russia—

Where the rich and fertile fields,
Through the bounty of their soil,
Bring the tiller fat crop yields
In exchange for his slight toil;
Where in meadows, fresh and green,
Springs purl flowing toward the glade,
Herds of wild mares may be seen
Roaming proud and unafraid.

But alas! It seems that there, too, things are quite different
from those about which the poet dreamed in that land: not only
in exchange for "slight toil" but even for heavy work, the tiller
is not going to harvest "fat crops." Likewise, as regards those mares,
the description should be considerably tuned down. By the way,
recently, in *The Moscow Gazette,* I came across an article on the
Crimea—on the eviction from the Crimea of the Tartars and on
"the desolation of the region." *The Moscow Gazette* sets forth a
bold idea—to the effect that there is no need for pitying the Tartars:
let them be evicted and, in their place, Russians had better be
colonized. Unhesitatingly, I call this a bold thought: this is one
of those ideas, one of those questions, about which I spoke in the
June issue of the *Diary*—the moment they arise "there forthwith
ensues general discordance among us." In fact, it is difficult to
decide whether everybody will agree with the opinion of *The Moscow Gazette,* with which I wholeheartedly agree, since I have long
been thinking the same way concerning "the Crimean question."
Decidedly, this is a *risky* opinion, and it is a question whether it
will be shared by liberal opinion, which has the last say in everything. True, *The Moscow Gazette* expresses the desire that "the
Tartars be not pitied," etc.—not only because of the political aspect
of the matter, not only for the consolidation of the border regions—
but, likewise, because of the economic needs of that region. It sets
forth the fact that the Tartars have proved their inability rationally to cultivate the Crimean soil, and that Russians—specifically
the South Russians—are much more fitted for this task, and, as
proof of this, it points to the Caucasus. Generally, if the colonization
(of course, gradual) of Russians in the Crimea should necessitate
some extraordinary expenditures even on the part of the state,
such disbursements are well worth risking and would prove very
profitable. In any event, should Russians fail to settle in the Crimea,
the Jews without fail would fall upon her and would exhaust her
soil.

The journey from Petersburg to Berlin is a long one—it lasts almost forty-eight hours—and, for this reason, I took with me, for any eventuality, two pamphlets and several newspapers. Precisely "for any eventuality"—because I am always afraid to stay in a crowd of strange Russians of our educated class; this, everywhere —be it in railroad cars or on boats, or in any kind of gatherings. This, I confess, is a weakness which I attribute, in the first place, to my personal suspiciousness. Abroad, in a crowd of foreigners, I always feel more at ease: there, everybody walks quite direct to the place of his destination, but our Russian walks and keeps looking around: "What"—thinks he—"will people say about me?" However, his appearance is firm and unshaken—yet, in reality, there is nothing more wavering and less self-confident than he. A Russian stranger, if he starts a conversation with you, always speaks to you in a remarkably confidential and cordial manner. However, beginning with his very first word, you perceive profound mistrust —and even hidden suspicious irritation—which, the moment anything goes against his grain, promptly leaps out of him in the form of a caustic remark, or even rudeness, notwithstanding all his "upbringing," and—what is most important—for no reason whatsoever. Everyone, as it were, wishes to revenge himself upon somebody for his nullity; and yet he may be not at all an insignificant man—at times he is just the reverse. No man oftener than a Russian is ready to repeat: "What do I care what people will say about me?" or: "I don't give a rap about public opinion." And there is no man more than a Russian (again, a civilized one) who would be more afraid of, and intimidated by, public opinion and what people will say or think about him. This is precisely caused by disrespect for himself, deeply rooted in him, of course, despite unlimited self-conceit and vainglory. These two contradictions are rooted in *virtually* every intelligent Russian; he is the first to whom they are unbearable, so that each one of them carries "hell in his soul." It is particularly painful to be meeting Russian strangers abroad somewhere, face to face, so that it is no longer possible to run away in the event of some calamity—for instance, if you were locked up with him in one and the same car. And yet—it would seem—"it is so nice to meet one's compatriot in a foreign country." Even the conversation usually begins with this very phrase. Upon finding out that you are Russian, the compatriot without fail begins: "You are Russian? How nice to meet a compatriot in a foreign country! I, too, am here . . ."—and, right away, frankness ensues, precisely, in a most cordial, so to speak, brotherly tone befitting two compatriots who have embraced each other in a foreign land. But don't trust this tone: even though the compatriot is smiling, nevertheless he is looking at you with suspicion;

this you can see from the expression of his eyes, from the way
he lisps when he speaks to you and gently scans his words. He
is taking your measure; he is already afraid of you; he is ready
to start lying. After all, he cannot help but look at you with suspicion and lie exactly because you also are a Russian and, willy-
nilly, he compares you with himself, perhaps, because you really
deserve this. It is also noteworthy that invariably—at least, not
infrequently—the Russian stranger abroad (there oftener, almost
invariably), after the first three sentences, hastens to interject a word to the effect that just a few minutes before he
met So-and-so, or that he heard something from So-and-so—
i.e., from some of our eminent or distinguished Russian men—
but he interjects this in the nicest and most familiar tone, just
as a friend—not only his friend but yours, too: "Of course, you
know the poor fellow is wandering from one local medical celebrity
to another; they are ordering him to watering places; why, the
man is in absolute despair. Are you acquainted with him?"—Should
you answer that you don't know him at all, the stranger will
promptly discover in this circumstance something offensive to himself: "You might have thought that I meant to brag to you about
my acquaintance with a prominent man." You can read this question in his eyes, and this, in fact, could have been the case. On
the other hand, if you answer that you know the man, the stranger
will feel still more offended—why?—I have really no idea. Briefly,
insincerity and animosity are growing on both sides and, suddenly,
the conversation breaks up and comes to an end. Your compatriot
turns away from you. He is ready to go on conversing all the time
with some German baker sitting opposite him, rather than with
you—and, specifically, he wishes you to notice this. Having begun
in such a friendly manner, he severs all relations and connections
with you, and rudely notices you not at all. When night comes,
he stretches out on the cushions, if there be room, reaching you
with his feet—perhaps, purposely touching you with his feet—and
when the journey is over, he leaves the car without even nodding
toward you. "Why did he get so offended?"—one thinks with sorrow and perplexity.

Best of all is to meet Russian generals. A Russian general
abroad is, above all, concerned with the fact that Russians meeting
him should not venture to talk to him, ignoring his rank, on the
alleged ground that "we are abroad and, therefore, we are all
equals." For this reason, beginning with the very first moment, he
sinks into a stern, marble silence, and this is good—at least, he
disturbs no one. By the way, a Russian general proceeding abroad
is sometimes very fond of donning civilian clothes, which he orders

from one of the most fashionable Petersburg tailors. On his arrival at a spa, where there are always so many pretty dames from all over Europe, he loves to flaunt himself. At the end of the season, he lets himself be photographed, with particular delight, in civilian attire so as to make presents of his picture to his acquaintances and to make some devoted subordinate of his happy with the gift. But, at any rate, the book or the newspaper brought along is of great help during the journey, precisely as a protection against Russians: "You see, I am reading. So leave me alone."

2

ON THE PUGNACITY OF THE GERMANS

Just as soon as we reached German soil, all of the six Germans in our compartment—the moment we had been locked up in it —started conversing among themselves about war and Russia. To me, this appeared curious; and, although I knew that in the German press, just now, there is a great deal of talk about Russia, nevertheless I did not think that they too would be discussing the question in public squares. These were by no means "upper-class" Germans; no doubt, among them there was not a single baron, and even not a single army officer. Besides, they were not discussing *la haute politique,* but merely the actual strength of Russia—more particularly, her military strength—with reference to the immediate present. With triumphant, and even somewhat haughty, calmness they told each other that at no time in the past had Russia been so weak from the standpoint of armaments, etc. A grave and tall German, who was on his way from Petersburg, announced in a most competent tone that, supposedly, we possess not more than two hundred and seventy thousand decent repeating rifles, while the rest are merely negligently remodeled old firearms, and that the aggregate number of repeating rifles does not reach half a million; that our supply of metal cartridges is not over sixty mil-lions—*i.e.,* only sixty cartridges per soldier, if the total war-time army be reckoned at the figure of one million men. However, they conversed pretty merrily. It should be noted that they were aware that I was a Russian but, apparently judging by the few words which I exchanged with the conductor, they must have concluded that I did not know German. But even though I speak bad German, nevertheless I do understand it. After a while I deemed it my "patriotic" duty to retort as calmly as possible—in accord with their tone—that all their figures and data were exaggerated in a negative sense; that already four years ago the equipment of our troops had reached a very satisfactory level, and that since then it has constantly been improved and that this is being continued uninterruptedly, so that we are able to compete with anyone. They listened to me attentively, despite my poor German, and even prompted me with this or that German word every time I would forget it, stopping short in my speech, and encouragingly nodded their heads, indicating thereby that they understood me. (N.B. If you speak poor German, you will be the more easily understood the more educated your German listener is. It is altogether different with a crowd in the street or, for instance, with servants: these are slow in understanding you, though you might have forgotten only one word in a whole sentence, and especially if you should happen to use, instead of some common word, a less customary one: at times, you would not be understood at all. I don't know if this is true about Frenchmen and Italians, but it was told and reported about Russian Sebastopol soldiers that they conversed —of course, by means of gestures—with the captured French soldiers in the Crimea and were able to understand them. Thus, had they known only half of the words spoken by the Frenchman, they would have fully understood him.)

The Germans made not even one refutation; they merely kept smiling at my words—not haughtily, perhaps, even approvingly— fully convinced that I, as a Russian, was speaking merely in defense of Russian honor; but I could see from the expression of their eyes that they did not believe a single word I was saying and that they continued to adhere to their own opinion. However, five years ago, in 1871, they were by no means as polite. I was then living in Dresden, and I remember how the Saxon troops returned after the war. The city then arranged for their triumphant entry and an ovation. I also remember the same troops one year before that, when they were just going to war, and when, suddenly, on all street corners and in all public places posters appeared with the words: *"Der Krieg ist erklärt!"* ("War has been declared!")—printed in large type. I then beheld these troops, and willy-nilly, I admired them: what vigor in those faces, what a serene, cheerful and, at the same time, grave expression in their eyes! They were all young men and, when looking at some marching company, it was impossible not to admire their wonderful military drill, their orderly step, their rigidly punctilious alignment, and, at the same time, the remarkable freedom which I had never before observed in a soldier, the conscious resoluteness which manifested itself in every gesture, in every step of these brave lads. It could be perceived that they were not driven, that they were going of their own accord. There was nothing stiff, nothing that would remind one of the corporal's rod. And that, in Germans—those very Germans from whom, when under Peter we organized our army, we borrowed both the corporal and the rod! No, these Germans marched without being driven with a rod—as one man, with perfect resoluteness and full certitude in victory. The war was a popular one: in the soldier there gleamed the citizen, and, I confess, I felt afraid for the French, despite the fact that I was still firmly convinced that they would beat the Germans. After that it is easy to imagine how these same soldiers had entered Dresden one year later after the victories which they had won over the French, from whom, throughout the whole century, they had endured all kinds of humiliations. Add to this usual German boastfulness—their nation-wide boundless self-conceit in case of some success, their petty bragging bordering on childishness and invariably attaining in Germans the level of arrogance, which is a rather unbecoming and almost surprising characteristic in this people. They have too much right to pride themselves over many a thing—even when compared with any other nation—to be displaying such triviality. It was apparent that this honor was so novel to them that they themselves had not expected it. And, in fact, they then became so drunk with success that they began to insult the Russians. At that time there were many Russians there, and later quite a few of them reported that everyone—even a shopkeeper— the moment he would start talking to a Russian—say, walking into his shop to buy something—would forthwith try to interject a remark such as this: "Now that we have finished with the French, we will get ready for you!" This malice against the Russians in those days broke out among the people spontaneously, notwithstanding everything the papers used to say then which understood Russia's policy during the war—a policy without which, perhaps, the Germans would not have been crowned with laurels. True, this was the first blaze of their military success—indeed, so unexpected —yet, the fact is that in that ardor they immediately recalled the Russians. This animosity against the Russians, which manifested itself almost spontaneously, at the time surprised even me, although I knew all my life that the German always and everywhere, ever since the time of the German Village in Moscow, has disliked the Russian. A Russian lady, Countess K., who in those days resided at Dresden, was sitting in one of the seats provided for the public on the occasion of the triumphal ovation to the troops marching into the city. Behind her several excited Germans began to scold Russia in a most awful manner. "I turned to them and abused them, using plebeian language"—she later told me. The Germans remained silent; they are very polite to the ladies, but, had it been a Russian man, they would have come back. At the time

I myself read in our newspapers that bands of drunken Germans, residents of Petersburg, used to provoke quarrels and fights at some drinking bouts with our soldiers, precisely under the pretext of "patriotism." By the way, most of the German newspapers are at present full of raging outbursts against Russia. Referring to this fury of the German press, alleging that the Russians seek to seize the East and the Slavs and, after strengthening themselves, to start an onslaught against European civilization, *The Voice* observed in one of its recent editorial articles that all this raging chorus is all the more surprising as it started, as if on purpose, immediately after the friendly conventions and meetings of the three Emperors, and that the matter, to say the least, was strange. This is a subtle remark.

3

THE VERY LAST WORD OF CIVILIZATION

Yes, in Europe there is gathering something seemingly un- avoidable. The Eastern question is growing and rising as a tidal wave and, perhaps, in reality it will ultimately engulf *everything* so that no peaceableness, no prudence, no firm determination not to incite war will be able to withstand the pressure of circum- stances. But the thing which is most important is that even now the dreadful fact is revealed—the fact that this is the last word of civilization. This last word has been uttered and revealed; now it is known, and it is the result of the whole development of eighteen centuries—of the whole humanization of humanity. All Europe, at least her leading representatives—those same men and nations who vociferated against slavery; who abolished Negro trade; who destroyed their domestic despotism; who proclaimed the rights of men; who created science and astounded the world with its power; who animated and captivated the human soul with art and its sacred ideals; who kindled enthusiasm and faith in the hearts of men by promising them in the very near future justice and truth—these same peoples and nations, suddenly at this instant, all of them (nearly all) are turning their backs on millions of unfortunate beings—Christians, men, their own brethren—who are perishing, who have been dishonored, and who are waiting, waiting hopefully and impatiently, till, one after another, they will all be crushed like reptiles, like bugs; till, finally, their desperate clamor and appeals for their salvation are silenced—clamors which annoy and disturb Europe. Precisely—like reptiles and bugs; even worse: tens, hundreds of thousands of Christians are being massacred as pernicious scabs, are being obliterated from the face of the earth, to their very roots. In the presence of their brothers, sisters are being assaulted; in the presence of their mothers, infants are being thrown up into the air to be caught on rifle-bayonets; villages are being annihilated; churches smashed into splinters; everything, without exception, is being *exterminated*—and this by a savage, disgusting Mohammedan horde, the sworn enemy of civilization. This is systematic extermination; this is not a gang of robbers which accidentally jumped out in the midst of a rebellion and war chaos but which is still afraid of the law. No, here we are faced with a system, a war method practiced by a huge Empire. Robbers are acting pursuant to ukases and instructions of ministers and rulers of the state—of the Sultan himself. And Europe, Christian Europe, the great civilization, looks on with impatience. . . . "When are these bugs going to be crushed, one after another?" Moreover, in Europe facts are being disputed; they are being denied in people's parliaments; they do not believe —a pretense is made that they do not believe. Each one of those leaders of the people knows that this is all true, but all of them, *à qui mieux mieux,* hasten to divert the other one's attention: "This is not true; this did not happen; this is an exaggeration! It is they themselves who have massacred sixty thousand of their own Bulgarians to lay the blame on the Turks!" "Your Excellency, she has flogged herself!" The Khlestakovs, the Skvoznik-Dmukhanovskys are in trouble! But why is this? What are these people afraid of? Why don't they want to see and listen, but instead are lying to themselves and disgracing themselves? But, you see, here Russia comes into play: "Russia would be strengthened; she would occupy the East, Constantinople, the Mediterranean, the ports; she would seize the trade. Russia, as a barbarian horde, would precipitate herself against Europe and would destroy civilization!"—(that very civilization which tolerates such barbaric things!) This is what they are shouting in England, in Germany, and, again, they are lying by the wholesale; they themselves do not believe a single word of these accusations and apprehensions. All these are but words designed to incite hatred in the popular masses. There isn't a man in Europe, though slightly reasoning and barely educated, who would believe today that Russia intends or is able to destroy civilization. Let them not believe in our disinterestedness; let them attribute to us every bad intention: this is intelligible. Yet it is incredible that, after so many examples and experiences, they should believe that we are stronger than all Europe combined. It is incredible that they should be ignorant of the fact that Europe is twice as strong as Russia, even if the latter held Constantinople in her hands; that Russia is exceedingly strong only at home, when she is defending her land against an invasion, but that she is four times weaker in an offensive. Oh, all this they know perfectly well, but they fool, and continue to fool, everybody and themselves solely because there, in England, there are several merchants and manufacturers who are pathologically suspicious and pathologically greedy when their interests are involved. But even these men know perfectly well that Russia, even under circumstances most advantageous to her, would nevertheless be unable to overpower their industry and commerce; that is still a matter of centuries to come. Yet even the most negligible expansion of anybody's trade, the slightest strengthening of anybody's sea power, causes alarm among them—a panic, anguish for profits. This is why the whole "civilization" suddenly turns out to be nothing but a puff. Well, but what is the Germans' concern? Why is their press sounding an alarm? —Because Russia stands behind their backs and ties their hands; because it was due to her that they missed the *opportune* moment once for all to obliterate France from the face of the earth so as never in the future to have to bother about her. "Russia hinders; Russia must be pushed back into her boundaries. But how is one to squeeze her in if, at the other end, France still stands *intact?*" Yes, Russia is guilty because of the fact itself that she is Russia, and that Russians are Russians—that is, Slavs. Hateful is the Slavic race to Europe—*les esclaves,* so to speak, slaves; and the Germans have so many of these slaves: who knows, they might rebel. And thus eighteen centuries of Christianity, humanization, science and progress suddenly—the moment the weak spot is touched—proves mere humbug, a fable for schoolchildren, an A B C moral. But therein is the trouble—the horror that this is "the last word of civilization," that it was uttered, it was not ashamed of being uttered. Oh, don't point out that in Europe, too, in England herself, public opinion did protest and appeal for monetary contributions for the relief of slaughtered mankind. This is all the more sad; all these are but individual cases; these merely go to prove how impotent they are over there against their general, state, national tendency. The questioning man stands perplexed: "Where is truth? Is it possible that the world is still so far from it? When will an end be put to strife? Will men ever get together? What stands in their way? Will truth ever be so strong as to subdue the depravity, cynicism and egoism of man? Where are the truths which have been evolved and acquired with so much pain? Where is humaneness? Indeed, are these truths at all? Aren't they mere exercises for 'lofty' sentiments, or for schoolboys to keep them under control, whereas the moment it comes to *real* business—

practical business—everything seems to be tossed aside, and to the devil—all ideals!"

Ideals are humbug, poesy, verses! And it is true that once more the Jew has enthroned himself everywhere! Why, not only has he "enthroned himself," but he never ceased to reign![1]

· CHAPTER II

1

Idealists-Cynics

AND DOES anyone remember the article by the unforgettable professor and unforgettable Russian—Timofei Nikolaievich Granovsky—on the Eastern question, which he wrote—if this be true—in the year 1855, in the very midst of our war with Europe, when the siege of Sebastopol had already begun? I took it with me on the train, and I have reread it precisely now in view of the fact that the Eastern question is being raised anew; and this old respectable article suddenly appeared to me extraordinarily curious, much more so than when I read it for the first time and when I was in full accord with it. This time I was struck by one particular consideration: first, by the view of a Westerner of those days concerning the people; and, secondly—and this is the important point—by the, so to speak, psychological significance of the article. I cannot refrain from conveying my impression to the reader.

Granovsky was the purest of all men of those days; he was irreproachable and beautiful. An idealist of the Forties—in the loftiest sense—he possessed the most individually peculiar and original nuance among our progressives of a certain pattern of his time. He was one of the most honest Stepan Trofimovichs (a character of an idealist of the Forties portrayed by me in the novel *The Possessed,* which our critics considered correct; and I love Stepan Trofimovich and profoundly respect him)—and, maybe, without the slightest comical trait rather inherent in this type. But I said that I was impressed with the *psychological* significance of the article, and this thought struck me as being amusing. I don't know if you will agree with me, but when our Russian idealist, an unquestionable idealist who knows that he is taken merely for such—so to speak, for a "patented" preacher of "the beautiful and the lofty"—suddenly finds it necessary to state or record his opinion on some matter (but a "real," practical, current matter, and not

[1]This article was written as early as in July.

on some question of poetry—on some momentous and *serious*, almost civic, matter), and to record it not somehow in passing, but in order to express a decisive and weighty judgment, and one which by all means may be influential—unexpectedly, by some miracle, he turns not only into an ardent realist and prosaist, but even into a cynic. Moreover, of that cynicism and prosaism, he is particularly proud. He records his opinion, and he almost cracks with his tongue. Ideals—let's toss them aside; ideals are humbug, poesy, verses; let's have in their stead nothing but "realistic truth." Yet he manages to over-salt it, to the point of cynicism. He seeks and presumes realistic truth in cynicism. The coarser, the drier, the more heartless it is—the more, in his judgment, realistic it is. Why is this so?—Because, in a case such as this, our idealist, without fail, will be ashamed of his idealism. He will be ashamed and will fear that he might be told: "Look here, you idealist: what do you understand in 'business'?—Go ahead, and preach there *the beautiful*, but leave it to us to judge 'business' matters." This trait was present even in Pushkin: time and again, the great poet used to feel ashamed of the fact that he was *only* a poet. Perhaps this trait may also be found in other nations, but I don't think so—at least, not in such a degree as in us. Over there, owing to the long-standing and common habit of work, occupations and significations of men, over a period of centuries, had the time to sort themselves, and almost everyone knows, understands and respects himself in his own profession and capacity. In Russia, however, in view of the two-hundred-year lack of habit of any work, the situation is somewhat different. Concealed, profound inner disrespect for oneself does not miss even such men as Pushkin and Granovsky. And, in truth, having found it necessary to turn suddenly from a professor of history into a diplomatist, this most innocent, most truthful man, in his judgments, denies the very possibility of Austria's gratitude to us for the fact that we helped her in her strife with the Hungarians and literally saved her from disintegration. And he denies this not because Austria was "crafty" and we should have known this in advance; no, he perceives no cunning and directly asserts that Austria could not have acted differently. Even more than that: he states that she *should not have* acted differently, and, on the contrary, that she should have acted as she did and that, for this reason, our hopes for Austria's gratitude merely constitute an unpardonable and ridiculous blunder of our policy. A private person—he implies—is one proposition, and the state—a different one. The state has its supreme immediate aims, its own advantages, so that it is simply ridiculous to demand gratitude even to the prejudice of that state's own interests. "In

Russia"—says Granovsky—"Austria's craftiness and ingratitude have become commonplace. But to speak of ingratitude and gratitude in political matters merely signifies lack of understanding. A state is not a private person; it cannot, because of gratitude, sacrifice its interests—all the more so as in political matters magnanimity itself *is never disinterested*." (That is, it should not be disinterested. Is this so?—This is precisely the thought.) Briefly, the esteemed idealist has uttered a whole lot of clever, but chiefly *realistic*, things. "You see, we are not merely composing verses!" True, this is clever—all the more so as it is not new; it is as old as the times when diplomats came into existence; even so, to justify so ardently Austria's act—and not only to justify it but to prove directly that she *should not have* acted otherwise—say what you will, but this somehow cuts the mind in two. Here there is something with which one cannot agree, which one loathes to accept, despite the extraordinary practical and political cleverness so unexpectedly expressed by our historian, poet and priest of the beautiful. For this admission of the sacredness of immediate advantage, of direct and hasty gain; this avowal of the justness of spittle upon honor and conscience merely for the sake of snatching a tuft of wool—may lead one very far. This, perhaps, may vindicate Metternich's policy on the ground of supreme and *realistic* state aims. Besides, do only practical advantages and immediate profits constitute a nation's real benefit and, therefore, its "supreme" policy as opposed to all these "Schiller" sentiments, ideals, and so forth? That's the question. On the contrary, isn't the best policy of a *great* nation precisely a policy of honor, magnanimity and justice, even if seemingly it is (in reality, it never is) detrimental to its interests? Is it possible that our historian was not aware of the fact that precisely these great and honest ideas (and not mere profit and a tuft of wool), in the long run, triumph over peoples and nations, despite all their apparent impracticability, and notwithstanding all their idealism, so humiliating in the view of the diplomatists, the Metternichs; and that the policy of honor and disinterestedness is not only the supreme but, perhaps, the most *advantageous* policy for a great nation, exactly because it is great? The policy of current practicality and of continually throwing oneself where there is more profit and where it is more practical reveals triviality, inner impotence of a state—an unfortunate condition. The diplomatic mind, the mind of practical and *vital* gain, invariably proved inferior to truth and honor, while truth and honor, at length, always triumphed. And if they did not triumph, they will—because men have invariably and eternally sought this and are seeking this. When Negro trade was about to be abolished, were not profound and wise objections raised to the effect that this "abolition" was impractical, that it would be detrimental to the vital and most essential interests of the nations and the states? People went so far as to assert that Negro trade was a matter of moral necessity; it was justified by the natural racial differences, and the inference used to be drawn that a Negro is almost not a man. . . .

When the North American colonies of England rebelled against her, did not people in practical England shout, year after year, that the liberation of the colonies from England's possession would mean the ruin of English interests, violent commotion, calamity?

When peasants were about to be liberated in Russia, weren't the same shouts heard in provincial districts? Didn't "profound and practical minds" assert that the state was embarking upon a bad road, unexplored and dreadful; that this would shake the state to its foundations; that not such should be a supreme policy looking to realistic interests and not those derived from modish economic considerations and theories, which have not been empirically assayed, as well as those founded on "sentimentality"?

Well, why should one be looking so far away?—Here we are faced with the Slavic question. Should we, at this time, forsake the Slavs for good?—Even though Granovsky insists that we are merely seeking to strengthen ourselves with the Slavs, and that we are acting only for our practical advantage, nevertheless, to my way of thinking, here he made a slip. Indeed, what is our practical benefit with them, even in the future? And how are we going to strengthen ourselves?—Through the Mediterranean in some future time? Or through Constantinople "which will never be ceded to us"? But this is nothing but a crane in the sky: even if we should manage to catch him, we would be merely adding to our troubles—for a whole millennium. Is this prosperity? Is this a wise man's view? Is this real practical interest?—There is nothing but bother and trouble with the Slavs—especially now when they are not yet ours. It is because of them that Europe, for a hundred years, has been looking askance at us. And at present not only is she looking at us askance, but at our slightest move she draws her sword and sights a gun at us. Simply, let us forsake them for good, and once and forever appease Europe. And we should not only forsake them: possibly, Europe would not believe that we did forsake them; no, we should have to forsake with proof in hand; we should throw ourselves upon the Slavs and crush them in a brotherly fashion in order to give our support to Turkey: "Can't you see, dear Slavic brethren, a state is not a private person; it cannot, for the sake of magnanimity, sacrifice its interests. Didn't you know this?"—And how many benefits—practical, real and immediate benefits, and not some visionary future ones—would Russia derive at once! Forthwith the Eastern question would come to an end; Europe, even though only for a while, would restore her confidence in us. As a result, our military budget would be curtailed; our credit would be improved; our ruble would be quoted at its real exchange rate—and not only this: the crane would fly away nowhere; he would keep circling right here! Well, just now we will act against our conscience; we will wait awhile: "The state is not a private person; it should not be sacrificing its interests—but in the future . . . Well, if the Slavs are destined not to get along without us, they themselves will join us when the time is ripe, and then we will again stick to them with love and brotherhood."

However, Granovsky perceives precisely this in our policy. He specifically asserts that during the whole last century our policy did nothing but oppress the Slavs, "denouncing and betraying them to the Turks"; that our Slavic policy has always been a policy of seizure and violence, and that it could not have been different. (Does this mean that it should have been such? Indeed, he does vindicate the others for such a policy! Why shouldn't he vindicate us?)

But is it really true that such was our traditional policy in the Slavic question? Is it possible that even now it has not been clarified?—That's the question!

2

IS IT SHAMEFUL TO BE AN IDEALIST?

Of course, Granovsky was ambitious, but I believe that ambition, at times—even hot-tempered ambition—must have been prevalent in all our capable men of those days—precisely owing to the absence of work; because of the impossibility of finding an occupation, so to speak, because of anguish for work. It used to come to the point where people seemingly engaged in some pursuit (a professor, for example, or a writer, a poet, even a great poet) placed little value on their profession—not merely because of the constraint in which they found themselves and their profession, but also because virtually each one of them was inclined to presume in himself a touch of some other vocation which, in his opinion, was higher, more useful, more civic than the one in which he was engaged. Irritableness of ambition in our best progressive and capable men (in some of them, of course) is extraordinary even nowadays and, invariably, it is due to the same cause. (However, I am speaking only of capable and gifted men and, for the time being, I make no mention of the ugly, impermissibly irritable self-conceit and vainglory of so many inept and vain contemporaneous "workers" who imagine themselves geniuses—although this phenomenon is particularly conspicuous in our day.) This anguish for work—this perpetual quest of occupation—which is exclusively caused by our two-hundred-year-long indolence and which has gone so far that at present we do not even know how to approach a task—moreover, even to determine where the task is and what it consists of—greatly irritates men in Russia. There appears self-conceit—sometimes even indecent self-conceit, taking into account the moral level of the man—which makes him almost ludicrous. But all this is caused precisely by the fact that this lofty moral person was never able to gauge himself, to ascertain his forces and his significance, to determine, so to speak, his own specific gravity and his real value in practical matters, in work. Had he ascertained all this, as a highly spiritual man, he would not deem it humiliating to admit that he has no aptitude for certain things. Nowadays, however, he is touchy and, owing to his irritableness, oftentimes embarks upon work for which he is not fitted.

Granovsky's article—I repeat—is cleverly written, although it contains political errors which subsequently were proved in Europe by facts which certainly could be specified, but I am not speaking of these mistakes and, besides, it is not for me to judge Granovsky in this respect. This time I was merely impressed with the extraordinary irritableness of the article. Oh, I am not attributing it to ambition, nor am I *attacking* a certain tendentiousness of the article. I can readily understand the *"cri du jour"* which is reflected in this paper, the feeling and sorrow of a citizen. After all, there are moments when even the most just man cannot be impartial. . . . (Alas, Granovsky did not live to see the liberation of the peasants, and he could not have imagined it even in his dreams!) No, I am not attacking this. But why does he, in this *Eastern Question* of his, look so contemptuously upon the people, and why does he not give them what is due to them? In this matter he refuses to perceive the people's participation, their thought. He positively asserts that concerning the cause of the Slavs and the contemporaneous war, the people held no opinion whatever and merely felt the burden of requisitions and taxes. It seems that the people should have had no opinion. Says Granovsky:

"In the first place, it is necessary to set aside the thought that this war (i.e., of 1853–'54–'55) is a holy war. The government sought to convince the people that it rose in defense of the rights of the co-religionists and of the Christian Church. The defenders of Orthodoxy and of the Slavic race *hoisted this banner with gladness* and preached a crusade against the Mohammedans. *But the age of crusades has passed: in our day no one will be prompted to rise in defense of the Holy Sepulchre* [and in defense of the Slavs, too?]; *no one regards the Mohammedans as eternal enemies of Christianity;* the keys to the Bethlehem temple serve as a mere pretext for the attainment of political aims." [In another place this is also directly stated concerning the Slavs.]

Of course, we are also willing to agree that in the Slavic question the Russian policy, during this last century, was perhaps, at times, not flawless. At certain moments it may have been too reserved and cautious, and for this reason, in somebody's impatient view, it may have seemed insincere. Perhaps there may have been excessive concern about current interests, ambiguity caused by certain external diplomatic pressure, half-measures, suspense; yet, essentially, on the whole, Russia's policy was hardly concerned *only* about bringing the Slavs under her domination in order thereby to increase her power and political influence. Of course, this was not so, and *in substance* our policy in the Slavic, *i.e.*, the Eastern, question, even through the entire Petersburg period of our history, hardly differed from our most ancient historical covenants and traditions, and from the popular opinion. And our government was always firmly aware of the fact that the moment the people would hear its appeal in this matter, they would wholeheartedly respond to it, and this is why in Russia the Eastern question was always essentially a popular question.

However, Granovsky does not at all admit it. Oh, Granovsky had a profound affection for the people! In his article he expresses sorrow and laments about their sufferings during the war, about the burdens endured by them. Indeed, can men like Granovsky fail to love the people? In this compassion, in this love, his beautiful soul was fully revealed. At the same time, however, involuntarily was revealed the opinion concerning the people of a sworn Westerner, always ready to admit in the people admirable beginnings, but merely "in a passive state," and on the level of a "secluded idyllic mode of existence," whereas "one had better refrain from speaking about their actual and potential activity." To him, the people, under all circumstances are a backward and a mute mass. And what would you think: we—almost all of us—in those days, believed him. This is why I do not venture to "attack" Granovsky, and I am merely accusing his times—and not him. His article passed from hand to hand, and it exercised influence. . . . That's the point: more than by anything, I was impressed with the parallel between this remarkable article, with its remarkable point of view, and our current, present moment. No, even the Westerner Granovsky today would be amazed and, possibly, would *believe*: these voluntary sacrifices and the people's contributions to the Orthodox Slavs; these sacrifices of the Old-Believers who, through their congregations, are sending sanitary units; these donations of artel workers collected from their last pennies, or subscriptions, initiated by communal resolutions, by whole villages; donations of soldiers and sailors out of their salaries; finally—Russians belonging to all classes, who go to fight and shed their blood for their oppressed Orthodox brethren—no, this is something manifest, something that cannot be called passive and which must be reckoned with. The movement has been exposed and it cannot be denied. Women, prominent ladies, are collecting alms in the streets for our Slavic brethren, and the people are gravely and fondly observing this penomenon which is novel to them: "This means that once more we all are getting together; that not always are we drifting apart; that we are all Christians."—This is what the people certainly feel and, perhaps, what they already think. And, of course, the news does reach them: they listen when newspapers are read to them; they themselves begin to read them. And, no doubt, they have heard and prayed in church for the repose of the soul of Nikolai Alexeevich Kireev who gave his life for the cause of the people. And—who knows?—they might compose their folksong about that death and that sacrifice—

> Though he did fall, he still will live
> Forever in the people's thought—
> For all he bravely chose to give,
> For his free soul, for all he'd fought!
> Death for the people is a glorious death!

Yes, this was a "death for the people," and not only for the Slavic people, but also for the common Orthodox and Russian cause, and the people will always understand it. No, our people are not materialists and, spiritually, they have not yet been corrupted to the point where they would be thinking only about material profits and positive interests. At heart they are glad when there arises a great goal and they accept it as spiritual bread. And is it possible that the people now, at this minute, do not realize that further developments in this "Slavic cause" may threaten with war even

us, that they may precipitate war?—If so—just as twenty years
ago, during the Eastern war—the people would have to endure
requisitions and burdens. But look at them now: are they afraid of
anything?—No, in our people there are more spiritual and active
forces than some of our "connoisseurs" are inclined to think. Better
had Granovsky left this opinion to others, to that multitude of
"connoisseurs of the people" and, perhaps, to some of our writers
about the people who, although they have buried themselves in
the Russian peasant, have forever remained foreigners.

In conclusion, I repeat: in Russia, idealists often forget that
idealism is in no sense a shameful thing. In both the idealist and
the realist, if only they be honest and magnanimous, the substance
is identical—love of mankind—and their object is identical—man;
it is only the *forms* of the representation of the object that are
different.

There is no reason for being ashamed of one's idealism: this
is the same road to the same goal. So that, in substance, idealism
is as realistic as realism, and it can never vanish from the world.
It is not for the Granovskys to be ashamed of the fact that they
come into being specifically for the purpose of preaching "the beautiful and the lofty." And should even the Granovskys become
ashamed and, for fear of the scoffing and haughty sages of the
Areopagus, should side with those who are next to the Metternichs
—who, then, would be our prophets? And it is not for *Granovsky,
the historian,* to be ignorant of the fact that to the peoples there
is nothing more precious than to possess and preserve ideals, and
that some sacred idea, no matter how weak, impractical and
ridiculous it may appear to the sages, will always carry an appeal
to some member of the Areopagus and to "the woman named
Thamar" who, from the very start, will believe in it and will believe the preacher; who will join the noble cause, not fearing
severance from the sages. And thus a negligible, untimely, impractical "tiny idea" begins to grow, to expand, and, at length, it con-
quers the world and the wise men of the Areopagus are silenced.

3

THE GERMANS AND WORK. INCOMPREHENSIBLE TRICKS.
ON WIT.

Ems is a brilliant and fashionable place. Sick people, pre-
eminently with chest ailments, with "catarrhs of the pulmonary
tract," come here from all over the world and are successfully

cured at her springs. Every summer there are some fourteen or fifteen thousand visitors—of course, mostly rich people or, at least, those who are in a position not to deny themselves the privilege of taking care of their health. But there are also poor people who *go* there *on foot* to take the cure. Of these, there are about one hundred persons and, maybe, they too do not come on foot but use some other means of locomotion.

I became very much interested in the *fourth*-class cars inaugurated on German railroads—only I don't know if they are designed for everybody's use. At some stop on the journey I asked a conductor (almost all conductors on German railroads are not only men of executive ability but they are also attentive and kind to the passengers) to explain to me what that fourth class meant. He showed me an empty car which had nothing but walls and a floor. It developed that passengers must stand on their feet.

"Perhaps, they sit down on the floor?"

"Oh, of course, people do as they please."

"How many places are there in a car?"

"Twenty-five."

Upon measuring mentally the dimensions of this vacant car for twenty-five persons, I concluded that they must necessarily be standing—even, shoulder to shoulder. So that in case they might actually crowd in twenty-five people—that is, to full capacity—not one of them could sit down, despite the "as they please." Of course, everyone must be holding his baggage in his hands. However, they probably have but small bundles with them.

"Yes, but here prices are half of what they are in the third class, and this is quite an advantage for a poor man."

Well, that's really worth something.

So, "the poor" arriving in Ems are not only medically treated but even maintained at the expense of . . . why, I don't know at whose expense. Shortly after one's arrival there, and when one has occupied a lodging at a hotel (in Ems all houses are hotels), without fail on the second or third day two collectors of donations, with books for recording them, one after the other, will call on you. They are of humble and patient appearance, but with some self-respect. One of them collects for the maintenance of these destitute sick people. Appended to the book is a printed appeal of the Ems doctors to their patients to remember the poor. You make a contribution within your means and inscribe your name in the book. I looked through it and I was amazed by the scantiness of the contributions: one mark, half a mark, rarely three marks, and very rarely five marks. And yet, it would seem that here the public is not being annoyed with requests for contributions: aside from these two collectors, there are no others. While you are making your contribution and recording your name in the book, the functionary (well, let's call him that) is humbly standing in the middle of your room.

"Do you collect much in the course of the season?"—I asked.

"Up to one thousand taler; but this is too small a sum compared with the need: there are many of them, up to a hundred persons, and we fully maintain them—we treat and feed them, and provide lodgings for them."

Verily, this isn't much. One thousand taler is equal to three thousand marks. If some fourteen thousand people be visiting the place, what would the per capita contribution amount to? Thus, there must be people who contribute nothing; they refuse to give and expel the collector (they actually *expel* him, as I subsequently learned). And yet this is a brilliant, most brilliant, public. Go out and look at that crowd when they are drinking mineral waters or when the music is playing.

By the way, as far back as in the spring I read in our papers that we, Russians, have contributed very little to the insurgent Slavs (of course, this was reported before the present contributions had been made), and that, compared with us, everybody in Europe has contributed much more, not to speak of Austria which contributed many (?) millions of guldens for the maintenance of the families of the insurgents who, by the tens of thousands, have made their way into her territory; that in England, for example, people have contributed much more than we—even in France and in Italy. However, say what you may, I do not believe in the enormity of these European contributions to the Slavs. Much has been said about England; however, it would be curious to learn the actual amount of her contributions which, it would seem, no one knows precisely.

As for Austria, which from the very beginning of the uprising has been contemplating the acquisition of a portion of Bosnia (this matter is already being discussed in diplomatic circles), her contributions were thus not disinterested, having been made with a view to her future interests. Besides, this was not a public contribution but simply a governmental appropriation. Yet, even here "the many" millions of guldens may be questioned. There have been contributions—more correctly, monetary appropriations—but whether the actual relief was substantial, is a matter which may be ascertained only in the future.

The other functionary—I mean, the Ems collector of donations—who invariably calls immediately after the first one, is collecting for *"blödige Kinder,"* *i.e.,* little idiot-children. Such is the name of the local institution. Of course, it is not only Ems that supplies the establishment with idiots; and it would be most unbecoming for so small a town to be begetting so many idiots. There is a government appropriation for the maintenance of this institution, but apparently it also has to resort to charity. A brilliant man or a gorgeous lady is cured and restored to health, precisely owing to the local mineral springs, and not from gratitude to this place, but as a souvenir they leave two or three marks for these destitute, forsaken, unfortunate little creatures. In this second book the contributions also amount to one mark, two marks, and only very rarely does there appear a contribution of ten marks. This second functionary collects in the course of the season fifteen hundred talers: "Things used to be better: formerly people contributed more liberally"—he added sadly.

In this book my attention was arrested by one contribution, so to speak, with a "tendency": 5 pfennigs (1½ silver copeck). This reminded me of a donation of a certain Russian State Councillor, recorded in the book at Piatigorsk for the erection of a monument to Lermontov: he contributed *one silver copeck,* and he signed his name. About a year ago this was reported in the press, but the name of the donor was not revealed, and, in my opinion, with no good reason since he had personally signed his name—and, perhaps, precisely dreaming about fame. However, the State Councillor apparently meant to reveal his mental vigor—his point of view, his orientation: he protested against art, against the nullity of poetry in our age of "realism," steamships and railroads, *i.e.,* against everything which is usually being denounced by the liberal (more correctly—echoing somebody else's liberal ideas) rabble of the lowest order. But this one—the local *Blödige,* what did he mean to express by his five pfennigs?—I really fail to understand wherein is the tendency in this case. *Blödige Kinder* are little unfortunate creatures, outcasts of the poorest families. Why should one be displaying wit in a matter such as this? "And if you give a poor wretch but one glass of water, even this will be credited to you in the Heavenly Kingdom." However, what am I talking about?—A glass of water at Ems certainly does not cost more than five pfennigs —by no means—so that even for five pfennigs one may be admitted to Paradise. Precisely, the fellow has estimated the minimum expense for admission to Paradise. "What's the use of paying extra?" —Simply, a child of his age! Nowadays, don't you see, no one can be duped!

Ever since my first visit to Ems—three years ago—ever since the first day of my sojourn there, I have been intrigued with one fact; it continues to interest me on each one of my visits. The two most popular springs at Ems—even though there are others—are Krenchen and Kesselbrunnen. Over these springs a house has been erected, and the springs themselves are fenced off from the public by a balustrade. Behind it stand several girls—three at each spring—courteous, young and neatly dressed. You hand them your glass which they promptly fill with the water. During the two hours designated for the morning drinking thousands of patients come to the balustrades; in the course of these two hours, each patient drinks several glasses—two, three, four—as many as are prescribed for him. The same takes place during the evening drinking hours. Thus, each one of the three girls fills and hands a great number of glasses. Yet not only is this being done in perfect order—unhurriedly, with poise, methodically, so that no one is ever being delayed—but what is most surprising is the fact that each of the girls, in my opinion, possesses almost supernatural apprehension. Only once, the first time after your arrival, you say to her: "Here is my glass. I have to have so many ounces of Krenchen and so many ounces of milk"—and during the whole month of your cure not even once will she make a mistake. Moreover, she knows you "by heart" and she recognizes you amidst the crowd, which is dense; people stand in several rows; everyone is stretching out his hand with his glass; she takes them—six or seven glasses at a time—fills them in some quarter of a minute and, without spilling or breaking them, returns the glass to each patient without a mistake. She hands you your glass herself and, amidst the thousands of glasses, she knows that this one is yours, that one —somebody else's, and she remembers by heart how many ounces of water and how many ounces of milk should be poured into it, and how many glasses you have to drink according to the prescription. Never does even the slightest mistake occur: I myself have been watching, and I have been making specific inquiries. And the principal thing: here there are several thousands of patients. Possibly this is a most ordinary thing in which there is nothing surprising, but to me, for the third year, it seems almost incomprehensible, and I still regard this as an inconceivable legerdemain. And even though it is ludicrous to be surprised at anything, this problem I am positively unable to solve. Apparently, it is necessary to conclude that these German women possess an extraordinary memory and quickness of apprehension; on the other hand, perhaps, this may be nothing but habit of work, adaptation to work from early childhood, or, to employ a metaphor, *victory over work*.

As far as work specifically is concerned, the observing Russian also feels perplexed. Living one month in the hotel—(strictly speaking, not in a hotel: here every house is a hotel, and the majority of these hotels, with the exception of several big ones, are simply apartments with service and board by stipulation)—I kept wondering at our maidservant. In the hotel where I lived there were twelve apartments, all of them occupied; in some of them whole families were living. Everyone rings the bell; everyone orders something; everyone has to be served; many times during the day she has to run up and down the staircase. And for all this there was in the hotel only one servant—a nineteen-year-old girl. Moreover, the hostess sent her around on errands: to fetch wine for dinner for this tenant, to a pharmacy—for that one; to the laundry—for the third one; to the grocery—for the hostess herself. That hostess, a widow, had three children; somehow they had to be taken care of, served; in the mornings they had to be dressed for school. Every Saturday the maid had to wash all the floors in the house; every day every room had to be cleaned, bed and table linen had to be changed, and each time after the departure of a tenant his entire apartment had to be immediately washed and cleaned, without waiting for Saturday. The girl went to bed at half past eleven in the evening, and in the morning the hostess would wake her up with a bell at five o'clock. All this is literally so, as I am stating it, and I do not exaggerate in the least. Add to this the fact that she worked for a most modest remuneration—inconceivable in Petersburg—and, on top of that, she had to be neatly dressed. Please note that there was nothing contrite or oppressed in the appearance of that maidservant: she was cheerful, bold, healthy—with a perfectly contented air and an unperturbed calmness.

Nay, in Russia people do not work this way: for no amount of money will our Russian maidservant accept such a "hard-labor" position. Besides, the quality of her work is different: a hundred times will she forget things; she will spill something; she will fail to bring things; she will break something; she will make a mistake; she will grow angry or "fresh." Whereas here, during the whole month, there was absolutely nothing to complain about.

To my way of thinking, this is remarkable and, as a Russian, I don't know whether this should be lauded or censured. Well, I will venture to laud it, although here there is something to think about. Here, everyone has accepted his status as it is, and is satisfied without envying, apparently without ever suspecting anything —at least, this is true of the overwhelming majority. Nevertheless, work is tempting—settled work which, in the course of centuries, has become crystallized; work with a manifest method and manner which is given to everyone almost at his birth. For this reason everyone knows how to approach his task and to completely *master* it. Here, everybody knows his task, although nothing but his task. I am saying this because here everybody works—not only maid-servants, but also their employers.

Look at a German functionary, say, a postoffice employee. Everybody knows what Russian functionaries are—especially those among them who are in daily contact with the public: a Russian functionary is something of an angry and irritable creature; and even if, at times, irritation is not manifest, yet one feels that it is concealed, and this may be guessed by his expression. He is presumptuous and haughty, something on the order of Jupiter. This is particularly noticeable in the tiniest midgets—say, among those who are givng information to the public, or who are receiving money, issuing tickets, and the like. Look at one of them: he is busy, he is "at work." The public gathers in a crowd; a line is formed; everyone is anxious to obtain his bit of information, to receive an answer, to get his receipt, to purchase his ticket. And here, he pays not the slightest attention to you. Finally, you are "next"; you are standing there, you speak to him—he doesn't listen, he doesn't look at you; he turns his head and talks to a functionary sitting behind him; he picks up some paper and checks something, but you are ready to suspect that he is merely pretending, and that there is nothing he needs to check. However, you are prepared to wait. Presently he gets up and walks out. Suddenly the clock strikes, and the office closes. Public, get out!

Our functionary, compared with the German, spends much less time at his work. Rudeness, inattention, neglect, *animosity* against the public for the sole reason that it is the public, and most of all—petty Jupiterism. He is anxious by all means to prove to you that you depend upon him. "Look at me: you there, behind the balustrade, you can do nothing to me, and I can do to you whatever pleases me, and if you grow angry, I shall call a guard and you will be ejected." He seeks to take vengeance upon someone for some kind of offense, to take vengeance upon you for his nothingness.

Here, at Ems, in the postoffice there are usually two, a maximum of three, functionaries. During the season there are months (for example, June and July) when visitors gather by the thousands. One can imagine what a mass of correspondence must be accumulating and what a volume of work the postoffice must be handling. Except for some two hours for dinner, the functionaries work all day long. Correspondence has to be received and dispatched; a thousand persons are coming to claim their *poste restante* or to make some inquiry. For each one the functionary looks through heaps of letters; he listens to everybody and gives him information or explains something; and he does all this patiently, kindly, politely—at the same time preserving his dignity. From a tiny midget he is being converted into a man, and not vice versa. . . . After my arrival in Ems, for a long time I did not receive a certain letter which I was impatiently awaiting; and every day I inquired about it at the *poste restante* window. One morning, after returning to my hotel from the "water-drinking," I found that letter on my desk. It had just arrived, and the functionary who remembered my name, but did not know where I was stopping, made a special search for my address in a printed list recording the arrivals of visitors and their addresses, and sent me this letter by special delivery, despite the fact that it was addressed *"poste restante"*—all this solely because on the eve when I came to inquire he had noticed my great anxiety. Well, would anyone of our functionaries do this?

As regards German wit and German apprehension, which have come to my mind specifically in connection with German work and everything I have stated above about it, there exist several opinions. The French, who even before never liked the Germans, always have considered, and now regard, the German mind as being a bit tight but, of course, by no means blunt. They perceive in the German intellect, as it were, some inclination to avoid always the straight issue in everything, and, on the contrary, an invariable desire to resort to something intermediary, to make out of a single proposition something bisyllabic, biarticulate. Among us, Russians, there has always circulated a great number of anecdotes about the tightness and dullness of the Germans, notwithstanding all our sincere admiration of their learnedness. But it seems to me that the Germans merely possess too strong a distinctiveness, too obstinate a national peculiarity, to the degree of haughtiness, which, at times, makes one indignant, and which, for this reason, leads to erroneous conclusions regarding them. However, at first, on a foreigner—especially if he is a newcomer in Germany—the German, in truth, sometimes, produces a strange impression in social intercourse.

On my way from Berlin to Ems the train made a four-minute stop at a certain station. This was at night-time: I was tired of sitting in the car, and I wanted to take at least a brief walk and to smoke a cigarette in the open air. In all the cars everybody was asleep, and no one but myself came out of the entire long train. Presently the bell rang and I suddenly noticed that, owing to my usual absentmindedness, I had forgotten the number of my car, the door of which, when I was leaving it, I myself shut. Perhaps only a few seconds were left; I was about to go to the conductor who stood at the other end of the train when, suddenly, I heard someone signalling: "Pst! Pst!"—"This must be my car!" I said to myself. In point of fact, Germans sitting in the cars in their small compartments which accommodate a maximum number of eight persons, are watchfully observing each other during the journey. When the train stops at a big station, where dinner or supper is being served, a German, on leaving his car, without fail goes to the trouble of waking up his sleeping neighbor so that he won't be sorry that he slept through supper, etc. So I thought it was one of my awakened companions in my car who called to me, noticing that I had lost my seat. I came up, and an anxious German face looked out.

"Was suchen Sie?" ("What are you looking for?")

"My car. Am I sitting with you? Is this my car?"

"No, this isn't your car, and your seat is not here. But where is your car?"

"That's the point: I've lost track of it!"

"Nor do I know which is your car."

Only at the very last second the conductor, who had come to my rescue, showed me my car. The question arises: why did that German call and interrogate me? But if you should stay awhile in Germany, you would learn that every German would act in the same manner.

Some ten years ago I went to Dresden. Next day, upon leaving my hotel, I intended to go straight to the picture gallery. I did not inquire about my way to it. The Dresden picture gallery is such a remarkable institution, in the whole world, that I was sure every Dresden resident, belonging to the educated class, would show me my way. And so, having passed a certain street, I stopped a German with a very serious and educated countenance.

"Permit me to ask you—where is the picture gallery here?"

"The picture gallery?"—said the German, pondering over my question.

"Yes."

"The Royal Picture Gallery?" (He laid particular emphasis on the word: "Royal.")

"Yes."

"I don't know where that gallery is."

"But . . . is there any other gallery?"

"Oh no, there is no other gallery."

CHAPTER III

1

The Russian or the French Language

WHAT A CROWD of Russians there are at all these German spas—particularly at the fashionable ones, such as Ems. Generally, Russians are very fond of taking cures. Even at Wunderfrau's, the sanatorium near Munich, where, by the way, there are no mineral springs, it is said that the main contingent of patients is provided by Russia. True, this *Frau* is frequented mostly by solid persons, so to speak, of the rank of generals; they send along their bathing paraphernalia in advance, and they entreat for reservations in that institution as early as in the winter. This *Frau* is a formidable and unyielding woman.

At Ems, naturally, you recognize Russians above all by the manner in which they talk, that is, by that Russian-French dialect which is characteristic only of Russia and which is beginning to startle even foreigners. I say: "is beginning to startle," since up to the present we have only been praised for it. I know, people will argue that it is terribly out of fashion to attack Russians for their French language, and that both this theme and its moral are altogether too worn out. But, to me, the surprising fact is not that Russians should not be speaking Russian among themselves (it would be even strange if they should be speaking Russian), but that they imagine that they speak good French. Who knocked this silly prejudice into our heads? No doubt, it persists only because of our ignorance. Russians who speak French (that is, the overwhelming majority of the educated Russians) may be divided into two general categories: those whose French is undeniably bad, and those who imagine that they speak like genuine Parisians (our whole *beau monde*), whereas their French is undeniably just as bad as that of the first category. Russians of the latter class border on absurdities. For example, during a solitary evening walk on the border of the Lanne, I once met two Russians—a man and a lady, both elderly people—who conversed with a most preoccupied air about some family matter which, to them, was apparently of great import and which interested and even disturbed them both a good deal. They spoke in an agitated tone, but in French, expressing themselves very poorly, bookishly, in dead, clumsy phrases at times, experiencing great difficulty in formulating a thought, or a nuance of a thought, so that impatiently they prompted one another. This they did, yet they were utterly unable to grasp the fact that they should start conversing in Russian. On the contrary, they preferred to express themselves poorly, even at the risk of being misunderstood so long as they spoke French. Suddenly I was startled with this, and it appeared to me as incredible nonsense, even though I had observed these things a hundred times in my life. Most important is the fact that in cases such as this there is no preference—even though I have just said "they preferred to express themselves"—or any choice of the language: simply they speak bad French by habit, as a matter of custom, even without raising the question in which language it is easier to converse. In this inept, dead speech the coarse, inept and dead pronunciation is disgusting.

The Russian-French dialect of the second category, that is, of the beau monde, is also characterized above all by the pronunciation. In fact, seemingly, a fellow speaks like a Parisian, whereas this is not at all so: deceit betrays itself from the very first sound —and in the first place precisely by that strained handling of the pronunciation, by the coarseness of the counterfeit, by the exaggerated rolling of "r's"—the *grasseyment*—by the indecent pronunciation of the letter "r," and, finally, by the moral aspect: that insolent self-conceit with which they pronounce those trilling letters; that childish vanity, not even concealed from each other, with which they flaunt one before the other the imitation of the language of the *garçon* in a Petersburg hairdresser's shop. Here the self-conceit with all this servility is repulsive.

Say what you will, but even though all this is obsolete, it continues to be surprising precisely because living people, in the bloom of health and vigor, venture to use an emaciated, withered, sickly language. Of course, they themselves do not realize the pitifulness and misery of that language (*i.e.*, not the French, but the one they speak), and, owing to lack of mental development, the abortiveness and scantiness of their thoughts, temporarily, they are awfully pleased with the material which they choose for the expression of their petty thoughts. They are unable to comprehend that, once they were born and grew up in Russia, it was forever impossible for them fully to degenerate into Frenchmen, despite the fact that, aping their nurses, they did lisp their very first words in French, and at a later age they practiced it when being taught by their tutors and in society; and that, for this reason, this dialect of theirs must always be a dead, and not a live, one—an unnatural, fantastic, insane language, precisely because it is taken for a genuine one; briefly—not at all the French language, since Russians, just like any other foreigners, are impotent to adopt all the principal generic elements of the living French language, since they were not born French; and since they are merely adopting an alien jargon and, at most, a hairdresser's insolence of phrase, and after that —perhaps insolence of thought. This is, as it were, a stolen language, and, for this reason, not one of the Russian Parisians is able to beget in his whole life a single expression of his own, a single original word which might be caught and start circulating in the street—a thing, however, which any hairdresser's *garçon* is fully capable of achieving.

Turgenev, in one of his novels, tells an anecdote about one such Russian who, in Paris, entering the Café de Paris, shouted: *"Garçon, beftek aux pommes de terre!,"* while another Russian who had already managed to ape the novel manner in which beefsteak is being ordered, came in and shouted: *"Garçon, beftek-pommes!"* The Russian who gave the order in the old-fashioned manner: *"aux pommes de terre,"* was in despair because he didn't know and had missed the new expression: *"beftek-pommes,"* and because he feared that now, perhaps, the *garçons* might look at him with contempt.

Apparently this story is an account of a true event. Slavishly crawling before the forms of the language and the opinion of the *garçons,* Russian Parisians, naturally, are also slaves to French thought. Thereby they doom their poor heads to the sad lot of never in their lives having a single thought of their own.

Yes, the discussion of the harm in adopting, since early childhood, an alien language instead of one's own, is unquestionably a ludicrous and old-fashioned theme—naïve to the point of inde- cency—yet it does seem to me that this topic is not worn out to the extent that one should not be attemping to say a few words concerning it. Besides, there is no such old theme about which something new could not be said. I do not pretend at anything *new* (how could I?), but I shall risk it—just for the sake of clearing my conscience: even so, I will say it. I am very eager to set forth my arguments in a most popular style in the hope that some dear mama of the beau monde may read them.

2

What Language Should a Future Pillar of His Motherland Speak?

I would ask dear mama the following question: does she know what a language is, and how does she understand the purpose for which the word was created? Undeniably, the language is the form, the flesh, the membrane of the thought (I am not explaining what thought is), so to speak, the last and concluding word of organic evolution. Hence, it is clear that the wealthier the material—the forms provided for the thought which I adopt for its expression— the happier I shall be in life, the more distinct and intelligible I shall be to myself and to others, the more sovereign and victorious; the quicker I shall say to myself that which I wish to say, the deeper I shall express it and the deeper I myself shall comprehend that which I sought to express, the firmer and the calmer will my spirit be, and—it stands to reason—the wiser I shall be.

And, again, does mama dear know that, even though man is capable of thinking with the velocity of electricity, in fact he does not think so quickly, but in an infinitely slower tempo, though infinitely more quickly than, for example, he speaks. Why is this so?—Because nevertheless, of necessity, he thinks in some language. Verily, we may not be conscious of the fact that we are thinking in some particular language, yet this is so; and if we are not think- ing in terms of words, that is, by uttering words, be it only mentally —nevertheless we think, so to speak, by "the elemental underlying power of that language" in which we choose to reason, if it be permitted to express it this way. Of course, the more flexibly, the more wealthily, the more multilaterally we master that language in which we choose to think, the more easily, the more multilaterally we shall express our thought in it. Essentially, why do we learn Euro- pean languages—French, for instance? First, simply to be able to read French and, secondly, to be able to converse with the French when we happen to come in contact with them—yet, under no circum- stance, to converse with Russians and with one's self. For a loftier life, for depth of thought, a foreign language is insufficient precisely because it always will remain alien to us; for this purpose one's native tongue is required, with which—so to speak—one is born. But right here we stumble over a difficulty: Russians—at least those belonging to the upper classes—have long ceased to be born with a live language; only subsequently do they acquire some kind of an artificial language, while they get to learn Russian virtually in school, by the grammar. Why, certainly, with eager desire and much diligence, one may, in the long run, re-educate oneself and, to a certain extent, learn the live Russian tongue, having been born with a dead one. I used to know a certain Russian writer who won a name for himself. He had learned not only the Russian language but even the Russian peasant and, in later days, he wrote novels dealing with peasant life. This comical case is not uncommon among us. At times, it assumed formidable proportions: the great Pushkin, according to his own admission, had been compelled to re-educate himself, and he learned the popular language and the people's spirit, *inter alia,* from his nurse Arina Rodionovna. The expression *"to learn the language"* is particularly fitted to us, Russians, because we, the upper class, are sufficiently detached from the people, that is, from the living language ("language" and "people," in our tongue, are synonymous, and what a wealthy, profound thought this is!).

However, it may be said: if we have to "learn" a live language, it makes no difference whether we learn Russian or French. But therein is the point: to a Russian, the Russian tongue is nevertheless easier, despite the governesses and the mise-en-scène; and, by all means, one has to take advantage of this ease, while there is time. In order to master the Russian tongue in a more natural way, without special strain, and not merely scientifically (of course, by science I mean not only the school grammar), it is necessary, following the example of Arina Rodionovna, to borrow it from early childhood from Russian nurses without fearing that these might impart to the child various prejudices—for instance, about the three whales (Good Lord! what of it if these whales should remain during one's whole life!). In addition, it is necessary not to fear the common people, even servants, against whom parents are warned by some of our performers. After that, while in school, one must by all means memorize specimens of the Russian tongue beginning with the most ancient epochs—from annals, legends, even from the Church-Slavic language—precisely to learn these by heart notwithstanding the backwardness of the method of memorizing. Having thus mastered our native tongue—*i.e.*, the one in which we think—to the best of one's ability, at least to the extent that it resembles something living, and having necessarily accustomed ourselves to think in it, we shall thereby derive a benefit from our peculiar Russian ability to learn European languages, from our polyglottism.

Indeed, only after having mastered with the utmost perfection the prime material—*i.e.*, one's native tongue—is one in a position to master, also with the utmost perfection, a foreign language, but not prior to that. We shall then imperceptibly appropriate from a foreign language several forms, alien to our tongue, and, also imperceptibly and involuntarily, we shall bring them in accord with the modalities of our thought, and we shall thereby broaden it.

There is a significant fact: in our unorganized and youthful language we are able to translate the most profound manifestations of the spirit and thought of the European languages: all European poets and thinkers are translatable and expressible in Russian, and some of them have already been most perfectly translated. At the same time, a great many specimens of the Russian popular tongue and of our belletristic works have, thus far, remained untranslatable and inexpressible in European languages—particularly, in French.

I cannot recall without laughing a translation into French (now a bibliographical rarity) from Gogol, which was made in the middle of the Forties by Mr. Viardot, the husband of the famous singer, in collaboration with a certain Russian, now a deservedly famous author—then, merely a beginner. Instead of Gogol some galimatias was produced. Much of Pushkin is also untranslatable. I believe that were one to attempt to translate such a thing as *The Narration* by archpriest Avvakum, the result again would be nonsensical—or, more correctly, nothing would come of it. Why is this so?—It is dreadful to say that, perhaps, the European spirit is not as multifaceted and is more peculiarly secluded than ours, notwithstanding the fact that it is undeniably more structuralized and that it has been revealed more graphically than ours. But if this is a dreadful statement, at least one cannot help but admit with hope and gladness that the spirit of our language is unquestionably multifaceted, wealthy, universal and all-embracing, since even within its unorganized forms it has proved able to express the gems and treasures of European thought, and we feel these have been expressed correctly and with precision. And it is of such "material" that we ourselves are depriving our children. What for?—Unquestionably, to make them unhappy. We despise this material, we consider it a coarse, "under-hoof" language in which it is unbecoming to express the beau-monde feeling or the beau-monde thought.

By the way: exactly five years ago we inaugurated the so-called classical reform of education. Mathematics and the two ancient languages—Latin and Greek—were recognized as the most effective means of mental, and even spiritual, development. It was not we who recognized and invented this: this is a fact, an undeniable fact, empirically ascertained by the whole of Europe in the course of centuries. We merely adopted it. But here is the point: along with the most intense teaching of these two great ancient languages and mathematics, the teaching of Russian had been virtually suppressed. The question arises: if the Russian language is in neglect, how, by what means, through the medium of what material are our children going to master the forms of those two ancient tongues? Is it possible that the mere mechanics of the instruction (and this—by Czech teachers) of these two languages constitute their developmental force? Besides, even the mechanics cannot be mastered without a parallel most intense and profound instruction in the *living* language. The whole morally developmental effect of these two ancient languages, these two most perfectly structuralized forms of human thought—which, in the course of centuries, have lifted the barbarian West to the highest level of civilization—this whole effect will, naturally, be missed by the new school precisely because of the decline in it of the Russian tongue. Or did our reformers imagine that we do not have to study Russian, except as to where one should be employing the letter *"yat,"* because we are born with it? But therein is the whole point: in the upper classes we are ceasing to be born with the living Russian language —and this has existed for a long time. But the living Russian tongue will come into being not prior to the time when we completely merge with the people. But I got excited: I began to talk to mother dear, and I shifted to the classical reform and to the merger with the people.

Of course, mother dear is weary of listening to all this: indignantly she waves her pretty little hand, and scoffingly she turns away. To mama it makes not a particle of difference in which language her sonny is going to think, and if it is going to be in the Parisian dialect—why, all the better: "It is more elegant, more clever, there is more taste!" But she even fails to understand that for this one has to be fully reborn into a Frenchman, whereas with the help of governesses and tutors this happiness cannot be attained, and that one may possibly reach only the first station—*i.e.*, to cease to be a Russian. Oh, dear mama does not know what poison she is injecting into her child beginning at the age of two by engaging a governess for him. Every mother and every father is aware, for instance, of a certain dreadful childish physical habit which is acquired by some unhappy children as early as at the age of ten, and which, if neglected, may sometimes convert them into idiots, into flabby, decrepit old men while they are still in their youth. I venture to state directly that a governess—*i.e.*, the French language from early childhood, from the very first lisping of the babe—is equivalent, in a moral sense, to the physical effect of this dreadful habit. All right if he is by nature stupid or dreadfully dull: if so, he will even live his whole life with his French, jestingly, with short little ideas, with a hairdresser's mentality, and he will die without ever noticing that all his life he was a fool. But what if he be an able man, with thoughts in his head and with magnanimous impulses in his heart? Can he be happy?—Without possessing the material for the structuralization within him of the whole depth of his thought and his spiritual quests; all his life possessing a dead, sickly, stolen language, with timid, mechanically learned, coarse forms which will not expand before him—he will eternally agonize as a result of an unceasing effort and strain, both mental and moral, in the endeavor to express himself and his soul. (Good heavens, is it so difficult to comprehend that this is a dead and unnatural language!) Painfully, he himself will notice that his thought is abortive—lightweight and cynical—precisely cynical because of its abortiveness, by reason of the insignificance and triviality of the forms in which it has been expressed all his life. Finally, he will observe that his heart, too, is corrupt. Debauch will come as a result of anguish. Oh, of course, his career will not suffer: all of these, born with governesses, are unfailingly designated by their mamas for the role of future pillars of their motherland, and they entertain the pretension that they are indispensable. He will glitter, issue orders and "prompt"; he will introduce new rules and he will know how to manage things. Briefly, very often he will even be very much pleased with himself, especially when he will be delivering long addresses replete with other people's ideas and alien phrases in which there will be *plus de noblesse que de sincérité*. And yet, if he be only slightly human, on the whole he will be unhappy. He will continually agonize as a result, as it were, of some kind of impotence, precisely like those youthful old men who suffer from premature exhaustion of virility caused by that bad habit.

But—alas—mama dear will not believe me that all these misfortunes may be caused by the French language and the governesses! I have the presentiment that it is not only mama who will tell me that I am exaggerating, and yet, strictly speaking, I have told the truth without exaggeration. It may be argued that, on the contrary, it is even better that one lives with an alien language; that one is apt to live with it in an easier, more lightweight and agreeable manner; that precisely these questions and quests of life should be avoided, and that it is precisely the French language that furthers all this—not the French language, as such, but as an alien tongue adopted instead of one's own. "What do you mean? This brilliant young man, this *charmeur* of the salons, this coiner of bons mots, will be unhappy? He is so elegantly dressed, his hair is so smartly combed, his face is of such an aristocratic color; he wears such a lovely rose in his buttonhole!" Mama dear is contemptuously smiling.

Even so, even without it—I mean, without French education—educated Russians, the overwhelming majority of them, are still nothing but intellectual proletarians, creatures without solid ground under their feet, with neither soil nor principle, international mental "neither-here-nor-there" men driven by any stray European wind. But this one who has gone through the experience of governesses and tutors, even at his best—even if he happens to think about something or to feel something—is, nevertheless, essentially hardly anything more than a gorgeously-gloved young man who, maybe, has swallowed a few fashionable *"ouvrages,"* but whose mind is continually groping in obscurity, while the heart is craving for

nothing but *"argent."* Of course, he is going to become a pillar of
his motherland, if he should rise to the proper rank.

Well, to mama dear, it's enough for the time being; but only
to mama. . . .

CHAPTER IV

1

Which Gives Relief at Spas: Mineral Water or Bon Ton?

I SHALL NOT describe Ems; besides, there are most detailed
descriptions of Ems in Russian—for instance, Dr. Hirschhorn's
booklet *Ems and Her Mineral Springs,* published in Petersburg.
From this booklet everything may be learned, beginning with
medicinal data concerning the springs, and including the minutest
details about hotel life, hygiene, walks, sites, and even about the
public. As for myself, I am not skilled in descriptions, and were
I—now that I have returned home—compelled to describe Ems, I
should in the first place recall the bright sun, the truly scenic gorge
of Taunus, in which Ems is situated, the huge elegant cosmopolitan
crowd, and my profound, most profound solitude amidst that crowd.
Nevertheless, despite the solitude I even like such crowds—of course,
in a peculiar way. In the Ems crowd I found a Russian acquaintance
of mine, that very *paradoxicalist* who, in days past, long ago, when
arguing with me, defended war—perceiving in it every kind of
virtue and truth which cannot be found in present-day society
(see the April issue of the *Diary*). It is well known that we, Russians—more correctly, Petersburg residents—have so arranged our
lives that we see strangers and, at times, mingle with God only knows
whom, whereas—even though not forgetting our friends—can a
Petersburg denizen forget anything or anybody?—We simply do
not see them, sometimes year after year. At Ems my friend also
drank some kind of water. He is about forty-five, maybe younger.

"You are right"—he said to me.—"One somehow likes this
local crowd, even without knowing why. True, one likes a crowd
everywhere—of course, a fashionable crowd, the cream. One may
not be trafficking with anyone among this society, but as yet there
has been nothing better in the world."

"Go on! . . ."

"I am not arguing with you. I am not arguing"—he hastened
to agree with me. "When a better society comes into being on
earth, and man makes up his mind to live, so to speak, more

rationally, we shall not deign to look at, or give a thought to, this present-day society, mentioning perhaps merely two words about it in a world history. But, today, what better society can you produce in its stead?"

"Is it true that even nowadays it is impossible to conceive of anything better than this idle crowd of well-to-do people—people who, were they not jostling at spas, as now, would not know what to undertake or how best to waste their days? Isolated persons are good; this is so; they may also be found in this crowd, but, on the whole—not only does it not deserve special commendation but even not special attention! . . ."

"You speak like a profound misanthrope, or simply in accordance with the prevailing vogue. You say: 'They wouldn't know how best to waste their days!' Believe me, each one of them has his own occupation, and even one on which he has wasted his whole life, and not merely a day. Certainly you cannot blame each one of them for the fact that he was unable to carve a paradise out of his life, and that, in consequence, he is suffering. Well, it pleases me to look at these sufferers here, and to watch them laughing."

"Don't they laugh out of mere politeness?"

"They laugh by force of habit which breaks them all and compels them to play their part in the 'game of paradise,' if you wish to call it so. They do not believe in paradise, and they are playing this game reluctantly, but still they are playing it, and this amuses them. The habit is too deeply rooted. Here you will find some people who are taking it seriously—and, of course, this is all the better for them: they feel as if they were in a real paradise. If you love them all (and you must love them), you must rejoice over the fact that they are given a chance to rest and forget themselves, even though in a mirage."

"Why, you are laughing! And why should I be loving them?"

"But this is mankind; there can be no other mankind, and how can one fail to love humanity?—Here there is a Russian lady who is very fond of mankind. Nor am I laughing at all. And so as not to persist on this topic, I shall directly tell you in conclusion that every bon-ton society—this fashionable crowd, for instance— possesses some positive merits. For example, every fashionable society is good by the very fact that, although it is caricatural, nevertheless it comes in closer contact with nature than any other social group—let us say, even the agricultural one which, in its majority, is still living quite unnaturally. I don't mention factories, troops, schools, universities: all these represent the climax of unnaturalness. But these people here are freer than the rest because they are

wealthier and, at least, they can live as they please. Of course,
they come in contact with nature only as far as politeness and
bon ton will permit. To expand, to become dissolved in, or to
open themselves fully to, nature—to that golden ray of sun over
there, which shines on us sinners, without discrimination, from
the blue sky—whether or not we are worthy of it—this, no doubt,
would be unbecoming, at least in the measure you and I, or some
poet, would like it at this moment. A small steel lock of bon ton,
as heretofore, hangs over each heart and each mind. Even so, one
has to admit that bon ton has taken a little step along the road
of touching nature, not only in the course of this century but
even in our generation. I draw a direct conclusion from my personal
observations: in our age people are more and more awake to the
fact that contact with nature is the last word of all progress—
of science, common sense, taste and perfect manners. Go and sink
your thought into that: you will see joy and cheerfulness on their
faces. They all speak with one another kindly, that is, very politely;
everybody is benign and cheerful. One may think that the whole
happiness of that young man with a rose in his buttonhole is to
cheer that fat, fifty-year-old lady. In fact, what makes him try
so hard to please her? Is it possible that he really wishes her happiness and cheerfulness?—Of course not: unquestionably there are
some special and purely personal reasons—they do not concern us
—which make him try so hard. But the most important point is
that, perhaps, nothing but bon ton compels him to act this way—
without any particular and personal reasons—and this in itself is
an important fact: it shows to what an extent in our age bon ton
can tame even the unruly nature of some lad. Poetry produces the
Byrons, and they produce the Corsairs, the Harolds, the Laras.
But look: how little time has elapsed since their appearance, and
yet all these personages have already been discarded by bon ton
and declared to be a most disreputable company. This is all the
more true of our Pechorin and the Caucasian Captive: these turned
out to be altogether—*mauvais ton;* they proved only to be Petersburg bureaucrats who for a brief moment have been in vogue.

"Why were these discarded?—Because these personages are
indeed wicked, impatient and are candidly looking exclusively to
their own interests; they disturb the harmony of bon ton which
by all means has got to pretend that each one lives for all, and
all live for each one. Look, flowers are being brought: these are
bouquets for the ladies, and those single roses—are for the gentlemen's buttonholes. Look: how cultivated, how neatly selected the
roses are, how they are sprayed with water! Never will a maiden
of the fields and meadows select or cut anything so elegant for

her peasant lad sweetheart. And yet these roses are brought for sale at five and ten German groschen, and the maiden of the fields has never even touched them.

"The golden age is a matter of the future, while this is an age of industry. But what is your concern? And does it make any difference to you whether it is 'Paradise' or 'like Paradise'? And yet, think: how much taste! What a sound idea! What is more appropriate to the drinking of mineral water—*i.e.*, to the hope of a cure, to health—than these flowers? Flowers are hopes. How much taste in this idea! Please recall the words: 'And why take ye thought for raiment? Consider the lilies of the field, how they grow . . . even Solomon in all his glory was not arrayed like one of these. Wherefore . . . shall God not much more clothe you? . . .' I do not recall the exact text, but what beautiful words! In them is the whole poesy of life, the whole truth of nature. However, while we have to wait for the time when the truth of nature shall reign and men, in the simplicity and gladness of their hearts, shall crown each other with flowers of sincere human love—all this may be bought and sold for five groschen without love. Again, I ask you, what difference does it make to you?—To my way of thinking, this way it is handier, because, in truth, from some love one is apt to scamper away because it demands too much gratitude, while here you take out a penny—and we are square. And yet in reality we get a semblance of the golden age; and if you are a man with imagination, you are satisfied.

"Yes, present-day wealth should be encouraged even though at other people's expense: it brings luxury and bon ton—things the remaining mass of mankind can never give. Here I have with me a beautiful painting which gladdens me, and one must always pay for diversion. Gladness and joy were always the most expensive things, whereas I, a poor man, without paying anything, am able to take part in general rejoicing at least, by cracking with my tongue. Listen: music is beginning to sound; people are laughing; the ladies are elegantly dressed, of course, like no one in the days of Solomon. And even if all this is but a mirage, still you and I are rejoicing. And, after all—speaking honestly—am I a decent man? (I am speaking only of myself.)—Owing to mineral water, I am in company with, so to speak, the cream of the cream of humanity. And with what appetite you will now go to drink your abominable German coffee! This is what I call the positive aspect of good society.

"Well, you are laughing! Besides, this is not new at all!"

"I am laughing. But tell me, has your appetite improved since you came here to drink the water?"

"Oh, very much so."

"Thus, the positive aspect of bon ton is so strong that it even affects your stomach?"

"What do you mean?—This is the effect of the mineral waters, and not of bon ton!"

"Unquestionably, the effect of bon ton, too. So that it is not certain which helps more at spas—mineral water or bon ton. Even the local physicians are in doubt as to which of the two deserves more credit. And, generally, it is difficult to express what an enormous, progressive stride medicine has made in our age: at present it is even begetting ideas, whereas in days past it used to have nothing but medicaments."

2

ONE OF THOSE BENEFITED BY MODERN WOMAN

Of course, I am not going to record all my conversations with this old-fashioned man. I knew, however, that to him the most ticklish theme was—women. And so, on one occasion we started a discussion about women. He remarked to me that I was staring attentively at something.

"I am staring at the Englishwomen; and I am doing so with a special object. I took with me for the journey to Ems two pamphlets by Granovsky—one on the Eastern question—and the other, on women. In the latter pamphlet there are several excellent and most mature thoughts. But can you imagine, one sentence perplexed me. The author writes: 'And yet, it is known to the world at large what an Englishwoman is: she represents a lofty type of feminine beauty and feminine spiritual qualities, and our Russian women cannot compete with this type.' Why, I cannot agree with this. Is it really possible that Englishwomen represent so high a type compared with our Russian women? I profoundly disagree with this."

"Who is the author of the pamphlet?"

"Since I have not commended the things which deserve praise in the pamphlet, and because I extracted from it only one sentence with which I disagree, I shall not reveal the name of the author."

"Probably the author is a bachelor, and he did not have the opportunity of finding out all the qualities of the Russian woman."

"Although you said this from a desire to be sarcastic, nevertheless you spoke the truth about the 'qualities' of the Russian woman. Indeed, it is not for a Russian man to renounce his women. In what sense is our woman inferior to any other?—I shall not

point to the crystallized ideals of our poets, beginning with Tatiana
—to Turgenev's and Tolstoy's women, even though this, in itself,
is strong evidence: if ideals of such beauty were incarnated in art,
they must have come from somewhere; they were not created out
of nothing. Therefore, such women exist in reality. Nor shall I
speak of the wives of our Decembrists, of thousands of other
generally known examples. And how can we, who are familiar with
Russian reality, fail to know about thousands of women, about
thousands of their unheralded exploits—seen by no one—and, at
times, amidst such a shocking setting, in such dark, dreadful
corners and dens, amidst such vices and horrors! Briefly, I shall
not defend the rights of the Russian woman to a high place among
the women of all Europe, but I shall merely say this: isn't it true
that there seems to exist a natural law among peoples and nations
by virtue of which every man must pre-eminently look for and love
the women of his people and nationality? If a man begins to place
women of other nations above his own and be pre-eminently fascinated by them, there must ensue an era of vacillation and decomposition of that nationality. God knows, here in Russia, during the
last hundred years something of the kind has begun to develop,
precisely in proportion to our severance from the people. We used
to be fascinated by Polish, French and even German women. Nowadays there are people eager to place Englishwomen above our
own. In my judgment, there is nothing comforting in this symptom.
Here there are two possibilities: either spiritual detachment from
one's nationality or else—simply a harem taste. It is necessary to
return to our woman, to learn our woman if we have unlearned to
understand her. . . ."

"I am readily willing to agree with you in everything, although I don't know if there is such a law of nature or nationality.
But let me ask you: why did you think that I sarcastically remarked that the author, being a bachelor, probably had no opportunity to learn all the highest qualities of the Russian woman?—
On this point there can be not even the slightest sarcasm on my
part because of the one fact that I myself was, as it were, benefited
by a Russian woman. Well, whoever I be, whatever I may seem to
you, during a certain period of my life I was the fiancé of a Russian
woman. This girl was, so to speak, socially more prominent than
I; she was surrounded by suitors; she was in a position to select,
and she . . ."

"Chose you? Excuse me, I didn't know . . ."

"No, she did not choose me, but precisely she discarded me,
but therein is the whole point. I will be frank with you: so long
as I was not yet her fiancé, everything was all right, and I was

happy in the mere fact that I was able to see the girl almost daily. I will even venture to remark—though quite in passing—that I did not produce an altogether unfavorable impression. I will add that the girl was given much freedom in her home. And one day, at a strange moment—which, I daresay, was unlike anything I have known—she suddenly promised to marry me. You wouldn't believe what I felt then. Of course, all this was kept secret by us, but when on that day, in a state of amazement, I returned to my apartment, the thought that I should be the possessor and the other half of so glamorous a creature crushed me like a weight. My glance skimmed over my furniture, over all those shabby belongings of a bachelor and little things of mine—which, however, were indispensable to me—and I felt so ashamed of myself, of my position in society, of my figure, my hair, and of these trifling possessions of mine, of the narrowness of my mind and heart, that I was even ready to curse my lot a thousand times at the thought that I, the most insignificant of all men, should possess treasures which suited me so little. I am telling you all this in order to note a rather unknown aspect of marital truth—or, more correctly, a feeling which, unfortunately, is all too rarely conceived by fiancés—*i.e.*, that in order to marry one must have in store a great deal of the silliest haughtiness, a great deal, you know, of some most stupid and trivial pride—and all this, coupled with a most ridiculous tone to which a delicate man can never get used. How can one, even for a moment, compare oneself with such a creature—a socially prominent girl, with such refined perfection, beginning with her upbringing, her curls, her tulle gowns, her dancing, her innocence, with that naïve, but at the same time socialite, charm in her judgments and feelings? And only to imagine that all this will enter my apartment, and I shall be in my morning gown—you are laughing? And yet, this is a dreadful thought! And then there is also this problem—one may be told: 'If you are afraid of such perfection, and if you consider yourself not suited for her—choose an outcast (*i.e.*, in no event a moral outcast).' Oh, but this, one refuses to do —even with indignation; one is not prepared to lower his bid.

"Well, I am not going to describe the details—they are all alike. For instance, when I lay down on my couch (I must say— the worst couch in the whole world, bought at a rag-fair, with broken springs) the following insignificant little thought occurred to me: 'Now, I am going to marry and, at least, there will always be around tiny pieces of cloth, say from patterns—to wipe pens.' Now, what is there, it would seem, more ordinary than this thought, and what is there dreadful in it? No doubt, it flitted through my mind unexpectedly, in passing—this you will understand yourself;

since God only knows what thoughts, at times, may flash through one's soul, and even at a moment when that soul is being dragged to a guillotine. This thought occurred to me probably in consequence of the fact that I hate, to the point of a nervous fit, to leave the steel pens unwiped—a thing which, however, is indulged in by everybody in the world. And would you believe, I bitterly reproached myself for this thought that same minute: in anticipation of an event of so great a magnitude, to be dreaming about rags for wiping pens, to be giving thought to such a trivial commonplace idea—'after that, what are you worth?'—Briefly, I perceived that my whole life would be now spent in self-reproach for every thought, for my every action.

"And then, a few days later, when suddenly she declared to me, with a smile on her face, that she had jested and that, on the contrary, she was going to marry a certain man of high rank, I—I . . . Why, at this juncture, instead of joy, I got so frightened, I felt such a degradation, that she herself got scared and ran for a glass of water. I recovered but my fright served me to good purpose: she understood how I loved her . . . and how highly—yes, how highly—I valued her. . . . 'And I thought'—she said to me later, after she got married—'that you were so proud, so learned, and that you would be despising me.' Ever since, I have had a friend in her, and, I repeat, if there was anyone who has ever been benefited by a woman—rather, by a Russian woman—this is certainly I, and this I shall never forget."

"So you became a friend of that person?"

"In the highest degree, but we see each other seldom—once a year, and even less frequently. Russian friends usually see each other once every five years, and many of them would not be able to stand more frequent meetings. At first, I did not call on them because her husband's standing in society was higher than mine; at present, however . . . at present, she is so unhappy that I find it difficult to look at her. To begin with, her husband is an old man of sixty-two and, a year after their wedding, a criminal charge was brought against him. In order to make up a deficency in government funds, he was compelled to surrender virtually his entire fortune. While his case was being tried, his feet failed him and now he is being wheeled around in Kreuznach, where I saw them both some ten days ago. While he is being pushed in a wheel chair, she always walks beside him at his right side, thereby complying with the lofty duty of a contemporary woman. And note, all the time and incessantly she has to listen to his malignant reproaches. I found it so painful to look at her—more correctly, at both of them— since even up to this day I don't know which one I should be pitying the more—that promptly then and there I left them and came here. I am very glad that I did not mention her name to you. Besides, even during that brief interview I had the misfortune to make her angry—and, perhaps, forever—by candidly stating to her my view on the happiness and duty of the Russian woman."

"Of course, you could not have found a more opportune occasion."

"You criticize me? But who would have told her this? On the contrary, it always seemed to me that, at least, to know why one is unhappy is the greatest happiness. And permit me—as long as this came up in our conversation—to state also to you my opinion on the happiness and duty of the Russian woman. At Kreuznach I did not complete my statement."

3

CHILDREN'S SECRETS

But, for the time being, I shall stop here. I merely meant to characterize the man and to introduce him to the reader in a preliminary way. Besides, it was my intention to characterize him only as a narrator, as I am in no way in accord with his views. I have already explained that he is a "paradoxicalist." And his view on "the happiness and duty of the Russian woman" even glitters with originality, despite the fact that he outlines it almost with anger. One is inclined to think that this is his sorest spot. Simply—according to his understanding—a woman, in order to be happy and to fulfill her duty, must by all means marry and, while she is married, she must bear as many children as possible, "not two, not three, but six, ten children, to the point of exhaustion, to the point of impotence. . . . Only then will she come in contact with real life and will come to know it in all its diverse manifestations."

"For goodness sake—without leaving her bedroom!"

"On the contrary! On the contrary! I foresee and know in advance all objections. I have weighed everything: 'universities, higher education, etc., etc.' But even leaving aside the fact that among men only one out of ten thousand becomes a scientist, I will ask you seriously: in what way can the university obstruct marriage and child-bearing? On the contrary, all women should be attending universities—both future scientists and simply educated people, but after the university—'marriage, and bear children.' As yet, there has been invented nothing cleverer in the whole world than bearing children. For this reason the more learning one accumulates for this purpose, the better things will turn out. Indeed, was it not Tchatzky who proclaimed that

> . . . to bear children,
> Whose mind has ever proved unequal?

"And he did so proclaim because he himself was a highly uneducated Moscow denizen, vociferating all his life—as an echo of someone else's voice—about European education, so that, as it turned out later, he did not even know how to write a will, leaving his estate to an unknown person—'to my friend, Sónechka.' This witticism about 'whose mind has ever proved unequal?' persisted over a period of fifty years because throughout these fifty years we had no educated people. At present, thank God, educated people are beginning to appear also in Russia. And, believe me, before anything else, they will grasp the fact that to bear and have children —is the principal, the most serious, thing in the world; it always has been and never ceased to be. 'Whose mind has ever proved unequal!' Can you imagine?—Well, it does prove unequal: the modern woman in Europe has ceased to bear children. For the time being, I shall keep silent about our women."

"What do you mean by 'ceased to bear children'?"

At this point I will remark in passing that in this man there is one unexpectedly strange trait: he is fond of children, he is a connoisseur of children, precisely of those babies who still retain "the angels' rank." He loves them so much that he runs after them. At Ems he has even become notorious in this respect. What he likes most is to walk in those avenues whither children are brought or taken out. He got acquainted with them, even with one-year-old ones, and succeeded in having many of them recognize him—awaiting him, smiling at him and extending to him their tiny hands. He always finds out from the German nurse the age —in years or months—of the child, he praises it and, indirectly, he also compliments the nurse, which flatters her. In a word, in him this is sort of a passion. He was always particularly delighted when every morning, in avenues at the springs, suddenly among the public there appeared crowds of children going to school—all dressed up, with sandwiches in their hands and with little knapsacks on their backs. One has to admit that these crowds of youngsters are truly very pleasant, especially those composed of four-, five-, and six-year-old children—that is, the youngest ones.

"*Tel que vous me voyez*, today I bought two reed pipes"— he told me one morning, with an extremely pleased air—"not for these, not for the school children, these are big ones, and only yesterday I had the pleasure of striking up an acquaintance with their schoolmaster—he is the most worthy man that could be imagined. No—for two little fatties, two brothers—one of the age of three, and the other one a two-year-old boy. They stopped before a kiosk with toys, their mouths wide open, in that state of silly and charming childish delight which is the most pleasing thing that exists. The storekeeper, a sly German woman, promptly guessed what my glance meant and, in a jiffy, she thrust a reed pipe into each one's hand. I had to pay two marks—yes, sir! The fatties' delight was beyond description: they walk and keep on piping. This was an hour ago, but just now I went there to make inquiries: they still keep on piping.

"Some time ago, when referring to the local society, I said to you that for the time being the world can produce nothing better. I told you a lie, and you believed it—don't deny it—you did believe it. On the contrary, here is what is best, here is where perfection is: the crowds of Ems children, with sandwiches in their hands and knapsacks behind their shoulders going to school. . . . Well, the sun, Taunus, children, their laughter, sandwiches and the elegant crowd of lords and marquises from all over the world—all these combined are charming. Did you notice the crowd always admires the children: this is a symptom of taste and an urge for seriousness. But Ems is stupid; Ems cannot help but be stupid; this is why she continues to bear children, whereas Paris has already suspended child-bearing."

"What do you mean—suspended?"

"There is in Paris an enormous industry known as *Articles de Paris* which, along with silk, French wines and fruits, has helped to pay the five-billion contribution. Paris greatly reveres that industry and is so busily engaged in it that she even forgets to produce children. And Paris is backed by the whole of France. Every year the Minister solemnly announces to the Chambers that '*le population reste stationnaire.*' You see, children are not being born, and if they are born, they do not last. 'As against this, however,'—adds the Minister with commendation—'our old men enjoy longevity.' But, to my way of thinking, if only they would all die, I mean the old ones . . . with whom France loads her Chambers. Much is there to rejoice over their longevity! Is so little sand strewn over there?"

"I still don't understand you. What's the point about *Articles de Paris?*"

"This is simple. However, being a novelist, you may not know one of the muddiest French writers and idealists of the old school—Alexander Dumas-fils. He has generated several, so to speak, movements. He insists that the French woman be bearing children.

Moreover, he directly announced a secret, known by everybody, that women belonging to the well-to-do bourgeoisie in France, uniformly, bear two children. Somehow they manage to arrange things with their husbands in such a way as to bear just two children—no more and no less. They bear two, and then they go on a strike. All of them—and the secret spreads with remarkable speed. Even two descendants constitute posterity, and besides two will acquire a larger estate than if it were to be divided between six. That's one thing. Well, secondly, the woman preserves herself for a longer period: beauty and health last longer; more time is left for social affairs, dresses and dancing. And, as regards parents' love—so to speak, the moral aspect of the question—one loves, they say, two children even more than six; the six might get naughty; they might become annoying; they might break something—go and busy yourself with them! Start reckoning what their shoes alone would cost —it would make you sick and tired! And so on, and so forth.

"However, the point is not that Dumas is angry; the point is that he openly ventured to declare the existence of the secret: two—no more, no less—and besides they live with their husbands *maritalement* to their heart's pleasure, in a word—everything is saved. Malthus, who was so afraid of the increase of the world's population, could not have conceived, even in his dreams, this kind of means. Well, all this is altogether too seductive. In France, as is known, there are an awful lot of property-owners—urban and rural bourgeoisie. To them this is a godsend. This is their invention. But this find will overstep the boundaries of France. Not more than a quarter of a century will elapse, and you will see that even stupid Ems will grow wiser. It is rumored that Berlin, in this respect, has already become very much wiser.

"However, even though the number of children is decreasing, nevertheless the Minister in France would have failed to notice the difference, were this confined to the bourgeoisie alone—*i.e.*, the well-to-do class—and were there not another angle to the matter. The other angle—the proletarians—eight, ten, perhaps as many as twelve million proletarians, unbaptized and unmarried people, living, instead of in wedlock, in 'rational associations'—'to avoid tyranny.' These, unhesitatingly, throw their children out into the street. Gavroches are born, they die, they do not survive; however, when they do survive, they fill the foundling institutions and the prisons for the under-aged criminals. Zola, a so-called realist, in his novel *Le Ventre de Paris*, has a very vivid depiction of the contemporary workers' marriage, *i.e.*, of marital cohabitation. And note: the Gavroches are no longer Frenchmen; but the most remarkable thing is that those, in the upper class, who are born property-owners, by twos and in secret—they, too, are not French-men. At least, I venture to assert this—so that both ends, the two opposites, meet. This is the first result: France begins to cease to be France. (Indeed, is it possible to maintain that these ten millions regard France as their fatherland!) I know there will be some who will say: 'All the better—the French will be obliterated, but human beings will remain.' But are they human beings? Let's say they are, but they are future savages who will swallow up Europe. By-and-by, but firmly and undeviatingly, out of them the insensible rabble is being hatched. That the generation is deteriorating physi-cally and growing impotent and vile, in my opinion, there can be no shadow of doubt. Well, and the physique drags morality behind it. Such are the fruits of the reign of the bourgeoisie. To my way of thinking, the whole cause is—land, *i.e.*, soil and its present-day distribution. All right, I will explain it to you."

4

The Land and the Children

"Land is everything"—my paradoxicalist continued. "I am drawing no line between the land and the children; this inference of mine comes of its own accord. However, I am not going to enlarge upon this point; you will understand it yourself if you give thought to it. The whole point is the result of an agrarian error; even all the rest—all the other human misfortunes—they all are, perhaps, derived from that agrarian error. Millions of paupers do not possess land, especially in France, where there is a scarcity of land anyhow. And so there is no place where they could be giving birth to children—they are compelled to bear them in base-ments, and not children but Gavroches, half of whom cannot name their fathers, while the other half—even their mothers. This is at one end. At the other—the upper end—I believe, is also the agrarian error, but of a different kind, an opposite one. It dates back, per-haps, to the times of Clovis, the conqueror of Gaul: there, each one has too much land; the usurpation is too great, dispropor-tionate; besides, they have too strong a hold on the land; they refuse to make any concessions, so that both here and there—there is abnormality. Something is liable to happen; something must change, because everybody must have land, while children must be born on the soil and not on the pavement. I don't know—I really don't—how this is going to be remedied; but I do know that over there there is no place where children can be begotten.

"I believe it is all right to work in a factory: the factory also is a legitimate proposition; it arises beside cultivated land—such is the law. But let every factory hand know that somewhere there, there is a garden under the golden sun and the vineyards—his own garden, or, to be more correct, a common, *i.e.*, communal, garden—and that in this garden lives his wife, a fine woman—not from the pavement—who loves him and waits for him; and with his wife are his children, who play 'little horses,' and all of whom know their father. *Que diable!* Every decent healthy urchin is born simultaneously with a 'little horse'; every decent father must know it if he wishes to be happy.

"Thus, the factory worker will bring thither the money which he earns, and he will not squander it on drinks in 'pubs' with females picked up on the pavement. And although, in the long run, that garden (in France, for example, where land is so scarce) cannot provide subsistence for himself and his family, so that the factory cannot be avoided, still let him know at least that there his children are growing up in association with the soil, the trees, the quails which are being caught; that they are attending school, and that the school stands in a field, and that he himself, after having worked all his life, will still go there to rest and, later—to die.

"And—who knows?—perhaps that garden will provide full subsistence and, besides, maybe the factory should not be feared because it will be built amidst the garden. Briefly, I have no idea how all this will shape itself, but this will come to pass; remember my word —it will come to pass even if it be a hundred years hence; and then recall the fact that I told you these things at Ems, amidst an artificial garden and amidst artificial people.

"Mankind will be regenerated in the Garden, and the Garden will restore it—such is the formula. You see how all this happened: at first, there were castles, and beside them—mud huts. The barons lived in the castles—and the vassals, in the mud huts. Thereupon the bourgeoisie began to rise behind fenced towns—slowly, on a microscopic scale. Meanwhile, the castles came to an end, and kings' capitals came into existence—big cities with kings' palaces and court hotels; this has lasted up to our century. In our century a dreadful revolution took place, and the bourgeoisie came out victorious. With the bourgeoisie there arose horrible cities which were never even dreamed of. Cities, such as sprang up in the Nineteenth Century, mankind had never seen before. These are cities with crystal palaces, with international exhibitions, banks, budgets, polluted rivers, railway platforms, with all kinds of associations—and, around them, factories and mills. At present people are awaiting the third phase: the bourgeoisie will expire and a regenerated mankind will come in its wake. It will distribute the land among communes, and will start living in the Garden. 'It will be regenerated in the Garden, and the Garden will restore it.' Thus—castles, cities and the Garden. If you wish to understand the full meaning of my idea, I will say that, in my judgment, children—I mean, real children—must be born on the soil, and not on the pavement. Later on, one may be living on the pavement, but a nation—an overwhelming portion of it—should be born and should be *sprouting* on the land, on the soil upon which corn and trees grow. But, in our day, European proletarians—all of them—are nothing but the pavement.

"In the Garden, however, little children will be springing straight from the earth, like Adam, and at the age of nine, when they are still eager to play, they will not be sent to factories; they will not be breaking their spines bending over a lathe, nor dulling their minds facing the wretched machine—which the bouregois worships—tiring and ruining their imagination in front of an endless row of gas lamps, and their morality by factory debauch which exceeds that of Sodom. And those are urchins and little ten-year-old girls! And where?—All right here—but in Russia where there is so much land; where factories are still nothing but a joke, where miserable little towns are built to accommodate just a handful—say, three—of petty government clerks!

"Even so if I perceive anywhere the kernel or the idea of the future—it is in Russia. Why so?—Because we have a principle, which still persists in the people, that land is *everything* to them; that they derive everything from, and out of, the land—and this is true of the overwhelming majority of the people. But the principal thing is that it is precisely the normal law of man. In the earth, in the soil, there is something sacramental. If you wish to regenerate mankind into something better, if you wish to make men virtually out of beasts—give them land, and you will achieve your purpose. At least in Russia, the land and the commune—I admit they are in a most miserable state—constitute the great nucleus of the future idea; and therein is the whole trick. At least, it is my opinion that in, and from, soil order is derived, and thus it is everywhere in mankind as a whole. All order in every country—political, civic, any kind of order—is always connected with the soil and with the character of its agriculture; everything else has been evolved within the frame of that character. If, in Russia, at present there prevails the greatest disorder, it is in the sphere of landownership, in the relations between the owners and the workers, and between the latter among themselves, as well as in the character of the cultivation of the soil. And so long as these are not going to be put on a right basis, don't expect solid organization in the rest. You see, I am blaming no one and nothing—it is a matter of world history, we understand. In my judgment, we have paid so small a ransom for ridding ourselves of serfdom because of the *consensus* of the country. On this 'consensus' I am staking everything; it is one of those popular principles which up to this day are being denied by our Potugins. Well, and as regards all our railroads, those new banks of ours, associations and credits—all these, to my way of thinking, are still nothing but twaddle. Among all our railroads I admit but the strategic ones. All this should have come after the settlement of the land problem; then it would have come naturally, whereas at present it is but stock-exchange speculation, the awakening of the Jew. You are laughing; you do not agree—all right. But just recently I read the memoirs of a certain Russian landowner, which he wrote in the middle of our century. As early as in the Twenties he made up his mind to liberate his peasants. In those days this was a rare and novel thing. Apropos, having visited his village, he established there a school and began to teach the peasant children choral church singing. His neighbor, also a landowner, called on him and listened to the choir. Then he said: 'You have conceived a clever idea; if you train them, you will find, without fail, a buyer who will purchase the whole choir. People love it, and you will get good money for the choir.'

"Thus, at the time when it was still possible to sell 'for export' choirs of little children, tearing them away from their fathers and mothers, setting the peasants free was still a perplexing and novel proposition in Russia. Presently, he started talking to the peasants about that novelty. They listened, began to wonder and grew frightened. Long did they discuss the matter, and they came to him. 'Well, what about the land?'—'The land is mine: you will have your huts, your farm buildings, while annually you will have to till my land on a fifty-fifty basis.' They scratched their heads: 'No, let it be as of old: we are yours, and the land is ours.' Of course, this surprised the landowner: 'Well, one might say—a savage people; in their moral degradation, they even refuse to accept liberty, liberty—that first blessing of man . . .' etc., etc. Subsequently, this saying—'We are yours, and the land is ours'—became generally known; it surprises no one, especially nowadays.

"However, the main question is: whence could this idea have come? Whence could there have arisen such an 'unnatural and unparalleled' conception of world history, if one compares it with that of Europe? And, mind you, it was just then that among our wise fellows war had been raging with particular fury on the question: 'Are there really in Russia such principles of the people as would merit the attention of our educated men?' No, sir, permit me to say: this means that the Russian, from the very beginning, could not imagine himself without land. But the most surprising thing is that even after the abolition of serfdom the overwhelming majority of the people has retained the essence of this formula and can still not imagine themselves without land. Now if they rejected freedom without land, this means that land to them is the principal thing—the basis of everything. Land is everything, and everything else emanates from it, *i.e.*, liberty and life and honor and family and children and order and church—in a word, everything that is precious. It was owing to this formula that they have retained such an institution as the commune. And yet what is the commune?—At times, it is a heavier burden than serfdom! Everybody has been discussing back and forth communal land-ownership; everybody knows how strongly it impedes, say, economic progress. At the same time, does it not contain the grain of something new, a better future ideal which awaits all men, as to which no one knows how it will come to pass, but which only we possess in embryo, and which can come to pass only in Russia, since it will come not through war and rebellion—but again, by great and universal consensus. Yes, consent—because even now great sacrifices are made for the achievement of that 'something.'

"And so little children will be born in the Garden; they will be set right, and no longer will ten-year-old girls be drinking bad liquor at inns with factory workers! Yes, sir, it is difficult, in our day, for children to be growing up! Indeed, I did disturb you! But little children—they are the future, and one loves only the future! Who bothers about the present?—Of course, not I and, certainly, not you. This is why one loves children more than anything. . . ."

5

A PECULIAR SUMMER FOR RUSSIA

Next day I said to my odd fellow: "You keep talking about children, and in the casino I just read in the Russian newspapers, around which—I may remark—all local Russians are crowding, a news item about a certain mother, a Bulgarian woman, over there in Bulgaria where people have been massacred by whole counties. She is an old woman living in a village; she lost her mind and wanders about amidst her ash-heaps. When she is being asked how all this happened, she does not answer in ordinary words, but at once presses her right hand against her cheek and begins to sing and—in a sing-song manner, in improvised verses—she tells the story about how she used to have a house, a family, a husband—about her six children and how the elder ones also had little chil-

dren, her grandsons. Then her torturers came and burned to death
her old man at the wall, slaughtered her falcon-children, assaulted
a little girl, abducted the other one—a beauty—ripped the infants'
stomachs with yataghans, and threw them all into the raging fire.
All this she had witnessed and she had heard the babies' shrieks."

"Yes, I too have also read about this"—said my queer friend.
"Remarkable, very remarkable. The principal thing—in verses. And
in Russia, our Russian critics, though at times they did laud verses,
still invariably they were inclined to believe they were created
mostly for mischief. It would be curious to trace the spontaneous
epic poetry, so to speak, in its elemental inception. This is a question of art."

"Stop pretending. However, I have observed that you are
not all too fond of speaking about the Eastern question."

"No, I also sent my contribution. If you insist, it is true
that there are certain things which do not appeal to me in the
Eastern question."

"Precisely what?"

"Why, abundance of love, for example."

"Look here, I am sure . . ."

"I know, I know: don't finish; and you are absolutely right.
Besides, I sent my contribution in the very beginning. You see,
in Russia the Eastern question is still, so to say, a question of
love, and it used to emanate from the Slavophiles. In fact, on sentimentality many a people have made good, especially last winter
with the Herzegovinians; there even ensued several sentimental
careers. Please note that I am saying nothing; besides, sentimentality, in itself, is a most excellent thing; but even a jade may be
wearied to death. This is what I have been fearing ever since spring,
and this is why I did not believe it. Later, in the summer, even
here, I was afraid that suddenly all this brotherliness might somehow be washed away from us. But at present—now I am no longer
afraid. Yes, Russian blood has been shed, and spilled blood is an
important thing—a uniting thing!"

"And is it really possible that you thought that our brotherliness might be washed off?"

"I plead guilty: I did think so. And how otherwise could
it be supposed? However, now I am no longer thinking so. You
see, even here, in Ems, some ten versts from the Rhine, news was
received, so to speak, straight from Belgrade. Tourists arrived, and
they themselves heard that in Belgrade Russia was blamed. On the
other hand, I myself have read in *Temps* and in *Débats* that after
the Turks had invaded Serbia, people in Belgrade cried: 'Down
with Cherniaiev.' However, other correspondents and eyewitnesses,

on the contrary, maintain that all this is nonsense, and that the
Serbians adore Russia and are expecting everything from Cherniaiev.
You know, I believe the news on both sides; surely, there must
have been cries of all kinds: Serbia is a young nation; she has no
soldiers; they don't know how to fight; there is a lot of magnanimity
and no business sense whatsoever. There Cherniaiev was compelled
to build an army, but I am sure they—the overwhelming majority
—fail to realize what a task it is to build an army in so short a
time and under existing circumstances. Later they will understand,
but then it is going to be world history. However, even though
far from all, nevertheless among their wisest ministerial heads there
are some to whom it does seem that Russia is treacherous; that
she is just dreaming of conquering and swallowing them. And so
I was fearing that all this might pour cold water on our brotherliness. Yet the contrary happened—so contrary that even to many
a Russian it was unexpected. Suddenly the whole of Russia arose
in commotion, and promptly she uttered her principal word. Soldier,
merchant, professor, God's little old woman—they were all unanimous. And mind, not a sound about usurpation: 'Here,' they said,
as it were, 'here's my contribution to the Orthodox cause.' And—
not only pennies for the Orthodox cause—each one is ready right
away to sacrifice his life. And, again, please note the words: 'for
the Orthodox cause'—this is a most momentous political formula
both in our day and in the future. It may even be said that it is
the formula of our future. And that there is not a sound from
anywhere about 'usurpation' is most peculiar. Europe under no
circumstance could have believed it because she herself would have
been acting not otherwise than with usurpation, so that—strictly
speaking—she cannot be blamed for her outcries against us—do you
know that?"

"In a word, this time it is the beginning of our final conflict
with Europe, and . . . could it have begun otherwise than with a
perplexity? To Europe, Russia is a perplexity, and Russia's every
act is a perplexity, and thus it shall be to the very end. Yes, it
has been long since Russia has manifested herself so consciously
and so accordantly; besides, in truth we did find our kinsmen and
brethren, and this is no longer elevated style; these we found not
merely through the Slavic Committee, but verily through our land
at large. Now, to me, this was unexpected, and this I would never
have believed. Even if anyone would have predicted it, it would
have been difficult to believe in our general and, so to speak, *sudden*
consensus. And yet what happened—did happen. You were telling
me about that ill-starred Bulgarian mother, but I know that this
summer another mother made her appearance: Mother Russia has

found her own new babies, and a great compassionate outcry has sounded. Precisely—babies, and precisely—great motherly lamentation. And, mind you, here again we have a grand political indication for the future: 'their mother, and not their mistress!' And even though it so happened that the new babies, failing to understand things—for only a brief moment, however—should start repining at her, she should not be listening or paying attention to it; she should continue to be charitable with infinite and patient motherhood as every real mother should. Do you know that this present summer will be recorded in the annals of our history? Well, it was not spent in vain! And what a number of Russian perplexities were cleared at once; to what a number of Russian questions answers will at once be received! For Russian consciousness, this summer was almost an epoch. We are prepared to exercise charity and, perhaps, even to spill our blood, and yet, do you know, we ourselves have acquired much. What do you think?"

Post-Scriptum

"At times, the Russian people conspicuously fail to be *verisimilar*."—This little phrase I have also heard this summer and, of course, again because, to the man who uttered it, much of that which happened this summer was unexpected and, perhaps, in fact, did not have the appearance of "verisimilitude." However, what was there new in what had occurred?—On the contrary, everything that was revealed, has it not been long, even always, present in the heart of the Russian people?

First of all, there arose the popular idea, and the popular sentiment was revealed: the sentiment of disinterested affection for their unfortunate and oppressed brethren, while the popular idea was the "Orthodox cause." And verily, in this alone something unexpected was revealed. Unexpected (however, by no means to all) was the fact that the people had not forgotten their great idea, their "Orthodox cause"; that they have not forgotten it in the course of their two-hundred-year slavery, dark ignorance, and in recent times—of despicable debauch, materialism, Jewry and alcohol. Secondly, unexpected was the fact that with the popular idea, the "Orthodox cause," were allied virtually all shades of opinion of the most educated strata of Russian society—those very elements which we regarded as completely detached from the people. In this connection one should note the extraordinary enthusiasm and unanimity of our press. . . . God's little old woman tends her copper coin for the Slavs, and she adds—"for the Orthodox cause." The journalist catches this word and records it in the newspaper with

genuine veneration, and one can see that with all his heart he favors
that same "Orthodox cause"; one feels it, when reading his article.
Perhaps, even our utter disbelievers have finally come to understand what, in substance, Orthodoxy and the "Orthodox cause"
mean to the Russian people. They have grasped the fact that this
is by no means mere ritual churchism and, on the other hand, by
no means *fanatisme réligieux* (as people in Europe are beginning
to call this present common Russian movement), but that it is
precisely human progress, universal humanization of man—specifically thus conceived by the Russian people, who, deriving everything from Christ and incarnating their whole future in Christ and
in His truth, are even unable to imagine themselves without Christ.
Liberals, deniers, sceptics, as well as preachers of social ideas, they
all—their majority at least—suddenly turned out to be ardent Russian patriots.

Well, this means that they were such. However, can it be asserted that we have known this all along?—On the contrary, is it
not true that until recently many bitter mutual reproaches have
been made—reproaches which, in many respects, have proved futile?
Of Russians, of real Russians, there proved to be an infinitely
greater number than had been estimated even by genuine Russians.
What is it, then, that has united these men, or—more correctly—
what is it that has showed them that in the main, in the essential,
even heretofore, they had not been disunited?

But herein is precisely the point: the Slavic idea, in its loftiest
sense, has ceased to be merely a Slavophile idea; suddenly, under
the pressure of circumstances, it has thrust itself into the very heart
of Russian society; it has graphically revealed itself in common
consciousness, while in the *live* sentiment it has coincided with the
popular movement. But what is this "Slavic idea in its loftiest
sense"? It became clear to everybody what it is: above all—*i.e.*,
prior to any historical, political, etc., interpretations—it is a sacrifice, even a longing for self-sacrifice in behalf of one's brethren,
a feeling of voluntary duty on the part of the strongest among
the Slavic tribes to intercede in defense of the weaker, in order
to make him equal in liberty and political independence to him
—the strongest—and thereby, henceforth, to establish the great all-
Slavic communion in the name of Christ's truth, *i.e.*, for the benefit,
love and service of mankind as a whole, for the defense of all
the weak and oppressed throughout the world.

This is by no means a theory: on the contrary, in the present
Russian movement—disinterested and brotherly to the point of
deliberate readiness to sacrifice its most vital interest, even including peace with Europe—this has been revealed as a fact, while, in

the future, can the all-Slavic communion come to pass for any other purpose than for the defense of the weak and for service to mankind? This must be so because the majority of the Slavic tribes have themselves been brought up and developed through nothing but suffering. Now, we wrote above that we are wondering how it is that the Russian people—who have been kept in serfdom, in ignorance and oppression—did not forget their great "Orthodox cause," their great Orthodox duty; how it is that they have not become completely bestialized; that they have not been converted into gloomy, secluded egoists looking to nothing but their personal advantage. But, probably, such is their nature as Slavs, that is, their ability to rise spiritually in suffering, to gain political strength under oppression, and—amidst slavery and humiliation—to unite in mutual affection and Christ's truth.

> Thee, my land, in days distressing,
> Christ, our Lord, in slavish dress,
> Burdened with the crucial stress,
> To and fro traverséd, blessing.

Precisely because the Russian people themselves have been oppressed and, over many centuries, have endured the crucial burden, they have not forgotten their "Orthodox cause," and their suffering brethren; this is why the people rose spiritually with perfect readiness in their hearts to help the oppressed in every way. This is what our elite intelligentsia has grasped—wholeheartedly backing the people's aspiration. And, having joined them, it suddenly and completely felt in communion with them. The movement, which seized everybody, was a magnanimous and humane one. Every sublime and cohesive idea, every sound cohesive sentiment, constitutes the greatest happiness in the life of a nation. This happiness was bestowed upon us. We could not help but clearly perceive the increased consensus, the clarification of many a former perplexity, our augmented self-consciousness. All of a sudden the political thought, clearly conceived by society and the people, was revealed. Alert Europe at once discerned this, and is now watching the Russian movement with extraordinary attention. To her, a conscious political thought in our people comes as a complete surprise. She forebodes something new which must be reckoned with; we have grown in her respect for us. The very rumors about the political and social disintegration of Russian society, as a national entity, which have been accumulating in Europe, must at present, in her opinion, unquestionably become subject to strong refutation. It developed that, when necessary, Russians know how to unite. Besides, our disintegrating forces—should she be persisting in her belief in them—must naturally assume a different orientation and face a different outcome. Indeed, as a result of this epoch, many a view will henceforth have to be modified. Briefly, this general and accordant Russian movement bears witness, in a considerable measure, to our national maturity, and cannot help but command respect for it.

Russian officers are going to Serbia, and they are sacrificing their lives there. The flow of Russian officers and veteran Russian soldiers into Cherniaiev's army has been continually growing and, progressively, continues to increase. It may be said: "Those are lost people who had nothing to do at home and who went just to go somewhere—careerists and adventurers." However (according to many accurate data), aside from the fact that these "adventurers" have received no monetary gains, and that the majority of them have barely managed to reach their destination—some of them, who were still in active service, unquestionably must have suffered a loss as a result of at least temporary retirement. But whoever they may be—what do we hear and read about them?—They are dying by the dozens on battlefields and are heroically performing their task. The young army of insurgent Slavs, built up by Cherniaiev, is already firmly relying on them. They glorify the Russian name in Europe and, with their blood, they unite us with our brethren. This blood that has been heroically shed will not be forgotten and will be placed to their credit. Nay, they are not adventurers; they are the conscious initiators of a new epoch; they are the pioneers of the Russian political thought, of the Russian aspirations, of the Russian will which they have declared before Europe.

One other Russian personage has come to light—gravely, calmly and even majestically: this is General Cherniaiev. His military operations, up to the present, have been developing with alternate success but, as yet, on the whole to his advantage. In Serbia he has built up an army; he has revealed a stern, firm, undeviating character. In addition, when proceeding to Serbia, he staked his whole military renown, which he had acquired previously in Russia, and, consequently, his future also. As it has recently become known, he agreed to assume command in Serbia merely of a separate detachment, and only lately has he been confirmed in the rank of commander in chief. The army with which he took the field consisted of the militia, of recruits who had never seen a rifle, of peaceful citizens—taken straight from the plow. The risk was very great and success was doubtful: verily, this was a sacrifice for a great cause. Having created the army, trained and organized it as well as possible, General Cherniaiev began to operate more firmly, more boldly. He succeeded in scoring a very considerable victory. Of late, he has been compelled to retreat under the pressure of an enemy three times stronger. But he carried out the retreat in time—saving the army, unbeaten and strong—and he occupied a formidable position which the "victors" did not dare to attack. Judging strictly, General Cherniaiev is only beginning his major operations. However, his army can no longer expect support from any source, whereas the enemy army can still substantially increase its strength. Besides, political considerations of the Serbian government may greatly handicap him and prevent him from completing his task.

Nevertheless, this personage has already been firmly and clearly revealed: his military talent is unquestioned, while his character and the lofty impulse of his soul, no doubt, stand on the level of Russian aspirations and aims. However, the full story about General Cherniaiev is yet to be told. It is noteworthy that after his departure to Serbia he acquired extraordinary popularity in Russia; his name became popular. And no wonder: Russia understands that he has initiated, and is pursuing, a cause coinciding with her best and most heartfelt aspirations, and that by his act he has declared her intentions to Europe. No matter what may happen later, he can already be proud of his work and Russia will not forget him, but will love him.

SEPTEMBER

CHAPTER I

1

Piccola Bestia

ABOUT SEVEN years ago I happened to be spending all summer, up to September, in Florence. In the opinion of the Italians, in summer Florence is the hottest—and in winter the coldest—city in all Italy. They consider summer far more tolerable in Naples than in Florence. And so, once, in the month of July, in the apartment which I rented from a landlord, an alarm broke out: all of a sudden two maidservants, led by the mistress, burst into my room —they had just seen a *piccola bestia* running into my room from the corridor outside; it had to be found and killed by all means. *Piccola bestia* is a tarantula.

Presently they began to search under the chairs, under the

tables, in all corners, in the furniture; thereupon they started sweeping under the cupboards and stamping their feet to frighten it and, thereby, to lure it out of its hiding place. Finally, they rushed into the bedroom, continuing their search under and in the bed, in the linen, and . . . —they did not find it. The tarantula was found only the next morning when the room was being swept and, it stands to reason, it was promptly executed. Even so, I had to spend my night in bed with the uncomfortable feeling that in my room, keeping me company, a *piccola bestia* was also spending the night.

It is said that the sting of a tarantula is rarely deadly, even though I did know, in my days at Semipalatinsk, exactly fifteen years before my sojourn at Florence, about a case when a line Cossack died of a tarantula's sting, despite medical treatment. As a rule, however, the sickness is confined to a burning fever or ordinary fever attacks, while in Italy, where there are so many physicians, it may be an even less serious matter. I don't know— I am not a doctor; even so, that night I felt "jittery." At first, I tried to banish the thought; I even laughed when I recalled and recited by heart Kuzma Prutkov's didactic fable *The Conductor and a Tarantula* (a perfect gem *sui generis*), and finally I fell asleep. But my dreams were decidedly unpleasant: about the tarantula, I did not dream at all, but I did dream about something most unpleasant, painful and nightmarish; I awoke frequently, and only in the morning, after sunrise, did I begin to sleep more quietly.

Do you know why this little anecdote came to my mind at present?—In connection with the Eastern question! . . . However, I am not wondering in the least: nowadays, what only do people not write and talk about the Eastern question!

I think this way: in connection with the Eastern question, there has run into Europe some *piccola bestia* which does not give to all good, peace-loving people a chance to calm down—people who love mankind and wish to see it flourishing, all those who are longing for that bright moment when, finally, *at least* this primitive, coarse strife of the nations will come to an end. In fact, if one gives thought to it, it does *seem* that with the final solution of the Eastern question, all other political strife in Europe will be terminated; that the formula—"the Eastern question"—comprises, perhaps unknowingly to itself, all other political questions, perplexities and prejudices of Europe. In a word, there would ensue something quite new, and, for Russia, an altogether different phase, since now it is obvious that only after the final settlement of this problem would Russia finally be in a position—for the first time in her whole history—to come to terms with Europe and to become intelligible to her. And now, precisely some *piccola bestia* stands in the way of all this happiness. It was always there but since the Eastern question arose, it keeps running into the rooms themselves. Everybody is in a state of waiting; everybody is alarmed; some kind of a nightmare hangs over everybody; everybody has bad dreams. But who or what that *piccola bestia* is, which causes such confusion, is impossible to determine because of the condition of general madness: everyone conceives it in his own way, and no one understands the other. And yet it seems that all have already been stung. The sting immediately causes most extraordinary fits: in Europe, one might think, people cease to understand each other, just as at the time of the Tower of Babylon; moreover—everyone ceases to comprehend what he himself wants. There is but one thing that everybody agrees upon: at once everybody points to Russia and everybody is sure that the pernicious vermin invariably runs out of there. And yet only in Russia is everything bright and clear, except, of course, for the great sorrow over her Eastern Slavic brethren—a sorrow which, however, illuminates the soul and lifts the heart. Every time the Eastern question is raised in Russia things shape themselves in a manner directly opposite to that of Europe: each one begins to understand the other more clearly; everyone correctly perceives what he wants, and all feel that they are in accord with one another. The poorest peasant knows what he should be longing for as much as the most educated man. The beautiful and noble feeling of disinterested and magnanimous assistance to brethren, crucified on the cross, promptly unites all Russians. Europe, however, believes neither in Russia's nobleness nor in her disinterestedness. That "disinterestedness" is precisely the whole source of the uncertainty, of the temptation, of everything that tends to cause the confusion —a condition which is repulsive and hateful to everybody; this is the reason why no one wants to believe it and everyone is, somehow, inclined to doubt it. Were it not for "disinterestedness," the matter would immediately have become ten times simpler and more understandable to Europe, whereas, in the presence of this disinterestedness, everything is darkness, uncertainty, puzzlement, mystery! Oh!—those who are stung are in Europe! And it stands to reason that in the conception of those who are stung the whole mystery is in Russia alone which, they argue, refuses to divulge anything to anyone, and which is firmly and undeviatingly pursuing some aim —craftily and silently deceiving everybody.

Already for two hundred years Europe has been living with Russia, which forced her entry into the family of European nations —into civilization. But Europe, foreboding evil, always has looked askance upon Russia, as upon a fatal riddle which arose God only knows whence—but which, however, must be solved *quand-même.*

And thus, precisely, every time the Eastern question arises, this
uncertainty—this perplexity of Europe as regards Russia—increases
to a pathological degree, and yet nothing is being solved. "Indeed,
who and what is it in the long run? And when shall we learn it?
Who are they—those Russians?—Asiatics, Tartars? At least, it would
be nice were the matter clear! But no—it isn't. That's the point—
it isn't clear, and we have to confess this to ourselves. And yet they
resemble us so little. . . . Besides, what is that communion of the
Slavs? What is it for, and what are its aims? What will—what can
—this perilous alliance tell us that is new?" And they wind up, as
hitherto and as always, by solving these questions in accordance
with their own yardsticks: "Usurpation, seizure"—they claim—
"means conquest, dishonesty, craftiness, future annihilation of civilization, a united Mongol horde, Tartars!"

However, hatred itself of Russia is impotent fully to unite those
who have been stung: every time the Eastern question arises, the
apparent wholeness of Europe begins, much too obviously, to fall
apart into personal, segregatedly national egoisms. There, everything
is derived from the false idea that somebody wants to seize and
grab something: "I should be in this, too, because—see—everybody
is grabbing, and I'm getting nothing!" So that every time this fatal
question appears on the scene, all former inveterate political conflicts and ailments of Europe begin to ache and fester. For this
reason, naturally, everybody seeks to quench the question—at least
temporarily; principally—to quench it in Russia, somehow to divert
Russia from it—somehow to exorcise, to conjure, to scare her.

And so Viscount Beaconsfield—an Israelite by birth (né
Disraeli)—in an address at some banquet, suddenly divulges to
Europe an extraordinary secret, to the effect that all those Russians,
headed by Cherniaiev, who rushed into Turkey to save the Slavs—
that they all are Russian socialists, communists, communards—
briefly, all those Russian destructive elements with which Russia
is supposedly loaded.—"Indeed, you may believe me for I am
Beaconsfield, the Premier, as I am called in Russian newspapers
in order to give more weight to their articles; I am the Prime
Minister; I have secret documents, so that I know better than you,
and I know very much."—This is what glimmers through every
phrase of that Beaconsfield. I am convinced that it was he who
invented for himself this family album name—reminiscent of our
Lenskys and Gremins—when he was entreating the Queen for his
noble rank, since he is a novelist.

By the way, when, a few lines above, I wrote about the mysterious *piccola bestia*, it suddenly occurred to me: what if the reader
should imagine that in this allegory I sought to depict Viscount

Beaconsfield?—I assure you that this is not so: *piccola bestia* is merely an idea, and not a person; besides, it would be granting too much honor to Mr. Beaconsfield, although one has to admit that he does very much resemble a *piccola bestia*.

Asserting in his speech that Serbia, having declared war upon Turkey, has perpetrated a dishonest act, and that the war which Serbia is waging at present is a dishonest war—and having thus spat into the face of the whole Russian movement, the whole Russian enthusiasm, the sacrifices, the aspirations, the entreaties about which he could not help but know—that Israelite, that new judge of the honor of England, continues thus (I am quoting him verbatim):

"Of course, Russia was glad to get rid of all these destructive elements by sending them into Serbia, although she failed to take into account that there they would unite their forces, achieve cohesion, reach an understanding, organize and grow into a power." . . . "Europe should take notice of this threatening force."—Beaconsfield stresses, menacing the English farmers with future socialism in Russia and in the East. "Also in Russia will they take notice of this insinuating phrase of mine"—of course, he says to himself. "Russia, too, has to be scared."

Spider, spider—*piccola bestia;* indeed, he awfully resembles it—indeed, a small, shaggy *bestia!* And how swiftly does he strike! For it was he who permitted the massacre of the Bulgarians; nay, more—he also plotted it, for he is a novelist, and this is his *chef-d'œuvre*. And yet, he is seventy years old, and soon he will have to retire into the earth—this he knows himself. And how he must have rejoiced over his rank of viscount! Surely, he must have dreamed about it all his life, when he was still writing his novels! What do these people believe in? How do they manage to sleep at night? What kind of dreams are they dreaming? What do they do in solitude with their souls?—Oh, their souls must be full of elegance! . . . Day in and day out they eat such delightful dinners in company with such refined and witty interlocutors; in the evenings they are fondled in the cream of society by such lovely ladies —oh, their lives are so respectable; their digestion—so wonderful; their dreams—so light, like those of infants! . . .

Recently, I have read that bashi-bazouks crucified two priests; they died after twenty-four hours of tortures surpassing all imagination. Even though, in the beginning, Beaconsfield had denied in Parliament any kind of tortures, even the slightest—of course, to himself, he knows about these two crosses, too, "since he has documents." No doubt, he chases away these trivial, trashy, even filthily indecent, pictures; however, these two black contorted corpses on the crosses may suddenly leap into the head at a most unexpected

moment—say, for example, when Beaconsfield, in his gorgeous bedroom, feels ready to fall asleep with a serene smile, recapitulating
in his mind the brilliant evening which he has just spent, and all
those delightful, witty things which he has said to this or that
gentleman, to this or that lady.

"Well"—Beaconsfield might think—"these black corpses on
the crosses . . . hm . . . of course . . . However, 'the state is not
a private person; it cannot, from mere sentimentality, sacrifice its
interests, all the more so as in political matters magnanimity itself
is never disinterested.' It is wonderful, what beautiful mottoes there
are"—Beaconsfield ponders—"even so refreshing, and principally—
so well-proportioned! . . . Indeed, isn't the state . . . But I had
better go to bed. . . . Hm . . . After all, what are these two
priests? Two 'popes'?—They call them 'popes,' *les popes.* It's their
own fault that they happened to be around! Why didn't they hide
somewhere . . . under a soft . . . *mais, avec votre permission, mes-
sieurs les deux crucifiés,* I am terribly tired of you with your silly
adventure, *et je vous souhaite la bonne nuit à tous les deux."*

And Beaconsfield falls asleep sweetly, gently. He dreams all
the time that he is a viscount, and all around him are roses and
lilies of the valley, and lovely, lovely ladies. Presently he makes
a most delightful speech: what *bons mots!* Everybody applauds!
He has just crushed the coalition. . . .

And now, all our captains and majors, veteran Sebastopolians
and Caucasians, in their crumpled old suits, with little white crosses
in their buttonholes (so many of them have been described!)—they
all are socialists?—Of course, some of them will take a drink; we
have been hearing about this: in this respect the service man is
rather weak, yet this is in no sense socialism! As against this,
please behold how he is dying in battle; what a dandy, what a hero
he is at the head of his battalion, glorifying the Russian name and,
by his personal example, converting even cowardly recruits into
heroes! So, according to you, he is a socialist?—Well, and what
about these two youths whom their mother brought by the hand
(this fact, too, did take place!)—are they communards?—And that
old warrior over there with his seven sons—does he really seek to
burn down the Tuileries?—These elderly soldiers, these Don Cossacks, these Russian contingents arriving with sanitary units and
field chapels—is it possible that they are dreaming about nothing
but shooting an archbishop? These Kireevs, these Raievskys—they
all are our destructive elements whom Europe has to dread? And
Cherniaiev, this most naïve of all heroes,—in Russia, former editor
of *The Russian World*—he, too, is a ringleader of Russian socialism?
Fie, how incredible! Had Beaconsfield known how, in Russia, all

this sounds ill-proportioned . . . and shameful, he would, perhaps, not have ventured to interject so ridiculous a passage in his speech.

2

WORDS, WORDS, WORDS!

Several opinions—both our own and European—on the solution of the Eastern question are decidedly surprising. By the way, in our journalistic world there are also some who, as it were, have been stung. Oh, I shall not enumerate all my impressions—this would make me tired. "Administrative autonomy" also is apt to cause paralysis of one's brain. Do you see, if things could be arranged so as to grant Bulgaria, Herzegovina and Bosnia equal rights with the Mohammedan population, and forthwith to find means how to guarantee their rights—"we definitely see no reason why the Eastern question could not be brought to a close," etc., etc. This opinion, as is known, enjoys particular authoritativeness in Europe. Briefly, a combination is conceived, the realization of which is more difficult than to create all Europe anew, or to separate water from earth, or anything else you please; and yet people believe that they have settled the problem, and they feel calm and content.

Nay, Russia has agreed to this only *in principle,* but the execution of this scheme she wants to supervise herself, and *in her own way;* and, of course, Messrs. Idle-Talkers, she would not let you derive the benefits therefrom. "To grant autonomy"?—"To find a combination"?—Why, how can it be done? And who is going to do it? Who is going to obey? And who is going to enforce obedience? Finally, who rules Turkey? What parties and what forces? Is there even in Constantinople, which is still better educated than the rest of the Turks, a single Turk who in reality, by inner conviction, would recognize a Christian community to such an extent equal to himself that anything factual could come of that "autonomy"? I say—"a single man" . . . And, if so—if there is not even one—how is it possible to conduct negotiations and enter into treaties with such a people?—"Organize supervision, find a combination"—guides keep insisting. Go ahead, try to find a combination! There are problems of such a nature as are absolutely impossible precisely of that solution for which people crave at a given moment. It was impossible to disentangle the Gordian knot with fingers, and yet people kept wracking their brains over how to disentangle it precisely with their fingers. But Alexander came and dissected it with a sword and, in this way, solved the riddle.

Then, for example, there is a certain journalistic opinion—

in truth, not only a journalistic one: it is an old diplomatic opinion
—as well as an opinion shared by many scientists, professors, feuilletonists, publicists, novelists, Westerners, Slavophiles, and so forth,
to wit: that, eventually, Constantinople will belong to nobody; that
she is going to be something on the order of a free international
city—in a word, something like a "common place." She is going
to be guarded by "European equilibrium," etc. Briefly, instead of
a direct and clear solution—the only one which is possible—there
comes some complicated and unnatural scientific combination. Now,
to ask but one question: what is European equilibrium?—Up to the
present, such an equilibrium has been conceived in relation to several
most powerful European states—say, five, for example—of equal
weight (*i.e.*, it was presumed, so to speak, from delicacy that they
were of equal weight). Thus, five wolves will lie down around the
choice piece (Constantinople), and each one of the five will be
engaged in nothing but guarding the prey against the others. And
this is being called a chef-d'œuvre, a *Meisterstück* of the solution
of the problem! But does this solve anything?—The fact alone is
that all is based upon a primitive absurdity, upon a fantastic, nonexistent and even unnatural fact—upon equilibrium. In reality, has
political equilibrium existed in the world at any time?—Positively
not! This is merely a tricky formula invented by crafty men in
order to cheat simpletons. And although Russia is not simple-
minded, yet she is honest, and, for this reason—I believe—she, more
frequently than the rest, has believed in the inviolability of the
truths and laws of that equilibrium, and many a time has she sincerely complied with them and acted as their protectress. In this
respect Europe has most impudently exploited Russia. As for the
others—suspended in a state of equilibrium—it seems that not one
of them has been giving serious thought to these equilibrial laws,
even though, for the time being, complying with formalities; however, as soon as, according to one's calculations, some gain was in
sight, he violated that equilibrium without concern for anything
else. The funniest part of it is that such tactics invariably succeeded,
and "equilibrium" would again ensue. However, when Russia, too,
without violating anything, gave a little thought to her own interests—at once all other equilibriums got together and moved
against Russia: "thou violatest the equilibrium!"

Well, the same is going to happen in the case of an international Constantinople: five wolves will be lying around baring their
teeth at each other, and each one will be silently inventing a combination—how to unite with the neighbors and how, after exterminating the other wolves, to divide the choice piece in a most advantageous manner. Is this a solution?—Meanwhile, among the

wolves-guardians, there arise *sui generis* new combinations: suddenly, one of the five wolves—and even the grayest one—on a certain day and hour, by some mishap, is converted from a wolf into a little lap dog which cannot even bark. There you are: the equilibrium is shattered! Moreover, in the future of Europe, it may happen that out of five powers of equal weight simply two will be formed, and in this case where will your combination be, Messrs. Wise-Heads? . . . By the way, I venture to set forth the following axiom: "Never will there be such a moment in Europe, never such a political state of things, when Constantinople would not be *somebody's, i.e.,* that she would not belong to someone." Such is the axiom, and it seems to me that it cannot be otherwise. And if you will permit a little joke, I might say that at the eleventh hour, at the last decisive moment, Constantinople will suddenly be seized by the English, just as they have seized Gibraltar, Malta, and so forth. And this will happen precisely at a time when the powers will still be entertaining the idea of the equilibrium. Precisely, these very Englishmen who, with such tender motherly care, are at present guarding the inviolability of Turkey, who prophesy to her the possibility of a great future, of civilization; who believe in her creative principles—precisely these Englishmen, when they perceive that the matter has come to an issue, will swallow the Sultan, together with Constantinople. This is in line with their character and orientation —so akin to their customary impudent arrogance, their oppression, their malice! Of course, just now all this is but a jest, and I am giving it out as such. However, it wouldn't be a bad idea to remember this joke: it smacks so of truth. . . .

3

COMBINATIONS AND COMBINATIONS

Thus, in the solution of the Eastern question all sorts of combinations are being admitted with the exception of the clearest, sanest, simplest, the most natural, one. It may even be said that the more unnatural the solution that is being suggested, the quicker is public opinion and common opinion to seize upon it.

Here, for example, is another "unnaturalness": it is suggested that "should Russia openly declare her disinterest, so that all Europe could hear it, the matter would at once be solved and settled." But happy he who believes! Should Russia not only declare, but *de facto* prove, her disinterest, this, perhaps, would still more confuse Europe. What if we should annex nothing—what if we should "bestow benefits" and should return without having taken advantage of anything, merely proving to Europe our disinterestedness?—Why, Europe would feel still worse: "The more disinterestedly you have benefited them, the more strongly you have proved to them that you are not seeking to violate their independence, the more devoted to you they will become—henceforth they will justly regard you as their sun, as a summit, as a zenith, as their Empire. What of it that they would be autonomous, and not your subjects? Still, in their souls they would deem themselves your subjects; unconsciously and involuntarily they would adopt this attitude." It is precisely this inevitability of the moral affiliation of the Slavs with Russia—sooner or later—this, so to speak, naturalness, the legitimacy of this fact, so dreaded by Europe, that constitutes her nightmare, her principal future fears. On her part, it is only forces and combinations—whereas, on our part, it is a law of nature, naturalness, kinship, truth. Now then, to whom will the future of Slavic countries belong?

Meanwhile, there is precisely in Europe a certain combination based upon a directly opposite principle, and such a *probable* one that, perhaps, it may have a future. This new combination is also "made in England"; this is, so to say, a corrective to all errors and slips of the Tory Party. This combination is based upon the idea that England herself forthwith bestow benefits upon the Slavs, on condition, however, that they be converted into eternal enemies and haters of Russia. It is suggested to renounce the Turks, to exterminate them as a lost people, good for nothing, and to form a union of all Christian peoples of the Balkan Peninsula, with Constantinople as its center. The liberated and grateful Slavs would, naturally, lean toward England as their savior and liberatress, which then would open their eyes on Russia: "She"—they would say—"is your worst enemy; under the guise of concern for you, she is dreaming of swallowing you and of depriving you of your inevitable glorious political future." Thus, when the Slavs would become convinced of Russia's treacherousness, they would at once form a new and powerful bulwark against her, and "then Constantinople will slip out of Russia's hands; they will not permit her thither—never."

At first glance it might seem that nothing cleverer, nothing more to the point, can be conceived. The main thing is that this is so simple and is based upon an existing fact. In passing, I have already mentioned that fact. It comes down to this: among a certain portion of the Slavic intelligentsia, among certain outstanding representatives and leaders of the Slavs, there dwells in truth a concealed mistrust of Russia's aims, and, as a result of this—even animosity against Russia and the Russians. Oh, I am not speaking of the people, the masses. To the Slavic peoples—the Serbians, the Montenegrins—Russia is still their sun, their hope, their friend, their mother and their protectress, their future liberatress! But the Slavic intelligentsia is a different proposition. Of course, I am not speaking of the intelligentsia as a whole; I would not even venture, or take it upon myself, to speak of all of them. "However, *even though far from all*, nevertheless among their wisest ministerial heads (as I expressed myself in my August *Diary*), there are some to whom it does seem that Russia is treacherous; that she is just dreaming of conquering and swallowing them." There is no point in concealing from ourselves that, perhaps, quite a large number of educated Slavs do not like us, Russians, at all. For instance, they still consider us ignorant, almost barbarians, compared with them. They are by no means greatly interested in the progress of our civic life, our internal organization, our reforms, our literature. Perhaps only the very learned among them know about Pushkin, and even among those who do know about him, only a few would agree to recognize him as the great Slavic genius. Many educated Czechs, for instance, are convinced that they had forty poets like Pushkin. Besides, all these Slavic segregations, in that state in which they are at present, are politically ambitious and irritable, as inexperienced nations which do not know life. Among such ones the English combination could meet with success provided it could come into vogue. And it is difficult to conceive why it shouldn't if, with the Whig victory in England, that combination were placed on her agenda. And yet how much artificiality, unnaturalness and deceit there is in that combination—how impossible it is!

To begin with, how is one to unite such disparate ethnographic units of the Balkan Peninsula, and at that—with a center in Constantinople?—There, there are Greeks, Slavs, Rumanians. To whom will Constantinople belong?—To all? That would be the beginning of friction and dissension, say, between the Greeks and the Slavs— to start with (even if it should be presumed that all Slavs be in accord among themselves). It may be said: it is possible to appoint a sovereign, to found an Empire—thus, it seems, it is contemplated in the dreams of the project. But who is going to be emperor—a Slav, a Greek, or maybe one of the Hapsburgs? In any event there would at once ensue dualisms, bifurcations. The important thing is that the Greek and Slav elements are incompatible: either element has enormous, altogether incommensurate and false, dreams about its forthcoming glorious political future. No, should England really make up her mind to forsake the Turks, she will fix all these things on a more solid foundation. Right here, so it seems to me, that combination might be put over which I have earlier denoted as a jest—that is, England herself might swallow Constantinople "for the benefit, so to speak, of the Slavs."—"I shall form of you, Slavs, a union and a bulwark in the North against the Northern colossus so as not to let him into Constantinople, for once he should seize Constantinople, he would also seize all of you. In such an event you would be deprived of your glorious political future. Also you, Greeks, don't you worry: Constantinople is yours. Precisely, I want her to be yours, and this is why I am occupying her. This I am doing merely in order not to give her to Russia. The Slavs will be protecting her from the North, and I—from the sea, and we shall let no one in. And I shall stay in Constantinople only for the time being until you gain strength and form a firm and mature federal Empire. But until that time comes, I shall be your leader and protectress. Are the places few where I have stayed? I have Gibraltar, Malta. . . . And didn't I return the Ionian Islands? . . ."

In a word, should this Whig product come into vogue, it would be difficult, I repeat, to doubt its success—of course, only a temporary one. Moreover, that time could be prolonged for many a year, but . . . all the more inevitably would all this collapse when the natural limit is reached; then it would be a final collapse since the whole combination is based upon calumny and unnaturalness.

The deceit is in the fact that Russia was calumniated. No fog can withstand the rays of truth. There will come a time when even the Slavic nations will comprehend the whole truth of Russian disinterest, and by then their spiritual communion with us will have been consummated. For our active communion with the Slavs has begun very recently, but now—now it will never cease and will continue stronger and stronger. At length, the Slavs will convince themselves—despite any kind of calumnies—of Russian brotherly affection for them. They will become affected by the irresistible witchery of the great and mighty Russian spirit which is akin to them. They will perceive that they cannot develop spiritually within petty coalitions, dissensions and envies, and that this is possible only on a full, all-Slavic scale. The enormity and might of the Russian communion will no longer frighten them; on the contrary, they will be irresistibly attracted by that enormity, and that might, as toward a center and a beginning. The religious concord will also serve as a very strong bond. Russian religion, Russian Orthodoxy, is everything the Russian people regard as their sanctity: in it are their ideals, the whole truth and rectitude of life. And what united and what kept the Slavic nations alive in the days of their distress, during the four centuries of the Mohammedan yoke—what but their religion? They have endured for it so much suffering that this alone must have made it dear to them. Finally, Russian blood was already shed for the Slavs, and blood is never forgotten.

Crafty people have overlooked all this. The possibility of calumniating Russia to the Slavs inspires them with success and with faith in the firmness of success. But such a success is of no long duration. Temporarily, however—I repeat—it may be realized. The combination decidedly may come into vogue if the Whigs should triumph, and this has to be taken into account. The English will risk it simply to anticipate Russia when the final hour strikes: "We ourselves shall manage to bestow benefits."

By the way, speaking of bloodshed. What if our volunteers, even without Russia's declaring war, should finally defeat the Turks and liberate the Slavs? It is rumored that so many volunteers come from Russia, and contributions flow so uninterruptedly, that, perhaps, in the long run, a whole Russian army might be formed under Cherniaiev. In any event, Europe and her diplomats would be very much surprised with such a result: "If volunteers alone defeated the Turks, what would have happened if the whole of Russia would have taken up arms?" An argument such as this would not be missed in Europe.

God bless the Russian volunteers with success!—It is rumored that Russian officers by the dozens are again being killed in battle. You, dear ones!

It is not out of place to make one more little remark which, in my judgment, is rather pressing. As the number of Russian volunteers in Serbia increases and in view of their many heroic deaths on battlefields, our papers have started collections under a new heading: *"For the benefit of families of Russians fallen in the war with the Turks for the liberation of the Balkan Slavs."* Contributions begin to flow. *The Voice* has already collected under this heading up to three thousand rubles, and the more people contribute—the better, of course. There is only one thing which is not quite all right: to my way of thinking, the formula for the collection is framed incompletely. Contributions are being received only for the benefit of families of Russians *fallen* in the war, etc. And what about the families of men who had been crippled? Is it possible that they will receive nothing? Yet these families might be in a more difficult position than those of the killed. He who has fallen—has fallen; he is being mourned; but that one came home a crippled man, without his feet, without his arms, or so badly wounded that henceforth his health will always require increasing care and medical attention. Besides, even though he is crippled, nevertheless he eats and drinks, and, consequently, in a poor family an extra mouth is added. Besides, in my opinion, there is one more erroneous indeterminateness: *"For the benefit of families of Russians fallen . . ."* etc. But there are well-to-do or less needy families; on the other hand, there are quite destitute and very needy families. If money is distributed among all, the poor will receive much too little. Therefore, it seems to me that the wording of the heading should be changed thus: *"For the benefit of the needy families of Russians fallen or crippled in the war with the Turks for the liberation of the Balkan Slavs."*

However, I am merely setting forth an idea, and if someone should succeed in framing a more accurate formula—of course, all the better. It is only to be hoped that contributions under this heading may accumulate more quickly and more abundantly. This is most useful, quite indispensable, and it may exercise a strong moral influence upon our magnanimous volunteers who are fighting for the Russian idea.

4

Morning Gowns and Soap

Among the opinions on the Eastern question I came across a perfect oddity. Recently, there appeared in the foreign press a strange argument: in ardent, virtually fantastic, terms people began to speculate as to what would happen to the world should Turkey be annihilated and pressed back into Asia. It was claimed that a calamity, a terrible repercussion, would ensue. Predictions were even made to the effect that in Asia, somewhere in Arabia, there would arise a new caliphate; that fanaticism would be resurrected, and that once more the Mohammedan world would make an onslaught against Europe. More profound thinkers confined their opinion to the argument that to evict a whole nation from Europe into Asia is an impossible and altogether unthinkable proposition. When I was reading all this, I somehow felt very surprised; even so, I was unable to guess what this actually meant. But, suddenly, I understood that all these diplomat-dreamers *de facto* are putting the question in a literal sense, *i.e.*, that concretely it comes down to the proposition that after the political destruction of the Turkish Empire, actually, literally and physically, all the Turks should be taken and transported somewhere to Asia.

How a thing of this sort could have been conceived—I simply cannot understand. Yet at banquets and meetings people were unquestionably scared by the prediction: a terrible repercussion, a calamity will ensue. Even so, it seems to me that nothing at all would happen, and that not a single Turk would have to be deported to Asia. In Russia something of this kind did happen once. When the Tartar Horde came to an end, the Kazan Czardom unexpectedly began to increase in strength, and this to such an extent that there was a time when it would have been difficult to predict to whom the Russian land would belong—to Christianity or Mohammedanism. That Czardom ruled the present-day Russian East; it was in communication with Astrakhan; it held the Volga in its hands, while at Russia's flank there appeared a most welcome ally of Kazan in the person of the Khan of the Crimean Horde—a terrible robber and plunderer from whom Moscow had suffered much. The situation was pressing, and the youthful Czar Ivan Vasilievich—at that time not yet Terrible—made up his mind to settle the Eastern question of those days by capturing Kazan.

The siege was a terrible one, and subsequently Karamzin described it most eloquently. The Kazan residents defended themselves desperately, perfectly, stubbornly, tenaciously and unwaveringly. However, their saps were blown up, and the Russians stormed Kazan and captured her. Well, what did Czar Ivan Vasilievich undertake when he entered Kazan? Did he order a wholesale extermination of her inhabitants—as he later did in the case of Novgorod the Great—so that henceforth they should not be in his way? Did he deport them to the steppes in Asia?—Not in the least: not even a single Tartar urchin was deported; everything remained as hitherto, and the heroic, formerly so dangerous, Kazan residents became pacified forever. And this came to pass in a most simple and most peculiar manner: just as soon as the city had been captured, the icon of the Mother of God was carried into it; for the first time since Kazan's foundation a Te Deum was officiated. Thereupon the foundation of an Orthodox church was laid; arms were assiduously confiscated from the inhabitants; Russian administration was inaugurated, while the Czar of Kazan was sent to a proper place—that's all. And the whole thing came to pass in just one day. A little while after that Kazan inhabitants began to sell us morning gowns, and still later—also soap. (I believe that this took place precisely in the indicated order—first came the morning gowns, and then—the soap.) Such was the end of the whole affair. Exactly in the same manner the matter would also be settled in Turkey, should the happy thought be conceived finally to abolish the Caliphate politically.

First a Te Deum would be officiated in the Saint Sophia Church; thereupon the Patriarch would consecrate it anew; by that day, I believe, a bell would have been brought from Moscow; the Sultan would be sent to a proper place—and this would be the end of everything. True, the Turks have a law, almost a dogma of the Koran, to the effect that only a Mohammedan may and shall carry arms, while a Gentile is denied this right. Of late, however,

they have begun to grant permission also to Gentiles to possess
arms, but only subject to a high tax, and in this way they even
invented a new source of state revenue; still, comparatively speaking, there are but very few who actually carry arms. Well, perhaps,
this one law could be amended on the very first day—*i.e.*, on the
day of the first Te Deum at Sophia—in the reverse sense that only
a Gentile may and shall carry arms, whereas a Mohammedan shall
be denied this right altogether, even for a high tax. Now, then, this
would be all that would be needed to assure peace and quiet; I
insist, nothing more would be required. After a little while, Turks
would also start selling us morning gowns, and later—also soap,
perhaps even of a better quality than that of Kazan. As regards
agriculture, tobacco industry and wine manufacture—these branches,
I believe, under the new administration and under new laws, would
improve so quickly and so successfully that, by-and-by, of course,
they would make it possible to pay the irredeemable debts of the
former Turkish state to Europe. Briefly, nothing would happen
except the best and most suitable things; there would be even
not the slightest repercussion, and—I repeat—not even a single Turkish urchin would have to be evicted from Europe.

Nor would anything happen in the East. True, perhaps, a
caliphate would arise somewhere—somewhere in the Asiatic steppes,
in the sands. However, to carry out an onslaught against Europe
in our age, so much money, so many pieces of artillery of the latest
design, so many rifles equipped with the repeating mechanism, so
many baggage-transports, so many equipment factories and plants
are required that not only Mohammedan, but even English, fanaticism itself would be impotent in whatever manner to come to the
assistance of the new caliphate. In a word, absolutely nothing but
good would ensue. And God grant us this good as quickly as possible
for, indeed, there is so much that is bad!

CHAPTER II

1

Antiquated People

"EVERY SUBLIME and cohesive idea, every sound cohesive
sentiment, constitutes the greatest happiness in the life of a nation.
This happiness was bestowed upon us. We could not help but
clearly perceive the increased consensus, the clarification of many
a former perplexity, our augmented self-consciousness."

This is what I expressed in the concluding article of the preceding, August, issue of my *Diary*. A sound cohesive sentiment in the life of nations is, indeed, happiness. If there was something in which I was mistaken, it was, perhaps, only in that I have somewhat exaggerated the degree of our "augmented accord and self-consciousness." But even on that point I am not ready to accede. He who loves Russia has long felt painfully that alienation of the upper Russian strata from the lower ones—from the people and their life—which, as an actual fact, at present is doubted by no one. Now, this alienation, according to my view, has partly given way and weakened in the face of the genuine all-Russian movement of the current year in connection with the Slavic cause. It stands to reason that it is impossible to conceive that our detachment from the people should have definitely come to an end and been cured. It will persist for a long time; still, such historical moments as we have lived through this year, no doubt, help both "our augmented accord and the clarification of perplexities"; in a word, they help us more clearly to understand the people and Russian life, on the one hand, while—on the other—they help the people themselves to become better acquainted with men, as it were, alien to them, not Russians, as it were—with "masters," as the people still call us.

It must be admitted that in this all-Russian movement of the current year the people have revealed themselves in a saner, clearer and more precise aspect than many persons belonging to our intelligent class. In the people a direct, simple and strong sentiment has manifested itself, and—what is most important—with a remarkable consensus and accord. Among them there was even no argument as to "why the Slavs should be helped."—"Should they be helped?" "Who should be helped more and better and who should not be helped at all?" "Shall we not, perchance, corrupt our morality, and shall we not impede our civic progress by giving too much help?" "With whom should we fight, and is it necessary to fight at all?"—and so on, and so forth. In brief, thousands of perplexities did, however, arise among our intelligentsia—particularly in certain of its portions, specifically among those which still maintain a haughty attitude toward the people, despising them from the heights of European education (at times, altogether imaginary). There—in those upper "segregations"—there were revealed quite a few extraordinary dissonances, instability of opinion, a strange lack of understanding of the most elementary things, almost ridiculous vacillation on the questions—what to do and what not to do, etc. "Should the Slavs be helped or should they not? And if they should be helped, why should they? And on what ground

is it more moral, more graceful, to help—on this or on that?"—
All these traits, at times most surprising, were actually reflected
in conversations, in facts and in literature. However, no stranger
article along these lines have I read than the one in the current
September issue of *The Messenger of Europe,* in the section entitled
"Domestic Survey." The article specifically treats of the present-
day current Russian movement, apropos of brotherly help to the
oppressed Slavs, and seeks to express on the subject as profound
an opinion as possible. The portion of the article dealing with the
Russian people and with society is not long—four or five short
pages; therefore, I shall venture to dwell upon them, so to speak,
one after another, without, of course, quoting everything. To my
way of thinking, these pages are extraordinarily curious, and they
constitute, as it were, a document. The object of my undertaking
will become apparent of its own accord, at the end of my review,
so that, I believe, it will not be necessary to draw any special moral.

However, in the way of brief information, I may merely mention the fact that the author obviously belongs to that antiquated
school of the theoretical Westerners which, a quarter of a century
ago, formed, so to speak, the zenith of our educated forces. At
present, however, it has grown so obsolete that in its pure primitive
state it is encountered very rarely. Those are, as it were, fragments
—the last Mohicans of the theoretical Russian Europeanism—detached from the people and from life, which, though at the time it
did have its place and the necessary causes of its existence, has
left in its wake, in addition to its *sui generis* usefulness, a great
deal of most harmful, prejudicial fiddle-faddle which continues to
be damaging even to the present day. The principal historical usefulness of those men was a negative one and it lay in the extremity
of their inferences and final judgments (for they were so haughty
that they pronounced their judgments not otherwise than in a final
form), in those farthest pillars of Hercules which they have reached
in their ecstatic theories. This extremism, willy-nilly, tended to sober
the minds, and it brought about the shift toward the people and
the merger with them. At present, after a whole quarter of a century, after so many new and hitherto unheard-of facts have been
revealed through practical study of Russian life, these "last Mohicans" of the antiquated theories, of necessity, appear in a comic
light, despite their exaggeratedly respectable deportment. Their
main comic trait lies in the fact that they still continue to regard
themselves as the youthful and sole guardians and, so to speak,
"sign-bearers" of those paths along which, in their opinion, real
Russian life should be developing. But they are so far behind life
that they definitely cease to recognize it, and for this reason they

are dwelling in a wholly fantastic world. This is why it is so very curious and so instructive, at a moment of so strong a public enthusiasm, to trace to what an extent this theoretical Europeanism has falsely alienated itself from the people and from society, to what an extent its views and dicta, at certain extraordinary moments of public life—though presumptuous and haughty as heretofore—are, essentially, weak, unsteady, obscure and erroneous in comparison with the clear, simple, firm and unflinching inferences of the popular sentiment and mind. But let us turn to the article.

However, in all justice to the author it must be said that he also admits—rather agrees to admit—the popular and public movement in favor of the Slavs, and he concedes that it is sufficiently sincere. Of course, how could he not have conceded this! —Even so, for so antiquated a "European," this is no slight merit. And yet for some reason all the time he seems to be displeased with something; true, he does not directly state that he is dissatisfied with the fact that this movement has come into being; but, as against this, he keeps grumbling and cavilling at details. I believe that Granovsky, one of the purest initial exponents of our theoretical Westernism, who in his own time also wrote on the Eastern question, and on the popular movement during the war of 1854–1856—only partly akin to the present one (see my article on Granovsky in the August issue of my *Diary*)—Granovsky, I say, would also, I believe, have been displeased with our present popular movement. And, of course, he would have preferred to perceive our people as heretofore, in the form of a motionless and backward mass, rather than to see them revealing themselves in such partly undeveloped and, so to speak, primitive forms unfit for our European age. And, generally, even though all these old theoreticians were fond of the people (however, this is not quite certain), yet they were fond in theory only, *i.e.*, in those fanciful representations and forms in which they wished to perceive them, so that, in substance, they did not love the people at all. But it should be admitted in their defense that they did not know the people at all, never deemed it necessary to know them or to have intercourse with them. Not that they *distorted the facts*, but they simply did not understand them at all, so that on many—all too many—occasions, the purest gold of the people's spirit, reason and lofty sentiment was attributed by them to insipidness, ignorance and dull Russian imbecility. Had the people revealed themselves, though slightly, not in those guises and images which pleased them (mostly—in the guise of the Parisian mob), they would probably have renounced them altogether. "First of all"—exclaims Granovsky, in his brochure on the Eastern question—"the thought should be altogether discarded that this is a sacred war. In our day no one is going to be prompted to a crusade. This is a different age: no one will move to redeem our Lord's sepulchre,"—and so on, and so forth. The theoretician of *The Messenger of Europe* adopts an identical attitude: he is displeased with the headings, he cavils at them. For instance, he is quite disappointed with the fact that the people and our society are not sending their contributions under the heading he would like. He would rather have a view, so to speak, more suited to our age, more enlightened. But, again, we have deviated from the subject.

I am omitting the beginning of the portion of the article with the Russian movement in support of the Slavs—a beginning which, in a sense, is quite characteristic, but I cannot be dwelling upon every line. Here is what the author states further.

2

KIFO-MOKIEVSCHINA

"However, the fact cannot be denied that among the many statements which have appeared in this connection in our newspapers, there have been some strange and tactless ones. Leaving aside those which indicated a desire to show off one's own personality—since this is of no importance—we must point to those which reveal inquisition as regards the sentiments of Russian citizens—not Great Russians. It is to be regretted that we have still been unable to rid ourselves of this bad habit, whereas the very nature of the matter in question necessitates special caution with regard to other nationalities which form part of the general Russian population. Let us also remark that, speaking generally, one should not be attributing to the movement in support of the Slavs too religious a character, constantly mentioning 'our fellow-believers.' To prompt Russian society to give help to the Slavs, those motives which can unite all citizens are quite sufficient, whereas such motives as may cause discord among them are superfluous. Should we seek to explain our sympathy with the Slavs, primarily by the fact that they are our fellow-believers, what attitude should we adopt toward those of our Mohammedans who would start collections for the benefit of the Turks, or who would declare their desire to join the Turkish army? . . . Agitation which has been recorded in certain localities of the Caucasus should remind us of the fact that the Orthodox Great Russian is living in a family, that he is the elder but not the only son of Russia."

Even this one passage would suffice to show the extent of the rupture with the public sense, the level of idle "Kifo-Mokievschina" that can be reached, in our day, by certain "sign-bearers" grown old in the obstinacy of their Europeanism. The author propounds to us, and has vexed himself with, questions which astound one by their artificiality and fictitiousness, by their extreme fantastic theoreticalness and—above all—by their aimlessness. "If we donate because we embrace the same religion, what should be our attitude toward those of our Mohammedans who would start collections for the benefit of the Turks, or who would declare their desire to join the Turkish army?" Now, is any such question possible, and can there be the slightest hesitation in answering it? Any ordinary, not twisted, Russian would promptly give you a most precise answer. And not only a Russian but any European, any North American, would give you a clear answer—only a European, perhaps, before replying, would gaze at you with extreme surprise. In passing, it may be observed that, generally, our Russian Westernism—*i.e.*, Europe-aping—taking root in Russian soil, quite frequently, little by little, assumes a nuance which is far from European, so that certain European ideas imported to us by "the guardians of signs" become altogether unrecognizable because they have undergone radical changes, in the process of being ground down by Russian theories and their application to Russian life, which, besides, our theoretician does not know at all and which he does not deem necessary to know. Do you see—"what attitude should we adopt toward our Mohammedans who," etc.? A very simple one: first, if we be at war with the Turks, and, for instance, our Tartars should begin to help the Turks with money, or should start joining the Turkish army—before society would have time to adopt any kind of attitude, the government itself, I daresay, would adopt toward them such an attitude as toward traitors to their country, and, no doubt, would manage to stop them in time. Secondly, if war should not yet have been declared, and the Turks should start massacring the Slavs, with whom all Russians are equally in sympathy, then, in case Russian Mohammedans should begin to contribute to Turks either money or men—do you think that any Russian would treat such a fact otherwise than with an insulted feeling and with indignation? . . . In your opinion, the whole trouble lies in the religious character of the contributions, *i.e.*, if only a Russian is helping a Slav, *as his fellow-believer*, how can he, without violating civil equality and justice, prohibit a Russian Tartar from making a similar contribution for the benefit of his co-religionist, the Turk? On the contrary, he may have, and has, a full right to do so, because a Russian, when extending help to a Slav against the Turks, has not the slightest thought of becoming an enemy of the Tartar or of waging war against him. However, a Tartar, by helping the Turk, severs his relations with Russia, becomes a traitor to Russia, and, by placing himself in the ranks of the Turks, wages a direct war against her. Besides, when I, a Russian, send my contribution for the benefit of a Slav, fighting the Turk, even because I am his co-religionist, I am hoping for his victory not because the Turk is a Moslem, but only because he is massacring the Slavs, whereas a Tartar, joining the Turks, can do so for the sole reason that I am a Christian, and that I allegedly seek to destroy Mohammedanism. Yet I am not at all seeking to destroy it—what I want is to protect my fellow-believer. . . . By helping the Slav, not only do I not attack the Tartar's religion, but I am even indifferent to the Mohammedanism of the Turk himself: let him be a Moslem as long as he wishes, on condition that he does not attack the Slavs. Perhaps, it may be argued: "If you assist your co-religionist against the Turks, you are thereby opposing the Tartars and their religion since they have a 'shariat,' and the Sultan is the caliph of all Moslems. A Gentile, however, on the strength of the Koran itself, cannot be free and have equal rights with a Moham-medan; by helping the Gentile to acquire equal rights, the Russian thereby, in the opinion of every Moslem, opposes not merely the Turks but Mohammedanism as a whole." But such being the case, not I, but the Tartar, is the instigator of the religious war, and you must concede that this is an argument of an altogether different nature, and that no tricks or headings can help the situation.

Now, it is your contention that the whole trouble lies in the fact of the commonness of religion, and that were I to conceal from the Tartar that I am helping the Slav as my co-religionist, and, on the contrary, were I to stress the fact that I am helping him under some other caption—say, because he is oppressed by the Turk, deprived of freedom, "that first blessing of man"—the Tartar would believe me. But I venture to assert that in the view of any Moslem, help given to a Gentile against a Mohammedan, no matter under what pretext, is absolutely equivalent to help given to a Gentile on the ground of religion. Didn't you really know this? And yet this is what you are precisely writing: "To prompt Russian society to give help to the Slavs, those motives which can unite all citizens are quite sufficient, whereas such motives as may cause discord among them are super-fluous. . . ." Here you are specifically referring to commonness of religion as a motive tending to bring about discord, and—to Russian Moslems—this you have actually explained. You are suggesting "fight for freedom," as the best and loftiest pretext—or "motive," as you put it—for Russian contributions for the benefit of the Slavs; and, apparently, you are fully convinced that "the Slavs' struggle

for freedom" would greatly appeal to the Tartar and would forthwith appease him. But again I assure you that to a Russian Mohammedan—if he be a man who would venture to go and help the
Turks—all motives are equal, and that no matter under which particular caption war be started, nevertheless, in his view, it would
be a religious war. However, it is not the Russian's fault that the
Tartar holds such a view. . . .

3

Continuation of the Preceding

I am really sorry that I had to go to all this length. Were a
war between France and Turkey at any time possible, and, in this
connection, were agitation to begin among Moslems belonging to
France—Algiers Arabs—do you really believe that the French would
not promptly subdue them in a most energetic manner? Would the
French resort to kid gloves and shamefully conceal their best and
noblest "motives" from fear that their Moslems, perchance, might
take offense and feel insulted? You are writing in a stately language a moral for the whole of Russia: "Agitation which has been
recorded in certain localities of the Caucasus [N. B., by the way,
thus you admit that there has been agitation] should remind us of
the fact that the Orthodox Great Russian is living in a family, that
he is the elder, but not the only, son of Russia." Let us admit that
this is expressed grandly—however, what would the Great Russian
have to do should the Caucasians really grow rebellious? What is
the fault of that elder son in the family that the Mohammedan Caucasian, that youngest son in the family, is so touchy about his
faith and that he holds the view that the elder son, by opposing the
Turks, *eo ipso* opposes Mohammedanism as a whole?—You fear
that "the elder son in the family" (the Great Russian) might, perchance, hurt the feelings of the youngest son (the Tartar or the
Caucasian). Indeed, what a humaneness, what an anxiety full of
enlightenment! You are stressing the point that the Orthodox Great
Russian "is the elder but not the only son of Russia." What is this,
may I ask?—The Russian land belongs to the Russians, to the
Russians *alone;* it is Russian land, and in it *there isn't an inch of
Tartar land.* The Tartars are the former tormentors of the Russian
land; they are aliens in this land. But the Russians, having subdued the Tartars, having recaptured from them their land and having conquered them, did not punish the Tartars for the tortures
of two centuries; they have not humiliated them in the manner in
which the Moslem Turks have humbled the Gentiles who have never

offended them; on the contrary, the Russians have granted the Tartars such full civic equality as, perhaps, you will not find in the most
civilized countries of the West, which, according to you, is so enlightened. Perhaps the Russian Mohammedan, at times, has even
abused his high privileges to the detriment of the Russian—the
owner and master of the Russian land. . . . Nor did the Russians
humble the Tartars' religion; they have neither persecuted nor
oppressed them. Believe me, nowhere in the West, nowhere in the
whole world, will you find such a broad, such a humane, religious
tolerance as in the soul of a real Russian. Believe me also that it is
rather the Tartar who is inclined to shun the Russian (precisely
because of the former's Mohammedanism) than vice versa. This
will be corroborated by anyone who has lived among the Tartars.
Nevertheless, the master of the Russian land is the Russian (Great
Russian, Little Russian, White Russian—they are all the same).
Thus it shall always be. And, believe me, should it ever become necessary for the Orthodox Russian to fight the Mohammedan Turk,
never will the Russian tolerate that anyone should *veto* him on
his own land. But, to handle the Tartars with such genteelness
that one would have to fear to reveal to them the most magnanimous
and spontaneous feelings, which are offensive to no one—feelings of
compassion for the jaded Slav, though he be a co-religionist; and,
moreover, to conceal carefully from the Tartar all that constitutes
the designation, the future, and—this is the main point—the mission
of the Russian—why, such a demand is ridiculous and humiliating
to a Russian. . . . In what way do I insult a Tartar by being in
sympathy with my religion and with my co-religionist? And where
is my fault if, according to his conceptions, each war of ours with
the Turks necessarily assumes a religious character? Certainly,
Russians are impotent to change the fundamental conceptions of
Mohammedanism as a whole. You say: "If so, be genteel, conceal,
and try not to insult. . . ." But if, indeed, he is so touchy, he may,
perhaps, be insulted by the fact that in the same street where his
mosque is, there also stands our Orthodox church.—Why not de-
molish it so that he may not feel insulted? Certainly, the Russian
doesn't have to run away from his own country! Certainly, he
doesn't have to crawl somewhere under a table, so that he shouldn't
be heard or seen, because of the fact that the youngest brother, the
Tartar, lives in the Russian land!

You started talking something about *"inquisition."*—"We must
point to those [articles in the Russian newspapers] which reveal
inquisition as regards the sentiments of Russian citizens—not Great
Russians. It is to be regretted that we have still been unable to rid
ourselves of this bad habit, whereas the very nature of the matter

in question necessitates special caution with regard to other nationalities which form part of the general Russian population." What
is this habit of ours?—I venture to assure you that this is merely
a false note of antiquated theoretical liberalism which is even incapable of applying sensibly a liberal idea imported from Europe.
No, sir, it is not for you and me to teach the people religious tolerance or to deliver lectures to them on freedom of conscience. In
this respect the people can teach both you and the whole of Europe.
However, you speak of newspapers, of Russian journalism. Now,
then, what is this inquisition? And what inveterate *habit of ours*
are you regretting?—The habit of inquisition in our literature? But
this is a fantasy which has no foundation in reality. I assure you
that in Russia no one was ever denounced in literature for either
religion or any local patriotic sentiments. And even if there may
have been individual cases, these were so isolated and exceptional
that it is sinful and shameful to raise them to the level of a general
rule: "We have still been unable to rid ourselves of this habit."
Besides, what is denouncement or inquisition? There are facts about
which it is impossible not to speak. I do not know to what articles
you are referring and what you are insinuating. I do recall reading
something about disturbances of fanaticism which flared up in the
Caucasus. But you yourself have just written about these disturbances in the sense of *a fact which has actually occurred*. It is rumored that preachers of fanaticism also came from Turkey to the
Crimea; however, whether any disturbances actually did or did not
take place, I shall not discuss—and, in truth, I myself do not know
for certain. I shall merely ask you: is it possible that, should some
newspaper report such a rumor, or actual fact, this could be called
"inquisition as regards the sentiments of our dissidents"? Supposing these facts of disturbances did actually occur, how would it be
possible to keep silent about them, especially in a newspaper whose
object it is to report facts? Thereby the newspaper prevents a
danger. For, were silence maintained and were the matter—I mean,
fanaticism—permitted to grow, both the fanatics and the Russians
living in their midst would suffer. Of course, should a newspaper
deliberately report false facts in order to *denounce* to the government and to instigate persecution, this would be inquisition and
denouncement. Yet, if the facts are correct, should one keep silent
about them? Besides, who has ever persecuted aliens in Russia for
their religion, even for certain "religious sentiments" or simply
feelings in the broadest sense of the term?—On the contrary, in this
respect, almost always things were rather lax in Russia—not at all
as, for example, in certain most enlightened European countries.
As regards religious sentiments, even schismatics nowadays are being

persecuted in Russia by virtually no one—not to speak of aliens. And if, of late, there have been several rare, quite isolated, cases of persecution of Stundists, these were forthwith sharply condemned by our entire press. By the way, shouldn't we agree with certain German newspapers which have been, and still are, accusing us of tormenting and persecuting our Baltic Germans for their religion and *sentiments?*—It is very, very regrettable that you do not specify the article and the fact so as to be sure to what inquisition you are referring. One must know and understand the usage of words and one should not be jesting with such words as "inquisition."

What particularly displeases you is the heading "commonness of religion." Go and help him, but for other motives—but not because of commonness of belief. But, to begin with, this "motive" is not invented; it has not been searched for; it came and revealed itself of its own accord; it was revealed by everybody at once. This is an historical motive, and its *history* persists up to the present day. You write: "One should not be attributing to the movement in support of the Slavs a religious character, constantly mentioning 'our fellow-believers.' " But, what shall we do about history and actual life? Should or should one not be attributing religious character, it appears of its own accord. Please consider: the Turk slaughters the Slavs because the latter—being a Christian, a Gentile—dares to seek equal rights with him. Were a Bulgarian to embrace Mohammedanism, the Turk would forthwith cease to torture him; on the contrary, he would at once recognize him as his kinsman—thus it is according to the Koran. Consequently, if Bulgarians are enduring such ferocious tortures, of course it is because of their Christianity; this is as clear as daylight. How, then, can a Russian, sending his contribution to the Slav, avoid "the religious question"? Why, to a Russian, it will not even occur to avoid it.

And, aside from the historical and current necessity, the Russian knows nothing, and even can conceive nothing, loftier than Christianity. He has denoted his entire land, all commonnesss, the whole of Russia, as "Christianstvo," "Krestianstvo."[1] Please give thought to Orthodoxy: it is by no means merely churchism and ritualism. It is a live sentiment which, in our people, has become one of those basic living forces without which nations cannot exist. Strictly speaking, in Russian Christianity there is no mysticism at all—there is humaneness, the mere image of Christ; at least, this is the essential.

In Europe, clericalism and churchism have long and justly been viewed with apprehension: over there, particularly in certain

[1]In Russian the word "Christianity" is "Christianstvo"; the word "peasantry"—"Krestianstvo." (B. B.)

localities, they are impeding the free course of life, every progress of life, and—it goes without saying—religion itself. But does our calm, humble Orthodoxy resemble the prejudicial, gloomy, plotting, intriguing and cruel clericalism of Europe? How, then, can it not be dear to the people? Popular aspirations are generated by the whole people, and they are not concocted in the journalistic editorial offices. "Should one or should one not"—the thing is going to be as it actually is.

For instance, you write further: "The noble cause of freedom perceived in the ranks of its defenders—Russians. From this viewpoint alone, which is even more exalted than sympathy resulting from common belief and even commonness of race, the Slavic cause is a sacred cause."—You are right: this is a very lofty motive; however, what does the motive of common belief express? It specifically signifies a jaded, crucified unfortunate, and it is against his oppression that I am rising with indignation. This means: "Give thy life for the oppressed, for thy neighbor; no nobler deed exists" —this is what the motive of common faith expresses!

Besides, I venture to remark—this, however, merely in general—that it is dangerous to seek "captions" and "headings" for good deeds. If, for instance, I am helping a Slav, as my fellow-believer, this is not a heading at all; this is merely a designation of his historical status at a given moment: "He is a fellow-believer—consequently, a Christian—and because of this he is being oppressed and tortured." But if I should say that I am helping him because of "the noble cause of freedom," thereby, as it were, I am setting forth the reason for my help. And if the reason for help be sought, Montenegrins, for instance, and Herzegovinians, who have manifested the noble longing for freedom more than the rest, would prove more worthy than others; Serbians—a little less, while Bulgarian men and women did not rise at all for liberty, except, perhaps, in the beginning, in small bands in the mountains. They simply howled when finger after finger—with intervals of five minutes to prolong the torture—was chopped off their little children by their tormentors, and this in the presence of the fathers and mothers. They even did not defend themselves and, merely wailing and agonizing, as if in a state of madness, they kissed the feet of the brutes—to make them cease their torture and restore to them their poor beloved ones. Well, maybe, these should be helped least since they have only suffered, and did not rise to the level of the noble cause of freedom —"this first blessing of man." Let us admit that you will not reason so nastily, but you should concede that, by introducing reasons and "motives" for humaneness, one is almost always apt to arrive at conclusions somewhat of this kind. It is best to help simply because a man is unhappy. Help, to a co-religionist, means precisely this. I repeat: the word "fellow-believer," in Russia, does by no means signify a clerical caption, but merely a historical designation. Believe me, "commonness of religion," too, is quite devoted to, and cherishes, the noble and great cause of freedom. Moreover, it is and always will be ready to die for it, when the need comes. And at present I am only voicing my opposition to the erroneous application of European ideas to Russian reality. . . .

4

FEARS AND APPREHENSIONS

The funniest part is that the esteemed theoretician forebodes in the contemporaneous enthusiasm for the Slavs a serious danger to us, and exerts his efforts to hasten to warn us against it. He believes that in a moment of self-seduction we will issue to ourselves a "certificate of maturity" and will go to sleep on the oven. Here is what he writes:

"In this sense we deem dangerous all deliberations—frequently coming to our notice—apropos of contributions for the benefit of the Slavs to the effect that: 'these facts reveal in Russian society a comforting animation; they prove that Russian society has grown mature. . . .' The inclination to admire ourselves in a mirror, apropos of international questions and declarations of sympathy with this or that nationality, then to be falling asleep as soundly as hard-working men who have fulfilled their duty, is so great in us that all such deliberations, though partly correct, are positively dangerous. For we did triumph over our readiness for sacrifices at the beginning of the Crimean War; we did celebrate our public maturity in connection with the communiqués of our Chancellor in 1863, and the cordial welcome given by us to the officers of the North American battleship, and the collection for the benefit of the Candiots, and the ovations given to Slavic writers in Petersburg and Moscow. Read what had been written in the newspapers at that time, and you will be convinced that certain phrases at present are being literally reiterated. . . . Let us ask ourselves: what has come of all those 'maturities' which we celebrated one after another, and did those moments in which we celebrated them advance us? . . . But we should remember that by following an inclination we do not acquire the rights to the issuance to us of 'a certificate of maturity' . . ."

To begin with, everything here—from the first word to the last—is in discord with reality. "The inclination to be falling asleep as soundly as hard-working men who have fulfilled their duty, is so great in us," etc. This "inclination to be falling asleep" is one of the most prejudicial and erroneous accusations of antiquated theory, which was fond of chattering much and of doing nothing, and which precisely always lay on the oven preaching morals from the top of it and, in self-enchantment with its beauty, continually looked at itself through the mirror. This prejudicial, and at present incredibly bureaucratized, accusation came into being at a time when the Russian, even if he lay on the oven or did nothing but play cards, acted in this way solely because he was not permitted to do anything; he was prevented from doing anything and prohibited from doing anything. But the moment fences in Russia were pushed asunder, the Russian forthwith revealed feverish restlessness and impatience for, and even perseverance in, work rather than the desire to get up on the oven. However, if work is still lagging, it is not because it is not being done but because in the face of a two-hundred-year desuetude from any work it is impossible to acquire at once the faculty of grasping business and approaching it correctly, and the ability to handle it. In accordance with the old custom, you delight in preaching morals and in scolding the Russian. I am say-ing this to the old theoreticians, who from the heights of their gran-deur never deigned to give thought to Russian life, to learn at least something of it, or, say, to check and correct their prejudicial views of days long gone by.

However, this apprehension is quite worthy of Kifa Mokievich —I mean concerning "the certificate of maturity." We—it is argued—shall issue to ourselves a certificate of maturity, and then we shall rest and fall asleep. This is antiquated theoretism which, on the contrary, has long ago issued to itself a certificate of maturity, which is inclined to self-adoration, to preaching morals and to sweet half-slumber. But such youthful, beautiful, unifying movements, carried on by society *in toto*, as have been registered this year, are apt to prompt further progress and perfection. Such moments leave in their wake nothing but a beneficent trace.

And whence could you deduce that Russian society is inclined toward self-admiration and looking at itself in a mirror?—All the facts contradict this contention. On the contrary, it is the most self-distrusting and self-castigating society in the whole world! . . . Not only did we sympathize with the Slavs: we have also liberated the peasants. Yet, look: has there ever in the history of the Russian people been a more sceptical, a more self-analyzing moment than that which we have lived through during these last twenty years?—During these years, in the distrust of ourselves, we have reached pathological extremes, inadmissible scoffing at ourselves, undeserved contempt for ourselves, and certainly we were far removed from self-enchantment with our perfection. You say that we sympathized with the Cretans, that we gave welcome to a battleship, and that on every occasion we wrote about our maturity, whereas nothing came of it. After that, you are ceasing to understand the most everyday phenomena not only of Russian but of universal life. For if, at the time, we have somewhat exaggeratedly rejoiced over ourselves and our successes—this is so natural in a youthful society longing for life, still too credulous of life and seriously looking upon its mission! This happens to any people, always and everywhere. Take any ancient book in the world—and you will see that such an identical *first* youthful delight with one's own success was peculiar even to the most ancient peoples, and, therefore, it has existed since the beginning of the world, provided these peoples were young and full of life and of the future. We may have experienced a too premature joy caused by our successes and by the fact that, finally, we did give up playing cards and began to attend to business. However, is this in the least dangerous, as the warner declares with anxiety?— On the contrary, these very men who accept actual life seriously and joyously, with such a feeling and such a heart—these very men will not let themselves fall asleep through over-confidence. Believe me that life which has been once aroused and which has started gushing forth as a hot spring, shall not stop. Self-enchantment will instantly vanish, and the stronger it was, the surer the salutary sobering is going to ensue to the accompaniment of the forward, and ever forward, motion. But though we shall grow sober, nevertheless we shall respect our recent salutary, youthful, noble and innocent delight. You ask: what has come of these "maturities"? What do you mean?—Perhaps this present moment is their outcome. And if there had been no enthusiasm about the Cretans and the reception of the Slavic guests—nothing would have ensued at present. Society has grown more serious; it became acquainted with a certain cycle of ideas and conceptions. For goodness' sake, everything in the world is forming gradually; the peoples, too, are forming gradually and are not born, ready-made, petty, sober-minded little pedants. And what makes you angry?—"We"—you allege—"are too excited about the movement." But premature wisdom, pedantry in youth playing the part of old men, is more dangerous. You dislike every live movement; you prefer didacticism—well, this is your taste. Oh, of course, you immediately cite the example of Europe: "France"— you say—"has done far more for Italy than we are presently doing for the Slavs. However, did French society, after the liberation of Europe, consider itself maturer than theretofore?" This is what you write. Now, this is impossible! Whom did you find for us as an example of modesty?—France?—But when did a Frenchman not look

at himself through a mirror? When did he not admire himself?—
Under Napoleon I, for instance, the French incited general European
hatred against themselves by their intolerable haughty air, their
boundless self-contentment and their all-embracing beatitude. Strictly
speaking, such they were always, till the very year of 1871. However, at present France is internally too disunited a nation and, for
this reason, it is difficult to survey her in this respect. Well, what
would you say about the English and, in particular, the Germans?
—How they dislike to look at themselves in a mirror! How they
dislike to brag—especially the Germans! And how sound are your
historical inferences: "France"—you claim—"has done far more for
Italy than we are presently doing for the Slavs. . . ." I assure you
that France, as such, has done nothing at all for Italy. Napoleon III
has liberated Northern Italy in accordance with his own political
schemes, and we do not know at all whether the French people,
of their own accord, would have liberated Italy without Napoleon
III and his political considerations. At least, it is very difficult to
determine whether the liberation of the Italians would have been
for their liberation or for a political usurpation of a certain kind. . . .
Now, we still believe that both Napoleon III and France herself,
subsequently, have been beholding, without any too great admiration,
the exploits of Cavour, and when that very loud *"Jamais!"* of the
French government had sounded, with respect to the further claims
of the Italians to Rome, the French people listened to this *"jamais,"*
perhaps, very approvingly.

Of course, nevertheless, it is true that France did more for
Italy than we, Russians, so far have done for the Slavs. The matter
is not yet closed, and its subsequent results are known only to God.
Still, it is difficult to suppose that a movement so sincere, a movement full of love and already supported by exploits of the greatest
self-denial—the Russian movement in support of the Slavs—should
need such instructive examples of valor as the liberation of Northern
Italy by Napoleon III. . . .

However, you are setting forth to the Russian people as an
example of magnanimity even the Hungarians. Particularly now the
Hungarians are lovely and magnanimous! Are they? What a narrow hatred they nourish against any thought of the alleviation of
the lot of the Slavs! What a hatred against Russia! How could
such an example and such a people come to your mind? . . .

Post-Scriptum

I repeat: I regret very much that I have dwelt at such length
on this subject, but in these words—quite innocent—of the unques-

tionably clever and kind, but somewhat antiquated, author—in the
tone in which these words were uttered, I seem to have discerned
sounds of voices, perhaps of the very near and bad future, and, for
this reason, I could not restrain myself. . . . Of course, these future
potential voices have nothing in common with the voice from *The
Messenger of Europe,* but somehow I seem to have heard them.

Indeed, should it so happen that by force of circumstances all
this kindly, noble Russian movement in support of the Slavs should
come to naught, that the cause should prove a failure and everybody, then, return and keep silent—oh, what new outcries we
should then be hearing, and in what a victorious and triumphant
tone, no longer innocent but sarcastic—malignant outcries, celebrating victory! Then, voices would freely sound, which at present—for
the time being—are hushed or which sing in unison with "the noble
impulse." Laughter would burst out straight into the face of this
noble impulse, and men of the noble impulse would again grow shy
and timid, while quite a few of them would believe—"yes, this
should have been anticipated"; this what they, poor things, would
say. "Aha, did you win, you believers?"—would vociferate the victorious ones. "What came of your communion, of your 'unifying
thought'? You were duped, you valiant knights! Clever men knew
in advance how the thing was going to end! Could this have been
otherwise? The cause is not worth a broken egg-shell! So, you have
issued to yourselves a certificate of maturity—eh? Have you now
grown more mature, gentlemen? No, brother, recoil to your corner
and keep giggling into your hand as heretofore—that will be better!"
This is what is going to sound, and also many other things—all of
which cannot be recorded. And how much cynicism would again at
once appear, how much incredulity in our forces—incredulity in Russia herself. Once more a requiem would be sung over her. And how
many rascals would appear! And how many youths pure in heart
would run away from society! Again—disunion! Again—vacillation!

By the way, Viscount Beaconsfield, when speaking of our
destructive elements, of course, knew he was lying. Perhaps he may
have foreboded that even if we have destructive elements, they must
assume a new orientation as a result of the new impulse of Russia.
And such a thought would be rather vexing to Viscount Tarantula.
Now, however—I mean, in case of failure of the "impulse"—the
tarantula would feel very happy—he knows why! But . . . but does
this resemble truth? Will this come to pass? What a bad dream!
A dream—that's all. . . .

OCTOBER

CHAPTER I

1

A Simple but Tricky Case

ON OCTOBER 15 the court rendered a decision in the case of that stepmother who, five months earlier, in May, threw her little stepdaughter, a child of six, out of the window on the fourth floor. Through some miracle the girl was unharmed and remained in good health. That stepmother, a peasant woman, Ekaterina Kornilova, of the age of twenty, was married to a widower who, according to her testimony, used to quarrel with her; he did not permit her to visit her relatives, and did not receive them at home; he reproached her over his late wife—for the fact that when the latter was alive his business was better, etc. In a word, "he drove her to the point where she ceased to love him," and, in order to take revenge upon him, she made up her mind to throw out of the window his daughter by his former wife, about whom he reproached her—and this she did. Briefly—leaving aside the miraculous salvation of the child—the story appears to be rather simple and clear. The court has considered the case from this viewpoint—*i.e.*, from the standpoint of its "simplicity"—and very simply, too, has sentenced Ekaterina Kornilova, "who at the time of the perpetration of the crime was older than seventeen and younger than twenty years, to forced labor for a term of two years and eight months, and upon the expiration of that term —to exile to Siberia for life."

However, despite all the simplicity and clearness, there is in the case something, as it were, unexplained. The defendant (a woman with a rather pretty face) was tried in the last period of her pregnancy, so that, for any eventuality, a midwife had been summoned into the courtroom. As early as in May, when this crime took place, I wrote in the May issue of my *Diary* (however, only cursorily and in passing, when discussing the routine and bureaucratic methods of our bar) the following words: "Precisely, it is abominable. . . . whereas the act of this monster stepmother is, indeed, too queer, and, perhaps, it warrants a subtle and profound analysis which might even tend to alleviate the lot of the delinquent woman." This is what I wrote at the time. Now, please examine the facts.

First, the defendant pleaded guilty—and this immediately after the commission of the crime: she had reported it herself. At that time she told at the police station that already on the eve she made up her mind to get rid of the stepdaughter whom she began to hate because of her malice against her husband, but in the evening on that eve she had been prevented from carrying out her design by the presence of her husband. Next day, however, when he went to work, she opened the window, removed the flower pots to one side of the window sill, and then ordered the girl to climb up on it and to look down through the open window. Naturally, the girl obeyed, even readily so, thinking that she might see below the window—God only knows what. But as soon as she had climbed onto the window sill, kneeled down and, leaning with her hands against the window, looked down through it, the stepmother lifted her legs from behind, and the child fell into the open space. According to her own story, the delinquent woman, after looking down upon the fallen child, closed the window and went to the police station to report the above. Such are the facts. What, it would seem, is simpler than this—and yet how fantastic! Isn't it?—Our jurors have been accused, and often so, of some very fantastic acquittals of defendants. At times even, so to speak, the moral feelings of perfect strangers were incensed. We understand that one may pity a criminal, nevertheless it is impossible to call evil good in so important a matter as a court of justice. And yet, there have been acquittals of this kind, *i.e.*, when evil was *virtually* called good—at least, not far from it. There appeared either false sentimentality or the lack of understanding of the principle itself of justice—lack of understanding of the fact that in court the first thing, the major principle, consists of defining evil, of specifying it, if possible, and of branding it as evil, *urbi et orbi*. Afterwards, the mitigation of the criminal's lot, care for his correction, etc. —all these are different problems, very profound and great problems, but altogether different from the cause of justice, and belonging to other departments of public life, departments which, one has to admit, have not yet been clearly defined or which, in Russia, have not even been formulated. It may be said, perhaps, that with respect to these branches of public life not even the first word has been uttered.

Meanwhile, these two *different ideas* are being confused in our courts, and there has ensued God only knows what. It develops that a crime is not at all being recognized as such. On the contrary, it is, as it were, proclaimed to society—and this by the court itself— that there is no such thing as crime, that crime, don't you see, is merely sickness caused by the abnormal condition of society—an idea which, *in certain individual applications* and in specific categories of phenomena, is correct to the point of ingeniousness, but wholly erroneous in its application to the total and general, since here there is a certain line which cannot be transgressed without altogether depriving man of his individuality; without taking away from him all his selfhood and life; without placing him on the level of a tiny bit of down depending upon any stray gust of wind—briefly, without proclaiming some kind of a new nature of man which has just been discovered by some novel science. However, now there exists no such science, even in its inception. So that all these merciful jurors' verdicts (save in rare cases when they were verily appropiate and unmistakable) in which, at times, a clearly proved crime substantiated by a full confession of the criminal was directly denied: "No, not guilty; he did not commit it; he did not murder"—all these merciful verdicts surprised the people, arousing scoffs and perplexity in society.

And now, having just read about the fate of the peasant woman Kornilova (two years and eight months of forced labor), it has suddenly occurred to me: "Here is one time when they should have acquitted; here is one time when they should have said: 'There was no crime; she did not murder; she did not throw anyone out of the window.'" However, I shall not dwell upon abstractnesses and sentiments in order to expound my thought. *Simply* it seems to me that here there was a most legitimate ground for the acquittal of the defendant—specifically, her pregnancy.

It is a well-known fact that during pregnancy a woman (especially with her first child) is subject to certain strange influences and impressions which strangely and fantastically affect her psyche. These influences, at times—however, in rare cases only—assume extraordinary, abnormal, almost absurd, forms. But what of the fact that this occurs rarely (*i.e.,* as exceptional phenomena)? In the present case, to those who had to decide upon the fate of a human being, it should have been sufficient that they do occur, and even only that they may occur. Doctor Nikítin, who examined the delinquent woman (after she had committed the crime), declared that in his opinion Kornílova committed her crime *consciously,* even though irritation and affect may be admitted. But, to begin with, what is the significance here of the term—*consciously?* People rarely do things unconsciously, save in a state of lunacy, in delirium, in delirium tremens. Isn't medical science itself cognizant of the fact that an act may be perpetrated, though quite consciously, nevertheless irresponsibly. Let us take the insane: the majority of their insane acts are perpetrated quite consciously, and they remember them; moreover, they can render an account of them; they will defend these acts; they will argue with you about them, and sometimes so logically that you might be nonplussed.

Of course, I am not a medical man, but I recall, for instance, a story which I heard in childhood about a certain Moscow lady

who, each time she was pregnant, and during certain periods of her
pregnancy, used to be affected by an irresistible passion for theft.
She stole articles and money from acquaintances whom she came to
visit, in shops where she would be buying something. Afterward,
these stolen articles used to be returned to their respective owners
by her family. That lady, however, was by no means poor; she was
educated and she belonged to good society. After the laspe of several
days of this strange passion, it would not even have occurred to her
to commit a theft. Even so, it stands to reason that she stole consciously and with full knowledge. Consciousness was fully retained
—only she was unable to resist the impulse. It may be presumed that
even at present, concerning these phenomena, medical science is
hardly in a position to assert anything with certainty—I mean, with
respect to their psychic aspect: subject to what specific laws do
there occur in the human soul such crises, such submissions and influences, such insane impulses without insanity; and what, strictly
speaking, does consciousness signify in these phenomena and what
role does it play? It suffices that the possibility of influences and
extraordinary submissions during a woman's pregnancy seems incontestable. . . . And what—I repeat—of the fact that these excessive
influences occur rarely? To the conscience of the judge, in cases of
this kind, it must be sufficient that, nevertheless, they may occur.
True, it may be argued: She did not intend to steal, as that other lady;
nor did she conceive anything extraordinary. On the contrary, she
did everything specifically *pertinent to the matter, i.e.,* she avenged
her hated husband by means of the murder of his daughter by his
former wife, about whom she, the defendant, had been reproached.
Still, you must admit that although this is intelligible, nevertheless
it is not simple; even though it was logical, yet you must concede
that had there been no pregnancy, this logic, perhaps, would not
have developed at all. This, for instance, might have taken place:
alone with her stepdaughter, after having been beaten by her husband, incensed by malice against him, in a state of bitter irritation,
she might have said to herself: "Wouldn't it be nice, just to punish
him, to throw that nasty little girl out of the window!"—this might
have occurred to her, *and she would not have done it.* She might
have sinned mentally, but not by deed. However, in the condition of
pregnancy, *she did it.* In either case the logic would have identical,
but the difference would have been great.

At least, if the jurors had acquitted the defendant, they could
have relied on something: "Although such pathological affects are
rare, nevertheless they do occur. What if in the present case, too,
there was an affect of pregnancy?" This is something to be considered.
At least, in such a case, mercy would have been intelligible to every-

body and would not have produced mental vacillation. And what if there should have been an error?—Better an error in mercy than in castigation—all the more so since in a case such as this nothing could have been verified. The delinquent woman is the first to consider herself guilty: she confessed immediately after having committed the crime; she also confessed six months later in court. Thus, perhaps, she will go to Siberia, sincerely and profoundly deeming herself guilty; thus she might also die, repenting in her last hour, and considering herself a murderess. And it will never occur to her or to anyone in the world that there is such a thing as a pathological affect which occurs in the condition of pregnancy, which precisely may have been the cause of everything, and that, had she not been pregnant, nothing would have happened. . . . Nay, of two errors it is better to select the error of mercy. One will sleep more peacefully. . . .

But what am I talking about?—A busy man cannot be thinking of sleep. A busy man has a hundred similar cases, and he falls asleep soundly just as soon as he hits the pillow in a state of fatigue. It is the idle fellow who, during a whole year, happens to run into one or two such cases, who has much time for deliberation. It is to him, perchance, that a thought of this kind may occur—just from indolence. In a word, indolence is the mother of all the vices.

By the way, a midwife was sitting in the courtroom: having convicted the delinquent woman, they also convicted with her her unborn infant. Isn't this strange? Let us say that this is not true; but you must concede that this seems to be very much like the truth—the fullest truth, too. In fact, even before his birth he is sentenced to Siberia with his mother, who must bring him up. If he goes with his mother, he will be deprived of his father; and should things turn out in such a way that the father would take him (I don't know whether he could do it now), he would be deprived of his mother. . . . Briefly, even prior to his birth he has been deprived of family—this is to begin with. And later, when he grows up, he will learn everything about his mother, and he will . . . However, many a thing may happen. It is best to take a *simple* view of the case. If one looks at it simply, all phantasmagorias will vanish. Thus it should be in life. I even think that all these things which appear so extraordinary are, in fact, handled in a most ordinary, a most prosaic manner—to the point of indecency. Indeed, look: this Kornilov is again a widower; his marriage is dissolved by the exile of his wife to Siberia. And now his wife—not his wife—in a few days will bear him a son (because she will certainly be permitted to deliver the child before she starts on her journey), and while she will be recovering she will be kept in the prison hospital or wherever she may be sent for that period. I'll bet you that Kornilov will visit her in a most prosaic fashion and—who knows—perhaps with that same little girl who flew out of the window. They will get together and they will be speaking about the simplest, everyday things —say, about some miserable cloth, or warm shoes and felt boots for her journey. Who knows if they will not, perhaps, get together in the heartiest manner, now that they have been divorced? And formerly they used to quarrel. Perhaps there will be no word of mutual reproach—just a bit of sighing about fate and, compassionately, one about the other. And this little girl who flew out of the window, I repeat, she will, without fail, be daily running on errands—from her father to "mama dear," bringing her "kolaches."[1] "Here, mama dear, papa is sending you a kolach, together with tea and sugar; tomorrow he will come to you himself." Perhaps the most tragic thing that is going to happen will be when bidding each other farewell at the railroad station, at the last moment, between the second bell and the third, they will start howling at the top of their voices. Following their example, the little girl will be howling, too, with her mouth wide open. Without fail, husband and wife, one after the other, will make low bows to each other: "Forgive me, *mátushka* Katerina Prokofievna; don't nourish a grudge against me!" And she, in turn: "Forgive me, too, *batiushka* Vasily Ivanovich (or whatever his name may be). I'm culpable before you. My guilt is great. . . ." At this juncture the nursling—who most certainly will be there—will start vociferating, no matter whether she takes him with her or he be left with the father. In a word, with our people there will never ensue a poem—isn't this so? They are the most prosaic people in the world, so that in this respect one feels ashamed of them. How differently all this would transpire, for instance, in Europe. What passions! What revenge! And how much dignity!— Just try to describe this case in a novel, step by step, beginning with the young bride's life at the widower's home up to the minute when she throws the girl out of the window, up to the moment when she peeps out of the window to see if the child is hurt and hastily goes to the police station; up to the time when she is sitting in the courtroom with the midwife at her side and these farewells and bows. . . . And imagine—I was about to write: "and nothing would come of it," whereas, perhaps, it might come out better than all our poems and novels, with their heroes "full of sublime foresight, whose lives are torn asunder." You know, I really cannot understand what our novelists are looking for: here is a theme for them, and let them describe it step by step—the whole truth! However, I for-

---

[1] "*Kolach*"—special white loaves which used to be very popular in Russia. (B. B.)

got the old saying: not the subject but the eye is the main thing. If one has an eye one will always find a subject. If, in you, the eye is missing, if one is blind, one will find nothing in any subject. Oh, the eye is all-important: what to one eye appears to be a poem, to another one will be merely a heap. . . .

And is it true that at present this Kornilova's verdict could not be mitigated? Is it altogether impossible? Verily, here there might have been an error. . . . I keep thinking that it was an error!

2

A FEW REMARKS ON SIMPLICITY AND SIMPLIFICATION

Now—about another thing. Now, I should like to state something about simplicity in general. I recall a little old incident which happened to me. Some thirty years ago, during our most "confused" epoch, which in some people's view was the most "rectilinear"— once upon a time, in winter, I stopped at a certain library in my neighborhood, on Meschanskaia Street (as it was then called). I was at the time pondering over a critical article, and I needed a certain novel by Thackeray—for quotations. At the library I was met by a certain miss (a damsel of those days). I asked for the novel. She listened to me with a stern expression:

"We don't keep such trash"—she cut me short with indescribable contempt, which, honest to God, I did not deserve.

Of course, this did not surprise me, since I understood what this meant. In those days there appeared many such phenomena; they sprang up somehow suddenly—with enthusiasm and spontaneity. An idea was launched into the street and assumed a most street-like appearance. It was then that Pushkin got a terrible scolding, and "boots" were exalted. Nevertheless, I made an attempt to talk the matter over:

"Do you really regard Thackeray as trash?"

"You should be ashamed of yourself for asking me this. Nowadays, olden times are a thing of the past. At present, there is rational demand for . . ."

And thus I walked out, leaving the damsel very pleased with herself and with the lesson she taught me. However, the simplicity of the view produced an awful impression on me, and it was precisely then that I started pondering over *simplicity* in general, and our Russian eagerness for generalization, in particular. This satisfaction of ours with the simple, the small and the petty, to say the least, is surprising. It may be argued that it is an insignificant and trivial incident, that the damsel was a little undeveloped fool, and—

what is most important—an uneducated girl, so that it was not worth while to recall the anecdote, especially as the girl could easily have imagined that before she came into existence everybody and Russia as a whole were fools, and then suddenly all people, including herself, had grown wise. I know all this, and I am also aware of the fact that, judging by the expression on the girl's face, she surely was able to utter nothing but those words about "rational demand" and Thackeray—and even that much was merely an echo of somebody else's opinion. Even so, the incident has ever since been retained in my memory as a comparison, an apology, almost an emblem.

Please give thought to present-day opinions, to the contemporaneous "rational demand" and to current judgments—not only on Thackeray but also on the Russian people as a whole: what a *simplicity!* What a rectilinearness! What a ready disposition to acquiesce, without further verification, in the little and the trivial! What a general impetuosity for the sake of appeasing oneself as quickly as possible, of pronouncing a judgment so as never to be bothered about it in the future! And, believe me, all this will persist in our midst for a long time. Look: everybody believes in the sincerity and effectiveness of the popular movement of this year. And yet faith seems already insufficient, and something simpler is sought. A member of a certain committee told in my presence that he had received quite a few letters with questions such as these: "Why are Slavs so essential? Why do we support the Slavs as Slavs? If Scandinavians had been in the same position, would we be helping them as we are helping the Slavs?"—In a word, what is the use of this "Slavs" caption? (Do you recall the concern about the heading of common belief in *The Messenger of Europe,* about which I spoke in the preceding issue of my *Diary?*) At first glance it would seem that here we are faced not with simplicity, not with an endeavor to simplify things: on the contrary, in these questions there sounds restlessness. However, in this case, simplicity resides precisely in the attempt to attain the *nihil* and the *tabula rasa*—consequently, in a way, to become composed. And what is simpler, more pacifying, than a zero? Also please note that in these questions—though indirectly—there begins to sound "the rational demand" and "you should be ashamed of yourself."

No doubt, there are a great many most intelligent and, so to speak, highly educated Russians who were very much displeased with this calm and humble, but firm and potent, popular dictum— and not because they failed to understand it but, on the contrary, because they understood it all too clearly, so that they were even puzzled. Unquestionably there are symptoms of a strong reaction. I am not referring to the innocent voices which could also be heard before, in the form of involuntary mumbling and disagreement due to antiquated petty principles concerning some old themes—for instance, "one shouldn't be hurrying so much and be so enthusiastic over such a cause as the support of the Slavs, who are coarse and unenlightened anyway, on the ground that they are some kind of 'brethren' of ours," etc. Nay, I am not speaking of these sensibly liberal little old men who are chewing obsolete phrases.—I am referring to the real reaction against the popular movement which, according to all indications, will very soon raise its head. This reaction naturally and unwittingly sides with those gentlemen who, having long ago simplified their view on Russia to the extreme limits of lucidity, are ready to say: "The whole phenomenon should be prohibited so that everything will be lying, as hitherto, in an inert order." And imagine that all these simplifiers are displeased with this "phenomenon" not because of its fantasticalness—*i.e.*, for example, in the sense that such an inert and dull simplicity suddenly should have dared to raise its voice as if in reality it were something conscious and live. Well, such a view would be intelligible: simply, they felt offended—nothing more. On the contrary, they are displeased with this phenomenon because suddenly, instead of being fantastic, it became so intelligible to everybody: "How did it dare to become suddenly intelligible to everybody? How did it dare to assume such a simplified and sensible appearance?" It is precisely this kind of indignation, as stated before, that also found its support in our intelligent little old men who are exerting their efforts in an endeavor to "simplify" and drag the "phenomenon" down from the conscious plane to something elemental, primordial, and, though good-natured, yet ignorant and potentially injurious. Briefly, reaction, above all, is trying its best and is resorting to every means to bring about simplification. . . .

However, as a result of such an excessive simplification of views on certain phenomena, the cause itself is at times being lost. In some cases simplicity is apt to harm the simplifiers themselves. Simplicity does not change; it is "rectilinear," and, in addition— haughty. Simplicity is the enemy of analysis. Very often it winds up in one's ceasing—because of his simplicity—to understand the subject or not perceiving it at all, so that the reverse ensues—*i.e.*, one's view from a simple one, *eo ipso*, turns into a fantastic one. In our midst this is caused by the mutual, prolonged and ever-increasing detachment of one Russia from the other. Our detachment originated precisely because of the *simplicity of one Russia's view of the other one*. It came into existence, as is known, quite a long time ago—as early as during Peter's epoch when, for the first time, there had been evolved an extraordinary simplification of upper

Russia's view of the people's Russia. Since then, from generation to generation, this view has steadily persisted in its simplification.

3

Two Suicides

Recently I happened to discuss with one of our writers (a great artist) the comicalness in life and the difficulty of defining a phenomenon by its proper word. Before that I had made the remark that I, who have known *Woe from Wit* for almost forty years, only this year have properly understood one of the most vivid characters in the comedy, namely, Molchalin—after this same writer with whom I conversed had explained to me Molchalin when, unexpectedly, he had portrayed this character in one of his satirical sketches. (Some day I am going to dwell on Molchalin. It is a great theme.)

"Do you know"—suddenly said my interlocutor, who apparently had long ago been impressed with his idea—"do you know that no matter what you might write or depict, no matter what you might record in a belletristic work, you would never be equal to reality? No matter what you might delineate, it would always be weaker than actual life. You might think that in some work you have reached the maximum of comicalness in this or that phenomenon of life, that you have caught its most ugly aspect—not at all! Reality forthwith will reveal to you such a phase along similar lines that you have never suspected, and one that exceeds everything your own observation and imagination was able to create!. . ."

This I had known ever since 1846, when I started writing—perhaps even before that. Time and again I used to be impressed with this fact, and the apparent impotence of art made me wonder about its usefulness. Indeed, trace a certain fact in actual life—one which at first glance is even not very vivid—and if only you are able and are endowed with vision, you will perceive in it a depth such as you will not find in Shakespeare. But the whole question is: *compared with whose vision, and who is able?* Indeed, not only to create and write artistic works, but also to discern a fact, something of an artist is required. To some observers all phenomena of life develop with a most touching simplicity and are so intelligible that they are not worth thinking about or being looked at. However, these same phenomena might embarrass another observer to such an extent (this happens quite often) that, in the long run, he feels unable to synthesize and simplify them, to draw them out into a straight line and thus to appease his mind. He then resorts to a different kind of simplification and *very simply* plants a bullet in his brain so as to extinguish at once his jaded mind, together with all its queries. Such are the two extremes between which the sum total of human intelligence is enclosed. But it stands to reason that never can we exhaust a phenomenon, never can we trace its end or its beginning. We are familiar merely with the everyday, apparent and current, and this only insofar as it appears to us, whereas the ends and the beginnings still constitute to man a realm of the fantastic.

By the way, last summer one of my esteemed correspondents wrote me about a strange and unsolved suicide, and all the time I have been meaning to speak about it. In that suicide everything is a riddle—both from the outside and from within. Of course, conforming to human nature, I sought somehow to unravel the enigma so as to stop at something and "to appease myself." The suicide was a young girl of twenty-three or twenty-four, the daughter of a well-known Russian emigrant; she was born abroad, of Russian parents, but almost not a Russian at all by upbringing. I believe there was a vague mention of her in the newspapers at the time, but the details are most curious: "She soaked a piece of cotton in chloroform, tied it around her face and lay down on the bed. . . . And thus she died. Before she died, she wrote the following note:

" 'Je m'en vais entreprendre un long voyage. Si cela ne réussit pas qu'on se rassemble pour fêter ma résurrection avec du Cliquot. *Si cela réussit,* je prie qu'on ne me laisse enterrer que tout à fait morte, puisqu'il est très desagréable de se réveiller dans un cercueil sous terre. *Ce n'est pas chic!'* "

Which means:

"I am undertaking a long journey. If I should not succeed, let people gather to celebrate my resurrection with a bottle of Cliquot. *If I should succeed,* I ask that I be interred only after I am altogether dead, since it is very disagreeable to awake in a coffin in the earth. It is not *chic!*"

In this nasty, vulgar *"chic,"* to my way of thinking, there sounds a protest, perhaps indignation, anger—but against what? Simply vulgar persons destroy themselves by suicide only owing to a material, visible, external cause, whereas by the tone of the note one may judge that no such cause could have existed in her case. Against what, then, could the indignation be?—Against the simplicity of the visible, against the meaninglessness of life? Was she one of those well-known judges and deniers of life who are indignant against the "absurdity" of man's appearance on earth, the nonsensical casualness of this appearance, the tyranny of the inert cause with which one cannot reconcile himself? Here we seem to be dealing with a soul which revolted against the "rectilinearness" of the phenomena, which could not stand this rectilinearness conveyed to her since childhood in her father's house. The ugliest thing is that, of course, she died devoid of any distinct doubt. It is most probable that her soul was devoid of distinct doubt or so-called queries. Likewise, it is quite probable that she implicitly believed, without further verification, everything which had been imparted to her since childhood. This means that she simply died of "cold, darkness and tedium" with, so to speak, animal and un-accountable suffering; she began to suffocate as if there were not enough air. The soul unaccountably proved unable to bear rectilinearness, and unaccountably demanded something more complex. . . .

About a month ago there appeared in all Petersburg newspapers a few short lines, in small type, about a Petersburg suicide: a poor young girl, a seamstress, jumped out of a window on the fourth floor "because she was utterly unable to find work for her livelihood." It was added that she jumped and fell to the ground, *holding a holy image in her hands*. This holy image in the hands is a strange, as yet unheard-of, trait in a suicide! This was a timid and humble suicide. Here, apparently, there was no grumbling or reproach: simply it became impossble to live, "God does not wish it"—and she died, having said her prayers.

There are certain things—much as they may seem *simple*—over which one does not cease to ponder for a long time; they come back in one's dreams, and one even thinks that he is to be blamed for them. This meek soul which destroyed itself involuntarily keeps vexing one's mind. It was precisely this death that reminded me of the suicide of the emigrant's daughter, which was communicated to me last summer. But how different are these two creatures; they seem to have come from two different planets! How different these two deaths! and which of these two souls had suffered more on earth—if such an idle question is becoming and permissible?

4

The Verdict

Apropos, here is the deliberation of a suicide *out of tedium*—of course, a materialist.

"... Indeed, what right did this nature have to bring me into this world pursuant to some of her eternal laws? I am created with consciousness and I did *conceive* nature: what right had she, therefore, to beget me without my will, without my will as a conscious creature?—Conscious implies suffering, but I do not wish to suffer, since why should I consent to suffering? Nature, through the medium of my consciousness, proclaims to me some sort of harmony of the whole. Human consciousness has produced religions out of this message. Nature tells me—even though I know well that I neither can nor ever shall participate in this 'harmony of the whole,' and besides, that I shall never even comprehend what it means—that nevertheless I must submit to this message, abase myself, accept suffering because of the harmony of the whole, and consent to live. However, if I were 'to make a conscious choice, of course I should rather wish to be happy only that moment when *I* exist, whereas I have no interest whatever in the whole and its harmony after *I* perish, and it does not concern me in the least whether this whole with its harmony remains in the world after me or whether it perishes simultaneously with me. And why should I bother about its preservation after I no longer exist?—that's the question. It would have been better to be created like all animals—*i.e.*, living but not conceiving myself rationally. But my consciousness is not harmony, but, on the contrary, precisely disharmony, because with it I am unhappy. Look: who is happy in this world and what kind of people *consent* to live?—Precisely those who are akin to animals and come nearest to their species by reason of their limited development and consciousness. These readily consent to live but on the specific condition that they live as animals, *i.e.*, eat, drink, sleep, build their nest and bring up children. To eat, drink and sleep, in the human tongue, means to grow rich and to plunder, while to build one's nest pre-eminently signifies—to plunder. Perhaps I may be told that one may arrange one's life and build one's nest on a rational basis, on scientifically sound social principles, and not by means of plunder, as heretofore.—All right, but I ask: What for? What is the purpose of arranging one's existence and of exerting so much effort to organize life in society soundly, rationally and righteously in a moral sense? Certainly no one will ever be able to give me an answer to this question. All that could be said in answer would be: 'To derive delight.' Yes, were I a flower or a cow, I should derive delight. But, incessantly putting questions to myself, as now, I cannot be happy even in the face of the most lofty and *immediate* happiness of love of neighbor and of mankind, since I know that tomorrow all this will perish: I and all the happiness, and all the love, and all mankind will be converted into naught, into former chaos. And on such a condition, under no consideration, can I accept any happiness—and not because of my refusal to accept it, not because I am stubbornly adhering to some principle, but for the simple reason that I will not and cannot be happy on the condition of being threatened with tomorrow's zero. This is a feeling—a direct and immediate feeling—and I cannot conquer it. All right: if I were to die but mankind, instead of me, were to persist forever, then, perhaps, I might nevertheless be consoled. However, our planet is not eternal, while mankind's duration is just as brief a moment as mine. And no matter how rationally, happily, righteously and holily mankind might organize its life on earth—tomorrow all this will be made equal to that same zero. And even though all this be necessary, pursuant to some almighty, eternal and fixed law of nature, yet, believe me, in this idea there is some kind of most profound disrespect for mankind which, to me, is profoundly insulting, and all the more unbearable as here there is no one who is guilty.

"And, finally, even were one to presume the possibility of that tale about man's ultimate attainment of a rational and scientific organization of life on earth—were one to believe this tale and the future happiness of man, the thought itself that, because of some inert laws, nature found it necessary to torture them thousands and thousands of years before granting them that happiness —this thought itself is unbearably repulsive. And if you add to this that this very nature which, finally, had admitted man to happiness will, for some reason, tomorrow find it necessary to convert all this into zero despite all the suffering with which mankind has paid for this happiness and—what is most important— without even bothering to conceal this from my consciousness, as it did conceal it from the cow—willy-nilly, there arises a most amusing, but also unbearably sad, thought: 'What if man has been placed on earth for some impudent experiment—just for the purpose of ascertaining whether or not this creature is going to survive on earth?' The principal sadness of this thought is in the fact that here, again, there is no guilty one; no one has conducted the experiment; there is no one to damn, since everything simply came to pass as a result of the inert laws of nature, which I do not understand at all, and with which my consciousness is altogether unable to reconcile itself. *Ergo:*

"Inasmuch as to my questions on happiness I am receiving from nature, through my own consciousness, only the answer that I can be happy not otherwise than within the harmony of the whole, which I do not comprehend, and which, it is obvious to me, I shall never be able to understand——

"Inasmuch as nature not only does not admit my right to demand an account from her, but even gives me no answer whatsoever—and not because she does not want to answer, but because she is unable to give me an answer——

"Inasmuch as I have convinced myself that nature, in order to answer my queries, designates (unconsciously) *my own self* and answers them with my own consciousness (since it is I who say all this to myself)——

"Finally, since, under these circumstances, I am assuming both the roles of a plaintiff and of a defendant, that of an accused and of a judge; and inasmuch as I consider this comedy, on the part of nature, altogether stupid, and to be enduring this comedy on my own part—even humiliating——

"Now, therefore, in my unmistakable role of a plaintiff and of a defendant, of a judge and of an accused, I sentence this nature, which has so unceremoniously and impudently brought me into existence for suffering, to annihilation, together with myself. . . . And because I am unable to destroy nature, I am destroying only myself, weary of enduring a tyranny in which there is no guilty one.

N. N."

CHAPTER II

1

A New Phase in the Eastern Question

THE EASTERN question has entered its second period, while the first period has come to an end, but not because of the alleged defeat of Cherniaiev. In this way also Suvorov was defeated in Switzerland, since he was compelled to retreat: but can we concede that Suvorov was defeated?—He was not to be blamed for the fact that he led the Russian people to France under impossible circumstances. We are not comparing Cherniaiev with Suvorov; we merely wish to say that there are circumstances in which even the Suvorovs retreat. True, at present in Petersburg some of our future army chiefs are loudly criticizing the military operations of Cherniaiev, while politicians are beginning to vociferate that he is specifically guilty of the fact that he led the Slavs and the Russian people into battle "under impossible circumstances." However, all these future army chiefs of ours have

not, as yet, experienced the pressure to which Cherniaiev was
subjected. All these military men are still civilians who seek to
invent powder, never having smelled it. And, as for politicians, they
had better recall the legend about the Suvorov ditch in Switzerland,
into which he jumped, ordering the soldiers to fill it up with earth
"if they refuse to obey him and follow him." Our good soldiers
burst into tears, took him out of the ditch and began to follow
him. Well, it seems that it is the Russian people who will extricate
Cherniaiev from the ditch which the Serbian intrigue has dug
for him. You have forgotten, gentlemen, that Cherniaiev is a popular
hero, and it is not for you to bury him in a ditch.

The Eastern question has entered its second period as a
result of the thunder-word of the Czar which resounded in the
hearts of all Russians, as a benediction—and in the hearts of all
enemies of Russia, as dread. The Porte yielded and accepted the ultimatum, but what will happen further is now more unknown than
ever. There are rumors of a conference in Constantinople (or
wherever it may be—what difference does it make?)—of a diplomats'
convention. Thus, again it is diplomacy—to the joy of those who
adorn it!

And now, after Russia's thunder-word, the European press
will again begin to preach to us. For even the Hungarians, on the
eve of our ultimatum, wrote and printed about us that we were
afraid of them and that, for this reason, we were manœuvring before
them, not daring to announce our intent. Once more the English
will start intriguing and telling us what we should be doing,
imagining that we are so afraid of them. Even a France of some
sort, even she with a haughty and bombastic air, will utter her
word at the conference, stating "what she wants and what she
doesn't want," whereas what do we care about France, and why
the devil should we be interested in what she wants or doesn't
want? At present, it is not 1853 and, perhaps, never has there
been a moment when Russia's enemies have been more harmless
to her than in our day. But let diplomacy begin to reign, to the
consolation of its Petersburg amateurs. However, Bulgaria, the
Slavs—what is going to happen to them in the course of these two
months? This is a pressing matter which cannot be postponed even
for a minute. What is going to happen to them in the course of
these two months? Perhaps Bulgarian blood will flow again! For
the Porte has to prove to her softas that it was not from cowardice
that she accepted the ultimatum. And Bulgaria will have to pay for
this: "You can see we are not afraid of the Russians if we slaughter
the Bulgarians at the time of the conference itself!" Now, what
are we going to do in an event which is so probable? Shall we

THE DIARY OF A WRITER

declare our indignation right there—at the conference?—But the Porte will immediately deny the massacre, will put all the blame on the Bulgarians themselves, and, perhaps, she will assume a nobly offended air, and will promptly appoint an investigating committee: "You can see for yourselves, gentlemen-representatives of Europe, how I am being affronted and how Russia keeps nagging at me!" Meanwhile, they will keep slaughtering the Bulgarians and, maybe, the European press will once more lend its support to the bashi-bazouks; it may contend that Russia keeps nagging because of her amour-propre; that she is deliberately intriguing against the conference, that she wants war and . . . And it is very possible that Europe will again suggest a peace which would be worse than war—an intensely armed peace, a peace fraught with restlessness and agitation of the peoples, with gloomy expectations—and this, perhaps, for a whole year! . . . Again, a whole year of uncertainty! . . . Well, and in a year—after such a peace—of course there will be war. The Slavs are in need of peace but not of such a peace. Nor is peace at all needed at present—but simply an end.

However, voices have been raised against Cherniaiev—and these are but first skirmishes. Wait: later the chorus will grow larger and stronger. The main point here is not Cherniaiev: this is a reaction against the movement of this year as a whole. *The Petersburg Gazette,* in an excellent article, in rebuttal to the attacks against Cherniaiev, foretold to *The Stock-Exchange Gazette* that it would lose its subscribers and that the public would turn away from it. At present this will hardly come to pass: nowadays there are a great many people with whom *The Stock-Exchange Gazette* is singing in unison. "Those are the very people in whom, during this year, there has accumulated much bitterness—angry and irritated people who call themselves pre-eminently men of order. To them the whole movement of this year is nothing but disorder, while Cherniaiev is merely a scoundrel: 'a lieutenant-general, and yet he rushed to seek adventure like some condottiere!' These, however, are men, so to speak, of bureaucratic order. But there are other amateurs of order, men belonging to the upper strata of the intelligentsia, who perceive with a bleeding heart that so many forces are wasted on such a medieval cause, so to speak, whereas schools, for example . . .," etc. Those attacking Cherniaiev are vociferating that Russian blood has been spilled in vain *without any profit to Russia. The New Time* admirably retorted on the question of profit, and what profit means—it retorted directly and in plain words, without being ashamed of the *idealism* of the words, of which everybody is so ashamed.

As early as in June, at the inception of the movement, I

happened to write in the *Diary* on the subject of how, in this case, the profit to Russia should be conceived. Such a lofty organism as Russia is should also be radiating an enormous spiritual meaning. Russia's gain is not in the seizure of Slavic provinces, but in a sincere and animated concern about them—in their protection, in brotherly union with them, and in the conveyance to them of our spirit and view on the reunion of the Slavic world. Such a lofty organism as Russia cannot be satisfied with mere material gain—with "bread" alone. And this is not an ideal, not phrases: the Russian people *in toto* and their whole movement of this year are proof of this. This is a movement which is unprecedented in other peoples in its self-renunciation and disinterestedness, in its devout religious thirst for *suffering for a right cause*. Such a people cannot inspire fear with respect to order; this is not a people of disorder but a people of firm views and indomitable principles, cherishing sacrifice and seeking truth; a people who know where truth is; a meek, but strong, honest people, pure in heart, like one of their lofty ideals—that valiant knight Ilya-Murometz, who is venerated as a saint. The heart of the Keeper of such a people should rejoice when beholding them—and it does rejoice, and the people know it! No, there was no disorder here. . . .

2

CHERNIAIEV

At present, even Cherniaiev's defenders regard him *not as a genius* but merely as a valiant and a brave general. However, the fact itself that in a Slavic cause he has headed the whole movement constitutes ingenious foresight, and only an ingenious force is capable of resolving such problems. The Slavic cause, of necessity, had to *begin* at last—*i.e.*, to embark upon its active phase —and without Cherniaiev it would not have reached such development. It might be said that herein lies the trouble—that he gave it a push, that he has swelled it to such proportions; that herein is his fault, and that he has started it at an inopportune moment. Even so, the great Slavic question had to be raised, and, in truth, I do not know whether it is possible to argue about its opportuneness. But once the Slavic cause has started, who, if not Russia, should have headed it?—Herein is Russia's mission, and Cherniaiev grasped it and hoisted the banner of Russia. To make this decision, to take this step—nay, nay, this could not have been done by a man devoid of a special power.

It may be said that all this was caused by ambition—that

he is an adventurer, seeking to distinguish himself. Yet, in such cases, ambitious men prefer to play a sure game, and even if they do take any risk, it is to a certain extent only: in circumstances threatening sure failure, they immediately forsake the cause. A sure failure of *immediate* military success, with no one but the Serbs and without the help of the Russians, Cherniaiev has, of course, anticipated long ago. At present too much is already known, too much has been fully explained in this story, for entertaining any doubts concerning this point. But he was unable to desert the cause since it is not confined to *immediate* military success: the future of both Russia and the Slavic countries resides in this cause. At any rate, his hope for Russia's immediate help was not mistaken since Russia has finally uttered her great decisive word. Had it been uttered only a little earlier, Cherniaiev would have erred in nothing. Indeed, in his place many a man would have refused to wait so long—namely, ambitious men and careerists. I am convinced that not a few among his critics would not have suffered half of the things which he has endured. However, Cherniaiev was serving an enormous cause and not merely gratifying his ambition, and he preferred to sacrifice everything—his fate, his fame, his career, perhaps his very life—rather than to forsake the cause, since he was laboring for the honor and *benefit* of Russia, and of this he was conscious. For the Slavic cause is the Russian cause, and *ultimately* it must be settled by Russia alone and in accord with the Russian idea. He stayed also because of the Russian volunteers who had converged under his banner for the sake of an idea which he represented. Certainly he could not have left them alone—and, again, in this there is an element of magnanimity. How many of his critics would have abandoned everything and everybody—the idea, and Russia, and volunteers, as many of them as there might be! For one must tell the truth.

Cherniaiev is also criticized by the military. However, to begin with, these military were not in Cherniaiev's position; and, secondly, after all, the task which Cherniaiev has actually accomplished "under impossible circumstances," could not, perhaps, have been achieved by any one of his critics. These "impossible circumstances," which exercised such a strong influence upon the military developments, also belong to history. Still, their salient traits are already known, and they are so typical that they cannot be overlooked even from a strategic standpoint. If it is true that the intrigue against Cherniaiev has reached the point where the highest bureaucrats of the country, in their distrustful hatred against a Russian general suspected by them, at the most critical moments have left his most urgent requests and demands for the army *without*

answer, and even on the eve of the last and decisive battles left
him without artillery shells—is just criticism of the military operations possible without the elucidation of this point?—All these intrigues, all this irritation, are unprecedented: anyhow, this general,
suspected by them, was the leader of their armed forces, and he
defended the doorway to Serbia. And, swayed by anger and hate,
they sacrificed everything—the army and even their fatherland—
merely for the sake of destroying a man disagreeable to them. At
least, such is the situation according to most accurate information.

The unquestionable fact of an intrigue is certified by all
correspondents and all European papers: it started in Belgrade
and all the time emanated thence, ever since Cherniaiev's arrival
in Serbia. This intrigue was strongly fostered by the English as
a matter of politics; it was also furthered by certain Russians—
why by these no one knows. It is very possible that in the beginning Cherniaiev in some way piqued the amour-propre of the
Serbian bureaucrats. However, no doubt, the main source of their
distrustful and unquenchable irritation against him was that about
which I have already spoken before—*i.e.,* the preconceived idea
entertained by many Serbs that should the Slavs be liberated by
the Russians, this would be done solely for Russia's benefit, and
that Russia would annex them and deprive them of "their so
eminent and indubitable political future." As is known, they ventured to declare war on Turkey even prior to Cherniaiev's arrival,
precisely because they dreamed of heading the Slavic movement,
and—after the defeat of the Sultan—of forming a united Slavic
Serbian Kingdom with a population of several millions and "with
so eminent a future." A large and influential Serbian party has
been dreaming of nothing but that. Briefly, those were dreamers
resembling little seven-year-old children who put on toy epaulets
and imagine themselves generals. Cherniaiev and the volunteers,
naturally, must have frightened the *party* "by the ensuing seizure
by Russia coming in their footsteps." And, no doubt, at present,
after the recent military reverses, there will arise among them—it
has already arisen—strong friction. All these dreamers will now
silently—and, perhaps, even aloud—begin to abuse the Russians,
asserting that it was precisely due to the Russians that calamity
befell them. Still, after a while, salutary reaction will set in, since
all these suspicious Serbs are, nevertheless, ardent patriots. They
will recall the Russian dead who gave their lives for their Serbian
country. The Russians will depart but the great idea will remain.
The great Russian spirit will leave its imprint in their souls, and
out of the Russian blood which has been shed for them, their own
valor will grow. For some day they will convince themselves that

Russian help was disinterested and that none of the Russians, who were killed for them, had any idea of annexing them!

However, all this should not alienate us from the Slavs. There are two Serbias: the upper Serbia, impetuous and inexperienced, which as yet has neither lived nor acted, but which is passionately dreaming about the future—the Serbia already having her parties and breathing with intrigues which, at times, reach such proportions (again because of impetuous inexperience) as cannot be encountered in any nation which has lived long and which is infinitely greater and more independent than Serbia. But alongside this upper Serbia, which is in such haste to live politically, there is the popular Serbia which deems the Russians only to be their saviors and brethren, and the Russian Czar their sun—the Serbia which loves the Russians and trusts them. It is impossible to formulate the view on this subject better than did *The Moscow Gazette,* undeniably our best political newspaper. Here are its words:

"We are convinced that the sentiments of the Russian people toward Serbia will not change as a result of the success of the intrigue inimical to both sides. The Serbs of the dukedom are an agricultural and peaceful people who, in the course of a long period of peace, have forgotten their militant traditions, and who have not yet had the time to evolve a firm popular consciousness such as cements every historical nation. Lastly, the Serbs of the dukedom cannot be called a people: they are but a fragment of a people devoid of organic significance. However, we cannot forget that the Serbs enthusiastically and unanimously arose in support of their consanguineous brethren who are being villainously tortured. . . . The Russian people will not desert the Serbs at this moment so terrible to them, and the blood shed by the Russians has proved how pure their sympathy was, how heroically disinterested their sacrifice was and how absurd are the hostile calumnies to the effect that Russia seeks to derive for herself some profits from Serbia's plight. Let the memory of the valiant Russian men who gave their lives for Serbia become a link of brotherly love between two peoples so close to each other by blood and religion."

In conclusion, I will say: admitting that we, Russians, have suffered, in addition to all *troubles* (?), material damages—having expended, maybe, tens of millions which, however, were spent for the organization and improvement of our armed forces (which, of course, is also good); nevertheless, the fact itself that as a result of the movement of this year we have learned who our *best men* are—this fact alone is an incomparable achievement. Oh, if only all the peoples, even the grandest and most intelligent peoples in

Europe, would firmly know and would unanimously agree as to who should be considered their genuinely best men—would Europe and European mankind appear in its present state?

3

BEST MEN

Best men—this is a theme on which it is worth while to say a few words.

Best men are they without whom no society and no nation can live and stand even in the face of the broadest equality of rights. Best men are, naturally, of two kinds: (1) those before whom the people themselves and the nation itself voluntarily of their free accord bow, revering their valor; and (2) those before whom everybody, or very many of the people or the nation, bow by reason, so to speak, of a certain coercion, and even if they conceive them to be "best men," they are doing so to a certain extent conditionally, and not altogether and as a matter of fact.

One should not repine at the existence of this "conditional" class of best men, officially recognized as such because of the supreme considerations of order and stability of administration, since this sort of "best men" exist by reason of an historical law and, thus far, they have always, from the beginning of the world, existed in all nations and states, so that no society could have formed itself and united into an entity without a certain voluntary autocoercion. Every society, in order that it may survive and live, has got to respect somebody and something, and—what is most important—society as a whole, and not as a matter of individual choice. Inasmuch as the best men of the first class—they who are genuinely valiant, before whom everybody, or the overwhelming majority of the nation, bows heartily and unhesitatingly—are, at times, somewhat elusive because they are ideal (at times they are hardly definable, are queer and peculiar, and outwardly not seldom have even a slightly incorrect appearance), in their stead best men are inaugurated *conditionally* in the form of a caste of best men under official patronage: "These you must respect." And if, besides, these "conditional" ones actually coincide with the best men of the first class (since not all men in the latter class have an incorrect appearance) and are genuinely valiant, not only is the aim achieved but it is doubly achieved. In Russia such best men, initially, were the members of the prince's bodyguard; later, the boyards and the clergy (but only the highest dignitaries), and even some eminent merchants—of these, however, there were very few.

It should be noted that both in Russia and elsewhere, *i.e.*, in Europe, these best men always elaborated for themselves a rather harmonious code of valor and honor, and even though this code on the whole was, of course, pretty contingent and, at times, greatly at variance with the ideals of the people, nevertheless in certain points it used to be quite lofty. For instance, the "best" man was unconditionally bound to give his life for his fatherland whenever such a sacrifice was required of him, and he did actually die as a matter of duty and honor "since otherwise great dishonor would be cast upon my family." And it goes without saying that this was incomparably better than the right to dishonor where a man, in a moment of danger, deserts everything and everybody and runs into hiding: "Let everything on earth perish so long as my life is safe." Thus it prevailed in Russia during a very long time; and it should also be observed that these conditional best men quite often, and in many a thing, agreed in their ideals with the unconditional, or popular, best men. Of course, not in everything—far from it—but at least it may be positively asserted that in those days there was infinitely more moral solidarity between the Russian boyards and the Russian people than almost anywhere else in Europe at that time—between the conquerors-tyrants, the knights, and the vanquished slaves—the people.

All of a sudden, however, there occurred in the organization of our best men a certain radical change: by virtue of a Czar's ukase, all best men were divided into fourteen categories, under the names of "classes," one higher than the other—in the form of a ladder—so that there came into existence fourteen grades of human valor bearing German names. In its subsequent development this change partly failed to attain the initial purpose for which it had been organized, since the former "best men" promptly occupied and filled all of the fourteen classes—only, instead of boyards, they began to be called "nobility." However, to a certain extent this change did attain its purpose because it has considerably stretched out the old fence: there ensued an influx of new forces from the lower strata of society—according to our terminology: democratic forces—especially from among seminarians. This influx has brought about, in the ranks of the best men, much that proved vivifying and productive, since there appeared gifted people with new conceptions, with a level of education which in those days was still unheard-of, who, at the same time, however, greatly despised their origin and avidly hastened to transform themselves, by the acquisition of titles, into full-blooded noblemen.

It should be noted that, aside from seminarians, only a few

individuals from among the people and the merchants found their
way into the category of "best men," and the nobility continued
to head the nation. This class was strongly organized, and whereas
in all Europe money, property, the gold bag, were honestly and
wholeheartedly conceived as everything that is valiant and best
in and among people, in Russia—and this even we can remember—
a general, for instance, was so highly esteemed that even the richest
merchant deemed it a great honor to lure him into his home for
dinner. Even recently I read an anecdote—which I should not have
believed if I had not known that it was perfectly true—about a
Petersburg lady belonging to the beau monde who, at a concert,
publicly drove from her seat a merchant-woman, worth ten millions,
occupied her place and, in addition, gave her a scolding—and this
occurred only some thirty years ago!

However, the fact should be noted that these "best" men,
who had so firmly planted themselves in their seats, acquired several
good rules—for example, virtual *obligation* for them to have some
education—so that this whole caste of best men became pre-eminently Russia's educated class, the guardian and bearer of Russian
enlightenment, whatever it may have been. It goes without saying
that it was also the sole guardian and bearer of the rules of honor
—however, quite in accord with the European standard, so that
the letter and form of the rules, in the long run, subdued the sincerity of the content: there was much honor, but of honest men
there finally remained but few.

During that period, particularly at its close, the class of "the
best" had already forsaken its ideals of "the best men," taken from
the people, so that it began to scoff openly at almost all popular conceptions of "the best." But suddenly there occurred one of the
most colossal and sweeping changes ever experienced by Russia:
serfdom was abolished and everything underwent a profound transformation. True, the fourteen classes remained as hitherto, yet the
"best men" began, as it were, to vacillate. All of a sudden the
former reverence among the rank and file of society was lost and
the conceptions of "the best" somehow changed. True, they also
partly changed for the better. Moreover, in the understanding of
what is best there ensued something altogether confusing and indeterminate. Nevertheless, the former view was no longer satisfactory,
so that in the minds of a great many people most momentous
questions arose: "Who, then, should be conceived as the *best* ones
and—most important of all—whence should they be expected, where
are they to be found, who will take it upon himself to proclaim
them as the best, and on what grounds? Finally, are these new

grounds known, and who will believe that they are precisely those ones on which so much has to be erected?" Verily, these questions began to arise in the minds of a great many people. . . .

4

ABOUT THE SAME

The whole thing was that the patronage of authority had been, as it were, withdrawn from the former "best men" and officialism was destroyed. Thus, there was this immediate consolation, that even though the former caste pattern of "the best men" had not been completely demolished, nevertheless it had considerably yielded and expanded so that any one of them, if he should seek to retain his former significance, willy-nilly, had to pass from the "conditional" best men to the category of the "natural" ones. There arose the beautiful hope that the "natural" ones would thus, little by little, assume the places of all the former "best men." But how this would come to pass remained, of course, a riddle. However, to many respectable, but impetuous and liberal, people here there was no riddle at all. In their camp everything had been decided, as though by statute, while some of them believed that everything had actually been achieved, and that if today the "natural" man has not yet assumed the first place—tomorrow, with the first rays of dawn, he will assume it without fail. Meanwhile, more reflective people kept pondering over questions arising out of the former theme: "Who are they—the natural ones? Does anyone know how they are called at present? Haven't we completely lost their ideal? Where is the generally acknowledged 'best man'? What and whom should society *in corpore* revere and whom should it imitate?"

Perhaps all these questions were not specifically framed in such terms and were not expressed in the form of these questions, nevertheless undoubtedly all this "agitation" has been felt by our society in some form or other. Ardent and enthusiastic people shouted to the sceptics that "the new man" exists, that he has been found, defined and given. Finally, it was decided that this new and "best" man is simply the enlightened man, a man of science and one *devoid of former prejudices*. This opinion, however, was unacceptable to many people by reason of this most simple consideration: that an educated man is not always honest and that science does not guarantee valor in man. At that moment of general vacillation and indeterminateness there were men who were about to suggest that we should apply to the people and resort to popular principles. But, to many of us, the term itself "popular principles" has been repulsive and hateful for a long time. Besides, the people, after their liberation, somehow did not hasten to reveal themselves in their valiant aspect, so that it was doubtful whether it would be possible to seek in them a solution to these queries. On the contrary, there were rumors about disorderliness, depravity, dreadful alcoholism, unsuccessful self-government, about kulaks and bloodsuckers of peasants, who have taken the place of the former landowners, and, finally—about the Jew. Even the "cleverest" writers have announced that the kulak and the bloodsucker are reigning supreme over the people and, besides, that the people themselves accept them as their genuine "best" men.

Finally, there came into being even a perfectly liberal view—in the strict sense of the term—to the effect that our people *cannot be* competent in the moulding of the ideal of a best man; that not only are they themselves incompetent, but they are impotent to participate in this exploit; that first they have to be taught how to read and write; that they have to be humanized and developed; that schools must be built, etc. It should be confessed that many a sceptic felt nonplussed, not knowing how to answer these contentions. . . .

Meanwhile, a new storm was coming up, a new calamity was arising—"the gold bag!" In lieu of the former "conditional" best men, a new *contingency* ensued which, in Russia, all of a sudden has acquired an awful significance. It goes without saying that "the gold bag" existed also in the past: it always existed, in the form of the merchant-millionaire; however, at no time in the past has it been placed so high—never has such a significance been attributed to it as in our day. Our former merchant, notwithstanding the role which everywhere in Europe capital and the millionaires have played, in Russia, comparatively speaking, occupied a rather insignificant place in the social hierarchy. To tell the truth—he did not deserve anything better. I will say in advance: I am speaking only about rich merchants, while the majority of them, who had not yet been corrupted by wealth, were living in the fashion of Ostrovsky's characters. Perhaps they were not worse than many others, again speaking comparatively, while the lowest and most numerous merchants virtually merged with the people. But the richer the former merchant grew, the worse he became. Essentially, he was nothing but a peasant—merely a corrupted peasant.

The former millionaire-merchants were divided into two classes: some of them continued to wear beards, despite their millions, and, in spite of the mirrors and inlaid floors in their huge mansions, lived somewhat swinishly—both in a moral and in a physical sense. The best that there was in them was their love of church bells and of vociferous deacons. However, notwithstanding this love, morally they were already detached from the people. It is difficult to conceive anything morally more contrasting than the people, on the one hand, and certain merchant-manufacturers, on the other. It is said that Ovsiannikov, when he was recently transported through Kazan to Siberia, kicked out with his feet the donated copper coins which the people naïvely threw into his carriage: this is the ultimate degree of the moral alienation from the people—a complete loss of the least understanding of the people's thought and spirit. And never have the people been in a worse bondage than in the factories owned by some of these gentlemen!

The other class of our millionaire-merchants was characterized by dresscoats and shaven chins; by the gorgeous European furnishings of their houses; by the upbringing of their daughters with the French and English languages, with pianos, and—not infrequently—by some badge acquired as a result of substantial donations; by intolerable scorn for everyone lower than they; by contempt for an ordinary "dinner"-general, and, at the same time, by the most servile humiliation before a high dignitary, especially whenever that merchant succeeded—God only knows through what intrigues and by what devices—in enticing such a dignitary to a ball or dinner which, needless to say, was given for him. This preoccupation with the problem of giving a dinner for a dignitary became the program of life. This was anxiously looked for: it was virtually for this alone that the millionaire lived on earth. It stands to reason that this former rich merchant worshipped his million as God: in his view the million was everything; the million had extricated him out of nothingness and had made him impressive. In the vulgar soul of this "corrupted peasant" (he continued to be that, despite all his dress-coats) there never could be conceived a single thought, a single feeling, which, though for a second, would raise him in his consciousness above that million of his. Naturally, despite the outward polish, the family of such a merchant grew up without any education. The million not only was not conducive to education but, on the contrary, it used to constitute in such cases the principal cause of ignorance: why should the son of such a millionaire study in a university if, without any study, he could have everything, especially since these millionaires, upon acquiring their million, quite often acquired the rights of nobility. Aside from debauch since the earliest youthful years, and the most distorted conceptions of the world, the fatherland, honor and duty, wealth contributed nothing to the souls of that carnivorous and arrogant youth. And the distortion of the world outlook was monstrous since, above all, there prevailed the conviction which assumed the form of an axiom: "With money I can buy everything, every distinction, every valor; I can bribe everybody and I can bail myself out of everything." It is difficult to imagine the extent of the aridness of heart in youths who grew up in those rich families. From boastfulness and a desire not to lag behind others, such a millionaire, at times, donated enormous sums for the benefit of the fatherland—for instance, in the case when it was threatened with danger (although this occurred but once, in 1872)—yet he made these donations in anticipation of rewards, while he was always ready, any minute of his existence, to join the first stray Jew, in order to betray everybody and everything, provided this yielded profit: patriotism, the feeling of civic duty, is almost non-existent in these hearts.

Oh, of course, I am speaking of our Russian commercial millionaire merely as a class. There are exceptions always and everywhere. In Russia, too, merchants can be pointed out who possessed European education and who distinguished themselves with worthy civic deeds. However, of such there are very few among our millionaires; every one of them is known by name. Because of exceptions, a class does not lose its character.

Now, the former limits of the merchant of days gone by were suddenly, in our day, widely set asunder. Suddenly he became affiliated with the European speculator, hitherto unknown in Russia, and the stock-exchange gambler. The contemporaneous merchant no longer needs to entice to his "dinner party" a "dignitary" or to give balls in his honor. He affiliates himself and fraternizes with the dignitary at the stock exchange, at a shareholders' meeting, in a bank which he establishes together with the dignitary. Nowadays he himself is somebody; he himself is a dignitary. The main point is that all of a sudden he found himself decidedly in one of the highest places in society, which in Europe has already long ago been officially and sincerely assigned to the millionaire. And, of course, he did not doubt that he was actually worthy of the place.

Briefly, he becomes more and more wholeheartedly convinced that it is precisely he who nowadays is "the best" man on earth, in lieu of all the former ones. But the pending calamity is not that he entertains such nonsense, but the fact that others also, it would seem (and already quite a few), begin to reason in the same way. In our day, the bag is unquestionably conceived by a *dreadful* majority to be the best of everything. Of course, these fears will be disputed. However, our present-day factual veneration of the bag is not only indisputable, but, by reason of the proportions it has assumed, it is also unprecedented. I repeat: also in the past the power of the bag was understood in Russia by everybody, but never until now has the bag been regarded as the loftiest thing on earth. In the official classification of Russians—in the social hierarchy—the former merchant's bag could not outweigh even a bureaucrat. At present, however, even the former hierarchy, without any coercion from the outside, seems to be ready to remove itself to the second place, ceding its place to the lovely and beautiful novel "condition" of the best man "who for so long a time and so erroneously did not assume his true rights." The present-day stock-exchange gambler enlists in his service littérateurs; the advocate pays court to him. "That young school turning out shrewd minds and dry hearts—a school distorting every sane feeling, whenever occasion calls for such distortion; a school of all sorts of challenges, fearless and irresponsible; a continual and incessant training, based on offer and demand"—this youthful school already has fallen in line with the stock-exchange gambler and begun to sing hymns of praise in his honor. Please do not think that I am hinting at "the Strusberg case"; advocates in that case who proclaimed their "pinched" clients as ideal men, who sang hymns to them as "the best men in all Moscow" (precisely, something of the kind)—these advocates have missed their mark. They have proved that they themselves are men devoid of the least serious conviction and even of poise, men with no sense of measure; and if they are playing in our midst the role of "European talents," it is solely because in the kingdom of the blind the one-eyed is king.

In fact, even as diplomats, they have charged the highest possible fee in order to obtain the maximum for the minimum: "Not only are they not guilty—they are holy!" It is rumored that at one point the public even began to hiss. However, an advocate, to begin with, is not a diplomat: the comparison is essentially erroneous. It would have been more correct, far more correct, to ask—pointing at the client—the question propounded in the Gospel: "Gentlemen of the jury, who among you is 'he that is without sin'?"—Oh, I am not criticizing the verdict; the verdict is just—and I bow before it; it had to be rendered if it were only against the bank. Precisely this case was of such a nature that to convict by "public conscience" this "pinched," ill-starred Moscow Loan Bank meant to convict at the same time all our banks, the whole stock exchange, all stock-exchange gamblers, even though they had not yet been caught—what difference does it make? Who is without

sin, without that same sin?—Honestly, who? Somebody has already
said in print that they were leniently punished.—I must explain
that I am not referring to Landau: he is really guilty of something extraordinary which I have no intention of even discussing.
But, in all conscience, Danila Schumacher, convicted of "swindling,"
got a terrible punishment. Let us look into our hearts: are there
many among us who would not have committed the same thing?—
One needn't confess aloud, but let him tacitly admit it. However,
long live justice!—All the same, they were jailed!—"Take that, for
our stock exchange and depraved times; take that, as a reward for
the fact that we are all egoists, that we all profess such villainous
materialistic views on happiness in life and its delights; for our arid
and treacherous feeling of self-preservation!" Nay, it is useful to
convict even one bank for our own sins. . . .

My God! Whither have I wandered? Is it possible that I,
too, am writing "about the Strusberg case"? Enough! I hasten to
cut this short. For I was speaking about "the best man," and I
merely meant to draw the conclusion that in Russia the ideal of
the real best man, even of the "natural" pattern, is in great danger
of growing muddy. The old has either been destroyed or is worn out;
the new is still borne on the wings of fantasy, whereas in actual life
we behold something abominable which has reached unheard-of proportions. The fascination which is being attributed to this new force
—the gold bag—even begins to inspire fear in some hearts, which
are all too suspicious, for instance, as regards the people. Indeed,
even though we—the upper stratum of society—might be seduced
by the new idol, nevertheless we should not vanish without leaving
a trace: not in vain has the torch of education been shining for us
throughout two centuries. We are armed with enlightenment, and
we should be able to repel the monster. At a moment of most filthy
debauch, didn't we convict the Moscow Loan Bank? But our people
—that "inert, corrupt, insensible mass"—into which the Jew has
thrust himself, what are they going to set against the monster of
materialism, in the guise of the gold bag, marching on them?—
Their misery? Their rags? Their taxes and their bad harvests?
Their vices? Liquor? Flogging? We were afraid that the people
would forthwith fall prostrate before the increasing power of the
gold bag, and that before even one generation should pass they
would be enslaved worse than ever before—and that they would
be driven into submission not only through coercion, but that they
would submit morally, with their whole will. We were afraid that
it is precisely they, before anyone else, who would say: "This is
the main thing; here is where power, tranquillity and happiness
reside! This is what we shall worship and follow!"

Such were the things of which one could have been justly afraid—at least for a long while. Many people started pondering—and suddenly . . .

Suddenly something happened last summer which I shall discuss in the next issue of the *Diary*. I want to speak about it without "humor," but wholeheartedly and more *plainly*. That which happened last summer was so touching and gladdening that it is even incredible.—Incredible because we had already given up the people for lost and we considered them grossly incompetent to utter their word on the question: what should the Russian "best man" be? We believed the whole organism of that people was already contaminated by material and spiritual debauch; we believed that the people had already forgotten their spiritual tenets, that they had not preserved them in their hearts, having lost or distorted them amidst misery and debauch. And suddenly all this "uniform and inert mass" (*i.e.,* in the opinion of our wiseacres, of course) which, in its hundred-million bulk, noiselessly and breathlessly stretched itself out on a surface of many thousands of versts, in a state of perpetual begetting, and recognized eternal impotence to say or perform anything—in the guise of something everlastingly elemental and obedient—all of a sudden all this Russia awoke, rose and humbly but firmly uttered *urbi et orbi* her beautiful word. Moreover, Russians, taking their staffs, in scores of hundreds, escorted by thousands of people, started on some novel crusade (thus the movement is already being called; the English were the first to compare the Russian movement with a crusade) to Serbia in support of some brethren of theirs because rumors had reached them that those brethren over there were being tortured and oppressed. A father—an old soldier—instead of living in peace, suddenly takes up arms and proceeds on foot, inquiring about his way, thousands of versts away, to fight the Turk in support of his brethren, taking along with him his nine-year-old daughter (this is a fact): "Christians will be found who will care for my daughter while I am wandering"—says he, in answer to questions—"but I will go and serve God's cause." And thus he goes. . . . And there are thousands of such cases!

Now, had anyone told ahead of time—say, last winter—that this would happen in Russia, we should not have believed it —we should not have believed in this "crusade" which, however, has actually begun (but is by no means ended). Even now, though one sees it openly, willy-nilly one asks oneself at times: "But how could this happen? How could such a wholly unforeseen event occur?" Russia has proclaimed aloud everything—what she reveres and what she believes in; she has stated what she deems to be "best" and what men she considers "best." Now, it is the discussion of the question—"what kind of people are these men and what ideals have been revealed?"—that I am postponing till the next issue of the *Diary*. Essentially, these ideals, these "best men" are clear and may be perceived at the first glance: in the conception of the people, "the best man" is he who has not bowed before material temptation; who is incessantly seeking work for God's cause; who loves truth and, whenever the occasion calls for it, rises to serve it, forsaking his home and his family and sacrificing his life. I mean to state specifically why we, the educated ones, at present can boldly and firmly hope that not only has the image of "the best man" not been lost in Russia, but that, on the contrary, it is radiating more brightly than at any time in the past; that its provider, guardian and bearer nowadays is precisely the common people whom we, in our enlightened haughtiness— and, at the same time, naïve ignorance—have considered so "incompetent." More particularly, I should like to dwell upon the question how the quests and requirements of our "enlightenment" even now could be brought into full accord with the people's conception of "the best man," notwithstanding the obviously naïve and artless forms in which the people express that conception. Not the form but the content is essential (even though the form, too, is beautiful). The content, however, is incontestable. This is why we can joyously embrace the new hope: our horizon has cleared and our new sun rises all too brightly. . . .

And if only it might prove possible that we should all agree and share the people's understanding of whom henceforth we should consider "the best man"—perhaps, beginning with this last summer, a new period in Russian history would come into existence.

NOVEMBER

THE MEEK ONE

A FANTASTIC STORY

The Author's Foreword

I APOLOGIZE to my readers that this time, instead of the "diary" in its usual form, I am merely printing a story. However, the greater part of the month I was occupied with this story. In any event, I ask the readers' indulgence.

Now—about the story itself. I called it "fantastic," although I consider it real in the highest degree. However, actually, there is in it an element of the fantastic—specifically, in its form—and this I deem necessary to explain in advance.

The point is that it is neither a story nor a diary. Please imagine a husband whose wife, a suicide, is lying on a table; several hours earlier she threw herself out of the window. He is in a state of consternation and, as yet, he has been unable to compose his thoughts. He keeps walking around in his rooms and is endeavoring to rationalize the event, "to collect his thoughts into one focus." At that, he is an inveterate hypochondriac—one of those who talk to themselves. And thus he talks to himself; he relates the event, and *rationalizes* it to himself. Despite the seeming consecutiveness of the speech, several times he contradicts himself—both in the logic and in his sentiments. He at once justifies himself and accuses her, and embarks upon other *obiter dicta:* we perceive here vulgarity of thought and heart, and also—profound feeling. Little by little, he actually rationalizes the affair to himself and collects "his thoughts into one focus." A range of reminiscences evoked by him irresistibly leads him, at length, to truth, and truth irresistibly exalts him—his mind and heart. By the end the tone itself of the narrative changes, compared with its incoherent beginning. Truth reveals itself to the unhappy man rather clearly and distinctly—at least, so it appears to him.

Such is the theme. It stands to reason that the process of the narrative lasts several hours, with interruptions and interludes, in a confused form: now he speaks to himself, now he addresses, as it were, an invisible listener—some kind of a judge. Thus it also takes place in real life. If a stenographer could have eavesdropped on him and transcribed everything after him, the sketch would have been rougher and less polished than it appears in my version; nevertheless, it seems to me that the psychological order would, perhaps, have been the same. Now, this supposition relative to the stenographer who had recorded everything (after whom I have edited his record) is what I denote as fantastic in this story. However, something partly similar to this has been resorted to several times in art. For example, Victor Hugo—in his masterpiece *The Last Day of a Man Condemned to Death*—has resorted to an almost identical device; and although he did not portray a stenographer, nevertheless he has introduced a still greater unreality when he presumed that a man condemned to death would have been able (and would have had the time) to keep a diary not only on his last day, but even in his last hour—and, literally, during his last minute. However, had he not resorted to this fantasy, the work itself would have been nonexistent—the most realistic and verisimilar of all his writings.

CHAPTER I

1

WHO WAS I AND WHO WAS SHE?

. . . NOW, AS LONG AS she is here—everything is still all right; I come up and look at her every minute; but tomorrow she will be carried away—and how shall I remain alone? Now she is on a table in the hall—two card tables were put together—while the coffin will be here tomorrow, a white one—white "gros-de-Naples."— However, this is not the point. . . . I keep walking, and I want to explain it to myself. I have already kept walking for six hours, yet I am still unable to collect my thoughts into one focus. The point is that I keep walking, walking, walking. . . . This is how it transpired. I will simply relate it in the order it happened. (Order!) Gentlemen, I am far from being a littérateur, and you can see it; let it be so, but I shall relate it as I understand it myself. Therein is my whole horror—that I comprehend everything!

If you wish to know, that is, if I should start from the beginning, she simply called on me then to pawn some articles in order to pay for an "ad" in *The Voice*—to the effect that So-and-so, a governess, was prepared to accept an out-of-town position and also to give lessons at private residences, etc. This was in the very beginning and, of course, I did not distinguish her from the others: she came like the rest—well, and so forth. Later, I began to distinguish. She was so lean, fair—medium tall in size; with me she was always rather clumsy, abashed (I believe she was the same with all strangers and, of course, to her I was just like any other, that is, considered not as a pawnbroker but a man). As soon as she would get the money she would turn around and go away. And she always kept silent. Others would argue, beg, bargain to get more; this one—no; what she would get . . . It seems, I am all confused. . . . Yes—first of all, I was impressed by her ornaments: silver, gilded earrings, some miserable locket —twenty-kopeck articles. She herself knew that their value was little, but from the expression on her face I saw that to her they were precious and, in fact, these were all that was left by her father and mother—this I learned later. Only once did I permit myself to smirk at her things. That is, you see, this I never permit myself in my dealings with the public; with the public I maintain a gentleman's tone: few words—polite and strict. "Strict, strict, strict." But once, unexpectedly, she ventured to bring some remnants (literally so) of a hare-mantelet—and I couldn't restrain myself, and suddenly I uttered something on the order of a witticism! Heavens! How she flared up! Her blue, big, pensive eyes—how inflamed they grew! But she didn't utter a single word; she took her "remnants" and walked out. It was just then that I noticed her especially for the first time, and I thought about her something of this kind—that is, something of a special kind. Yes, I recall also another impression—that is, if you please, the main impression, the synthesis of everything: specifically that she was awfully young, as if she were fourteen, whereas at that time she was already almost sixteen—only three months younger than that. However, it isn't this that I meant to say: the synthesis lay not in this at all. Next day she came again. Later I found out that she had been at Dobronravov's and Moser's with that mantelet, but they accept nothing but gold; they even refused to talk. But once I took a cameo from her (a pretty miserable one), and thereupon, having thought the matter over, I felt surprised: I, too, accept nothing but gold and silver, yet I allowed her to pawn a cameo. This, then, was my second thought about her—this I remember, very clearly and distinctly.

This time—that is, after Moser—she brought an amber cigar-holder, a thing so-so, amateurish, but to us, again, it was worth nothing because we're interested only in gold. Because she came after yesterday's *refusal,* I received her sternly. My sternness is dryness. However, when handing her two rubles, I could not restrain myself and told her, as it were, with some irritation: "This is only *for you,* and Moser would not accept such an article from you." The words *"for you"*—I emphasized particularly, and precisely *in a certain sense.* I was angry. Again, she flushed upon hearing this *"for you"; she* didn't say anything; she didn't throw the money back; she took it—well, that's poverty! But how she flared up! I understood that I had stung her. When she had left, suddenly I asked myself: "Is it possible that this triumph over her costs me two rubles?—Hee, hee, hee!" I specifically recall repeating this question twice: "Is it worth it? Is it worth it?" And, laughingly, I answered this question to myself in the affirmative. I was quite amused at the time. But this wasn't an evil feeling; it was deliberate, intentional: I meant to test her because suddenly certain thoughts in connection with her began to rove

through my mind. This was my third *special* thought about her.
. . . Well, this was the beginning of everything. Of course,
at once I sought to find out indirectly all circumstances, and I
awaited her visit with particular impatience. For I had a presentiment that she would come soon. When she came, I started an amiable
and most polite conversation. I am not badly brought up and I
have manners. Hm! It was then that I guessed that she was kind
and meek. The good and meek ones do not resist long, and though
they do not readily reveal themselves, nevertheless they are absolutely unable to evade a conversation: they give curt answers, but
still they answer, and the further—the more, only don't get tired
yourself, if there is anything you need from them. Naturally, at
that time she told me nothing. It was later that I found out about
The Voice and about everything. In these days she went to the limit
in her advertising campaign—at first, naturally, in a presumptuous
tone: "Governess, ready to accept out-of-town position. Offers to
be mailed in sealed envelopes."—And later: "Willing to do anything
—teach, act as companion, take care of the household, nurse a
sick lady; able to sew," etc.—old stuff! Of course, all these ads
were full of variations, but at length, when she had reached the
point of despair, the ad read: "Without salary—for food." No, she
couldn't find a position! Then I decided to test her for the last
time. Suddenly I took that date's issue of *The Voice* and showed
her an ad: "Young person; fatherless and motherless orphan; desires position as governess of minor children; may be useful in
household."

"You see, this person placed her ad in the morning, and in
the evening she will find a position without fail. This is how one
should advertise!"

Once more she flared up; again her eyes grew inflamed; she
turned around and forthwith walked out. This pleased me very
much. However, by that time I was certain of everything, and I
was not afraid: no one was going to accept cigarette-holders. Meanwhile, she had even disposed of these. To be sure: two days later
she came—so pale, so agitated: I guessed that something must have
happened at home, and something had happened. In a minute I shall
explain what actually happened, but now I wish merely to recall
how suddenly I assumed airs and how I grew in her opinion. All
of a sudden I conceived this intention. The point is that she brought
that holy image (she took the resolution to bring it). . . Oh, but
listen! Listen to me! Now it begins, because all along I keep
faltering. . . . The point is that now I want to recall everything,
every detail, every wee trait. All along I am endeavoring to collect

my thoughts into a focus—and I can't, and now these tiny traits, these little traits . . .

The image of the Mother of God. The Mother of God with the Infant—a domestic, ancient family image with a silver gilded trimming. Cost?—Well, about six rubles. I see—she treasures the image; she pawns the whole image without removing the trimming. I say to her: "Would be better to take off the trimming, and take back the image because, somehow, you know, nevertheless it's an image."

"Is this prohibited to you?"

"No, not that it is prohibited, but so . . . perhaps, you yourself . . ."

"Well, remove it."

"You know, I am not going to remove it; instead, I shall place it over there—in the image case"—I said, after deliberation—"along with the other images, under the image lamp"—ever since I had opened my pawnshop, the image lamp has been kept lit—"and simply pay ten rubles."

"I don't need ten rubles. Give me five. I'll redeem it without fail."

"And you don't want ten? The image is worth it"—I added, again noticing a flash in her eyes. She kept silent. I brought her five rubles.

"Don't think ill of me. I myself have been in such straits, even in worse ones, and if today you find me engaged in this kind of occupation . . . this is after everything I have endured. . . ."

"You are avenging society? Yes?"—she unexpectedly interrupted me with a rather caustic smile in which, however, there was much innocence (I mean—indifference, because at that time most decidedly she did not distinguish me from others, so that she said it almost inoffensively).—Ah!—I said to myself—this is the kind you are: character manifests itself—one of the new orientation.

"You see"—I promptly remarked, half-jestingly, half-mysteriously—"I am part of that part of the whole which seeks to do evil and does good. . . ."

Quickly and with great curiosity—in which, however, there was much that was childish—she glanced at me.

"Wait . . . What is this thought? Whence is it?—I have heard it somewhere . . ."

"Don't ransack your brain: in these words Mephistopheles introduces himself to Faust. Have you read *Faust?*"

"Not . . . not attentively."

"In other words—you haven't read it all. You should read

it. However, again I see a sarcastic twist of your lips. Please do not suspect in me so little taste that I am trying to veil my role of pawnbroker by introducing myself as a Mephisto. A pawnbroker remains a pawnbroker. We know it."

"Somehow, you are strange . . . I didn't mean at all to tell you anything . . ."

She meant to say: "I didn't expect that you would be an educated man." But she didn't say it; however, I knew that this was her thought. I gratified her immensely.

"You see"—I observed—"in every profession one may be doing good things. Of course, I am not referring to myself: let's admit that I am doing nothing but evil things but . . ."

"Of course, in every station in life one may be doing good" —said she, looking at me with a quick and penetrating glance. "Exactly—in every station"—she added suddenly.

Oh, I remember—I remember all these moments! And I wish to add that when youth, dear youth, wants to utter something clever and penetrating, suddenly, all too sincerely and naïvely it betrays by the expression of its face that thought, "you see, I am now telling you something clever and penetrating," and not from vainglory, as we; but one perceives that youth itself treasures all this very highly and believes and respects it, convinced that you, too, respect it even as itself. Oh, sincerity! This is how they conquer! And in her everything was so charming!

I remember. I forget nothing! When she left, at once I made up my mind. That same day I embarked upon my final investigations and I learned all the rest of her current "ins and outs"; all her former secrets I already knew through Lukeria, who was then their servant and whom, several days before, I had bribed. These "ins and outs" were so dreadful that I fail to understand how she could have managed to laugh, as just now, and to take an interest in the words of Mephistopheles, when she herself was facing such a horror. But—that's youth! It is precisely this that I then thought about her with pride and gladness, since here there was also magnanimity: "See, I am on the brink of perdition, but still Goethe's great words are shining!" Youth is always—at least, a bit—magnanimous, be it even in a crooked direction. That is, I am speaking about her, about her alone. And the main thing—even then I was looking at her as if *mine*, and I didn't doubt my power. Do you know, this is an awfully sensual thought when one no longer doubts?

But what is the matter with me? If I go on this way, I shall never collect everything into one focus. Let's hurry, let's hurry!— This is not the point at all. Oh, God!

2

Marital Proposal

I shall explain in a few words the "ins and outs" which I learned about her: her father and mother had died long ago, three years before that, and she had to stay with disorderly aunts. It is not enough to call them disorderly: one aunt, a widow, with a large family—six children, one much younger than the others; the other aunt, an old maid, and bad. Both bad. Her father was a functionary, a former scribe; he was but a personal, and not a hereditary, nobleman. Briefly—everything suited me. I came, as it were, from a higher plane: anyhow, a retired captain of a brilliant regiment, a hereditary nobleman, independent, and so forth—and, as for the pawnshop, the aunts could regard this with nothing but respect. At her aunts' she had been kept a slave for three years; nevertheless, she managed to pass some kind of examination, snatching the time for this, despite the merciless daily toil;—and this certainly meant something: it was evidence of her longing for the sublime and noble! Why did I want to marry her?—However, I don't give a hoot about myself; this comes later. . . . And is this the point?—She gave lessons to her aunt's children; she sewed—at the end not only underwear—and she washed the floor, and her with a bad chest! In plain language—they even beat her and used to reproach her for every piece of bread. At length they sought to sell her. Pshaw!—I am omitting the filthy details! Later she told me everything in detail. All this had been observed during a whole year by a fat shopkeeper —not an ordinary shopkeeper, but the owner of two grocery stores. He had already buried two wives and was on the lookout for a third one, and his choice fell on her: "She is gentle"—said he—"she grew up in poverty, and I will marry her for my orphans." It is true—he did have orphans. He started courting her and began to negotiate with the aunts. Besides—he was a man of fifty. She was horror-stricken. It was at this juncture that she began to frequent me in order to pay for her ads in *The Voice*. Finally, she asked that her aunts grant her a wee bit of a respite to think the matter over. This wee bit she was granted, but only one; she was refused the second one. They nagged and nagged her: "We don't know what we shall be eating ourselves—even without an extra mouth!" I was already aware of all this, and that day—after the morning incident—I had made up my mind. In the evening the shopkeeper called on her; he brought a pound of candies from his store, at fifty kopecks. She was sitting with him, and I called Lukeria out of the kitchen and told her to go back and to whisper to her that I was waiting at the gate, and that I wished to tell her something without any delay. I was pleased with myself. And, generally, all that day I was awfully content.

Right there at the gate, in the presence of Lukeria, much to her amazement—she was amazed by the fact itself that I had called her out—I explained to her that I would deem it a happiness and an honor . . . Secondly, that she should not be surprised at my manner—that this was taking place at the gate: "I am a straight-forward man"—said I—"and I have studied the circumstances of the case." And I wasn't lying that I was straightforward. Oh, hang it! And I spoke not only politely—that is, showing that I was a man of good manners—but also with originality—and this is the essential thing. Well, is it a sin to be admitting this? I wish to judge myself and I am so judging. I must speak pro and con, and this is what I am doing. Even later I was recalling the incident with delight, although this was silly. Straightway, without fluttering, I announced, first, that I was a man of no great talent, not too clever, perhaps even not very kind—a rather cheap egotist (I re-member this expression: I devised it on my way to her, and I was pleased with it), and that it was quite possible that I had many unpleasant qualities also in other respects. All this was uttered with some sort of pride—well, you know how such things are said.

It stands to reason that I had enough taste—after having nobly announced my shortcomings—not to embark upon the enu-meration of my merits: "As against this"—as people say—"I have this, that and the other to my credit." I could see that she was still terribly afraid, but I didn't soft-pedal anything; moreover, seeing that she was afraid, I deliberately strengthened my statements: I told her directly that she would have enough to eat, but as for gowns, theatres, balls—there would be nothing of that, unless in some future time when my aim would have been attained. Decidedly this stern tone fascinated me. I added—and this as much *en passant* as possible—that I had chosen this occupation, meaning the pawn-shop, because I had a certain goal—there was, so to say, a particular circumstance. . . . But I had the right to speak this way: I actually did have a goal, and there was a circumstance. Wait, gentlemen: I was the first to hate that pawnshop all my life but, substantially —even though it is silly to speak to oneself in mysterious phrases —I was "avenging society"—verily, verily so! So that her morning witticism about my "avenging" was unjustified. You see, had I directly told her in so many words: "Yes, I am avenging society," she would have burst into laughter, as in the morning, and the thing would, in fact, have appeared amusing. Well, but through an indirect hint, by uttering a mysterious phrase, it proved possible to trick the imagination. Besides, by that time I was already afraid of nothing; I knew that the stout shopkeeper was in any event more repulsive to her than I and that, standing there at the gate, I would appear to her as her liberator. Indeed, this I did understand. Oh, man understands villainies particularly well! But were these villainies? How can a man be judged in a situation such as this? Didn't I already love her then?

Wait: of course, then I didn't mention to her even a word about benefaction; on the contrary, oh, on the contrary: "It is *I*" —I implied, as it were—"who is overwhelmed with benefits—not *you*." So that I even expressed this specifically in words—couldn't restrain myself—and, perhaps, it came out stupidly, because I noticed a fleeting wrinkle in her brow. But, on the whole, I decidedly won. Wait, if one is to recall all this filth, I shall also mention the last swinishness. I was standing there, and the thought occurred to me: you are tall, well-built, good-mannered and, finally—speaking without swagger—you are handsome. This is what flashed through my mind.

Naturally, then and there, at the gate, she said "Yes" to me. But . . . I must add: right there, at the gate, she pondered for a long while before saying "Yes." She grew so pensive, so pensive, that I was ready to ask her: "Now, what's your answer?" In truth, I could not restrain myself, and actually asked her with a little ostentation in the tone—"Now, what's your answer?"

"Wait, I'm thinking."

And so serious was her dear little face, so serious that even then I could have read! . . . And—imagine—I felt hurt: "Is it possible"—as I asked myself—"that she is choosing between me and that shopkeeper?" Oh, then I did not yet comprehend! Then I understood nothing—nothing at all! Not until today have I understood!

I remember, Lukeria came running after me, when I had left; she stopped me in the street, and hurriedly she said: "God will reward you, sir, for sheltering our dear girl! Only, don't tell her that—she is so proud!"

Well, proud! I am fond of the proud ones myself. The proud ones are particularly beautiful when . . . when you no longer doubt your power over them.—Eh? Oh, mean, maladroit man! Oh, how pleased I was! You know when she stood there, at the gate, deep in thought about answering "yes" to me, and I kept wondering— do you know that she may have been pondering over this thought: "If it is misfortune there and here, wouldn't it be better to choose

directly the worst, that is, the shopkeeper—let him, in a drunken
fit, beat me to death!" Eh? What do you think?—Could such a
thought have occurred to her?

But even now I don't understand; even now I understand
nothing! Just a moment ago I said that this thought may have
occurred to her—to choose between two misfortunes, the worst one
—meaning the shopkeeper. But who of the two was worse to her
at that time—I or the shopkeeper?—The shopkeeper or the pawnbroker reciting Goethe? This is still a question! What question?—
Even this I don't understand: the answer lies on the table, and
yet I say—"question"! Well, I don't give a rap about myself! I
am not the point at all. . . . By the way, what is it to me now
whether I am the point or not? This, to be sure, I can't settle at all.
I had better go to bed. I have a headache. . . .

3

THE NOBLEST OF MEN—BUT I DON'T BELIEVE IT MYSELF

Couldn't fall asleep. How could I?—Something raps in my
head, like a pulse. Wish I could master all this—all this filth. Oh,
what filth! Out of what filth I extricated her at that time! Certainly, she must have understood this, and should have prized my
action! I also liked certain thoughts—for instance, that I was forty-
one, and she—only sixteen. This captivated me—I mean, this feeling
of inequality; it is very delightful, very delightful.

Now, for example, I intended to arrange our wedding à l'an-
glaise—that is, no one but the two of us, save, perhaps, two witnesses
of whom Lukeria would be one. And immediately after that—I was
planning to take a train, say, for Moscow (where, by the way, I
had some business to attend to), stopping at a hotel for a fortnight or so. She protested; she would not permit it, and so I was
compelled to pay my respects to the aunts, as her relatives from
whom I had taken her. I gave in and the aunts got what was due
them. I even gave these creatures a hundred rubles each and
promised to give more—naturally without mentioning it to her, in
order not to sadden her with the meanness of the mis-en-scène. The
aunts immediately became as sweet as honey.

There also was an argument about the trousseau: she had
nothing—almost literally so—but she didn't insist on anything. However, I succeeded in proving to her that it wouldn't do for her to
bring nothing, and so I bought her the trousseau—since who else
would have bought it for her? Well, I don't give a hoot about
myself! Nevertheless, right then, I did convey to her some of my

ideas, so that at least she was aware of them. Perhaps I even hastened
to do so. The main thing is that from the very beginning, much
as she tried to restrain herself, she threw herself at me with love;
every evening when I came home she used to meet me at the door;
with delight she would tell me in her lisp (that charming lisp of
innocence) about her whole childhood—her infancy, her parents'
home, her father and mother. But at once I threw cold water on all
this ecstasy. Precisely therein was my idea. I reacted to these
transports with silence—benevolent, of course. . . . Still, she soon
perceived that I was an enigma. And it was the enigma that I
principally aimed at! Maybe it was for the purpose of proposing
a riddle that I perpetrated this stupidity! First, sternness—it was
in the spirit of sternness that I admitted her to my home. In a
word, even though I was content, at that time I devised a whole
system. Oh, it developed without any strain, of its own accord.
Besides, it was impossible to have had things otherwise; I was
compelled to devise a system owing to a circumstance beyond my
control.—What the devil do I slander myself for! It was a genuine
system. No, just listen—if a man is to be judged, his case should
be laid bare. . . . Listen!

How should I start, since it is very difficult? Just as soon
as I began to exculpate myself—the difficulty arose. You see: youth,
for instance, despises money. So I started at once to stress the
money question; I pressed that question. And I stressed it so strongly
that she grew more and more silent—she would open her eyes wide,
she would listen and look at me, and she would grow silent. D'you
see, youth is magnanimous—I mean, good youth—magnanimous
and impulsive, but it possesses little tolerance: the moment anything goes against their grain, they grow contemptuous. But I sought
breadth, I meant to inoculate breadth straight into her heart, into
her heartfelt views—isn't it so? I'll take a trivial example: how,
let's say, could I have explained my pawnshop to a character such
as hers? Naturally, I did not directly bring up the subject because
it might have appeared as though I was apologizing for the pawnshop: no, I acted, so to speak, with pride—I spoke almost tacitly.
And I am a master at speaking tacitly: all my life I have spoken
tacitly, and silently I have lived through whole tragedies. Oh, indeed, I was unhappy! I was cast out by everybody, thrown out
and forgotten. Not a soul, not a single soul knows it. And all of
a sudden this sixteen-year-old one got possession of certain details
about me—from mean people—imagining that she knew everything,
whereas the secret lay concealed in the breast of that man! All
the time I kept silent, especially with her—till yesterday. Why did
I keep silent?—Why?—Just because I am a proud man. It was

my desire that she should learn of herself, without me, but not from
the tales of mean people; that she should *herself guess* everything
about that man and that she should comprehend him! Admitting
her to my house, I desired full respect. I wished that she should
look at me worshipfully for all my suffering—and I deserved it. Oh,
I was always proud, and I always sought either everything or nothing!—Because I'm not a half-way man where happiness is concerned,
for this reason was I then compelled to act as I did: "Guess yourself"—so to say—"and appraise!" Because you must concede that
had I myself started explaining to her and prompting her, had I
started wriggling and soliciting respect, it would have been the
same as if I should be begging alms. . . . However . . . however,
why do I speak about this?

Stupid, stupid, stupid and stupid! Directly and mercilessly
(I emphasize the fact that it was mercilessly) I explained to her
in a few words that youth's magnanimity is delightful, but that
it isn't worth a penny. Why isn't it worth anything?—Because they
acquire it cheaply; it comes about without their having lived; it
is, so to speak, "the first impressions of existence"; but let's look
at you in process of work! Cheap magnanimity is always easy;
even to give one's life—even this is cheap, since it is nothing but
boiling blood, an over-abundance of energy, a passionate craving
for beauty! No, assume a deed of magnanimity which is difficult,
tranquil—one about which nothing is heard, one without glamour,
one entailing calumnies, in which there is much sacrifice and not
a drop of glory in which you—radiant man—are represented to everybody as a villain, whereas you are the most honest man on earth
—now, just take a try at this sort of a deed! Nay, you will refuse
it! And I—all my life I have been doing nothing but carrying out
such a deed. At first she argued—how hotly!—but later she left off
speaking and, finally, she grew quite silent; only, when listening,
she would open her eyes awfully wide—such big, big eyes, so attentive. . . . And . . . and, besides, suddenly I noticed a smile—a distrustful, silent, wicked smile. Now, it was with this smile that I
admitted her to my house. It is also true that she could have gone
nowhere else. . . .

4

All Plans and Plans

Which one of us was it that started it first?

No one. It started by itself from the first step. I said that
I admitted her to my home in the spirit of sternness. However,
I softened that spirit from the very first step. Even when she was

still my fiancée I told her that she would be in charge of accepting articles in pawn and paying out money, and then she said nothing (please note this fact). Moreover, she began to work, even with zeal. Well, of course, the apartment and furniture—all this remained as heretofore. The apartment—two rooms: one—a big hall with a balustrade, behind which the cash office is situated; the other one —also a large room, our common room, which also serves as a bedroom. Mine is scanty furniture; even at the aunts' it was better. My image case, with an image lamp, stands in the hall where the cash office is situated; in my room there is a cupboard in which there are several books and my linen; I have the key for it.—Well, the bed, tables, chairs. I told her, when she was still my fiancée, that one ruble, and no more, was appropriated for our subsistence —I mean, food—that is, for me, her and Lukeria, whom I had lured over into my service. "I need"—I said—"thirty thousand in three years; otherwise, one can't make money." She did not object, but I myself increased the appropriation by thirty kopecks. Same thing about the theatre. I told my fiancée that there would be no theatre, and yet I conceded the theatre once a month, and in a decent way, too—in the orchestra. We went together, and we were there three times. We saw *Pursuit of Happiness* and *Singing Birds*—so I think. (Oh, I don't give a rap! I don't give a rap!) We went there and returned home silently. Why is it that from the very beginning we kept silent?—For, at first, there were no quarrels, and yet silence was maintained. I remember she kept looking at me stealthily, as it were. The moment I noticed this I made my silence still more persistent. True, it was I who had been stressing silence—not she. On her part, once or twice there were outbursts when she would start kissing me; since, however, these outbursts were of a pathological, hysterical character—whereas I needed solid happiness, together with her respect—I reacted coldly. And I was right: after every outburst, the next day there was a quarrel.

Then again, there were no quarrels, but there was silence— and an increasingly arrogant air on her part. "Rebellion and independence"—that was the thing; only she didn't know how to go about it. Yes, this meek face grew more and more impertinent. Would you believe it? I had become repugnant to her—this I learned. And the fact that she would lose her temper in outbursts could not be doubted. Well, for example, how could the fact be accounted for that, having emerged from such filth and poverty, having washed floors, she started sniffing at our poverty?—You see, this was not poverty but economy, and only in certain things—even luxury, say, in linen, in cleanness. Even in days gone by, I always used to believe that cleanness in the husband appeals to the wife. However, she turned up her nose not at poverty but at my alleged stinginess in economy: "He pursues some purpose; he makes a display of his firm character." Suddenly she herself renounced the theatre. And that mocking look became more and more pronounced. . . . And more and more intense silence on my part.

Certainly I wouldn't try to exculpate myself!—The main thing was that pawnshop. Permit me to say that I knew that a woman —a sixteen-year old woman—could not help but completely submit to a man. There is no originality in women; this is an axiom. Even now, even now, to me this is an axiom! What does it matter that she lies there, in the hall: truth is truth, and Mill himself can do nothing about it! While a loving woman—oh, a loving woman deifies even the vices and villainies of her beloved one. He himself couldn't find such excuses for his villainies as she manages to frame. This is magnanimous but not original. Women were ruined solely through lack of originality. And what does it matter, I repeat, that you are pointing to that table over there? Well, is the thing on the table original? Oh!—Oh!

Now, listen: I was always convinced of her love. Even then, didn't she fling herself at my neck?—This means that she loved— more correctly, sought to love. Yes, thus it was: she wished—she sought—to love. And, what is most important, in this case there have been no villainies for which she should have been finding justification. You say "pawnbroker"—everybody says it. And what of it? This means that there must, indeed, have been reasons why a most magnanimous of all men became a pawnbroker. You see, gentlemen, there are ideas . . . that is, you see, if a certain idea be expressed in words, it would sound perfectly silly. One would be ashamed of himself. And why?—For no reason whatsoever. Because we are all good-for-nothings; we cannot tolerate truth—or just why, I don't know. I just said—"most magnanimous of all men." This sounds ridiculous, and yet this was so. But this is true—that is, the most truthful truth! Yes—at that time *I had the right* to provide for myself and to open the pawnshop: "You, people, you have renounced me; you drove me away with contemptuous silence. You answered my passionate impulse toward you with an offense that will be felt by me all my life. Therefore, now I have the right to protect my-self against you by a wall, to raise thirty thousand rubles and to finish my life somewhere in the Crimea, on the Southern Shore, in the mountains and among vineyards, on my own estate bought with this thirty thousand, and—what's most important—far away from all of you, but with no anger against you, with an ideal in my soul, with a beloved woman next to my heart, with a family—should God bless me with one—helping the neighboring farmers."

Naturally, it is good that I am now saying this to myself, but what could be more ridiculous than if I should have then said all these things aloud?—This is why there was proud silence; this is why we were sitting without uttering a word. Because how much would she have understood?—Sixteen years! Early youth!—Indeed, what could she have comprehended of my justifications, of my sufferings? Here were straightforwardness, ignorance of life, cheap youthful convictions, chicken blindness of "beautiful hearts"—and the main thing, here was the pawnshop, and basta! (was I a villain in the pawnshop—didn't she see how I acted and how I overcharged people?). Oh, how dreadful is truth on earth! This charming one, this meek one, this celestial one—she was a tyrant, an intolerable tyrant of my soul, and a torturer! I should calumniate myself if I did not tell this! You think that I did not love her? Who can say that I did not love her? You see, there was irony here—the wicked irony of fate and nature! We are damned; generally, man's life is damned! (Mine in particular!) At present, I understand that here I did make some mistake!—Somehow things developed here not as they should have. Everything was clear; my plan was as clear as the sky. "Severe, proud and needing no moral consolations by anyone; suffering silently." Thus it really was: I didn't lie, I didn't! "Later she herself will perceive that here was magnanimity—only she proved unable to notice this!—and the moment when some day she guesses this, her esteem will be ten times greater; she will fall prostrate, worshipfully folding her hands." Such was the plan. But right there I forgot something, or failed to take something into consideration. I proved unable to do some one thing. But enough, enough! . . . What's finished is finished. Be bolder, man! And be proud! Thou art not guilty! . . .

Well, I will tell the truth; I will not be afraid to face the truth: *she* is guilty. *She* is guilty! . . .

5

THE MEEK ONE REBELS

Quarrels started because of the fact that all of a sudden she decided to loan the money according to her ideas, to appraise the articles in excess of their value—and on two occasions she even deigned to start arguing with me on the subject. I did not agree with her. But at this juncture a captain's widow happened to come into the picture.

An old woman—a captain's widow—came with a locket, a present from her late husband—well, of course, a souvenir. I gave her thirty rubles. She started lamenting and begging that the article be preserved—why, of course, we would preserve it. Well, briefly, all of a sudden—some five days later—she came to exchange the locket for a bracelet which was not worth even eight rubles. Naturally, I refused. Probably she must have then guessed something by the expression in my wife's eyes, and so she came again in my absence, and my wife exchanged the locket.

Having learned this that same day, I started talking mildly, but firmly and reasonably. She was sitting on the bed, with her eyes fixed on the floor and her right toe striking against the rug (her gesture); a wicked smile was on her lips. Then, without in the least raising my voice, I calmly told her that the money was *mine;* that I had the right to look at life through *my* eyes, and that, when I invited her to my house, I concealed nothing from her.

Suddenly, she jumped to her feet, her body trembling all over—and what would you think?—She started stamping her feet at me. This was a beast; it was a fit; it was a beast in a fit. I grew numb from amazement: never did I expect anything of the kind. But I didn't lose my head; I didn't even move—and, again, in the former calm voice I told her directly that from then on I was depriving her of the right to participate in my business. Straight to my face, she burst into laughter and left the apartment.

The point is that she had no right to go out of the apartment. Without me—nowhere; such was the stipulation when she was still my fiancée. In the evening she came back. On my part—not a word.

Next morning she went out again, and also the following day. I locked the pawnshop and went to the aunts. At the time of the wedding I had severed my relations with them: ever since neither did I invite them nor did I call on them. It developed that she had not been to see them. They listened to me with curiosity, and they laughed at me—straight in my face: "This is what you deserve." But I expected their laughter. Right then and there I bribed the younger aunt, the maiden, with one hundred rubles, and I gave her twenty-five on account. Two days later she came to me: "Here"—she said—"an officer, a Lieutenant Efimovich—your former regimental mate—is involved." I was quite amazed. That Efimovich had caused me most of the trouble in the regiment, but—being a shameless man—about a month ago, under the pretext of pawning something, he had come to the pawnshop once, then a second time, and I recall that he began to laugh with my wife. Right then I went up and told him that, considering our former relations, he shouldn't dare to call on me. However, I didn't even dream about any such thing, and I merely said to myself that he was an impudent fellow. Yet now the aunt informed me that my wife had already had a rendezvous with him and that the whole affair was being handled by a former acquaintance of the aunts, Ulia Samsonovna, a widow—and, besides, a colonel's widow. "It is she"—she said—"whom your wife now frequents."

I shall cut this picture short. This business cost me up to three hundred, but two days later it was so arranged that I should be standing in the next room, behind a closed door, and I should be listening to the first eye-to-eye rendezvous of my wife with Efimovich. However, in anticipation of this, on the eve there had occurred between us a brief—but, to me, a rather significant—scene.

She had come home toward evening; she sat down on the bed looking mockingly at me and stamping her little foot on the rug. While I was looking at her the thought flashed through my mind that all during the last month, or rather the last two weeks, her disposition was altogether not her own; it may even have been called—an inverted disposition: here was a turbulent, aggressive—I wouldn't say, shameless—but disorderly creature deliberately looking for trouble. Meekness, however, stood in her way. When such a creature begins to revolt, even if she exceeds the limit, still one can see that she is merely coercing herself, that she is prompting herself, but that she herself is impotent to overcome her chastity and shame. This is why such ones, at times, exceed all limits so that you refuse to believe your own observing mind. On the contrary, a soul accustomed to debauch will always soft-pedal things, will act more filthily but in an orderly and respectable manner, with a pretense of superiority.

"And is it true that you were kicked out of the regiment because you were afraid to accept the challenge to a duel?"—she asked suddenly, out of a clear sky, and her eyes glistened.

"It is true: I was asked to leave the regiment in consequence of the decision of the officers' court, although before that I had already sent in my resignation."

"Kicked out as a coward?"

"Yes, they decided I was a coward. But I refused the duel not because I was a coward, but because I refused to submit to their tyrannical decision to challenge a man when I myself perceived no offense. You should know"—I couldn't refrain from stating at this point—"that to oppose such a tyranny by action and to accept all its consequences meant to manifest more courage than to participate in any kind of a duel."

I couldn't restrain myself: by uttering this phrase I started, as it were, exculpating myself, and this was all she needed; what she needed was to humiliate me once more. She laughed angrily.

"And is it true that after that you were loitering for three years in the streets of Petersburg, as a vagabond—begging for dimes and spending nights under billiard tables?"

"I also used to spend nights in the Sennaia, at the Viazemsky house. Yes, this is true: after the regiment there was much disgrace in my life, much degradation, but not moral degradation because even then I was the first to despise my actions. This was merely degradation of my will power and of my mind, caused by the despair over my situation. But this has passed."

"Oh, now you are a personage—a financier!"

That was a hint at the pawnshop. But by that time I was able to compose myself. I could see that she was craving for my humiliating explanations which I did not give. At this juncture a pawner rang the bell and I went to him, into the hall. An hour later, when unexpectedly she got dressed to leave the house, she stopped in front of me and said:

"However, before the wedding you didn't tell me a thing about it?"

I did not answer, and she left.

Thus, the next day I was standing in that room, behind the door, and I was listening: my fate was being decided, and I had a pistol in my pocket. She was dressed up. She sat by the table while Efimovich kept making wry faces. And what happened?— The thing (this I say to my honor), exactly the thing which I dreaded and supposed—without, however, realizing that I was dreading and supposing it. I don't know if I am making myself clear.

The following happened. I was listening for a whole hour, and during that entire hour I was present at a contest between a most noble and lofty woman and an aristocratic, depraved, blunt creature with a cringing soul. And where—I was asking myself in a state of amazement—did this naïve, this meek, this taciturn one learn all this? The wittiest author of a beau-monde comedy could not have conceived that scene of mockeries, naïve laughter and sacred contempt of virtue for vice. And how much brilliancy was there in her words and casual expressions; what witticisms in the perspicacious replies, what truth in her condemnation! And at the same time how much of an almost girlish naïveté! She laughed to his face at his avowals of love, at his gestures and his proposals. Having come with a coarse approach to the task and anticipating no resistance, he suddenly sank.

At first I was ready to suppose mere coquetry on her part— "coquetry on the part of a creature, although depraved yet witty, to exact a higher bid." But no: truth began to shine as the sun, and it was impossible to doubt. It was from fancied and impulsive hatred against me that she, the inexperienced, could have ventured to arrange this rendezvous, but just as soon as it came to business, at once her eyes were opened. She was simply a creature tossing about with one aim in her mind—to insult me at any cost; but, having embarked upon this kind of filth, she felt unable to stand the disorder. And was it she, the sinless and chaste, cherishing an ideal, whom Efimovich, or any other of these beau-monde creatures, could have seduced?—On the contrary, he merely made her laugh. The whole truth rose from her soul, and indignation evoked sarcasm from her heart. I repeat: this jester, at length, grew quite grave and sat there knitting his brow, scarcely answering her, so that I began to fear that he might venture to insult her from mean vengeance. And I repeat once more: to my honor, I listened to that scene almost without surprise—as if I had encountered something familiar. I went there as though for the purpose of encountering it. I had come believing nothing, no accusation, despite the fact that I took the pistol—this is the truth! And could I have imagined her different? Indeed, for what did I love her? Why did I esteem her? Why did I marry her?—Oh, it stands to reason that I became only too well convinced how she hated me; still I also became convinced how chaste she was. Suddenly I opened the door, and thus cut the scene short. Efimovich jumped to his feet. I took her by the hand and asked her to leave with me. Ready-witted, Efimovich burst into loud and rolling laughter:

"Oh, I'll not argue against the sacred marital rights! Lead her away! Lead her away! And, do you know"—he shouted to me as I was leaving—"although a gentleman should not be duelling with you, nevertheless out of respect for your lady, I am at your service . . . if, however, you'll risk it. . . ."

"You hear!"—I stopped her for a second at the threshold.

After that not a word was said till we got home. I led her by the hand, and she did not resist. On the contrary, she was awfully surprised—but only up to the time we reached the house. But when we arrived home, she seated herself on a chair and began to gaze at me. She was terribly pale; although her lips creased themselves into a mocking smile, she was looking with a solemn and severe challenge and, during the first few minutes, I believe, she was seriously convinced that I would shoot her with the pistol. However, I silently took out the pistol and put it on the table. She looked at me and then at the pistol. (Note: this pistol was familiar to her. I had bought it and loaded it at the time itself when I had opened the pawnshop. It was then that I decided neither to keep enormous dogs nor to employ a robust footman, as Moser did. At my house visitors are admitted by the cook. However, people engaged in our kind of business cannot be deprived—for any eventuality—of the means of self-protection. And so I bought a loaded pistol. The first days—after she had entered my house—she took a lively interest in this pistol; she asked questions about it, and I even explained to her the mechanism and its system. Moreover, once I persuaded her to shoot at a target. Note all this.) Paying no attention to her frightened air, I lay down on the bed, half-dressed. I was quite exhausted. It was about eleven o'clock. She remained sitting in the same place, without moving, for another hour or so; then she blew out the candle and she, too, lay down, without undressing, on the couch near the wall. It was the first time that she did not lie down beside me—please note this, too.

6

THE DREADFUL REMINISCENCE

Now, this dreadful reminiscence. . . .

I woke up in the morning—I believe, shortly after seven—and the room was almost light. I awoke at once, with full consciousness, and suddenly opened my eyes. She was standing by the table holding the pistol in her hand. She did not notice that I had awakened and that I was looking at her. And, suddenly, I saw that she started moving toward me with the pistol in her hand. Instantly I closed my eyes, pretending that I was sound asleep.

She came up to the bed and stood over me. I heard everything, and though there ensued dead silence, I could hear that silence. At this moment there occurred a spasmodic movement, and all of a sudden, irresistibly, against my will I opened my eyes. She looked straight into my eyes, and the pistol was already at my temple. But we looked at each other for just a second. I forced myself to close my eyes again and that very moment I decided, with all the power of my will, that I wouldn't move and wouldn't open my eyes—no matter what might be awaiting me.

In fact, it does happen that a man who is sound asleep suddenly opens his eyes, even raises his head for a second, looks around the room and, thereupon, after an instant, unconsciously places his head on the pillow and continues to sleep, without remembering anything. When, having met her gaze and felt the pistol at my temple, I instantly closed my eyes without moving—as a man sound asleep—and most decidedly she could have supposed that I was actually sleeping, that I saw nothing, all the more so as it would have been altogether incredible to close one's eyes at *such* a moment after having seen what I had beheld.

Yes, incredible. Nevertheless she could have guessed the truth, and this suddenly—that same moment—flashed through my mind. Oh, what a whirl of thoughts and feelings rushed past through my brain in less than an instant, and long live the electricity of the human thought! In this case (I felt), if she had guessed the truth, known I was not sleeping, I should have crushed her by my readiness to accept death, and now her hand might waver. The former determination might be shattered by a new extraordinary impression. It is said that people standing on an altitude are drawn, as it were, of their own accord downward into the abyss. I believe that many suicides and murders have been committed for the sole reason that the pistol had been taken in the hand. This is also an abyss—a forty-five degree slope on which one has got to slip down, and one is irresistibly impelled to pull the trigger. However, the realization of the fact that I had seen everything, that I know, and that I am silently awaiting death at her hand, might keep her back on the slope.

Silence persisted, and suddenly I felt about my temple, at my hair, the cold touch of iron. You may ask: did I firmly hope that I would be saved? I will answer you as before God: I had no hope—save, perhaps, one chance in a hundred. Why, then, was I accepting death? But I will ask you: what did I need life for after the pistol had been pointed at me by the creature beloved by me? Besides, I knew with all the force of my being that, at that same moment, between us there was a struggle in progress, a dreadful combat for life or death, a duel involving that very coward of yesterday, kicked out for cowardice by his mates. I knew this and so did she—provided she had guessed the truth that I was not sleeping.

Perhaps this did not happen; perhaps I did not even think about these things at that time; nevertheless this must have happened, though without thought, since, thereafter, every hour of my life, I have been doing nothing but thinking about this.

But you will again ask me: why did I not save her from the crime?—Oh, thousands of times I have asked myself this question —every time when, with a cold sweat on my spine, I have been recalling that second. However, then my soul was in gloomy despair: I was perishing, I myself was perishing—so whom, then, could I be saving? And how do you know that I had the intention of saving anyone? Who knows what I could then have felt?

All the same, consciousness was astir; seconds passed; there was dead silence. She was still standing over me—and, suddenly,

I shivered from hope! Quickly I opened my eyes. She was no longer in the room. I got up from my bed: I had conquered—and she was forever vanquished!

I came out for tea. The samovar was always served in the front room, and she always poured the tea. Silently I took my seat at the table and accepted a glass of tea from her. After about five minutes I glanced at her. She looked dreadfully pale, even more pallid than yesterday, and she was looking at me. And suddenly—suddenly seeing that I was looking at her, she smiled wanly with pallid lips, with a timid question in her eyes. "This means that she is still doubting and asking herself: 'Does he or doesn't he know? Did he or didn't he see?' . . ." Indifferently I turned my eyes away. After tea I locked the pawnshop, went to the market and bought an iron bed and a screen. Upon my return home, I ordered that the bed be placed in the hall, enclosing it with the screen. This was a bed for her but I didn't say a word to her. She understood without words, by reason of that very bed, that I "saw everything and knew everything," and that there could be no further doubt. For the night I left the pistol, as usual, on the table. When night came, she lay down silently on this new bed of hers: the marriage was dissolved—"vanquished but not forgiven." During the night she became delirious, and in the morning brain fever developed. For six weeks she was confined in bed.

CHAPTER II

1

The Dream of Pride

LUKERIA HAS just announced that she is not going to stay with me, and that just as soon as the mistress has been buried, she will quit. I have prayed on my knees for five minutes, but I meant to pray an hour; but I keep thinking and thinking, and all thoughts are ill thoughts, and the headaches—what's the use of praying?—Nothing but sin!—It is also strange that I don't want to sleep: in a deep, very deep sorrow, after the first strongest outbursts, one always wants to sleep. It is said that those condemned to death sleep soundly on the last night. Yes—so it should be; this is in accord with nature, otherwise one couldn't endure it. . . . I lay down on the couch but didn't fall asleep. . . .

. . . During the six weeks of her illness we nursed her day and night—I, Lukeria and a trained nurse from a hospital, whom

I had engaged. I wasn't counting the money, and I even wanted to spend it on her. I invited Doctor Schroeder and paid him ten rubles for every visit. After she regained consciousness, I began to come more rarely into her sight. However, why do I describe this?—When she had completely recovered, quietly and silently she seated herself at a special table which I also bought for her then. . . . Yes, it is true—we kept absolutely silent; that is, later we did begin to talk—but only about ordinary things. Of course, on my own part, I deliberately refrained from talking too much, but I distinctly observed that she, too, was glad, as it were, not to utter a superfluous word. This seemed to me quite natural on her part: "She is too upset and too vanquished"—I used to say to my-self. "Of course, she must be given time to forget and to get accus-tomed to things." And thus we kept silent, but every minute I kept silently preparing myself for the future. I thought that she was doing the same, and it intrigued me awfully to conjecture: "What, precisely, is she now thinking about?"

I will also say: oh, of course, no one knows how much I have endured groaning over her during her sickness. But I groaned silently, suppressing the groans in my breast even from Lukeria. I couldn't imagine, I couldn't even suppose, that she might die without learning everything. However, when she was no longer in danger and her health began to come back—this I remember—I calmed down, and quickly so. Moreover, I decided *to postpone our future* as long as possible, leaving everything temporarily in its present state. Yes, at that time there occurred to me something strange and peculiar—I don't know how to call it otherwise: I grew triumphant, and the very knowledge of it proved sufficient to me. Thus winter passed. Oh, I was content as never before—and this, all winter.

You see, in my life there was one dreadful external circum-stance which, up to that time—*i.e.*, up to the very moment of my wife's catastrophe—weighed heavily upon me every day and every hour, namely—the loss of reputation and the retirement from the regiment. Briefly, it was a tyrannical injustice against me. True, my mates were not fond of me because of my difficult disposition, although it often happens that a thing which seems lofty and sacred to you, which is revered by you, for some reason makes the crowd of your associates laugh. Oh, I was never liked, not even in school. Always and everywhere, I was disliked. Even Lukeria is unable to like me. And the incident in the regiment, though unquestionably it was accidental, was a consequence of the dislike for me. I am telling this because there is nothing more offensive and intolerable than to perish as a result of an accident which might not have happened—as a result of an unfortunate conglomeration of circumstances which might have passed by as clouds. To an intelligent person this is humiliating. This was the incident.

In a theatre, between the acts, I went to the refreshment room. Suddenly a hussar, A—v, entering the room, in the presence of all the officers and public assembled there, started loudly telling two of his mates, also hussars, that Captain Bezumtzev of our regiment had just caused a scandal in the corridor, and that "he seemed to be drunk." The conversation died away and, besides, it was a mistake, since Captain Bezumtzev was not intoxicated and, strictly speaking, the scandal was not a scandal. The hussars began to talk about something else, and that was the end of it. However, the next day the story reached our regiment, and forthwith people started telling that I alone of all the regiment had been in the refreshment room and that when the hussar A—v made an impudent reference to Captain Bezumtzev, I did not come up to A—v and did not stop him with a reprimand. But why should I have? If he had a grudge against Bezumtzev, this was their personal affair, and why should I have become embroiled in it?—Meanwhile, the officers maintained that this was not a personal matter but one which also concerned the regiment, and since of all the officers of our regiment I was the only one present there, I thereby proved to all the officers and public assembled in the refreshment room that in our regiment there are officers who are not too touchy about their honor and that of their regiment. I could not agree with such a judgment. I was informed that I could remedy the situation should I at least now—even though belatedly—have a formal talk with A—v. I didn't want to do so and, since I was irritated, I refused with haughtiness. Thereupon I immediately sent my resignation—and this is the whole story. I resigned—proud but with a shattered spirit. My will power and my mind grew weak. It so happened that at that time my sister's husband had squandered our modest fortune, including my share in it—a microscopic share, but I found myself in the street without a penny. I could have accepted private employment, but this I didn't do: after my brilliant uniform I found it impossible to take a position at some railroad. And so—if it's shame, let it be shame; if it's disgrace—let it be disgrace; if it's degradation—let it be degradation; the worse, the better—this is what I chose. Then came three years of gloomy reminiscences, including the Viazemsky house.

Some eighteen months ago a wealthy old woman, my godmother, died in Moscow, and unexpectedly she left me, among others, three thousand in her will. I thought the matter over and at once chose my fate. I decided to open a pawnshop, without

asking people's forgiveness: money, a home and a new life away
from the former reminiscences—such was my plan. Nevertheless
my gloomy past and the reputation of my honor, lost forever, oppressed me every hour, every minute. But then I married. Was
it by accident or not?—I don't know. But, in admitting her to
my house, I thought that I was admitting a friend: I needed a
friend too badly. But I clearly perceived that the friend should
be prepared, that a finishing touch should be added to her and
that she should even be conquered. And could I have explained
anything at once to this sixteen-year-old and prejudiced one?—For
instance, how could I—without the accidental help brought about
by the dreadful catastrophe with the pistol—have made her believe
that I was no coward, and that in the regiment I was unjustly
accused of cowardice? But the catastrophe came at the proper
time. Having endured the pistol, I had avenged my whole gloomy
past. And although no one has learned about this, nevertheless *she*
learned it, and to me this was everything because she herself was
everything to me—my whole hope for the future, in my dreams!
She was the only human being whom I had been building up for
myself, and no one else was needed—and now she had learned everything; at least she found out that unjustifiably she had hastened
to join my enemies. This thought delighted me. No longer, in her
opinion, could I have remained a coward—maybe, just a queer man;
yet even this thought—after everything that happened—did not
displease me at all: queerness is no vice; on the contrary, sometimes it even attracts women. In a word, I deliberately postponed
the denouement: for the time being, that which did take place
was quite enough for my peace, and it comprised many a picture,
much material for my dreams. Therein is the nastiness—that I am
a dreamer; there was enough material for me, and, as for her, I
reasoned that she could *wait*.

Thus passed the whole winter, in anticipation of something.
I liked to look stealthily at her when she would be sitting by her
table. She was occupied with some work, mending linen, and in
the evenings, at times, she read books which she took from my
cupboard. The selection of the books in the cupboard must have
borne witness in my favor. However, she went out hardly anywhere. Daily before dusk, after dinner, I took her out for a walk,
for exercise, but not altogether silently as heretofore. I sought to
pretend that we did not maintain silence but were conversing
understandingly; however, as stated before, we did it in such a
way as not to speak too much. I did it deliberately and, as to
her, I thought she had to be "given time." Of course, it was strange
that not once, almost till the end of winter, did the thought occur

to me that while I liked to look stealthily at her, never throughout the whole winter did I catch even a single glance of hers at me! I thought that this was timidity on her part. Besides, she looked so timidly meek, so exhausted after her illness. No, it was better to wait—and "suddenly, of her own accord, she will come up to thee. . . ."

This thought irresistibly delighted me. I will add one thing: at times, as though deliberately, I excited myself and actually worked up my spirit and my mind to the point where, as it were, I began to feel offended by her. And thus it lasted for some time. But my hatred was never able to ripen and to strike root in my soul. Besides, I myself felt that this was merely a game. Even then, though I had dissolved the marriage, having bought the bed and the screen, never was I able to perceive in her a delinquent woman. And this not because I judged her crime lightmindedly, but because I had a reason for forgiving her completely, from the very first day—even before I had bought the bed. In a word, this was queerness on my part, because morally I am stern. On the contrary, in my view she was so vanquished, so humbled, so crushed that at times I painfully pitied her, notwithstanding the fact that in the face of everything I was sometimes pleased with the idea of her humiliation. The idea of this inequality of ours pleased me. . . .

That winter I purposely perpetrated several good deeds. I cancelled two debts and gave a poor woman some money without taking any pawn. I told my wife nothing about it, and I did this in such a way that she should not learn of it. But the woman, of her own accord, came to thank me almost on her knees. In this way the matter became known. I was under the impression that she learned with pleasure about the incident with the woman.

But spring was approaching. It was already the middle of April; the storm windows had been removed and the sun, in bright patches, began to light our taciturn rooms. But a shroud was hanging before me, blinding my mind. That fatal, dreadful shroud! How did it happen that all of a sudden it all dropped from my eyes, and I recovered my sight and grasped everything? Was it by accident, or had the destined day come, or was it a ray of sun that kindled the thought and the guess in my blunted mind?—No, it wasn't a thought or a guess; it was a little vein, a tiny, almost atrophied vein; it began to shiver and came to life, and it illuminated my dulled soul and my diabolical pride. I then, as it were, jumped from my seat. Besides, it happened all of a sudden, unexpectedly. This happened toward the evening hour, around five o'clock, after dinner. . . .

2

SUDDENLY THE SHROUD FELL

But first—two words. Even a month ago I observed in her a strange pensiveness, not silence but precisely pensiveness. This I also noticed unexpectedly. She was sitting at work—her head bent over some sewing; she did not see that I was looking at her. And, right then, I was suddenly struck by the fact that she had grown so thin, so lean; that her face was so pale and her lips had become white; all these combined, together with her pensiveness, struck me suddenly and extraordinarily. Even before that I had heard a little dry cough, especially at nighttime. Right away I got up and, without telling her anything, I went to summon Schroeder.

Schroeder came the next day. She was quite surprised and kept looking now at Schroeder, now at me.

"Yes, I feel well"—said she, with an indeterminate smile.

Schroeder did not examine her too attentively (these physicians sometimes are haughtily negligent), and he merely told me in the other room that this was the after-effect of her illness and that, it now being spring, it would be a good idea to take her somewhere to the seashore or, if this were impossible, to go away for the summer to some country place. In a word, he said nothing except that she was weak—or something of the sort. After Schroeder had left, suddenly she said again, looking at me with a very serious expression:

"I feel well—quite well."

However, after having said this, she suddenly blushed—apparently for shame. Apparently, this was shame. Oh, now I understand: she was ashamed that I, still *her husband,* was concerned about her just as if I were a real husband. But then I did not understand, attributing her blush to humility (shroud!).

And so, a month later, after four o'clock in the afternoon, in the month of April, on a bright sunny day, I was sitting at the cash desk checking some accounts. Suddenly I heard her, sitting in our room by the table and working, begin to sing gently, gently. This produced upon me an overwhelming impression which, even now, I cannot comprehend. Prior to that, I almost never heard her sing, save in the very first days after I had admitted her to my house, when we still could be merry and shoot at the target with the pistol. At that time she still had a rather strong and sonorous voice, which, though not true, was very agreeable and healthy. Now, however, her little song was weak—not exactly melancholy (this was some canzonet), but in the voice there was something half-split, broken—as though the little voice was out of control—and the song itself was a sickly one. She sang in a lowered voice which, having risen, suddenly broke off—such a poor little voice and it broke off so pitifully! She coughed, and thereupon began to sing in a faint voice. . . .

People may laugh at my agitation, but no one will ever understand why I felt so troubled! No, I was not yet sorry for her; this was something altogether different. In the beginning—at least in the first few minutes—I was perplexed and terribly surprised; it was an awful and strange surprise—pathological and almost spiteful: "She sings—and in my presence! *Did she forget about me?*"

All upset, I remained motionless and then, suddenly, I got up, took my hat and walked out, as if unconscious. At least, I didn't know why and where I was going. Lukeria began to help me with my overcoat.

"She is singing?"—I said to Lukeria automatically. She didn't understand me and looked at me still at a loss to comprehend the meaning of my question. True, I was unintelligible.

"Is it the first time she has been singing?"

"No, sometimes she does sing in your absence"—answered Lukeria.

I remember everything. I descended the staircase, got out in the street and went along without thinking whither I was going. I walked to the corner and began to gaze—I don't know in what direction. People passed by, pushed me, but I didn't feel it. I hailed a cabman and told him to drive me to the Police Bridge—God knows what for. After a while, however, I suddenly got out of the cab and gave the coachman twenty kopecks:

"This is because I disturbed you"—I told him, insensibly laughing at him, but in my heart some kind of ecstasy began to rise.

I turned back home, and walked with ever more rapid strides. The half-split, poor, broken little note again began to ring in my soul. Something took my breath from me. The shroud was falling off my eyes! If she started singing in my presence, this means that she forgot about me—this was clear and dreadful. It was the heart that sensed it. Yet ecstasy gleamed in my soul, overcoming fear.

Oh, irony of fate!—Indeed, all winter there was, and could have been nothing in my soul but this ecstasy! But where was I all winter? Was I in communion with my soul?—I ran up the staircase, in a great hurry; I don't know whether I entered timidly or not. I only remember that the whole floor was undulating and I was drifting, as it were, downstream. I entered the room; she was sitting in the same place sewing, her head bent down, but she was no longer singing. Casually and indifferently she glanced at me, but it was not a glance—it was a mere gesture, an ordinary and indifferent gesture, as when somebody enters a room.

Straightway I came up and, like a madman, I sat down on the next chair, quite close to her. Quickly she looked as though frightened. I took her hand, and I don't remember what I said to her—*i.e.*, what I meant to say—because I even could not speak correctly. My voice broke down and wouldn't obey me. In fact, I didn't know what to say. I was merely out of breath.

"Let's have a talk. . . . You know . . . say something!"—I babbled something stupid. . . . Oh, well, could I think of reason?—She shivered and shook herself away from me in great fear, looking into my face. But, suddenly, her eyes expressed *stern surprise*. Yes, surprise—and *stern* surprise. She looked at me with big eyes. That sternness, that stern surprise, with one blow shattered me into pieces. "So you also are after love?"—such was the question in that astonishment of hers, even though she remained silent. But I read everything, everything. Everything quivered in me, and I fell down at her feet. She promptly jumped to her feet, but with extraordinary force I held her by both of her hands.

And I fully realized my despair—oh, I understood it! But would you believe that ecstasy was boiling in my heart so irresistibly that I thought I should die. I kissed her feet in a state of rapture and happiness. Yes, happiness—infinite and boundless—and this, fully comprehending my hopeless despair! I wept, I was uttering something, but I could not refrain from talking. Fear and astonishment suddenly gave way in her to some anxious thought, some extraordinary question, and she was strangely—even wildly—looking at me; she sought to grasp something as quickly as possible, and she smiled. She felt awfully ashamed that I was kissing her feet, and she tried to draw them away, but immediately I began to kiss that spot on the floor where her foot had been resting. She saw it and, unexpectedly, she started laughing from shame (you know how people laugh when they are ashamed). Then she was seized with an hysterical fit; I saw her hands shudder—I wasn't thinking about this, but I kept muttering that I loved her, that I would not get up: "Let me kiss your dress . . . let me pray to you all my life. . . ." I don't know, I don't remember. Suddenly, she broke into tears and began to be convulsed. There ensued a dreadful fit of hysterics. I had frightened her.

I carried her to the bed. When the fit was over, she sat up in the bed and, with a desperate air, she seized my hands, entreating me to calm down. "Please stop, don't torture yourself, calm down!"—and again she began to cry. All that evening I didn't leave

her even for a moment. I kept telling her that I would take her
to Boulogne for sea-bathing right away, in a fortnight; that her
little voice was so shaky; that I just heard it; that I would close
the pawnshop and sell it to Dobronravov; that a new life would
begin, but the main thing—Boulogne, Boulogne! She was listening
to me, but all the time with apprehension. Her dread grew stronger
and stronger. Yet to me this was not the important point; the main
point was that more and more irresistibly I longed to lie at her
feet and to kiss the ground upon which her feet stood, and pray
to her; "and I shall ask nothing, nothing more from you"—I kept
repeating every minute.—"Don't answer anything; don't notice me
at all, and only permit me to look at you from the corner! Convert
me into a thing of yours, into a dog! . . ." She wept.

   "And I thought you would leave me so"—this suddenly and
involuntarily burst out of her, so involuntarily that, perhaps, she
didn't notice at all that she had said it. And yet, this was the
most important, the most fatal, the most intelligible word of hers
during that evening, and it slashed, as it were, my heart as a
knife! It explained everything to me, but so long as she was there,
at my side, before my eyes, I was irresistibly hoping and was
terribly happy. Oh, that evening I tired her out awfully, and I
understood it, but I kept incessantly thinking that I would at once
transform everything. Finally, late in the evening she became quite
exhausted, and I persuaded her to go to sleep—and, promptly and
soundly, she fell asleep. I was expecting that she would grow
delirious, but there was but the slightest delirium. During the night
I got up almost every minute; quietly, in my slippers, I came to
look at her. I wrung my hands over her, beholding the ill creature
on this cheap little cot—this iron bed which I had bought for
three rubles. I knelt before her, but I didn't dare to kiss her feet
(without her will!). I was on my knees and prayed God, but then
again I jumped to my feet. Lukeria was gazing at me, and time
and again she came out of the kitchen. I went to her and told her
to go to bed, and that tomorrow "something altogether new" would
begin.

   And I believed in this blindly, insanely, awfully. Oh, ecstasy,
ecstasy deluged me! I was only waiting for tomorrow. What was
most important—I did not believe in any calamity despite the
symptoms of it. Reason had not yet returned to me completely,
notwithstanding the fallen shroud, and it didn't return for a long,
long time—oh, till today, till this very day! And how could it
have returned then? indeed, then she was still alive; she was here
before me, and I—before her: "Tomorrow she will wake up and
I will tell her everything, and she will perceive everything." At the

time such was my way of reasoning, simple and clear—and ecstasy! The main thing was that journey to Boulogne. Somehow, I thought all the time that Boulogne was everything, that there was something final in Boulogne. "To Boulogne! To Boulogne! . . ." Insanely, I was waiting for the morning.

3

I UNDERSTAND TOO CLEARLY

And this was only several days ago—five days, only five days, last Tuesday! No, no, if only she had waited just a little longer, I should have dispelled the darkness!—And didn't she calm down? For the next day she listened to me with a smile, despite the confusion. . . . Most important of all was the fact that during all that time—all five days—there was confusion, or shame, in her. She was also afraid, very much afraid. I'm not going to argue; I'm not going to contradict like a madman. "There was fear, but how could she not have been afraid?"—Because it was so long that we had been estranged, separated one from the other, and suddenly all this. . . . But I disregarded her fear: the new life was gleaming! . . . The truth, the unquestionable truth is that I did make a mistake. Just as we awoke the next day, that very morning (this was on Wednesday), suddenly I made a mistake: suddenly, I made her my friend. I hastened much too much, but confession was imperative—why more than confession! I didn't conceal even that which all my life I hid even from myself. I told her frankly that all winter long I had been fully convinced of her love. I explained to her that the pawnshop was but a degradation of my will and my reason, a personal idea of self-flagellation and self-praising. I explained to her that then, in that refreshment room, I actually did get scared—owing to my disposition, my suspiciousness: I was struck by the mis-en-scène, by the refreshment room; I was struck by the thought: how am I going to come forward? Will it not be ridiculous? . . . I grew cowardly not over the duel, but over the thought that it would be ridiculous. . . . And, later, I did not wish to admit this, and kept torturing everybody; and it was for this that I had been torturing her, too, and that I married her in order to torture her for this. Generally, I spoke mostly like a person in delirium. She herself took me by my hands and asked me to stop: "You are exaggerating . . . you are torturing yourself!"—and again there were tears, again almost fits! She kept entreating that I shouldn't be telling all these things, that I shouldn't be reminiscing.

I disregarded the entreaties, or I paid insufficient attention to them: Spring—Boulogne! Over there, there is sun, our new sun!—This is what I was telling her all the time! I would close the pawnshop, turning over the business to Dobronravov. Suddenly I suggested giving everything away to the poor, except the initial three thousand, inherited from my godmother, which we would expend for the journey to Boulogne; and then, upon our return, we would start a new, working life. Thus it was decided because she said nothing . . . she merely smiled. And, it seems, she smiled more from sensitiveness, so as not to offend me. For I did see that I oppressed her: don't think that I am so stupid and so egoistic that I didn't see it. I saw everything to the last dot; I saw and knew better than anyone: all my despair stood out clearly!

I told her everything about myself and about her. Also, about Lukeria. I told her that I wept. . . . Oh, I also changed the conversation; I tried by all means not to remind her about certain things. She even grew animated once or twice—indeed, this I remember, I do! Why do you say that I looked but saw nothing? Had only *this* not have occurred, everything would have been resurrected. Didn't she tell me—only two days ago, when the conversation turned to the topic of reading and what she had read that winter—didn't she recall with a laugh and tell me about that scene of Gil Blas with the Archbishop of Granada. And what a childish, charming laugh that was! Just like the time when she was my fiancée (an instant! an instant!). And how glad I was! However, I was awfully surprised—I mean, about the Archbishop: thus she did possess so much serenity of spirit and so much happiness that she could laugh when she sat reading a masterpiece that winter! This means that she was then beginning to be completely appeased; that she believed I would leave her *so*. "And I thought you would leave me *so*"—this is what she had uttered on Tuesday! Oh, this was the thought of a ten-year-old girl! And, indeed, she believed, actually believed, that everything would remain *so:* she by her table, I—at mine; thus the both of us, till the age of sixty. And suddenly—here I come forward, I, the husband, and a husband needs love! Oh, what a misunderstanding! Oh, this blindness of mine!

It was also a mistake that I was looking at her with transport: I should have restrained myself, because ecstasy was frightening. But I did restrain myself, since no longer did I kiss her feet. Not once did I make it appear that I was a husband—this never even came to my mind—I merely worshipped! still, it was impossible to keep absolutely silent! It was impossible not to talk at all!

Suddenly I told her that I was delighted with her conversation, and that I considered her incomparably better educated and more intelligent than myself. She blushed deeply and, with embarrassment, she said that I was exaggerating. At this juncture, being unable to restrain myself, I stupidly told her with what delight, standing there behind the door, I had listened to her duel—the duel of innocence—with that creature, and how I enjoyed her intellect, the brilliancy of her, coupled with such childish naïveté. She shivered all over, as it were, again muttering something to the effect that I was exaggerating, but suddenly her whole face darkened; she covered it with her hands and broke into tears. . . . No longer could I restrain myself: again I fell at her feet, kissing them—and, once more, she had a fit even as on Tuesday. This occurred yesterday evening—and this morning . . .

In the morning? Oh, madman, this was today, this morning, only recently, only recently!

Please listen and think: when only a few hours ago we met at tea with the samovar on the table (after yesterday's fit) she even astonished me by her composure—thus it was! And I trembled all night from fear over yesterday's incident. Suddenly she came up to me, stood before me and, crossing her hands (so recently, so recently), she started telling me that she was a delinquent woman; that she knew this; that her crime weighed upon her all winter, that it also tormented her at present . . . that she valued highly my magnanimity. . . . "I will be your faithful wife, I will respect you. . . ." Then I jumped to my feet and, like a lunatic, embraced her! I kissed and kissed her face, her lips, like a husband —the first time after a long estrangement. And why did I leave her—for two hours only . . . our foreign passports. . . . Oh, God! Had I returned only five minutes earlier! . . . And then this crowd at our gate . . . those looks at me . . . Oh, Lord!

Lukeria says (oh, now, under no circumstance will I let her go; she knows everything, she stayed with us all winter; she will be relating everything to me)—she says that after I left the house, and only about twenty minutes before I came back, she unexpectedly went to the mistress in our room, to ask her about something—I don't remember what—and she saw that her ikon (that same image of the Mother of God) had been taken out of the image case, and was standing on the table before the mistress, and that it was her impression that she, the mistress, had been just praying before it. "What is it, madam?"—"Nothing, Lukeria, you can go!—Wait, Lukeria"—she went and kissed her.—"Are you happy, madam?"—asked Lukeria.—"Yes, Lukeria."—"Long ago my master should have come to you and asked your forgiveness. . . .

Thank God that you have made up."—"All right, Lukeria"—she said—"go now," and she smiled, but strangely somehow—so strangely that some ten minutes later Lukeria went back to look at her: "She was standing near the wall, quite close to the window, pressing her hand against the wall and her head against her hand. She stood there musing. And so deep in her thoughts was she that she didn't hear me and notice that I stood looking at her from the other room. I saw that she was smiling, as it were; she stood there pondering and smiling. I looked at her, quietly turned around and walked out wondering. Presently I heard the window being opened. Immediately I returned and said to her: 'It is cool outside, madam; beware of catching a cold.' Suddenly, I saw that she got up on the window sill, standing upright at the open window, with her back turned to me, holding the ikon in her hands. My heart sank, and I cried, 'Madam! Madam!' She heard me, made a move to turn toward me but didn't turn, took a step, pressing the image to her breast—and leaped out of the window!"

I remember only that when I entered the gate she was still warm. The main thing—they were all gazing at me. First, they were shouting, but then they all grew silent and gave way before me . . . and she lay with the ikon. I dimly recall that I approached and kept looking at her for a long while. They all gathered around me and were telling me something. Lukeria was there but I didn't see her. She said she spoke to me. I only remember that commoner: he kept shouting at me: "A handful of blood!"—pointing to blood on the stone. I believe, I touched the blood with my finger and stained it; for I looked at my finger (this I remember), while he kept saying: "A handful, a handful!"

"And what's that about a handful?"—I cried at the pitch of my voice and, so they say, I lifted my arms and started at him. . . .

Oh, how odd, how odd! Misunderstanding! It's untrue! Impossible! . . .

4

I Was Only Five Minutes Late

Isn't this so? Is this plausible? Can it be said that it is possible? Why?—For what reason did this woman die?

Oh, believe me, I understand. . . . Yet, for what reason did she die?—This is still a question. Did she become afraid of my love and did she seriously ask herself whether or not to accept it, and, being unable to bear this question, did she prefer to die? I know, I know—there's no point in cracking the brain: she gave too many promises, she grew frightened lest she wouldn't be able to keep them—that's clear. Here there are several circumstances which are perfectly horrible.

Because what did she die for? This question still stands unanswered. This question hammers, hammers away at my brain. And I would have left her *so* if she should have wished that it remain so. She didn't believe it—that's it! No—no, I am lying— it's not at all this. Simply because with me it had to be honest: if it were love, it had to be full love—and not the kind of love she would be meting out to the shopkeeper. And inasmuch as she was too chaste, too pure to accede to such a love as would have satisfied the shopkeeper, she did not wish to deceive me. She didn't want to deceive me with half- or quarter-love, under the guise of love. They are too honest—that's the point! I meant to inculcate breadth of heart—you remember?—Queer thought!

I'm awfully curious to know this: did she respect me? I don't know whether she despised me or not. I don't think she despised me. Awfully strange: why is it that throughout the whole winter the thought never occurred to me that she despised me? I was firmly convinced of the contrary till that very moment when she looked at me with stern surprise. Stern—precisely. Then, at once, I grasped that she despised me. I grasped this irrevocably, forever! Ah, would that she had despised me even for the rest of my life, but would that she had lived, lived! Only recently she walked, she conversed. I'm quite at a loss to understand how she could leap out of the window! And how could I have supposed it even five minutes before I called Lukeria. For nothing in the world shall I now let Lukeria go!

Oh, we still could have reached an agreement. Only during the winter we got frightfully alienated from each other—but couldn't we have become accustomed? Why, why couldn't we have gotten together and started a new life? I am magnanimous, and so was she—and here was the junction point! A few more words—two days, no more—and she would have understood everything.

The thing that is most offensive is that this is all an accident —a simple, barbarous, inert accident! This is the offense! Five minutes, only five minutes late was I! Had I come five minutes earlier—the instant would have floated away as a cloud, and later it would never have occurred to her. And it would have come to the point where she would have grasped everything. And now— again these empty rooms, again I am alone. The pendulum is swinging; to it it makes no difference; it regrets no one. There's nobody —that's the trouble!

I keep pacing and pacing. I know, I know—don't prompt me:

to you it seems funny that I am complaining of the accident and of the five minutes? But this obviousness. Think: she didn't even leave a note to the effect: "Don't blame anyone for my death"—as they all do. Is it possible that she could not reason out that they might cause trouble even for Lukeria: "You were alone with her"—they might have said—"and you must have pushed her." At least, they might have worn her out were it not for the fact that, from the windows in the wing of the building and in the courtyard, four people saw how she stood with the ikon in her hands and leaped out of her own accord. But this, too, is an accident—that people were standing there and witnessing the scene. No, all this was an instant, merely an unaccountable moment. Suddenness and fantasy! What does it matter that before that she had been praying before the ikon? This did not mean—before death. The entire spell lasted, maybe, some ten minutes only—the whole resolution—precisely as she was standing at the wall, leaning, with her head in her hand, and smiling. The thought flew into her head, it started whirling—and she was unable to withstand it.

Here is an obvious misunderstanding—say what you please. She still could have lived with me. And what if it was anæmia?—Simply from anæmia, from exhaustion of vital energy?—She grew tired that winter, that's it. . . .

I was late! ! !

How lean she is in the coffin! How sharp her little nose has become! Her eyelashes lie like arrows. And she only fell—she didn't fracture or break anything! Only "a handful of blood"—that is, a little dessert spoonful. Internal concussion. Strange thought: what if it were possible not to bury her? Because if she should be carried away, then . . . Oh, no: it is almost impossible that she be carried away! Oh, I know that she must be carried away—I am not a lunatic, and I am not at all in delirium. On the contrary, never before has my mind been so clear.—But how is it going to be?—Again there will be nobody in the house. Again, the two rooms—and I alone with those pawned articles. Delirium, delirium—that's delirium! I wore her out—that's it!

Now, what do I care about your laws? What use have I for your customs, your habits, your life, your state, your religion? Let your judge judge me; let them take me into your court, your public court, and let them declare that they reject everything. The judge will shout: "Keep silent, officer!" And I will shout to him: "What authority do you possess which would now compel me to obey you? Why did dark inertia smash to pieces that which was dearest of all? What use have I now for your laws?—I segregate myself." Oh, it's all the same to me.

She's blind, blind! Dead! She hears nothing! You don't know with what paradise I would have surrounded you. Paradise would have been in my soul, and I would have planted it all around you! All right, you wouldn't love me—all right. What of it? And everything would have been *so;* everything would have remained *so.* You would be conversing with me as a friend—and we should be rejoicing, laughing happily and looking into each other's eyes. And thus we should be living. And even if you should love someone else—all right, all right! You would be walking with him and laughing, and I should be beholding you from across the street. . . . Let everything be as it may—only let her once again open her eyes!—For a moment, for one instant only! Would that she would glance at me only, as she did so recently when she stood before me and took the vow that she would be my faithful wife! Oh, in one glance she would have grasped everything!

Inertia! Oh, nature! Men on earth are alone—this is the calamity! "Is there in the field a living man?"—shouts the valiant Russian knight. I—not a knight—am shouting too, and no one responds. People say that the sun vivifies the universe, and look at it—isn't it a corpse? Everything is dead, and everywhere—nothing but corpses. Only men and, around them, silence—such is earth. "Love each other."—Who said this? Whose covenant is this? The pendulum is swinging insensibly and disgustingly. It's night—two o'clock. Her little shoes stand by her dear little bed, as if awaiting her. . . . No, seriously—tomorrow, when they carry her away, what will I do?

DECEMBER

CHAPTER I

1

Again About a Simple but Tricky Case

EXACTLY TWO months ago, in the October issue of my *Diary,* I made some comments on an unfortunate criminal woman, Katerina Prokofieva Kornilova—that very stepmother who, in the month of May, prompted by anger against her husband, cast out of the window her six-year-old stepdaughter. This case is particularly notorious, due to the fact that the little stepdaughter who was thrown out of the window on the fourth floor, was not hurt—she was not injured, and she is now alive and in good health.

I shall not recapitulate in detail my October article; perhaps the readers have not forgotten it. I shall only remind them of the object of that article: from the very beginning I felt that the case was altogether too extraordinary, and I at once became convinced that it should not be treated *too simply*. The ill-starred delinquent woman was pregnant; she was irritated by her husband's nagging, and she languished. But it was not this—*i.e.*, the desire to take vengeance upon her reproachful and offensive husband—that was the cause of the crime, but "the affect of pregnancy." In my opinion, at that time—during several days or weeks—she had been living through that peculiar, quite unexplored, but undeniably existent state, affecting certain pregnant women, when in a woman's soul there occur strange twists, queer submissions and influences—insanity without insanity which, sometimes, may reach the proportion of conspicuously potent and ugly abnormalities. I cited a case, which I have known since childhood, of a Moscow lady who, invariably, during a certain period of her pregnancy, acquired a strange desire and submitted to a queer whim—of stealing. And yet that lady had a carriage of her own and did not at all need those articles which she stole; however, she did this deliberately—fully conscious of her acts. Consciousness was fully retained, but she was unable to resist the strange impulse.

This is what I wrote two months ago and, I confess, I wrote this with the most remote, almost hopeless, aim to help somehow and in some manner, and to alleviate the fate of, the unfortunate woman despite the dreadful sentence imposed upon her. I was unable to refrain in my article from stating that if our jurors have given verdicts of acquittal so many times, mostly to women, notwithstanding their full confessions of the crimes they had committed, and despite the obvious evidence of those crimes ascertained by the court—it would seem that they could also have acquitted Kornilova. (Precisely several days later, after the verdict in the case of poor, pregnant Kornilova who was sentenced to forced labor and exile to Siberia for life, the strangest criminal, a murderess Kirilova, was acquitted altogether.) However, I shall quote what I wrote at the time.

"At least, if the jurors had acquitted the defendant, they could have relied on something: 'Although such pathological affects are rare, nevertheless, they do occur. What if in the present case, too, there was an affect of pregnancy?' This is something to be considered. At least, in such a case mercy would have been intelligible to everybody and would not have produced mental vacillation. And what if there should have been an error? Better an error in mercy . . ."

Having written all this, lured by my thoughts, I started meditating and I added in my article that this poor twenty-year-old delinquent woman, who at the time was about to give birth to a child in prison, had perhaps already made up with her husband. Maybe the husband (who is now free and has the right to marry again) calls on her at the prison, while she is waiting to be transferred to the hard-labor penitentiary, and they are both grieving and crying. Perhaps the victim—that little girl—also visits her "Mama," having forgotten everything, and caresses her wholeheartedly. I even pictured the scene of their farewell at the railroad station. All these "meditations" came from my pen not for the sake of effect and not for mere delineation, but simply because I felt the living truth, consisting of the fact that although they both, husband and wife, unquestionably consider her a criminal woman—he, his wife, and she, herself—nevertheless, as a matter of fact, they could not help but forgive each other and reconcile themselves with each other—and not only because of the Christian feeling, but precisely as a result of an involuntary instinctive sentiment that the perpetrated crime—so obvious and unquestionable to their simple way of thinking—essentially, *perhaps, is not a crime at all,* but something that has strangely occurred and has been strangely perpetrated, as if not by their will, but by God's judgment—for the sins of both of them. . . .

Having finished that article and having brought out the issue of the *Diary*—and being still under the impression of all my meditations—I made up my mind, by all means, to interview Kornilova while she was still in the local jail. I confess that I was very curious to ascertain whether there was any truth in my conjectures about Kornilova and in my subsequent dreams concerning the case. It so happened that there soon occurred a circumstance which enabled me to visit Kornilova and make her acquaintance. Now, I myself was surprised that at least three-quarters of my meditations proved to be true: my guesses were as correct as if I had been present at what actually happened. The husband, in fact, did call on her and continues to visit her; the two, in truth, are weeping and lamenting over each other; they are bidding farewell—one to the other—and they are forgiving. "The little girl would have come to see me"— Kornilova herself told me—"but at present she is in some school where pupils live as inmates." I regret that I am not in a position to relate everything I learned about the life of this disintegrated family, even though here there are some very curious traits—well, of course, *sui generis.* Indeed, in certain things I was mistaken, but not in the essential ones: for instance, whereas Kornilov is a peasant, he wears German clothes; he is much younger than I supposed he was; he works as a scooper[1] at the Government Printing Office, and his monthly wages are rather substantial for a peasant; this means that he is much better off than I presumed in my conjectures. And she is a seamstress; she was a seamstress, and even now, in jail, she is engaged in sewing; she gets orders and is earning good money. In brief, it is not all "cloth and felt boots for her journey, or tea and sugar"; the conversation is on a somewhat higher plane. When I first went to visit her, she had already given birth to a child—not a son, however, but a daughter, etc. These are slight disparities but, in the main, in the essentials, there was no mistake.

At that time, during the period of her accouchement, she was kept in a special compartment, and she was sitting in a corner; beside her, on a bed, lay the newly-born child who had been christened only on the eve. When I came in, the infant gave a faint cry, with that singular little crack which is peculiar to all newly-born. By the way, for some reason, this jail is not called a prison but a "house of preliminary detention of criminals." However, they keep there quite a few criminals, especially of certain peculiar categories, about whom, perhaps, in due course of time I shall have something to say. But I may add apropos that I have gained a very comforting impression—at least, in this women's division—from observing unquestionable humaneness in the relations between the inspectresses and the women inmates. Later I visited other cells—for instance, the one in which criminal women with nurslings are kept in common. I myself saw the concern, attention and care accorded to them by their respectable immediate mistresses. And even though I had been observing them but a short while, nevertheless there are such traits, such words, such actions and movements, as are at once indicative of many a thing.

The first time I stayed with Kornilova about twenty minutes: she is a very young, good-looking woman, with an intelligent expression on her face, but very naïve indeed. In the beginning, the first couple of minutes, she was somewhat surprised over my visit, but soon she believed that she beheld beside her one of *her own,* who sympathized with her, as I introduced myself to her when I came in, and then she became quite frank with me. She is not very loquacious; nor is she too perspicacious in conversation, but what she does say she says firmly and clearly, apparently truthfully and invariably kindly, without any sugar-coating and servility. She spoke to me not exactly as her equal, but almost as one of her own. At that time, probably still under the influence of recent childbed, and also the recent verdict in her case (in the very last days of her pregnancy), she was somewhat excited and she even began to weep when

[1]One who ladles out the liquid in which bank notes are dyed.

she recalled certain testimony given against her in court—about some alleged words which, supposedly, she had uttered on the day of her crime, but which in reality she never did utter. She was very grieved over the injustice of that testimony but the thing that struck me was the fact that she spoke without the slightest bitterness, and only once did she exclaim: "Thus, such was my fate!" When immediately I brought up the subject of her newly-born daughter, at once she began to smile: "Yesterday"—she said—"we christened her."—"What's her name?"—"Just as mine—Katerina." That smile of a mother sentenced to hard labor, at her child who was born in prison immediately after the sentence and who, while still unborn, had been convicted together with her mother—that smile produced on me a strange and painful impression. When, cautiously, I started questioning her about her crime, the tone of her answers pleased me very much. She answered everything clearly, in a straightforward manner, not at all evasively, so that I perceived at once that no special precautions were needed. She fully confessed that she was a criminal guilty of everything of which she had been accused. It also struck me that when speaking about her husband (in a state of anger against whom she had pushed the girl out of the window) not only did she say nothing—not even a bit—spiteful or accusatory, but on the contrary there was kindness in her tone.—"Well, how did all this come to pass?"—And she frankly said to me: "I meant to commit something wicked; only here it was not my will, as it were, but somebody else's." I remember she added (in answer to my question) that even though she did go at once to the police station to report the incident, nevertheless "I didn't want to go, but somehow I went there—I don't know what for—and I confessed to everything of my own volition."

Even on the eve of my visit, I learned that her lawyer, Mr. L., had filed a cassation complaint. Thus there was still some hope—though only a faint one. However, in my mind I entertained another hope about which, for the time being, I shall keep silent, but which, at the end of our interview, I conveyed to her. She listened to me without much reliance on the success of my project, but she believed wholeheartedly in my sympathy for her and, right then, thanked me for it. In answer to my question as to whether I could be useful to her in any way—promptly guessing what I had in mind—she said that she needed nothing, that she had both money and work. However, in these words there sounded no touchiness whatsoever, so that, had she been without money, perhaps she would not have refused to accept from me a small contribution.

Subsequently, I called on her a couple of times. Among other things, I spoke to her once about the full acquittal of the murderess

Kirilova, which took place only several days after her, Kornilova's, conviction—but I noticed not even the slightest envy or murmur on her part. Positively she is inclined to consider herself a grave criminal. Observing her more closely, involuntarily I noticed that at the bottom of this rather curious feminine character there was much steadiness, orderliness and—this aroused my particular interest—cheerfulness. Nevertheless, apparently, reminiscences weigh heavily on her: with sincere grief she regrets that she had been stern with the child—"I took a dislike to her";—that she beat her after listening to her husband's incessant nagging on the subject of his late wife, of whom, as I guessed, Kornilova was jealous. She is noticeably disturbed by the thought that now her husband is free and may even marry, and it was with great pleasure that she told me that once when her husband had recently visited her, he said to her: "Is it possible, under these circumstances, to think about marriage!" Thus—I said to myself—she must have been the first to bring up this subject. I repeat: she fully realizes that after the sentence imposed upon her, her husband is no longer her husband and that the marriage is annulled. The thought occurred to me that some truly peculiar rendezvous and conversations must be taking place between them.

In the course of these visits I had occasion to speak about Kornilova with several prison inspectresses and with Madam A. P. B.—the assistant to the warden. I was surprised by the apparent sympathy which Kornilova has aroused in all of them. Among other things, Madam A. P. B. conveyed to me a curious observation, namely: when Kornilova (shortly after the crime) had been admitted to the prison, she was an altogether different creature—discourteous, malicious, quick at wicked answers. However, in less than two or three weeks she changed suddenly and completely: she grew kind, naïve, meek—"and thus she still is." This statement seemed to me very relevant to the *case*. The trouble is that the case has already been adjudicated and the sentence pronounced. But the other day I was informed that the court's verdict, which had been appealed, was rescinded (because of the violation of Section 693 of the Code of Criminal Procedure), and that the case will be tried by a jury in another division of the court.

Thus, at the present moment Kornilova is again a defendant, and not a hard-labor convict; and again she is the legitimate wife of her husband, and he—her legitimate husband! This means that hope again is gleaming upon her. Let us pray God that this youthful soul, which has already endured so much, be not completely crushed by a new "guilty" verdict. It is hard for a human soul to endure such shocks: they are akin to a situation where a man condemned to die before a firing squad would suddenly be untied from the post; hope would be restored in him; the bandage would be removed from his eyes; once more he would be seeing the sunlight—but five minutes later he would again be tied to the post.

Indeed, is it possible that not the slightest attention will be paid to the fact of the pregnancy of the defendant at the time of the commission of her crime? Naturally, the most important part of the prosecution consists of the fact that, nevertheless, she had *consciously* committed the crime. But I am asking again: what role does consciousness play in such a case as this? Consciousness may have been fully retained and, despite the most lucid consciousness, she was unable to resist the insane and perverted pathological affect. In fact, does this seem so impossible? Had she not been pregnant at the moment of her angry irritation she would, perhaps, have said to herself: "Bad girl—she should be thrown out of the window; that would stop him from reproaching me every hour over her mother." Thus she might have reasoned, and still might not have done it, whereas in a pregnant state she *could not resist*, and did it. Couldn't this have transpired precisely in this way? And what does it matter that she herself testified that already on the eve she had made up her mind to throw the child out of the window, but that she was prevented by the presence of her husband?—Even so, all this criminal deliberation, so logically and firmly conceived, and next morning so methodically put into effect (including the removal of the flower pots, etc.), under no circumstance can be attributed to ordinary intentional villainy: here there happened something unnatural and abnormal.

Think about one thing: having pushed the girl out of the window and having looked through it to see how the girl fell (the first moment she fainted and was unconscious, so that looking at her through the window, Kornilova, of course, could have considered her dead), the murderess closed the window, got dressed and went to the police station to denounce herself. However, what would have been the purpose of denouncing herself if she might have planned the crime firmly and calmly, with cold-blooded deliberation? Who and where were the witnesses to the fact that she had thrown the child out, or that the girl herself fell owing to incautiousness?—She could also have convinced her husband, upon his return, that the little girl fell due to her own fault, and that she, Kornilova, was guilty of nothing (thus she would have injured her husband and at the same she would have exonerated herself). Even if she had then—after looking through the window—become convinced that the child was not hurt and was alive, so that it might later testify against her—even so Kornilova would have had nothing to fear:

what significance could have attached at the trial, to the testimony of a six-year-old girl to the effect that she had been lifted from behind by her feet and pushed out of the window?—Any medical expert could have contended that it might have seemed to the girl at the moment when she had lost her balance and was falling (*i.e.*, if in fact she should have fallen through her own fault), that someone from behind had seized her by her little feet and pushed her downward. And if this be so, why did the criminal woman go forthwith to denounce herself?—Of course, it might be said: "She was in despair and sought to commit suicide one way or another." In fact, no other explanation can be found; yet this explanation itself shows in what state of psychic tension and derangement was this *pregnant* woman. Her own words are curious: "I didn't want to go to the police station, but somehow I went there all the same." This means that she acted as if in delirium—*"as if not by her own will,"* despite the full confession.

On the other hand, the testimony of Madam A. P. B. also explains a whole lot: "This was an altogether different creature—rude and angry—and suddenly, two weeks later, she changed radically: she became meek, placid, kind." Why so?—Precisely because a certain pathological period of pregnancy had come to an end—a period of sick will and of "insanity without insanity"; with it the pathological affect came to an end, and a new creature came into being.

Look here: once more she will be sentenced to hard labor; again she, who has already been so shocked and who has endured so much, will be shocked and crushed by the *second* sentence, and she, the twenty-year-old one, who has almost not yet begun to live, with a nursling in her arms, will be cast into a hard-labor penitentiary. And what will be the result? Will she derive much from hard labor? Will not her soul harden? Will it not be depraved and exasperated forever? Whom and when did hard labor ever reform? And the most important thing—all this in the presence of an utterly unexplained and not refuted doubt concerning the pathological affect of her pregnant condition at the time.

Again I repeat, just as two months ago: "better to err in mercy than in chastisement." Acquit the unfortunate and, perhaps, a young soul will not perish—a soul which, maybe, has so much life in the future and in which there are so many good potentialities therefor. In prison all this will unfailingly be ruined, since the soul will be depraved, whereas now the terrible lesson, already endured by her, will guard her, perhaps, for her whole life, against an evil deed; and —what is most important—it will help to develop and ripen those seeds and beginnings of good which apparently and unquestionably are present in this youthful soul. And were her heart truly hard and spiteful, mercy would unfailingly soften it. But I assure you, it is far from being hard and spiteful, and I am not the only one to bear witness to this. Is it not possible to acquit her—to *risk* acquitting her?

2

BELATED MORAL

That October issue of my *Diary* has also caused me trouble—in a way, of course. In it there is a short article *The Verdict,* which had left me in some doubt. That *Verdict* is the confession of a suicide, recorded by himself immediately before he shot himself with a pistol—recorded for his justification and, maybe, as a moral. Several of my friends, whose opinion I treasure most highly, even praised the article but corroborated my doubts. They praised it for the fact that actually a formula, as it were, of suicides of this pattern had been found—a formula which clearly expressed their basic ideology. But these friends of mine were wondering if the object of the article would be understood by each and all of my readers. Wouldn't it, contrariwise, produce on someone some altogether opposite impression? Moreover, wouldn't some of them—those very people who had already begun to dream about the pistol or the noose—wouldn't they be seduced by the reading of my article, and wouldn't they feel even more confirmed in their unfortunate intentions? In a word, doubts were expressed which were identical with those that had earlier occurred to me. And, as a result, I came to the deduction that it would have been necessary to give, directly and simply, in clear words at the end of the article, the author's explanation of the object with which it had been written—and even to add a moral.

With this I was in accord. Besides, while I was writing the article I myself felt that a moral was necessary, but somehow I was ashamed to write it. I felt ashamed to presume, even in a very naïve reader, so much simplicity that he wouldn't guess the *underlying motive* of the article, its object, its moral. To me this object was so clear that, willy-nilly, I supposed it to be equally clear to everybody. I proved to be wrong.

Correct is the observation which was made several years ago by a writer to the effect that in days gone by it was considered a shame to admit the lack of understanding of certain things because it was direct proof of the dullness of him who made such an admission, of his ignorance, of the defective development of his mind and heart, of the weakness of his mental faculties. At present, on the contrary, the phrase—"I don't understand it"—is often being uttered almost with pride or, at least, with an important air. This phrase promptly places the man, in the opinion of his listeners, on a pedestal, and—what is still more comic—in his own opinion, too; and he isn't in the least ashamed of the cheapness of the pedestal thus acquired. Nowadays the words: "I understand nothing about Raphael," or "I have purposely read all of Shakespeare and, I confess, I found absolutely nothing particular in him"—these words today may be accepted not only as a sign of profound intellect, but even as something valiant, virtually as a moral exploit. And is it only Shakespeare or Raphael who is subjected to such judgments and to such doubts?

This observation concerning uppish ignoramuses, which I have recorded here in my own words, is rather correct. In point of fact, the pride of the ignoramuses has become boundless. Poorly developed and dull people are not ashamed of these unfortunate qualities of theirs; on the contrary, a situation has developed where these very qualities "add zest" to them. I have also often observed that both in literature and in private life there have developed great segregations, and many-facetedness of knowledge has disappeared: people who vehemently challenge their adversaries throughout whole decades have not read a single line of the latter's writings: "I have different convictions"—they say—"and I am not going to read nonsence." Verily—a penny's worth of ammunition and a ruble's worth of ambition. Such an extreme one-sidedness and isolation, such segregation and intolerance, have developed only in our day—*i.e.*, preeminently during the last twenty years. Coupled with these, there arose in many a man some sort of impudent boldness: men of negligible knowledge laugh—and even to one's face—at people possessing ten times more learning and understanding. And what is worst of all —as time goes on "rectilinearness" develops in an ever-increasing measure: for example, the instinct for adaptation, for metaphor, for allegory, begins to disappear. Noticeably, people cease (generally speaking) to understand jest, humor—and this, according to the observation of a certain German thinker, is one of the surest symptoms of the intellectual and moral degradation of an epoch. Instead, there come into being gloomy blockheads with frowning brows and narrow minds moving in one direction only—along the straight line toward one fixed point. Do you think that I am speaking only of the young ones and the liberals?—I assure you that I am referring also to old fellows and conservatives. As though in imitation of the young ones (at present already gray ones), some twenty years ago there came into being queer single-track conservatives—irritated old men who understand nothing about current affairs, about the new people and the younger generation. Their rectilinearness, if you please, was sometimes even more rigorous, more cruel and more obtuse than that of "the new men." Oh, possibly, all this developed in them as a result of the superfluity of good intentions and of magnanimous feelings which, however, had been vexed with the latest follies. Nevertheless, at times they are blinder than the modern rectilinearists. However, I am afraid that, while denouncing rectilinearness, I myself have digressed much too far.

The moment my article had been printed I was swamped—by letters and personal calls—with inquiries as to the meaning of my *Verdict.* "What do you mean to say, and is it possible that you are justifying suicide?" Some of the people—so it seemed to me—were even rejoicing over something. And the other day a certain author, a Mr. N. P., sent me a brief and politely denunciatory article of his which he had published in the Moscow weekly *Recreation.* I do not subscribe to this periodical, and I do not suppose that its editor sent me this issue; therefore, I ascribe its receipt to the courtesy of the author himself. He condemns my article and ridicules it:

"I received the October issue of the *Writer's Diary;* I read it and began to ponder over it: there are many good things in this issue, but also many *strange* ones. Let me state my perplexity in the briefest terms. For instance, what was the purpose of printing in this issue the 'deliberations' of a suicide from tedium? Positively, I fail to understand the reason. These 'deliberations'—if thus may be denoted the delirium of a half-crazy man—are well known, of course, somewhat differently worded, *by everybody whose concern this is,* and, therefore, their appearance, *in our day,* in a diary of such a writer as F. M. Dostoievsky, serves as a ridiculous and miserable anachronism. Ours is an age of *cast-iron* conceptions, positive opinions—an age which displays on its banner the motto: 'To live by all means!' It stands to reason that everywhere and in everything there are exceptions: there are suicides *with* and *without* deliberation, but nowadays no one pays the slightest attention to this trivial heroism, since this heroism is altogether too silly! There was a time when suicide, particularly *with deliberation,* used to be raised to the level of the greatest 'consciousness'—only of *what?*—and of heroism, consisting of no one knows what; however, these *rotten* times have irrevocably passed—and, thank God, there is nothing to regret about them.

"Every suicide who dies with deliberation similar to that recorded in Mr. Dostoievsky's *Diary* deserves no sympathy; he is a coarse egoist, a man seeking honors, and a most harmful member of human society. He is even unable to perpetrate his stupid act without being talked about; even here he fails to adhere to his role, to his fancied character: he writes a deliberation even though he could easily have died without any deliberation. . . . Oh, Falstaffs of life! Stilted knights!"

Having read this, I was even seized with despondency. Good Lord, is it possible that I have many such readers, and can it be that Mr. N. P., in asserting that my suicide does not deserve sympathy, seriously maintains that I depicted him for the purpose of arousing his, Mr. N. P.'s, "compassion"?—Of course, Mr. N. P.'s isolated opinion would be of little importance. But the point is that in this case undoubtedly he expresses a whole type, a whole collection of fellows of his own pattern, an impudent type in a way akin to that about which I spoke above—impudent and bigoted—a type of those very "cast-iron conceptions" to which Mr. N. P. himself refers in the lines which I have quoted from his article. This is a suspicion concerning a whole collection. Honest to goodness—I am scared. Of course, maybe I am taking the matter too seriously. However, I will state this: notwithstanding my great susceptibility, I would not have given an answer even to the "collection," and not because of disdain for it—why should one not have a little chat with people?—but simply because space is scarce in this issue. Thus, if I am now answering and sacrificing space, I am doing so in answer to my own doubts—as it were, to myself. I see that to my October article there should, without delay, be appended a moral, that its purpose should be explained and defended. At least, conscience will be clear. That's it.

3

ARBITRARY ASSERTIONS

My article—*The Verdict*—refers to the basic and loftiest idea of human existence—the necessity and inevitability of a belief in the immortality of the human soul. The underlying idea of this confession of a man perishing as a result of "a logical suicide" is the necessity of the immediate inference that without faith in one's soul and its immortality, man's existence is unnatural, unthinkable, impossible. Now, it seemed to me that I have clearly expressed the formula of a logical suicide, that I have discovered it. In him there is no faith in immortality; this he explains in the very beginning. Little by little, the thought of his aimlessness and his hatred of the muteness of the surrounding inertia lead him to the inevitable conviction of the utter absurdity of man's existence on earth. It becomes clear as daylight to him that only those men can consent to live who resemble the lower animals and who come nearest to the latter by reason of the limited development of their minds and their purely carnal wants.

They agree to live specifically as animals, *i.e.*, in order "to eat, drink, sleep, build their nests and raise children." Indeed, eating, sleeping, polluting and sitting on soft cushions will long attract men to earth, but not the higher types. Meanwhile, it is the higher types that are, and always have been, sovereign on earth, and invariably it so happened that, when the time was ripe, millions of people followed them. What is the loftiest word, the loftiest thought? This word, this thought (without which mankind cannot exist) is often uttered for the first time by the poor, imperceptible people without any significance, who even frequently are persecuted and who die in exile and in obscurity. But the thought, the word uttered by them, never dies, never disappears without leaving a trace; it can never vanish if it has once been uttered; and this is noteworthy in mankind. And in the next generation, maybe twenty or thirty years later, the thought of the genius is embraced by everything and everybody—it lures everything and everybody—and the result is that not the millions of people, not the material forces, apparently so dreadful and immutable, not money, not the sword, not might are triumphant—but the thought imperceptible at first, and often the thought of an apparently most insignificant man. Mr. N. P. writes that the appearance of such a confession in my *Diary* "serves—[serves what?] —as a ridiculous and miserable anachronism," since "ours is an age of cast-iron conceptions, positive opinions, an age which displays on its banner the motto: 'To live by all means!' . . ." (Quite so! Quite so! Probably this is the reason why in our day suicides among the educated class have so increased.) I assure the esteemed N. P. and people of his type that this "cast iron," when the time comes, is converted into down in the face of some idea—no matter how insignificant it might seem in the beginning to fellows of "cast-iron conceptions." However, to me personally, one of the most dreaded apprehensions for our future—even our near future—is the fact that, in my view, in much too large a portion of our Russian educated stratum, by some strange . . . well, let us say, predestination—there is spreading with ever-increasing rapidity complete disbelief in one's soul and in its immortality. And not only does this disbelief strengthen itself by a sort of conviction (as yet we have but few convictions of any kind) but also by some strange universal indifference —at times even scoffing at this loftiest idea of human existence. God knows by virtue of what laws it spreads among us, and it is indifference not only toward this particular idea but toward everything that is vital—for the truth of life, for everything that generates and nourishes life, that brings health, that annihilates decomposition and fetidness. In our day, this indifference—compared, let us say, with the feelings of other, European, nations—is almost a Russian peculiarity. It has long ago penetrated the Russian educated family, having almost destroyed it.

Neither man nor nation can exist without a sublime idea. And on earth there is *but one* sublime idea—namely, the idea of the immortality of man's soul—since all other "sublime" ideas of life, which give life to man, *are merely derived from this one idea*. On this point I may be contradicted (that is, on the question of this unity of the source of everything sublime on earth), but as yet I am not going to argue, and I am setting forth my idea arbitrarily. In one breath it is impossible to explain it, so it is better to elucidate it by degrees. For this, there will be time in the future.

My *felo-de-se* is precisely a passionate exponent of his idea—*i.e.*, the necessity of suicide—and not an indifferent, not a cast-iron man. He really suffers and is tormented, and, it would seem, this I have expressed clearly. To him, it is quite obvious that he cannot live, and he knows only too well that he is right and that it is impossible to refute him. Irresistibly, there stand before him the loftiest, the most pressing questions: "What is the use of living if he has already conceived the idea that for man to live like an animal is disgusting, abnormal and insufficient? And what, in this case, can retain him on earth?" He cannot solve these questions and he knows it, since even though he realizes that there is what he calls a "harmony of the whole," still he says: "I do not understand it, I shall never be able to understand it, and of necessity I am not going to partake of it; this comes of its own accord." Now, it is this lucidity that finished him. Well, where is the trouble? In what was he mistaken?—The trouble is solely in the loss of faith in immortality.

However, he himself ardently seeks (that is, he was seeking while he was living, seeking sufferingly) conciliation; he meant to find it in "love for mankind."—"Not I but, perhaps, mankind will be happy and some day may attain harmony. This thought could retain me on earth"—he drops the word. And, of course, this is a magnanimous thought and one full of suffering. But the irresistible conviction that the life of mankind—just as his own—is, substantially, a fleeting moment, and that on the morrow of the realization of "harmony" (if one is to believe that this dream can be realized) mankind will be reduced to the same zero even as he, by the force of the inert laws of nature, and that—after so much suffering endured for the attainment of that dream—this thought completely stirs his spirit; this sets him in revolt precisely because of his love of mankind; it insults him on behalf of mankind as a whole, by the law of the contagion of ideas; it even kills in him love itself of mankind. Similarly it has been observed many a time that in a family dying from starvation, father and mother—when at length the suffering of their children grew intolerable—began to hate them, those hitherto beloved ones, precisely because of the *intolerableness* of their suffering. Moreover, I assert that the realization of one's utter impotence to help, to render some service, or to bring alleviation to suffering mankind—and at the same time when there is a firm conviction of the existence of that suffering,—*may convert in one's heart love for mankind into a hatred of it.* Gentlemen of cast-iron ideas, of course, will not believe this and will be utterly unable to understand it: to them, love of mankind and its happiness are such cheap things; everything is so conveniently fixed; everything has been set and described so long ago that these things are not worth being given a thought to. But I intend to make them really laugh: I assert (again, as yet, without producing any proof) that love of mankind is unthinkable, unintelligible and *altogether impossible without the accompanying faith in the immortality of man's soul.* Those who, having deprived man of the faith in his immortality, are seeking to substitute for it—as life's loftiest aim—"love of mankind," those, I maintain, are lifting their arm against themselves, since in lieu of love of mankind they are planting in the heart of him who has lost his faith seeds of hatred of mankind. Let pundits of cast-iron ideas shrug their shoulders at this assertion. But this thought is wiser than their wisdom, and unhesitatingly I believe that some day humankind will embrace it as an axiom although, once more, I am setting forth this idea without any supporting proof.

I even assert and venture to say that love of mankind *in general, as an idea,* is one of the most incomprehensible ideas for the human mind. Precisely as an idea. Sentiment alone can vindicate it. However, sentiment is possible precisely only in the presence of the accompanying conviction of the immortality of man's soul. (Another arbitrary assertion.)

It is clear, then, that suicide—when the idea of immortality has been lost—becomes an utter and inevitable necessity for any man who, by his mental development, has even slightly lifted himself above the level of cattle. On the contrary, immortality—promising eternal life—ties man all the more strongly to earth. Here there is a seeming contradiction: if there is so much life—that is, if in addition to earthly existence there is an immortal one—why should one be treasuring so highly his earthly life? And yet, the contrary is true, since only with faith in his immortality does man comprehend the full meaning of his rational destination on earth. However, without the faith in his immortality, man's ties with earth are severed, they grow thinner and more putrescent, while the loss of the sublime meaning of life (felt at least in the form of unconscious anguish) inevitably leads to suicide.

Hence, the reverse moral of my October article: "If faith in immortality is so essential to man's existence, it is, therefore, a normal condition of the human race and, this being so, the immortality itself of the human soul exists undeniably." In a word, the idea of immortality is life itself—"live life," its ultimate formula, the mainspring of truth and just consciousness for humankind. Such was the object of my article, and I supposed that, willy-nilly, everyone who had read it would so comprehend it.

4

A Few Words About Youth

Well, by the way. Perhaps it may be pointed out to me that in our age suicide is being committed by men who have never dwelt upon any abstract problems; nevertheless, they kill themselves mysteriously, without any apparent reason. In truth, we do perceive a great number of suicides (their abundance is also a mystery *sui generis*), strange and mysterious, committed not by reason of poverty or some affront, without any apparent reasons and not at all because of material need, unrequited love, jealousy, ill-health, hypochondria or insanity—but God only knows why. In our day, such cases constitute a great temptation, and since it is impossible to deny that they have assumed the proportions of an epidemic, they arise in the minds of many people as a most disturbing question. Of course, I am not venturing to explain all these suicides—this I cannot do[1]—but I am firmly convinced that the majority of the suicides, *in toto*, directly or indirectly, were committed as a result of one and the same spiritual illness—the absence in the souls of these men of the sublime idea of existence. In this sense our indifference, as a contemporary Russian illness, is gnawing all souls. Verily, in Russia there are people who pray God and go to church but who do not believe in the immortality of their souls—*i.e.*, not that they do not believe in it, but they simply never think of it. Even so, at times they are by no means people of the cast-iron, the bestial, pattern. However, as stated above, the whole sublime purpose and meaning of life, the desire and the urge to live, emanate only from this faith. I repeat, there are many people desirous to live without any ideas, without any sublime meaning of life—simply to pursue an animal existence, as

[1] I am receiving a great many letters giving the facts pertaining to suicides, with questions: how and what do I think about these suicides, and how do I explain them?

some lower species. And yet there are many individuals—what is most curious, apparently extremely coarse and vicious ones—whose nature, however, perhaps without their knowledge, has long been craving for sublime aims and the lofty meaning of life. These will not be appeased by love of eating, by the love of fish-pies, beautiful trotters, debauch, ranks, bureaucratic power, the adoration of their subordinates and the hall porters at the doors of their mansions. Men of this caliber will precisely shoot themselves apparently *for no reason*, and yet it will be necessarily because of anguish, unconscious perhaps, for the sublime significance of life which they have found nowhere. On top of that, some of them will shoot themselves after having preliminarily perpetrated some scandalous villainy, abomination or monstrosity. Of course, looking at many of these cases it is difficult to believe that they committed suicide because of the longing for the sublime aims of life: "Why, they never thought about any aims; they never spoke about any such things, and they merely committed villainies!"—such is the common opinion. But let us admit that they were not concerned about these things and that they did perpetrate villainies: do you positively know how, by what devious ways, in the life of society this sublime anguish is being conveyed to one's soul and contaminates it?—Ideas soar through the air but necessarily in accordance with some laws; ideas live and spread in accordance with laws which are too difficult for us to record; ideas are contagious. And do you know that in the general mood of life a certain idea or concern or anguish, accessible only to a highly educated and developed intellect, may suddenly be imparted to an almost illiterate, coarse creature who was never concerned about anything, and may contaminate his soul with its influence? Again, I may be told that in our age even children are committing suicide, or such raw youths as have had no life experience. Even so, I am secretly convinced that it is our youth that suffers and agonizes because of the absence of sublime aims of life. In our families practically no mention is made about the sublime aims of life, while not only do they not give the slightest thought to the idea of immortality but much too frequently a satirical attitude is adopted toward it—and this in the presence of children from their early childhood, and perhaps with an express didactic purpose.

"But we have no family at all"—recently remarked one of our most talented writers, when arguing with me. Well, this is partly true: with our universal indifference for the sublime aims of life, perhaps in some strata of the nation our family is already in a state of decomposition. At least it is obviously clear that our young generation is destined to seek ideals for itself, and the loftiest

meaning of life. But its segregation, this abandonment of youth
to their own resources—this is what is dreadful. This problem is
all too important at this moment of our existence. Our youth is so
placed that absolutely nowhere does it find advice as to the loftiest
meaning of life. From our brainy people and, generally, from its
leaders, youth—I repeat—can borrow merely a rather satirical view,
but nothing *positive, i.e.,* in what to believe, what should be respected and adored, what should be sought; and yet all this is so
needed, so indispensable to youth; there is, always has been, craving for all this in all ages and everywhere! And even if in the family
or at school youth could still be given some sound advice, nevertheless, again, the family and the school (of course, not without
exceptions) have grown too indifferent to these things because of
many other more practical and contemporaneously interesting problems and aims. The youths of December 6, at the Kazan Square,
were undoubtedly but "a driven herd" in the hands of some crafty
swindlers, judging at least by the *facts* made public in *The Moscow
Gazette.* What will come of this affair, what is going to be revealed
—I do not know. No doubt, here there was folly—wicked, immoral,
apish imitativeness of somebody else's behavior; nevertheless, they
could have been brought together only by the conviction that they
had been convened in the name of something lofty and beautiful,
in the name of some remarkable self-sacrifice for the greatest aims.
Even if only a very few of them possessed this "quest of one's
ideal," still these few would reign over the rest and lead them—
this much is clear. Now, who is guilty that their ideal is so ugly?
—Of course, they themselves are guilty, too, but not they alone.
No doubt, even the present reality surrounding them could have
saved them from their ugly segregation from everything essential
and real, from their coarsest lack of understanding of the simplest
things; but the point is that apparently the time has arrived when
detachment from the soil and from the people's truth in our younger
generation must astound and terrify even "the fathers" themselves
who have so long ago detached themselves from all that is Russian
and who are finishing their lives in beatific tranquillity and peace
as superior critics of the Russian land.

Now, this is a lesson—a lesson to the family, to the school
and to the blissfully convinced critics: they themselves do not
recognize *their consequences* which they renounce. However, again,
can they—those "fathers"—can they be *completely* blamed? They
themselves—aren't they products and consequences of some peculiar
fatal laws and predestinations which have been hanging over the
entire educated stratum of Russian society for almost two centuries, virtually until the time of the great reforms of our reign?

Nay, it seems that the two-century-long detachment from the soil and *from work of every kind* cannot remain unpunished. It is insufficient to blame; one has to seek remedies.

To my way of thinking remedies are still available: they are in the people, in their sanctities and in our communion with the people. But . . . this is something for the future. I embarked upon my *Diary* partly for the purpose of speaking about these remedies as long as strength will permit.

5

On Suicide and Haughtiness

But it is time to finish up with Mr. N. P. To him happened the thing which happens to many people of his "type": what is clear to them and what they can most readily comprehend they conceive to be stupid. They are much more inclined to despise lucidity than to praise it. It is different if a flourish or a fog accompanies something: "This we don't understand—therefore, it is deep."

He says that the "deliberation" of my suicide is merely "the delirium of a half-crazy man," and that that is "well known." I am very much inclined to believe that the "deliberation" became "known" to him only after he had read my article. As to the "delirium of a half-crazy man" (is this known to Mr. N. P. and the whole collection of the N. P.'s?), it—*i.e.*, the inference of the necessity of suicide—is too much to many people in Europe, as it were, the last word of science. I have expressed this "last word of science" in brief terms, clearly and popularly, with the sole purpose of refuting it—not by reasoning or logic, since it cannot be refuted by logic (I challenge not only Mr. N. P. but anyone to refute logically this "delirium of the insane"), but by faith, by the deduction of the necessity of faith in the immortality of man's soul; by the inference of the conviction that this faith is the only source of "live life" on earth—of life, health, sane ideas and sound deductions and inferences. . . . And, in conclusion—something altogether comic. In the same October issue I reported the suicide of an emigrant's daughter: she soaked a piece of cotton wool in chloroform, tied it around her face and lay down on the bed. And thus she died. Before death she wrote a note: "I am undertaking a long journey. If I should not succeed, let people gather to celebrate my resurrection with a bottle of Cliquot. *If I should succeed,* I ask that I be interred only after I am altogether dead, since it is very disagreeable to awake in a coffin in the earth. This is not *chic!*"

Mr. N. P. haughtily grew angry with this "vain little" suicide, and came to the conclusion that her act "deserves no attention whatsoever." He also grew angry with me for my "exceedingly naïve" question as to which one of the two suicides had suffered more on earth. At this juncture there ensued something comical. Unexpectedly he added: "I daresay that a man who desires *to greet* his return to life with a champagne glass in his hand—[of course, in his hand]—did not suffer much in this life if, with such triumph, once more he enters it without changing in the least its conditions, and even without thinking about them. . . ."

What a funny thought and what a ludicrous consideration! Here he was mostly tempted by champagne: "He who drinks champagne cannot suffer." But were she so fond of champagne, she would have continued to live so as to drink it, whereas she wrote about champagne before her death—*i.e.*, real death—knowing well that she would die without fail. She could not have believed much in the chance of her recovery to life; nor did this chance present anything attractive to her, because recovery, of course, would have meant to her recovery to a new suicide. Thus, here champagne was of no consequence, *i.e.*, not at all for the purpose of consuming it—and is it possible that this has to be explained? And she wrote about champagne from the desire, when dying, to. perpetrate some cynicism as abominable and filthy as possible. And she selected champagne precisely because she could not conceive a filthier, more abominable picture than this drinking bout at the time of her "resurrection from the dead." She had to write this in order to insult, with this filth, everything she was forsaking on earth, to damn earth and her whole earthly life, to spit on it and to declare that spittle to her relatives whom she was leaving behind.

Whence such a spite in a seventeen-year-old girl? (N. B. She was seventeen, and not twenty, as I erroneously put it in my article. Subsequently I was corrected by those who know this incident better.) And against whom was that spite directed? No one had offended her; she was in need of nothing, and she died apparently also for no reason whatever. But precisely this note; precisely the fact that at such a moment she was *eager* to perpetrate such a filthy and spiteful cynicism—and this is obvious—this precisely leads one to think that her life was immeasurably more chaste than this filthy twist; and that spite, the boundless exasperation of that twist, on the contrary, bears witness to the suffering and painful mood of her spirit, to her despair in the last moment of her life. If she had died of some apathetic weariness, without knowing why, she would not have perpetrated this cynicism. One has to take a more humane attitude toward such a spiritual condition. Here, suffering was obvious and certainly she died of spiritual anguish, having greatly suffered.

What could have tormented her so much at the age of seventeen?—But herein is the dreadful question of our age. I have set forth the hypothesis that she died of anguish (too premature an anguish) and of aimlessness of life, only because of the upbringing, perverted by theory, at her parents' home—an upbringing involving an erroneous conception of the sublime significance and aims of life, a deliberate extermination in her soul of all faith in its immortality. Let this be only my supposition. Yet certainly she did not die merely for the purpose of leaving after her that abject note—to cause surprise, as Mr. N. P. seems to think. "No man shall hate his flesh." Self-extermination is a serious thing despite any chic or display, while epidemic self-extermination, assuming ever-increasing proportions among the educated classes, is all too momentous a phenomenon which deserves relentless observation and study.

Some eighteen months ago a highly talented and competent member of our judiciary showed me a batch of letters and notes of suicides in their own handwriting, collected by him—notes which had been written by them immediately before, *i.e.*, five minutes before, death. I remember two lines written by a fifteen-year-old girl. Likewise, I recall pencil scrawls written in a carriage in which the suicide shot himself before he had reached his destination. I believe that even if Mr. N. P. could have perused this intensely interesting batch, perhaps even in his soul there would have come a change, and consternation would have penetrated his tranquil heart. But this I do not know. In any event one should be dealing with these facts more humanely and not so haughtily. Perhaps we ourselves are guilty of these facts, and in the future no cast iron is going to save us from the calamitous consequences of our placidity and haughtiness—that is, when time comes for these consequences.

Enough, however. I have given my answer not to Mr. N. P. alone, but to many Messrs. N. P. . . . .

CHAPTER II

1

An Anecdote from Children's Lives

I SHALL tell it so as not to forget it.

On the outskirts—and even farther than the outskirts—of Petersburg there lives a mother with her twelve-year-old daughter.

This is not a well-to-do family, but the mother has a job and earns her livelihood by her work, while the daughter attends school in Petersburg, and every time she goes to school or returns home from school she uses a public carriage which departs from the Gostiny Dvor and goes as far as the place where they live, and back, several times a day at fixed hours.

And once upon a time, recently—some two months ago—when suddenly and quickly winter set in and the first sledging began, during a whole week of calm, bright days, with two or three degrees of frost—the mother, looking at her daughter, said: "Sasha, I see you are not learning your lessons. I have been observing this several evenings. Do you know your lessons?"

"Oh, dear Mama, don't worry: I have prepared everything; I have prepared everything even a week in advance."

"If so—all right."

The next day Sasha went to school, and shortly after five o'clock in the afternoon the conductor of the public carriage in which Sasha was due to return, as he was driving by their gate, jumped off the coach and presented a note to "dear Mama," reading as follows:

"Dear Mama, all this week I have been a bad girl. I received three zeros and I kept deceiving you. I am ashamed to come back to you, and I shall not return to you. Adieu, dear Mama, forgive me. Your Sasha."

One can imagine what the mother must have experienced. Of course, her first impulse was to leave work at once and to proceed as quickly as possible to the city in order to find Sasha through some traces. But where? How?—A close acquaintance happened to be there at the time; he took the matter close to his heart and volunteered to go at once to Petersburg and there, after making inquiries at the school, to search and search at the homes of all her acquaintances—if necessary, all night long.

The main consideration—that Sasha, repenting her decision, might meanwhile return and, not finding mother home, might perhaps again slip away—induced the mother to stay home and to place her trust in the hearty sympathy of a kind man. It was decided that should Sasha not be found by the following morning, the police would be notified at dawn. Having remained home, the mother spent several painful hours which I am not depicting here since they will be understood without description.

". . . And presently"—relates the mother—"around ten o'clock, suddenly I heard the familiar little steps on the snow in the courtyard, and then—on the staircase. The door opened—and there was Sasha."

"Dear Mama—oh, dear Mama, how glad I am that I came back to you! Oh!"

She folded her hands, then covered her face with their palms and sat down on the bed. She was so tired, so exhausted. Well, of course, then ensued the first exclamations, the first questions. Mother was cautious; to begin with, she did not dare to reproach her daughter.

"Oh, dear Mama, just as soon as I lied to you yesterday about the lessons, I made up my mind to attend school no longer and not to return to you; because how would it be: I shouldn't be going to school and I should be lying every day to you that I was attending school?"

"Well, what would you be doing with yourself? If you weren't at school and not at home with me, where would you be?"

"I thought—in the street. Every day, from early morning, I meant to walk in the streets. My little fur coat is warm, and should I feel cold I would go to the Passage. And, instead of my dinner, I decided to buy a loaf of bread every day, and as for drinking—I should have managed one way or the other; at present there's snow. One loaf would suffice. I have fifteen kopecks; three kopecks a loaf; this would make five days."

"And then?"

"After that, I don't know—I hadn't thought of it."

"But where would you be spending your nights? Now, where?"

"Spending my nights?—I thought about that. As it would be growing dark and late, I was planning to go to the railroad, far beyond the railroad station, where there is no one, and where there are an awful lot of cars. I would climb into one of these cars which, I would notice, would not be moved anywhere, and I would sleep there till morning. And I did go. I went thither, far beyond the station, and there there was no one, and I saw cars standing at the side, such cars as are quite different from those in which everybody is riding. Now, I thought, I will climb into one of these cars and no one will see me. Just as I started to climb, suddenly a watchman shouted at me:

"'Where are you climbing? In these cars corpses are transported.'

"I heard this, jumped off and, by that time, I saw him approaching me. 'What do you want here?'—he said. But I started running and running; he shouted something but I ran away. I went along quite scared. I returned to the street and, as I walked, I suddenly saw a house—a big, stone house—under construction; still nothing but bricks, without glass in windows or doors, which were barred with boards; around the house—a fence. I thought if

I could manage to get into the house somehow, no one would see me there because it was dark. I went along a by-lane and discovered a spot through which, though it was barred, I could climb. This I did and I found myself straight in a ditch—still full of earth. I went gropingly along the wall toward the corner, and there there were boards and bricks. 'Here'—I said to myself—'I will spend the night on the boards.' And so I lay down. Only, all of a sudden I heard something, as if people were talking in very low voices. I raised myself, and right in the corner I heard a conversation in low voices, and saw eyes as though gazing at me from there. I was very much frightened, and again I ran into the street through the same door, and I heard them call me. But I managed to slip away. And I had thought that the house was empty.

"When I came out again, suddenly I felt tired. So tired, so tired. I walked through the streets; people were moving around, and I didn't know what time it was. Presently I got out on the Nevsky Prospect and went by the Gostiny Dvor, my eyes full of tears. 'How nice it would be'—I said to myself—'if a kind man would pass by and pity a poor little girl who has no place to spend a night.' I would confess to him and he would say to me: 'Come and spend a night at our home.' While I was thinking about all this, suddenly I saw our bus standing and ready to start on its last trip in our direction, whereas I thought that it had left long ago. 'Ah'—I said to myself—'I will go to Mama!' I got in, took a seat, and now, dear Mama, I'm so glad I came back to you! Never more will I deceive you, and I'll study diligently! Ah, dear Mama! Dear Mama!"

"I asked her"—the mother went on with her story—"Sasha, is it possible that you have invented all this yourself—meaning, not to go to school and to live in the streets?"

"You see, dear Mama, long ago I struck up an acquaintance with a girl of my age; but she attends another school. Only, would you believe that she almost never does go to school, and at home, day after day, she tells everybody that she attends school. And she told me that she got weary of studying, whereas in the streets she felt cheerful. 'The moment I leave the house'—says she—'I keep walking, and already for two weeks I haven't showed up at school; I am looking at the stores through the windows; I go to the Passage; I eat but one loaf of bread till evening when it is time to go home.' And when I learned all this from her, I said to myself: 'I wish I did the same,' and I began to feel weary at school. Only I wasn't determined until yesterday, and yesterday—after I had lied to you—I made up my mind. . . ."

This anecdote is a true story. Of course, at present, measures have been taken by the mother. When this was related to me, I thought that it would not be superfluous to publish it in the *Diary*. I received permission to do so—naturally, subject to full incognito. Without question, I shall be immediately told: "This is an isolated case, and simply because the girl is very stupid." But I know for sure that the girl is by no means stupid. I know also that in these youthful souls, already emerged from early childhood but still far from having ripened to any, even preliminary, maturity, at times there may take birth astonishing, fantastic conceptions, dreams and resolutions. This age (twelve or thirteen years) is extraordinarily interesting in girls—even more so than in boys. By the way, speaking of boys: do you remember a report, published four years ago in newspapers, about three very young pupils in the first years of high school who sought to run away to America; they were caught quite a distance away from the city, and at the same time a large pistol in their possession was seized. Generally, in days gone by, one or two generations back, dreams and fantasies may have been roaming in the heads of these very youthful folks, just as in the contemporary ones. However, present-day youngsters are somehow more resolute and much less inclined toward doubts and reflections. The former ones, having conceived a project (well, for example, to escape to Venice, after having read about Venice in the novels of Hoffmann and George Sand—I knew one such fellow), nevertheless did not proceed with the fulfillment of these projects, and at the utmost confided them under oath to some schoolmate, whereas the contemporary ones, having conceived something, put it into effect. However, the former ones used to be restrained by a sense of duty, by the feeling of obligation toward their fathers and mothers, toward certain convictions and principles. But, nowadays these ties have undeniably grown somewhat more lax. There is less restraint in them, both outward and inward. This, perhaps, is the reason why the brain also works more one-sidedly, and, of course, all this is caused by something.

And the principal thing is that those are by no means isolated cases resulting from stupidity. I repeat, this most curious age requires special attention on the part of pedagogues who, in our day, are busying themselves so much with pedagogy, and by parents who are so busy both with "business" and with things not related to business. And how easily all this may happen—*i.e.*, everything most to be dreaded—and to whom?—To our own children! To think only of that passage in this narrative of the mother—where the little girl "suddenly felt *tired*"; where she was walking and weeping and dreaming of meeting a kind man who would pity her because she had no place where she could spend the night and who would ask her to come along with him. To think only that this

desire of hers, bearing witness to her youthful innocence and
immaturity, could have been so easily realized since the streets
and our wealthiest homes swarm precisely with such "kind fellows"!
Well, and after that? Next morning?—Either the hole in the ice or
the shame of confessing; and as a sequence of that shame—the
ensuing ability, after concealing everything within one's self, *to get
used to the reminiscence,* and after that to start pondering over
it but now from a different standpoint, and to keep thinking and
thinking, but now with an extraordinary variety of images, and
all this—little by little, of its own accord. Well, and at length—
perhaps the desire to repeat the experience, and then all the rest.
And this—at the age of twelve! And everything carefully concealed. Indeed, carefully concealed in the strict meaning of the
word! And that other girl who, instead of attending school, spends
her time on "window-shopping" and visits to the Passage, the one
who taught our girl! In days gone by I used to hear something
of the kind about boys who were weary of studying but to whom
vagabondage was amusing. (N. B. Vagabondage is a habit, a pathological one and partly our national one, one of our distinctions from
Europe—a habit which is eventually converted into a pathological
passion and which frequently takes its inception from early childhood. Without fail, later on I shall speak about this national passion of ours.) But it now appears that *vagrant* girls are also possible. And let us say that here it is still complete *innocence;* yet
let her be innocent as a primitive creature in paradise, nevertheless
she will not evade "the knowledge of good and evil," at least a
wee bit of it—at least, in imagination, meditatingly. For the street
is such a brisk school. And the most important thing—I repeat
again and again—is that highly curious age, an age which still
retains the most touching infantile innocence and immaturity, on
the one hand—and, on the other, which has already acquired an
avidly quick faculty of apperceiving and readily familiarizing itself
with such ideas and conceptions as, according to the conviction
of many parents and pedagogues, this age cannot even conceive.
This split, these two so dissimilar halves of these young creatures,
in their blending, constitute a great deal of critical danger in their
lives.

2

Explanation Concerning My Participation in the
Forthcoming Publication of the Magazine—"Light"

In *A Writer's Diary* (again in the same October issue) I
printed an advertisement concerning the publication in the year

1877, by Professor N. P. Wagner, of a new magazine *Light*. And just as soon as this announcement appeared, I began to receive inquiries about the forthcoming magazine and my participation in it. To everyone whom I had a chance to answer I stated that, at the request of N. P. Wagner, I have promised to contribute to that magazine one story, and that this is *all* that my participation in it will consist of. However, now I feel it necessary to state this in print since inquiries continue to be received. Daily I am getting letters from my readers from which I clearly perceive that for some reason they suddenly became convinced that my participation in the magazine *Light* would be much more elaborate than stated in Professor Wagner's announcement, *i.e.*, that I am almost *switching over to Light,* embarking upon a new activity and expanding my former one, and that if I am not a co-publisher or co-editor of the forthcoming periodical, unfailingly I am a participant in its idea, design, plan, etc.

In answer to this, I hereby state that in the coming year 1877 I shall be publishing only the *Writer's Diary,* and that my *entire* work as an author will be dedicated to the *Diary,* much as in the past year. As to the new publication *Light,* I am not going to participate either in its plan or as co-editor. Even the idea itself of the future journal is not fully known to me, and I am awaiting the appearance of its first issue in order to familiarize myself with it. I believe that my close affiliation with the magazine *Light* was inferred from the fact that the initial announcement concerning it was printed in the *Writer's Diary,* and subsequently it so happened that for a considerable time this advertisement has not been repeated in any other periodical.

At any rate, the promise to contribute a story to some other publication does not mean that I am going to relinquish my own, and switch over to that other, periodical, while my sincere wish to the esteemed N. P. Wagner for success to the venture is merely based upon my personal hope and even my conviction that in his journal there will be something new, original and useful. As to the rest and to any further details, I know nothing regarding the magazine *Light*. Its publication is alien to me, and thus far it is as little known to me as to any other person who has read the newspaper advertisement concerning it.

3

WHERE DOES THE BUSINESS STAND?

A year has elapsed, and this twelfth issue brings to a close the first year of the publication of the *Writer's Diary*. On the part of my readers I have met most flattering sympathy, and yet I have not expressed even a hundredth part of what I have meant to express, while, as I see now, many of the things which I have stated I have not succeeded in expressing clearly from the start, so that I have even been misunderstood—for which, of course, I am mostly blaming myself. However, even though I have managed to say but little, nevertheless I hope that from what has been expressed during the current year my readers have grasped what the character and the orientation of the *Diary* will be in the forthcoming year. Thus far, the main object of the *Diary* was to explain, as far as possible, the idea of our national spiritual independence, elucidating it in concrete facts as they appear. In this sense, for instance, in the *Diary* there has been considerable discussion of our sudden national and popular movement of this year in connection with the so-called "Slavic problem." Let me say in advance: the *Diary* does not pretend to set forth monthly political articles; but it will endeavor to find and, as far as possible, to point out our national and popular point of view also in current political events. For example, from my articles on the "Slavic movement" of this year the readers may have understood that the *Diary* merely sought to elucidate the substance and the meaning of this movement pre-eminently as far as we, Russians, are concerned; to emphasize the fact that for us the problem is not confined to Slavism and to its political aspect in the contemporary sense. Slavism—*i.e.*, the communion of all Slavs, in fellowship among themselves and with the Russian people—as well as the political phase of the Eastern problem, *i.e.*, the questions concerning the frontiers, the border regions, the seas and the straits, Constantinople, etc.,—all these questions, even though undoubtedly they are of the utmost importance to Russia and her future destinies, nevertheless they alone do not exhaust for us the substance of the Eastern problem, *i.e.*, from the standpoint of its solution in our popular sense. In this sense these questions of major importance retreat to the second plan since the substance of the whole matter, as it is understood by the people, resides undeniably and entirely only in the destinies of Eastern Christianity, that is, Orthodoxy. Our people know neither Serbians nor Bulgarians: the Russian people are helping with their pennies and volunteers—not the Slavs and not Slavism; but rumors have reached them that Orthodox Christians, our brethren, are suffering for Christ's faith, from the Turks —the "godless Agarians." This is why—and this is the sole reason why—there originated this year a popular movement. In the present and future destinies of Orthodox Christianity lies the whole idea of the Russian people; therein is their service to Christ and their

thirst for the exploit on Christ's behalf. This is a genuine thirst—
a great and unceasing thirst—which has been burning in our people
since the most ancient times, and this is an extremely important
fact as it characterizes our people and our state. Moscow old-
believers have donated and equipped a complete (and excellent)
sanitary unit which they have dispatched to Serbia; and yet they
knew perfectly well that Serbians are not old-believers and yet that
their religion is the same as ours even though they are not in
communion in matters relating to faith. Here there manifested
itself precisely the idea of the future and ultimate—even though
remote—destinies of Orthodox Christianity, and the hope for the
future communion of all Eastern Christians. This means that, coming to the assistance of the Christians against the Turks, the oppressors of Christianity, despite temporary differences they regarded the Serbians—like themselves—as genuine, be it even in
the future, Christians. In this sense the donation has even a historical significance, arousing comforting thoughts and partly corroborating our statement that in the destinies of Christianity lies
the whole object of the Russian people, notwithstanding the fact
that temporarily they are disunited by certain fictitious religious
differences. Undeniably, there lives in the people the firm belief
that Russia exists for the sole purpose of serving Christ and protecting ecumenic Orthodoxy *as a whole*. If this thought will not
be directly expressed by everyone among the people, nevertheless
I assert that it will be quite consciously formulated by many of
them, and these unquestionably exercise an influence upon the
rest of the people. So that it may be said that in the people at
large this is almost a *conscious* idea and not one that is merely
concealed in popular sentiment. Thus, the Eastern question is intelligible to the Russian people in this sense alone. This is the
principal fact.

However, this being so, the view of the Eastern question
must assume, to all of us, an incomparably more definite aspect.
Russia is strong owing to her people and their spirit, and not merely
by education or, for example, by her wealth, enlightenment, etc.,
as certain European states which, as a result of their decrepitude
and the loss of the live national idea, have become altogether
artificial and, as it were, even unnatural. But if the people conceive
the Slavic—and, generally, the Eastern—question only in the light
of the destinies of Orthodoxy, it is clear that it is no longer an
accidental, or temporary, or merely political matter, but one which
relates to the very substance of the Russian people, which means
that it is eternal, perpetual, till its final solution.

Russia, in this sense, can no longer renounce her *Drang nach*

Osten and cannot alter its objective lest she be renouncing herself. And if temporarily, in accordance with circumstances, this problem may, and unquestionably *must* have at times assumed a different orientation; even if, at times, we wished, or were forced, to yield to circumstances, to restrain our aspirations, nevertheless, on the whole this problem, as the essence of the very life of the Russian people, unfailingly must some time attain its fundamental aim, *i.e.,* the unification of all Orthodox groups in Christ and brotherhood, without distinction between the Slavs and the other Orthodox peoples. This communion may not be political at all, while the Slavic question in the narrow sense, as well as the political question, also in the narrow sense (*i.e.,* the seas, the straits, Constantinople, and so forth), of course, will be automatically solved in a way which is in the least discord with the solution of the basic problem. Thus, I repeat, this question—from the standpoint of the people—assumes a firm and everlasting aspect.

In this respect Europe, failing to comprehend completely our national ideals, or rather—applying to them her own gauge and merely attributing to us the thirst for usurpation, violence, conquest of countries—at the same time comprehends very well the essential meaning of the matter.

From the standpoint of Europe, it is of no consequence that at present we are not going to seize any countries and that we promise not to conquer anyone; to her, it is far more important that, even as heretofore and always, we are inflexible in our determination to help the Slavs, and that we have no intention of ever renouncing this help. And should this happen now, should we come to the assistance of the Slavs, in the eyes of Europe we should be adding another stone to that fortress which we are gradually erecting in the East—as Europe is convinced—against her. Since, by helping the Slavs, we are thereby continuing to affirm and consolidate the Slavs' faith in Russia and her might, and we are accustoming them more and more to look upon Russia as their sun, as the center of the whole Slavdom and even of the entire East. And the consolidation of this idea, in Europe's opinion, is worth the conquests, despite all concessions which Russia, honestly and faithfully, is ready to make for the pacification of Europe.

Europe understands only too well that in this *planting of the idea,* so far, is the basic substance of the matter—not merely in the material acquisition of the Balkan Peninsula. Europe also comprehends that Russian policy, too, distinctly conceives the essence of its task. And if so, how can Europe fail to be afraid?— This is the reason why Europe sought by all means to take the

Slavs under her tutelage, so to speak, to steal them from us, and, if possible, to set them forever against Russia and the Russians. This is why she wants the Paris Treaty to continue as long as possible. Hence also, all these projects about Belgians, about European gendarmerie, etc., etc. Oh—anything, only not the Russians; only to remove Russia from the eyes and thoughts of the Slavs; to eradicate her from their memory! This is where the matter stands now.

4

A LITTLE WORD ABOUT "PETER THINKING FOR A DAY"[1]

Of late, there has been much talk about the fact that among our educated strata the summer ecstasies were followed by alleviation, by incredulity, cynicism and even irritation. Aside from intense haters of our Slavic movement, all the others, I believe, can be divided into two general categories. The first category comprises the, so to speak, *Judaizers*. They keep hammering about the harm of war in the economic aspect: they scare people with bank failures, the lowering of exchange rates, depression in commerce, even our military impotence—not only as compared with Europe but even with the Turks, forgetting that the Turkish bashi-bazouk is the torturer of the unarmed and the defenseless, the beheader of dead bodies—and, according to the Russian proverb—"a brave fellow against sheep, but against a brave fellow—himself a sheep," which unfailingly will prove true.

Now, what are the *Judaizers* after? The answer is clear: first and mainly, they were disturbed in their comfortable seats; but without dwelling upon this moral aspect of their case, let us turn to—"secondly": utter nullity of the historical and national understanding of the forthcoming task. The affair is conceived by them as a mere fleeting little caprice which may be terminated any given moment: "You frisked, so to say, and now—enough; now let's go back to business"—of course, stock-exchange business.

The second category comprises the *Europeanizers;* this is our inveterate Europeanizing. From this camp we still hear the most "radical" questions: "What do we care about the Slavs? Why should we love the Slavs? Why should we fight for them? By chasing after the useless, shall we not harm our own development, our schools? Racing after nationality, shall we not harm cosmopolitanism? Finally, shall we not provoke religious fanaticism in Russia? And so on, and so forth. In a word—although these

[1]The expression *"obodniat"* is untranslatable; this is the closest version of the sense in which Dostoievsky uses it. (B. B.)

are radical questions, nevertheless they are long-worn-out questions. The main point here is the old, ancient, senile and historical fright before the insolent thought about the possibility of Russian independence. Formerly, in days gone by, they were all liberals and progressives and they were rated as such. But their historical time has passed, and at present it is difficult to conceive anything more reactionary than they. Meanwhile, in the blissful inertia of their ideas of the Forties and Thirties, they still consider themselves progressive. Formerly they were regarded as democrats, but at present it is difficult to conceive more squeamish aristocrats in their relation to the people. It may be said that they have denounced in our people only the dark traits; but the point is that, while denouncing the dark, they have ridiculed also everything that is bright, and it may even be said that it is precisely in brightness that they perceive darkness. They fail to discern what is bright and what is dark! Again, indeed, if all conceptions of our Europeanizing intelligentsia be scrutinized, it would be impossible to conceive anything more hostile to the sane, just and independent development of the Russian people.

And all this—in the fullest innocence of their hearts. Oh, they, too, love the people but . . . in their own way. And what does it matter that some day in Russia everything will come to an accord and will find its explanation?—In the meantime great events may occur and they may take our intelligentsia unawares. Will it then not be too late? The proverb says: "Catch Peter at morn; if you give him the day to think, he'll begin to stink." The proverb is a coarse one and it is not elegantly expressed, but what it expresses is true. Will not the same thing happen to the Russian Europeanizing man which happens to Peter when he has been thinking too long? Hasn't he already been thinking too long? That's exactly the point: it seems that something of the kind is beginning to happen. . . .

And yet, to me it is almost an axiom that all our Russian isolations and segregations, from their very inception, have been based on nothing but the coarsest misconceptions and that there is nothing essential in them. The most vexing thing is that it will still take a long time before this is made clear to everybody. This is also one of our most curious themes.

1877

January

CHAPTER I

1

Three Ideas

I WILL begin my new year where I left off last year. The last sentence in the December issue of my *Diary* was to the effect that "virtually all our Russian isolations and segregations have been based on nothing but coarsest misconceptions in which there is nothing essential and unsurmountable." I repeat once more: all quarrels and segregations were caused only by the errors and deviations of the mind, and not of the heart, and it is this definition that comprises the whole essence of our segregations.

This essence is rather comforting. The mistakes and perplexities of the mind vanish more quickly and imperceptibly than the errors of the heart; they are cured not so much by disputes and logical explanations as by the irresistible logic of the events of the live, real life which very often bear in themselves the necessary and correct inference and indicate the straight road, even if not all at once, at the very moment of their occurrence, then, at any rate, at very early dates, sometimes even without awaiting the appearance of new generations.

Different is the situation relating to the errors of the heart. These constitute a very momentous thing: there is a contaminated spirit, at times, the spirit of the whole nation, which is frequently accompanied by such a degree of blindness that no facts can cure, no matter how persistently these point to the straight road. On the contrary, this kind of blindness remodels facts to its own taste and assimilates them with its own contaminated spirit; and it even happens that a whole nation would rather deliberately die, that is, holding onto its blindness, than be cured, refusing the cure. Let people not laugh at me in advance for my contention that the errors of the mind are all too lightly and quickly effaceable. And it would be most ridiculous for any one—not to speak of myself—to assume in this respect the role of an effacer firmly and calmly convinced that words are capable of bringing one to reason or of reversing the convictions prevailing in society at a given moment. I realize all this. Nevertheless, one shouldn't be ashamed of his convictions; at present there is no necessity for this, and he who has some word to utter, let him say it without fearing that people will not listen to him or even that he will be ridiculed and that he will produce upon the minds of his contemporaries no impression whatsoever.

In this respect the *Writer's Diary* will never deviate from its path, will never yield to the tendencies of the age, to the power of the reigning and prevailing influences should it consider them unjust; it will not seek to adapt itself to them, to flatter and to use cunning. After a whole year of publication we believe it permissible to make this statement. Indeed, also last year we understood well and were fully aware of the fact that many things about which we wrote with ardor and conviction, only harmed us substantially, and that it would have been far more profitable had we with equal ardor sung in a different unison.

We repeat: it would seem to us that at present *all people* should be expressing themselves as candidly and directly as possible, without being ashamed of the naïve nakedness of some thought. In fact, perhaps, extraordinary and enormous events are awaiting us, that is, all Russia. "Suddenly great events may occur and may take our intelligentsia unawares. Will it then not be too late?"—as I said when winding up my December issue of the *Diary*. By this statement I did not mean merely political events in this "nearest future," although even these events cannot help but arrest the attention of the scantiest and most "Judaized" minds which are concerned about nothing except themselves.

In point of fact, what awaits the world not only in the last quarter of the century but even (who knows?) perhaps, this year? Europe is restless; of this there can be no doubt. But is it temporary, momentary restlessness?—Not at all: apparently the time has come for something sempiternal, millenarian, for that which has been moulding itself in the world ever since the beginning of its civilization.

Three ideas are arising before the world, and it seems that they are in a state of final formulation. On one side at the extremity of Europe—the condemned Catholic idea, awaiting in great suffering and perplexity—is it to be or not to be? Is it still going to live or has its end come? I am referring not merely to the

Catholic religion but to the whole *Catholic idea,* to the destiny of the nations which for a millennium have been shaping themselves under the influence of this idea and which are saturated with it through and through. In this sense France, for example, through the ages has been, as it were, the fullest incarnation of the Catholic idea,—the head of this idea which of course was inherited from the Romans and in their spirit. That France, which *in toto* has now lost *virtually all* of her religion (the Jesuits and the atheists there are one and the same); which several times has closed her churches and which on one occasion subjected God himself to ballot in the Assembly; France which has evolved from the ideas of 1789 her own peculiar French socialism, *i.e.,* the pacification and organization of human society without and beyond Christ, as Catholicism has sought but failed to organize society in the name of Christ; that same France with her revolutionists of the Convention, with her atheists, with her socialists and with her present-day communards,—is, continues to be, in the highest degree, fully and altogether, a Catholic nation, completely contaminated with the spirit and letter of Catholicism, which by the mouths of her most arrant atheists is proclaiming: *Liberté, Egalité, Fraternité— ou la mort, i.e.,* exactly as this would be proclaimed by the Pope himself were he compelled to formulate the Catholic *liberté, egalité, fraternité* in his style, in his spirit, in the genuine style and spirit of a medieval Pope. The present-day French socialism itself—seemingly an ardent and fatal protest against the Catholic idea on the part of all men and nations tortured by and strangulated with it, who desire by all means to live, and to continue to live, but now without Catholicism and without its gods—this protest itself which actually began at the end of the last century (in fact, much earlier) is nothing but the truest and most direct continuation of the Catholic idea, its fullest, most final realization, its fatal consequence which has been evolved through centuries. French socialism is nothing else but a *compulsory* communion of mankind,—an idea which dates back to ancient Rome and which was fully conserved in Catholicism. Thus, the idea of the liberation of the human spirit from Catholicism became vested there precisely in the narrowest Catholic forms borrowed from the very heart of its spirit, from its letter, from its materialism, from its despotism, from its morality.

On the other side there arises the old Protestantism, which over a period of nineteen centuries has been protesting against Rome and her idea—the ancient pagan idea and the renovated Catholic idea—against her idea of possession of man on earth, both morally and materially; against her civilization; Protestantism which has been protesting ever since the time of Arminius and the Teutoburger

Wald. This is the German who blindly believes that in him alone, and not in the Catholic civilization, resides the rejuvenation of mankind. Throughout his whole history he has been dreaming of, and thirsting for, his unification, for the proclamation of his proud idea which had been powerfully formulated as early as the time of Luther's heresy, whereas now, five years after the debacle of France, the leading, principal and most Christian Catholic nation, the German is already fully convinced of his triumph and that no one can assume his place at the head of the world and of its renaissance. He believes in this haughtily and undeviatingly; he believes that there is nothing on earth higher than his spirit and his word, and that only Germany can utter it. To him it is even ridiculous to suppose that there be in the world, though merely in embryo, anything which Germany, predestined to lead the world, would fail to contain. And yet it is not out of place to remark, though only in parentheses, that through the nineteen centuries of her existence Germany herself which has been doing nothing but protesting, has never uttered her own *new word* but has been living all along by negation and protest against her enemy. Thus, the strange event may very well occur that when Germany scores the final victory and destroys that against which she has been protesting nineteen centuries, suddenly, she herself will have to die spiritually, right after her foe, because there would be nothing to live for, *there would be nothing to protest against*. For the time being, let it be my chimera, nevertheless Luther's Protestantism is already a fact: his is a protesting and merely *denying* faith, and just as soon as Catholicism disappears from the earth, Protestantism will unfailingly disappear, too, because there is going to be nothing to protest against, and it will turn into straight atheism, and that will be the end. But let us say that as yet this is merely my chimera.

The German despises the Slavic idea just as much as the Catholic idea with that difference only that the latter he always evaluated as a strong and powerful enemy, whereas the Slavic idea not only did he deem worth nothing but, up to the very last moment, he even did not admit it at all. However, of late, he begins to look askance upon the Slavs with great suspicion. Even though up to now it seems ridiculous to him to suppose that they may possess any aims and ideas whatsoever, any hope "of uttering anything to the world," nevertheless ever since France's debacle his uneasy suspicions have been increasing, while last year's events and current events, of course, could not have alleviated his mistrust.

At present Germany's situation is somewhat embarrassing: at any rate, before any Eastern ideas, she has to finish her task in the West. Who will deny that France, only half-slaughtered France, does not and did not cause anxiety to the German—all these five years following her pogrom—specifically because he has failed to slaughter her to death? In 1875, this anxiety had assumed in Berlin extraordinary proportions, and Germany unfailingly would have rushed, as long as there still was time, to strike a death-blow at her immemorial enemy, but certain extraordinarily strong circumstances prevented her from so doing. And now, this year, there is no doubt that France, which has been growing stronger every year, frightens Germany even more than two years ago. Germany knows that the enemy will not die without a struggle; moreover, that when he feels that he has completely recovered, he will start the battle himself so that three years, five years, hence, it will be already too late for Germany.

And now, in view of the fact that the European East is so completely absorbed by the idea which suddenly arose there, and that it is too busy with its own affairs,—it may very well happen that Germany, temporarily, finding her hands free, will make her final onslaught against her Western enemy, against the dreadful nightmare which tortures her,—and all this may come to pass in the nearest future. It may be generally said that if the situation in the East is strained and difficult, Germany is, perhaps, even in a worse position; she is faced with almost more anxieties and different scares notwithstanding her immeasurably haughty tone. This, at least, should be particularly noted by us.

Meanwhile in the East there really begins to kindle and shine with unprecedented and never-heard-of light the third world idea —the Slavic idea—an idea which is coming into being,—perhaps the third future possibility of the solution of European and human destinies. At present it is clear to everybody that with the settlement of the Eastern question, a new factor, a new element, will penetrate mankind, an element which, thus far, has been passive and in a state of inertia, and which, to say the least, cannot fail to exercise a potent and decisive influence upon world destinies.

What is this idea? What does the Slavs' communion bring with it? All this is still too indeterminate, but that something new must be introduced and uttered,—this virtually no one doubts.

And these three enormous world ideas almost at one and the same time have come together to their denouement. All this is, of course, no caprice, nor a war for some heritage or some dispute of two prominent dames, as in the last century. Here we have some-thing universal and final, which, though by no means solving *all* human destinies, brings with it the beginning of the end of the whole former history of European mankind,—the beginning of the solution of its further destinies, which are in the hands of God and about which man can guess almost nothing although he may forebode them.

Now, there arises this question: Can such events be arrested in their course? Can ideas of this magnitude be subjected to petty, Judaized, third-rate considerations? Can their solution be post-poned, and, finally, is it or is it not useful to do so?—No doubt, wisdom must guard and protect the nations and must serve hu-maneness and humankind; still certain ideas possess their own inert, mighty and all-engulfing power. It is impossible to arrest with the hand the summit of a rock which has torn away and is fall-ing. Of course, we Russians possess two dreadful powers, worth all others in the world—the unity, the spiritual indivisibility of the millions of our people, and their closest communion with the Monarch. The latter, no doubt, is incontestable; yet not only do our "Peters thinking for a day" not comprehend the popular idea, but they do not want to understand it.

2

MIRAGES: STUNDISM AND REDSTOCKISTS

But is it only the "Europeanizing" and the "Peters thinking for a day" who do not wish to understand?—There are others who are much more malignant. The "Peters," at least, acknowledge our popular movement of this year in support of the Slavs, whereas the others do not. The "Peters" commend this movement—of course in their own way—although much in it is not to their liking; but the others deny the movement itself, contrary to Russia's testi-mony: "There was nothing"—they say—"and that's the end of it." Not only was there nothing; nothing could have been. "The people" —they claim—"were nowhere clamoring and declaring a desire for war." Well, our people are never vociferating and coming out with declarations; our people are reasonable and calm; besides, they do not want war at all, not in the least; but with all their burning heart and soul they do sympathize with their brethren oppressed for Christ's faith. However, if it should prove necessary; should the Czar's great word sound, they all will rise—the whole hundred million mass of them—and will do everything within the power of such a hundred million mass inspired by one impulse, in accord, as one man. So that in view of the mysterious future of the proximate destinies of all Europe, it is impossible not to value this power of cohesion, not to contemplate it in moments of our involuntary considerations and conjectures. And God forbid war! Who wants it?—Although in parentheses it may be remarked that blood shed "for a great cause" means much; it may cleanse and wash many a thing; it may vivify many things, and it may lift anew much that has been thus far downtrodden and polluted in our souls.

However, these are but "words and thoughts." I merely mean to say that there are all-engulfing historical events which cannot be shaken off by either will or cunning, just as it is impossible to arrest a sea tide and order it to return. Still this present triumphant cynicism after the summer ecstasies is insulting—this joy of cynicism, a joy over something nasty which allegedly has triumphed over men's enthusiasm; insulting are these triumphant speeches of men not merely despising but even altogether denying our people *in toto*, and, it would seem, conceiving them, as heretofore, merely to be an inert mass and working hands, just as they have been regarded for two consecutive centuries until the great day of February nineteenth. "Should I imitate such people? What kind of idea do they have? Where did you find it?"—those are questions which nowadays are heard incessantly. This disbelief in the spiritual force of the people, naturally, is a disbelief in the whole of Russia. No doubt, here there are admixed many different factors guiding the deniers but would you believe it, there is much sincerity in them! And what is most important of all—there is utter ignorance of Russia.

Now, is it conceivable that some of them rejoice over our Stundism, that they are glad for, in behalf of, the people, for their benefit and their good? "Nevertheless [they argue] this is something higher than the former popular beliefs; nevertheless this can, at least, in some degree, ennoble the people." And don't think that these are but rare and isolated arguments.

By the way, what is this ill-starred Stundism?—Several Russian workers employed by German colonists grasped the fact that the Germans are better off than the Russians, and that is so because theirs is a different order. Pastors who happened to be there explained that theirs is a better order because of the difference in religion. Thus groups of ignorant Russian people got together; they began to listen to the interpretation of the Gospel; they themselves started reading and discussing,—and there ensued something which usually occurs in such cases. A vessel is carried with some precious vivifying liquid. But presently people get up on their feet and begin to shout: "Blind men! Why do you kiss the vessel?—It is only the content, and not the container, that is precious; you are kissing glass, mere glass; you are adoring a vessel; you are attributing all the holiness to glass, so that you are forgetting its precious content! Idolaters! Throw away the vessel!

Break it! Worship only the liquid, and not the glass!" And they break the vessel and the vivifying liquid, the precious content, is spilled on the earth and, of course, vanishes there. The vessel is broken and the liquid is lost. However, while the liquid has not yet entirely vanished in the soil, there ensues a hubbub: to save something that still remains in the broken potsherds, people begin to shout that a new vessel should be promptly brought; there arises a dispute as to how and in which form it should be made. The dispute arises *from the very start,* and promptly, beginning with the first two words, the altercation becomes confined to the letter of the matter. People are inclined to worship this letter even more than the former one so as only to acquire a new vessel as quickly as possible. But the dispute grows sharper; men break up in antagonistic groups, and each group carries away for itself a few drops of the precious liquid, in special multiformed cups picked up at random, and the groups no longer communicate one with the other. Idolatry grows stronger in proportion to the number of the fragments of the broken vessel.

This is an eternal story, a very old one which began much before the time of Martin Ivanovich Luther; but pursuant to historical laws almost an identical story repeated itself in our Stundism: it is known that they are already breaking up, disputing about letters, interpreting the Gospel, each one in accordance with his understanding, and the main point is that this is taking place *from the very start.* Poor, unfortunate, ignorant people! And yet how much sincerity! How many good beginnings! How much determination to endure, even suffering! How much helpless stupidity and petty pedantic hypocrisy, egoistic ambition, sweet gratifying haughtiness in this new rank of "saints," even roguery and chicaneries; but the main thing—"from the very start," *i.e.,* ever since the creation of the world, since the questions have arisen: What is man and what is woman? What is good and what is evil? Is there or is there not a God?

And would you believe that the very fact that they are so helpless, that they have to begin from the beginning, precisely this fact appeals to many of them, and especially—to some of them: "They will start living in accordance with their own ideas which means that without fail they will come to some kind of understanding." What an argument! So that the precious heritage, acquired through ages, which should be explained to these ignorant people in its great true meaning, and not thrown away upon the earth as useless old rags of the past centuries, essentially has been irretrievably lost for them. Development, light, progress are again pushed far back from them, since from now on isolation will ensue for them,—segregation and seclusion of sectarianism, and instead of the anticipated new "sensible" ideas, there will be erected old, most antiquated, generally familiar and very nasty idols,—and now try to smash them!

However, there is no reason whatsoever to fear Stundism even though it certainly should be pitied. This Stundism has absolutely no future; it will not expand widely; it will come to a halt and, unfailingly, it will merge with some obscure sect of the Russian people, with the Khlystis, presumably this most ancient of all sects of the world which undeniably has its meaning and which conserves it in two ancient attributes: whirling and prophecy. Even the Templars were prosecuted for whirling and prophesying; and the Quakers are whirling and prophesying; and Pythia in ancient times whirled and prophesied; and people used to whirl and prophesy at the home of Tatarinova; and it is very possible that our Redstockists will wind up with whirling, while it seems that even now they are already prophesying. Let the Redstockists take no offense because of this comparison.

By the way: many people laugh at the synchronous coincidence of the origination in Russia of the two sects—Stundism among the common people, and the Redstockist in our most fashionable society. And yet here there is much which isn't funny. As regards the coincidence of the origination of our two sects, undoubtedly they arose out of one and the same ignorance, *i.e.*, the utter ignorance of their religion.

3

Foma Danilov—the Russian Hero Tortured to Death

In the spring of last year all newspapers reprinted the news which appeared in *The Russian Invalid* about the martyr's death of a non-commissioned officer of the 2nd Turkestan Rifle Battalion, Foma Danilov; he was taken a prisoner by the Kipchaks and barbarously murdered by them on November 21, 1875, at Margelan, after having been subjected to many refined tortures because he had refused to enter their service and to embrace Mohammedanism. The Khan himself promised him pardon, reward and honors on condition that he renounce Christ. Danilov answered that he could not betray the Cross, and that as a subject of the Czar, though in captivity, he had to abide by his duty toward the Czar and Christianity. The torturers, having tortured him to death, were astonished by the force of his spirit and gave him the name of "bogatyr," which means "valiant knight."

At the time this news item, though printed in all newspapers, caused but little comment in society, while the papers having published it in the form of a usual newspaper *entre-filet*, did not deem it necessary to dwell upon it *particularly*. In a word, in the case of Foma Danilov "it was quiet" in stock-exchange parlance. Subsequently, as is known, the Slavic movement came into being; then came Cherniaiev, the Serbians, Kireev, donations, volunteers, and the tortured-to-death Foma was completely forgotten (*i.e.*, by the newspapers), and recently additional details amplifying the earlier account have been received. It is reported that the Samara governor has made inquiries about the family of Danilov, who was a peasant of the village Kirsanovka of the Buguruslan county of the Samara province, and it was found that he was survived by his wife Evfrosinia of the age of twenty-seven and a six-year-old daughter Oulita who were in a destitute condition. Relief was given to them on the noble initiative of the governor, who applied to several persons requesting them to help the widow and the daughter of the martyred Russian hero, and to the Samara provincial zemstvo assembly—with the proposal to place Danilov's daughter as a stipendiary in one of the educational institutions. Thereupon 1320 rubles were collected; 600 rubles were set aside till the daughter's majority, the remainder of the sum was turned over to the widow, and the daughter was placed in a school. In addition the Chief of the General Staff notified the governor that the Emperor gracefully ordered that an annual life pension of 120 rubles be paid by the State Treasury to the widow. Thereupon . . . thereupon the matter probably will be again forgotten in view of the current anxieties, political fears, enormous problems awaiting their solution, bankruptcies, and so on, and so forth.

Oh, I do not mean to say that our society took an indifferent attitude toward this striking act as one not worthy of attention. It is merely a fact that little was said, or, more correctly, almost no one spoke about it *particularly*. However, perhaps, people somewhere did speak among themselves, among merchants, among the clergy, for instance, but not in society, not among our intelligentsia. Of course, the people will not forget this great death: this hero has suffered tortures for Christ and he is a great Russian. The people treasure this and will not forget, have never forgotten, such deeds.

And now I already hear, as it were, those voices so familiar to me: "No doubt, this is force; this we admit; nevertheless it is an obscure force which manifested itself in so-to-speak antediluvian, bureaucratized forms, and, therefore, why should we be *particularly* talking about the matter? It does not belong to our world; it would have been different had this force revealed itself intelligently, consciously. There are, you see, also other sufferers and other forces; there are infinitely loftier ideas, for instance, the idea of cosmopolitanism. . . ."

Notwithstanding these sensible and intelligent voices, it seems to me permissible and altogether justifiable to say something *particular* about Danilov. Moreover, I even venture to maintain that our intelligentsia would have by no means humiliated itself had it dealt with this fact more attentively. For instance, first of all I am surprised that no astonishment was revealed—precisely, astonishment. I am not speaking of the people: among them no astonishment is needed and there will be none: Foma's deed cannot seem to them extraordinary for the mere reason of their great faith in themselves and in their soul. They will react to this heroic exploit only by a strong sentiment and a great emotion. However, were a similar fact to occur in Europe, that is, the manifestation of such a great spiritual force among the English or the French, they would have certainly heralded it all over the world. Nay, listen, gentlemen, do you know how I represent to myself this obscure soldier of the Turkestan battalion?—Indeed, this is, so to speak, the emblem of Russia, of all Russia, of all our popular Russia, the true image of that very Russia in which our cynics and profound sages are now denying the great spirit, every possibility of enthusiasm and of the revelation of a great thought and great feeling. Listen, none the less you are not those cynics, you are merely intelligently Europeanizing, that is, essentially, the kindest folk: in fact, you do not deny that in summer our people, here and there, did manifest extraordinary spiritual potency: men left their homes and children, and went to die for religion, for the oppressed, God knows whither and God knows with what means, exactly as the first crusaders nine centuries ago in Europe,—those very crusaders whose reappearance Granovsky, for example, would have considered almost ridiculous and offensive "in our age of positive problems, progress," etc. Let this summer movement of ours be, in your opinion, a blind and even insensible movement, a so-to-speak "crusaders'" movement. Nevertheless, it cannot be denied that it was firm and magnanimous—if it be viewed from only a slightly broader standpoint. A great idea was awakening, an idea which, at once, has lifted, maybe, hundreds of thousands and millions of souls from inertia, cynicism, debauch and ugliness in which, prior to that, these souls had been submerged. You know, of course, that our people are considered kindhearted and even intellectually most gifted, but still an ignorant elemental mass devoid of consciousness, almost solidly addicted to vices and prejudices, almost solidly indecent. But you see, I will venture to express, so to speak, an axiom:

in order to judge the moral force of a people and what they are
capable of in the future, one has to take into account not that
level of indecency to which, temporarily, even though in their
majority, they have sunk, but that elevation of the spirit which
they are capable of attaining when the time comes. Indecency is
a temporary misfortune, always dependent upon past and transitory
circumstances, upon slavery, secular oppression, inveterateness,
whereas the gift of magnanimity is a perpetual, elemental gift
which is born with a people, one which is all the more to be valued
if, despite centuries of slavery, oppression and misery, it is still
preserved intact in the hearts of the people.

Seemingly, Foma Danilov was one of the most ordinary and
inconspicuous specimens of the Russian people, inconspicuous as
the Russian people themselves. (Indeed, to still quite a few they
are altogether inconspicuous.) Perhaps, in days past, he had been
leading a loose life; he may have been fond of drinking; maybe,
he even did not pray much, although, of course, he always remembered God. And all of a sudden he is being ordered to change his
religion under the threat of a martyr's death. In this connection
one has to recall what these tortures, these Asiatic tortures are!
He faces the Khan himself, who promises him his favors, and
Danilov understands perfectly that his refusal unfailingly will
anger the Khan, will vex the ambition of the Kipchaks because
"this Christan dog dares to despise Islam to such a degree." Yet,
notwithstanding everything that awaits him, this inconspicuous
Russian man endures the cruelest tortures and dies astonishing
his torturers. You know, gentlemen, that none of us would have
done this. To assume martyrdom in public, at times, is even sightly;
but here the thing transpired in utter obscurity, in a remote locality; no one was looking at him; besides Foma himself could
not have thought, and certainly did not suppose, that his heroic
deed would be heralded all over Russia. I believe some of the
martyrs, even during the first centuries of the Christian era, when
enduring their tortures, were partly consoled and alleviated by the
conviction that their death would serve as an example for the timid
and oscillating ones, and would increase the number of the followers of Christ. For Foma even this great consolation could
not have existed: who would find it out?—He was alone among his
torturers. He was still young. Over there, somewhere, were his young
wife and daughter. Never is he going to see them again. But be
it so: "Wherever I may be, I will not act against my conscience,
and I will endure the tortures."—Indeed, this is truth for truth's
sake, and not for the sake of ostentation! And no iniquity, no
sophism with conscience: "I shall embrace Islam ostensibly; I shall

not yield to temptation; no one is going to see. Later I shall pray
for forgiveness; life is long. I shall perpetrate good deeds." There
was nothing of the kind: astounding, primitive, elemental honesty.
Nay, gentlemen, we should hardly have acted in this manner!

But this is—we, whereas to our people Danilov's exploit, I
repeat, is, perhaps, even not surprising. Therein is the point that
precisely here we have, as it were, the portrait, the full picture
of the Russian people. This is precisely what makes the thing
dear to me and, of course, to you. Likewise our people love truth
for its own sake and not for ostentation. And let them be coarse
and ugly and sinful and inconspicuous, but when their time comes,
and a cause of general popular truth arises, then you will be
astounded by that measure of spiritual freedom which they will
reveal despite the pressure of materialism, passions, pecuniary and
material greed, and even in the face of dread of the cruelest martyr's
death. And they will do and manifest all this simply, firmly, without claiming any reward or commendation, without making a display of themselves: "That in which I believe, I confess." In this
respect even the most obdurate wranglers about "reaction" in the
people's ideals have nothing to say, since it is unimportant whether
or not an ideal is reactionary; the important point is the ability
to reveal the strongest will for the sake of a magnanimous exploit.
(This ridiculous little idea about "reaction" I introduced here for
the sake of complete impartiality.)

You know, gentlemen, the question must be put squarely: I
maintain that we have nothing to teach such a people. This is a
sophism but sometimes it does come to my mind. Why, of course,
we are more educated than the people, but the trouble is—what are
we going to teach them! Of course, I am not speaking of trades,
technique, mathematics; these may be taught even by hired travelling Germans, if we should fail to teach them. But what are we
going to impart? For we are Russians, brethren of this people, and
this means that we must *enlighten* them. And yet what do we have
to impart to them from among the things that are moral and lofty?
What shall we explain to them? With what shall we illume their
"obscure" souls? The enlightenment of the people—this, gentlemen,
is our right and our duty,—this is a right in the highest Christian
sense: he who knows the good, the true word of life, must, is duty-
bound, to convey it to him who knows not, to his brother groping
in darkness—thus it is according to the Gospel. Now, what shall
we convey to the groping that he does not know better than we?

Of course, first of all,—teaching is useful, and one has to
learn. Isn't this so? But the people, even before us, said: "Knowledge is light, ignorance is darkness." Eradication of prejudices,

for instance, or the casting down of idols? But within ourselves there is such a mass of prejudices, and we have placed before ourselves so many idols, that the people will unhesitatingly tell us: "Physician, heal thyself." (And they know our idols; they are quite able to discern things!)—Well, is it self-respect? Personal dignity?—But our people as a whole respect themselves far more than we; they respect and understand their dignity much more deeply than we. In fact, we are awfully ambitious, yet we do not respect ourselves at all, nor is there in us the feeling of personal dignity,—in no respect whatsoever. Well—to give an example—is it for us to teach the people respect for other men's convictions? Our people, even prior to Peter, have proved their respect for other men's convictions, whereas we, even among ourselves, do not forgive one another the slightest deviation from our convictions, and those even slightly disagreeing with us we consider scoundrels, forgetting that he who is apt to lose respect for others, to begin with, does not respect himself. Is it for us to teach the people faith in ourselves, in our strength? The people have their Foma Danilovs— thousands of them, whereas we do not believe in the least in Russian strength, and, besides, we regard this disbelief as sublime enlightenment and virtually as prowess.

What is it, finally, that we can teach? We loathe to the point of wrath everything that our people love and respect, for which their heart longs. So what sort of demophiles are we? It may be argued that we love the people all the more if we loathe their ignorance wishing them good. Nay, gentlemen, not at all: In fact, if we truly loved the people—and not merely in articles and books —we should come closer to them; we should take pains to study that which at present, altogether without thinking, abiding by European patterns, we seek to exterminate in them. If we should do this, perhaps, we ourselves might learn so many things that at present we cannot even imagine.

However, we have one consolation, one great superiority to our people, and this is why we so despise them: it is that they are nationally-minded and adhere to this with all their strength, whereas ours are cosmopolitan convictions, and, for this reason, we have lifted ourselves far above them. Now, herein is our whole dissension, our detachment from the people. And I directly proclaim: should we settle this point, should we find the point of reconciliation, at once our whole discord with the people would come to an end. Such a point exists; and it is very easy to find it. I repeat decisively that even our most radical disagreements, essentially, are nothing but a mirage.

CHAPTER II

1

A Conciliatory Dream Without Science

FIRST OF ALL, I shall set forth the most controversial, the most ticklish proposition, and I begin with it:

"Every great people believes, and must believe if it intends to live long, that in it alone resides the salvation of the world; that it lives in order to stand at the head of the nations, to affiliate and unite all of them, and to lead them in a concordant choir toward the final goal preordained for them."

I assert that it has been thus in the case of all great nations of the world; the most ancient and the youngest ones; that only this faith has raised them to the possibility, each one of them at its own time, of exercising an enormous influence upon the destinies of mankind. Such undeniably was the case of ancient Rome; so it was likewise in the case of Rome during the period of her Catholic existence. When the Catholic idea had been inherited by France the same happened there, and during almost two centuries France, till her most recent debacle and despondency, all the time and undeniably considered herself the mistress of the world at least in the moral domain, and at times also in the political field; the leader of its progress and the guide of its future. However, Germany has been dreaming about the same, and as against the universal Catholic idea and its authority, she set forth as her banner Protestantism and the unlimited freedom of conscience and exploration. This—I repeat—is more or less the case of all great nations in the zenith of their development.

I may be told that all this is an error, and the *confession* of those very nations may be cited, the admissions of their scientists and thinkers, who have been specifically writing about the joint significance of the European nations which, jointly, participated in the creation and consummation of European civilization, and, of course, I am not going to deny these admissions. However, leaving aside the fact that such final inferences of the admissions, generally, constitute the end of the active life of the peoples, I shall merely note that these very thinkers and confessors, no matter what they may have been writing about the universal harmony of nations, at the same time and in most cases, with their immediate, live and sincere sentiment, *continued to believe,* exactly as the masses of their peoples, that in that choir of nations which constitute world harmony, and the jointly evolved civilization, they (the French, for instance) are heading the union; that they are the most progressive ones who are destined to lead, while the rest merely follow their leadership; that suppose they even borrow something from the other nations, nevertheless it is only a tiny bit, whereas the other peoples will borrow from them everything, the most essential; that these other nations can live only by their, the leaders', spirit and idea, and that they cannot act otherwise than embrace, in the long run, their spirit, and, sooner or later, merge with it.

Even in present-day France, despondent and spiritually dismembered, there is one such idea which, to our way of thinking, constitutes a new, perfectly normal phase of development of her former universal Catholic idea; virtually fifty per cent of the French believe even in our day that therein is concealed not only their salvation but that of the world, too,—that is, their French socialism. Of course this idea—their French socialism—is an erroneous and desperate one. However, at this juncture, it is not its quality that is important but the fact that it exists, that it actively lives, and that those who profess it entertain no doubts and are not despondent as the overwhelming portion of France.

On the other hand, look at virtually any Englishman, whether of the highest or lowest status, whether a lord or a worker, whether learned or uneducated, and you will be convinced that every one of them, above all, seeks to be an Englishman, to preserve himself as such in all phases of his life—private and public, political and cosmopolitan, and that he even endeavors to love mankind not otherwise than in the guise of an Englishman.

It may be said that even if this were true, if everything were as I maintain, nevertheless self-intoxication and self-conceit would be humiliating to those great nations; that their significance would be reduced by their egoism, by stupid chauvinism, and that not only would these fail to add to them vital energy, but, on the contrary, they would corrupt the life from the very beginning. It may be also argued that such insane and haughty ideas deserve not imitation but, on the contrary, extermination by the light of reason which destroys prejudices.

Now, let us say that, on the one hand, this is very true. Nevertheless the matter necessarily has to be examined in its other aspect, and then it will appear not only not humiliating, but quite the reverse. What is there in the fact that a youth with no life experience is dreaming of some day becoming a hero? Believe me that such haughty and arrogant ideas are, perhaps, more vivifying and useful to that lad than the certain prudence of a boy who already at the age of sixteen believes in the wise rule: "happiness is better than knighthood." Believe me that the life of that former youth, even after the misfortunes and failures through which he might live, on the whole will still be more satisfying than the pacified existence of the prudent companion of his childhood even though he be destined to sit all his life on velvet. Such a faith in one's self is not immoral and not at all trivial boasting.

The same is true of the nations: let there be prudent, honest, moderate pacific peoples devoid of any impulses—merchants and shipbuilders—living opulently and in extreme tidiness. Well, God bless them, but all the same they will not go far; unfailingly, it will be mediocrity which in no way will serve the human race: such nations lack that energy, that great self-confidence, those three moving whales[1] upon which all great peoples stand. The belief that one wishes and can utter the last word to the world; that it can be revived through the abundance of one's vital force; faith in the sacredness of one's ideals, in the strength of one's love, of one's thirst for serving mankind—nay, such a faith is a guaranty of the loftiest life of the nations, and it is only through this faith that they are in a position to render to humanity the full measure of that service which at the time of their inception, they have been destined to render by nature herself, and to bequeath to future mankind. Only a nation fortified with such a faith is entitled to sublime life.

The ancient legendary knight believed that all obstacles would fall before him—all phantoms and monsters; that he would conquer everything and everybody; that he would achieve everything if only he abided by his vow of "justice, chastity and poverty." You may say that all these are legends and songs in which only Don Quixote can believe, and that the laws of actual life are quite different. If so, I will deliberately trap you, gentlemen, and I will prove that you are Don Quixotes yourselves; that you yourselves possess an identical idea in which you believe and through which you seek to revive mankind.

In fact, in what do you believe?—You believe (and I share your belief) in cosmopolitanism, *i.e.*, that the natural barriers and prejudices which until now have impeded the free intercourse of nations by the egoism of their national aspiration, some day will fall before the light of reason and consciousness, and that the peoples will then start living in one congenial accord, like brethren, sensibly and lovingly striving for universal harmony. Gentlemen, what can be loftier, more sacred, than this faith of yours? And the main thing is that nowhere in the world will you any longer find

[1]This refers to the Norse legend in which the universe is pictured as resting on the backs of three huge, moving whales.

this faith, for instance, in no people in Europe, where the individualities of the nations are circumscribed very sharply; where, if such a faith is to be found, it exists not otherwise than in the form of a metaphysical conception; true, an ardent and burning conception but nevertheless an abstract one. And in you, gentlemen, *i.e.*, not only in you but in all us Russians, this is a universal, live, fundamental faith. In Russia everybody believes in this consciously and simply, both the educated strata and, through live instinct, the common people to whom also religion prescribes belief in these same things. Yes, gentlemen, you think that you alone of all the Russian intelligentsia are cosmopolitans, while the rest are merely Slavophiles and nationalists. But this isn't so: Slavophiles and nationalists believe in identically the same things as you, and even more firmly than you!

I shall refer only to the Slavophiles: indeed, what have they been proclaiming through the mouths of their men of action, founders and representatives of their doctrine?—In direct, clear and precise statements they have been asserting that Russia, in conjunction with Slavdom, and at its head, will utter to the whole world the greatest word ever heard, and that that word will precisely be a covenant of universal human fellowship, and no longer in the spirit of personal egoism by means of which at present men and nations unnaturally, because of the struggle for existence, unite with each other in their civilization, setting moral boundaries to the free spirit by positive science, at the same time digging ditches for each other and spreading about each other lies, blasphemy and calumnies. The Slavophiles' ideal was communion in the spirit of true and broad love, devoid of deceit and materialism, and on the basis of the individual magnanimous example which the Russian people, at the head of the free all-Slavic communion in Europe, is destined to set.

You will tell me that you do not believe in this at all; that all these are abstract speculations. Yet here the important matter is not the question how one believes, but the fact that in Russia, despite all the discordance, people still agree and concur in this ultimate general idea of the universal fellowship of men. This fact is undeniable and, in itself, is surprising because this feeling, in the form of so vivid and fundamental an urge, exists in no other people. And if this be so, this means that in us, in all of us, there is a solid and specific national idea—precisely, *national*. Consequently, if the Russian national idea, in the last analysis, is but the universal fellowship of men, this signifies that our whole benefit should reside in the endeavor to finish, for the time being, our dissensions, and become Russians and national as quickly as possible. Our whole salvation is not to quarrel in advance about the question how, in what form, this idea will be realized, in yours or in ours, but for all of us to pass from the drawing-room directly over to business.

But precisely here lies the difficulty.

2

In Europe We Are Mere Canaille

Now, how did you get down to business? You started long ago, quite some time ago; however, what did you accomplish for cosmopolitanism, for the triumph of your idea? You began with aimless vagabondage throughout Europe led by the avid desire to be reborn into Europeans, at least outwardly. Throughout the entire eighteenth century we were doing nothing but imitating a guise. We were absorbing European tastes; we were even eating all sorts of filth, trying not to knit our brows: "See what an Englishman I am; I can eat nothing without cayenne pepper!" You think I am jeering?—Not in the least. I understand only too well that it was impossible to begin differently. Even prior to Peter, still under the Moscow czars and patriarchs, one young Moscow dandy of those days, one of the progressives, donned a French costume with a sword hooked at his side.

Precisely, we had to start with contempt for our own and for ours. If during two whole centuries we have remained at this point, without moving either backward or forward, such must have been the term fixed for us by nature. True, we did also move: contempt for everything that was our own as well as for ours has been increasing more and more, especially when we began to understand Europe more fully. However, the sharp segregation of nationalities and the sharply fixed patterns of national characters, in Europe, caused no confusion among us. We began precisely with a direct "elimination of all contrasts," and we thus evolved the cosmopolitan type of a "European," *i.e.*, from the very beginning we discerned the *general* which unites them all,—this is quite characteristic.

Thereupon, as time went on, having grown cleverer, straightway we laid hold of civilization, and at once we adopted a blind and faithful belief that, precisely, in civilization resides that "universality" which is destined to unite mankind. Even Europeans, looking upon us, aliens and newcomers, used to express surprise at the enthusiastic faith of ours, all the more so as they themselves—alas—began to lose, little by little, this faith in themselves. We greeted with rapture the advent of Rousseau and Voltaire; together with the travelling Karamzin we touchingly rejoiced in 1789 over the convocation of the "Etats Généraux," and if later, at the end of the first quarter of the current century, we, in accord with the progressive Europeans, despaired over their vanished dreams and shattered ideals, nevertheless we did not lose our faith, and we even used to console the Europeans themselves. Even the "whitest" Russians at home, in their fatherland, forthwith grew red in Europe, which is also a most characteristic trait.

Then, in the middle of our century, some of us gained the honor of joining French socialism, accepting it without the slightest hesitation as the ultimate solution of cosmopolitan communion, *i.e.*, as the realization of that dream of ours which till then had rarely tempted us. Thus we mistook for the realization of our aim that which was the climax of egoism and barbarity; the pinnacle of economic muddle and confusion; the culmination of the calumny of human nature, and utter eradication of men's freedom. But this did not trouble us in the least. On the contrary, perceiving the sad perplexity of certain profound European thinkers, we, with utmost flippancy, forthwith called them scoundrels and blockheads. We completely believed—and still believe—that positive science is fully capable of determining the *moral* boundaries between the individual entities and the nations (as if science, were it capable of this, could reveal these mysteries prior to *the completion of the experiment, i.e.*, prior to the realization of all destinies of man on earth).

Our landowners sold their peasant serfs and proceeded to Paris in order to publish socialistic magazines, and our Rudins died on barricades. Meanwhile we became so detached from the Russian soil that we lost every conception of how much this doctrine differed from the soul of the Russian people. In truth, not only did we consider the Russian people's character as worthless but we even denied the existence of any character in them. We forgot to think of it, and with full despotic calmness we were convinced (even without raising any questions) that our people would immediately accept everything which we told them, in fact, ordered them. In this connection there circulated among the people several very amusing anecdotes. Our cosmopolitans in every respect have remained landowners in their relation to the people—even after the peasant reform.

And what did we achieve?—Strange results: mainly that in Europe everybody looked upon us mockingly, while the best and unquestionably clever Russians were viewed with haughty condescension. Not even emigration from Russia, that is political emigra-

tion, and the fullest renunciation of Russia, saved them from that
haughty condescension. Europeans did not want to recognize us
as their own despite anything, despite any sacrifices,—under any
circumstances. This meant: *Grattez le Russe et vous verrez le
Tartare.* And thus it stands up to the present. Among them we
became proverbial. And the more, to please them, we despised our
nationality, the more they despised us. We wriggled before them;
subserviently we professed our "European" opinions and convictions, and they haughtily did not listen to us, and usually added
with a polite smile—as if seeking to get rid of us as quickly as
possible—that we "did not properly understand them." Specifically
they were surprised at the fact that we, being such Tartars (*les
Tartares*) utterly failed to become Russians, whereas we never were
able to explain to them that we sought to be not Russians but
cosmopolitans. True, of late, they managed to understand something. They came to realize that we want something which they
fear and which is dangerous to them; they grasped the fact that
there are many of us, eighty millions; that we know and comprehend all European ideas, while they do not know our Russian ideas,
and that should they even come to know them, they would not
understand them; that we speak all languages, while they—only
their own.—Well, they began to surmise and suspect also many other
things. It came to the point where they directly called us enemies
and the future destroyers of European civilization. This is how
they understood our passionate aim to become cosmopolitans!

And yet, under no circumstance can we renounce Europe.
Europe is our second fatherland, and I am the first ardently to
profess this; I have always professed this. To us *all* Europe is
almost as dear as Russia; in Europe resides the entire tribe of
Japheth, and our idea is the unification of all nations descending
from that tribe; even much farther—down to Shem and Ham. Now,
what's to be done?

First of all and above all to become Russians. If cosmopolitanism is a Russian national idea, then every one of us must become a Russian, *i.e.*, himself. Then everything will change—from
the very first step. To become a Russian means to cease to despise
one's own people. And just as soon as the European perceives that
we have begun to respect our people and our nationality, he will
at once begin to respect us. Indeed, the stronger, the more independent we grow in our national spirit, the more strongly and
closely shall we reflect ourselves in the European soul, and having
become related to it, we shall at once become more intelligible
to it. Then they would no longer haughtily turn away from us
but would listen to us. Then we should even change our outward

appearance. Having become ourselves, we should at last acquire a human, and not apish, countenance. We should acquire the appearance of free men, and not that of slaves, lackeys, of Potugin. Then we should be taken for human beings, and not for international outcasts, not for "the canaille" of Europeanism, liberalism and socialism. We should even talk to them more intelligently than at present because we should find in our people, in their spirit, new words which unfailingly would become more intelligible to Europeans. Besides, we ourselves should then understand that much of what we used to despise in our people is not darkness but precisely light; not stupidity but reason. And having grasped this, unfailingly, we should utter in Europe such a word as has never been heard before. We should then become convinced that the genuine social truth resides in no one else but our people; that their idea, their spirit contains the living urge of universal communion of men, a fellowship with full respect for national individualities, for their preservation, for the maintenance of complete liberty of men, with the indication of what liberty comprises, *i.e.*, loving communion, guaranteed by deeds, by the living example, by the factual need of brotherhood, and not under the threat of the guillotine, not by means of chopping off millions of heads. . . .

However, did I really intend to convince anyone?—This was merely a joke. But man is weak: maybe, some lad belonging to the young generation will read this.

3

RUSSIAN SATIRE. *Virgin Soil. Last Songs.* OLD
REMINISCENCES

This month I was also occupied with literature, *i.e.*, with belles-lettres, "elegant literature," and I read certain things with fascination. By the way, recently I have read a foreign opinion on Russian satire, *i.e.*, on our present-day, contemporaneous satire. It was expressed in France. There is one remarkable deduction—I forget the exact words but this is the meaning: "Russian satire is afraid, as it were, of a good deed in Russian society. When it encounters such a deed, it begins to feel disturbed and does not calm down until it discovers somewhere, in the underlying motive of that deed,—a scoundrel. At this juncture the satire at once starts rejoicing and shouts: 'This is in no sense a good deed; there is absolutely nothing to be glad of. You can see for yourselves that here, too, there sits a scoundrel!'"

Is this opinion just? I do not believe it is. I know only that our satire has brilliant representatives who are very much in vogue. The public is very fond of satire; nevertheless, it is at least my conviction that this very public is much more fond of positive beauty, that it craves and thirsts for it. Count Leo Tolstoy, unquestionably, is the most beloved writer among the Russian public of all shades.

Our satire, no matter how brilliant, does in truth suffer from a certain indeterminateness—this, perhaps, may be said about it. At times, it is impossible to conceive, *in toto* and generally, what exactly our satire seeks to express. It does seem that it has no underlying motive; yet can this be so? The things in which it believes, in the name of which it condemns—these seem to be submerged in the darkness of uncertainty. It is impossible to determine what the satire itself considers to be good.

And, strangely, one begins to ponder over this question.

I have read Turgenev's *Virgin Soil,* and I am awaiting the second part.

By the way, I have been writing for thirty years, and throughout this whole period I have been struck by this amusing observation: all our critics—and I have been following literature almost forty years—those who are no longer and those still living, in a word, all those whom I remember; the moment they would start writing, with a touch of solemnness, some review of the current Russian literature—this is equally true of the present and of days past—(formerly our magazines used to give in January annual reviews), they would more or less invariably, and with great delight, resort to one and the same phrase: "In our day, when literature is in a state of such decadence," or "in our day when Russian literature is in a state of such stagnation," or "in our literary ill times," or "wandering through the deserts of Russian literature," etc.—The same thought twisted a thousand different ways.

Yet in the course of these forty years there appeared the last works of Pushkin; Gogol came and went; we had Lermontov; Ostrovsky, Turgenev, Goncharov and at least ten or more other most talented belles-lettrists who made their appearances. And this—in belles-lettres only! It may be positively asserted that in so short a period, never, in any literature, did there appear so many gifted writers as in Russia,—all along, without intervals. Even so, now, it must have been only last month, I was reading about stagnation in Russian literature and the "deserts of Russian belles-lettres."

However, this is merely an amusing observation—an altogether innocent thing which has no significance whatsoever. But it deserves a smile.

Naturally, I am going to say nothing about *Virgin Soil;*

everybody is awaiting the second part. Besides, it is not for me to speak. The artistic merit of Turgenev's creations is unquestioned. I shall only remark that on the top of page 92 of the novel (see *Messenger of Europe*) there are fifteen or twenty lines in which, in my opinion, is condensed, as it were, the whole idea of the work, the author's view of his subject. It is to be regretted that this view is quite erroneous, and I profoundly disagree with it. Those are the few words which the author says about Solomin, one of the characters in the novel.

In the January issue of *The Domestic Records* I have read Nekrasov's *Last Songs*. Passionate songs and words not fully told, as always in Nekrasov, but what painful moans of a sick man! Our poet is very sick and—this he told me himself—he sees clearly his situation. But somehow I don't believe it. . . . His is a strong and susceptible constitution. He is suffering terribly (he has some kind of an intestinal ulcer—a sickness which is even difficult to diagnose), but I refuse to believe that he will not survive till spring, and then he can go to some spa abroad, with a different climate, and his health will be restored—of this I am convinced.

Strange things happen to people. We rarely saw each other; we also had misunderstandings, but there was in our lives one incident which I could never forget, namely, our first meeting. And imagine, recently I called on Nekrasov, and he, the ailing and the jaded, from the very first words began to tell me that he remembered those days. Then—this was thirty years ago!—there happened something so youthful, so fresh and good which is forever preserved in the hearts of those who have lived through this experience. We were both slightly over twenty years old. I was then residing in Petersburg; one year before I resigned from the engineers' corps, not knowing why, full of vague and uncertain aspirations. This was in May, 1845. Early in the winter, suddenly, I began to write *Poor Folks*, my first novel; before that I had never written anything. Having finished the novel, I did not know what to do with it, and to whom it should be submitted. I had no literary acquaintances whatever, save D. V. Grigorovich; but in those days he, too, had written nothing except a short article *Petersburg Hurdy-Gurdy Men* for one of the almanacs. If I am not mistaken, he was about to leave for his estate for the summer, meanwhile living in Nekrasov's apartment. Having called on me, he said: "Bring your manuscript: [as yet he had not read it] Nekrasov intends to publish an almanac for the coming year; I will show it to him." I brought my manuscript. Nekrasov I saw but for a moment; we shook hands. I was perplexed by the thought that I had come with

my composition, and I quickly left having scarcely said a word
to Nekrasov. I gave little thought to success, and I was afraid of
"the party of The Domestic Records," as people used to call it
in those days. I had been reading Bielinsky with enthusiasm for
several years, but he seemed threatening and dreadful, and, at times,
I would say to myself: "He will ridicule my *Poor Folks!"*—but
only at times. I wrote the novel passionately, almost with tears.
"Is it possible that all this, all these minutes through which I have
lived with pen in hand working on this novel,—can it be that all
this is a lie, a mirage, a wrong sentiment?"—But, of course, thus
I thought only now and then, and doubt forthwith returned to me.

In the evening of the same day that I submitted the manuscript, I went far off to visit a former friend of mine. All night
we spoke about *Dead Souls* and read the novel for how long a time
—I don't remember. In those days it used to be this way among
young men; two or three of them would get together: "Gentlemen,
shall we read Gogol?"—They would sit down and read, sometimes,
all night. Then among the youth there were many who, as it were,
were penetrated with something and were awaiting something.

I returned home at four o'clock, in a white Petersburg night,
bright as a day. The weather was beautiful and warm, and upon
entering my apartment I did not go to bed, but opened the window
and seated myself in front of it. Suddenly I heard the bell ring.
This surprised me very much. Presently Grigorovich and Nekrasov
rushed upon me and in a perfect transport started embracing me,
and both were almost crying.

In the evening they came home early, took my manuscript
and began to read it, just for a test. "We shall be able to judge
from the first ten pages." But having read ten pages, they decided
to read ten more pages, and thereupon, without interruption, they
sat all night till morning reading aloud and taking turns when one
grew tired. "He is reading about the student's death,"—Grigorovich
later told me, when we were alone—"and suddenly I notice, in that
place where the father runs behind the coffin, Nekrasov's voice
begins to falter, once, then a second time, and then, losing control
over himself, he raps upon the manuscript with his palm, exclaiming: 'The rascal!'—meaning you. And thus all night."

After they had finished reading (112 pages in all), they
unanimously decided to call on me immediately: "What does it
matter that he is sleeping! We'll wake him up. *This* is more important than sleep!" Subsequently, having studied Nekrasov's disposition, I often wondered about this incident: his is a reserved,
almost suspicious character, cautious and uncommunicative. At

least, this is how I always sized him up, so that the minute of our first meeting was in truth the manifestation of a most profound feeling.

They stayed with me half an hour, or so, and during that time we managed to discuss God knows how many topics, understanding each other from the first syllable, hastening, with exclamations. We spoke about poetry and truth and "the existing situation," and, it goes without saying, about Gogol, quoting from *The Revizor* and *Dead Souls,* but principally—about Bielinsky. "I will give him your novel today, and you will see—what a man! What a man! You will get acquainted; you will see what a soul he has!"—Nekrasov was telling me enthusiastically, with both hands shaking me by my shoulders. "Well, now sleep, sleep! We are leaving you, and tomorrow—come to us!" How could I sleep after their visit! What ecstasy! What a success! And principally —the sentiment was dear. I remember distinctly: "A fellow meets with success, he is praised, people meet him, congratulate him; but they came running with tears, at four o'clock, to wake me up because this is more important than sleep . . . Ah, how nice!" This is what I was thinking. How could I sleep!

That same day Nekrasov brought the manuscript to Bielinsky. He worshipped Bielinsky, and it seems that he loved him more than any one else in his life. At that time Nekrasov had not yet written anything as important as the things which he wrote shortly thereafter—one year thence. As far as I know, Nekrasov happened to come to Petersburg, all alone, at the age of sixteen. He also started writing almost at that age. I know little about his acquaintance with Bielinsky, but Bielinsky discovered him from the very beginning, and, perhaps, has exercised a strong influence upon the mood of his poetry. Notwithstanding Nekrasov's youthfulness in those days, and the difference in age between them, there must have transpired such moments, and such words must have been uttered as have a lasting effect and bind people with indissoluble ties.

"A new Gogol has appeared!"—exclaimed Nekrasov entering Bielinsky's apartment with my *Poor Folks.*—"Gogols grow like mushrooms in your midst"—severely remarked Bielinsky; but he took the manuscript. When, in the evening, Nekrasov again called on him, he found him in a state of real agitation: "Bring him, bring him along as soon as possible."

And now (this, then, was already the third day) I was brought to Bielinsky. I recall that, at first glance, I was struck by his appearance, his nose, his forehead. For some reason I imagined him—"this awful, this dreadful critic"—quite differently. He met me very gravely and with reserve. "Well,"—I said to myself—"thus it should be." However, it seems that not one minute had passed when the picture radically changed: it was gravity of an individual, of a great critic meeting a twenty-two-year-old author—beginner, but, so to speak, gravity coming from his respect for those feelings which he sought to convey to me as quickly as possible. He began to speak ardently with burning eyes. "But do you, yourself, understand"—he repeated to me several times, screaming, as was his habit, —"what you have written!" He always screamed when he spoke in a state of great agitation. "You may have written, guided by immediate instinct, as an artist, but did you yourself rationalize all this dreadful truth which you have pointed out to us? It is impossible that at your age of twenty you could have understood it. Now, this unfortunate functionary of yours—why, he has so long and desperately sweated in service, he has reduced himself to such a state that he does not even dare to consider himself unlucky—from humility, and he is almost inclined to treat the slightest complaint as an act of free-thinking; he does not even dare claim his right to misfortune, and when a kind man, his general, gives him that hundred rubles,—he is crushed, annihilated by amazement that one like himself could be pitied by 'their excellency'—not 'his excellency' but 'their excellency' as he expresses himself in your novel! And that torn-off button! That minute when he kisses the general's hand,—why, this is no longer compassion for this unfortunate—this is horror, horror! In this very gratitude is his horror! This is tragedy! You have touched upon the very essence of the matter; by one stroke you have indicated the main thing. We, publicists and critics, we merely deliberate; we try to explain this with words, but you, an artist, with one trait, with one stroke, in an image, you set forth the very gist, so that one can feel it with one's own hand, so as to enable the least reasoning reader to grasp everything at once! This is the mystery of art! This is the truth of art! This is the artist's service to truth! To you, as an artist, truth is revealed and declared; it came to you as a gift. Treasure, then, your gift, be faithful to it, and you will become a great writer!" . . .

All this he was telling me then. All this he later told about me also to many others who are still living and who can corroborate my account. In a state of ecstasy I left him. I stopped at the corner of his house, looked at the sky, at the bright day, at passersby, and with my whole being I felt that a solemn moment had occurred in my life, a break forever; that something altogether new had begun, something I had not anticipated even in my most impassioned dreams. (And in those days I was an awful dreamer.) "And am I in truth so great?"—I was bashfully asking myself in

a state of some timid ecstasy. Oh, don't you laugh! Later, never
did I think that I was great, but then—was it possible to resist?
—"Oh, I shall prove worthy of this praise.—And what men! What
men! It is here that one finds men! I shall earn this praise! I
shall endeavor to become as beautiful as they! I shall remain
'faithful'! How lightminded I am! And if only Bielinsky knew
what nasty, shameful thoughts dwell within me! And yet people
keep saying that these littérateurs are haughty and ambitious. True,
such men are to be found only in Russia; they are lone, but only
they possess the truth, and truth, the good, veracity always conquer and triumph over vice and evil. We shall triumph!—Oh, I long
for them! I long to be with them!"

I was thinking all this; I recall that moment with fullest
lucidity. Thereafter I never could forget it. This was the most
delightful minute in my whole life. When I was serving my term
of hard labor it fortified me spiritually every time I recalled it.
Even now invariably I recall it with ecstasy.

And now, after thirty years, as I recently sat at the bed
of the sick Nekrasov, I recalled the whole minute, once more living
through it. I did not remind him of it in detail; I reminded him
only of the fact that these minutes of ours did exist, and I could
see that he remembered them. I knew that he did remember them.
When I returned from Siberia he showed me a poem in his book.
"At that time, this I wrote about you"—said he. Yet we have lived
our whole lives apart. On his sick-bed he is now recalling his friends
who are no longer:

> Their prophetic songs have been silenced:
> They fell victims of treason and spite
> In the blossom of youth, and their portraits
> Look on me with reproach and with blight.

"With reproach"—indeed, these are painful words. Did we remain
"faithful"? Did we? Let everyone answer the question according
to his own judgment, his own conscience. But do read these suffering sons yourselves, and let our beloved and passionate poet be
revived in your hearts! A poet with passion for suffering! . . .

4

The Boy Celebrating His Saint's Day

Do you remember Count Tolstoy's *Childhood and Youth?*
There, there is a little boy, the hero of the story. But he is not
an ordinary boy, not like other children, and not like his brother

Volodia. He is only about twelve years old, yet such thoughts and feelings come to his mind as are not akin to those of children of his age. He gives himself passionately to his meditations and feelings, but he knows already that it is better to keep them to himself. Bashful chastity and lofty pride prevent him from revealing these dreams and sentiments. He envies his brother and considers him incomparably superior to himself, especially as far as alertness and the features of the face are concerned, and yet he has a secret presentiment that his brother in all respects is inferior to him; he tries to banish this thought which he regards as meanness. All too frequently he looks at himself in the mirror, and he comes to the conclusion that he is very ugly. The thought glimmers in his mind that nobody loves him, that he is despised. In a word, this is a rather unusual boy, and yet one belonging to that type of family of the middle-upper nobility strata of which Count Leo Tolstoy, in accordance with Pushkin's bequest,[1] was the full-fledged poet and historian.

Now, guests gather at their house, a large Moscow family house; the boy's sister celebrates her saint's day. Adults are accompanied by their children, boys and girls. Games are started; then dancing begins. Our hero is sluggish; he dances worse than the rest. He seeks to distinguish himself by wit, but in this he does not succeed,—and, as chance would have it, there are so many pretty girls here—and coupled with this is his perpetual thought, the persistent suspicion that he is the worst among all the others. In despair, he resolves to do something so as to astound everyone. In the presence of all the girls and all those uppish elder boys, who look down on him with utter neglect, suddenly, beside himself with disheartenment, with that feeling with which one leaps into an abyss forming itself under one's feet, he shows his tongue to the tutor and with all his strength he strikes him with his fist! "Now everybody knows what he is! He has made a display of himself!" Disgracefully he is dragged into a closet, and there he is locked up. Deeming himself lost forever, the boy begins to meditate: he will run away from home, he will enlist in the army; in a battle he will kill many Turks, and then fall wounded. Victory! "Where is our savior?"—cries everybody; he is kissed and embraced. Now he is back in Moscow. He strolls along the Tverskoy Boulevard with his bandaged arm. He meet the Emperor. . . . And suddenly the thought that the door will be opened and the tutor will enter with rods dispels those dreams like dust. Other dreams begin. All of a sudden he invents the reason why "everybody dislikes him

[1]Dostoievsky made a mistake: Leo Tolstoy was born in 1828; Pushkin died in 1837.

so": probably he is a foundling, and this is being concealed from him. . . . The whirlwind increases in strength: now he is dying; people enter the closet and find his body; "Poor boy!" Everybody pities him. "He was a good boy! It is you who ruined his life"— the father says to the tutor. . . . Tears choke the dreamer. . . . This whole story winds up with the child's illness, fever, delirium. This is a most serious psychological essay dealing with a child's soul. It is wonderfully written.

I have recalled this essay in detail intentionally. I received a letter from K—v in which the death of a child—also a twelve-year-old boy—is depicted. And . . . possibly there is something similar here. However, I shall quote parts of the letter without changing a single word in the quotations. The *topic* is curious.

"On November 8, after dinner, the news spread in town that a *suicide* had taken place: *a twelve- or thirteen-year-old boy,* a high-school pupil, had hanged himself. Here are the circumstances of the case. A school-master teaching a subject, the lesson of which, that morning, the deceased boy failed to learn, punished the boy by retaining him at school till five o'clock in the evening. The pupil walked around for a while; then he untied a rope from a pulley which he happened to notice; he tied the rope to a nail on which usually the so-called golden or red plate hangs which, for some reason, had been removed that day, and hanged himself. The watchman who had been washing the floor in the adjacent rooms, upon discovering the unfortunate boy, hastened to the inspector. The inspector came running; the suicide was extricated from the noose, but they failed to revive him. . . . What was the cause of the suicide? The boy was not inclined toward violence and bestiality; generally speaking, he studied well, and only of late he had received several unsatisfactory marks from his school-master, and for this he was punished. . . . It is rumored that both the boy's father, a very severe man, and the boy himself, that day celebrated their saint's day. Perhaps the youngster, with childish delight, was meditating how he would be greeted at home—by his mother, father, little brothers and sisters. . . . And now he has to sit all alone, hungry, in an empty building and ponder over the father's dreadful wrath which he will have to face, over the humiliation, shame and, perhaps, punishment which he will have to endure. He knew about the possibility of committing suicide (and who among children of our epoch do not know this?). One feels terribly sorry for the deceased boy, for the inspector, an excellent man and pedagogue, whom the pupils adore; one also feels afraid for the school within whose walls such phenomena take place. What did the classmates of the deceased and other children studying there, among whom in the preparatory classes there are perfect little darlings, feel when they learned about the incident? Isn't this too harsh a training? Isn't too much significance attached to marks—to twos and ones, to golden and red plates, on the nails of which pupils hang themselves? Isn't there too much formalism and dry heartlessness in the matter of our education?"

Of course, one feels awfully sorry for the little boy celebrating his saint's day, but I will not enlarge upon the probable causes of this sad *incident,* and particularly upon "marks, twos, and excessive severity," etc. All these also existed before, and there were no suicides, so that the cause is not to be sought here. I took the episode from Count Tolstoy's *Youth* because of the similarity of the two cases; yet there is also an enormous difference. No doubt Misha, who celebrated his saint's day, killed himself not from anger and not merely from fear. Both these feelings—anger and pathological fear—are too simple, and these would more probably find *an outcome in themselves.* However, fear of punishment could have exercised some influence, especially in the presence of pathological suspiciousness. Nevertheless, even in this case the feeling could have been much more complex, and again it is very possible that there transpired something similar to what was depicted by Count Tolstoy, *i.e.,* suppressed, not yet conscious, childish queries, a strong feeling of some oppressive injustice, an early suspicious and painful perception of personal nullity, a pathologically developed query: "Why does *everybody* so dislike me?" a passionate desire to compel people to pity one, *i.e.,* a passionate thirst for love *on the part of them all,* and a multitude, a multitude of other complications and nuances.

The point is that these or other such nuances, unfailingly, were there, but there were also traits of some new reality, altogether different from that which prevailed in the pacified and firmly, long ago structuralized landowner's family of the middle-upper stratum of which Count Tolstoy was our *historian,* and apparently at that very epoch when the former order of nobility established upon the earlier landowners' foundations, was affected by some new, still unknown but radical change,—at least by some enormous regeneration into novel, still latent, almost utterly unknown forms. There is here in this incident of the boy celebrating his saint's day one particular trait distinctly belonging to our epoch. Count Tolstoy's boy could meditate with valetudinary tears of effete emotionalism in his soul that *they* would enter the closet and would find him dead, and that they would begin to love and pity him, and blame themselves. He could even have meditated about suicide, but only meditated: the rigorous order of the historically formed noble family would have had its effect, even upon a twelve-year-old child, and would have prevented the *dream* from being converted into reality, whereas here—the boy *meditated* and *acted* accordingly.

However, in pointing this out, I am speaking not only about the present-day epidemic of suicides. One feels that here something is not so; that an enormous part of the Russian order of life was left entirely without observation and without a *historian*. At least, it is clear that the life of our middle-upper stratum of nobility, so graphically depicted by our belles-lettrists, already constitutes an insignificant and segregated little corner of Russian life. Who will be the *historian* of the other little corners, apparently, quite numerous? And if, in this chaos which has long prevailed—but which is particularly noticeable at present—in our social life, as yet, the normal law and guiding thread cannot be discovered, perhaps, even by an artist of Shakespearean magnitude,—who is going to elucidate at least a fraction of this chaos, even without the hope of finding the leading thread?

The principal thing is that, as yet, no one seems to be concerned about this matter,—that it is still premature even to our greatest artists. Unquestionably there is in Russia a life which is in a state of decomposition, and consequently this brings about a disintegrating family. However, we have the essential and a life forming itself anew, on novel foundations. Who will discern and indicate them? Who is in a position to determine and express— even though slightly—the laws of both this decomposition and the new construction? Or is this still too early? However, has even the old been fully noted?

From the Editor's Office

Despite my categorical statement in the preceding December issue of the *Diary,* people still keep sending me letters with the question: "Am I or am I not going to publish the new magazine *Light?*" and they enclose postage for replies. Once more, and for the last time, I am advising all inquirers that not I, but Nikolai Petrovich Wagner, is publishing the periodical *Light,* and that I am taking no part in its editorship.

Madam O. A. A—va, who wrote to Editor's Office concerning her work in connection with examinations, is requested to send her correct address. The former one, given by her, on Mokhovaia Street, proved erroneous.

FEBRUARY

CHAPTER I

1

Self-Appointed Prophets and Lame Coopers who Continue to Construct the Moon on Gorokhovaia Street. One of the Most Unknown Great Russian Men

THE EASTERN question, as heretofore, is before everybody's eyes. Much as we have tried to forget about it and divert ourselves with everything that happened to be around—with butterweek, *Virgin Soil*, bankruptcies, avowed scoundrels,—much as we endeavored to embrace cynicism, assuring everybody—and in the first place ourselves—"That nothing at all has happened; that everything was fabricated and counterfeited"; much as we sought to bury our heads under the pillow—like little children—to avoid seeing the grim phantom,—the phantom is still before our eyes; it did not depart anywhere; it stands and threatens as hitherto. Everyone—the wrathful cynic and the sincere citizen and the debaucher serenely diverting himself and the mere idler—everyone feels and remembers that there is this something,—something that has by no means been settled or finished, and yet pressing and necessary which, sooner or later, will unfailingly call and summon us for the dénouement and that without fail

> Something surely must be done,
> Somehow this must be concluded.

And the least we can do is to undertake something, or to conclude the thing somehow, and it would be best to conclude the thing in the best way.

Meanwhile time rolls and rolls; spring is on the way, and what is spring going to bring us? Some people cry that it is too late. This only God knows: there is always time for a good deed. Perhaps something may work itself out at least by spring. Maybe something will be finally settled, that is, at least for one year. For at present no one makes plans in Europe in connection with the Eastern question for more than one year, all the more so as Turkey herself can hardly last one year. And the point is not in Turkey, but what will remain after her. These final European decisions for one year are, perhaps, advantageous; well, to others—not very. And what is going to happen to the others, especially those others who are beyond the Danube? However, only the Russian people think about them.

Yes, they do think. And say what you may, much as we have been exerting all our efforts, denying all winter our summer movement, yet, in my opinion, it did continue all winter throughout Russia, exactly as in the summer—undeviatingly and faithfully, but calmly and with the hope for the Czar's decision. And, of course, it will continue to the very end, despite our prophets who managed to discern—and precisely last summer—in the image of Russia only a sleeping, hideous, drunken creature which extended itself from the "icy Finnish rocks to the flaming land of Colchis," with a colossal bottle in its hands. To my way of thinking, even if these prophets of ours fail to see what gives life to Russia, so much the better: they will not meddle and hinder; and even should they start meddling, they would miss the target.

You see, here the point is that our Europeanism and our "enlightened" European view on Russia—is the same old moon which the same journeyman lame cooper is constructing on Gorokhovaia Street, and he is making it as badly as before,—this he is proving every minute. Only the other day he has also proved it. Henceforth he will be making it still more incompetently. Well, let him: a German, besides, a lame German. One has to have compassion.

And what does Russia care about such prophets? Nowadays we wouldn't even scratch our noses—past times have passed.

Some time ago there was mention in the newspapers that this winter more than one party of poor little children, total orphans belonging to families disrupted by the war, was brought to Moscow from the Slavic lands. They are being placed in private homes and institutions. It would be nice if, at length, all this should continue and be organized all over Russia on the largest possible scale: well, this is only a favor, while these little ones must be looked after for they are all *future* Slavs.

Apropos. I asked myself several times: how did those several hundred thousand mouths feed themselves—those Bulgarians, Bosnians, Herzegovinans and others who have fled from their torturers, after massacres and ruin, to Serbia, Montenegro, Austria and elsewhere at random? Taking into account the amount of money required for their subsistence and knowing that neither the Serbians nor the Montenegrins have at their disposal such sums and that at present they themselves have hardly anything to eat,—one fails to understand how these hundreds of thousands could feed themselves with their little children, how they managed to clothe themselves and their children in winter.

It is said that recently another "party of little ones," between the ages of three and thirteen years, was brought to Moscow; they were adopted by the Pokrov Community of the Sisters of Charity. It is also reported that the Sisters have placed these little Serbian girls together with Bulgarian girls who arrived earlier, and that they are supervised by a Sister who speaks the Serbian language, which makes the children glad and happy. Of course, the children are kept warm and comfortable, but a friend of mine who recently returned from Moscow related to me a most characteristic anecdote about these same children: the Serbian girls are sitting in one corner, and the Bulgarian girls in another, and they refuse either to play together or to speak to each other. When the Serbian girls are asked why they do not want to play with the Bulgarian girls, they answer: "We gave them arms to fight the Turks with us, but they hid the arms and did not go to fight the Turks." In my opinion, this is very curious. If eight- and nine-year-old babies speak this language, they must have picked it up from their fathers, and if such words of the fathers pass on to the children, this means that there is an unquestionable and awful discord between the Balkan Slavs. Yes, that eternal discord among Slavs! They perpetuate it in their traditions and preserve it in their songs, and without their enormous unifying center—Russia, there can be no Slavic accord, the Slavs will vanish altogether from the face of the earth—no matter what Serbian intelligentsia and European-civilized Czechs might be dreaming. . . . There are still many dreamers among them. Well, almost all of them are dreamers. . . .

Do you remember in Pushkin's *Songs of the Western Slavs* —*The Song about the Battle at Great Zenitza?* There, the insurgents, headed by Radivoy, started a campaign against the Turks.

> And Dalmatians, beholding our army,
> Turned up their long mustaches,
> Put their hats on awry
> And said: "Take us along with you!" . . .

> Beglerbey with his Bosnians
> Against us marched from Banialuki
> But as soon as their horses started neighing,
> And their crooked swords flashed in the sun
> On that sunny morn at the Great Zenitza,
> The Dalmatian traitors dispersed shamelessly!

By the way, I asked: "Do you remember *The Songs of the Western Slavs,*" etc. I can answer in advance for everybody that nobody remembers either *The Song about the Battle at Great Zenitza* or Pushkin's *Songs of the Western Slavs* themselves. Well, save some specialists, philologists, or some very old men. Perhaps I am badly mistaken, but of this I am firmly convinced. And yet, do you know, gentlemen, that *The Songs of the Western Slavs* is Pushkin's masterpiece among his masterpieces, not to speak of the prophetic and political significance of these verses which appeared fifty years ago. The fact of the appearance in those days of these *Songs* in Russia is important: this is a presentiment of the Slavs on the part of the Russians; this is the Russians' prophecy to the Slavs about future brotherhood and communion. Even so I have never read in any criticism concerning these "Pushkin's compositions" that they were his *chef d'œuvre*. They were considered— so-so, whereas they are precisely a masterpiece, all that is sublime by reason of its significance.

In my judgment as yet, we have not begun to understand Pushkin: he is a genius who was many years ahead of Russian consciousness. He was already a Russian, a real Russian, who, by the power of his genius reshaped himself into a Russian, whereas we are still taking our lessons from the lame cooper. Pushkin was one of the first Russians who fully conceived in himself the Russian; who drew the Russian out of himself, and showed by his example how the Russian should look upon his people, and the Russian family and Europe, and the lame cooper, and the brethren Slavs. No Russian has ever held a more humane, a loftier, a saner view than Pushkin.

However, for the time being, I shall not enlarge upon this, but about *The Songs* I may merely remark that, as is known, they were borrowed by Pushkin from the French, from Merimée's book, *La Gouzla,* which, according to his own admission, he wrote haphazardly, without leaving Paris. This most talented French writer, subsequently a sénateur, almost a relative of Napoleon III, who is now dead, depicted in that *Gouzla* under the guise of Slavs, of course, only Frenchmen—even the French Parisians: they don't know how to write differently. To a real Frenchman there exists in the world nothing but Paris. Having read the book, and having addressed an inquiry to its author in Paris, Pushkin composed from it his *Songs, i.e.,* from the French depicted by Merimée he restored the Slavs, and of course, now these *Songs of the Western Slavs* are songs of genuine Slavs who even became related to the Russians.

It stands to reason that no such songs exist in Serbia; the Serbians have other songs, but this makes no difference: Pushkin's are all-Slavic, popular songs, which poured out of the Slavic heart, expressing the spirit of the Slavs, their image, their meaning, their customs, their history. I would show to those highly educated Serbians, who last summer have been looking upon the Russians so distrustfully, for instance, Pushkin's song about *Georgi the Black* or that *Song about the Battle at Great Zenitza.* These two master-pieces among *The Songs* are diamonds of the first magnitude in Pushkin's poetry, and precisely because of this they are utterly unknown in our schools not only by the pupils but most probably also by the teachers who will be astonished to hear, for the first time, that these songs, and not *The Caucasian Captive,* not *The Gypsies,* are such masterpieces. And yet it would have been a good idea, at least during last year, to popularize *The Songs* in our schools.

However, judging by the course of events, it is doubtful that the Serbians will soon learn about this most unknown of all great Russian men. Thus, I believe, one can define our great Pushkin about whom thousands and tens of thousands among our intelligent-sia do not know, that he was a poet, a Russian of great magnitude, for whose monument, up to the present, we were unable to collect the necessary sum,—this trait will be noted in our history. And the Serbians, upon reading these *Songs,* of course, would perceive what we think about their liberty, whether or not we respect it, whether or not we are rejoicing over it, and whether or not we seek to subject them to our rule and to deprive them of that liberty.

However, enough has been said about poetry. And let people not smile haughtily at me: "See, what trifles he is talking about!" This is no trifle: in Russia it is still necessary to speak much about Pushkin, and this for a long time in the future.

2

HOME-BAKED GIANTS AND THE HUMILIATED SON OF THE "NEST." AN ANECDOTE ABOUT THE SKIN STRIPPED FROM THE BACK. THE SUPERIOR INTERESTS OF CIVILIZATION AND "LET THEM BE DAMNED IF THEY ARE TO BE BOUGHT AT SUCH A PRICE"

The Serbian Skupshtina which convened last month for one moment (for one hour and one-half—the papers reported) at Bel-grade to decide upon one question only: "To conclude or not to conclude peace?"—that Skupshtina, as it is rumored, did not reveal a mood as exaggeratedly hasty and pacific as has been anticipated —taking into account all circumstances. It is said that it agreed to peace only because of some trick, some ministerial intrigue. At any rate, if it is in the least true that the Skupshtina was not afraid of the continuation of the war, and taking into account their desperate situation, one, willy-nilly, asks himself: "Why did we shout so loudly about the cowardice of the Serbians?" I have been receiving letters from Serbia and I have talked with those arriving from there, and I particularly remember a letter from a youthful Russian, who remained there, who wrote about the Serbians with enthusiasm, expressing indignation over the fact that in Russia there are men who believe that Serbians are cowards and egoists. The enthusiastic Russian emigrant exculpates the self-mutilation of the Serbian soldier under Cherniaiev and Novoselov: you see, they are so tenderhearted a people, they love so dearly their "nest," where each one has left behind a wife, children, or a mother, sisters, brothers, a horse and a dog, that they forsake everything, mutilate themselves, shoot off their fingers, in order to become unfit for service and to return to their beloved nest as quickly as possible! Imagine, I can understand this tenderheartedness, and I also understand this whole process, and of course, in this case they are too tenderhearted a people, although, at the same time, they are rather dull children of their fatherland so that they do not themselves understand what their hearts are longing for.

In his tenderheartedness the Serbian inhabitant of the "nest," in my opinion, reminds me very much of those children whom most probably you remember since your childhood: suddenly, from a family, or even from a disrupted family, they find themselves in a school. Up to then the boy has lived only at home and has known nothing but his home; and suddenly—a hundred schoolmates, strange faces, noise, hubbub, everything quite different from things at home. God, what a torture! At home, perhaps, it was cold and he was hungry; still, he was loved, and even if he wasn't loved, nevertheless there it was *home*, he was alone at his home and by himself, whereas here—not a word of endearment on the part of the superiors; severity on the part of the tutors; such difficult subjects; such long corridors, and such inhuman mad-caps, affronters and mockers; how merciless are his schoolmates: "As if they were devoid of heart! As if they had neither father nor mother!" Thus far, he has been told that it was awful and disgraceful to lie and to offend, but here they all lie, cheat, offend and on top of that they laugh at his horror. For some reason here they took a dislike to him, because he weeps about his nest, he "pollutes the class." Presently the whole class begins to beat him mercilessly, all the time, with no reason, without anger—just for diversion.

I may note that in my childhood I met many such unfortunate children in various schools. And at times, what crimes of this kind are perpetrated in our educational institutions of every name and grade,—precisely crimes! And let a boy stupidly venture to lodge a complaint, and he will be beaten almost to death (yes, even to death). School children beaten mercilessly and heedlessly. For years they will tease him by calling him an "informer"; they will refuse to talk to him and will make him a pariah. And at the same time —what heartlessness and merciless indifference on the part of the superiors! In my childhood I do not recall a single pedagogue; nor do I suppose there are many of them at present—only functionaries receiving salaries.

And yet these very children who when entering school yearn for their families and their native nests,—precisely they in many cases subsequently develop into unusual, talented and gifted men. On the other hand, those children who, taken away from their families, quickly adapt themselves to any given order, who instantly get used to everything, who never yearn for anything, and even at once begin to lead others,—they, as a rule, turn out inept or simply bad people, cunning fellows and intriguers ever since the age of eight. Of course, I am judging too generally; nevertheless, in my opinion, he is a bad child who, when entering school, does not secretly yearn for his family, save in a case where he had no family at all, or the family was a thoroughly bad one.

Willy-nilly, I compared such a boy, suffering during his first days at school, with the Serbian recruit—self-mutilator. I was unable to explain his unfortunate, unreasoning, almost animal-like desire to throw down the rifle too hastily and flee home otherwise than by the same feeling. The only difference is that in this desire, incredible, phenomenal dullness is revealed. He brushes aside, as it were, the thought that if everybody, even as he, is going to disperse, there would be no one left to protect the country, and thus some day the Turks would come to his "nest" too, and would destroy that beloved "nest" of his, and would slaughter his mother and fiancée and sister, and their horse and dog. In fact, in much too many Serbian hearts the suffering for the native nest did not attain the level of suffering for the native land, which is a strange phenomenon. True, now that their war is finished and peace is concluded, it may be remarked that the hearts of the upper Serbian intelligentsia far from always attained the level of suffering for their fatherland; however, this was due to a different cause than in the case of the lower hearts. In the upper stratum this is caused, perhaps, by an excessively strong political ambition. Thus, because

of the "superior" interests of their native land these superior hearts
had almost no time to occupy themselves with the lower, popular,
so commonplace interests.

However, concerning the lower Serbian, I believe, it is nevertheless possible to make one curious remark. Indeed, one cannot
attribute his self-mutilations, his flights from the battlefield, to
anything but tenderheartedness and dullness of the mind. It seems
to me that, when deserting his colors and fleeing home, he was
quite able to understand that he was doing a bad thing, and very
possibly he was the first to blame himself. At the same time, he
never believed that, if he deserted, his native country would be left
defenseless and without protection: "Oh, heroes will remain,—the
Kireevs, Cherniaievs, the Russians, will remain, and even his stern
Serbian superiors, while what is he?—An imperceptible particle,
trash—nothing else. He will quit, and no one will even miss
him . . ."

To my way of thinking this was the feeling that dwelt in
him. This is very curious; it is characteristic of the people: at
the top, braggarts, civilized Europeans dreaming about the subjugation of all Slavs into one Serbia, intriguing even against Russia,
in a word, genuine Europeans, the Khorvatovichs and the Mari-
novichs just like the Moltkes and the Bismarcks. At the other end,
side by side with these giants,—the humiliated son of the "nest,"
precisely humiliated by four centuries of slavery: it is due to this
humiliation that he considers himself a nullity, an imperceptible
particle: "The giants will stay where they are and no one will
notice me. I am so tiny, while they are such eternal masters. . . ."

I was reading somewhere that some of these stern masters,
beholding a lower Serbian ready to desert his colors, straightway
shot his head off with a pistol: "See, what iron dukes we too
could manage to become!" It would seem that they are treating
their common people over there somewhat haughtily.

Generally, the upper Slavs "with a glorious future"—in any
event are extraordinary curious folk in political, civic, historical
and all sorts of respects.

At present, when Cherniaiev has already departed from there,
and volunteers have been sent away, they, i.e., their military men,
express a strategic thought about which we have heard nothing
heretofore. They maintain that their Serbian is altogether unfit for
service in a regular army in open battle, whereas the popular Serbian
war is "the small war," i.e., guerrilla warfare, warfare conducted by
bands in forests, passes, from behind stones and rocks. Well, this
may be so. However, because they have already concluded peace,

it is now hardly possible to verify this. At least, they will remain with this strategic conviction. Well, this too is a consolation in misfortune.

Will this peace last long?—But to say a farewell word about this Serbian war in which we Russians, almost to the last man, so sincerely participated with our hearts, it seems to me that the Serbians are parting with us and with our assistance with even greater suspiciousness than they have been greeting us at the beginning of the war. One may also conclude that this suspiciousness toward us will be increasing as long as they themselves develop and grow mentally,—this means a very long time. This also means that above all we should be paying no attention to their suspiciousness and that we should be acting as we see fit.

Concerning the Eastern question, we must relentlessly bear in mind one truth: that the main Slavic problem is not merely the liberation of the Slavs from their torturers but that this liberation be accomplished, though with the assistance of the Russians (for it cannot be otherwise—if only they could do without the Russians!) yet at least, so as to remain indebted to the Russians as little as possible.

It is said—this was told to me by that same friend who returned from Moscow—that among the Slavic children brought to Moscow there is a child, a little girl of the age of eight or nine years, who often faints, and she is being specially cared for. She is fainting from a reminiscence: she saw with her own eyes how last summer Circassians stripped the skin from her father—they tore it off completely. This reminiscence clings to her tenaciously, and quite probably will last forever, with years, perhaps, growing milder, although I wonder if in such a case it can be softened. Oh, civilization! Oh, Europe, whose interests would so suffer should she earnestly forbid the Turks to strip the fathers' skins in the presence of their children! Of course, these superior interests of European civilization are: commerce, maritime navigation, markets, factories —what in the eyes of Europe can be more important? These are interests which not only fingers but even thought is not allowed to touch, but "let them be damned—the interests of European civilization!" This is not my exclamation. This is what *The Moscow Gazette* exclaimed, and I deem it an honor to second this exclamation: Yes, yes, let them be damned—these interests of civilization, and even civilization itself if for its preservation it be necessary to strip the skin from men. However, this is a fact: for the preservation of civilization it is necessary to strip the skin from human beings.

3

ABOUT STRIPPING SKINS IN GENERAL AND VARIOUS ABER-
RATIONS IN PARTICULAR—HATRED OF AUTHORITY COUPLED
WITH LACKEYISM IN THOUGHT

"From men? From what men?—Only from a tiny portion of
human beings—somewhere there, in a little corner, from a Turkish
subject about whom no one would even have heard had the Russians
not heralded it. As against this, an enormous part of the organism is
alive, healthy and thrives—trades and manufactures!"

This story about the little fainting Bulgarian girl was related
to me in the morning, and that same day I happened to be on the
Nevsky Prospect. There, shortly after three o'clock in the afternoon, mothers and nurses take out children, and suddenly an involuntary thought weightily fell upon my mind: "Civilization!"—
I was saying to myself—"Who dares to speak against civilization?"
Nay, civilization does mean something: at least, these children
of ours peacefully walking here, on the Nevsky Prospect, will not
see how the skin is being stripped from their fathers; nor will
mothers behold how these children will be thrown up into the air
and caught on bayonets, as happened in Bulgaria. At least this
advantage of ours must be credited to civilization! And let it exist
only in Europe, *i.e.*, only in one little corner of the globe, a corner
which is rather small compared with the surface of our planet (a
dreadful thought!). Nevertheless it does exist, even though in a
little corner—it exists, true, at the high price of skinning our own
brethren somewhere there, at the border; nevertheless, here, at
least, it exists. To think that only formerly, even recently, solidly,
civilization existed nowhere, not even in Europe, and if now we
have it in Europe, it is for the first time since this planet has come
into existence! Nay, after all, this has already been achieved and
can never be retracted. This is an extremely important consideration
which involuntarily penetrates one's soul; it is not at all so small
that it wouldn't be deserving of one's attention, all the more so
as the world is still, as hitherto,—a mystery, despite civilization
and its acquisitions. God knows with what things the world is
pregnant, and what may happen in the future, even in the immediate future.

And as I was about to exclaim to myself with rapture: "Long
live civilization," suddenly I began to doubt everything: "Well,
has this been really achieved for these children on the Nevsky
Prospect? Say, isn't this a mirage even here, and are we not merely
being deceived?"

Do you know, gentlemen, I came to the conclusion that it

was a mirage, or—to put it more mildly—almost a mirage. And if skins are not stripped from the fathers in the presence of their children on the Nevsky,—well, this is only by accident, so to speak "owing to circumstances beyond the public's control" and, of course, also because policemen are standing on the corners.

Oh, I hasten to explain: By no means am I alluding to some allegory; nor am I hinting at the suffering of some present-day proletarian, or at a parent who says to his seven-year-old son: "Here's my covenant: if thou stealest five rubles, I shall damn thee; if thou stealest one hundred thousand I shall bless thee." Nay, I am using my words literally. I mean literally skinning, that very stripping of skins which took place last summer in Bulgaria, and in which, it appears, the victorious Turks are so eager to indulge. And it is about this skinning that I am asserting that if it does not occur on the Nevsky, it is "only by accident, owing to circumstances beyond our control," and, principally, because for the time being it is prohibited, whereas if we had our own way, perhaps this would be transpiring notwithstanding all our civilization.

To my way of thinking, if one were to tell the whole truth, they are simply afraid of some custom, some rule accepted without proof,—almost of a prejudice. However, if some "competent" men would "prove" that, at times, it is useful to the common cause to strip the skin from a certain back, and that even though this is repugnant, nevertheless "the aim justifies the means,"—were one to start saying these things in a competent style and in the presence of opportune circumstances, believe me, forthwith performers would appear, and besides,—from among the jolliest.

Let this be a very droll paradox of mine! I am the first to subscribe to this definition with my two hands, nevertheless, I assure you that precisely this would take place. Civilization exists; its laws exist; there is even faith in them. Yet were a new vogue to appear, a multitude of men would promptly change. Of course, not all of them; still there would remain such a tiny handful of them that you, my reader, and I should be surprised, and who knows where we ourselves should land—among the skinners or the skinned.

Naturally, people will start shouting straight to my face that all this is trash, that never can such a vogue come into existence, and that this much, at least, civilization did attain. Gentlemen, what naiveté on your part! You are laughing? Well, and what about France in 1793 (not to peep into more recent events)? Hasn't there been firmly established there this very vogue of stripping skins—and this under the guise of the most sacred principles of civilization;—this after Rousseau and Voltaire! You may say that all this is not at all so; that this was very long ago. Still, please observe that, perhaps, I am resorting to history solely for the purpose of avoiding discussion of current things. Believe me, the most complete aberration both in the minds and hearts of men is always possible, and in Russia, specifically in our time, not only is it possible but, judging by the course of events, it is inevitable. Look: are there many among us who agree as to what is good and what is bad? And this refers not only to so-called "truths" but even to any question taken at random. And how swiftly changes and metamorphoses are taking place among us! What are the Moscow "jacks of hearts"? It seems to me that they merely represent that fraction of Russian nobility which was unable to endure the peasants' reform. Even if they are not landowners themselves, they are the children of landowners. After the peasants' reform, they fillipped their cravats and started whistling. Nor was the peasants' reform the sole cause here: simply, they could not manage to endure the "new ideas." "If all the things we were taught were prejudices, what then shall we follow? If there is *nothing*, this means that one may do *everything*—that's the idea!" Please note that this is an incredibly common idea: nine-tenths of the adherents of the new ideas are professing it; in other words, nine-tenths of the progressives are even unable to understand them differently. In our midst Darwin, for example, is promptly converted into a pickpocket—that is what a "jack of hearts" is.

It stands to reason that mankind has stored a great number of humane rules which have formed themselves in the course of centuries, and some of these rules are taken as inviolable. But what I wish to say is that despite all these rules, tenets, religions, civilization, only the most imperceptible minority of mankind is saved by them. True, they are those who prove to be victors, but this—only in the long run, whereas in contemporaneous things, in the current course of history, men, as it were, remain always identical, *i.e.*, in their overwhelming majority, they are devoid of the slightest firm conception of the sense of duty, of the sense of honor; so that were a new vogue to come into existence, they would all start running about naked,—and with what pleasure!

Rules are there, but men are in no manner ready for them. I might be told that it is not necessary to get ready, and that it is only necessary to discover what these rules are. But is this so? Are these rules, no matter what they be, likely to survive for a long time if one is so eager to run about naked?

I think this way: it is possible to rationalize and to perceive a thing correctly and at once, but to become a man at once is impossible: one has to mould oneself into a man. Here discipline is required. But it is precisely this relentless self-discipline that our present-day thinkers reject; they say: "There was too much despotism; liberty is needed." However, this liberty leads the overwhelming majority to nothing but lackeyism before another man's thought, since people are awfully fond of things which are offered them ready-made. Moreover, thinkers are proclaiming general laws, *i.e.*, such rules as will suddenly make everybody happy, without any refinement: let only these rules come into existence. Why, even if this ideal were feasible, no rules, even the most obvious ones, could be put into practice with *unfinished* men. Now, it is in this relentless self-discipline and uninterrupted work on one's self that our citizen could reveal himself. And it is with this magnanimous work on one's self that one has to begin in order to lift our *Virgin Soil*, otherwise there is no need of lifting it.

Is this so?—But the main thing is that we do not know what's good and what's bad. We have lost every instinct in this respect. We have smashed to pieces all former authorities and we have inaugurated new ones. Yet he among us who is slightly cleverer than the rest, does not believe in them, while he who is bolder spiritually becomes "a jack of hearts." Moreover, honest to God, he will begin to strip the skin, and on top of it, he will proclaim that this is useful to the general cause, and therefore sacred. How then, in what sense, can one start working for self-improvement if it is not known what's good and what's bad?

4

THE METTERNICHS AND THE DON QUIXOTES

But in order not to speak abstractly, let us turn to this theme. Now, we actually do not strip the skins. Moreover, we do not like it. (Only, God knows: the amateur oftentimes hides; he is little known; he is bashful—for the time being, he is "afraid of prejudice.") However, if we don't like it at home and *never do it,* we should hate it in others. And it is not enough to hate: we must not permit anyone to strip the skins; yes, we simply must not permit it. And yet is this so in reality?—The most indignant among us are not as indignant as they should be. I am speaking not only about the Slavs: if we are so compassionate, we should be acting in the measure of our compassion, and not within the limits of a ten-ruble contribution. I might be told that it is impossible to give away everything. With this I agree, although I don't know why. Indeed, why not everything? Precisely, that's the point: one does understand absolutely nothing even in one's own nature. And suddenly the question of "the interests of civilization" is set forth with enormous authority.

The question is put directly, clearly, scientifically and with candid cynicism. "The interests of civilization are production, wealth, tranquillity required by capital. Enormous, uninterrupted and progressive production at lower prices is needed in view of the great increase in the number of proletarians. By giving employment to the proletarian, we are thereby placing at his disposal articles of consumption at reduced prices. The calmer it is in Europe, the lower are prices. Consequently, tranquillity must prevail in Europe. The bustle of war will chase away production. Capital is cowardly; it will be scared by the war and will go into hiding. If one were to restrain the Turks' right to strip the skin from the back of the Gentile, it would be necessary to start a war; and if war were to break out, at once Russia would come forward; this would mean such a complication in the prosecution of the war as would drag the whole world into it. Then— good-by production, and the proletarian would be thrown out into the street. But the proletarian in the street is dangerous. In parliamentary speeches it is already being stated directly and candidly, aloud so that the whole world hears it, that the proletarian is dangerous, that among proletarians there is unrest, and that they listen to socialism. No, better let them there, somewhere in the wilderness, strip the skin. The inviolability of the Turkish rights must be upheld. It is necessary to quench the Eastern question and permit the skinning. Besides, what are these skins? And are two or three some such skins worth the tranquillity of Europe—well, let's say—twenty, all right—thirty thousand skins—what's the difference? If we want, we will hear nothing; we'll stop our ears . . ."

Such is the opinion of Europe (perhaps, her decision). Such are the *interests of civilization,* and, again—let them be damned! And all the more damned as the aberration of the minds (Russian minds in particular) is inevitable. The question is put squarely. What is better—that many tens of millions of workers be thrown out into the street, or that only units of the millions of Gentiles should suffer at the hands of the Turks?—Numbers are set forth; people are being scared with figures. In addition, politicians and wise teachers come forward: there is such a rule—they claim—such a doctrine, such an axiom which reads that the morality of one man, of one citizen, of a single unit—is one thing, and the morality of the state—another thing. Thus, that which in a single unit, in a single individual, is regarded as villainy, in the case of an entire state may acquire the guise of greatest wisdom!

This doctrine is very popular and antiquated, but be it also damned. Principally, let them refrain from scaring us with figures. Let Europe have it as she pleases, but let it be different with us.

It is better to believe that happiness cannot be purchased with villainy than to feel happy, knowing that villainy has been tolerated. Russia has never been able to produce her real Metternichs and Beaconsfields. On the contrary, during her whole European life she has lived not for herself, but for alien, precisely "cosmopolitan interests."

Indeed, in the course of these two hundred years, perhaps, there may have been instances when, at times, she has endeavored to imitate Europe and has set up at home her Metternichs, but somehow it always turned out in the long run that a Russian Metternich suddenly—much to the surprise of Europe—proved to be a Don Quixote. Naturally, the Don Quixote was ridiculed. But it seems that now the time has come, and the Don Quixote begins not to amuse but to frighten. The point of the matter is that he has undeniably rationalized his status in Europe, and he is no longer going to fight against windmills. As against this he has remained a faithful knight, and this, to them, is the most dreadful thing.

As a matter of fact, people shout in Europe about "Russian usurpations and Russian cunning"; but this is done for one purpose only—to frighten her mob whenever necessary, whereas the bawlers themselves do not believe this at all—they never did. On the contrary, in the image of Russia, they are perplexed and frightened by something truthful, something too disinterested, honest, loathing both graft and grab. They have a presentiment that Russia cannot be bribed with, and induced by, any political advantage to a covetous or violent act—save, perhaps, by deceit. However, even though Don Quixote is a great knight, nevertheless, at times, he can be awfully sly so that he will not let himself be deceived. England, France, Austria—in fact, is there over there even a single nation with which an alliance could not be formed, at an opportune moment, for a political gain with a forcible covetous aim?— It is only necessary not to miss the moment at which the bribed nation can sell herself at the highest price. Alone Russia cannot be lured into any unjust alliance,—at any price. And inasmuch as, at the same time, Russia is terribly strong, and her organism is obviously growing and maturing not by days but by hours, which is perfectly understood in Europe (despite the fact that, at times, they are shouting that the colossus has been undermined),—how can they not be fearing?

Apropos: this view on the incorruptibleness of Russia's foreign policy and her perpetual service to the interests of mankind as a whole, even to her detriment, is vindicated by history, and to this special attention should be paid. Herein is our distinction from

Europe. Moreover, this view of the character of Russia is so little known, that even in our midst there are but few who would believe it. Of course, *errors* of Russian policy should not be charged to Russia's account, since we are dealing here only with the spirit and ethical character of our policy, and not with its successes in the past and long past. In the latter respect, in ancient times, we actually did have windmills, but I repeat, it seems that their time has passed forever.

Nay, speaking seriously: what is there in prosperity which is bought at the price of untruth and skinning? Let that which is truth to man as an individual be also truth to the nation as a whole. Yes, of course, one may be temporarily put to a loss, one may be impoverished for the time being, deprived of markets; one's production may be curtailed and the cost of living may increase. But let the nation's organism remain morally healthy, and the nation will undoubtedly gain more, even materially.

Let it be noted that Europe has unquestionably reached the point where she treasures most the current gain, the gain of the actual moment—even at any price,—since over there, they are living merely from day to day, by the present minute only, and they even do not know themselves what is going to happen to them tomorrow. However, we—Russia—we still believe in something lasting, which moulds itself in Russia, and therefore we seek permanent and essential gains. It is also for this reason that we, as a political organism, have always believed in eternal morality, and not in a relative one, good but for a few days.

Believe me, Don Quixote, too, knows his gains and knows how to calculate: he knows that he will gain in his dignity and in the cognizance of it if only, as heretofore, he remains a knight. Besides, he is convinced that, by following this road, he will not deprive himself of the sincerity in the quest of the good and truth, and that this knowledge will fortify him in his further career. Finally, he is convinced that such a policy is also the best school for the nation. It is imperative that the "jack of hearts" should not dare to tell me straight to my face: "Why, with you, too, everything is relative and based upon gain." It is necessary that also the enthusiastic lad should come to love his nation instead of going to seek truth and the ideal on the outside and without society. And when the time of our hard—terribly hard—school is over, he will end by loving his nation. Truth, even as the sun, cannot be hidden. Russia's mission, in the long run, will become clear even to the most distorted minds both in our midst and in Europe. Why are, at present, in Russia, such aberrations of the minds possible as nowhere else?—Because, owing to an order of things that has lasted a century and a half, our intelligentsia *in toto* did nothing but disaccustom itself from Russia, and it finished by a complete disacquaintance with her, maintaining relations with her only through the bureaucratic chancery. With the reforms of the present reign a new era came into existence. The work has started and it cannot stop.

And Europe has read the autumnal manifesto of the Russian Emperor and has memorized it; she has memorized it not only for the current moment but for a long time to come, for future current moments. If necessary, we shall draw the sword on behalf of the oppressed and unfortunate, even though to the detriment of our immediate advantage. But let at the same time our faith grow still firmer that precisely herein lies Russia's genuine mission, her strength and truth, and that the self-sacrifice for the oppressed and forsaken by everybody in Europe, in the interests of civilization, is a real service to its actual and true interests.

Nay, it is necessary that in political organisms the same Christ's truth be recognized as by any believer. Somewhere at least this truth must be preserved; some nation at least must radiate. Otherwise what would happen? Everything would be dimmed, distorted and would be drowned in cynicism. Otherwise you would be unable to restrain the morality of individual citizens, too, and in this event how is the entire organism of the people going to live? Authority is needed. It is necessary that the sun shine. The sun appeared in the East, and it is from the East that the new day begins for mankind. When the sun is shining in its full glory, then it will be understood what the real "interests of civilization" are. Otherwise the banner bearing the inscription *"Après nous le déluge"* will be hoisted. Is it possible that this supposedly so glorious "civilization" will lead the European man to such a motto and will be done with him? It comes to this.

CHAPTER II

1

One of the Principal Contemporaneous Questions

PERHAPS MY readers have already observed that in publishing my *Writer's Diary*, now over one year, I endeavored to speak as little as possible about the current events in Russian literature, and even when I did venture to say a few words on this subject, they were in an enthusiastically eulogistic tone. And yet, in this

voluntary abstinence of mine—what an untruth! I am a writer, and
I am writing *A Writer's Diary*. Why, perhaps I, more than anyone,
have been interested all this year in the things that have been appearing in literature: is it necessary to conceal?—Maybe these were
the strongest impressions. "You are a writer, a belles-lettrist yourself,"—I would say to myself—"and therefore your every opinion on
belletristic literature, with the exception of unconditional eulogy,
would be regarded as partial; unless you speak about phenomena
of the remote past." This was the consideration which has been
restraining me.

Even so, this time, I shall venture to disregard this consideration. I shall discuss nothing in a purely belletristic and critical sense
unless I am forced to do so,—"apropos." And now there arises a
pretext. The point is that a month ago I came across so serious
and characteristic a work in current literature that I have read
even with surprise because I have long ceased to expect in fiction
anything of this kind, and on such a scale. In a writer—artist *par
excellence,* pre-eminently a belles-lettrist, I read three or four pages
of genuine "topics of the day"—everything that is of the greatest
moment in our Russian political and social problems being as it
were brought into one focus. And what is most important—with the
utterly characteristic nuance of the current moment, precisely as
this question is being put at this very moment,—as it is being put
and is being left unsolved. I am referring to several pages in *Anna
Karenina* by Count Leo Tolstoy, in the January issue of *The Russian Messenger.*

Concerning the novel itself I shall say only a word, and this
only in the way of a most necessary preface. I started reading it,
as we all did, very long ago. At first, I liked it. Later, though the
details continued to please me—so that I was unable to tear myself
away from them—on the whole I began to like the novel less: I
kept thinking that I had already read it somewhere—precisely in
Childhood and Youth, by the same Count Tolstoy, and in his *War
and Peace,* and that there it was even fresher. The same story of
a Russian noble family, although the plot was different: characters,
such as Vronsky (one of the heroes of the romance), who can speak
of nothing but horses, and who is even unable to find a subject for
conversation other than about horses, are, of course, curious from
the standpoint of ascertaining their type, but very monotonous
and confined to a certain caste only. For instance, it seemed to
me that the love of this "stallion in uniform," as a friend of mine
called him, could have been depicted only in an ironical tone.
However, when the author began to introduce me seriously into
the inner world of his hero, I seemed to be bored. And then, sud-

denly, all my prejudices were shattered: the scene of the heroine's
death (later she recovers) explained to me the essential part of the
author's design. In the very center of that petty and insolent life
there appeared a great and eternal living truth, at once illuminating
everything. These petty, insignificant and deceitful beings suddenly
became genuine and truthful people, worthy of being called men,
solely because of a natural law, the law of human death. Their
shell vanished, and truth alone appeared. The last ones developed
into the first, while the first ones (Vronsky) all of a sudden became
the last, losing their halo in humiliation; but having been humbled,
they became infinitely better, worthier, more truthful than when
they were the first and the eminent. Hatred and deceit began to
speak in terms of forgiveness and love. Instead of worldly, beau-
monde conceptions there appeared humaneness. They all forgave and
acquitted one another. Caste and exclusiveness suddenly vanished
and were rendered impossible, and these paper people began to
resemble genuine human beings! There proved to be no guilty ones:
they all accused themselves unconditionally, and thereby they at
once acquitted themselves. The reader felt that there is a living
truth, a most real and inescapable truth, which has to be believed,
and that our whole life, all our troubles, both the petty and disgraceful ones and those which we often consider as our gravest
ones,—they all are mostly but petty and fantastic vanity which
falls and disappears even without defending itself before the moment of the living truth.

The most important thing was the indication that such a
moment actually exists, although it rarely appears in its glaring
fullness, and in some lives it does not appear at all. This moment
was found and revealed to us by the novelist in all its terrible truth.
He proved that this truth actually exists not merely as a matter
of belief, not only as an ideal, but inevitably, inescapably, obviously. It seems that this is precisely what the novelist sought to prove
to us when he was conceiving his novel. The Russian reader has
to be often reminded about this eternal truth: in Russia many
people begin to forget it. This reminder was a good act on the
part of the author—to say nothing about the fact that he executed
it as a sublime artist.

After that the romance continues to follow its course. But
somewhat to my surprise, in the sixth part of the novel I came
across a scene reflecting the real "topic of the day," and what is
most important—it appeared not intentionally, not tendentiously
but it arose precisely from the artistic essence of the novel. Nevertheless, I repeat, this, to me, was unexpected and I was somewhat
astonished. Somehow, I didn't think that the author would venture

to lead his heroes, in their development to such "pillars." True, the whole purport of reality is in these "pillars," in this extremeness of the deduction. Without it the novel would even have assumed an indeterminate appearance, in no way conforming to either the current or the essential Russian interests: there would be designed some little corner of life, with a deliberate neglect of the main and most disturbing element in that life.

However, it seems that I am most decidedly embarking upon criticism, and this is no business of mine. I merely mean to point to one scene. It is nothing but two characters revealing themselves precisely in that aspect in which at present they may be most typical for us, and thereby that type of men, to which these two persons belong, is shown by the author in the most curious light from the standpoint of their contemporaneous social designation.

They are both noblemen, hereditary noblemen and original landowners. Both are depicted after the peasant reform. Both used to be "serf landowners," and the question arises: What remains of these noblemen—in the sense of their noble status—after the peasant reform? Inasmuch as the type of these two landowners is very common, the question is partly settled by the author. One of them is Stiva Oblonsky, an egotist, a refined Epicurean, a Moscow resident and a member of the English Club. As a rule these men are regarded as innocent and amiable fast livers, pleasing egoists, standing in no one's way, witty, and living for their own pleasure. Not seldom these men have large families: they treat their wives and children kindly but they give little thought to them. They are very fond of easy women,—of course, of the respectable pattern. They are little educated, but they love elegant things, arts, and they like to converse about everything. When the peasant reform came, this nobleman at once grasped its meaning: he calculated and understood that even so something had been left to him, and consequently, that there was no need to change his habits, and—*après moi le déluge*. He does not bother to think about the fate of his wife and children. By the remnants of his fortune and by his connections he is saved from the fate of a "jack of hearts." However, were his fortune ruined and were it impossible to receive a salary for nothing, perhaps, he would have become a "jack," naturally, exerting every effort of his mind—at times, a very sharp mind—to become a most respectable high life "jack." Of course, in olden days, when he had to pay a card debt or his mistress, now and then, he would send his men away as recruits. But such reminiscences never perplex him and, besides, he forgot them altogether. Even though he is an aristocrat, he never did attach any significance to his noble birth, and when serfdom was abolished, he began to regard this fact as a vanished thing. Among all people there remained to him only the *lucky man,* the bureaucrat beginning with a certain rank and the rich man. The railroad man and the banker, having become powers, he promptly established relations and friendship with them.

And the conversation itself begins with Levin, his relative and a landowner (but of a wholly opposite type who lives on his estate), reproaching him for the fact that he frequents railroad men, attends their dinners and festivals, men, who in Levin's opinion, are equivocal and harmful. Oblonsky caustically refutes him. And, generally, after they had become related, there developed between them rather caustic relations. Besides, in our day, a scamp refuting an honest man is always stronger because he bears the appearance of dignity derived from common sense, whereas the honest man, resembling an idealist, looks like a fool.

The conversation takes place at a hunting party, on a summer night. The hunters are spending the night in a peasant's barn and they are lying on hay. Oblonsky is arguing that contempt for railroad men, for their intrigues, profiteering, their entreaties for concessions, speculations—is meaningless; that they are men like any other; that they work and use their brains, as the rest, and as a result—they build a road.

"But any acquisition in disproportion to work spent is dishonest"—says Levin.

"But who is going to determine the proportion?"—Oblonsky continues. . . . "You did not draw a line between honest and dishonest work. The fact that I am receiving a higher salary than my head-clerk, even though he knows the business better than I— is this dishonest?"

"I don't know."

"Well, I'll tell you: the fact that you are receiving for your work on the estate an extra of, say, five thousand, whereas this peasant, no matter how much he may labor, will get not more than fifty rubles, is as dishonest as the fact that I am getting more than the head-clerk. . . ."

"No, wait"—Levin continues—"You say that it is not fair that I am getting five thousand, and the peasant, fifty rubles: this is true. It is unfair, I feel it, but . . ."

"Yes, you feel it, but you do not give away your estate to him," said Stepan Arkadievich as though on purpose to provoke Levin. . . .

"I do not give it away, because no one is demanding this from me, and even if I wanted to, I couldn't give it away . . . and there is no one to whom I could give it away."

"Give it to this peasant; he would not refuse to take it."

"Well, how am I going to give it away to him? Shall I go with him and execute a deed?"

"I don't know; but if you are convinced that you have no right . . ."

"I am not at all convinced. On the contrary, I feel that I have no right to give it away, that I have obligations toward both the land and the family."

"No, wait; but if you consider that this inequality is unjust, why don't you act accordingly? . . ."

"I do act, only negatively, in the sense that I am not going to seek to increase that difference in the status which exists between me and him."

"No, if you forgive me, this is a paradox . . ."

"That's it, my friend. It should be one way or the other: either to consider that the present organization of society is just, and then to defend one's rights, or to confess that one is enjoying unjust privileges, *as I do, and to enjoy them with pleasure.*"

"No, if it were unjust, you couldn't enjoy these benefits with pleasure,—*at least, I couldn't; to me, the most important thing is to feel that I am not guilty.*"

2

"TOPIC OF THE DAY"

Such is the conversation. And you must admit that this is "the topic of the day," even the most pressing thing in our topic of the day. And how many most typical, purely Russian traits! To begin with, some forty years ago these ideas were hardly coming into existence even in Europe; even there, were there many who knew Saint-Simon and Fourier—the original "idealistic" interpreters of these ideas?—And in our midst—in our midst there were hardly fifty men in all Russia who knew about this new movement which had begun in Western Europe.

And now, suddenly, these "questions" are being discussed by landowners at hunting parties spending the night in a peasant's barn, and they are being debated in a most characteristic and most competent manner so that at least the negative side of the question is settled and signed by them irrevocably. True, these are landowners of the beau monde; they speak at the English Club, they read newspapers, they follow the trials through newspapers and other sources. Even so, the fact itself that such idealistic trash is recognized as a most vital topic for conversation among men who are by no means professors or specialists, but simply society people, Oblonskys and Levins,—this trait, I say, is one of the most characteristic peculiarities of the present-day state of the Russian minds.

The second most characteristic trait in this conversation noted by the artist-author is the fact that the justice of these new ideas is being judged by a man who wouldn't give a penny for them, *i.e.*, for the happiness of a proletarian, a poor fellow, and who, on the contrary, if occasion should arise, would bark him as a lime-tree. Yet, with a light heart and the jocundity of a punster, with one stroke, he attests to the bankruptcy of the whole history of mankind, declaring its present order the climax of absurdity. "I am"—he says, as it were—"in full agreement with this." Please note that these Stivas are always the first to agree with all this. With one stroke he has condemned the whole Christian order, the individual, the family—oh, this costs him nothing. Also, please bear in mind that in Russia science is non-existent; yet these gentlemen, with utter shamelessness realizing the fact that they have no science, and that they began to speak about this only yesterday, and echoing somebody else's voice, are nevertheless deciding upon problems of such a magnitude without the slightest hesitation.

But we have here a third most characteristic trait. This gentleman openly declares: "It should be one way or the other: either to consider that the present organization of society is just, and then to defend one's rights, *or to confess that one is enjoying unjust privileges, as I do, and to enjoy them with pleasure.*" In other words, having in substance signed a sentence on the whole of Russia and having condemned as well his family, the future of his children, he openly declares that this does not concern him; he says, as it were: "I admit that I am a villain, but I shall remain a villain for my pleasure. *Après moi le déluge.*" He is calm because he still has a fortune, but should it happen that he lost it,—why wouldn't he become a "jack"?—this is the straightest road.

This, then, is the citizen, the family man, the Russian—what a characteristic, purely Russian trait! You might say that even so he is an exception. What exception? And can this be so?— Please recall how much cynicism we have perceived during these last twenty years; what ease in conversations and metamorphoses; what an absence of fundamental convictions, and what promptness in adopting the first passer-by only to sell him out tomorrow for a kopeck. No moral fund, except—*Après moi le déluge.*

But it is most curious that side by side with this very numerous and prevailing type, there stands another type of Russian nobleman and landowner, a directly opposite one,—there can be nothing more opposite.—This is Levin. But of Levins, there is a vast multitude, almost as many as Oblonskys. I am not speaking about his face, his figure, which the artist created in his novel. I am referring merely to one trait of his essence, but the most basic one, and I assert that this trait is unbelievably widely diffused among us, *i.e.*, among our cynicism and Kalmuck attitude toward work. For some time this trait has been manifesting itself every minute. Men of this pattern convulsively, almost pathologically, seek to receive answers to their queries; they are firmly hoping, passionately believing, despite the fact that they are unable to settle almost anything. This trait is perfectly revealed in Levin's reply to Stiva: "No, if it were unjust, I couldn't enjoy these benefits with pleasure,—*at least, I couldn't; to me the most important thing is to feel that I am not guilty.*"

And, in fact, he will not calm down until he settles the question whether or not he is guilty. Do you know to what extent he will fail to compose himself? He will go to every extreme, if only it be necessary; if he proves to himself that this is the thing to do, Levin, in opposition to Stiva, who says: "Even though as a villain, I continue to live for my own pleasure,"—will become a Nekrasov's "Vlas" who, in a fit of great emotion and fear, gave away his fortune, and

> . . . went forth, in footfall measured,
> To collect God's churches' share.

And if he is not going "to collect God's churches' share," he will do something on a similar scale and with an equal zeal. Please note—I hasten to repeat what I said concerning this trait: there is a great multitude of new men, Russians, of this new root who *thirst for truth*, truth alone without the conventional deceit, and who, in order to attain that truth, will give away everything. These men came into being during the last twenty years, and their number is steadily increasing, even though they could have always been anticipated—even before Peter's epoch.

This is the forthcoming, future Russia of honest people who need nothing but the truth. Oh, there is also in them great intolerance: because of inexperience they reject all conventions, even all explanations. But I strongly emphasize the fact that they are swayed by a genuine sentiment. Another characteristic thing about them is that there is a great deal of dissension among them, and, temporarily, they belong to most divergent strata and they hold all sorts of convictions; we see among them aristocrats and proletarians, clergymen and disbelievers, rich men and poor,

learned men and ignoramuses, old men and little girls, Slavophiles
and Westerners. The discord in convictions is great, but the aspiration for honesty and truth is unshakable and inviolable: for the
word of truth any one of them will forsake his life and all his
privileges, and will—I reiterate—become a Vlas.

Perhaps people might start shouting that this is a wild
fantasy; that in our midst there isn't so much honesty and *search
for honesty*. However, I specifically assert that side by side with
terrible debauch, I foresee these future men to whom the future
of Russia belongs; that no longer can one fail to perceive them,
and that the artist who juxtaposed that outlived cynic, Stiva,
with his new man Levin, compared, as it were, this doomed, depraved, very numerous Russian society which, however, committed
suicide by its own verdict,—with the society of the new truth
which refuses to bear in its heart the conviction of its culpability,
and which will give anything to clear its heart of its guilt.

It is remarkable in this connection that our society actually
is divided virtually only into these two categories,—to that extent they are numerous and do completely embrace Russian life—
of course, if the altogether lazy, inept, and indifferent ones be
disregarded. But the most typical, most Russian trait in the "topic
of the day," pointed out by the author, consists of the fact that
his new man, his Levin, does not know how to settle the question
perplexing him. That is, he has *almost* settled it in his heart—
and not in his favor—*suspecting* that he is *guilty,* but something
firm, straight and concrete rises in protest from his whole nature,
and restrains him, for the time being, from pronouncing the final
judgment. Stiva, on the contrary, to whom it makes no difference
whether or not he is guilty, settles the question without the slightest hesitation; he even feels that it is to his advantage: "If everything is absurd and there is nothing sacred, this means that everything is permitted, while I still have much time ahead of me,
since doomsday is not coming tomorrow." It is curious that exactly this weak side of the question has perplexed Levin, bringing
him to an impasse: this is strictly in line with the Russian fashion,
which has been quite correctly noted by the author. The whole
point of the matter is that all these ideas and questions in Russia
are mere theory imported to us from an alien order of things;
from Europe, where they have long acquired their historical and
practical aspects. What is to be done?—Both our noblemen are
noblemen, and it is not easy for them to rid themselves of European authority; here, too, they have to pay tribute to Europe.
Now Levin, with his Russian heart, confuses the purely Russian,
and the only possible, solution of the question with its European

construction. He confuses the Christian solution with the historical "right." To make the thing clear, let us imagine this little picture:

Levin stands, buried deep in his thoughts, after his night conversation with Stiva at the hunting party, and painfully—because his soul is honest—seeks to solve the question which has perplexed him, and which, consequently, must have been perplexing him heretofore.

"Yes,"—he argues, half solving his query—"yes, speaking honestly, by what right do we, as Veselovsky said the other day, eat, drink, hunt, do nothing, and the poor man is eternally, eternally working? Yes, Stiva is right, I *must* share my fortune with the poor and go to work for them."

Beside Levin stands a "poor man," and he says:

"Quite so, you really should and must give away your fortune to the poor, and you must go and work for us."

Of course, by deciding the matter, so to speak, in a superior sense, Levin will be perfectly right, and the "poor man" altogether wrong. But herein is the whole difference in the approach to the question, since its moral solution should not be confused with the historical one; otherwise there is going to be an everlasting confusion, which actually persists, especially in the theoretical Russian heads—in the heads of the scamp Stivas and in the heads of the pure-in-heart Levins. In Europe, life and practice have put the question—although absurdly, in the form of its ideal solution, nevertheless realistically as far as its current course is concerned, no longer confusing the two conflicting views—the moral and the historical—at least, as far as possible.

Let me explain my thought, though in a few words.

3

The Topic of the Day in Europe

In Europe there was feudalism and there were knights. However, in the course of one thousand years, or more, the bourgeoisie gained strength, and finally, everywhere, it delivered a battle, defeating and driving away the knights, and planted itself in their place. Thus the saying, *"Ôte-toi de là, que je m'y mette"* ("Get out of there so that I may place myself there") was fulfilled. But having placed itself in the stead of its former masters and having seized their property, the bourgeoisie completely disregarded the people, the proletarian, and having refused to recognize him as its brother, it converted him, in exchange for his daily bread, into a working force for its own welfare.

Our Russian Stiva decides for himself that he is wrong; yet deliberately he wishes to remain a scamp, because he is living fatly and comfortably. The foreign Stiva does not agree with ours, considering himself altogether right, and on this point, in his own way, he is more logical, since in his opinion there is here no *right* whatsoever—there is only *history,* a historical course of events. He took the place of the knight because he conquered the knight by force, and he understands perfectly that the proletarian, who at the time of his, Stiva's, struggle against the knight was still insignificant and weak, may well gain in strength and is even growing stronger every day. He has a clear presentiment that when the proletarian gains full strength, he will displace him just as he, the bourgeois, had displaced the knight, will tell him exactly the same thing. "Get out of there so that I may place myself there." Where, then, is there right? There is here nothing but history. Oh, he would be ready to compromise, somehow to make up with the enemy. He has even endeavored to do so. Inasmuch, however, as he has guessed, and, moreover, knows from experience, that the enemy is under no circumstance prepared to make peace; that he is unwilling to share, but wants *everything;* furthermore, that if he, Stiva, were to cede something, he would thereby merely be weakening himself,—he resolved to cede nothing, and he is getting ready for the battle. Perhaps his situation is hopeless; still because it is in accord with human nature to fortify one's spirit in anticipation of a battle,—he does not despair; on the contrary, he is fortifying himself for the battle with ever increasing energy, resorting to all means and exerting all his efforts, so long as he has the strength to do so; he is weakening his adversary, and, for the time being he is doing nothing but that.

Here is how the matter stands in Europe. True, recently, quite recently, over there, too, there was a *moral* approach to the problem: there were Fourierists and Cabetists; there were inquests, disputes, and debates on various very delicate subjects. At present, however, the leaders of the proletariat, for the time being, have discarded all this. They simply seek to prepare for the battle; they are organizing an army; they are mustering it into regiments, they are raising funds, convinced of their victory: "And then, after the victory, everything will shape itself in a practical way, even though, possibly, after rivers of blood have been shed." The bourgeois understand that the leaders of the proletarians are tempting them with sheer plunder, and this being so, it isn't even worth while setting forth the moral aspect. However, even among the present-day chiefs there are ringleaders who are preaching also the moral right of the poor. Strictly speaking, too, the commanders tolerate these ringleaders as a matter of flourish, in order to embellish the affair and to convey to it a guise of supreme justice. Among these "moral" ringleaders there are many intriguers, but there are also many who are great and fervent believers. They openly declare that they are seeking nothing for themselves and that they are laboring for humanity; that they seek to establish a new order of things for its happiness. At this juncture they are met by the bourgeois on a rather firm ground, and it is openly pointed out to them that they wish to compel him, the bourgeois, to become a brother of the proletarian and to make him share his property with the latter—by club and blood. Although this rather resembles the truth, the ringleaders answer him that they do not consider the bourgeoisie capable of becoming brethren of the people, and it is for this reason that they are employing force against them, altogether excluding them from brotherhood; "Brotherhood"—they say—"will ensue later, from among proletarians, whereas you—you are the one hundred million heads doomed to extermination, and nothing more. We are finished with you—for the happiness of the human race."

Other ringleaders openly declare that they do not need any brotherhood at all; that Christianity is nonsense, and that future mankind will be organized on scientific foundations. Naturally, all this cannot shake and convince the bourgeois. He understands and answers that this society on scientific foundations is pure fantasy; that they are representing man to themselves not at all as he has been created by nature; that it is difficult for man to renounce unconditionally the right of property, the family and liberty; that they are demanding too great a sacrifice from their future man, as an individual; that man can be reduced to this state only by means of terrible violence and on condition that dreadful espionage and unceasing control by a despotic government are established over him. In conclusion he challenges them to point to that force which would be capable of uniting the future man into an accordant, and not forcible, society.

In answer to the above the ringleaders set forth utility and necessity which are conceived by man himself, and that he, of his own accord, will voluntarily agree to make all the required concessions in order to save himself from destruction and death. They are being told that utility and self-preservation alone never can generate a complete and harmonious fellowship; that no utility will ever replace willfulness and the rights of the individual; that these factors and motives are too weak, and that, therefore, all this, even as before, remains uncertain; that were they to resort merely to the moral aspect of the matter, the proletarian wouldn't even listen to them, and if he is following them and is organizing for the battle, this is solely because he is tempted by the promised plunder and is excited by the anticipation of the battle and the destruction. Therefore, in the long run, the moral aspect of the question should be altogether discarded since it does not stand the test of mildest criticism,—and one should simply be getting ready for the combat.

Such is the European approach to the matter. Both sides are terribly wrong, and both will perish in their sins. I repeat, to us Russians, the most painful thing is that in Russia even the Levins ponder over these questions, whereas their only possible solution, a specifically Russian one, and not for Russians only, but for mankind as a whole, is the moral, *i.e.,* Christian approach to them. In Europe such an approach is inconceivable, although even there, sooner or later—after floods of blood and one hundred million heads— they will have to recognize it because in it alone lies the solution.

4

THE RUSSIAN SOLUTION TO THE PROBLEM

If you have felt that it is painful to you "to eat, drink, do nothing and engage in hunting," and if you have really felt it and you are genuinely sorry for "the poor," of whom there are so many, give them your property; if you wish, make your contribution to the common cause, go and work for all men, and "you will be rewarded in heaven where they neither hoard nor covet." Go, even as Vlas, whose

> . . . whole soul's enormous power
> On a godly task was spent.

And if you do not wish, like Vlas, to make a collection for God's church, take care of the enlightenment of the soul of that poor man, enlighten him, teach him. Even were everybody, like you, to give away their property to "the poor," all the distributed riches of the rich of this world would be merely a drop in the sea. Therefore, it is necessary to pay more attention to enlightenment, science and enhancement of love. Then wealth would be really increasing, real wealth, since it is not to be sought in golden garments, but in the joy of general communion and in the firm hope that everybody will extend a helping hand to him whom misfortune has befallen and to his children. And do not say that you are but a weak unit, and that should you alone give away your property and go to serve, you would thereby accomplish and rectify nothing.

On the contrary, even if there should be only a few like you,—even then things would start moving.

Besides, as a matter of fact, it is not necessary to conceive the giving away of property as a *binding* condition, since in the matter of love *constraint* resembles a uniform, fidelity to the letter. The conviction that one has complied with the letter leads to haughtiness, formalism and indolence. One has to do only that which one's heart dictates: if it orders a man to give away his fortune —let him give it away; if it orders him to go and work for all men —let him go and work. But even here, don't follow the example of certain dreamers, who straightway get hold of a wheelbarrow and say: "I am not a nobleman—I want to work as a peasant." The wheelbarrow, too, is a uniform.

On the contrary, if you feel that you will be useful to everybody in the capacity of a scientist, matriculate in a university and obtain some means therefor. Neither the giving away of property, nor the wearing of a peasant coat are obligatory: all this is mere letter and formality: *only your resolution to do everything for the sake of active love,* everything within the limits of your possibility, everything which you sincerely consider possible for yourself—is obligatory and important. However, to think that all these endeavors will render you one of the people is nothing but an assumption of a false guise which is discourteous to them and which humiliates you. You are too complex to become one of them; besides, your education will prevent you from becoming a peasant. Better raise the peasant to your "complexity." Only be sincere and artless: this is better than any kind of assumed "commonness." But above all—don't scare yourself; don't say: "one man in the field is no soldier," etc. Anyone who sincerely seeks truth is awfully strong. Nor should you imitate certain idle talkers who keep repeating all the time so that people will hear them: "We are not permitted to do anything; our hands are tied; we are driven to despair and disillusionment!" and so on, and so forth. They all are pompous talkers, heroes of *mauvais ton* poems, show-off idlers. He who wishes to be useful, can accomplish a world of good even if literally his hands are tied. The genuine worker, having embarked upon a certain course of action, at once perceives so much work before himself that he is not going to complain that he is not permitted to act, and unfailingly he will find and succeed in accomplishing something. All real workers know it. In our midst the mere study of Russia will take so much time, since only the rarest man among us knows our Russia.

Complaints about disillusionment are perfectly stupid: joy resulting from the contemplation of the edifice which is being erected must quench every soul's thirst, everybody's, even if, for the time being only minute grains of sand be brought for the construction of the edifice. You have but one reward—love, should you deserve it. Let us say that you are seeking no reward; however, you are engaged in a work of love,—how, then, can you refrain from soliciting love?

But let no one tell you that you should have done all this even without love, so to speak, because of a personal interest, and that otherwise you would have been compelled by force. Nay, in Russia different convictions should be propagated, especially relative to the conceptions of liberty, equality and brotherhood. In the present aspect of the world, liberty is conceived as license, whereas genuine liberty is only in the mastering of one's self, of one's own will in order that one may eventually attain a moral condition where, at any given moment, one is a real master of himself. License of desires leads only to your enslavement.

This is why almost the whole present-day world is conceiving liberty in financial security and in laws guaranteeing it: "I have money, therefore, I can do what I please; I have money, therefore, I am not going to perish and I will not solicit anyone's help, and not to be soliciting anyone's help is the supreme liberty." And yet, substantially, this is not freedom but, again, slavery, slavery based on money. On the contrary, supreme freedom is not to hoard money and not to base one's security upon it, but "to distribute one's property among all people and to go and serve everybody." If a man is capable of this, if he is capable of overcoming himself to such an extent—isn't he free after that? This is the supreme manifestation of will-power!

Next, what is equality in the contemporaneous civilized world? Jealous watchfulness of one over the other, self-conceit and envy: "He is clever, he is a Shakespeare, he prides himself on his talent. Let's humiliate and exterminate him." However, genuine equality says: "What is it to me that thou art more talented than I, cleverer, handsomer?—On the contrary, I am glad of it because I love thee. But even though I am less important than thou, yet, as a man, I respect myself, and thou knowest this, and thou thyself respectest me, and I am happy over thy respect. If by reason of thy capabilities, thou renderest me a hundred times more service than I can render thee, I bless thee for that, I admire thee and thank thee, and in no way do I regard my admiration as something to be ashamed of. On the contrary, I am happy because I am grateful to thee, and I am working for thee and for everybody in the measure of my weak capabilities—it is not at all with a view to getting square with thee, but because I love all of you."

Were all men to speak thus, most certainly they would become brethren, and not for the mere sake of economic gain but because of the fullness of joyous life, because of the fullness of love.

It may be said that this is a fantasy, that this "Russian answer to the problem" is "the Kingdom of Heaven," and is only possible in the Kingdom of Heaven. Yes, the Stivas would grow very angry were the Kingdom of Heaven to come. However, the fact itself should be taken into account that this fantasy of "the Russian solution to the problem" is incomparably less fantastic and infinitely more plausible than the European solution. Such men, *i.e.*, "Vlases," we have already seen, we rather often perceive them now among all classes; but, thus far, we have seen nowhere their "future man," and he himself promised to come only after crossing rivers of blood. Besides, even if there existed an order and principles which would permit organization of society in a faultless manner; and were it even possible to achieve it before testing it,—just so and *a priori*, deriving it from mere meditations of the heart and "scientific" figures borrowed at that from the former social order,—with unready, unfinished people, no rules would survive or could be put into effect, and, contrariwise, they would be felt only as a burden.

However, I boundlessly believe in our future men, in those who already begin to appear, about whom I spoke above; as yet, they have not reached any accord; with respect to their convictions they are broken up into little groups and camps. As against this they all are seeking truth above everything else, and if they could only learn where truth is, they would be prepared to sacrifice for its attainment everything including life itself. Believe me: once they finally find the path of truth, they will inspire the rest to follow them—and not by violence but freely.

This is what individuals can accomplish to begin with. This is the plow which can break our "virgin soil." Before preaching to the people "what they should be,"—show it to them through your own example; fulfill it yourselves, and everybody will follow you. What is there Utopian or impossible in this proposition?—I don't understand! True, we are very depraved, very pusillanimous, and therefore we do not believe and are inclined to scoff. However, at present we are almost of no import; it is the future ones who really count. The people are pure in heart; what they need is education—this is the most momentous thing! In this we should believe above all, and this we should learn to discern. And to those pure in heart there is one advice: self-control and self-mastery before any first step. Before compelling others, fulfill it yourselves—herein is the whole mystery of the first step.

An Answer to a Letter

The editorial office of the *Writer's Diary* has received the following letter:

"Dear Fedor Mikhailovich:

On January 12 I mailed you 2 rubles 50 kopecks, requesting you to send me your publication *A Writer's Diary*. I learned through the newspapers that the first issue came out on February 1; today is the 25th but, as yet, I have not received it! I am most curious to learn the reason for this. I don't know how you feel about the matter, but to me such an attitude toward the subscribers seems more than strange!

Should you make up your mind to send me your publication some time, please address it to Dr. V. V. K—n of the Zemstvo Municipal Hospital, City Novokhopersk. February 25, 1877."

The following is the answer of the editorial office:

"Dear Sir:

Much to our regret, complaints about the non-receipt of the issues are being received by us rather frequently, especially in the beginning of the year. Upon checking in our books, we always find that the respective copies have been duly mailed long ago. Therefore, they are being lost en route. Of course, the percentage of these losses in relation to the number of subscribers is very small; nevertheless, they do invariably happen, and not only in the case of our publication but also in that of other periodicals. As a rule, without entering into explanations, and in order to satisfy the subscribers as promptly as possible, we send duplicate copies, since how is one to trace a missing copy! In the middle of the year things begin to straighten out, and by the end of the year there are practically no losses.

However, you, sir, among all the conjectures as to why the copy has not reached you, unhesitatingly chose one, namely fraud, on the part of the editorial office. This is clear from the tone of your letter, and especially from the words: '*Should you make up your mind to send your publication some time, please,*' *etc.* Thus, you directly suppose that the editor deliberately held back your copy, and you do not refrain from expressing the doubt that you will ever receive it. In view of the above the editorial office hastens to return to you your 2 rubles and 50 kopecks and requests you not to bother it in the future. It is compelled to do so because of an intelligible and natural motive which, sir, probably will not astonish you."

MARCH

CHAPTER I

1

Once More on the Subject that Constantinople, Sooner or Later, Must Be Ours

LAST YEAR, in the June issue of the *Diary*, I stated that Constantinople, "sooner or later, must be ours." That was a fervent and glorious time: all Russia, her spirit and heart, was rising, and the people voluntarily went to serve Christ and Orthodoxy against the pagans for the cause of our brethren by faith and blood, the Slavs. Even though I have denoted that article of mine as "a Utopian conception of history," nevertheless I myself firmly believed in my words and did not regard them as a Utopia, and, besides, I am now ready to reiterate them literally.

"Yes, the Golden Horn and Constantinople—they will be ours. To begin with, this will come to pass of its own accord, precisely because the hour has come, and even if it has not yet arrived, indeed it will come in the near future; all symptoms point to this. This is a natural solution—so to speak, the word of nature herself. If this has not occurred before, it has been precisely because the time has not been ripe."

Thereupon I explained my contention why the time was not, and could not have been, ripe. "Had even the thought then occurred to Peter," I wrote in that issue, "to seize Constantinople instead of founding Petersburg, I believe that, after some deliberation, he would have abandoned this idea—granted that he was powerful enough to crush the Sultan—since in those days the time was inopportune and the project could even have brought ruin to Russia.

"If in Finnish Petersburg we did not elude the influence of the neighboring Germans who, though useful, have paralyzed Russian progress before its genuine path had been ascertained, how then in Constantinople—so enormous and original, with her remnants of a most powerful and ancient civilization—could we have managed to elude the influence of the Greeks, men far more subtle than the coarse Germans, men who have infinitely more points in common with us than the Germans, who do not resemble us at all—numerous courtiers who would promptly have surrounded the Throne and who, ahead of the Russians, would have become educated and learned, who would have captivated Peter himself, not to speak of his immediate successors, taking advantage of his weak spot by their skill in seamanship.

"Briefly, they would have captured Russia politically; they would forthwith have dragged her along some new Asiatic path—again into a seclusion of some sort—and the Russia of those days, of course, could not have endured this. Her Russian strength and nationality would have been arrested in their development. The mighty Great Russian would have remained in estrangement in his grim, snowy North, serving merely as material for the regenerated Constantinople, and, perhaps, in the long run, he would have made up his mind not to follow her at all. At the same time the Russian South would have been captured by the Greeks. Moreover, there might have occurred a schism in Orthodoxy itself which would have been divided into two worlds—the regenerated world of Constantinople and the old Russian. . . . In a word, this would have been a most untimely event. At present things are quite different.

"At present," I wrote, "Russia could take possession of Constantinople even without transferring thither her capital, which in Peter's times and long thereafter could not have been avoided. Now Constantinople could be ours, not as Russia's capital, but," I added, "also not as a capital of Slavdom as some people are dreaming. Slavdom without Russia would exhaust itself there in its struggle with the Greeks, even in the event that it might succeed in forming from its parts some political whole. But for the Greeks alone to inherit Constantinople is at present altogether impossible: it is impossible to surrender to them so important a spot on the globe; this would be something altogether out of proportion.

"However, in the name of what, in the name of what *moral* right could Russia be aspiring for Constantinople? Basing herself upon what superior aims could Russia claim Constantinople from Europe?

"Precisely," I wrote, "as a leader of Orthodoxy, as its protectress and guardian—a role designated to her ever since Ivan III, who placed her symbol and the Byzantine double-headed eagle above the ancient coat of arms of Russia, a role which unquestionably revealed itself only after Peter the Great when Russia perceived in herself the strength to fulfill her mission and factually became the real and sole protectress of Orthodoxy and of the peoples adhering to it. Such is the ground, such is the right to ancient Constantinople, which would be intelligible and not offensive even to Slavs most sensitive to their independence, even to the Greeks themselves. Besides, thereby would be revealed the true essence of those political relations which inevitably must develop between Russia and all other Orthodox peoples—whether Slavs or Greeks makes no difference. Russia is their guardian, or even their leader, perhaps, but not their sovereign; their mother, but not their mistress. Even if she were to become their sovereign some time in the future, it would be only by their own election and subject to the preservation of everything by which they themselves would define their independence and individuality."

Naturally, all these considerations were conceived by me in the article of last June by no means as something which was subject to immediate fulfillment, but merely as something which unquestionably has got to come when the historical moment and the predestined time arrive, the proximity or remoteness of which cannot be predicted but may nevertheless be foreseen.

Since then nine months have elapsed. I believe, it is not necessary to recall these nine months: we all remember those enthusiastic days, in the beginning full of hopes, and thereafter—so strange and disturbing, a period which up to the present has come to no solution, so that God only knows (I believe it is only in this way one may express oneself) what it will come to; shall we draw the sword, or will the matter once more be postponed by some compromise? But no matter what happens, for some reason, precisely now I wish to state a few additional and explanatory words in connection with my June meditations concerning the fate of Constantinople. No matter what happens—whether there is going to be peace, or new concessions on the part of Russia are made —sooner or later, Constantinople will be ours. This is what I wish to reiterate precisely at this time, but now from a certain new viewpoint.

Yes, she must be ours not only because she is a famous port, not only because of the straits, "the center of the universe," "the navel of the earth"; not from the standpoint of the long-conceived necessity for a tremendous giant, such as Russia, finally, to get out of his locked room—in which he has already grown up to the ceiling—into free spaces where he may inhale the free air of the seas and oceans. I wish to set forth but one consideration, also of major importance, why Constantinople cannot evade Russia. I am setting forth this particular consideration in preference to others because it seems to me that no one takes this viewpoint into account, or, at least, people have forgotten to consider it, whereas, perhaps, it is the most important one.

2

The Russian People, from Their Standpoint, Have Fully Grown Up to a Sane Conception of the Eastern Problem

Although this may sound absurd, nevertheless it is true that the four centuries of Turkish oppression in the East, in a certain sense, were even useful to Christianity and Orthodoxy there,—negatively, of course, and yet fostering their consolidation, and what is most important—their communion and unity, much in the same way as the two centuries of the Tartar yoke had helped in the past the consolidation of the Church in Russia. The oppressed and jaded Christian population of the East has perceived in Christ, in faith in Him, its sole consolation, and in the Church the only and last remnant of its national individuality and distinction. This was its last and sole hope, the last splinter of a wrecked ship, since the Church, in spite of everything, was preserving these tribes as a nationality, while the faith in Christ prevented them—at least a portion of them—from merging with the conquerors and forgetting their origin and their past history. The persecuted peoples themselves felt and fully understood all this and rallied closer around the Cross.

On the other hand, ever since the conquest of Constantinople, the entire enormous Christian East, willy-nilly and suddenly threw its glance at remote Russia which had just then shaken off the Tartar yoke, and, as it were, foreboded her future might and the future all-uniting center of its salvation. And Russia forthwith unhesitatingly accepted the banner of the East, having placed the Byzantine double-eagle over and above its ancient coat-of-arms, thereby assuming, as it were, the obligation to Orthodoxy as a whole: to guard all the peoples professing it against final destruction.

At the same time, the whole Russian people fully confirmed the new mission of Russia and their Czar in the future destinies of the entire Eastern world. Ever since that time the people have been—and still are—perceiving, firmly and undeviatingly, the beloved title of their Czar in the word "Orthodox," "Orthodox Czar." Having thus named their Czar, the people, as it were, acknowledged in this appellation his designation—the designation of a guardian and unifier, and when God's command thunders—also the designation of the liberator of Orthodoxy, and Christianity *in toto* professing it, from Mohammedan barbarism and Western heresy.

Two centuries ago, especially beginning with Peter the Great, the beliefs and hopes of the Eastern peoples commenced to come true: Russia's sword has several times been shining in the East for its protection. It goes without saying that the peoples of the East, too, could not help but perceive in the Czar of Russia not only their liberator but also their future Czar. However, in the course of these two centuries there came to them European education and European influence. The upper, educated, portion of the people, their intelligentsia, both in Russia and in the East, little by little, grew more indifferent to the Orthodox idea; it even began to deny the fact that in this idea resides the regeneration and resurrection to a new grand life of both the East and Russia. In Russia, for instance, the overwhelming part of her educated class ceased and even, as it were, disaccustomed itself, to perceive in this idea the main mission of Russia, the covenant of her future and her vital force. Contrariwise, all these began to be perceived in novel ideas. Many people, in a purely Western fashion, began to see in the Church nothing but dead formalism, segregation, ritualism, and starting with the end of the past century—even prejudice and hypocrisy: the spirit, the idea, the living force was forgotten. There appeared economic conceptions of the Western pattern, new political doctrines, new morality which sought to correct and supersede the former one. Finally, science made its appearance, and it could not help but introduce disbelief in the former ideas. . . . Besides, in the peoples of the East there began to awaken pre-eminently national ideas: suddenly there arose a fear that, after having shaken off the Turkish yoke, they would fall under the yoke of Russia.

However, among the many millions of our common people and in their czars the idea of the liberation of the East and of the Church of Christ was never dead. The movement which seized the Russian people last summer proved that they forgot nothing of their ancient hopes and beliefs; it even surprised the overwhelming mass of our intelligentsia to such an extent that they adopted a skeptical and scoffing attitude toward it, assuring everybody—and above all themselves—that the movement was invented and counterfeited by disreputable men who were seeking to come to the forefront to occupy a showy place.

Indeed, who, in our day, among our intelligentsia—save a small portion of it which detached itself from the general chorus—could admit that our people are capable of *consciously* comprehending their political, social and ethical mission? How could it be conceived that this coarse common mass, which only recently was kept in bondage and which now half-killed itself with vodka, knew and was convinced that its destiny was to serve Christ, and that of its Czar—to guard the Christian faith and to liberate Orthodoxy? "Even though this mass always called itself Christian, nevertheless it has no conception of either religion or even Christ; it knows not even the most ordinary prayers." This is what is usually being said about our people. Who is saying this? You think—a German pastor who has organized our Stundism; or a travelling European; a correspondent of a political newspaper; or some educated top Jew, from among those who do not believe in God and of whom suddenly nowadays so many have been propagated in our midst; or, finally, one of those Russians residing abroad who pictures to himself Russia and her people not otherwise than in the guise of a drunken peasant woman with a square bottle in her hand?—Oh, no! Thus thinks an enormous part of our Russian, very best society. Yet they do not suspect that even though our people do not know prayers, nevertheless the essence of Christianity, its spirit and truth, are conserved and fortified in them—despite their vices—as strongly as, perhaps, in no other people in the world.

True, an atheist or a Russian European indifferent to religion even does not understand it otherwise than in the shape of formalism and hypocrisy. However, in the people they behold nothing akin to hypocrisy, and, therefore, they infer that the people understand nothing in religion; that they pray, whenever they deem it necessary, to a board, but that, essentially, they are indifferent and their spirit is killed by formalism. They do not at all discern in the people the Christian spirit, perhaps, because they have long ago lost it and do not know where it resides and where it blows. However, this "depraved" and ignorant people of ours loves the humble man and God's holy fool: in all their traditions and legends the people have preserved the belief that the weak and the humbled, unjustly suffering for Christ, will be raised above the eminent and the strong when God's judgment and ordainment are pronounced. Our people are also fond of telling the story of the renowned and grand life of their great, chaste and humble Christian Knight, Ilya-Murometz, the champion of truth, the liberator of the poor and weak, the meek and modest, the faithful and pure in heart.

And possessing, revering and loving such a valiant knight, how can our people fail to believe in the triumph of oppressed peoples and our brethren in the East? Our people revere the memory of their great and humble hermits and saints; they are fond of reciting to their children the stories about the great Christian martyrs. They have learned and know these stories, and it was from them that I first heard them; they were told with deep understanding and reverence and they became engraved in my heart.

Besides, every year, there arise from the people's midst great repenting "Vlases" who give away all their property and who, with touching emotion, engage in the humble and great exploit of truth, work and poverty. . . .

However, I will postpone my comments on the people: some day they will succeed in making themselves understood, or at least, in being taken into consideration. It will be comprehended that the people, too, are of some import. Finally the momentous fact will be realized that not even once, in the great or only slightly important moments of Russian history, could Russia do without her people; that Russia is popular; that Russia is not Austria; that in every significant moment of our historical life the issue has invariably been determined by the people's spirit and view, by the czars of the people in sublime communion with the latter. This extremely important historical fact is usually almost disregarded by our intelligentsia, and it is always being recalled suddenly somehow, when the historical date rumbles.

But I digressed. I was speaking about Constantinople.

3

The Most Opportune Thoughts at the Present Time

The Eastern Church, its representatives—the ecumenic patriarchs—during all the four centuries of their enslavement lived in peace among themselves and with Russia—I mean, in matters concerning religion: there have been no disturbances, heresies, schisms —for these there was no time.

However, during the current century, especially during the last twenty years, after the great Eastern war, one, as it were, could smell there the putrescent odor of a decomposing corpse: the presentiment of death and decomposition of "the sick man" and of the ruin of his czardom have become the main feeling. Oh, of course, the final liberation can be brought about only by Russia, that Russia which also now, at the present moment of general colloquies about the East, alone raises her voice in Europe on their behalf, whereas all other nations and kingdoms of the enlightened European world, naturally, would be glad if all these oppressed peoples of the East would not exist at all. But—alas—virtually all the Eastern intelligentsia, while appealing for Russia's help, are nevertheless afraid of her, perhaps, as much as of the Turks: "Although Russia will liberate us from the Turks, still she will absorb us, even as 'the sick man,' and will prevent the development of our nationalities"—such is their *idée fixe* poisoning all their hopes! Besides, the moment the first ray of education fell upon them, ever increasing national antagonisms began to harass them. The recent Greek-Bulgarian church strife, under the guise of an ecclesiastical conflict, was, of course, but a national one, constituting, as it were, a prophecy for the future. The ecumenic Patriarch, censuring the Bulgarians for disobedience and excommunicating their arbitrarily elected Exarch, pointed out that in religious matters the canons of the Church and church discipline must not be sacrificed to "the new and perilous principle of nationality." However, the Patriarch himself, being a Greek, by promulgating the excommunication of the Bulgarians, was serving the same principle of nationality—only in favor of the Greeks against the Slavs.

In a word, it may be predicted with probability that were "the sick man" to die, forthwith antagonisms and consternation would ensue among them—to begin with, specifically of an ecclesiastical character, which would cause unquestionable harm even to Russia; harm would be caused even in case Russia, by force of circumstances, should be compelled to withdraw from participation in the settlement of the Eastern question. It may even be said that these dissensions, perhaps, would be felt by Russia all the more painfully should she withdraw from active and predominant participation in the destinies of the East.

And yet suddenly people begin to shout (and not only in Europe, but even many of our superior political minds) that should the Turks happen to expire as a state, Constantinople must be regenerated not otherwise than as an "international city," *i.e.*, as some kind of a half-way, free settlement, so as to avoid disputes concerning her. No more erroneous thought can be conceived.

First of all, because such an excellent spot of the terrestrial globe will simply not be permitted to become international, that is, nobody's; unfailingly and promptly, let's say, the British will intervene with their fleet, in the capacity of friends, specifically, in order to protect and guard this "internationality," but, in fact, for the purpose of taking possession of Constantinople for their benefit. And wherever they settle it is difficult to evict them thence —they are an adhesive people.

Moreover, the Greeks, Slavs and Mohammedans of Constantinople would call the English in, would clutch at them with both hands, and would not let them thence, the reason for it again being Russia: "They will protect us"—they would say—"against Russia, our liberatrix." And this would have been all right had they not perceived and understood what Englishmen, and Europe in general, are to them. Oh, even *now* they know better than anybody that no one in Europe, except Russia, cares anything about their happiness, *i.e.*, the happiness of the entire Christian community under the Mohammedans. That entire community knows perfectly well that were it possible to repeat the Bulgarian horrors of last summer (and this it would seem is quite possible) somehow silently and stealthily, the English would be the first in Europe to wish the repetition—be it even ten times—of these massacres, and not because of bloodthirstiness, not in the least: there the people are humane and enlightened, but because these slaughters, were they repeated ten times, would completely exterminate the Christian community, so thoroughly that there would be no one left on the Balkan Peninsula to engage in uprisings against the Turks. And herein is the essence of the matter: only the dear Turks would remain, and Turkish securities would at once go up on all European stock-exchanges, while Russia "with her ambition and aggressive plans" would have to withdraw deeper into her own domains, because of the absence of any one to protect.

The Christian community is perfectly cognizant that at present it may be expecting from Europe precisely this sort of sentiment. However, the situation would be quite different were "the sick man" finally to die, whether of his own accord or by Russia's sword. In this event Europe would promptly contract the fondest love for the regenerated peoples and would immediately rush "to save them from Russia."

It may be presumed that Europe would be the first to introduce the idea of "internationality" into their new organization. Europe will grasp the fact that over the corpse of "the sick man" confusion, dissension and antagonism would arise among the liberated peoples,—and this is precisely what she wants: a pretext for intervention, and most important of all—a pretext for inciting them against Russia which, no doubt, will not permit them to quarrel over the heritage of the sick man. And there would be no calumny which Europe would not launch against us. "It is because of the Russians that we haven't helped you against the Turks"—the English would then say to them. Alas, the peoples of the East are fully aware of this even now; and they know that "England will never participate in their liberation, and will never give her consent thereto, if such consent be deemed necessary, because she hates those Christians by reason of their spiritual tie with Russia. It is England's intention that Eastern Christians should start hating us as strongly as she herself hates us. . . ." (*Moscow Gazette, No. 63.*)

This is what these peoples know and what meanwhile they are silently memorizing, and this is what they have, of course, already charged to the future account of Russia. And yet we think that they adore us.

In the international city, aside from the English protectors, the Greeks—the original masters of the city—will nevertheless be the hosts. It may be presumed that the Greeks look upon the Slavs even with greater contempt than the Germans. However, inasmuch as the Slavs will be dreaded by the Greeks, contempt will be replaced by embitterment. Of course, they will not be in a position to wage war against each other, or to be declaring war on one another, at least, in a serious sense, because the protectors will not permit it. Well, but precisely in view of the impossibility of an open and honest scuffle, there will arise among them all sorts of other dissensions which, in the first place, will acquire an ecclesiastical character. This will be the start, since this would be the handiest way. And it is this that I meant to point out.

I am maintaining this because the program has already been set forth: the Bulgarians and Constantinople. From this standpoint the Greeks are in a strong position, and they understand it. And yet there can be nothing more dreadful in the future to the entire East, and also to Russia, than another church dissension which, alas, is so possible should Russia, even for one moment, withdraw her protection and rigid supervision.

Even though all this belongs to the future and is even nothing but conjecture, yet it would be unpardonable to overlook it even as a mere conjecture. Indeed, should we too desire the continuation of the Turkish rule and good health to "the sick man"? Is it conceivable that we too will come to this point? Is it not clear that were this sick man to expire, and—what is most important—were Russia even partly to withdraw her final and predominant influence upon the destinies of the East, were she to make this concession to Europe—it is more than probable that church unity of so many centuries would be rocked on the Balkan Peninsula and, maybe, still farther in the East. It can even be put this way: whether or not dissensions would ensue, but should the sick man die, it is very probable that *in any event* a great church *sobor* for the settlement of the newly regenerated Church would be unavoidable. Why has this to be anticipated? During these four centuries of persecution and oppression the representatives of the Eastern Church have always followed Russia's advice. However, should they tomorrow be liberated from the Turkish yoke, and, in addition, should Europe extend protection to them, they would forthwith adopt a different attitude toward Russia.

The moment Russia sided with the Slavs, the representatives of the Eastern Church, *i.e.*, principally, the Greeks, would probably declare to her that they have no further need of her or her advice. They would hasten to make such a declaration precisely because during four centuries they have been looking on Russia with arms folded in prayer. And Russia's situation would be virtually the most difficult one: those very Bulgarians would immediately start vociferating that a new, Eastern, Pope had ascended the throne at Constantinople, and—who knows?—maybe they would be right. In truth, international Constantinople could serve, even though temporarily, as a pedestal for the new Pope. In this event were Russia to back the Greeks, it would mean that she would be losing the Slavs; and should she come out in support of the Slavs, it would mean, perhaps, that she might be contracting most embarrassing and most serious church troubles.

It is clear that all this can be avoided only "in good time in advance" by Russia's firmness in the Eastern question and her undeviating adherence to the great traditions of our ancient, secular Russian policy. In this matter we must make no concessions to any kind of Europe and for no considerations whatsoever, since this cause is our life or death. Sooner or later, Constantinople must be ours, be it only for the avoidance of painful and embarrassing church dissensions which may so easily arise between the young and inexperienced peoples of the East, and which have been exemplified by the dispute—with so sad an outcome—between the Bulgarians and the ecumenic Patriarch.

Once we take possession of Constantinople nothing of the kind can occur. The peoples of the West who are so jealously watching Russia's every step, at this moment, do not know and suspect these as yet fanciful but all too plausible combinations. Should they even learn about them at this time, they would not understand them and would attach to them no special significance. However, subsequently, when it is too late, they will perfectly grasp these combinations and will attach significance to them.

The Russian people who conceive the Eastern question not otherwise than in the sense of the liberation of Orthodox Christianity, as a whole, and of the future grand unity of the Church, should they contrariwise, observe new dissensions and discord, would be painfully shocked, and perhaps any new solution of the matter would affect them and their whole mode of existence, particularly if at length it were to assume pre-eminently an ecclesiastical character. For this reason alone we cannot, under any circumstances, relinquish or weaken our secular participation in this great problem. Not the excellent port alone, not only the road leading to the seas and oceans, binds Russia so closely with the solution of the destinies of this fatal question, nor even the unification and regeneration of the Slavs. . . . Our task is deeper, immeasurably deeper. We, Russia, we are really necessary and unavoidable to Eastern Christianity *in toto*, to the whole future fate of Orthodoxy on earth, and to its unity. This was always conceived so by our people and their czars. . . .

Briefly, this dreadful Eastern question constitutes almost our whole future fate. Therein lie, as it were, all our tasks, and what is most important—our only exit into the plenitude of history. In this question is also our final conflict with Europe and our ultimate communion with her but only upon new, mighty and fertile foundations. Oh, how can Europe at this time grasp the fatal and vital importance to ourselves of the solution to this question?—In a word, no matter what may be the outcome of the present, perhaps quite indispensable diplomatic agreements and negotiations, nevertheless, sooner or later, *Constantinople must be ours*, let it be only in the future, in a century!

This, we Russians, all of us, must always and undeviatingly bear in mind. This is what I meant to state, particularly at the present European moment. . . .

CHAPTER II

1

"The Jewish Question"

OH, PLEASE don't think that I mean to raise "the Jewish question"! I wrote the title jestingly. To raise a question of such magnitude as the status of the Jew in Russia, and the status of Russia which among her sons has three million Jews—is beyond my power. The question exceeds my limits. Still, I can have a certain opinion of my own, and it now appears that some Jews begin to take interest in it. For some time I have been receiving letters from them in which they seriously and with bitterness have reproached me for the fact that I am attacking them, that "I hate the Yiddisher," that I hate him not for his vices, "not as an exploiter," but specifically as a race, *i.e.,* somewhat along the line that "Judas sold out Christ." This is being written by "educated" Jews, meaning, by such ones as (this I have noticed, but by no means do I generalize my remark, and this I am emphasizing in advance) always, as it were, endeavor to advise you that, because of their education, they long ago ceased to share "the prejudices" of their nation; that they do not comply with their religious rituals, like other petty Jews; that they deem this below the level of their enlightenment, and that, besides, they do not believe in God.

I shall observe, parenthetically, that to all those gentlemen from among the "top Jews" who are such staunch advocates of their nation, it is much too sinful to forget their forty-century-old Jehovah and to renounce him. And this is sinful not only because of national sentiment but likewise for other momentous reasons. And strangely: a Jew without God is somehow inconceivable; a Jew without God cannot be imagined. However, this is a vast theme, and for the time being we shall leave it aside.

The thing that surprises me most is how, on what grounds,

have I been classed as a hater of Jews as a people, as a nation?
To a certain extent I am permitted by these gentlemen themselves
to condemn the Jew as an exploiter and for some of his vices,—
but only ostensibly: in fact, it is difficult to find anything more
irritable and susceptible than the educated Jew, more touchy than
he, as a Jew. But, again, when and how did I declare hate against
the Jews as a people?—Since there never has been such a hatred
in my heart, and those Jews who are acquainted with me and have
dealt with me know it, from the very outset and before I say a
word, I withdraw from myself this accusation, once and forever,
so as not to make special mention of it later.

Am I not accused of hatred because sometimes I called the
Jew "Yiddisher"? But, in the first place, I did not think that this
is so abusive, and secondly, as far as I can remember, I have
always used the word "Yiddisher" in order to denote a certain idea:
"Yiddisher, Yiddishism, Yiddish reign," etc. This denotes a certain
conception, orientation, characteristic of the age. One may argue
about this idea, and disagree with it, but one shouldn't feel offended
by a word.

I shall quote certain passages from a long, and in many respects, beautiful letter, addressed to me by a highly educated Jew,
which aroused in me great interest. It is one of the most typical
accusations of my hatred of the Jew, as a people. It goes without
saying that the name of Mr. N. K., the author of this letter, is
kept strictly anonymous.

". . . But I intend to touch upon a subject which most decidedly I am unable to explain to myself: this is your hatred of
the 'Yiddisher' which is revealed virtually in every issue of your
Diary.

"I should like to know why are you protesting against the
Yiddisher, and not the exploiter in general? I, not less than you,
cannot tolerate the prejudices of my nation,—not little have I suffered from these—but I shall never concede that there dwells shameless exploitation in the blood of this nation.

"Is it possible that *you* are unable to lift yourself to the
comprehension of the fundamental law of any social life to the
effect that *all* citizens of a state, without any exception, if they are
paying all taxes required for the existence of the state, must enjoy
all rights and advantages of its existence, and that for the violators
of the law, the harmful members of the society, there must be one
and the same measure of punishment, common to all? . . . Why,
then, should all the Jews be restricted in their rights, and why
should special penal laws exist for them? In what manner is alien
exploitation (the Jews are nevertheless Russian subjects) by Ger-

mans, Englishmen, Greeks, of whom there is so great a number in Russia, better than Yiddish exploitation? In what way is the Russian Orthodox kulak, peasant-exploiter, inn-keeper, blood-sucker, who has propagated so profusely *all over* Russia, better than the one from among Yiddishers, who nevertheless is operating within a limited area? Why is this one better than the other? . . ."

[At this juncture my esteemed correspondent compares several notorious Russian kulaks with Jewish ones in the sense that the Russians are just as bad. But what does this prove? Indeed, we take no pride in our kulaks and we do not set them as examples for imitation, and on the contrary we agree wholeheartedly that both are no good.]

"I could propound to you such questions by the thousand.

"Meanwhile, speaking about the 'Yiddisher,' you include in this term the whole terribly destitute mass of the three-million Jewish population in Russia, of which at least 2,900,000 are engaged in a desperate struggle for existence, a mass which is morally purer not only than the other nationalities but also than the Russian people deified by you. Likewise, you have included in this term that considerable number of Jews with higher education who are distinguishing themselves in all fields of state life. Take, for instance . . ."

[Here there are again several names which, with the exception of that of Goldstein, I do not deem myself entitled to print, since some of them perhaps would be displeased to read that they are of Jewish origin.]

"Take, for example, Goldstein [who died heroically in Serbia for the Slavic idea] and those who labor for the good of society and of mankind. Your hate of the 'Yid' extends even to Disraeli . . . who, probably, knows not himself that his ancestors some time in the past were Spanish Jews, and who, of course, does not direct English conservative policy from the standpoint of a 'Yiddisher.'

"No, unfortunately, you know neither the Jewish *people* nor their life—neither their spirit nor, finally, their forty-century history. Unfortunately—because you are, at any rate, a sincere, absolutely sincere, man; yet, unconsciously you are causing harm to an enormous mass of destitute people, whereas influential 'Yids' who receive in their salons the potent ones of this world, naturally, are afraid of neither the press nor even the impotent wrath of the exploited. But enough has been said on this subject. Hardly will I sway you to my view, but I am very anxious that you should convince me."

Such are the excerpts. Before I answer anything (because I don't want to bear so grave an accusation) I shall call attention to the vehemence of the attack and the degree of touchiness. Positively, during the whole year of the publication of my *Diary* there has been no slur against the "Yiddisher" of such dimensions as would justify so strong an attack. Secondly, it should be also observed that my esteemed correspondent, having also touched in these few lines of his upon the Russian people, could not bear, could not refrain from adopting toward the poor Russian people a somewhat too haughty attitude. True, in Russia even Russians have not left a spot not bespat (Schedrin's expression), so it is all the more excusable for a Jew. However, in any event, this animus clearly shows how the Jews themselves look upon the Russians. Indeed, this was written by an educated and talented man (only I don't think that he is devoid of prejudices). What, then, should one be expecting from uneducated Jews, of whom there are so many, —what sentiments for the Russian? I am not saying this accusingly: all this is natural! I wish only to indicate that for the motives of our disagreement with the Jew, perhaps not only the Russian should be held responsible, and that, of course, these motives have accumulated on either side, and it is a question—on which side more.

Having noted the above, I shall say a few words in my defense, and generally, as to how I view this matter. And even though, as stated, this question is beyond my capacity, nevertheless I too can express at least something.

2

Pro-and-Con

True, it is very difficult to learn the forty-century-long history of a people such as the Jews; but, to start with, this much I know, that in the whole world there is certainly no other people who would be complaining as much about their lot, incessantly, after each step and word of theirs,—about their humiliation, their suffering, their martyrdom. One might think that it is not they who are reigning in Europe, who are directing there at least the stock-exchanges, and therefore politics, domestic affairs, the morality of the states. Let noble Goldstein be dying for the Slavic idea. Even so, if the Jewish idea in the world had not been so strong, maybe, that very "Slavic" question (of last year) would long ago have been settled in favor of the Slavs, and not of the Turks.

I am ready to believe that Lord Beaconsfield has, perhaps, forgotten about his descent—some time in the past—from Spanish Yiddishers (for sure, however, he hasn't forgotten); but that during last year he did "direct English conservative policy" *partly* from the standpoint of a Yid is, in my opinion, impossible to doubt. "Partly"—cannot but be admitted.

But let all this be merely verbalism on my part,—light tone and light words. I concede. Nevertheless, I am unable fully to believe in the screams of the Jews that they are so downtrodden, oppressed and humiliated. In my opinion, the Russian peasant, and generally, the Russian commoner, virtually bears heavier burdens than the Jew. In another letter my correspondent writes me:

"In the first place it is *necessary* to grant them [the Jews] all civil rights (think, up to now they are deprived of the most fundamental right—of free selection of the place of residence, which leads to a multitude of awful restrictions for the whole Jewish mass) as to all other alien nationalities in Russia, and only after that may it be demanded from them that they comply with their duties toward the state and the native population."

But Mr. Correspondent, you who write me in the same letter, on the next page, that you "are far more devoted to, and pity more, the toiling mass of the Russian people, than the Jewish mass" (which, to be sure, for a Jew, is too strongly expressed) you, too, should remember that at the time when the Jew "has been restricted in the free selection of the place of residence," twenty-three millions of "the Russian toiling mass" have been enduring serfdom which was, of course, more burdensome than "the selection of the place of residence." Now, did the Jews pity them then?—I don't think so: in the Western border region and in the South you will get a comprehensive answer to this question. Nay, at that time the Jews also vociferated about rights which the Russian people themselves did not have; they shouted and complained that they were downtrodden and martyrs, and that when they should be granted more rights, "then demand from us that we comply with the duties toward the state and the native population."

But then came the Liberator and liberated the native people. And who was the first to fall upon them as on a victim? Who preeminently took advantage of their vices? Who tied them with that sempiternal gold pursuit of theirs? By whom—whenever possible— were the abolished landowners promptly replaced, with the difference that the latter, even though they did strongly exploit men, nevertheless endeavored—perhaps in their own interest—not to ruin the peasants in order to prevent the exhaustion of labor, whereas the Jew is not concerned about the exhaustion of Russian labor: he grabs what's his, and off he goes.

I know that upon reading this, the Jews will forthwith start screaming that this is a lie; that this is a calumny; that I am lying; that I believe all this nonsense because I "do not know the forty-century-old history of these chaste angels who are incomparably purer morally not only than the other nationalities but also than the Russian people deified by me" (according to the words of my correspondent. See above).

But let, let them be morally purer than all the peoples of the world, nevertheless I have just read in the March issue of *The Messenger of Europe* a news item to the effect that in America, in the Southern States, they have already leaped *en masse* upon the millions of liberated Negroes, and have already taken a grip upon them in their, the Jews', own way, by means of their sempiternal "gold pursuit" and by taking advantage of the inexperience and vices of the exploited tribe. Imagine, when I read this, I immediately recalled that the same thing came to my mind five years ago, specifically, that the Negroes have now been liberated from the slave-owners, but that they will not last because the Jews, of whom there are so many in the world, will jump at this new little victim. This came to my mind, and I assure you that several times during this interim I was asking myself: "Well, why doesn't one hear anything about the Jews there; why do not newspapers write about them, because the Negroes are a treasure for the Jews; is it possible that they would miss it?" And at last my expectation came true, the newspapers have written it up,—I read it.

Now, some ten days ago I read in *The New Times* (No. 371) a most characteristic communication from Kovno to the effect that: "the Jews there have so assaulted the local Lithuanian population, that they almost ruined all of them with vodka, and only the Roman Catholic priests began to save the poor drunkards threatening them with the tortures of hell and organizing temperance societies." True, the enlightened correspondent strongly blushes on behalf of his population which still believes in its priests and in the tortures of hell, but he adds in this connection that following the example of the priests, enlightened local economists began to establish rural banks specifically with the object of saving the people from the Jew—the money lender, and also rural markets where "the destitute toiling mass" could buy articles of first necessity at real prices, and not at those set by the Jew.

Well, I have read all this, and I know that instantly people will start shouting that this proves nothing; that all this is caused by the fact that the Jews themselves are oppressed; that they are poor themselves; that all this is but a "struggle for existence"; that only a fool would fail to understand it, and that were the Jews not so destitute themselves, were they, contrariwise, to grow rich,— they would instantly reveal themselves in a most humane light so that the whole world would be astounded. However, it goes without saying that all those Negroes and Lithuanians are even poorer than the Jews who are squeezing the sap out of them, and yet, the former (only read the correspondence) loathe the kind of trade for which the Jew is so eager.

Secondly, it is not difficult to be humane and moral when one rolls in butter, but the moment "the struggle for existence" comes into play,—don't you dare reproach me. To my way of thinking, this is not a very angelic trait.

Third, of course, I am not setting forth these two news items from *The Messenger of Europe* and *The New Times* as capital and all-decisive facts. If one should start writing the history of this universal tribe, it would at once be possible to discover a hundred thousand of analogous and even more important facts, so that one or two additional facts would mean nothing in particular. However, it is curious in this connection that the moment you should require —say, in the course of an argument or in a minute of silent irresolution—information about the Jew and his doings,—don't go to public libraries; don't ransack old books or your own old notes; don't labor, don't search, don't exert your efforts, instead, without leaving your chair, stretch out your hand to any newspaper at random which happens to be near you, and look at the second or third page: unfailingly, you will find something about Jews, and unfailingly—that which interests you; unfailingly—that which is most characteristic, and unfailingly—one and the same thing, *i.e.*,—the same exploits!

Now, concede that this does mean something; it does indicate and reveal to you something, even though you be an absolute ignoramus in the forty-century-long history of this tribe. No question, I will be told that everybody is hatred-stricken, and therefore everybody is lying. Of course, it may happen that everyone to the last man is lying; but if this be so, there arises at once a new question: if everybody without exception is lying and hatred-stricken, whence did this hatred arise? Since this universal hatred does mean something; as Bielinsky exclaimed once: "indeed, the word *everybody* does mean something!"

"Free selection of the place of residence!" But is the "native" Russian absolutely free in the choice of the place of residence? Is it not true that also in the case of the Russian commoner, up to the present, the former restrictions in the complete freedom of the selection of the place of residence continue to persist,—those undesirable restrictions which are survivals of the times of serfdom and which have long been attracting the attention of the government? And as far as Jews are concerned, it is apparent to everybody that in the last twenty years their rights in the selection of the place of residence have been very considerably expanded. At least, they have appeared throughout Russia in places where they have not been seen before. However, the Jews keep complaining of hatred and restrictions.

Let it be conceded that I am not firm in my knowledge of the Jewish modes of living, but one thing I do know for sure, and I am ready to argue about it with anyone, namely, that among our common people there is no preconceived, *a priori*, blunt religious hatred of the Jew, something along the lines: "Judas sold out Christ." Even if one hears it from little children or drunken persons, nevertheless our people as a whole look upon the Jew, I repeat, without a preconceived hatred. I have been observing this for fifty years. I even happened to live among the people, in their very midst, in one and the same barracks, sleeping with them on the same cots. There there were several Jews, and no one *despised* them, no one shunned them or persecuted them. When they said their prayers (and Jews pray with screams, donning a special garment) nobody found this strange, no one hindered them or scoffed at them,—a fact which precisely was to be expected from such a coarse people—in your estimation— as the Russians. On the contrary, when beholding them, they used to say: "such is their religion, and thus they pray"; and would pass by calmly, almost approvingly.

And yet these same Jews in many respects shunned the Russians, they refused to take meals with them, looked upon them with haughtiness (and where?—in a prison!) and generally expressed squeamishness and aversion towards the Russian, towards the "native" people. The same is true in the case of soldiers' armories, and everywhere—all over Russia: make inquiries, ask if a Jew, as a Jew, as a Yiddisher, is being abused in armories because of his faith, his customs. Nowhere is he being abused, and that is also true of the people at large. On the contrary, I assure you that in armories, as elsewhere, the Russian commoner perceives and understands only too well (besides, the Jews themselves do not conceal it) that the Jew does not want to take meals with him, that he has an aversion toward him, seeking as much as possible to avoid him and segregate himself from him. And yet, instead of feeling hurt, the Russian commoner calmly and clearly says: "such is his religion; it is because of his faith that he does not take meals with me and shuns me" (*i.e.*, not because he is spiteful). And having comprehended this supreme cause, he wholeheartedly forgives the Jew.

However, at times, I was fancying: now, how would it be if in Russia there were not three million Jews, but three million Russians, and there were eighty million Jews,—well into what would they convert the Russians and how would they treat them? Would they permit them to acquire equal rights? Would they permit them to worship freely in their midst? Wouldn't they convert them into slaves? Worse than that: wouldn't they skin them altogether? Wouldn't they slaughter them to the last man, to the point of complete extermination, as they used to do with alien peoples in ancient times, during their ancient history?

Nay, I assure you that in the Russian people there is no preconceived hatred of the Jew, but perhaps there is a dislike of him, and especially in certain localities, maybe—a strong dislike. Oh, this cannot be avoided; this exists; but it arises not at all from the fact that he is a Jew, not because of some racial or religious hate, but it comes from other causes of which not the native people but the Jew himself is guilty.

3

STATUS IN STATU. FORTY CENTURIES OF EXISTENCE

Hatred, and besides one caused by prejudice—this is what the Jews are accusing the native population of. However, if the point concerning prejudices has been raised, what do you think: does the Jew have fewer prejudices against the Russian than the latter against the Jew? Hasn't he more of them?—I have given you examples of the attitude of the Russian common people toward the Jew. And here I have before me letters from Jews, and not from common ones, but from educated Jews. And so much hatred in these letters against "the native population"! And the main thing is: they write without realizing it themselves.

You see, in order to exist forty centuries on earth, *i.e.*, virtually the entire historical period of mankind, and besides, in such a close and unbroken unity; in order to lose so many times one's territory, one's political independence, laws, almost one's religion,—to lose, and again to unite each time, to regenerate *in the former idea*, though in a different guise, to create anew laws and almost religion—nay, such a viable people, such an extraordinarily strong and energetic people, such an unprecedented people in the world, could not have existed without *status in statu* which they have always and everywhere preserved at the time of their most dreadful, thousand, long dispersions and persecutions. Speaking of *status in statu*, I am by no means seeking to frame an accusation. Still, what is the meaning of this *status in statu?* What is its eternal, immutable idea? Wherein is the essence of this idea?

It would be too long and impossible to expound this in a brief article; besides, it would be impossible for the same reason that, despite the forty centuries, not all *times and seasons* have arrived, and mankind's last word on this great tribe is still to come. However, without fathoming the essence and depth of the subject, it is possible to outline, at least, certain symptoms of that *status in statu,*—be it only externally. These symptoms are: alienation and estrangement in the matter of religious dogma; the impossibility of fusion; belief that in the world there exists but one national entity—the Jew, while, even though other entities exist, nevertheless it should be presumed that they are, as it were, nonexistent. "Step out of the family of nations, and form your own entity, and thou shalt know that henceforth thou art the only one before God; exterminate the rest, or make slaves of them, or exploit them. Have faith in the conquest of the whole world; adhere to the belief that everything will submit to thee. Loathe strictly everything, and do not have intercourse with anyone in thy mode of living. And even when thou shalt lose the land, thy political individuality, even when thou shalt be dispersed all over the face of the earth, amidst all nations,—never mind, have faith in everything that has been promised thee, once and forever; believe that all this will come to pass, and meanwhile live, loathe, unite and exploit, and—wait, wait. . . ."

Such is the essence of that *status in statu,* and, in addition, there are, of course, inner and, perhaps, mysterious laws guarding this idea.

You say, gentlemen—educated Jews and opponents—that all this is certainly nonsense, and that even if there be a *status in statu* (*i.e.,* there has been, but at present, according to them, only the dimmest traces of it remain), it is solely because persecution has brought it about; religious persecution since the Middle Ages, and even earlier, has generated it, and that this *status in statu* came into existence merely from the instinct of self-preservation. However, if it continues, especially in Russia, it is because the Jew has not yet been given equal rights with the native population.

But this is how I feel: should the Jew be given equal rights, under no circumstance would he renounce his *status in statu.* Moreover, to attribute it to nothing but persecution and the instinct of self-preservation—is insufficient. Besides, there would not have been enough tenacity in store for self-preservation during forty centuries; the people would have grown weary of preserving themselves for so long a time. Even the strongest civilizations in the world have failed to survive half of the forty centuries, losing their political strength and racial countenance. Here it is not only self-preservation that constitutes the main cause, but a certain compelling and luring idea, something so universal and profound that on it, as stated above, mankind is perhaps still unable to utter its last word. That we are here dealing with something of a pre-eminently religious character—there can be no doubt. That their Providence, under the former, initial name of Jehovah, with his ideal and his covenant, continues to lead his people toward a firm goal—this much is clear. Besides, I repeat, it is impossible to conceive a Jew without God. Moreover, I do not believe in the existence of atheists even among the educated Jews: they all are of the same substance, and God only knows what the world has to expect from the educated Jews! Even in my childhood I have read and heard a legend about Jews to the effect that they are supposed to be undeviatingly awaiting the Messiah, all of them, both the lowest Yiddisher and the highest and most learned one —the philosopher and the cabalist—rabbi; that they all believe that the Messiah will again unite them in Jerusalem and will bring by his sword all nations to their feet; that this is the reason why the overwhelming majority of the Jews have a predilection but for one profession—the trade in gold, and at the utmost—for gold-smithery; and all this, so it is alleged, in order, that, when Messiah comes, they should not need to have a new fatherland and to be tied to the land of aliens in their, the Jews' possession, but to have everything converted into gold and jewels, so that it will be easier to carry them away when

> The ray of dawn begins to shine:
> Our flute, our tabor and the cymbal;
> Our riches and our holy symbol
> We will bring back to our old shrine,
> To our old home—to Palestine.

All this—I repeat—I heard as a legend, but I believe that the substance of the matter unfailingly is there, in the form of an instinctively irresistible tendency. But in order that such a substance of the matter might be preserved, it is, of course, necessary that the strictest *status in statu* be preserved. And it is being preserved. Thus, not only persecution was and is its cause, but another *idea*. . . .

If, however, among the Jews there exists in reality such an inner rigid organization as unites them into something solid and segregated, one almost may well give thought to the question whether equal rights with the native population should be granted to them.

It goes without saying that everything required by humaneness and justice, everything called for by compassion and the Christian law must be done for the Jews. But should they, in full armor of their organization and their segregation, their racial and religious detachment; in complete armor of their regulations and principles utterly opposed to that idea abiding by which the whole European world, at least up to the present time, has been developing;—should they demand complete equalization in *all possible* rights with the native population, wouldn't they then be granted something greater, something excessive, something sovereign compared with the native population?

At this juncture, the Jews will, of course point to other aliens: "now, these have been granted equal, or almost equal, rights, whereas the Jews have fewer rights than all other aliens; and this —because people are afraid of us, Jews: because we are supposedly more harmful than all other aliens. And yet in what sense is the Jew harmful? Even if there be bad qualities in the Jewish people, this is solely because these are being fostered by the Russian people themselves—by Russian ignorance, by the Russians' unfitness for independence, by their low economic development. The Russian people themselves demand a mediator, a leader, an economic warden in business, a creditor; they themselves are inviting him and surrendering themselves to him. On the contrary, look at things in Europe: there the nations are strong and independent in spirit; they are peoples with strong national sentiment, with a long-standing habit and skill for work, and there they are not afraid to grant all rights to the Jew! Does one hear in France anything about the harm resulting from *status in statu* of the local Jews?"

Apparently, this is a strong line of reasoning; however, in this connection there arises in one's mind a notion—in parentheses, namely: Thus, Jewry is thriving precisely there where the people are still ignorant, or not free, or economically backward. It is there that Jewry has a *champ libre!* And instead of raising, by its influence, the level of education, instead of increasing knowledge, generating economic fitness in the native population,—instead of this, the Jew, wherever he has settled, has still more humiliated and debauched the people; there humaneness was still more debased and the educational level fell still lower; there inescapable, inhuman misery, and with it despair, spread still more disgustingly. Ask the native population in our border regions: What is propelling the Jew—has been propelling him for centuries? You will receive a unanimous answer: *mercilessness*. "He has been prompted so many centuries only by pitilessness for us, only by the thirst for our sweat and blood."

And, in truth, the whole activity of the Jews in these border regions of ours consisted of rendering the native population as much as possible inescapably dependent on them, taking *advantage of the local laws*. They always managed to be on friendly terms with those upon whom the people were dependent, and, certainly, it is not for them to complain, at least in this respect, *about their restricted rights compared with the native population.* They have received from us enough of such rights over the native population. What, in the course of decades and centuries, has become of the Russian people where the Jews settled is attested by the history of our border regions. What, then?—Point to any other tribe from among Russian aliens which could rival the Jew by his dreadful influence in this connection! You will find no such tribe. In this respect the Jew preserves all his originality as compared with other Russian aliens, and, of course, the reason therefor is that *status in statu* of his, the spirit of which specifically breathes with pitilessness for everything that is not Jew, with disrespect for any people and tribe, for every human creature who is not a Jew. And what kind of justification is it that in Western Europe the nations did not permit themselves to be overwhelmed, and that thus the Russian people themselves are at fault? Because the Russian people in the border regions of Russia proved weaker than the European nations (and exclusively as a result of their secular cruel political circumstances), for this sole reason should they be completely crushed by exploitation, instead of being helped?

And if reference is made to Europe, to France, for example, —there too, hardly has their *status in statu* been harmless. Of course, there, Christianity and its idea have been lowered and are sinking not because of the Jew's fault, but through their own fault; nevertheless, it is impossible not to note also in Europe the great triumph of Jewry which has replaced many former ideas with its own.

Oh, it goes without saying that man always, at all times, has been worshipping materialism and has been inclined to perceive and understand liberty only in the sense of making his life secure through money hoarded by the exertion of every effort and accumulated by all possible means. However, at no time in the past have these tendencies been raised so cynically and so obviously to the level of a sublime principle as in our Nineteenth Century. "Everybody for himself, and only for himself, and every intercourse with man solely for one's self"—such is the ethical tenet of the majority of present-day people,[1] even not bad people, but, on the contrary, laboring people who neither murder nor steal. And mercilessness for the lower masses, the decline of brotherhood, exploitation of the poor by the rich,—oh, of course, all this existed

[1] The fundamental idea of the bourgeoisie which, at the end of the last century, took the place of the former concept of a world order,—an idea which has become the focal idea of the present century throughout the whole European world.

also before and always; however, it had not been raised to the level of supreme truth and of science—it had been condemned by Christianity, whereas at present, on the contrary, it is being regarded as virtue.

Thus, it is not for nothing that over there the Jews are reigning everywhere over stock-exchanges; it is not for nothing that they control capital, that they are the masters of credit, and it is not for nothing—I repeat—that they are also the masters of international politics, and what is going to happen in the future is known to the Jews themselves: their reign, their complete reign is approaching! We are approaching the complete triumph of ideas before which sentiments of humanity, thirst for truth, Christian and national feelings, and even those of national dignity, must bow. On the contrary, we are approaching materialism, a blind, carnivorous craving for personal material welfare, a craving for personal accumulation of money by any means—this is all that has been proclaimed as the supreme aim, as the reasonable thing, as liberty, in lieu of the Christian idea of salvation only through the closest moral and brotherly fellowship of men.

People will laugh and say that this is not all brought about by the Jews. Of course, not only by them, but if the Jews have completely triumphed and thriven in Europe precisely at the time when these new principles have triumphed there to the point of having been raised to the level of a moral principle, it is impossible not to infer that the Jews, too, have contributed their influence to this condition. Our opponents point out that, on the contrary, the Jews are poor, poor even everywhere, especially in Russia; that only the very summit of the Jews is rich—bankers and kings of stock-exchanges—while the rest, virtually nine-tenths of the Jews, are literally beggars, running about for a piece of bread, offering commissions and anxiously looking for an opportunity to snatch somewhere a penny for bread. Yes, this seems to be so, but what does this signify? Does it not specifically mean that in the very toil of the Jews (*i.e.*, at least, their overwhelming majority), in their very exploitation there is something wrong, abnormal, something unnatural carrying in itself retribution. The Jew is offering his interposition, he is trading in another man's labor. Capital is accumulated labor; the Jew loves to trade in somebody else's labor! But, temporarily, this changes nothing. As against this, the summit of the Jews is assuming stronger and firmer power over mankind seeking to convey to it its image and substance. Jews keep vociferating that among them, too, there are good people. Oh, God! Is this the point?—Besides, we are speaking not about *good* or bad people. And aren't there good people among those? Wasn't the late James Rothschild of Paris a good man?—We are speaking about the whole and its idea; we are speaking about *Judaism* and the *Jewish idea* which is clasping the whole world instead of Christianity which "did not succeed." . . .

4

But Long Live Brotherhood

But what am I talking about and what for? Or am I an enemy of the Jews? Indeed, is it true, as a noble and educated Jewish girl writes me (of this I have no doubt—this can be perceived from the letter, from the ardent sentiments expressed in this letter), is it true that I am—to use her words—an enemy of this "unfortunate" tribe which I am "so cruelly attacking on every opportune occasion." "Your contempt for the Jewish tribe which 'thinks about nothing except itself,' etc., is obvious." Nay, I protest against this obviousness, and besides, I deny the fact itself. On the contrary, I am saying and writing that "everything required by humaneness and justice, everything called for by compassion and the Christian law,—all this must be done for the Jews." These words were written by me above, but now I will add to them that despite all considerations already set forth by me, I am decidedly favoring full extension of Jewish rights in formal legislation, and, if possible, fullest equality with the native population (N. B., although, perhaps, in certain cases, even now they have more rights, or—to put it better—*more possibilities of exercising them* than the native population itself).

Of course, the following fantasy, for instance, comes to my mind: "Now, what if somehow, for some reason, our rural commune should disintegrate, that commune which is protecting our poor native peasant against so many ills; what if, straightway, the Jew, and his whole kehillah should fall upon that liberated peasant,—so inexperienced, so incapable of resisting temptation, and who up to this time has been guarded precisely by the commune?—Why, of course: instantly, this would be his end; his entire property, his whole strength, the very next day, would come under the power of the Jew, and there would ensue such an era as could be compared not only with the era of serfdom but even with that of the Tartar yoke."

Despite all the "fantasies" and everything I have written above, however, I favor full and complete equalization of rights because such is Christ's law, such is the Christian principle. But if so, what was the point of writing so many pages, and what did I intend to express if I am so *contradicting* myself?—Specifically, the fact that I am not contradicting myself, and that from the

Russian native side I see no difficulties in extending Jewish rights; I do, however, assert that these obstacles are incomparably greater on the part of the Jews than on the part of the Russians, and that if up to the present the thing which one wishes wholeheartedly has not come to pass, the blame therefor is infinitely less on the Russian than on the Jew himself. Similarly what I was telling about the common Jew who refuses to maintain intercourse and share his meals with the Russians who were not angry with him, who did not retaliate but, on the contrary, at once grasped the situation and forgave him, saying: "this is because such is his religion,"—similarly this we often perceive in the intelligent Jew—a boundless and haughty prejudice against the Russian.

Oh, they do shout that they are fond of the Russian people; one of them even wrote me that he was sorry that the Russian people were devoid of religion and understood nothing in their Christianity. This is too strongly put for a Jew, and there merely arises this question: Does this highly educated Jew himself understand anything about Christianity?—But self-conceit and haughtiness are qualities of the Jewish character, which to us Russians, is very painful. Who, as between the two of us—the Russian or the Jew—is more incapable of understanding the other?—I swear, I would rather exonerate the Russian: at least, he has no (positively no) religious hatred of the Jew. And who has more prejudices of other kinds? Now, the Jews keep vociferating that they have been oppressed and persecuted for so many centuries, that they are being oppressed and persecuted at present, and that this much, at least, should be taken into account by the Russian when analyzing the Jewish character. All right, we do take this into account, and this we can prove: among the educated strata of the Russian people on more than one occasion voices have been raised in favor of the Jews. Well, what about the Jews?—Did they, and do they, take into account, when blaming, and complaining against, the Russians, all the oppression and persecution which the Russian people themselves have endured? Is it possible to maintain that the Russian people, "in the course of their history" have endured fewer misfortunes and ills than the Jews wheresoever it may have been? And is it possible to assert that the Jew very frequently has not allied himself with the persecutors of the Russian people, taking a lease on them from their oppressors, and becoming himself their persecutor?—Indeed, all this did happen, it did exist; indeed, this is history, an historical fact. But we have never heard that the Jewish people repented for this, and yet they keep accusing the Russian people of the fact that they do not love the Jews enough.

Still, "let it come to pass, let it come to pass!" Let there be full moral unity of the tribes and no discrimination in their rights! And for this purpose, in the first place, I implore my opponents and my Jewish correspondents to be more indulgent and just toward us Russians. If their haughtiness, their perpetual "sad squeamishness" toward the Russian race is merely a prejudice, an "historical excrescence," *and is not concealed in some much deeper mysteries of their law and organization,*—let all this be dispelled as soon as possible, and let us come together in one spirit, in complete brotherhood, for mutual assistance and for the great cause of serving our land, our state and our fatherland! Let the mutual accusations be mollified; let the customary exaggeration of these accusations, hindering the clear understanding of things, disappear! One can pledge for the Russian people: oh, they will accept the Jew in the fullest brotherhood, despite the difference in religion— and with perfect respect for the historical fact of such a difference. Nevertheless, for complete brotherhood—*brotherhood on the part of both sides is needed.* Let the Jew also show at least some brotherly feeling for the Russian people so as to encourage them. I know that even at present there are plenty of men among the Jewish people who are seeking and craving for the elimination of the mis-understandings, men who, besides, are humane, and I shall not keep silent on this fact so as to conceal the truth. It is precisely in order that these useful and humane persons should not grow despondent and low-spirited, and with a view to weakening, at least somewhat, their prejudices, thereby facilitating their first steps, that I should favor a full extension of rights to the Jewish race, at least, as far as possible, specifically, in so far as the Jewish people themselves prove their ability to accept and make use of these rights without detriment to the native population. It would even be possible to make an advance concession, to make more steps forward on the part of the Russian side. The only question is: to what extent would these new, good Jews succeed and how far are they themselves adapted to the new and beautiful cause of genuine brotherly communion with men who are alien to them by religion and blood?

CHAPTER III

1

"The Funeral of the 'Universal Man' "

IN THIS March issue of my *Diary* I meant to discuss many things. And now again, somehow, it so happened that the things about which I had intended to say but a few words absorbed the entire space. And how many themes there are which all the year I have been planning to dwell upon, and still I am unable to come to them. Indeed, about certain matters it would be necessary to say much, and inasmuch as it develops that much cannot be told, one does not embark upon the discussion of the subject in question.

This time, leaving aside these "important" topics, I meant to say, in passing, at least a few words on art. I have seen Rossi in *Hamlet,* and I came to the conclusion that, instead of Hamlet, I saw Mr. Rossi. But it is better not to start talking if I do not intend to say everything. I wanted also to discuss (a little) Semi-radsky's picture, but most of all I intended to interject a few words on idealism and realism in art, on Repin and Mr. Raphael—but I see that all these will have to be postponed until a more opportune time.

Furthermore it was my intention to write—but this somewhat more elaborately—about some letters, particularly anonymous, which I have been receiving during the whole period of the publication of the *Diary.* Generally speaking, I am not in a position to answer all letters which I am receiving, especially the anonymous ones, and yet, during these eighteen months I have derived from this correspondence (on our common themes) several observations which, at least in my opinion, are noteworthy: in any event, it becomes possible to make several special notes, based on experience, concerning our present-day Russian intellectual mood—the things in which our not idle minds are interested and toward which they are bent, and who exactly are these not idle minds. In this connection curious traits may be recorded representative of age, sex, social status and even of this or that locality of Russia.

I believe that some space should be devoted in one of the future issues of the *Diary,* for instance, to anonymous letters and their characteristics; in my opinion this wouldn't be too boring since these writings reflect variety of every kind. Of course, not everything—perhaps, not even the most curious—can be told and recorded. For this reason,—and not knowing whether I can manage to cope with this theme—I hesitate to embark upon it.

However, at this time I want to refer to a letter, not an anonymous one, from Miss L., a very young Jewish girl whom I know well and with whom I made my acquaintance in Petersburg. She writes me from the city of M. Almost never did I converse with esteemed Miss L. on the subject of "the Jewish question," in spite of the fact that she seems to be one of those strict and serious-minded Jewesses. I see that her letter strangely fits into the whole chapter on the Jews which I have just finished writing. It might be too much to dwell again on the same subject, but this is a different theme, or even if it is the same theme, nevertheless it reveals the opposite aspect of the question, and even, as it were, a hint at its solution.

Let Miss L. magnanimously forgive me for taking the liberty of quoting here in her own words that part of her letter in which she describes the funeral of Dr. Hindenburg in the city of M., and which contains these most sincere and touchingly truthful lines written under the first impression of what she has seen. I did not wish to conceal the fact that this was written by a Jewess, and that these sentiments are those of a Jewess. . . .

"I am writing this under the fresh impression of a funeral. It was the funeral of *Dr. Hindenburg,* aged eighty-four. Because he was a Protestant, his body was first taken to a Protestant church, and only after that—to the cemetery. Never did I see at a funeral such sympathy, such warm tears; never did I hear words which sprang so spontaneously from the soul. . . . He died in such poverty that there was no money to take care of his burial expenses.

"He has been practicing in M. for fifty-eight years and how much good he did during that time. If you only knew, Fedor Mikhailovich, what a man this was! He was a doctor and an obstetrician; his name will live here in posterity; legends about him are already being told. All the common people called him 'father,' they loved and adored him, and only when he died did they comprehend what they have lost in this man. While his body lay in the coffin (in the church), I think there wasn't a single person who did not come up to weep over him and to kiss his feet, particularly poor Jewesses whom he has helped so much; they wept and prayed that he be taken straight to Paradise. Today our former cook, an awfully poor woman, called on us, and she said that when her last child was born he, seeing that there was no food in her room, gave her thirty kopecks—to cook soup, and thereafter every day he came to see her leaving twenty kopecks for her; and when she began to recover, he sent her two partridges. Also, once having been called to a dreadfully poor woman in childbed (and such were the women who used to call him), he, seeing that there was no cloth in which the baby could be wrapped, took off his upper shirt and handkerchief (he always wore a handkerchief on his head), tore them up and gave them to the woman.

"He also cured a poor Jew, a wood-cutter; after that his wife and then her children fell sick. Every God's day, twice a day he called on them, and when he had put them all on their feet, he asked the Jew: 'How are you going to pay me?' The Jew said that he had absolutely nothing, except a she-goat which he would sell that day. This he did; he sold the goat for four rubles, and brought the money to the doctor who, through his man-servant, gave twelve rubles, in addition to the four, ordered him to buy a cow, and meanwhile he told the wood-cutter to go home. An hour later the cow was brought to the latter, and he was informed that the doctor found that goat-milk was not good for them.

"Thus he lived all his life. On some occasions, he would leave with the poor as much as thirty or forty rubles; he also gave money to the poor peasant women in villages.

"But he was buried like a saint. All the poor people closed their stores and ran after the coffin. It is a custom among Jews that at funerals little boys sing psalms, but it is forbidden to sing them when a person of non-Jewish faith is being buried. In this case, however, at the funeral procession boys marched before the coffin and sang these psalms. In all synagogues prayers were said for his soul, and bells in *all* churches pealed during the procession. There was a band of military music, and Jewish musicians called on the son of the deceased and begged—as for an honor—to be permitted to play during the procession. All the poor people gave five or ten kopecks, while the rich Jews contributed much, and a gorgeous, enormous wreath of fresh flowers was ordered, with white and black ribbons at its sides on which in gold lettering his principal services were recorded, for instance, the foundation of a hospital, etc. I was unable to decipher what was written there, and besides, is it possible to enumerate all his merits?

"At his grave orations were delivered by a pastor and a rabbi. Both wept, and he lay there in his old, worn-out uniform; his head was tied with an old handkerchief—that dear head of his, and it seemed that he was merely sleeping so fresh was the color of his face. . . ."

2

An Isolated Case

"An isolated case"—people might say. Well, gentlemen, once more I plead guilty: again I perceive in an isolated case almost the beginning of the solution of the whole question . . . that same "Jewish question" with which I have entitled the second chapter of the *Diary*. By the way, why did I call the little old doctor a "universal man"? He was rather a common man, and not a "universal man." This city of M. is a big provincial town in the Western region; it has a large Jewish population; there are also Germans,

Russians, of course, Poles, Lithuanians; and all these nationalities have recognized the righteous old man as their own. He himself was a Protestant and specifically a German, fully a German: the way he bought the cow and sent her to the poor Jew—this is a typically German *"Witz."* First, he baffled him: "How are you going to pay me?" And it stands to reason that when the poor fellow was selling his last goat in order to pay his "benefactor," he did not repine in the least; on the contrary, in his soul he was bitterly sorry that the goat was worth only four rubles, while "the poor old man laboring for all the poor folks has also got to live, and what is four rubles for all the favors he has bestowed upon the family?" Well, the little old man was no fool; he smiled, and his heart said: "Now, I'll show him, the poor fellow, our German *Witz!*" And how heartily he must have laughed to himself when the cow was taken to the Jew, and he might have spent that night in a miserable shanty of some poor Jewess in childbed. And it would have been nice for the eighty-year-old man to get a good night's sleep, to give his old bones a little rest.

Were I a painter, I would have painted this "genre," that night at the Jewess' childbed. I am awfully fond of realism in art, but in the pictures of some of our modern realists *there is no moral center,* as a mighty poet and a refined artist expressed himself the other day, conversing with me about Semiradsky's canvas. I believe that here, in the subject suggested by me for the "genre" there would be such a center. And for the artist it would be a gorgeous subject. First, the ideal, impossible, fetid misery of a poor Jewish shanty. Here much humor could be expressed and in a most opportune sense: humor is wit of a profound feeling, and I like this definition very much. With a refined feeling and intellect the artist may achieve much by the mere reshuffling of the roles of all these miserable household articles in a poor hut, and by this *amusing* reshuffle he can at once touch your heart. Besides, light could be made interesting: on a warped table a greasy guttered candle is burning out, while through the hoary tiny window, covered with ice, glimmers the dawn of another difficult day for poor folks. Women subject to painful accouchement often bring forth the child at dawn: all night long they suffer great pains, and in the early morning they deliver the child. Presently, the tired little old man, turning for a moment from the mother, takes hold of the child; there is nothing to swathe him with; there is even no duster (gentlemen, I swear that such misery exists; it does exist, it's pure realism, realism reaching the level of the fantastic). And the righteous old man takes off his worn-out uniform, then he also removes from his shoulders his shirt and tears it up for swaddles. The expression of his face is stern and concentrated. The poor newborn tiny Jewish baby squirms before him on the bed; a Christian takes the little Jew into his hands and wraps him with a shirt from his shoulders.

Gentlemen, this is the solution to the Jewish question: the eighty-year-old naked torso of the doctor, shivering from morning dampness, may assume a prominent place in the picture, not to speak of the face of the old man and that of the exhausted young woman in childbed looking at her new-born, and the doctor knows it: "This poor little Yiddisher will grow up, and, perhaps, he himself will take his shirt off his shoulders and, remembering the story of his birth, will give it to a Christian"—with naïve and noble faith ponders the old man. Will this come to pass?—Most probably not. However, this may come to pass, and there is nothing better on earth than to believe that *this* may and will come to pass. And as for the doctor, he has the right so to believe since in his case it has already materialized. "I did it, and someone else will do it. In what sense am I better than another?"—he encourages himself.

The tired old Jewess, the mother of the woman in childbed, in rags, busies herself at the stove. The Jew, who has been out to fetch a bundle of chips, opens the door of the hut, and chilly vapors, like a cloud, for an instant, break into the room. On the floor, on a felt bedding, two little Jewish boys are sound asleep. In a word, the *mise-en-scène* could be worked out very well. Even the thirty kopecks in copper on the table which the doctor has left for the soup of the woman in childbed might constitute a detail —a small copper pile of three-kopecks coins, methodically put together, and by no means tossed hither and thither. Even mother-of-pearl could be delineated, just as in Semiradsky's picture in which a piece of mother-of-pearl is wonderfully painted: indeed, sometimes doctors are given pretty little presents (so as not to pay much in cash),—and the doctor's cigar case made of mother-of-pearl lies there, next to the copper heap. Yes, it's all right, the picture would come out with a "moral center." I suggest that it be painted.

Isolated case! Some two years ago it has been reported that somewhere (I have forgotten where) in the south of Russia, a certain doctor who on a hot morning had just come out of a bathing house refreshed and invigorated, and who was anxious to go home as quickly as possible for a cup of coffee, refused to give assistance to a drowned man who had been taken out of the water nearby, despite the fact that a crowd of people urged him to do so. I believe he was prosecuted for this. And yet, perhaps, he was an educated man with new ideas, a progressive, but one who "reasonably" demanded new general laws and rights for everybody, neglecting isolated cases. He might even have believed that isolated cases are rather harmful because they postpone the general solution to the problem, and that as far as these single cases are concerned, the principle "the worse—the better" should be in force. However, general rights cannot very well be put into effect in the absence of isolated cases.

The common man, though he may have constituted an isolated case, succeeded in uniting at his grave a whole town. The Russian peasant women and the poor Jewesses kissed his feet, crowding around him and weeping all together. Fifty-eight years of service to humanity in this town; fifty-eight years of unceasing love, united everybody, at least once, at his coffin in common ecstasy and tears. The population of the whole town turned out at his funeral; the bells of *all* the churches were pealing; prayers were sung in all languages. The pastor in tears delivered his oration over the open grave. The rabbi, standing by, waited for the pastor to finish his eulogy, and then he made his speech shedding tears, in turn. Indeed, at this moment this very "Jewish question" has been almost solved! Since the pastor and the rabbi became united in common love; they almost embraced each other at this grave in the presence of Christians and Jews. What of it, if, after parting, each one embarked upon his old prejudices: the drop grinds the stone, and it is these "common people" who are conquering the world by uniting it. Prejudices will grow dimmer after every isolated case and, finally, will disappear.

Legends will survive the little old man, writes Miss L., also a Jewess, one who also has wept over that "dear head" of the humanitarian. And legends—why, they are the first step toward work, this live reminiscence and continual reminder about these "conquerors of the world" to whom the future of the world belongs. And once you believe that they are the conquerors and that "they shall inherit the earth," you are almost united in everything.

All this is very simple. It seems, however, that one thing is difficult: to become convinced that without these units the sum total can never be arrived at; everything will fall apart, but these will unite everything. These suggest the thought; they inspire us with faith; they constitute a living example and, therefore, a proof. And it is not at all necessary to wait until everybody becomes as good as they, or a great many: only very few of such men are needed to save the world—thus strong they are. And if so, how can one fail to hope?

To Our Correspondents

Novocherkassk. U. G. Please send the article on Stundism.

* * *

Mrs. N. N. is requested to proceed with the fulfillment of her promise to send information on events in the life of the peasants and on the Zemstvo work in her region.

* * *

This time we apologize to all those who have sent advertisements about their periodicals for publication in the *Diary:* owing to the lack of space we were unable to fill their orders.

APRIL

CHAPTER I

1

War. We Are Stronger than the Rest

"WAR! WAR has been declared!"—people were exclaiming in Russia two weeks ago. "Will there be war?"—others were asking. "It has been declared, declared!"—people replied to them. "Yes; declared, but will there be war?"—they kept asking. . . .

Indeed, such questions did arise; perhaps they are still being asked. And it was not only because of long diplomatic procrastination that people have utterly lost their faith; here there was something different—the instinct. Everybody feels that something final has begun; that some kind of an end of something that has been in the past is nearing,—of some long, protracted past, and that a step is made in the direction of something altogether new which splits the past into two, which regenerates and resurrects it for a new life . . . and that this step is being made by Russia! Precisely herein is the incredulity of the "wise" fellows. There is instinctive presentiment but disbelief persists: "Russia! But how can she? How does she dare? Is she ready? Is she ready inwardly, morally—not only materially? . . . Over there is Europe; easy to say—Europe! While Russia . . . What is Russia? And such a step!"

However, the people believe that they are ready for this regenerating and great step. It is the people themselves led by the Czar who have risen for war. When the Czar's word had sounded, the people poured into churches, and thus it was all over Russia. When the Czar's manifesto was being read, the people were crossing themselves and they all *congratulated* one another upon the declaration of war. We saw this with our own eyes, we heard it, even here, in Petersburg. And again the same things, the same facts arose as last year. Peasants in volostis are making, to the limit of their means, money contributions; they give carts with horses. And suddenly, these thousands of men, as one man, began to exclaim: "What do those donations and those carts mean! Everyone of us will go to war!"

Here, in Petersburg, we have donors for wounded and sick soldiers; they give as much as several thousand rubles each, and they insist that their gifts be listed as *anonymous*. Such instances are very numerous; there will be tens of thousands of similar cases, and they will surprise no one. They merely signify that the people have risen for the truth, for a sacred cause, that they, as a whole, have risen for the sake of war and that they mean war.

Oh, the wiseacres will deny even these facts as they did those of last year; the wiseacres, even as of late, continue to ridicule the people although their voices have noticeably abated. Whence do they derive so much self-reliance? Why do they laugh? Precisely because they still consider themselves a power without which nothing can be done. And yet their power is coming to an end. They are nearing a terrible debacle, and when it breaks out they too will start speaking a different language, but then everybody will perceive that they are not muttering their own words but merely echoing somebody else's voice; then people will turn away from them and will hopefully turn toward the Czar and his people.

We ourselves need this war; not merely because our "Slavic brethren" have been oppressed by the Turks. We are also rising for our own salvation. The war will clear the air which we breathe and in which we have been suffocating, closeted in spiritual narrowness and stricken with impotence of decay. The wiseacres are shouting that we are perishing from our own domestic disorganization, and that, for this reason, not war but lasting peace should be sought so that we may be transformed from beasts and blockheads into human beings, so that we may learn order, honesty and honor:—"then go ahead and help your Slavic brethren"—thus they wind up their song in accordant chorus.

In this connection it would be curious to know how they conceive that process by means of which they expect to improve. And how can they acquire honor by means of flagrant dishonor? Finally, it would be curious to find out how and by what means they would vindicate their severance from the universal and ubiquitous popular sentiment?—Yes, the contention seems justified that truth can be acquired only through martyrdom. Millions of men are moving and suffering and are passing away without leaving a trace, as it were, predestined never to learn the truth. They are living by somebody else's ideas, seeking ready-made words and examples, and clinging to causes suggested from without. They are shouting that they are being backed up by authorities, by Europe. They are hissing at those who are not in accord with them, who despise lackeyism of thought and who believe in their own and in their people's independence. In fact these masses of vociferating men are predestined to constitute an inert means for enabling but scattered individuals in their midst to approach the truth, though slightly, or, at least, to get a presentiment of it. It is these individuals who lead the masses, who dominate the movement, conceiving the idea and bequeathing it to these tossing multitudes of human beings. We also have had such individuals. Some of us—even many—already understand them. Yet, the wiseacres continue to laugh and still believe that they are a great power. "They'll take a walk and come back" —they say, referring to our troops which have crossed the border; they speak so even aloud. "There will be no war. War! How can we conduct a war!—This is merely a promenade and manœuvres at the cost of hundreds of millions for the purpose of upholding honor." Such is their intimate view of the affair. At that—is it only an intimate view?

But even if it could so happen that we should be beaten, or though after beating the enemy, under pressure of circumstances, we should, nevertheless, have to make a trifling peace,—oh, then, of course, the wiseacres would triumph. And what hissing, rows and cynicism would again ensue for several years, what a bacchanalia of self-contempt, blows on the face and self-provocation— and this not for inspiring resurrection and vigor, but precisely for the sake of the triumph of their own dishonor, faithlessness and impotence! And the new nihilism, just as the former one, would begin with the negation of the Russian people and their independence. And the main thing is that it would acquire so much strength, it would become so fortified that it would unquestionably insult, even aloud, Russia's sacred things. And youths would again be spitting upon their families and homes; again they would start running away from their old people repeating over and over the mechanically learned old boring words about European greatness, and about our duty to be as impersonal as possible. And what is most important— the old song, old words, and nothing new for a long time!

Nay, we need war and victory. With war and victory the new word will be uttered, and a new life will begin—not merely, as heretofore, deadening chit-chat,—why, gentlemen,—not only as heretofore, as we have it now!

But we must be ready for everything, and even if the worst, the impossibly worst, outcome of the war, which has begun now, be supposed, much bad experience as we may have to endure; much as we may have to suffer from that old grief with which we are bored to death,—nevertheless the colossus is not going to be undermined, and sooner or later he will take his own. This is not merely a hope, but a full certitude, and in the impossibility of undermining the colossus is our whole strength in the face of Europe, where virtually everybody is afraid that their old edifice will be undermined and the ceilings will crash upon them.

This colossus is our people. And the beginning of this present *popular* war as well as all recent facts preceding it have graphically demonstrated, to those who know how to behold things, the integrity and freshness of our people and the extent to which they remained immune to that decay which has putrefied our sages.

And what service they have rendered to us in Europe! Only recently they have been vociferating to the whole world that we were poor and negligible; scoffingly they have been assuring everybody that we had no such thing as popular spirit since there was no *people,* and that the people and their spirit have been invented by the fantasies of the home-baked Moscow dreamers; that eighty million Russian peasants were merely inert, drunken taxation units; that there was no unity between the Czar and the people; that this was only text-book stuff; that, on the contrary, everything was undermined and gnawed through by nihilism; that our soldiers would throw down their rifles and would start running as so many sheep; that we had neither cartridges nor provisions, and finally, that we ourselves perceived that we have been bluffing, that we have gone too far, and that we exerted all our efforts to find a pretext for a retreat without getting most ignominious blows on our face— which "even we were unable to endure," and that we were praying that Europe might invent such a pretext for us.

This is what our wiseacres have been swearing to, and one is almost unable to be angry with them, since such are their genuine views and conceptions. And in truth, in many a thing we are poor and pitiful. Yes, it is true: there is so much that is bad in Russia that a wiseacre, particularly if he is *our* "wiseacre," could not "betray" himself and could not help but exclaim: "That's the end of Russia, and there is nothing to regret!" Well, these familiar ideas of our wiseacres have spread throughout Europe, especially through European correspondents who have invaded Russia on the eve of the war in order to investigate us on the spot, to inspect

us with their European eyes, and to estimate our strength with
their European gauges. And it goes without saying that they have
been listening only to our "wise and sensible" ones. They have all
overlooked the people's strength, the people's spirit, and all over
Europe the news has spread that Russia was perishing, that Russia
was nothing at all, that she has been nothing, that she is nothing
and will be reduced to nothing.

But the hearts of our traditional enemies and haters whom
for two centuries we have been vexing in Europe began to quiver
—the hearts of many thousands of European Jews and of the millions of "Christians" Judaizing in accord with them, the heart of
Beaconsfield—when he was told that Russia would endure everything, including a most shameful blow in the face, but would not
resort to war—such was, so to speak, her "peaceableness." But having made them all blind, God saved us: too firmly were they convinced of Russia's ruin and nothingness. But they did overlook the
cardinal thing. They have overlooked the Russian people as a whole,
as a living force, and the colossal fact—the union of the Czar with
his people! *Only this is* what they have overlooked!

Besides, they were utterly unable to understand and believe
the fact that our Czar was really peaceable and that he, in truth,
had such compassion: they thought that this was mere "politics."
They see nothing even at present: they are clamoring that it is
only manifest that "patriotism has suddenly arisen in our midst."
"Is this patriotism?"—they ask. "Is this Czar's communion with
the people for the sake of a great cause—is it *only* patriotism?"
Our principal strength is precisely in the fact that they do not
understand Russia at all—they understand nothing about Russia!
They do not know that nothing in the world can conquer us; that
we may, perhaps, be losing battles, but that nevertheless we shall
remain invincible precisely because of the unity of our popular
spirit, and by reason of the people's consciousness; that we are
not France, which is all in Paris; that we are not Europe, which
is altogether dependent upon the stock-exchanges of her bourgeoisie
and the "tranquillity" of her proletarians which is being purchased
—and this only for one hour—with the last resorts of their local
governments. They do not comprehend and know that, if it be our
will, neither the Jews of all Europe nor the millions of their gold
—not even the millions of their armies, can conquer us; that if it
be our will, it is impossible to compel us to do something we do
not wish, and that there is no such power on earth which could
compel us.

The only trouble is that these words will be laughed at not
only in Europe, but at home, too, and not only by our wise and

sensible ones, but even by genuine Russians of our educated strata —to such an extent we do not understand ourselves and our native strength which, thank God, has not yet been broken.

These good men fail to understand that in our immense and most peculiar land, which does not resemble Europe, even war tactics (a thing so common!) may be quite different from those of Europe; that the basis of European tactics—money and scientific organizations of six hundred thousand men—strong military invasions—may stumble over our land and knock against a new force unknown to them, whose foundation lies in the nature of our boundless Russian land and of our all-united Russian spirit.

However, let our many good men, *for the time being,* fail to understand this (they do not know and are timid). Yet our Czars are aware of this and the people feel this. Alexander I was cognizant of this peculiar force of ours when he said that he would grow a beard and retire with his people to the depths of the forests rather than lay down his sword and submit to Napoleon's will. And, of course, in a collision with such a force all Europe would be smashed because for such a war she would not have sufficient money, unity and organization.

When all our Russian men learn that we are so powerful, then we shall achieve a condition where we shall not have to conduct wars; then Europe will begin to believe in us and she will then, for the first time, *discover* us, as in the past she has discovered America. But for this it is necessary that we, ahead of them, discover ourselves, and that our intelligentsia understand that it can no longer segregate and detach itself from its people. . . .

2

Not Always Is War a Scourge. Sometimes It Is Salvation

But our wiseacres have also seized upon another aspect of the matter: they are preaching philanthropy and humaneness; they are lamenting over blood that has been shed, over the fact that in the course of the war we shall grow still more bestial and defiled and that thereby we shall be still farther removed from domestic progress, from the right road, from science.

Yes, of course, war is a calamity; still, there is much fallacy in these arguments, and, what is most important—we are surfeited with these bourgeois morals! The exploit of bloody self-sacrifice for the sake of everything that we regard as sacred, is, of course, more moral than the whole bourgeois catechism. The enthusiasm of a nation inspired by a magnanimous idea is a progressive impulse and not bestialization. It stands to reason that we may be mistaken in what we consider a magnanimous idea, but if that which we deem to be our sanctity is disgraceful and vicious, we cannot evade punishment which will be conferred upon us by nature herself: ignominy and vice carry in themselves death, and, sooner or later, they punish themselves. For example, a war undertaken for the sake of acquisition of wealth, prompted by the insatiable greed of the bourse, may actually be derived from the same law of the development of one's national individuality, common to all peoples,—nevertheless there is a limit to this development which should not be exceeded; beyond this limit any acquisition, any progress, signifies excess carrying in itself disease followed by death. Thus, were England, in this present Eastern struggle, to back Turkey, completely neglecting, for the sake of her commercial profits, the groans of oppressed mankind,—no doubt, she would be drawing the sword against herself, and, sooner or later, that sword would fall on her own head.

On the contrary, what is purer and more sacred than the exploit of a war such as Russia is undertaking at present? It may be said: "But Russia, too, although she really undertakes the war only for the purpose of liberating the tortured tribes and restoring their independence, nevertheless, thereby acquires in these tribes future allies and, therefore, she is gaining strength, so that all this, naturally, expresses the same law of development of national individuality which England seeks to enforce. And inasmuch as the concept of 'Panslavism,' by its very immensity unquestionably may be intimidating Europe, she has the right, by virtue of the law of self-preservation, to stop us just as much as we have the right to go ahead, disregarding her fears and being guided in our movement by nothing but political foresight and prudence. Thus, in all this there is nothing either sacred or vicious,—merely the eternal animal instinct of the peoples by which all insufficiently and inadequately developed earthly tribes, without any exception, are abiding. Nevertheless, accumulated consciousness, science and humaneness, sooner or later, unfailingly are apt to weaken the eternal bestial instinct of the imprudent nations, inspiring all the peoples with the desire of peace, international fellowship and humane progress. Therefore, peace, and not blood, should nevertheless be preached."

Holy words! But in this case, somehow, they are inapplicable to Russia, or—to put it better—Russia at this historical moment constitutes, so to speak, an exception. This is really so.

In fact, should Russia, which rose so disinterestedly and truthfully for the salvation and regeneration of the oppressed tribes, strengthen herself in the future with them, nevertheless, even in this case, she would constitute a most exceptional example which Europe in no way expects since she is measuring things with her own yardstick. Russia, by even greatly strengthening herself as a result of her alliance with the tribes liberated by her, would not fall upon Europe with the sword; she would neither seize nor take away anything, as Europe, unfailingly, would do, if it were possible for her to unite all nations against Russia. In fact, all nations in Europe have been doing so throughout their whole histories whenever the possibility arose of strengthening themselves at the expense of their neighbors.

This has been the case from the most savage primordial times down to the recent contemporaneous Franco-Prussian war. And what became then of their whole civilization?—The most learned and enlightened of all nations fell upon another equally learned and enlightened nation, and seizing upon the opportunity, devoured it as a wild beast, drank its blood, squeezed out of it all its sap, in the form of billions in indemnity, and chopped off its whole side, in the form of its two best provinces.

In truth, after all this, can Europe be blamed for being unable to understand Russia's mission? Can they—these uppish, learned and strong ones—comprehend and presume, be it only in fantasy, that perhaps Russia has been predestined and created for their own salvation, and that it is she which, perhaps, will finally utter this word of salvation?

Oh, yes, of course, not only shall we not seize and take away anything from them, but the fact itself that we shall greatly strengthen ourselves (through the alliance of love and brotherhood, and not usurpation and violence) will, finally, enable us not to draw the sword, but, on the contrary, in the tranquillity of our might—to reveal an example of sincere peace, international fellowship and disinterestedness.

We shall be the first to announce to the world that we seek to achieve our own welfare not through the suppression of national individualities alien to us, but, on the contrary, that we perceive our welfare in the freest and most independent development of all other nations and in brotherly communion with them. One nation will be amplifying the other; we shall be grafting upon ourselves their organic peculiarities, and, on our part, we shall give them our own twigs for grafting. We shall maintain spiritual intercourse with them, teaching them and learning from them, up to the time when mankind, as a grand and beautiful tree, having attained full maturity and universal brotherhood through the fellowship of all peoples, shades with itself the happy earth!

Let our present-day "universal men" and self-renouncers laugh at these "fantastic" words, but we cannot be blamed for the fact that we believe in these things, *i.e.,* that in this respect we are in full accord with our people who also believe in them. Ask the people; ask the soldier: Why are they rising? Why do they go to war and what are they expecting from it?—Everyone of them, as one man, will tell you that they are going in order to serve Christ and to liberate the oppressed brethren, and not one of them is thinking about usurpation.

Quite so: precisely during this war we shall prove our idea concerning Russia's future mission in Europe; specifically we shall prove it by the fact that after liberating the Slavic countries we shall acquire for ourselves not even a scrap of land (as Austria is dreaming on her behalf), and that, on the contrary, we shall watch over their own mutual accord and protect their liberty and independence, be it even against all Europe. This being so, ours is a sacred idea, and our war is not "the eternal bestial instinct of imprudent nations," but specifically the first step toward the realization of that perpetual peace in which we are happy to believe,— toward the attainment *in reality* of international fellowship and of *truly* humane welfare!

Thus, it is not always that peace and only peace must be preached, and salvation is not always only in peace *quand-même* but sometimes also in war.

3

DOES SPILLED BLOOD SAVE?

"But blood, but nevertheless blood!"—the wiseacres keep saying. And truly all these bureaucratic phrases about blood are nothing but an array of most insignificant bombastic words for specific purposes. Stock-exchange brokers, for instance, nowadays are very fond of talking about humaneness. And many among those who are talking about humaneness are merely trading in it. Meanwhile, without war, perhaps, even more blood would be shed.

Believe me that in certain, if not in all, cases (save in the case of civil wars) war is a process by means of which *specifically* international peace is achieved with a minimum loss of blood, with minimum sorrow and effort, and at least more or less normal relations between the nations are evolved. Of course, this is a pity, but what can be done if this is so? And it is better to draw the sword once than to suffer interminably.

And in what manner is present peace, prevailing among the civilized nations, better than war? The contrary is true: peace, lasting peace, rather than war tends to harden and bestialize man. Lasting peace always generates cruelty, cowardice and coarse, fat egoism, and chiefly—intellectual stagnation. It is only the exploiters of the peoples who grow fat in times of long peace. It is being repeated over and over again that peace generates wealth, but only for one-tenth of the people, and this one-tenth, having contracted the diseases of wealth, transmits the contagion to the other nine-tenths who have no wealth. And that one-tenth is contaminated by debauch and cynicism.

As a result of an excessive accumulation of riches in the hands of a few, coarseness of feeling is being generated in the owners of wealth. The sense of the elegant is converted into thirst for whimsical excesses and abnormalities. Voluptuousness spreads awfully. It generates cruelty and cowardice. The ponderous and coarse soul of the sensualist is more cruel than any other, even vicious, soul. A sensualist who faints at the sight of blood from a cut finger, will not forgive a poor devil and will send him to jail for the smallest debt. On the other hand, cruelty generates intense and cowardly anxiety concerning one's own security which at times of lasting peace, invariably very soon converts itself into panicky fear for one's self and transmits itself to all social strata; this generates an awful thirst for the acquisition and accumulation of money. The faith in the solidarity of men, in their brotherhood, in the help of society disappears, and the motto "each one for himself" is being loudly proclaimed. The poor fellow sees clearly what the rich man is and what kind of brother to him he is, and so all men begin to isolate and segregate themselves.

Egoism kills magnanimity. Art alone fosters in society the higher aspirations of life and seeks to wake the soul which during the periods of protracted peace falls asleep. This is the reason why it has been suggested that art can flourish only in times of lasting peace. But this is a gross error: art, meaning *genuine* art, develops during the periods of protracted peace precisely because it is opposed to the ponderous and vicious slumber of the souls. In such times artistic creations always invoke an ideal; they generate protest and indignation; they disturb society and not seldom they compel those to suffer who are anxious to awake and to get out of the stinking ditch.

Thus it appears that, in the long run, the lasting bourgeois peace itself, almost invariably generates a war urge; peace creates this urge as a miserable consequence of itself, however, not in the name of some great and just cause worthy of a great nation, but for the sake of some trivial stock-exchange interests, some new markets sought by exploiters; for the sake of the acquisition of new slaves needed by the owners of gold bags,—in a word—for reasons which are not justified even by motives of self-preservation but which, on the contrary, bear witness to the whimsical and pathological condition of the national organism. These interests, and the wars which are undertaken for their sake, debauch and even completely ruin the nations, whereas a war for a magnanimous cause, for the liberation of the oppressed, for a disinterested and sacred idea,—such a war merely clears the air contaminated with miasmas, cures the soul, chases away cowardice and indolence, sets forth and proclaims a firm aim, launches and clarifies the idea which this or that nation must put into effect.

Such a war fortifies every nation with the realization of self-sacrifice, and the spirit of the entire nation—with the realization of mutual solidarity and unity of all members of which it is formed; principally, however, with the realization of an accomplished duty and a noble deed: "We are not quite degraded and debauched if something humane is left in us!"

And look: With what did our recent preachers of peaceableness and humaneness begin their sermon?—They began it with an outright inhuman cruelty. Not only did they themselves refuse to come to the assistance of the martyrs who were appealing to them, but they kept others back and prevented them from doing so. Ostensibly so humane and sensitive, they cold-bloodedly and scoffingly denied the necessity of self-sacrifice and of enterprise on our part. They sought to push Russia on a most trivial road, unworthy of a great nation,—not to speak of their contempt for the people who have recognized in the Slavic martyrs their brethren—and consequently of their haughty severance from the will of the people above whom they have placed their false "European" enlightenment. Their pet motto was: "Physician, heal thyself." "You are endeavoring to heal and save others, whereas you haven't even built schools at home," they argued. Well, we are going to heal ourselves. Of course, schools are important, but they require spirit and orientation; so we are going now to provide ourselves with the spirit and to acquire a sane orientation. And we shall acquire it if God sends us victory. We shall come back with the conviction of a task disinterestedly performed by us, with the conviction that we have gloriously served humanity with our blood and that we have restored our energy and strength, and all this—in the place of the recent disgraceful vacillation of our thought, in the place of our deadening stagnation insensibly borrowed from Europeanism. And what is most important—we shall more closely affiliate ourselves with the people, because in them, and in them alone, we shall find the cure for our two-century-old illness and unproductive weakness.

And, generally, it may be said that if society is infected and sick, even so good a thing as protracted peace, instead of benefiting it, becomes injurious to it. This is also applicable to Europe as a whole. It is not without reason that in European history, as far back as it can be remembered, no single generation has lived without a war.

Thus it appears that war, too, is needed for some purpose, that it is salutary and that it alleviates mankind. This is abominable, if conceived abstractly, but in practice this seems to be so, and precisely because to an infected organism even so beneficial a thing as peace becomes harmful.

Nevertheless, only that war proves useful which is undertaken for an idea, in the name of a sublime and magnanimous principle, and not for the sake of material interests, greedy usurpation and haughty violence. Such wars merely led nations along false roads and invariably ruined them. If not we, our children, will see how England is going to end. At present for everybody in the world "the time is close at hand." Well, it is time, too.

4

The Opinion of the "Gentlest" Czar on the Eastern Question

I received an excerpt from a book which was published last year in Kiev, *The Moscow State under Czar Alexei Mikhailovich and Patriarch Nikon according to the records of Archdeacon Pavel of Aleppo*, by Ivan Obolensky. Kiev, 1876 (pages 90–91).

This is a page from somebody else's work, but it is so characteristic for this current minute of ours, while the book itself, probably, is so unknown to the bulk of the public, that I have made up my mind to print these few lines in the *Diary*. This is the opinion of Czar Alexei Mikhailovich on the Eastern question,—also a "Gentlest" Czar, but one who lived two centuries ago,—his lamentation over the fact that he could not be a Czar-Liberator.

"It was said that on Holy Easter (of the year 1656) the Czar, when kissing the Greek merchants in commemoration of Christ's resurrection, among other things asked them: 'Do you wish and do you expect me to liberate and ransom you from captivity?' And when they answered: 'How can it be otherwise? How can we help but wish so?'—he added: 'Quite so. Therefore when you return to your land, ask all the monks and bishops to pray to God and celebrate liturgies for me, so that through their prayers I be given the strength to cut off the head of their enemy.' And having shed abundant tears, he then said, turning to the magnates: 'My heart grieves because of the enslavement of these poor people who are groaning in the clutches of the enemies of our faith. God, on the day of Judgment, will call me to account *if, being in a position to liberate them, I were to neglect my duty.* I do not know how long these bad conditions in state affairs are going to last, but ever since the times of my father and his predecessors, patriarchs, bishops, monks and simple beggars have been coming to us with complaints about the oppression of the enslavers, and not even one of them has come for any reason other than because he felt oppressed with severe sorrow and had to flee from the cruelty of his masters. *I am afraid of the questions which the Creator, on that day, will propound to me. And I have decided in my mind that, if such be the will of God, I shall use all my troops, I shall drain my treasury, and I shall shed blood to the last drop in an endeavor to liberate them.'* To all this the dignitaries answered the Czar: 'Oh, Lord, grant thy heart's desire.' "

CHAPTER II

The Dream of a Strange Man

A FANTASTIC STORY

1

I AM A STRANGE man. Now they call me insane. It would have been a promotion in rank should I still have remained to them just queer, as before. But at present I am no longer angry; at present they all are dear to me, even when they laugh at me—then, for some reason, they are even particularly dear. I should myself laugh with them—not exactly at myself, but loving them—if I did not feel so sad looking at them. I am sad because they don't know the truth, and I know it. Oh, how painful it is to know the truth in solitude! But this they won't understand. No, they won't.

But in days gone by I used to agonize because I seemed strange. Not seemed—but was strange. I was always funny, and I have been aware of this, perhaps ever since my birth. Perhaps already at the age of seven I knew that I was strange. After that I attended school, then a university, and what?—The more I studied the more I became convinced that I was funny. So that, to me, my whole university training, in the long run, existed, as it were, only for the purpose of proving and explaining to me that I was strange.

The thing which happened in the case of my studies repeated itself also in life.

With every new year there grew and strengthened in me the conviction of my odd appearance in all respects. I was always laughed at by everybody. But no one knew or even suspected that if there was a man on earth who, more than anybody, knew that I was strange, this was I, myself, and precisely this was the most offensive thing to me,—the fact that they didn't know it. However, this was my own fault. I was always so proud that never, for anything in the world, would I have consented to admit this. With the years this pride has been growing in me, and if it were ever to come to the point that I should permit myself to confess to anyone that I was strange,—it seems that right then and there, that same evening, I should have blown my brains out with a revolver.

Oh, how I suffered in my youthful years fearing that I might give way and suddenly confess to my schoolmates. But from the time I became a young man, even though year after year I became more and more conscious of my dreadful quality,—for some reason I felt slightly calmer. Precisely—"for some reason," because even up to the present day I am at a loss to understand why. Perhaps it was because there was growing in my soul a horrible anguish as a result of one fact which was infinitely greater than anything I was able to conceive, namely, the conviction which has formed itself in me that everywhere in the world *nothing matters*. This I foreboded long before, but the full conviction arose somehow suddenly during the last year. All of a sudden, I felt that to me it would make *no difference* whether the world existed or whether there was nothing anywhere. I began to hear and feel with all my being that *around me there was nothing*. At first, it seemed to me that in the past there had been much, but later I guessed that in the past, too, there had been nothing, and only that, for some reason, there had seemed to be. Little by little I also became convinced that never will there be anything. Then suddenly I stopped being angry with people and almost didn't notice them. Truly, this manifested itself even in most insignificant trifles: for instance, at times I would happen to be walking in the street and knocking against people—not on account of pensiveness: what had I to think about? In those days I ceased to think altogether: it made no difference to me. And this would have been all right had it solved the questions. Oh, I haven't solved a single one, and yet how many there were! But I began to feel that *nothing mattered,* and all the questions withdrew from me.

And now it was after that that I learned the truth. I learned it last November, to be exact—on the third of November, and from that time on I can recall my every moment.

It was a gloomy evening—the gloomiest that can ever be. Shortly after ten I was going home, and I specifically remember that the thought occurred to me that there could be no gloomier time. Even in a physical sense. Rain was pouring all day long, and this was the coldest and gloomiest rain—even some kind of a threatening rain—that I could recall,—full of obvious animosity toward men. Suddenly, shortly after ten o'clock, it stopped raining, and an awful humidity ensued—colder and more humid than when it was raining. Everything emitted some sort of vapor—every stone in the street and in every by-lane if one looked into its farthest end, away from the street.

Presently I began to imagine that were gas to be extinguished everywhere it would be more pleasant, whereas with gas one's heart feels sadder because it illumines all this.

That day I hadn't had my dinner, and all evening, from the early hours, I spent at the apartment of an engineer and there were two friends of his besides. I kept silent all the time, and I believe they were bored with me. They were speaking about something provocative, and, suddenly, they even grew excited. But it made no difference to them—this I saw—and they kept up their excitement —only so. And suddenly I told them: "Gentlemen, this makes no difference to you." They took no offense, but they all laughed at me. This was because I made my remark without any reproach, and simply for the reason that it made no difference to me. And they did see that it made no difference to me, and this made them feel jolly.

When, in the street, the thought about gas occurred to me, I looked up at the sky. It was awfully dark, and yet I could clearly discern torn clouds, and between them—bottomless black spots. Suddenly I noticed in one of them a tiny star and I started gazing at it. This because that little star suggested to me a thought: I decided to commit suicide that night. This I had firmly resolved two months ago and, poor as I was, I bought an excellent revolver which I loaded that same day. But two months had elapsed, yet it was still lying in the drawer; however, to such an extent it made no difference to me that—for what reason I don't know—I sought to catch at last a moment when I should feel less indifferent. And, thus, throughout these two months, every night, as I was going home, I thought that I should shoot myself. All the time I was waiting for the moment.

And now that tiny star suggested to me the thought, and I made up my mind that *unfailingly* this is going to take place that very night. And why that star had suggested the thought—I don't know.

While I was thus looking at the sky, that little girl seized me by the elbow. The street was deserted, and there was almost no one around. In the distance a cabman was sleeping in his droshki. The girl was about eight years old; she wore a handkerchief on her head and nothing but a shabby little dress; she was all wet; but I noticed particularly her wet torn shoes; I remember them even now; somehow they struck my eye. Suddenly she began to pull me by the elbow and to call to me. She did not cry, but she kept uttering in a broken voice some kind of words which she was unable to pronounce correctly because she was shivering and shaking with cold. For some reason she was panic-stricken and she shouted desperately: "Dear mama! Dear mama!" I was about to turn my face to her but I didn't say a single word and kept on walking; however, she continued to run behind me pulling me by my arm. In her voice I heard a sound which in very frightened children signifies despair. I know that sound. Even though she did not pronounce her words distinctly, nevertheless I understood that her mother was dying somewhere or that something had happened to them there, and now she had run out into the street in order to summon someone or to find something to help mama. But I didn't follow her; on the contrary, the thought suddenly occurred to me to drive her off. First I told her to find a policeman. But sobbing, out of breath, she kept running by my side, and then suddenly she folded her tiny hands as if in supplication. She wouldn't leave me. It was then that I stamped and shouted at her. She merely cried out: "Sir! Sir!" left me and precipitately ran across the street; there, there appeared some passer-by, and she must have rushed to him.

I went up to my fifth floor. I am living in a rooming house. Mine is a poorly furnished small room with one semicircular garret window. In my room there is an oil-cloth couch, also a table on which I keep my books, two chairs and an old, old—and yet Voltairian—armchair.

I sat down, lighted the candle and started thinking. In the room next to mine, behind a partition, the havoc continued. It had already lasted two days. That room is occupied by a retired captain; he had visitors—maybe six civilians; they were drinking vodka and playing "faro" with old cards. Last night an affray broke out there, and I know that two of them, for quite a while, pulled each other by the hair. The landlady meant to lodge a complaint but she is terribly afraid of the captain. In our establishment there is but one other tenant—a skinny little lady, an army officer's wife, from out of town, with three little children who fell sick after they had moved into their lodging. But the lady and the children are afraid of the captain to the point of fainting; at night they keep trembling and crossing themselves, and the youngest child was so frightened that he was seized with some sort of fit.

I know for sure that this captain sometimes stops passers-by on the Nevsky and asks alms. People refuse to give him any employment, but strange to say (this is the point I am driving at), during all this month that he has been living here, he has never aroused in me any feeling of vexation. Of course, from the very beginning, I have declined acquaintanceship with him, and, besides, from the start he felt bored with me. Yet no matter how much they might have been shouting behind their partition, no matter how many of them might have been there,—it always made no difference to me. I sit all night long, and, truly, I don't hear them—to such an extent that I forget about them. Every night I don't sleep till dawn, —this has lasted for about a year. I sit all night in the armchair by the table doing nothing. I read books only in the daytime. I sit and I don't even think—just so: some kind of thoughts wander through my mind, and I let them loose. In the course of the night the whole candle burns up.

Calmly I sat down by the table. I took out the revolver and put it before me. When I did so, I remember, I asked myself: "Right?" and quite positively I answered: "Right." Meaning that I would shoot myself. I knew that that night I would unfailingly shoot myself, but how long I should sit by the table—that I didn't know. And, of course, I would have shot myself had it not been for that little girl.

2

You see: even though it made no difference to me, nevertheless I did feel pain. Should anyone have struck me, I should have felt a pain. The same—in the moral sense: should anything pitiful have occurred, I should have felt pity exactly as in the days when I had not yet felt that "it made no difference." Just now I also felt pity: most certainly I would have helped a child. Why, then, did I not help that little girl?—Because of a thought which occurred to me: as she was pulling and calling me, suddenly a question arose before me, and I couldn't solve it. It was an idle question but I grew angry. I grew angry because of the belief that, once I had decided that I would commit suicide that night, everything in the world, more than ever, should have made no difference to me. Why, then, all of a sudden, did I feel that not everything was a matter of indifference to me and that I was pitying the little girl?

I recall that I felt great pity for her—to the point of some strange pain, which was quite incredible in my situation. Truly, I am unable to describe better that fleeting feeling but it also persisted at home, while I was already sitting by the table, and I was much irritated,—as I haven't been for so long. Deliberations followed one another. It seemed clear that if I were a man, and not yet a zero, and while I was not yet reduced to a zero, I was living, and, therefore, I could suffer, be angry and feel ashamed of my actions. All right. But if I should kill myself, say, in two hours, what would the little girl be to me, what would shame and everything in the world matter to me?—I am being reduced to a zero—an absolute zero. And is it possible that the realization of the fact that in an instant I shall be completely nonexistent, and that, therefore, nothing will exist, could have exercised no influence upon the feeling of pity for the little girl and the feeling of shame for the villainy which I have committed?—For I stamped at the unfortunate child and shouted at her in a brutal voice because I said to myself: "Not only do I feel no pity, but even should I commit an inhuman villainy,—now I can commit it because in two hours everything will be extinct." Would you believe that this was the reason why I began to shout? At present I am almost sure of that.

It seemed clear that now life and the world were, so to speak, dependent on me. It may even have been said that the world has been created for me alone: I will shoot myself, and the world will not exist, at least for me. Not to speak of the fact that, perhaps, after me in reality nothing will exist for anyone, and that the moment my consciousness is extinguished the whole world, too, will vanish as a phantom, as an adjunct of my consciousness, and will become nonexistent, since, perhaps, this whole world and all these men are nothing but I myself.

I recall that while I was thus sitting and deliberating, I turned all these new questions, which crowded in my mind, one after another, in an altogether different direction and conceived something radically new. For example, suddenly, a strange thought occurred to me: What if formerly I had lived on the moon or on Mars, and if there I should have perpetrated the most shameful and dishonest act that could possibly be conceived; and, further, that if over there I should have been abused and dishonored in a manner that may be conceived and felt only in a dream, in a nightmare; and if subsequently, finding myself on the earth, I should continue to be conscious of the act I had committed on the other planet, and, besides, that I should know that never, under any circumstance, should I return thither,—then, looking from the earth at the moon, would it, or would it not, *make a difference?* Should I, or should I not, feel ashamed of my act?

These were idle and superfluous questions since the revolver lay already before me, and with all my being I knew that *this* would unfailingly occur, yet they excited me and made me mad. Now—it seemed—I should be unable to die without having first solved something.

In a word, that little girl saved me since, because of the questions, I had postponed the shot. Meanwhile, in the captain's room things began to quiet down: they finished their card game and now they were settling down for the night, and in the meantime they kept grumbling and were idly continuing to abuse one another. At this juncture, suddenly, I fell asleep in the armchair by the table, which has never happened to me before. I fell asleep quite imperceptibly to myself. Dreams, as is known, are very strange phenomena: one thing appears with awful lucidity, with jewelled finish of detail; but other things are skipped, as it were, quite unnoticed—for instance, space and time.

It would seem that dreams are generated not by the intellect but by desires, not by the brain but by the heart. And yet, at times, what extremely complicated things did my mind perform in sleep! For instance, my brother died five years ago. Sometimes I see him in my dreams: he participates in my affairs; we take a great interest in them; even so, through the whole dream, I distinctly know and remember that he died and was buried. Why am I not surprised that, though dead, he is still right here, at my side and busies himself together with me? Why does my reason admit all this?

But enough. I am turning to my dream. Yes, I saw this dream, my dream, on the third of November! They are teasing me by insisting that this was only a dream. But is it not all the same whether or not this was a dream, if it has enunciated to me the Truth? For once you have learned the Truth, you have beheld it, you know that it is the Truth, that there is and can be no other Truth whether you be sleeping or waking. All right: let it be a dream; let it; but that life which you are so extolling, I sought to extinguish with suicide, and my dream, my dream—oh, it has enunciated to me a new, great, regenerated, vigorous life!

Listen!

3

I have stated that I fell asleep unconsciously and even, as it were, continuing to deliberate upon the same subjects. Suddenly I dreamed that I was taking the revolver, and, seated, I was pressing it straight against my heart,—my heart, and not my head. Before that I decided to shoot myself through my head, specifically—

through the right temple. Having aimed at my chest, I waited a second or two, and suddenly my candle, the table and the wall opposite me, started moving and rocking. I quickly fired the shot.

In sleep, at times, you are falling down from an elevation, or you are being cut or beaten, but you never experience any pain unless, somehow, you actually hurt yourself in your bed: in this case you will feel the pain, and almost always you will wake up from the pain.

Thus it was also in my dream: I felt no pain, but it seemed to me that after my shot everything within me shook, and suddenly everything became extinguished and grew terribly dark around me. I became blind and numb, as it were. Now I am lying stretched out upon my back on something hard. I see nothing and I am unable to make the slightest motion. People around are walking back and forth and shouting; the captain is speaking in his bass; the landlady is screaming,—and then suddenly, again an interval, and now I am being carried in a closed coffin. And I feel how the coffin is rocking, and I am deliberating upon this. But all of a sudden, for the first time, I am struck by the thought that I died, completely died; I know it. I do not doubt it. I neither see nor move, and yet I feel and reason. However, soon I become reconciled to this, and, as it usually happens in sleep, I accepted reality without arguing.

Presently I am being interred. Everybody goes away. I am alone; all alone. I do not move. Whenever in the past, in a waking state, I used to think how I should be buried in a grave, strictly speaking, I had associated with the grave only the sensation of dampness and cold. Now, too, I felt very cold, especially in the tips of my toes; otherwise I felt nothing.

I lay, and, strange, I waited for nothing, accepting without challenge the fact that a dead man has nothing to wait for. But it was damp. I don't know how much time had elapsed—one hour, or several days, or many days. Suddenly, however, a drop of water, which oozed through the cover of the coffin, fell on my closed left eye; then after a minute—another one; again,—after a minute,—a third one, and so on, and so forth—with intervals of one minute. Profound indignation flared up in my heart, and all of a sudden I felt a physical pain in it: "This is my wound—I said to myself —it's the shot, it's the bullet there." . . . And drops continued to fall—every minute—on my closed eye. Then, all at once, I appealed —not with my voice since I was motionless—but with all my being, to the Sovereign of everything that was happening to me:

"Whosoever Thou may be, but if Thou art; if there exists something more sensible than that which is transpiring at present, grant that it be here. However, if Thou avengest my foolish suicide with the ugliness and absurdity of continued being,—know that no torture to which I may be subjected will ever compare with that contempt which I shall silently experience be it during millions of years of martyrdom!" . . .

I made the appeal and grew silent. Profound silence lasted almost one minute, and even one more drop fell, but I knew, boundlessly, inviolably I knew and believed that everything would forthwith change. And suddenly my grave was thrown open. That is, I don't know whether it had been opened or excavated, but I was grasped by some dark creature, unknown to me, and we found ourselves in open spaces. Suddenly I recovered my sight: it was a dark night; never, never was there such darkness! We swept through space—already far away from the earth. I asked nothing of the one who was carrying me; I was proud. I assured myself that I was not afraid, and I almost fainted from delight with the thought that I was not afraid. I do not remember how long we soared, and I cannot conceive it: everything transpired, as always in a dream, when one skips over space and time and the laws of being and reason, and stops merely on those points about which the heart is meditating.

I remember that unexpectedly I noticed in the darkness a tiny star: "Is this Sirius?"—I asked suddenly, failing to restrain myself, because I didn't want to ask any question. "No, this is that same star which you have observed amidst the clouds when you were on your way home"—answered the creature which carried me away. I knew that it possessed, as it were, a human image. Strange thing: I did not like the creature; I even felt profound disgust. I had expected complete nonexistence, and it was for this purpose that I shot myself through the heart. And now I was in the hands of a creature—of course, not a human one—which *was*, which existed. "So, there is life also beyond the grave!"—I thought with the strange lightmindedness of a dream, but the essence of my heart remained with me in all its depth: "If it is necessary to *be* again"—I said to myself—"and to live again by somebody's inflexible will, I don't want to be vanquished and humiliated!"— "Thou knowest that I am afraid of thee, and because of this thou hast contempt for me"—I said suddenly to my fellow-traveller, again failing to refrain from the humiliating question which contained an admission, and sensing, as a pin's prick, humiliation in my heart. The creature made no reply but I felt that I was not being despised or scoffed at, and that I was even not being pitied, but that our journey had a purpose—unknown and mysterious—which concerned me alone.

Fear was growing in my heart. Numbly but painfully, as if

piercing me, it was being conveyed to me by my silent companion. We were sweeping through dark and unknown spaces. I had long ceased to perceive the constellations familiar to my eyes. I knew that there were stars in the heavenly expanse whose rays reached the earth in thousands and millions of years. Perhaps we had already flown beyond these spaces. I was awaiting something with dreadful anguish which oppressed my heart. And suddenly some familiar and highly appealing sensation shook me: suddenly I saw our sun! I knew that this could not have been *our* sun which had generated *our* earth, and that we were removed from our sun at an infinite distance; yet, with all my being, for some reason, I gathered that this was a sun identical with ours, its duplication, its alter ego. A sweet, appealing sensation filled my soul with ecstasy: the germane force of light, that which begot me, was reflected in my heart and resurrected it, and for the first time after my grave I felt life, former life.

"But if this be the sun, if it is a sun absolutely identical with ours"—I exclaimed—"where then is the earth?" And my fellow-traveller pointed at a tiny star which with emerald luster, shone in the darkness. We were directly sweeping toward it.

"And are such duplications really possible in the universe? Is such, indeed, the natural law? . . . And if the earth is yonder, is it possible that it is an earth identical with ours . . . absolutely identical—unfortunate, poor and eternally beloved, generating even in its most ungrateful children a painful love of itself?"—I kept exclaiming shaken with irresistible, ecstatic love of that germane, former earth which I had abandoned. The image of the poor little girl, whom I have offended, flickered before me.

"Thou shalt see everything"—said my companion, and some kind of a sorrow sounded in his words.

But we were swiftly approaching the planet. It grew in its dimensions in my sight; I was already discerning the ocean, the outline of Europe, and suddenly a strange feeling of some great, holy jealousy flared up in my heart. How can there be such a duplication? What for? I love, I can be loving, only that earth which I have left, upon which there remains the spray of my blood when I, the ungrateful, with a shot through my heart, extinguished my life. Yet, never, never did I cease to love that earth, and on that night when I was parting with it, perhaps, I loved it even more painfully than ever.

Is there suffering on this new earth?—On our earth we can truly love only with suffering, only through suffering! We do not know how to love otherwise and we know no other love. I am longing for suffering in order to love. I long, I thirst, this very minute, for an opportunity to kiss with tears in my eyes, only that earth which I have left, and I do not want, I do not accept life on any other earth! . . .

However, my fellow-traveller had already left me. Suddenly, quite unnoticeably, I stood on this other earth in bright sunlight of a day as beautiful as paradise. I believe, I was standing on one of those isles which on our earth form part of the Greek Archipelago, or somewhere on the coast of the mainland adjacent to that Archipelago. Oh, everything was exactly as on our earth, but it seemed that everything around radiated with some holiday, and with great, holy and finally achieved triumph. The calm emerald sea gently splashed against the shore embracing it with manifest, apparent, almost conscious love. Tall, beautiful trees stood there in full luxury of their bloom, and their countless leaflets—I am sure of it—welcomed me with their gentle, kind murmur, uttering, as it were, words of love. The grass sparkled with bright fragrant flowers. Little birds, in flocks, flew through the air, and, unafraid of me, alighted on my shoulders and hands, joyfully beating at me with dear little trepidating wings.

And, finally, I saw and got to know the people of that happy land. They came to me themselves, they surrounded and embraced me. Children of the sun, of their sun,—oh, how beautiful they were! Never did I see on our earth such beauty in man. Perhaps only in our children of tenderest age it is possible to find a remote reflection of that beauty. The eyes of these happy people were full of bright glitter. Their faces radiated with intelligence and some kind of consciousness which had reached the level of tranquillity; yet these faces were cheerful. Innocent gladness sounded in the words and voices of these men.

Oh, at once, at the first glance at their faces, I grasped everything, everything! This was an earth not defiled by sin; upon it lived men who had not sinned; they lived in a paradise similar to that in which, according to the tradition of all mankind, lived our fallen forefathers, with the only exception that here the whole earth, everywhere, was one and the same paradise. These men, laughing joyously, crowded around me and caressed me. They took me to their homes, and each one of them sought to assuage me. Oh, they asked me no questions, but it seemed to me that they knew everything, and they sought as quickly as possible to drive away suffering from my face.

4

Again, look here: All right, let this have been nothing but a dream! But the feeling of love of these innocent and beautiful people stayed within me forever, and I feel that their love pours thence upon me even now. I have seen them myself, I got to know them; I became convinced; I loved them and subsequently I suffered for them.

Oh, I understood at once, even then, that in many respects I should not comprehend them at all. To me, a contemporaneous progressive and hideous Petersburg resident, it seemed incredible, for instance, that they, who knew so much, did not possess our science. But soon I came to understand that their knowledge was amplified by, and derived from, revelations which differed from those on our earth, and that their aspirations were also altogether different. They had no desires and they were placid; they did not aspire to the knowledge of life, as we seek to comprehend it, because their life was complete. Yet their knowledge was deeper and higher than that of our science, since the latter seeks to explain what life is; science itself endeavors to conceive it in order to teach others how to live; they, however, knew how to live even without science, and this I understood; but I was unable to comprehend their knowledge. They showed me their trees, and I failed to understand the measure of love with which they beheld them, as if they were speaking of creatures akin to them. And do you know that, perhaps, I am not mistaken when I say that they conversed with them! Yes, they did discover their language, and I am convinced that the trees understood them.

Thus they also looked upon the whole of nature,—on animals which lived peacefully with them and never attacked them; they loved those men conquered with their own love. They pointed at stars and spoke to me something about them which I was unable to grasp, but I am sure that through some means they communicated, as it were, with these celestial bodies,—only not through thought but through some live medium.

Oh, these men did not even endeavor to make me understand them; they loved me without this; on the other hand, I knew that they would also never understand me, and for this reason almost never did I speak to them about our earth. I merely embraced in their presence that earth on which they lived, and adored them without words; they saw this and permitted themselves to be adored, without being ashamed of being adored by me because they themselves loved much. They did not suffer on my behalf when, at times, with tears I kissed their feet, gladly knowing in their hearts with what force of love they would respond to me.

Sometimes I asked myself with surprise: How did they manage, all that time, not to insult one like me, and not even once to arouse in one like me a feeling of jealousy and envy? Many a time

I asked myself how was I, a braggart and a liar, able to refrain from speaking to them about my learning, about which, of course, they had no conception? How was I able to refrain from speaking in a manner which would surprise them with that learning of mine, at least, by reason of my love of them.

They were vivacious and joyous like children. They roamed through their beautiful groves and forests; they sang lovely songs; they subsisted on light food, on fruits from their trees, on honey from their woods, on the milk of the animals which loved them. They labored but little and slightly for their food and clothing. They were endowed with love and children were born to them, but never did I observe in them those impulses of *cruel* voluptuousness which affect virtually everybody on our earth,—everybody, and which are the sole source of almost all sin in our human race. They rejoiced over their newborn as new participants in their felicity. They never quarrelled and there was no jealousy among them; they did not even understand what these things meant. Their children were common children because they all formed one family. There were virtually no diseases among them, although there was death. However, their old men passed away gently, as though falling asleep, surrounded by men bidding them farewell, blessing them, smiling to them; and they departed accompanied by serene smiles. On these occasions I perceived no sorrow, no tears; there was merely love grown to the level of ecstasy, but calm, composed, meditative ecstasy. One could imagine that they continued to communicate with their dead even after their death, and that the earthly communion between them was not interrupted by death.

They were almost unable to understand me when I asked them about eternal life; yet they were so unaccountably convinced of it that it did not constitute a question to them. They had no temples, but in them there was some kind of a daily, live, unceasing communion with the whole of the universe. They had no religion, yet they possessed a firm belief that when they reach in their earthly gladness the full measure of earthly nature, there will ensue for them, both for the living and the dead, a still greater expansion of their communion with the whole of the universe. They awaited this moment with joy, but without haste, without suffering about it, keeping it, as it were, in the anticipations of their hearts which they communicated to each other. In the evenings, before going to sleep, they were fond of singing in concordant choirs. In these songs they expressed all sentiments derived from the passing day; they glorified it and bade it farewell. They glorified nature, the earth and seas and forests. They were fond of composing songs about one another; they praised each other like children. Those were the simplest songs but they were evoked from the heart and penetrated it. And not only in songs but it seemed that they were spending all their lives in admiring each other. It was a sort of mutual complete and universal enamoredness. Some of their solemn and ecstatic songs I almost could not understand at all. Comprehending their words I never was able to penetrate their full meaning. It remained inaccessible to my mind; but my heart, as it were, was moved, more and more permeated with it. Often I told them that all this I had sensed long before; that all this joy and this glory were vaguely expressed in me on our earth in the form of an appealing anguish which, at times, reached the level of unbearable sorrow; that in the dreams of my heart and in the visions of my mind I anticipated them all and their glory, and that often, on our earth, I was unable to behold without tears the setting sun . . .; that in my hatred of men on our earth there has always been anguish: "Why was I unable to hate them without loving them? Why was I unable not to forgive them? And why was there anguish in my love of them? Why was I unable to love them without hating them?"—They listened to me, and I could see that they could not comprehend the things I was telling them; yet I did not regret my telling these things to them: I knew that they understood the full measure of my anguish for those whom I had abandoned. Yes, when they looked at me that dear expression of their eyes was permeated with love; when I felt that in their presence my heart, too, became as innocent and truthful as theirs, I did not regret that I was unable to understand them. Breath failed me because of the sensation of the fullness of life, and silently I worshipped them.

Oh, everybody is openly laughing at me, assuring me that even in a dream it is impossible to have seen such details as I am recounting now; that in my dream I saw or foresaw nothing but a sentiment generated by my own heart in a state of delirium, and that, on my awakening, I invented the details myself. And when I opened my mouth to tell them that perhaps all this was so in reality,—God, how they burst into laughter right to my face, and what merriment I caused among them.

Oh, yes, of course, I was vanquished by the mere sensation of that dream, and it alone was spared in my wounded and bleeding heart. As against this, the actual images and forms of my dream, that is, those which I have actually seen at the time of my dream, reached such a state of harmony; they were so fascinating and beautiful, and they were so truthful that when I awoke I was, of course, unable to express them in our weak words. Thus they must have been, as it were, dimmed in my mind, and, for this reason, perhaps, I was in truth unconsciously compelled to invent those details, of course, distorting them especially because of my passionate desire to express them in one way or another as quickly as possible.

However, how can I help but believe that all this did take place? It might have been a thousand times better, brighter and more joyful than what I am telling here.

Let this be a dream, but all this must have taken place. Do you know, I will tell you a secret: all this, perhaps, was not at all a dream! Since here there occurred something so awfully real that it could not have been dreamed in a dream. Let us admit that my heart has generated the dream. However, could my heart alone have generated such a dreadful truth as has subsequently occurred to me? How could I have invented or fancied it with my heart? Is it conceivable that my trivial heart and my whimsical, petty mind could have raised themselves to such a revelation of truth! Oh, judge for yourselves: up to the present I have been concealing the full truth, but now I am going to complete my story. The point is that I have . . . debauched them all!

5

Yes, yes, it ended in the fact that I debauched them all! How this could have happened,—I don't know. The dream has soared through millennia, and only in me it has left a feeling of wholeness. I merely know that I was the cause of the first apostasy. Much like a filthy trichina, or a pestilential germ infecting whole countries, so I contaminated with myself that happy earth which was innocent prior to my coming into being. They have learned to lie, they became fond of the lie and they perceived its beauty. Oh, perhaps this started innocently, with a jest, with coquetry or an amorous intrigue,—perhaps just with an atom, but this atom of deceit penetrated their hearts and pleased them. Shortly after that voluptuousness was born; voluptuousness generated jealousy, jealousy—cruelty. . . . Oh, I don't know, I don't remember,—very soon the first blood spurted: they were astonished and terrified, and they began to part one from the other and segregate themselves. Unions appeared, but unions against one another. Then abuses and reproaches ensued. They became cognizant of shame, which they extolled as a virtue. The conception of honor was born, and each union hoisted its own banner. They began to torture the animals which fled from them to the forests and became their enemies. A struggle for segregation began—for disjunction, for individuality, for "mine and thine." They began to speak different languages. They became cognizant of sorrow and they became accustomed to loving it; they craved for suffering and claimed that Truth can be attained through suffering only. Then science came into existence. When they became wicked they started speaking about brotherhood and humaneness and grasped the meaning of these ideas. When they grew criminal they invented justice and enacted for themselves codes for its maintenance, and for the enforcement of their codes they used the guillotine. They could hardly recall that which they had lost. They even refused to believe that sometime in the past they were innocent and happy. They went so far as to ridicule the very possibility of their former happiness which they denoted as a fancy. They were even unable to imagine happiness in forms and images, but strangely and remarkably—having lost all faith in their former happiness, having called it a fairy-tale, so ardently did they begin to wish to become again innocent and happy that they fell prostrate before the desires of their heart, they erected temples in which they worshipped their own idea, their own "desire," with tears of adoration, fully believing at the same time in the impossibility of its fulfillment.

However, should it so happen that they could return to that state of innocence and happiness which they had lost, or if someone should show it to them and ask them whether they would like to return to it, they would certainly refuse to do so. They used to tell me: "Let us admit that we are deceitful, wicked and unjust; we *know* it and we deplore this and torment ourselves for this; we castigate and rack ourselves harder, perhaps, than that merciful Judge who will be judging us and whose name we know not. But we have science at our command, and through it we shall again find the Truth which we shall then embrace consciously. Knowledge is superior to feeling; cognition of life is superior to life. Science will give us wisdom; wisdom will reveal the laws, and the knowledge of the laws of happiness is superior to happiness."

This is what they used to tell me, and after such words each one began to love himself more than the rest. Nor could they have acted differently. Each one became so jealous of his individuality that he exerted all his efforts merely to humiliate and belittle it in the others, conceiving this to be the aim of his life.

Then came slavery—even voluntary slavery: the weak readily submitted to the strong on condition that the latter help them to oppress those who were still weaker than they themselves. There appeared godly men who went in tears to these people, and spoke to them about their haughtiness, about the loss of harmony and measure, about the loss of shame by them. These righteous men were subjected to ridicule and stoned. Their holy blood was spilled at the thresholds of the temples. As against this, there appeared men who began to conjecture how to unite again all men so that each one, without ceasing to love himself above all others, at the same time should not hinder anyone and that all men might be thus living in a concordant society. Wars were waged for the sake of this idea. At the same time all the belligerents firmly believed that science, wisdom and the instinct of self-preservation, in the long run, would compel men to unite in a harmonious and rational society. In the meantime, in order to expedite matters, "the wise" sought to exterminate "the imprudent," those who could not understand their idea, so as not to impede its triumph.

However, soon the sense of self-preservation began to grow weaker: there came haughty men and sensualists who straightway demanded either everything or nothing. For the acquisition of everything they resorted to villainy, and if they failed in it—to suicide.

Religions sprang up which preached the cult of nonexistence and self-destruction for the attainment of eternal peace in nothingness. Finally, these men grew tired of senseless labor, and suffering appeared on their faces; then they proclaimed that suffering was beauty, because only in suffering there was thought. They exalted suffering in their songs. I moved among them wringing my hands and shedding tears over them, but I loved them, perhaps, even more than before when there was no suffering on their faces and when they were innocent and so beautiful. I grew fonder of their earth desecrated by them than when it was a paradise, for the sole reason that sorrow appeared on it.

Alas, I always loved grief and sorrow, but only for myself, for myself, while I wept pitying them. I stretched my arms toward them in despair, accusing, damning and despising myself. I told them that I, I alone did all this; that it was I who brought to them debauch, contagion and deceit! I implored them to crucify me; I taught them how to make the cross. I could not, I had no strength to kill myself, but I wanted to suffer tortures inflicted by them; I craved for torture; I was anxious that my blood, to its last drop, be shed in these tortures. But they merely laughed at me and, finally, they began to consider me crazy. They defended me and said that they had received that which they had wished themselves, and that everything which existed now could not have not existed.

Finally, they announced to me that I was beginning to be dangerous to them and that they would place me in an insane asylum if I shouldn't keep silent. Then sorrow penetrated my soul with such force that my heart contracted, and I felt that I should die. And then . . . well, then I awoke.

It was already morning, that is, it wasn't daylight, but it was after five o'clock. I woke up in the same armchair. The candle had burned down to the end. In the captain's room people were sleeping, and all around there was silence such as is rare in our lodging.

First of all, I jumped to my feet extremely surprised: nothing of the kind had ever happened to me—even as far as trifles and details were concerned: for instance, never did I thus fall asleep in my armchair. Presently, as I was standing trying to collect my thoughts, my eye caught sight of the revolver, ready and loaded. Instantly I pushed it away from me! Oh, now I craved for life, life! I raised my arms and appealed to eternal Truth. I did not appeal but I wept. Ecstasy, immeasurable ecstasy lifted my whole being. Yes, life, and—preaching! I decided upon preaching that same moment—and for all my life! I am going to preach; I want to preach—what?—Truth, since I beheld it; I beheld it with my own eyes; I beheld its whole glory!

Well, from that time on I have been preaching! Besides, I love all those who are laughing at me more than the rest. Why this is so—I don't know, I cannot explain, but let it be thus. They say that even now I am confused, meaning that if even now I am so confused, what's going to happen in the future? Very true: I am confused and, maybe, in the future it will be worse. And, of course, I shall become disconcerted several times before I find out how to preach, that is, with what words and deeds, since this is very difficult to achieve. Even now I see all this as clearly as daylight, but listen: who doesn't get confused! And yet all men are headed toward one and the same thing, or, at least, they all strive for the same thing—from the sage to the last robber, only they follow different roads. This is an old Truth, but here is what's new in it: even I cannot be greatly confused. The reason is that I saw Truth and I know that men can be beautiful and happy without losing their faculty of living on earth. I refuse and am unable to believe that evil is a normal condition in men. Yet they all laugh at this belief of mine. But how can I help but have faith: I saw Truth—my mind did not invent it, and I saw, saw it, and its *live image* filled my soul forever.

Thus, why should I be led astray? Of course, I may deviate— even several times; I may even be echoing in my words somebody else's thoughts, but not for a long while: the live image of what I saw will always stay with me, and it will always correct and guide me.

Oh, I am brave and brisk. I am on my way even were my journey to last a thousand years. Do you know that at first I meant to conceal the fact that I have debauched everybody, but this was a mistake—here was the first mistake! But Truth whispered to me

that I was *lying*, guarded and led me. But how to establish paradise
—I don't know because I can't express it in words. After my dream
I lost the words—at least, all most important and relevant words.

But be it so: I will proceed, and I will be speaking incessantly
because all the same I beheld the thing with my own eyes, even
though I am unable to recount what I have seen. However, this
is precisely what the scoffers don't understand: "You saw"—they
say—"something delirious, an hallucination." Now, now! Is this
clever?—Yet, they take such great pride! Dream? What's a dream?
And isn't our life a dream?—I'll go further: let, let this never come
true and let paradise never come to pass (this much I understand),
—well, nevertheless I will be preaching.

Meanwhile, this is so simple: in one day, *in one hour*, everything would be at once established! The main thing is—love thy
neighbors as thyself. This is the cardinal point; that's all, and
nothing further is needed; it would be at once discovered how
things should be arranged. And yet this is but an old truth which
has been reiterated and read a billion times! Even so, it did not
manage to stay with us! "Cognition of life ·is superior to life;
knowledge of the laws of happiness is superior to happiness"—this
is what has to be combated! And I will combat it. If only everybody would desire it, everything could at once be arranged.

And I have found that little girl. And I will go! I will!

Discharge of Defendant Kornilova

On the twenty-second day of April of the current year the
case of defendant Kornilova was tried for the second time at the
local Circuit Court by new judges and a new panel of jurors. The
former court verdict, rendered last year, has been rescinded by the
Senate on the ground of the insufficiency of the medical tests.

Perhaps most of my readers have a clear recollection of this
case. A young step-mother (at that time still not of age), being
in a state of pregnancy, prompted by anger against her husband,
who kept reproaching her with his former wife, and after a violent
quarrel with him, pushed her six-year-old step-daughter out of the
window from the fourth floor (5½ sagenes), her husband's daughter,
and almost a miracle occurred: the child was not killed; she sustained neither fractures nor injuries, and soon regained consciousness. At present the little girl is alive and in good health.

Having waked up in the morning when the husband had
already gone to work, she let the child sleep; then she dressed the
girl and gave her coffee. After that she opened the window and
threw her out. Without even looking through the window to ascer-

tain what had happened to the child, she closed the window, got dressed and went to the police station. There she reported the incident, answering questions in a rude and strange manner. When, several hours later, she was told that the child was alive, she, expressing neither joy nor vexation, quite indifferently and cold-bloodedly, as if in a state of pensiveness, remarked: "How strong she is!"

Thereupon, for almost six weeks, while confined in two prisons, she continued to be morose, rude and uncommunicative. And, suddenly, all at once, all this disappeared: throughout the remaining four months till she was delivered of a child, as well as the rest of the time, during and after the trial, the mistress of the women's division of the prison was never tired of praising her: her disposition became even, calm, kind and serene. However, all this I have described before. Briefly,—the former verdict has been rescinded, and subsequently, on the twenty-second of April, a new verdict was announced by virtue of which Kornilova was acquitted.

I was present in the court room, and I gathered many impressions. It is only a pity that I am unable to record them, and that literally I am compelled to confine my account to but a few words. Besides, I am giving an account of this case solely because in the past I have written about it *in extenso*, and, therefore, I deem it not superfluous to inform the readers about the outcome of the case.

The trial lasted twice as long as the former one. The composition of the jurors was particularly remarkable. A new witness— the mistress of the women's division of the prison—was asked to take the stand. Her testimony concerning Kornilova's character was very weighty and favorable to her. Likewise the testimony of the defendant's husband was quite remarkable: with extreme honesty he concealed nothing—neither the quarrels nor the offenses on his part. He defended his wife and he spoke cordially, straightforwardly and candidly. He is only a peasant; true, he is wearing European clothes; he reads books and he receives a monthly salary of thirty rubles.

Furthermore, the selection of expert witnesses was also remarkable. Altogether, six experts were summoned—all men of repute and celebrities in medical science. Five of them took the stand. Three experts unhesitatingly testified that a pathological condition peculiar to a pregnant woman *could have* caused the commission of the crime in this case. Only one—Dr. Florinsky—dissented from this opinion, but, fortunately, he is not a psychiatrist, and his opinion proved of no consequence. The last man to testify was our noted psychiatrist Dukov. He spoke for almost one hour answering the questions propounded to him by the prosecutor and the presiding justice. It is difficult to conceive a more refined understanding of the human soul and its pathological states. I was also amazed by the wealth and variety of extremely curious observations gathered by him over a long period of years. As for myself, decidedly, I listened to certain statements of this expert with admiration. His opinion was altogether in favor of the defendant: he stated *positively* and *conclusively* that in his opinion the defendant, at the time of the perpetration by her of the dreadful crime, was in a pathological psychic state.

In conclusion, the prosecutor himself withdrew the charge of premeditation, *i.e.*, the main malice in the indictment. Attorney-at-law Lustig, the attorney for the defendant, very adroitly warded off several accusations, and one of the most important ones—the alleged hatred of the step-mother toward her step-daughter—he managed to reduce to naught, revealing in it nothing but back-yard gossip.

After a long charge by the presiding judge, the jurors retired to the jurors' room, and in less than fifteen minutes they rendered a verdict of acquittal which was greeted almost with enthusiasm by the numerous public. Many people crossed themselves, others congratulated and shook hands with each other. The husband of the acquitted that same evening, after ten o'clock, took her home, and she, in a happy mood, returned to her home after an absence of almost one year, with the impression of a lesson learned for all her life and of manifest divine fate in this whole case—beginning with (to mention but one fact) the miraculous salvation of the child.

To My Readers

I am asking my readers for great indulgence. Last year, owing to my summer journey to Ems for the cure of my disease, I was forced to bring out the July and August issues of the *Diary* on August thirty-first, under one cover, of course with a double number of pages. This year, because of the aggravation of my illness, I am compelled to publish the May and June issues jointly, under one cover, at the end of June or in the very early part of July. Thereafter the July and August numbers, as last year, will also be published in August. Beginning with the month of September the *Diary* will be issued regularly on the last day of each month.

Leaving Petersburg, following the doctor's advice, I wish to state that although the premises of the editorial office will be closed in Petersburg until September, nevertheless all out-of-town (*as well as Petersburg*) subscribers and readers, in case of need, may apply *by mail* to the editorial office much in the same way as hitherto.

These letters will be forwarded forthwith by the office manager, and every complaint, misunderstanding, etc., as in the past, will be taken care of as soon as possible. Likewise all letters addressed to me will be immediately forwarded. Concerning this matter the editorial office has been given most explicit instructions. Subscriptions will continue as hitherto: subscriptions will be immediately taken care of.

I don't know if my readers and subscribers to *A Writer's Diary* will excuse me. In the face of such an unforeseen circumstance as a complication of one's illness, it is difficult to plan everything in advance. The overwhelming majority of my readers up to the present have maintained a benevolent attitude toward me, of which I am convinced by solid facts. I venture to rely upon their kindness also at this time.

MAY–JUNE

CHAPTER I

1

From the Book of Predictions by Johann Lichtenberger,
in the year 1528

I HAVE received a very strange document. This is an ancient, true, a hazy and allegorical, prediction concerning current events and the present war.

One of our young scientists has discovered in London, in the Royal Library, an ancient folio-volume, *The Book of Predictions—* "*Prognosticationes*" by Johann Lichtenberger, edition 1528, in Latin. This is a rare, perhaps even the only existing, copy. In this book the future of Europe and of mankind is set forth in hazy pictures. This is a mystical book. I am reproducing here only those lines which were conveyed to me, *and merely as a fact* not devoid of certain interest.

Following the prognostications about the French Revolution (1789) and Napoleon I who is called in the book—"the great eagle" (*aquila grandis*), the following is stated concerning the future European events:

"Post haec veniet altera aquila quae ignem fovebit in gremio sponsae Christi et erunt tres adulteri unusque legitimus qui alios vorabit.

"Exsurget aquila grandis in Oriente, aquicolae occidentales moerebunt. Tria regna comportabit. Ipsa est aquila grandis, quae

dormiet annis multis, refutata resurget et contremiscere faciet aqui-
colas occidentales in terra Virginis et alios montes superbissimos;
et volabit ad meridiem recuperando amissa. Et amore charitatis
inflammabit Deus aquilam orientalem volando ad ardua alis duabus
fulgens in montibus christianitatis."

("After that a new eagle shall come who shall kindle fire in
the bosom of Christ's bride, and there shall be three natural issues
and one legitimate issue, and he shall devour the others. A great
eagle shall arise in the East, and the Western islanders shall start
wailing. He shall capture three kingdoms. This is the great eagle
who sleepeth many a year; though wounded he shall arise, and
shall compel the Western sea-bound inhabitants of the land of the
Virgin and the other proud summits to tremble, and he shall fly
southward to retrieve that which had been lost. And God shall
kindle the Eastern eagle with love of mercy so that he may fly on
his two wings to accomplish that which is difficult, flashing upon
the peaks of Christianity.")

Of course, this is a bit foggy; you must concede, however,
that the great Eastern eagle who sleepeth many a year; *wounded*
(N. B.—Isn't this our war with Europe 22 years ago?) he shall
arise and shall compel to tremble the Western sea-bound inhabitants,
—you must concede that somehow this is suggestive of the present,
on condition, of course, that we disregard our Europeanizing wiseacres who, contrary to the prophecy, still continue to tremble, as
it were, before "the sea-bound inhabitants" at a time when the eagle
has already flown away "flashing with his two wings." But it is only
the wiseacres who are trembling—not the eagle.

Furthermore, "the Western sea-bound inhabitants of the land of
the Virgin" obviously signify England, if Johann Lichtenberger's
prophecy be applied to the contemporary events. However, what in
this case is the meaning of "the land of the Virgin"?—In 1528 Queen
Elizabeth had not yet been reigning. Doesn't Lichtenberger's allegory signify a land (British Isles) which has never been subjected
to invasion in the sense in which in days gone by Napoleon expressed himself about European capitals which had suffered from
his invasion: "A capital subjected to an invasion resembles a maiden
who has lost her virginity."—However, according to the prophecy,
the eagle will also compel other "proud summits" to tremble; he
will fly southward to retrieve that which had been lost, and—this
is most remarkable—that "God shall kindle the Eastern eagle with
love of mercy so that he may fly on his two wings to accomplish
that which is difficult, flashing upon the peaks of Christianity."
Concede that this is something very suggestive. Didn't our eagle
take to his wings kindled with mercy for the oppressed and hurt?

Was it not Christ's mercy that has prompted our whole people "to a difficult task"—both in the past and this year? Who is going to deny this? This people, these soldiers recruited from the people, who do not thoroughly know their prayers, used to pick up in the Crimea, near Sebastopol, wounded Frenchmen, and carried them to have their wounds dressed *before* their own Russians. "Let these lie and wait; anyone will pick up a Russian, but the French chap is a stranger—he should be pitied first." Isn't this Christ, doesn't Christ's spirit sound in these naïve and magnanimous jestingly uttered words?

Thus, isn't Christ's spirit in our people, backward but kind, ignorant but not barbarian? Yes, Christ is their strength—our Russian strength—now that the eagle has flown to achieve "the difficult task." And what does some single anecdote about Sebastopol soldiers mean compared with thousands of manifestations of Christ's spirit and "the fire of mercy" in our people, in reality, in full view and in everybody's sight, despite the wiseacres' endeavor to suppress the thought and bury the fact of our people's participation, through their spirit and heart, in the present-day destinies of Russia and the East?

And don't start pointing at "the bestiality and dullness" of the people, at their ignorance and backwardness by reason of which they are supposedly unable to understand the things which are transpiring at present. They do perfectly understand the essence of the matter; rest assured that they have been comprehending it for four centuries. Were they to learn about contemporaneous diplomats, these they wouldn't understand at all. But who will understand them? Indeed our great people were brought up like beasts; they have suffered tortures ever since they came into being, throughout the millennium of their existence,—tortures such as no other people in the world could have endured, because they would have disintegrated and perished, whereas our people merely grew stronger and became more compact amidst their misfortunes. Do not, then, reproach them for "bestiality and ignorance," Messrs. Wiseacres, since you—precisely you—have done nothing for them. On the contrary, you abandoned the people two centuries ago, you have forsaken them and alienated them from you; you have converted them into a taxation unit, into a quit-rent item for your own benefit. The people have been growing—gentlemen, enlightened Europeans, —forgotten and downtrodden by you, driven by you as a beast into a haunt. But their Christ was with them, and it was with Him alone that they lived to that great day when, twenty years ago, the Northern eagle, kindled with the flame of mercy, flapped and spread his wings and blessed the people with these wings. . . .

Yes, there is much bestiality in people, but do not point at it. This bestiality is the mire of centuries; it will be cleansed. And the trouble is not in the fact that there still is bestiality but in a condition where bestiality would be extolled as virtue.

I have seen robbers who had committed many bestialities and who, by reason of their depraved and weakened will-power, had fallen lower than the lowest depths. Yet these debauched and degraded beasts knew—at least within themselves—that they were beasts, and they felt how low they had fallen, and in pure and serene moments, which God sends even to beasts, they knew how to condemn themselves, even though often they were no longer able to rise.

It is different when bestiality is placed above everybody, as an idol, and people worship it considering themselves virtuous precisely because of this. Lord Beaconsfield—and after him all Beaconsfields—both our domestic and European ones—stopped their ears and closed their eyes to the bestialities and tortures to which entire human tribes are being subjected; they have betrayed Christ for the sake of "the interests of civilization," and because of the fact that the oppressed tribes are called Slavs, i.e., because they carry within themselves something new. All the more reason, then, that they should be crushed to death—also for the sake of the antiquated rotting civilization.

Now, this is bestiality—educated and extolled as virtue—which is being worshipped as an idol both in the West and still at home, in Russia. And didn't "the most beatific Pope, the infallible vicar of God," when passing away, during his last days on earth, didn't he pray for victory for the Turks, the torturers of Christianity, over the Russians who arose in Christ's name in defense of Christianity, for the sole reason that, according to his *infallible* judgment, the Turks are nevertheless better than the Russian heretics who do not recognize the Pope? Isn't this bestiality? Isn't this barbarism?

Indeed, Johann Lichtenberger's prophecy is strongly suggestive of the present moment. And should we not conceive the Pope among other "proud summits" whom the eagle, flapping his wings, will compel to tremble? By the way, to wind up with the prophecy: What did Johann Lichtenberger mean when speaking of the eagle "who shall kindle fire in the bosom of Christ's bride, and there shall be three natural issues and one legitimate issue, and he shall devour the others"?—In religious and mystical parlance the expression "Christ's bride" has always meant the Church in general. What, then, are the three natural and one legitimate issues?—It seems that if he should be considered a prognosticator,—three religions: Catholicism, Protestantism and . . . which is the third illegitimate? And which is the legitimate religion?

However, let us leave Johann Lichtenberger. It is difficult to speak seriously about all this. All this is but a mystical allegory though somewhat resembling the truth.

And aren't there quite a few coincidences? True, all this has been written and printed in 1528, and this is curious. In those days there must have often appeared works of this kind, and although that time preceded the wars of the great Protestant reformation, there had been already many Protestants, reformers and prophets. It is also known that later, especially in Protestant armies, there have always been many "ecstatic" prophets among the warriors—prognosticators and convulsionaries.

If I have recorded this Latin excerpt from an ancient book (which, I repeat, unquestionably exists), it is solely as a significant fact,—not as a miracle. Besides, are only miracles miraculous? Not seldom, most miraculous are things which occur in reality. Nearly always we perceive reality as we *wish* to perceive it, as we wish to interpret it to ourselves. If, at times, we start analyzing, and if in the visible we perceive not that which we sought to perceive but that which it is *in reality,* unhesitatingly we take that which we have perceived for a miracle. This happens quite often, and, at times, I swear, we would rather believe in a miracle and in an impossibility than in the truth *which we do not wish to see.* This always happens on earth—therein is the whole history of mankind.

2

About Anonymous Abusive Letters

I did not go abroad and I am now in the province of Kursk. My physician, having learned that I had an opportunity of spending the summer in the country, and, besides, in such a province as that of Kursk, prescribed that I should drink in the country Essentuki water, adding that this would be far more beneficial to me than Ems, to whose water, supposedly, I became accustomed. I deem it my duty to state that I have received from my readers a great many letters with the expression of sincere sympathy in connection with the announcement of my illness. And generally, I wish to mention, by the way, that during all the time of the publication of my *Diary* I have been, and still am, receiving many signed and anonymous letters so gratifying to me, so approbative of, and so encouraging to, my work, that I must unhesitatingly state that I have never either expected so general a sympathy or

considered myself worthy of it. These letters I shall keep as a
treasure, and what is there hypocritical in the fact that I am stating so in print? Indeed, is it bad that I appreciate and treasure
this general attention accorded to me? But it might be said that
now I am praising myself and boasting. Let them say so, but, inwardly, I know that the fact that I am merely expressing my
gratitude, my sincere feeling, does not mean bragging; besides, I
am no longer young enough to fail to understand how this statement will irritate certain gentlemen. It seems, however, that of
these there aren't too many.

Among several hundreds of letters received during the eighteen
months of the publication of the *Diary,* there were at least one
hundred (but surely more than that) anonymous ones, but out
of this number only two letters were absolutely hostile. There were
people disagreeing with my convictions, but then they directly set
forth their objections, always seriously, sincerely, without the slightest personal insinuations—this is true of both the signed and unsigned letters,—and I only regret that because of the large numbers
of letters which are being received, I am utterly unable to answer
each one of them.

However, these two letters are exceptions. They were written
not for the purpose of raising objections but for abuse. Now, these
gentlemen, composers of these letters—will be irritated with my
statement of thanks. The last of these letters deals precisely with
the announcement of my illness. My anonymous correspondent was
seriously angry: how, he maintains, did I dare to announce in print
so private and personal a matter as my illness, and in his letter
to me he wrote a most discourteous and rude parody on my announcement. But leaving aside the main object of the letter—abuse,
willy-nilly I became interested in the following question: if, for
instance, by reason of ill health, I was compelled to go away for
a cure, and on this account I was deprived of the possibility of
publishing the May issue of the *Diary* on time, but jointly with
the June issue; and inasmuch as every time, in each issue of the
Diary, I have been announcing the date of the publication of the
next number,—well, it seemed to me that a mere unmotivated announcement, devoid of any explanations, to the effect that the next
issue of the *Diary* is going to appear jointly with the June one,
would have been somewhat unceremonious. And, after all, why
shouldn't I have explained the reason why this was to take place?
And have I, indeed, dwelt so much on my announcement of my
illness?—Of course, all this is but a trifle, and were the matter to
emanate from a person seriously shocked in his feeling of literary
and public decorum, there would have arisen a curious, yet, per-

haps, in a way, respectable specimen of a gentleman, although standing outside of the literary profession, nevertheless one who, so to speak, burns with the commendable craving for compliance with literary decorum, and who although carrying his aspirations to the point of scrupulousness, nevertheless derives them from a worthy and curious source. But invectives spoiled the whole thing: it became clear that the whole object lay in them.

No doubt, it wouldn't have been worthwhile to dwell here upon all this; but I have been thinking for quite a long time of saying a few words about anonymous letters in general, *i.e.*, abusive anonymous letters, and I am glad that the opportunity presented itself.

The point is that I have long been under the impression that in our epoch, so vacillating and so transitional, so full of changes and so unsatisfactory (as, indeed, it must be),—certainly there must have appeared a great multitude of, so to speak, neglected, forgotten, slighted and vexed people: "Why are *they* everywhere, and not I? Why don't people pay attention to me, too?" In this state of personal irritation and, as it were, of dissatisfied ideal, a certain fellow is likely, at times, to take a match and commit arson,—to such an extent is this feeling painful. This I quite understand, and before condemning him one should arm himself with humaneness rather than with indignation. However, to be using matches for arson is the utmost limit and, so to speak, the lot of mighty Byronic characters. Fortunately, there are less horrible outlets for characters not as mighty. Such an outlet is simply to do a certain dirty action, —well, to calumniate, to belie, to spread gossip or to write an anonymous letter.

In a word, I have been long suspecting, and I still suspect, that our epoch, though unquestionably one of great reforms and events, must at the same time be an era of intense anonymous letters of an abusive character. As regards literature, this is true beyond a shadow of doubt: anonymous abusive letters constitute, as it were, an inviolable part of contemporaneous Russian literature and accompany it in all directions. And who, among editors and writers, is not receiving them? I even made inquiries in some periodicals, and in one of them—precisely in one of those which suddenly met with good fortune, created an impression and pleased the public so greatly that they themselves did not expect such a success—an active contributor told me that they were receiving such a mass of abusive anonymous letters that they weren't read at all,—they were merely opened. He was about to relate to me in detail the contents of some of such epistles, but he burst into laughter.

Thus it must be: our inexperienced anonymous scribes still do not suspect that the more their letters are abusive, the more innocent and harmless they are. This is a good trait: it signifies that although our anonymous writers are ardent, they lack composure, and they do not understand that the more courteous and dignified the tone of a sarcastic anonymous letter is, the more biting it is and the stronger its impression. This means that Jesuitism as yet has made no progress among us, and that the matter has not yet reached its second, *superior* phase. Therefore, it is still in its inception, and, consequently, it is merely the fruit of unbridled ardor, and not of a deliberated and strictly trained spiteful sentiment. This is not, so to speak, Spanish vengeance, which, for the attainment of its goal, is even ready to make great sacrifices, and which has learned composure.

Our anonymous abuser is still far from being that mysterious stranger in Lermontov's drama *The Masquerade,* a colossal figure, who having once upon a time received a blow on his face from a certain officer, retired into the wilderness where he spent thirty years deliberating upon his vengeance. No, it is still that same Slavic nature of ours which is anxious to resort to abusive language as quickly as possible, and finish with it (and at that—even to make peace right then and there). Concede that all this is in a certain sense gratifying because here, too, everything is green, young and fresh,—something on the order of life's spring, even though— it must be confessed—a most disgusting spring.

I deem it my duty to add one more observation: it seems that our young generation, *i.e.,* very young, raw youths, do not write anonymous invective letters. I am receiving a lot of letters from young people, and they are all signed. Only those of them are unsigned in which too cordial feelings are expressed. But those youths who disagree with me in this or that always sign their names. (However, it is all too easy—on the strength of many indications and devices resorted to—to find out that an anonymous abusive letter has been written not by one belonging to the young generation, not by a raw youth.)

Thus, our youth, apparently, understands that, to begin with, it is possible to write even a very sharp letter but that the signature under it conveys to the wording a great value; and that the whole character of the letter is improved by the fact of the signature since it adds to it a spirit of straightforwardness, courage and readiness to defend and bear the consequences of one's convictions. Besides, the very sharpness of the expressions is merely indicative of the ardor of the conviction and not of the desire to insult.

Thus, it is clear that a scolder who does not sign his name seeks above all to use unprintable invectives; he wishes to give himself this pleasure, and he has no other aim. And he knows himself that he is doing a dirty thing, that he is harming himself, *i.e.*, the importance of his letter; yet such is the urge for calling names. This trait, meaning—this urge, is worth noting since it still predominates among our educated society. And let people ridicule me for my belief that this trait is *predominant* in our midst. I am convinced that I am not exaggerating, and that we, so to speak, *en masse* are standing at present on this level of development.

Besides, take also into account the fact that it is possible not to write a single anonymous letter, and yet to carry all life long the soul of an anonymous scolder. This is an important consideration. And what is there in the fact that during eighteen months I have received only two abusive letters?—This merely goes to prove my innocence and negligibleness as well as the limited sphere of my activities, besides,—that I am dealing with decent people. However, other workers who are more in the public eye than myself (and on this ground alone—more guilty than I) and who, in addition, by the very nature and character of their periodicals, are compelled to operate in a much wider sphere, are, perhaps, receiving every eighteen months two hundred, and not two, abusive letters.

Briefly, I am convinced that European civilization has inoculated into us very little humaneness, and that there are, perhaps, so many people in our midst who are willing to use invectives quickly and immediately at every opportunity that one is really afraid. And there are still more of those who are inclined to use abusive language with impunity, anonymously and safely, from behind the door. And it is precisely the anonymous letter which provides them with such a possibility: a letter cannot be thrashed and it blushes not.

In olden days we had no European honor. Our boyards used to scold each other and even fought each other openly, and a box on the ear was not regarded as a great and irreparable injury to one's dignity. As against this they had their own honor though not in a European form—yet not less sacred and solemn than that in Europe. For the sake of this honor the boyard, at times, renounced his whole fortune, his standing at the court, and even the Czar's graces. However, with the change in our clothing and the introduction of the European sword, there ensued in Russia a new European honor, and during two centuries it has failed to take firm root. Thus the old has been forgotten and spat at while the new has been adopted suspiciously and sceptically. It was adopted mechanically, so to speak, whereas spiritually we forgot what honor meant, and the heart-felt need for it was lost, and this—dreadful though this admission be—with only very few exceptions.

During these two centuries of our European and, so to speak, "sword period," honor and conscience, strange to say, were mostly, and even entirely, preserved in our people who have hardly been affected by the sword period of our history. Let it be admitted that the people are dirty, ignorant and barbarous. Let people mercilessly ridicule my presumption, but it is my life-long conviction that our people are incomparably purer in heart than our upper classes, and that the people's mind is not bifurcated to such an extent as to cherish, side by side with a noble idea, its dirty little antithesis. This we frequently see in our intelligentsia. Besides, they entertain both ideas at one and the same time, not knowing which to believe and give preference to in practice, denoting this state of their mind and soul as "wealth of development" and "blessings of European civilization." And they would rather die with this "wealth" of tedium and disgust than stop strongly ridiculing our people, not yet contaminated with an alien civilization, for their naïveté and the uprightness of their beliefs. . . .

But this is a broad subject. I shall simply say: I am sure that the coarsest among the people would be ashamed of some of the thoughts and impulses of some of our "superior workers," and would turn away with disgust from most of the actions of our educated men. I am convinced that he does not understand—and will not understand for a long time to come—that it is permissible, in solitude, behind closed doors, when nobody sees it, to be committing filthy things and considering them morally quite regular for the sole reason that there are no witnesses and nobody spies on him. And yet, among our educated strata this sort of thing is being practiced on an alarmingly large scale, quite shamelessly and frequently even with the supreme satisfaction of the mind and the higher faculties of an enlightened spirit. According to the people's conception that which is filthy in public is equally nasty behind closed doors. However, we specifically regard the people as ribald, vile men and reactionary scolders who delight in cursing and invectives.

In this connection it is not out of place to recall the following —all the more so as this has changed and passed long ago. In the days of my youth, the majority of our military men were convinced that the Russian soldier, as coming from the people, is extremely fond of using obscene language and ribaldries. On this ground some regimental commanders, in order to gain popularity, permitted themselves during drills, for instance, to curse, resorting to such phrases and indecencies that the soldiers literally blushed and sought to forget in their barracks the things which they had heard from their superiors, shouting down the fellow who ventured to repeat them. *I personally witnessed this.* And how glad at heart were these regimental commanders, imagining that they succeeded in mimicking the Russian soldier's spirit!

Why, even Gogol in his *Correspondence with Friends* counselled a friend of his, when publicly scolding a peasant serf, to use by all means strong language; he went so far as to specify the words which should be used on such occasions, namely those which were strongest and contained, so to speak, more than outward ribaldry,—more "refinement."

Yet even though, unfortunately, the Russian people do use obscene language, yet not all of them do so, far from all,—in fact, the negligible minority (will it be believed?). The main thing, however, is that they revile automatically rather than with moral "refinement"; by force of habit rather than with deliberation. Revilement with deliberation is observed only in very rare specimens of vagabonds, drunkards and all sorts of good-for-nothing idlers despised by the people. Although the latter do resort to vituperation by force of habit, they know themselves that this is a bad habit, and they condemn it. Thus, to break this habit of the people is simply a matter of mechanical disuse and not of a moral effort.

Generally, this idea that our people are fond of using obscene language, in my opinion, has been implanted in our educated stratum at the time when its final moral break with the people became an accomplished fact, which, as we know, resulted in the present-day misconception of the latter on the part of the former. It was at that time that there also appeared many other erroneous ideas about the Russian people.

Even though my assertion, that the people are by no means such convinced scolders, may be disbelieved, nevertheless it is justified. And those hopes which I place in the people I place also in our young generation. The people and the young generation of our intelligentsia will suddenly come together and agree on many things, and they will understand each other much more successfully than our generation in its own times. There is seriousness in our youth, and I pray God only that it be directed more intelligently.

By the way, speaking of youth: recently, a very young man in a letter addressed to me wrote me a very sharp rebuttal in connection with a topic which I am not going to mention, and not only did he sign this sharp (but by no means discourteous) epistle *en toutes lettres,* but he also gave his address. I asked him to come and see me in order to clear up the matter. He came, and I was

impressed with the ardor and seriousness of his attitude toward the
problem in question. He agreed with me on certain points, and he
left in a state of hesitation.

I may add that our young men evince a greater ability in
arguing than our old men, *i.e.*, in the manner in which they argue:
they listen and let people speak. This is due to the fact that, to
them, the elucidation of a matter is more important than their
personal ambitions. When that young man was leaving me, he
expressed his regrets for the sharpness of his letter, and he did this
with natural dignity.

Our youth is devoid of leadership—that's the point! And yet,
how badly they need it! How often did they run with enthusiasm
after men who were not worthy of it but only slightly sincere!
And who will the future leader or leaders be—whoever will it be?
And will our Russian fate send us such men?—Such are the questions!

3

The Plan of a Satirical Novel Dealing with Con-
temporaneous Life

But I am not yet through with the anonymous scolder. The
point is that such a man may become a most serious literary character—in a romance or in a novel. The principal thing is that one may
and must approach the matter from a different point of view—
from a broad and humane standpoint coordinating it with Russian
character in general, and the contemporaneous, current causes of
the appearance in our midst of this type in particular.

In fact, the moment you begin to analyze this type, you are
compelled to admit that at present we cannot help but have such
men, or, to be more precise, that, in our day, it is this kind of
men that we mostly must expect, and that if of them there are still
comparatively few, this is due to a special grace of God.

Indeed, they all are men who have been brought up in our
recent vacillating families, by discontented, sceptical fathers who
have bequeathed to their children nothing but indifference for the
present, and hardly anything more than some vague anxiety concerning some fantastic future on which, however, even so-called
ready realists and frigid haters of our present are inclined to pin
their faith. In addition, these fathers, of course, bequeathed to their
children sceptical, impotent laughter, though scarcely conscious yet
always all-complacent. In the last twenty or twenty-five years was
it only a few children who grew up in the families of these wicked

envious men who, having spent the last pennies of their redemption money, bequeathed to their children misery and the covenant of villainy—have there been few such families?

Now, suppose such a young man takes up some employment. He cuts no figure; he is devoid of wit; he has no connections. He has an innate mind which, however, any man possesses. But because his mind was brought up on idle sneering—which for twenty-five years has been conceived as liberalism—our hero, naturally, takes his mind for genius.

Oh, God! How is it possible not to expect boundless selfishness in a man who grew up without the slightest moral support? At first, he swaggers dreadfully; however, because he nevertheless has a mind (for the type, I prefer to take a man intellectually somewhat above the average rather than below the average, since it is only in these two cases that the appearance of this type is conceivable),—he soon discovers that sneering is a negative thing which leads to nothing positive; and that if it satisfied his father, this was due to the fact that he was a blockhead, even though a liberal fellow, whereas he, the son, is neverthless a genius who merely for the time being finds it difficult to reveal himself. Oh, of couse, in his soul he is ready for most any emphatic villainy, "since why shouldn't villainy be resorted to for business? And who, in our age, is able to prove that villainy is villainy?"—etc.

In a word, he has been brought up on these ready-made questions. But he also soon guesses that even in order to resort to villainy he must wait long for an opening, and, besides, that, perhaps, even to him it is a long distance between the moral readiness to commit a villainy and its actual commission, so that, first, he must, so to speak, "get into line" in a practical sense. Of course, if he were more stupid, he would settle down in a jiffy: "Down with those higher aspirations! The thing to do is to ingratiate oneself with this man or that, to follow him, and to toil hard, obediently, with conviction,—and in the long run the career will be made." However, personal ambition and the conviction that he is a genius for a long while stand in his way: even in his thoughts he cannot put his supposedly so brilliant fate on the same level with the lot of some Mr. So-and-So, or Mr. So-and-So: "No, sir: as yet we are in opposition, and if they want me, let them come to me and beg me!"

Thus, he is waiting for someone to come and beg him; he is angry; he is full of keen resentment, and he waits. Meanwhile, right next to him Mr. So and So has managed to outpace him; another fellow has already settled down; a third oaf has now become his boss,—that very chap whom he himself had nicknamed in that "superior school" of theirs and on whom he had composed an epigram in verse at the time when he was editing the hand-written school magazine and was reputed to be a genius.

"Nay, that's an affront! Why he and not I? And everywhere everything is occupied! No"—says he to himself—"my career is else-where. And what's the use of being employed? It's only blockheads who stick to employment! My career is—literature." Presently he begins to mail his compositions to editorial offices—first incognito, and then—giving his full name. Naturally, people don't answer him. Seized with impatience, he begins to besiege in person one editorial office after another. Occasionally, when a manuscript is returned to him, he indulges in witticisms and bilious sneering, so to speak, to alleviate his heart. But all this doesn't help. "No, apparently, here, too, every place is occupied!"—he says to himself with a sad smile.

Chiefly, he is kept tortured with the fatal trouble of finding always and everywhere as many men as possible who are worse off than he. Oh, he would never be able to understand how one may rejoice over the fact that there are people better off than he! Well, it is at this juncture that the thought occurs to him for the first time to mail to some editorial office, the one where he had been most strongly affronted, a spiteful unsigned letter. He writes and mails it; he does it a second time—the thing pleases him. Even so, nothing happens: much as hitherto everything around remains deaf, dumb and blind. "Nay, what kind of career is this!"—he decides at length, and, finally, he makes up his mind "to ingratiate himself."

He picks a *person*, namely, his boss—the director. In this, perhaps, chance and connections come to his aid. Even Gogol's Poprischin made his debut by distinguishing himself in the business of sharpening pens: for this purpose he had been summoned to his excellency's apartment, where he saw the director's daughter for whom he sharpened two pens. However, the epoch of the Poprischins has passed; besides, in our day, pens are no longer being sharpened. Nor can our hero betray his own character: not pens but most daring thoughts dwell in his mind. In brief, in the shortest time, he becomes convinced that he has captivated the director's daughter, and that she languishes for him. "Well, here's the career,"—he muses —"and what would be the use of women if a clever man couldn't make a career through them? Realistically considered, this is the gist of the feminine problem. And the main thing is that this isn't anything to be ashamed of: are there few men who found their road through women?" But then at this juncture, just as in Popri-schin's case, an adjutant turns up! Poprischin reacted to this in accordance with his character: he grew insane over the fancy that he was the King of Spain. How natural! What was there left to humilated Poprischin without any connections, without a career, without boldness or any kind of initiative, especially during the Petersburg period, other than to embark upon most desperate fancying and to believe in his visions? Our Poprischin, however, our contemporaneous Poprischin, would not believe for anything in the world that he is the same kind of Poprischin as the original one, merely one who has been duplicated thirty years hence. His soul is full of thunder and lightning, contempt and sarcasms,—and so he, too, embarks upon fancying but of a different kind. He recalls the fact that in this world there are anonymous letters, and that once upon a time he had resorted to them. And thus he risks his pretty little letter; but now no longer is it addressed to an editorial office; now it is a more daring venture: he feels that he is embarking upon a new—practical phase. Oh, how carefully he locks himself up from his landlady in his tiny room! How he trembles lest he be spied upon! Yet he scribbles and scribbles, changing his handwriting! He composes four pages of calumnies and invectives! He reads them over and over again, and having spent the whole night in this occupation, at dawn he seals the letter and addresses it to the fiancé-adjutant. He has altered his handwriting, and he is not afraid.

Now he counts the hours: by this time the letter must have been received—the letter to the suitor about his fiancée. Why, of course, he will repudiate her! He will be scared!—For this is not a letter but a "chef-d'œuvre"! And our young friend is fully aware of the fact that he is a wicked little villain; but he is only glad of it: "Now is the time for the bifurcation of thought, and breadth. Nowadays one cannot thrive by rectilinear thought!"

It goes without saying that the letter produces no result: the wedding takes place; yet the beginning has been made, and our hero, as it were, has hit upon his career. A mirage *sui generis* takes possession of him—much as in the case of Poprischin. With ardor he hastens to devote himself to the new activity—the writing of anonymous letters. He finds out things about his general; he muses; he pours out everything that has accumulated during the many years of disappointing service, vexed personal ambitions, bile and envy. He criticizes each and every action of the general; he ridicules him in a most merciless manner, and this in several letters, in a whole series of them. And how pleased he is in the beginning! The actions of the general, his wife, his mistress, and the stupidity of their whole Ministry—all these, everything is depicted in his letters. By and by he turns to state considerations. He composes

a letter to the Minister in which, unceremoniously, he suggests that
Russia be remodelled. No, the Minister cannot help but be struck:
genius will impress him, and his letter might be brought to the
attention of . . . of such a person that . . . In a word: *courage,
mon enfant!* and they'll start looking for the author; then, at once,
I shall reveal my name, so to speak, without bashfulness.

Briefly, he is intoxicated with his compositions, and every
minute he visualizes how his letters are being opened, and what
is reflected upon the faces of those persons. . . . In such a mood,
at times, he even indulges in a joke: jestingly he writes letters to
some of the oddest fellows; he does not neglect some Egor Egoro-
vich, his old head-clerk whom he really drives almost insane by
anonymously assuring him that his wife is having a love-affair with
the local police lieutenant (the main thing is that this may be
half true).

Thus some time elapses, but . . . but suddenly a strange
thought occurs to him, namely, that he is Poprischin, nothing but
Poprischin, that same Poprischin, only a million times viler, and that
all these pasquinades from around the corner, his whole anonymous
potency, in substance is a mirage and nothing more, besides,—a
foul petty mirage, a filthy and disgraceful mirage, even much nastier
than the fancy about the Spanish throne.

At this point there occurs a serious thing—not something disgraceful: "What's disgrace?—Disgrace is nothing! Only apothecaries
are afraid of disgrace!"—but a really dreadful thing, quite dreadful! The point is that, although our hero has a mind, nevertheless
he cannot restrain himself, and at the time of his intoxication with
his new career—specifically, after his little epistle to the Minister
—he lets a word slip about his letters, and to whom?—To that
German landlady of his—well, not everything—she would not have
understood everything; of course, just a trifle, so, from the fullness
of his heart. Yet how great is his surprise when, a month later,
a gentle functionary in another Ministry, who occupies a remote
roomlet in the apartment of the same landlady, a spiteful and
taciturn little chap, having suddenly grown angry with something,
intimates to him, as he is passing through the corridor, that he
—the timid fellow—is "a moral man, and that he does not write
anonymous letters, as certain gentlemen do." Just think! At first
our hero is not greatly scared. Moreover, having interrogated the
functionary—for this express purpose having humiliatingly made up
with him—he convinces himself that the latter knows virtually nothing. Well . . . but what if he does know?—Besides, for some time
rumors have been rampant in his department to the effect that
somebody has been busy writing and sending through the local

mails abusive letters to the superiors, and that for sure this must have been someone of the employees.

The poor fellow begins to ponder; he even doesn't sleep at night. In a word, one may graphically imagine the torments of his soul, his suspiciousness, his slips. Finally, he is almost fully convinced that everybody knows everything; that he is not being told so only for the time being; that his discharge from service has been decided upon, and that, naturally, this will not be the end of it. In a word, he is almost driven insane.

One day, as he is sitting in the department, boundless indignation against everybody and everything arises in his heart: "Oh, wicked, damned men!"—he exclaims to himself—"Is it possible to pretend to such an extent! They know that *this is I;* everyone of them knows it! Whisperingly, they tell this, one to the other, when I happen to be passing by! They are also aware of the document concerning me which lies ready there, at the office. . . . And they are all pretending! They all conceal it from me! They seek to enjoy it; they want to see how I am going to be dragged off. . . . No, this shall not come to pass! No!"

An hour later, accidentally, he brings some paper to the office of his excellency. He walks in; respectfully, he places the paper on the desk. The general is busy; he pays no attention. Our hero turns around; he is about to leave the room noiselessly; he touches the handle of the door, and suddenly, as if he were falling into an abyss, he throws himself at the feet of his excellency, a second before that not even having suspected that he would do this: "All the same, I have to perish! Better to confess of my own accord!" "Only be calm, your excellency! Please be still, your excellency, so that no one may hear us outside! I will tell you everything, everything!"—he implores like a madman the dumbfounded excellency, foolishly clasping his hands before the general.

And presently, by fits and starts, incoherently, he confesses everything, to the greatest amazement of his excellency who entertained no suspicions whatsoever. But here, too, our hero remains fully faithful to his character, because why does he throw himself at the feet of the general? Of course, from illness, from suspiciousness, but *mainly because* he—he who got scared, he, the humiliated and the self-denouncing one—nevertheless much as heretofore, hopes like a little fool intoxicated with self-conceit, that, perhaps, his excellency, having listened to him, and, so to speak, impressed with his genius, will open his arms and stretching out those hands with which he has signed so many papers for the benefit of the fatherland, will embrace him: "Is it possible that you have been driven to this point, unfortunate but gifted young man! Oh, it is

I who am to be blamed for everything! I overlooked you! I assume the full guilt! Oh, God! Here is what our talented youth is compelled to resort to as a result of our antiquated order of things and prejudices! But come, come to my heart, and share my office with me. And we . . . we shall turn the department topsy-turvy!"

But it did not happen thus. Later, a long time thereafter, in disgrace and humiliation, recalling the kick which he received from the toe of the general's boot, which directly fitted into his face, he accused fate and men almost sincerely: "Once in my life I fully opened my arms to embrace people, and what did I receive?"

Some most natural and contemporaneous finale may be conceived: for instance, our hero, already dismissed from service, is hired, for one hundred rubles, for a fictitious wedding, after which he departs in one direction, and she in another—to her grocer: "lovely and noble," as Schedrin's police lieutenant expresses himself in a similar situation.

In a word, it seems to me that the character of an anonymous scolder is not a bad theme for a novel. And a serious one. Of course, here, Gogol would be needed, but . . . I am glad at least that accidentally I have come across this idea. Perhaps I shall really try to introduce it into a novel.

CHAPTER II

1

Former Agriculturists—Future Diplomats

BUT WHITHER did I deviate from my subject? I started telling that I was in the country and was glad of it. It is quite a long time since I have lived in the country in Russia. However, I shall postpone the discussion about country life, and here I shall only mention that, among other reasons, I am glad that I am in the country and not abroad because I could not see Russians sauntering there.

As a matter of fact, in our times—so popular, so concordant and patriotic—when one is expressly looking at home for Russians, waiting and longing for them, needing them,—in such times it is too painful to behold abroad—whither for twenty years, year after year, our intelligentsia have been expatriating themselves and colonizing—the transformation of the purely Russian, raw and perhaps excellent material into a pitiful international canaille—faceless, devoid of character and nationality, without a fatherland. I am not speaking of the fathers,—they are incorrigible and God be with them—but of their unfortunate children whom they are ruining abroad. As to the fathers, in the long run they begin to look ridiculous even to our notorious Russian Europeans.

Mr. Burenin, who is now a war correspondent, tells in one of his letters about an amusing meeting with one of our Europeans of the Forties, "with gray respectable curls," permanently residing abroad, but who came expressly to observe the war (of course, from a very safe distance), "the spectacle of the struggle." In the railroad car he started to make witticisms concerning all the things at which these genlemen have been poking fun now for forty years, *i.e.*, the Russian spirit, the Slavophiles, and so forth.

According to him, the reason why he is residing abroad is that in Russia "there is still nothing a serious-minded and respectable man can do." (N. B. I am citing from memory.) One of his most successful witticisms was that "orders already have been issued to the railroads to ship in a special car—in view of the entry of our troops into Bulgaria and the regeneration of the Slavs—the shadow of Khomiakov." But it may be remarked to this gray-curled gentleman that he is himself very much akin to the shadow of some, perhaps, quite respectable Western liberal babbler of the Forties who—if after so many years he had lived to see his gray curls and had started repeating the same things at which he had stopped in his Forties, were he Granovsky himself—would certainly look exactly like this buffoon, this fellow who spoke about the order to ship to the theatre of war in a railroad car the shadow of Khomiakov, and about the alleged fact that a decent man had still nothing to do in Russia.

Twenty years ago it was mostly landowners who emigrated (I retain this word) from Russia. Since then emigration has persisted year after year. It goes without saying that among the emigrants there were many who were not landowners; there were all sorts of people. Still, the overwhelming majority, if not all of them, more or less hated Russia: some of them hated her on moral grounds, because of the conviction that "there was nothing such respectable and clever men as they could be doing in Russia"; others simply hated her without any convictions, so to speak, naturally, physically—because of her climate, her fields, her forests, her status, her liberated peasants; because of Russian history,—in a word, hated her for everything.

I wish to note that such a hatred may also be quite passive, very calm and indifferent to the point of apathy. And at this juncture redemption moneys began to pass through their hands. In addition, a great many of them suddenly became convinced that with the liberation of the peasants everything was lost—the village, landownership, the nobility, and Russia. True, with the liberation of the peasants, rural labor was left without sufficient organization and protection, and individual landownership, naturally, grew scared and perplexed as in no historical revolution in the past. And so landowners began to sell their lands, and part of them (quite a large part) rushed abroad. But no matter what they may be setting forth in their defense, nevertheless they cannot conceal from their countrymen and their children the fact that the principal cause of their emigration was also the lure of egoistic *far niente*.

Now, ever since those days Russian individual landownership has been in a state of utter chaos: land is sold and resold; owners change every minute; even the appearance of the land is changing; it is being deforested,—and what is it going to be reduced to? who will ultimately own it? of whom is the renovated Russian landowning class going to be composed? what form will it finally assume?—all these things are difficult to predict. And yet, if you please, this is the principal question of the Russian future.

It is a natural law of some kind—not only in Russia but all over the world: those who own the land in a country are its masters—in every respect. Thus it has been always and everywhere. It may be said, however, that in Russia, in addition, we have the commune,—so they are the masters. But is the question of the commune one of those which we have finally settled? Hasn't this question, too, passed fifteen years ago into a different phase like everything else?

However, I shall reserve the discussion of all these things for the future. Meanwhile I shall wind up my thought without supporting evidence: if landownership in a country is *seriously* organized, in that country everything is going to be serious—in all respects both in a general sense and in all particulars. For instance, we are busying ourselves with education, with public schools. And yet I am of the opinion that only then will our schools be seriously and solidly organized when landownership and agriculture are established on a serious and solid foundation, and that productive agriculture will be the result not of the school, but, on the contrary, a good school will come in consequence of productive agriculture, *i.e.*, nationally organized landownership, and under no circumstance prior to that.

Parallel to this example is everything else: domestic affairs, laws, morality, the very genius of the nations. Finally, every correct function of the national organism can be organized only when solid landownership is firmly established. The same may also be said of the character of landownership: let it be aristocratic or democratic, but the character of landownership determines the character of the nation.

But at present our former landowners keep roaming abroad, in all the cities and spas of Europe, screwing up prices in restaurants and dragging after them, as rich men, governesses and nurses for their children, dressed in laces and English costumes; with bare legs, exhibiting them to Europe. And Europe looks at this and wonders: "See, how many rich people there are there! And—what's most important: how many educated people, craving for European enlightenment! It was due to despotism that up to the present time they have been denied foreign passports! And, suddenly, look: how many landowners, capitalists and retired *rentiers* they have! —Yes, more than in France where there are so many *rentiers!*"

And try to explain to Europe that this is a strictly Russian phenomenon; that there is nothing of the *"rentier"* business here; that, on the contrary, this is the devouring of fundamental capital; the burning of the candle at both ends,—of course, Europe would not believe a phenomenon which is impossible there; she would simply not understand it.

And the important point is that these Sybarites sauntering in German spas and on the shores of the Swiss lakes; these Luculluses spending their fortunes in the restaurants of Paris,—they know themselves and even forebode with pain that they will finally eat up their funds, and that their children—these little cherubs in English dresses—perhaps, will have to beg in Europe (and they will beg!) or that they will become French and German workers (they will become French and German workers!). "But"—they say to themselves—*"après nous le déluge.* And who's to blame?—Again it's our Russian order of things, our ponderous Russia where there still is nothing a decent man can be doing." This is how they reason, while the most liberal of them, those who may be called the sublimest and purest Westerners of the Forties, say, perhaps, to themselves: "Well, what of it if the children be left destitute! As against this, they will inherit the idea, the noble leaven of the true and sacred mode of reasoning. Brought up away from Russia, they will not know the 'popes' and the stupid word 'fatherland.' They will understand that the fatherland is a prejudice—one of the most pernicious in the world. They will acquire noble cosmopolitan minds. We, and only we Russians, will initiate these new minds. By the fact itself that we are squandering abroad our redemption moneys we are laying the foundation of the new forthcoming international citizenship which, sooner or later, will reform Europe, and all the honor therefor is ours because we have started ahead of all others."

True, thus speak only the "gray-curled," *i.e.,* only very few,

since are there many progressives, indeed?—The more practical,
even from among the "gray-curled," *those who are not so noble,*
in the long run, are still pinning their hopes on "connections." "It
is true that we are here squandering our fortunes, nevertheless
we are gaining something—well, acquaintances, connections which
later on will prove useful in the 'fatherland.' Besides, even though
we are bringing up our children in a liberal spirit, nevertheless we
are bringing them up as gentlemen, and this, after all, is the main
thing. They will hover in exclusive and high spheres, while liberalism
in these spheres has always signified and accompanied gentility,
because a gentlemen's liberalism is useful to the highest conservatism, so to speak: in Russia this has always been recognized. And
what's there in the fact that we are bringing up our children abroad?
—This precisely means that we are training them for the diplomatic
service. How delightful are all these positions in conjunction with
the embassies and consulates! How innumerable are these handsome positions and how delightfully they are situated! These will
suffice for our children: easy, nice, moneyed and solid; besides, the
service always commands the public eye: clean, dandyish, gentle-
manly service! As to the work—well, it's a soft job; what one
has to do is to strike up acquaintances with Russians abroad—
from among those who are more respectable; but those who are
up to mischief and who seek consular protection, we shall treat
haughtily, as authoritatively as possible: we shan't even listen to
them: 'We don't believe you! You're causing trouble! You imagine
that you're still in our dear fatherland, whereas this is a clean
place. Because of fellows like you we're likely to run into disagreeablenesses, and is it worthwhile to trouble the foreign authorities!
Look at yourselves in a mirror—and you will see to what state
you're reduced!' Therein is the whole service! Briefly, our little
children will know how to make their way. Yes, sir. Connections
—that's what the parent's heart has to be concerned about; the rest
will come of its own accord when need arises."

Thus, all the less noble—from among those squandering their
fortunes abroad—are counting on connections. Yet what are these?
—Well, even if they mean something, nevertheless this *cloth* wears
out very quickly. And it wouldn't be a bad thing at all, in addition
to connections, to have in store, say, a little knowledge of Russia
and a mind of one's own—for any eventuality. At present, however,
in the epoch of reforms and new principles, in Russia, as if on
purpose, everyone wishes to be guided by his own mind; this
is what everybody wants. To be sure, this is an enlightened idea,
but the trouble is that at no time has there been in Russia less
independent thought than in our day and this—in the face of a

universal desire to have it. Why this is so—I will not venture to
decide; besides, this would be difficult. Still, I do positively know
one of the reasons why our little cherubs will unquestionably turn
out to be fools: and even though this is an old factor, I shall
specify it.

However, this is the same thing which I have pointed out
last year. The reason lies in the Russian language, *i.e.*, the insufficiency of the Russian native tongue because of upbringing abroad,
with foreign governesses and nurses. This has always been prevalent
in our midst, meaning, this deficiency; but never to such an extent
as now when so many little cherubs are being brought up abroad.
Let us say that they are being trained for the diplomatic service,
and, as we know, French is the diplomatic language, while it is
sufficient to know the Russian language merely grammatically. But
is this so? Much as this question is obsolete to the point of triviality,
nevertheless it is still so unsettled that recently it has been discussed in the press, though indirectly, apropos of Mr. Turgenev's
work in French.

The opinion has been expressed that "what difference would
it make to Mr. Turgenev to write in either Russian or French," and
that "in that there would be nothing prohibitory." Of course, there
is nothing prohibitory, especially to so great a writer and connoisseur of the Russian language as Turgenev. And if it be his
fancy, why shouldn't he write in French, particularly because he
knows it almost as well as the Russian tongue? On this ground—
not a word about Turgenev.

But . . . but I see that I am decidedly repeating myself; last
year I said exactly the same, referring to the same subject, and
also in the same months spent abroad, when I was conversing with
an outlandish Russian mama concerning the harm of the French
language to her little cherubs. However, mama is now bringing up
her darling ones for a diplomatic vocation, and, strictly, speaking,
it is only diplomacy that I intend to touch upon, and although
I feel it unpleasant to repeat myself, nevertheless I shall risk dedi-
cating to it a few words.

"But French is the diplomatic language," mama interrupts
me—this time even without giving me a chance to begin. Alas, since
last year she has been preparing for this, and she treats me haughtily.

"Quite so, madam"—I answer her—"yours is a strong argument, and I am in perfect accord with you. But, to begin with,
that which I have said about the knowledge of the Russian tongue
is equally applicable to French—isn't this so? For in order to be
able to express the wealth of one's being in French one has got
to master it, too, in a perfect manner. Well, you should know that

there is such a mystery of nature, her law, by virtue of which man can have a perfect knowledge of that language only with which he is born, *i.e.*, that which is spoken by the people to whom he belongs." You knit your brows; I have offended you. You look scoffingly at me. You wave your little hand, and you assure me that you have already heard this last year, and that I am repeating myself.

"Very well, I concede this; besides, it is not a *ladies'* theme. I will simply concede and will agree with you that a Russian, too, may acquire a perfect knowledge of the French language, subject, however, to an all-important condition: that he be born in France, that he grow up there, and that, from the very first hour of his life, he be transformed into a Frenchman.

"Oh, you are put into good humor! You are smiling. However, please observe, madam, that even for you this will not be quite possible to effect as concerns your little cherub, notwithstanding all conveniences, *i.e.*, emigration, redemption monies, the Parisian nurse, and the like. Besides, you should also take into account the faculties inborn, so to speak: indeed, in the matter of these faculties, your little cherub, for example, cannot be compared with Mr. Turgenev. Tell me, are many Turgenevs born? . . . .

"Ah, no, now, what do I say!—Again, I made a mistake, my tongue slipped: without fail, your little cherub will become a Turgenev, or three Turgenevs at once. Let's leave this, but . . ."

"But"—you suddenly interrupt me—"all diplomats are clever anyway, so why should one be so concerned about intellect? Believe me: connections—that's the only thing needed. Mon mari . . ."

"You are quite right, madam,"—I hasten to interrupt her—"connections—that's the thing, but leaving your husband as much aside as possible, I shall nevertheless observe that, in addition to connections, it wouldn't be bad to have a bit of brains. And, to begin with, diplomats are clever not because they are diplomats, but because they were clever men even before they became diplomats. Believe me also that there are a great many diplomats who are remarkably stupid men."

"Ah, not at all, no!"—You interrupt me impatiently—"All diplomats are always clever; they all occupy such excellent positions! And this is the noblest kind of service!"

"Madam, madam!"—I exclaim—"You say: connections, knowledge of languages. But connections can merely provide one with a position, and after that? . . . Now, please visualize: your little cherub is growing up in the midst of European restaurants. He is leading a fast life in the company of young cocottes, foreign viscounts and our Russian counts, but after that—what? . . . Well, he knows all languages, and for this reason alone—not a single one. Deprived of his native tongue, he, naturally, catches but the fragments of thoughts and sentiments of all nations; his mind, ever since his youthful years, has been shaken up into some sort of a muddy concoction; he becomes an international neither-here-nor-there creature with short, abortive meagre ideas, with a dull narrowness of judgment. He is a diplomat, but, to him, the history of nations somehow shapes itself in a burlesque manner. He does not see, nor does he even suspect, how nations and people live, what laws govern their organisms, and whether there is wholeness in these laws, whether some general international law can be perceived in them. He is ready to deduce all world events from the mere fact that this or that queen has angered the favorite mistress of this or that king, and thus a war has broken out between two kingdoms. . . .

"Let me please reason from your point of view. All right, let's say 'connections.' . . . But to acquire connections character is needed—amiability of the character, mildness, kindness, and at the same time—firmness, perseverance. . . . For a diplomat has to be captivating; he must, so to speak, charm, conquer,—isn't this so? Well, will you believe me or not if I tell you directly and most positively that without the knowledge of one's native tongue, without having mastered it, it is entirely impossible to build up a character, even if the little cherub is naturally well and richly gifted. In due course of time, thoughts, ideas and feelings will arise in him; these ideas and sentiments will, so to speak, press upon him from within, seeking and demanding expression for themselves. Yet without the rich, ready forms of expression contracted since childhood, i.e., without the language, without its cultivation, without its fineness, without the mastery of its nuances,—your son will always be dissatisfied with himself. Fragments of thoughts will no longer satisfy him; the material accumulating in the mind and in the heart will demand elaborate expression. . . . The young man will become preoccupied and absentminded, aimlessly pensive, and later—he will grow surly, intolerable; he will lose his health; perhaps he will even be affected with indigestion.—Would you believe it? . . .

"But I see you bursting into laughter. Well, once more I was carried away—I admit. (And yet, good Lord,—how true the things I am saying!) However, permit me to finish. Permit me to remind you that just now I gave in and agreed with you, for form's sake, that diplomats are nevertheless clever; but you have driven me, madam, to the point where I am compelled not to conceal from you the most secret underlying reason for my view on the subject.

Several times in my life, madam, as if on purpose, the thought has occurred to me that in diplomacy at large, among all nations, there have been but very few clever men. It is even surprising. On the contrary, the dullness of this caste in the European history of the present century . . . That is, you see, they are all clever—more or less—this is undeniable; they are all witty, but what are their minds? Has a single one of them penetrated the substance of things and foreseen those mysterious laws which lead Europe toward something unknown, strange, dreadful, which, however, is already obvious at present, which is taking place quite evidently in the sight of those who are at least a little capable of foresight? No, madam, it may be positively asserted that in this respectable and most privileged caste there wasn't a single diplomat, not a single mind of this caliber! (Of course, in making this statement, I am excluding Russia and everything domestic since, by our very essence, in this respect we are 'a different story.') Quite the reverse is true: throughout this whole century there appeared the craftiest diplomatic minds—this I admit; intriguers with a pretense at the most realistic understanding of things. And yet none of them perceived anything beyond their noses and beyond current interests (at that—the most superficial and erroneous ones!). To tie a torn little thread, to put a little patch on a hole, 'to screw up the price, to gild a thing so it be taken for something new'—that's our job, that's where our work lies!

"There are good reasons for all this: in my opinion the major reason is the disunity of the principles, the alienation from the people and the segregation of the diplomatic minds in too fashionable a sphere detached from mankind.

"Take the instance of Count Cavour,—wasn't his a great mind? Wasn't he a diplomat?—I am citing him because his genius is generally recognized and also because he is dead. Yet what did he do, look: Oh, he did achieve his aim, he did unite Italy, but what was the result?—For 2,000 years Italy bore in herself a universal unifying idea—not some abstract idea, not a speculation of some theoretical mind, but a realistic, organic idea; the fruit of the national and universal life. This was the unification of the whole world—first, the ancient Roman and later—the papal unification. The peoples who have been growing and disappearing in Italy in the course of these two and one-half millennia, understood that they were the bearers of a universal idea, while those who did not understand it felt and divined it. Science, art—everything was invested and permeated with this universal significance. Oh, let us admit that, at length, this universal idea became worn out and wasted there (although hardly so!). But what—in the long run—

has come in its stead? Upon what can Italy be congratulated?
What advantage has she achieved after Count Cavour's diplomacy?
—There rose a united second-rate little kingdom which had lost
every kind of a universal aspiration; which exchanged it for the
most worn-out, bourgeois principle—the thirtieth repetition of this
principle since the French revolution—a kingdom fully content with
its unity which means nothing, a mechanical, and not a spiritual
unity (*i.e.*, not the former universal unity), and on top of that—
a kingdom burdened with insolvent indebtedness, and, in addition,
—one specifically content with its own second-rateness. This is what
came of it; such was Count Cavour's creation!

"In a word, the contemporaneous diplomat is precisely 'a
great beast for petty affairs.' Count Metternich was considered
one of the subtlest and most profound diplomats in the world;
and, undeniably, he did exercise an influence over the whole of
Europe. And yet what was his idea? How did he understand his
epoch, which in his days was just marking its beginning? How did
he foresee the future?—Alas, he decided to use police measures in
dealing with all the fundamental ideas of the century which were
coming into being, and he was quite sure of success!

"Let's turn to Prince Bismarck,—this one is undeniably a
genius, but . . ." *"Finissons, monsieur"*—sternly Mama interrupts
me, haughtily, with an air of profoundly insulted dignity. It goes
without saying that I am at once awfully scared. Of course, I am
not understood: one shouldn't touch upon such themes with the
mamas, and I have made a terrible lapse. But with whom, in our
day, may one speak about diplomacy?—That's the question.—And
yet what an interesting theme, and specifically—in our day! However . . .

2

DIPLOMACY IN THE FACE OF WORLD PROBLEMS

And what a grave theme! For what is the characteristic
trait of our present time? All those endowed with wisdom maintain that ours is pre-eminently a diplomatic epoch, a time when
all world destinies have to be settled by diplomacy alone. It is
asserted that supposedly somewhere there is a war in progress.
I have even heard that there actually was a war in progress, but
I am told—this I read everywhere—that if somewhere there is
something on the order of a war,—all this is understood in a wrong
sense. . . .

At all events, it has been decided that the war will impede
nothing, that is, no healthy functions of the nation which—accord-

ing to the latest views of everything that is called "supreme wisdom"—are pre-eminently and solely centered in diplomacy; and
that all these military promenades, manœuvres, and so forth—ad-
mittedly necessary—in truth, constitute but one of the phases of
superior diplomacy,—nothing else.

Thus we have to believe. For my own part, I am very much
inclined to believe so, since all this is quite reassuring. However,
this is what is curious and awfully conspicuous: The Eastern question arose in Russia; simultaneously, and even earlier it has also
arisen throughout Europe, and this is quite understandable: everybody and even non-diplomats (especially they) know that the
Eastern question is, so to speak, one of the world questions, one
of the fundamental *divisions* of the international and immediate
settlement of human destinies, their new and forthcoming phase.
It is known that the matter concerns not only the East of Europe,
not only the Slavs, the Russians and the Turks, or specifically
some sort of Bulgarians, but also Western Europe as a whole; and
that it is confined not only to seas and straits, entrances and exits,
but that it is much deeper, more fundamental, more elemental,
more vital, more essential, more primordial. Therefore, it is understandable why Europe is alarmed and why diplomacy is kept so
busy.

But what is diplomacy's business?—This is my question!
With what is diplomacy (pre-eminently at present) occupied in the
Eastern question?—The business of diplomacy (otherwise it wouldn't
be diplomacy) at present is to suppress the Eastern question in
all respects, and promptly to assure everybody concerned and not
concerned, that no question at all has arisen, and that all these
things are merely little manœuvres and promenades; and also to
assure, if possible, that not only has the Eastern question not
arisen, but that it has never existed; that it only comes to the
fact that a century ago fog has been spread—also on diplomatic
grounds—and that this unexplained fog continues to persist.

Frankly speaking, this could even be believed were it not
for a certain riddle, but no longer a diplomatic one (that's the
trouble!) since diplomacy never, under any circumstance, tackles
such riddles; moreover, it turns away from them with contempt,
considering them mere fantasies unworthy of superior minds. This
riddle could be formulated thus: Why was it always so, especially
of late, *i.e.*, beginning with the middle of the nineteenth century
—and the more lately the more graphically and concretely—why
is it that the moment there arises in the world a matter concerning
something universal, at once, side by side with such a universal
question, parallel to it, *all the other* universal questions arise?

Thus, it doesn't suffice that at present there arises in Europe one universal question,—nay, suddenly, and unexpectedly, side by side with it, Europe raises in France another world question—the Catholic question. And this one not on the alleged ground that the Pope is soon going to die, and that France, as the representative of Catholicism, should see to it that nothing should change in its centuries-old organization, but also because, apparently, Catholicism has been chosen as a common banner for rallying the whole old order of things,—the product of nineteen centuries. This is an alliance against something new and forthcoming, vital and fatal,— against the impending renovation of the universe through a new order of things; against the social, moral and fundamental revolution in the whole Western European life. Or, at least, if there is going to be no revival, the alliance is to be directed against the dreadful concussion and the colossal revolution which undeniably threatens to shake all the bourgeois states throughout the world, wherever the bourgeoisie has organized and flourished after the French pattern of 1789, and to overthrow it and to take its place.

By the way: I shall deviate for a moment from my theme in order to make a *nota bene* because I have a presentiment that to some wiseacres, particularly the liberal ones, it will seem funny that in the very midst of the nineteenth century I call France a Catholic state and a representative of Catholicism! For this reason, in the way of explanation of my thought, I will state—as yet without supporting evidence—that France is a country which, even if there shouldn't remain in it a single person believing in the Pope or even in God, will nevertheless continue to be a pre-eminently Catholic country, the representative, so to speak, of the entire Catholic organism, its banner; it will continue to be that for a long time, perhaps, incredibly long, when France ceases to be France and is transformed into something different.

Moreover, socialism itself will begin in France in accordance with the Catholic pattern, with Catholic organization and leaven; not otherwise—to such an extent that country is Catholic! At present I am not going to prove these things in detail. For the time being I shall merely point, for instance, to the following: Why was it that MacMahon was suddenly, for no apparent reason, prompted to raise, precisely, the Catholic issue? This brave general (however, almost everywhere beaten, and who in diplomacy distinguished himself with the brief phrase: "J'y suis et j'y reste"), it would seem, is by no means one of those men who are able to raise *consciously* an issue of this kind. And yet, he did raise the most basic of the old European questions, and precisely in the form it had to be raised. But what is more important: Why was it raised exactly at the time when in another corner of the world another world issue had been raised—the Eastern question? Why does one issue press itself upon the other? Why does one question generate another notwithstanding the fact that between them there is no apparent connection?

And not only these two issues were raised simultaneously: together with the Eastern question other questions were raised, and still others will be brought forward if the former issue develops correctly. Briefly, the fundamental problems of Europe and of mankind in our age are always set up simultaneously. And it is precisely this synchronism that is impressive. The condition that all questions necessarily arise simultaneously constitutes the riddle!

But why am I saying all this?—Because diplomacy looks upon these specific problems with contempt. Not only does it not recognize any such coincidences but it refuses even to think about them. According to diplomacy these are all mirages, nonsense and trifles: "There are no such things, and simply Marshal MacMahon, or rather his wife, had some sort of a whim, and that's how it happened." And on this ground, even though at the beginning of this chapter I did proclaim that ours was pre-eminently a diplomatic epoch, while everything else was a mirage, nevertheless I am the first who must disbelieve this. Nay, here we are faced with a riddle! Nay, here it is not only diplomacy that settles the issue but also something else. I confess that I am very much perplexed with this inference: I was so inclined to believe in diplomacy! And all these new questions are but new bothers, and nothing else. . . .

3

NEVER WAS RUSSIA MORE POWERFUL THAN AT PRESENT —NOT A DIPLOMATIC DECISION

Forsooth, I have merely put the question, but thus far I have dwelt upon it without supporting evidence. But I have always thought, and long before the present question was raised (i.e., the one dealing with the synchronism of the origin of all world issues the moment one of them is raised), about another, incomparably more simple and most natural question to which—precisely because it is so simple and natural—men in their wisdom are paying virtually no attention.

This is the other question: All right, if diplomacy is,—has been, and will be in the future, always and everywhere—the arbitratrix of all the fundamental and most important issues of mankind, nevertheless does the final settlement of European problems always depend upon diplomacy? Isn't it, on the contrary, true that in every question there comes a phase, a point, when it can no longer be settled by appeasing diplomatic means, that is—by little patches? Undeniably, from the diplomatic standpoint, and consequently from the standpoint of common sense, all world questions are always explained by the mere fact that such and such states sought to expand their borders; or this or that brave general had this or that desire; or that some prominent lady was displeased with this or that, etc. (Let this be undeniable; I will concede it because this is superlative wisdom.) Nevertheless, even were we to accept these realistic causes and explanations, isn't there a certain moment, a certain point in the progress of human affairs, a certain phase, when suddenly there appear some strange forces—true, incomprehensible and mysterious forces—which take possession of everything, seizing everything at once, and which drag everything irresistibly, blindly, as it were, downhill or, perhaps, into an abyss?

Essentially, I should like to know if diplomacy is always so reliant upon itself and its resources that it is not in the least afraid of these forces, and points and phases, maybe not suspecting their existence at all?—Alas, it would seem—always. And therefore: how am I going to believe in it and trust it? And am I able to accept diplomacy as the final arbitratrix of the destinies of still so whimsical and licentious a mankind?

Alas, in Kaidanov's detailed history there is one of the greatest phrases, specifically where, in modern history, he begins the description of the French Revolution and the appearance of Napoleon I. This phrase marks the beginning of a chapter, and my mind has retained it all my life. Here it is: "Profound silence reigned throughout Europe when Frederick the Great shut his eyes forever; but never did such a silence precede so great a storm!"

Tell me, do you know a greater phrase?—In fact, who in Europe in those days, i.e., when Frederick the Great shut his eyes forever, could have foreseen—even in a remote manner—the things which would happen to men and to Europe in the course of the subsequent thirty years?—I am not speaking about some ordinary educated people, or even writers, journalists, professors. They all, as we know, were baffled at the time: for example, Schiller wrote a dithyramb on the opening of the National Assembly; young Karamzin, who was then journeying in Europe, beheld the same event with a touching quiver in his heart, while in Petersburg long before that a marble bust of Voltaire adorned his home.

No, I shall directly turn to superlative wisdom—I shall ask the arbitrators of human destinies, that is, the diplomats themselves this question: Did they in those days foresee anything of what was to happen in the next thirty years?

But here is the dreadful thing: Had I asked this question of the diplomats (and please note that almost all European diplomats were using "Kaidashka's" textbook), and if they had deigned to listen to me, they surely would have answered with haughty laughter that *"accidents* cannot be foreseen, and that complete wisdom consists of preparedness for any accidents."

How do you like that! No, I shall tell you: this is a typical answer even though I conceived it myself, since I haven't bothered a single diplomat with questions (and I don't care to). But what I find horrible is that I am convinced that such precisely would have been their answer, and this is why I called it typical. For what —pray tell me—were, if not *accidents,* the events of the end of the last century in the opinion of the diplomats? They were and are. And Napoleon, for instance, was an arch-accident. Had he died over there, in Corsica, at the age of three of scarlet fever, the *tiers état* of mankind, the bourgeoisie, would not have proceeded, with its new banner in hand, to change the whole face of Europe (a procedure which continues up to the present time); would have stayed home in Paris, and, perhaps, would have died away in the very beginning!

The point is that, to my way of thinking, the present period, too, will end in Old Europe with something colossal, *i.e.,* perhaps, not literally identical with the events which brought to an end the eighteenth century, nevertheless equally gigantic, elemental and dreadful,—and also entailing a change of the face of the whole world, or, at least, in the West of Old Europe.

Now, should our wiseacres assert that it is impossible to foresee *accidents,* etc., moreover, if nothing concerning such a finale has occurred to them, then . . .

In a word: little patches, little patches and little patches!

Well, let's be prudent. Let's wait. For patches, if you please, are also necessary, useful, prudent and practical things. All the more so, as patches may, for instance, deceive the enemy.

At present we are at war, and should it so happen that Austria should make a hostile move against us, she could be deceived by a "little patch," and she would readily fall in love with the deception, since what is Austria?—She is at the point of death, she is ready to collapse; she is as much "a sick man" as Turkey is, even worse, perhaps. She is a specimen of all sorts of dualisms, of every kind of internal hostile combinations, nationalities, ideas, different discords and conflicting tendencies: there, there are Hungarians and Slavs and Germans, and there, too, is the kingdom of the Jews.

Now, owing to the fact that diplomacy is courting her, she may, in truth, conceive the idea that she is a power which really means much, and which is capable of achieving much in the general settlement of destinies. Such a deceit of imagination, generated precisely by courtship and little patches, is useful from the standpoint of the settlement of the Slavic destinies; it is useful, since, for awhile it may divert the enemy, whereas by the time of the decision, when he suddenly sees that nobody is afraid of him, and that he is no power at all,—the deceit may bring him to a state of dejection, or simply perplex him.

England is a different proposition: she is something more weighty, and besides, at present she is terribly preoccupied with her own basic ventures. This one will not be lulled to sleep by wooing and little patches. Whatever she may be told, she will never, under any circumstance, believe that an enormous nation, at present the most powerful nation in the world, which has drawn its mighty sword, which has unfolded the banner of a great idea and which has already crossed the Danube, might in reality consent to solve the problems which it intends to tackle to its obvious detriment, solely for England's benefit. For every improvement in the destinies of the Slavic nations constitutes *at all events* a conspicuous damage to England: no one, under any circumstance, is going to be cajoled by patches—they will not believe them! The point is that in England nobody will believe anything. Besides, what arguments can convince her?—Is it, for instance, the allegation "I will *begin* just a bit, and I will not finish"? But in politics the beginning is everything, since, naturally, sooner or later, the beginning must lead to the end. What is there in the fact that the end is not going to be achieved today?—All the same, it will come tomorrow.

In a word: they will not believe, and for this reason we, too, should not believe the English, or, at least, we should believe them as little as possible—of course, secretly. It would also be a good thing if we should guess that at present England is in a more critical situation than ever. It can be formulated in a precise manner in one word: *Isolation*. For never before, perhaps, has England been in so dreadful an isolation as she is at present. Oh, how glad she would be now to find in Europe an alliance, some *entente cordiale*. But the trouble is that in Europe there has never been a time at which it was more difficult to form an alliance, since precisely now everything in Europe has arisen simultaneously—all world issues at once, and at the same time—all world controversies, so that every nation or state *has its hands full with its own domestic affairs*. And inasmuch as England's interest is not a world interest but one which has long ago been segregated from everybody and which exclusively concerns England alone,—for the time being, at least, she will remain in absolute isolation.

Of course, for the sake of mutual benefits England would be in a position to reach an accord even with those pursuing a conflicting aim: "I will give thee this, and thou give me that." However, by reason of the nature of the present European troubles it would be difficult to form an *entente cordiale* of this kind—at least, at this moment,—and England will have to wait long for the time when, in the subsequent course of events, somehow, she will get a chance to fit into the picture with her alliance.

Besides, England above all, needs a profitable alliance, *i.e.*, one in which she will take everything, in return giving, if possible, *nothing*. Well, such a profitable alliance at present is least to be expected, and so England is in a state of isolation. Oh, if only we could successfully take advantage of this isolation! But at this juncture we may utter another exclamation: "Oh, if we were less sceptical, and if only we could believe in the fact that there are world questions, and that they are not a mirage!"

The main point is that in Russia a very considerable part of our intelligentsia is, somehow, always inclined to perceive and accept Europe not realistically as it is constituted at present but as an antedated conception, from a retarded viewpoint; it does not look into the future but is rather inclined to judge Europe by her past, even by her remote past.

And yet world problems do really exist, and how can one—especially we—fail to believe in them: Two of these issues have already arisen, being driven no longer by human wisdom but by their own elemental force, by their organic necessity. These can no longer be left without solution despite all the speculations of diplomacy.

But there is likewise a third question, also a world question; it is also arising and has already almost arisen. In particular, it may be designated the Germanic question; essentially, however, it is conspicuously an all-European one, and it is insolubly and organically merged with the fate of Europe as a whole and with all other world issues. But to all appearances nothing can be more pacific and serene than present-day Germany: in the calmness of her terrible force she looks, observes and waits. Everybody more or less needs her; everybody is more or less dependent on her.

And yet all this is a mirage! Therein is the whole point: at present everybody in Europe is preoccupied with his own business; everybody is faced with his own problem of such paramount importance as almost entails his very existence—to be or not to be. A similar problem has also arisen in Germany precisely at the moment when all other world issues have arisen, and—anticipating things—I may add that this condition of Europe is most beneficial to Russia at the present minute! For never has she been so needed by Europe, never has she been so powerful in Europe's opinion; and yet never so completely segregated from the questions arising in Old Europe—most capital and dreadful questions, but *her own,* peculiar only to her, that Old Europe,—and not to Russia.

And at no time would an alliance with Russia have been more treasured by Europe than at present; at no time could Russia have congratulated herself with more joy upon the fact that she is not the Old, but the New Europe; that she is *in se* a separate and mighty world for which the time has now come to enter a new and superior phase of her potency, and to become more than ever independent of other, *their,* fatal questions with which decrepit Europe has bound herself!

CHAPTER III

1

The Germanic World Problem. Germany Is a Protesting Country

BUT WE started speaking about Germany, her present aim, and her present fatal problem, at the same time a world problem. What is this aim? And why is it only now turning into such a troublesome problem for Germany, and why was it not so before, recently, a year ago or even two months ago?

Germany's aim is one; it existed before, always. It is her *Protestantism*—not that single formula of Protestantism which was conceived in Luther's time, but her continual Protestantism, her continual protest against the Roman world, ever since Arminius,—against everything that was Rome and Roman in aim, and subsequently—against everything that was bequeathed by ancient Rome to the new Rome and to all those peoples who inherited from Rome her idea, her formula and element; against the heir of Rome and everything that constitutes this legacy.

I am convinced that some readers, upon reading these lines, will shrug their shoulders and will start laughing: "Why, is it possible in the nineteenth century, in the age of new ideas and science, to talk about Catholicism and Protestantism—as if we were still living in the Middle Ages! And, perhaps, if there be religious people, even fanatics, they survive as an archæologic rarity; they are confined to specific localities and corners, condemned and ridiculed by everybody, and—what is most important—there are so few of them, just a miserable handful of backward folk. Thus, is it possible to regard them as a something in so high a matter as world politics?"

However, I speak not of the religious *protest*. I am not dwelling upon the temporary formulæ of the ancient Roman idea nor upon the eternal German protest against it. I am referring merely to the basic idea which originated two thousand years ago, and which has survived ever since, gradually transforming itself into different guises and formulæ. Precisely in our day this extreme Western European world, which has inherited the Roman legacy, is in labor with a new metamorphosis of that inherited ancient idea. To those who can see, this is so obvious that it needs no explanations.

Ancient Rome was the first to generate the idea of the universal unity of men, and was the first to start thinking of (and firmly believing in) putting it practically into effect in the form of universal empire. However, this formula fell before Christianity —the formula but not the idea. For this idea is that of European mankind; through this idea its civilization came into being; for it alone mankind lives.

Only the idea of the universal *Roman* empire succumbed, and it was replaced by a new ideal, also universal, of a communion in Christ. This new ideal bifurcated into the Eastern ideal of a purely spiritual communion of men, and the Western European, Roman Catholic, papal ideal diametrically opposite to the Eastern one.

This Western Roman Catholic incarnation of the idea was achieved in its own way, having lost, however, its Christian, spiritual foundation and having replaced it with the ancient Roman legacy. Roman papacy proclaimed that Christianity and its idea, without the universal possession of lands and peoples, are not spiritual but political. In other words, that they cannot be achieved without the realization on earth of a new universal Roman empire now headed not by the Roman emperor but by the Pope. And thus it was sought to establish a new universal empire in full accord with the spirit of the ancient Roman world, only in a different form.

Thus, we have in the Eastern ideal—first, the spiritual communion of mankind in Christ, and thereafter, in consequence of the spiritual unity of all men in Christ and as an unchallenged deduction therefrom—a just state and social communion. In the Roman interpretation we have a reverse situation: first it is necessary to achieve firm state unity in the form of a universal empire, and only after that, perhaps, spiritual fellowship under the rule of the Pope as the potentate of this world.

Since that time, in the Roman world this scheme has been progressing and changing uninterruptedly, and with its progress the most essential part of the Christian element has been virtually lost. Finally, having rejected Christianity spiritually, the heirs of the ancient Roman world likewise renounced papacy. The dreadful French revolution has thundered. In substance, it was but the last modification and metamorphosis of the same ancient Roman formula of universal unity. The new formula, however, proved insufficient. The new idea failed to come true. There even was a moment when all the nations which had inherited the ancient Roman tradition were almost in despair. Oh, of course, that portion of society which in 1789 won political leadership, *i.e.*, the bourgeoisie, triumphed and declared that there was no necessity of going any further. But all those minds which by virtue of the eternal laws of nature are destined to dwell in a state of everlasting universal fermentation seeking new formulæ of some ideal and a new word indispensable to the progress of the human organism,—they all rushed to the humiliated and the defrauded, to all those who had not received their share in the new formula of universal unity proclaimed by the French revolution of 1789. These proclaimed a new word of their own, namely, the necessity of universal fellowship not for the equal distribution of rights allotted to a quarter, or so, of the human race, leaving the rest to serve as raw material and a means of exploitation for the happiness of that quarter of mankind, but, on the contrary—for universal equality, with each and every one sharing the blessings of this world, whatever these may prove. It was decided to put this scheme into effect by resorting to *all* means, *i.e.*, not by the means of Christian civilization—without stopping at anything.

Now, what has been Germany's part in this, throughout these two thousand years? The most characteristic and essential trait of this great, proud and peculiar people—ever since their appearance on the historical horizon—consisted of the fact that they never consented to assimilate their destiny and their principles to those of the outermost Western world, *i.e.*, the heirs of the ancient Roman tradition. The Germans have been *protesting* against the latter throughout these two thousand years. And even though they did not (never did so far) utter "their word," or set forth their strictly formulated ideal in lieu of the ancient Roman idea, nevertheless, it seems that, within themselves, they always were convinced that they were capable of uttering this "new word" and of leading mankind.

They struggled against the Roman world as early as the times of Arminius, and during the epoch of Roman Christianity they, more than any other nation, struggled for the sovereign power against the new Rome.

Finally, the Germans protested most vehemently, deriving their formula of protest from the innermost spiritual, elemental foundation of the Germanic world: they proclaimed the freedom of inquiry, and they raised Luther's banner. This was a terrible, universal break: the formula of protest had been found and filled with a content; even so it still was a negative formula, and the new, *positive* word was not yet uttered.

And now, the Germanic spirit, having uttered this "new word" of protest, as it were, fainted for a while, quite parallel to an identical weakening of the former strictly formulated unity of the forces of his adversary. The outermost Western world, under the influence of the discovery of America, of new sciences and new principles, sought to reincarnate itself in a new truth, in a new phase.

When, at the time of the French Revolution, the first attempt at such a reincarnation took place, the Germanic spirit became quite perplexed, and for a time lost its identity and faith in itself. It proved impotent to say anything against the new ideas of the outermost Western world. Luther's Protestantism had long outlived its time, while the idea of free inquiry had long been accepted by universal science. Germany's enormous organism more than ever began to feel that it had no flesh, so to speak, and no form for self-expression. It was then that the pressing urge to consolidate itself, at least outwardly, into a harmonious organism was born in Germany in anticipation of the new future aspects of her eternal struggle against the outermost Western world.

At this point a rather curious coincidence should be noted: both traditionally adverse camps, both contestants of old Europe for sovereignty over her, simultaneously (or nearly so) seized upon and carried out virtually one and the same task. The new, still meditated, future formula of the outermost Western world, *i.e.*, the regeneration of society on new social foundations, a formula which almost throughout this century has been propagated only by dreamers, by its scientific representatives, all sorts of idealists and castle-builders, suddenly in recent years has changed its guise, its course, and resolved: To abandon, for the time being, the theoretical definition and elaboration of its task, and to embark at once, prior to any fancying, upon its practical phase, *i.e.*, to begin the struggle. For this purpose—to start combining all future champions of the new idea into one organization, meaning the whole *fourth* estate defrauded in 1789, all the needy, all workers, all beggars, and, having achieved this organization—to hoist the banner of a new, unheard-of world revolution.

Thus the International came into existence; there ensued international intercourse among the beggars of this world, meetings, conventions, new regulations, laws,—in a word, *throughout the whole of old Western Europe* there was laid the foundation of a new *status in statu* designed to engulf the old order of this world prevailing throughout Western Europe.

And now, while this was transpiring in the enemy camp, Germany's genius grasped the fact that it was the German task, too,—prior to any other business or undertaking, prior to any attempt at a "new word" against the adversary who had reincarnated himself from the ancient Catholic idea—to complete her own political consolidation and the restoration of her political organism, and, only after having completed that—to face her eternal enemy.

Thus it came to pass: having completed her unification, Germany attacked her enemy, embarking upon a new phase of her struggle against her, which she began with blood and iron. The iron business is finished, and now it has got to be completed spiritually, essentially.

But, suddenly, Germany finds herself faced with a new concern, with a new, unexpected turn of events terribly complicating the task. Now, what is this task and what is this new turn?

2

A CERTAIN INGENIOUSLY SUSPICIOUS MAN

This task, this new *unexpected* concern of Germany, if you please, has long been seeking to come out into the open. At present, however, the whole trouble is caused by the fact that this concern suddenly sprang up into the limelight in consequence of the unexpected clerical revolution in France. This concern, in a way, may be formulated in the form of the following doubt: "Has, in truth, the German organism, been consolidated into one whole? On the contrary, is it not, as heretofore, dismembered in spite of the ingenious efforts of the German leaders during the last twenty-five years? More than that: Has it become consolidated, at least politically? Is it not a mirage, despite the Franco-Prussian war and the promulgation thereafter of the new, hitherto unheard-of, German Empire?" Such is the difficult question.

The whole difficulty of this question lies, principally, in that until quite recently it was even not supposed to be existent, at least, by the overwhelming majority of the Germans. Self-intoxication, pride and absolute faith in their immense might, after the Franco-Prussian war, made almost all Germans drunk, without exception. A people who have rarely been vanquishers but who have been so strangely often vanquished,—that people unexpectedly conquered an enemy who nearly always conquered everybody! And inasmuch as it was clear that they could not help but conquer because of the exemplary organization of their innumerable army, on altogether novel principles, and, besides, because it was headed by such ingenious leaders,—the German could not help but grow proud to the point of intoxication. In this connection it is not even necessary to take into account the habitual self-complacent boastfulness of every German—that inveterate trait of the German character.

On the other hand, from a so recently dismembered political organism there suddenly arose such a harmonious whole that the German could not doubt the fact—and fully believed in it—that the consolidation had been achieved, and that a new brilliant and great phase of development had begun for the Germanic organism.

Thus not only pride and chauvinism but almost levity came into being. What kind of questions could there arise—not merely to some pugnacious shopkeeper or shoemaker, but even to a professor or minister? Even so, there was a handful of Germans who very soon—almost immediately after the Franco-Prussian war—began to doubt and ponder. It was unquestionably Prince Bismarck who stood at the head of the most remarkable members of that small group.

No sooner had the German troops evacuated France than he clearly perceived the fact that too little had been accomplished with "blood and iron" and that—bearing in mind the magnitude of the goal—at least twice as much should have been accomplished—taking advantage of the situation. True, the German side has received immeasurably more military benefits, and these for a long time to come. After the cession of Alsace and Lorraine, territorially France has become so small a country for a great power that, in the case of a new war, after two or three battles successful to the German side, the German troops will at once be in the center of France, and from a strategic standpoint she will be lost.

However, are victories so certain? Is it possible to count certainly upon these two victorious battles?—In the Franco-Prussian war, strictly speaking, the Germans conquered not the French but only Napoleon and his administration. Not always will France have troops so poorly organized and so incompetently commanded. Not always will there be usurpers who, in dynastic interests, needing partisan generals and civil servants, will be compelled to tolerate such lamentable defects as render the existence of a regular army impossible. Not always will Sedan be repeated, since, in truth, Sedan was an accident which happened only because of the fact that Napoleon could no longer have returned to Paris otherwise than by the grace of the Prussian King. Not always will there be such inept generals as MacMahon, and such traitors as Bazaine!

Intoxicated with triumph so unheard of in their case, the Germans—each one of them—of course, could conceive the belief that all this had been achieved exclusively by their talents. However, the doubting group could have thought differently, especially when the conquered foe, who only recently had been so disorganized and shaken, had suddenly, in one lump, paid three billion in indemnity, without even knitting his brows. Naturally, this has greatly saddened Prince Bismarck.

On the other hand, the doubting group faced another, perhaps more important question: Has the political and civil unification within the organism been fully achieved?—Everybody in Europe, and particularly we in Russia, have as yet never doubted this. Generally speaking, we Russians have accepted the things which transpired in Germany during the last ten or fifteen years as something final, not in the least accidental, but natural; as something which must not change. The accomplished facts inspired us with extraordinary respect. However, in the opinion of such ingenious men as Prince Bismarck, hardly everything that had to be accomplished had acquired final solidity. That which today may seem durable is, maybe, nothing but a fantasy. It is difficult to suppose that so inveterate a habit of political disunity will disappear among the Germans as suddenly and as easily as one drinks a glass of water. The German by his nature is headstrong. Besides, the present generation of the Germans has been bribed with successes; it is intoxicated with pride, and is restrained by the iron hand of its leaders. Still, perhaps, in the not distant future, when these leaders pass into another world, ceding their place to other men, the questions and instincts which have temporarily been suppressed will be brought to the foreground. It is also quite probable that the energy of the initial impulse of the consolidation will be exhausted, and, instead, the oppositional energy will again be restored, and that it will undermine that which has been accomplished.

There will arise a tendency for disintegration and segregation at the very moment when, in the West, the dreadful enemy fully recovers from the blow, the enemy who even now is neither sleeping nor drowsing and who will begin with something that may be anticipated.

And, in addition, there appears a law of nature, so to speak:

all the same, in Europe Germany is a *middle* country: no matter how strong she is, on one side is France, and the other—Russia. True, as yet the Russians are courteous. But what if suddenly they should grasp the fact that they are in no need of an alliance with Germany, whereas Germany needs an alliance with Russia; and, moreover, that *the dependency upon an alliance* with Russia especially after the Franco-Prussian war, seems to be Germany's fatal destiny. Therein is the point: that even a man as firmly convinced of his strength as Prince Bismarck cannot believe in too ardent a deference to Russia.

True, until the last unexpected adventure in France which has suddenly changed the whole aspect of the matter, Prince Bismarck has still been hoping that the extraordinary esteem of Russia for a long time would remain unshaken. And suddenly—that adventure! In a word, something extraordinary happened.

Extraordinary—to everybody, but not to Prince Bismarck! Now it appears that his genius had anticipated this whole "adventure." Tell me, was it not his genius, his ingenious eye, that so long ago has discerned the principal adversary? Precisely why did he develop such an intense hatred of Catholicism? Why has he for so many years been pursuing and persecuting everything emanating from Rome (*i.e.*, from the Pope)? Why did he so foresightedly strive for the Italian *alliance* (it may be thus expressed)—if not for the purpose of crushing, with the assistance of the Italian government, the papal principle on earth when the time of the election of a new Pope comes? He persecuted not the Catholic faith but its Roman foundation.

Why, of course, he has been acting as a German, as a Protestant; he has been acting against the principal element of the external Western world which has always been hostile to Germany. Nevertheless, a good many most ingenious and liberal European thinkers regarded this campaign of the great Bismarck against the insignificant Pope as a struggle of an elephant against a fly. Some people were even inclined to explain all this by the queerness of genius, by the caprices of an ingenious man. The point, however, is that the ingenious politician *was able*—perhaps he alone among the politicians of the whole world—to evaluate the strength of the Roman tradition within itself and among Germany's enemies, and to perceive that it may serve in the future as a dreadful cement for the consolidation of all these adversaries into one force. He was able to divine that, perhaps, the Roman idea alone may find such a banner and at the fatal (and—in Bismarck's view—inevitable) moment will unite all the enemies of Germany, already crushed by him, into one dreadful whole.

And now the ingenious conjecture suddenly proved true: all parties in vanquished France, from among those which could have initiated a movement against Germany, were dismembered; not one of them was able to triumph and to seize the power in France. Nor were they able to combine, each one of them pursuing its own aims,—and, suddenly, the banner of the Pope and the Jesuits has united everything. The enemy arose, and the enemy is no longer France but the Pope himself. It is the Pope leading everybody and everything to whom the Roman idea had been bequeathed, who is ready to assault Germany. However, in order to give a clearer account of what has happened, let us examine more attentively the camps of Germany's adversaries.

3

BOTH ANGRY AND STRONG

The Pope is dying. He will very soon pass away. The whole of Catholicism which accepts Christ in the guise of the Roman idea has long been in a state of awful agitation. The fatal moment is approaching. No error should be committed since it would spell the death of the Roman idea.

It may so happen that the new Pope, under the pressure of all European governments will be elected "not freely," and he who is going to be proclaimed as Pope will consent to renounce forever, and as a matter of principle, mundane possessions and the title of the earthly Sovereign which Pius refused to renounce. (On the contrary, at the fatal moment when he had been deprived of both Rome and the last parcel of land, and when only the Vatican had been left in his possession,—at that same moment, as if on purpose, he proclaimed his infallibility, and at the same time the thesis: Without mundane possessions Christianity cannot survive on earth; *i.e.,* strictly speaking, he proclaimed himself Sovereign of the world, having set Catholicism—now dogmatically—the direct aim of a universal monarchy for which he ordained it to strive for the glory of God and of Christ on earth.)

Oh, of course, at the time he made all wits laugh: "Angry but not strong—Khlestakov's brother." And now should the newly elected Pope unexpectedly be bribed, and should even the conclave itself, under the pressure of Europe, be compelled to enter into an agreement with the adversaries of the Roman idea,—well, then that would be its death. If once the regularly elected, infallible Pope should renounce in principle the title of the earthly Sovereign, this would signify that thus it would remain forever.

On the other hand, should the Pope newly elected by the conclave firmly, and *urbi et orbi,* proclaim that he intends to renounce nothing, and that he fully adheres to the former idea; should he start with an anthema against all enemies of Rome and Roman Catholicism,—the governments of Europe might fail to extend recognition to him, and in this case, too, there may occur in the Roman Church a fatal and violent commotion whose consequences would be innumerable and unpredictable.

Oh, isn't it true that this would sound funny and insignificant to politicians and diplomats of Europe! The downtrodden Pope, imprisoned in the Vatican, appeared to them during the last years as such a nullity that it would have been a shame to pay any attention to him. Thus many progressives of Europe have been reasoning, especially the witty and liberal ones. The Pope delivering allocutions and issuing syllabuses, receiving devotionalists, damning and dying—in their view resembled a buffoon performing for their entertainment. The thought that an enormous universal idea which had been conceived in the brain of the devil when he was tempting Christ in the wilderness; an idea which has been organically living in the world one thousand years; that this idea, nevertheless, would die in an instant—was taken for granted.

Of course, here the mistake lay in the religious meaning of that idea, in that two meanings were intermixed: "It is so rare that men believe in God, especially in the Roman interpretation of God, while in France even the people do not believe in Him,—maybe only the upper class,—and even they do not believe but merely make wry faces,—what significance, then, can the Pope and Roman Catholicism have in our enlightened age?" This is what wits are convinced of even in our day.

However, the religious idea and the papal idea are essentially different. Now it was this papal idea which in our day, only two months ago, suddenly manifested such a viability, such a force that it has caused in France a most radical political revolution, has put a bridle upon her and slavishly dragged her along in its wake.

In recent years in France the parliamentary majority has been republican. Republicans conducted their affairs decently, honestly, quietly, with no commotions. They improved the army, allocating huge sums without raising any objections. However, they did not even think about war, and everybody understood both in France and in Europe that if there was a peaceable party it certainly was the republican party. Its leaders evinced restraint and extraordinary prudence. Essentially, however, they all were abstract men and idealists. They were incorrigible and quite impotent people. These were liberal, gray-haired old men making themselves look younger and imagining themselves still young. They congealed in the ideas of the first French revolution, *i.e.*, in the triumph of the *tiers état,* and they are an incarnation of the bourgeoisie in the strictest meaning of the term. This was exactly the same as the July monarchy with the difference only that it was called a republic and that there was no king (*i.e.*, of course, a "tyrant"). The only new thing they introduced was the promulgation, in 1848, of universal suffrage, which the July royal government was so afraid of and which had produced nothing dangerous; on the contrary, it had contributed to the bourgeoisie much that was distinctly useful. Subsequently this idea proved very useful to the government of Napoleon III.

In their parlance the word "republic" was something comically idealistic. It would seem that this innocent party could have fully satisfied France, *i.e.*, the urban bourgeoisie and the landowners. However, the contrary proved true. In fact, why has the republic always seemed in France an unreliable government? And if the republicans were not always hated, they were always despised by the overwhelming majority of the bourgeoisie for their impotence. Likewise the people almost never believed in them. The point is that every time a republic had been established in France, everything lost there its solidity and self-assurance. Up to the present time the republic has always been some kind of a provisional interim—between social endeavors of the most dreadful dimensions, on the one hand, and some, at times most impudent, usurper. And inasmuch as this happened almost invariably, society became used to viewing the republic accordingly. And just as soon as a republic came into existence, everybody always felt, as it were, in a state of interregnum; and no matter how prudently republicans governed, the bourgeoisie, under their administration, was always convinced that, sooner or later, the red rebellion would thunder, or some kind of a monarchy would be proclaimed.

It came to the point where the bourgeoisie took a greater liking to the monarchical form of government than to the republic, notwithstanding the fact that the monarchy, for example under Napoleon III, made attempts, as it were, to enter into an agreement with the Socialists, whereas no one on earth is more hostile toward socialists than the strict republicans. These are content with the mere word "republic," whereas socialists are concerned not about words but only about deeds. According to the principles of the socialists, it makes no difference whether it be a republic or a monarchy, whether they be French or Germans, and, in truth, if somehow it came to the point where the Pope should be of some service to them, they would also acclaim the Pope. Above all, they are concerned about *their own business, i.e.,* about the triumph of the fourth estate and the equal distribution of rights to the blessings of the world, and as to the particular banner—that's unessential, let it be despotism itself.

It is noteworthy that Prince Bismarck hates socialism no less than popery, and that particularly of late the German government began to fear socialistic propaganda all too greatly. Unquestionably this is due to the fact that socialism deprives the national principle of its individuality, undermining the very foundations of nationality; however, the principle of nationality is the fundamental, all-important idea of German unity, of everything that has occurred in recent years. But it is quite possible that Prince Bismarck takes even a deeper view, *i.e.,* that socialism is the forthcoming power for all of Western Europe, and should papacy ever be forsaken and rejected by the governments of the world, it is more than likely to throw itself into the arms of socialism and merge with it.

On foot and barefooted, the Pope will go to all the beggars, and he will tell them that everything the socialists teach and strive for is contained in the Gospel; that so far the time had not been ripe for them to learn about this; but that now the time has come, and that he, the Pope, surrenders Christ to them and believes in the ant-hill.

Roman Catholicism does not need Christ. (This is all too clear.) What it strives for is universal sovereignty. It will say: "What you need is a united front against the enemy. Unite, then, under my power, since I alone—among all powers and potentates of the world —am *universal;* and let us go together!" Probably Prince Bismarck foreshadows this picture, because he alone among all diplomats was so quick-sighted as to prefigure the viability of the Roman idea and that energy with which it is determined to defend itself regardless, by any means. It is inspired with a devilish desire to live, and it is difficult to kill it—it is a snake! This is what Prince Bismarck alone—the principal enemy of papacy and of the Roman idea— realizes to the fullest extent.

But the little old fellows who try to appear younger than they are—the republicans—are unable to comprehend this. From mere liberalism, they hated clericalism, but they considered the Pope to be impotent and despicable, and the Roman idea—altogether obsolete. It did not even occur to them to live on good terms with the dreadful clerical party—at least, politically—in order to fortify themselves. For the time being, at least, they shouldn't have irritated the clericals, they shouldn't have provoked them with so intentional a strife; they might even have promised them some assistance in connection with the election of the new Pope. Yet they did precisely the reverse either because of ideal honesty or simply from light-mindedness. Of late, they have been persecuting the clericals with particular vigor,—and this at the very moment when France alone was left as a support of papacy which otherwise had to face the dreadful chance of dying together with Pius IX. Since who else, in Europe, in case of need, could draw the sword in defense of the "freedom" of the election of the Pope and the freedom of the elected Pope?—Besides, this must be a strong, a mighty sword. Save for France with her million-strong army, there was no other choice. And now, France is at the head of the enemies!

True, Marshal MacMahon is obedient, but he is in their clutches, and he does not know how to extricate himself: the majority in the Chamber is republican and liberal, and no other party is in a position to replace it. In a word, it is impossible to overthrow the republican majority, and, all of a sudden, those despised and impotent clericals come to Marshal MacMahon's aid, revealing to the whole world such a potency as no one had any longer expected from them. They announce to the parties that they can unite only under the clerical banner, and these, impressed with the obviousness, at once agree with them.

In fact, both to the legitimists and the Bonapartists the principal and nearest foe is the republican majority. If each of these parties works apart for itself, it can achieve nothing; yet, jointly, they can become a power conquering everything and disperse the republicans. And after they have crushed the republic, each party can take care of itself, and, of course, each of them will have all the more chance of success, the more it gratifies the clericals. The latter have reckoned all this mathematically; the junction did take place, and the clerical majority of the Senate gave MacMahon permission to disperse the republicans.

4

THE BLACK ARMY. THE LEGIONS' OPINION AS A NEW ELEMENT OF CIVILIZATION

Having manifested such unexpected strength and adroitness, the clericals, no doubt, will go further. At a moment which will be decisive for them, they will declare war on Germany—and this is what Prince Bismarck realized at once! They have already achieved the main thing. MacMahon has agreed to throw France into a policy of adventure. Will the clericals stop at this juncture?—Certainly, they don't have to pity France!—They need France, as everything else in the world, only as long as she is useful to them.

Oh, they might have pitied her: that country is their only hope and it has served them so many centuries! At present, however, they stand before the most critical moment in the whole millennium, and if it is France that happens to be around, why shouldn't they suck her sap out, even if it kills her? Why not risk her very existence? It is imperative to take from her everything she can give. And what is more important still: it is impossible to tarry even for a minute—a little later and for them unquestionably it will be too late. So that precisely now the attempt should be made to check Bismarck, since, if anyone will be harmful at the time of the election of the Pope certainly it is he. And on top of that, Bismarck, as if on purpose, is alone precisely at this minute, alone, without allies. Russia (his whole hope) is now busy in the East.

Finally, if they succeeded in taming Bismarck, though temporarily, it would be necessary, as quickly as possible and in advance, to lay the foundation for the *future*. It would be necessary to take advantage of the successful moment, and once and forever to create out of France a faithful ally, obedient and ready to do anything. And for this purpose it would be indispensable to effect in France a revolution, but a *serious* one—radical and secular. No doubt, in all this there is much risk, but let others waver—not the Jesuit fathers.

The main thing is that at this moment they have no choice other than to risk and risk. . . .

They positively cannot confine themselves to the clerical *coup d'état* accomplished in France without a war with Germany and a *serious* revolution in France. They have precisely reached this state of affairs. They have to have everything or nothing: should they merely take a wee bit, confining themselves to the exercise of some sort of an influence in government circles, this would bring them no advantage whatsoever since at present their needs are great! For this reason they must venture a most conspicuous and arrogant risk, because they must take the whole *va-banque*. Should the risk fail, for instance, should the Germans again conquer and crush France, all the same the clericals' situation wouldn't be worse than at present (*i.e.*, had they kept quiet and had they not started their *coup d'état*): they would keep what they have, what they had prior to the beginning of the "adventure"; in other words, they would be in a most miserable situation which couldn't grow worse.

The case of France is different: should she again be conquered she would perish. But are Jesuits such fellows as to retreat before a contingency of this sort?—They know that were France victorious they would get *everything* and they would grow so strong in France that it would become impossible to exterminate them there. And for this they possess their special means, as yet unheard of in France.

All other revolutionists, even the most rabid and reddest ones, having accomplished a *coup d'état,* would nevertheless take into account—in a way, at least—certain general things which existed before, even lawful things. However, the Jesuit revolutionists cannot act lawfully, they can act only *uncommonly.* This black army standing without the boundaries of mankind and its civic status, without civilization, emanates exclusively from within itself. This is a *status in statu;* this is the Pope's army. It seeks but the triumph of *its own* idea,—and after that let everything standing in its way perish; let all the other factors wither and perish; let everything standing in discord with them die—civilization, society, science! Unquestionably it will be their task to cultivate France in a new and final manner if chance be on their side, and to sweep out of her all *litter* with such a mop as was unheard of, so as to eliminate every suggestion of resistance, conveying to the country a new organic constitution under the strictest Jesuit tutelage—for ever and ever.

All this, at first glance, may seem quite nonsensical. In the French papers (as well as in ours) all well-intentioned people are firmly convinced that the clericals will unfailingly break their legs at the next election of the French Chamber. The French republicans, in the innocence of their soul, are also fully convinced that all the *activité dévorante* of the newly appointed prefects and mayors will achieve nothing; that all former republicans will be reelected, and that they will form the previous majority, vetoing all of MacMahon's schemes; after that the clericals will be thrown out, and, perhaps, MacMahon himself with them.

However, this confidence is altogether unfounded, and certainly in this respect the clericals are not very much worried. The point is that the naïve and pure-in-heart little old fellows, in spite of their long experience, still seem not fully to comprehend the sort of people they are dealing with. For should the election prove even slightly unfavorable to the clericals, they would oust the new Chamber, too, notwithstanding all its constitutional and legal rights. It may be objected that this would be unlawful and, therefore, impossible.—This is so, but what do laws matter to them, to that black army? They will certainly suggest—and there are already facts tending to support this contention—to the obedient Marshal MacMahon the desperate resolution of resorting to such a device as has never yet been employed even in France, namely—*military despotism.* People will exclaim that this is an old device; that it

has been resorted to several times—by the Napoleons, for instance!
—Even so, I venture to remark that all this was different: this
device *in all its candor* has never been employed in France. Marshal
MacMahon, having enlisted for himself the devotion of the army,
would be in a position simply with bayonets to disperse the new
forthcoming Assembly of the French representatives, *should it oppose him,* after which he would announce to the whole country
that *such was the will of the army.* Much like a Roman emperor
of the epoch of the decadence of the Empire, he could declare that
henceforth "he would take into consideration only the opinion of
the legions." Then a general state of siege and military despotism
would be inaugurated,—and you will see, you will, that these will
please many people in France! And believe me that, if this should
prove necessary, there would be plebiscites which *by a majority
vote of all France* would authorize war and would appropriate the
funds needed therefor.

In his recent address to the troops Marshal MacMahon spoke
precisely in this spirit, and it was very favorably received by the
army. There can be no doubt that the army is rather in favor of
him. Besides, now he has gone so far that he cannot stop lest he
lose his post, whereas his whole policy is expressed in one phrase:
"J'y suis et j'y reste," that is, "Here I am, and here I'm going to
stay." As is known, he did not go further than this phrase, and,
of course, for the triumph of this motto he may even, perhaps, risk
the very existence of France.

Once, at the time of the Franco-Prussian war, he already
proved his readiness for such a risk, when, under the influence of
the Bonapartists, he deliberately ventured to deprive France of
her army, from devotion to Napoleon's dynasty. The clericals, no
doubt, have guaranteed him his *"J'y suis et j'y reste."*

Having united the parties, *i.e.,* the legitimists and the Bonapartists, under their banner, certainly they must have been able
adroitly to *point out* to MacMahon that, if necessary, it would be
possible to do without both Chambord and Bonaparte; that it
would not be necessary at all to call them,—under no circumstance
—but that simply he, Marshal MacMahon, should remain dictator
and permanent ruler—that is, not for the term of seven years, but
forever.

This is how the motto *"J'y suis et j'y reste"* will come to
pass—on condition of the army's consent; however, France's subsequent acquiescence is inevitable because a firm dictatorial hand at
the head of the government will appeal to the taste of quite a few.

Such flattering *suggestions,* no doubt, have been made. Perhaps doubt will be expressed that a man such as MacMahon would

be able to undertake and achieve all these things. But, to begin with, he did undertake and achieve the first half of the task, that half which was in no way easier, from the standpoint of resoluteness, than the second future one. Secondly, it is precisely such men, not at all enterprising *in se,* if, suddenly, they fall under somebody's supreme and decisive influence, who are capable of revealing enormous and fatal resoluteness,—not because of great genius but precisely on account of the opposite reason.

In this connection the main thing is—not reasoning, but simply —the push; and once they are well pushed, they push on in one direction till they either break the wall with their head or break their horns.

5

A Rather Unpleasant Secret

All this is well understood in Germany. At least, all semi-official organs of the press, influenced by Prince Bismarck, are firmly convinced of the inevitability of war. Who is going to assault first and precisely when is not known, but there is much chance that war may break out. Of course, the storm may still blow over. The whole hope rests in the possibility that Marshal MacMahon, like Ajax in the past, might unexpectedly grow afraid of everything he has assumed, and, perplexed, he might stop in the middle of the road. In this event he would risk perishing, and it is inconceivable that he should not understand this. And as for the chance of perplexity in the middle of the road—even though it is a possibility, one can hardly firmly rely upon it.

For the time being Prince Bismarck is watching with feverish attention everything transpiring in France: he is watching and waiting. To him the crux lies precisely in the fact that the affair has not begun at the moment he had expected. At present his hands are tied. But most troublesome is the fact that the ulcers, which had been carefully concealed, have come to light. I have already spoken about the major ulcer of all the Germans—about their fear that Russia might suddenly realize how mighty she is, and what weight her decisive word may acquire precisely at this moment, and principally that *"the dependency upon an alliance with Russia, especially after the Franco-Prussian war, seems to be Germany's fatal destiny."* This German secret may now be suddenly revealed, and this from the standpoint of the Germans would be rather awkward.

Much as Germany's policy *during recent years* toward us was frankly hostile, nevertheless all Germans did adhere to the secret.

In this respect the press in particular was active. Until now the Germans assumed the quiet and haughty appearance peculiar to a power that needs no one's help. At present, however, this weak spot has to come to light. For should clerical France embark upon the fatal struggle, it would not suffice to conquer her, or merely to repulse her assault—should she be the first to attack—but it would be imperative to render her impotent forever, actually to crush her, taking advantage of the occasion—such would be the task! And inasmuch as France has an army of one million men, the task would have to be achieved without a hitch, it would have to be *secured*, since otherwise it shouldn't be undertaken at all. But there is no guaranty other than the guaranty of Russia's decisive word.

Briefly, the most unpleasant thing is that all this comes so suddenly. All former calculatons are mixed up, and now events govern the calculations, and not vice versa. France might start today, tomorrow, just when she is restoring domestic order though only a little. She has embarked on a policy of adventure; this is obvious to everybody, and this being so, who knows where the adventures will come to a stop? Where is the wall, the boundary line?—This is very disagreeable: so recently did the Germans display such an independent air, especially last year! Let us recall that during that year Russia, too, has been trying to ascertain who in Europe were her friends, and the Germans knew about Russia's troubles, and they assumed a triumphant air appropriate to the occasion.

Of course, every Slavic movement has always been somewhat disturbing to Germany; even so, it may be distinctly stated that in Russia's declaration of war two months ago there was, perhaps, something pleasant to Germany: "Nay, now, under no circumstance, will they guess"—thus people reasoned in Germany two months ago—"that it is we who need them. On the contrary, at present, when they stand facing the Danube—a German river, they are fully convinced that they need us awfully, and that at the end of the war our weighty word cannot be avoided. And it is good that the Russians think so. This will be useful to us in the future."

No doubt, many shrewd Germans have been thus thinking about us: their whole press has been so thinking and writing,— and now, all of a sudden, that clerical mood has turned everything upside down: "Oh, now they will guess; they will guess everything! And, besides, it is necessary that Russia finish and free herself in the East as soon as possible. However, it would be disadvantageous to bring pressure upon her. Maybe, she will take fright of England and Austria, but this is hardly to be expected. One should not even be thinking of combining with England and Austria to bring pressure upon Russia: later these won't help, while Russia will be angry. Strange situation! Wouldn't it be an idea to help Russia so that she may finish quickly. This could be done without drawing the sword—by mere political pressure upon Austria, for example. . . ." This is how the same politicians are reasoning at present, and it is very likely that all this is so in reality.

In a word, I merely seek to express my conviction, my faith, that not only is Russia strong and powerful, as she always has been, but at present especially so; she is the mightiest of all European countries, and never has Europe attached more weight to her decisive word than at this moment. Let Russia be occupied in the East, nevertheless her one decisive word may now, by her desire and will, turn the scales of European policy.

Of course even England herself understands that in view of the *possibility* of most troublesome events in extreme Western Europe, she, too, may lose two-thirds of her prestige in the opinion of the Russians; that at length even the most suspicious Russians will grasp the fact that under no circumstance will she risk a war in the face of Russia's firm resolution to pursue her task, and that she, England, would rather count on the division of the heritage after "the sick man" than risk an open war in his defense at so troublesome a moment in Europe.

Indeed, should it so happen that something unexpected and fatal should break out in Western Europe, England would never venture to interfere wholeheartedly with such a troublesome affair so different from the usual character of her interests. No doubt, in such an event she would adopt an attitude of keen watchfulness, awaiting, as is her custom, a convenient moment when she might snuff somewhere a division of spoils in order to become at once a party to it. And to undertake at present (*i.e.*, prior to the final clarification of these Western events) something really serious with regard to Russia would be too imprudent on the part of England.

On the other hand, left *alone,* what can Austria do?—Besides, it seems incredible that the clerical complications in the extreme West of Europe should not have perplexed her, at least, to some extent. And, of course, much like all others, she awaits the further development of events, so that her hands, like those of the rest, are partly tied. Everybody's hands are bound, and only Russia's hands are free. This means that something *unexpectedly* favorable to us has ensued. After all, how can one fail to rely upon the *unexpected* in the determination of human destinies?

The world is ruled by God and His laws, and should anything new and complex break over Europe, this signifies that, sooner or later, this inevitably had to come to pass. But I pray the Lord that I am mistaken; that the gathering cloud may be dispersed, and that all my presentiments merely prove my own "ardent" fantasies— fantasies of a man understanding nothing in politics.

The question comes to this: are all semi-official organs of the press in Germany right when they await and prognosticate war? On the other hand, all the ministers of MacMahon, even before any accusations have been framed, exert their efforts to assure the French and the whole world that France will not start the war. You must concede that all this is, at least, suspicious and that the clarification of the doubts, by the mere course of events, may come in the very near future.

But now what if so much depends upon "the legions' opinion"? It would be bad if it came to this: this would be the end of France. However, this could happen only in France—nowhere else in the whole world. And I pray the Lord that this shall not happen there, either: the beginning is bad; the next step would be still worse.

CHAPTER IV

1

Lovers of the Turks

WELL, IN RUSSIA there have appeared quite a few lovers of the Turks—of course, apropos of the war with them. In days past never in my life did I hear anyone begin a conversation in order to eulogize the Turks. At present, however, I hear quite often about their defenders. I have even met some of them: they get quite excited. Of course, we are dealing here with an urge to appear original. Even so, those lovers are scientists, teachers, professors.

"The Mohammedan world has contributed to Christian science. The Christian world was sunk in the darkness of ignorance when science had already been shining among the Arabs."

You see, here, Christianity is supposed to have been the cause of ignorance. That's Buckle, even Draper. Thus, it appears that Islam is light and Christianity—the beginning of darkness. What a unique logic! This is probably why at present Mohammedanism is so enlightened compared with Christianity. Why did they extinguish their torch so soon?

"Yes, they, however, have monotheism, whereas Christians . . ."

This eulogy of the Mohammedans for monotheism, *i.e.*, the purity of the doctrine of the unity of God, supposedly higher than the Christian, is a hobby-horse of many lovers of the Turks. But here the main point is that these lovers have detached themselves from the people and do not understand them. And having dissociated themselves from the people, they have managed to form some strange conceptions about what transpires in the head of the Russian plebeian. Meanwhile the Russian plebeian, "understanding nothing in matters of religion and not knowing his prayers"—as people are wont to speak about him—quite frequently, if not always, forms in his mind and in his soul a most peculiar but *correct* and precise conviction, fully satisfying him, about the things in which he believes, notwithstanding the fact that only a rare plebeian is able clearly and consistently to express his beliefs in words.

This "intelligent" Russian who has dissociated himself from the people would be surprised to hear that the illiterate peasant fully and unwaveringly believes in the unity of God, that there is but one God, and no God other than He. At the same time the Russian peasant knows and reverently believes (every Russian peasant knows it) that Christ is his true God; that He was begotten of God the Father and was born of the Virgin Mary.

To begin with, the educated Russian who has detached himself from the people will refuse to admit the very possibility that the Russian peasant, who has learned nothing, should possess such a knowledge: "He is so uneducated, so ignorant; he is being taught nothing. Where is his teacher?" That educated fellow will never understand that the teacher of the peasant "in the matter of his faith" is the soil itself, the whole Russian land; that these beliefs, as it were, are born with him and are fortified in his heart together with life.

But to some of those Russian thinkers most incredible is the fact that the Russian common people cannot be led astray as regards their convictions! He himself, having long lost every conception of what the great, immediate and ardent faith of the people is, is unable to admit that reverently believing in the great Christian mystery of the incarnation of the Son of God, the plebeian at the same time adheres to the strictest monotheism. He is rather inclined to attribute this firmness of the *immediate* convictions of the Russian plebeian to the lack of the habit of reasoning, to the habit of confounding conceptions because of indolence and dullness of thought and the absence of the critical faculty in his mind. And he will attribute the "lamentable" state of the plebeians' intellect to his downtroddenness, poverty, debauchery, serfdom, etc. To this the Russian scientist, studying the Russian people, firmly clings.

By the same process of reasoning, Orthodox Russians may be condemned, for example, for their worship of ikons. A Lutheran pastor is at a loss to understand how it is possible to believe in the true God and, at the same time, to worship a "board," an image of a saint, and to avoid idolatry. The Russian educated man more often than not is inclined to agree with this argument of the pastor. And yet, there is not a single Russian peasant—whether man or woman—who, worshipping an ikon, would confuse, though slightly, the "board" with God Himself, notwithstanding the fact that the people, at the same time, believe in the miraculousness of some ikons. But there isn't *a single Russian* who would attribute the miraculous force of an ikon to the ikon itself, and not to the will of God. And this is altogether different. Now, this view of the Russian common people neither the pastor nor the Russian who has detached himself from the people will ever admit. Well, they will even not believe that this is so.

However, they had better recall Mohammed's paradise in order to amplify their conviction about the purity of Turkish conceptions dealing with the unity of God. Of course, I am saying all this not for the purpose of starting a theological dispute with the admirers of Turkish monotheism. Nor, in fact, did I start it. These admirers are rather concerned about the *sane* conceptions of the people, while they themselves, perhaps, don't give a rap who is going to believe or how. This is why I have discussed the question merely from the popular point of view.

2

GOLDEN DRESS-COATS. THE PIG-HEADED ONES

In addition to the lovers of the Turks, there has appeared a great number of men with an urge for a *separate opinion:* "It's all nonsense; there is no movement. Addresses are nothing but humbug. This is not in accord with the Russian manner. Sanitary units are fiddle-faddle. This is not Russian style. Sentimentalism. Slavs were fabricated. Bulgarians were fabricated. The Turks are better than the Bulgarians. It's all rubbish. I love the Turks. . . ."

This sort of thing has not the malignantly shrewd design of the *"haute politique."* We do have a *"haute politique"*—this is undeniable; but this is simply personal ambition. Ambition of two kinds: (1) either extremely suppressed, and as a result—the pressing urge of appearing original, just so as to distinguish, or somehow to manifest oneself, and (2) ambition caused by extraordinary grandeur.

The Russian "great man" more often than not is unable to bear his grandeur. Truly, were it possible to put on a golden dress-coat made, say, of brocade, so as not to resemble all the rest, he would candidly don it and he wouldn't be ashamed. I am convinced that if, as yet, I haven't seen any of our "great men" in golden dress-suits, it is, probably, because the tailors refuse to make them. "I am cleverer than the rest. I am great. They all think about themselves *this way;* well, I don't want it their way. I'll prove that I am great. . . ."

I am eager to speak especially about the golden dress-coat, the characteristically Russian social and psychological sources of its origin, the typical examples, and so on, and so forth.—This is a pet theme of mine. However, leaving the golden dress-coat in peace for the present, I shall say a few words about the pig-headed ones. There are all sorts of pig-headed ones—good and bad, clever and stupid, honest and dishonest, etc. Of these we have many. These aim at one point from which it is impossible to divert them: *J'y suis et j'y reste.* They are Russian MacMahons.

News is reaching us from the army about the heroism and self-sacrifice of the Russians, both soldiers and officers. This is our youth. So recently there prevailed disbelief in the youth—our hope. Many people perceived in them nothing but cynicism; they were accused of blunt negation, coldness, indifference, dull suicides, and now, suddenly, the air apparently has been cleared: these same young folks are manifesting magnanimity, thirst for heroic impulse, duty, honor and sacrifice. They march at the head of the soldiers; they are the first to brave danger . . .

"Yes, but it is only a drunken person or a lunatic who can deliberately throw himself into the arms of death. There is no other explanation."

"What? Don't you suppose there is in him the magnanimous realization of the fact that he is sacrificing himself for Russia, that he is serving her? . . ."

"With his fist?"

"What do you mean? In a war one has to fight. How else could he be useful?"

"Hm. Schools, for example."

"Schools—at a proper time. Subsequently he will bring with him into the school the realization of a fulfilled duty; a magnanimous reminiscence; rapprochement with the people.

"In general, solidarity for a common cause. Soldier and officer live *over there* in one spirit, in a common feeling. The intelligentsia allies itself with the people; it returns to the people in deed, and not in theory; it learns to respect the people from whose midst this soldier has been recruited, and it teaches the people to respect it— no longer as chiefs or masters, but as men, spiritually. The recent

story of a plebeian who, in tears, embraced General Cherniaiev
in the Assumption Cathedral, is significant. You wish to educate
the people; but you will educate them more quickly by making
them respect your ideas, your deeds, and by attracting their hearts
to you. The more the people *personally* respect educated man, the
more surely will public education be achieved. Thus, by earning the
respect of the people, you are already serving the cause of public
education, those very schools about which you are so concerned."

"To earn respect through the fist? To make the people respect
the fist?"

"Here it is not only the fist. Above all, here is magnanimity,
sacrifice of one's own life in everybody's sight. In public even
death has its attraction. Now, you are asking me, what can compel
a man in the prime of his life to sacrifice it almost with certainty?
You are baffled,—otherwise it is impossible to explain your words
about the drunk and the lunatic: this is but an allegory, a mode
of expression. What can compel a man?—Thirst for fame, for an
honest deed; thirst for earning a good reputation, the praise of
all fellow-countrymen who are now watching his deeds; for revealing his personality, for glorifying his name."

"Aha, to make a career!"

"But all these sentiments and impulses are magnanimous.
There are thousands of them, and they are all combined. Man is
not composed of some one impulse; man is a whole world: let only
the basic impulse in him be noble. His own blood spilled, readiness to spill it, ennobles a man, conferring upon him for all his subsequent life the duty of honor. In our press fear has already been
expressed that these men may subsequently take an upper hand;
that self-satisfaction and haughtiness may appear; that they may
despise education, humble civilians; that they may behave violently, and that these ideas may penetrate society. But these are
futile fears. When is all this going to happen?"

"How is it possible that the Kopeikins, who 'so to speak, have
been spilling their blood,' should fail to appear?"

"Quite so, but these fellows will only make people laugh and
will harm themselves. However, the moral benefit will be boundless. The distress of cynicism will vanish, there will arise respect
for honest achievement. . . ."

"And for the fist."

"We are dealing here not with mere pugilists. Here we find
virtually children, children pure in heart. He has just been com-
missioned, and he throws himself forward for an exploit, with the
thought: Far away, what will his mother, his sister say, they with
whom he had just parted? . . . Is this merely funny and senti-

mental?—Finally, why not admit in these heroes superior conscious-ness? They understand that Russia has taken upon herself a dif-ficult task, and that it may become even more complex. They see that Russia is waging a war not only against Turkey; that the Turkish armies are commanded by English generals; that English officers, with English money, are building numerous fortifications; that the English fleet is encouraging Turkey to continue the war; finally, that English troops have already appeared (in Asiatic Turkey) . . . They are aware of all these things, and they rush to their death, realizing that the time has come to render Russia a faithful service. I am not even mentioning the Bulgarians, the oppressed 'Slavic brethren,' tortured and insulted. To our shame this theme has already grown obsolete . . . but not in their hearts. Don't you really perceive in many of them superior consciousness, the thought that they are serving mankind, the oppressed and the insulted?. . ."

"Serving mankind with the fist!"

"Permit me, apropos, to tell you an anecdote. I have already once reported that in Moscow, in one of the homes in which little Bulgarian children, orphans, are kept, who have been brought to Russia after the debacle over there, there is a girl, about ten years old, who has seen (and this she is unable to forget) the Turks skinning her live father. Well, in that same home there is also another invalid Bulgarian girl—she, too, is about ten years old—and people were recently telling me about her. Hers is a strange illness: a gradual but ever increasing weakness and a continual desire to sleep. She sleeps all the time; but sleep does not make her stronger, rather the opposite. It is very serious. This little girl may have already died. She has one unbearable recollection. The Turks seized her little brother, an infant of two or three years; first they poked his eyes out with a needle, and then they impaled him. The child screamed long and terribly, until he died. This is an absolutely true story. Well, the little girl is unable to forget this: all this took place in her presence, in her sight. Maybe, nature sends sleep to such an afflicted heart, because in a waking state she would be unable to live with such an uninterrupted memory. Now, imagine that you had been present there, at the moment the child's eyes had been poked out. Tell me, wouldn't you have rushed to stop them, even with your fist?"

"Yes, but nevertheless, the fist."

"All right, don't beat them, if you wish. But take their yataghans away from them. Can this be done without resorting to force?"

Apropos. Is it possible that among us there are such lovers

of the Turks as would not wish to take their yataghans away from them? I think and I believe that there are none such.

JULY—AUGUST

CHAPTER I

1

*A Conversation with a Moscow Acquaintance of Mine.
—A Note Apropos of a New Book*

HAVING ISSUED in Petersburg my belated May-June number of the *Diary,* on my way back to the province of Kursk, passing through Moscow, I had a chat about this and that with an old Moscow acquaintance of mine whom I see rarely but whose opinion I treasure greatly. I am not recording our conversation *in toto* even though in the course of it I learned certain curious things relating to the current situation which I had not suspected.

However, as I was parting with my interlocutor, I mentioned, among other things, that I intended to make en route a small detour, some hundred and fifty versts from Moscow, in order to visit the place of my early childhood and boyhood,—a village which, in days gone by, belonged to my parents, but which has long ago become the property of one of our women relatives. I have not been there for forty years; although many times I sought to go there, yet I was always unable to do so, despite the fact that that small and inconspicuous spot had left a deep and strong impression upon me for my whole life, and that there everything to me was full of dearest memories.

Well, we have such memories and such spots; we all did have them. It would be curious to know: What will be precious in their recollections to our present-day youth, our present-day children and raw youths? Will there be anything precious? Chiefly —precisely what? Of what character?

That our contemporary children will also have such sacred memories there can be no doubt, since otherwise "live life" would cease. Man cannot even live without something sacred and precious carried away into life from the memories of childhood. Some people, apparently, do not think about this; nevertheless, unconsciously, they do preserve such recollections. They may even be painful and bitter; however, even suffering endured in one's life may subsequently transform itself into a sanctuary of the soul. Generally speaking, man has been so created that he loves his past suffering. Besides, man, of necessity, is inclined to mark points, as it were, in his past in order to be subsequently guided by them and to deduce from them something whole—as a matter of routine and for his own edification.

The strongest and most influential recollections are those produced in childhood. Therefore, unquestionably, those memories and impressions—possibly the strongest and most sacred ones—will be carried into life also by present-day children. However, what will there be in those memories, precisely what will they carry into their lives, what form will this precious stock assume? All these, of course, are curious and grave questions. Were it possible to foreshadow, to a certain extent at least, an answer to them, many of the disturbing contemporary doubts could be quenched, and perhaps many people would gladly place trust in the Russian youth. What would be most important, however,—if it were possible—would be to feel, even though faintly, our future, our Russian future, which is so enigmatic. But the trouble is that at no time has there been an epoch in our Russian life which yielded less data for presentiment and foreknowledge of our always enigmatic future than the present one.

Besides, never has the Russian family been shaken so loose, more distintegrated, more unsorted and more uninformed than at present. Where will you now find such "childhoods and boyhoods" as have been depicted so harmoniously and graphically, for instance, by Count Leo Tolstoy when he portrayed *his* epoch and his family, or those portrayed in his *War and Peace?* At present all these creations are *nothing more than historical pictures of times long past*. Oh, I do not mean to say that these were such beautiful pictures. In our day I should not like to see them repeated, and I am not speaking about this at all. I merely speak about their *character*, about the completeness, precision and explicitness of their character, those qualities which made it possible to give such a clear and graphic representation of the epoch as we have in both creations by Count Tolstoy.

Nowadays this does not exist; there is no explicitness, no clearness. The contemporary Russian family is becoming more and more *casual*. Precisely *casual*—such is the definition of the present-day Russian family. It has lost its old features, somehow suddenly, even unexpectedly, while its new face . . . will it be able to create for itself a new, desirable face satisfying the Russian heart?—Some, even serious-minded, people positively maintain that at present the Russian family "does not exist at all." Of course, all this is being said about the educated Russian family, *i.e.*, of the upper strata and not of the common people. Of the latter's family, however, is it not also a question?

"This is what is indisputable,"—my interlocutor told me. "It is undeniable that in the very near future new questions will arise among the people; in fact, they have already arisen,—a heap, a whole mass of new, formerly nonexistent questions, never heard of by the people, and all this is natural. But who is going to answer these questions? Who in Russia is ready to answer them? And who is going to be first to do so? Who is waiting and getting ready for this? Such are the questions—our questions—which, besides, are of paramount importance."

No doubt, they are of prime importance. Such a decisive break in our life as the reform of February nineteenth, as all subsequent reforms, and especially—literacy (even the faintest contact with it),—all these unquestionably will raise—have already raised—questions, and later they may convey a form to them, group them together, communicate stability to them. And who, in fact, will answer these questions? Who stands nearest to the people? The clergy? But they have long ceased to answer the questions of the people. Except for some priests who still burn with zeal for Christ —often imperceptible and utterly unknown precisely because they seek nothing for themselves, living only for their flock. Except for these, and alas it would seem very few others, the rest, when pressed for answers, may, perhaps, respond to them with denouncements. Still others to such an extent alienate their flock from themselves by altogether incommensurate levies that no one would even think to come to them with questions. This theme could be greatly elaborated, but I shall speak more about it later.

Next, rural teachers are about the nearest to the people. But what are our rural teachers good for and what are they ready for? So far, what has this new profession exhibited? True, it is still merely in a state of formation; nevertheless, by reason of its significance, it is all-important for the future. What can these men answer?—It is better not to answer this question.

Thus there remain casual answers—in towns, at stations, on roads and in streets, in marketplaces, by passers-by, by vagabonds, and finally by former landowners. (It stands to reason that I am not mentioning the authorities.) Oh, of course, there will be many answers, perhaps, even more than questions, good answers and bad, foolish and wise. Still, it seems that their principal effect will be that each answer will raise three new questions, and this will go crescendo. The result will be chaos. Well, chaos wouldn't be so bad: precocious solutions are worse than chaos.

"And what is most important—there is nothing to talk about. The people will stand it."

Of course, they will stand it; they will stand it even without us—with or without the respondents. Russia is mighty. She has managed to endure things even worse than these. Besides, not such is her mission and aim that she should deviate without reflection from her secular path. Moreover,—not such are her dimensions. He who believes in Russia knows that she will endure absolutely *everything*—even the questions—and, essentially, she will remain the same, our holy Russia, as heretofore. And no matter how much her face may change, this should not be feared. Nor is it at all necessary to delay or remove the questions. He who believes in Russia should even be ashamed of entertaining such thoughts. Her mission is so lofty and her inner presentiment of that mission is so clear (particularly in our epoch, especially at this moment) that he who believes in this mission, must be above all doubts and apprehensions. "Here is patience and faith of the Saints," as it is said in the Holy Scripture.

That morning I saw for the first time an advertisement in the papers about the separate publication of the eighth and last part of *Anna Karenina* which had been rejected by the editor of *The Russian Messenger* in which the novel has been appearing beginning with its first part. Everybody also knows that this last, eighth, part was rejected because its orientation was in discord with that of the magazine and the convictions of the editors; specifically apropos of the author's opinion on the Eastern question and the war of last year. I immediately decided to buy the book, and as I was bidding good-by to my interlocutor, I asked him about it, knowing that he has been long familiar with its content. He began to laugh.

"The most innocent thing there can be!"—he answered—"I can't understand at all why *The Russian Messenger* did not publish it. Besides, the author had granted the right to any exceptions and annotations if the editors disagreed with him. Therefore, they should have simply made a footnote to the effect that the author . . ."

However, I will not record here the contents of the footnote which my interlocutor had suggested, all the more so as he expressed it while he was still laughing. But at the end he added seriously:

"Notwithstanding his enormous artistic talent, the author of *Anna Karenina* possesses one of those Russian intellects which see clearly those things only which stand directly before their eyes, and therefore, they push on toward that one point. Apparently, they are deprived of the faculty of turning the neck to the right or to the left in order to discern also that which is on the side:

they have to turn the whole body. Then, maybe, they start saying something entirely different, since, at all events, they are always
strictly sincere. This twist may not occur at all, but it may also
occur a month later, and then the respected author will begin
to cry with equal passion that volunteers should be dispatched
and lint should be plucked, and he will be saying everything we
are saying. . . ."

I bought that book, read it and found it in no way as "innocent" as that. Despite my whole aversion to embarking upon a
criticism of contemporary writers and their works, I have made
up my mind without fail to discuss the book in my *Diary* (perhaps
even in this issue). I deemed it not out of place to record also my
conversation with my interlocutor to whom I apologize for my indiscretion. . . .

2

THIRST FOR RUMORS AND THE THINGS "CONCEALED."—
THE WORD "CONCEALED" MAY HAVE A FUTURE, AND
THEREFORE MEASURES SHOULD BE TAKEN IN ADVANCE.
AGAIN ON A CASUAL FAMILY

These "places of my childhood," whch I intended to visit,
are only one hundred and fifty versts from Moscow, of which one
hundred and forty versts are by railway. However, I was obliged
to spend almost ten hours covering this distance: there are many
stops; one has to change trains several times, and at one station
one has to wait three hours before boarding the next train. And
all this on top of the disagreeablenesses of a Russian railroad and
the virtually haughty attitude toward one and one's needs on the
part of conductors and "the authorities."

Everybody knows well the motto of the Russian railway:
"The road does not exist for the public, but the public exists for the
road." There isn't a single railroad man, from the conductor to
the director, who would doubt this axiom, and who wouldn't look
at you with derisive surprise should you begin to tell him that
the railroad exists for the public. But the main thing is that they
won't listen.

By the way, this summer I have travelled at least four
thousand versts, and this time everywhere en route I was particularly impressed with the people: everywhere they speak about
the war. Nothing can be compared with the interest and eager
curiosity with which the common people inquired about, and listened
to, the accounts concerning the war. In railroad cars I even noticed
several peasants reading the papers, mostly aloud.

Several times I chanced to be sitting next to them: some commoner would cautiously look you over; and, especially if he saw a newspaper in your hands or lying beside you, he would promptly and extremely politely inquire whence you came. And if you answered that you came from Moscow or from Petersburg (and, still more interesting to him—if you came from the South, from Odessa, for example), he would unfailingly ask: "What's the news about the war?"

Thereupon if you inspired him—even a little—with confidence in your reply and your readiness to answer his questions, he would at once, although still cautiously, change his curious air to a mysterious one, and drawing closer to you and lowering his voice, he would ask: "And isn't there, so to speak, anything special?" meaning, extra special, not reported in the papers, something concealed. I may add that among the people there are none discontented with the government for the declaration of war,—even among the most malevolent types. And there are those who are malevolent. For instance, you walk down the station platform during a stop, and suddenly you hear: "Seventeen thousand of our men were killed— a telegram was just received!" You see a young fellow making a speech; on his face there is an expression of ominous ecstasy, and not because he is glad that seventeen thousand of our men were killed; nay, this is something different, as if a man's property were destroyed by fire—everything was destroyed—hut, money, cattle: "Look, Orthodox Christians!—Everything perished! I'm in rags, all alone in the world!" At such moments on the face of the poor devil there also is an expression of some malevolent self-intoxication.

However, speaking of the "seventeen thousand" there is also something additional: "there is such a telegram; only it is being delayed, concealed, not yet released . . . we saw it, we read it ourselves . . ."—such is the meaning.

All of a sudden, I couldn't restrain myself, approached the group and said that it was all rubbish, foolish rumors, that seventeen thousand of our men could not have been slain, that everything was all right. The lad (he seems to have been a commoner, perhaps even a peasant) was somewhat abashed—very little though: "We are ignorant people. We are not uttering our own words—this is what we have heard."—The crowd promptly dispersed, and then the station bell rang.

Now I find this incident curious because it occurred on July 19, around five o'clock in the afternoon. On the eve, that is July 18, the Plevna battle took place. What kind of a telegram could have been received by whomsoever, not to speak of anyone among those

railroad passengers? Of course, this was a mere coincidence. I do
not think, however, that the lad himself was the spreader and
inventor of false rumors: it is most probable that he had actually
heard the story from somebody. I presume that this summer in
Russia there must have appeared a lot of fabricators of false, and
of course malicious, rumors about reverses and misfortunes; such
rumors have a design and they are being spread not from mere
fondness of lying.

In view of the ardent patriotic mood of the people during
this war; further taking into account that discernment concerning
the meaning and the aims of this war which since last year has
been revealed by our people; finally, because of the fervent and
reverent faith of the people in their Czar,—all these delays and
secrets in the war communiqués not only are not useful, but they
are .positively harmful. Naturally, no one can either demand or
desire that strategic plans, the numbers of troops, military secrets,
etc., be revealed, before an action had been carried out. It is at
least desirable that our papers be given information before it appears in the Viennese press.[1]

Sitting in the station where I had to wait three hours to
change trains, I was in a most miserable mood, and was vexed
with everything. Because there was nothing to do, suddenly it
occurred to me to analyze: why was I vexed, and wasn't there, in
addition to general causes, some accidental immediate cause?—I
didn't have to look long for it, and having found it I began to
laugh. The cause lay in a recent encounter which I had in the
railroad car, two stations earlier. A certain gentleman entered the
car, a perfect gentleman, very much resembling the type of Russian
gentlemen roving abroad. He came in leading his little son, a boy
who could not have been more than eight years old—even younger
perhaps. He was very neatly dressed in a most fashionable European
children's costume, in a charming little jacket, wearing elegant
shoes and batiste linen. Apparently, the father took good care of
him. No sooner had they been seated than he said to his father:
"Papa, give me a cigarette"! Papa promptly reached into his
pocket, took out a mother-of-pearl cigarette case, picked two cigarettes, one for himself, the other for the boy, lighted them, and
they began smoking with a most habitual air obviously suggesting
that this sort of thing, to them, was a common happening. The
gentleman began to think about something, while the boy kept
looking through the window of the car, smoking and inhaling. He

[1] At present in the main, this has been rectified: hardly a day passes
without the public receiving wire communiqués from the Commander-in-
Chief.

puffed up his cigarette very quickly. Scarcely fifteen minutes later, he said again: "Papa, give me a cigarette"!—and again both started smoking. During the time they sat in the car with me—and we passed only two stations—the boy had smoked at least four cigarettes.

Nothing of the kind have I ever witnessed before, and I was greatly astonished. The weak, tender and quite undeveloped chest of so little a child was already inured to such a horror. And whence could such an unnaturally precocious habit develop?—Of course, it was the father's example: children are so imitative. But how could the father allow his child the use of such poison?—Consumption, catarrh of respiratory tracts, of the cavity of the lungs—this is what is inevitably threatening the unfortunate boy; thus it is in nine cases out of ten; this is clear, known to everybody. And yet it is the father himself who encourages in his child an unnaturally precocious habit!

What did this gentleman mean to prove thereby?—Disdain of prejudices? Did he intend to emphasize the novel idea that everything hitherto prohibited was nonsense and that, on the contrary, everything was permitted?—I can't understand it. This case remains unexplained to me; it is almost a miraculous case. Never in my life have I encountered such a father and, probably, I never shall meet such a one again. We come across strange fathers in our day!

However, I promptly ceased to laugh. I laughed only because I had discovered so quickly the cause of my bad mood. Presently, however, without any connection with the incident, I recalled yesterday's conversation with my interlocutor relating to the question: What will contemporary children carry into life which was dear and sacred in their childhood? After that I began to think about my idea of the *casualness* of the present-day family . . . and again I sank into most disagreeable musing.

It may be asked: What is that *casualness?* What do I mean by this term? I answer: To my way of thinking, the casualness of the contemporary Russian family consists of the loss by the modern fathers of every general idea about their families, an idea general to all fathers, tying them all together, which they themselves believe in, and which they would teach their children to believe, conveying to them this faith for their lives.

Please note: This idea, this faith may, perhaps, be erroneous so that the best of the children may subsequently renounce it, or, at least, correct it for their own children. Even so, the very existence of such a general idea binding society and the family is already the beginning of order, *i.e.*, moral order, which, naturally, is subject to change, progress, correction, I admit—but—order just the same. Nowadays, however, there is no such order because there is nothing general and binding, nothing in which all fathers believe. Instead there are: first, wholesale, sweeping renunciation of the past (renunciation and nothing positive); second, attempts to say something positive, yet neither general nor binding, but everyone in his own way,—attempts parcelled into units and individuals, devoid of experience, practice, even without full faith in them on the part of their inventors. At times these attempts have an excellent nucleus but they are unseasoned, abortive, and, occasionally—even ugly, in the form of a sweeping admission of everything heretofore prohibited on the theory that all that is old is stupid—this to the point of the silliest notions, such as the permission given to seven-year-old children to indulge in smoking tobacco.

Finally, an indolent attitude toward work: apathetic and in-dolent fathers, egoists: "Eh, let things come as they will! Why should we worry!—Children will grow up like the rest. They'll adjust themselves. But they are a great bore! Better had they been nonexistent." Thus, as a result—disorder, parcelling and casual-ness of the Russian family, while hope is virtually in God alone: "Let's trust that He may send us some little general idea, so that we may again unite!"

Of course, order of this kind produces disconsolateness; the latter, in turn, increases indolence, and in hot-headed individuals cynical, angry indolence. However, even at present there are many by no means indolent but, on the contrary, very diligent fathers. These are mostly fathers with ideas. Some fellow listens, for in-stance, to some things which in themselves are not stupid at all; he reads two or three clever books, and all of a sudden he decides to reduce the whole upbringing and all his duties toward the family to nothing but beefsteak: "Underdone beef-steak; and, of course, Liebig . . .," etc. Another, most honest man *in se*, who in days gone by used to be considered a wit, has discharged three of his children's nurses: "These rascals are quite impossible: I strictly forbade it. And can you imagine, yesterday I walked into the chil-dren's room and I saw her putting Lízochka in the cradle, crossing her, and I heard her teaching the child that prayer *'Mother of God'*; 'Forgive papa and mama . . .' This I strictly forbade! I have decided to engage an English woman. But will she be better?" A third chap is busy trying to find a mistress for his son who is scarcely fifteen years old: "Otherwise, you know, he may develop those dreadful habits, or else someday he might pick up someone in the street . . . contract a venereal disease . . . No, it's better to take care of this matter beforehand." A fourth one initiates his seventeen-year-old boy into the most progressive "ideas," and the lad in a most natural manner (since what can come of certain knowledge prior to the acquisition of life experience?) reduces these progressive ideas (often very good ones) to the formula: "If there is nothing sacred, this means that one may perpetrate any villainy."

Granted, in these cases the fathers are hot-headed; yet, is it in many of them that this ardor is justified by something serious-minded, by reasoning and suffering? Do we have many such fathers? —Mostly it is nothing but liberal giggling, echoing somebody else's voice. And thus the child carries into life, aside from everything else, a comical memory of his father, his droll image.

But these are the "diligent" ones, and there aren't so many of them. The lazy ones are incomparably more numerous. Every transitional and disintegrative state of society generates indolence and apathy, since in such epochs only very few are capable of seeing clearly what is ahead of them and of not being led astray. The majority, however, is confused, loses the thread, and, finally, gives it all up: "Eh, to hell with everything! What are those duties when we ourselves are unable to say anything intelligently! I wish I myself could manage to pull through life somehow, and why should I bother about duties!" And now, these indolent fellows, if they happen to be rich, are even complying with their duties in a suitable manner: they dress and feed their children well; they hire governesses and after that teachers; finally, their children matriculate in universities, but . . . there is no father, there is no family; the lad enters life alone because his heart has not lived, it is not bound with the youth's past, with family or childhood.

However, this refers only to the rich ones; these are well-off, but are there many who are well-off?—The majority, the over-whelming majority, are poor. Therefore, in the face of the fathers' indolence as regards the family, the children are altogether left to the mercy of chance! Poverty, the troubles of their fathers are reflected in their hearts in gloomy pictures, in memories at times of a most venomous character. Till a very advanced age the children keep recalling their fathers' pusillanimity, quarrels in their families, accusations, bitter reproaches, even curses upon them, for extra mouths; and what is still worse,—sometimes the baseness of their fathers, mean acts perpetrated for the sake of obtaining a position or acquiring money, foul intrigues, hideous servility. And long after, maybe all their lives, the children are inclined blindly to accuse these men, having derived nothing from their childhood that might mitigate that filth of their memories, and to size up truthfully, realistically, and, therefore, *acquittingly*, those now elderly people in whose midst their early years dragged out so sadly.

These, however, are still the best children; whereas the majority of them carry into their lives not only the filth of *memories*, but the filth itself; these deliberately provide themselves with it; they fill their pockets with it in order to make practical use of it—no longer with gnashing of pain, like their parents, but with light hearts. "Everybody"—they say—"lives in dirt. Only dreamers rave about ideals; to be sure, it's more handy to be surrounded with filth. . . ."

"But what do you wish? What are those memories which children should have derived from childhood in order to sterilize the dirt of their families and to acquire an *'acquitting'* attitude, as you say, toward their fathers?" I answer: What can I, singlehanded, say if society *in toto* has no reply to it?—There is nothing common among contemporary fathers, said I; there is nothing binding them together. There is no great idea (it has been lost), no great faith in their hearts in such an idea. And it is only such great faith that is capable of generating *the beautiful* in children's memories —decidedly!—despite the cruelest surroundings of their childhood, poverty and even moral filth itself which surrounded their cradles!

Oh, there are instances when even the most degraded father, but one who has preserved in his soul even a remote former vision of the great faith in the idea, has managed to transplant its seed and the great sentiment into the susceptible and thirsting souls of his pitiful children, and later he has been wholeheartedly forgiven by them because of this benefit, despite everything else.

Man should not step out of childhood into life without the embryos of something positive and beautiful; without these a generation should not be permitted to start on its life journey. Look: do not the contemporary fathers, from among the ardent and diligent, believe in this? Oh, they fully believe that without a cohesive, general moral and civic idea it is impossible to bring up a generation and let it start on its life journey! But they themselves have lost the general idea, and they are dismembered. They are united only in the negative, and even this in a negligent manner. They are disunited in the positive; besides, essentially, they do not even believe in themselves, since they are echoing somebody else's voice, they have joined an alien life, an alien idea, and they have lost all connection with their native Russian life.

However, I repeat, there are a few ardent ones; there are infinitely more of those who are indolent. By the way, do you remember the Djunkovskys' trial? This is quite a recent trial. It took place only on June 10 of the current year at the Kaluga Circuit Court. Amidst the thunder of the current events, perhaps, only very few took notice of it. I have read the account of it in

The New Times, and I don't know if it has been reported in other papers. This was a case of the Przemysl landowners, Major Alexander Afanasievich Djunkovsky, fifty years old, and his wife Ekaterina Petrovna Djunkovsky, forty years old, charged with cruel treatment of their young children,—Nikolai, Alexander and Olga. . . . At this point it may be noted that the children in question were of the following ages: Nikolai, thirteen years old; Olga, twelve years old, and Alexander, eleven years old. And—anticipating things —I may add that the defendants were acquitted by the court.

In my judgment, this trial graphically reveals much that is typical in our present-day life, and yet the banality of it is the most surprising thing. One feels that there is nowadays an extraordinarily large number of precisely such Russian families, of course, not exactly identical; not everywhere does one find such accidentals as *scratching of heels* (this will be discussed further), but the essence of the matter, the fundamental trait of many similar families, is identical. This is precisely the type of an "indolent family," to which I have just referred;—if not a complete and not a wholly correct type (especially judged by certain most exceptional and characteristic details), nevertheless a very remarkable specimen of that type. However, let the readers judge for themselves. The defendants were committed to trial by decree of the Moscow Court of Appeals. Now, let me remind the readers of the indictment. I am reprinting it from *The New Times,* as it was stated there, *i.e.,* in an abridged form.

3

The Case of the Parents Djunkovsky and Their Own Children

"The defendants Djunkovsky, possessing a certain fortune, and employing a suitable number of servants, have placed their children Nikolai, Alexander and Olga in a position altogether different from that of their other children. Not only did they fail to treat them as parents, and fondle them, but having left them without supervision, they gave them poor subsistence (living quarters, clothing, beds and meals), compelling them to such occupations as scratching their heels, etc., thus inciting and maintaining in the said children a feeling of discontent and irritation, which led them to perpetrate upon their deceased sister an act which will be referred to further. All this combined could not fail to exercise a harmful influence upon the health of the children. It appears, for example, from the case, that Olga is suffering from epilepsy.

"Besides not contributing by either supervision or care to the moral development of these children, the defendants have been resorting to measures which cannot be termed mild corrective measures for young children. Thus, the defendants used to lock up their children for a considerable time in the toilet room, left them home in a cold room, almost without food, or had them take dinner and sleep in a servant's room, thus placing them in company with persons hardly capable of contributing to their correction; finally, the defendants frequently beat their children with anything that happened to be around—even with fists, rods, switches, with a whip intended for horses—with such cruelty that it was frightful to behold and (according to the testimony of the boy Alexander) so that the child's back ached five days after one of these castigations. Such beatings came as a result not always of some mischef, though trifling, but just incidentally—of mere caprice.

"A soldier's widow, Sergeeva, who was employed by the Djunkovskys as a laundress, among other things, testified that the defendants disliked their children Nikolai, Alexander and Olga, who slept separately from the other children, downstairs, in one room, on the floor, on felt; that they were covered haphazardly (they had one torn blanket); that they were given servants' meals, resulting in their continual hunger. They were shabbily clothed: in summer they wore different kinds of shirts, and in winter—short fur cloaks. To these children Mrs. Djunkovsky was worse than a step-mother; she beat them, especially Alexander, with whatever happened to be around, and at times simply with her fists. When she flogged Nikolai, it was horrible to behold. The children were naughty, but merely as children are. They were treated particularly badly in the evenings, when they had to scratch their mother's heels; this lasted an hour, or longer,—till the mother fell asleep. Formerly this used to be done by the servants, incluming Sergeeva, who at length refused to engage in this occupation because her hands swelled!

"From the testimony of Ousachkova it appears that Alexander and Olga wallowed on the floor, on dirty pillows, generally they were kept in a dirty state—in a pig's haunt it's cleaner than in their room.

"Nobleman Lubimov, who lived as a tutor with the Djunkovskys until August 1875, asserted that Nikolai, Olga and Alexander were kept poorly, and that, at times, they had to go barefooted. From a statement by Miss Shishova—a graduate of the Nicholas Institute, who, until August 1874, was employed as governess of the defendants' children, and whose deposition, because of her non-appearance, was read at the trial—it appeared that Mrs. Djunkovsky was an egoistic woman, who, just like her husband, never fondled her children Alexander and Nikolai. Shishova explained the general absence of order at the home of the defendants and their indifference to their children by the neglect of the defendants of everything, even of themselves. Their business affairs were always embroiled, and they were continually in trouble; they were incapable of keeping house. Mrs. Djunkovsky, who was anxious not to be bothered with anything, entrusted her husband with the task of punishing the children, which he did. And even though that witness had never been present at the castigations, nevertheless she stated that in punishments there was no cruelty. It happened—further stated pedagogue Shishova—that Mrs. Djunkovsky, or even I, locked up the children for mischief in a room where there was a water closet, but that room was no colder than the other rooms in the apartment, and it was heated. Shishova herself punished the children with a leather lash, but it was a small lash. To the knowledge of the witness, the children have never been denied food for several days.

"The boys Nikolai and Alexander made reserved depositions to the examining magistrate; however, from them it appears that they had been flogged with a leather lash used for horses, as well as with a switch, which was also employed by their tutor Lubimov. On one occasion Alexander's back ached for five days after he had been flogged by his mother because he had brought some potatoes from the kitchen to his sister Olga for her lunch.

"Djunkovsky in his defense referred to the fact that his children were utterly spoiled, and in support of his contention he related the following incident: when his eldest daughter Ekaterina died, and while her body was lying on a table, the boys Nikolai and Alexander cut some twigs in the garden, beat the deceased on her face with them, and kept saying: Now, we'll make fun of you for complaining against us!

"At the trial the defendants pleaded 'not guilty.' Defendant Djunkovsky asserted that he was spending more money for the upbringing of his children than his means permitted; that he felt very sad that he had failed to achieve his aim, and that his children were growing from bad to worse.

"The eldest son, Nikolai, before he had entered high school, used to be a good boy, but after he had attended school for a certain time he learned to steal. Prior to his matriculation he used to know his prayers, but subsequently he forgot them—for the reason that in high school he declared himself a Catholic and received no religious instruction whatsoever, in spite of the fact that Nikolai's certificate of birth had been produced, and therein it was stated that he was of Orthodox faith.

"In her last speech Mrs. Djunkovsky stated that she had employed several governesses for her children, that unfortunately she

had misjudged them all, as well as the tutor, but that now the
father himself was taking care of the upbringing of the children,
and that she hoped that they would be completely reformed."

Such was the case. As stated above, the defendants were
acquitted. Why not? The remarkable thing is not that they were
acquitted but that they were brought to trial and tried. What court
could have found them guilty, and of what? Oh, certainly there
is a court which can find them guilty, clearly specifying their guilt,
but not a criminal court with jurors who judge on the strength
of statutory law. And in written law nowhere is there a provision
making it a punishable offense for fathers to treat their children
indolently, incompetently and heartlessly. Otherwise it would be
necessary to condemn half of Russia—nay, far more than that!
Besides, what is "heartless treatment"? It would have been different had there been cruel tortures—something dreadful and inhuman. But I recall in the trial of Kroneberg, who was accused of
inhuman treatment of his child, the lawyer opened the Code of
Laws and read some sections dealing with cruel treatment, brutal
torture, etc., with a view to proving that the acts of his clients
were not subject to any of them, in which it is clearly defined
what is to be understood as cruel and inhuman torture. And I also
recall that these definitions were so cruel that decidedly they were
akin to the tortures of the Bulgarians by the bashi-bazouks, and
if there was no impaling or cutting strips out of one's back, there
were broken ribs, arms, legs—and what not?—so that some leather
lash, a small one at that according to Miss Shishova's statement,
most certainly does not conform to that section of the Code of Laws
and give ground for indictment. "They flogged with a rod"—they
say. Well, who doesn't flog children with rods? Nine-tenths of
Russia practices this. By no means can this be subject to the provisions of criminal law. "They flogged for no good reason, for potatoes."—"No, sir, not for potatoes"—Mr. Djunkovsky might have
replied—"here, everything came together: for depravity, because
they, the brutes, beat the deceased daughter Ekaterina on her
face."—"We did lock them up in the toilet room. But the toilet
room was heated—what more do you want? A lock-up is always a
lock-up."—"Why, then, did you feed them with servants' food, and
why have you made them sleep virtually in a pigs' sty, on some
sort of spread, with one torn blanket?"—"Well, sir, this was also
punishment, and besides, it is immaterial whether or not the blanket
was full of holes. I am spending on the education of my children
more than my means permit, and the law doesn't have to dig into
my pockets to count my money."—"This, then, is the reason why
you didn't fondle your children?"—"Now, wait, show me please a
section in the Code of Laws which would prescribe to me, under

threat of punishment, to fondle my children—especially such naughty, heartless, miserable pilferers and brutes!"—"Finally, is it for the same reason that you have adopted a wrong system of bringing up your children?"—"Well, what system of upbringing does the criminal law prescribe under threat of punishment? Besides, it isn't the business of the law . . ."

Briefly, I maintain that it was impossible to drag the Djunkovskys' case into a criminal court. And thus it came to pass: they were acquitted, and nothing came of their prosecution. And yet the reader feels that there may—perhaps, already did—ensue a real tragedy. Oh, this is a case for a different court. What court?

What?—Well, for example, Miss Shishova, a pedagogue—she makes her deposition and in it she renders a verdict. Let us note that this Miss Shishova—even though she herself did flog the children with a leather lash ("only it was a small one"), nevertheless seems to be a clever woman: it is impossible to define the Djunkovskys' characters more precisely and in a more clever way than she did it. "Mrs. Djunkovsky"—says she—"is an *egoistic woman*. The Djunkovskys' house is *in disorder . . . because of the defendants' neglect of everything, including even themselves*. Their business affairs are always embroiled; they are always in trouble; they do not know how to keep house, they suffer, and yet, more than anything, they seek tranquillity: Mrs. Djunkovsky, who has been continually avoiding any disturbance, entrusted even the punishment of the children to her husband. . . ." In a word, Miss Shishova, having lived with the Djunkovskys, formed an opinion that they were heartless egoists, and mainly—indolent egoists. Of course indolence was the cause of eternal disorder in their house, disorder also in their affairs, despite the fact that there was nothing they sought more than tranquillity: "Eh, to hell with you! Would that we could only pull ourselves through life!"

From whence do their indolence and apathy come?—God knows! Is it because they suffer from the contemporary chaos of life, in which it is so difficult to understand anything? Or has contemporary life given so little response to their spiritual aspirations, wishes and quests? Or, finally, is it because of the failure to comprehend the things taking place all around, that their own conceptions became disintegrated, so that they no longer could be collected, and disillusionment ensued?—I don't know, I don't know, but apparently they are educated people who in days past—maybe even now—used to love things beautiful and lofty. The scratching of heels would not contradict this; it is precisely something on the order of lazy, apathetic disillusionment, an indolent pastime, a thirst for solitude, repose and warmth. Here we are dealing with nerves,—and precisely not so much idleness as craving for rest and solitude, *i.e.*, segregation from all duties and obligations. Yes, of course, here there is egoism, and egoists are capricious and cowardly in the face of duty: in them there is a perpetual, cowardly aversion to binding themselves with any duty.

It should be borne in mind that this continual and passionate craving to avoid any duty almost always generates and fosters in the egoist the conviction that, contrariwise, everyone with whom he is in contact is to be charged as regards him with some obligation, tax or liability. No matter how silly this fantasy is, nevertheless, in the long run, it takes root and develops into irritable discontent with the whole world, and into a bitter and often angry feeling toward everything and everybody. Noncompliance with these imaginary obligations is felt by the heart as an affront, so that you will never in your whole life surmise why a certain egoist is perpetually angry with you. This peevish feeling extends also to his own children—oh, to the children par excellence. Children are the predestined victims of this whimsical selfishness; besides, they are the nearest at hand, and what is most important—there is no control: "They are my own children!"

Don't be surprised that this hateful feeling, constantly irritated by the reminder of the neglected duty toward the children, and the constant sticking before your eyes of these new little individuals demanding everything from you, and impudently (alas,—not impudently but in a childish manner!), not understanding that you need your repose, and attaching to it not the least significance, —don't be surprised, I say, that this spiteful feeling even for one's own children may, at length, transform itself into real vengefulness, and, encouraged and provoked by impunity—even into bestiality. Indeed, indolence always generates bestiality and culminates in it; bestiality not from cruelty, but precisely from laziness. These are not cruel, but specifically, indolent hearts.

And now this lady who is so fond of repose, to the point of insisting that her heels be scratched, having finally grown irascible because *she alone* never has peace, everything around her being in a state of disorder and requiring her constant presence and attention,—this lady jumps from her bed, seizes a switch and flogs, flogs her own child unquenchably, insatiably, malignantly so that "it is horrible to look at her"—as the maid-servant testified—and why, for what reason? Because the boy brought from the kitchen to his hungry little sister (suffering from epilepsy) a few potatoes; that is, she beats him for a kind act, for the fact that the child's heart has not yet been depraved, has not yet grown callous. "All the same, I forbade it, but you did it. Now, then, don't do your kind thing, but do my wicked thing!" Nay, this is hysterics!

The children sleep in filth; "in a pigs' sty it is cleaner," with one torn blanket for the three of them: "Never mind, they deserve it"—reasons their own mother—"they don't let me rest!" And she reasons thus not because her heart is cruel,—no, perhaps by nature her heart is kind and good,—but, see, they don't let her rest; she can't attain tranquillity in her life; the further it goes, the worse it grows, and here, on top of it, are these children ("What for? Why were they born?"); they grow, they are naughty, and every day they require more and more work and attention! Nay, if this be hysterics it has been accumulating over a period of whole years.

Side by side with this sick mother of the family (brought to the state of sickliness), stands before the court the father, Mr. Djunkovsky. Well, maybe he is even a very good man; it seems that he is an educated man, not at all a cynic; on the contrary, he understands his fatherly duty to such a point that his heart is afflicted. Almost with tears he complains in the court room about his young children; he stretches out his arms: "I did everything for them, everything: I hired tutors, governesses. I spent more money on them than my means would permit, and they, the brutes, began to steal, they beat their deceased sister on her face." In a word, he considers himself right.

The children stand right there, nearby. It is noteworthy that they made "reserved, cautious depositions," *i.e.*, they complained little, and defended themselves but slightly, and I don't think that was due to mere fear of the parents, to whom they would have to return just the same. On the contrary, it would seem that the fact itself that their father was being tried for his cruel treatment of them might have made them bolder. Simply, they felt uneasy participating in a trial against their father, to be standing at his side and testifying against him, whereas he, heedless of the future, and without giving thought to the feelings which henceforth would remain in the hearts of these children, not even suspecting what they would carry into their future from the experience of that day,—he accused them and revealed everything that was bad in them, their shameful deeds,—complaining to the court, to the public, to society.

Even so, he considers himself right, while Mrs. Djunkovsky fully, unhesitatingly, believes in the future. She declares to the court that *everything* is the fault of bad tutors and governesses; that she is disillusioned with them, but that now when her husband expects to take charge of their children's upbringing they "will be completely reformed." (Quite! Quite!) However, God help them.

By the way, let me note something concerning the mischief of the young Djunkovskys.

The fact that they beat their deceased sister on her face with rods is, of course, disgusting and repulsive. But let us try to be impartial, and I swear that we shall find that even this is merely children's mischief—precisely childish "fantasticality." This is something caused by children's imagination and not by depraved hearts. Children's imagination, by its very nature, particularly at a certain age, is extremely susceptible and inclined toward fantastic things. This is especially true of those families in which—though people live in close proximity to one another, each one always before the eyes of the other—but in which, nevertheless, the children are segregated into a group apart—by reason of their fathers' perpetual troubles and lack of time. "Learn your lessons! Stick to your books! No mischief!"—This is what they hear all the time; and they sit over their little books, in their designated corners, not even daring to swing their feet. At night, in their pigs' sty, when falling asleep, or when learning their weary lessons, or while locked up in the toilet room, the little Djunkovskys might have accustomed themselves to strange fantasies—both kind, heart-felt and spiteful ones, or simply in a children's fashion—to fairy, fantastic ones: "Now, were I older"—thus the boy might have been fancying—"I would go to war, and then I would come back here. That despicable fellow, the tutor, would ask: 'Where have you been? How did you dare to leave the class-room?'—And I would pull the order of Saint George out of my pocket, and would insert it into my button-hole! He would be scared and would fall on his knees!"

When the sister died, one of the three, trying to warm himself under the edge of his torn blanket, while falling asleep, could have invented this: "Do you know what, Kolia, God has deliberately punished her because she was wicked, and informed on us. Now she sees from above; she would like to denounce, but she can't. Let's beat her tomorrow with rods. Let her look from above, let her see it and be angry that she can't complain!"

I swear that perhaps, a few days later, the kids repented in their hearts that they had perpetrated such a disgusting stupidity. Children's hearts are tender. In this connection I know this little incident. A certain mother of seven children died. One of the kids, a little seven- or eight-year-old girl, seeing her dead mama, began to wail desperately. She wept so much that she had to be carried to the children's room almost in an hysterical condition. People didn't know how to console her. A foolish woman, a hanger-on who happened to be there, comforting the little girl, suddenly told her: "Don't cry! Why do you cry so bitterly?—She didn't like you. Do you remember how she punished you? How you had to stand in the corner? Don't you remember?"—The fool tried to make things better; she must have thought that the child would stop crying and would quiet down.—She did achieve her aim: suddenly the girl stopped crying. Moreover, both next day, and at the funeral, she displayed an indifferent, restrained, offended air, as if implying: "She didn't like me!" The thought that she was an offended, persecuted, disliked child appealed to her imagination. Will you believe it, this happened to an eight-year-old child. However, the child's "fantasticality" did not last long: several days later the little girl again began to grieve for her mother so strongly that she fell sick. After that, all her life, the daughter could think of her mother not otherwise than with reverence.

It goes without saying that the little Djunkovskys should have been punished for their offense in connection with their late sister. But this was a childish, silly, fantastic offense which did not signify any depravity of their hearts. As to the prank of the boy Nikolai at high school declaring himself a Catholic in order to avoid religious instruction, it was a childish prank par excellence: he was showing off to impress his schoolmates: "See, you have to receive religious instruction, and I got rid of it; I fooled all of them thanks to the fact that my family name sounds Polish." Decidedly, this was but a *school-trick*—a foolish and bad one, for which he should have been severely punished; still, one shouldn't be despairing of the boy and imagining that he was so debauched that he had turned into a rogue. But Djunkovsky, the father, seems to have believed this; otherwise he would not have complained so lamentingly in court.

It happens in our courts that when defendants are acquitted (especially, when they are obviously guilty, but are freed only through the mercy of the court) the presiding judge, announcing the defendant's discharge, sometimes utters a few words for their edification on the subject of how they should accept that acquittal, what they should derive from it for their lives and how they should behave to avoid trouble in the future. In cases of this kind, the presiding justice speaks, as it were, on behalf of society as a whole, in the name of the state.

Perhaps the verdict of acquittal was announced to the defendants Djunkovskys without any such admonition.—This I do not know, but I am simply imagining what the presiding judge might have told them when announcing to them their discharge. This is what I believe he might have told them.

4

THE IMAGINARY SPEECH OF THE PRESIDENT OF THE COURT

"Defendants, you are acquitted. But remember that in addition to this court, there is another court—that of your own conscience. Act so as to make that other court, too, acquit you, even though at some future time.

"You have declared that now you yourselves intend to take charge of the upbringing and education of your children: had you done so previously, probably there would have been no trial involving your children such as you have stood here today. But I am afraid: Do you possess sufficient strength for putting into effect your good intention? It is not enough to venture upon such a task; one has to ask oneself: Will there be sufficient zeal and patience to accomplish it? I do not wish, I do not dare, to say that you are heartless parents who hate your children. Besides, to hate one's own children is almost an unnatural thing, and therefore impossible. And to hate children who are still so little is a nonsensical and even ridiculous thing. However, indolence, indifference, lazy desuetude of such prime, natural and highly civic duty as the upbringing of one's own children in reality are apt to generate even a dislike of them, almost hatred, virtually a feeling of some personal vengeance upon them, especially as they grow older, as their natural needs increase,—in the measure of your own realization of the fact that much must be done for them, much labor has to be invested, which means that much of one's own self-sufficient segregation and repose has to be sacrificed.

"Moreover, ever increasing mischief of the neglected children,—the inculcation in them of bad habits,—the apparent distortion of their minds and hearts finally may implant a direct aversion to them even in parents' hearts. In your fervent, tearful complaints about the vices of your children we all heard here and perceived your profound, genuine sorrow,—sorrow of all ill-starred father offended by his children. However, think a little and reason: what could have made them better?—For instance, it developed at the trial that for their indolence and pranks you used to lock them up, at times, for several hours, in the toilet room. Of course: a lock-up is a lock-up, and, besides, your toilet room was *heated* so that here there was no cruel torture. However, is this so?—While sitting there, feeling his humiliating and shameful situation, the child could be growing spiteful; most fantastic perverted and cynical visions could have passed through his mind; he could have completely lost his love—love of his own nest and even of you, his parents, since it could have seemed to him that you do not value his feelings for you at all, nor his human dignity, whereas even within a child, the smallest child, there is structuralized human dignity. This you should remember. It appears that you have given no thought whatsoever to the fact that these thoughts—mainly these strong, though childish, impressions of his—he will later carry into his life and will bear them in his heart, perhaps, till his very grave.

"In the first place, have you yourself done at least something to avoid the humiliating necessity of placing the child in such a place, thereby shaming him and holding him up to ridicule?—For later on in life, he will unfailingly raise this question, putting it squarely before himself. You maintain that you have done *everything* for your children, and it seems that you yourself are convinced of this. But I don't believe that you have done everything; and when you uttered these words with such sorrowful feeling, I am sure that concerning this point you had grave doubts. You have stressed the fact that you have been hiring tutors and spending money in excess of your means.

"No doubt children need a tutor, and in employing a tutor you have acted as a zealous father. However, to hire a tutor to teach the children certain subjects, of course does not mean to *deliver* the children to him, to forget all about them, to get rid of them, so that they may be of no further bother to you. It seems that you have done precisely this, believing that, having paid money, you have done everything, even more, *everything* in excess of your means; whereas I wish to assure you that you have done the minimum of what you could have done for them. You merely ransomed yourself with money from a debt, from a parent's obligation, in the belief that you have already accomplished everything. You forgot that their childish little souls require constant, uninterrupted contact with your parents' souls; that spiritually you always will be for them, so to speak, on a mountain as an object of love, of genuine respect and beautiful imitation. Science is one thing, but a father must always be to his children a good, conspicuous example of that total moral inference which their minds and hearts derive from science. Your heart-felt and invariably apparent care for them, your love, would warm, like a clement ray, everything sown in their souls, and of course this would yield an abundant and good crop. But it seems that having sown nothing yourself, and having delivered them to a sower alien to your family, you demanded a crop, and unaccustomed to this task, you demanded it too soon, and, having failed to get it, you grew irascible and angry with . . . kids, your own children,—and also much too soon!

"All this is because the upbringing of children is a labor, a duty—sweet to some parents even despite troubles, scarcity of means, poverty, and to others, to quite a few well-to-do-parents, a most oppressive and burdensome duty. This is why they seek to free themselves from it with money, if money is available. However, if money doesn't help, or if, as in the case of many, there is none, they usually resort to severity, cruelty, torture—to rods. I shall tell you what a rod is: In the family it is a product of the parents' indolence,—its inevitable result. Everything that could be achieved by labor and love, incessant training of children; everything that could be accomplished by reasoning, explanation, admonition, patience, upbringing and example,—all these things, weak and impatient fathers, as a rule, hope to achieve by the rod: 'I shall not explain, but shall order; I shall not suggest, but shall compel.' Now, what is the result? A sly, secretive child will unfailingly submit; he will deceive you, and your rod will not reform but merely deprave him. A weak, timid and kind-hearted child will be scared by your rod. Finally, a good-natured, naïve child, with straightforward and candid heart, will first be offended and then embittered and you will lose his heart.

"It is difficult, often very painful, for a child's heart to tear itself from one it loves; however, once it does tear itself loose, there arise in it awful, unnaturally precocious cynicism, bitterness; and the feeling of justice becomes distorted. Of course, all this takes place only when cruelty is caused by the parents' egoism,—when the owner of the field, having failed to sow it, expects a rich harvest. In such cases cruelty and injustice on the part of the fathers, unrestrained, keep increasing—this is the usual course. 'Don't do the good that is yours, but do the bad which is mine.'—This is what, at length, becomes the motto, and the child is punished even for a good deed, for those potatoes which he brings to his sister from the kitchen.—How can the heart fail to grow embittered? How can its conceptions fail to become distorted?

"Not being cruel and even loving your children, you punished them by your neglect of them, by humiliating them: they slept in a filthy room, on some sort of a spread; they ate their meals not from your table, but with the servants. And of course you believed that, finally, they would feel their guilt and would be reformed. In the reverse case, one would have to suppose that you did so from hatred of them, from vengeance upon them—in order to wrong them. However, the court refused to find it so, and attributed your actions to the erroneous calculation of an educator. Now you intend to bring them up and tutor them: this is a difficult task, despite your wife's belief that it is an easy one.

"Your children are not in the court room. I ordered them to be shown out, and, therefore, I am at liberty to touch upon the main point in this difficult task. The principal thing is that both sides will have to forgive much. They must forgive you the bitter and painful impressions of their children's hearts, their embitterment and their vices. On your own part, you must ask them to forgive your egoism, your neglect of them, the distortion of your feelings toward them, your cruelty, and, finally, the fact that you were here standing trial because of them. I am saying so, since, upon leaving the court room, you will put the blame for everything not upon yourselves, but unfailingly upon them—of this I am sure! Thus, embarking upon the difficult task of bringing up your children, ask yourselves: Can you accuse yourselves, and not them, of all the offenses and crimes which were your fault and not theirs? —If you can, you will succeed in your task! This would mean that God has cleansed your sight and enlightened your conscience. If you can't, you had better not undertake your task.

"The second difficult thing with which you will be faced in your work is the necessity of overcoming, exterminating and modifying in their hearts many a former impression and memory. However, so much has to be obliterated, so much created anew, that I am wondering—how are you going to achieve it?—Oh, if you should learn to love them,—of course, you would succeed in everything. Still, even love is a labor, even in love one has to learn,— would you believe it? Finally, do you believe, are you convinced, that in your beautiful undertaking you will not be stopped by some petty, most primitive and trivial every-day trouble, about which at present, perhaps, you are not even thinking but which may constitute a most important obstacle to your good intentions. Every zealous and sensible father knows, for instance, how important it is in every-day family life to restrain himself in the presence of his children from negligence, so to speak, in family relations, from a certain laxity and licentiousness, from bad and ugly habits, and, principally from inattentiveness to, and neglect of, their childish opinion of yourselves, the disagreeable, ugly and comical impression which so easily may form itself in them when they behold haphazardness in family life.

"Would you believe that, at times, a conscientious father must radically re-educate himself for his children? Oh, if parents are kind, if their love for their children is zealous and fervent, children will forgive them much and will later forget many a comical and ugly thing, and they will not unconditionally condemn them even for some of their altogether bad deeds; on the contrary, their hearts will unfailingly find extenuating circumstances. But in discordant and spiteful families it might be quite different. Your wife, as it developed at the trial, has a pathological habit of having her heels scratched before her sleep. The maid-servant has testified that even to her this duty was painful, that 'her hands swelled.' Now, imagine that boy, that son of yours, who is compelled to do the scratching instead of the maid-servant! Oh, if the mother had loved him sincerely and tenderly, and he were convinced of this, now and in the future he would recall this weakness of a person dear to him with a good-natured smile, even though he might have felt angry at the time when he was forced to scratch. But I imagine how he must have felt, what thoughts came to his mind, when he had been sitting for an hour or longer engaged in this ridiculous occupation before a creature who did not love him, who was ready every minute to jump up and start flogging him for no reason whatever. In this case, the insistence upon this service unfailingly must have seemed to him humiliating, disdainful and despicable. He could not fail to realize—or, to put it more correctly, to feel—that his mother did not need him as a son; that as a son she despised him, forgot him, compelling him to sleep on some sort of a spread; and if she remembered him, it was only in order to beat him, and that, therefore, she needed him not as a son but merely as some sort of a curry-comb!

"And yet you are complaining that the children became corrupted, that they are callous monsters, that 'they learned to steal!' Strain your imagination a little; try to visualize your son in the future, say, at the age of thirty, and think with what disgust, with what spiteful feeling and contempt, he will recall this episode of his childhood . . . That he will remember it till his death hour, there can be no shadow of doubt. He will not forgive, he will begin to hate his memories, his childhood; he will curse his parents' former nest and those who, at the time, were with him in that nest!

"At present, without fail, you will have to exterminate these memories, to transform them, to drown them with other, new, potent and sacred sensations—what a colossal task! Dreadful to think of it! Nay, the task which you are about to undertake is much more difficult, far more difficult, than it seems to your wife!

"Don't be angry, don't take offense at my words. In addressing you, I am performing a pressing duty. I am speaking on behalf of society, in the name of society, the state and the fatherland. You are parents; they are your children; you are contemporary Russia; they are future Russia. What would happen to Russia should the Russian fathers evade their civic duty, seeking solitude or—more correctly—indolent and cynical segregation from society, from their people and from their prime duties toward the latter?

"The most dreadful fact is that this is so common: you are not the only ones, even though others may be committing the same errors as yours under different formulae. Still more significant is the fact that you are not only not the worst, but in many respects the best among contemporary fathers, since in your hearts the realization of your duty is not dead, even though you have failed to comply with it. In you there is no absolute negation of the duty.

You are not cold egoists. On the contrary you are irritated—whether against yourselves or against your children I shall not venture to ascertain. However, you have proved capable of taking to your hearts your failure and of being profoundly grieved by it!

"And so, let God help you in your determination to correct your failure. Seek love, and store love in your hearts. Love is so omnipotent that it even regenerates ourselves. It is only with love, and not with our natural authority over our children that we can buy their hearts. Besides, nature herself, among all our obligations, helps us most in our duties toward children, having so provided that it is impossible not to love them. And how can one fail to love them?—Should we cease to love children, whom then could we love? And what would then become of us?—Recall that it was only for the sake of children, for the sake of their little golden-haired heads, that our Saviour promised us to curtail 'the times and the seasons.' It is for their sake that the suffering in the regeneration of human society into a more perfect one shall be curtailed. Let this perfection come to pass, and let the suffering and perplexities of our civilization come to an end!

"And now you may go,—you are acquitted. . . ."

CHAPTER II

1

Again Segregation. The Eighth Part of Anna Karenina

NOWADAYS, MANY of the educated Russians are wont to say: "What people? I am the people myself!" In the eighth part of *Anna Karenina,* Levin, the beloved hero of the author of the novel, says about himself that *he himself is the people.* Some time in the past, speaking of *Anna Karenina,* I have called that Levin "pure in heart Levin." Still adhering to my belief in the purity of his heart, I do not believe that he is "the people." On the contrary, at present I perceive that he, too, is ardently seeking segregation. I became convinced of this after reading this eighth part of *Anna Karenina* about which I began to speak in the opening pages of the current July-August issue of my *Diary.*

It stands to reason that Levin, as a matter of fact, is not an actually existing person but merely a fiction of the novelist. Nevertheless that novelist, a man of immense talent, endowed with a considerable intellect and very much respected by educated Russia, —that novelist portrays in this ideal, *i.e.*, in a fictitious character,

partly also his own view of our contemporary Russian reality,—
which is clear to anyone who has read this remarkable work. Thus,
when dwelling upon the nonexistent Levin, we shall thereby dwell
upon the actual view of current Russian life of one of the most
noted contemporary Russian men. This is a momentous subject
for discussion even in our thunderous epoch permeated with so many
colossal, horrible and quickly shifting events.

This view of so renowned a Russian writer, precisely on a
matter of so considerable interest to all Russians as the all-Russian
national movement of the past two years in connection with the
"Eastern question," is comprehensively and finally revealed in this
eighth and last part of his work, which was rejected by the editor
of *The Russian Messenger* as a result of his disagreement with the
convictions of the author, and which recently was published in
separate book form. The substance of this view, as I understood it,
mainly comes down to this: First, that the so-called national movement is by no means shared by our people, who do not even understand it. Second, that all this was deliberately fabricated in the
beginning by certain individuals; that subsequently it has received
the support of journalists prompted by motives of profit—to have
their periodicals read. Third, that all volunteers were either lost
men, or drunkards, or else—simply stupid fellows. Fourth, that this
whole so-called enthusiasm of the Russian national spirit in support
of the Slavs not only has been fabricated by certain individuals and
supported by mercenary journalists, but that it has been counterfeited contrary to, so to speak, our fundamental principles; and
Fifth, that all the barbarities and unheard-of tortures perpetrated
against the Slavs are incapable of inciting in us Russians an immediate sentiment of compassion, and that "such an immediate feeling
for the oppression of the Slavs *does not and cannot exist*." The latter
is expressed finally and categorically.

Thus "the pure in heart Levin" has embarked upon a segregation, deviating from the overwhelming mass of the Russians. However, his view is neither novel nor original. It would have been
quite useful and much to the taste of many people in Petersburg
who last winter reasoned along the same lines. They were socially
rather prominent men, and it is to be regretted that the book has
appeared somewhat belatedly.

What has caused such a gloomy segregation in Levin and
such a gruff deviation on his part I cannot determine. True, he is
an ardent, "restless" man, addicted to all-embracing analysis, and,
strictly speaking, a man who does not believe anything within himself. Nevertheless, he is a man "pure in heart." This I maintain—
even though it is difficult to conceive by what mysterious, and at

times ridiculous, paths a most unnatural, a most artificial and ugly feeling may penetrate the sincerest and purest heart. However, I may also remark that although many people assert—and as stated above, I clearly perceive it myself—that in the person of Levin the author in many respects expresses his own convictions and views, thrusting them into Levin's mouth almost forcibly, sometimes obviously even sacrificing the artistic element, nevertheless I am by no means confounding the person of Levin, as portrayed by the author, with the person of the author himself. I am saying this in a state of a somewhat bitter perplexity, since although much of what the author expresses in the person of Levin obviously concerns only the latter, as an artistically delineated character, nevertheless this is not what I had expected from such an author.

2

CONFESSIONS OF A SLAVOPHILE

Yes, not this. Here I am compelled to express some of my feelings, notwithstanding the fact that when I began to publish my *Diary* last year I made up my mind that literary criticism would have no place in it. But I shall reveal the feelings of a non-critic even though apropos of a literary production.

In fact, I am writing a *Diary, i.e.,* I am recording my impressions apropos of everything that strikes me most in current events. This is why, for some reason, I prescribe for myself an artificial obligation to conceal, *quand-même,* perhaps the strongest impressions I experience only on the grounds that they pertain to Rusian literature. Of course, at the bottom of this decision there was also a correct thought, nevertheless a literal adherence to it is incorrect. This I see, for the reason itself that this is but the letter of the proposition. Besides, the literary work, on which thus far I have kept silent, to me is no longer simply a literary product, but a whole *fact* bearing a different significance.

Perhaps I shall express myself too naïvely; still I venture to say this: this fact of an impression from a novel, from fiction, from a poem, last spring coincided in my soul with the enormous fact of the declaration of the current war. And both facts, both impressions, have found in my mind a real mutual connection and a point of mutual contact which, to me, is striking. Instead of laughing at me, you had better listen to me.

In many respects I hold Slavophile convictions, even though I am not quite a Slavophile. In Russia, Slavophiles up to the present are conceived differently. To some people, even in our day, much

as in the past,—for instance, to Bielinsky—the Slavophile doctrine
signifies nothing but kvas and radish. *Actually* Bielinsky did not go
beyond this conception of it. To others (and let me note to a great
many, almost to the majority of the Slavophiles themselves) it
means the desire to liberate and unite all the Slavs under the sovereign rule of Russia—a rule which may not even be strictly political.

Finally, to others still, the Slavophile doctrine, in addition to
that assimilation of the Slavs under the rule of Russia, signifies
and comprises a spiritual union of all those who believe that our
great Russia, at the head of the united Slavs, will utter to the
world, to the whole of European mankind and to civilization, her
new, sane and as yet unheard-of word. That word will be uttered
for the good and genuine unification of mankind as a whole in a
new, brotherly, universal union whose inception is derived from
the Slavic genius, pre-eminently from the spirit of the great Rus-
sion people who have suffered so long, who during so many centuries have been doomed to silence, but who have always possessed
great powers for clarifying and settling many bitter and fatal misunderstandings of Western European civilization. Now, I belong to
this group of the convinced and the believing.

Again, in this connection there is nothing to banter and laugh
at: these are old words and an old faith, and the fact itself that
this faith does not die and that these words continue to sound,
that on the contrary they grow increasingly stronger, that they
expand, acquiring new partisans, new convinced workers,—this fact
alone should finally compel adversaries and mockers of this *doctrine* to envisage it at least a little more seriously and to abandon
vain and ossified animosity against it. But for the time being enough
has been said.

The point is that last spring our great war for the great exploit
began. Sooner or later, despite all temporary reverses postponing
the settlement of the matter, this exploit will be brought to an
end, even though specifically during the present war it may not
prove possible to carry it to its full and desired conclusion. This
exploit is so great, and the aim of the war is so incredible to Europe,
that of course she must be indignant over our *cunning,* she must
disbelieve the declarations which we made when beginning the war,
and she must in every way, by all means, harm us, and by allying
herself with our enemy—though not through an open, formal political accord—struggle against us, even if only clandestinely, in
anticipation of an open war. And all this, it goes without saying,
is the result of our declared intentions and aims!

"The great Eastern eagle, shining with his two wings on the

peaks of Christianity, soared over the world." He seeks no conquest
or acquisition, no expansion of his borders; but the liberation of
the oppressed and the downtrodden, giving them new life for their
benefit and that of mankind. For, no matter how one may reason,
no matter how sceptically one may view the matter,—essentially,
such is our aim, and it is this that Europe refuses to believe. And
I assure you that Europe fears not so much the possible growth
of Russia's strength as she fears the fact that Russia is capable of
undertaking such tasks. This you should particularly bear in mind.
To undertake something not for one's direct benefit seems to Europe
so unusual, so in discord with international customs, that Russia's
act is naturally regarded by Europe not only as the barbarity of
"a backward, bestial and unenlightened nation" capable of *vileness
and stupidity*, of embarking in our age upon something on the order
of the crusades of the dark ages, but even as a most immoral fact
fraught with danger to Europe and supposedly threatening her
great civilization.

Look, who in Europe likes us, especially at present?—Even
our *friends*—our notorious formal friends, so to speak—even they
candidly announce that they are *glad of our reverses*. A defeat of
the Russians, to them, is more delightful than their victories: it
cheers them, flatters them. However, in the event of our success,
these friends have already agreed to exert all efforts to derive from
it more benefits than Russia herself might derive. . . .

But this, too, is to be discussed later. I began to speak principally about the impression which last spring, after the declaration
of war, must have been felt by all those who believe in the great,
universal significance of Russia. This unheard-of war for the weak
and the oppressed, for the sake of giving them life and liberty—
and not for the purpose of usurping them,—this aim of the war,
long unheard-of in the world, suddenly became to all of us who
believe in Russia a fact significantly and solemnly reaffirming our
faith. This was no longer a dream, a conjecture, but a reality *which
began to come true*. "Once it begins to come true, it must come
to an end, to that great, new word which Russia, heading the Slavic
union, will utter to Europe. And even that word is already about
to reveal itself, despite the fact that Europe still does not understand and will long refuse to believe it. All this is in full accord
with the things which the believers have been maintaining."—Yes,
the impression was a solemn and significant one, and of course
the faith of the believers must have been still more tempered and
strengthened.

However, so grave was the matter that even in the minds
of the believers disturbing questions began to arise: "Russia and

Europe! Russia draws her sword against the Turks; yet, who knows, she may come to blows with Europe.—Wouldn't this be too early? A conflict with Europe is something different from a conflict with the Turks, and it must come to pass not through the sword alone." —This is what the believers have always understood. But are we ready for that other conflict?—True, the word already began to reveal itself; even so, leaving Europe aside,—does everybody understand it in Russia? Now, we, the believers, are prophesying, for instance, that only Russia possesses those elements which are capable of solving the fatal all-European problem of the small fry, without battle and blood, with neither hatred nor spite, but that Russia will utter that word when Europe is already stained with blood, since prior to that no one in Europe would hear our word; even should they hear it, they would altogether fail to understand it.

Yes, we, the believers, believe in this. Meanwhile, what do our own Russians in Russia answer?—We are told that these are but ecstatic conjectures, convulsionism, mad dreams, fits. We are asked for proofs, firm indications and accomplished facts. At present to what shall we point in corroboration of our prophecies? To the liberation of the peasants,—to a fact which is still so little understood by us as a measure of the manifestation of Russian spiritual strength?—To the innateness in us and naturalness of our brotherhood, which in our day is clearly brought to light, emerging from everything that for centuries has been keeping it down, despite the litter and filth which it encounters, which smear and distort its features to the point of unrecognizability? But suppose we should point to these facts: we should again be told that they all are convulsionism, mad dreams, and not facts at all; that they are being interpreted differently and confusedly, and that, as yet, they can serve as a proof of nothing.

This is what virtually everybody would tell us. And yet we who understand ourselves so little and who have so little faith in ourselves—we come in conflict with Europe! Europe—but it is a dreadful and sacred thing—Europe! Oh, do you know, gentlemen, how this very Europe, this "land of sacred miracles," is dear to us, Slavophile dreamers,—according to you, haters of Europe! Do you know how these "miracles" are dear to us; how we love and revere with a stronger than brotherly feeling, those great nations inhabiting her, all the great and the beautiful which they have created! Do you know what tears we shed, what pangs of the heart we feel when we suffer and fret over the destinies of that dear and *kindred* land of ours; how the dark clouds, overcasting more and more its horizon, frighten us!—Never did you, gentlemen—our Europeans and Westerners—love Europe as strongly as we love her, we—Slavophile dreamers and, according to you—her inveterate enemies!

Nay, that land is dear to us; dear is the peaceful victory of the great Christian spirit preserved in the East. . . . And in our fear of colliding with Europe in the course of the present war, we are more than anything else afraid of the possibility that Europe may not understand us, that even as heretofore, as always, she may face us with haughtiness and contempt, with her sword, still as wild barbarians unworthy to speak in her presence.

Yes, we have asked ourselves, what should we tell her, what should we show her so that she might understand us? Apparently, we still have so little of anything which is *intelligible* to her and for which she can respect us.—Our fundamental key idea, our emerging "new word"—she will not understand for a long, long time. She needs intelligible facts *now,* intelligible from her *present* point of view. She will ask us: "Where is your civilization? Does one perceive harmony of your economic forces in that chaos which we all see in Russia? Where is *your* science, *your* art, *your* literature?"

3

Anna Karenina AS A FACT OF SPECIAL SIGNIFICANCE

And it was precisely at that time, *i.e.,* last spring, one evening, that I happened to meet in the street one of our writers most beloved by me. We meet very rarely, once in several months, and always accidentally, mostly in the street. He is one of the most eminent members of that group of five or six of our belles-lettrists whom in their conjunction, for some reason, people are used to call "the Pleiad." At least, critics, after the public, have specially segregated them from the rest of the belles-lettrists; this has been in effect for some time—the same group of five, and "the Pleiad" does not increase in number.

I like to meet this kind romancer of whom I am so fond, and it gives me pleasure to prove to him, among other things, that I flatly refuse to believe he has grown antiquated—as he maintains —and that he is not going to write anything else. From my brief conversation with him I always carry away some fine, perspicacious word.

That time there were plenty of topics for conversation: the war had already begun. But at once and directly he turned to *Anna Karenina.* I had just then finished reading the seventh part, with which the novel came to a close in *The Russian Messenger.* In his appearance, my interlocutor is not an enthusiastic man. But on that occasion he impressed me with his firmness and ardent insistence upon his opinion of *Anna Karenina*.

"This is an unheard-of, outstanding thing. Who among our writers can match him? And in Europe, who can exhibit at least anything equal to his? Has there been in their literature, in recent years, and long before, a work which would be comparable to his?"

In this verdict—which I fully shared—I was chiefly impressed with the fact that this reference to Europe precisely fitted in with the questions and perplexities which, at that time, arose of their own accord in the minds of so many people. The book in my opinion directly assumed the proportions of a fact capable of giving Europe an answer on our behalf, of that long-sought fact which we could point out to Europe. Of course, people will start vociferating scoffingly that this is only literature, a novel of some kind; that it is ridiculous to exaggerate so greatly and appear in Europe with nothing but a novel. I know that people will vociferate and laugh, but this doesn't trouble me: I am not exaggerating and I am looking at things soberly. I know myself that, as yet, this is but a novel; that this is but a drop of what is needed; however, to my way of thinking the principal thing is that this drop already exists, it is given, it is here in reality and in truth. Therefore, if it exists; if Russian genius has proved capable of generating this *fact*, it is not doomed to impotence; it can create; it can give something which is its *own*; it can originate its *own* and finish uttering it when the times and the seasons come to pass.

Besides, this is far from being only a drop. Here, too, I am not exaggerating: I am fully aware of the fact that not only in some individual member of the Pleiad, but in the Pleiad as a whole, strictly speaking, you will not find that which is called ingenious, creative force. In all our literature there have been but three unquestioned men of genius with an unquestioned "new word"—Lomonosov, Pushkin and partly Gogol. And this whole Pleiad (including the author of *Anna Karenina*) emerged directly from Pushkin, one of Russia's greatest men, who, however, is still far from being understood and explained.

In Pushkin there are two principal, or guiding, ideas, and both comprise the symbol of the whole future character, of the whole future mission of Russia, and, therefore,—of our whole future destiny. The first idea is the *universality* of Russia, her responsiveness and actual, unquestioned and most profound kinship with the geniuses of all ages and nations of the world. This thought was expressed by Pushkin not as a mere suggestion, doctrine or theory; not as a dream or prophecy, but it was *actually* fulfilled by him, embodied forever in his ingenious creations and proved by the latter. He was a man of the ancient world; he was a German; he was an Englishman, profoundly cognizant of his genius, of the anguish of his aspirations (*Feast During the Plague*), and he was also the poet of the East. He said and proclaimed to all these peoples that Russian genius knew them, understood them,—was contiguous with them, that, as a kinsman, it could fully *reincarnate* itself in them; that universality was given only to the Russian spirit —the future mission to comprehend and to unite all the different nationalities, eliminating all their contradictions.

Pushkin's second idea is his turn toward the people, his sole reliance upon their strength; his covenant that in the people, and only in them, we shall fully discover our Russian genius and the cognizance of its destiny. And again, not only did Pushkin point this out, but he was the first actually to achieve it. It was with him that in Russia began the conscious turn toward the people, which was unthinkable before him, ever since the time of Peter's reform. All our present-day Pleiad has been laboring pursuant to his dictates, and after Pushkin it has uttered nothing *new*. All embryos were in him, and were indicated by him. Besides, the Pleiad has elaborated only the tiniest part of the things indicated by Pushkin. As against this, they elaborated that which they did with such opulence of power, with such depth and precision that Pushkin, of course, would have recognized them.

It stands to reason that *Anna Karenina,* in its idea, is not a new or unheard-of thing in Russia. On the contrary we could directly point out to Europe that its source is Pushkin, himself the brightest, firmest and most undeniable proof of the independence of Russian genius and its right to the greatest, most universal, pan-human and all-assimilating significance in the fuutre. (Alas, no matter how much we might point out, our writers would not be read in Europe for a long time to come; and even should the Europeans start reading them, they would not understand and prize them. In fact, they are altogether unable to prize them, not because of the paucity of their intellectual faculties, but because we constitute to them a wholly different world, as if we had descended from the moon, so that it is even difficult for them to admit our very existence. All this I know, and I speak of "pointing out to Europe" only as my own conviction of our right to our independence in the face of Europe.)

Nevertheless *Anna Karenina,* as an artistic production, is perfect. It has appeared at an opportune moment, and in our epoch no work in European belles-lettres can compare with it. Secondly, by its idea, the novel is something inherently ours, our *own*, specifically something constituting our Russian peculiarity as distinguished from the European world, our national "new word," or, at least, its beginning—precisely such a word as one doesn't hear in Europe, which, however, she needs so badly, despite all her haughtiness.

I am unable to embark here upon literary criticism, and will merely say a few words.

In *Anna Karenina* is expressed a view of human guilt and criminality. People are portrayed in abnormal circumstances. Evil existed before them. Caught in the whirl of deceit, people commit crime and fatally perish. It will be perceived that this is a thought dealing with the most beloved and antiquated European themes. However, how is this problem solved in Europe? Everywhere in Europe it is solved in a twofold manner.

First solution: The law has been laid down, framed, formulated and conceived during millennia. Evil and good are defined, weighed, measured, and their degrees have been historically ascertained by the sages of mankind by means of uninterrupted training of the human soul and highly scientific elaboration of the extent of the cohesive force of human intercourse. It is ordered to abide blindly by this enacted code. He who fails to abide by it, he who violates it, pays for it with his freedom, his property, his life, pays literally and inhumanly. "I know"—says their own civilization—"that this is blind, cruel, impossible, since a final formula of behavior cannot be elaborated while mankind is still in the middle of the road; however, since there is no other solution, one has to abide by the written code,—abide literally and inhumanly; without this it would be worse. At the same time, despite all the abnormality and absurdity of the organization which we call the great European civilization, let the forces of the human spirit be healthy and intact; let not society be shaken in its belief that it is headed for perfection; let it not dare to think that the ideal of the beautiful and the lofty has been dimmed; that the conceptions of good and evil are being distorted and twisted; that normality is continually replaced by conventionalism; that simplicity and naturalness are perishing, being continually suppressed by accumulating deceit!"

The second solution is the reverse: "Inasmuch as society is abnormally organized, it is impossible to make the human entity responsible for its consequences. Therefore, the criminal is irresponsible, and at present crime does not exist. To overcome crime and human guilt, it is necessary to overcome the abnormality of society and its structure. Since it takes long to cure the existing order of things, and besides, inasmuch as no medicine has been discovered, it is necessary to destroy society *in toto* and to sweep away the old order, as it were with a broom. After that everything has to be started anew, upon different foundations, which are still unknown, but which nevertheless cannot be worse than the existing order and which, contrariwise, comprise many chances for success. The main hope is in science."

Such, then, is the second solution: people are looking forward to the future ant-hill, and meanwhile the world will be stained with blood. No other solutions of guilt and human delinquency are being offered by the Western European world.

However, in the Russian author's approach to culpability and human delinquency it is clearly revealed that no ant-hill, no triumph of "the fourth estate," no elimination of poverty, no organization of labor will save mankind from abnormality, and therefore,—from guilt and criminality. This is expressed in an immense psychological analysis of the human soul, with tremendous depth and potency, with a realism of artistic portrayal hitherto unknown in Russia. It is clear and intelligible to the point of obviousness that evil in mankind is concealed deeper than the physician-socialists suppose; that in no organization of society can evil be eliminated; that the human soul will remain identical; that abnormality and sin emanate from the soul itself, and finally, that the laws of the human spirit are so unknown to science, so obscure, so indeterminate and mysterious, that, as yet, there can neither be physicians nor *final* judges, but that there is only He who saith: "Vengeance belongeth unto me; I will recompense." He alone knows the *whole* mystery of the world and man's ultimate destiny. And man, as yet, with the pride of infallibility, should not venture to solve anything—the times and the seasons have not yet come. The human judge himself must know that he is not the final judge; that he himself is a sinner; that in his hands—scales and measures will be an absurdity, *if* holding the scales and the measures he fails to submit to the law of the still insoluble mystery and to resort to the only solution— to Mercy and Love. And that man should not perish in despair of the ignorance of his paths and destinies, of the conviction of the mysterious and fatal inevitability of evil, he has been given a solution. It is cleverly traced by the poet in the ingenious scene of the penultimate part of the novel,—in the scene of the mortal illness of the heroine, when criminals and enemies are suddenly transformed into superior beings, into brothers, who have forgiven each other everything; beings who by mutual all-forgiveness, have removed from themselves deceit, guilt and crime, and thereby at once acquitted themselves with full cognizance of the fact that they have become entitled to acquittal.

But later, at the end of the novel, in a dark and dreadful picture of the degradation of the human spirit, traced step by step,

in the delineation of that fatal condition when evil, having taken
possession of man binds his every move, paralyzes every desire of
resistance, every thought, every wish to combat darkness, invading
the soul, which deliberately, with delight, with a passion for vengeance, is conceived by the soul as light,—in that picture there is
so much edification for the human judge, for him who holds the
scales and the measures that, of course, he will exclaim with fear
and perplexity: "Nay, it is not always that vengeance belongeth
unto me, and not always I who shall recompense." And he will
not cruelly accuse the gloomily fallen criminal of having neglected
the light of the solution,—always pointed out to him—and of having
deliberately rejected it. At least, the human judge will not cling
to the letter of the law.

If we possess literary works of such power of thought and
execution, why couldn't we *later* have *our own* science, our economic
and social solutions? Why does Europe deny us independence, *our
own* word?—These questions arise of their own accord. Indeed, one
cannot presume the ridiculous thought that nature has bestowed
upon us merely literary gifts. All the rest is a matter of history,
of circumstances and of conditions of time. Thus, at least, our
Europeans should be reasoning in anticipation of the judgment of
the European Europeans. . . .

4

A Landowner Procuring Faith in God from a Peasant

Now that I have expressed my feelings, perhaps it will be
understood how I was affected by the apostasy of such an author,
by his segregation from the all-Russian great cause, and his paradoxical untruth attributed by him to the people in his ill-starred
eighth part of the novel, separately published by him. He simply
robs the people of everything that is most sacred to them, depriving
them of the principal sense of their life. It would have been far
more agreeable to him should our people everywhere fail to rise
with their hearts in defense of their brethren oppressed for their
faith. It is only in this sense that he denies a fact despite its obviousness.

Of course, all this is merely expressed by the fictitious character of the novel; yet, I repeat, the author himself is too clearly
visible by his side. True, this is a sincere book, and the author
speaks from his heart. Even the most ticklish things (and in the
book there are ticklish things) are fitted into it, as if by chance, so
that despite all their ticklishness, you accept them at their face
value without admitting the possibility of any crookedness in them.

Even so, I do not regard this book as such an innocent one. Naturally, at present it exercises—and can exercise—no influence whatever, save, perhaps, that it might once more sound as a "yea" to a certain secluded group. But the fact that such an author writes thus is very sad. This is sad for the future. But I had better get to business: I mean to object and to state precisely what has struck me.

First, however, I shall deal with Levin—obviously, the principal hero of the novel: in him the positive element is expressed in opposition, as it were, to those abnormalities which caused ruin and suffering to the other characters of the novel. Apparently, Levin was intended by the author to express all this. And yet, Levin is still not perfect; he still lacks something. This should have been dealt with and settled so as to eliminate all doubts and questions as to who Levin is. The reader will later understand why I am dwelling on this and why I am not turning directly to the main subject.

Levin is happy. The novel winds up with his glorification, but still he lacks inner, spiritual peace. He is tormented with the eternal problems confronting mankind: of God, eternal life, good and evil, and the like. He suffers because he is an agnostic and because he is unable to be appeased with the things which appease everybody, *i.e.*, with personal benefit, self-adoration, or worship of one's own ideals, ambition, etc. This is a sign of magnanimity—is it not? But nothing less could have been expected of Levin. By the way, it appears that he is well-read; he is familiar with the works of philosophers, positivists and simple naturalists. But nothing satisfies him. On the contrary, he becomes more confused, so that in his leisure hours, when he is not occupied with husbandry, he seeks refuge in woods and groves; he even prizes his Kitty less than she deserves.

And, unexpectedly, he meets a peasant, who, speaking about two morally different peasants, Mitiukha and Fokanych, expresses himself thus:

"How can Mitiukha fail to get what's due him! He'll bring pressure and collect his due. He has no pity for a peasant. But Uncle Fokanych,—is he going to skin a fellow? Now he'll grant a loan; now he'll let it go. This way, at times, he fails to collect his due in full, 'cause he's human."

"Why should he let it go?"

"No matter. See,—people are different: one fellow lives for no other purpose than his needs; take Mitiukha, for one; he stuffs his belly—that's all. But Fokanych is a truthful old man. He lives for his soul, he remembers God."

"What do you mean 'remembers God'? How does he live for his soul?" Levin almost shrieked.

"Why, that's simple:—according to truth, in God-like manner. People are different . . . You for one, you'll not harm a man."

"Yes, yes! So long!"—muttered Levin, losing his breath from emotion, and turning away, he took his cane and speedily went home.

However, again he ran to the forest, lay down under aspens and began to think almost in a state of rapture. The word has been found; all the eternal riddles have been solved,—and this by a simple peasant's word: "To live for one's soul; to remember God." Of course, the peasant has told him nothing new; he has known this for a long time. Nevertheless the peasant led his thought and prompted the decision at the most ticklish moment.

Then there ensues a series of Levin's deliberations which are quite correct and pointedly expressed. This is the thought: Why should one seek with the intellect that which is already given by life itself, that with which every man is born, and by which (even against his will) every man abides and must abide? Every man is born with conscience, with the conception of good and evil; therefore he is born with a direct aim in life—to live for the good and to abhor the evil. With this the peasant and the master, the Frenchman, the Russian, the Turk are born—they all revere the good (N. B. although many in an awfully peculiar manner of their own). And I—says Levin—sought to perceive all this through mathematics, science, reason; or else—I was waiting for a miracle, whereas this was given me gratuitously,—it was born with me. And there is direct proof that it was given gratuitously: everybody in the world understands, or is able to understand that: *"Thou shalt love thy neighbor as thyself."* Essentially, this knowledge comprises man's whole *law*, and so it was enunciated to us by Christ Himself. And yet this knowledge is innate; therefore, it is given gratuitously, since reason under no circumstance could have given it.—Why?— Because to "love one's neighbor," from the standpoint of reason, is unreasonable.

"Whence did I get this?"—Levin asks himself—"Was it by reason that I arrived at the conclusion that one has to love his neighbor and not oppress him?—This I was told in my childhood, and I *believed it gladly,* because I was told that which was in my soul. And who revealed it?—Not reason. Reason discovered the struggle for existence and the law requiring that everybody who hinders the satisfaction of my desires should be oppressed. Such is the inference of reason. But to love one's neighbor could not have been conceived by reason since this is unreasonable."

Furthermore, the recent scene with the children came to Levin's mind. The children began to roast raspberries in cups, over lighted candles, pouring milk, as from a fountain, into their mouths. The mother, having caught them in *flagrante delicto,* began to reprimand them, explaining that if they should spoil the plates and dishes and spill the milk, there would be neither vessels nor milk. Apparently, however, the children did not believe it, because they were unable to conceive "the full extent of that which they enjoyed, and therefore they were unable to understand that that which they were destroying was the very thing by which they lived."

"This comes of its own accord"—so they reasoned—"there is nothing interesting or important in this, since this has always existed and always will exist. And everything is always the same. We don't have to think about it; all this is ready. But we want to invent something which is ours, something new. And so we thought of putting the raspberries into a cup and roasting them over a candle, pouring milk, as from a fountain, straight into our mouths. This is merry and new, and in no sense worse than drinking from a cup."

"Aren't we doing the same thing; wasn't I doing it, when I was endeavoring to discover through reason the meaning of the forces of nature and the sense of man's life?"—continued Levin.

"And aren't all philosophical theories doing the same thing when they seek to lead man, by means of strange reasoning, unnatural to him, to the knowledge of that which he has known long before, with such certainty that he could not have lived without it? Isn't it clear in the exposition of the doctrine of every philosopher that he knows in advance, as indubitably as the peasant Fedor,—and in no way more clearly than he—the principal meaning of life; and that he merely seeks to return by a doubtful rational path to that which is known to everybody?

"Now, what if children be let loose so that they may buy things themselves, manufacture plates and dishes, milk cows, and so forth? Would they engage in mischief?—Why, they would die of hunger. Well, what if we be let loose, with our passions, thoughts, bereft of the conception of the one God and Creator! Or without the conception of what is good, without the explanation of moral evil!

"Well, try to build something without these conceptions! We are merely destroying, because spiritually we are satiated. Precisely —children!"

In a word, doubts are dissipated and Levin begins to believe.

—In what? As yet, he has not strictly ascertained this, but he believes. However, is this faith? Joyously he puts this question to
himself: "Is it possible that this is faith?"—Presumably not. Moreover: men such as Levin can hardly possess final faith. Levin likes
to call himself "the people," but he is a nobleman's son, a Moscow
nobleman's son, of the middle-upper stratum whose historian Count
Tolstoy pre-eminently has been.

Even though the peasant has told Levin nothing new, nevertheless he has suggested an idea, and with this idea faith has begun.
This alone should have demonstrated to Levin that he was not
quite "the people," and that he had no right to speak thus about
himself: "I myself am the people." But this I shall leave for further
discussion. I merely wish to say that men like Levin, no matter
how long they be living amidst, or side by side with, the people,
never will fully become the people. Moreover, in many ways they
will never understand the people at all. Self-conceit, or an act of
will—besides, so whimsical a will—is not enough to become the
people of one's volition. Let him be a landowner, an industrious
landowner; let him be familiar with peasants' pursuits; let him
mow and know how to yoke horses to a cart; let him know that
fresh cucumbers are served with honey. All the same, hard as he
may try, there will remain in his soul a shade of what I believe
may be denoted as *sauntering*, that very sauntering—physical and
spiritual—which, much as he may resist it, was bequeathed to him,
and which, of course, the people perceive in every nobleman, as,
fortunately, they do not see things with our eyes.

However, this too comes later. And he will again destroy his
faith; he will destroy it himself; it will not persist long: some
new twig will appear, and at once everything will fall apart. Kitty
started to walk and stumbled. Now, why did she stumble? If she
stumbled, this means that she could not have not stumbled; it is
only too clear that she stumbled for such and such a reason. It is
clear that in this case everything depended upon laws which may
be strictly ascertained. And if this be so, this means that science
governs everything. Where, then, is Providence? What is its role?
Where is man's responsibility? And if there is no Providence, how
can I believe in God? And so on, and so forth. Take a straight line
and extend it into infinity. In a word, this honest soul is a most
idle, chaotic soul, otherwise he wouldn't have been a contemporary
Russian educated nobleman, and besides, of the middle-upper
stratum of the nobility.

This he brilliantly proves, hardly later than an hour after the
acquisition of faith; he argues that the people do not at all feel
that which men in general are capable of feeling; with one stroke

he destroys the soul of the people in a most willful manner. More-over, he announces that he has no pity for human suffering. He proclaims that "no immediate feeling of compassion for the op-pressed Slavs exists or can exist," *i.e.*, not only in him, but in all Russians. "I am, so to speak, the people." Indeed, they value the Russian people much too cheaply. Well, they are old appraisers. Hardly an hour had elapsed after the acquisition of faith, when raspberries again started roasting over the candle.

CHAPTER III

1

Irritability of Amour-Propre

CHILDREN CAME running in and announced to Levin that guests had arrived. "One of them swings his arms this way." It developed that guests had come from Moscow. Levin seated them under the trees; honey and fresh cucumbers were served to them, and the guests at once embarked upon honey and the Eastern ques-tion.

All this, you see, dates back to last year. You recall: Cher-niaiev, the volunteers, donations. Conversation promptly flares up because everybody is irresistibly attracted toward the main sub-ject. Aside from the ladies, the interlocutors are: first, a Moscow professor, a nice but somewhat stupid fellow. Then comes a man (he is portrayed for this specific purpose) of enormous intellect and learning—Sergei Ivanovich Koznyshev, Levin's half-brother, by the same mother. This character is skillfully delineated in the novel, and, at length, he becomes intelligible (a man of the Forties). Sergei Ivanovich has just thrown himself—altogether and with zeal —into the Slavic work. The Committee has conferred upon him so many tasks that, recalling last summer, it is difficult to imagine how he could leave the work and go to the country for two whole weeks. True, if he had not come, there would have been no con-versation at the apiary about the popular movement, and conse-quently,—there would have been no eighth part of the novel, which was written exclusively for this conversation.

You see, this Sergei Ivanovich, some two or three months prior to that, had published in Moscow some learned book on Russia, a book on which he had worked long and in which he had placed much hope. The book, however, proved to be a failure, and a shameful failure. No one said anything about it and it passed

unnoticed. At this juncture Sergei Ivanovich embarked upon the
Slavic work with such zeal as could not have been expected from
him. Thus it appears that he embarked upon it unnaturally: his
whole enthusiasm for the Slavs was but an *ambition rentrée,* and
one feels that Levin cannot fail to be a victor over such a man.
In the previous parts of the novel Sergei Ivanovich is very skillfully
portrayed in a comical light. But in the eighth part it becomes quite
clear that he has been conceived solely for the purpose of serving
at the end of the novel as a pedestal for Levin's greatness. Still this
character is delineated very successfully.

As against this—the old Prince is one of the least successful
characters. He also sits there and talks about the Eastern question.
He is unsuccessful throughout the whole novel—not only in the
part dealing with the Eastern question. This is one of the positive
types designed to express positive beauty,—of course without sinning
against realism: he has his weaknesses and almost comic traits, but
he is quite respectable. He is the kindhearted character in the
novel; he is also the incarnation of common sense; once he starts,
he acts like a trained donkey: common sense and nothing but common sense. Nay, there is also humor in him, and, generally, human
traits. The funny thing is that this old man is designed to represent
wit. Having gone through the school of life, this father of numerous
children, although they are well provided for in his old age, views
everything around him with the calm smile of a sage,—with a smile,
however, which is far from benign and inoffensive. He will give
advice, but beware of his *jeu d'esprit*—it is sharp as a razor.

But unexpectedly an unfortunate thing happens: this man designed to act as a wit; this man full of common sense, God knows
why, appears not only devoid of wit but is even somewhat trivial.
True, he keeps trying—as he does throughout the novel—to say
something witty, but absolutely nothing comes of his endeavors.
The reader, finally, from delicacy, is ready to accept these attempts
at wit, or, so to speak, throes of wit, for wit itself. But much more
disappointing is the fact that this very man, in the eighth part of
the novel,—true, published separately—expresses ideas which, I concede, though also not witty (in this respect the old Prince is consistent) are cynical and calumnious against a portion of our society
and our people. Instead of a kindhearted fellow, there appears some
sort of clubman who denies both the Russian people and everything
that is good in them; club irritation and senile bile sound in his
words. However, the old Prince's political theory is in no sense new.
It is a repetition for the hundred thousandth time of what, even
without him, we hear every minute: "Here I am"—said the Prince
—"I lived abroad, I read the papers, and I confess, prior to the

Bulgarian horrors, I was at a loss to understand why all Russians suddenly grew fond of their Slav brethren, whereas I feel no love for them. I was very grieved to think that I was a monster [this, you see, is a witticism: just fancy, he believes himself to be a monster!], or that Carlsbad affects me this way [double witticism!]. However, having come here, I calmed down [why, certainly!]. I see that, aside from myself, there are people who are interested only in Russia, and not in their Slav brethren."

That's where we perceive real depth! One has to take interest *only* in Russia. So that help given to the Slavs is directly declared to be a non-Russian task. Were he to conceive it to be a Russian task, he would not have said that one has to take interest *only* in Russia, because to take interest in the Slavs would then naturally have signified an interest in Russia and her mission. Thus, the character of the Prince's conception comes down to a narrow understanding of Russian interests. Of course, we have heard these things! A thousand times one may hear them! And in some circles one hears nothing but this!

However, here is something much more malignant. This is a conversation held a few minutes before that. The old Prince asks Sergei Ivanovich:

" '. . . For Christ's sake, explain to me, Sergei Ivanovich, whither are all these volunteers going? With whom do they fight?'

" 'With the Turks'—Sergei Ivanovich, smiling, calmly replied.

" 'But who has declared war upon the Turks?—Ivan Ivanovich Ragozov and Countess Lydia Ivanovna in company with Madam Staal?' "

[Here we are: he has betrayed himself. You understand that this was the purpose of his questions. Perhaps this is the reason he hastened to come from Carlsbad. But this is a different matter, and the fact that the Prince started talking about this, is, perhaps, even a good thing. Of course, this idea, too, is not new, but why is it reiterated?—Last winter quite a few people—those who needed it—kept asserting that somebody in Russia had declared war on the Turks. This was set forth. But this little idea started circulating and returned to its inventors. Since last year no one at all had declared war on the Turks, and such an assertion, to say the least, was an *exaggeration*. True, in the subsequent conversation Sergei Ivanovich gives joking replies, but naïve and honest Levin, like a real *enfant terrible*, directly expresses that which is on the Prince's mind:]

" 'No one has declared war; but people sympathize with the sufferings of their neighbors, and they seek to help them'—said Sergei Ivanovich.

" 'But the Prince speaks not of help'—said Levin, taking the side of his father-in-law—'but of war. The Prince says that private people have no right to take part in a war without the permission of the government.'

[Now you see what Levin's concern is? The question is put squarely; besides, it is clarified by the stupid sally of Katavasov. Here is what Levin says further:]

" 'Yes, my theory is this: on the one hand, war is such a beastly, cruel and awful thing that no man, not to speak of a Christian, can assume personal responsibility for its initiation; this may be done only by a government which is instituted therefor and which is led to war inevitably. On the other hand, according to both science and common sense, in state affairs, especially in the matter of war, citizens renounce their personal will.'

"Sergei Ivanovich and Katavasov, with ready objections, started speaking at the same time.

" 'But that's the point, my dear, that there may be cases when the government does not comply with the will of the citizens, and then society declares its will'—said Katavasov.

"Sergei Ivanovich, however, apparently, did not approve this objection."

In a word it is pointed out, and insisted upon, that last year somebody in Russia, disregarding the government, declared war on the Turks. Levin, with his intellect, could have guessed that Katavasov was a little fool; that Katavasovs may be found everywhere; that last year's movement was precisely opposite to Katavasov's ideas, since it was Russian, national, genuinely our movement, and not a game in some sort of opposition. But Levin insists on his own ideas; he pushes his accusation to the end. Not truth is dear to him but that which he has invented. Here are the arguments with which he winds up his thoughts on the subject:

". . . He [Levin] spoke, much as Mikhailych and the people who expressed their thought in the legend about the summoning of the Varangians: 'Rule over us and take possession of us. We gladly promise full obedience. We assume all labors, humiliations and sacrifices. But we shall not judge and render decisions.' And at present the people, according to Sergei Ivanovich, have *renounced this right which was bought at such a high price*. He also meant to say that if public opinion is an infallible judge, why, then, are revolutions and the Commune not as lawful as the movement in support of the Slavs?"

Do you hear? And no considerations will lead these gentlemen astray—no facts no matter how obvious. I have already said that it would have been better had the Prince and Levin refrained from such accusations. But who doesn't see that in one of them there is insulted *amour-propre*, while the other is a paradoxicalist. However, perhaps also in Levin there is piqued *amour-propre*, since no one knows what may suddenly pique man's vanity!

And yet it is clear that the accusation is nonsensical; besides, there can be no such accusation because it cannot exist. The facts were altogether different.

2

TOUT CE QUI N'EST PAS EXPRESSEMENT PERMIS EST DÉFENDU[1]

War on Turkey was declared last year not by or in Russia, but in Slavic countries by the ruling princes, *i.e.*, sovereigns—Prince Milan of Serbia and Prince Nicholas of Montenegro—who took up arms against Turkey because of the unheard-of persecutions, barbarities, plunder and massacres of her Slavic subjects, including Herzegovinans, who were compelled by these bestialities to rise against their oppressors. The incredible tortures and massacres to which Herzegovinans had been subjected became known in Europe. The news about these horrors also spread in Russia—first among the educated public, and later—among the people. Because it was incredible this news spread everywhere. Information was received that hundreds of thousands of human beings—old men, pregnant women, forsaken children, were leaving their homes, fleeing from Turkey to the bordering countries, anywhere, deprived of bread, shelter, clothing, driven by extreme fear and the instinct of self-preservation. The princes, the Church and its dignitaries raised their voices in defense of the unfortunate ones and began to collect alms for them. Our people, too, started sending them donations; contributions to specific centers—editorial offices of magazines, branches of the former Slavic Committees—and in this there was nothing unlawful, anti-governmental or immoral. On the contrary, it may be boldly asserted that in this there was nothing but good.

As to the Slavic princes who had started war against Turkey, neither Russia nor anyone in Russia was guilty of that. True, one of these ruling princes, namely, Prince Milan of Serbia, was not entirely independent; on the contrary, he owed the Sultan a certain vassal subordination so that in one of the Russian newspapers he was bitterly reproached for the fact that he was, so to speak, a rebel. And in order completely to abash him and put him to shame it was stated that he revolted against his "lord." But again, strictly

[1]Everything that is not expressly permitted is prohibited.

speaking, this is Prince Milan's personal affair, for which he alone can be held responsible. Neither Russia, however, nor any one in Russia, declared war last year, and therefore no one sinned against the Sultan.

Meanwhile donations continued to be sent, but this is altogether a different matter. Suddenly, one of the Russian generals, who at the time held no office, not yet an old man, only a major-general, but one with a certain reputation because of his former rather successful military operations in Central Asia, of his own accord, proceeded to Serbia and offered his services to Prince Milan. His offer was accepted and he was enlisted in the service; not, however, as commander-in-chief of the Serbian army, as it was rumored in Russia. This rumor persisted for a long time.

It was at this juncture that Russian volunteers came into being. Unquestionably, however, there were volunteers even before, *i.e.*, before Cherniaiev. Altogether, in the course of the past year, there were not so many volunteers, very few thousands, but they were seen off to Serbia decidedly by all Russia, especially by the people—the real people—and not by *drunkards,* as spiteful Levin particularly insists. He regards the volunteers also as *drunkards*. Yet this wasn't so; the thing did not transpire in some secluded corner: it was known to everybody; everybody could see it and be convinced; *i.e.*, all Russia decided that this was a good cause.

On the part of the people there was revealed so much that was noble, touching and sound, that the whole movement last year by the Russian people in support of the Slavs, unquestionably will remain one of the best pages in their history. However, to defend the people from the Levins; to prove to them that these were not drunkards, not seducers, but, on the contrary, men who knew what they were after,—to prove all this, in my opinion, is quite futile and unnecessary, and moreover, humiliating to the people.

The main point is that all this transpired openly, in everybody's sight. Facts have been reported which were remarkable and characteristic; they were recorded, memorized and will not be forgotten; they can no longer be challenged. But I shall speak about the people later.

As regards volunteers, it should have been expected that in their ranks, side by side with supreme self-sacrifice for one's neighbor (*e.g.*, Kireev), there would be mere boldness, impulse, bravado, and so forth. All this came to pass exactly as it happens always and everywhere. True, no one has as yet counted the number of those tipplers and drunkards, those roving idlers, if such have been among volunteers, who gave their lives there, far away, for a magnanimous cause, so that there is no ground for attacking them so censoriously, even invectively. However, the assertion that the volunteers of last year were *all* revellers, drunkards and good-for-nothing men is, to say the least, senseless, since—I repeat—the thing transpired not in some remote corner but in full view.

But, at all events, last year positively none of the Russians declared war on a neighboring state, in defiance of the government. Ivan Ivanovich Ragozov and Countess Lydia Ivanovna could not have declared war on the Turks had they even wished to do so. Moreover, they did not rouse the volunteers, they did not lure or hire anyone; everyone went *absolutely* voluntarily,—and this is known to everybody. But they did help the volunteers and, in addition, they did send money to the Slavic countries for the relief of the unfortunate, the exhausted and mutilated; they did help with money the insurgents who rose in defense of the sufferers. This did take place, yes, it did, and was even accompanied with the most ardent wishes that the Turks, the blood-suckers, should break their necks.—Yes, this did take place. But the whole question is whether this is a declaration of war. If it is not,—is it or is it not forbidden by the government, *i.e.*, is it forbidden to help with money those fighting for the Christians and to wish that the Turks should break their necks?—Again, I do not believe at all that this is interdicted, since the matter was an open one, everybody saw, everybody participated, while the volunteers received their foreign passports from the government itself.

However, I do not know; perhaps there is such a law "that private persons have no right to take part in a war without the permission of the government," *i.e.*, that they have no right, without a special permission of the government, to enlist in the service of foreign sovereigns. Perhaps there actually is some such law, a very antiquated one, which has not yet been repealed. But the government itself could have invoked it, so why should Levin worry? What has he got to do with all this? And yet he is worried precisely about this . . .

"*Pardon, monsieur, mais il me semble que tout ce qui n'est pas expressement défendu est permis.*"

"*Au contraire, monsieur: tout ce qui n'est pas expressement permis est défendu.*"

Which means:

"I beg your pardon, sir: it seems to me that everything that is not expressly prohibited is permitted."

"On the contrary, sir, everything that is not expressly permitted is prohibited."

This brief comical conversation of a man of order with a man of disorder took place in France. But this interpreter of order is appointed to keep order; he is its interpreter and defender; he is the proper person. But what is Levin's concern? What kind of specialist in such a matter is he? He keeps fearing that some kind of a right shouldn't be lost. Meanwhile the whole people, sympathizing with the oppressed Christians, were perfectly aware of the fact that they were right, that they did nothing contrary to the will of their Czar, and that in their hearts they were in accord with him. Yes, the people knew this. Those who were equipping the volunteers thought exactly in the same way. Not one of them consoled himself, even though secretly, with the foolish thought that he was acting against the will of the government. The Czar's word was awaited with patience and great hope; everybody had a presentiment of it, and they were not mistaken in it. In a word, the accusation dealing with the declaration of war is a fantastic one which falls of its own accord, and it cannot be sustained.

But Levin and the Prince themselves exonerate the people from this accusation. They directly deny the participation of the people in the movement of last year. As against this they directly assert that the people understood nothing, could understand nothing; that everything was artificially incited by journalists in order to enlist subscribers; that everything was deliberately fabricated by the Ragozovs, and so on, and so forth.

" 'Personal opinions have no significance here'—said Sergei Ivanovich.—'Personal opinions are of no import when all Russia—the people—expressed their will.'

" 'I beg your pardon. I don't see it. The people know *absolutely* nothing'—said the Prince.

" 'No, papa . . . What do you mean that they know nothing? And Sunday, in church?'—remarked Dolly, who was listening to the conversation.

" 'Well, what about Sunday in church? The priest was *ordered* to read. He read it. They *understood nothing;* they sighed as they do *at every sermon'*—the Prince continued. 'Then they were told that a collection was to be taken up in the church for a salutary cause, and they extracted a kopeck and gave it. But for what—*they don't know themselves.'* "

This nonsensical opinion, standing in direct conflict with the facts coming from the Prince, is easily explained: it emanates from one of the former guardians of the people, a former serf-owner who could not—no matter how good he was—help but despise his slaves, and consider himself immeasurably superior to them in understanding. "Well, they sighed a little, and understood nothing." But here is Levin's opinion. He, at least, is not portrayed as a former slave-owner.

" 'I don't have to inquire,'—said Sergei Ivanovich. 'We have seen and see hundreds and hundreds of men who have forsaken everything in order to serve the right cause; they come from every part of Russia, and directly, clearly express their thought and their aim. They bring their pennies, and they tell directly why they do so. What does this mean?'

" 'This means, to my way of thinking'—said Levin, who was growing excited—'that among a people of eighty million there will always be, not hundreds, as at present, but tens of thousands of men *who have lost their social status, reckless people, who are always ready to join a Pugachiov gang,* to head for Khiva, Serbia. . . .'

" 'I am telling you that not hundreds and not the reckless, but the best representatives of the people!'—Sergei Ivanovich said, with irritation as if he were defending the last bit of his property. 'And donations?—Here, the whole people are expressing their will.'

" 'The word "people" is so indeterminate,'—said Levin. 'Volost scribes, teachers of peasant parentage, perhaps one out of a thousand knows what the matter is about. The remaining eighty million, like Mikhailych, not only do not express their will, but they even haven't the slightest conception in what connection they should be expressing it. What right, then, do we have to say that this is the will of the people?' "

And, generally, it should be remarked, once and for all, that the term "the will of the people" in relation to the movement of last year is altogether out of place; it serves nothing because it expresses nothing. Last year it was not the will of the people that manifested itself but, first of all, their great compassion; secondly, their zeal for Christ; thirdly, their own repentance as it were, something on the order of a preparation for the sacrament; truly it could be thus expressed. I shall explain this further, but here I may add that I am very glad to hear Levin utter such expressions about the volunteers of last year as being ready *"to join a Pugachiov gang,"* etc. At least, now I can no longer, under any circumstance, attribute these thoughts to the author. Of this I am very glad since I clearly understand that the author has exercised his rights as an artist: he has felt strongly that the excited hypochondriac Levin, as a character artistically conceived by him, at this moment of the dispute, could not help but fully reveal his disposition, *i.e.,* wind up his comments on the volunteers and the Russian people, who saw them off—with a most insulting invective.

Nevertheless, inasmuch as the people were actually blamed for the movement of last year, and for their stupidity and dullness, and because these accusations were circulated, while the insinuation about the Pugachiov gangs was also ready to spring up,—I shall venture to explain here, as briefly as possible, how one should understand the riddle of the *consciousness* of our popular movement of last year in support of the Slavs. Since in certain circles this has actually grown into a riddle: "How"—they ask themselves—"how is it possible that the people who only yesterday, for the first time, heard about the Slavs; who know nothing about either geography or history, suddenly begin to rave madly about the Slavs, suddenly take such a liking for them!"

Aside from some specific circles, this theme was seized upon in clubs by gray-headed chaps, like the old Prince; apparently, it also appealed to Levin since it tended to lend support to the explanation he offered concerning the artificial fabrication of the movement by certain persons and for certain aims.

True as against Levin, Sergei Ivanovich is set forth as a defender of the consciousness of the popular movement. But he defends his cause poorly; he also grows excited, and generally, as stated, he is represented in a comical light. And yet the question of the consciousness and lucidity of the popular feeling for the oppressed Christians is so clear; it can be defined so precisely that I could not evade the temptation to explain, how, in my opinion, this matter should be understood in order to avoid confusion and especially *riddles*.

3

On the Unmistakable Knowledge of the Uneducated and Illiterate Russian People of the Quintessence of the Eastern Question

Since the beginning of the Russian people and their state, ever since the baptism of Russia, pilgrims began to journey to the holy lands—to the Holy Sepulcher, to Athos, etc.

As far back as the time of the Crusades, a Russian superior of a convent went to Jerusalem and was kindly received there by the King of Jerusalem, Baldwin, whom he eloquently depicted in the record of his journey. Thereafter pilgrimages to the East, to the Holy Land, have never ceased up to our days. Even at present among Russian monks in Russia there are quite a few who used to live in Athos. Thus, the backward, wholly illiterate Russian people, *i.e.*, the simplest village peasants, who know nothing about history and geography, are—and for a long time in the past have been—fully aware of the fact that the Holy Land and the local Eastern Christians have been conquered by the impious Mohammedans, the Turks, and that Christians in the whole East have been, and are, enduring a hard and difficult life.

The Russian people with afflicted hearts know this. And such is the Russian popular, historical, trait that the repentant exploits connected with pilgrimages to the Holy Land have always, since ancient times, been held in high esteem by our people. Penniless old men, discharged soldiers, old peasant women, without any knowledge of geography, have left their villages with beggars' sacks on their shoulders, and have reached—true, at times, after many misfortunes—the Holy Land. Upon their return home, the stories of their pilgrimages were reverently listened to.

Generally, stories about "the Divine" are very much liked by the Russian people. Peasants, their children, commoners in cities, even merchants, listen to these stories with fondness and sighs. Here is, for instance, a question: Who has read the *Acta Martyrum?* —Somebody in a monastery; among laymen—some professor as a matter of duty, or some odd old fellow who fasts and attends Vespers. It is even difficult to lay hands on this book: one would have to buy it, but try to borrow it in a parish—you would be refused. And now, would you believe that in the whole of Russia the knowledge of the *Acta Martyrum* is extremely widely diffused,— of course not of the book *in toto* but of its spirit, at least. Why so?— Because there are a great many tellers—men and women—of the lives of saints. They relate the stories from the *Acta Martyrum* with great skill, adding nothing of their own, and they are eagerly listened to. In childhood I heard these narratives myself, before I even learned to read. Later, I used to hear them even in prisons among robbers, and they listened to them sighingly.

These stories are not told from books, but they are memorized orally. To the Russian people there is something, so to speak, repentant and expiatory in these accounts about the Holy Places. Even bad, mean people, forestallers and oppressors, have often acquired a strange and irresistible desire to start on a pilgrimage so as to purify themselves through labor and exploit,—to comply with a vow made long ago. If they did not go to the East, to Jerusalem, they went to Russian Holy Places—to Kiev, to the Solovetzky thaumaturgists.

Nekrasov, when he conceived his great *Vlas*, as a great artist, could not even imagine him otherwise than wearing chains, in repentant roving. This is an historical trait in the life of our people which cannot be neglected if only for the reason that it is encountered in no other European nation. What will come of it is difficult to tell, all the more so as literacy and enlightenment are coming to our people through the schools, and no doubt new questions will arise which may cause many changes.

However, at present, only this trait can solve the whole *riddle*

of the consciousness of last year's movement of our people in support of the "Slavic brethren"—as they were officially denoted last
year and as they are almost scoffingly called now. It is true that
our people know next to nothing about the Slavs. Not only one out
of a thousand, as Levin says, but perhaps even one out of many
thousands may have cursorily heard that somewhere there are some
Serbians, Montenegrins, Bulgarians, our coreligionists. However, all
our people, or their *overwhelming majority,* have heard and know
that there are Orthodox Christians under the Mohammedan yoke;
that they suffer and are being oppressed, and that even the holiest
places—Jerusalem, Athos—belong to dissidents.

Even twenty or more years ago the people could have heard
about the tortured Eastern Christians and the enslaved holy places,
when the late Emperor was starting his war with Turkey, and later
with Europe, which led to Sebastopol. It was also then, in the beginning of the war, that the word came from above about the holy
places, a word which the people could have since then remembered.
Besides, long before our last year's enthusiasm for the Slavs, the
tortures of the latter had begun. This was discussed and publicized
in Russia for almost a whole year. I used to hear even in those
days questions asked by the people: "Is it true that the Turks are
again rising?"

Moreover (but this is a far-fetched consideration) it seems
to me that times favored the movement of last year. Relatively
speaking, the liberation of the peasants in Russia took place quite
a long time ago. Now, these years have elapsed, and what did the
people perceive in their midst?—Among other things they perceived
increased drunkenness, reinforced kulaks in increased numbers,
misery all around them, and often—the bestial image impressed on
themselves. Perhaps some kind of sorrow began to afflict many a
heart, repentant sorrow, sorrow of self-condemnation, the quest for
something better, sacred . . . Suddenly a voice sounded heralding
the oppression of Christians; martyrdom for the Church, for faith;
Christians giving their lives for Christ and ascending the cross,
since, had they consented to renounce the Cross and to embrace
Islam, they would all have been spared and rewarded.—This, of
course, was known to the people. Appeals for donations were
launched. After that the rumor spread about a Russian general
who had gone to help the Christians; then came the volunteers. All
these things shook the people. Precisely shook them, as I stated
above, *as an appeal to penitence, to preparation for the sacrament.*
He who was unable to go himself brought his pennies, but everybody, all Russia, saw the volunteers off.

The old Prince, sojourning at Carlsbad, was unable to understand this movement, and he came home at the very height of it—with a humorous smile on his lips. But what could the old clubman have understood about Russia and the Russians? Level-headed Levin could have understood much more than the old Prince, but he was led astray by the thought that the people did not know history and geography, principally, however, by spite because some fellows like the Rogozovs dared to declare war without his permission.

However, there was no declaration of war, while on the part of the people there was general touching repentance, thirst for participation in something holy, in Christ's cause, for the support of those who are zealous for His Cross. So that the movement was at once repentant and historical.

Please note that when I speak about this historical trait of the Russian people, *i.e.*, their zeal for "God's cause," the holy places, oppressed Christianity, and, generally, for everything repentant and Divine, I have no idea of commending them for this: I am neither praising nor blaming them. I am merely stating a fact *which can explain much*. What is to be done about the fact that we do possess such an historical trait? I don't know what will come of it, but it is quite certain that something will.

In the life of the people the most important things shape themselves in accordance with their most momentous and characteristic peculiarities. For example, temporarily, this historical trait of our people produced *every time,* when Russia was at war with the Sultan, a consciously national attitude of the people toward such a war. So that one shouldn't be surprised at the ardent sympathy of the people with such a war on the mere ground that they do not know history and geography. What they need—they know.

Oh, our people are illiterate, they are ignoramuses—this cannot be doubted. Even in a moral respect they could be taught many excellent and most enlightened things concerning this inveterate, ancient historical trait of theirs. It could be explained to these Russian men that all their rovings and pilgrimages merely point to a narrow understanding of their duties and obligations; that there is no need for journeying so far in order to acquire the good; that it would be better if they should forsake drunkenness, pay attention to the betterment of their welfare, to the accumulation of economic assets; if they should not beat their wives; if they should give thought to schools, highways, etc.,—in a word, that they should help in some way at least to make Russia, their fatherland, resemble other "enlightened European states." Finally, it could be explained to the pilgrim that his pilgrimages to the holy places are of no use to God at all; chiefly on the grounds that they are of no advantage either to himself or his family; that, on the contrary, a pilgrim, departing for a long time, leaving his home and father-land, does so, strictly speaking, for an egoistic motive, for the salvation of his soul, whereas God would be far more pleased if he should spend his leisure for some benefit to his neighbor, for instance, if he should spend a little time in his kitchen-garden, look after his calves, etc.

Briefly, it would be possible to say many beautiful things. But what is to be done if this historical trait and the quest of the good have assumed in our people *almost, exclusively this particular form, i.e.,* a *repentant* form in the guise of pilgrimage and sacrifice? —At least, in anticipation of "enlightenment," clever Levin could have credited the people with this *historical trait of theirs.* At least, he could have understood that many volunteers, and the people who saw them off, were prompted by a good motive, hoping to accomplish something good (this must be conceded!) and, therefore, at all events, they were good representatives of the people. Of course, they were not "flashing with education," and yet they were not lost or reckless men, not drunkards or idlers, but perhaps the best men among the people. They acted for Christ's cause, while in the innermost soul of a great many of them it was conceived as a purifying and repentant cause. And not one of them felt guilty about this before their Czar! On the contrary, they all knew the Czar's, the Liberator's, merciful heart was in full accord with his people. Everybody was awaiting with touching emotion and hope the expression of the Czar's will, his word, while we, sitting in our corners, were silently rejoicing over the fact that the great Russian people had vindicated our great and eternal hope in them.

For this reason how could the comparison with the Pugachiov gang, the Commune, etc., in any sense be applicable to the people and their noble and humble movement!—Precisely only a hypochondriac such as Levin, irritated to the point of commotion, could proclaim a thing of this sort. This is what touchiness means!

4

LEVIN'S COMMOTION. QUESTION: DOES DISTANCE EXERCISE INFLUENCE UPON HUMANENESS? CAN ONE AGREE WITH THE OPINION OF A CAPTURED TURK CONCERNING THE HUMANENESS OF SOME OF OUR LADIES? WHAT, THEN, ARE OUR TEACHERS TEACHING US?

But the commotion extends even farther: Levin is directly and intrusively proclaiming that that compassion for the suffering of the Slavs—*"the immediate feeling of sympathy for the oppression of the Slavs does not and cannot exist"*; Sergei Ivanovich says:

" '. . . Here there is no declaration of war but simply a manifestation of humane, Christian sentiment. Consanguineous brethren and fellow-believers are being slaughtered. Let us say—not even brethren, not fellow-believers, but simply—children, women, old men. The sentiment is aroused, and Russians run to help put an end to these horrors. Imagine that you were walking in the street and you saw that drunken people were beating a woman or a child. I take it, you wouldn't inquire whether or not war had been declared on these men, but you would rush upon them and you would protect the assaulted.'

" 'But I wouldn't kill'—said Levin.

" 'Yes, you would.'

" 'I don't know. If I saw this, I should be led by my immediate feeling. *But I cannot say in advance.* And such an immediate sentiment for the oppression of the Slavs does not nor cannot exist.'

" 'Perhaps in you it does not exist. But in others it does exist'—said Sergei Ivanovich, discontentedly knitting his brows.—'Legends of Orthodox people suffering under the yoke of "impious Agrarians" are alive in the people. The people heard about the suffering of their brethren, and they raised their voice.'

" 'Maybe'—said Levin evasively—'but I don't see it. *I am the people myself.* I don't feel it.' "

Again we come to: "I am the people myself." Once more I repeat: only two hours before Levin received his faith from a peasant; at least he intimated to Levin how one should believe. I am neither praising the peasant nor humbling Levin. Nor do I venture to decide at this time, who of the two believed better, whose psychic condition was superior and more developed, etc. But you should concede—I repeat—that from this fact alone Levin could have guessed that there was a *substantial* difference between him and the people. But here he says: "I am the people myself." Why is he so sure that he himself is the people? Because he knows how to yoke a horse to a cart, and knows that it is good to eat cucumbers with honey. Think of such men! And what self-conceit! What haughtiness and arrogance!

Still, this is not the main point. Levin asserts that immediate sentiment for the oppression of the Slavs *does not and cannot exist.* He is rebuked: "the people heard about the suffering of their brethren, and they raised their voice." But he replies: "Maybe, but I don't see it. I am the people myself, *and I don't feel it."*

Is that—compassion?—Please note that Levin's dispute with Sergei Ivanovich about compassion and the immediate sentiment for the oppression of the Slavs is conducted evasively, as it were, with the intent of winding it up with Levin's victory. For instance, Sergei Ivanovich exerts his efforts in arguing that were Levin to behold drunken people beating a woman, he would rush to protect her. "But I wouldn't kill!" retorts Levin. "Yes, you would kill"— Sergei Ivanovich insists. And, of course, he speaks nonsense, since who, when helping a woman beaten by drunken men, is going to kill them?—The woman may be protected without killing. But the main thing is that here we are not dealing with a street fight: the simile is incorrect and not homogeneous. They are conversing about the Slavs, about tortures, racks and murders to which they are being subjected, and Levin knows only too well that he is speaking about the Slavs. Therefore, when he says that he doesn't know whether he would help; that he sees nothing; that he *feels nothing,* etc., he specifically declares that he feels no compassion for the tortures of the Slavs (and not for the suffering of a woman beaten by drunken men) and he insists that no immediate sentiment for the oppression of the Slavs—and not for the oppression of a drunken woman—exists or can exist. Why, he literally expresses himself to this effect.

Here we have a rather curious psychological fact. The book was published two and a half months ago, when it was already positively known that all the countless stories about the innumerable torments and tortures of the Slavs were absolutely true, and that they had been attested to by thousands of witnesses and eye-witnesses of all nations. The things which we have learned in the course of these eighteen months about the tortures of the Slavs exceed any fantasy of the sickliest and most perverted imagination.

To begin with, it is known that these massacres are not accidental but systematic, deliberately instigated and encouraged by all means. People are exterminated by the thousands and tens of thousands. The refinements of the tortures are such that nothing of the kind has ever been printed or heard of. Live men are flayed in the presence of their children; infants are thrown up and caught on bayonets in the sight of their mothers; women are raped, and at the very moment when the woman is being raped, she is stabbed to death with a dagger, and what is most important—babies are tortured and slain.

Levin says that he feels *nothing!* and haphazardly asserts that no immediate sentiment for the oppression of the Slavs exists or can exist. But I venture to assure Mr. Levin that it can exist, and that I myself have repeatedly witnessed it. For example, I have seen a certain gentleman who does not like to speak about his sentiments, but who upon hearing about a two-year-old boy

whose eyes had been pierced with a needle, in the presence of his
sister, and thereafter impaled so that the child did not promptly
die but continued to scream for a long while,—upon hearing about
this incident, that gentleman almost became ill; he could not sleep
that night, and for two days he felt painfully depressed so that he
was unable to work.

In this connection I venture to assure Mr. Levin that this
gentleman is an honest and unquestionably respectable man, by no
means a drunkard and not a member of the Pugachiov gang. I
merely wish to state that an immediate, and even a very strong,
sentiment about the tortures of the Slavs can exist among all classes
of society. But Levin insists that it cannot even exist, and that he
himself feels *nothing*. To me this is a puzzle. Of course, there are
simply insensible, coarse and perverted people. Levin, however, it
would seem, is not a man of this kind; he is portrayed as a perfectly susceptible man. Doesn't mere distance in this case exercise
a certain influence? In fact, isn't this *psychological* peculiarity
present in certain characters?—"I don't see it myself; the thing is
transpiring far away; and I feel nothing." Leaving all jokes aside,
imagine that on the planet Mars there are men, and that there
infants' eyes are being pierced. Perhaps we, inhabiting our earth,
might feel no pity, at least, no great pity? The same, maybe, is
also true on earth when distances are very great: "Eh, it's in another hemisphere, not here!" That is, even though he does not so
directly express himself, that is what he feels, *i.e.*, he feels *nothing*.
In this case, if distance really exercises such an influence upon
humaneness, a new question arises of its own accord: "At what
distance does humaneness cease?" And Levin actually does constitute a great riddle from the standpoint of humaneness: he positively declares that *he does not know* whether he would kill:

"If I saw this, I should be led by my immediate sentiment,
but I can't say in advance."

This means that he does not know how he would act! And
yet he is a susceptible man, and as such he is afraid to kill . . .
the Turk. Let us imagine the following scene: Levin stands still
with a rifle and bayonet, and two steps from him a Turk is voluptuously getting ready to pierce the eyes of an infant whom he
holds in his arms. The seven-year-old little sister of the boy screams
and like an insane person rushes to tear her brother away from the
Turk. And here stands Levin in doubt, wavering:

"I don't know what to do. I feel nothing. I am the people
myself. No immediate sentiment for the oppression of the Slavs
exists or can exist."

No, seriously speaking, what would he have done after all

the things he has told us? How would it be possible not to rescue
the child? Is it conceivable that he would let him be tortured to
death and not snatch him from the hands of the Turkish villain?

"Yes, he should be snatched, but, maybe, it will become necessary to give the Turk a hard push?"

"Well, push him!"

"Hm, push! And what if he refuses to surrender the child and
draws the sword? Perhaps it will become necessary to kill the
Turk?"

"Well, kill him!"

"No, how is it possible to kill? No, one shouldn't kill a Turk!
No, better let him pierce the child's eyes and torture him to death,
and I'll go to Kitty."

This is how Levin would act; this is directly derived from
his convictions, from everything he utters. He positively says that
he *doesn't know* whether he would help a woman or a child if he
had to kill a Turk. And for the Turks he feels an awful pity.

"Twenty years ago we should have kept silent," says Sergei
Ivanovich—"but now we hear the voice of the Russian people who
are ready to rise as one man, and are ready for self-sacrifice for
the oppressed brethren: this is a great step and token of strength."

"But it's not only sacrifice: one has to kill the Turks"—
meekly says Levin. "The people send their donations and are ready
to sacrifice for their soul, and not for murder."

In other words: "Here, little girl, take this money, a donation
for the salvation of our soul. Well, and as for your little brother—
let them pierce his eyes. You see, one shouldn't kill a Turk. . . ."

And further this is what the author himself says about Levin:

"He was unable to agree that dozens of men, among them
his brother, had the right, on the basis of what hundreds of fine
speakers—volunteers arriving from the capital related to them, to
maintain that they, together with the newspapers expressed the
will and the thought of the people, such thought as *manifests itself
in vengeance and murder.*"

This is unjust: there is no vengeance whatever. Now we are
at war with these bloodsuckers, and yet we hear about nothing
but the most humane acts on the part of the Russians. It may be
boldly asserted that few of the European armies would act with
such an enemy as our army is acting now. Only recently the idea
has been suggested in two or three newspapers that, perhaps, it
would be expedient, precisely with a view to curtailing the number
of brutalities, to resort to reprisals against Turks arrantly guilty
of brutalities and tortures. After subjecting prisoners and the
wounded to unspeakable tortures, such as cutting off noses and

limbs, they kill them. Among them there have appeared specialists
for exterminating nurslings, real maestros who seize a nursling by
its two legs and at once rend it in half for the amusement and
fun of their comrades, the bashi-bazouks. This deceitful and vile
nation denies the brutalities it has perpetrated. The Sultan's ministers assert that there can be no killing of prisoners since "the
Koran forbids it." Only recently the humane German Emperor
indignantly rejected the official and deceitful wholesale complaint
of the Turks about the alleged Russian atrocities and declared that
he did not believe them. It would seem that one cannot act humanely toward this contemptible nation, and yet we do act humanely. I even venture to express my personal opinion that it would
be better not to resort to reprisals against Turks proved guilty of
killing prisoners and the wounded. This would scarcely diminish
their atrocities. It is said that even now, when they are taken
prisoners, they look frightened and suspicious, *firmly convinced*
that their heads will be promptly chopped off. Better not let the
magnanimous and humane conduct of the Russians be darkened by
reprisals. However, the piercing of infants' eyes must not be permitted, and in order to stop this villainy forever, it is necessary
to liberate effectively the oppressed, disarming the tyrants once and
for all. Don't worry, when they have been disarmed, they will be
manufacturing and selling morning-gowns and soap—even as our
Kazan Tartars, whom I have already discussed, but in order to
snatch the weapons from their hands, this has to be done in battle.
However, battle is not vengeance. Levin may be tranquil as regards
the Turk.

Even last year he might have been tranquil as regards the
Turk. Doesn't he know the Russian, the Russian soldier? Here it
is being reported that although the soldier in battle does stab the
monster-Turk, it has been observed that he has shared his soldier's
ration with the Turkish captive, fed and pitied him. And believe
me,—the soldier knew everything about the Turk; he knew that
were he himself to be taken prisoner by that captive Turk, the
latter would behead him, and together with the heads of other
executed prisoners he would pile up a crescent and in its center
he would fashion from other limbs of the body an obscene star.
The soldier knows all this, and yet he feeds the captive Turk exhausted by battle: "He is a man, after all, though not a Christian."
A correspondent of one of the English newspapers, having witnessed
similar incidents, said: "This is an army of gentlemen."

And better than many others Levin might have known that
this is really an army of gentlemen. When the Bulgarian in some
towns asked His Highness, the Commander-in-Chief, what they

should do with the property of the Turkish refugees, he told them: "Collect it, and keep it until their return; harvest the fields, keep the crop and take one-third of it as a reward for your labor." These are also a gentleman's words, and I repeat—Levin's mind might have rested in peace as regards the Turks: where is vengeance here? Where are the reprisals? Moreover, Levin whose knowledge of Russian society is so exquisite, might have guessed that the Turks will be also saved by our pseudo-Europeanism, and our foolish, artificial and narrow sentimentalism so common in our educated society. Has Levin heard about our ladies who throw flowers to Turkish war prisoners transported in railroad cars and welcome them with expensive tobacco and bonbons?—It has been reported that as the train pulled off, one of the Turks loudly hawked and energetically spat into the very midst of the humane Russian ladies who were waving their little handkerchiefs to the departing train. Of course, it is difficult to share fully the opinion of that insensible Turk, and Levin can comprehend that, on the part of our ladies, coddling the Turks was mere hysterical sentimentalism and pseudo-liberal Europeanism: "See, how humane we are, how Europeanized, and how well we express it!"

However, doesn't Levin himself preach and advocate the same narrow-mindedness, the same sentimental Europeanism?—Turks are killed in a war, in honest action, *without any vengeance* upon them, and solely *because* there is no other way of wresting from them their dishonorable arms. Thus things happened last year also. If arms are not wrested from them—so as to avoid killing them—if we walk away, they will again forthwith cut off women's breasts and pierce infants' eyes. What's to be done?—Let them pierce the eyes so as perchance not to kill a Turk? But this is a distortion of conceptions, the dullest and coarsest sentimentalism; this is fanatical narrow-mindedness, the fullest perversion of nature.

Besides, the soldier compelled to kill a Turk sacrifices his own life and, on top of that, he endures racks and tortures. Is it for mere vengeance, for mere killing, that the Russian people have risen? And when was it that assistance to the massacred, to those who are being exterminated by entire regions, to assaulted women and children in whose defense there is no one in the whole world to intercede,—was considered a callous, ridiculous and almost immoral act, a craving for vengeance and blood-thirst! And what insensibility side by side with sentimentalism!—In fact, Levin himself has a child, a boy! He loves him! When this child is bathed in a bathtub it is almost a family event! Why doesn't his heart bleed when he hears and reads about wholesale massacres, about children with crushed heads crawling around their assaulted, murdered mothers with their breasts cut off? This happened in a Bulgarian church where two hundred such corpses were found, after the town had been plundered. Levin reads all this, and there he stands and meditates:

"Kitty is cheerful; today she ate with an appetite; the boy was bathed in the tub, and he begins to recognize me: what do I care about things that are transpiring in another hemisphere?—*No immediate sentiment for the oppression of the Slavs exists or can exist*—because I feel *nothing*."

Is this how Levin brings to a close his epopee? Is it he whom the author seeks to set forth as an example of a truthful, honest man? Men, such as the author of *Anna Karenina,* are teachers of society, our teachers, while we are merely their pupils. What, then, do they teach us?

SEPTEMBER

CHAPTER I

1

Unlucky and Odd Fellows

IT IS difficult to conceive unluckier men than the French republicans with their French republic. Soon one hundred years will have elapsed since, for the first time, this institution came into existence. Since then every time (now it is the third time) adroit usurpers have confiscated the republic for their benefit, no one has risen in its serious defense, save some negligible group. Not even once has there been strong popular support. Besides, during those periods when the republic chanced to exist, only a few people regarded it as a final, and not a transitory thing. Nevertheless, no men are more convinced of the country's support than the French republicans.

However, during the first two attempts to create a republic in France—in the past century and in 1848—the republicans of those days may have had certain grounds, especially in the initial phases of these attempts, to expect that the country would support them. However, it would seem that the present-day republicans—those very republicans who in the near future are destined to be liquidated, together with their republic, for somebody's benefit—could have entertained no hopes for a steady future, even had the country some sympathy for them (very unsteady, to be sure,—since they now

exist merely negatively, according to the proverb: in the absence
of fish even a crawfish is a fish).

And yet on the eve of their almost certain downfall they are
convinced of their complete victory. What unlucky fellows they
are, and what an ill-starred republic this last and third has been.
And even though the late Thiers recognized it, yet specifically he
recognized it as a crawfish in the absence of fish!

Let us only recall how this republic came into existence. These
republicans waited almost twenty years for the "glorious" minute
of the downfall of the usurper, when "the country shall call them."
And what happened?—Having seized power after Sedan, these odd
fellows were compelled to load upon their shoulders a horrible war
which they did not want but which was handed to them by that
very usurper before he had departed for his charming Castle Wil-
helmshöhe—to smoke his cigarettes. And if this crafty usurper, while
promenading along the walks of the gardens of the German castle,
felt angry at them because again they had usurped his power, nevertheless, unfailingly, he must have smiled now and then—with that
spiteful smile—at the thought how he had punished them, throwing
his guilt upon their weak shoulders. Since, be that as it may, subsequently, France has nevertheless blamed them rather than him—
at least, them more than him—for continuing a hopeless war; for
their failure to restore peace immediately after assuming power;
for the surrender of two provinces; for the three billions; for the
devastation of the country; for the incompetent conduct of the
war; for their haphazard, disorderly administration lacking all control. Even up to this day Gambetta, the former dictator at the time,
is accused of all these things, even though he was innocent of them,
and, on the contrary, did everything that could have been done
under the then prevailing dreadful circumstances.

Briefly, this accusation of the republicans for their incompetence and the ruin of the country has persisted, and even still
persists, seriously and firmly. Much as everybody understands that
Emperor Napoleon was the prime cause of the calamity, "but why"
—it is argued—"didn't they manage to repair the situation once they
assumed the task? Moreover, they made things inconceivably so
much worse."—Such is the accusation. Not only that: along with
this accusation, something contemptuous and comical was cast on
them at the thought of what a mess they got into in the beginning,
when they seized power. And yet what else could they then have
done?—Not to accept the war and to sign an armistice in the very
beginning, immediately after assuming power, and after Sedan,
would have been altogether impossible: the Germans even then
would have demanded the cession of territory and an indemnity,

and what would have become of these republicans had they accepted an armistice on such terms? They would have been directly accused of pusillanimity, of disgracing the country, of the fact that, "still possessing an army," they offered no resistance and ignominiously capitulated. This would have been a nice stigma upon their new republic!

And inasmuch as to them the republic, its restoration in France, was far dearer than the salvation of the country, it constituted everything;—and so they were compelled to fight, almost obviously foreseeing that they would come to a still greater disgrace by the time of the termination of the war. Thus, disgrace was ahead of them, disgrace was behind them; this was not only an unfortunate, not only a tragic situation, but in some respects even a comical one, since it was not in this manner that they had dreamed to be enthroned after the tyrant!

This comicalness was aggravated by the fact that all the same they enthroned themselves with a light heart, despite everything. Not that they did not grieve about France—oh, among them there are excellent men, judging by their feelings, and even genuine servants of the fatherland, provided it is called a republic. Maybe there are two or three among them who are ready to place the republic itself in the background on condition that France be happy (although it is doubtful that there be such—to be precise, perhaps one or two, and not more).

However, the point is that just as soon as they had patched up some sort of peace with the Germans and begun to rule the country peacefully, at once they conceived the idea that the country had irrevocably fallen in love with them, and this—to say the least, —this is what was comical.

Most positively there dwells in every French republican the fatal conviction, dooming him, that the word "republican" suffices; that to call the country "a republic" suffices to make it happy— at once and forever. They always ascribe all the misfortunes of the republic to nothing but external unfavorable circumstances, to the existence of usurpers,—those wicked men; never did they give thought to the incredible weakness of those roots which bind the republic with the soil of France, and which during a whole century have failed to grow stronger and penetrate deeper. Besides, in the course of all these six years it has never occurred to them that their comical situation, inherited by them from Napoleon III, still persists; that if the old calamity has blown over, a new calamity, similar to the old one, is approaching, and that it will unfailingly place them in a *most* comical situation, so comical that they will no longer be able to retain their hold on France—perhaps, in the near future.

This new comicalness consists of the fact that in this future calamity, even as in the old one, their compliance with lofty duty, their service to the fatherland, *deliberately* leads to its detriment; further, that this calamity, just like the old one, is absolutely inevitable, constituting the same trap in which they were caught in 1871; and that—adding insult to injury—this predicament, much in the same way as the old one, was bequeathed to them by that very Napoleon III whom they so intensely hate and whose memory they so bitterly curse.

In fact, who in the world is now the most zealous supporter of the French republic? Who is the man favoring most its institution?—Unquestionably, Prince Bismarck. So long as the republic exists in France, the war of *revanche* is impossible. Just imagine that the republicans might venture to declare war on the Germans! —Prince Bismarck understands it. And yet it is clear as daylight that the enormous forty-million organism of France cannot perpetually remain under the disgraceful tutelage of Germany. The wounds will heal up; the debacle will be forgotten; new forces will come into being; health will be restored; assets and troops will be created and organized. And can a country, which for so long a time has been the political leader of the nations, fail to aspire anew to its former role, its former position in Europe?—Perhaps this moment is not far off: the surplus of inner energies must inevitably impel them to extricate themselves from Bismarck's tutelage and to restore their former *independence*. (At present France can still by no means be called independent.)

And now, France *in toto,* from her first step, has knocked her head against her republic. I reiterate: just imagine present-day republicans wishing to act in any way impertinently toward Prince Bismarck—to the extent of risking a war with him! To begin with,—who would follow them even if France herself should favor war? Secondly, there comes the inescapable consideration: What if the Germans should again defeat them? This would be the final fiasco of the republicans in France, because France would blame them for the failure and would expel them forever, forgetting that she herself sought a *revanche* and her former leading position. . . .

However, should the republicans adopt a firm attitude; should they neglect to listen to the new voices and screams; should they fail to declare war,—this would mean to oppose the aspirations of the country, and in this event, again, France would dismiss them and would surrender to the first adroit leader who appeared on the scene. In a word: Sedan is in the past, and Sedan is ahead! And yet, no doubt, they have not even started to ponder over this, notwithstanding the fact that the new outburst of the country, perhaps, is very close at hand. Nor did they ever consider the fact that, strictly speaking, they are nothing but Prince Bismarck's "protégés," and that France, year after year, must more and more comprehend this,—precisely as she restores and accumulates her energies; consequently, that she must more and more despise them —first, to herself and not very clearly, but subsequently much more clearly, and finally aloud, and not merely silently.

But the republicans do not recognize the comical aspect. They are pathetic people. On the contrary, precisely now they feel encouraged—after MacMahon, the president of the "republic," has driven them away and locked the Chamber till the October election. Now they are "the persecuted," and they feel as if they are in the aureole. They expect that all France will suddenly start singing the Marseillaise and shout: *"On assassine nos frères!"* ("Our brethren are being massacred!")—the notorious cry of all former Paris street revolutions, after which the mobs used to erect barricades. Anyway, they look forward to "lawfulness," *i.e.*, that the country, indignant against Marshal MacMahon, the prospective future usurper, will again elect the same republican majority, and besides will add new republican deputies, after which the newly convened Chamber will utter a stern "veto" to the Marshal, who, frightened with "lawfulness," will hide his tail and retire.

They are immovably convinced of the force of that "lawfulness," and not because of the paucity of their mental faculties, but because these good fellows are too much party men; they have been chewing the same cud and sitting in one and the same corner too long. They have been suffering too long for their beloved republic, and, on this ground, they are sure of retaliation.

It is surprising that also in Russia many of our newspapers believe in their forthcoming triumph and the inevitable victory of "lawfulness." But in what way is this "lawfulness" guaranteed if MacMahon should not deign to submit to it—as he has already announced to the country in his strange manifesto?—By the indignation and wrath of the country? But the Marshal would promptly find numerous supporters in that very country, as this has invariably happened in such cases in France. What is to be done then? Erect barricades? But with the modern rifle and modern artillery the former barricades are impossible. Besides, France would refuse to erect them even if she should earnestly desire a republic. Exhausted and worn out as a result of a century-old political disorganization, she would, in a most prosaic manner, calculate on which side strength lies, and she would submit to it. Strength is now in the *legions,* and the country foreshadows this. Thus, the whole question is: For whom are the legions?

2

A CURIOUS CHARACTER

In the May-June issue of my *Diary* I have already given an account of the legion, as a new power, which is destined to occupy a place of its own in European civilization; this was long before the promulgation of the manifesto of the Marshal-President. And now everything has happened as I then anticipated. In this manifesto, which surprised everybody, the Marshal, though promising to abide by lawfulness, though promising peace, etc.,—nevertheless directly stated that should the country disagree with his opinion and elect at the forthcoming elections the former republican majority, he, on his part, would be compelled to disagree with the opinion of the country and would not submit to its elections. Such a strange act of the Marshal must have some underlying motive. He could not have used such language and adopted such a tone in addressing the country (France is not a village of some sort!) had he not been firmly convinced of his strength and success.

Therefore, now it is clear that his whole hope is the army, of which he is quite sure. In fact, at the time of his summer excursions throughout France, in many towns and provinces the Marshal was received rather equivocally, but the army and the fleet everywhere manifested absolute loyalty and greeted him with sympathetic acclamation. Of course, the Marshal's good, so to speak, even innocent, feelings cannot be doubted. Even though he did act in discord with the custom by directly stating in advance that he would not submit to the lawful opinion of the country should the latter disobey him, nevertheless, this, of course, was due to the fact that he sought in his own way, to promote the welfare of his country and was sure that he would do so.

Thus, the moral qualities of the Marshal should not be doubted, but, perhaps, some other qualities . . . Indeed, the Marshal, it seems, is one of those characters who cannot help being under somebody's tutelage. From this standpoint his character possesses certain remarkable peculiarities. The question is: for whom does he labor at present? For whom does he so exert himself and for whom does he risk so much? No doubt, he is under absolute tutelage, and yet he alone in all Europe is fully convinced even today that he is under no tutelage at all, and that he is acting independently. Smart people who have got hold of him, probably —for the time being—support this conviction of his; they exert their efforts to appear to be mere yes-men, meanwhile leading him irrevocably in any direction they choose. All this becomes possible because they are perfectly familiar with this sort of character and his personal ambitions. However, such slick people may be found only in one party—true, in the strongest and most enormous Clerical party. The other political parties in France cannot boast of adroitness.

Indeed, here is the question: If the Marshal is under tutelage, —under whose tutelage is he? At present it is well known that Bonapartists are awfully disturbed: they have nominated a large number of candidates; the Marshal himself patronizes them; they are sure of their victory at the polls; they are sure of the army; the Imperial Prince is already on the Continent, and it is even rumored that he will go to Paris. However, is it to be believed that Marshal MacMahon, the President of the "Republic" so sure of himself, is assuming such a load of trouble and risks solely for the purpose of enthroning the Imperial Prince? It seems to me (and, again, this is but my personal opinion) that this is not so. Unless, perhaps, there are some quite special combinations—for instance, that newspaper rumor which was current about one month ago to the effect that the Marshal's daughter is supposed to have been betrothed to the Imperial Prince, etc. But if no such special secret combinations exist; if, as yet, there are no special agreements and contracts, it does seem to me that the Marshal is inclined to make the country happy in *his* favor rather than in anyone else's, and if he gives his support to the Bonapartist candidates, it is because nevertheless they are more trustworthy than the rest, and that later they would be led in whatever direction he desired.

God knows what ideas might be conceived by a mind such as his. It is not in vain that a certain Bishop in an address of welcome to the Marshal has already suggested that on his maternal side he is descended from Charles the Great. In a word, several years of presidency have planted in his soul certain irritating and fantastic impressions. Besides, he is a military man.

However, all these deliberations are but meditative attempts to explain a mysterious character. At present the truth is that the Marshal is in the hands of the Clericals and that they are leading him, even though, no doubt, he thinks that it is he who is leading them, and that they are in his hands, and not he in theirs. But it goes without saying that they are not in his hands, and it positively seems that the fate of France at this moment depends *on them alone*. No doubt, the dreadful underground intrigue still continues. And even though Europe has long been aware of this and has known, from the very start, that in the present-day Western European movement they were playing an important part, nevertheless—so it would seem—they are concealing, and succeeding in

keeping from sight, the *magnitude and strength of their role;* they
are maneuvering, and, for the time being, are hiding behind others,
for instance, the Marshal, the Bonapartists, and so it will continue
until they reach their goal.

Strictly speaking, it makes no difference to them who is
going to succeed—the Marshal or the Imperial Prince. They have
not, and must not have, any personal sympathies. Theirs is but one
aim: that France, as soon as possible, should draw her sword and
assault Germany. And it was for this aim that they have crushed
the Republicans incapable of rising in support of the Pope. At
present, however, they are waiting calmly and adroitly—who's going
to have more chances?—Should the Imperial Prince actually give
them more chances from the standpoint of the ability to declare
war, perhaps they would hang on to him and would usher him to
Paris without further thought about MacMahon. It seems, however, that, temporarily, they are still clinging to the Marshal.

By the way, it is said that only recently the Marshal, in the
course of a conversation, made the following remark aloud: "Rumors are being spread that I intend to destroy republican institutions, but, of course, people forget that, when accepting the presidency of the republic, I gave my word to preserve them." These
words fully corroborate the conjecture about the Marshal's moral
innocence, despite all the accusations of the republicans. Thus, as
an honest man and a soldier, he prizes his word of honor, and, of
course, he is not going to violate it. But if he preserves the republic
and at the same time drives away the republicans, this means
that he intends to continue the republic without the republicans.
It seems that such actually is his political program, and that he
has been assured that it is quite feasible. This program, coupled
with the motto: *"J'y suis et j'y reste"* ("I am here to stay") obviously constitutes the whole cycle of his political convictions up
to the year 1880, when the term of his presidency and, therefore,
that of his word of honor, expires.

At that time, however, the dream will begin: "The grateful
country, seeing that he is quitting the presidency, will offer him a
new office, say, that of Charles the Great, and then everything will
again run smoothly."

It stands to reason that the slick fellows steering him—should
he really wish to comply with his word of honor and preserve the
republican institutions—would forthwith exchange him for a Bonaparte, if the preserved republic, even though without the republicans, should impede their subsequent plans. It seems that it is for
this reason that they have swayed him to support the Bonapartist
candidacies, assuring him that this is to his advantage.

In any event, he continues to be under such a firm tutelage that he can no longer extricate himself from it. In a word, the world is confronted with some great and altogether new events; one can foresee the appearance of the legions and a formidable Catholic movement. It is reported that the Pope's health "is satisfactory." But it would be a calamity should the death of the Pope coincide with the elections in France or should it occur shortly thereafter. In this event the Eastern question might at once be converted into an all-European one. . . .

3

THIS BUT NOT QUITE. REFERENCE TO WHAT I WROTE THREE MONTHS AGO

In the summer May-June issue of my *Diary* I formulated my thought in some detail. However, no one paid attention to the principal part of my article, *i.e.*, to the contention that the key to the present and future events in all Europe *lies in the Catholic conspiracy,* and in the forthcoming, indubitable and formidable Catholic movement coinciding with the death of the Pope—which, apparently, is a matter of the very near future—and the election of the new Pope. And thus my article passed unnoticed (in the press).

And yet now, even more strongly and more firmly than three months ago, I adhere to the same opinion. Since that time so many events, corroborating my conjecture, have taken place that I can no longer doubt its correctness. Since those days, newspapers—our own and foreign—have begun to allude to this theme, without venturing, however, to formulate the final deduction. This is what was stated in *The Moscow Gazette,* in an excellent editorial article (*The Moscow Gazette, No. 235*). Among other things it cites the opinion of the English newspaper correspondents:

"English newspaper correspondents are offering very candid explanations. According to their interpretation, the key to European politics is in Germany's hand, and Germany is precisely inclined to side, even more firmly than before, with Russia—because of very intelligible calculations. First, it was perceived in Berlin that the reverses of Russian strategy have 'enlivened and encouraged Austria, which supposedly still nourishes a certain grudge against Prussia. Furthermore, Germany's major enemies—France and Catholicism, both these powers—are extending their full sympathy to Turkey. True, in the beginning of the Eastern complications France flirted with Russia somewhat. However, even if, at the time, there was some sympathy for us, not only has it grown cold at present, but it has decidedly turned toward the Turkish side. As for militant

Catholicism, as everybody knows, not only now but from the very start, it has decidedly and passionately taken under its protection orthodox Turkey as against schismatic Russia. The indecency of the ardent Clericals has reached such a point that one of them started commenting on the Koran with a degree of tenderness, so that even ultramontane *Germania* deemed it necessary to restrain such sallies with the remark that although one has to rejoice over the victories of the Turks over the hateful Russians, nevertheless it is awkward to express openly sympathy for Islam.

"Inasmuch as the *mot d'ordre* of Catholicism remarkably co-incides with the swing of public opinion in France in favor of the Turks; and since Austria, also a Catholic country, has interests conflicting with those of Russia, Berlin naturally fears the possibility of a Catholic and anti-Prussian league into which eventually the ultramontane and separatist interests of Southern Germany and 'even England' could be drawn. This is what the English correspondents are talking about, but the leading role in these intrigues unquestionably belongs to England. Thus, as heretofore, we are left alone face to face with Turkey."

All this is splendid. However, all this is still not quite the thing, not the real explanatory and last word which, surprisingly, no one, as it were, wishes to utter; which, as yet, no one seems to foresee in its proper completeness. Still, this article has raised the question of *militant Catholicism* and its significance from Bismarck's standpoint, of its present influence upon France, and finally even of a *league, i.e.*, that Berlin *"naturally fears the possibility of a Catholic and anti-Prussian league into which eventually the ultramontane and separatist interests of Southern Germany and 'even England' could be drawn."*

But I spoke about the league, about the *conspiracy* more than two months ago, before anyone had raised this point, as at present; still, I then uttered my concluding word, *i.e.*, that the whole matter resides in this conspiracy; that everything in Europe hinges on it, and that the Eastern war itself may, in the very near future, be converted into an all-European war solely because of this immense conspiracy of dying Catholicism.

Even so, it seems that these "correspondents' opinions" in the whole admirable article of *The Moscow Gazette* still refuse to admit this thought, and instead they even assert that "the leading role in these intrigues unquestionably belongs to England," and that *"as heretofore, we are left alone face to face with Turkey."* But is this so? Are we left alone? On the contrary, aren't we destined, in the very near future, to be left alone not with Turkey but with all Europe?

In fact, what then is "militant Catholicism" which is generally noticed and acknowledged in the present events? Whence this pugnacity to the point of "passion" with which Catholicism has taken under its "protection" orthodox Turkey as against schismatic Russia? Is it possible that it is merely because "Russia is a schismatic country"? At present Catholicism has so many troubles and pressing concerns that it has no time to think about all these ancient church feuds. And what is most important—whence this "Catholic league" which is so feared by Berlin?—It is precisely these things that I dwelt upon more than two months ago, seeking to explain them. And it was my inference that this league, which now is already recognized by others, is a solid and rigidly organized Catholic *conspiracy* aiming at the renovation of the Roman laic rule,—a conspiracy which at the moment is prevalent in all Europe; that it will exercise an enormous *influence* upon all current events in Europe, and that, consequently, the key to all contemporary *intrigues* is neither here nor there, not only in England, but unquestionably in the universal Catholic conspiracy!

Militant Catholicism vehemently and "passionately" sides with the Turks against us. And even in England, even in Hungary, at this moment, there are no haters of Russia as ardent as these militant Clericals.—Not some prelate, but the Pope himself, loudly and with joy, spoke at the Vatican Conferences about "the victories of the Turks prophesying to Russia a dreadful future." This dying old man, and besides—"the head of Christianity," was not ashamed to announce *urbi et orbi* that every time he hears with joy about Russian reverses. This awful hatred becomes quite intelligible if it is admitted that at present Catholicism is actually "militating," and that, by deed, *i.e., with the sword,* it is waging a war in Europe against its dreaded and fatal enemies.

But who in Europe is now the most dreadful enemy of Roman Catholicism, *i.e.,* the secular monarchy of the Pope?—Unquestionably, Prince Bismarck. Rome herself was taken away from the Pope at the very moment of Germany's and Bismarck's triumph when Germany had crushed France, then the principal defendress of papacy, thereby forthwith untying the hands of the Italian King, who immediately occupied Rome. Ever since, the whole concern of Catholicism has been the discovery of Germany's and Prince Bismarck's enemy and rival. For his own part, Prince Bismarck himself clearly understands the fact, in all its breadth—understood it long ago—that Roman papal Catholicism is, in addition, the eternal enemy of Protestant Germany, which for so many centuries has been protesting against Rome and her idea in all its manifestations, and against all its allies, protectors and followers. Moreover, he understands that Catholicism precisely now, *i.e.*, the most momentous hour for united Germany, is the most noxious of all elements impeding this unification of hers, *i.e.*, the completion of the edifice to the erection of which Prince Bismarck, all his life, has devoted so much labor.

Furthermore, Berlin fears "the possibility" of a Catholic and anti-Prussian league, into which eventually the ultramontane and separatist interests of Southern Germany could be drawn. Berlin also fears, and has long before anticipated, that Catholicism, sooner or later, unfailingly will serve as a pretext for the future rise of France against Germany, which has humbled, conquered and ruined her; that Roman Catholicism will offer this pretext sooner and more quickly than anyone else, and that, consequently, the major danger to unified Germany lies precisely in Roman Catholicism, and in nothing else.

And Berlin's foresight has emanated from the natural and necessary consideration that, first, at present, papacy has no defender in the whole world other than that same France; that it can solely rely upon her sword, *provided it can manage to seize it firmly and hold it in its own hand;* secondly, that Roman Catholicism is far from being a crushed enemy, that it is a thousand-year-old enemy; that it is an enemy passionately craving for life; that its viability is phenomenal; that it still possesses many forces, and that such an immense historical idea as the secular papal power cannot be extinguished in a minute. Briefly, Berlin has become cognizant not only of the enemy but also of his strength. In Berlin, enemies are not despised before battle.

However, if Catholicism's desire to live is so strong, and if it is necessary to go on living; and if the sword which can protect it is in the hands of France alone,—it clearly follows that France cannot be permitted to slip out of its hands, particularly if the moment should prove opportune. This opportune moment arose last spring; this was the Russian war with the Turks,—the Eastern question. Indeed, who is Germany's principal ally?—Of course, Russia. This Rome understands perfectly. This is why the Pope was so cheered by Russian "reverses." This means that the principal ally of the most dreaded enemy of the papal power has been drawn away by the war from his inveterate ally, Germany, and thus Germany is now alone. This further signifies that the moment, which Catholicism has so long been awaiting, has arrived: when, if not now, is the most convenient time for inflaming inveterate hatred and throwing France into a war of *revanche* against Germany?

Moreover, other seasons fatal to Catholicism are approach-

ing, so that it can't lose even a minute: the inevitable death of
the Pope and the election of a new one are to be expected very
shortly. And in Rome it is well known that Prince Bismarck is
going to use all his power, his best endeavors, to deliver the last
and most horrible blow against the papal authority, exercising his
utmost influence upon the election of the new Pope so as to convert
him—if possible with his own consent—from a secular sovereign and
potentate into a mere Patriarch, and thus, by dividing Catholicism
into two rival camps, to bring about once and forever its disintegration and the destruction of its claims and hopes.

Why, then, not hasten against Bismarck, resorting to all
means?—All the more so as the Eastern question comes in handy!
Oh, at last France is in a position to find allies whom for so long
a time she has failed to find! Now a whole coalition can even be
formed! Let all Europe be stained with blood, but as against this
the Pope will triumph, and for the Romish confessors of Christ—
this is everything.

And thus they have begun to work. First of all, it was imperative to make France support them. How was this to be achieved?
—Yet they did achieve this. At present all European politicians
and the whole European press agree that the May coup-d'état in
France was brought about by the Clericals; but—I repeat—no one
seems to perceive in this fact its fundamental significance. Everybody seems to think that four months ago the Clericals precipitated
a coup-d'état in France only for the purpose of gaining more freedom of action, certain advantages, privileges, expansion of their
rights. And yet it is impossible to believe that the coup-d'état was
not engineered for the most radical aims, i.e., in order to bring
about (in view of the forthcoming dissensions in the Roman Church,
following the death of the Pope) in the near future an inevitable
war between France and Germany—precisely war! And you will
see—regardless of what the outcome may be—they will achieve their
goal, they will precipitate a war as a result of which—should France
be victorious—the Pope will, perhaps, regain his secular power.

They accomplished the task in a most adroit manner, and
what is most important—they chose a moment when everything
seemed to converge toward their success. They had to begin with
the ousting of the republicans who, under no circumstance, would
have supported the Pope and risked a war with Germany. And they
did oust them. In addition, it was necessary to compel Marshal
MacMahon to make an irreparable—exactly irreparable—error in
order to set him on an irrevocable course. And he did commit this
error; he did oust the republicans, and he did announce to France
at large that they shall not return. Thus the foundation has been

firmly laid, and, for the time being, the Clericals are quiet: they know that should France again return a republican majority in the Chamber, the Marshal will send it back.

Gambetta has declared that the Marshal would either have to submit to the decision of the country or quit his post. In full accord with Gambetta all the republicans have come to the same conclusion, forgetting, however, the Marshal's motto: *"J'y suis et j'y reste"* ("I am here to stay"), and that he will not quit. It is clear that the Marshal's whole hope resides in the legions. The Clericals, too, intend to take advantage of the legions' devotion to the Marshal or to whomsoever they may. If only the coup-d'état could be brought to an end, they would manage to steer events in the needed direction. It is most probable that all this will come to pass: they will stand at the side of the usurper; they will guide him. And even should they not stand at his side, the thing would develop of its own accord since it has been set right: if only the coup-d'état be brought to an end. They know what a colossal impression *any political change in France* would produce upon Prince Bismarck. As early as the year 1875, he sought to declare war on France, fearing her steady annual reinforcement. However, every coup-d'état in France would, naturally, greatly disturb him. Especially at a moment when Germany is left without her natural ally, Russia; when Austria (also an old adversary of Germany), where there are so many Catholic elements hostile to Germany, has suddenly become cognizant of her importance, and when England, ever since the beginning of the Eastern war, with such irritable impatience, has been looking for an ally in Europe! "What if France" —thus they must be arguing in Berlin—"headed by its new government, around which the Clericals are sneaking, which they are guiding and which they own,—what if France should guess that if there is to be a war of *revanche*, she would never strike a more opportune moment than the present to begin it, and more formidable allies to support her! And what if the Pope should die at that time [which is quite possible]? What if the Clericals should compel the new French government to declare to Prince Bismarck that his views on the election of the new Pope are in discord with those of France [and this will inevitably happen if the Republicans are ousted]? What if, at the same time, the new French government should guess that were it to succeed [bearing in mind the possibility of finding powerful allies in Europe] in reconquering at least one of the provinces taken away from France in 1871, it would consolidate its authority and influence in the country, for at least twenty years!—Nay, in these circumstances, is it possible not to be nervous!"

And the most important point is that here there is one additional little fact: the German is arrogant and haughty; he will not tolerate disobedience. Up to the present France has been under the complete and obedient tutelage of Germany; she has given Germany a reply to all her inquiries, virtually concerning every one of her, France's, moves; she has had to explain and apologize for every additional army division, for every battery, and, suddenly, this France dares to raise her head! So that the Clericals may boldly presume that Prince Bismarck will virtually take the initiative in starting the war. Didn't he, in fact, seek to start it in 1875? Not to start war would be equivalent to letting France slip out of Germany's hands forever.

True, in 1875 the situation was different. But should Austria side with Germany . . . In a word, at the recent meeting of the Chancellors of Germany and Austria, probably not only the Eastern question was discussed. And if there be in the world a state in a most advantageous external political situation, it is precisely Austria!

4

What Does Austria at Present Think About?

It may be argued that there is agitation in Austria; that one-half of Austria does not want what its government is after. In Hungary manifestations are taking place; Hungary is eager to give support to the Turks against the Russians. Some Anglo-Magyar-Polish conspiracy has even been discovered. On the other hand, although at present the Slavic elements support the government, nevertheless the government of Austria looks on them askance and suspiciously, perhaps even more askance than on the Hungarians. If so, can it be maintained that, at this minute, Austria is in a political situation as advantageous as any European state can possibly be?

Yes, this is so. True, the Catholic work, unquestionably, is also on foot in Austria. The Clericals are farsighted. They are not ones to fail to understand the present-day significance of that country or to miss an opportunity! And it stands to reason that they are not missing the opportunity to incite in that Catholic and "most Christian" land all kinds of disturbances under every conceivable pretext, guise and form. But here is the point: who knows, although in Austria, of course, it is pretended that people are very angry about these disturbances, nevertheless, the contrary may be true: these disturbances are kept in store *for any eventuality* in anticipation of the fact that they may be useful in the very near future. However, in view of current events, Austria most probably, though considering herself in the happiest political situation, has not yet decided upon her *distant* and quite specific policy but still keeps looking around and waiting: what will *prudence* compel her to do? And even if she has made up her mind about anything, it is merely about the *immediate* policy,—and this only tentatively. Generally, she is in a beatific mood; she takes her time in reaching her decisions, knowing that everybody is waiting for her and that everybody needs her; she is taking aim at the prey which she picks herself and sensually licks her lips in anticipation of the forthcoming, inevitable blessings.

At the recent meetings of the Chancellors of the two German states, perhaps much of a "tentative" nature has been discussed. At least, the Austrian government has publicly announced that nothing in the East shall take place and be settled in violation of Austria's interests,—which is quite an elaborate idea. Thus Austria, without having even touched the sword, already feels certain that she will be given a substantial share in Russian successes, should these develop, and perhaps even a still greater share should no such successes ensue. And this—merely as a result of her immediate policies! And in the future?—Even at present everybody needs Austria, seeks her opinion, her neutrality; everybody makes promises, perhaps bribes her, and this—only because she sits and says: "Hm!" Indeed, that state which is now so fully aware of its value, cannot help relying upon the chances of its future policy, which still remains unknown, notwithstanding the cordial meetings of the Chancellors. —Of this I am fully convinced. Moreover, I am sure that this policy will remain generally unknown till the very last and fatal moment, —which would be quite in line with the customs and traditions of Austria's inveterate policy. Keenly, oh how keenly, she now watches France, awaiting her fate, expecting most interesting new facts.— And the main point is that Austria is in a most self-complacent mood.

Even so, she also cannot help being agitated: probably, very soon she will have to decide upon her future policy,—and irrevocably so. Of course, in her situation this is a pleasant but nevertheless intense agitation. Indeed, she must understand—and, perhaps, very keenly—that with every present-day coup-d'état in France (so close and so possible), even with every new government in France (save, again, the republican), the chances of Germany's conflict with France are *absolutely inevitable*,—even if the new rulers of France should not desire war, and, on the contrary, should exert every effort to maintain peace. Oh, Austria, perhaps, better than anyone, is capable of realizing the fact that there are moments in the lives of the nations when no longer will or calculation leads to a certain action but fate itself.

Now, I shall venture to set forth a fantastic dream (and, of course, only a dream). I shall venture to conjecture what Austria thinks, at this crucial and uncertain moment, about that *future* policy of hers, upon which, of course, she has not yet decided, since still not all facts are clear. However, somebody is already knocking at the door; this she hears; somebody wants to come in and is already turning the handle of the lock, but the door is not yet open, and who's going to come in?—As yet, no one knows. France is faced with a riddle which will be solved there, and meanwhile Austria sits and *ponders*. And how can she fail to ponder?—If swords are drawn; if Germany and France finally throw themselves upon each other, whom will she support? With whom is she going to side?—This is the *most distant* question, and yet perhaps she will have to answer it very soon!

Thus, how can she now help knowing her price! Because he on whose behalf she draws her sword will triumph. No one knows what has been said at the meetings of the Chancellors of both German Empires, but it is certain that hints have been exchanged between them. How could hints have been avoided?—Perhaps something more explicit than mere hints has been said and *suggested*. In a word, unquestionably, many gifts and presents have been promised her, so that she is quite sure that if she adheres to her alliance with Germany, in return for it she will receive . . . much. And this—as a reward for some sort of neutrality, for the mere fact that during some six months she would sit quietly without moving in anticipation of a reward for her good behavior—this is the most pleasant thing!—Since, I believe, no Chancellor would be able to enlist her active participation against France: Austria will make no such mistake. She is not going to beat France to death. On the contrary, at the last fatal moment, she might protect her by means of a diplomatic betrayal, thereby securing for herself an additional reward. For one cannot remain *quite without France* in the embrace of such a giant as Germany will become after her second victory over France. Who knows, the giant might later suddenly embrace her and squeeze her—unawares of course—so strongly that she would be crushed like a fly. Besides, that other Eastern giant—to her right—might, finally, arise from his secular bed. . . .

"Good behavior is a good thing"—Austria, perhaps, silently cogitates at present—"but" . . . In a word, another—true, most fantastic—dream must appear in her imagination. . . .

"The coup d'état in France may even begin this coming autumn, and, perhaps, it will come to a quick end. Should the republic perish, or should it be left in some nominal, absurd form, discord with Germany may begin in the winter. The Clericals would certainly see to it, all the more so as by that time the Pope will unfailingly die, and the election of a new Pope would forthwith furnish a pretext for misunderstandings and conflicts. However, even should the Pope fail to die, the possibility of misunderstandings and conflicts would still remain in force. And should Germany firmly make up her mind, the war would begin next spring. At the other end of Europe, the winter campaign against Turkey also seems inevitable, so that Germany's ally would still be busy by the spring of next year. Thus, should the war of *revanche* flare up, France would at once find two allies—England and Turkey."

Thus, Germany would be left alone with . . . Italy, *i.e.*, almost alone. Oh, of course, Germany is arrogant and mighty. But France, too, has managed to recover : she has an army of one million, and England would be of some help, after all : German maritime cities would have to be protected against her fleet, which would mean that some troops, artillery, arms and supplies would have to be set aside. Anyway, this would weaken Germany to some extent. "In a word, France, even without me, has enough chances to wage a successful war"—muses Austria—"at least twice as many as in 1870, since, surely, France will not commit the errors of those days. Furthermore, whether or not France be beaten, nevertheless I shall be compensated in the East, since there nothing is going to be settled in discord with Austria's interests. This has been decided upon and signed. However . . . what if, at the most decisive moment, prudently reserving for myself freedom of decision, I should side with France, and should even draw the sword!"

Indeed, what would happen then?

Austria would at once find herself among three enemies : Italy, Germany and Russia. Russia, however, would be terribly busy with her own war, and she would not be in a position to attack. Italy, at any rate, shouldn't be feared too much. There remains only Germany. But were she even to dispatch troops against Austria, she would thereby weaken herself; still, of course, it wouldn't be a large force because she would need all her troops against France. In fact, were Austria to risk an alliance with France, France would, perhaps, be the first to assault Germany, even if Germany did not wish to fight. France, Austria, England and Turkey—against Germany with Italy—this is a dreadful coalition! Success would be quite probable. And in the event of success Austria could recover everything she had lost at Sadowa, and even much more. Furthermore, in the East she would, under no circumstance, lose her benefits and everything that was promised her. But what is more important still—she would gain in influence in Catholic Germany. Should Germany be conquered, not even conquered, but should she emerge from the war not quite successful,—Germany's unity would at once be shaken. In Southern Catholic Germany, separatism would arise, which, besides, the Clericals would foster with all their strength, and of which Austria would naturally take advantage . . . to such an extent that then two Germanys, two German Empires, would come into being—a Catholic and a Protestant. Thereupon, by reinforcing herself with the German element, Austria might challenge her own "dualism," placing Hungary in her former, ancient and respectful relations toward herself, after which, of course, she would dispose of her own Slavs,—somehow forever! . . .

Briefly, there might be innumerable benefits! Finally, even in the event that she should not be victorious, it wouldn't be such a calamity, since she wouldn't be able to conquer such a powerful coalition *completely*, as in 1871, so that, unfailingly she would be beaten. Thus peace could be concluded without any too dreadful consequence. "Thus, with whom would it be better to side? What's better? With whom would it be more advantageous?"

In view of the present events in Europe, Austria, unquestionably, puts such radical questions to herself . . .

5

WHO'S KNOCKING AT THE DOOR? WHO WILL ENTER?
INESCAPABLE FATE

When I started this chapter, two facts and communiqués were still absent; now, suddenly, they have filled the whole European press, so that everything which I had written in this chapter as conjecture has now been most punctually corroborated. My *Diary* will be published next month, on October seventh; today is only September twenty-ninth, and my "predictions," so to speak, upon which I had embarked in this chapter, taking chances, as it were, will partly prove obsolete and accomplished facts from which I copied these "prophecies" of mine.

However, I venture to remind the readers of the summer May-June issue of my *Diary*. Virtually everything I wrote there concerning the immediate future of Europe has already come true, or *is beginning to be substantiated* at present. Even so, at the time, I heard opinions expressed (true, by laymen) in which my article was called an "ecstatic rage," a fantastic exaggeration. People were simply ridiculing the strength and significance of the Clerical conspiracy; besides, they would admit no conspiracy at all. Only two weeks ago I heard a "competent" man express the opinion that

the death of the Pope and the election of a new Pope would pass
in Europe without leaving any trace. But even today it is already
known what importance Bismarck is attaching to it and what he
had said about it in Berlin to Crispi.

In the May-June issue of my *Diary* I wrote that ever since the
time of the Franco-Prussian war Bismarck's genius had grasped the
fact that the most formidable enemy of the newly unified Germany
was Roman Catholicism, which, to begin with, would serve as a
pretext for a war of *revanche* that would engulf all Europe. This
was considered absurd, etc. And all this because I wrote these things
at a time when neither in Russia nor in the European press did
anyone even think to bother about them, notwithstanding the Eastern war, which was already thundering in the world and causing
concern to everybody. At that time it was the general consensus
that things would be confined to the East.

Well, perhaps even now no one believes in the *inevitability*
of a European war in the very near future. On the contrary, only
recently serious attention was paid to the opinion of competent
Englishmen (Northscot's speech) that pacification may be brought
about by winter. So that, perhaps, I am considering in vain this
present chapter of mine to be obsolete in advance. Even though
facts have already come to light; although their enormous importance is beginning to reveal itself; although something fatal,
dreadful and—what is most important—something near is already
soaring over all Europe,—notwithstanding all this, I am sure, many
people even now will consider my interpretation of these facts erroneous and ridiculous, fantastic and exaggerated, because everybody is taking the current events for something incomparably less
significant than they actually are.

For example, we shall see elections in France, and suddenly
she might return the former republican majority, as is quite possible. And I am convinced that people will at once start vociferating
that everything has come to a happy end; that the sky has cleared;
that no conflicts are in sight; that MacMahon has confessed his
guilt; that the *impotent* Clericals have disgracefully withdrawn to
the background, and that peace and "lawfulness" have been restored
in Europe. All my conjectures, as stated in this chapter, will again
seem but products of idle imagination. Again it will be said that
I have conveyed to facts—true, accomplished facts—an erroneous
meaning, and chiefly a meaning which is *nowhere attributed to
them*.

However, let us once more await the events, and we shall then
see where the more correct road is. And just as a matter of record,
I shall attempt in conclusion to indicate the points and landmarks

of this road which is already becoming visible to everybody, and which, willy-nilly, we shall all have to follow. This I am doing, as stated, just as a matter of record—for future verification. In fact —this is simply a summary of this chapter.

1. The road begins at Rome and leads from Rome, from the Vatican, where the dying old man, the head of a crowd of Jesuits standing by him, has mapped it long ago. When the Eastern problem arose, the Jesuits realized that the most opportune moment had come. Following the road thus traced, they broke into France, made there a coup d'état, and placed her in a position which makes her war with Germany in the near future virtually inevitable, even if she does not desire it. All this Prince Bismarck has long in advance understood and foreseen. In my opinion at least, he alone, several years prior to the current moment, discerned and sized up his principal enemy and the enormous universal importance of that last battle for its existence which in the very near future *dying papal Catholicism* will unquestionably fight against the whole world.

2. At the present moment this fatal struggle is already shaping itself, while the last battle is approaching with terrible speed. France has been chosen and designated for the dreadful battle, and the battle will take place. It is inevitable, this is certain. However, there is a slim chance that it may be postponed—but only for a short time. In all events, the battle is *inevitable and not far distant*.

3. The moment the battle begins it will be converted into an all-European battle. The Eastern problem and the Eastern war, by force of destiny, will merge with the all-European conflict in which Austria's final decision which side she is to lend her sword will be one of the most noteworthy episodes. However, the most essential and momentous aspect of this last and fatal struggle will consist in that, on the one hand, it will be the solution of the thousand-year-old question of Roman Catholicism, and on the other —that, by the will of Providence, it will be replaced with regenerated Eastern Christianity. In this way our Russian Eastern problem will assume the proportions of a universal and ecumenical one fraught with extraordinary predestined significance, even though this predestination should come to pass before blind eyes incapable to the last minute of perceiving the obvious and of comprehending the meaning of the preordained. Finally——

4. (And let it be called the most conjectural and fantastic of all my predictions—I concede this in advance.) I am convinced that the war will end in favor of the East, in favor of the Eastern alliance; that Russia has nothing to fear should the Eastern war merge with the all-European one, and that should the matter thus expand—it would be all for the better.

Oh, no doubt, this would be a dreadful affair should so much precious human blood be shed! But at least there is consolation in the thought that the blood thus shed would unquestionably save Europe from a ten times greater effusion of blood should the matter be again postponed and protracted. All the more so as the great struggle will unquestionably end quickly. Moreover, so many problems would be finally solved (the Roman Catholic problem, jointly with France's fate, the German, Eastern, Mohammedan problems); so many matters, altogether insoluble in the former course of events, would be settled; the face of Europe would be so changed; so many new and progressive things would ensue in human relationships that perhaps it is not necessary to suffer spiritually and to dread too much the last convulsive jerk of old Europe on the eve of her indubitable and great regeneration. . . .

Finally, I shall add one more consideration. Were one to make it a rule to judge all universal events of the greatest importance—even from a most superficial standpoint—by the principle: "today as yesterday, tomorrow as today,"—such a rule would be in obvious discord with the history of the nations and of mankind. And yet it is precisely what so-called realistic and sober common sense prescribes, so that virtually everyone who ventures to believe that tomorrow, maybe, the matter will appear to everybody in an altogether different guise than it seemed yesterday—is ridiculed and hissed at. For instance, even today, in the presence of all facts, does it not seem to quite a few that the Clerical movement is a most insignificant trifle; that Gambetta will make a speech, and everything will be restored to yesterday's status; that quite possibly our war with Turkey will be ended by winter, and then again, as hitherto, stock-exchange speculation and railroad business will begin, the ruble rate will rise, we shall be merrily travelling abroad, etc.

The impossibility of the continuation of the old order of things, in Europe, was an obvious truth to all her progressive minds, on the eve of the first European revolution which began in France at the end of the past century. Even so, who in the whole world, even on the eve of the convocation of the States-General, could have foreseen and predicted the form which, virtually on the following day, the event would assume, how it would begin . . . And after it had come to pass, who, for instance, could have predicted the advent of Napoleon I, who, in substance, was, as it were, the predestined executor of the first historical phase of the event which began in 1789?

Moreover, in the times of Napoleon I, perhaps it seemed to everybody in Europe that his appearance was positively a sheer external accident in no way connected with that universal law by virtue of which the former face of the world was destined, at the end of the past century, to assume a new guise.

And today somebody is knocking at the door; some new man with a new word seeks to open the door and enter. . . . But who is going to enter?—This is the question. Is it going to be an altogether new man, or again, one resembling all us old dwarfs?

CHAPTER II

1

A LIE IS SAVED BY A LIE

ONCE UPON a time Don Quixote, the well-known knight of the doleful image, the most magnanimous of all knights on earth, the simplest in soul and one of the greatest men in heart, while roaming in the company of his faithful armor-bearer Sancho in pursuit of adventures, was suddenly struck by a perplexity which made him ponder for a long while.

The point is that oftentimes ancient knights, beginning with Amadis de Gaula, whose life-histories survived in the most truthful books called romances of chivalry (for the purchase of which Don Quixote did not regret selling a few of the best acres of his small estate),—not seldom these knights, in the course of their famous wanderings, beneficial to the whole world,—would suddenly encounter whole armies—at times even one hundred thousand men strong—dispatched against them by the evil spirit, by wicked fairies who envied them and obstructed them in every possible way in the achievement of their great goal—to be united with their beautiful ladies.

Usually when a knight encountered such a monstrous and evil army, he drew his sword, invoking for his spiritual aid the name of his lady, and thereupon he hewed his way into the very midst of his enemies and annihilated them to the last man.

Apparently this was a simple matter, but suddenly Don Quixote started pondering.—Over what?—It appeared to him impossible that one knight—no matter how strong, and though he should keep swinging his sword untiringly twenty-four hours—should be able to kill at once, in just one battle, one hundred thousand men. Anyhow, even to kill one man time is needed. To kill one hundred thousand men much time is required, and regardless of how he swung his sword, this could not be accomplished in several hours, all at once, by one man. And yet these truthful books told that the incident occurred precisely in the course of one battle. How, then, could this happen?

"I have solved this riddle, my friend Sancho"—Don Quixote finally said. "Inasmuch as all these giants, all these wicked fairies, were but the evil spirit, their army, too, possessed the same magic and evil character. I believe that these armies were not composed of men exactly like us, for example. These men were but an illusion, a creation of magic, and probably their bodies did not resemble ours, but were rather akin to the bodies, for instance, of mollusks, worms and spiders. Thus, the solid and sharp sword of a knight, swung by his mighty hand, striking these bodies, instantly passed through them, almost without resistance, as if through the air. And if so, he could have actually with one blow passed through four or five, even ten, bodies if these stood in a compact group. It is intelligible, then, that the matter was greatly accelerated, and the knight was actually able to annihilate in several hours whole armies of these fairies and other monsters." . . .

Here the great poet and heart-reader discerned one of the deepest and most mysterious traits of the human spirit. Oh, this is a great book, not one of those such as are written nowadays. Such books are bequeathed to mankind once in several hundred years. And you will find such aspects of human nature discerned on every page of this book.

To take but one fact, that this Sancho—the personification of common sense, prudence, cunning, the golden mean—chances to become a friend and fellow-traveller of the insanest man on earth;— precisely he, and no other! He deceives Don Quixote continually; he cheats him like a child, and at the same time he fully believes in his great mind; he is tenderly fascinated by the greatness of his heart; he also gives full credence to the fantastic dreams of the valiant Knight, and not once does he doubt that the latter finally will conquer the island!

How desirable it would be for our youth to become thoroughly familiar with these grand works of world literature. I don't know what is being taught in the courses in literature, but acquaintance with this the grandest and saddest book conceived by the genius of man would unquestionably ennoble the soul of a youth with a great thought and would plant in his heart momentous queries, helping to divert his mind from the worship of the eternal stupid idol of mediocrity, self-complacent conceit and trivial prudence. This saddest of all books man will not forget to take along with him to the Lord's last judgment. He will point to the very deep and fatal mystery of man and of mankind revealed in it. He will show that the most sublime beauty of man, his loftiest purity, chastity, naïveté, gentleness, courage, and finally, the greatest are often—alas, much too often—reduced to naught, with no benefit to mankind, solely because all these the noblest and richest gifts with which man is frequently endowed have lacked one and the last gift— *genius* in order to administer the wealth of these blessings and all their power,—to administer and lead them along a truthful and not fantastic and insane path of action—for the benefit of the human race!

Genius, however, is so sparingly, so rarely allotted to tribes and peoples, that the spectacle of the cruel irony of fate which so often dooms the labors of the noblest men and most ardent friends of mankind to hisses and ridicule, to stoning, solely because they are unable at the fatal moment to discern the true meaning of things and to discover their *new word*,—this spectacle of the vain perdition of so many great and very noble forces may lead a friend of humanity to despair, no longer rousing him to laughter but stirring him to bitter tears, forever angering his hitherto pure and credulous heart with doubt. . . .

However, I merely meant to point out this most curious trait which along with hundreds of other profound observations, Cervantes discerned and revealed in man's heart. The most fantastic of all men, who embraced to the point of lunacy the belief in the most chimerical dream that can be imagined, suddenly is seized with doubt and perplexity which almost shatter his whole faith. And it is curious to note what proved capable of undermining it: not the absurdity of his initial aberration; not the irrationality of the existence of knights roaming for the benefit of mankind; not the nonsensicalness of those magic miracles which are recorded in "the most truthful books,"—nay, on the contrary—an outward, secondary, altogether isolated circumstance. The fantastic man suddenly begins *to crave for realism!* It is not the fact of the appearance of fairy armies that baffles him—oh, this cannot be doubted! Besides, how could these great and splendid knights have revealed their valor if all these trials had not been cast upon them, if there had been no envious giants and wicked fairies?—The ideal of the wandering knights is so grand, so lofty and useful, it has so fascinated the heart of the noble Don Quixote that to renounce faith in it completely became an impossibility for him; it would have been equivalent to the betrayal of the ideal, of duty, of love of Dulcinea and of mankind. (When he did renounce this ideal; when he recovered from his insanity and grew *reasonable*,—after he had returned from his second expedition, in which he was defeated by the level-headed and sensible barber Carasco, the negator and satirist,—he promptly passed away, calmly, with a sad smile, comforting weeping Sancho, loving the whole world with the full strength of love that dwelt in his holy heart, and yet realizing that there was nothing further for him to do in this world.)

Nay, he was perplexed merely with that surest mathematical consideration that no matter how the knight might swing his sword, and regardless of how mighty he might be, it is impossible to defeat an army of one hundred thousand men in the course of several hours, or even of one day, killing each one of them, to the last man. Even so, this is stated in the truthful books. This means that a lie is stated. And if there is one lie,—everything is a lie. How, then, is *truth* to be saved? Presently he invents for the salvation of truth another fancy, but twice, three times more fantastic, cruder, more absurd than the first one; he conceives hundreds of thousand of imaginary men possessing mollusk-bodies through which the sharp sword of the knight can pass ten times more effectively and quickly than through ordinary human bodies. Thus *realism* is taken care of, *truth is saved,* and now the first, principal fancy may be believed without any further doubts,—and this, again, owing to the second far more nonsensical vision, conceived for the salvation of the realism of the initial one.

Ask yourselves: didn't, perhaps, a thing such as this occur in your lives? Say that you took a liking to a certain fancy of yours, to an idea, to some inference of yours, a conviction, or some external fact which struck your imagination, finally to a woman who bewitched you. You rush after the object of your love with all the strength of your soul. True, no matter how you may be blinded, how your heart may be tempted, yet if in that object of your love there be deceit, illusion, something that you yourselves have exaggerated and distorted in it owing to your passion, your initial impetus—solely for the purpose of making of it your idol and worshipping it,—of course, secretly you will feel it, doubt will oppress you, tease your mind, roam in your soul, preventing you from living peacefully with your beloved fancy.

Now, then, don't you remember, wouldn't you admit, at least to yourselves: what would suddenly comfort you? Haven't you conceived a new vision, a new lie, perhaps, of the crudest kind, in which you hasten lovingly to believe only because it has solved your initial doubt?

2

MOLLUSKS TAKEN FOR HUMAN BEINGS. WHAT IS MORE ADVANTAGEOUS TO US: WHEN THE TRUTH IS KNOWN ABOUT US OR WHEN NONSENSE IS SPOKEN ABOUT US?

In our day virtually all Europe is in love with the Turks,— more or less. Formerly, say a year ago, even though Europe sought to discover in the Turks some sort of great national strength, nevertheless everybody understood within himself that they did this solely because of their hatred of Russia. Indeed, they could not help realizing the fact that in Turkey there are no forces, that there can be none, inherent in a normal, healthy organism; moreover, that perhaps there is no organism left—to such an extent is is undermined, contaminated and putrefied, that the Turks are but an Asiatic horde, and not a regular state.

At present, however, since Turkey has been at war with Russia, little by little, in certain European quarters there has arisen a real and serious conviction that that nation is not only an organism but one possessing great vigor and qualifications for development and future progress. This fancy has captivated many a European mind more and more, and finally this conviction has even drifted over to Russia: in Russia, too, some people have begun to speak of some unexpected national forces which Turkey has suddenly revealed. But in Europe this fancy took root as a result of hatred of Russia, whereas in our midst it is the result of pusillanimity and horrible haste in reaching pessimistic conclusions, which were always a characteristic trait of the educated classes of our society just as soon as somewhere and in some respect we began to have "reverses."

In Europe the same thing happened as transpired in the defective mind of Don Quixote, only in an inverted sense, although the substance of the fact is identical: to save the *truth* Don Quixote invented men with mollusk-bodies; whereas Europe, in order to save her fundamental vision, so comforting to her, concerning the negligibleness and impotence of Russia, converted a real mollusk into a human organism, bestowing upon it flesh and blood, spiritual vigor and health. At present the most educated European states are fervently disseminating perfect absurdities about Russia. Even in days gone by we were little known in Europe, so little that one used always to wonder that such enlightened nations took so flimsy an interest in the study of that people whom they hated so intensely and whom they have always feared. Up to the present, this paucity of European knowledge of us, and even a certain impossibility for Europe to understand us on many points, in a certain sense, were partly advantageous to us. Therefore, now also no harm will ensue.

Let them shout at home about "the disgraceful weakness of Russia as a military power," contrary to the testimony of dozens of their own correspondents from the firing line, who have expressed admiration at the fighting aptitude, chivalrous tenacity and marvelous discipline of the Russian soldier and officer; let them regard the possible mistakes, even grave mistakes, of the Russian staff in the beginning of the war not only as irreparable but as organic and customary defects of our army and nation (forgetting how often we have defeated them in the field during the last two centuries); finally, let their *most serious* political periodicals herald to Europe as an accurate truth the colossal uprising of the people, led by nihilists in Petersburg—on the Viborgskaia Storona, and that two regiments were dispatched at the instance of the authorities by railway from Dinaburg—to save Petersburg,—let them, in their blind wrath, say all these things. I repeat, this is even to our advantage, since they know not what they are doing. For it goes without saying that they would be eager to incite hatred against us everywhere abroad as against "dangerous enemies of their civilization." They already visualize us in a defeated condition, in disgracefully ridiculous impotence as a military power and a state organism. But he who is so weak and insignificant,—how can he arouse the fear of the coalition? And yet they feel it necessary to incite their society against us. Consequently, what they say is to their detriment, and if so they are not causing us harm but bestowing a benefit upon us. As for us,—we shall wait for the end.

But let us only imagine that they might receive the fullest, most precise and truthful information concerning the force of the spirit, the feeling, the unshakable faith of the Russian people in the justice of the great cause in defense of which their Emperor has drawn his sword, and in the indubitable triumph—sooner or later—of that cause. To imagine that Europe would, finally, comprehend that to Russia this is a national war *par excellence;* that our people are by no means a dead, inanimate mass, as Europe always imagines them to be, but a mighty organism, conscious of its strength, united as one man, by heart and will, inseparable from their army,—oh, what an alarm would this information rouse all over Europe! And, of course, it would tend more to bring about an actual coalition against us than their pet calumnies about our impotence and ruin. Nay, better for them to believe in the uprising on the Viborgskaia Storona. We should only be encouraged by the fact that they believe in it.

However, in Europe all this is intelligible, and one understands why this is transpiring there. But how can people at home vacillate, be troubled and even believe in some sort of newly and suddenly revealed vital force of the Turkish nation? How did it manifest this force? By fanaticism? But fanaticism is carrion and not strength. This has been preached a hundred times in Russia by those very men who now believe in Turkish strength. People speak about Turkish victories. Yet the Turks have merely once or twice beaten off our attacks, and these are, so to speak, negative and not positive victories. We, besieged in Sebastopol, on one occasion re-

pelled an assault of the French and English inflicting terrible losses
on them, but in those days Europe did not vociferate about our
victory.

The last two months we have been greatly outnumbered by
the Turks. . . . Well, have they taken advantage of this? Why didn't
they force us across the Balkans? Why didn't they drive us back
across the Danube?—On the contrary, everywhere we have retained
our main positions, and everywhere we have repelled the Turks.
On several occasions seven or eight of our battalions have defeated
twenty of theirs, as it recently happened on the Czerkovna. Convinced of the strength of the Turks, it is, however, pointed out that
their rifles and even artillery are superior to ours. Yet people
refuse to remember that, strictly speaking, we are fighting not only
against the Turks but also against the European powers; that many
Englishmen are serving as officers in the Turkish army; that the
Turks are armed with European money; that European diplomacy,
ever since the beginning of the war, has been opposing us in many
ways, having deprived us of the help of our natural allies and even
of our real roads of communication to Turkey. Besides, by her hatred
of us, Europe has encouraged the fanaticism of the Turks.

Finally, in Europe a conspiracy of whole organized, armed
and financed gangs has been discovered; their object is to attack
unexpectedly the rear of our army. On top of this, recently a Turkish
loan has been cooked up in Europe, to her own great financial detriment. This impossible loan was granted solely because Europe is so
fond of the fancy that Turkey, far from being a mollusk-state, is
an organism with flesh and blood just like the European states.
And this at a time when whole provinces of Turkey were stained
with floods of blood, when a regular conspiracy of the Turkish rulers
revealed the intent to annihilate the Bulgarians—to the last man!

The Turks are fighting us, feeding and supporting their army
with such requisitions of supplies, horses and cattle as inevitably
must completely ruin that richest Turkish province. And it is to
these destroyers and slaughterers of their own country that the enlightened English granted a loan, believing in their economic sol-
vency!

But let all this be so over there—in Europe! There, this is
somehow intelligible! But how can we regard the Turks as a force?
Is the utter destruction of their own country or the complete annihilation of the Christian population of the state—force? Such force will
not last them till the end of the war. The first turn of the war in
our favor,—and the fantastic edifice of their military and national
strength will instantaneously collapse and vanish like a genuine
phantom, together with its fanaticism, which will escape like steam
through an open valve.

Some clever fellows in Russia are cursing—both orally and in print—the Slavic problem. "What a fuss you are making about these Slavs and these fantasies of their unification! And who cast those Slavs upon our neck! What for?—To doom us to an everlasting discord with Europe, to her eternal suspiciousness and hatred of us, now and in the future?—Well, let them be damned, those Slavophiles!" and so on, and so forth.

However, it seems that these clamorous wiseacres are altogether misinformed on the Slavs and the Eastern question, and that many of them never took any interest in them—up to the very last moment. Therefore, it is impossible to argue with them. Indeed, they are not aware of the fact that the Eastern question (including the Slavic problem) was invented not at all by the Slavophiles, nor by anybody else; that it arose long ago of its own accord—long before the Slavophiles, before us, even before Peter the Great and the Russian Empire. It arose at the time of the initial consolidation of the Great Russian race into a unified Russian state, *i.e.*, simultaneously with the Moscow Czardom.

The Eastern question is a fundamental idea of the Moscow Czardom, of which Peter the Great took full cognizance, and which, when he left Moscow, he transferred to Petersburg. Peter fully understood its organic connection with the Russian state and the Russian soul. This is why this idea did not only survive in Petersburg but it was, as it were, recognized as a *Russian mission* by all the successors of Peter. This is why it can neither be forsaken nor modified.

To abandon the Slavic idea and to leave without solution the problem entailing the fate of Eastern Christianity (N. B. which is the substance of the Eastern problem)—would be equivalent to smashing Russia into pieces, and to inventing in her place something new, but not Russia at all. This would not even be a revolution, but simply destruction; therefore this would even be impossible, since such an entity cannot be destroyed and transformed into an altogether different organism. At present perhaps only the blindest of our Russian Europeans—and with them, to their shame, stock-exchange speculators—do not perceive and do not recognize this idea. I call tentatively stock-exchange speculators all those present-day Russians who have no other concern in Russia but their pocket-books, and who view Russia exclusively from the standpoint of the interests of their pockets. Now they are shouting in a chorus about commercial depression, the stock-exchange crisis and the decline in rate of exchange of the ruble.

However, were these stock-exchange gamblers so far-sighted as to understand anything outside their sphere, they would grasp the fact that should Russia have failed to begin the present war, they themselves would be worse off. In order that there be "business," even stock-exchange business, it is necessary that the nation live in reality, *i.e.*, a genuine live life abiding by its natural mission, and not as a galvanized corpse in the hands of Jews and stock-exchange speculators.

Had we not started the present war—after all the cynical and insulting provocations of our enemies,—had we not come to the rescue of the tortured martyrs, we should despise ourselves. But self-contempt, moral degradation, and ensuing cynicism impede even "business." Nations live by a great sentiment, a great all-unifying and all-illuminating thought; by cohesion of the people, and finally, on condition that the people, involuntarily, consider themselves to be in accord with their upper men. This generates national vigor. This is what nations live by, and not merely by stock-exchange speculations and by concern about the rate of the ruble. The wealthier a nation is spiritually, the richer it is materially . . . But, say, what obsolete words I am uttering!

3

A SLIGHT HINT AT THE FUTURE INTELLIGENT RUSSIAN MAN. THE UNQUESTIONABLE FATE OF THE FUTURE RUSSIAN WOMAN

Nowadays there are strange perplexities and odd concerns. Positively, there are Russians who are even *afraid* of Russian successes and victories. They are afraid not because they wish evil to the Russians; on the contrary, they are sincerely sorry about every Russian reverse; they are good Russians. Yet they are also afraid of Russian successes and victories "because, you see, after a victorious war self-reliance, self-conceit, chauvinism and stagnation will develop."

But the whole mistake of these good men consists in that they have always perceived Russian progress in self-bespitting. Why, at present, self-reliance is the thing which, perhaps, we need most! At length we need self-respect, and not self-bespitting. Don't worry—there will be no stagnation. The war will throw light on so many things and will make us change so many old things! This you would never be able to achieve by self-bespitting and mockery which, of late, have been turned into mere pastime. As against this, there will also be revealed much which used to be regarded by our wise denouncers as a mere trifle, which nevertheless constitutes our very essence in every respect. Nay, it is not our custom to indulge

in chauvinism and self-intoxication! When did this take place in
Russian society?—Those who claim this are simply ignorant of
Russian history. Much has been said about our self-intoxication
after Sebastopol; it was claimed that at that time self-confidence
had ruined us. However, at no time was educated society less self-
confident—even to the point of decomposition—than at the epoch
preceding Sebastopol.

I may remark in passing: among those who wrote about our
self-intoxication and taunted us with it after Sebastopol, there were
several new young writers who attracted to themselves a good deal
of public attention and roused in society much sympathy because
of their accusations. However, these sincerely well-wishing denouncers were at once joined by so many impudent and disreputable
fellows; there ensued so much unbridled sham; there appeared so
many men who understood nothing about the substance of the matter, and yet imagined themselves saviors of Russia,—moreover,
among them there appeared so many outspoken enemies of Russia
—that, at length, these men who had, *bona fide,* joined the cause
originated by the talented men, finished by harming it. At first,
however, they did meet with success, solely because the Russians,
pure in heart, who at that time really craved for regeneration, for
the new word, failed to discern in them scamps, inept, even venal
people without any convictions. On the contrary, these naïve Russians believed that the latter were for Russia, for her interests, for
regeneration, for the people and society. At length, the overwhelming majority of the Russians became disillusioned and turned their
backs upon the scamps. And it was after that that stock-exchange
gamblers and seekers of railroad concessions made their appearance . . . It seems that at present this mistake will not be repeated
because, unquestionably, new men, with a new vision and with
new power will appear.

These new men will not be afraid of self-respect, but they
will also not be afraid to follow the old course; nor will they be
afraid of the wiseacres. They will be modest, but they will know
many things, derived from practical experience, of which these wiseacres of ours have never dreamed. By practical experience they will
learn to respect the Russian man and the Russian people. This
knowledge they will unfailingly bring along with them, and in this
will be their main *point d'appui*. They will not attribute all our
misfortunes and *ineptitudes* exclusively to the characteristics of the
Russian man and the Russian nature. This, however, has become
a bureaucratic device of our wiseacres, since this is comfortable
and requires no brains.

They will be the first to attest the fact that the Russian spirit
and the Russian man are in no way to be blamed for the hundreds

of thousands of accusations heaped upon them; that wherever a
Russian is given direct access to a job he will do it not worse than
any other.

Oh, these new men, despite all their modesty, will, finally,
understand how often our wiseacres, even the purest in heart who
wished genuine benefit, have sat on two chairs, seeking to discover
the root of the evil. These new men, who unfailingly will appear
after the war, will be joined by many live forces from among the
people and the Russian youth. Even before the war they made their
appearance, but then we were unable to discern them. And when
here we all expected to perceive a spectacle of cynicism and corruption—over there, they revealed a spectacle of such conscious
self-denial and sincere sentiment, such faith in that cause for which
they had gone to give their lives, that we, here, merely kept wondering—whence did all this come?

Some correspondents of foreign newspapers have accused certain Russian officers of being ambitious, careerists, of seeking distinctions, forgetting the principal aim—the love of their fatherland
and that cause which they undertook to serve. However, if there
be such Russian officers, these correspondents would do well to
become acquainted with those young men or with those inconspicuous officers—even as far as their ranks are concerned—with
those modest servants of their fatherland and of the just cause for
which they valiantly died, side by side with their soldiers, with
absolute self-denial, and not at all for distinctions, not for show or
career, but only because they had great hearts and were staunch
Christians, inconspicuous great Russian men, of whom there are
so many—virtually to the last soldier—in our army.

Please note that when speaking of the future new man, I am
by no means pointing only to our warriors in anticipation of their
return. Innumerable others will appear,—*all those who in the past
have been craving for the belief in the Russian man*, but who were
unable to reveal themselves in opposition to the generally and mani-
festly prevailing negation and pessimism. But now, contemplating
the *faith* in his strength which the Russian has revealed *over there*,
willy-nilly, they will be encouraged and will believe that here, too,
there are real Russian forces: whence, if not from here, did they
spring up there? And having braced themselves, they will get together, and modestly but firmly they will turn to the real task
without fearing anyone's loud and bombastic words—these old, old
words! Yet, our clever little old men are still convinced that precisely they are the newest and the *young* men, and that they are
uttering the newest words!

However, the principal and most salutary regeneration of
Russian society unquestionably will be allotted to the Russian

woman. After the present war, during which the Russian woman has revealed herself so loftily, so lucidly, so sacredly, one can no longer doubt the lofty destination which awaits her in our midst. The secular prejudices will finally fall, and "barbaric" Russia will show what place she will allot to the "little mother," "little sister," of the Russian soldier, that self-renouncing martyr for the Russian man.

Can we continue to deny this woman, who has so visibly revealed her valor, full equality of rights with the male in the fields of education, professions, tenure of office, she in whom at present we place all our hopes, now, after her exploit, in connection with the regeneration and elevation of our society! This would be shameful and unreasonable, all the more so as at present this would be altogether dependent on us, since the Russian woman of her own accord has assumed a place to which she is entitled; of her own accord, she strode over those steps which until now had set the limit to her rights. She has proved what heights she can ascend, and what she is able to achieve.

However, in speaking so, I have in mind the *Russian woman,* and not those sentimental ladies who treated the Turks to candies. Of course, there is nothing bad in being kind to the Turks; still, this is not what *those women* over there accomplished. Therefore, *these* are only *old* Russian dames, whereas *those* are *new* Russian women. Nor do I speak only about those who there are sacrificing themselves for God's cause and for the service to humanity. Those proved to us by the fact of their appearance that in Russia there are many great women's hearts ready for public labors and self-denial, since, again, whence, if not from here, did those spring up there?

But I should like to say more, in a special article, about the Russian woman and her unquestionable immediate lot in our society, and therefore I shall return to this theme in the following October issue of my *Diary.*

OCTOBER

CHAPTER I

1

To Our Readers

ON ACCOUNT of ill-health which prevents me from publishing the *Diary* on strictly determined dates, I have decided to suspend its publication for one or two years. This I am doing with much regret because, when last year I embarked on the publication of the *Diary,* I did not expect that I should meet with so much sympathy on the part of the readers, which has lasted all the time, till this day. I am sincerely grateful for it. I owe my particular thanks to all those who have addressed me by mail: from these letters I have learned many new things. And, generally, the two-year publication of the *Diary* has taught me much, and in many respects reinforced me. But, regretfully, I am positively compelled to suspend publication. With the December issue the publication will come to an end. I hope that neither I nor the readers will forget each other.

2

An Old Eternal Military Rule

Much has been said and written, both in Europe and Russia, about our military mistakes during the present campaign. They now continue to be discussed. Of course, the correct and complete evaluation of our military actions belongs to the future, *i.e.,* at least, it can be made only upon the termination of the war. However, even now certain facts are revealed with sufficient completeness to permit one to render a more or less correct judgment.

I shall not venture to discuss our military mistakes, since I am hardly competent in these matters (although it seems that it is the incompetent ones who get most excited in Russia). I merely wish to point to a certain contemporary fact (and not an error) which, thus far, has been little observed and explained by military science, which has hardly been evaluated from the standpoint of its *contemporary* essence. It could have been guessed merely theoretically, but practically it has never been confirmed up to the present war.

This fatal fact, practically unconfirmed up to the present war, was destined, as if on purpose, to reveal itself inevitably, in all its strength, and final precision, in the course of the present campaign, because this strictly military fact precisely conforms to the national military character of the Turks, or, more correctly, to the principal distinguishing mark of their military character. Moreover, it may even be suggested that were it not for the Turks, this fact, perhaps, would not have been explained, at least in Europe, despite the recent wars (even such a huge war as the Franco-Prussian campaign). Indeed, this fact had not been explained since it did not have time to reveal itself.

At present, after the fatal experience of the current war, it will, naturally, become an element of military science and its significance will be evaluated. However, the *fatality* of this to us consisted in the fact that the Russian army, so to speak, stumbled against this military fact—not yet explained in a practical sense— and that we, Russians, were destined to interpret it to our enormous detriment, at least, as long as its meaning was not quite clear to us. Even so, many people both in Russia and Europe, up to this day, are inclined to regard this formidable detriment, sustained by us, as a result of this obscure fact, solely as our military mistake, whereas here there was something fatal and unavoidable, and not an error. Now, for instance, were the German army in our place, it would also have been hurt by this fact, although it might have evaluated it quickly and adopted corresponding counter-measures faster.

I merely mean to say that not all of our mistakes of this present campaign are in reality mistakes, and that the most important ones among them would have been committed by any European army in our place. I repeat: we stumbled against an obscure military fact, and prior to its elucidation we sustained a loss, which cannot be considered an absolute error. But what is this fact?

When in the days of my youth, I was studying higher military and engineering sciences at the Chief Engineering School and attended a six-year course there at the end of the Thirties and the beginning of the Forties, there was a conviction which was considered irrevocable,—an engineering axiom. (However, I hasten to remark in parentheses: so long ago have I forsaken engineering and military pursuits that I do not pretend to be in the least competent in this field. I matriculated in the Chief Engineering School and attended a six-year course there at the end of Thirties and in the beginning of the Forties. Thereupon, having graduated from the School and left it, I served as engineer only one year. I tendered my resignation and embarked upon literature. Totleben graduated three or four years earlier than I; I remember Kaufman in the officers' classes. I was in the same class with the younger Kaufman —in the Conductors' classes. Radetzky, Petrushevsky and Yolshin were only one year my seniors. Only three of my classmates have deviated from the straight road to choose an unsteady and uncertain path; namely, I, the writer Grigorovich and the artist Trutovsky. In a word, this was very long ago.)

That engineering axiom came down to the conviction that no fortress is, or can be, impregnable. In other words, no matter how skillfully a fortress may be fortified and defended, in the long run it must fall, and thus the military art of the assault of a fortress always exceeds the means and art of its defense. Of course, this was merely conceived generally and theoretically:—the essential qualities of both engineering arts, that of the attack and of the defense of fortresses, were examined as mere abstract propositions. Naturally, there is no rule without exceptions, and even in those days certain existent fortresses used to be mentioned which were supposedly impregnable—for instance, Gibraltar, about which, however, we had but a hear-say knowledge. Still, from a scientific standpoint no fortress should have been conceived as impregnable, and the axiom that the art of the assault of a fortress always exceeds the means and art of its defense—remained unshaken.

Of course, it is different in practice. A certain fortress, for instance, may acquire the character of an impregnable citadel (without being such) only because, owing to this or that circumstance, the enemy's main forces may be held up before it too long and exhaust themselves, thus it renders a service greater than that which can be expected. Totleben, for example, knew for certain that in the long run Sebastopol would be captured, no matter how skillfully he defended her. However, the Allies most certainly did not know, when they began to besiege Sebastopol, that she would require so great a strain on their part. On the contrary, probably, they supposed that Sebastopol would occupy them for but two months or so, and that her siege would be but a passing episode in a huge plan of countless blows which they were ready to deliver at Russia, apart from the capture of Sebastopol. And thus she served as an impregnable citadel, even though, at length, she was captured. By the protracted, ingenious defense of Totleben—unexpected by them—the Allied resources, both military and financial, had been so exhausted and shattered that, after the capture of Sebastopol, further blows could not even be thought of, and our enemies sought peace, at least, not less ardently than we! Would they have offered us such peace terms as they did, if they had succeeded in capturing Sebastopol in two months!

Thus, absolutely impregnable fortresses are *not needed:* by a skillful defense and by the heroic tenacity of the defenders a fortress by no means impregnable may break the enemies' forces. Nevertheless, ingenious as the defense of Sebastopol may have been, sooner or later—I repeat—she must have fallen because, given a certain equality in the strength of both adversaries, the force of the assault always exceeds the force of the defense, *i.e.*, again, speaking scientifically, and not in a practical sense, because, at times, the attackers have actually abandoned the siege of certain fortresses—even after a long siege—however, not because these were impregnable, but because they sought to deliver a blow elsewhere, with fewer losses,—if only such a solution presented itself.

3

THE SAME RULE—ONLY IN A NEW VERSION

Now, this military fact, this, so to speak, strategic axiom, during our present war with the Turks, has been suddenly shaken, as it were. By what?—Not by a *permanent* fortification, not by the impregnable citadel of a threatening fortress, but by a volatile field fortification, at most of a *temporary* character. In days gone by field defenses were not even taken into consideration; these were considered field fortifications which merely strengthened the scene of the battle. At Borodino we did construct redoubts which served their purpose, *i.e.*, fortified the scene; nevertheless, they were captured, although with losses to the enemy, but they were captured on the day itself of the battle.

Yet at Plevna something altogether new has occurred. A series of ordinary field fortifications, at most of a *temporary* character (in days past certainly not important things) has conveyed to the site the significance of an impregnable citadel, inconquerable with the employment of the traditional weapons, which has required on our part double, treble efforts, compared with those anticipated, and which, up to the present, has not been captured. Had this been a threatening series of fortifications defended only by traditional old defense means—could it have withstood the energetic, brilliant and unprecedented assault of the Russians?—Most certainly not: it would have served its purpose; of course, it would have made the attack more difficult; nevertheless 50,000 Russians, impetuously smashing ahead, as they did on the thirtieth of August, of course would have captured the redoubts and would have defeated the 50,000 army of Osman-Pasha, *i.e.*, in the presence of an equal number of troops the task would have been achieved and reinforcements would not have been required. At present, however, after two unsuccessful assaults, it has proved necessary at least to double our army, and this is but the first step in the realization of the task.

What, then, is the matter?—Of course it is to be accounted for by the present-day rifle. The Turk, covering himself with a hastily thrown-up bank, is able to fire such a mass of bullets that it is not impossible for the assaulting column, before it has even reached the breast-works, to be exterminated to the last man. Oh, of course, it is possible to capture Plevna by resorting to the traditional method, *i.e.*, to the frontal attack without any fortification works, exactly as the redoubts were captured at Borodino. *And our Russians would have done it!* Perhaps no European army would have ventured this, but they would have done it. But here is the

trouble: experience proved that for this it would have been necessary to sacrifice tens of thousands of Russians so that, having captured the redoubts by frontal attack, disposing in the beginning
of an equal number of men as Osman, by the end we should have
been numerically so weakened that we should have been unable to
check Osman, who would have lost behind his trenches ten times
fewer men than we.

Thus, after two unsuccessful assaults, finally, it proved necessary: first, to double our forces; secondly, with Totleben's assistance,
to start engineering work, *i.e.*, something virtually resembling an
atack against the strongest permanent fortresses; third, to begin
the siege of Plevna, to occupy the roads, to interrupt communications, to cut off the flow of supplies to the enemy. In a word, a
group of most ordinary, temporary field defenses have acquired,
from the standpoint of the enemy, the significance of a first-class
fortress. And even though Plevna will be captured—for sure—or to
put it more correctly, even though Osman will be caught when he
tries to force his way through in order to extricate himself from
his own trap so as to avoid starving to death in it (and once he
attempts to force his way he will *uncover himself,* and abandoning
the defense, he will asume the role of an attacker, and to us—herein
is the whole trick! Thus, he would lose at once all advantages
of the deadly and invincible fire behind closed defenses); even so,
the result is that Plevna has already served its purpose to the enemy;
it has checked the initial victorious march of the Russians, compelling them to double and treble their efforts and losses (of which even
Europe considered Russia incapable). And—who knows—perhaps
Osman, even without so dreadful an ultimate result to himself,
hopes to snatch at least half of his army from the hands of the
Russians, and to flee at its head, so as again to dig in somewhere,
throwing up a new Plevna, provided only he is given a chance to
achieve all this. However, everybody has the right to hope, and
Osman is an energetic and proud man.

It may even be said that if he who defends himself possesses
entrenching implements and disposes of some twenty thousand soldiers—given the modern rifle—by means of a series of ordinary
former field fortifications, any number of which can be scattered
in the course of one night in a selected locality, he will increase
the strength of these twenty thousand men to an army fifty or sixty
thousand strong so that, if circumstances do not favor manœuvring,
one does not know how to handle the situation.

Thus, this series of light defenses, at times, proves to him who
defends himself even more beneficial than the most threatening and
impregnable fortress because, when he retreats, he transports it

with him to any chosen site, as if it were a mere entrenching implement. At length you will capture it from him by sacrificing thousands of soldiers in the course of the assault, but tomorrow you encounter in your path another such fortress, provided the enemy is given time to escape from you.

At present there is in Turkey not just one Plevna, but each Turkish army, even each detachment, digs in, and on the morrow it installs behind the trenches its deadly rifles, saying to the Russians: "Come up in double numbers, and incur losses ten times as great as you anticipated in the beginning of the war." In order to match his forces with the assaulted, there remains nothing for the attacker but to stop opposite him and dig in too. But this cannot be done, because he is the attacker; he came to attack and to march forward. He cannot be sitting behind fortifications; he came to storm them. . . .

People who know will understand that I am speaking merely theoretically, that I am dwelling upon attack and defense in general, setting aside all other eventualities of war, which change every minute the course of events, swaying it hither or thither. I merely wish to express the formula that *with the modern rifle,* assisted by field fortifications, every army on the defensive, *in any European country,* has unexpectedly gained a terrible advantage over the attacking army. Now the force of defense exceeds the force of attack, and it is unquestionably more advantageous to him who defends himself to conduct a war than to him who is attacking.

Such is the fact which, thus far, has not been fully elucidated in strategy, which is even quite *unexpected,* against which we, the Russians, were destined to stumble, which we were destined to solve to our great detriment. And this is not at all our *mistake,* but merely a new military fact which suddenly revealed itself and became clear. . . .

4

The Most Enormous Military Mistakes Sometimes May Not be Mistakes at All

Well,—people will say—what kind of a new fact did you discover here? Didn't we know before the beginning of the campaign what the new rifle was and its deadly effect? Besides, it is not new; it was old long ago, so that not only were we in Petersburg in a position to calculate but we were in duty bound to calculate and prepare ourselves for its deadly action, particularly from behind a closed fortification. But the point is that practice does not coincide with theory, and that we actually *could not* calculate and prepare. Only to civilians this seems easy, to those sitting in their drawing-rooms and criticizing our military operations.

Indeed, I am not denying the mistakes; I admit that there have been, and had to be, mistakes. But I merely do not wish to deem this one *fact* to be our absolute mistake, and I declare that up to this war *in all its overwhelming effect,* it was an obscure and even unknown fact. No doubt, it would have been possible to calculate and know in advance that with the modern rifle the defender, covering himself with the lightest fortification, might inflict upon the attacker twice as much harm as before. To learn and calculate is an easy matter requiring no strategic science. But here is what was infinitely more difficult to calculate and foresee, *i.e.,* the fact that with the present rifle the defender, covering himself with a fortification, would inflict not *twice,* but *five times* more harm than in former times, while in the face of such an energetic defense as we have met on the part of the Turks (it was excusable not to have taken it into account)—*ten times* more. Let us admit that that fact was known, yet its effect, its dimensions were unknown. No one knew that, even though the present-day rifle had strengthened the attacker, nevertheless it had reinforced the defender *infinitely more.* This *excess* of the reinforcement was unknown to us, and it was precisely this which constitutes the new, unexpected fact against which we stumbled.

It was not known, nor could it have been known, because nowhere, prior to this war with the Turks, had it been so fully revealed. Believe me that were the German army in our place, it would also have *stumbled* against this fact and would have sustained great losses. I repeat: perhaps the German army would have been quicker than we to evaluate its significance fully and would have adopted necessary counter-measures: in some cases the German is more cautious and circumspect than the Russian; as against this, the Russian possesses such a self-denying discipline, such absolute self-sacrifice, such strength of energy, tenacity and impetuosity that, verily, it is difficult to decide which of the two is superior in military matters. Naturally, our competent men, knowing the Russian soldier, in the beginning, prior to the experience with the modern rifle, even from behind fortifications, could have given the matter but cursory thought, and even if the modern rifle were *not only twice but three times* as deadly as the former rifle, they could have feared it little. Yet it developed that the modern rifle used from behind a fortification was *five,* and even *ten times* more powerful than the former one. This, however, could have been ascertained only by practical experience. . . . And up to the present in this respect there had been no practical experience in European wars.

Indeed, with the appearance of the modern rifle apparently many more simpler facts have not been elucidated. For instance, only now have we come to life when our troops have received Berdan rifles, whereas, in the beginning, the army was equipped with other kinds of rifles—slow and short-range ones. This, unquestionably, was a mistake. However, the fact to which I am pointing was not a mistake: in all its completeness it could not have been anticipated; nor was it possible, prior to practical experience, to make accurate calculations.

The Franco-Prussian war, a war between two so highly educated nations, which are so equal in regard to inventions and military equipment (the French had a better rifle than the Germans, and the latter were compelled to accept it, without delay, while the war was still in progress)—the Franco-Prussian war which has introduced so many novel elements into strategy, almost bringing about a revolution with it, had *in no way* elucidated *our fact*. And yet it could have thrown light upon it. But there occurred special circumstances which prevented this, and the conqueror of France up to the present, up to the Turkish war itself, remained ignorant of the fact that the Frenchman, defeated by him, possessed a colossal weapon with which to check the German onslaught in 1871, but failed to make use of it owing to special circumstances which resulted in the fact that the power of this weapon could not even have occurred to the Frenchman. By no means did the Germans conquer the French; they conquered the then prevailing French state of affairs—first, of the Napoleonic regime, and later of the republican chaos.

In the beginning of the war, the French army—whose national characteristic is frontal attack at half-sword with the enemy—was dreadfully amazed and morally depressed by the fact that instead of crossing the Rhine and invading Germany, it was compelled to defend its own territory at home. Several battles took place which the Germans won. However, the thought that with the use of their magnificent *chassepot* several more dreadful Plevnas could be thrown up at once in order to stem the terrible onslaught of the enemy,—that thought did not occur to the Frenchman at all. He kept endeavoring to smash ahead, and up to Sedan itself he refused to believe that he was conquered. Then came Sedan, and the bulk of the regular army—because of considerations which by no means were military considerations—was withdrawn from the field. There was left the defense of Paris by the madman Trochu. Gambetta flew out of Paris in a balloon, *descendit du Ciel* (descended from heaven) in one of the provinces—as a certain historian wrote about him, proclaimed a dictatorship and began to recruit new armies. These little resembled regular troops and were made up of all sorts of riff-raff, for which, however, Gambetta could not be blamed. At the time, they themselves wrote that the majority of their soldiers did not know how to load a rifle and to take aim; why, they were not even concerned about such things; they did not want to fight and were anxious to be left in peace.

Then came winter, with its cold and hunger. How could they have guessed that suddenly they could grow three, four times stronger than their enemy—by resorting to their *chassepots* and trenching implements?—Well, did they have these implements? The siege of Paris—which had a political rather than a military significance—was also an obstacle. In a word, the French failed to make use of the dreadful *new* military fact, and did not discover its effect. In the course of our present Turkish war this fact has been *fully* revealed, and it stands to reason that Germany's politicians and military men have taken cognizance of it with anxiety.

Indeed, should this fact be dealt with by science, by tactics, in every army, perhaps the French will also take advantage of it, when Germany again assaults them. And if the French brush aside their military prejudices (which is very difficult); if they fully embrace the conviction, derived from the Turkish war, that defense with the modern rifle and trench implements is now much stronger than attack, which requires a double number of men, the following may be stated: the French have an army of one million men; but there is a general military rule that it is far easier for the assaulted to concentrate his forces if he is fighting on his own territory—even if a country possesses such a disadvantageous military borderline as Russia,—whereas the attacker, should he even dispose of an army of two million men (which is never the case), could never invade the assaulted country with more than six or seven hundred thousand troops.

Now, imagine that this whole million of defenders should resort to trench implements as energetically and broadly as nowadays the Turks do; imagine a talented general and excellent engineers,—in this event Germany would have to dispatch to France—not just a million, but a minimum of a million and a half! Undoubtedly, someone in Germany is now thinking about this.

5

WE MERELY STUMBLED AGAINST A FACT, BUT THERE WAS
NO MISTAKE. TWO ARMIES—TWO OPPOSITES. THE PRES-
ENT STATE OF AFFAIRS

Precisely the Turks were destined to discover the new fact in all its completeness. Other nations, other armies, would long

have failed to discover it *practically in such completeness*. The
Turks have long refrained from attacking Europe, and they are
specifically used to defense. This is the principal national characteristic of the Turkish army. Behind fortifications the Turk is
tenacious and energetic, and during this war Europe, as if on purpose, encouraged him, helped him with armaments, engineers, with
huge sums of money, and finally, by inciting him against us, she
aroused his fanaticism. Had he even been ignorant of the fact,
there would have been plenty of people to inform him of it; but
it so happened that the fact was in full accord with his national
spirit. He promptly grasped the meaning of the trenching implement, coupled with the magazine rifle, and the resulting immense
preponderance in strength of defense over attack. And as if on
purpose, the Russians were destined to stumble against this, *i.e.*,
that army which, in accordance with ancient, secular tradition, has
adopted as its method of attack—fiery assault, breast to breast, in
close formation, suddenly converting a thousand men into one being.

From these two opposites the new axiom has revealed itself
in all its completeness. I repeat: it was possible to anticipate and
calculate that the strength of the new rifle behind a covering trench
exceeds twice, even three times, the effort of the attacker. Relying
upon the tenacity and unheard-of energy of the Russian soldier,
we had the right to regard this *"twice and three times"* with contempt (for a long time we did so regard it). However, the thing
proved not twice or three times, but ten times stronger. This could
not have been anticipated and quickly learned despite even practical
experience.

Of course, to civilian strategists all this will sound ridiculous.
Nor do they recognize the existence of the fact itself: "We should
have foreseen—that's all. Everybody knows that the Peabody rifle
emits ten to twelve cartridges per minute. Well, it should have been
understood that a Turk sitting behind a trench with such a rifle
will mow down an attacking column to the last man." But, I repeat,
theoretically, before the experiment, this could not have been fully
evaluated.

There are extremely simple things which the most ingenious
generals have been unable to guess beforehand. A French historian
bitterly criticizes Napoleon I for the fact that disposing in 1815
of an army of 170,000 (only that many) and being fully aware that
he could not count on recruiting a single additional soldier in France
—because France was exhausted to that extent as a result of
twenty years of wars—he nevertheless ventured to attack his enemies,
i.e., risked a foreign war, instead of a domestic one. This historian
seeks to prove that, even had Napoleon won the battle of Waterloo,

this would not have saved him from ultimate debacle in that same campaign because of the overwhelming numerical preponderance of the coalition. Napoleon's whole mistake, according to this historian, consisted in that he continued, as hitherto, to consider one French soldier worth two German soldiers. Had it been so, he would, of course, have made up for the want of the men with whom he proceeded to fight all Europe. But in 1815, claims the historian, this was no longer so: after twenty years the Germans had learned how to fight, improving the quality of their soldiers to the point where they were fully equal to the French soldiers.

Thus, even ingenious Napoleon made such a seemingly simple mistake: he failed to guess a thing which he should have known long ago, and which his critic perceived so clearly. However, it is easy to criticize, and it is easy to be a great general sitting on a sofa. It is remarkable that Napoleon and we were *mistaken* in one and the same point, *i.e.*, by erroneously attributing an excessive significance to certain national peculiarities of our armies.

In conclusion I shall reiterate, again and again, that everything stated here has but a general, scientific meaning (be it correct or incorrect—let everyone judge for himself). In practice, however, the results may greatly vary. For instance, in the beginning of the war the Turks did let us cross the Danube and the Balkans; they did surrender their fortresses and cities; they did flee before our advancing troops, without giving any thought to their trench implements and to the effect of their Peabody rifle. It also seems that at that time they were not yet possessed with fanaticism. Strictly speaking, it was only at Plevna that they fully guessed *wherein lay the trick*. Only there did they discover for the first time all the tactical advantages possessed by the attacked.

It may happen, however, that Plevna will be captured in a week, and with it *"the whole"* Osman, *i.e.*, perhaps he will not succeed in carrying out a retreat if he attempts a break-through. Then, suddenly, for example, the Turks may reveal the former sinking of the spirits; they will forget Adrianople and Sofia; they will throw down their trench implements, hurriedly fleeing in the face of the Russian offensive. In a word, many things may happen. However, all this does not at all change the significance of the new axiom in its general sense, *i.e.*, that with modern equipment the strength of the defense exceeds the force of the attack not as hitherto but *exceedingly* so.

Let us refer to another example: somewhere there is a war, and a general locks himself up with his troops in a strong fortress. Having calculated all data, *i.e.*, the quantity of provisions; the position and strength of the fortifications, engineering science is able (I believe) to ascertain almost precisely how long the fortress may resist the siege and thereby render undeniable service to its country by tying down around its walls, at the hottest moment of the campaign, the two times stronger attacking enemy. Let us suppose the length of time is six or seven months. Unexpectedly the general who has locked himself up in that fortress, capitulates—for some special reasons of his own—not after seven, but after two months.

Briefly, practice may bring about countless variations. Even so—given modern military equipment—the axiom of the *excessiveness* of the preponderance (about which, up to our present war with the Turks, no one has ever dreamed) of the strength of the defense over the force of the attack retains its force. (Once more I emphasize: it was not the preponderance of the strength that could not have been anticipated but such excessiveness of it.)

However, at present, practice is already operating to our advantage, and we shall commit no *such* error in the future. At present Todleben is over there. What he is doing we do not exactly know; but, perhaps, the ingenious engineer, by some new ingenious discovery, will find a means to shatter the *axiom* (not only in this particular case but in general), to eliminate *excessiveness* and to balance the forces (that of the attack and of the defense). Europe is attentively and eagerly watching his actions, awaiting not merely political but also scientific inferences.

Briefly, our military horizon looks brighter and, once more, there is much hope. In Asia a great victory has brought the matter to an end. And our Balkan army is numerically strong and magnificent; its spirit is equal to its great goal. The Russian people—I mean the people—as a whole, as one man, desire that the great aim of the war in defense of Christianity may be achieved. Mothers cannot refrain from shedding tears over their children leaving for the battlefields: this is nature. But the conviction of the holiness of the cause retains its full force. Fathers and mothers know whither they send their children: the war is a popular one. This is being denied by some people who do not believe; they gather contradicting facts, but, for instance, such news items as the following appearing in the papers in small type remain virtually unnoticed:

"It is reported to *The Odessa Messenger* from the station Birzula that 2800 convalescent soldiers have been transported through that station to the army in the field. They were accompanied by six convalescent officers. It is noteworthy that from among the wounded *not even one* wished to take advantage of his right to be transferred to the reserve forces. They all hasten to go back to the front." (*The Moscow Gazette*, No. 251.)

How do you like this news item? Indeed, it would seem that facts such as these bear witness to the character of the cause! After that, how can it be asserted that the war is not a popular war, and that the people stand aloof? But this is not an isolated fact; there is a multitude of such facts. They will all be gathered, they will begin to shine, and they will become part of history. . . . Fortunately most of these facts have been attested to by numerous European eye-witnesses; no longer can they be changed, counterfeited and presented in a stock-exchange or *Roman Clerical* light.

CHAPTER II

1

Hartung's Suicide and Our Eternal Question: Who Is to Be Blamed?

OF LATE, all Russian newspapers have been—and still are—discussing General Hartung's suicide in Moscow during the session of the Circuit Court, a quarter of an hour after he had heard the jurors' verdict which found him guilty. Therefore, I believe that all the readers of *The Diary* are already more or less conversant with this extraordinary and tragic incident, and so I don't have to explain anything in detail.

The general purport comes down to this: a man of considerable rank and belonging to select society becomes friendly with a former tailor, subsequently a money lender, Sanftleben, and not because he has to borrow money from him, but, as it were, as a matter of friendship, assuming incidentally, and quite readily, the role of his executor. Then, upon Sanftleben's death, certain heinous things begin to transpire: the promissory notes ledger disappears, no one knows whither; in violation of the procedure prescribed by law, promissory notes, papers and documents are removed by Hartung to his apartment. It develops that Hartung has entered into collusion with one group of the heirs to the detriment of the others (even though he may not have suspected this himself). Thereupon one of the heirs rushes into his apartment, and the poor executor learns that he is mixed up with bad company. Direct accusations are brought forward;—he is accused of the theft of bills of exchange, the bills of exchange ledgers, of false endorsement of the latter, of the disappearance of documents, involving a loss of property in the sum of over one hundred or even two hundred thousand rubles. . . . Then comes the trial. The prosecutor is even glad of it and of the

fact that a general is in the dock, side by side with a plebeian, thus
giving the Russian Themis an opportunity to proclaim the equality
of the strong and the notable with the humble and the insignificant
before the law.

However, the trial proceeds quite normally (whatever may be
said about it) and, finally, the jurors pronounce an almost inevitable
condemnation, the meaning of which is: "guilty—he did embezzle."
The Court retires to frame the sentence, but General Hartung did
not choose to wait for it: stepping out—so it is reported—into the
adjoining room, he seated himself by a table, grasped his poor
head with both hands, and then, suddenly, a shot sounded: he shot
himself through the heart with a revolver which he had brought
along with him and which he had loaded beforehand. On his person a
note—also written beforehand—was found, in which he "swears by
Almighty God that in this case he embezzled nothing, and that he
forgives his enemies." Thus, he died convinced of his innocence
and his gentlemanliness.

Now, this death has aroused everybody in Moscow and all
the newspapers in Russia. It was said that the judges and the
prosecutor came out of their chambers with pallid faces, and that
the jurors, too, were abashed. The papers began to vociferate about
"the obviously unjust verdict." Some of them noted that no longer
can the Russian courts be accused of lenient and conniving verdicts:
"Here"—they implied—"is an example: an innocent man perished!"
Others justly observed that it is impossible not to give credence to
such solemn and last words of a man on earth, and thus, almost
unquestionably the inference could be drawn that in this case a
lamentable judicial error was committed. Well, much has been said
and written in the papers.

It must be admitted that some of the newspaper comments
were strange: some sort of falsity sounded in them,—they may have
been ardent and sincere, if you please,—but nevertheless,—false. One
feels sorry for Hartung; but here it is rather a tragedy (very deep
tragedy)—the destiny of Russian life, than an error on anyone's part.
Or to put it better: here everybody is guilty: the habits and customs of our educated society; the characters which have developed
and formed themselves, and finally, the habits and customs of
our adopted, young and insufficiently Russified courts.

However, if everybody around is guilty this means that individually and singly no one is guilty. Among all the newspaper comments I liked most that which appeared in *The New Times*. It so
happened that on the eve I conversed with one of our astute jurists
and connoisseurs of Russian life, and it developed that he and I
were in full accord. Very shrewdly my interlocutor pointed out the

tragic character of this case and its causes. Next day in the *Stranger's* feuilleton I read many things quite akin to those which we had discussed on the eve. Therefore, if I say a few words, it will be merely in general and apropos.

2

The Russian Gentleman. A Gentleman Must Remain a Gentleman to the End

The point is that the old characters have not yet disappeared, and, it seems, they will persist for a long while because everything requires time and nature prevails everywhere. I am speaking about the characters of our educated society. At this juncture I might persistently and obstinately add that it would not be good should we suddenly shift like weather cocks, since the most obnoxious trait of our educated characters is precisely their flippancy and meaninglessness. It reminds one of something lackeyish, of a lackey donning his master's clothes. For instance, one of the characteristics of our gentlemanliness—if once, for some reason, we associate ourselves with the rich and the prominent, and particularly, if we manage to be admitted to their circle—is *imposing deportment,* the urge to establish ourselves on a grand scale.

Please note that at present I am not saying a word personally about Hartung; I do not know his biography at all. I merely mean to record several traits of the generally well-known character of our educated people to whom, under certain circumstances, exactly the same thing might happen which happened to General Hartung. For instance, an insignificant man, of low rank, without a penny in his pocket, suddenly finds himself in fashionable society, or, for some reason, begins to be associated with it. Presently the poor devil, who has possessed nothing but the ability to worm his way into the beau monde, acquires a carriage; he rents an apartment in which he can "live decently"; he hires lackeys, buys clothes, gloves and so forth. Perhaps he seeks to make a career, to become somebody, but more often he simply wants to ape: "Well, everybody lives this way, why shouldn't I?" There is in him some kind of shame which cannot be overcome. In a word: honor and decency are conceived in a strange manner.

I believe that parallel to this lack of understanding of such a fundamental thing as the feeling of self-respect is only the lack of understanding on the part of virtually the entire educated European age of the conception of liberty and of what it consists.—But this will be discussed later.

The second and again almost tragic trait of our educated Russian is his yielding temper, his readiness to compromise. Oh, there are many kulaks and stock-exchange gamblers, repulsive but steadfast scoundrels. There are even good steadfast people, but these are awfully scarce, whereas in the majority of the decent Russians there rather prevails this yieldingness—the urge to concede, to compromise. And this is by no means due to good nature or to cowardice; nay, this is some kind of delicacy, or God knows what.

How often, for example, in a conversation with an opinionated man who presses you, insisting that you make your comment, you agree with him and change your opinion, or even surrender your vote at some meeting, despite the fact that within yourself you are not at all inclined to do so. Likewise, the Russian is very much influenced by the word *"everybody"*: "I am like everybody else"; "I am in accord with the general opinion"; "Let us all proceed, hurrah!" But there is here another strange thing: the Russian is very fond of seducing and tempting himself, of being swayed and persuaded. He does not want to do this or that, for instance to become Sanftleben's executor; yet he persuades himself: "Well why shouldn't I? . . ."

In this stratum of educated Russians there are even most attractive types, but they are specifically endowed with these unfortunate traits of Russian gentlemanliness to which I have just alluded. Some of them are almost innocent, virtual Schillers. Their ignorance of "business matters" conveys to them something almost touching; but they possess a strong sense of honor: such a man will shoot himself, just like Hartung, if, in his judgment, he loses his honor. Of these there is a rather large number. Even so, these people hardly ever know the sum of their indebtedness. Not that they are all spendthrifts; on the contrary, some of them are admirable husbands and fathers; but money may be as thoughtlessly squandered by a man who lives fast as by an excellent father. Many of them begin life with scanty remnants of their former hereditary estates, which promptly vanish in their early youth. Then comes marriage, then—a rank and a comfortable government position, which is so-so; nevertheless, it yields some income and provides a foundation for life, something solid as distinguished from the beau-monde vagabondage of earlier days. But debts accumulate uninterruptedly; of course he pays them because he is a gentleman, but he pays them by means of incurring new debts. It may be positively asserted that many of them when they ponder, at times, to themselves, in solitude, over their situation, can say boldly and with great dignity: "We have stolen nothing; nor do we want to steal anything."

Meanwhile, this little thing may happen: on some occasion he is capable of borrowing—well, in view of some urgent necessity —from his children's nurse, say ten rubles she has saved. After all, why not?—Not seldom the old nurse is a close, intimate associate who has lived many years with the family. She is almost a member of the family; she is indulgent; she is even entrusted with the most important keys. The good general, her master, has long ago promised to provide her, when old age comes, with a lodging in an alms-house; but all these business affairs have prevented him from taking care of this matter despite the fact that long ago he should have put in a word for her. The nurse, on her own part, is afraid to remind him of his promise; only once a year, maybe, she mentions something about the alms-house; she shivers at the thought of annoying such a nervous and always bothered man as her general. "They are good; they will remember"—she thinks at times, as she puts her old bones to rest on her bed. And as for the ten rubles, she is even ashamed to remind him of them; she has her own conscience—the good old woman. Suddenly the general dies, and the old woman is left without either lodging or ten rubles.

All this is, of course, a trifle, an awful bagatelle. But should the general be reminded in the world beyond that the nurse was never paid her ten rubles, he would blush terribly: "What ten rubles? This can't be! Oh, yes, indeed, four years ago! *Mais comment, comment* could this happen!" And this debt would weigh upon him even more heavily than some ten-thousand-ruble debt he left on earth! He would feel awfully ashamed: "Oh, believe me, this was unintentional! Believe me. I didn't even think of it; I just forgot to think!" However, only the angels would be listening to the poor general (for unfailingly he would be taken to Paradise) whereas the nurse on earth would still be deprived of the ten rubles. Sometimes the good old woman feels sorry for him: "Well, God be with him; it is a sin to cast such a thing upon his memory. He was a most precious man, a righteous master."

One more thing: were this delightful man somehow to return to earth and be incarnated in the former general—would he or would he not return the ten rubles to the nurse?

However, not all of them keep borrowing. Here is a friend, that very noble Ivan Petrovich; he asks someone to execute in his favor a bill of exchange for six thousand rubles. "I will discount it"—says he—"at my bank; I will discount it, and here, my dearest friend—take this counter bill for six thousand." What is there to think about? The bills are executed. Thereupon he frequently meets Ivan Petrovich in the club; but it stands to reason that both have forgotten about these bills of exchange, because both are, so to speak, the very flower of respectable people in our society. Suddenly, six months later, the total six thousand falls upon the general's shoulders: "You have to pay it, your excellency!" Well, it is on such occasions that they turn to fellows such as Sanftleben and instruments of indebtedness are issued with one hundred per cent interest.

Again, I ask you to believe me that in my narrative I do not venture—not even in the least—to accuse the late General Hartung: I did not know him at all, and about him personally I have heard nothing. I have merely ventured to present a light sketch of the character of one of the members of this society. However, were he to be placed in an embarrassing position, similar to that of Hartung in his relation to Sanftleben, exactly the same thing might happen to him which happened to Hartung, including suicide. This is destiny, tragedy: up to his last moment General Hartung considered himself innocent, and he left a note. . . .

"Well,"—some people might say—"here is that note! It is impossible that at such a moment a man—even a religious man, as it developed—should lie. This means that he embezzled nothing if he solemnly declared that he did not do so. Moreover, in this case, there could be no compromise, not even with his conscience: no matter how shaky and obscure was the man's reason on account of all this entanglement, still if he says: 'I did not embezzle,' he cannot fail to know whether or not he did embezzle. This is strictly a human affair. The question is simply this: Did he, or did he not steal? How could he have failed to know if he did steal?"

—All this is quite correct, but here there might have been— and surely was—the following! He wrote only about himself: "I have embezzled nothing, and I did not think of embezzling." Even so—others could have embezzled.

"Absolutely impossible,"—it will be objected. "If he permitted other people to embezzle, and knowing this, in his capacity as guardian, kept silent, this would mean that *he,* in collusion with others, *did embezzle!* General Hartung could not fail to understand that this made no difference."

To this I will answer: first, the argument: "If he knew and permitted others to embezzle, this means that he, too, embezzled" may be contradicted; secondly, here, unquestionably, there is a difference. And, third, General Hartung could have written the note merely in this literal sense about which we speak, *i.e.,* "Personally I did not steal, *and did not want* to steal anything; others did it against my will. I am guilty only of weakness, but not of embezzlement, because I did not want to steal anything from anybody, and I even resisted it. Others did it." . . . He could have written his fatal words precisely in this sense. However, being honest and noble, he would never have conceded that "If I permitted others to steal, *ergo* I stole myself." He was departing to God, and he knew that he wanted neither to steal nor permit others to steal, but it just so happened that property had been stolen.

Besides, please observe: under no circumstance could he have more clearly explained these words in his note, *i.e.*, "I am guilty of indulgence, and not of embezzlement," etc. Indeed, he, a gentleman, could not have denounced others, particularly in so solemn a moment when he "forgave his enemies."

Finally,—and this is the most plausible explanation—perhaps, even to his own heart he could not confess his indulgence, his weakness, good-natured connivance. Perhaps here there was a net of circumstances which, to the very last moment, he was unable to comprehend, thus he departed to the world beyond. "The bills of exchange ledger disappeared." And now level-headed people, whom he implicitly trusts, convince him, from the very start, that this is a mere trifle, that it disappeared somehow of its own accord, because no one needed it anyway. They prove to him by figures, mathematically, that the ledger would be detrimental, and in no sense useful, to the interests of the heirs themselves. (In fact, this very argument was subsequently set forth at the trial by the defense, and it seems that it was correct.)

All the rest could have been shown and explained to Hartung in the same sense. For he was not familiar with business matters and he could be persuaded by everything they may have told him: "Believe us, we, too, are noble people. Just like you, we don't want to steal anything from the heirs; yet Sanftleben left his affairs in such a ticklish state that should they (the heirs) find out about the bills of exchange ledger and other things, they might directly accuse us of swindling, and, therefore, this should be concealed from them."

Naturally, these "irregularities" of Sanftleben came to light not at once but gradually, so that Hartung learned the truth, or, to put it more accurately—lost the truth and was drawn into deceit, gradually, day by day. Suddenly, one of the heirs rushes into Hartung's apartment, and virtually shouts that Hartung is a thief. This heir walked in triumphantly, with a victorious and wicked smile, fully convinced that now he dared to perpetrate any nastiness in the General's apartment. It was only then that the General fully discovered in what a hole he was. Thereupon he became quite disorientated: he began to suggest compromises, settlements, and, of course, got himself still more entangled, whereas the accusing side avidly seized upon new facts which discredited him in connection with those compromises and settlements. All these became part of the case.

Briefly, Hartung died convinced of his complete innocence. Even so, strictly speaking, there was no error . . . no judicial error. This was destiny; a tragedy occurred: blind force, for some reason, chose to punish Hartung alone for the *vices* which are so common in his circle. There are, perhaps, ten thousand men such as he, but Hartung alone perished. This innocent and scrupulously honest man, with his tragic denouement, of all these ten thousand people, was able to arouse the maximum of sympathy, while his trial got the maximum of publicity throughout Russia and came as a warning to "the vicious." But it is doubtful if fate, that blind goddess, counted on this when she smote him.

3

DECEIT IS NECESSARY TO TRUTH. DECEIT MULTIPLIED BY
DECEIT PRODUCES TRUTH. IS THIS SO?

And yet I wish to share with my readers a former impression which resurrected itself in my mind, even though it is, perhaps, very naïve. This is something about our courts in general. A public jury trial is regarded throughout the world virtually as an achieved perfection. "This is, so to speak, a victory, the loftiest fruit of reason." I believe in this, together with the others, since you might be told: "Well, invent something better!"—and you would be unable to do so. Consequently, one has to agree for this sole reason that nothing better can be invented.

Meanwhile, the prosecutor mounts the stage . . . I mean the platform. Let us suppose that he is an excellent and clever man, conscientious, educated, with Christian convictions, one who knows Russia and the Russian as only few people in Russia do. Well, this highly conscientious man begins directly with the statement that he is "even glad that this crime has been committed, because, at last, that villain will be punished, that defendant yonder; because if you only knew, gentlemen of the jury, what a rascal he is!" That is, he is not going to mention the word "rascal," but this makes no difference: in a polite, mild and most humane manner, at length, he will make him appear worse than any conceivable rascal. With sorrow in his heart, in most delicate terms, he states that the defendant's mother was of the same kind; that, finally, he could not fail to steal because basest debauchery drew him ever so strongly into the abyss. He perpetrated everything consciously and in a most premeditated manner. Please recall how well the fire in a

neighboring street served him at the moment of the commission
of the crime, because the fire, by causing alarm, diverted the attention of the house-porters and of everybody in the neighborhood.
"Oh, of course, I am far from *directly* accusing him of arson! But,
gentlemen of the jury, you must admit that here the strange coincidence of two circumstances inevitably suggests a certain thought.
. . . Well, I'll keep silent, mute. . . . But you will, it stands to
reason that you will, send away this thief and murderer (because
he would have unfailingly murdered had he encountered someone
in the apartment!) and, finally,—this incendiary, this arrant, proved
incendiary,—send him as far as possible, and thereby enable decent
people to breathe freely, the housewives to leave their apartments
peacefully, to buy food, and the landlords—not to tremble for their
property even if it be insured by this or that insurance company.
However, the main point is that I am dwelling in vain on all these
things: Look at him! He sits there and does not dare to look straight
into the eyes of honest people! And isn't one glance at him sufficient
to convince you that he is a thief, a murderer and an incendiary!
I solemnly regret but one thing: that he did not manage to commit
ten times more such thefts of laundry, to murder ten such housewives and to set afire ten such houses, because then the very immensity of the crime would shake our civically sleepy society and
would, finally, compel it to resort to self-defense and awake from
its criminal civic slumber." . . .

Oh, we know that the prosecutor will speak in a far nobler
style. Our words are but a caricature fit for some Sunday comic
sheet with parodies and couplets.—I admit that. Let us even suppose that this is one of those cases which raise grave social and
civic questions, and what is more important—that it is fraught with
psychological motives, and it is known that even in all Europe
prosecutors are extraordinarily eager about psychology. Well, even
so, the deduction would be identical, *i.e.*, that it is to be regretted
that instead of one poisoning, there had not been ten, thirty, five
hundred poisonings, because then your hearts would quiver and you
would arise, as one man, etc.

But it may be objected that there is nothing in this. True,
quite a few prosecutors are not orators at all, but, in the first place,
a prosecutor is a functionary who has to act in compliance with
the duties of his office, and, secondly, prosecutors are always exaggerating accusations, and in this there is nothing prejudicial, but
on the contrary—all this is useful. Precisely thus it should be. And
in opposition to the prosecutor the defendant has a defense counsel
who is given the full right to refute the former. Moreover, even in
all Europe it is permitted to prove—of course, with the utmost

politeness—that the prosecutor is stupid, nonsensical, somewhat mean, and that "if anyone set two houses on fire in one day on the Third Line on Vasilevsky Island, it was precisely this particular prosecutor because at that very time he attended on the Vasilevsky Island a Saint's day party at the house of General Mikhailov, a most admirable and noble creature. And that it was he who set the house afire there can be no doubt for the sole reason (again, psychology!) that had he not set this house afire, prompted by rancor against the landlord merchant Ivan Borodaty, such a stupid, nonsensical and trivial accusation of the defendant of arson for the purpose of diverting the attention of all the inhabitants in that street and committing this imaginary and nonsensical crime never would have occurred to him. The prosecutor's own arson precisely suggested to him the thought of accusing the defendant of it."

Finally, take into account that the defense lawyer is permitted to make gestures, shed tears, gnash his teeth, pull his hair, rap the chairs (but not to pretend to hit anyone with them), and finally to faint, if he is altogether too noble and cannot endure injustice. However, this is not permitted to the prosecutor, no matter how noble he may be, because it would seem somewhat strange that a functionary in uniform should faint and fall on his back. This is never practiced.

Again, everything I am saying is a caricature, nothing but a caricature, and none of these things ever takes place. Everything is carried out in a most respectable fashion, I concede (even though chairs used to be rapped and lawyers, at times, did faint!). But I am merely concerned with the essence of the matter since the same point may be reached by the most dignified parlance, as well as by the least dignified.

"What do you mean?"—I may be asked.—"This is exactly what is needed: exactly exaggeration is needed—on both sides! Sometimes the juror is not a very educated man; besides, he is busy, —he has his shop, his business; sometimes he is absent-minded, and sometimes he is simply unable to concentrate. For this reason he must be helped to concentrate; he must be shown all the phases of the case, even the most impossible ones, so that he may be absolutely sure that the prosecution has exhausted every possibility that can be imagined, and there is nothing more to think about it; also, that the defense has set forth everything conceivable and inconceivable for whitewashing the defendant and making him look whiter than snow on a mountain. Then yonder, in that special room of theirs, they will know, mechanically so to speak, exactly what must spring out, a plus or a minus, so that at least their conscience may be quite calm. To sum up—it is clear that all this is necessary in order that truth may be arrived at, *i.e.,* vehement attacks and vehement defense; even more—a vehement attack on the part of the prosecutor—speaking in the strictest sense—is even more beneficial to the defendant than to the prosecutor, so that, again, nothing better can be invented."

In a word, the modern court not only constitutes a victory, or the loftiest fruit of the mind, but is also a most tricky thing. One has to concede this. Besides, it is a public court: the public gathers there by the hundreds. And is it possible to suppose that they crowd it from mere idleness, for the show of it?—Of course not. But whatever prompts them to attend a trial, it is necessary that they should leave the court room with a sublime, strong, edifying and wholesome impression. Meanwhile they sit there and see that, essentially, there is some deceit there.—Oh, not in the trial itself, not in the meaning of the verdict, but simply in some habits, for instance, which we have borrowed with such a felicitous lightness from Europe, and which have implanted themselves in our representatives of both defense and prosecution.

I go home, and there I think to myself: I know personally Ivan Khristoforovich, the prosecutor; he is a very clever and kind man, and yet, he lied and knew that he was lying. A case which should involve some reprimand or a two-month jail sentence he managed to stretch out to twenty years of exile to the remotest regions. Let this be necessary for the clarification of the case, nevertheless he did deliberately lie in a case involving a man's neck. How can this be reconciled, especially if he is a talented man, since *il en reste toujours quelque chose,* all the more so, if the defense is somewhat weak and is good for nothing but rapping chairs. True, here Ivan Khristoforovich's *amour-propre* was aroused—a purely human treat, to be sure—yet is it excusable in so important a case? Whither did man disappear—the sublime, humane, civilized man?

Finally, let truth emerge from all this—mechanically, so to speak, in a shrewd manner—but the public attending the trial, perhaps, will actually gather for the purpose of witnessing a show, for the contemplation of a mechanical and very shrewd device, and, listening with delight to, say, how ably the talented defense counsel lies against his conscience, they are ready to applaud him from their seats: "Why, how well the fellow lies!" But in the bulk of the public this generates cynicism and falsity which take root imperceptibly. Not truth is craved for but talent; let it only make people merry, let it amuse them! The humane sentiment grows dull, and it cannot be restored by fainting somersaults. Well, and please suppose, again, that the liar is actually a man with great talent!

I know that on my part all this is but idle lamentation. But listen: a public jury trial is not a Russian institution; it was copied from foreign patterns. Is it not possible to hope that Russian nationality, the Russian spirit, some day will smooth out the asperities, will eliminate the falsity of bad habits, and that everything will be conducted in full accord with veracity and truth?—Indeed, at present this is impossible: precisely in our day defense and prosecution display these bad habits, since the former is looking for money, and the latter—for a career. However, in some remote future the prosecutor may even be able to plead the cause of the defendant instead of accusing him, so that should the defense lawyers argue that the minute fraction of the accusation of the defendant which the prosecutor still has brought forth against him is inapplicable to him—the jurors would simply disbelieve them.

I even think that such a method would more quickly and more expeditiously tend to ascertain the truth than the former mechanical method of exaggeration, consisting of inordinateness of prosecution and bestiality of defense. Of course, I shall be told that this is absolutely impossible, and inasmuch as the same prevails in Europe, my method should not be adopted, and that *"the more mechanical —the better."*

Now, this mechanism, this mechanical method of dragging out truth to the surface, perhaps will be replaced in Russia . . . simply by truth. Artificial exaggeration will disappear on either side. Everything will be sincere and truthful, and there will be no game at the discovery of truth. On the stage there will be no show, no game, but a lesson, an exemplification—edification. True, lawyers will be paid much less. However, all the Utopias will come to pass only when we grow wings and all people are converted into angels. But then there will also be no courts. . . .

CHAPTER III

1

Roman Clericals in Russia

RECENTLY, IN an editorial article of *The Moscow Gazette* (No. 262) there appeared the following statement:

"Two days ago we called attention to some party in the interior of Russia which acts in accord with Russia's enemies and which is ready to help the Turks in their struggle against her,—a party of Anglo-Magyars which hates every manifestation of our national spirit, every act of our government in harmony with it, and which places Russian patriotism on a par with nihilism and revolution,—a party which feeds the foreign press, hostile to us, with most abominable dispatches. No sooner was our article sent to press than a telegram from our Petersburg correspondent gave the gist of a communiqué made public in *The Messenger of the Government* revealing new stratagems of this party. At the very moment when between Plevna and Orchanje our army was scoring brilliant successes, in Petersburg the intrigue spread rumors about the defeat which those same victorious troops had supposedly suffered—with a view to causing despondency among the public. The intrigue is so strenuously at work that the government has deemed it necessary to warn the public against such malicious rumors."

The very next day *The New Times* observed in this connection, though merely in passing, that *The Moscow Gazette* had slightly exaggerated the matter, and that, possibly, *The Messenger of the Government* simply referred to some chit-chat among the public which had no such significance. (I am stating the thought expressed in *The New Times* in my own words, from memory.)

It is quite possible that *The Messenger of the Government* actually referred to some "chat-chat." Even so, the supposition of *The Moscow Gazette* is well-founded. Only who are these Anglo-Magyars whom *The Moscow Gazette* mentions?—In our border regions and also in the interior we shall find our Roman Clericals. We are no longer in the month of May: today everybody knows and writes about the universal Clerical conspiracy; even our most liberal newspapers concede the fact that such a conspiracy exists. Indeed, it would have been strange if the Vatican conspiracy should have missed our Roman Clericals and should have failed to make use of them. Sedition in the rear of the Russian armies would be very useful to the Vatican, especially, at this time.

Here is another extract—now from *The New Times*, No. 587. In its section, entitled "Among Newspapers and Magazines," it quotes the opinion of *The Voice* expressed apropos of certain articles in the English *Morning Post* and in several Polish periodicals published abroad. This is the quotation:

"In the issue of October 22nd of *The Morning Post* there appeared an article—curious because of its unexpectedness—in which that Turkophile newspaper reported parleys which had supposedly begun between Russia and Germany in connection with the cession of the region adjoining the Vistula up to that river itself. It goes without saying that in the opinion of *The Morning Post* this is the result of an agreement by virtue of which Germany undertook to support 'Russia's acquisitions on the Balkan Peninsula.' The London paper further insists that the Poles in the region adjoining the

Vistula at present no longer contemplate an uprising, 'not wishing to fall into a still harsher enslavement,' that is, under Prussian domination; and that should some disturbances occur in 'Russian Poland,' these would be merely the result of 'Russo-Prussian intrigues.' . . . It is noteworthy that several days prior to the appearance of this article in *The Morning Post*, the *Dziennik Polski* spoke on the same subject, although in a somewhat different tone, alleging that the Russian government, when evacuating its troops from the Vistula region, disseminated there an appeal to the peasants urging them to organize a rural police guard from among their own midst for the surveillance of the landowners and the suppression of any attempt at rebellion. *The Voice*, reporting the contents of these articles, wondered why the *Dziennik Polski* and *The Morning Post* had suddenly become so zealous. Why was it necessary for them to allude to the nonsensical fable about the Russian appeal to the Vistula peasants and the Russo-Prussian *agents-provocateurs* supposedly seeking to incite 'an artificial uprising' in Poland?

"These unexpected sallies must have some definite object. The papers which have published them probably possess information which makes them fear an outbreak of disturbances in the Vistula region, and they seek to distort in advance the meaning of a movement the consequences of which are, apparently, disturbing to them. These tactics are not new. They were resorted to in 1863 by the Poles and their Western friends. This reminiscence itself leads one to admit that the articles in the *Dziennik Polski* and in *The Morning Post* are not devoid of significance, and that they have some mysterious connection with the earlier rumors in the Magyar press about the Poles' sympathy for the Turks, and their clandestine desire to complicate Russia's situation by revolutionary agitation on our Western border. It is noteworthy that these articles coincide with the report about the candidacy of Cardinal Ledohowski for the papal throne. . . ." "We"—says *The Voice*—"do not belong to those who are eager to attach exaggerated importance to all fantastic combinations which are seized upon by Russia's ill-wishers in the hope of impeding the favorable outcome of the present war. However, in this particular case the matter seems to us so serious that it is impossible to leave it without notice, meaning the unexpected, and apparently wholly uncalled for, appearance of the articles in the *Dziennik Polski* and in *The Morning Post*."

Thus, there is also in Russia something resembling the ramifications of a Clerical conspiracy. The report itself about Ledohowski's candidacy is unquestionably derived from a Polish source, since only the giddy head of a Polish propagandist abroad can seriously believe that the Roman Conclave, permeated with such refined intellects, could commit the blunder of electing Ledohowski: the new Pope would be doing nothing but restoring his fatherland instead of restoring the Roman universal power of the Popes.

However, let us leave this aside, and state that nevertheless the ramifications of the Clerical conspiracy in Russia are clearly visible. Besides, *The New Times* adds:

"The present-day persistent polemics of the *Journal de St. Petersbourg* against the Italian Clerical newspapers seem to indicate that there are signs of some agitation in our Western border region."

Well, by no means only "signs." Thus it is precisely that *party* which, according to *The Moscow Gazette*, "acts in accord with the enemies of Russia . . ., which hates every manifestation of our national spirit, *every act of our government in harmony with it,* and which places Russian patriotism on a par with nihilism and revolution—a party whch feeds the foreign press with the most abominable dispatches hostile to us. . . ."

Indeed, it is very possible that European dispatches from Russia are the work of this party. This rejoicing over Russian reverses and the giddy screams of delight over the alleged information that "Russia has proved weak, devoid of financial resources, with a demoralized army, with a discontented and repining people, with nihilism which has undermined society,"—all these fairy tales unmistakably bear the stamp of a well-known origin.

Oh, it stands to reason that Russian pens will also be found which are ready to write in unison with the Clericals; however, it seems that these dispatches abroad could not have been written by Russians: this would have been too mean. Nevertheless, it is possible that the Clericals without even overstraining themselves, are guiding Russian pens in Russia. Perhaps, they are not prompting them, and they do not enter into *direct* communications with them, because these bold liberal pens *sometimes* belong to most honest men who, if they had received a direct offer from a Clerical, would propel him down the staircase.

However, a Clerical, especially one who has lived long in Russia, knows perfectly well that he doesn't even have to call on the bold pen, because the bold pen will write everything gratis solely because he imagines (oh, you dear ones!) that this is honest and liberal. For instance, the bold pen is indignant at the Clericals who remain close to MacMahon in France, and he writes threatening articles against them. But at the same time, not only will he fail to notice a Russian Roman Clerical, but, at times, he will start singing in full unison with him. Such fellows exist,—they exist. And, maybe, our sly Roman Clericals even wonder at them: "What an inclination on their part to fall down this way between two

chairs!"—they ponder, nodding their heads. "And how disinterestedly! True, they must be liberal to the end. Why, they even
vociferate that Russia has no right to liberate the Slavs! Why, a
hundred thousand rubles would be too low a compensation to them!
And all this—between two chairs, every minute so! Why don't they
get hurt! Or does it heal up very quickly—in their case? . . ."

2

A SUMMER ATTEMPT ON THE PART OF OLD POLAND AT
RECONCILIATION

Early in the summer these Clerical agitators attempted to stage
their demonstration even through Russian periodicals. Wolves disguised themselves in sheep's clothing, and began to talk in a tone
of would-be ambassadors of the entire Polish "emigration" abroad.
They began to offer peace: "Accept us!"—they said.—"We also perceive that Slavic brotherhood is unquestionable, and we do not
wish to stay behind." They spoke with extreme tenderness and set
forth the following reasons:

"We have"—they said—"engineers, chemists, technologists, artisans, bookkeepers, agronomists, etc. Of these there are many in
the emigration. Let them in!"

In an article in issue No. 172 of *The St. Petersburg Gazette*
a resident of Lithuania asked: "Isn't work available in your midst
to that stratum which in days past gave a Tengoborski to Russia,
and a Wolowski—to France? And in the field of art, which tends
to make manners less crude and to ennoble character, Brotzki, the
sculptor and Matejko, the painter, are universally recognized as
representative of Polish society. Don't you need these men? And
what do you say about a whole mass of littérateurs, publicists, industrialists, manufacturers, and all kinds of workers? Do you also
have no need for them?" (*The New Times*, quoted from Kostomarov's article.)

Mr. Kostomarov, in *The New Times*, admirably answered all
these ingratiations. I regret that space does not permit me to print
excerpts from this excellent article. By clear and precise arguments
Mr. Kostomarov proved that all this was a mere trap set for us;
that they would send to Russia traitors, such as Conrad Wallenrod;
that the Pole, the native of Old Poland, instinctively, blindly, hates
Russia and the Russians. Mr. Kostomarov admits, however, that
there are excellent Poles who may even live on friendly terms with
this or that Russian, saving him from some calamity and helping
him financially. This is, of course, true; but let this Russian—even

after twenty years of friendship—express to that excellent Pole his political convictions concerning Poland in the Russan spirit,—that Pole would at once become an open or secret enemy of his Russian friend—for all his life, to the end—an irreconcilable, boundless enemy. This Mr. Kostomarov forgot to add.

This whole summer attempt at "reconciliation," which had its Russian advocates and so mighty an opponent as Mr. Kostomarov, was unquestionably a Clerical reconnaissance from Europe, a ramification of the all-European Clerical conspiracy. Oh, these Poles, natives of Old Poland, insist that they are in no sense Clericals, papists, Romans, and that we should have learned this about them long ago. But to imagine that "Old Poland," that Polish emigration, does not adhere to the Pope in a Jesuitical spirit, that it is far removed from Clerical fantasies—what a funny thought! Aren't they the ones who should adhere to the Vatican,—they who are—and always have been—fully cognizant of its strength?—Nay, they will not betray the Vatican, nor will the Vatican betray them.

The summer sally in connection with reconciliation was performed at a time when the entire emigration started moving against the Russians; when Polish legions were being recruited; when the aristocrats of the emigration went to Constantinople with enormous sums of money (of course, not their own!). All this reconciliation was nothing but cunning, as Mr. Kostomarov defined it.

By the way: they are offering us their scientists, technicians and artists, and they say: "Accept them. Don't you need them?" At this point it may be added that probably they consider us a savage people, but they are ignorant of the fact that we possess everything they are offering, and that ours is, perhaps, of a higher quality. But there is no ground for offense. The main point is: why don't they come? We did have several Poles who revealed their talents, and Russia esteemed and respected them, held them in high repute, in no way segregating them from the Russians. What is the purpose of these stipulations! Come!—Reconcile yourselves and submit, but know that there never will be an Old Poland. There is a New Poland, a Poland liberated by the Czar, a regenerated Poland, which unquestionably may expect in the future a lot equal with that of any Slavic tribe, when Slavdom is liberated and resurrected in Europe. However, there never will be an Old Poland, because she could not live in peace with Russia. It is her ideal to occupy Russia's place in the Slavic world. Her motto as applied to Russia is: *"Ôte-toi de là, que je m'y mette."*

It is noteworthy that the Polish advance skirmisher speaks only about scientists and artists. Well, what about the leaders of the emigration, the aristocrats?—Imagine only that Russia might yield to the flattering words and announce that she wants reconciliation. Then they would haughtily ask us: "What are your terms?" —Because if you suggest that we admit the emigrants to Russia, while they do not come here of their own accord,—*this means that they are awaiting terms*. And now imagine that suddenly Russia might recognize them as "something," as a belligerent party, and might start negotiations! Presently they would drift into Russia: the magnates at once would begin to find fault, demanding high positions and distinctions. Thereupon they would start shouting, so that all Europe could hear them, that they were deceived; and then they would instigate a Polish rebellion. . . . Would Russia be drawn into such a calamity! Would she make such a mistake!

Of course, the Poles themselves could not have believed that such a crude attempt would deceive Russia. Yet they did count upon the pure-in-heart Russian partisans. That this was a Clerical scheme, a Clerical move in the direction of Russia—there can be no doubt. The question may be asked: What was the object of that move?—Well, don't the Clericals need to reconnoitre the situation, to confuse the thoughts, to conceal their real designs, to acquire Russian pens, to agitate Russian Poland, etc. . . . ? Why, who can tell what other plans they may have had!

3

The Sally of "The Stock-Exchange Gazette." Not Bold but Wicked Pens

We were just speaking about "bold pens." But we have pens which are not bold but disgusting. They also whistle (and how they whistle!) in unison with the Polish nightingales, but the Poles do not even direct them. All this they do disinterestedly, knowing not what they do. Here we have malice pure and simple, betrayed hopes and piqued *amour-propre*. Such is the article in *The Stock-Exchange Gazette* (No. 257) about Mr. Ilovaisky. At least, they should have learned to write; instead, they make themselves ridiculous.

It is a matter of common knowledge that our scientist Mr. Ilovaisky was arrested and mistreated in Galicia. Passing through Galicia on a scientific mission, he applied, by mistake, to a Polish priest with the request to be shown certain local antiquities. Subsequently he found a Russian priest, but the malicious Polish priest promptly denounced him under the pretext that Mr. Ilovaisky was a Russian Panslavist, propagandist and agitator. Very unceremoniously he was arrested, searched, dragged from one prison to another, and finally, thanks to the intercession of a local scientist, he was deported to the Russian border.

This affair promptly became known in Russia: *The Moscow Gazette* printed an article concerning it. Our newspapers noted it, but without any ardor, merely as a curious incident. The fact that a Russian scientist, for no reason whatsoever, had been maltreated, appeared to everybody to be a very ordinary event. Mr. Ilovaisky himself printed in *The Moscow Gazette* a few lines in answer to the hostile press—meek, apathetic, somniferous lines. As against this, our stock-exchange gamblers—who view Russia only from the standpoint of their own pockets and to whom Russia is of no concern—rendered her a remarkable service. Here is the article which appeared in *The Stock-Exchange Gazette:*

". . . What queer thing did Mr. Ilovaisky embark upon in Galicia? What kind of propaganda did he start there? Is it possible that the misfortunes through which Russia is living at present are insufficient to chase folly out of the heads of our inveterate Panslavists? And can it be that after what has been happening now in full view of everybody, they still have the impudence to persist in their fanaticism and buffoonery with all this Panslavic fiddle-faddle, which paves the way for innumerable state calamities and with which we all have been satiated long ago? So long as our Panslavists, who have grown dull from indolence, confined themselves to the *export of Panslavic church bells,* this was nobody's business, and they could amuse themselves to their hearts' content. However, when they begin to export, together with those bells, their sacristans to ring them for church, the matter acquires a different meaning. Who had summoned, who had authorized, Mr. Ilovaisky to engage in his Panslavic propaganda? Does he, or does he not, understand what consequences it might entail, particularly now, at this moment? Gentlemen, you are showering invectives against Klapka on the ground that he is inciting the Magyars to help the Turks. But what are you doing yourselves? What is Mr. Ilovaisky doing under the guise of studying Slavic antiquities? Aren't you satisfied with the evil which your fanaticism of last year has brought about? What new mess are you trying to cook up? We know well that you are fully capable of throwing a stone into water. But you must remember that the stones which you throw, at times, have to be pulled out by the efforts of a whole nation, at the price of bloody sacrifices and national exhaustion. Then stop playing the fool: everything has its season. If up to the present you have aroused in all reasonable people nothing but ridicule, now you can expect only indignation."

These people speak about indignation! Listen, *how did you dare,* without knowing about the affair, to write so positively to all

Russia, to all Europe (since your article in Europe acquired a significance *of its own*),—how dared you to write about Mr. Ilovaisky: "who had summoned, who had authorized Mr. Ilovaisky to engage in his Panslavic propaganda?" And thereupon, after the ridiculous comparison of Mr. Ilovaisky with Klapka: "but what are you doing yourselves? What is Mr. Ilovaisky doing *under the guise of studying Slavic antiquities?*" How did you dare to write about this so *positively* when you knew *positively* that it was a lie? Do you really imagine that you will be permitted to betray Russia? Referring to Mr. Ilovaisky, you ask: "Does he, or does he not know?" But I will ask you, Mr. Publicist: Do you, or do you not, understand what you did?—Since in Austria they will not ask: What kind of man wrote this?—a clever or a stupid man? educated or uneducated? does he have any idea about Panslavism or does he know nothing? has he read anything about it? Indeed, in Austria it will be positively said: "So it is true that Russia is sending out agitators. If this were not true, how could a big, independent Petersburg daily newspaper so *positively* and so reproachfully have addressed the Panslavists, specifically corroborating the fact of the dispatch of emissaries for propaganda? Indeed, the man who wrote it is a Russian himself,"—they will say. "In the long run, patriotism would have stopped him and prompted him to conceal the crime. But in this instance he was unable to conceal the truth because the indignation of a patriot poured out against the Panslavists, who are thus actually plotting dreadful calamities for Russia by their reckless propaganda and agitation in Austria and the Slavic countries. In this situation, we don't have to apologize for the arrest of some fellow by the name of Ilovaisky; on the contrary, we have to make more arrests, keep all Russians in Austria under strict police surveillance. We should not send our apologies, but the Russian government must apologize to us for so openly permitting at home the work of noxious political societies directed against Austria, and continuously dispatching large numbers of agitators to incite the Austrian Slavs against their lawful government."

Unquestionably, this will be said in Austria, and no doubt, your article, Mr. Publicist, will be commented on precisely in this spirit. Don't you think that this is treason? Don't you betray Russia's interests to the Poles and the Austrians? Don't you give support to political sedition and don't you serve it?—For you know *certainly, fully, precisely* that no one has ever dispatched any emissaries whatever. How, then, did you dare to write that Mr. Ilovaisky went to foster sedition *"under the guise of studying Slavic antiquities"?* Is there anyone in Russia who would believe you? Moreover, your statements concerning this affair are as positive as if you knew it quite as well as your five fingers. Who, then, is sowing sedition?

Now, let us turn to another point. Having quenched your anger, having written an arrant lie, having so flagrantly betrayed the Russian interests to the Old Poles, the Austrians and every kind of European rabble which unceasingly and perpetually agitates against us, do you venture to hope that Russian readers will sympathize with you? Is it possible that you have so low an opinion of them?

And what a tone! What trepidation, what humiliation before Austria! "She may grow angry!"—so to speak. In Gogol an ataman says to the Cossacks: "The favors of a foreign king—not even a king, but the favors of a Polish magnate who kicks their faces with his yellow boot are dearer to them than any brotherhood." The ataman says this about traitors. Is it possible that you wish that the Russians, too, trembling in animal fear for their interests and money, should likewise bow before some yellow boot? Precisely now, at this moment, wouldn't, on the contrary, our best policy toward Austria be a policy of highest social and national dignity, and not the one you are advocating?—For the more humiliation—which you advocate—we manifest, the more, and in equal measure, we should strengthen and reinforce her demands. Besides, why should we fear Austria?—Never would she be in a position to draw her sword against us, even if such were her desire.

On the contrary, precisely now the time has come for a straight-forward and frank policy so as to avoid sad misunderstandings when the war comes to an end. We don't have to give promissory notes. In the same way we must look upon England. The English should, at least, understand that we have no reason to fear them, and that, contrariwise, we are in a position to cause them more harm than they can cause us. This they must know. Meanwhile they have some wrong information about us which is supported precisely by such sallies as we see in *The Stock-Exchange Gazette*.

Last summer was it not in Austria that people were made to believe that Russia's strength was a mirage which had deceived everybody, and that henceforth Russia could no longer be regarded as a strong military power? It was precisely then that Austria's tone became arrogant. Was it not England's opinion—also in her upper circles—that 10,000 English troops landed at Trebizond would once and forever settle our whole *problem* in the East and in the Caucasus? Certainly, we know them, but they, it appears, do not know us. But it is poor service to Russia to betray her interests to her enemies, and to picture her in a cowardly and humiliated guise, whereas this is not in the least true, and the whole thing is a lie.

NOVEMBER

CHAPTER I

1

What Does the Word "Strutzky"[1] Mean?

IN THE course of the two-year publication of my *Diary* I have used twice or three times the little known word "strutzky," and I received from Moscow and the provincial districts several inquiries what this word meant. I apologize for not having as yet answered this question: all the time I have meant to answer it, even though between the lines, in the *Diary.* Now, bringing its publication to a close, I shall devote a few lines to this incomprehensible Petersburg word, and if I begin the first page of the November issue with this trifle it is specifically because when I postpone the subject to the last page, as I used to do before, because of other topics, I never found space for the "strutzkys" and every time I had to postpone the explanation to the next issue.

The word "strutzky" is a plebeian word, one used exclusively by the common people, and it seems, only in Petersburg. I believe it was also coined in Petersburg. I say: *"it seems"* because, much as I have inquired of "competent" people, I have never been able to ascertain whence it came; what its phonetic origin is; if it is being used anywhere in Russia, except in Petersburg, and finally, if it was actually invented there. As for myself, again "it seems" to me (I cannot express myself more positively) that this is a purely Petersburg word coined by the common people, but by whom, when, how long ago—I don't know. On the basis of repeated inquiries, and as far as I understand, I may state that its meaning is as follows:

A "strutzky" is a vain, trashy man, a nullity. In most cases, perhaps, invariably, he is a drunkard, who dissipates his fortune in drinking, a lost fellow. However, it seems that in some cases even a man who is not a drunkard may be called a "strutzky." But the principal characteristics of this worthless and good-for-nothing drunkard, which have earned him a special name and as much as the invention of a new word, are: first, silliness, absurdity *sui*

[1] The Russian word "strutzky" is untranslatable; it is a derogatory, slangy word which broadly means "rabble." Sometimes it is used to denote the inferior social status of the civilians compared with that of the privileged military caste, in the sense the German junkers used to say with contempt, "Das ganze 'Civil' ist eine niedridge Rasse." (B. B.)

generis, brainlessness, economic worthlessness; clamorous nullity.
On a holiday, in the evening, drunken people are bawling; one can
hear them quarrelling. Then there sounds a violent outcry to summon the police. In the crowd, piled up in a heap, one hears distinctly
a protesting, appealing, complaining and threatening voice. There
is much pretended wrath. You approach the crowd, you inquire:
"What's the matter?"—In answer people laugh, wave their hands,
and walk away: "Oh, nothing—strutzkys!" In this connection the
word "strutzkys" is pronounced with disdain, with contempt—always with contempt. Should the shouting man even be beaten or
affronted,—even in this case, it seems, he would get no sympathy
for the sole reason that he is a "strutzky," *i.e.*, everything in him
is rubbish: the fact that he is shouting is trash; that he was beaten
—is trash—"the most worthless man" that can be imagined.

I may add that the "strutzkys" are usually shabbily dressed,
in clothes which are out of season, and they wear torn shoes. Furthermore "it seems" that only those who wear European clothes are
called "strutzkys." However, I would not swear to this, but it
seems that this is so.

The second essential characteristic of the dissipated drunkard,
called a "strutzky," aside from foolishness and worthlessness, is his
uncertain position in society. I believe that a man who owns money,
a house, property of some kind, also one who has even a somewhat
steady and fixed job, say, that of a factory worker, could not be
called a "strutzky." However, even if he has some business of his
own, say, a small shop, or the like, if somehow he conducts his
affairs unsoundly, without keeping accounts, he may be promoted
to the rank of a "strutzky."

Thus, a "strutzky" is a good-for-nothing fellow, who is unable
to live on good terms anywhere, to settle down; he is a worthless
and ignorant man; when drunk, he often acts insolently; he is loud-
mouthed; he is frequently affronted, mostly because he likes to feel
offended; he is one who calls the police, the authorities; he is the
one who cries: "help! help!" And all these things combined: trash,
nonsense, triviality, evoking contemptuous laughter: "Eh, that's
nothing—'strutzky'!"

I repeat, it seems to me that this is exclusively a Petersburg
word. Whether it is used in other parts of Russia, I don't know.
It is very much in use among the common people in Petersburg
where there are a great many migratory elements from the provincial
districts. For this reason it is quite probable that the term might
pass over to other provinces, if it hasn't already done so. Maybe
it will be accepted in literature: I believe that, aside from myself,
other writers also have employed it. To a littérateur, the attraction

in this word lies in the nuance of contempt with which the people
specifically use it only of the trashy, empty-headed, vociferating,
worthless, vile little fellows blustering in their despicable wrath.
Indeed, also among the educated strata there are many fellows of
this kind—aren't there? Not necessarily drunkards and not in torn
shoes, but therein is the only difference. How can one refrain from
calling these superior ones—"strutzkys," especially as the word is
ready-made and is tempting because of the nuance of contempt
with which the people pronounce it.

2

The History of the Verb "Stushevatsia"[1]

By the way, speaking of the origin and employment of new
words. In our literature there is in general use a word "stushevatsia,"
which, though it was not born yesterday, is of rather recent origin,
and which has existed not more than three decades: at the time
of Pushkin it was utterly unknown and was not used by anyone.
At present, however, it may be found not only among littérateurs,
belles-lettrists of every kind, from the most humorous to the most
serious, but also in scientific treatises, dissertations and philosophical
books. Moreover, it may be encountered in official departmental
documents, reports, accounts and even in ordinances: it is known
to everybody; everybody understands it and uses it. Even so, in
all Russia there is only one man who knows the precise origin of
this word, the time when it was invented and when it appeared in
literature. This man is myself, because it was I who, for the first
time, used this word in literature. For the first time it appeared in
print on January 1, 1846, in *The Domestic Records,* in my novel
The Double: Adventures of Mr. Goliadkin.

I began my first novel, *Poor Folks,* in 1844; it was finished;
it became known to Bielinsky, and was accepted by Nekrasov for
his almanac *Petersburg Collection* for the year 1845, which was
published in the latter part of that year. However, in that same
year, in the summer, after I had made my acquaintance with Bielinsky, I started working on my second novel, *The Double: Adventures
of Mr. Goliadkin.* Ever since the early autumn of 1845, Bielinsky
had shown a lively interest in this new work of mine. Even before
he had read it, he spoke about it to Andrei Alexandrovich Kraievsky,
for whose magazine he was then working, and to whom he also
introduced me. It was agreed between Kraievsky and myself that I

[1]The Russian word "stushevatsia" means to disappear, to vanish, to be
blotted out, to efface oneself. (B. B.)

should give him my new novel *The Double* for *The Domestic Records*: it was to appear in the first months of 1846.

Most decidedly, I did not succeed with that novel; however, its idea was rather lucid, and I have never expressed in my writings anything more serious. Still, as far as form was concerned, I failed utterly. Fifteen years later, I made considerable improvements in it for the then "Complete Collection" of my works; however, also at that time I came again to the conclusion that in this work I had not succeeded at all, and were I now to expound and express this idea, I should adopt an altogether different form. But in 1846, I failed to find it, and was unable to master the novel.

Even so, I believe, early in December, 1845, Bielinsky persuaded me to read at his house at least two or three chapters of that novel. For this purpose he even arranged a soirée—a thing he never did—to which he invited his intimates. I remember that Ivan Sergeevich Turgenev listened to one-half of what I read, praised it and left—he was very much in a hurry. The three or four chapters which I read greatly pleased Bielinsky (even though they were not worth it). However, he did not know the end of the novel, and was still under the spell of *Poor Folks*. It was precisely at that reading that I employed for the first time the word "stushevatsia," which became so popular. The novel was forgotten—this it deserved—but the new word was picked up, it was memorized and admitted in literature.

The word "stushevatsia"—"to disappear," "to vanish," "to reduce one's self," so to speak, "to naught," but to vanish not all of a sudden, not by crashing into an abyss with thunder and lightning, but, as it were, delicately, fluently, imperceptibly sinking into nullity. This resembles a vanishing shade on a strip of a drawing washed with Indian ink—from black gradually to lighter and lighter shades, and finally, to absolute white, "to *naught*." Probably, in *The Double* I employed this word pointedly in those first three chapters which I read at Bielinsky's soirée; there it referred to a sly and annoying little fellow who managed very appropriately to vanish from the stage (or something like that—I forget). I say this because the new word aroused no perplexity in the listeners. On the contrary, it was at once understood and noted. Bielinsky interrupted me precisely in order to commend that expression. All others among the audience (they all are still alive) likewise praised it. I distinctly remember that Ivan Sergeevich Turgenev also made a favorable comment on that word. Andrei Alexandrovich Kraievsky, for his part, subsequently lauded it very warmly. Aside from these men, there are other persons who will probably recall that, at the time, the new word aroused their interest—at least a little. However, it took root and penetrated literature not at once but very gradually and imperceptibly.

I remember that in 1854, after I was discharged from prison in Siberia, I began to peruse all the literary works which had appeared during the five years of my absence. (I read at one sitting and derived an enchanting impression from *The Sportsman's Sketches* —which had barely begun to appear in my young days—and Turgenev's early novels. True, then the sun of the steppes shone above me; it was early spring, and with it an altogether new life was coming into being—the end of forced labor, liberty!) Thus, having started reading, I was even surprised to find how frequently I began to encounter the word "stushevatsia." Later, in the Sixties, it had become an altogether familiar word in literature, while at present, I repeat, I even encounter it in official documents published in the newspapers, and also in scientific dissertations. And it is used precisely in that sense in which I employed it for the first time.

However, if I employed it for the first time in literature, nevertheless I did not coin it. This word was invented by my classmates in the Chief Engineering School. Maybe I also participated in its invention—I don't remember. Somehow it invented itself, of its own accord, and it came into usage.

In all six classes of the School we were required to draw plans for different fortifications and military architecture. The ability to sketch free-hand was strictly insisted upon and required of each one of us, so that those who had no predilection for drawing willy-nilly were compelled to endeavor *quand-même* to attain a certain skill in this field. Marks received for drawing plans were included in the sum total of one's marks, and thus affected the average mark. One could graduate from the senior officers' class, and enlist in the service, as an excellent mathematician, fortifier or engineer, but if his drawings were somewhat defective, the mark awarded for them, forming part of the sum total, could decrease the mean mark to such an extent as to deprive one, at the time of his graduation, of very substantial privileges, for example, of the next rank. For this reason everybody tried his best to master drawing.

All plans used to be drawn and shaded with India ink; among other things, we sought to acquire the skill of shading a given surface—coloring it—so that the shades gradually passed from darker hues to lighter ones, and finally,—to colorless white, to naught. Skillful shading conveyed to the drawing a stylish appearance.

On one occasion, suddenly in the class somebody would ask: "Where is So and So?"—"Eh, he vanished ('stushevatsia') somewhere." Or else, two classmates would be conversing, and one would say that he had to start learning his lessons, and then taking his books he would say to his mate: "Now, you just vanish, you must *'stushevatsia'!*" Again, for instance, a student of a higher grade, addressing a newly matriculated tyro, would say: "Not long ago I was calling you. Whither did you deign to vanish? ('stushevatsia')." This precisely meant "to withdraw," "to vanish," and the expression was derived from shading, from the passage from the dark hue "to naught." I distinctly recall that this word was in usage only in our class, and was hardly adopted by the other classes. It seems that when our class left the school, the word disappeared with it. Some three years later I recalled it and inserted it into my novel.

I have dealt so seriously and extensively with the history of so insignificant a word for the use of a future learned lexicographer, some future Dahl, and even if I have bored my readers, the future Dahl will thank me. So, let this be stated for him alone. However, if you please, for the sake of *clarity*, I shall fully confess: during my entire literary career what I liked *most* in this word was the fact that I have succeeded in introducing a new expression into Russian speech, and whenever I come across it in print, I always feel very much pleased. Well, now you will understand why I thought it possible to describe such a trifle in a special article.

CHAPTER II

1

Servility or Politeness?

IT IS known that all educated Russians are extremely polite, *i.e.*, whenever they deal with Europe, or if they think that Europe is looking at them, even though she is not looking at them at all. Oh, at home, among ourselves, we'll have it our own way—at home, Europeanism can be brushed aside. In passing let us refer, say, to our family relations, to our attitude—in an overwhelming majority of cases—toward civic matters, honor, duty. Well, who among our preachers of "European" ideas seriously believes in them?— Of course, only honest men, and, besides, necessarily kind-hearted men, so that they believe in them only because they are kind-hearted. But of these do we have many?

Strictly speaking, perhaps, there isn't a single European amongst us, because we are incapable of being Europeans. In Russia, progressive intellects, stock-exchange intellects and in every way leading intellects merely levy taxes on European ideas. And I believe, so it is everywhere. Naturally, I am not speaking of people with great common sense: those do not believe in European ideas, because there is nothing to believe in. In fact, nothing in the world was ever as obscure, vague, uncertain and indefinable as that *"cycle of ideas"* which we managed to accumulate in the course of the two centuries of our Europeanism; essentially, it is not a cycle, but a chaos of fragments of sentiments, of alien unintelligible ideas, inferences, habits, but particularly words, words, words—of course, most European and liberal words, but, as far as we are concerned,— nothing but words.

To explain all this by mere imitativeness is impossible. Nor can this be explained by servility of thought—by Russian ideological servility before Europe. In us there is much, even very much, servility of thought, but nevertheless the supreme cause of our European bondage is not servility but rather our innate Russian politeness toward Europe. Perhaps it may be observed that this is identical with servility. In many cases—it is, but not always. (It stands to reason that I am not speaking of the leading rogues whom I have mentioned above: these Europeans don't give a rap for Europe,—never did give a rap. As level-headed fellows, throughout these two centuries, they have been fishing in troubled waters.)

Here is, for instance, what the Englishman Gladstone says about the present Russian war with Turkey:

"Whatever may be said about some other chapters of Russian history, by liberating many millions of enslaved peoples from a cruel and humiliating yoke, Russia will render mankind one of the most brilliant services recorded in history, a service which will never be effaced from the grateful memory of the nations."

Honestly speaking, do you think that a Russian European could have pronounced these words?—Never in his life! He would have swallowed his tongue before he would have pronounced them. Out of politeness not only toward Europe but toward himself, he would blush should he read or hear this in Russian or from a Russian. "For goodness sake, how do we dare . . . to aspire to such honors! These are not meant for us! Our face is much too crooked to be venturing to 'liberate mankind'! And besides, what reactionary thoughts: 'Russia liberating the peoples!'—What an unliberal thought!"

Such is the sincere opinion of a Russian European of the pure type, and he would rather chop off his fingers than write something along Gladstone's lines. "Well, perhaps Gladstone can afford to compose such things. Besides he does not even understand anything about Russia, or he knows how to feather his nest: he composes for future plans."—This is what the European thinks. And some of those who are kinder and more ardent, on this occasion might add to themselves, not without pride: "Well, we Russian

Europeans are perhaps more liberal than European Europeans; we have gone farther than they. Who among our sober intellects would nowadays open his mouth to speak about some sort of liberation of the peoples? What a reactionary way of thinking! And Gladstone says such things without being ashamed!"

Well, gentlemen what shall we call all this?—Servility or politeness toward Europe?

I still insist that during the European period of our history politeness has played an enormous role. Indeed, among these Europeans of ours there are so many most honest, courageous people, men of honor, even though alien and adopted, perhaps unintelligible to the knight himself—since, say what you may to him, it is still European gibberish—nevertheless, honor,—men who personally will not permit anyone to tread upon their feet. Thus, how can they be directly called servile? Nay, it is politeness, and not servility, that is at the bottom of the trouble,—I repeat—politeness toward Europe. At home we will make up for any loss.

The ladies who enthusiastically treated the Turks to candies and cigars, unquestionably did so also from politeness: "See, how charmingly, tenderly, kindly, humanely, Europeanly we are enlightened!" At present these dames have learned better—partly from coarse people. However, before they had learned their lesson, say the day following the incident on the train transporting the Turks into which they were throwing bouquets and candies,—what if another train-load of Turks had arrived, and there had been aboard that bashi-bazouk who is said to be a special expert in rending nurslings asunder in a trice by seizing them by both legs, and in cutting strips out of a mother's back?—Why, I believe these good ladies would have welcomed him with enthusiastic screams, ready to give him not only candies but something even better than candies, after which, in their ladies' committee, they would, perhaps, have raised the question of endowing a scholarship bearing his name in the local high-school.

Oh, believe me, in Russia politeness may lead to anything, and mine is not in the least a fantastic supposition. Looking at themselves in a mirror, these ladies, I take it, fell in love with themselves: "What humane, what liberal dears we are!" And do you really think that this fantastic little picture could not come to pass?—That haughty glance which some Europeans now throw at our people and their movement, denying in our whole people every kind of thought or movement, "save some silly hysterical sallies of one fool out of thousands of common people,"—don't you think that such a view—the possibility itself of such a view—justifies the delineation of the above fantastic picture?

Among us politeness toward Europe is universal. Turkish war prisoners demanded white bread, and it was given them. Turkish war prisoners refused to work. Prince Meschersky, an eyewitness, relates in his *Diary* from the Caucasus:

"The prisoners departed from Tiflis. It was intended to transport them by relays of horses, but they revolted and deigned to announce that they would not go because they were not used to Russian carts. In view of this, postal coaches and carriages equipped with springs were provided for their transportation, each vehicle driven by six horses. They deigned to express their pleasure with this, and in view of the fact that an enormous number of horses had to be requisitioned for this purpose, the poor travellers along the Military Georgian road will be obliged to wait three days for horses. And an officer in the Russian service, accompanying the prisoners, is being paid 50 kopecks per diem for subsistence, and he is being seated not in a carriage but in a bus, just as servants travel. All this is humaneness!" (*The Moscow Gazette*, No. 273.)

Well, not humaneness but that very politeness in the matter of European opinion about us, sensitiveness, susceptibility: "Europe is looking at us. Therefore, we have to wear full uniform, and pashas have to be provided with carriages."

In another of its issues (No. 282) *The Moscow Gazette* further reports that in Moscow there was a real outburst of indignation when people saw the comfortable accommodations we provided for the transportation of the Turkish war prisoners:

"All captive privates were comfortably placed in third-class cars; officers—in second-class cars, while the pasha occupied a first-class compartment. Why such accommodations for them?"—could be heard in public.—"Our grenadiers were transported in horse-cars, whereas they are provided with special passenger trains."

"Why speak about grenadiers!"—says a merchant in the crowd. "Even wounded soldiers were transported in freight cars, and there was no time to lay straw under them. Look at the pasha —he's fat as a boar. He should be placed in a freight car—there he would lose a bit of his fat!"

"Over there, they have been killing our wounded, tendons were pulled out of them, they burned them on a slow fire and now they are being fondled for that! . . ."

"These are not solitary voices"—further observes *The Moscow Gazette*—"they are expressive of the general opinion of the people that it is painful to behold the comfortable accommodations provided for the bashi-bazouks and that whole Turkish rabble, robbed by their own pashas, compared with those assigned to our soldiers. . . ."

Strictly speaking, in this we find nothing particular: politeness or, so to speak, the uniform of politeness displayed before European opinion—that's all. But in Russia this has lasted two centuries—it's time we got used to this.

Speaking of anecdotes, I noted one in *The Petersburg Gazette* quoting a letter of Mr. V. Krestovsky which he wrote at the front, but I don't know to whom. Nor do I know whence *The Petersburg Gazette* borrowed it. This is the statement:

"In Mr. Krestovsky's letter a comical incident is cited: Near the retinue there appeared an Englishman wearing a cork helmet and a civilian overcoat of pea color. It is said that he is a member of Parliament who takes advantage of the recess period for writing correspondence 'from the front' for one of the large London papers (*The Times*). Others assert that he is simply an amateur, and still others—that he is a friend of Russia. Let all this be so, nevertheless it should be observed that this 'friend of Russia' behaves rather eccentrically: for instance, he sits in the presence of the Grand Duke when everybody, including His Highness, is standing; at dinner, attended by the Grand Duke, he gets up whenever he pleases, and today he even suggested to an officer, an acquaintance of his, that he might help him to pull on the sleeves of his pea overcoat. With a somewhat surprised look the officer glanced at the Englishman, measuring him from head to foot, smiled slightly, shrugged his shoulders, and without protest helped him to put on his overcoat. Of course, there was nothing else to do. In answer, the Englishman in a slight salute raised his hand to the cork helmet."

The Petersburg Gazette called this a comical incident. I regret to say that I find nothing comical in it; on the contrary, it is very vexing, and makes one's blood boil. Besides, from childhood, we have been accustomed to believe (probably, under the influence of romances and French vaudevilles) that every Englishman is a queer fellow and an eccentric. But what is a queer fellow?—He is not always a fool or so naïve that he cannot guess that not everywhere in the world are things run in the same way as somewhere at home, in his own corner. On the contrary, Englishmen are a level-headed nation with broad views. As navigators—and besides, enlightened ones—they have seen a great many people and customs in all countries of the world. They are extraordinary and gifted observers. At home they discovered humor, denoting it with a special word, and they explained it to mankind. How can such a man—besides, a member of Parliament—fail to know when he should be standing and sitting? Why, there is no country where etiquette is more rigidly observed than in England. For instance, English court etiquette is the most elaborate and refined in the world. If that Englishman is

a member of Parliament, naturally, he might have learned etiquette
from the very manner in which the lower House communicates with
the upper one, and precisely who may sit and who is obliged to
get up in the other's presence. If, in addition, he belongs to fashionable society; again, nowhere is there such etiquette as at the recep-
tions, dinners and balls of English aristocracy during their London
season.

Nay, judging by the way this anecdote has been related, here
we have something altogether different. Here is English haughtiness,
not simply haughtiness but *an arrogant challenge*. This "friend of
Russia" cannot be her great friend. He sits there, looks at Russian
officers and ponders: "Gentlemen, I know you are lion-hearted; you
undertake the impossible and carry it out. You have no fear of an
enemy; you are heroes; you are Bayards—each one of you, and the
sense of honor is fully familiar to you. Indeed, I cannot deny that
which I see with my own eyes. Nevertheless, I am an Englishman,
while you are only Russians; I am a European, and to Europe you
owe 'politeness.' No matter how lion-hearted you may be, nevertheless I am a man of a superior type. And it pleases me very much,
it pleases me particularly, to study your 'politeness' in relation to
myself, your *innate* and *irresistible* politeness, without which a Russian cannot look at a foreigner, all the more so, at a foreigner such
as myself. You think these are but mere trifles. Well, these trifles
comfort and amuse me. I went to take a trip. I heard that you were
heroes. I came to take a look at you. But nevertheless I shall go
home with the conviction that, as a son of Old England (at this
point his heart quivers with pride) I am the superior man on earth,
while you are but of second rank. . . ."

In the above account the last lines are particularly curious:
"With a somewhat surprised look, the officer glanced at the
Englishman, measuring him from head to foot, smiled slightly,
shrugged his shoulders, and without protest helped him to put on
his overcoat. *Of course, there was nothing else to do.*"

Why this "of course"? Why was there *nothing* else to do?—On
the contrary, something quite different, reverse, opposite could have
been done: it was possible "to glance at the Englishman, measuring
him from head to foot, smile slightly, shrug his shoulders,"—and
pass by, without so much as touching the overcoat.—This is what
could have been done. Could it not be noticed that the enlightened
navigator was playing a trick, that the most refined connoisseur of
etiquette was seizing upon the moment for the satisfaction of his
petty pride?—Therein is the whole point. Maybe, at that very
moment it was impossible to bethink one's self of the situation—
our enlightened "politeness" stood in the way—not toward that

member of Parliament wearing some sort of a cork helmet (what's this cork helmet?) but toward Europe, toward the obligation of European enlightenment in which we grew up, in which we have got stuck to the point of losing our independent personality, and from which it will take a long time to extricate ourselves.

Shipments of cartridges to the Turkish army from England and America are colossal. At present it is positively known that at Plevna a Turkish soldier, at times, fires 500 rounds of ammunition per day. Thus to equip the Turkish army the Turks had neither facilities nor money. The presence of the English and of their money in the current war is undeniable. Their ships are transporting ammunition and all that is needed. And yet some of our papers are vociferating—from "politeness": "Ah, please, don't say this! Ah, let's not raise this question! Let's pretend we don't hear about these things! Otherwise the enlightened navigators might grow angry, and then . . ."

Well, then what? What are you afraid of?—Much could be added on the subject of "politeness."

Even if there be some little promissory notes issued by us to Europe in the form of different promises made prior to the time of our crossing the Barbocz bridge, this, too, must have been done from politeness toward Europe and our admiration of her.

However, let us temporarily leave the subject of politeness. I shall only recall that in the beginning of the chapter, when I started speaking of politeness, I added: "this is politeness only toward Europe. At home we shall make up for any loss." Taking advantage of the occasion, I wish to point out how, at times, we manage to make up for the loss, and to take our *revanche*.

2

The Most Servile Incident Possible

Do you remember, gentlemen, that last summer, long before "Plevna," when we suddenly entered Bulgaria, and appeared beyond the Balkans, we were jolted with indignation. That is, not all of us—this must be stated in the first place—not even fifty per cent, but much less. Still there was a considerable number of those who grew indignant, and voices were raised—first, the voices of war correspondents, and later—voices in our press, especially in Petersburg. Those were ardent, convinced voices full of most virtuous indignation.

The whole incident arose in consequence of the fact that those who raised their voices went—as is known by the whole world and particularly by us—to save the oppressed, the crushed and exhausted.

I recall that even prior to the declaration of war I read in one of our most serious newspapers, that, in weighing the chances of war and the expenditures necessarily connected therewith, of course, "it would be necessary, upon entering Bulgaria, to feed not only our army but also the starving Bulgarian population." This I read myself, and I can state where.

Now then, with these ideas about the Bulgarians, for whose defense we went all the way from the shores of the Finnish gulf and all Russian rivers to shed our blood, unexpectedly we saw charming little Bulgarian cottages, surrounded with smiling gardens and flowers, cattle, cultivated land yielding almost hundredfold harvests, and, on top of that, three Orthodox churches to one mosque —this among those oppressed for faith! "How dare they!"—Indignation instantly flared up in the offended hearts of some liberators, and the blood of insult rose to their cheeks. "Besides, we have come to save them. Therefore, they should be welcoming us almost on their knees. But they are not on their knees; they look at us askance, and it even seems that they are not glad we are here! And this, in a case where we are involved! True, they welcome us with bread and salt, yet they do, they certainly do, look at us askance!"

And voices began to rise. Look here, gentlemen, what would you think: suddenly you receive a false telegram, or one erroneously understood by you, to the effect that a man dear to you—a friend, or a brother of yours—is sick; that somewhere far away he has been robbed or that he has been run over by a train, or something of the sort. You leave all your work and speed to that unfortunate brother. And much to your surprise you discover that nothing of the kind has happened: you meet a man who is in better health than you. He sits at the table and dines. Vociferously he asks you to join him, and he bursts out into laughter over your false alarm, over that *qui pro quo*. Whether or not you are very fond of the man, is it possible that you would be angry at him because he has not been robbed or run over by a train? Chiefly—because he has such red cheeks, that he so enjoys his dinner and his glass of wine? Certainly not. On the contrary, you should even be glad that he is alive and in better health than yourself. Why, being human, you might be a little angry—but not because his legs were not cut off by the wheels. Indeed, you would not start, straight after dinner, writing dispatches and anecdotes about him, vilifying his character, recording traits unfavorable to him. . . .

Well, in the case of the Bulgarians this has been done. "In Russia even a well-to-do peasant has not such good food as this oppressed Bulgarian." And others later inferred that the Russians were the cause of all Bulgarian misfortunes: had we not beforehand, without knowing the actual facts, threatened the Turks on behalf of the oppressed Bulgarian: had we not subsequently come to liberate these "robbed" rich fellows, they would be living, even up to the present day, in clover. This is still being asserted.

I am saying this only in the spirit that because of our "politeness" toward Europe and our enlightened Europeanism, we manage, at times, to make good, in our own way, at home, where Europe no longer sees and observes us and because she can't understand Russian. And Bulgaria means *"at home."* We have come to liberate them, which is the same as if we came *home*—they are ours. He has there a garden and an estate,—well, this is the same as if they were mine. Of course, I am not going to take anything away from him, because I am an honorable man, and true—also because I have no power to do this, nevertheless he should *feel* and be forever grateful, since I have entered his home,—well, this is the same as if *I made a present to him* of everything he possesses—I took it away from the Turk, his oppressor, and returned it to him. Indeed, he must understand this. . . . And suddenly it develops that nobody is oppressing him! What a vexing unpleasantness! Isn't it though?

What servility in lieu of enlightened politeness! Isn't it? And what a funny incident!—This is one of the most comical "makings up" "at home" in compensation for the tightness of the ill-fitting uniform of European politeness in which we are flaunting ourselves before Europe. A most servile incident occurred to these ardent gentlemen, catching *quite a few* of them unawares. This is more serious than unexpectedly to hold an overcoat for an Englishman.

Subsequently everything came to light, and the truth revealed itself to many of the indignant—even though not to all of them— up to this day. It developed, in the first place, that the Bulgarian is in no way guilty because of the fact that he is industrious and that his soil yields hundredfold harvests. Secondly, he can't be blamed for "looking askance." To consider only that he has been a slave for four centuries, and when he encounters new masters he does not believe them to be his brethren, but, on the contrary, believes them to be his new masters. Besides, he is afraid of his former masters, and painfully ponders to himself: "What if they should come back and find out that I have offered bread and salt?" —It was because of these inner questions that he looked askance. And he was right, he made a good guess—the poor fellow: after we had accomplished our first valiant onrush beyond the Balkans, we suddenly withdrew. The Turks again came back to them, and what they got from the Turks is a matter of record in world history! These neat little cottages, these savings, gardens, cattle—all these were plundered, reduced to ashes, erased from the face of the earth.

Not by the scores, not by the hundreds, but by the thousands and tens of thousands, Bulgarians were exterminated by fire and sword; their children were rent asunder and died in the throes of torture; dishonored wives and daughters were either beaten after they had been raped, or taken into captivity for sale, while the husbands—those same who welcomed the Russians, as well as those who never did welcome them but to whom the Russians might have come some day—they all smarted, for the Russians, on the gallows or bonfires. The beasts who tortured them nailed them for the night by their ears to fences, and in the morning they hanged all of them, to the last man, compelling one of them to hang the rest, and when he had hanged a score of culprits, in conclusion he had to hang himself amid the uproar of the sadistic beasts known as the Turkish nation who, subsequently, were so greatly admired by some of our most delicate ladies. . . .

N. B. Only recently, in the middle of November, reports were received from Pyrgos about the new atrocities of these monsters. When, in the course of a spirited skirmish there, the Turks temporarily succeeded in pressing us back so that we had no time to remove our wounded soldiers and officers, and that same day when in the evening we recaptured the ground, we found our wounded robbed, naked, with cut-off noses, ears, lips, carved-out stomachs, and finally burned to death on stacks of straw and corn to which our wounded, then still alive, were transported by the Turks, who thereupon set these stacks afire. Reprisals are a cruel thing, all the more so as, essentially, they lead to nothing, as I have already stated once in one of the preceding issues of the *Diary*. However, severity in dealing with the superiors of these beasts would not be out of place. The announcement could be made—publicly so that all Europe should hear it—that in case atrocities are committed, the immediate superiors of those Turks who order them, if they be captured, will be court-martialled and shot. (The Prussians unfailingly would have done this because they even dealt exactly in the same way with the French for reasons ten times less justifiable than in the case of the beasts with whom we are at war.)[1]

Such a warning, instead of carriages equipped with springs, would teach many of them. At present, however, that same "commander," captured and seeing how he is welcomed after his atrocities, really imagines himself infinitely superior to the "infidel Russian." I assure you that this Turk will never believe in our European

[1]N. B. I believe it would be easy to find out now or later who was the Turkish commander who, for instance, was in charge of the attack at Pyrgos.

politeness and in our fear of Europe. Besides, he would not understand this at all, nor would he conceive such a cause. The polite fear of Europe is a purely Russian thing and invention, and no one will ever comprehend it. And therefore, "if you are thus bowing to me"—argues the Turkish commander—"after I have permitted only yesterday my soldiers to cut off, maybe, your own brother's nose, this means that you feel that you are inferior to me, and that I am superior to you. So it should be, by the will of Allah, and there is nothing surprising in this!"

This is what the captive Turkish pasha must be, and unfailingly is, thinking.

Therefore, when those who grew indignant against the Bulgarians lived to see the sad denouement wrought upon the latter, willy-nilly they understood that Bulgarian life, essentially, is nothing but scenery; that all those cottages, and gardens, and wives and children; all these young boys and girls in those cottages,—that they all, in fact, belong to the Turk, who grabs them whenever he pleases. He grabs them also in times of peace,—he grabs money and cattle, wives and little girls, and if nevertheless everything continued to remain in a flourishing state, this was only due to the fact that the Turk did not want to bring utter destruction upon so fertile a field, expecting to exploit it also in the future. On the contrary, at times, and in certain localities, he permitted full blossoming precisely with a view to exploiting it in due time.

Of course, at present the Turks, having grown furious, are completely destroying Bulgaria. They regret that they have not done this before. If we capture Plevna and tarry in our advance, the Turks seeing that, perhaps, they may have to part with Bulgaria forever, will destroy everything that can possibly be destroyed—so long as there is time.

There are two remarkable opinions: our sages still keep asserting that, in the absence of Russian intervention, the Bulgarian would be living in clover, and that the Russians are the cause of all his misfortunes. Now, the Englishman Forbes, the correspondent of the newspaper *Daily News,* well-known for his excellent and comprehensive dispatches from the front, finally, candidly came out with his English truth. He *sincerely* believes that the Turks had "the full right" to exterminate the entire Bulgarian population to the north of the Balkans at the time when the Russian army had crossed the Danube. Forbes almost regrets (of course, politically) that this did not take place, and infers that the Bulgarians owe a debt of eternal gratitude to the Turks for the fact that the latter have not slaughtered everyone of them like so many sheep.

Recalling our Russian opinion about "the Bulgarian living in clover," and comparing it with the opinion of Forbes, we might as well address the Bulgarian with the following admonition. "How can you maintain that you are not living in clover seeing that you, Bulgarians, have not been slaughtered, head by head, to the last man!"

But there is one more strange thing: it stands out, and it will remain in history. Is it possible that so educated a man as Forbes, belonging to so great and enlightened a nation as England, can calmly and serenely admit such a right on the part of the Turks? And mind that of course he would not have expressed himself thus if, in lieu of the Bulgarians, the French or the Italians had been at stake. He did thus express himself because these were only Bulgarians, Slavs. What innate blood contempt for the Slavs, for the Slavic race, they all have in Europe! They consider them to be mere dogs!—The possibility and the reasonableness of slaughtering everyone of them, to the last man, the entire tribe, including women and children, are admitted.

And mind,—this is very important—this is being said not by Lord Beaconsfield: compelled by politics, by "English interests," he could have expressed such piratical and bestial convictions. But Forbes is an honest man, not a politician. The duty of complying with the interest of England *quand-même and at any cost* has not been conferred upon him. Such a man! So honest, talented, truthful, humane—judging by his former dispatches! Here we are dealing precisely with some sort of Western European aversion to everything bearing the name of Slavdom. These Bulgarians may be boiled in boiling water like those bugs' nests in the wooden beds of old women! Isn't there some kind of an instinct here, some presentiment that all Eastern Slavic tribes, after their liberation, will assume some day an enormous role in the new, future human race in the place of the old civilization, led astray from the right road? At present Western people can neither consciously conceive nor even admit this, just as they cannot conceive bugs' nests as something superior which is going to replace them.

But this is Russia! Obviously, here an altogether new idea for everybody's seduction and wrath has been launched—to everybody's surprise. Here the banner of the future has appeared. And inasmuch as Russia is not a "bugs' nest," as they consider the Bulgarians, but a giant and a power which it is impossible not to admit; and because Russia is also a Slavic nation,—how these Western fellows must hate Russia in their hearts, instinctively, unaccountably, rejoicing over every reverse, every calamity of hers! Precisely, this is instinct; we have here a presentiment of the future! . . .

3

An Altogether Special Word About Slavs Which I Meant to Say Long Ago

Apropos, I shall say a *special* word about the Slavs and the Slavic problem. I meant to say it long ago. Suddenly, everybody in Russia has started talking about the possibility of an early peace. Let us give freedom to fantasy, and let us suppose that all of a sudden the task has been accomplished, that owing to Russia's insistence, and with her blood, the Slavs have already been liberated; moreover, that the Turkish Empire exists no longer, and that the Balkan Peninsula is free and lives a new life.

Of course, it is impossible to foretell in all details what form, to begin with, will that Slavic freedom assume, *i.e.*, is it going to be a federation of the liberated small tribes (N. B.—it seems that for a long time to come there will be no federation), or will separate small principalities come into existence, in the form of small states with sovereigns called from various ruling houses? It is also difficult to conceive whether Serbia's boundaries will be enlarged, or whether Austria will prevent it; what territory Bulgaria will occupy; what will become of Herzegovina and Bosnia; what the relations will be between the newly liberated small Slavic nations, for instance, the Rumanians or even the Greeks—the Constantinople Greeks and those other Athenian Greeks; finally, whether these countries and small lands will be quite independent, or will be under the protectorate and supervision of "the concert of European powers," including Russia. (I believe that all these small nations will unfailingly solicit a European concert, be it even with Russia, solely as a matter of protection against the ambitions of Russia.)—None of these questions can be decided beforehand, and I do not venture to settle them.

However, even at present it is possible to know certainly two things: (1) that sooner or later all Slavic tribes on the Balkan Peninsula will, in the long run, unfailingly free themselves of the Turkish yoke, and that they will start a new, free and perhaps independent life, and (2) . . . Well, this "secondly" which will unfailingly come to pass, I meant to discuss long ago.

This "secondly" consists of the fact that according to my inner, my fullest and now irresistible conviction, Russia has never had such haters, enviers, calumniators and even open enemies as she will have in these Slavic tribes—just as soon as Russia has liberated them and Europe has consented to recognize their liberation! And let people raise no objections, let them not argue with me or shout

at me that I am exaggerating, that I am a hater of the Slavs!
—On the contrary, I like them very much; but I am not going
to defend myself because I know that this will come to pass precisely in the way I maintain, and not because of the base and
allegedly ungrateful character of the Slavs, not at all: in this respect
their character is akin to the character of all others, but precisely
because *such things* cannot come to pass otherwise on earth. I shall
not enlarge on this subject, but I know that by no means should
we expect gratitude from the Slavs; we should prepare for this in
advance.

I repeat: they will start their new life by soliciting from
Europe, from England and Germany, for example, a guaranty and
protectorate of their freedom. And even though Russia also participates in the concert of the European powers, nevertheless they
will act this way for protection against *Russia*. To begin with, they
will unfailingly announce to themselves and convince themselves—
tacitly if not aloud—that they owe Russia no gratitude whatever;
that, on the contrary, at the time of the conclusion of the peace,
they barely saved their skins from Russia's ambitions by the intervention of the European concert, and, had Europe not intervened,
Russia, having taken them away from the Turks, would have
promptly swallowed them "with a view to expanding her borders
and creating a great Pan-Slavic Empire in order to make the Slavs
slaves of the greedy, cunning and barbaric Great Russian race."

For a long, very long time they will be unable to recognize
Russia's disinterestedness and the great, holy, unheard-of act of
raising the banner of the greatest of all ideas by which man lives—
and once these ideas cease to animate him, he grows benumbed,
crippled, and dies of sores and exhaustion.

Now, do you think the Slavs have now finally understood this
present war, a war of the whole Russian people, headed by the
Czar, and launched against the monsters for the liberation of the
ill-starred nations? However, I shall not speak of the present moment. Besides, the Slavs still need us: we are liberating them.
But later, when we have liberated them and they have somehow
settled,—will they think of this war as a great exploit undertaken
for their liberation?—Decide for yourselves. Why, they will never
recognize this! On the contrary, they will assert, first as a political
and later as a scientific truth, that had there been no liberatrix
Russia during all these one hundred years, they would have managed
long ago to free themselves from the Turks by their own valor,
or with the help of Europe, which—again, had there been no Russia
in existence,—not only would have had nothing against their liberation but would have liberated them herself. This crafty doctrine

certainly must be entertained by them even at present, and in the future they will develop it into a scientific and political axiom. Moreover, they will speak of the Turks with even greater respect than of Russia.

Perhaps, during a whole century, or even longer, they will unceasingly tremble for their freedom and fear Russia's ambitions. They will ask favors of the European states; they will calumniate Russia, gossip about her and intrigue against her. Oh, I am not speaking of individuals: there will be some who will comprehend what Russia has meant, means and will always mean to them. They will understand the full greatness and sacredness of Russia's cause and of the great idea, of the banner, which she will raise amidst mankind. In the beginning, however, these men will be in such a pitiful minority that they will be ridiculed and subjected to hate and even political persecution.

The liberated Slavs will particularly enjoy announcing and heralding to the whole world that they are enlightened nations, capable of embracing the loftiest European culture, whereas Russia is a barbaric country, a grim northern colossus, not even of pure Slavic blood, an oppressor and persecutor of European civilization. It goes without saying that from the very beginning they will adopt a constitutional form of government; they will have parliaments, responsible ministers, orators and speeches. These will greatly comfort and delight them. They will be tickled to death to read telegraphic dispatches about themselves in the Paris and London papers, heralding to the whole world that, after a protracted parliamentary storm, the cabinet has finally fallen in Bulgaria, and that a cabinet has been formed by the liberal majority; or that some Ivan Chiftlik of theirs finally has consented to accept the portfolio of president of the council of ministers.

Russia must be well prepared to face the fact that all these liberated Slavs will enthusiastically rush to Europe; that they will be contaminated with the political and social European forms—to the point of losing their individuality, and that thus they will have to live through a long period of Europeanism before they are able to understand at least something about their Slavic significance and their special Slavic mission among mankind.

Among themselves, these petty countries will be perpetually quarrelling, envying each other and intriguing one against the other. It stands to reason that at a moment of some serious calamity they will unfailingly apply to Russia for help. No matter how much they may hate, gossip and calumniate us in Europe, coquetting with her and assuring her of their love, nevertheless they will always instinctively feel—of course at a moment of some calamity, and not before—

that Europe is, always was and will always remain, a natural enemy of their unity, and, if they do exist on earth, it is, of course, because of the fact that there stands a gigantic magnet—Russia—which, drawing all of them to herself, thereby preserves their wholeness and unity. There will even be moments when they will be able to concede—almost consciously—that had there been no Russia, the great Eastern center and the great attracting force, their unity would have instantly collapsed, been torn to pieces, so that their very nationality would have vanished in the European ocean, as a few drops of water vanish in a sea.

For a long while Russia will be left with the anguish and task of making peace among them, teaching them, and perhaps, occasionally, even drawing her sword in their defense. Naturally, there arises at once the question: wherein, then, is Russia's benefit? Why has Russia been warring on their behalf a whole century, sacrificing her blood, her strength, her money? Was it only for the purpose of reaping so much petty hatred and ingratitude? Oh, it stands to reason that Russia will always realize that she is the center of Slavic unity; that if the Slavs are enjoying a free national existence, it is because she willed and wishes so; that it was she who accomplished and created all this. However, aside from labors, vexations and perpetual concerns, what benefit can be derived by Russia from this realization?

At present it is difficult to answer this question, and the answer may not be clear.

First, as we all know, Russia will never, must never, think of enlarging her territory at the expense of the Slavs, of annexing them politically, of carving Russian provinces out of their lands, etc. Even now all Slavs, much like all Europe, suspect Russia of such aspirations; they will suspect them for a century hence. But God guard Russia against these aspirations, and the more political disinterestedness with regard to the Slavs she manifests, the more surely she will subsequently succeed in uniting them around herself —one hundred years hence. However, by providing the Slavs, from the very beginning, with as much political freedom, by withdrawing herself from tutelage and supervision of any kind; by merely announcing to them that she will always be ready to draw her sword against those who may threaten their freedom and nationality, Russia may thereby rid herself of the dreadful troubles and commotions of *enforcing* this tutelage and her political influence upon the Slavs, which, of course is hateful to them and always suspicious to Europe. Even so, by manifesting the fullest disinterestedness, Russia will thereby conquer and finally attract the Slavs to herself: at first they will apply to her in times of calamity, but subsequently, some day, they will come back to her, and they will all *press* themselves to her, with complete, childish trust. They will all return to their native nest.

Of course, even in our day, among Russians there are many learned and poetical conceptions. These Russians expect that the new liberated Slavic nations, resurrected to a new life, will begin by joining themselves to Russia as to their own mother and their liberatrix, and that, unquestionably, in the very near future, they will introduce into Russian life many new and unheard-of elements; that they will expand Russia's Slavdom, Russia's soul; that they will even exercise an influence upon the Russian language, literature, creative faculties; that they will spiritually enrich Russia and will reveal to her new horizons.

I confess that all this always has seemed to me nothing but learned enthusiasm. The truth is that something along these lines will not come to pass before, say, a century, but meanwhile, and, maybe, for one hundred years, there will be nothing which Russia can borrow from the Slavs, whether from their ideas or their literature. They are terribly young to be teaching us. On the contrary, perhaps throughout that forthcoming century, Russia will have to struggle against their narrowness and obstinacy; against their bad habits, their indubitable betrayal of Slavdom in the near future for the sake of the European forms of political and social organization which they will avidly adopt.

After the settlement of the Slavic question Russia will, obviously, have finally to settle the Eastern problem. It will take a long time before present-day Slavs will comprehend what the Eastern problem is! It will also take them a long time to understand Slavic fellowship in brotherly accord. To explain this to them incessantly by deed and great example will henceforth always be Russia's task. Again, it may be argued: What is all this for? Why should Russia assume such a task?—What for?—In order to pursue a superior, great life; in order to shine to the world with a great, disinterested and pure idea; in order to create, at length, a great and mighty organism of a brotherly union of nations; to create this organism not by means of political violence, not by the sword, but by persuasion, example, love, disinterestedness,—by light; to elevate those little ones to our level, so that they shall perceive in Russia her motherly mission—such is Russia's goal, such, if you please, are her benefits.

If nations fail to live by superior disinterested ideas, by the lofty aims of serving mankind, and merely serve their own "interests," they must unfailingly perish, grow benumbed, wear themselves out, die. And there is no loftier goal than that which Russia

will set for herself when she disinterestedly serves the Slavs, demanding no gratitude from them, serving their moral (and not merely
political) unification into one great whole. Only then will united
Slavdom utter its new salutary word to mankind. . . . No loftier
aims exist on earth. For this reason there can also be nothing more
"beneficial" to Russia than always to keep these aims before her,
more and more clarifying them to herself, more and more lifting
herself spiritually in this eternal, incessant and valiant labor of hers
on behalf of mankind.

Let the war end happily, and Russia indubitably will pass into
a new and superior phase of her existence.

CHAPTER III

1

*Peace Rumors. "Constantinople Must Be Ours."—Is This
Possible? Different Opinions*

AND SUDDENLY everybody has started talking about the
end of the war—not only in Europe, but also at home. People have
begun to debate the probable peace terms. It is gratifying that the
majority of our political newspapers now evaluate more or less correctly our labors, the blood which Russia has shed and her efforts,
suggesting peace terms if possible commensurate with her efforts.
It is particularly pleasing that the majority of those debating this
topic begin to recognize Russia's independence in the face of the
imminent European intervention at the time of the conclusion of
peace and her right to conclude a separate, independent, peace without appealing to Europe, and, if possible, without even taking great
heed of her. The lot of the Slavs is also being taken into account.
The question of indemnity is being considered, and people ardently
insist upon the surrender of the Turkish iron-clad monitors. Many
people concede our right to annex Kars and Erzerum.

However, even now there are people who feel offended by the
suggestion that we should have the impudence to annex anything
like Kars. As against this there are, finally, those who even talk
about Constantinople and that she must be ours.

These debates and discussions about peace and the peace terms
will always be renewed after each one of our major military operations. I merely wish to observe that in all—or nearly all—these
present-day deliberations of our periodicals there seems to be not
exactly an omission but an oversight. I mean—people regard Europe
as . . . Europe, *i.e.*, as she has been, with all sorts of variations,

throughout this century: the same great powers are taken for granted; the same political equilibrium, and so forth. Meanwhile, in our day, Europe is changing from hour to hour; she is no longer what she was six months ago. It is impossible, even three months in advance, to be sure what changes may take place and what she will look like by next spring. Colossal and fatal contemporary facts, which probably will have to be formulated and settled very soon, are still not evaluated on that scale on which, essentially, the world will have to envisage them. At present even the structure of that Europe which may intervene in our affairs at the time of the conclusion of peace cannot be ascertained unmistakably. On this ground it is a mistake, in my opinion, to discuss the peace terms, basing them upon former data, without fully evaluating the fact that all these previous conditions have been set in motion, that they are in a fluent state, that they slip away, presaging new evaluations. However, this is something for future discussion.

At this juncture, inasmuch as the question of Constantinople has been raised, I should like to note in passing a very strange and, to me, a rather unexpected opinion on the immediate "destinies of Constantinople," which was expressed by a man from whom one had the right to expect an altogether different judgment in view of the contemporary events which actually have taken place and which unquestionably are likely to happen.

Nikolai Yakovlevich Danilevsky, who eight years ago wrote an admirable book *Russia and Europe,* in which there is only one obscure and weak chapter concerning the future fate of Constantinople, has recently printed in the newspaper *The Russian World* a series of articles on the same subject. His final deduction concerning Constantinople is very original. I shall not analyze it in detail.

Following some excellent and sound deliberations to the effect that Constantinople—after the Turks have been driven out of her —by no means should become a free city—like Cracow, for example, in the past—lest she be converted into a nest of filth and intrigue, a harem for all conspirators of the world, a prey of the Jews, speculators, etc., etc.,—N. Y. Danilevsky asserts that some day Constantinople must become a city belonging to all Eastern peoples. According to him, they all will possess her, along with the Russians who will own her on an equal basis with the other Slavs.

To me, such a decision seems strange. What can be the comparison between the Russians and the Slavs? How can Russia share the possession of Constantinople on an equal basis with the Slavs if Russia in every respect is unequal to them—to every petty tribe separately and to all of them combined? The giant Gulliver, if he had wished, could have assured the Lilliputs that he was their equal in every respect. However, this would obviously have been absurd. What is the purpose of assuming an absurdity and compelling oneself to believe it?

Constantinople must be *ours*, conquered by *us*, Russians, from the Turks, and remain ours forever. She must belong to us alone, and possessing her we may, of course, admit into her all Slavs and, in addition, anyone whom we please, on the broadest basis. But this would not be federal possession of the city along with the Slavs.

One has merely to consider the fact that a whole century would be required before a federal union of the Slavs could be achieved. Russia will take possession of Constantinople and the necessary metropolitan area, as well as of the Bosphorus and the Straits; there she will maintain troops, fortifications and a fleet. And thus it should be for a long, long time.

Oh, people will start vociferating: "So, Russia's service to the Slavic cause was not so disinterested, after all!" To this it may be easily said that Russia's service to the Slavs is not going to be finished now; that it will continue throughout many centuries; that by Russia alone, by her great central power, the Slavs will manage to exist on earth; that nothing can ever repay her for such a service, and that if at present Russia occupies Constantinople, it is solely because among her aims and in her mission, in addition to the Slavic question, there is another problem, her greatest and ultimate problem,—specifically the Eastern problem which may be settled only in Constantinople. But the federal possession of Constantinople by various petty tribes may even kill the Eastern problem, whose solution, however, should be persistently sought because it is closely tied to the destiny and mission of Russia herself, and it can be solved by her alone.

I am not speaking of the fact that in Constantinople all these small nations would quarrel among themselves for power and for her possession. The Greeks will set them at variance. The western Slavs, too, will be envious of the fact that the eastern Slavs possess such a splendid spot of Europe and the terrestrial globe. . . . In a word, Constantinople would serve as a cause of dissension in the entire Slavic and Eastern world which would prevent the unity of the Slavs and would stop the normal course of their existence. In this situation the salvation would be in Russia's occupying Constantinople alone,—for herself, for her own account. Russia could then say to the Eastern peoples that she is taking possession of Constantinople "because not one of you has grown up to her, not all of you combined, but I, Russia have grown up." She has.

Precisely now the new phase of Russia's existence begins.

Constantinople is the center of the Eastern world, while Russia is its spiritual center and its head. At present it is necessary and even *useful* for Russia to forget Petersburg for a while—a little at least—and to visit the East because of the change of her fate and of all Europe, a change close at hand, standing "at the door."

But let us leave for the time being the analysis of all the inconveniences of a common possession of Constantinople, and even the harm which would result therefrom, especially to the Slavs. I shall merely say a few words about the fate in this event of the Constantinople Greeks and of Orthodoxy.

The Greeks would look upon the new Slavic element in Constantinople jealously and would hate and fear the Slavs more intensely than even the former Mohammedans. The recent controversy between the Bulgarians and the Patriarchal Throne may serve as an example of the future. The Orthodox dignitaries in Constantinople might degrade themselves to the level of intrigue, petty imprecations, excommunications, irregular sobors, etc., perhaps, even, heresy. And all this owing to national causes, national insults and vexations. "Why are the Slavs superior to us?"—all Greeks in accord may ask. "Why is their unconditional right to Constantinople recognized even though jointly with us?" At the same time, please observe that Russia's occupying that city, and possessing strength and unquestioned authority, would almost eliminate the possibility of such questions. Even the Greeks will not envy nor be greatly vexed by the fact that she possesses Constantinople precisely because Russia is so manifest a power and ruler of the destinies of the East.

Russia, possessing Constantinople, would be guarding the freedom of all Slavs and of *all Eastern* peoples without drawing a line between them and the Slavs. During all these centuries the Mohammedan rule over all these peoples has been not a unifying but an oppressive force; under that rule they did not even dare to move, which means that they have not lived like human beings at all. However, with the abolition of the Mohammedan rule, there might ensue among these peoples, who would suddenly leap out from under the yoke to freedom, awful chaos. So that not only a duly constituted federation but even ordinary accord among them is unquestionably but a dream of the future. Temporarily Russia would serve as a unifying force precisely by reason of the fact that she would firmly establish herself in Constantinople. Russia would save them from one another and would guard the freedom of the entire East and its future order.

Finally, Russia alone is capable of raising in the East the banner of the new idea and of explaining to the whole Eastern world its new mission. For what is the Eastern question?—In its essence, it is the solution of the destinies of Orthodoxy which are merged with Russia's mission. Now, what are these destinies of Orthodoxy?—Roman Catholicism, which has long ago sold Christ for earthly rule; which has compelled mankind to turn away from itself, and which was thus the prime cause of Europe's materialism and atheism,—that Catholicism has naturally generated socialism. For socialism has for its aim the solution of the destinies of mankind not in accord with Christ but without God and Christ. It was inevitably generated in Europe in a natural way in lieu of the deteriorated Christian principle and in the measure of its perversion and loss by the Catholic Church itself.

The lost image of Christ in all the light of its purity is conserved in Orthodoxy. And it is from the East that the new word will be uttered to the world in opposition to future socialism, and this word may again save European mankind. Such is the mission of the East and this is what the Eastern question means to Russia.

I know that many people will call this deliberation "religious mania," but N. Y. Danilevsky can well understand what I am saying. However, for the fulfillment of such a mission Russia needs Constantinople since the latter is the center of the Eastern world. Russia, with her people headed by the Czar, is tacitly cognizant of the fact that she is the bearer of the idea of Christ; that the word of Orthodoxy transforms itself in her into a great cause which has begun with the present war, and that ahead of her there lie centuries of self-sacrificing labor, of fostering the brotherhood of the peoples and of ardent motherly service to them as to dear children.

Yes, this is a great Christian cause; this is the new activity of Christianity—precisely in this war, because of it, whereas N. Y. Danilevsky still does not believe it—obviously because, as yet, he deems no one *worthy* of occupying Constantinople—not even Russia. Is it because the Russians have not grown up to her?—This is difficult to understand. Of course, it is difficult to establish an accordant possession of Constantinople *on the basis of equal rights*. The author of the article admits, however, that for the time being, temporarily, Russia alone might possess Constantinople, protecting her rather than venturing to possess her, on condition that subsequently the city be turned over to the joint possession of the small nations. (Why should it be thus transferred?) It seems that N. Y. Danilevsky believes that single-handed possession of Constantinople by Russia would be tempting and, so to speak, demoralizing; that this would arouse in her bad imperialistic instincts, etc. But it is time to acquire faith in Russia, especially after the exploit of the present war. Yes, she has grown up—even to Constantinople.

And now, unexpectedly, the author hesitates to entrust Constantinople to Russia *even for the time being*. And imagine how he winds up: he infers that *for the time being* it is necessary to prolong Turkey's existence (taking away from her all the Slavs, the Balkans, etc.); to leave Constantinople temporarily under the rule of the Turks; that *for the present* this would supposedly be the most advantageous solution for Russia, and that therein is the Divine fate. But why is it Divine fate? Why?—Of course, the author supposes that in this new existence of Turkey, Russia would exercise a controlling influence over her (Turkey's) dependence upon Russia, so to speak. But what is the purpose of *such* a masquerade? Please consider: Russia—the sovereign,—and yet, for the time being, Turkey should be left intact. I may remark that Europe would be even less inclined to give her consent to such a combination than to the complete conquest of Turkey because it is better to have a definite *fait accompli* than a still contested and protracted affair, threatening new wars in the very near future.

Thus, in the last analysis, the author is almost in accord with the opinion of Lord Beaconsfield, *i.e.*, that Turkey's existence is necessary and that she should not be destroyed.

"Of Turkey there will remain but a shadow"—says N. Y. Danilevsky; "nevertheless, for the time being this shadow *must* tinge the shores of the Bosphorus and the Dardanelles, since, temporarily, it is impossible to replace her with a *live*—not only live but healthy—organism!"

Do you hear? Russia, as yet, is not a healthy, not even a live, organism; she should not dare to replace in the capital of Orthodoxy the Turkish rot!—To me this is surprising (again, after the *exploit* of the present war!). I am sure that there is something here which I do not understand. Doesn't the author simply imply that as yet it is impossible to let Russia into Constantinople (for the purpose of sole possession or her subsequent transfer to the nations) because Europe will not consent to let her in? Perhaps the author does not believe that during this present war Russia has the power to achieve such a final result. Specifically, in one part of his article he says that "the *occupation* of Constantinople by the Russians will encounter a most decisive resistance on the part of the majority of the European powers." If so, his inference concerning the necessity of leaving the Turks in Constantinople, for the time being, becomes more intelligible. Nevertheless, apropos of "the resistance of the majority of the European powers" two points should be observed: (1) that, as I have stated above, Europe would, perhaps, perceive a more conciliatory solution in our occupation of Constantinople than in the formula suggested by Mr. Danilevsky, *i.e.*, in a Turkey deprived of her individuality, under Russia's complete tutelage, without the Balkans, without the Slavs, with demolished fortifications, without a fleet,—in a word, as the author expresses himself, a "shadow" of former Turkey. It stands to reason that it is not this kind of Turkey that "the majority of the European powers" would be inclined to see, and Europe would not be deceived if merely "the shadow of Turkey" were left on earth: "All the same, if not today, then tomorrow, you will enter Constantinople"—she would say to the Russians. For this reason the final solution would be preferable to her rather than a Turkey in the guise of a shadow. (2) It may also be observed that, *perhaps,* in reality there never has been (and never will be) so advantageous a moment for the occupation of Constantinople as at present, precisely in the course of this war, precisely at this moment, or a moment very close to it—because of the present political situation of Europe herself.

2

AGAIN, FOR THE LAST TIME, "PREDICTIONS"

You keep saying: "the majority of the European powers" will not permit it. But now what is "the majority of the European powers"? Can it be defined at this moment? I repeat what I have stated above: from hour to hour Europe is changing from what she used to be recently—from what she was only six months ago—so that one cannot even vouch three months ahead for her further immutability. The point is that we are on the eve of the greatest and most violent events and revolutions in Europe—and this *without exaggeration.* At this moment, now in November, that "majority of the European powers," which could in any respect issue to us their threatening *veto* at the time of the conclusion of peace, is confined to England, and, maybe, also to Austria, although England will at any cost drag her into an alliance, hoping even for an alliance with France. But we shall not be alone (now this is already obvious). In Europe there is Germany, and she is on our side.

Yes, immense cataclysms are awaiting Europe, perturbations which the human mind refuses to believe, conceiving their realization as something fantastic. Meanwhile many things, which only last summer were considered fantastic, impossible and exaggerated, by the end of the year literally came to pass in Europe. For instance, the opinion about the strength of the universal Catholic Conspiracy, an opinion which only last summer *everybody* was inclined to laugh at, or at least to ignore,—at present is shared by *everybody* and has been corroborated by facts.

I am calling attention to this solely in order that readers should also believe in our present "predictions" and should not deem them fantastic and exaggerated pictures, as probably quite a few people considered many of our predictions in May, June, July and August, which, however, came true to the letter.

The only statesman in Europe who, with his ingenious glance, penetrates the very bottom of facts, is indisputably Prince Bismarck. Long ago he perceived in Roman Catholicism and in the monster begotten by it—socialism (Germany is eaten through with socialism), the most dreadful enemy of Germany, of her unity and her future regeneration. Bismarck has got to crush Catholicism at the time of the election of the new Pope. Oh, he understands that he will not completely crush it and that he will merely place it in a certain new phase of the struggle. But as far as Catholicism is concerned, so long as France is alive, the old phase of the struggle continues to persist. So long as France is alive, Catholicism has a strong sword, and there is hope for a European coalition. As for France, her fate, in the view of Prince Bismarck, is doomed. To him there is but one question. Who is to live—she or Germany? Should France fall,—Catholicism, together with socialism, would enter a new phase. And while European politicians are watching MacMahon's interminable war with the republicans—wholeheartedly hoping for a republican victory, *still believing and accepting* as a fact that in France the republic is a popular government capable of uniting her—Prince Bismarck, in the meantime, fully comprehends that France has finished her term; that inwardly that nation has divided itself forever, and that it will never have a firm, all-unifying authoritative government, or a healthy national unifying center. And even though France's weakness may thus merely tend to encourage Germany, nevertheless, Prince Bismarck sees, I repeat, that so long as France is alive politically, Roman Catholicism continues to live, holding in its hand a drawn sword. Moreover, he understands that perhaps Catholicism may once more, *for a while,* serve this decayed country as a unifying idea, be it only outwardly and politically. For it is impossible that France, even headed by the republicans, should not, sooner or later, draw her sword in defense of the Pope and the destinies of Catholicism.

The republicans themselves would see that, should they forsake the Pope and Catholicism, their own existence in France would be rendered impossible. True, they might prove incapable of following this thought to its logical conclusion, and thus, to the last moment, they would remain not only Prince Bismarck's *protégés* (whom, however, to himself, he has condemned to death along with all other French parties which have the ambition to reunite France into one indissoluble whole)—but also Germany's slaves, surrendering to her all France, not only into political bondage but also into inner, essential and spiritual serfdom. This they are doing by depriving France of the most independent of her *political and historical* ideas,—by tearing away from her that banner which, during so many centuries, she has been holding high in the capacity of the representative of the Romanic element in European mankind.

Those, however, who will drive the inept and useless republicans out of their seats will unfailingly see to it (Bismarck knows it) that, for the last time, the Catholic banner is hoisted against Germany—a banner which France does not believe in and which she almost *in toto* denies, but which, politically, may serve her as a last point of support and unity against the fatal—and also last— onslaught of Protestant Germany, which has been eternally protesting against the principles inherited from ancient Rome by a whole half of European mankind.

For this reason probably Prince Bismarck has already predestined France's fate. The fate of Poland awaits France, and politically she will not live, or else Germany will cease to exist. Having achieved this, Bismarck will then compel militant Roman Catholicism (which will be waging war till the end of the world) to embark upon a new phase of its existence—and struggle for existence—a phase of underground, reptilian and conspiratory war. And he is anticipating Catholicism in this new phase. The sooner this comes to pass, the better for him, because he is awaiting the alliance of both enemies of Germany and of mankind, thereby hoping to crush them all the more easily—at once. . . .

3

It is Necessary to Seize the Moment

Just as soon as France falls politically, the alliance of both enemies will be formed. The two enemies have always been organically tied to France. Almost up to recent times Catholicism has been her cementing and integral idea, while socialism was begotten in it.

By depriving France of her political existence, Prince Bismarck hopes to deliver a blow at socialism. Socialism, as a heritage of Catholicism, and France are most hateful to a genuine German. It is excusable that Germany's representatives believe that it is so easy to master socialism by merely destroying France politically— as its source and beginning.

However, this is what is most probably going to happen should

France fall politically: Catholicism will lose its sword, and for the first time will appeal to the people whom it has been despising so many centuries, ingratiating itself with mundane kings and emperors. Now, however, it will appeal to the people, since there is nowhere else to go; specifically, it will appeal to the leaders of the most mobile and rebellious element of the people—the socialists. Catholicism will tell the people that Christ also preached everything the socialists are preaching to them. Once more it will pervert and sell them Christ as it has sold Him so many times in the past for earthly possessions, defending the rights of the Inquisition which, in the name of loving Christ, tortured men for freedom of conscience,—in the name of Christ to whom only that disciple was dear who came to Him of his free accord and not the one who had been bought or frightened.

Catholicism sold Christ when it blessed the Jesuits and sanctioned the righteousness "of every means for Christ's cause." However, since time immemorial, it has converted Christ's cause into a mere concern for its earthly possessions and its future political domination over the whole world. When Catholic mankind turned away from the monstrous image in which, at length, Christ had been revealed to them,—after many protests, reformations, etc., at the beginning of this century—endeavors arose to organize life without God, without Christ. Devoid of the instinct of a bee or an ant, unmistakably and with utmost precision constructing their hive and ant-hill, men sought to create something on the order of an unmistakable ant-hill. They rejected the unique formula of mankind's salvation, derived from God and announced through revelation to man: "Thou shalt love thy neighbor as thyself," and substituted for it practical inferences, such as *"Chacun pour soi et Dieu pour tous"* ("Each one for himself and God for all"), or scientific axioms, such as "the struggle for existence."

Bereft of the instinct which guides animals and enables them to organize their life faultlessly, men haughtily sought to rely upon science, forgetting that for such a task as the creation of society, science is still, so to speak, in swaddles. Dreams ensued. The future tower of Babylon became the ideal but also the dread of humanity. But after these dreams there soon appeared other simple doctrines, intelligible to everybody, for instance: "to rob the rich, to stain the world with blood, after which *somehow everything will again be settled of its own accord.*"

Finally, even these teachers were outstripped: there appeared the doctrine of anarchy, after which—if it could be put into effect— there would again ensue a period of cannibalism, and people would be compelled to start all over again as they started some ten thousand years ago. Catholicism fully understands all this, and it will manage to seduce the leaders of the underground war. It will say to them: "You have no center, no order in the conduct of the work; you are a force scattered all over the world, and now, after the downfall of France—also an oppressed force. I shall be your rallying center, and I shall attract to you all those who still believe in me."

One way or another, the alliance will be formed. Catholicism does not wish to die, whereas social revolution and the new social period in Europe are indubitable: two forces, unquestionably, will have to come to an understanding, to unite. It stands to reason that slaughter, blood, plunder, even cannibalism would be advantageous to Catholicism. Precisely then it may hope to catch once more its fish in troubled waters, foreseeing the moment when, finally, mankind, exhausted by chaos and lawlessness, will fall into its arms. Then, once more, it will become in reality the sole and absolute "earthly ruler and universal authority," sharing its power with no one. Thereby it will attain its ultimate goal.

Alas, this picture is not a fantasy. I positively assert that it is being foreshadowed in the West by quite a few people. Probably it is also being foreseen by the lords of Germany. Still the leaders of the German people are mistaken in one respect—in the easiness of conquering and crushing these two dreadful and united enemies. They are relying on the strength of regenerated Germany, on her Protestant spirit protesting against the tenets and *consequences* of ancient and modern Rome. But they will not stop the monster. It will be checked and vanquished by the reunited East and by the new word which it will utter to mankind. . . .

At all events one thing seems clear to me, that Germany *needs us* even more than we think. And she needs us not for a momentary political alliance but *forever*. The idea of reunited Germany is a broad and stately one; it goes back into the depth of ages. What has Germany to divide with us?—Her object is all Western mankind. She has selected for herself the European Western world where she seeks to inculcate her principles in lieu of the Roman and Romanic tenets, and henceforth to become its leader, leaving the East to Russia. Thus, two great peoples are destined to transform the face of this world. These are not contrivances of the mind or of ambition: the world itself shapes itself thus. There are new and strange facts; they are appearing daily.

At a time when in Russia it was even considered fantastic to speak and dream about Constantinople, in the German press many people began to discuss our occupation of her as a most ordinary matter. Compared with Germany's former attitude toward us, this is almost strange. It is to be supposed that Russia's friendship with Germany is not hypocritical but firm, that, as time goes on, it will grow stronger, gradually penetrating the consciousness of both nations. For this reason, for Russia, perhaps there never has been a more opportune moment for the final solution of the Eastern question than the present one.

Germany is awaiting the end of our war, perhaps even more impatiently than we. Meanwhile, it is actually true that nowadays one cannot vouch for what is going to happen even three months in advance. Shall we finish the war before the ultimate and fatal European disturbances take place? This is unknown. But whether or not we shall be in time to help Germany, at all events she counts on us not as on a *temporary* but an *eternal* ally.

As for the current moment,—again, the key to the situation is in France and in the election of the Pope. Here one has to expect a conflict between France and Germany which is all the more certain as there are provokers. England will be the one which will see to it, after which Austria perhaps will also move. But all these things we have discussed only recently. Since that time nothing has occurred that contradicts our former opinions. On the contrary they have been corroborated. . . .

In any event, Russia must seize the moment. Is our favorable European moment going to last long?—So long as the present great leaders of Germany act, it is *most probable* that this moment is guaranteed to us.

DECEMBER

CHAPTER I

1

The Final Explanation of a Previous Fact

CONCLUDING WITH this last December issue the two-year publication of the *Diary,* I deem it necessary once more to say a few words concerning a matter which I have discussed *in extenso.* I decided to mention it as early as May, but, owing to special considerations, I postponed the discussion of the subject precisely till the last issue.

This is again in reference to that stepmother Kornilova who, prompted by wrath against her husband, threw her six-year-old stepdaughter out of the window; the latter, having fallen from a five-sagene height, remained alive. As is known, the delinquent

woman was tried and convicted. Subsequently the sentence was
rescinded, and on April 22 of this year, at the second trial, she was
finally acquitted. (See *A Writer's Diary,* October, 1876, and April,
1877.)

I happened to take a certain part in this case. The president
of the court, and later also the prosecutor, publicly announced,
in the courtroom itself, that the first verdict by virtue of which
Kornilova had been found guilty, was quashed precisely because of
my suggestion set forth in the *Diary* that "the act of the criminal
woman may have been prompted by her pregnant state." I framed
and developed this idea as a result of extraordinary and strange
psychic peculiarities which irresistibly, of their own accord, struck
one's eyes and arrested one's attention during the perusal of the
details of the perpetrated act. However, all this is known to our
readers. Perhaps it is also known that, following a most rigid
investigation, and after most obstinate and persistent arguments of
the prosecutor, the jurors nevertheless acquitted Kornilova, having
stayed in the jurors' room not longer than ten minutes, and that
the public left the courtroom enthusiastically approving the acquittal.

Even so, at the time, that very day, the thought occurred
to me that in so important a case involving the highest motives
of civic and spiritual life, it is very desirable that everything be
explained in all minutest details so that in society and in the souls
of the jurors, who have rendered a verdict of acquittal, there no
longer remain any doubts, vacillations and regrets that an indubitably criminal woman was left unpunished. Here children are
involved, the children's lot (often dreadful in Russia, especially
among the poor class), and the problem of childhood—and yet, the
murderess of a child is acquitted, the public sympathizes with her!
And now—I myself (according to the statement of the court itself)
contributed to this! Of course, I acted in accordance with my conviction. However, after the verdict had been announced, suddenly
doubt began to torment me: Didn't the verdict leave a residue of
discontent, perplexity, distrust of justice, even indignation in society? In our press there was little comment on the acquittal of
Kornilova—people were occupied with other things: there was a
presentiment of war.

But in *The Northern Messenger,* a newspaper which had just
been started, I read an article full of indignation against the acquittal, and even anger against me for my participation in this
case. The article was written in an undignified tone. Well, I wasn't
the only one who was subjected to the indignation of *The Northern
Messenger;* Leo Tolstoy was also subjected to wrathful and un-

dignified scoffing in connection with *Anna Karenina*. Personally I should not have answered the author, but in that article I perceived exactly the thing I was afraid to encounter in a certain portion of our society, viz., confused impression, perplexity and indignation against the verdict.

And so I made up my mind to wait eight months in order to become, during this period, finally convinced that the verdict had exercised no bad influence upon the defendant; that, on the contrary, the mercy of the court, like a good seed, fell upon fertile soil; that the defendant *was really worthy* of compassion and mercy; that the impulses of incomprehensible, almost fantastic rage, in a fit of which she had committed her villainy, did not recur and *can never* return to her; that hers is a kindly and meek soul; that she is not a destroyer and murderess (of which I was convinced throughout the whole trial), and that the crime of that unfortunate woman had to be explained by a special, accidental circumstance, by illness, by an "affect," precisely by those pathological fits which occur rather often among pregnant women (of course in conjunction with other unfavorable conditions and circumstances) during a certain period of pregnancy, and finally,—that the jurors, society and the public, which was present in the courtroom and which listened to the verdict with ardent sympathy, should no longer doubt the expediency of such a verdict, and regret their mercy.

And now after all these eight months, I am in a position to communicate and add something in connection with this case, of which, however, everybody, maybe, has grown tired. I shall be replying as it were to society, *i.e.*, to that portion of it which, according to my supposition, may have disagreed with the verdict rendered, doubted it and grown indignant against it,—that is, if there has been such a portion of the dissatisfied in our society. And inasmuch as among all these dissatisfied I know (not personally, however) only that one "Observer" who wrote the threatening article in *The Northern Messenger,* I shall give him my answer. Most probably no arguments of mine will in any way convince him, but perhaps I shall be understood by my readers.

The "Observer," when referring in his article to Kornilova's case, attributed to it the highest significance. He pointed out with indignation the lot of children, defenseless children, and regretted the fact that the defendant had not been sentenced to the severest punishment. Thus it was a question of Siberia, of the exile of a twenty-year-old woman with her nursling born in prison (who would thus have been exiled with her to Siberia), and of the ruin of a young family.

In these circumstances—it would seem—it would have been

necessary, in the first place, to deal with the analyzed facts scrupulously, seriously and impartially. And yet (Would you believe it?)
this "Observer" *does not know* the case with which he is dealing;
he speaks without thinking; he invents non-existent circumstances
and throws them at the former defendant; *obviously* he was not
present in the courtroom; he did not listen to the pleadings; he was
not in court at the time of the announcement of the verdict.—Nevertheless he angrily demands punishment of a human being!

But here the fate of a human being is involved—of several
human beings at once; it is a question of tearing a human life
asunder—pitilessly, with blood. True, the ill-starred woman had already been acquitted when the "Observer" came out with his article.
But such attacks influence society, the courts, public opinion; they
may have a repercussion in a future case involving a similar defendant; finally, they offend the acquitted,—well, of course, she belongs to the common people, and therefore she is defenseless!

However, this is the article, *i.e.*, that portion of it which refers
to Kornilova's case. I am quoting the most essential parts, deleting
but very little.

2

EXCERPT

. . . .

"To the jurors it is far more difficult to imagine themselves in the
condition of a pregnant woman; even more so—in the condition of
a six-year-old girl whom that woman has thrown out of a window
from the fourth floor. One has to be endowed with all that power
of imagination in which, as is known, Mr. Dostoievsky excels among
us all, to comprehend fully the condition of a woman and to elucidate to one's self the irresistibility of the affects of pregnancy.

"He actually did penetrate that state; he went to see a certain
lady in the penitentiary; he was impressed with her humility, and
in several issues of his *Diary* he came out as her ardent advocate.
But Mr. Dostoievsky is too susceptible, and besides, 'the pathological
manifestation of volition' is an outright hobby of the author of
The Possessed, The Idiot, etc.; to him it is excusable to feel a
weakness for them. I look upon the case in a simpler manner, and
I assert that after such instances of exculpation of the cruel treatment of children—which in Russia, as also in England, is by no
means infrequent—there remains not even a shadow of deterrent to
this kind of behavior. How many cases of cruel treatment of children are there for each case that is subject to court examination?
There are children whose whole lives—morning, noon, and night—

are nothing but a succession of suffering. These are innocent creatures enduring a lot compared with which the labor of parricides
in the mines is happiness—with rest, with the absence of eternal,
unquenchable fear, with full peace of the mind in so far as it is
not disturbed by the pangs of conscience. Out of ten thousand, and
probably out of a hundred thousand, cases of cruel treatment of
children, only one reaches the courts—one which for some reason
attracts more attention. For example, a stepmother perpetually beats
an unfortunate six-year-old creature, and finally throws it out of
the fourth-floor window. When she learns that the hated child was
not killed, she exclaims: 'She is strong!' There is neither sudden
manifestation of hatred nor repentance after the commission of
the murder: everything is homogeneous and logical in the manifestation of one and the same evil will. And they acquit this woman!
If in such cases of cruelty to children, which are clear to the point
of obviousness, verdicts of acquittal are returned, what can be
expected in other cases, less clearly defined, more complex?—Of
course, acquittal, acquittal and acquittal. As stated, in England,
among the poorer classes in the cities, cases of cruelty to children
are not infrequent. But I wish I might be shown one example of
such an acquittal by English jurors. Oh, when there appears before
our jurors a schismatic who has dropped a disparaging remark
about a church dome—that's a different matter. In England he would
not even be arraigned, but in Russia—let him not expect an acquittal. Yet cruelty to a little girl—why, is it worth ruining a young
woman for this! Anyhow, she is nevertheless a stepmother, that
is, almost a mother of the victim! Anyhow, she feeds her, and beats
her more and more. But this will not surprise a Russian. A friend
of mine told me that the other day he was being driven by a cabman who continually lashed his horse. In answer to my friend's
remark to this effect, the cabman said: 'Such is its lot! It must be
eternally and mercilessly beaten.'

"Oh, Russia, this has been thy lot throughout the centuries!
For, maybe, that stepmother had also been beaten in her childhood.
And thou takest this into account and sayest: God be with her.
But thou shouldst not do so. Thou shouldst pity the little ones.
At present thou art not going to be beaten, and thou shouldst not
exculpate cruelty to him who is no longer born a serf.

"I may be told: 'You are attacking the institution of jurors,
when even without it . . .' and so forth. I am not attacking the
institution; I have no idea of attacking it; it is a good institution;
infinitely better than those courts in which public conscience did
not participate. But I am conversing with this conscience about
this or that of its manifestations. . . .

". . . But to beat a child for a whole year or so, and there-upon to throw her out to her almost certain death—this is a different matter. 'That same evening, after ten o'clock, the husband of the acquitted took her home, and she, in a happy mood, again returned to her home.' How touching! But woe to the poor child if it re-mained in that home which 'the happy one' entered. Woe to it, if it should ever chance to come back to its father's home.

" 'Affect of pregnancy'—well, a new, pitiful word has been invented. No matter how strong this affect may have been, never-theless, under its influence, the woman did not rush upon her hus-band or her neighbors. Her whole affect was reserved exclusively for that defenseless girl whom she had been torturing for a whole year without any affect. What, then, did the jurors rely upon in their acquittal?—Upon the fact that one psychiatrist admitted 'a pathological psychic state' of the defendant at the time of the com-mission of her crime. Three other psychiatrists merely stated that the pathological condition of the pregnant woman might have exer-cised an influence upon the perpetration of the offense, whereas one accoucheur, Professor Florinsky, who is, perhaps, best familiar with all symptoms of pregnancy, declared his dissent from such opinions. Thus four out of five experts did not admit that in the case at the bar the crime was positively committed in a state of 'affect of preg-nancy,' and subsequent irresponsibility. Yet the jurors acquitted. Eh, what an important matter!—The child was not killed, and as for the fact that it was beaten, well,—'such is its lot.' "

3

DISTORTIONS AND MANIPULATIONS—THIS COSTS US NOTHING

Such is the excerpt. Such is the accusation—there is also much indignation against me. But now I ask "The Observer": How could you so distort the facts in so important an accusation, setting them forth in such a deceitful and fictitious light? When was there beat-ing, *systematic* beating by the stepmother? You state directly and precisely:

"The stepmother perpetually beats an unfortunate six-year-old creature, and finally throws it out from the fourth floor . . ."

Then: "But to beat a child *for a whole year or so,* and there-upon to throw her out to her almost certain death . . ."

You exclaim—referring to the child:

"Woe to it, if it should ever chance to come back to its father's home."

And, finally, you put into the jurors' mouths a bestial phrase:
"Eh, what an important matter!—The child was not killed,
and as for the fact that it was beaten, well,—'such is its lot.'"

In a word, you misrepresented all the facts, picturing the
whole case as if the crime, according to you, were committed solely
because of the stepmother's hatred of the child, whom she had been
beating a whole year and finished by throwing it out the window.
You have purposely represented the defendant in the guise of a
beast,—of an insatiable, wicked stepmother, exclusively in order to
justify your article and to arouse the indignation of society against
the merciful verdict of the jurors. And we have the right to infer
that you have made this substitution solely for the purpose which
I have just indicated—we are justified in inferring this because you
could not—you had no right to—fail to ascertain the minutest details of the case in which you take it upon yourself to render a
verdict and to demand punishment.

However, there *never has been* any beast, that beastly stepmother hating the child and insatiable in its torture. This was positively ascertained by the investigation. It is true that, originally,
an idea was set forth to the effect that the stepmother tortured the
child and out of hatred decided to kill the girl. Subsequently, however, the prosecution relinquished this idea altogether: it became
too obvious that the crime had been committed because of motives
entirely different from the hatred of the child, motives which were
fully elucidated in the course of the trial and which had nothing
to do with the child. Besides, at the trial there appeared no witnesses who could testify to the cruelty of the stepmother—to the
beatings. There was but one testimony of a single woman who lived
right there, next to them, in the corridor (where many people were
living) that the stepmother used to flog the child very painfully,
yet even that testimony, as was subsequently shown by the defense,
proved "a corridor gossip" and nothing more. . . . There was that
which usually happens in families of this kind, taking into account
the level of their education and development, namely, that both
the father and the stepmother used to punish the child for mischief,
but only at times, *i.e.*, very rarely and not inhumanely, but "paternally," as they themselves described it. Unfortunately, this prevails in all such Russian families, throughout Russia, and this in the
presence of intense love and care for the children, which very often
is far greater and stronger than in certain educated, wealthy and
Europeanly enlightened Russian families. This is merely want of
knowledge, and not cruelty. Kornilova, however, was a good stepmother; she cared for the child and was attentive to her. Only once
was the punishment *cruel*: one morning, upon awakening, the step-

mother beat the girl *because she did not know how to take care of her natural wants at night.* Here there was no hatred of the child. When I remarked to her that one should not be punished for this; that the physical constitution of a child is different from that of an adult, and that a six-year-old child is too young to be always able to take care of its natural wants, she replied: "But I was told that this had to be done in order to break the habit, and that other-wise the child could not be induced to give it up." It was on that occasion that she struck the child with a rope "six times, so hard that scars were left." Now, that woman in the corridor, the only witness of that one case of cruelty, saw these marks, and it was about them that she testified in court. It was also for these scars that the husband, when he came home from work, promptly punished his wife, *i.e.,* gave her a beating. He is a severe, straightforward, honest and above all an inflexible man, although, as you see, partly adhering to customs of olden times. He beat his wife rarely and not cruelly (so she says herself), solely to uphold the principle of the husband's authority. He loved his child (though he punished the little girl for mischief oftener than did the stepmother). But he is not a man who would permit anyone, even his wife, to mistreat the child.

Thus the only case of severe punishment (scars) revealed at the trial, is converted by the accuser in his article in *The Northern Messenger* into systematic, bestial, stepmother's year-round beating, into stepmother's hatred which, progressively growing in intensity, culminated in her throwing the child out the window, whereas five minutes before the commission of her dreadful crime she was not thinking about the child.

Mr. Obeserver, you will start laughing and you will say: "Isn't punishment with rods, which leaves scars, a *stepmother's* beating?" Yes, it is bestial punishment. Quite so. But this case (the singleness of which was corroborated at the trial, and at present, in my opinion, positively) I repeat, is not systematic, relentless, bestial, stepmother's year-round beating. This was but an *accident* caused by want of knowledge of how one should educate, by a false conception of how one should teach a child and not at all by hatred, or because "such is the child's lot." Thus your description of this woman as a wicked stepmother, and the personality which was revealed at the trial, are radically different.

Yes, she pushed the child out. This is a dreadful and bestial crime; yet, did she do this as a cruel stepmother?—Such is the question in answer to your unfounded accusation. Why do you ad-here to such a ferocious accusation if you know yourself that it cannot be proved; that at the trial it was relinquished, and that there were no witnesses who could testify to it? Is it possible that you were merely after a literary effect! For by asserting that the stepmother with this murder brought to a climax year-round torture (altogether nonexistent) of the child, *eo ipso* you are distorting the facts for a reader little informed about this case; you are extorting from his soul compassion and mercy which, willy-nilly, he must feel, upon reading your article. And yet, had you not pictured to him this stepmother as a torturer of the child, she may have, perhaps, won in his heart a slight indulgence as a sick person, pathologically shocked, as an irritated pregnant woman, as is clear from the fantastic, wild and mysterious details of the event. Is it just, for a public man, to act this way? Is it human?

But you even say more. You wrote—and, again, positively and precisely—as an observer who had studied the case in all its minutest details:

" 'Affect of pregnancy'—well a new, pitiful word has been invented. No matter how strong this affect might have been, nevertheless, under its influence, the woman did not rush upon her husband or her neighbors. Her whole affect was reserved for that defenseless girl whom she had been torturing a whole year without any affect. What, then, did the jurors rely upon in their acquittal?"

But upon what did you yourself rely, Mr. Observer, when concocting such a complete distortion of the case? "She did not rush upon her husband!" But this was the one thing which had been testified to at the trial that in her quarrels with her husband (however, only during the last several days) she reached that state of madness, which prompted her to commit the crime. They were quarrelling not at all over the child, and literally the child had nothing to do with these brawls; *in those days she did not even think about it*. "Then I did not even need it"—as she put it herself.

Not for you but for my readers I shall try to trace these two characters, those of the husband and wife, involved in the brawls, since I understood them even prior to the verdict. They revealed themselves to me as a result of most attentive observation. In this there can be no great indiscretion, on my part, since much has already been revealed in the course of the trial. Besides, strictly speaking, I am doing this for their exoneration.

And so the point is this. Above all, the husband is a steady, straightforward, most honest and kind man (*i.e.*, even magnanimous, as he has proved subsequently), but too puritanical, too naïvely and even too rigorously abiding by a once-and-for-all adopted opinion and conviction. Here one has also to take into account a certain difference of age between him and his wife, he being much older than she, as well as the fact that he is a widower. He works all

day, and although he wears "German" clothes and has the appearance, as it were, of an "educated" man, nevertheless he has received
no special education. I may also remark that in his countenance
there is an obvious mark of self-respect. Let me add that he is not
very talkative, not very cheerful or risible. Perhaps his is a somewhat difficult disposition. He married her when she was still very
young. She is an honest girl, a seamstress by profession, who used
to earn good money.

I do not know how they met. She married him of her free will,
because she loved him. But very soon discord ensued, and although
for a long time things did not come to a head, nevertheless perplexity, alienation, and finally even irritation on both sides grew
slowly but steadily and undeviatingly. The point is—this may even
be the whole cause—that despite increasing irritation, they loved
each other very ardently, and this—to the very end. Love sharpened
the demands on either side, increased them, adding irritation to
them.

And on top of all this—her character. Hers is a rather reserved
and somewhat proud character. Both among men and women there
are those who, though nourishing in their hearts most ardent feelings, are nevertheless somehow bashful about revealing them: there
is little endearment in them, few caressing words; few embraces
and little fondling. If, as a result, they be called heartless and insensible, they shut themselves in even tighter. When they are accused they seldom seek to explain the matter; on the contrary, they
leave this concern to the accuser, as though saying: "Guess yourself: if you love, you must understand that I am right." And if he
fails to understand and grows more and more irritable, she, too,
grows more and more angry.

Now, this husband, from the very beginning, started admonishing, teaching her, reproaching her severely (though not at all cruelly)
with his former wife, and this was particularly painful to her. However, things did not go too badly. It always so happened that, in
answer to his accusations, she would start quarrelling and uttering
spiteful words, instead of seeking to clear up the misunderstanding
by some final explanation or indication of its underlying causes.
At length, such tactics were given up entirely. It came to the point
where feelings more morose, disillusionment in lieu of love, grew
up in her heart (in her heart first, and not in the husband's). All
this grew rather unconsciously.—Well, this is difficult toiling life;
there is not much time to think about sentiments. He goes to work;
she keeps house, cooks, even washes the floors. Along the extended
corridor in the government building there are small rooms, one for
each family of married workers employed in that state institution.

It so happened that, with the husband's permission, she went to a Saint's day party, in the family home of that artisan who taught her the sewing craft in her childhood and girlhood, and with whom both she and her husband continued to be acquainted. This time the husband, who had to attend to some work, stayed home. The Saint's day party turned out to be a jolly one; there were many invited; refreshments were served; people started to dance. The feast lasted till morning. Accustomed to a rather dull life at her husband's house, in one room, always toiling, the young woman, apparently, recalled the days of her girlhood, and enjoyed herself at the ball so long that she forgot the hour fixed for her return. All in all, she was persuaded to spend the night with the hosts, all the more so as it was a long way to her home. The husband, who for the first time spent the night without his wife, grew angry,—very much so: next day, quitting work, he went after her to her hosts, found her there, and right then and there, in the presence of the guests, he *punished* her. They went home silently, and for two days and two nights after that they did not speak to each other and did not take their meals together. All this I have learned in fragments, while she, despite my questioning, gave little explanation of her psychic state at the time. "I do not remember what I was thinking about those two days, but I kept pondering. *I did not even look at her at all* [meaning the little stepdaughter]. I remember everything as it happened but I couldn't tell you how I did it."

Early in the morning of the third day the husband left the house and went to work; the little girl was still sleeping. The stepmother busied herself around the stove. Finally, the girl woke up. The stepmother automatically, as usual, washed her, put on her shoes and dressed her, prepared her coffee . . . "and I didn't think about her at all." The child sat down, drank from her cup, and ate her breakfast—"and, all of a sudden, I looked at her."

4

SPITEFUL PSYCHOLOGISTS. ACCOUCHEURS—PSYCHIATRISTS

Listen, Mr. Observer, you assert—positively and precisely—that the whole affair occurred without vacillations, deliberately, calmly. You imply that she was beating the child for a whole year, and finally thought the matter over, made up her mind, and threw the infant out the window. "*There* is neither sudden manifestation of hatred"—you write with indignation—"nor repentance after the commission of the murder: everything is homogeneous and logical in the manifestation of *one and the same evil will*. And they acquit this woman!"

Such are your own words. But the prosecutor himself withdrew the charge of premeditation of the crime. Do you know this, Mr. Observer?—he withdrew it publicly, solemnly, at the most critical moment of the trial. And yet the prosecutor had been accusing the delinquent woman with cruel perseverance. How, then, Mr. Observer, do you assert, after the prosecutor's retreat, that there was no suddenness; that, on the contrary,—everything was homogeneous and logical in the manifestation of one and the same evil will? Homogeneous and logical!—Therefore, deliberate and premeditated.

Once more, let us briefly recapitulate: she ordered the girl to stand up on the window-sill and look out of the window, and when the girl did so, she lifted her by her legs and threw her out from the height of five and one-half sagenes. Then she shut the window, got dressed and went to the police station to denounce herself. Tell me, is this really homogeneous, logical, and not fantastic? And to begin with, what was the purpose of feeding the child, if the affair had been long before settled in her mind? Why wait for the child to drink her coffee and eat her bread?—How is it possible (and is it natural?)—not even to look out the window, after she had thrown out the girl? And, if you please, what was the purpose of self-denunciation? For, allegedly, everything was the result of spite, of hatred of the girl "whom she beat all year."—Why, having killed that girl, having finally conceived and perpetrated the murder—long ago and calmly premeditated—go at once to denounce herself?—Let death be the lot of the hated girl, but why should she ruin her own life? Besides, if in addition to hatred of the girl there was another motive for killing her,—the desire to take vengeance upon the husband by means of causing death to his child—she could have simply told him that the mischievous girl, on her own initiative, climbed the window and fell out. All the same, the aim would have been achieved; the father would have been astounded and shaken, while at that time no one in the world could have accused her of premeditated murder, even though she might have been suspected of it. Where was the evidence? Even should the girl have remained alive, who would have given credence to her lisping? Contrariwise, the murderess would have achieved everything which she set out to achieve; all the more completely, *i.e.*, much more cruelly and painfully, she would have avenged herself upon the husband who, though suspecting her of the murder, would have suffered even more from her impunity, seeing that she could not be brought to justice. On the other hand, by punishing herself, by ruining her life in a penitentiary, in Siberia, in the galleys, she would thereby be giving satisfaction to her husband.

What was the purpose of all this? And who in a case such as

this dresses himself up to go and ruin himself? Oh, I may be told that she simply meant to avenge the child and the husband; that she sought to end her marriage with her husband: "They will send me to the galley, and the marriage will be annulled!"—However, leaving aside the fact that the annulment of the marriage could have been conceived and brought about in a different manner, without ruining, at the age of nineteen, all one's life and freedom,—leaving this aside, you must concede that a person who deliberately ventures to throw himself into an abyss—heedlessly and unhesitatingly —you must concede that in such a human soul there must be at that moment a dreadful feeling, dark despair, an irresistible urge for perdition, for self-annihilation. This being so, can it be said— preserving common sense—that "there was neither *suddenness* nor repentance in the soul!"—If there was no repentance, there was gloom, damnation, madness. At least, it cannot be maintained that everything was logical and homogeneous, premeditated, without suddenness.

One has to be himself in a state of "affect" to assert this. Had she not gone to denounce herself; should she have stayed home; should she have lied to the people and to her husband that the child killed herself,—everything actually would have been logical and homogeneous, without suddenness in the manifestation of the evil will. However, immediate self-destruction—not forced but voluntary —of course, bears witness, at least, to the dreadfully disturbed psychic state of the murderess. The expression: "How strong she is!" was cited by the expert for the defense (and not the prosecution) for the purpose of showing to the court that the gloomy, cold, as if numb psychic state of the defendant after she had committed her crime, was not spiteful, frigid moral insensibility on her part.

My whole trouble was that, having, at the time, read the first sentence of the court, I was struck precisely by the strangeness and fantasticalness of all the details of the case; and having taking into account the fact of the fifth month of her pregnancy at the time of the commission of the murder—which was also reported in the papers—I was unable, quite involuntarily, not to start reasoning: wasn't pregnancy the prompting cause? *i.e.*, as I then wrote, didn't the thing happen this way: "She looked at the child, and spitefully thought: 'It would be nice to throw her out the window!'? Yet had she not been pregnant, maybe, she would have spitefully thought this, but would not have done it, would not have thrown the child out, whereas, being pregnant, she did it"? Now, this was my whole trouble: thus I reasoned at the time and thus I wrote.

But is it possible that the sentence was rescinded and that subsequently the murderess was acquitted as a mere result of these words? Mr. Observer, you scoff at the experts! You assert that only one of the five held that the delinquent woman was actually in a state that was an affect of pregnancy, while three others merely maintained that there could have been an influence of pregnancy, but did not positively say that such influence was present. From this you infer that only one of the experts *positively* exonerated the defendant, while four experts failed to do so. But this argument of yours is incorrect: you demand too much from human conscience. It suffices to say that three experts, apparently, did not want to exonerate the defendant *positively, i.e.,* to take this upon their conscience, but the facts were so impressive and obvious that these scientists nevertheless did waver, and finally were unable to say "no" directly and simply, but were *compelled* to say that "actually there might have been a pathological influence at the time of the commission of the crime." Well, to the jurors this was equivalent to a verdict: "If they were able to say: 'might have been,' this means, perhaps, that it actually was."

Such a strong doubt on the part of the jurors could not help influencing their verdict, and thus it should have been from the standpoint of sublime truth. Is it possible to kill a woman with a verdict, a woman whose full guilt was obviously doubted by three experts, while the fourth, Dukov, an expert specifically in psychic diseases, directly and firmly attributed the crime to the then disturbed psychic state of the delinquent woman?

But "The Observer" particularly seized upon the fifth expert, Mr. Florinsky, who dissented from the opinion of the other four experts, implying that he must know more about women's diseases. But why must he know more about psychic derangements than the expert psychiatrists? Is it because he is an accoucheur and practices not psychiatry but an altogether different thing?—This, too, is not quite logical.

5

An Incident Which to My Mind Explains Much

Now I will relate an incident which, to my mind, may finally explain certain things about this case, and which may directly serve the purpose for which I embarked upon this article.

On the third day after the acquittal of the defendant Kornilova (April 22, 1877), they—husband and wife—came to see me in the morning. On the eve they both went to a children's home where the victimized little girl (the one who was thrown out) had been placed, and next day they were planning to visit her again. By the way, the lot of the child has been taken care of, and there is no reason for exclaiming: "Woe now to the child! . . ." etc. When his wife was taken to prison, the husband placed the child in that orphan asylum because, working all day long, from early morning to late in the evening, it was impossible for him to care for her. Upon the wife's return, they decided to leave the girl in the home since there she is well taken care of. But during the holiday season they frequently took her home. At Christmas time, she stayed with them at their home. Despite her work, from early morning till late at night; despite the nursling (who was born in prison), the stepmother manages now and then to find time to visit the girl at the home, to bring her little presents, and so forth. While she was still in the penitentiary, when recalling how she had abused the child, she frequently dreamed that she might see her, and do something so as to make the little girl forget the incident. These fantasies were somewhat strange on the part of so reserved and even so little trusting a woman as was Kornilova all the time during the trial. Still, these fantasies were to come true. On Christmas, about a month ago, not having seen the Kornilovs for about six months, I stopped at their apartment, and Kornilova, before anything else, told me that the girl "jumps with joy and always embraces her whenever she, Kornilova, calls on her at the children's home." And when I was leaving them, suddenly she told me: "She will forget. . . ."

Thus, they came to see me on the third day after her acquittal. . . . But I keep deviating; I shall deviate once more—just for a minute. "The Observer," in his article, humorously and spitefully scoffs at me for my visits to Kornilova in prison. "He actually did penetrate that state" (meaning, the condition of pregnancy)—says he about me. "He went to see a certain lady in the penitentiary; he was impressed with her humility, and in several issues of his *Diary* he came out as her ardent advocate."

To begin with, what is the meaning of the word "lady"? Why this vulgar tone?—For "The Observer" is fully aware of the fact that it is not a dame or a lady, but a simple peasant woman, a worker from early morning till late at night; she cooks, washes the floors and does some sewing for outside customers, if she can manage to snatch a moment of leisure. I visited her in the penitentiary once a month, staying with her ten, at the utmost fifteen, minutes, usually in a common cell for women awaiting trial and having nurslings. If I observed this woman with curiosity and sought to comprehend her character,— is anything wrong with this,—does it deserve ridicule and scoffing? But let us go back to my story.

And so they came to visit me; they both sat in a concentrated, serious mood. Until then I had known the husband but little. And

suddenly he said: "Two days ago, when we returned home"—(this
was after the acquittal; thus it must have been after eleven o'clock
in the evening, and she wakes up at five in the morning)—"at once
we seated ourselves at the table, I took the Gospel and began to
read it to her." I confess: when he said this, looking at him I
thought, "Yes, he couldn't have done otherwise: this is a type, an
intact type,—this could have been guessed." In a word, he is a
puritan, a most honest, most serious man, unquestionably kind and
magnanimous, but one who will yield nothing and surrender none
of his convictions. This husband looks upon marriage with full
faith, precisely as upon a sacrament.

He is one of those husbands who can still be found in Russia,
and who abiding by the ancient Russian custom and tradition, upon
returning home from the wedding and retiring to the bedroom with
his newly wed wife, first of all, throws himself upon his knees before
a holy image and prays long, asking God that He bless their future
life. Kornilov acted then in a similar manner: once more accepting
his wife and renewing his marriage with her, which had been severed
as a result of the dreadful crime, first of all, he opened the Gospel
and began reading it to her without being in the least restrained
in his manly and serious determination by the consideration that
the woman was almost collapsing from fatigue; that she was dreadfully shaken even when she was getting ready for the trial, and that
on that last fatal day of the trial she had endured so many crushing
impressions—moral and physical—that it would have been excusable,
even to such a rigorous puritan as he, to let her rest a bit, and
collect herself, and that this would have conformed more to the
aim which he had when he had opened the Gospel. His act seemed
to me almost awkward—all too inflexible, because it might have
failed to produce the desired result. A very guilty soul—especially
if it vividly realizes its guilt and has already endured much pain—
should not be too obviously and *hastily* reproached for its guilt,
lest a reverse effect be produced, especially when it repents anyway.
In circumstances such as these, the man upon whom the woman
depends, exalting himself over her in the aureole of a judge, appears
to her as something merciless, too autocratically breaking into her
soul, and sternly repulsing her repentance and the good sentiments
regenerated in her: "Not rest, not food, nor drink, are needed for
one such as you. Sit down and listen to how one has to live."

As they were leaving, I succeeded in remarking in passing that
he should not be hurrying so and proceeding so inflexibly, and that,
perhaps, this method would prove more expedient. I spoke briefly
and plainly. Even so, I thought he might, perhaps, fail to understand me. Unexpectedly, in answer to my remark, he said: "But

right then, as soon as we entered the house, and when we started reading, she told me everything, how, during your last visit, you taught her to be good, should she be sentenced to Siberia, told her how she should live there. . . ."

This is how the thing happened. It is true that exactly on the eve of the trial, I visited her at the prison. No one, neither I nor her defense lawyer, had any firm hopes for her acquittal. Neither had she. I found her apparently composed. She was sitting and stitching something. Her child was slightly indisposed. Yet she was not exactly sad, but, as it were, oppressed. As for myself, I had in my mind several gloomy thoughts concerning her. I called on her precisely to tell her a few words. We firmly hoped that she might be exiled only to a penal settlement. And so a woman scarcely of full age, with a nursling, would start for Siberia. Her marriage would be annulled. In a strange country, alone, defenseless, still rather pretty-looking, and so young—how could she withstand temptation?—This is what I was thinking. Truly, fate would be pushing her into the arms of debauch.—For I know Siberia: there, there are a great many men eager to seduce; many unmarried men—employees and speculators—are journeying thither from Russia. It is easy to be seduced, and the Siberians—plebeians and commoners—are absolutely merciless toward a fallen woman. No one will stand in her way, but a woman whose reputation has once been soiled can never restore it: she is doomed to everlasting contempt, reproaches, scoffing, and so—till old age, to her very grave. She will be specially nicknamed. And the child (a girl) would be *compelled* to inherit her mother's career: the girl, coming from a family with a shady reputation, would be unable to find a decent and honest fiancé. It would be different, however, if an exiled mother lived an honest and chaste life in Siberia: a young woman who manages to live a chaste life enjoys boundless respect: everybody is ready to defend and please her; everybody takes off his hat to her. Such a woman may be sure to find a husband for her daughter. Moreover, with time, when people begin to know and trust her, she may, perhaps, contract a second honest marriage and enter an honest family.[1]

It was this that I meant to convey to the young woman, scarcely of full age. On purpose, I selected precisely that last day before the trial because—I was saying to myself—it would more

[1]In Siberia, people rarely are curious about one's past, *i.e.,* for what crime one has been exiled. This is equally true of prison inmates and of the population in general. Perhaps this is due to the fact that in the course of the last three centuries virtually the whole population of Siberia was descended from exiles and it became populated with them.

FEODOR DOSTOIEVSKY: 1877

vividly impress itself upon her mind and would more deeply be engraved in her soul.

Having listened to my admonitions as to how she should live in Siberia, should she be exiled, she thanked me gloomily and seriously, hardly raising her eyes to me. And now, tired, exhausted, shaken with this horrible impression of the long trial, and at home having been made to listen to the Gospel, she did not think to herself: "At least, he should pity me! Why doesn't he postpone this until tomorrow? Why doesn't he give me something to eat and let me rest!" Nor was she offended by the fact that *she was being treated so disdainfully.* (N. B. The offense of being treated disdainfully may be felt by the most dreadful criminal, fully cognizant of his crime, and even by a deeply repentant criminal.) On the contrary, she had nothing better to say to her husband than *promptly* to inform him that also in the penitentiary people taught her to be good and that she should live in the strange country honestly and chastely. Obviously, she did so because she knew that this story would please her husband, that it would be in line with his tone and would encourage him: "This means"—he would think—"that she was really repenting, that she truly made up her mind to live a decent life." And he actually did so think, while in answer to my advice not to scare her with too hasty severity toward her, he directly told me, of course, with joy in his heart: "There's no reason to fear for her and to be cautious, since she herself is glad to be honest. . . ."

I don't know, but it seems to me that all this is intelligible. The readers will understand why I am recording these things. At present it may be at least hoped that the great mercy of the court did not spoil the delinquent woman more, but that, on the contrary, it struck good soil. For even in days past, in prison, as well as now she considered and continues to consider herself an indubitable criminal, while she attributes her acquittal exclusively to the great mercy of the court.

She herself does not understand "the affect of pregnancy." And verily she is an indubitable criminal; she was in possession of full memory when committing her crime; she remembers every incident, every minute trait of the perpetrated offense, and she only does not know and cannot even explain to herself, until this day: *"How she could have done it then and how she could have ventured it!"*

Yes, Mr. Observer, the court pardoned an actual criminal, despite the now unquestionable and fatal "affect of pregnancy," so ridiculed by you, and of which, at present, I am profoundly and firmly convinced. And now decide for yourself. Had they annulled

the marriage; had they torn her away from a man whom she unquestionably loved and loves, and who constitutes to her her whole
family; had they banished her to Siberia,—her the solitary, helpless,
twenty-year-old one, with her nursling—dooming her to debauch
and infamy (for in Siberia the fall would have unfailingly happened);—tell me, what would have been the sense of ruining and
corrupting a life which at present, it would seem, has returned to
truth, in consequence of a severe purge and repentance, with a
regenerated heart? Isn't it better to reform, discover and restore a
human being than simply to chop off his head? It is easy, abiding
by the letter of the law, to cut off one's head, but it is always far
more difficult to examine a case in accordance with truth, humanely
and paternally.

Finally, you knew that together with the young, twenty-year-
old mother, *i.e.*, with an inexperienced woman,—in the future unfailingly a victim of want and debauch—her baby was to be banished.
. . . But let me tell you a few special words about babies.

6

AM I AN ENEMY OF CHILDREN? WHAT DOES THE WORD
"HAPPY ONE" MEAN AT TIMES

Your whole article, Mr. Observer, is a protest "against the
exculpation of the cruel treatment of children." Of course, the fact
that you are raising your voice in defense of children is to your
credit, but your attitude toward me is too haughty. You say:

One has to be endowed with all that power of imagination
in which, as is known, Mr. Dostoievsky excels among us all to
comprehend fully the condition of a woman and to elucidate to
one's self the irresistibility of the affect of pregnancy. . . . But
Mr. Dostoievsky is too susceptible, and besides, 'the pathological
manifestation of volition' is an outright hobby of the author of *The
Possessed, The Idiot,* etc.; to him it is excusable to feel a weakness
for them. I look upon the case in a simpler manner, and I assert
that after such instances of exculpation of the cruel treatment of
children,—which in Russia, as also in England, is by no means infrequent—there remains not even a shadow of deterrent to this kind
of behavior," and so on, and so forth.

In the first place, referring to "my weakness for the pathological manifestations of volition," I will merely tell you that it
seems that in my novels and stories I did, at times, actually succeed
in discovering certain people who considered themselves sound, and
then proved to them that they were unsound. Do you know that

a great many people are ill because of their boundless confidence
in their normalcy, and, *eo ipso* they are infected with awful self-
conceit, impossible narcissism, which sometimes reaches the level
of the conviction of one's infallibility?

Well, precisely such ones I used to call to the attention of
my readers and even prove that sturdy fellows are far from being
as healthy as people think; that, contrariwise, they are very sick
and should be placed under medical care. In this I see nothing
wrong, but "The Observer" is too harsh toward me because his phrase
about "the exculpation of the cruel treatment of children" is also
aimed at me. He merely softens it "a little" by saying that "to him
it is excusable."

His whole article is written as a direct proof that because of
my predilection for "the pathological manifestation of volition"
common sense has been so distorted in me that I am inclined to
pity the torturer of a child, that beastly stepmother, rather than
her tortured victim, the weak, miserable little girl,—beaten, insulted
and, finally, murdered. This, to me, is offensive.

In contradistinction to my pathological inclination, "The Observer" directly, hastily, and candidly points to himself, setting his
sound health as an example: "I"—he implies—"look upon the case
more simply [than Mr. Dostoievsky], and I assert that after such
instances of exculpation of the cruel treatment of children . . .,"
etc. Thus I am justifying cruel treatment of children—what a dreadful accusation! In this case permit me to defend myself.

I shall not point to my former thirty years of literary work
in order to settle the question whether I am a great enemy of children and an advocate of their cruel treatment, but I shall merely
remind the readers of the last two years of my authorship, that is,
the publication of *A Writer's Diary*. At the time of the Kronebergs'
trial, despite my predilection for "the pathological manifestation
of volition," it so happened that I came out in defense of the child,
the victim, and not of the torturers. Consequently, Mr. Observer,
sometimes, I, too, side with common sense.

At present I even regret, Mr. Observer, that then you did not
come out in defense of the child; surely you would have written
a most ardent article. But somehow I do not recall a single ardent
article in defense of the child. Consequently, at the time, you did
not deem it necessary to intercede. Thereupon, recently,—last summer,—I happened to raise my voice in defense of the young children
of the Djunkovskys, who had also been subjected to torture in their
parents' home. Again, about the Djunkovskys you wrote nothing.
True, no one has written anything. This is easy to understand:
everybody was occupied with such important political problems!

Finally, I could refer not to one but to several instances when, in the course of these two years, I have spoken in the *Diary* about children, their upbringing, their sad lot in our families; about delinquent children in our correctional institutions. I even mentioned a certain little boy at Christ's Christmas tree—of course, a fictitious incident—which, however, does not exactly prove my insensibility or my indifference for children.

Mr. Observer, I will tell you this: when I first read in the newspapers about Kornilova's crime, about her inexorable sentence, and when, willy-nilly, I was struck by the thought that, perhaps, the criminal woman was not as guilty as she appeared to be (please note, Mr. Observer, that even then virtually nothing had been mentioned in the newspaper accounts of the trial about "*the stepmother's* beating," and even at that time this charge was no longer pressed by the prosecution)—having made up my mind to write something in favor of Kornilova, I understood only too clearly what I was embarking upon. At present, I candidly admit this to you. I fully understood that I was writing an unsympathetic article; that I was raising my voice in defense of the torturer, and against whom?— Against a little child. I foresaw that *certain people* would accuse me of insensibility, self-conceit, even of sickliness: "He is defending a stepmother, the murderess of a child!" I clearly foresaw this inflexibility of accusation on the part of some judges—for instance, on yours, Mr. Observer—so that, for a while, I hesitated, but in the end, I made up my mind: "If I believe that here is the truth, is it worth while to serve deceit for the sake of gaining popularity?"— this is what I finally said to myself. Besides, I was encouraged by the faith in my readers: "In the long run, they will understand"— I thought to myself—"that it is impossible to accuse me of the desire to exculpate torture of children, and if I now raise my voice in defense of the murderess, setting forth my suspicion of her pathological and insane state at the time of the commission of her villainy, thereby I am not defending the villainy itself, nor am I rejoicing over the fact that the child was beaten and killed. On the contrary, perhaps, I have the greatest compassion for the child, not less than that of any other. . . ."

Caustically you ridiculed me, Mr. Observer, for one sentence in my article on the acquittal of the defendant Kornilova:

"That same evening, after ten o'clock, the husband took her home, and she, in a happy mood, again returned to her home after an absence of almost one year, *with the impression of an enormous lesson derived by her for her whole life and of manifest Divine Providence in the whole case, beginning with the miraculous salvation of the child . . .*"

You see, Mr. Observer, I am ready to make a reservation and to apologize to you for the reproach which I have just made for my cut-in-half sentence. In fact, I can see now that it is not as clear as I had hoped, and that one may be mistaken about its meaning. Here, the whole point comes down to my understanding of the word "happy."

I conceived the defendant's happiness not only in the fact that she had been freed but in that "she returned home with the impression of an enormous lesson derived by her *for her whole life* and with a presentiment of Divine Providence guiding her." For there is no greater happiness than to become convinced of people's mercy and of their love of one another.—This is faith, full faith for one's whole life! And what happiness is superior to faith? Can this former criminal woman ever doubt people, people as mankind, as a whole, their goodness and sacred character? For a person on the verge of ruin and perdition to enter her own home with such a potent impression of a new faith is the greatest conceivable happiness. We know that often noble and lofty people have suffered from disbelief in the practical goodness of the great character of men, in their kindness, in their ideals, in their Divine origin, and died in a state of sad disillusionment.

Of course, you will smile at me and, perhaps, say that I am again indulging my fancy; that in a person as ignorant and coarse as Kornilova, descended from the common people and deprived of education, there can be no such disillusionment nor such emotions in the soul. This is not true!—These ignorant people do not know how to express all this in our way, in our tongue; but quite often they feel as deeply as we, the "educated people," and experience these feelings of theirs with the same happiness or with the same sorrow and pain as we.

Much as in ourselves, in them there may be disillusionment and mistrust of people. Had Kornilova been exiled to Siberia she would have fallen there and perished. Don't you think that in some better moment of her life she would feel the whole horror of her degradation, and would carry away in her heart—to her very grave —exasperation, all the more bitter because to her it would have been aimless, since, aside from herself, she could not have blamed anyone, because, I repeat, she is fully convinced—even to this moment —that she is an *indubitable criminal,* and she merely does not know how it all happened to her at the time. At present, however, believing herself a criminal and considering herself such, but suddenly forgiven by men, overwhelmed with benefits and pardoned, how can she fail to feel a regeneration to a new life superior to the former? —It was not some single person that pardoned her, but *everybody—*

the court, the jurors, which means society as a whole, bestowed mercy upon her. After that, how could she have failed to bear in her soul a feeling of an immense indebtedness—for her whole life —to all those who pitied her, that is, to all men on earth?

Every *great* happiness bears within it a certain sorrow because it arouses in us superior consciousness. Grief, rarer than great happiness, arouses in us such a lucidity of consciousness. Great, that is, sublime happiness lays an obligation on the soul. (I repeat: there is no greater happiness than to acquire faith in men's kindness and their love of one another.)

When the woman taken in adultery, condemned to stoning, was told: "Go and sin no more," is it possible that she went home to sin? Therefore, also in the case of Kornilova the whole question is: On what soil did the seed fall? This is why it now occurred to me to write this article. Mr. Observer, having read your attack against me seven months ago, I decided to postpone my answer to you so as to amplify my data. Now it seems to me that judging by the impressions I have gathered, I can unmistakenly state that the seed fell upon good soil, that a human being has been resurrected; that no harm was done to anyone; that the soul of the criminal woman is crushed at once with repentance and with the eternally beneficial impression of the boundless mercy of men, and that now, after having experienced so much kindness and love, it would be difficult for her heart to grow wicked. And I repeat to you, Mr. Observer, that she has no idea of excusing herself with the unquestionable "affect of pregnancy" which arouses in you such indignation.

In a word, it seemed to me not without point to convey all this, not only to you, Mr. Observer, but to my readers, and to all those merciful men who have acquitted her. And don't you worry, Mr. Observer, about the little girl and do not exclaim: "Woe to the child!" At present her fate has been rather well taken care of —and "she will forget." There is sound hope for this.

CHAPTER II

1

The Death of Nekrasov. On What Has Been Said at His Grave

NEKRASOV IS dead. The last time I saw him before his death was one month ago. Then he looked so much like a corpse that

it was strange to see that he could speak and move his lips. Yet not
only did he speak but he preserved full lucidity of the mind. It
seems that he still did not believe in the proximity of a near death.
A week before his passing he had a stroke which paralyzed the
right side of his body, and on the morning of the 28th[1] I learned
that he had passed away on the eve, on the 27th, at eight o'clock
in the evening. That same day I went to see him. His face, terribly
macerated and disfigured as a result of suffering, somehow struck
me most. When leaving, I could hear the psalmist reading over the
deceased in a distinct but slow voice: "There is no man who has
not sinned." Having returned home, I was unable to start working.
I took Nekrasov's three volumes and began to read them, beginning
with the first page. I sat reading all night till six o'clock in the
morning, and once more I lived through those thirty years. The
first four poems, with which the first volume of his works begins,
appeared in the *Petersburg Collection* in which my first novel was
also published.

Thereupon, as I kept reading—and I read one poem after another—my whole life passed rapidly before me. I recognized and
recalled those of his poems which I first read in Siberia, when having served my four years of imprisonment, and having been discharged from the penitentiary, finally I received permission to lay
my hands on a book. I also recalled the impression produced on
me at the time. Briefly, that night I read virtually two-thirds of
everything Nekrasov wrote, and literally, for the first time, I understood how much Nekrasov, as a poet, had meant in my life!—Of
course, as a poet.

We met rarely, and only once with a wholly unrestrained,
warm feeling, namely, at the very outset of our acquaintance, in
1845, at the time of *Poor Folk*. But this I have already recorded.
A few moments passed then between us during which, once and
for all, this mysterious man revealed himself to me in the most
essential and concealed aspect of his spirit. As I at once guessed
then, his was a heart wounded in the very early days of his life,
and it was *that wound which never did heal* that was the inception
and source of his whole lifelong passionate and suffering poetry.
With tears he spoke to me about his childhood, about the ugly life
which oppressed him in his parents' home, about his mother;—and
the way he spoke of her, that force of emotion with which he recol-
lected her, even then gave rise to the presentiment that if there
was going to be anything sacred in his life, anything that could
save him and serve him as a beacon, as a guiding star in the darkest

[1]December 28, 1877. (B. B.)

and most fatal moments of his life,—of course, it would only be the earliest infantile recollection about the infantile tears and sobbings, together with her, somewhere stealthily, so as not to be seen (as he told me) with his martyred mother, who loved him so ardently. I believe that no subsequent attachment could have exercised so potent an influence upon his will and some obscure irresistible urges of his soul, which obsessed him throughout his life, as his devotion to his mother.

And even then one could discern these obscure psychic impulses. After that, very shortly, I recall—we parted: our mutual intimacy lasted not longer than several months—thanks to misunderstandings, external circumstances, and the meddling of good people. Thereafter, many years later, when I returned from Siberia, even though we disagreed frequently, nevertheless, despite the difference in our convictions which was then beginning to manifest itself, when we met, at times, we said to each other strange things, as though actually something that had begun in our youth, in 1845, persisted in our lives; as though this refused to be interrupted, and could not be, notwithstanding the fact that sometimes we did not see each other for years and years. Thus, once upon a time—I believe it was in 1863—when handing me a little volume of his poems, he pointed to one piece, *The Unfortunate*, and said impressively: "When I wrote this, I was thinking about you [*i.e.*, about my life in Siberia]. This was written about you." And finally, of late, we again began to see each other, when my novel *Raw Youth* was being published in his magazine.

Nekrasov's funeral was attended by several thousand of his admirers. There were many students. The funeral procession began at nine o'clock in the morning, and it was only at dusk that people left the cemetery. At his grave many orations were delivered, but only a few littérateurs spoke. Among other things, somebody's beautiful poem was read. Deeply impressed, I made my way to the still open grave strewn with flowers and wreaths, and in my weak voice I said a few words. I began precisely with the statement that his was a heart wounded once for his whole life, and that this bleeding wound was the source of his whole poetry—passionate to the point of tortured love of everything suffering from violence, from the cruelty of unrestrained will—everything that oppressed the Russian woman, the child in our Russian families, the common man in his lot, which is often so bitter. I also expressed my conviction that in our poetry Nekrasov was last in the line of those poets who appeared with their "new word."

In fact—leaving aside the question of the artistic power of

his poetry, and its scope—Nekrasov, in truth, was very original and he did come with "a new word." For instance, in the past, there had been Tutchev, a greater and more artistic poet, and yet he will never occupy so conspicuous and memorable a place in our literature as will unquestionably be assumed by Nekrasov. In this sense, among the poets (*i.e.*, who appeared with "a new word") he must be placed right next to Pushkin and Lermontov. When I expressed this thought aloud, there occurred a little incident: a voice in the crowd shouted that Nekrasov was *greater* than Pushkin and Lermontov, and that these two were merely "Byronists." Several voices caught it up, shouting: "Yes, greater!"

However, I did not mean to discuss the relative greatness of the three poets. But here is what subsequently developed: Mr. Skabichevsky, in *The Stock-Exchange Gazette*, in his message to the young people on Nekrasov's significance, referring to the fact that when *someone* (*i.e.*, I) at the grave of Nekrasov "ventured to compare his name with those of Pushkin and Lermontov, all of you (*i.e.*, college youth) *in unison, in a chorus*, shouted: 'he was greater, greater than they!'" I wish to assure Mr. Skabichevsky that he has been wrongly informed, and I remember distinctly (I hope I am not mistaken) that first there sounded only one voice: "greater, greater than they," adding at once that Pushkin and Lermontov were "Byronists"—in a supplementary remark which is much more characteristic of and natural to one voice or opinion than to *all* those present shouting at one and the same moment, that is, to a chorus composed of a thousand people. This fact, then, tends to support my version of the incident. And it was only after the first outcry that several other voices sounded, but only several, and I did not hear any thousand-man-strong chorus. This I reiterate, and I hope I am not mistaken.

I insist on this point because to me it would have been painful if *all* our youth had committed such an error. Gratitude to the departing great names should dwell in a young heart. No doubt, the ironical outcries about Byronists and "greater, greater," did not come as a result of the desire to start a literary dispute at the grave of the dear deceased—which would have been out of place. This was merely an ardent impulse to express as strongly as possible the sentiment of emotion, gratitude and ecstasy, accumulated in one's heart for the great poet who used to move us so deeply and who, though in his grave, was still so close to us (whereas those great old men are so far from us!).

However, this whole incident, then and there, aroused in me the desire to elucidate my idea in the next issue of *The Diary* and to state in detail my views on so remarkable and extraordinary a phenomenon in our life and poetry as Nekrasov, explaining the specific significance of this phenomenon, as I understand it.

2

PUSHKIN, LERMONTOV AND NEKRASOV

And first of all, one shouldn't use the word "Byronist" as an invective. Byronism, though a momentary phenomenon, was a great, sacred and necessary one in the life of European mankind and, perhaps, in that of the entire human race. Byronism appeared at a moment of dreadful anguish, disillusionment and almost despair among men. Following the ecstatic transports of the new creed in the new ideals proclaimed at the end of the last century in France, then the most progressive nation of European mankind, the outcome was very different from what had been expected; this so deceived the faith of man that there has never perhaps been a sadder moment in the history of Western Europe. The new idols—raised for one moment only—fell not only as a result of external (political) causes, but because of their intrinsic bankruptcy—which was clearly perceived by the sagacious hearts and the progressive minds. The new *outcome* was not yet in sight; the new valve was not yet revealed, and everybody was suffocating under the weight of a former world, which drew and narrowed itself down over mankind in a most dreadful manner. The old idols lay shattered.

It was at this very moment that a great and mighty genius, a passionate poet, appeared. In his melodies there sounded mankind's anguish of those days, its gloomy disillusionment in its mission and in the ideals which had deceived it. It was a novel, then unheard-of, muse of vengeance and sorrow, malediction and despair. The spirit of Byronism, as it were, swept mankind as a whole, and everything responded to it. It was precisely as if a valve had been opened: at least, amidst the universal and dull groans—mostly unconscious—this was a mighty outcry in which all the cries and moans of mankind combined and merged in one chord. How could it not have been felt in Russia and particularly by so great, ingenious and leading a mind as that of Pushkin?—In those days also, in Russia no strong mind, no magnanimous heart could have evaded Byronism. And not only because of compassion from afar for Europe and European mankind, but because precisely at that time in Russia, too, there arose a great many unsolved and tormenting questions, a great many old disillusionments. . . . However the greatness of Pushkin, as the leading genius, lay precisely in the fact that he, surrounded by men who virtually failed to understand him, so soon

found a firm path, *a great and keenly looked for outcome for us
Russians, and indicated it.* This outcome was—"populism,"[1]—*the
worship of the Russian people's truth.*[2]

"Pushkin was a great and extraordinary phenomenon." He
was "not only a Russian, but the first Russian." For a Russian not
to understand Pushkin means to be deprived of the right to call
himself a Russian. Pushkin understood the Russian people and
grasped their mission so deeply, on such a grand scale, as no one
had ever done. I am not mentioning the fact that by the universality
of his genius, by his faculty of responding to all the manifold aspects
of European mankind and of virtually reincarnating himself in the
genius of alien peoples and nationalities, he bore witness to the
humaneness and universality of the Russian spirit, thereby, as it
were, prognosticating the future mission of Russia's genius in the
midst of humankind as its all-unifying, all-reconciling and all-re-
generating element. Nor shall I touch upon the fact that Pushkin
was the first in Russia who, with anguish, in prophetic foresight,
exclaimed:

> "Shall I behold the free, the liberated people
> And serfdom fallen at the Czar's majestic nod!"

I shall speak now merely of Pushkin's love of the Russian people.
His was an all-embracing love, a love which prior to him no one
had ever manifested. "Don't love me, but love what's *mine*"—this is
what the people will always tell you when they want to be assured
of your love of them.

Every nobleman, especially one who is human and Europeanly
enlightened, is fully capable of loving the people, that is, pitying
them for their needs, poverty and suffering. But the people *need* to
be loved not for their suffering, but *for their own sake.* What does
it mean to love them *for their own sake?* "Well, you should love
what I love; you should revere what I revere"—this is what it means.
And it is only thus that the people will respond to you. Otherwise
they will never recognize you as their own, no matter how much
you may be sorry for them. Likewise they will always discern
falsity regardless of any pitiful words you may use to tempt them.

Pushkin loved the people precisely in this manner, in a way
required by the people; nor did he guess how the people should be
loved; he did not prepare himself therefor; he did not learn how
to act: suddenly he himself became the people. He bowed to the

---

[1]The Russian word "narodnost," derived from the word "narod"—"the
people," is untranslatable. Perhaps the nearest, though far from satisfactory, translation, is "populism." (B. B.)

[2]These are Gogol's words.

people's truth: he recognized it as his own truth. Despite all the vices of the people and many of their terrible habits, he succeeded in discerning the great substance of their spirit at a time when almost no one even looked upon the people. And he accepted the people's substance as an ideal of his own soul. And this—at a time when the most humane and Europeanly enlightened lovers of the Russian people candidly regretted the fact that our people were so mean that they were incapable of lifting themselves to the level of the Parisian street mob. Above all, they believed that the Russian people were slaves. By slavery they excused the people's degradation. Even so, they could not love a slave since, all the same, he was repugnant.

Pushkin was the first to declare that the Russian *is not a slave*, never was one, despite many centuries of slavery. There was serfdom but there were no serfs (of course, speaking generally, and not about exceptions)—such was Pushkin's thesis. Even from the gait of the Russian peasant he drew the inference that he was not and could not be a slave (even though he was in serfdom)—a trait which demonstrates in Pushkin a profound and direct love of the people. He also recognized in our people (again, taken as a whole, and disregarding the usual and inevitable exceptions) the lofty feeling of self-respect; he foresaw that calm dignity with which they would accept their liberation from serfdom,—a fact which, for instance, long after Pushkin, our most remarkable educated Russian Europeans did not understand, expecting from the people something quite different.

Oh, they loved the people sincerely and ardently, but in their own, European way. They vociferated about their bestial status in serfdom. Even so they wholeheartedly believed that our people were actually beasts. And suddenly that people became free with such manly dignity, without the slightest urge to avenge themselves upon their former owners: "You mind your business, we will mind ours. If you wish—come to us. For whatever good you may bring us, you will always be honored by us."

Yes, to many people our peasant, after his liberation, appeared to be a strange enigma. Many people even decided that this in him was the result of a want of mental development and dullness, an aftermath of former serfdom. And this we behold in our day.— What, then, must have been the feeling in Pushkin's times? Didn't I hear in the days of my youth the opinion expressed by progressive and "competent" people that the character of Savelyich, in Pushkin's *The Captain's Daughter*, the serf of the landowners Griniovi, who fell to Pugachiov's feet imploring him to spare the life of the nobleman's son, and "better to hang him, the old dotard,—for the sake of fear and edification,"—that not only is this character that of a slave, but that is an apotheosis of Russian slavery!

Pushkin loved the people not only for their suffering. One pities suffering, and so commiseration frequently goes parallel with contempt. Pushkin loved everything the people loved, revering everything they revered. He loved Russian nature, the Russian countryside, passionately, to the point of emotion. He was not a nobleman —merciful and humane—pitying the peasant because of his bitter lot. With his heart he incarnated in himself a man belonging to the common people, his essence, almost—his image. The depreciation of Pushkin, as a poet who was devoted to the people rather historically and archaically than factually, is erroneous and even senseless. In these historical and archaic motives there sounds a love, *an estimation of the people,* which belongs to them *eternally,* always—now and in the future—and not only to some historical people who have long ceased to exist.

Our people love their history principally because they find in it intact that same sanctity in which they preserve their creed even in our day, despite all their distress and lifelong sufferings. Beginning with the stately and immense figure of the chronicler in *Boris Godunov* and winding up with Pugachiov's fellow travellers —in Pushkin they all are the people in their most profound manifestations; they are all intelligible to the people as their own essence. And is this all? The Russian spirit is diffused in all the creations of Pushkin, the Russian vein pulsates everywhere. In the great, inimitable, incomparable songs, supposedly of the Western Slavs, which are obviously the product of the great Russian spirit, we find the expression of the Russian's conception of his Slavic brethren, therein is his whole heart; therein is revealed the whole philosophy of the people which, up to the present, is preserved in their songs, legends, traditions, stories,—everything the people love and hold sacred: the ideals of their heroes, their czars, national defenders and commiserators, the models of courage, humility, love and sacrifice. And those delightful jests of Pushkin, for instance, that chit-chat of the two drunken peasants, or that *Tale about the Bear* whose she bear was killed,—why, this is something amorous, charming and touching in his contemplation of the people.

Had Pushkin lived longer, he would have bequeathed to us such treasures for the understanding of the people as would have— through their influence—unfailingly curtailed the times and seasons for the transition to the people's truth, their vigor, the realization of their mission by our whole intelligentsia, which still exalts itself over the people by its Europeanism.

Now, it is this worship of the people's truth that I perceive (alas, perhaps, I alone among all his admirers) in Nekrasov, in his

best creations. I treasure—very much so—the fact that he was "the
commiserator for the people's sorrow"; that he spoke so much and
so passionately about the people's grief. But still dearer to me is
the fact that in the great, painful and ecstatic moments of his life
—despite all the opposing influences and even his own personal convictions—he bowed before the people's truth with all his being, a
fact to which his loftiest creations bear full witness. It is in this
spirit that I spoke about him, who, after Pushkin and Lermontov,
came much as the latter two, partly with a new word (for Pushkin's "word," to us, is still new. And not only new but one which,
as yet, has not been understood and deciphered, and which is regarded as most obsolete rubbish).

Before I turn to Nekrasov, I shall say a few words about
Lermontov in order to justify my contention that he also believed
in the people's truth. Of course, Lermontov was a Byronist, but
because of his great and original poetic power he was a peculiar
Byronist—some kind of sarcastic, capricious, surly Byronist, perpetually distrusting even his own inspiration, his own Byronism.
But if he had stopped fussing about the personality of the educated
Russian tormented by his Europeanism, no doubt he would, just
like Pushkin, have found the solution in the worship of the people's
truth. In support of this there are strong and precise indications.
However, in his case, too, death arrested the natural course.

As a matter of fact, in all his poems he is gloomy, capricious;
he wants to speak the truth, but more often than not he lies, and
he knows it and suffers because he is lying. However, the moment
he touches upon the people, he is serene and lucid. He loves the
Russian soldier, the Cossack, and he reveres the people. And he
writes that immortal song about the young merchant Kalashnikov
who kills for an outrage the Czar's bodyguard Kiribeevich, and,
summoned to appear before Czar Ivan the Terrible, he answers him
that he killed the Czar's servant Kiribeevich "of his own free will
—not by accident."

Gentlemen, do you remember "the slave Shibanov"? He was
the slave of Prince Kurbsky, a Russian emigrant of the Sixteenth
Century, who kept writing protesting and virtually abusive epistles
to the same Czar Ivan—from abroad, where he found safe refuge.
Having written one of these letters, he summoned his slave Shibanov
and ordered him to deliver it to Moscow and to hand it personally
to the Czar. The slave Shibanov acted as he was ordered. In the
Kremlin Square he stopped the Czar, who was leaving the cathedral,
escorted by his retinue, and handed him the epistle of his master,
Prince Kurbsky. The Czar lifted his staff with a sharp ferrule, and
with all his might drove it into Shibanov's foot, and leaning upon
his staff, he started reading the letter. Shibanov, with his pierced

foot, did not move. Subsequently, when answering Prince Kurbsky's letter, the Czar, among other things, wrote: "Thou shouldst be put to shame by thy slave Shibanov." This meant that he, the Czar himself, was put to shame by the slave Shibanov. The character of this Russian "slave" must have impressed Lermontov's soul. His Kalashnikov speaks to the Czar without any reproach about Kiribeevich, fully aware of the execution awaiting him; he tells the Czar "the whole genuine truth" that he killed his favorite "of his own free will—not by accident."

I repeat, had Lermontov lived, we should have had a great poet who would have acknowledged the people's truth, and maybe a genuine "commiserator for the people's sorrow." But this title was conferred upon Nekrasov.

Again, I am not comparing Nekrasov with Pushkin. I am not measuring with a yardstick who is taller and who is shorter, since here there can be no comparison, nor even a question of comparison. By the grandeur and depth of his Russian genius Pushkin up to this day shines like a sun over our whole Russian intelligent world outlook. He is a great prophet who is still not understood. Compared with him, Nekrasov is but a tiny dot, a small planet which, however, emerged from that great sun. And leaving aside all measurements—who is taller or shorter—immortality, fully deserved immortality, belongs to Nekrasov, and I have already explained why: for his worship of the people's truth which, in him, was not a result of some kind of imitation, nor even of a fully conscious process— it was an urge, an irresistible impulse. And in Nekrasov this was all the more remarkable as all his life he had been under the influence of people who, perhaps, very sincerely loved and pitied the people but who never acknowledged any truth in them, and who always placed European enlightenment far above the truth of the people's spirit. Without inquiring into the Russian soul and not knowing what it expects and craves for, these men frequently wished our people—with all their love for them—that which might have been detrimental to them. Was it not they who in the Russian popular movement of the last two years almost completely failed to acknowledge that exaltation of the enthusiasm of the national spirit which the people have been revealing for the first time with such completeness and so forcefully, thereby proving their sane, mighty and steady unity in one and the same great idea and their prescience of their future predestination. And not only do they refuse to recognize the truth of the popular movement, but they virtually consider it reaction, something bearing witness to the impassable want of consciousness and backwardness of the Russian people, which has grown inveterate in the course of centuries.

Despite his remarkable and extraordinarily keen intellect,

Nekrasov, however, lacked serious education; at least it was limited. All his life he was unable to rid himself of certain influences—he had no strength to do so. Yet he possessed an original psychic power of his own which never left him, a genuine, passionate—and what is most important—direct love of the people. With all his soul he commiserated with their suffering, perceiving in them not merely an image degraded by slavery—a bestial image—but through the force of his love he was able to grasp almost unconsciously the beauty of the people, their strength and intellect, their suffering humility, and partly even to believe in their future predestination. Oh, intellectually, Nekrasov could be mistaken in many a thing. In an impromptu, recently published for the first time, contemplating with alarmed reproach the people liberated from serfdom, he found it possible to exclaim:

". . . But are the people happy?"

The great instinct of his heart revealed to him the people's sorrow, but if he had been asked: "What should one wish for the people? How can it be done?"—he might have given a quite erroneous, perhaps even detrimental answer. And, of course, he could not be blamed: in Russia there is still extremely little political sense, while Nekrasov, I repeat, was all his life under alien influences. But with his heart, with his great poetic inspiration, in some of his grand poems, irresistibly he merged with the very essence of the people. In this sense he was a popular poet. Everyone descending from the people, even with a minimum of education, will understand much in Nekrasov, provided, however, he is educated. The question whether the Russian people as a whole can understand him is obviously a senseless one. What will the "common people" understand in his masterpieces: *The Knight for an Hour, Silence, Russian Women?* Even in his great *Vlas,* which might be intelligible to the people (but which in no way would inspire them, since this poetry has long been divorced from life itself) they would unfailingly discern two or three false traits. What would the people make out of one of his mightiest and most appealing poems—*On the Volga?* This is Byron's genuine spirit and tone.

Nay, as yet, Nekrasov is merely a poet of the Russian intelligentsia who spoke with love and passion to the same Russian intelligentsia about the people and their suffering. I am not speaking of the future: in the future the people will take notice of Nekrasov. Then they will understand that once upon a time there lived a kind Russian nobleman who shed lamenting tears over their popular grief, and who could find nothing better, when running away from his wealth and from the sinful temptations of his nobleman's life, in his very distressful moments, than to come to the

people, and, in his irresistible love of them, cleanse his tormented
heart, since Nekrasov's love of the people was but *an outlet of his
personal sorrow about himself.*

However, before I explain how I understand this "personal
sorrow" of our dear deceased poet about himself, I feel that I must
call attention to one characteristic and peculiar circumstance which
was recorded in virtually all our newspapers immediately after
Nekrasov's death—in practically all articles dedicated to him.

3

THE POET AND THE CITIZEN. GENERAL COMMENTS ON
NEKRASOV AS A MAN

All newspapers—just as soon as they began to speak about
Nekrasov, about his death and funeral, just as soon as they began
to define his significance—forthwith added, all of them without exception, certain considerations regarding a kind of low "practicality"
in his character, certain defects and even vices, some sort of duplicity in the image which he left behind. Some papers merely hinted
at this, very slightly, in a couple of lines, but the important fact
is that all the same they did hint, apparently owing to some necessity which they could not avoid. But in other periodicals, which
dwelt on Nekrasov in greater detail, the thing appeared even more
strangely. In fact: without framing any accusations in detail, and,
as it were, avoiding them out of profound and sincere respect for
the deceased, nevertheless they set out to exculpate him, so that
the matter became still more incomprehensible. "Well, what do you
exculpate him of?"—involuntarily one would ask oneself: "If you
know something, there is no reason for hiding it; but we wish to
know if he actually needs your apologies." This was the question
which arose in one's mind. However, they did not want to formulate
any accusations, but they hastened with their apologies and reservations, as if seeking to forewarn somebody and mainly, again, as if
they could not avoid this, even though, maybe, they did not wish
to embark upon the subject.

Generally speaking, this is an extremely peculiar case. Still,
if thought be given to it, you and everyone else—whoever he may
be—unquestionably would come to the conclusion that this is a
perfectly normal case, since, once you start speaking about Nekrasov
as a poet, it is verily impossible to avoid speaking about him as
an individual, for the reason that in Nekrasov the poet and citizen
are so closely combined, so inexplicable one without the other, and
taken together they explain one another so clearly that when you

begin to speak about him as a poet, willy-nilly, you turn to the citizen. And you feel that you are compelled to do so and that you cannot avoid it.

But what can we say and what specifically do we see? The word "practicality" is uttered, *i.e.*, the ability to take care of one's business—that's all. But right away people hasten with their apologies: "He suffered,"—they say. "Ever since childhood he was oppressed by his milieu"; as a youth—homeless and forsaken—he endured much grief in Petersburg, and, accordingly, he became "practical" (*i.e.*, as if he could not help becoming practical). Others go still farther, insinuating that without this "practicality" Nekrasov, perhaps, would not have accomplished obviously useful things for the public benefit, for instance, that he would have been unsuccessful with the publication of the magazine, etc. Well, is it implied that for good ends bad means should be justified?—And this —speaking of Nekrasov, who, with his poems, made hearts quiver, evoking ecstasy and emotion for the good and the beautiful!

Of course, all this is being said by way of apology. But it does seem to me that Nekrasov does not need any such exculpation. In apologies of this kind there is always something humiliating, dimming and degrading to the image of him who is being exculpated to the level of triviality. In fact, the moment I start justifying "the duplicity and practicality" of a person, thereby I am insisting, as it were, that in certain circumstances such a duplicity is natural and almost necessary. If so, one has to reconcile oneself completely, when he, repenting, beats himself against the slabs of his own church, and cries: "I have fallen! I have fallen!"—And this—in verses of unfading beauty which he writes down that very night, while on the morrow, just as soon as the night is over and tears dry up, he embarks again on "practicality" on the alleged ground that it is something altogether apart and that it is a *necessary* thing. Well, what then do these groans and cries, expressed in verses, mean?—Art for art's sake—nothing more, even in its most trivial sense, because he lauds these verses himself, he admires them, he is quite pleased with them, he publishes them and counts upon them: they will add brilliancy to the periodical; they will make young hearts beat more strongly.

Nay, if all this is justified without proper explanation, we risk committing a grave error and generating perplexity. And then in answer to the question: "Whom are you burying?" we, who attended his funeral, should be compelled to say: "We are burying the most brilliant representative of art for art's sake." And yet was this so? Nay, *in truth this was not so:* we did bury a "commiserator of the people's sorrow," an eternal sufferer for himself, one who was never able to appease himself and who, with disgust and self-castigation, rejected cheap reconciliation.

The matter has to be clarified sincerely and impartially, and whatever is ascertained should be accepted for what it is worth regardless of any personality and any further considerations. In this case, if possible, the essence of the matter has to be scrutinized so as to reconstruct with the utmost precision the personality, the character, of the deceased. Our hearts insist on this so that there may be left no perplexity whatsoever such as involuntarily smears the memory, not seldom leaving an unworthy shadow even on a noble image.

Personally, I have known little of the "practical life" of the deceased, and for this reason I am in no position to embark on the anecdotal aspect of the matter. But were I even in a position to do so, I would refuse it because I should be plunging into what I myself consider to be gossip. Because I am (and also formerly was) convinced that of everything that has been said about the deceased, at least half—and, maybe, three-quarters—is a pure lie. Lies, rubbish and gossip. A man as original and remarkable as Nekrasov was bound to have enemies. And the things which were true, which did happen, were likely, at times, to be exaggerated. However, even taking all this into account, nevertheless there remains a residue. What is it?—Something gloomy, sombre and undeniably painful, since what do these groans mean, these cries and tears of his, these avowals that he "has fallen," this passionate confession in the presence of his mother's shadow?—Again, I am not going to dwell upon the factual aspect of the matter; I believe, however, that the essence of that gloomy and painful half of our poet's life was foretold by himself, at the dawn of his days, in one of his earliest pieces, which, if I am not mistaken, were jotted down prior to his acquaintance with Bielinsky, and only later moulded into the form in which they appeared in print. Here are these verses:

> "The evening lights were about to be lighted,
> The wind roared fiercely and the rain fell hard,
> When en route from Poltava I finally sighted
> That capital city—after vexing retard.
> I carried a stick—long and bulky,
> And also a wallet that was empty and torn,
> An old sheepskin coat I wore, and sulky
> I felt,—unhappy and almost forlorn.
> Bereft of money, of name, situation,
> Short of stature and looking so queer . . .
> But forty years lapsed—and what transformation—
> I have that million, it's mine, it is here."

Money—that was Nekrasov's demon! Well, he did love gold, luxury, delights, and was it in order to possess these that he resorted to "practicality"?—No, it was a demon of a different kind—a gloomy and most degrading devil. His was a demon of haughtiness, of thirst for security, of a desire to wall himself off from people, and calmly look down on their wrath and threats. I believe that this demon entered his heart when he was but a child, a child of fifteen years, who found himself on the Petersburg pavement and who had almost fled from his father. The timid and proud soul was hurt and stung; it did not wish to look for patrons, to enter into any agreements with that alien rabble. Not that distrust of people stole into his heart at so young an age,—it was rather a sceptical and too precocious (and therefore erroneous) attitude toward them. Let them not be so spiteful and horrid as they are reputed to be (he must certainly have thought); nevertheless they all are such weak and cowardly trash. Accordingly, they will ruin one even without ill-will the moment their interests are at stake. It was then, perhaps, that Nekrasov's meditations began and the verse: "I have that million, it's mine, it is here" formed itself in his mind—right there, in the street.

His was a thirst for a gloomy, sullen, segregated security with a view to dependence on no one. I believe I am not mistaken, since I recall something to this effect on the occasion of my first acquaintance with him. At least, so it seemed to me all my life. However, his was a foul demon. Was it for this kind of security that Nekrasov's soul could have been craving, a soul capable of responding to everything sacred, a soul that never lost faith in itself? Is it with this kind of security that so gifted a soul protects itself? Such people start on their journey barefooted, with empty hands, with serene and lucid hearts. Their security is not in gold. Gold is coarseness, violence, despotism! Gold may seem to constitute security precisely to that weak and cowardly rabble which Nekrasov himself despised. Is it possible that the pictures of violence, and—later—of sensuality and debauch could live on good terms in the heart of a man who was capable himself of appealing to one: "Forsake everything. Take thy staff and follow me!"

"Lead me away to the camp of the perishing
For the glorious cause of affection and love . . ."

But the demon overpowered the man: he stayed on the spot and went nowhere. For this he paid with suffering all his life. In fact, we know nothing but his verses. But what do we know about his inner struggle with his demon, a struggle which undoubtedly must have been painful and which lasted all his life?—I am not even speaking about Nekrasov's good deeds: he did not advertise them, and yet, unquestionably, there were good deeds: people already begin to bear witness to the humaneness and kindliness of that "practical" soul. Mr. Souvorin has already made public certain things. I am sure there will appear many more favorable comments: it cannot be otherwise.

"Oh,"—I may be told—"you are also exculpating, and even in a cheaper manner than we." No, I am offering no apologies: I am merely explaining, and I have succeeded in framing the question—the final and all-explanatory question.

4

A WITNESS IN NEKRASOV'S FAVOR

It was already Hamlet who wondered at the tears of the actor who, when reciting his part, wept over some Hecuba: "What's Hecuba to him?"—Hamlet asked. Now, this is the direct question: Was Nekrasov a similar actor, one who was capable of *sincerely* weeping over himself and that spiritual sanctity of which he had been depriving himself, then of pouring out his sorrow (genuine sorrow) in verses of unfading beauty, and next morning actually consoling himself with their beauty—with the beauty of the verses —and nothing but that? Moreover: was he capable of perceiving this beauty of the verses as a "practical" proposition which was likely to bring him profit, money, fame, and to make use of it in this spirit? Or, on the contrary, did not the poet's sorrow pass by after writing these verses and was it not assuaged by them? Did the beauty and power, expressed in them, oppress and torment him? And if, being unable to overcome his eternal demon, his passions which subdued him all his life, he fell again, did he calmly reconcile himself with his degradation? Didn't his groans and outcries grow still stronger in the secret and sacred moments of repentance? Didn't they re-echo and grow stronger in his heart every time that he convinced himself of the cost of his demon and the high price he had paid for those benefits which he had received from that demon? In a word, even if he was able *instantly* to reconcile himself with his demon, and even started justifying his "practicality" in his conversation with people, was this a lasting reconciliation or assuagement, or, on the contrary, did it instantly vanish from the heart, leaving as its aftermath a still more burning pain, shame and remorse? Then—if only this question could be settled—what would be left to us?—We should merely have to condemn him for the fact that being unable to overcome his temptations, he did not take his life as, for instance, that ancient Pechersk martyr who, being also unable to contend with the serpent of passion which tormented him, dug himself into the earth up to his waist and died, and if he did not succeed in casting out his demon, certainly he did conquer him. In this event we ourselves—each one of us—should find ourselves in a humiliating and ridiculous situation should we venture to assume the role of judges pronouncing such verdicts. Nevertheless a poet who wrote about himself:

> "You do not have to be a poet—
> But citizen you've got to be,"

thereby, as it were, recognized the fact that he might be judged by people as a "citizen." As individuals we should feel ashamed to judge him. Who are we anyhow—each one of us? We merely do not speak about ourselves aloud, concealing our nastiness, with which, within ourselves, we are fully reconciled. Perhaps the poet lamented such of his deeds as would not make us knit our brows had we committed them. For we know about his degradations, about his demon, from his own verses, which he, in his repentant sincerity, did not hesitate to publish. This and everything else that has been said about him, as a man, about his "practicality," and so forth,—all these would have died naturally and would have been effaced from the memory of men; all this would have been reduced to the level of simple gossip so that he would have needed no apology.

I may observe in passing that so practical a man, who knew so well how to take care of his business, indeed was not practical at all in making public his repentant groans and wailings. Therefore, perhaps, he was not so practical as some people maintain.

Nevertheless—I repeat—he has to face the judgment of citizens since he himself recognized this tribunal. Thus, if the question propounded above: Was the poet satisfied with his own verses in which he clothed his tears; did he come in accord with himself to the state of calmness which again enabled him to embark upon "practicality" with a light heart? or, on the contrary, were these reconciliations but momentary, so that, perhaps, he despised himself for their infamy, suffering all the more and all the more bitterly and thus, all his life?—Should these questions—I repeat—be settled in the latter sense, of course we could also at once reconcile ourselves with the "citizen" Nekrasov, since his own sufferings, in our view, would have fully cleansed his memory. Naturally, there arises forthwith this objection: If you are unable to settle these questions (for who can settle them?) they should not have been raised at all. There is, however, a witness who is in a position to answer them. This witness is the people.

That is, love of the people! To begin with, why did so "practical" a man have to be so fascinated with love of the people? Everybody attends to his own business: one is occupied with practicality, the other—with sorrow for the people. Well, suppose it is merely a whim: all right, one can toy with it, and then give it up. But Nekrasov kept it up all his life. It may be said that, to him, the people were something on the order of "Hecuba," a subject of tears clothed in verses, and yielding an income. I am not speaking about the fact that it is difficult to counterfeit such sincerity of love as sounds in Nekrasov's poetry (this may be endlessly debated), but I shall merely say that to me it is clear why Nekrasov loved the people so much; why he was so attracted to them in the difficult moments of his life; why he went to them and what he found in them. It is because—as I stated above—in Nekrasov love of the people was, as it were, *an outcome of his own sorrow for himself.* Once you suppose and admit this, the whole Nekrasov—both as a poet and a citizen—will be intelligible to you. In the service of the people with his heart and talent he perceived his self-purification. The people were his inner need not only for the sake of poetry. In his love of them he found his own exculpation. By his sentiments for the people he elevated his own spirit. But still more important is the fact that among the people who surrounded him he failed to find an object of love, nor did he find it in the fact that these people respected and worshipped him. Moreover: he detached himself from them and went to the insulted, to the suffering, to the naïve and humiliated—in those minutes when he was seized with disgust with that life to which, at times, he yielded faint-heartedly and viciously: he beat himself against the slabs of his own poor village church, and he was healed. He would not have chosen such a solution *had he not believed in it.* In the love of the people he felt something steady, a firm and sacred outcome of everything that tormented him. He knew of nothing holier, steadier and more truthful which he could worship. Indeed, he could not have perceived his whole self-exculpation in mere verses about the people. And further, this being the case, he worshipped *the people's truth.* If, in his whole life, he found nothing worthier of love than the people, this means that he did recognize *both the people's truth and truth in the people,* and also that truth does exist and is preserved in the people. If he did not quite consciously or rationally recognize this, with his heart he accepted this irresistibly and absolutely. In that vicious peasant, whose humiliated and humiliating image tormented him so strongly, he thus perceived something genuine and sacred which he could not help esteeming, to which he could not help responding with all his heart.

It is in this sense that, speaking above of Nekrasov's literary significance, I classed him among those who recognized the people's truth. And his eternal quest for that truth, his unceasing striving for it, obviously bear witness to the fact—this I repeat—that he was attracted to the people by an inner and supreme urge, and that, therefore, this craving must indicate that perpetual inner anguish which could not be quenched with any crafty arguments of temptation, with any paradoxes or practical exculpations. If so, he must have suffered all his life. . . . In this case, what kind of judges are we?—Even if we be judges, we are not accusers.

Nekrasov is a Russian historical type,—one of the great examples of the extent of contradictions and bifurcations in the realm of morality and rational convictions which a Russian can reach in our sad transitional epoch. But this man stays in our hearts. His impulses of love so often were sincere, pure and naïve! His longing for the people was so lofty that it places him as a poet in a superior station. As for the man, the citizen, by his suffering for them, he exculpated himself and he redeemed much if actually there was anything to redeem. . . .

5

To the Reader

The December and last issue of *The Diary* comes with great delay for two reasons: because of my ill health throughout the month of December, and on account of the unexpected transition to a new printing plant from the former one which ceased to exist. In a new and unfamiliar place things were inevitably delayed. In any event, I assume the responsibility, and I ask my readers for indulgence.

In answer to numerous queries of my subscribers and readers whether, at least from time to time, I could publish *The Diary* in the forthcoming year, 1878, without binding myself with monthly terms,—I hasten to state that for many reasons I am unable to do so. Perhaps I shall venture to publish one issue, and once more to talk to my readers. Indeed, I have been publishing my periodical for myself, as much as for others, because of the irresistible urge to express my views in so peculiar and characteristic an epoch as ours. Should I publish even a single issue, I shall make this fact known through the newspapers. Nor do I contemplate writing for other periodicals. In the latter I could publish only a story or a novel.

In the course of the forthcoming year of rest from the *periodical* publication I expect, indeed, to engage in belletristic work which imperceptibly and involuntarily moulded itself during the two years of the publication of *The Diary*. But I firmly hope to renew its publication one year hence. With all my heart I wish to thank all those who have paid me so sincere a tribute. To those who wrote me that I am suspending my publication at so hot a time, I may remark that one year hence the time may, perhaps, be still hotter and more characteristic, and then, once more, we shall serve together a good cause.

I say *together,* because I actually regard my numerous correspondents as my collaborators. I was greatly helped by their communications, comments and advice and by that sincerity with which they applied to me. How I regret that, owing to lack of time and ill health, I am unable to answer so many of them! Again, I ask all those whom I have not yet answered for their kind and good-hearted indulgence. I feel particularly guilty before those who have written me during the last three months. To that person who wrote me about "the anguish of those poor boys, and that she does not know what to tell them" (the person who wrote this will probably recognize herself by these expressions), I am now taking this opportunity to tell her that I was wholeheartedly interested in her letter. If it were only possible I should have published my reply to this letter in *The Diary*. I had to abandon this thought only because I found it impossible to print her letter *in toto*. And yet it does graphically bear witness to the ardent and noble mood of the majority of our youth, to their sincere desire to serve every good cause for the general benefit. I shall say only this to my correspondent: perhaps it is the Russian woman who is destined to save us all, our whole society, through the new energy which is regenerated in her, through her very noble thirst *to serve the cause* even to the point of sacrifice and heroism. She will put to shame the inactivity of the other elements and will captivate them, and will turn those who have been led astray on the right path. But enough has been said: I am answering my much estemed correspondent here, in *The Diary,* because I suspect that the former address given by her is no longer valid.

I was unable to answer very many of my correspondents for the reason that such momentous and live subjects as interest them cannot be answered by letters. On such topics—not letters but articles, even whole books, must be written. A letter must inevitably contain omissions, perplexities. There are themes on which it is absolutely impossible to correspond.

To the person who asked me to state in *The Diary* that I have received her letter about her brother killed in this war, I hasten to say that I was sincerely touched and moved by her sorrow for her deceased friend and brother, and also by her delight that he had served so beautiful a cause. I am pleased to advise my correspondent that I have met here a young man who had personally known the deceased and who corroborated everything she wrote me about him.

I heartily shake the hand and thank the correspondent who wrote me a long letter (five pages) about the Red Cross, and I ask him henceforth to continue corresponding with me. I shall unfailingly send him the thing he asked for.

Several correspondents who recently made inquiries *point by point* I shall answer separately, as well as him who asked me: "Who is a strutzky?" (I hope these correspondents will recognize themselves by these expressions.) I apologize particularly to my correspondents from Minsk and Vitebsk that I have so delayed my answers to them. After taking a rest, if possible I shall answer everybody. Thus let people not complain and wait.

My address will be the same. I only ask you to give the house number and the street, and not to address the mail to the editorial office of *A Writer's Diary*.

Once more I thank everybody. I hope for a happy au revoir in the near future. This is a glorious but difficult and fatal time. How much hangs by a hair at this very minute, and how we shall be discussing these things a year hence!

P. S. The publisher of a new book which has just appeared, *The Eastern Question: Its Past and Present, A Defense of Russia*, by Sir T. Sinclair, Baronet, an English M.P.; translated from the English—asked me to print in this issue of *The Diary* an advertisement about this book. However, having looked through and familiarized myself with it, I wish to recommend it personally to the readers, instead of inserting a regular advertisement. It is difficult to write a more popular, more interesting and sensible book than this one. At present we are much in need of such a book, and there are few men so well informed on the Eastern question. And yet, in our day, *everybody* should be familiar with this question. This is needed and necessary. Sinclair is a defender of Russian interests. In Europe he has long been known as a political writer. The compact volume of 350 printed pages costs only 1 ruble (postpaid— 1 ruble 20 kopecks). The book is sold in all book-stores.

1880

1880

August

CHAPTER I

Explanatory Word Concerning the Address on Pushkin Printed Below

MY ADDRESS on Pushkin and his significance, printed below and constituting the substance of the contents of the present issue of *The Writer's Diary* (the only one for the year 1880[1]) was delivered on June 8 of the current year at the solemn exercises of *The Society of Lovers of Russian Literature,* before a large audience, and it created a considerable impression. Ivan Sergeevich Aksakov, who then said about himself that everybody considers him as it were a leader of the Slavophiles, stated from the tribune that my address "constituted an event." I recall this here not for the purpose of boasting but in order to say this: If my address constitutes an event, it is from one and only one standpoint, which I shall explain later. It is for this purpose that I am writing this preface. In the address itself I meant to emphasize the following four points in my discussion of Pushkin's significance to Russia.

1. That Pushkin, with his profoundly perspicacious and ingenious mind and purely Russian heart, was the first to detect and record the principal pathological phenomenon of our educated society, historically detached from, and priding itself on, the people. He indicated and graphically set before us our negative type—the restless man, refusing to be reconciled, having no faith in his own soil and in the native forces, denying Russia and ultimately himself (*i.e.,* his own society, his educated stratum which grew up on our native soil), refusing to co-operate with others and sincerely suffering. Aleko and Onegin subsequently generated in our belles-lettres a number of related characters: they were followed by the Pechorins, the Tchitchikovs, the Rudins, the Lavretzkys, the

[1]If health permits me, I hope to renew the publication of *The Writer's Diary* in the forthcoming year, 1881.

Bolkonskys (in Leo Tolstoy's *War and Peace*), and many others
whose very appearance bears witness to his immense intellect and
genius, to the *truth of the idea originally conceived by Pushkin. To
him belong the honor* and the glory, for having spotted the principal
sore of the society which came into existence after Peter's great
reform. It is to his ingenious diagnosis that we owe the knowledge
of our disease, and he was also the first to comfort us, by giving
us the great hope that this is not a mortal illness; that Russian
society can be cured, reformed and resurrected if it embraces the
people's truth;

2. That he was the first—precisely the first, and there was no
one prior to him—to discern and give us the artistic types of Russian
beauty directly emerging from the Russian spirit,—beauty which
resides in the people's truth, in our soil. This is borne out by the
character of Tatiana, a purely Russian woman, who managed to
guard herself against this earthly deceit, as well as by historical
types, such as those of the Monk and others in *Boris Godunov;*
by *genre* types, for instance, in *The Captain's Daughter,* and by
many other images scattered through his poems, stories and notes,
even in *The History of Pugachiov's Rebellion.* The point which must
be particularly noted is that all these types of Russian positive
beauty, of the Russian soul, were fully derived from the people:
it was not in our present civilization; not in the so-called "European" education (which, it may be noted in passing, we never did
possess); not in the deformities of the outwardly adopted European
ideas and forms,—that Pushkin found this beauty but exclusively
in the people's spirit, and *in it alone.* Thus—I repeat—having diag-
nosed the disease, he inspired us with a great hope: "Believe in the
people's spirit; await salvation from it alone, and you will be saved."
Having penetrated Pushkin, it is impossible not to draw such an
inference.

3. The third point which I meant to emphasize in speaking of
the significance of Pushkin, is that peculiar and most characteristic
trait of his artistic genius, which is to be found nowhere and in
no one else; it is the faculty of universal susceptibility, and fullest,
virtually perfect reincarnation of the genius of alien nations. I stated
in my address that Europe has brought forth the greatest universal
artistic geniuses—the Shakespeares, the Cervanteses, the Schillers—
but that in none of them do we perceive that faculty which is revealed in Pushkin. It is not only a question of susceptibility, but
precisely of amazing completeness of reincarnation. In my evaluation of Pushkin I could not help emphasizing this faculty as the
most characteristic aspect of his genius, which, among all universal
artists, belongs only to him, and by which he differs from all of

them. But it was not for the depreciation of European geniuses of such a magnitude as Shakespeare and Schiller that I said this. Such a silly inference from my words could be made only by a fool. The universality, the all-comprehensive, the unexplored depth of the world types of man belonging to the Aryan race conceived by Shakespeare I do not doubt in the least. And had Shakespeare actually created his Othello as a *Venetian* Moor, and not as an Englishman, he would have merely conveyed to him the halo of a local national character, but the universal significance of this type would have remained identical, since he would have expressed also in an Italian that which he sought to express—and with equal potency.

I repeat: I did not mean to challenge the universal significance of the Shakespeares and Schillers when pointing out the most ingenious faculty of Pushkin to reincarnate in himself the genius of alien nations. I merely sought to emphasize in that faculty and in its completeness a great and prophetic prognostication to us.

4. This is altogether a Russian, national faculty which Pushkin merely shares with our whole people; and, as a most perfect artist, he is also the most perfect exponent of this faculty, at least in his work—in the work of an artist.

Our people bear in their soul this proclivity for universal susceptibility and all-reconciliation; and on more than one occasion they have revealed it during the two centuries since Peter's reform. When indicating this faculty of our people, I could not help, at the same time, setting forth in this fact our great future consolation, and perhaps our greatest hope shining for us in the distance. More particularly, I emphasized the fact that our longing for Europe, even despite all its enthusiasm and extremes, *in its foundation,* was not only legitimate and reasonable, but also popular, fully coinciding with the aspirations of the popular spirit, and that, in the last analysis, it has unquestionably a superior aim. Of course in my brief address—all too brief—I was unable to expound my thought in all its completeness, but I believe that at least that which is stated in it is clear.

One should by no means be indignant at my statement that "our destitute land will, perhaps, at length speak a new word to the world." Likewise, it is ridiculous to maintain that before this new word is given to the world "we have to develop economically, scientifically and civically, and only after that start dreaming about 'new words' addressed to such perfect (would-be) organisms as the European peoples." In my address I am precisely stressing the fact that I do not attempt to compare the Russian people with the Western nations in the sphere of their economic or scientific glory. I merely say that among all nations the Russian soul, the genius of the Russian people is, perhaps, most apt to embrace the idea of the universal fellowship of man, of brotherly love,—that sober point of view which forgives that which is hostile; which distinguishes and excuses that which is desperate; which removes contradictions. This is not an economic or any other trait; this is merely a moral characteristic, and who can deny or refute it in the Russian people? Can anyone say that the Russian people are merely an inert mass doomed to serve *economically* the advancement and progress of our European intelligentsia, priding itself on our people, whereas the intelligentsia carries within itself dead inertia from which there is nothing to expect or hope?—Alas, many people maintain this, but I ventured to declare something different.

I repeat that, of course, I was unable to prove comprehensively and fully "this fantasy of mine," as I myself called it, but at the same time I could not refrain from pointing to it. But to assert that our destitute and confused land cannot comprise such lofty aspirations so long as it is not economically and civically equal to the West—is sheer nonsense. Essentially, the fundamental spiritual treasures are not dependent upon economic assets. Our destitute and unorganized land, aside from its upper stratum, stands as one man. All the eighty millions of its population represent such a spiritual unity as is, of course, nonexistent—and cannot exist—anywhere in Europe. For this reason alone it cannot be said that our land is unmanageable, and, strictly speaking, it cannot be maintained that it is destitute. On the contrary, in Europe, where so much wealth is accumulated, the entire civic foundation of all her nations is undermined, and may tomorrow collapse once and for all without leaving a trace. In its stead there will ensue something altogether new and unheard-of, something in no way resembling former things. And no treasures accumulated by Europe will save her from her collapse because "wealth, too, will instantly vanish."

And yet it is precisely that undermined and contaminated civic order of hers that is being pointed out to our people as an ideal to which they should aspire, and only after having attained it may they dare to lisp to Europe some word of theirs. But I assert that it is possible to embrace and embody a loving and all-unifying spirit not only in the face of our present economic destitution, but a much worse one, such as we had after Batyi's invasion and the devastation of the Troubled Epoch when Russia was saved exclusively by the all-unifying spirit of the people.

And finally, if it be really necessary in order to have the right to love mankind and to be endowed with an all-unifying soul, to possess the faculty of not hating alien peoples because they do not resemble us; to refrain from the desire to segregate oneself in one's own nationality from all others so as to acquire everything for that nationality, regarding all other nations as a mere lemon which may be squeezed out (and in Europe there are peoples possessing such a spirit!)—if indeed, for the realization of all this it be necessary to become a rich people and to drag home the European civic order, is it possible that we must slavishly copy that European order (which tomorrow will collapse in Europe)? Is it possible that in this case the Russian organism will not be permitted to develop in a national fashion, by means of its own organic strength, that it must necessarily be deprived of its individuality and slavishly ape Europe? But where is the Russian organism to be hidden? Do these gentlemen understand what an organism is?—And yet they keep talking about natural sciences! "The people will not permit it"—said an interlocutor two years ago to a meddlesome Westerner apropos of something. "Then annihilate the people!"—calmly and haughtily replied the Westerner. Nor was he an insignificant "nobody,"—he was one of the representatives of our intelligentsia. This is a true story.

In these four points I have indicated Pushkin's significance to us, and my address—I repeat—produced an impression, not by its merits (this I emphasize), not by the talent of its delivery (I agree with all my adversaries, and I am not boasting), but by its sincerity and, I daresay, by a certain irrefutability of the facts I set forth despite its brevity and incompleteness.

However, wherein is "the event," as Ivan Sergeevich Aksakov expressed himself?—Precisely in that the Slavophiles, or the so-called Russian party (Good Lord, we have a "Russian party"!) made an immense and, perhaps, final step toward reconciliation with the Westerners, since the Slavophiles declared the legitimacy of the Westerners' longing for Europe, even the legitimacy of their extremest lures and inferences, explaining that legitimacy by our purely Russian popular aspiration which coincides with the spirit itself of the people. And the Slavophiles justified that enticement by historical necessity, historical fate. So that should there some time in the future be a balance drawn, in the last analysis it would appear that Westerners have served the Russian land and the aspirations of its spirit just like those genuine Russians who sincerely loved their own land and who, perhaps, too jealously guarded it against all temptations of "the Russian aliens."

Finally, it was declared that all perplexities and bitter disputes between the two parties constituted but one great misunderstanding. This, then, could have, perhaps, become an "event," since the Slavophiles right then and there, after my address, expressed their full accord with its inferences. On my own part I state—I have also so stated in my address—that the merit and honor of this new step (if the sincerest desire of reconciliation constitutes an honor) does by no means belong to me alone, but to the whole Slavophile doctrine, to the whole spirit and orientation of our "party"; that this was always clear to those who inquired impartially into that doctrine; and that the idea which I expounded has more than once been, if not expressed—then indicated by the Slavophiles. I merely managed to strike the opportune moment.

Now, then, this is my deduction: Should the Westerners accept our inference and agree with it, all misunderstandings between both parties would, in truth, be obliterated so that "the Westerners and Slavophiles would have nothing to quarrel about," as Ivan Sergeevich Aksakov put it, "since henceforth everything would be explained." Of course, it was in this sense that my address was an "event." But, alas, the word "event" was uttered in a state of sincere enthusiasm by only one party; but will it be accepted by the other side, or will it remain merely an ideal?—this is an altogether different question. The moment I had left the chair, side by side with the Slavophiles who embraced me and shook my hand, Westerners came to the platform to shake my hand, and not the rank and file, but the outstanding representatives of Westernism, particularly those who were, at the time, playing the leading roles. They shook my hand with the same ardent and sincere enthusiasm as the Slavophiles; they called my address "ingenious," several times stressing this word. I am afraid, however, very much afraid, that this was said on the spur of the moment of enthusiasm. Oh, I am not afraid that they will reject their opinion that my address was ingenious: I know myself that it was not ingenious, and I wasn't in the least seduced by the commendations, so that I shall wholeheartedly forgive them their disillusionment in my ingeniousness. But this is what may happen; this is what the Westerners may say after a little reflection. (*Nota bene:* I am not speaking about those who shook my hand; I am referring to Westerners in general. This I wish to emphasize.)

"Ah,"—the Westerners will perhaps say (do you hear?—only "perhaps"—nothing more) "finally, after protracted disputes and wrangles, you have conceded that our longing for Europe was legitimate and normal; you have admitted that there was truth also on our side; you have lowered your banners. Well, we cordially accept your admission, and we hasten to state to you that this wasn't so bad on your part: at least, this serves as an indication that there is some intelligence in you, which, however, we,—save the dullest among us for whom we do not wish to and cannot hold ourselves responsible—have never denied in you; but, you see, there arises here a new predicament which must be explained as promptly as possible. The point is that your thesis, your inference to the effect that in our temptations we supposedly coincided with the popular spirit and were mysteriously guided by it,—this thesis remains to us more than dubious, and, therefore, an agreement between us again becomes impossible. Know that we were guided by Europe, by her science and by Peter's reform, and not at all by the spirit of our people, which we never did encounter or scent on our way. On the contrary, we left it behind and hastily ran away from it. From the very beginning we have been proceeding independently, and not at all guided by a supposedly impelling instinct of the Russian people for universal susceptibility and fellowship of mankind,—well, for all the things about which you have spoken so much. Since the time has come to speak quite candidly, we say that much as heretofore, we perceive in the Russian people merely an inert mass from which we have nothing to learn, a mass which impedes Russia's progress and which must be remodelled and recreated, if it is impossible organically, at least mechanically, *i.e.*, compelling them, once and for all, to obey us—for ever and ever. And in order to achieve such obedience it is necessary to introduce a civil order identical with that prevailing in European countries. Strictly speaking our people are destitute and fetid—and thus they always have been; they can possess neither individuality nor idea. The whole history of our people is an absurdity from which you have been deducing the devil only knows what, whereas only we viewed it soberly. A people such as ours should have no history, while that which they possessed under the guise of history should be forgotten by them with disgust,—everything *in toto*. Only our educated society should have its history while the people should serve society with their labor and energies.

"Please don't get excited and don't shout: speaking of obedience we do not intend to enslave our people—of course not! Please don't draw such an inference: we are humane, we are Europeans, you know this only too well. On the contrary, we wish to educate our people, little by little, in an orderly fashion and to crown our edifice by lifting them to our level and by reshaping their nationality into a different one which will mould itself of its own accord after they have been educated. Their education we will base upon and begin with those very things with which we ourselves began, *i.e.*, with the negation of their whole past and the damnation which they themselves will invoke upon it. The moment we have taught a man to read and write we shall make him take a sniff of Europe; we shall forthwith tempt him with her, say with the refinement of her ways of living, her decorum, clothes, drinks, dances,—in a word we shall make him feel ashamed of his former bast shoe and kvass, of his ancient songs; and even though among them there are several most beautiful and musical ones, nevertheless we shall make him sing rhymed vaudeville songs regardless how angry you may feel about this. Briefly, for the sake of a good goal, in the first place we shall press upon the sensitive part of his character—just as we used to be pressed to resort to all sorts of means—and then the people will be ours. They will grow ashamed of their past and will damn it. He who damns his past is ours—such is our formula! We shall fully apply it when we start lifting the people to our level. However, should the people prove incapable of education,—'they should be eliminated,' since then it would be clear that our people are an unworthy, barbaric mass which should be compelled to obey. What is to be done?—Truth resides only in the intelligentsia and in Europe. Therefore, even though you may have eighty million people (of which, it seems, you are boasting) yet all these millions, in the first place, must serve that European truth, because no other exists or can exist. The number of millions will not scare us.

"Such is our usual inference, but now you have it in all its nakedness. We adhere to it. Indeed, should we accept your deduction, we could not join you in your conversations about such strange things as, for example, le Pravoslavie (Orthodoxy) and its alleged particular significance. We hope that you will, at least, not demand this from us, especially now when the last word of Europe and European science, in its general synthesis, is atheism, enlightened and humane, and we can no longer refrain from following Europe.

"On this ground, that part of your address in which you are praising us we may, perhaps, accept with certain reservations,—all right, we shall grant you this courtesy. As to the other half of the address which relates to you and to all your "principles"—we beg your pardon: we cannot accept. . . ."

Such may be the sad inference. I repeat: I should not dare attribute it only to those Westerners who shook my hand, but even to many, quite a few of the most enlightened Westerners, Russian workers and genuine Russians, who, despite their theories, are respectable and esteemed Russian citizens. As against these, the mass of apostates, the mass of your Westerners, the mediocrity, the street through which the idea is being dragged, all those plebeians of the "orientation" (and they are as numerous as sand grains on the sea shore)—they will unfailingly say something on this order—perhaps they have already said it. (N. B. For instance, concerning religion, one of the periodicals, with its inherent wit, has already stated that the aim of the Slavophiles is to rebaptize all Europe into Orthodoxy.)

However, let us set aside gloomy thoughts and let us place

hope in the leading representatives of our Europeanism. And should they accept at least one half of our inference and of our reliance upon them, theirs be honor and glory for this, and we should greet them with a delighted heart. Should they accept only one half, *i.e.*, should they, at least, admit the independence and individuality of the Russian spirit, the legitimacy of its being and its humanitarian, all-unifying aspiration,—there would be almost nothing to quarrel about, at least nothing essential and fundamental. In this case my address might actually serve as a basis for a new event. The address itself—this I repeat for the last time—was not an event (it does not deserve such an appellation); the great Pushkin festivities were what produced the event of our fellowship—a fellowship of all educated and sincere Russians for the sake of the future beautiful aim.

CHAPTER II

Pushkin

(A Sketch)

Delivered on June 8 at a Meeting of the Society of Lovers of Russian Literature.

"PUSHKIN IS an extraordinary, and perhaps a unique, phenomenon of the Russian spirit," said Gogol. For my own part, I will add: and a prophetic one. Yes, in his appearance, to all us Russians, there is something indisputably prophetic. Pushkin appeared precisely at the very inception of our true self-consciousness, which was then just coming into being and which originated in our society after a whole century following Peter's reform; and his appearance greatly helped to illuminate our obscure path with a new guiding light. It is in this sense that Pushkin is a prophecy and a revelation.

I divide the activity of our great poet into three periods. I am not speaking now as a literary critic: when referring to Pushkin's creative work, I merely wish to explain my conception of his prophetic significance to us, and my understanding of this word. In passing, I may remark, however, that it seems to me that between the periods of Pushkin's activity there are no clearly defined lines of demarcation. To my mind the inception of *Eugene Onegin,* for instance, belongs to the first period, while its concluding part should be placed in the second period, when Pushkin had already found his ideals in his own country, and had fully and affectionately absorbed them in his loving and perspicacious soul. It is said that, in his first period, Pushkin imitated the European poets—Parny,

André Chénier and others—but particularly—Byron. Yes, no doubt, the poets of Europe did exercise a strong influence upon the development of his genius; and maintained it throughout his life. Nevertheless, not even his earliest poems were mere imitations, so that even in them the extraordinary independence of his genius was revealed. In imitations one never finds such personal suffering and such depth of self-consciousness as Pushkin revealed, for instance in his *Gypsies,* a poem which I ascribe entirely to the first period of his creative life. I do not speak of the creative potency and impetuosity which could not have been expressed so strongly had it been merely imitative.

In the character of Aleko, the hero of the poem *Gypsies,* there is already revealed a strong, deep and purely Russian concept, which was subsequently expressed in such harmonious perfection in *Eugene Onegin,* where virtually the same Aleko is shown not in a fantastic light but in a palpably real and intelligible guise. In Aleko, Pushkin had already discerned and ingeniously noted that unhappy wanderer in his native land, that traditional Russian sufferer detached from the people who appeared in our society as a historical necessity. And, of course, Pushkin found him not only in Byron. Aleko's is a true and unmistakably conceived character, a lasting character long since native to our Russian land. These homeless Russian ramblers are wandering still, and it seems it will be long before they disappear. If, in our day, they no longer visit Gypsy camps with their wild and odd mode of living in a quest for their universal ideals and in order to seek refuge in the bosom of nature from the confused and incongruous life of our Russian educated society—all the same they embrace socialism, which did not exist in Aleko's times, and with their new creed they journey to another field, eagerly tilling it, believing, even as Aleko, that through this fantastic labor they will attain their goal and happiness not for themselves alone but for all men. A Russian sufferer in order to find peace needs precisely universal happiness: with nothing less than that is he content—of course, as long as the proposition is confined to theory. Essentially, it is the same Russian who appeared in a different epoch.

This character, I repeat, came into being among our educated society detached from the people's might in the beginning of the second century after the great reform of Peter. Oh, an overwhelming majority of Russian intellectuals served peacefully in the days of Pushkin—just as now—as civil servants, in the government or on railroads and in banks, or otherwise earned their livelihood, or were even engaged in scientific work, in lecturing—in a regular, leisured and peaceful fashion, receiving salaries, playing preference,[1] with no

[1] A game of cards popular in Pushkin's time.

inclination to take refuge whether in Gypsy camps or in other places more suited to our time. At the utmost they play at liberalism "with a tinge of European socialism" to which a certain benign Russian flavor is conveyed, but, after all, this is merely a matter of time. What of the fact that one man has not even begun to worry while another, encountering a locked door, has already smashed his head against it?—In due time all men will meet the same destiny, unless they choose the salutary road of humble communion with the people. And even if not all men meet this destiny: it suffices if "the chosen," one tenth, start worrying; the great majority will lose peace through them.

Of course, Aleko as yet does not know how to express correctly his anguish: in him all this is still an abstract mood: yearning for nature; complaints against fashionable society; universal aspirations; laments over truth, somewhere and somehow lost, which he can nowhere find. In this there is something akin to Jean-Jacques Rousseau. Wherein that truth is, in what form and where it can appear, and precisely when it was lost, of course, he does not know himself, but his is sincere suffering. A fantastic and impatient creature, he still awaits salvation pre-eminently from external things, as needs he must: "Truth," it is implied, "is somewhere without him, somewhere in other lands—European, perhaps—with their solid historical order, with its settled social and civic mode of life." Nor will he ever comprehend that first of all truth is within himself. How can he understand this?—He is an alien in his own country; for a whole century he has been unaccustomed to work; he is devoid of culture; he has grown up as a damsel in a convent within closed walls; he has fulfilled strange and unaccountable obligations associated with this or that of the fourteen classes into which Russian educated society is divided. He is still nothing but a blade of grass torn from its roots and blown about by the wind. This he feels; this makes him suffer—not seldom quite acutely! What if, perhaps belonging to hereditary nobility and possibly owning serfs, taking advantage of his noble birth, he, for once, allowed himself to indulge in a little whim of taking a fancy to people living "without laws" in a Gypsy camp, leading a bear which performs? Naturally a woman, "a wild woman," as the poet calls her, more than anyone could inspire him with the hope of deliverance from his anguish, and so, with light-minded but passionate credulity he throws himself into the arms of Zemphira: "Here"—says he—"is my escape; here, perhaps, is my happiness—here, in the bosom of nature, far from fashionable society; here—among men without civilization and without laws!"

And what is the outcome?—At his first encounter with the

conditions of wild nature he fails to restrain himself, and he stains his hands with blood. The poor dreamer proves unequal not only to universal harmony but even to those Gypsies who cast him away without vengeance, without malice, in naïve dignity:

> "Depart from us, thou haughty man:
> We're wild, we have no binding laws,
> We neither punish nor torment."

Of course, all this is fantastic, but "the haughty man" is genuine and is cleverly conceived. First he has been conceived in Russia by Pushkin;—and this should be remembered. Quite so: the moment something goes against his grain, he is ready to devour his adversary to avenge his offense, or—which is still handier—recalling his appurtenance to one of the fourteen classes, he may appeal (this did happen) to the chastising and torturing law, provided his personal wrong be thus avenged.

Nay, this is an ingenious poem—not an imitation! Here, indeed, we have the Russian answer to the "accursed question" in terms of the people's faith and truth: "Humble thyself, proud man; above all, break thy haughtiness! Humble thyself, idle man, and, first of all, labor on thy native land!"—Such is the solution according to the people's truth and wisdom. "Truth is within—not without thee. Find thyself within thyself. Not others shouldst thou subdue; subdue thyself; be master of thyself—and thou shalt perceive truth. Not in things, not outside thee nor overseas is this truth, but above all in thine own labor for self-betterment. If thou conquerest thyself, if thou humblest thyself, then wilt thou be free beyond dreams; thou wilt labor upon a great task; thou wilt make others free and thou wilt find happiness, since thy life will be full, and thou wilt, finally, understand thine own people and their sacred truth. Neither with the Gypsies nor elsewhere is universal harmony provided if thou thyself art unworthy of it—if thou art given to malice and pride, if thou demandest life as a gift without even comprehending that it has to be paid for."

This solution of the question is clearly indicated in Pushkin's poem. It is expressed still more clearly in *Eugene Onegin*, a poem which is no longer fantastic but tangibly realistic, in which genuine Russian life is incarnated with such creative potency and completeness as have never been witnessed either before or, perhaps, also since Pushkin.

Onegin arrives from Petersburg—necessarily from Petersburg: it is imperative for the poem, and Pushkin could not miss such an important realistic trait in the biography of his hero. Onegin—I re-

peat—is the same Aleko, particularly where he later exclaims in
anguish:

> "Oh, why, like Tula's poor assessor,
> Am I not lying paralyzed?"

However, in the beginning of the poem, he is still half a dandy
and half a man of the world; as yet, he has not lived long enough
to be completely disillusioned in life. Even so, "the noble fiend of
secret boredom" begins to visit and annoy him.

It stands to reason that in the remote heart of his motherland
he is in exile, not at home. He knows not what to undertake, and
feels as if he were a guest in his own home. Later, when he roams,
seized with anguish for his own land, in foreign countries and
among strangers, as an unquestionably clever and sincere man he
feels even more a stranger to himself. True, he, too, loves his country, but he does not trust it. Of course, he has heard about its ideals
but he has no faith in them. He merely believes in an utter impossibility of any kind of work in his native land, and he looks upon
the few—now as heretofore—who believe in this possibility with a
sad smile. He killed Lensky out of mere spleen—which may have
been an outgrowth of a longing for some universal ideal: this is so
typical of us, so plausible.

Quite different is Tatiana: hers is a strong character, firmly
standing on her own soil. She is deeper than Onegin, and of course
wiser than he. With her noble instinct she foresees where and in
what truth resides, and this is revealed in the finale of the poem.
Perhaps Pushkin might have done better had he called his poem
by the name Tatiana, and not Onegin, since she is undeniably its
protagonist. She is a positive, not a negative, character; she is a
type of real beauty and an apotheosis of Russian womanhood, and
it is to her that the poet assigned the task of expressing the idea
of the poem in the famous scene of her last meeting with Onegin.
It may even be said that so beautiful and genuine a type of Russian woman has virtually never reappeared in our literature—save,
perhaps, for the image of Liza in Turgenev's *A Gentlefolk's Nest*.

However, the habit of looking down upon people accounts for
the fact that Onegin altogether failed to understand Tatiana when,
in a remote place, he met her first, in the humble guise of a pure and
chaste girl, so abashed by his presence. He was unable to discern
perfection in that poor girl, and perhaps he even took her for a
"moral embryo." She—an embryo! And this—after her letter to
Onegin! If there is a moral embryo in the poem it is, of course,
Onegin himself—this is undeniable. Nor was he capable in the least
of comprehending her, for did he know the human soul?—All his

life he was an abstract man, a restless dreamer. And again he failed
to appraise her later in Petersburg as a *grande dame* when, according to his own words in his letter to Tatiana, he began "to comprehend her full perfection." But these were only words: unrecog-
nized and unappreciated she passed through his life, and therein lay
the tragedy of their love. Oh, had only Childe Harold, at the time,
in that country place, at their first meeting, or by some chance
Lord Byron himself, arriving from England and taking notice of
her timid, modest charm, pointed it out to him—oh, then Onegin
would have been at once astonished and struck with admiration;
for there is, at times, in these universal sufferers a good deal of
spiritual servility! But this did not happen, and this seeker of universal harmony, having read to her his sermon and, after all, having
honestly dealt with her, started off with his *Weltschmerz*, and with
his hands stained with blood spilt in senseless anger, to roam in
his native land forgetful of Tatiana, full to the brim with health
and strength, exclaiming with a curse:

> "Oh, I am young, and full of vigor!
> On naught but anguish can I figure!"

This Tatiana understood. In immortal strophes of his romance
the poet shows her visiting the dwelling of that man who was then
still fascinating and mysterious to her. I need not speak here about
the artistic perfection and inimitable beauty of these lines. Here she
is shown in his study. She examines his books, his various possessions. She seeks, through them, to divine his soul—her riddle—and
finally "that moral embryo," after a wistful pause, with a strange
smile, foreseeing the solution of the enigma, gently whispers: "Isn't
he a parody perchance?"

Yes, this she had to whisper—she did divine him. Long afterwards in Petersburg, when they had met once more, she had completely comprehended his quality. By the way, who was it that said
that life in the *beau monde* and at court had a pernicious effect upon
her soul and that the position of a lady of fashion and the newly
engendered ideas of fashionable society were partly the cause of
her refusal of Onegin? No, this is not so. No, it is the same, the
former rustic Tanya! She is not spoiled; on the contrary, half-
broken, she suffers and feels oppressed by the pomp of Petersburg
life. She hates her position as a lady of fashion, and he who judges
her differently utterly fails to understand what Pushkin sought to
express. With firmness she tells Onegin:

> "Pledged to another husband, I
> To him stay loyal, till I die."

She says this precisely as a Russian woman; therein is her apotheosis. She expresses the truth of the poem. Oh, I shall not say a
word about her religious convictions, about her attitude toward the
sacrament of marriage—upon this I shall not touch. Well, did she
refuse to follow him, despite having said to him: "I love you," because "as a Russian woman"—and not a Southern or some French
woman—she is incapable of so bold a step, or has no strength to
break her chains, to sacrifice the lure of honors, riches and her
social position, the conventions of virtue?—Nay, brave is the Russian woman. She will boldly follow that in which she believes—and
this she has proved. But "having been pledged to another man," she
will be "loyal to him unto death." To whom, to what is she faithful? To what obligations?—To that old general whom she cannot
love, since she loves Onegin, and whom she married because "her
mother wept, adjured, besought her," while in her offended and
wounded soul there was then only despair, and no hope, no ray of
light?—Yes, she is loyal to that general, her husband, an honest
man, who loves and respects her and takes pride in her. Even though
her mother did "beseech" her, it was she, Tatiana, and no one but
her, who gave her consent, and it was she who swore to be his faithful wife. Even though she married him in despair, now he is her
husband, and perfidy on her part would disgrace and shame him
and this would be his death. But can one's happiness be founded
upon another's unhappiness?—Happiness is not confined to the mere
delights of love; it also involves the supreme harmony of the spirit.
What will assuage the spirit if there is in the past a dishonest,
merciless, inhuman act? Dare she run away for the only reason that
here might be her happiness?—But what kind of happiness would
it be if it were based upon somebody's unhappiness?—Please suppose that you yourself are erecting an edifice of human destiny in
order to bestow upon men at last tranquillity and peace. And
imagine, further, that for this end it is necessary and inevitable to
torture to death only one human creature, moreover—not even so
worthy a creature, which to some people may even seem ridiculous
—not some Shakespeare, but simply an honest old man, the husband
of a young wife whose love he blindly trusts, without, however,
knowing her heart at all; whom he respects; of whom he is proud—
a husband who is happy with her and who has found his peace. And
now it is he who must be dishonored, disgraced and tortured to
death in order to erect upon the suffering of this disgraced old man
your edifice! In these circumstances would you agree to be the
architect of such an edifice?—That's the question. And can you conceive, though for an instant, that men, for whom this edifice was
erected, would agree to accept from you happiness if it were founded

upon the suffering, let us say, of some negligible creature but one
mercilessly and unjustly tortured to death; or, if they accepted it,
that they would forever stay happy?—Tell me, could Tatiana with
her lofty soul, with her heart so ennobled by suffering, have answered
otherwise?—Nay, a pure Russian heart gives this reply: "Let me
alone be deprived of happiness; let my unhappiness be immeasurably greater than that of this old man; finally, let no one ever,
including the old man, learn about and appreciate my sacrifice, but
I refuse to be happy by ruining another man!"—This is tragedy: it
does transpire, and Tatiana sends away Onegin.

It may be argued that Onegin is also unhappy; that by saving
one man she ruined the other!—Well, perhaps this is the cardinal
point in the poem. By the way—the question why Tatiana refused to
follow Onegin has, at least in our literature, a rather peculiar history. That is why I deemed it possible to elaborate on it. What is
most characteristic is that the moral solution of this question has
for a long time been in doubt. I reason this way: even if Tatiana
had become free; even if her old husband had died and she had become a widow—even then she would not have gone away with Onegin.
One has to comprehend the essence of her character: she knows
who he is: he, the eternal wanderer; he meets by chance the woman
whom he had formerly neglected, in a new, brilliant, unattainable
setting. Why, perhaps the essence of the matter is in that setting:
the young girl whom he virtually used to despise, is now worshipped
by the *beau monde*—that terrible authority to Onegin, who, despite
his universal aspirations, throws himself, dazzled, at her feet! "This"
—he exclaims—"is my ideal! Here is my salvation! This is my
escape from my anguish, I failed to notice it and yet . . . 'So possible was happiness, so near!' "

And even as Aleko in the past turned to Zemphira, Onegin is
now drawn to Tatiana, seeking all solutions in his new whimsical
fantasy. And doesn't Tatiana perceive this in him? Hasn't she appraised him long ago? She is firmly convinced that, strictly speaking, he merely loves his new fancy, and not her, the hitherto humble
Tatiana! She knows that he takes her for something different—not
for what she actually is; that it is not she whom he loves; that he
is even incapable of loving anyone, despite the fact that he suffers
so acutely!—He loves his fantasy. But he himself is but a fantasy!
Were she to follow him, the very next day he would be disillusioned
and would regard his infatuation scoffingly. He is devoid of any
soil; he is a blade of grass caught in a gust.

Tatiana is very different!—Even in despair, in the agony of her
lucid recognition of the fact that her life is ruined—she is herself
solid, unshakeable, something upon which her soul relies. These are

the reminiscences of her childhood, of her birthplace, in a rural
wilderness, where her humble and pure life began,

> "Ay, of that burial-ground so quiet,
> Where my poor nurse reposes now
> Beneath her cross and shadowing bough."[1]

Oh, these reminiscences, these pictures of the past, to her are
now more precious than anything else; these images—nothing else is
left to save her soul from ultimate despair. Nor is this a bagatelle;
nay, there is much in this, because this is a whole foundation, something indestructible and solid. Here is the link with the motherland, with her own people, with their sanctity.

And what, by contrast, has he to offer? Who is he?—Certainly
she would not follow him from mere compassion, to gratify him, to
give him out of boundless loving pity, for a while at least, illusive
happiness, knowing certainly in advance that tomorrow he would
deride it. Nay, there are deep and firm souls which, even though
from infinite compassion, will not surrender their sanctity by dooming it to dishonor. Nay, Tatiana never could have followed Onegin.

Thus, in *Onegin,* in that immortal and inimitable poem, Pushkin, as no one ever before him, revealed himself as a great national
writer. With one stroke, in a most precise and perspicacious manner,
he indicated the innermost essence of the upper stratum of our society
standing above the level of the people. Having traced the type of the
Russian wanderer of all time; having been the first—by reason of
his ingenious instinct, his historical fate, his immense significance
to our future destinies—to place side by side with this type a character of positive and unquestioned beauty in the person of a Russian woman, Pushkin—also first among the Russian writers in his
other creations of the same period—showed us a whole gallery of
genuinely beautiful Russian characters which he discovered in the
Russian people. Their principal beauty lies in their incontestable
and tangible truth, so that it is impossible to deny them, and they
stand there as though sculptured.

Once more, I reiterate: I am not speaking as a literary critic,
and for this reason I shall not dwell in any literary detail upon
these ingenious creations of our poet. For instance, it would be possible to write a whole book about the character of the annalist-
monk, revealing the great importance and significance to us of this
stately Russian figure unearthed by Pushkin in the Russian soil.
He revealed and moulded it, forever placing it before us in its in-

[1] *Evgeny Onegin* by A. S. Pushkin. Translated by Oliver Elton. The
Pushkin Press. London, 1939.

disputable, humble and spiritually noble beauty as evidence of that potent spirit of Russian national life which is capable of producing characters of such incontestable truth. This character has been established; it is here; it cannot be denied by the assertion that it is mere fiction or a fantasy and idealization of the poet. You contemplate it, and you admit: yes, this exists. Therefore, the spirit of the people that conceived it must exist, and it is great and boundless.

Everywhere in Pushkin there sounds a faith in the Russian character, in its spiritual might, and where there is faith there is hope, great hope for the Russian:

> "With hope for all the good and glory,
> I look ahead, devoid of fear,"

said the poet himself, referring to another subject; yet these words are directly applicable to his entire national creative work. And never was any Russian writer, either prior to Pushkin or since, so wholeheartedly and germanely at one with his people as he. It stands to reason that we have many writers who are connoisseurs of the people; they write about the people with much talent, pointedly and lovingly; and yet, compared with Pushkin, they are verily, with one or at most two exceptions, among his latest followers, merely "gentlemen" writing about the people. In the most talented among them, even in these two exceptions just mentioned, now and then, suddenly there appears something haughty, something belonging to a different world and mode of living, something of an effort to lift the people to these writers' level and thereby to bestow happiness on them. In Pushkin, however, there is precisely something *genuinely* akin to the people which reaches in him the point of almost naïve emotionalism. Take his story about *The Bear* and the peasant who killed his "lady bear's mate"; or recall the verses "Kinsman John, when we start drinking," and you will understand what I mean.

All these artistic treasures and gems of creative insight were left by our great poet as mere landmarks for future artists and workers in the same realm. It may be positively asserted that had there been no Pushkin the men of talent following him would be nonexistent. At least they would not have revealed themselves so potently and so clearly, despite their great gifts, as they did reveal themselves later, in our day.

Still, the point is not confined to poesy alone, to mere artistic creation: had there been no Pushkin, perhaps our faith in our Russian individuality, in our national strength, and our belief in our future independent mission in the family of the European nations, would not have manifested itself with so unyielding a force as it did later (although not in everybody but only in very few). This exploit of Pushkin becomes particularly clear when what I call the third period of his creative work is examined.

As stated, there are no clear-cut divisions between these periods. For instance, certain works of the third period could even have appeared at the very beginning of the creative work of our poet, since Pushkin was always, so to speak, a complete and homogeneous organism bearing within it at once all the beginnings, and not acquiring them from without. External stimuli merely called forth in him what lay hidden in the depth of his soul. Even so, that organism developed, and the stages of its development may actually be traced; in each one of them its intrinsic character may be indicated and the gradual transformation from one period to another may be discerned.

Thus, that group of his works may be placed in the third class which pre-eminently reflects universal ideas, poetic images of other nations in which their genius is incarnated. Some of these works appeared only after Pushkin's death. It is in this period that our poet reveals something almost miraculous and unheard-of, something never before recorded in any nation. In fact, in European belles-lettres there were geniuses of immense creative magnitude—Shakespeare, Cervantes, Schiller. But please point to even one of these geniuses who possessed such a universal susceptibility as Pushkin. And this faculty, the major faculty of our nationality, Pushkin shares with our people, and by virtue of this he is pre-eminently a national poet. Even the greatest of the European poets were never able to embody in themselves with such potency as Pushkin the genius of an alien, perhaps neighboring people—their spirit, its hidden depth, its longing for its predestination. In dealing with foreign nations it may be said, on the contrary, that the European poets reincarnated in them their own nationality, interpreting them from their own national point of view. Even in Shakespeare, his Italians, for instance, are almost invariably Englishmen. Pushkin alone—among all world poets—possesses the faculty of completely reincarnating in himself an alien nationality. Take his *Scene from Faust, The Covetous Knight*, or his ballade *Once There Lived a Poor Young Knight.* Read again his *Don Juan*, and had it not been signed by Pushkin you would never have guessed that it was not written by a Spaniard. What deep, fantastic images in the poem *A Feast During the Plague!* But in these fantastic images one discerns the genius of England: this admirable song about the plague sung by the hero of the poem; and *Mary's Song*, with those verses

"Our children's cheerful voices
In the noisy school were heard,—"

these English songs, this anguish of British genius, its lamentations, its suffering presentiment of its future. Recall the strange poem:

"When wandering once amidst a valley wild . . ."

This is almost a literal rendition of the first three pages of a strange mystical book, written in prose by an ancient English sectarian—but is it a mere rendition?—In the sad and ecstatic music of these verses there sounds the soul of northern Protestantism, of an English sectarian leader, a boundless mystic with his dull, gloomy and irresistible aspirations and unrestraint of mystical reverie. When reading these queer verses, one feels the spirit of the age of the Reformation; one begins to understand the militant fury of early Protestantism, history itself; and one grasps it not only rationally, but as if one were physically present there, as if one had walked through an armed camp of sectarians, had sung their hymns with them, wept with them in their religious ecstasies and shared their creed with them.

Apropos: compare this religious mysticism with the religious strophes from the Koran, or *Imitations of the Koran:* isn't this a Mohammedan? Isn't this the very spirit of the Koran, its sword, the naïve stateliness of its creed and its threatening power?

And again—here is the ancient world, here are *The Egyptian Nights;* here are the earthly gods who seated themselves as such on the people's backs, gods already despising the genius of the people and their aspirations, no longer believing in that genius—gods who in fact became segregated gods, who grew mad in their isolation, who in their weariness foresaw death, and who in their agony sought diversion in fantastic brutalities, in the voluptuousness of creeping things, of a female spider devouring its male.

Nay, I assert emphatically that never has there been a poet with such a universal responsiveness as Pushkin. But it is not only a matter of susceptibility but also of its amazing depth—that reincarnation in his spirit of the spirit of foreign nations, an almost complete, and therefore miraculous, reincarnation. This phenomenon has been revealed in no other poet in the world. This we find in Pushkin alone, and in this sense he is a unique and unheard-of phenomenon, and to my mind a prophetic one . . . since it is exactly in this that his national, Russian strength revealed itself most —the national character of his poetry, the national spirit in its future development and in our future, which is concealed in that which is already present—and this has been prophetically revealed by Pushkin. For what else is the strength of the Russian national spirit than the aspiration, in its ultimate goal, for universality and all-embracing humanitarianism? Having become fully a national poet, having come in contact with the people and their vigor, Pushkin at once began to foresee their future destiny. In this he was a diviner and a prophet.

In fact, what has Peter's reform meant to us, not only from the standpoint of its effect upon the future but even in that which has already come to pass and stands in full view? What was the meaning of this reform?—Surely, it was not a mere adoption by us of European dress, habits, inventions and science. Let us scrutinize the matter, let us examine it attentively. Yes, it is very possible that at first Peter conceived the reform in this narrow utilitarian sense. Later, however, in the subsequent elaboration of his idea, he certainly must have obeyed a certain concealed instinct which impelled him in his work to aspire unquestionably for future, greater aims than mere utilitarianism. Likewise, the Russian people accepted the reform not from mere utilitarian motives, but, no doubt, because they at once felt an infinitely loftier goal than mere utilitarianism. I repeat: they felt it unconsciously, and yet in a direct and vital manner. Indeed, at once we began to strive impetuously for the most vital universal all-humanitarian fellowship. Not inimically (as it would seem it should have happened) but in a friendly manner, with full love, we admitted into our soul the genius of foreign nations, without any racial discrimination, instinctively managing—almost from the first step—to eliminate contradictions, to excuse and reconcile differences, thereby manifesting our readiness and proclivity to enter into an all-embracing, universal communion with all the nationalities of the great Aryan races.

Yes, the Russian's destiny is incontestably all-European and universal. To become a genuine and all-round Russian means, perhaps (and this you should remember), to become brother of all men, *a universal man,* if you please. Oh, all this Slavophilism and this Westernism is a great, although historically inevitable, misunderstanding. To a genuine Russian, Europe and the destiny of the great Aryan race are as dear as Russia herself, as the fate of his native land, because our destiny is universality acquired not by the sword but by the force of brotherhood and our brotherly longing for fellowship of men. If you analyze our history after Peter's reform, you will find traces and indications of this idea, of this fantasy of mine, in the character of our intercourse with European nations, even in our state policies. For what else has Russia been doing in her policies, during these two centuries, than serving Europe much more than herself? I do not believe that this took place because of the mere want of aptitude on the part of our statesmen.

Oh, the peoples of Europe have no idea how dear they are to

us! And later—in this I believe—we, well, not we but the future
Russians, to the last man, will comprehend that to become a genuine Russian means to seek finally to reconcile all European controversies, to show the solution of European anguish in our all-
humanitarian and all-unifying Russian soul, to embrace in it with
brotherly love all our brethren, and finally, perhaps, to utter the
ultimate word of great, universal harmony, of the brotherly accord
of all nations abiding by the law of Christ's Gospel!

I know, I know too well, that my words may sound ecstatic,
exaggerated and fantastic. Be it so: I do not feel sorry for having
uttered them. This had to be said, especially now, at the moment
of our triumph, of the celebration of the memory of our great
genius, who, in his creative work, incarnated precisely this idea.
Besides, it has been expressed before: I am saying nothing new.
What is most important—all this may sound conceited: "Is such
a destiny"—it might be said—"to be bestowed upon our crude land!
Are we destined to utter the new word to mankind?" Well, do I
speak of economic renown, of the glory of sword or science?—I am
speaking merely of the brotherhood of men and of the fact that
the Russian heart is more adapted to universal, all-humanitarian
brotherly fellowship than any other nation. I perceive this in our
history, in our gifted men, in the creative genius of Pushkin. Let
our land be poor, but this destitute land "Christ, in a serf's garb,
has traversed, to and fro, with blessing." Why shouldn't we embrace His ultimate word? Wasn't He Himself born in a manger?

I repeat: at least we are already in a position to point to
Pushkin, to the universality and all-humanitarianism of his genius.
For wasn't he capable of embracing in his soul foreign genius as
his own? In art, at least, in creative achievement, he has indubitably
revealed this universality of the Russian spirit, and this in itself is
a great indication. If my idea is a fantasy—at least it has its support in Pushkin. Had he lived longer, perhaps he might have revealed
great and immortal images of the Russian soul which would be
intelligible to our European brethren; he might have attracted them
to us much more than they are attracted at present; perhaps he
might have explained to them the whole truth of our aspirations,
and thus they would comprehend us better than at present and
might foresee our destiny; they would cease to look upon us as
suspiciously and haughtily as they still do. Had Pushkin lived
longer, perhaps there would have been among us, too, less strife and
misunderstanding. But God willed differently: Pushkin died in the
full bloom of his creative power, and no doubt he carried with him
into his grave some great secret. And now we, with him no longer
among us, are endeavoring to solve it.

CHAPTER III

Seizing upon an Occasion

Four lectures on different subjects apropos of one lecture read to me by Mr. Gradovsky. With an address to Mr. Gradovsky.

1

CONCERNING ONE MOST IMPORTANT MATTER

I WAS about to wind up my Diary, confining it to my *Address* delivered in Moscow on June 8 and the preface to it that I wrote anticipating a row which, in fact, burst out in our press after my *Address* had appeared in *The Moscow Gazette*. But having read your criticism, Mr. Gradovsky, I delayed the publication of *The Diary* in order to supplement it with my reply to your attacks. Indeed, my presentiments came true: a terrible row did break out. I was called "a coward," "a haughty man," "a Manilov," "a poet." It was suggested that police be summoned to restrain the public's outbursts—of course, moral, liberal police. But why not actual police? —In Russia they are not less liberal than those liberals who started howling at me. Well, there is little difference between the former and the latter!

For the time being, however, let us leave this aside. I shall turn directly to my reply to your points. I must confess from the very outset that personally I have nothing in common with you, and there is nothing for me to discuss with you: it is impossible for me to agree with you. For this reason I do not in the least intend either to convince or to dissuade you. Even in the past, when read-·ing some of your articles, I used to wonder at the trend of your thoughts. Why, then, do I answer you now?—Solely because I have others in mind, *i.e.*, readers, who will settle our controversy. It is only for them that I am writing.

I feel, I foresee, I can even perceive that there are new elements thirsting for a new word, weary of the obsolete liberal giggling at any word of hope for Russia; sick and tired of the former liberal toothless scepticism—of the old corpses which, by oversight, have not been buried, and which still regard themselves as the young generation—of the antiquated liberal leader and savior of Russia whose character has fully revealed itself during the last twenty-five years, and who, according to the popular saying, is "a man aimlessly shouting in a marketplace." In a word, I wish to state *many a thing,* aside from my reply to your remarks, so that in giving my answer, I am, as it were, seizing upon an occasion.

In the first place, you raise the question—and even reproach me for not having expressed myself more clearly: Whence did our "wanderers," about whom I spoke in my *Address,* come? Well, this is a long story which one should begin from afar. Besides, no matter what I might reply in this connection, you would not agree with me because you have your own preconceived and ready solution: "Because"—you would say—"they were disgusted at living side by side with the Skvoznik-Dmukhanovskys, and also on account of the civic sorrow which they felt for the peasants, who, at that time, had not yet been liberated." Such an inference would be worthy of the contemporary liberal man, who, speaking generally, when it comes to Russia, has everything settled and signed with that extraordinary ease typical only of a Russian liberal. Nevertheless this is a more complicated question than you think—much more complicated—despite your categorical solution. In due time I shall speak about "the Skvozniks" and "the civic sorrow." But first, permit me to refer to a most characteristic statement of yours, which you also express with a lightness bordering on frivolity, and about which I cannot keep silent. You say:

"In one way or another, for two centuries we have been under the influence of European enlightenment, which strongly affected us because of 'the universal susceptibility' of the Russian which Mr. Dostoievsky regards as our national trait. There is no way in which we can escape this enlightenment; nor is there any need for this. This is a fact which cannot be helped, for the reason that a Russian who desires enlightenment *necessarily* acquires it from a Western European source because of the total absence of Russian sources."

Of course, this is sportively said, but you uttered an important word: "enlightenment." I wish to ask you what you mean by it? Western science, useful knowledge, handicrafts, or spiritual enlightenment? The former, *i.e.,* science and trades, in truth, should not evade us, and there actually is no reason for us to seek to evade them. I am also in full accord with you that these can be acquired only from Western European sources, for which Europe deserves praise and our eternal gratitude. But my conception of enlightenment (and I believe that no one can have a different conception) coincides with what this word literally implies, *i.e.,* spiritual light illuminating the soul, enlightening the heart, guiding the mind and indicating to it the road of life. If this be so, I wish to state to you that there is no reason for us to borrow such an enlightenment from Western European sources because Russian sources are fully available—and not absent. You are surprised? You see, in disputes I like to begin with the very essence of the matter, with the most controversial point.

I assert that our people have long been enlightened, having embraced in their hearts Christ and His teachings. It may be argued that the people do not know the teachings of Christ, and that no sermons are preached to them. But this is a vain objection: they know everything, precisely everything that they have to know, although they could not pass an examination in catechism. The people acquired their knowledge in churches where, for centuries, they have been listening to prayers and hymns which are better than sermons. They have been repeating and singing these prayers in forests, fleeing from their enemies, as far back as the time of Batyi's invasion; they may have been singing: *"O mighty Lord, be with us!"* It may have been then that they memorized this hymn because at that time nothing but Christ was left to them; yet in this hymn alone is Christ's whole truth. And what is there in the fact that few sermons are preached to the people and that chanters are muttering unintelligibly?—This is the most colossal accusation against our Church invented by the liberals, coupled with that of the inadequacy of the Church-Slavonic language supposedly incomprehensible to the common people! (And what about the Old-Believers?—Oh, God!) As against this, the priest reads: "God and Lord of my being," etc. —and in this prayer *the whole essence of Christianity* is contained, its entire catechism, and the people know this prayer by heart. Likewise they know by heart the life-histories of many a saint; they relate them and listen to them with emotion.

However, the principal school of Christianity from which they have graduated is—those centuries of innumerable and interminable sufferings which they have endured in the course of their history, when, forsaken and oppressed by everybody, toiling for everybody, they remained with no one but Christ—the Consoler Whom they then embraced forever in their soul, and Who, as a reward for this, has saved their soul from despair!

However, why am I telling you all this! Is it conceivable that I seek to convince you?—My words—this goes without saying—will sound childish to you, almost indecent. But I repeat—now for the third time—I am not writing for you. Besides, this is an important theme: there is still much that has to be specially said about it, and I shall speak of it so long as I can hold the pen in my hand. At present, however, I shall express my thought only in its essential thesis: If our people have long been enlightened by the fact of their acceptance of the quintessence of Christ and His teachings, together with Him, they have embraced *genuine* enlightenment. With this fundamental supply of enlightenment, Western sciences will become a real blessing to the people. They will not dim the image of Christ as in the West, where, however, it was dimmed not by science, as liberals maintain, but by the Western Church itself, which distorted it by transforming itself into a Roman state, having embodied the latter in the form of papacy. Indeed, in the West there is no longer Christianity, there is no Church, notwithstanding the fact that there still are many Christians who will never disappear. Catholicism, in truth, is no longer Christianity; gradually it is transforming itself into idolatry, while Protestantism with gigantic strides is being converted into atheism and into vacillating, fluent, variable (and not eternal) ethics.

Of course, you will at once retort that Christianity and the worship of Christ do not at all exhaust the whole cycle of enlightenment; that they are but one aspect; that, on the contrary, there is need of sciences, civic ideas, progress, etc. To this I have nothing to say to you—arguing would be unbecoming, since, even though you are right to a certain extent, for example, as far as science is concerned, nevertheless you will never admit that the Christianity of our people *must prevail forever,* that it must always be the principal and vital foundation of their enlightenment! In my address I said that Tatiana, having refused to follow Onegin, acted in a Russian fashion, in accordance with the people's truth, whereas one of my critics, indignant at the idea that the Russian people possess truth of their own, unexpectedly retorted with the question: "What about incest?"—Can such critics be answered? Primarily, they feel insulted by the fact that the people can have a truth of their own, and therefore be genuinely enlightened. Why, is incest prevalent among the people as a whole, and does it exist as *truth?* Indeed, our people are coarse, but by no means all of them—oh, not all of them; I swear to this as a witness because I have observed them, I know them, I lived with them a number of years, sharing my meals and sleeping with them; I "was personally classed with villains"; I worked with them performing actual manual labor at a time when others were "dipping their hands in blood,"[1] toying with liberalism and giggling at the people, proclaiming in their lectures and journalistic feuilletons that there was "an impress of the beast" upon the people.

So, don't tell me that I do not know the people! I know them: it was because of them that I again received into my soul Christ Who had been revealed to me in my parents' home and Whom I was about to lose when, on my own part, I transformed myself into a "European liberal."

[1]Nekrasov's verse, from *A Knight for an Hour.*

But let us concede that our people are sinful and crude, that theirs is still a bestial image:

> "On his mother's back, funning,
> Sonny's taking a gay ride,
> While his young wife's running,
> Like a filly alongside—"

Well, there must have been a reason for this folk song! All Russian songs are derived from some actuality—have you noticed this? —But be fair just for once, you liberal fellows: try to recall what the people have endured in the course of so many centuries. Recall who is most to be blamed for their bestial image, and don't condemn them!—Indeed, it is silly to accuse the peasant of the fact that his hair wasn't dressed in a French hairdresser's parlor on the Grand Morskayia!—And yet virtually such accusations are propounded when our European liberals begin to rise against the Russian people and start *denying* them; claiming that they have failed to develop their individuality, and that they are devoid of nationality!

Oh, Lord!—And in the West, wherever you please, among any people—is there less drunkenness and stealing? Not the same brutality?—And besides—embitterment (which is absent in our people) and real, hundred-per-cent ignorance, thorough want of enlightenment, because, at times, it is combined with such lawlessness that it is no longer considered a sin, but it is actually treated as truth.

Even so, let us concede that bestiality and sin are present among our people. But one thing is incontestable: in their mass at least (not merely in ideal but in actual reality) the people do not accept —never will—their sins for truth! They sin, but sooner or later, they always say: I did perpetrate an untruth. Even if he who sinned does not say it, somebody else will say it for him, and truth will be thus restored. Sin is stench, and stench is dispelled when the sun rises. Sin is a transient matter, whereas Christ is eternal. Daily the people sin and commit villainies; yet in their best moments, when they turn to Christ, they never err in truth. What is important is the thing in which the people believe as their truth; in what they conceive and perceive in it; what they recognize as their loftiest aspiration; what they love; what they are asking from God; what they worshipfully lament. And the people's ideal is—Christ. With Christ there comes, of course, enlightenment, and in their superior, critical moments our people always settle national matters—always have been settling them—in a Christian spirit.

You may observe mockingly: "Lamenting and sighing are not enough: one has to do things—one has to exist."—Well, gentlemen,

Russian enlightened Europeans, have you many righteous men in your ranks? Point to your righteous men whom you seek to substitute for Christ. But you should remember that among the people there are also righteous men. There are positive characters of inconceivable beauty and power who have not come within the range of your observation. Yes, there are righteous men and sufferers for the truth—whether or not we happen to see them. It seems to me that he who is capable of seeing, of course, will see and understand them; he, however, who perceives nothing but the image of the beast will see nothing. The people at least know and believe that righteous men exist; this knowledge fortifies the people, inspiring them with the hope that at the eleventh, fatal hour these men will save them. And, in fact, how many times the people did save our fatherland!—Only recently the people, though sinking in sin, drunkenness and lawlessness, the people, as a whole, were spiritually gladdened by the last war for Christ's faith of the Slavs trampled upon by the Mohammedans. The people accepted this war, they seized upon it as upon an expiatory sacrifice for their sins and lawlessness; they sent their sons to give their lives for a holy cause, and they did not vociferate that the ruble was going down, and that the price of meat was going up. They listened avidly to war news, they eagerly inquired and read about it, and we all witnessed this.

I know: the people's spiritual enthusiasm, and particularly the motives behind it are being denied by our liberals; they scoff at this idea. "These rascals"—they imply—"have a constructive idea; they have a civic sentiment, a political thought!—Can this be conceded?" Why is it that our European liberalism so often adopts a hostile attitude toward the people? Why is it that in Europe those who call themselves democrats invariably stand in defense of the people, or at least rely on them, whereas our democrats are frequently aristocrats, and, in the last analysis, almost always they come out in support of everything that tends to suppress the people, and they wind up with sheer domineering? Oh, I am not asserting that they are conscious enemies of the people, but the tragedy lies in the lack of consciousness. You will be incensed with these queries of mine. Be it so. To me all these are axioms, and, of course, I shall not cease to explain and expound them as long as I continue to write and speak.

Thus, let us finish: science is one thing, but we do not have to borrow "enlightenment" from Western-European sources, lest we adopt such social formulæ as: *"Chacun pour soi et Dieu pour tous"* or *"Après moi le déluge."* People will at once start shouting: "Don't we have similar sayings? Don't we have the adage: 'Old hospitality is not remembered,' and hundreds of other aphorisms

of the same kind?"—Quite so, the people have different by-words:
the mind of the people is broad; so is their humor. Developing consciousness always prompts negation; yet all these are mere *by-
words,* and the people do not believe in their moral truth, they joke
about them and scoff at them; the people reject them—at least the
people as a whole. But would you venture to assert that *"Chacun
pour soi et Dieu pour tous"* is a mere adage and not a social formula commonly adopted in the West which *everybody* serves and
believes?—at least all those who rule the people, keep them in check,
who own the land and the proletarian, who stand on guard over
"European enlightenment"?—Why do we have to have such an
enlightenment? Let us try to find at home a different kind of enlightenment. Science is one proposition and enlightenment another.

With faith in the people and their strength, we may develop
some time in the future our Christian enlightenment in its full
brightness and radiance. It stands to reason that you will tell me
that all this is but protracted and idle talk, and not an answer to
your criticism. Be it so. I consider this an introduction, and a necessary one. Just as you find and note in my *Address* such points of
disagreement as, from your own standpoint, are the most important,
so I, for my part, have noted and set forth that point in your
article which I consider the main point of our disagreement, as it
serves as an obstacle to reaching an accord with you. However, the
preface is finished, and let us turn to your criticism, this time without further deviations.

2

ALEKO AND DERJIMORDA. ALEKO'S SUFFERING FOR THE
PEASANT SERF. ANECDOTES

Criticizing my *Address,* you write:
"But Pushkin portraying Aleko and Onegin with their negation did not show precisely what they 'deny,' and therefore it is
extremely hazardous to assert that they specifically deny 'the people's truth,' the fundamental principles of the Russian world outlook. This is perceived nowhere."

Whether or not it is perceived; whether or not it is hazardous
to make the above assertion—will be discussed forthwith. First,
however, let us deal with your statement about the Dmukhanovskys
from whom Aleko supposedly fled to the Gypsies:

"But it is true that the world of the roamers of those days"—you
write—"was one renouncing another world. For the interpretation of
these characters other characters have to be considered which Push-

kin did not portray, although at times he referred to them with burning indignation. The nature of his talent prevented him from sinking
into that gloom and treating these owls and bats, filling the basements
(even more so, perhaps, the upper stories) of the Russian abode
as 'pearls of creation': This was done by Gogol—the great reverse
side of Pushkin. He told the world why Aleko made his escape to
the Gypsies; why Onegin felt bored; why there came into being
'superfluous men' immortalized by Turgenev, Korobochka, Sobakevich, Skvoznik-Dmukhanovsky, Derjimorda, Tiapkin-Liapkin—this
is the shadowy side of Aleko, Beltov, Rudin and many others. This
is the background without which the characters of the latter are
unintelligible. And Gogol's heroes were Russian—oh, how genuinely
Russian! There was no *Weltschmerz* in Korobochka; Skvoznik-
Dmukhanovsky managed to perfection to deal with the storekeepers; Sobakevich knew his peasants from A to Z, and they clearly
saw him through. Of course Aleko and the Rudins neither saw nor
comprehended all this; they simply fled wherever they could: Aleko
to the Gypsies, Rudin to Paris to give his life for an altogether
alien cause."

You see, they *simply* fled. Oh, the journalistic ease of the
solution! How simply everything transpires in your opinion; how
ready and predetermined!—Verily, yours are ready-made words.
By the way, why did you start dwelling upon the subject that
Gogol's heroes were Russians—"oh, how genuinely Russian!"—This
is quite irrelevant to our controversy. Besides, who does not know
that they were Russians? Aleko and Onegin, too, were Russians;
you and I are Russians. Likewise Rudin was a Russian, a full-
fledged Russian, who ran away to Paris to give his life for a cause
which, according to you, was quite alien to him. He was a Russian
in the strictest sense precisely for the reason that the cause for
which he died in Paris was by no means so alien to him as it would
have been to an Englishman or a German, since a European, universal, all-humanitarian cause has long ceased to be alien to a
Russian. This is Rudin's distinguishing mark. Strictly speaking,
Rudin's tragedy lay in the fact that he found no labor to perform
on his own soil, and died in a foreign land, but not as foreign as
you maintain.

This is, however, the point: despite the fact that all these
Skvozniks and Sobakevichs were Russians, nevertheless they were
corrupted Russians, detached from their soil; although they were
familiar with one aspect of the people's mode of living, still they
knew nothing about its other aspect; they did not even suspect its
existence—this is the whole point. They did not even suspect the
existence of the people's soul, the things for which the people were

thirsting and praying, because they profoundly despised the people. They denied in the people any soul, save for the purpose of the census. You claim that "Sobakevich knew his peasants from A to Z." This is impossible: he perceived in his Proshka nothing but a labor unit which he could sell to Tchitchikov. You say that Skvoznik-Dmukhanovsky managed to perfection to deal with the merchants. For goodness' sake! Read the bailiff's monologue to those store-keepers in the fifth act: in this manner one speaks, perhaps, to dogs, but not to human beings. Does this mean to deal with the Russian "to perfection"? Is it possible that you are praising him?—Why, he had really better have smacked them on their faces or pulled them by their hair!

In my childhood I saw once on a highway a state courier in uniform with flaps, wearing a three-cornered hat with a feather sticking in it, brutally with his fist beating the driver on his nape, while the latter madly whipped the steaming troika racing at full speed. Of course this courier was Russian by birth, but one so blinded, so alienated from the people that he did not know how to deal with a Russian otherwise than with his heavy fist in lieu of conversing with him in any manner whatsoever. And yet he spent all his life in the company of postboys and Russian commoners of every kind. However, the flaps of his uniform, his feathered hat, his polished Petersburg boots, to him were spiritually dearer not only than the Russian peasant, but perhaps than Russia *in toto,* which he crossed from one end to the other, in which, probably, he found nothing remarkable or worthy of note other than his own fist or the kick of his polished boot. The whole of Russia represented itself to him merely in the guise of his superiors, outside of whom virtually nothing was worthy of existence. How could such a fellow understand the people's essence and their soul! Although a Russian, he was a "European" Russian, only one who had embarked upon his Europeanism not with education but with debauchery, just in the same way as many others did. Yes, sir, this debauchery on many occasions was held in Russia to be the surest means of converting Russians into Europeans. Indeed, the son of that state-messenger might have become a professor, *i.e.,* a patented European.

And so, don't speak about their understanding of the people's essence. We had to have Pushkin, the Khomiakovs, the Samarins, the Aksakovs before we could begin to speak about the people's essence. (Although prior to them this subject used to be discussed but in a somewhat pseudo-classical and histrionic fashion.) And when they began to speak about "the people's truth," everybody looked upon them as epileptics and idiots whose ideal was "eating radishes and writing denouncements." At first their appearance and opinions surprised everybody to such an extent that liberals began to wonder: aren't these men about to start denouncing them?—It is up to you to decide whether or not our contemporary liberals have much advanced from that silly view on Slavophiles.

But let us turn to business. You state that Aleko fled to the Gypsies from Derjimorda. Let us concede that this is true. But the worst thing is that you, Mr. Gradovsky, with full conviction admit Aleko's right to such surliness. You imply: "He could not have failed to flee to the Gypsies because Derjimorda was too repulsive." But I assert that in a certain sense Aleko and Onegin were also Derjimordas, and perhaps even worse than these, with that difference only that I am not accusing them in the least, fully realizing the tragedy of their fate, whereas you are lauding them for their escape. "Such great"—you seem to imply—"such interesting men were unable to live on good terms with such monsters." You are awfully mistaken. You infer that Aleko and Onegin did not in the least alienate themselves from their native soil and did not deny the people's truth. Moreover, you seem to say: "they were by no means haughty!"—This is what you maintain. Well, in this case haughtiness is a logical and unavoidable consequence of their abstraction and their detachment from their own soil. Indeed, you cannot deny the fact that they did not know their soil, that they grew and were brought up as if in a convent. They acquired their knowledge of Russia in Petersburg, through bureaucratic channels, and their relations with the people were those of a master with his serf. Let us even admit that at times they lived in the country, in proximity to the peasant. My state messenger, all life long, rubbed shoulders with postilions, and admitted that they were worthy of nothing but his fist. Aleko and Onegin behaved in Russia haughtily and impatiently like all men who live in a small group segregated from the people, fully provided for, *i.e.*, supported by the peasant's labor and depending on European education, which they also received gratuitously. The very fact that our educated classes, as a result of historical preparation, virtually throughout our whole national existence have been converted into lazy creatures, explains their abstraction and alienation from their native soil. They perished not because of Derjimorda as such but because they were unable to explain to themselves the phenomenon of Derjimorda and its origin. For this they were too proud. But having failed to find the meaning of Derjimorda, they deemed it impossible to toil on their native soil, regarding those who believed in such a possibility as blockheads or as Derjimordas themselves.

These roamers exalted themselves not only over the Derji-

mordas but over Russia as a whole, because Russia, in their last analysis, was populated only with serfs and Derjimordas, whereas if there
were nobler elements there, they were composed of Alekos and
Onegins, and of no one but them. This line of reasoning inevitably
leads to haughtiness: dwelling in a state of segregation they naturally began to wonder at their own nobility and superiority over
the vile Derjimordas whom they were unable to comprehend. Had
they not been uppish they would have perceived that they were
Derjimordas themselves, and having comprehended this they might
have found a way to reconciliation. With regard to the people there
was on their part a feeling not merely of haughtiness but of aversion, and this was the general rule.

You will not believe all this. On the contrary, while admitting
that in the Alekos and Onegins certain traits are truly unbecoming,
you haughtily start reproaching me for the narrowness of my view
that "it is hardly reasonable to cure the symptoms leaving the root
of the disease intact." You assert that when I say: "Humble thyself, haughty man," I am thereby accusing Aleko of his personal
qualities, overlooking the root of the matter, "as if the essence of
it resides in the individual qualities of those exalting themselves
and refusing to humble themselves." "The question has not been
decided"—you say—"over what did these wanderers exalt themselves. Equally, another question remains unanswered: Before what
should they humble themselves?"—On your part, all this is very
presumptuous. It is apparent that I clearly inferred that "the roamers" were a product of the historical course of development of our
society. This means that I am not placing the full blame upon
them *personally* and upon their personal qualities. You have this
in my *Address* which was written and published. Why, then, do
you distort my views? Quoting my tirade: "Humble thyself," you
write:

"In these words Mr. Dostoievsky has expressed 'the holy of
holies' of his convictions, that which at once constitutes both the
strength and weakness of the author of *The Brothers Karamazov*.
These words comprise a great *religious* ideal, a potent sermon of
personal morality, but they contain no inkling of *social* ideals."

And after these words you begin at once to criticize the idea
"of personal betterment in the spirit of Christian love." I shall turn
in a minute to your opinion of "self-betterment," but first I will
unfold for you your underlying idea, which it seems you seek to
conceal: You grew angry at me not only because I accused "the
wanderer," but because I do not perceive in him an ideal of moral
perfection, a sound, healthy Russian which he can and must be!
When you admit that in Aleko and Onegin there are "unbecoming

traits" you are merely dodging the issue. According to your inner conviction, which for some reason you do not wish to reveal completely, "the wanderers" are normal and beautiful, beautiful in the fact itself that they have fled from the Derjimordas. Your indignation is at once aroused the moment one ventures to perceive in them the slightest defect. You state specifically: "It would be nonsensical to maintain that they perished because of their uppishness and their refusal to be humbled before the people's truth." Finally you are ardently arguing, and insisting, that they were the ones who liberated the peasants. You state:

"I will say more: If there was any thought conserved in the souls of the best of 'those wanderers of the first part of our century,' it was precisely the thought about the people, while their most burning hatred was directed against serfdom which oppressed the people. Even though they loved the people and hated serfdom in their own, if you please 'European,' way, nevertheless, who but they prepared our society for the abolition of serfdom?—They, too, have served their 'native soil' as best they could—originally as preachers of liberation and later as peace mediators of the first period."

Therein is the point that "the wanderers" hated serfdom "in their own European way." The point is in the fact that they hated serfdom not for the sake of the Russian peasant who worked for them and fed them, and whom they, among others, oppressed. If civic sorrow was so painful to them that they had to flee to the Gypsies or to the barricades in Paris—who prevented them from simply liberating their peasants with land, and in this way from removing that civic sorrow, at least from their personal responsibility? But we heard little about such liberations, whereas there was quite a bit of civic howling. The implication is that "the milieu ruined their souls; and, besides, why should one be deprived of his capital?" Well, why shouldn't they have been deprived of their capital if their sorrow for the peasants was so intense that they had to run away to the barricades?—Therein is the point that in that "little spot called Paris" money was needed, even though one took part in the fight on the barricades, so that serfs had to send their poll-tax anyway. Why, these gentlemen acted even in a simpler manner: they pledged, sold or exchanged (what's the difference!) their peasants, and having thus raised money, they went to Paris and financed there the publication of French radical newspapers and magazines for the salvation of mankind, and not just of the Russian peasant.

You assure us that sorrow for the peasant serf devoured all of them. Not really for the peasant serf, but abstract sorrow about

slavery prevailing in mankind. "This shouldn't be! This is unenlightened. Let's have *Liberté, Égalité et Fraternité!*" As for the
Russian peasant in particular, sorrow for him, maybe, did not torment these great hearts at all. I know and have memorized many
sayings of the most "enlightened" men of the good old times.
"Slavery"—they used to say, in their intimate talks among themselves—"is unquestionably a great evil. But taking everything into
account, are our people—a people? Are they akin to the Paris people of 1793? Why, they are used to slavery; their faces, their forms,
are the expression of slavery. Or take the rod, for instance. Generally speaking, of course, it is an awful abomination. But, really,
the Russian still needs it: the good little peasant has to be flogged;
he would start agonizing should he not be flogged. Such is our nation!"—In days gone by I used to hear such conversations, and
I swear, opinions of this kind used to be expressed even by quite
enlightened men. This is sober truth. Perhaps Onegin did not flog
his house-servants, although I would not swear to this. But Aleko,
I am sure, now and then flogged his serfs—and not because of the
cruelty of his heart but almost from compassion, for a good end:
"Why, he needs it; he can't live without being flogged a little. He
comes of his own accord and begs: 'Master, do please flog me, make
a man of me! I'm completely spoiled!' Well, what's to be done
with such a nature, I ask you; so one has to satisfy him and administer a little flogging!"

I repeat, their feeling for the peasant often bordered on
squeamishness. And to think of the number of contemptuous anecdotes about the Russian peasant which circulated among them—
despicable, obscene anecdotes about his slavish soul, his "idolatry,"
his priest, his woman. And all these were told with a light heart
sometimes by people whose own family life reminded one of a
brothel. Of course, this was not always due to something evil; at
times this resulted from a too enthusiastic susceptibility to the
latest European ideas *à la Lucrezia Floriani,* for instance, interpreted and embraced with Russian impetuosity. They were Russians
in everything!

Oh, the Russian lamenting roamers, at times, were great
rogues, Mr. Gradovsky. Now, these very anecdotes about the Russian peasant and the contemptuous attitude toward him almost
always alleviated in their hearts the sharpness of their civic sorrow
caused by serfdom, thus conveying to it an abstract universal character with which one can live on very good terms, spiritually feeding oneself·on the contemplation of one's moral beauty and on the
largesse of civic thought, while feeding the body—and feeding it
well—with the poll-tax levied from those same peasants! One doesn't

have to go far: only recently an oldtimer told an anecdote in a magazine about outstanding Russian liberals of those days, and universal minds, meeting a Russian peasant woman. Those were arrant, so to speak, patented wanderers who became known as such in history. You see, once upon a time, in the summer of 1845, there gathered a great multitude of guests in a gorgeous suburban Moscow villa where, according to the same oldtimer "colossal dinner parties" used to be given: among the guests there were many most humane professors, most renowned lovers and connoisseurs of the fine arts and of some other things, most famous democrats, subsequently noted politicians of universal importance, critics, writers, and intellectually most charming ladies. Presently the whole company, after a champagne dinner with fish-pies and bird-milk[1] (there must have been a reason for calling these dinners "colossal"!), went for a stroll into the fields. In a remote part of a corn-field they encountered a woman reaper. We all know what harvest time is: peasants—men and women—get up at four o'clock in the morning, and they go to gather the crops, toiling till late at night. Reaping, having to stoop down for twelve hours, is hard work; the sun burns mercilessly. When a woman reaper works in a corn-field, one can't even see her. Well, it was there, amidst the corn, that our distinguished company came across the woman reaper, and, imagine —she "in a primitive costume" (with only a shirt on her!). How dreadful! Universal humane sentiment is aroused at once, and an insulted voice sounds: "Among all women it is only the Russian woman who is ashamed of nobody!" And, of course, the inference is readily drawn: "Only the Russian woman is of a kind before whom nobody is ashamed of anything." (Does it mean that one shouldn't be ashamed of anything?)—There ensued a dispute: some came out in defense of the peasant woman. But what kind of defenders were they, and with what arguments did they have to contend? . . .

Such were the opinions and contentions which prevailed among a crowd of roaming landowners, drunk with champagne and feasting on oysters—and on whose money? Well, on money earned by that very woman reaper! Why, it was for you, universal wanderers, that she toiled; it was through her labor that you got satiated. Because, amidst the corn, where nobody sees her, tormented by the sun and sweat, she took off her linen skirt, with nothing but a shirt on her—because of this you called her shameless, and your delicate sense of shame was insulted? "The most shameless among all women!" Eh, you chaste fellows! What about your Parisian "diversions"! What about your sportiveness in that "little spot called

[1] An ironic Russian phrase, connoting a very choice meal.

Paris"! And that neat little cancan at the Bal-Mabille, which made Russian fellows thaw from the very account of it! And that charming little song:

> "Ma commère, quand je dance,
> Comment va mon cotillon?"

with a graceful lifting of the petticoat and jerking of the posteriors —does all this incense our chaste Russian fellows?—On the contrary, it captivates them. "We beg your pardon—they stage it so gracefully—that little cancan, those sportive little jerks—indeed, this is a most elegant *article de Paris, sui generis,* whereas here, what is there?—A peasant woman, a Russian peasant woman, a log, a block!"

Nay, here we have not merely a deep belief in the nastiness of our peasant and our people: here the sentiment has grown to the point of personal squeamishness toward the peasant, oh, of course, involuntary, almost unconscious, not even noticed on their part.

I confess, Mr. Gradovsky, that I utterly disagree with your cardinal thesis: "Who but they prepared our society for the abolition of serfdom?"—Perhaps, by means of abstract chit-chat with an effusion of civic sorrow according to all the rules!—Well, of course, this was added to the sum total, and may have served the cause. However, the liberation of the peasants was fostered, and those working for their liberation were helped, by men of the type of Samarin, for example, and not by your roamers. Mr. Gradovsky, there appeared a multitude of men of Samarin's pattern—which does not in the least resemble that of the wanderers—who offered their services to the great work of those days. But, of course, there is not a word about them in your article. As for the roamers, they evidently very soon grew tired of it, and, again, they began to pout squeamishly. They would not have been roamers had they acted differently. Having received their redemption payments, they began to sell their lands and forests for extermination and deforestation to merchants and kulaks, they expatriated themselves, inaugurating absenteeism. . . .

It stands to reason that you, Mr. Professor, will not agree with my opinion. But what can I do?—Under no circumstance can I consent to recognize the character of this Russian superior liberal man—so dear to your heart—as the ideal of a genuine, normal Russian, which supposedly he actually was, is and must be in the future. During the last decades nothing very constructive has been accomplished by these men on their native soil. This is a more correct statement than your dithyramb glorifying these gentlemen of days gone by.

3

Two Halves

Now I am turning to your views on "individual self-betterment in the spirit of Christian love" and on its alleged utter insufficiency in comparison with "social ideals," and, principally—with "social institutions." You begin with the statement that this is the cardinal point of our disagreement. You write:

"Now we come to the most important point of our disagreement with Mr. Dostoievsky. Insisting on humility before the people's truth, before the ideals of the people, he accepts this 'truth' and these ideals as something ready-made, immutable and eternal. We venture to tell him—no! The social ideals of our people are still in the process of formation, development. The people have to labor much upon self-betterment in order to be worthy of being called a great people."

Partly, in the beginning of my article, in its first subdivision, I have already answered you on the question of "truth" and the ideals of the people. This truth and these ideals you positively consider insufficient for the development of Russia's social ideals. Religion—you imply—is one proposition, while the social cause is a different one. With your scientific knife, you are cutting a live, homogeneous organism into two separate halves, and you assert that they must be altogether independent one from the other. Let us scrutinize the matter more closely, let us analyze each half separately, and perhaps we shall arrive at something. First, let us deal with the half pertaining to "self-betterment in the spirit of Christian love." You state:

"Mr. Dostoievsky urges that we start working upon ourselves and that we humble ourselves. Of course, individual self-betterment in the spirit of Christian love is the major premise of any activity, whether great or small. But from this it does not follow that men *personally perfect in a Christian sense* necessarily form a perfect society. Let us cite an example.

"The Apostle Paul instructed slaves and their masters concerning their mutual relations. Both the former and the latter may have obeyed, and usually did obey, the Apostle's words; *individually* they were good Christians; nevertheless, slavery thereby was not made sacred, and it continued to be an immoral institution. Equally, Mr. Dostoievsky, like every one of us, used to know admirable Christian landowners and peasants. *Serfdom*, however, continued to be an abomination in God's judgment, and the Russian Czar-Liberator came forward as a champion not only of *personal*, individual morality but also of *social* morality, of which in olden times there were no adequate conceptions, notwithstanding the fact that there were, perhaps, more 'good men' than at present.

"Individual and social morality do not constitute one and the same thing. From this it follows that no *social* improvement can be achieved *only* through the betterment of the personal qualities of men constituting a society. I shall again cite an example. Let us suppose that beginning with the year 1800 a number of preachers of Christian love and humility had started to improve the morality of the Korobochkas and Sobakevichs. Could it be presumed that they would have succeeded in abolishing serfdom, that this 'phenomenon' could have been eliminated without the utterance of the *Imperial* word? On the contrary, Korobochka would have begun to argue that she was a true Christian woman and a genuine 'mother' of her peasants, and she would have clung to this conviction despite all the arguments of the preacher. . . .

"Men's betterment in a *social* sense cannot be accomplished by mere work 'upon oneself.' One may work upon self-improvement and subdue one's passions in a wilderness and on a desert island. But as *social* beings men develop and improve in working *beside each other, one for the other* and *one with the other*. This is why social progress is so greatly dependent upon *social institutions* which mould in man if not Christian, then civic virtues."

See how much I have quoted from you! All this is awfully haughty and "individual self-betterment in the spirit of Christian love" certainly has got "a black eye": in civic matters—you imply —it is virtually good for nothing. Verily, you understand Christianity in a most curious way! Presuming that Korobochka and Sobakevich might have become true, *perfect* Christians (you speak yourself about perfection)—could they be induced to renounce serfdom? This is the crafty question which you propound, and which—it goes without saying—you answer: "No, it is impossible to induce Korobochka, even though she be a perfect Christian."

This I shall answer directly: Had Korobochka become, or could she have become, *a true,* perfect Christian, there would have been no serfdom on her estate, so that there would be nothing to bother about, notwithstanding the fact that all deeds and bills of sales would still be kept in her trunk. Another thing: Korobochka has been a Christian all along, she was born a Christian. Thus, when you speak about the new preachers of Christianity, you mean Christianity, though identical in substance with the former one, yet intensified, *perfect,* so to speak, one that has attained its ideal. Well, if so, what slaves, what masters can there be?—One has to have at least a bit of understanding of Christianity! And what difference would it have made to Korobochka, a *perfect* Christian, whether her peasants were serfs or freemen?—She would have been their mother, a real mother, who would have promptly dismissed the former "mistress." This would have come to pass of its own accord. The former mistress and the former slave would have vanished like mist in the rays of sun, and altogether new human beings would have come into existence, and quite new, hitherto unheard-of relations would have ensued between them. Besides, an unheard-of condition would arise: *everywhere* there would appear perfect Christians, of whom formerly there had been so few that they were almost imperceptible.

Mr. Gradovsky, you have set forth yourself this fantastic supposition, and having embarked upon such phantasms, you have to take the consequences. I assure you that in this event Korobochka's peasants themselves would not have left her, for the simple reason that everybody sees where he can be better off. Where would he be better off?—in your institutions?—or in the home of his loving landowning mother?—Also, I venture to assure you that if slavery prevailed in the days of the Apostle Paul, this was precisely because the churches which originated then were not yet *perfect,* as we perceive from the Epistles of the Apostle himself. However, those members of the congregations who, individually, attained perfection, no longer owned or could have had slaves, because these became brethren, and a brother, a true brother, cannot have a brother as his slave. But, according to you, the preaching of Christianity was impotent. At least you maintain that slavery was not made sacred as a result of the Apostle's preaching. And yet many other men of science, especially European historians, have reproached Christianity for having allegedly sanctified slavery. This means a lack of understanding of the essence of the matter. Just imagine that Mary of Egypt owned peasant serfs and refused to liberate them! What an absurdity!—In Christianity, in genuine Christianity, there are and always will be masters and servants, but a serf is inconceivable. I am speaking of true and perfect Christianity. But servants are not slaves. The disciple Timothy served Paul when they journeyed together. Yet read Paul's Epistles to Timothy: does he write to a slave, or even a servant?—Precisely he is his "own son in faith," his "dearly beloved son"!—Such will be the relations between masters and their servants when both the former and the latter become perfect Christians! There will be servants and masters, but masters will no longer be masters nor will servants be slaves.

Please imagine that in a future society there will be a Kepler, a Kant, a Shakespeare: they are engaged in a great work for all men, and everybody realizes this and reveres them. Shakespeare has no time to interrupt his work in order to clean his room and remove the garbage. And, believe me, some other citizen, of his own volition, will come to serve him, and will remove Shakespeare's garbage. Well, would this humiliate him? Would this make him a slave?—Certainly not. He knows that Shakespeare is infinitely more useful than he. "Honor and glory to thee!"—he will say to Shakespeare—"I am glad to serve thee: at least in a slight way I shall thereby serve the common cause, because I shall save thy time for thy great work. But I am not a slave. By the fact itself that I am admitting that thou, Shakespeare, art superior to myself in genius, that I came to serve thee, I have proved that from the standpoint of human moral dignity, I am in no sense inferior to thee, and, *as man*, am equal to thee." Why, then he would not even have to say all these things, for the sole reason that then no such questions would arise; they would be simply inconceivable, for, verily, all men would be new men, Christ's children, while the former beast in man would be vanquished.

Of course, you will say that this is again a fantasy. Yet I was not the first to embark upon fastasies.—You were the one: you started picturing Korobochka as a *perfect* Christian with "serf *children*" whom she refuses to liberate. This is more paradoxical than my fantasy.

Clever people will start laughing and will say: "What's the use, then, to advocate self-betterment in the spirit of Christian love, if true Christianity does not exist on earth, or there is so little of it that it is well-nigh imperceptible, since otherwise (according to my own words) everything would be instantly settled and slavery of every kind would be abolished: the Korobochkas would be transformed into lucid spirits and there would be nothing left but to start singing a hymn to God?" Yes, of course, gentlemen-scoffers, there are still very few true Christians (although there are some). But how do you know how many of them are needed to preserve the Christian ideal among the people—and with it the people's great hope? Apply this to civic conceptions: how many true citizens are needed to preserve civic virtue in society? This question, too, you cannot answer. In this respect there is a political economy of its own, of an altogether different kind, unknown to us, unknown even to you, Mr. Gradovsky.

Again, it might be said: If there are so few confessors of the great idea, what use is there in it?—And how do you know to what benefit, in the last analysis, it will lead? Apparently, thus far, the only thing that was needed was that the great idea should not expire. The situation is different at present when something new is arising in the world, and when one has to be prepared. Besides, it is not a matter of benefit but of truth. For if I believe that truth is here, precisely in what I believe, what do I care if even the whole world should refuse to believe in my truth, should ridicule me and should choose a different road?—Therein is the strength of a great moral idea that it cements men into a most solid union; that it is not measured in terms of benefit but makes men aspire to the future, to eternal aims and absolute gladness. How will you unite men for the attainment of your civic aims if there is no foundation in the form of an initial great moral idea? But all moral ideas are identical: they are all based upon the principle of absolute individual self-betterment in the future, in an ideal which comprises all aspirations, all longings, and, consequently, all our civic ideals emanate therefrom. Just try to cement men into a civic society with the sole aim of "saving their skins"!—You will derive nothing but the moral formula: *"Chacun pour soi et Dieu pour tous."* With such a formula no civic institution can live long, Mr. Gradovsky.

But I will go further: I intend to surprise you. Please be advised, learned Professor, that there are no social, civic ideals, as such, not originally tied to moral ideals, and existing independently in the form of a separate half, chipped off from the whole with your scientific knife, ideals which can be borrowed from without and successfully transplanted into any new spot in the form of a separate "institution." There are no such ideals, they never have existed, never can exist!

Besides, what is a social ideal? How is one to understand this term?—Of course, its essence resides in the attempt of men to find a formula of social organization, faultless, if possible, and satisfying everybody. Isn't this so? But men do not know such a formula. Men have been looking for it during six thousand years of their historical existence, and they have failed to find it. The ant knows its ant-hill formula; the bee the formula of its beehive (even though they do not know them in a human way; they know them in their own way, and this is all they need). Man however, does not know his formula.

If so, whence can the ideal of civic organization in human society be derived?—Trace it historically and you will forthwith perceive whence it is derived. You will see that it is solely the product of moral self-betterment of individual entities; it has its inception there. Thus it has been from time immemorial, and thus it always will be. In the origin of every people, of every nationality, the moral idea invariably preceded the origination of the nationality itself, *since the former created the latter.* The moral idea always emanated from mystical ideas, from the conviction that man is eternal, that he is not a mere earthly animal, but that he is tied to other worlds and eternity. Invariably and everywhere these beliefs assumed the form of religion, the form of a confession of the new idea. And just as soon as a new religion came into being, a new civic nationality came into existence. Look at the Hebrews and the Mohammedans: Jewish nationality came into being after the Mosaic law, even its beginning can be traced to the law of Abraham, while the Mohammedan nationalities arose only after the Koran.

To preserve the acquired spiritual treasure, men are forthwith attracted to each other, and only then do they zealously and anxiously, *"working beside each other, one for the other, one with the other"* (as you eloquently put it) begin to investigate how they should organize so as to preserve the treasure without losing any part of it; how to find such a *civic* formula of common existence as would help them to promote throughout the world the acquired moral treasure in its full glory.

And please observe that just as soon as after centuries and ages—here there is also a law of its own, unknown to us—the spiritual ideal of this or that nationality begins to loosen and weaken, the nationality begins to degenerate, together with its civic constitution, and the civic ideals which had moulded themselves within it become extinct. The civic forms of a people assume the character in which their religion is expressed. Therefore the civic ideals are always directly and organically tied to the moral ideals, and—what is most important—the former indisputably are derived only from the latter. Civic ideals never appear *of their own accord* because when they do appear they have as their only object the consummation of the moral aspirations of the given nationality, in the form and in so far as these moral aspirations have moulded themselves in that nationality.

On this ground "self-betterment in a religious sense" in the life of the peoples is the foundation of everything, since self-betterment is *the confession of the acquired religion,* whereas "the civic ideals," devoid of this longing for self-betterment, never do appear, and never can come into being.

You might retort, perhaps, that you said yourself that "individual self-betterment is the beginning of everything," and that you have not used your knife to divide anything. But therein is the point that you did cut a live organism into two halves. Individual self-betterment is not only "the *beginning* of everything," but also its continuation and outcome. It—and it alone—embraces, creates and preserves the national organism. It is for the sake of self-betterment that the civic formula of a nation exists, since it came into being only for its preservation as an initially acquired treasure.

When, however, a nationality loses the urge of individual self-betterment *in the spirit which procreated it,* gradually, all "civic institutions" begin to disappear because there is nothing more to preserve.
Therefore it is altogether impossible to maintain what you have
framed in the following sentence:

"This is why social progress is so greatly dependent upon
social *institutions* which mould in man, if not Christian, then civic
virtues."

"If not Christian, then civic virtues"! Doesn't one see here
the scientific knife dividing the indivisible, cutting a homogeneous
live organism into two separate dead halves—the moral and civic?
You may say that "social institutions" and the dignity of "citizen"
may comprise a very great moral idea; that "the civic idea" in ripe
and developed nations always replaces the initial religious idea which
degenerates into the former and which it legitimately inherits. Quite
so, this is being maintained by many people, but thus far we have
never seen this fantasy realized. When in a nation the moral or
religious idea wears itself out, there always comes the panicky,
cowardly urge to unite for the sole purpose of "saving the skins":
then no other aims of civic unity exist. At present, for instance, the
French bourgeoisie sticks together only for the purpose of "saving
its skin" from the fourth estate which tries to break into its door.
But "the saving of skins" is the most impotent and lowest of all
ideas uniting mankind. This is the beginning of the end. People
pretend to stick together, but at the same time they are on a sharp
look-out for the first moment of danger, ready to disperse. And
what, in this case, can an "institution," as such, save? If there be
brethren, there will be brotherhood. But if there are no brethren
no "institution" will ever produce brotherhood. What is the sense
of establishing an "institution" and inscribing on it: *Liberté, Égalité,
Fraternité!* Nothing will be achieved by an "institution," so that
it will become necessary, quite inevitably, to add to these three
"constituent" words, three new ones: *"ou la mort," "fraternité ou
la mort,"* and brethren will start chopping off the heads of their
brethren in order to achieve brotherhood through "the civic institution."

This is merely an example, but a good one. You, Mr. Gradovsky, just like Aleko, seek salvation in things and external phenomena: "Let there be in Russia fools and rogues, no one but they"
(according to certain views this is so); it is sufficient, however, to
transplant from Europe into Russia some "institution," and, in your
opinion, everything will be saved. The mechanical transplantation
to Russia of European forms (which tomorrow will collapse there),
alien and not suited to our people, is, as we know, the most mo-

mentous notion of Russian Europeanism. By the way, Mr. Gradovsky, when condemning our want of order, shaming Russia for it,
and pointing out Europe to her, you state the following:

"Meanwhile at home we are even unable to cope with such
discords and contradictions as have been settled long ago in Europe . . ."

You mean Europe has settled them? Who could have told you
this?—Why, Europe is on the eve of a general and dreadful collapse. The ant-hill which has been long in the process of construction without the Church and Christ (since the Church, having
dimmed its ideal, long ago and everywhere reincarnated itself in
the state), with a moral principle shaken loose from its foundation,
with everything general and absolute lost—this ant-hill, I say, is
utterly undermined. The fourth estate is coming, it knocks at the
door, and breaks into it, and if it is not opened to it, it will break
the door. The fourth estate cares nothing for the former ideals;
it rejects every existing law. It will make no compromises, no concessions; buttresses will not save the edifice. Concessions only provoke, but the fourth estate wants everything. There will come to
pass something wholly unsuspected. All these parliamentarisms, all
civic theories professed at present, all accumulated riches, banks,
sciences, Jews—all these will instantly perish without leaving a trace
—save the Jews, who even then will find their way out, so that this
work will even be to their advantage. All this is "near, at the door."
—You laugh? Blessed be those who laugh. God grant you time to
live longer; you will see it yourself. Then you will be surprised.
You will tell me with sarcasm: "What is your love of Europe if
you are making such prophecies to her!"—Do I rejoice?—I merely
foresee that the balance has been struck. The final settlement, the
payment due, may occur much sooner than the most vivid fantasy
can conceive. The symptoms are dreadful. The long-standing abnormal political status of the European countries may serve as a
beginning of everything. How can this status be normal, if abnormality is laid in its very foundation and has been accumulating
during centuries? One small part of mankind cannot own the rest
of mankind as slaves. Yet it was for this sole purpose that, up to
the present, *all* civic institutions (long not Christian) of Europe,
now altogether pagan, have been inaugurated. This abnormality,
and these "insoluble" political questions (however generally known)
unfailingly must lead to a colossal, final, partitioning, political war
in which everybody will be involved, and which will break out in
the course of the current century, and, perhaps, even in the coming
decade.

What do you think: Will society over there endure *at present* a long political war?—The manufacturer is cowardly and easily scared; likewise the Jew. Factories and banks will all close down should the war drag out even slightly or should it threaten to be prolonged, and millions of hungry mouths, outcast proletarians, will be thrown into the streets. Perhaps you are relying on the prudence of the politicians, and on the fact that they will not start a war? But when was it possible to rely on such a prudence? Perhaps you are relying on legislative bodies, that they will refuse to make appropriations for the war, anticipating its consequences. But when did these chambers over there ever anticipate consequences and refuse to appropriate funds to a more or less persistent leader?—And now the proletarian is in the street. Do you think that, as heretofore, he will patiently wait, dying of starvation?—After political socialism? After the International? After social conventions and the Paris Commune?—Nay, at present it is not going to be the way it used to be: the proletarians will rush upon Europe, and the entire old order will collapse forever. The waves will break only against our shores, and then it will be arrantly revealed to everybody to what an extent our national organism differs from the European. Then you too, gentlemen doctrinarians, will come to your senses, and will begin to seek at home those "people's tenets" which now you are merely ridiculing.

But now, gentlemen, you are pointing to Europe and suggesting that those very institutions which will collapse tomorrow as an outworn absurdity be transplanted to Russia, institutions in which many wise men in Europe have long ceased to believe, which hold out and exist there by mere inertia.

And who, except an abstract doctrinarian, could take the comedy of bourgeois unity, which we are witnessing in Europe, for a normal formula of human fellowship on earth? "They"—you say —"have solved their problems long ago!"—And this—after twenty constitutions and scarcely less than ten revolutions!—Oh, only then, perhaps, liberated for a moment from Europe, we ourselves, without European tutelage, shall dwell upon our social ideals, necessarily derived from Christ and individual self-betterment, Mr. Gradovsky.

You will ask: What social and civic ideals of our own can we have outside of those of European origin?—Well, our social and civic ideals are better, more solid and even—oh, *horribile dictu!*—more liberal than your European ideals! Yes, they are more liberal because they emanate directly from our people's organism, and they are not a slavishly impersonal transplantation from the West. Of course, here I cannot enlarge upon the subject because my article has grown too long anyway.

By the way, please recall: what was the ancient Christian

Church? What did it strive to be?—It came into existence immediately after Christ. It was formed by a handful of men, and forthwith, almost in the very first days after Christ, it began to seek after its "civic formula," fully based upon the moral hope of quenching its spirit in accordance with the principles of individual self-betterment. Christian communes—churches—arose, following which a new, hitherto unheard-of nation began to form itself—all-brotherly, all-humanitarian in the form of an Oecumenical Church. But it was subjected to persecution; its ideal was moulded underground, while on the earth's surface a huge edifice, an enormous ant-hill, was being erected—the ancient Roman Empire, which was also, as it were, an ideal and a solution of the moral aspirations of the ancient world: there arose the demigod; the Empire itself embodied the religious idea providing an outlet to all moral aspirations of the ancient world. The ant-hill, however, did not come to pass, having been undermined by the Church. A collision of two diametrically opposed ideas occurred: the man-god encountered the God-man, Apollo of Belvedere encountered Christ. A compromise took place: the Empire embraced Christianity, while the Church accepted the Roman law and the Roman state. A small part of the Church retired into the wilderness and continued there its original work: Christian communes again came into existence, and later monasteries. But these were merely tests, which continue even to our day. As we know, the remaining overwhelming portion of the Church subsequently split into two parts. In the Western part the state, at length, subdued the Church altogether. Papacy arose—a continuation of the ancient Roman Empire in a new incarnation. In the Eastern half, however, the state was conquered and destroyed by the sword of Mohammed, and there remained only Christ detached from the state. That state which embraced and again raised Christ has endured such dreadful secular sufferings from its enemies, the Tartars, want of order, serfdom, Europe and Europeanism—is still enduring so much suffering—that actually no real social formula in the spirit of love and Christian self-improvement has yet been elaborated in it. But it is not for you, Mr. Gradovsky, to reproach that state for this fact. Temporarily our people are only Christ-bearers and they place their entire hope in Him alone. They called themselves "Krestianin,"[1] i.e., "Christian"; and this is not only a matter of words; this comprises the idea of their whole future. You, Mr. Gradovsky, are mercilessly reproaching Russia for her want of order. But who has prevented her from establishing order during these last two centuries, and, particularly, during the last forty

[1] The Russian word "Krestianin" means peasant; the Russian word "Christianin" means Christian.

years?—Well, Russian Europeans, akin to yourself, Mr. Gradovsky, who have never ceased to exist during the last two centuries, and who, in our day, are pressing us ever so hard. Who is hostile to Russia's organic and independent development based upon its national principles? Who scoffingly refused even to admit or notice the existence of these tenets? Who sought to remodel our people, fantastically "raising them to the level of the reformers," or simply to convert them into so many liberal European creatures, just like the reformers themselves, from time to time snatching from the people's masses this or that man, perverting him into a European even though with mere flaps on his uniform?—In stating this, I do not mean to say that the European is perverted. I merely mean to say that to remodel a Russian into a European is oftentimes equivalent to actual perversion. And yet of this alone consists the whole ideal of the program of their work: precisely—tearing away one man after another from the masses—how absurd! They seek to tear away all the eighty millions of our people and to remodel them. Do you really believe that the whole mass of the Russian people will consent to such an impersonality as these Russian European gentlemen?

4

HUMBLE THYSELF—TO ONE; EXALT THYSELF—TO THE OTHER. A TEMPEST IN A TEA-POT

Thus far, I have been merely wrangling with you, Mr. Gradovsky, but now I want to accuse you of a deliberate distortion of my thought, of the principal point of my *Address*. You write:

"There sticks in them (*i.e.*, in our people) too much untruth, residues of secular serfdom, for them to be entitled *to demand that we should worship them* and, in addition, for them to attempt to turn all Europe to the right road, as Mr. Dostoievsky predicts.

"Strange thing! A man who condemns haughtiness in individual wanderers, urges a whole people, in whom he perceives some kind of a universal apostle, to take pride in themselves. To these he says: 'Humble Yourselves!' to those—'Exalt Yourselves!'"

And further:

"And now, without having evolved a proper nationality, all of a sudden we are to dream about a universal role! Isn't this too early? Mr. Dostoievsky is proud of the fact that during two centuries we have been serving Europe. We confess that this 'service' does not rouse in us a joyous feeling. Can the time of the Congress of Vienna and, generally, the epoch of Congresses be a subject of our 'pride'? The time when, serving Metternich, we were suppressing the national movement in Italy and Germany, and were even looking askance at the Greeks—our coreligionists? And what hatred we contracted in Europe precisely for this 'service'!"

First, I shall dwell upon the latter trifling, almost innocent misquotation: When I said that "during the last two centuries we have been serving Europe, perhaps, more than ourselves,"—did I commend *the way* we served?—I merely meant to note the fact of the service, which is correct. However, the fact of the service and *the way* we served are two altogether different propositions. We may have committed a number of political blunders—the Europeans, too, are committing many an error, almost daily—but I was not commending our mistakes: I merely noted the fact of our service (almost always disinterested). Don't you understand that these are two different matters? "Mr. Dostoievsky is proud of the fact that we served Europe"—you say. I said this without any pride: I merely pointed to a trait of our national spirit, a very significant trait. Thus to discover a beautiful, healthy trait in a national spirit necessarily means to exalt oneself?

And why are you talking about Metternich and the Congresses?—It is you who venture to teach me! Even as a student I spoke about our service rendered to Metternich, using stronger language, and precisely for these words about our faulty service to Metternich (of course, among other words) thirty years ago, I paid my respective penalty. Why did you make this distortion?—Well, in order to demonstrate: "See what a liberal I am! And that poet, that enthusiastic admirer of the people, do you hear what reactionary stuff he is babbling, priding himself about our service to Metternich!"—*Amour propre*, Mr. Gradovsky!

However, this is, of course, but a trifle. Yet the following is not a bagatelle.

Thus, when I say to the people: "Lift up your spirit!" it means that I am telling them: "Exalt yourselves!"; that I am urging them to be haughty; that I am teaching them uppishness?—Suppose, Mr. Gradovsky, you tell your own children: "Children, lift up your spirit! Be noble!"—does this really mean that you are teaching them to exalt themselves, or that teaching them, you are exalting yourself?—And what did I say?—I spoke about the hope that "at length, they will be brethren of all men," with an emphasis on the words "at length." Is the serene hope that some day brotherhood will be achieved by our suffering mankind, and that perhaps *we shall be permitted* to become brethren of all men—is this hope equivalent to pride, to an appeal to haughtiness? Why, in the latter part of my *Address* I stated explicitly: "Do I speak of economic renown, of the glory of sword and science?—I am merely speaking about

brotherhood of men, and of the fact that the Russian heart is more
adapted to universal all-humanitarian brotherly fellowship than any
other nation. . . ." Such are my words. And is this an appeal to
pride? Immediately after the said words in my *Address* I added:
"Let our land be poor but this destitute land Christ, in a serf's garb,
has traversed to and fro with blessings. Why shouldn't we embrace
his ultimate word?" Now, does this Christ's word signify an appeal
to haughtiness, and is the hope that we may embrace this word
—uppishness?

You state indignantly that "it is too early to demand that
we be worshipped." But where is there such a demand—for goodness'
sake! This desire of universal service, the desire to become servants
and brethren; to serve them with our love—does this mean to demand
universal worship? If there be such a demand, the sacred, disinterested desire of universal service at once becomes an absurdity! No
one bows to a servant, and a brother does not expect genuflection
on the part of his brother.

Imagine, Mr. Gradovsky, that you have performed some good
deed, or that you are about to perform it. Now, on your way, you
begin to ponder fondly: "How glad the poor devil will be to receive
the unexpected help which I shall give him! How his spirit will be
braced!—Why, he will be resurrected! He will tell about his joy to
his family, to his children! He will cry with them." Pondering about
these things, you will naturally be moved yourself, you may even
start shedding tears (is it possible that this never happened to
you?), and suddenly a prudent voice begins to whisper into your
ear: "You are exalting yourself, imagining all this! You are shedding tears from haughtiness!"—For goodness' sake! The hope itself
that we Russians may mean something to mankind, and that at
length we shall be worthy of rendering brotherly service to it—this
hope itself aroused delight and evoked tears of enthusaism among
the thousands of listeners. I am not bragging, and it is not from
haughtiness that I am recalling this: I am merely recording the
solemnity of the moment. Serene hope was given that we, too, may
mean something to mankind; that we may become *merely* brethren
to other men, and now this one ardent hint united everybody into
one thought, into one sentiment. Strangers embraced each other,
swearing that henceforth they would try to be better. Two old men
came up to me and told me: "We've been enemies for twenty years;
we've been harming one another, and now, under the influence of
your words, we have made peace."

One of the newspapers hastened to observe that this enthusiasm
meant nothing; that this was simply a momentary mood accompanied by "the kissing of hands"; that the orators ascended the

platform in vain, and that in vain did they speak and finish their addresses. "No matter what they said, there would have been the same enthusiasm, for such happened to be the goodhearted mood in Moscow at the time!" Had that journalist gone there and spoken something on his own behalf, would people have rushed to him as they did to me? Why was it that three days earlier addresses were delivered and the speakers were given great ovations, but the thing which took place after my address occurred there to no one before? This was a unique moment in the Pushkin celebration, and it did not repeat itself.

Honestly, I am saying this with no idea of bragging; yet the moment was too solemn and I cannot keep silent on it. Its solemnity consisted of the fact that new elements clearly and graphically revealed themselves in society—men thirsting for a worthy adventure, for a comforting idea, for the promise of a cause. This means that society is no longer satisfied with our mere liberal giggling at Russia, that the doctrine of Russia's eternal impotence has grown repulsive! Only one hope, one hint, kindled in the hearts a holy thirst for an all-humanitarian cause, for a universal brotherly service and adventure. Was it haughtiness that kindled those hearts and made people cry? Did I urge them to be uppish! Ah, you! . . .

You see, Mr. Gradovsky, the seriousness of that moment suddenly frightened many people in our liberal tea-pot, all the more so as it came so unexpectedly. "What! Thus far, we have been so pleasantly and so usefully giggling and spitting upon everything, and now suddenly . . . Why, this is a rebellion! Let's call the police!" Several frightened gentlemen jumped up: "Well, what's going to happen to us now? We have also been writing . . . Where are they going to stick us now? The thing has got to be effaced, as quickly as possible, so that no trace be left! We have to explain promptly to all Russia that this was merely a complacent mood in hospitable Moscow, a charming little moment after a series of dinners—nothing more! And as for the rebellion, let the police quell it!"

And they set to work: I am a coward; I am a poet; I am insignificant; the significance of my address is naught—in a word, people acted imprudently on the spur of the moment. The public, however, might not have believed all these things. So the matter had to be handled skillfully; it had to be tackled coolheadedly: something could even be praised in my *Address:* "Well, there is nevertheless a certain flux of ideas," and thereupon, little by little, everything should be spat upon and effaced to the satisfaction of everybody.

In brief, they acted not so skillfully. There appeared a gap; it had to be filled as promptly as possible. And so forthwith there came forth a weighty, experienced critic combining the irresponsibility of his attacks with *comme il faut* appearance. You are this critic, Mr. Gradovsky: you wrote your article, people have read it, and everything has calmed down. You have served a common and admirable cause; at least your views were reprinted everywhere: "The speech of the poet does not stand the test of acid criticism. Poets are poets, but level-headed men always stand on guard, ready at any moment to pour a bucket of cold water on the dreamer."

In the concluding part of your article you ask me to forgive you those expressions which I may consider sharp. In concluding my article, I am not asking your forgiveness, Mr. Gradovsky, for the sharp expressions if there be such; I was answering not Mr. Gradovsky personally, but Mr. Gradovsky the publicist. Personally I have no reason whatsoever not to respect you. If, however, I do not respect your opinions and cling to this, how could I mollify things by asking your forgiveness?—But it was painful to see that a very serious and significant moment in the life of our society was represented in a distorted manner and was erroneously interpreted. It was painful to see that the idea which I am serving is being dragged through the streets. It was you who dragged it.

I know that on every side I shall be told that it was not worth while and it was ridiculous to write such a long article in answer to your article, which is short compared with mine. I repeat, however, that your article served merely as a pretext: I meant to express certain things in general. Beginning with next year I am planning to resume the publication of *A Writer's Diary*. So let this present issue serve as my *profession de foi* for the future; let it be, so to speak, a "test" issue.

Perhaps it may also be said that this answer of mine annuls the whole meaning of my *Address* delivered at Moscow, in which I appealed to both Russian parties to unite and to bring about a reconciliation, recognizing the legitimacy of either party. Not at all: the meaning of my *Address* has not been annulled; on the contrary, it has been reinforced, since in my answer to you I specifically state that both parties, in their mutual alienation, in their hostility one to the other, are placing themselves and their work in an abnormal situation, whereas united and in accord with each other, they might rise and save everything, set in motion boundless forces and lead Russia to a new, sound, grand, as yet unheard-of life!

1881

January

CHAPTER I

1

Finances. A Citizen Insulted in the Person of Thersites.
Crowning from Below and the Musicians.
The Chatter-Mill and Chatterboxes

GOOD LORD! Is it possible that after three years of silence I shall come out in my resumed *Diary* with an economic article? Am I an economist or a financier? Never was I either. Even despite the modern trend, I am not infected with economism. And yet, following the common mood, I am coming out with an economic article. That the trend is towards economics there can be no shadow of doubt. Nowadays all are economists. Every new magazine seeks to be recognized as an economic periodical and introduces itself in this spirit. Why, how can one fail to be an economist? Who can afford not to be one in the face of the drop of the rate of exchange of the ruble and the deficit? This all-round economic trend has become particularly noticeable in Russia in the last years, after our Turkish campaign. Of course, also in days gone by we used to discuss finances back and forth, but during and after the war everybody rushed headlong into finances. And this was only natural: the ruble dropped, war loans, etc. But aside from the ruble exchange, there was in this case an element of revenge which continues in our day, revenge for the war: "We"—such is the implication—"told you, we predicted!" Most busily engaged in economism are those who in 1876 and 1877 maintained that money was better than magnanimity; that the Eastern question was nothing but mischief and fiction; that not only was there no national enthusiasm, not only was the war unpopular and not national, but that, strictly speaking, there were no people, and that instead there was an inert, dumb and mute mass organized for taxation purposes and the maintenance of the intelligentsia, a mass which, even though it contributes pennies to the church, does so because the priest and the authorities have issued respective orders. All Russian Thersites—and of these there are many among the intelligentsia—were then awfully offended in their best sentiments. In the person of Thersites the citizen was insulted. So they began to take vengeance by blaming finances. Little by little they were joined by non-Thersites and even former "heroes." Everybody began to pout—true, some people not too seriously. It must be admitted that the disadvantageous peace, the Berlin Conference, contributed to this condition.[1]

Here I merely wish to state that at present everybody is writing about the ruble and the deficit: partly, in this there is a gregarious element: everybody is writing, everybody is alarmed— why shouldn't I be alarmed?—People may think that I am a poor citizen, that I am not interested. However, here and there one finds genuine civic anxiety, pain, painful doubts concerning the future. This I do not wish to conceal. Nevertheless, even genuine civic anxiety is almost invariably linked to the theme: Why is it that at home everything is so different from things in Europe? "In Europe the thaler is everywhere quoted favorably, whereas our ruble stands low. Why are we not Europe? Why are things at home different from those in Europe?—It's because our edifice is not crowned!"

And so everybody started vociferating about "crowning the edifice," forgetting that as yet no edifice has been erected, so that there is actually nothing to crown; that in lieu of an edifice we have but several white waistcoats who imagine that they constitute the edifice, and that, if the crowning is to be started at all, it should be begun from below—from the peasant's overcoat and the bast-shoe, and not from the white vest. At this point it is necessary to make a reservation: of course, at first glance, crowning from below seems an absurdity, at least, in an architectural sense, and stands in conflict with everything that has existed and does exist in Europe in this respect. However, inasmuch as in Russia everything is peculiar, different from what we see in Europe, and, at times, altogether topsy-turvy—so important a matter as the crowning of the edifice may be effected in a manner contrary to that in Europe—to the great surprise and indignation of our Russian European minds. For, to Europe's surprise, our lower stratum, our peasant's overcoat and

[1]N. B. By the way, speaking about the Berlin Conference: in those days in a remote provincial district, on a by-road, a peasant woman, the hostess of a small inn, unexpectedly asked me: "Dear sir, tell me, how did they decide upon our case abroad? Any news about this?" I wondered at the woman. However, this, *i.e.*, the question of popular enthusiasm, I shall discuss later.

bast-shoe, is actually an edifice of its kind—not only the foundation, but precisely the edifice itself—though not completed, yet solid and firm, erected in the course of centuries, in fact, foreseeing the whole genuine, though not fully developed, idea of the future architecturally completed edifice.

Well, if the whole truth is to be told, these outcries of our Europeans about the crowning, as stated, bear rather a gregarious and mechanically-appeasing than a truly civic, morally civic, character. And the reason why everybody has jumped at this new consolation is that all these external, precisely *mechanically*-appeasing devices are always easy, agreeable and extremely handy. "What we need is the European formula—and everything will be saved. It has to be applied, taken out of a ready-made chest, and forthwith Russia will become Europe, and the ruble—a thaler." The thing which is particularly pleasant in these mechanical consolations is the fact that one doesn't have to think at all—still less suffer or be perplexed. I am speaking about the herd—and I am not referring to righteous men. These may be found everywhere, even among European Russians, and I esteem them. But you must concede that in Russia, in most cases, all this transpires dancingly, as it were: What's the use of thinking and cracking one's brains! One may contract a headache! Nay, take something ready-made from somebody else, and forthwith you will have music, an accordant concerto—

If seated in a row
Our skill we'll surely show.

Well, what if as musicians you are good for nothing, and this, gentlemen, is true of the overwhelming majority of you. What if nothing but a chatterbox-mill comes out of the white vests! What if the colossal majority of the white vests shouldn't be admitted at all to the crowned edifice (at least in the first instance) if ever it should happen to be crowned! That is, they could and should be let in because, after all, they are Russians—many of them good fellows—on condition that they should consent, jointly with the country at large, to give their advice humbly in some great common cause. But the trouble is that they would refuse to give their advice jointly with their country; they would start exalting themselves over it. Up to our day, for two whole centuries, they have kept aloof—and all of a sudden they would unite with the people!—This is not vaudeville; this requires history and culture, but we neither have culture nor ever had it.

Look at the excitement of a European Russian—at times a most innocent and amiable one—scrutinize the absurd, venomous and criminal excitement, with foam at his mouth, and reaching the point of calumny, with which he wrangles about his cherished ideas, precisely those which are pre-eminently in discord with the people's world outlook, their holiest hopes and most sacred beliefs! Why, such a gentleman, such an idler, before he could unite with his native land, which smells of the peasant's coat and the bast-shoe, would have to give up some of his most revered European books and convictions. But this he would not do because he is, *malgré lui*, squeamish toward the people and haughty toward Russia. "We"—they would say—"are the only ones who are capable of giving advice, whereas the rest (*i.e.*, the country at large) for the time being should be content with the fact that we are educating them, and thereby gradually raising them to our level and 'teaching the people their rights and duties.'" (It is they who plan to teach the people their rights, and especially their duties!—What wags!)

"Russian society"—they will further say—"cannot stay in the county jail side by side with the ragged people wearing their national bast-shoes." Setting out in such a mood, it is possible—even inevitable—to revert to serfdom, to the enslavement of the peasant's coat and the bast-shoe, not in the form of the former bondage, but by means of enlightened tutelage with its political consequences: "And again we shall enchain the people!"

Well, naturally, they will wind up by instituting the chatter-box mill for themselves alone. But so instituted, at first, they will not recognize and understand one another.—This will unfailingly happen. Roaming in the dark they would bump each other's heads. Don't feel offended, gentlemen: this has happened to societies, not even like ours—which for two centuries has been detached from any kind of work and which is devoid of any original culture—when the occasion arose to give advice for the first time; this has happened among the most enlightened nations. However, because they had to their credit a secular culture and since they always relied, more or less, on the people, they promptly recovered and embarked upon a firm road, of course not without some preliminary bumps on their foreheads.

And you, our Europeans—what will you be relying upon? How are you going to reach an accord?—Is it only by means of seating yourselves, side by side, in a row? And what a breed of chatter-boxes we have in our midst!—As if they were really getting ready for action! At times, one of those progressive and didactic fellows sits down and starts talking: there is neither end nor beginning, everything is muddled up and twisted into a ball. He keeps talking for an hour and a half, and he talks so sweetly, so smoothly, as if a bird were singing! And you ask yourself: Well, is he a clever fellow? What is he anyway?—And you can't make up your mind. Every word, taken separately, seems to be intelligible and clear, but you can make nothing out of the whole. You fail to understand whether henceforth eggs are going to hatch the hen, or, as heretofore, the hen is going to hatch the eggs: one can only see that an eloquent hen hatches, in lieu of eggs, perfect rot. At length, one's eyes begin to bulge and fog sets in in one's head. This is a newly born type; it has not yet been reflected in our belles-lettres. Many a thing relating to contemporary current events has not yet been touched upon in literature; many a thing has been overlooked and is badly lagging. Mostly literature keeps toying with characters of the Forties, at the best, of the Fifties. Perhaps literature has embarked upon the historical novel because it has lost the sense and meaning of the current moment.

2

CAN WE DEMAND FOR RUSSIA EUROPEAN FINANCES?

"Well, what about finances? Where is that financial article of yours?"—I may be asked. But, again, what kind of an economist or financier am I? I do not even dare to write about finances. Why, then, did I venture and why am I about to write such an article? —for the simple reason that, starting to write on finances, I shall deviate to something altogether different, and thus it will not be a financial but some wholly different article. This encourages me. Nor am I even worthy of dwelling upon financial matters since I know that I am viewing our finances by no means from the European standpoint; moreover, I do not believe that it can be made applicable to us—for the specific reason that we are in no way Europe, that, compared with her, everything is so peculiar in Russia that we seem to be dwelling on the moon.

In Europe, for instance, the slavish, feudal relations between the lower and upper castes for centuries were in the process of liquidation until, finally, a revolution broke out. In a word, everything happened historically and in a cultured fashion. In Russia, however, serfdom, with all its consequences, collapsed instantaneously, and, thank God, without even the slightest revolution. One wonders: Whence should there have come a concussion, I mean a great capital concussion? True: everything that falls suddenly falls dangerously, with a great concussion. I shall, of course, not regret that it fell suddenly. On the contrary, it is excellent that this abominable historical sin of ours was at once abrogated by the great word of the Liberator. Nevertheless the law of nature cannot be evaded, and

there was a great concussion. Would that it had been only great!
But why so enormous? Naturally everything has to abide by the
laws of history, and no doubt there are many people who now clearly
perceive why everything happened as it did.

Without enlarging upon this subject (it is a colossal theme
with which, perhaps, a historian of the next century will be able
to cope), without adding a word, I shall merely point to certain
particulars which strike one's attention and cause confusion.

Take, for instance, this: serfdom collapsed; it stood in the
way of everything; it even impeded the progress of agriculture. It
might have seemed that at last the time had come for the peasant
to blossom out and grow rich.—Nothing of the kind happened: in
agriculture the peasant sank to the minimum of what the land is
capable of yielding. And the main trouble is that one does not know
whether there be such a force (and of what it specifically consists)
as would prompt the peasant to venture to raise himself above that
minimum which the land yields to him and to ask it for a maximum.

Wiseacres may say: This is a vain question which is understood by everybody. But I am firmly convinced that this question
is far from having been settled, and that it is of a vastly more far-
reaching significance than people suppose. Furthermore, consider
this: former noble landownership has deteriorated to a pitiful level.
At the same time, apparently, we are witnessing the degeneration
of the whole former landowning class into something different, into
an educated class, since into what else can it degenerate?—Well, it
would seem, what could be better? The people need the intelligentsia as their leaders; the people themselves crave for the intelligentsia and seek them. Unfortunately, this, too, as yet is an
ideal, which looks like a delightful heron soaring through the skies.
In reality it is far from this. Will the caste, the former landowners,
endeavor to become the educated *people?*—This is the question and,
you know, the major, most cardinal question with which we are
faced at present, one upon which perhaps our whole future depends!
Even so, this question is far from being settled, and it cannot even
be conceived how it is going to be solved. Will not the caste take
an uppish attitude and become again an authoritative power, of
course not in the former sense of servitude but by endeavoring, for
instance, in lieu of uniting with the people, taking advantage of its
education, to create a new domineering discordant force and to place
itself above the people as an intellectual aristocracy and establish
a tutelage over them? Will this caste henceforth and forever sincerely recognize the people as its brother by blood and spirit? Will
it respect the things our people revere? Will it agree to love, even
more than itself, that for which the people feel affection?—Without

this the intelligentsia will never merge with our people, because what they respect and love is a matter of their firm conviction, and they will never yield or renounce it, regardless of any intelligentsia, much as they may thirst for the latter.

All this is of vital importance and yet altogether unsettled. And generally everything in Russia is replete with questions. And the main thing is that all this requires time, history, culture, generations, whereas we have to solve this in one moment. Therein is our main difference from Europe—that in Russia much happens not as a result of historical and cultural process, but somehow suddenly, by an altogether unexpected decree of government authority. It stands to reason that no one is to be blamed for everything that happens; in a way this is also an historical process. Even so, you must concede that Europe has never had and known such a history. How then can one demand that we be Europe, and in addition—with her financial system?—For example, I believe as in an economic axiom that land is *possessed* not by railroad men, not by industrialists, not by millionaires, not by banks, not by Jews, but in the first instance—only by agriculturists; that he who cultivates the land leads everything, and that agriculturists actually constitute the state, its kernel and its core. But is this so in Russia? Aren't things inside out at this moment? Where is our kernel? In whom? Don't the railroad man and the Jew own our economic assets? We are constructing railroads. But it is a fact that they are being built as nowhere else: Europe has been covering herself with her railroad net virtually during a whole half century, notwithstanding her wealth. Yet we have built the last fifteen or sixteen thousand versts of our railways in the course of ten years—and this in the face of our poverty, and at such an economically disturbed time as the period which immediately followed the abolition of serfdom! And, of course, the railroads attracted all capital at a time when agriculture needed it most. The railroads were built at the expense of the destruction of agriculture.

Again, have we solved the problem of individual private landownership? Will it survive side by side with peasant landownership? Will it be based upon a sound and solid labor force—and not upon the proletariat and the pot-house?—And yet without a sound solution of this problem what sober consequences can be expected? We need sober solutions. Lacking these we shall never have tranquillity, whereas tranquillity is the source of all great power. How, then, can we demand a European budget and orderly finances?—It is not a case of why we have no European economy and sound finance, but—how we manage to survive.—We have survived through the solid, unifying force of the whole people.

We have little tranquillity, especially spiritual peace, *i.e.*, the main thing, since without spiritual peace no peace is possible. This is particularly neglected, and only temporary, material smoothness is sought. There is no peace of mind, and this is true of all strata; there is no calmness in our convictions, in our opinions, in our nerves, in our appetites. Work and the recognition of the fact that through work alone one will be saved—are altogether absent. There is no sense of duty. And whence should it be derived?—No right culture has existed for a century and a half—perhaps no culture whatsoever. "Why should I work if through my culture I have been brought to the point where I deny everything around me? And if there are blockheads who hope to save the edifice by some European contrivances—I deny the blockheads, and I believe in the principle: the worse—the better, and this is my whole philosophy."

I assure you that nowadays many people say this—at least to themselves—and some of them—even aloud. And yet the fellow who utters such aphorisms is made of bones and of flesh. "The worse —the better"—says he; but this applies only to others, to everybody, whereas as far as he is concerned he believes in the motto: "Let me have the best." This is how he conceives his philosophy. He has a wolf's appetite. A man of the size of a bear, he has woman's nerves, deranged and spoiled. He is cruel and sensual; he can endure nothing: "Why should I take the trouble to endure this?" With no more restaurant dinners and cocottes—what's the use of living?— And he drives a bullet through his brain. It is all right if he only shoots himself: what if he defrauds another man, abiding by all legal formalities? Time does not wait—poverty is spreading everywhere. Merchants are complaining everywhere that no one buys anything. Factories are curtailing production. Go into a store and ask: "How is business?"—They tell you: "In days past for the holiday a fellow bought at least half a dozen shirts; but nowadays they all buy just one shirt at a time." Take even fashionable restaurants, since this is the last place where poverty puts in an appearance. "No"—they will tell you—"there is no more lavish spending as in days gone by; they all sit tight; at best a fellow comes and orders a regular dinner"—and this is the former fop and dandy. Redemption monies are spent. At present there remain only forests which are being hewn down; but after these have been done with, there will be nothing left. When travelling on a railroad, please observe fire-wood at the stations: in days past they used to cut logs, whereas at present one often sees some kind of thin sticks instead of fire-wood; not trees but bushes, so to speak, striplings, or undergrowth, are being cut. Of course, to you this observation may seem trifling in the face of all other colossal problems of our time. But our financiers absolutely ignore the question of our forests; they don't want to know anything about them, as if on principle. And yet deforestation, if one gives thought to it, will most harmfully affect our finances. Despite this, there seems to be a general tacit agreement to skip over the surface of the timber problem as long as the catastrophe has not yet come. It will come suddenly because everybody is satisfied with the fact that the market price of timber is adequate, people refuse to take heed of the fact that the price is artificial, due to intense selling on the part of those who are cutting down forests, bushes included, because they have spent all their money. There will come a moment when there will be nothing more to cut and nothing to sell. But let us leave this for further discussion. I began to speak about general poverty and its opposite—increase in appetite.

In passing, I merely wish to note that there have appeared an awful lot of Captain Kopeikins, in countless varieties, beginning with real ones and including those belonging to fashionable and perfumed sets. They all grind their teeth at the treasury and at public funds. Of course they will soon turn, if not into highway robbers like the real Captain Kopeikin, at least into industrial pickpockets—some in legalized guise, while others will not even bother to protect themselves with legal formalities. Some of these fellows may even proudly declare: "I am such because I deny everything, and I am fostering negation." Indeed, aren't Kopeikins liberals? They fully comprehend that liberalism is in vogue, and that it may be used to one's advantage. Who has not seen them?—a cosmopolitan liberal, a cheap atheist, exalting himself over the people by his education, is worth a kopeck. He is the most trivial of all vulgar manifestations of our pseudo-liberalism. Even so, he is endowed with unquenchable appetite, and for this reason he is dangerous. It is men of this type who are the first to embrace the idea of all sorts of transplantations from without for mechanical cures; they gather in groups and form a crowd, which is often led by most honest men, who, strictly speaking, should not be blamed for this fact: "Let there be any change whatsoever, so long as it entails no work," says liberal Kopeikin.—"A change, whatever it be, will be to my advantage, since surely, at first at least, I shall manage to derive some profit for myself." From this standpoint he is dangerous, although he is only a Kopeikin. But let us leave Kopeikin. All that I have said is but a tiny fraction of the subject of the absence of tranquillity at home. I can see for myself that my introduction is much too long. So let me turn directly to finances!

3

LET US FORGET CURRENT THINGS IN ORDER TO RENDER THE ROOTS HEALTHY. BECAUSE OF INABILITY I EMBARK UPON SOMETHING SPIRITUAL

Such is my nature that I shall begin with the end, and not with the beginning, and straightway I shall set forth my idea. I have never been able to write in a measured fashion, gradually reaching the conclusion, formulating it only after having preliminarily explained it in detail and, if possible, proved it. I had no patience; my temper stood in the way, and thereby, of course, I harmed myself, because some inferences formulated directly without preparation and preliminary proof, at times, are apt to cause surprise and confusion, or even make people laugh. And I know in advance that my inferences are precisely such as may make the reader laugh if he has not been prepared beforehand. My idea, my formula, is as follows: "In order to establish a sound financial system in a state which has experienced a violent commotion, do not ponder too much over current needs no matter how pressing, but think only about rendering the roots healthy—and this will produce sound finances."

Of course people will start laughing: "Everybody knows this much"—they will say. "There is nothing new in your formula. Who is ignorant of the fact that roots should not be famished; that if the roots dry up there can be no fruit, etc.?" However, let me explain my thought; as yet I have not fully expounded it, and—alas —my trouble is that were I ever to write a whole book in an endeavor to develop my idea—even then (I foresee) I should fail to explain it in a way which would make it intelligible *in its entirety*. This is due to the fact that there is a certain predetermination in this idea.

You see, it stands to reason that everybody knows that roots must be kept healthy. What Minister of Finance did not take care of them, especially the present one? The tax on salt has already been abolished. Other extraordinary, capital reforms are pending, reforms actually affecting the "roots." Besides, also in former times, ten years ago, different measures were applied for rendering the roots healthy. Audits were instituted; committees were appointed for the study of the economic status of the Russian peasant, his industrial pursuits, his courts of justice, his institutions of self-government, his diseases, customs, habits, and so on, and so forth. Committees formed subcommittees for the collection of statistical data, and everything progressed rather smoothly, in the best administrative sense.

However, I started speaking about altogether different matters. In my opinion, not only subcommittees but even such cardinal reforms as the abolition of the salt tax and the forthcoming great reform of the tax system, are mere palliatives, external things which do not begin with the roots. This is what I want to emphasize. We shall begin with roots when we forget—if not completely, half-forget at least—the current things, the headline news, the crying needs of our budget, our foreign indebtedness, the deficit, the ruble, even bankruptcy, which, however, we shall never have, despite all the malevolent prophecies of our foreign friends. In a word, when we forget all current things and turn our exclusive attention to the treatment of the roots, only then shall we reap an abundant and healthy crop. At that time we may revert to current things, or, more correctly—to new current things, because one may expect that during this intermission the things of the past (*i.e.*, the contemporary, our present-day current things) will change and transform themselves so radically that we shall not recognize them.

And yet, of course, I understand that what I have just said may sound fantastic; that it is impossible not to think about the ruble, about payments on loans, bankruptcy, the army; that these expenditures must be met in the first instance. But I assure you that I understand this. I must confess that I set forth my idea squarely, extending my desiderata almost to the point of an impossible ideal. I thought that by starting out with an absurdity I might be better understood. And I said, "If only we could force ourselves to half-forget current things and divert our attention to something wholly different, to that depth into which, honestly speaking, thus far, we have never looked because we sought to find it on the surface." But I am ready to mitigate my formula, and in lieu of it I propose: let us not *half-forget* the current things—I renounce the half—but let us forget only one twentieth of them, on condition (on the binding condition), however, that, having begun with one twentieth of oblivion of the current things, we add each subsequent year another one twentieth, attaining in this way, say, three quarters of the oblivion. In this matter it is not the fraction that is important but the *principle* which one adopts and by which one undeviatingly abides.

Well, we are faced with the same question: What shall we do with the present?—We can't discard it as something nonexistent! But I do not propose to discard it. I know myself that the existent cannot be made nonexistent. And yet, gentlemen, sometimes it can be. For should we annually diminish by only one twentieth our pathologically anxious attention to current things, turning it in the same ratio to something else, the proposition would not appear so fantastic. On the contrary, it would seem plausible; all the more so, I repeat, as there is no need to worry about the present annually neglected one twentieth, for the simple reason that it will not be lost or eliminated, but will naturally transform itself into something different; something much better; it will submit to the new principle and will become part of its spirit.

It may be said that I am speaking in riddles. But this is not so. By way of an example I shall first say a few prefatory words on the subject of how one may begin the transition from the current things to the "treatment of the roots."

For instance, what if Petersburg, by some miracle, should suddenly agree to diminish her haughty attitude toward Russia!— Indeed, this would be the first glorious and sound step towards "the treatment of the roots"! Look at Petersburg. She has gone so far as to believe that she is all Russia, and this belief grows increasingly from generation to generation. In this spirit Petersburg follows, as it were, the example of Paris, despite the fact that she does not resemble Paris at all! Paris formed herself historically, of her own accord, so as to absorb France, the whole significance of her political and social life, her whole purport. Take Paris away from France, and what will remain of France?—Nothing but a geographical definition. Now, some of us imagine, even as in Paris, that Petersburg has absorbed all Russia. But Petersburg is by no means Russia. To the overwhelming majority of the Russian people the significance of Petersburg is confined to the fact that the Czar resides there. However, from generation to generation, our Petersburg intelligentsia have comprehended Russia less and less, because, having closeted themselves in their Finnish marsh, they have been changing their view of Russia more and more, so that, finally, she has narrowed down to the microscopical dimensions of some Karlsruhe. But peep out of Petersburg and you will behold an ocean of Russian land, an immense bottomless sea. Even so, a son of Petersburg parents calmly denies the sea of the Russian people and takes it for something inert and unconscious, spiritually negligible and extremely backward. "Russia is massive"—says he—"but stupid. She is only good for maintaining us so that we may educate her and teach her the meaning of state order."

The future sons of our fatherland are moulded in Petersburg in the process of dancing and polishing inlaid floors, whereas "the servile rats," as Ivan Alexandrovich Khlestakov used to call them, are studying their fatherland in chanceries; naturally, they manage to learn something, but not Russia—something altogether different, at times, very strange. And this "something different and strange" they obtrude upon Russia. Meanwhile the sea of the people lives in its own peculiar manner with every new generation spiritually more and more segregating itself from Petersburg. And don't tell me that, though the pulse of the people's life beats mightily, theirs is an unconscious existence, as is still believed not only by Petersburg residents but even by some of the few Russians who understand Russia. Oh, if only you knew how incorrect this is; how much consciousness has accumulated in the Russian people even during the present reign! Yes, consciousness is steadily growing, and so much has been grasped and rationalized by the people that Petersburg gentlemen would not believe it. This is perceived by those who know how to see; this can be foreseen; it merely does not manifest itself in its totality; yet it can even be clearly observed locally, in remote corners, in peasants' abodes. And how can it be revealed in its totality? How can it be revealed in an ocean? But when some day consciousness manifests itself, or only begins to reveal itself, how dumbfounded will the educated Petersburg gentleman be! True, for a long time he will deny it; he will refuse to believe his five senses! For a long time the European homunculus will refuse to surrender,—some of them will die without surrendering.

In order to avoid great future misunderstandings, how desirable it would be—I repeat—that Petersburg, at least her best representatives, should tone down a bit their haughty attitude toward Russia! More understanding, more humility before the great Russian land, before the ocean of Russia—this is what we need. And what a sure first step this would be toward "the treatment of the roots!" . . .

"If you please"—I may be interrupted—"as yet all this is nothing but obsolete worn-out Slavophile rubbish; there is nothing real in it—it is something on the spiritual order. What is this 'treatment of the roots'?—Thus far you haven't explained this. What are these roots? What do you mean by them?"

You're right, gentlemen, quite right.—Let's begin with the "roots."

4

THE FIRST ROOT. INSTEAD OF A FIRM FINANCIAL TONE I
AM LAPSING INTO OLD WORDS. THE OCEAN. THIRST FOR
TRUTH AND THE NECESSITY OF TRANQUILLITY SO USEFUL
TO FINANCE

The first root, the most essential root, which must by all means be rendered healthy is, no doubt, the Russian people, that ocean about which I have just spoken. I am referring here to our common people, the plebeian and the peasant, the source of taxation, the callous laborers' hands,—to the ocean. Oh, don't I know what our government has done—is incessantly doing—for them during the present reign, beginning with their liberation from serfdom? Yes, the government takes care of their needs, of their education, of their medical treatment; at times, it even forgives them their arrears,—in a word, it does and cares much,—and who does not know this? Yet I intend to speak about a different thing: I mean spiritual health of this great root which is the basis of everything. Yes, the people are spiritually sick—not mortally: the core of their soul is healthy. Nevertheless it is a painful disease. What is it called?— This is difficult to define in one word. It might be described as "unquenched thirst for truth." The people are continually seeking truth, an outlet to it, and they do not find it.

I wish I could confine myself to the financial aspect of this malady, but I shall have to add a few obsolete words. Ever since the liberation from serfdom, there has arisen in the people an urge, a thirst, for something new, something that was not an aftermath of the past; a thirst for the whole truth, for complete civic resurrection to a new life following their great liberation. There ensued an urge for a new word; new sentiments began to boil, and there arose a profound belief in a new order. After the initial period of the first mediators, suddenly there came to pass something different from what the people had expected. There arose an order in which the people would have been glad to believe but which they understood little. In fact, they could not understand it at all; they were losing themselves, and, therefore, were unable to believe in that order. There came something external, as it were alien to them, something not their own. There is no point in ruminating on a subject which has been thrashed out long ago: others will tell the story better. Read it, for instance, in the magazine *Rus*. Then reckless drunkenness began to spread, as if a drunken sea overflowed Russia. And even though it is still raging, the people have not lost their longing for the new truth, for the whole truth, notwithstanding the fact that they continue to abuse liquor. Perhaps at no time have the people been more susceptible to certain influences and tendencies, more defenseless against them than at present. Take, for instance, Stundism, and observe its popularity among the masses. What does it signify?—Quest after truth and anxiety for it. Precisely,—anxiety. The people, in our day, are morally "disturbed." I am convinced that if, thus far, nihilistic propaganda has failed to find its way to the people, this has been exclusively due to the incompetence, stupidity and unpreparedness of the propagandists, who did not even know how to approach the people. However, with the slightest skill they would have penetrated the people just as Stundism has. Oh, one must guard the people. "The time will come to pass when ye shall be told: Here is Christ, or yonder. Do not believe it." At present something similar is transpiring, and not only among the people, but, perhaps, also among our upper strata. Aren't the people disturbed by various unusual rumors about the new partition of the land, about new "gold charters"? Recently, in churches, announcements were made to the effect that people should not believe these rumors; that nothing is going to happen. But, would you believe it? precisely after these announcements, in different localities, belief grew stronger that something would "transpire": "They would not be reading in vain: if they start reading, this means that something will 'transpire.'" This is how people began to talk immediately after the announcements had been read,—at least, here and there. I know of one instance: peasants were negotiating with a neighboring landowner for the purchase of his land; the parties agreed upon the price, but after that announcement the peasants would not go through with the deal: "We'll get that land without paying for it." They smile and wait.

I am merely referring to rumors, to the eagerness to listen to them, indicating the state of moral disturbance of the people. And this is the most important point: the people are left alone, dependent solely upon their own strength; spiritually they are supported by no one. There is the zemstvo, but they are "bosses." There are courts, but these, too, are "bosses." Finally, there is the peasants' commune, the peasants' village assembly; however, these seem to exhibit a tendency of turning into something akin to "the authorities." Newspapers are full of descriptions of the manner in which the people elect their deputies in the presence of "the authorities," of some government official, and what comes of it. There are thousands of these anecdotes, and I shall not recapitulate them. A simpleton starts looking around, and unexpectedly draws the conclusion that only the kulak or the peasants' blood-sucker manages to prosper; everything seems to serve only him: "Well, then, I shall also try to become a kulak!"—And this he becomes. Another more timid fellow turns into a thorough drunkard, not because he is overcome by poverty but because he is disgusted with lawlessness. What is to be done?—This is predestination.

The people were given an administration; officers were appointed,—well, it would seem that this ought to have settled matters. And yet, for some reason, the contrary happened. It has been reckoned that at present there are some twenty government officials specially appointed for the people, standing above the people protecting and guarding them. Everybody is the poor man's boss anyway, and yet here we have no additional group of special appointees! This makes the people's freedom of movement equal to that of a fly caught in a plate full of molasses. Not only from a moral but also from a financial point of view such a "freedom of movement" is harmful. And the main thing is that the people are alone, without any advisers. They have only God and the Czar; these two forces, these two great hopes are the people's only support; while all other counselors pass them by without any effect. For example, the whole progressive intelligentsia passes the people by because even though there are many level-headed men among our intelligentsia, only a few of them have any understanding of the people. In Russia there is nothing but negation and incessant complaints: "Why isn't society 'vivified'? Why can't it be 'vivified' by some means? What's the riddle?"—Society cannot be animated because you do not rely upon the people; spiritually, the people are not with you, and they are alien to you. You are constituting, as it were, an upper stratum above the people enveloping Russia; and, according to your own statements and writings, it was for you that the Reformer left the people in servitude in order that, by serving you with their labor, they might enable you to acquire European enlightenment. During these two centuries you have become enlightened, but the people have alienated themselves from you, and you have segregated yourselves from them. "But aren't we"—you will say—"sorrowing for the people? Don't we keep writing about the people? Don't we appeal to them?"—Quite so. You are doing all this. But, for some reason, the Russian people are convinced that you sorrow not for them but for some other people who do not resemble the Russian people, whom you actually despise. This disdainful attitude toward the people, in some of us, is quite unconscious, so to speak, altogether involuntary. This is an aftergrowth of serfdom. It took its inception at the time when civically the people were put to death for the sake of our European enlightenment. This aftergrowth unquestionably persists in us till this day when the people have been resurrected. And do you know that it is no longer possible for us to unite with the people unless some miracle happens in Russia? Here I shall repeat my own words which I uttered long ago: The overwhelming mass of the Russian people is Orthodox; it lives by the idea of Orthodoxy in all its completeness despite the fact that rationally and scientifically they do not comprehend this idea. *Essentially,* save for this "idea" there dwells no other in our people; everything is derived from it,—at least this is what the people want wholeheartedly and with deep conviction. They want precisely everything they possess and everything that is given them, to emanate exclusively from this idea.

This is true in spite of the fact that many things happening among the people nonsensically are derived not from this idea but from fetid, foul, criminal, barbaric sources. But even the criminal and the barbarian, although they sin, nevertheless, in the loftiest moments of their lives, they pray God that their sins and abominations may come to an end, and that everything may be again derived from their beloved "idea."

I know that our educated men ridicule me: they refuse even to recognize "this idea" in the people, pointing to their sins and abominations (for which these men themselves are responsible, having oppressed the people for two centuries); they also emphasize the people's prejudices, their alleged indifference to religion, while some of them imagine that the Russian people are simply atheists. Their great error consists of the fact that they refuse to recognize the existence of the Church as an element in the life of the people. I am not speaking of church buildings, or the clergy. I am now referring to our Russian "socialism,"[1] the ultimate aim of which is the establishment of an œcumenical Church on earth in so far as the earth is capable of embracing it. I am speaking of the unquenchable, inherent thirst in the Russian people for great, universal, brotherly fellowship in the name of Christ. And even if this fellowship, as yet, does not exist, and if that church has not completely materialized,—not in prayers only but in reality—nevertheless the instinct for it and the unquenchable, oftentimes unconscious, thirst for it, indubitably dwell in the hearts of the millions of our people.

Not in communism, not in mechanical forms is the socialism of the Russian people expressed: they believe that they shall be finally saved *through the universal communion in the name of Christ*. This is our Russian socialism! It is the presence in the Russian people of this sublime unifying "church" idea that you, our European gentlemen, are ridiculing. There are many other "ideas" in the people which you will never embrace and which you, in your European world outlook, conceive as outright Tartar ideas. At this time I shall not even mention these other ideas, although they are extremely important; their truth you do not comprehend at all.

Here I am merely speaking about this focal idea of our people—about their hope for the future œcumenical Church which, by Divine Providence, moulds itself in their hearts. At this juncture the following formula may be set forth: He who fails to comprehend in our people their Orthodoxy and its ultimate aims never

---

[1]Strange as it may seem, I am using this term, descriptive of something diametrically opposed to everything the Church represents, for the purpose of elucidating my thought.

can understand the people themselves. Moreover, he is incapable of loving the people (even though the hearts of many of our Europeans are pure and longing for justice and love). They will love them only in the guise that they conceive and desire. Inasmuch, however, as the people will never become such as our wiseacres would like to see them, and will always remain such as they are, an unavoidable and dangerous conflict may be anticipated in the future. Indeed, the formula, framed above, has also a reverse significance, *i.e.*: Never will the people take such a European Russian for their own. "First, learn to love my sanctity; begin to revere that which I revere,—then you will be, even as I, my brother, irrespective of the fact that you dress differently, that you are a gentleman, a boss, and that, at times, you don't know how to express yourself decently in Russian."—This is what the people will tell you, since the people are clever and there is liberality in them. At times, they will even esteem and take a liking to a good man, though he does not believe in their sanctity; they will listen to him, if he is level-headed, will thank him for his advice and will take advantage of it. The Russian people can live on good terms with anyone, because they have seen many a sight, they have noticed and memorized many a thing in the course of their long and difficult life of the last two centuries. However, you do not even concede the fact that the people have noticed and memorized many a thing, and that, consequently, they are cognizant of them; and that, on this ground, they are not merely an inert mass and a source of taxation, as you have defined them. Even so, to live on good and even loving terms with a man is one thing, and to recognize him as *one's own* is an altogether different proposition. Without such a recognition, however, there can be no fellowship.

I merely wish to state that the forces alienating us from the people are very great; that the people are left to themselves, in their great segregation, and that, save for the Czar, in whom they inviolably believe, they expect support from no one and from nowhere. They would be glad to perceive such a support but it is difficult to discern it. And yet, what a mighty, creative, blissful and new—wholly new—force would arise in Russia should a communion of our educated classes with the people come to pass! I mean—spiritual communion. O, gentlemen Ministers of Finance, then you would be computing your annual budgets quite differently from those which you are now drawing! Rivers of milk would be flowing in our Czardom, and all your ideals would be attained at once! "Well, how is this to be done? Is it possible that our European enlightenment is to be blamed for this?"—Oh, not at all enlightenment. To tell the truth, as yet there is none; nevertheless segregation persists, as it were, in the name of European enlightenment which we don't have. But genuine enlightenment is not to be blamed for this condition. I even reason this way: had we genuine enlightenment there would have been among us no segregation, since the people, too, crave enlightenment. But having acquired our enlightenment, we flew away from the people to the moon, and we lost our road to them. How, then, can we, such detached individuals, assume the task of making the people healthy? What can be done in order that the people's spirit, languishing and everywhere disturbed, should be braced and pacified? Capital itself, its mobility, requires *moral* tranquillity, bereft of which it either hides or remains unproductive. What is to be done in order that the spirit of the people may be assuaged by truth, by perceiving the truth?— There is even truth at present, but it is necessary that the people should believe in it. How is one to inculcate in their souls the conviction that truth exists in our Russian land, and that its banner soars high? What is to be done, for example, to make the people believe in their courts, in their representation, and to make them feel that these are flesh of their flesh and bone of their bone?—I am not going into details. How can I? If one were to start explaining and describing everything, I believe "that even the world itself could not contain the books that should be written."

However, if only truth could be guaranteed to the people in the future so that they should firmly believe that it will unfailingly come; if the fly should extricate itself—at least a bit—out of the plate of molasses,—even then an unaccountably great thing would come to pass. I state directly: the whole trouble is the result of the old alienation of our educated class from the lower stratum, from our people. How is one to restore peace between the upper stratum and the grand ocean? How is one to pacify the ocean so as to avoid a great commotion?

5

LET THEM SPEAK FIRST. FOR THE TIME BEING LET US STAND ASIDE IN ORDER TO LEARN SENSE AND REASON

For this there is a magic word: "Show faith." Yes, our people can be trusted, they are worthy of confidence. Summon the gray peasants' coats, and ask them about their needs, and they will tell you the truth, and, perhaps, for the first time, we shall hear the real truth. And there should be no elaborate preparations: the people could be questioned locally, in counties, in peasants' huts, since even if scattered locally they would say exactly the same thing which they would say if they were assembled in one place, because their spirit is one. Scattered or brought together they are one, since their spirit is one. Each locality would merely add its local peculiarity, but *in toto* everything would be in accord and one. It should only be observed that, for the time being, precisely the peasant, the genuine peasant, should be given a chance to express himself. True, alongside the peasant you will find the kulak and the bloodsucker; but they, too, are peasants, and in so great a cause they will not betray their land and will utter a true word.—Such is, indeed, our national peculiarity.

How is this to be achieved?—Well, men in power are in a better position to decide this question. I merely believe that the matter would require no special formulae. Our people are not particular about forms, especially, ready-made, foreign forms, which they do not need at all, because they have different things on their minds; they never were, never will be, interested in forms because on this matter they have their own, quite peculiar opinions. Indeed, in this case a people such as ours can be fully trusted. For who has not seen them beside, near and with the Czar? They are true, loyal children of the Czar, and he is their father. Is the saying that "the Czar is their father" a mere phrase, an empty sound in Russia? He who so believes understands nothing about Russia! Nay, this is a profound and most original idea,—a live and mighty organism of the people merging with their Czar. This idea is a force which has been moulding itself in the course of centuries, especially the last two centuries, which were so dreadful to the people, but which we so ardently eulogize for European enlightenment, forgetting the fact that this enlightenment was bought two centuries ago at the expense of serfdom and a Calvary of the Russian people serving us. The people waited for their liberator, and he came. Why, then, shouldn't they be his own, true children? The Czar to the people is not an extrinsic force such as that of some conqueror (as were, for instance, the dynasties of the former Kings of France), but a national, all-unifying force, which the people themselves desired, which they nurtured in their hearts, which they came to love, for which they suffered because from it alone they hoped for their exodus from Egypt. To the people, the Czar is the incarnation of themselves, their whole ideology, their hopes and beliefs.

So recently these hopes have been completely realized. Would the people renounce their further hopes? Wouldn't the latter, on the contrary, be strengthened and reinforced, since after the peasants' reform the Czar became the people's father not merely in hope but in reality. This attitude of the people toward the Czar is the genuine, adamant foundation of every reform in Russia. If you wish, there is in Russia no creative, protective and leading force other than this live organic bond of the people with their Czar, from which everything is derived. For instance, who would even have ventured to dream about the peasants' reform without knowing and believing in advance that the Czar was a father to the people, and that precisely this faith of the people in the Czar as their father would save and protect everything and stave off the calamity? Alas, incompetent is that reformer-economist who shuns the genuine and living national forces because of some prejudice or foreign belief. Why, we are not with the people, we do not understand them for the one reason that, even though we know and comprehend their attitude toward the Czar, yet we are unable to embrace in all its completeness the cardinal and essential element in our destinies, *i.e.*, that this attitude of the Russian people toward their Czar is the most peculiar trait which distinguishes our people from all other peoples of Europe and of the whole world; that in Russia this is not merely a temporary, transitory phenomenon, not a mere symptom of national infancy or the people's growth, as some wiseacre may think, but a secular, perpetual fact which will never—at least, not for a very long time—change.

How, then, is it possible to maintain that our people are not different from all other nations, and that they do not bear within themselves an idea of their own? Is it not, on the contrary, clear that the Russian people bear within themselves the organic embryo of an idea which differs from any idea in the world? And this idea comprises in Russia so mighty a force that it will naturally exercise an influence upon our whole future history. Inasmuch, however, as this idea is quite peculiar and is encountered nowhere else, *our history cannot resemble the history of other European nations;* even less can it be a slavish copy of the latter.

This is what our wise fellows fail to comprehend, they who believe that everything in Russia will transform itself into a Europe, devoid of any individuality, and who hate individuality. This may result in a calamity. And the fact that in Russia all fundamentals are different from anything in Europe may be demonstrated by the following example: Civil liberty may be established in Russia on an integral scale, more complete than anywhere in the world, whether in Europe or even in North America, and precisely on the same adamant foundation. It will be based not upon a written sheet of paper, but upon the children's affection of the people for the Czar, as their father, since children may be permitted many a thing which is inconceivable in the case of contractual nations; they may be entrusted with much that has nowhere been encountered, since children will not betray their father, and, being children, they will lovingly accept from him any correction of their errors.

How, then, can confidence be denied to such a people?—Let them speak about their needs, let them tell the whole truth about them. But, I repeat, first, let them speak alone, while we, "the people's intelligentsia," for the time being, humbly stand aside and look at them, listening to what they have to say. Oh, it is not on some political grounds that I am suggesting that our intelligentsia be temporarily set aside. Do not attribute to me these motives. I am suggesting this, if you will pardon me, for purely *pedagogical* motives. Yes, let us stand aside and listen to the people; let us find out how clearly and intelligently they will express their truth without our assistance, precisely a matter genuinely their own, how they will hit the target, without offending us, should we be involved in the discussion. Let us stand there and let us learn the people's humility, their business-like reasoning, the concreteness of their mind.

You may retort: "You said yourself that the people are apt to listen to nonsensical rumors.—What kind of wisdom, then, can we expect from them?"—Quite so. But rumor is one thing, and fellowship in a common cause is an altogether different proposition. Wholeness will ensue, which, in turn, will exercise an influence upon itself and will produce reason. Indeed, it will be a school for us all, a most beneficial school. Perceiving in the people such a serious, business-like approach to their problems, we shall be surprised. And, of course, some of us will not believe our eyes. Of these, however, there will be very few, since all those who are genuinely sincere, who really thirst for truth and principally for common benefit,—those will all support the wise utterances of the people. But all those who are insincere will forthwith reveal themselves and their content. Should there remain sincere men who even then fail to believe in the people, such old-believers and doctrinaires of the Forties and Fifties, such old incorrigible children will merely be ridiculous and harmless. Aside from these, all others will clear their eyes and cleanse their understanding.

This might be an event of major importance from the standpoint of its consequences, since . . . it is in this form that the beginning, the first step in the direction of a merger of our whole educated class, so uppish toward the people, with the latter would start. I am speaking merely about a spiritual merger. This is all we need, and this will greatly help everything, will regenerate everything and provide us with a new idea. I believe that our serene and fresh youth will be the first to surrender their hearts to the people and will understand the people for the first time. The reason I am placing so much hope in our youth is that they also suffer from "the quest after truth" and agonize for it; therefore they, more than anyone, are akin to the people, and they will at once understand that the people are seeking the truth. And having closely familiarized themselves with the soul of the people, they will relinquish the radical nonsense which was about to captivate so many of them who imagined that they had found the truth in the extreme European doctrines.

Oh, I believe that I am not dreaming, and that I am not exaggerating those beneficial consequences which could be derived from so good a cause. Haughtiness would vanish and respect for the native land would arise. An altogether new idea would enter our souls, illuminating in them everything that, thus far, has remained in the dark; its light would expose deceit and banish it. Who knows?—This might be the beginning of a reform the significance of which would even surpass that of the peasants' reform: here there would also be a "liberation"—a liberation of our minds and hearts from European serfdom *sui generis* in which, during two centuries, we have been dwelling, just in the same way as the peasant has recently been our slave. If only this second reform could begin and be realized, it would merely be the consequence of the first great reform of the beginning of the present reign. At that time the two-century-old wall which separated the people from the intelligentsia fell materially, and now this wall would fall spiritually. And what can be loftier and more profitable to Russia than this spiritual merger of the social classes? Kinsfolks for the first time would come to learn their kin. Those who, till now, used to be ashamed of our people as a barbaric people impeding progress, would become ashamed of their former shame; they would humble themselves before many a thing and would begin to esteem many a thing which they formerly did not respect but despised. And when the people have given their reply, when they have given a full account of themselves, and their humble word has been uttered, ask then our intelligentsia their opinion on what the people have said, and you will at once see the results. Then the word of the intelligentsia will also be productive, since, after all, they are educated people and theirs should be the last word. Even so, the example of the people who have uttered their word first, at all events would guard us against many an error, much foolishness we were about to speak before the people had spoken. And then you would see that our intelligentsia would say nothing contradictory to the people, merely expressing their truth in scientific language and developing it to the full breadth of their education, since science, or its fundamentals, is in the possession of the intelligentsia, and the people are in bad need of science. Moreover, even if there be someone who disagrees with the basic tenets of the people, he will not dare to oppose the national spirit,—and this is rather important.

It is very possible that spiritual tranquillity would begin precisely with this step. There would arise common, undivided hope, and our aims would reveal themselves to us clearly. This is all the more desirable as our educated men do not know at all, or know indistinctly, what our future national and state aims are. This is our weak point, especially at this moment. And this confusion, this ignorance, is unquestionably the source of great anxiety and want of order. This is true not only of the present but also of the infinitely more bitter future. All this could be elucidated, or at least might serve as an indication how things should be interpreted and envisaged.

Well, enough has been said on this subject. I have expressed myself as best I could. Even though not everything may be understood—if I have proved unable to make myself understood, I accept the blame for this—nevertheless, that which will be comprehended should be accepted in a peaceful, inoffensive spirit. I merely wish that it may be impartially understood; that above all I am for the people; that I believe as in a sanctity in their soul, in their great forces, which no one among us knows in their full compass and grandeur. Primarily, I believe in the people's salutary destiny, in their conservative and creative spirit. And my only desire is that this should be perceived by everybody. The moment this is perceived everything else will begin to be understood.

Why should all this be a dream?—I am not speaking of the immensity of the task, but only of the peasant, his own, initial affairs, affecting him alone. Doesn't he have such special problems, pertaining to him alone, as should become known, so to speak, as a matter of taking initiative or by way of an introduction to any even very grand reform? Great benefits would be derived from such a knowledge: we should have facts; we should learn the truth about many a thing; precious material would be gathered which would guard many of us against fantastic hopes, distortions in the European fashion, and exaggerations. Most important of all—I repeat—we shall find the proper tone and spirit, that very spirit which alone may generate future things on an even greater scale. This task will bear a national and profoundly conservative impress. No one, not even the most fantastic minds, will be able to avoid in the future the consequences of this impress; even these fantastic minds will be tempted and will voluntarily accept it.

CHAPTER II

1

A Witty Bureaucrat. His Opinion on Our Liberals and Europeans

BUT HAVING finished this first chapter, I shall interrupt my article on finance, since I feel that what I write is very boring. But I am interrupting it only for the time being. I should like to dwell upon other "roots" and other elements which in my judgment could be made healthy. I am suspending my article also for the reason that I should be unable to squeeze it *in toto* into the thirty-two pages of *The Diary,* so that willy-nilly, I should have to postpone it till the subsequent issues.

"There's no point in this. Not necessary to continue it in the subsequent issues"—squeamish voices will interrupt me. (I anticipate these voices.)—"This has no bearing on finances; it's just . . . mischief. All this is not realistic [although I don't see why?]; all this has a mystical flavor, with no bearing upon concrete and current things! Give us a novel in your subsequent issues!"

Strange voices!—I am specifically insisting on the necessity of turning away from many a concrete and current thing in order that we may create a different reality much more concrete than our present one upon which we have embarked and in which we are sticking—if you will pardon me—also like that fly in the molasses.—Therein is my whole idea, *i.e.,* that we should turn our heads and eyes in an altogether different direction. Such is my thought.

Those in power could start the thing, and from this standpoint by fancies become not at all as fantastic as they may seem, because should the authorities take the initiative, much could be accomplished at once. Some of our principles would be radically changed; flies would be extricated from the molasses and freed. This idea appears to be unpopular: we have long been used to immobility, while it feels so sweet to be sitting in molasses.

True, I am again deviating, and I may be curtly reminded that, having written so much, I have failed, thus far, to explain what are the current and present things I am referring to, and what kind of future I prefer. This is precisely what I intend to explain in the future issues of my *Diary.* However, in winding up the present discussion, I shall say a few words about a meeting which I had with a rather witty bureaucrat who told me a curious thing precisely dealing with certain principles pertaining to the changes in our present-day "current" affairs.

In a certain society the conversation turned to finances and economy, but specifically in the spirit of frugality in saving our financial resources, and expending them in such a way as to prevent the loss of a single kopeck or that it should be spent for no fantastic appropriations. At present we speak almost incessantly about this kind of economy, and the government, on its own part, is preoccupied with the same problem. We have established control, and year after year we have been curtailing our staffs. Of late, people even started speaking about the curtailment of the army. In newspapers a specific figure has even been suggested, namely, that our standing army be reduced by 50,000 men, while in other quarters it was proposed to reduce it by one half, and it was claimed that this would entail no harmful consequences. This might have been excellent, but the following consideration involuntarily comes to one's mind: to begin with we might reduce the army by 50,000 men; even so, money thus saved would slip through our fingers— hither and thither—of course for state needs, but such as are not worthy of so radical a sacrifice as this. We shall never be able to restore these 50,000 men, or, at any rate, this could be done only with a great effort, because, having once made the reduction, it would be difficult to restore it, whereas we greatly need an army, especially just now, when everybody is ready to retaliate against us. It would be dangerous to embark upon this road but only *at present*, with current things as they are. Were we to adopt rigid, gloomy economy, in the spirit and resolution of Peter should he have made up his mind to economize, only then could we be sure that this precious money would be expended on a genuinely worthy cause. But are we capable of this in the face of the "crying" needs of the current moment with which we have bound ourselves?

I may remark that should we do this—start economizing—this would be one of the first turning steps from the fantastic past of the current things toward the new, realistic and relevant tasks. For example we have often reduced the personnel of government employees, but the result is that their staffs seem to be increasing. Are we capable of a curtailment which would reduce their number from forty to four? That four functionaries can oftentimes accomplish what forty were engaged in there can be no shadow of doubt, especially should the paper office routine be curtailed and the present bureaucratic methods radically reformed.—Such was the subject which was brought up in the conversation of our company. It was observed that this, to say the least, would require a thorough reorganization. Others retorted that we had much more radical reforms than this one. Still others maintained that the salaries of those four employees who had replaced the forty, could even be trebled, and that they would work willingly, without repining; and, further, that should their salaries be trebled, their subsistence would amount to that of twelve present employees, which would reduce the present appropriation by three quarters.

At this juncture I was interrupted by my bureaucrat. First, I wish to remark that much to my surprise he did not object to the possibility of replacing forty functionaries with four, thus implying that business could be conducted by those remaining four. But he did object to something else, namely, to the principle itself; to the erroneousness and criminality of the principle. I am recording here his objections, not verbatim, but in my version. I am recording them because, I repeat, to me, they sounded strange, in a certain sense, and comprised an almost piquant idea. Of course, he did not deign to answer me in detail since in a matter such as this I am not a specialist, and "understand little"—which I hasten to admit.—The principle, however, he hoped, I should be able to understand.

"The reduction of the number of government employees from forty to four"—thus he started sternly and with conviction—"not only is not useful but is essentially harmful, despite the fact that state expenditures would actually be considerably curtailed. Not only is the reduction from forty to four harmful, but even from forty to thirty-eight for the following reason: thereby you would be challenging the fundamental principle itself, because for almost two hundred years, ever since Peter, we have constituted in the state *everything*. Strictly speaking, we are the state, while *everything* else is merely an appendix. At least, such was the situation until recently, till the liberation of the peasants. All former elective offices, those of the nobility, for instance, were automatically imbued with our spirit, so to speak. Perceiving this, we were not disturbed in the least, since the principle laid down two centuries ago was in no sense violated. True, after the peasants' reform a new tendency began to manifest itself: self-government came into existence, the zemstvo, and the like. . . . It is now clear that these new institutions at once began to assume our guise, our soul and body; they, too, began to reincarnate themselves. And this happened by no means under our pressure (this is an erroneous idea) but automatically, since it is difficult to rid oneself of secular habits; nor is it at all necessary, if you please, especially in so great and fundamental a national task. You may not believe me, but if you are capable of rationalizing this, of course you will understand me. For what are we?—Even to this day we are *everything*, we continue to be everything,—and, again, without any effort on our part, without exerting ourselves in the least, precisely automatically, in the natural course of events. People have long been shouting that ours is a bureaucratic, not a live but dead, paper proposition, and that Russia has outlived it. Maybe she has outlived it, but, as yet, we alone are holding, building and preserving her lest she fall apart. For that which you call bureaucratic carrion, *i.e.*, we ourselves, as an institution, and our whole work,—all these, to use a simile, constitute the skeleton in a living organism. Scatter the skeleton, the bones, and the live body will perish. Granting that the work is being performed in a dead manner, yet it develops in accordance with a system, with a great principle. This is what I want to tell you. Let the work be done in a bureaucratic fashion, even badly and incompletely, nevertheless it is being performed somehow, and what is most important—everything stands erect without falling apart, and the fact that it does not fall is the main thing. I agree with you, and perhaps I am ready to concede that as a matter of fact we are not *everything*: we are clever enough to understand that we do not constitute everything in Russia, especially, in our day. All right, conceding the fact that we are not everything,—we are *something, i.e.*, something real, actually existent, though partly incorporeal. Now, what have you with which to replace us so that we could safely withdraw; what kind of 'something' have you which would replace us so that nothing would fall?—All your self-governments and zemstvos are nothing but beautiful herons soaring in the skies, who have never, as yet, alighted on earth. Therefore, they are zeros, even though beautiful zeros, whereas we may not be beautiful, we may be boring, but we are *something,* and by no means zeros.

"You all keep blaming us for the heron: Why hasn't he alighted to this very day? You claim that we are to be blamed for this and for the alleged fact that we seek to transform the beautiful heron into our guise, endowing him with our spirit. Of course, on our part it would have been very laudable had this actually been entirely our fault, since this would have proved that we are backing a secular, fundamental and noble principle, and seeking to transform a useless zero into a useful something. But believe me, of this we are in no way guilty, or, at least, too little guilty: the beautiful heron himself is in a state of hesitation; he knows not what he should ultimately become: whether he should assume our guise or become really independent. He vacillates; he does not trust himself; he is almost lost. I assure you that he would have come to us by his own free will without any pressure on our part. Thus, it appears that we are, so to speak, a natural magnet to which everything is still being drawn—and will be drawn for a long time.

"Again, you seem to be sceptical, you laugh. But I am willing to bet. Just try to unfold the wings of your beautiful wee birdie; give him a free choice! Send your zemstvo a formal, stern decree, bearing a file number: 'Henceforth thou shalt be independent, and not a bureaucratic heron,' and, believe me, all these herons, of their own volition, would try to come to us and would wind up by becoming genuine bureaucrats imbibing our spirit and assuming our guise; they would copy us in everything. Even the elected peasant would knock at our door; this would greatly flatter him. Not in vain have tastes moulded themselves for two centuries.

"And yet, you wish that we, that is, something steady, standing on its feet, would exchange ourselves for this riddle, this charade, this beautiful heron of yours! Nay, better let us hold the titmouse in our hands. Better let us cope with the task in our own way. We shall improve, clean ourselves; why, we may introduce something new, so to speak, more progressive, conforming more to the spirit of the age. Perhaps we may even become more virtuous. But we will not exchange our present, the real *something* for a ghost, for a suddenly dreamed of dream, since there is none and nothing to replace us. This is correct. We resist annihilation, so to speak, by inertia. This inertia in us is precious, because, in truth, in our day, everything is held together by it alone. Therefore, to be reduced to thirty-eight from forty—not to speak of the reduction from forty to four—is a most harmful and even immoral proposition. You will gain pennies, but you will destroy a principle. Just try to cut out or change your formula, if conscience would permit you to venture such a thing: why, this would be a betrayal of our whole Russian Europeanism and enlightenment,—do you know this? This would be a negation of the fact that we are a state, that we are Europeans. This would be treason to Peter! And do you know that your liberals (well, ours too) who in the newspapers are so ardently supporting the zemstvo against bureaucracy, strictly speaking are contradicting themselves. Why, the zemstvo, all these novelties, this 'popularism'—they are, indeed, those very 'popular principles or their inception,' about which 'The Russian Party' (you may have heard that it has been thus nicknamed in Berlin) so hated by our Europeans, is so loudly vociferating, which are so furiously denied by our Russian liberalism and Europeanism; which they so bitterly ridicule, the very existence of which they refuse to admit! Liberalism is very much afraid of these principles! What if they should ever be realized!—In a sense this certainly would be a surprise!

"This means that, strictly speaking, all your Europeans are with us, and we are with them, and this they should have understood long ago and dutifully memorized. If you please, not only are we supporting the same things as they, but we and they are one and the same thing! Our guise and our spirit reside in them, in your Europeans. This is actually so! Here is what I am going to add: Europe—I mean Russian Europe, or Europe in Russia—this is we, we alone. We are the incarnation of the whole formula of Russian Europeanism; it resides *in toto* in us. We alone are also its interpreters. And I can't see why they shouldn't be receiving duly established decorations for their Europeanism if we are merging with them so innocently! They would wear them with pleasure, and they might even thereby be attracted to us. But we don't know how to do these things. And they keep scolding,—verily, kinsfolk fail to recognize their own kin!

"To wind up the discussion about your zemstvos and all these innovations, I shall tell you once and for all: No, sir! This is a long and not a short story. This requires a preliminary culture, its own, perhaps, two-hundred-year-long history. Be it only a century- or half-century-long history, since ours is an age of telegraphy and railroads, which accelerate and facilitate all communications. Even if it is only fifty years, nevertheless it is not forthwith. 'Forthwith and right away' are abominable Russian words. Right away nothing can come to pass, save men akin to us. And thus it will be for a long time."

At this point my bureaucrat, with proud deportment, ceased speaking. And would you believe it, I did not argue with him, since there was "something" in his words, some kind of a sad truth, something actually existent. Of course, inwardly, in my soul I did not agree with him. And the tone with which these departing men speak! . . . Even so, there was "something" in his words. . . .

2

AN OLD KRYLOV FABLE ABOUT A CERTAIN PIG

And to finish with all this—once and for all, I shall quote a short and very pretty little fable by Krylov which is probably forgotten by everybody, since what has our busy and tossing age to do with Krylov? This little fable involuntarily came to my mind when I was about to start writing my article on finances and the task of rendering our roots healthy. It has an admirable moral, but on a different theme, on the subject of other roots. However, this makes no difference,—it is applicable to our situation. This is the fable:

"A Pig beneath an ancient oak
Upon the acorns gorged and stuffed all day,
Then in the shadow snoring lay.
At last, with heavy eyes, the Swine awoke,
Got up, and with his snout the roots began to poke.
'Dost thou not see? This hurts the tree!'
A Raven from the oak called out reproachfully.
'If thou lay'st bare the roots, thou'lt make the tree decay.'
Says Pig: 'Well, let it! As for me,
That doesn't disturb me anyway!
It's not much use that I can see,
And if it went for good, I'd never fret for that:
It's acorns that I want; it's they that make me fat!'
'Ungrateful, thou!' the Oak replied in tone severe,
'If thou shouldst raise thy snout and look up here,
Then thou wouldst see
That all these acorns grow on me.' "[1]

Isn't this a good fable? And are we willing to resemble this portrait?

3

GEOK-TEPE. WHAT IS ASIA TO US?

Geok-Tepe is captured. The Turkomans are defeated, and although they are not yet quite pacified, our victory is indubitable. Society and the press are jubilant. But was it long ago that society, and partly also the press, took a most indifferent attitude toward this affair?—Particularly after the failure of General Lomakin and in the beginning of the preparations for the second offensive. "Why should we go there? What is Asia to us?—So much money has been expended, whereas we have a famine, diphtheria, we have no schools, etc." Yes, such opinions were expressed; we heard them. Not everybody shared them—far from it. Even so, one has to admit that, of late, many people began to adopt a hostile attitude toward our aggressive policy in Asia. True, the lack of information concerning the expedition undertaken was a contributing factor to this mood. Only quite recently news began to slip into Russia from the foreign press, whereas Skobelev's telegrams were printed throughout Russia when the undertaking was practically all over. Nevertheless, one can hardly maintain that our society has a clear conception of our mission in Asia,—what specifically she means to us now and

[1] From *The Fables of Krylov,* translated by Sir Bernard Pares, published by Jonathan Cape Limited, London, 1926.

in the future. Generally speaking, our whole Russian Asia, including Siberia, still exists to Russia merely in the form of some kind of an appendix in which European Russia has no desire to take any interest. "We are Europe,"—it is implied.—"What is our business in Asia!" There even sounded very harsh voices: "Oh, this Russian Asia of ours! We are even unable to establish order and settle properly in Europe, and here we have to meddle with Asia! Why, Asia is quite superfluous to us! How can we get rid of her!" Even in our day such opinions are expressed by our wiseacres,—of course, out of their great wisdom.

Skobelev's victory resounded all over Asia to her remotest corners: "Another fierce and proud orthodox people bowed before the White Czar!" And let this rumor echo and re-echo. Let the conviction of the invincibility of the White Czar and of his sword grow and spread among the millions of those peoples,—to the very borders of India and in India herself. After General Lomakin's failure throughout Asia there must have spread doubt as to the invincibility of our sword, and Russian prestige was unquestionably jeopardized. This is why we cannot stop on this road. The peoples may have their khans and emirs; in their imagination England, whose strength they admire, may stand as a menace, but the name of the White Czar must soar above those of the khans and emirs, above the name of the Caliph himself. Such is the conviction that must prevail in Asia! And, from year to year, it does spread there. And we need it because it prepares them for the future.

What for? What future? What is the need of the future seizure of Asia? What's our business there?

This is necessary because Russia is not only in Europe but also in Asia; because the Russian is not only a European but also an Asiatic. Moreover, Asia, perhaps, holds out greater promises to us than Europe. In our future destinies Asia is, perhaps, our main outlet!

I anticipate the indignation with which this reactionary suggestion of mine will be read. To me, however, it is an axiom. Yes, if there is one of the major roots which has to be rendered healthy, it is precisely our opinion of Asia. We must banish the slavish fear that Europe will call us Asiatic barbarians, and that it will be said that we are more Asiatics than Europeans. This fear that Europe might regard us as Asiatics has been haunting us for almost two centuries. It has particularly increased during the present nineteenth century, reaching almost the point of panic, something on the order of the trepidation which the "enigmatic" words "metal" and "fiend" cause among the Moscow merchants' wives. This erroneous fright of ours, this mistaken view of ourselves solely as

Europeans, and not Asiatics—which we have never ceased to be—this shame and this faulty opinion have cost us a good deal in the course of the last two centuries, and the price we have had to pay has consisted of the loss of our spiritual independence, of our unsuccessful policies in Europe, and finally of money—God only knows how much money—which we spent in order to prove to Europe that we were Europeans and not Asiatics.

However, Peter's shock which pushed us into Europe, at first necessary and salutary, proved too strong, and for this we cannot be fully blamed. And was there a limit to our efforts to make Europe recognize us as *hers*, as Europeans, solely as Europeans, and not Tartars! Continually and incessantly we have annoyed Europe, meddling with her affairs and petty business. Now, we scared her with our strength, dispatching our armies "to save the kings," now we bowed before Europe—which we shouldn't have done—assuring her that we were created solely for the purpose of serving her and making her happy. In 1812, having driven Napoleon out of Russia, we did not make peace with him, as certain perspicacious Russians advised us to do, but moved into Europe as a solid wall in order to make her happy and to liberate her from her aggressor. Of course, this was a lustrous picture: on the one hand was the despot and the aggressor, while on the other—the peacemaker and the resurrector. Still, in those days our political fortune consisted not in the picture, but in the fact that that aggressor had been placed, for the first time during his whole career, in a position where he would have made peace with us,—a sincere, lasting peace, maybe, forever. On condition that we should not hinder him in Europe, he would have given us the East, so that our present Eastern problem—the menace and calamity of our present and of our future—would have been settled long ago. The aggressor later said it himself, and surely he did not lie, since he could have done nothing better than to be our ally on condition that the East should be ours, and the West—his. Then he certainly would have mastered the European nations, whereas the latter, including England, were then still too weak to stop us in the East. Subsequently, Napoleon, or his dynasty after his death, would, perhaps, have fallen, but the East nevertheless would have been ours. (Then we should have had access to the sea, and we could have met England on the seas.) But we gave all this up for a little show. What was the result?—All these nations we liberated, before they had even dispatched Napoleon, began to look on us with most obvious malevolence and the bitterest suspicion. At the Congresses at once they all united against us, as a solid wall, grabbing everything for themselves. And not only did they leave nothing to us, but they exacted from us certain obligations—true, these were voluntary obligations—which, however, subsequently proved to be very costly ones.

Later, despite this lesson,—what did we do throughout the subsequent years of our century, up to this very day? Didn't we contribute to the consolidation of the German states? Didn't we strengthen them to such an extent that today they are, perhaps, stronger than we?—Indeed, it is no exaggeration to say that we have contributed to their growth and strength. Didn't we, in answer to their appeals, go to quell their strifes? Didn't we protect their rear when calamities threatened them? And now, contrariwise, didn't they threaten our rear when we were faced with a calamity, or didn't they threaten to appear in our rear, when we were menaced with other dangers? It came to the point where everybody in Europe, every tribe and every nation, held in their bosom a stone stored against us long ago, merely waiting for the first conflict. This is what we have gained in Europe by serving her.—Nothing but her hatred! We have played the part of Repetilov, who, racing after fortune, "In dowry got but naught, in service—no advancement."

But why this hatred against us? Why can't they all, once and for all, start trusting us and become convinced of our harmlessness? Why can't they believe that we are their friends and good servants, and that our whole European mission is to serve Europe and her welfare? (For is it not so? Haven't we been acting so throughout this century? Have we done or achieved anything for ourselves?—Everything was spent on Europe!) Nay, they cannot place trust in us. The main reason is that they are altogether unable to recognize us as *theirs*.

Under no circumstance will they believe that we can in truth, on an equal basis with them, participate in the future destinies of their civilization. They consider us alien to their civilization; they regard us as strangers and impostors. They take us for thieves who stole from them their enlightenment and who disguised themselves in their garbs. Turks and Semites are spiritually closer to them than we, Aryans. All this has a very important reason: we carry to mankind an altogether different idea than they—that's the reason. And this, despite the fact that our "Russian Europeans" exert their efforts to assure Europe that we have no idea whatsoever, and that we can have none in the future; that Russia is incapable of possessing an idea of her own, being capable of mere imitation; that we shall always imitate, and that we are not Asiatics, not barbarians, but just as they—Europeans.

Europe, however, for once, at least, did not believe our Russian Europeans. On the contrary, in this matter her inferences coincide with those of our Slavophiles, although she knows them not,—

at best she might have merely heard something about them. The coincidence is precisely that Europe believes, much as the Slavophiles believe, that we have an "idea" of our own,—a peculiar, not a European idea; that Russia can have, is capable of possessing, an idea. Of course, as yet, Europe knows nothing about the essence of our idea, since did she know it she would forthwith be pacified and even gladdened. But some day she will unfailingly come to know this idea, precisely when the critical moment in her destiny arrives. At present, however, she does not believe: admitting the fact that we possess an idea, she is afraid of it. Finally, she is quite disgusted with us, even though, at times, she is polite to us. For instance, they readily admit that Russian science can already point to several remarkable workers; that it has to its credit several good works which have even rendered service to European science. But under no circumstance will Europe now believe that not only scientific workers (even though very talented) may be born in Russia, but men of genius, leaders of mankind, such as a Bacon Kant or Aristotle. This they will never believe, since they do not believe in our civilization, while, as yet, they do not know our future idea. In truth, they are right: we shall have no Bacon, no Newton, no Aristotle so long as we fail to stand on our own road and be spiritually independent. The same is true of all other things, —of art and industry: Europe is ready to praise us, to stroke our heads, but she does not recognize us as hers, she despises us, whether secretly or openly; she considers us as an inferior race. At times, she feels aversion to us, especially when we fling ourselves on her neck with brotherly embraces.

However, it is difficult to turn away from "the window to Europe"; here is predestination. Meanwhile Asia may be, in truth, our future outlet! I reiterate this exclamation. And if we could only take cognizance of this idea, even though partially, what a root would be rendered whole! Asia, our Asiatic Russia,—why, this is also our sick root, which has to be not only refreshed but resurrected and transformed! A principle, a new principle, a new vision of the matter—this is what we need.

4

QUESTIONS AND ANSWERS

"What for? What for?"—irritated voices will sound.—"Our Asiatic affairs even now continually require from us troops and unproductive expenditures. And what is Asia's industry? What is her merchandise? Where shall we find there consumers of our goods?

And you suggest, no one knows why, that we should forever turn away from Europe!"

"Not forever," I continue to insist,—"for the time being, and not altogether: hard as we may try we shall never completely tear ourselves away from Europe. We should not abandon Europe completely. Nor is this necessary. She is a 'land of holy miracles'; this was uttered by a most ardent Slavophile. Europe, even as Russia, is our mother, our second mother. We have taken much from her; we shall again take, and we shall not wish to be ungrateful to her. Last year, at the Pushkin festivities in Moscow, I said a few words about the future great mission of the Russian people in Europe (in which I believe), and much mud was thrown at me, I was scolded, by everybody,—even by those who had then embraced me,—as though I had perpetrated an abomination, a nasty deed, having then uttered my word.

"However, perhaps, my word will not be forgotten. But enough has been said about this. Even so, we have the right to take care of our re-education and of our exodus from Egypt, since we ourselves created out of Europe something on the order of our spiritual Egypt."

"Wait,"—I shall be interrupted—"in what way will Asia contribute to our independence? There, we'll fall asleep in an Asiatic fashion, but we shall not become independent!"

"You see,"—I continue—"when we turn to Asia, with our new vision of her, in Russia there may occur something akin to what happened in Europe when America was discovered. Since, in truth, to us Asia is like the then undiscovered America. With our aspiration for Asia, our spirit and forces will be regenerated. The moment we become independent, we shall find what to do, whereas during the two centuries with Europe we lost the habit of any work; we became chatterers and idlers."

"Well, how are you going to arouse us for the Asiatic venture, if we are idlers? Who's going to be aroused first even if it were proved, as by two times two, that our happiness lies there?"

"In Europe we were hangers-on and slaves, whereas we shall go to Asia as masters. In Europe we were Asiatics, whereas in Asia we, too, are Europeans. Our civilizing mission in Asia will bribe our spirit and drive us thither. It is only necessary that the movement should start. Build only two railroads: begin with the one to Siberia, and then—to Central Asia,—and at once you will see the consequences."

"Indeed, yours is a modest desire!"—people will tell me laughingly.—"Where are the funds? And what shall we get in return?— Nothing but a loss to us!"

"First, had we in the last twenty-five years set aside only three million rubles annually (and three million rubles, at times, simply slip through our fingers),—by now we should have built seventy-five million rubles' worth of Asiatic roads, *i.e.*, over one thousand versts, no matter how you reckon. Then you speak about losses. Oh, if instead of us Englishmen or Americans inhabited Russia, they would show you what losses mean! They would certainly discover our America! Do you know that in Asia there are lands which are less explored than the interior of Africa? And do we know what riches are concealed in the bosom of these boundless lands? Oh, they would get at everything—metals and minerals, innumerable coal fields; they would find and discover everything—and they would know how to use these materials. They would summon science to their aid; they would compel the earth to yield fifty grains to one, —that same earth about which we here still think that it is nothing but a steppe naked as our palm. Corn would attract people; production, industry, would come into existence. Don't you worry: consumers would be found, and the road to them would be discovered; they would be found in the depths of Asia, where millions of them are slumbering now; to reach them new roads would be constructed!"

"Well, here you are eulogizing science, and at the same time you urge us to renounce science and enlightenment; you are suggesting that we become Asiatics!"

"There, we shall need science all the more"—I exclaim—"since what are we in science now?—Half-educated men and dilettanti. But there we shall become workers: necessity itself will compel us to it the moment the independent, enterprising spirit arises. In science, too, we shall become masters and not hangers-on, as we now are all too often. But the main thing is that our civilizing mission in Asia will be understood and learned by us from the very first steps,—this cannot be doubted. It will lift our spirit; it will convey to us dignity and self-consciousness, which at present we either lack altogether or possess in a trifling degree. Our longing for Asia, should it ever arise among us, would, in addition, serve as an outlet to many a restless mind, to those seized with anguish, to the lazy, to those who have grown tired of doing nothing. Give an efflux to water, and mustiness and stench will disappear. Once they are drawn into work, they will not feel bored; they will all be regenerated. Even the inept fellow with a piqued, aching *amour-propre,* would find there an outlet for himself, since it often happens that an incapable man in one place is resurrected almost as a genius in another place. This is also often observed in European colonies. And don't you worry: Russia will not be depopulated: the thing will start gradually. At first, only a few men will go, but after a while news from them will be received which will attract others. Even so, to the Russian Sea this will be imperceptible. Extricate the fly from the molasses; even straighten its wings as much as possible. Still, only a negligible percentage of the population will drift thither, so that the migration will remain unnoticed. Over there, however, it will be quite noticeable! Wherever a 'Uruss' settles in Asia, the land will forthwith become Russian land. A new Russia will arise which in due time will regenerate and resurrect the old one and will show the latter the road which she has to follow. This, however, requires a new principle and a turn. These would necessitate the least destruction and commotion. Let it be only slightly fathomed (but fathomed) that Asia is our future outlet, that our riches are there, that there is our ocean; that when in Europe, because of the overcrowded condition alone, inevitable and humiliating communism is established, communism which Europe herself will loathe; when whole throngs will crowd around one hearth, and gradually individual economies will be ruined, while families will forsake their homes and will start living in collective communes; when children (three quarters of them foundlings) will be brought up in foundling institutions,—then we shall still have wide expanses, meadows and forests, and our children will grow up in their parents' homes, not in stone barracks—amidst gardens and sowed fields, beholding above them clear, blue skies.

"Yes, Asia holds out to us many a promise, many an opportunity, the full scale of which we here cannot clearly conceive. Not only gold lies concealed in the earth. But we do need a new principle which, in turn, will provide us with moneys required for the work. Speaking truthfully why should we maintain, over there, in Europe, especially at this time, so many embassies with their costly gloss and lustre, with their refined wit and dinners, with their brilliant but expensive staffs? What are all these Gambettas and Popes to us, precisely now, even though Bismarck may be oppressing them? Would it not be better, for example, temporarily, to don a beggar's garb, to sit down by the roadside, placing a cap before us and to start collecting pennies. Let Europe think: *'la Russie se recueille'*. Meanwhile, at home, we should be getting ready and organizing things. People might say: 'Why should we be humbling ourselves?'—Well, we shall not humiliate ourselves in the least! When I mentioned the cap, I was speaking allegorically. Not only shall we not humble ourselves, but at once we shall elevate ourselves. This is what is going to happen. Europe is sly and clever: she will at once guess, and, believe me, she will forthwith begin to respect us. It stands to reason that, at first, our independence will puzzle her, but to a certain extent it will please her. Perceiving that we have embarked upon 'gloomy economy'; that we have decided to abide by the proverb 'they who cannot as they will, must will as they may'; that we have become frugal; that we are saving and valuing our ruble; that we are not making it of paper,—Europe will forthwith begin to value our ruble in her own markets. Why, if Europe sees that we are not afraid of deficits and bankruptcies, but that we go straight to our goal, she will come to us herself offering money; and she will offer it to us as serious, business-like people who have learned business and who know how to conduct it."

"Wait,"—I hear a voice—"you said something about Gambetta. But we are in no position to brush everything aside. Take, to begin with, the Eastern question: it remains pending. How are we going to evade it?"

"On the Eastern question at this time I would say: At this minute, in our political spheres there is, perhaps, not even one political mind which would consider it common sense that Constantinople must be ours (save in some remote, enigmatic future). If so, what is there to wait for?—At this minute the essence of the Eastern problem comes down to an alliance of Germany with Austria, plus the Austrian seizures in Turkey which are encouraged by Prince Bismarck. We can and, of course, will protest only in some extreme cases. However, so long as these two nations are united, what can we do without incurring very grave risks? Please observe that the Allies are waiting only until, at length, we should grow angry. However, as heretofore, we may love the Slavic nations, encourage them at times, even extend our help to them. Besides, they will not perish within a short time. And the term is likely to expire very soon. Let it suffice to say that we shall make it appear that we do not intend to meddle with European affairs, as heretofore; bereft of us, they will quarrel among themselves all the sooner. Indeed, Austria will never believe that Germany fell in love with her solely because of her beautiful eyes. Austria knows only too well that in the long run Germany must incorporate the Austrian Germans into the German union. But for no price will Austria cede her Germans—not even if Constantinople were offered her for them—so highly she values them. Therefore pretexts for discords are present there. And, on top of that, Germany is faced with the same insoluble French problem which, to her, has now become an eternal problem. Besides, Germany's unification itself appears to be incomplete and is apt to be undermined. It also appears that European socialism not only is not dead but continues to constitute a very grave menace.

"In a word, let us only wait and refrain from meddling,—even if we are invited to meddle. Just as soon as their discord comes to a crash, 'political equilibrium' will crack, and then the Eastern question will at once be solved. We should only have to choose the opportune moment, even as at the time of the Franco-Prussian slaughter, and we should suddenly declare, as we then declared concerning the Black Sea: 'We do not wish to recognize any Austrian seizures in Turkey!'—and all seizures will instantly vanish, perhaps, together with Austria herself. In this way we shall catch up with everything which ostensibly, for the time being, we let slip."

"What about England? You overlook England. When she observes our Asiatic aspirations, she will instantly grow alarmed."

"Paraphrasing the proverb, I retort: 'If one fears England one should sit at home and move nowhere.' Besides, nothing new is going to alarm her since she is also alarmed with the same old thing at present. On the contrary, now we are holding her in confusion and ignorance concerning the future, and she is expecting from us the worst things. When, however, she comes to understand the true character of all our moves in Asia, perhaps some of her apprehensions will be toned down. . . . Well, I concede: she will not tone them down; she is too far from this frame of mind. Still, I repeat: 'If one fears England, one should sit at home and move nowhere!' Therefore, let me exclaim once more: 'Long live the Geok-Tepe victory! Long live Skobelev and his good soldiers!' Eternal memory to those valiant knights who 'were eliminated from the rolls.' We shall record them on our rolls."

Notes
and
Index to the Diary

Notes

[A]

Aksákov, A. (Alexander) N., 1832–1903, author of several interesting articles on the theory of spiritism. His house in St. Petersburg was the meeting place where, in the Seventies, a number of spiritualistic séances were held.

Aksákov, Iván Sergéevich (1823–1886), son of Sergeí Timoféevich Aksákov and brother of Konstantin Aksákov, an outstanding publicist, an ardent patriot, one of the most influential Slavophiles, and a leading member of the Moscow Slavic Committee (1876–1878), whose views on the Eastern question, on Russia's role in the destinies of Slavdom and on the Russo-Turkish war of 1877–1878, agreed with those of Dostoievsky.

Aksákov, Konstantin Sergéevich (1817–1860), one of the most talented Slavophiles, brother of Iván Sergéevich Aksákov. In the Fifties K. S. Aksákov expounded his views in a Moscow weekly *The Rumor* (*Molvá*).

Aksákov, Sergeí Timoféevich (1791–1859), famous Russian diarist, father of Konstantin Aksákov and Iván Aksákov. His prose rivals that of Púshkin, Lérmontov (q.v.), and Turgénev (q.v.). Speaking of his writings, Maurice Baring says: "One is spell-bound by the charm, the dignity, the good nature, the gentle, easy accent of the speaker, who was a

gentleman by character as well as by lineage, one of God's as well as one of Russia's nobility." Aksákov's principal works, masterpieces rather, are *Family Chronicle* (1856), *The Years of Childhood of Bagróv the Grandson* (1858) and *Tales and Recollections of a Sportsman* (1855).

Alexeí Mikháilovich (1645–1676), Czar, the second Czar of the Románov dynasty, the father of Peter the Great (1699–1725).

Amadis de Gaula, or Amadis of Gaul, the hero of a famous cycle of romances of chivalry; these legends form the so-called "Amadis cycle," which is affiliated with the Arthurian cycle and the Knights of the Round Table. These romances were widely read in Western Europe in the XVIth and XVIIth Centuries.

Antón — The Poor Wretch — once a popular novel by Apollón Alexandróvich Grigoróvich (q.v.).

Apráksin shopkeepers, in St. Petersburg, reputedly the most backward, ignorant and vulgar group of the lower middle class.

Artél—in pre-Soviet Russia, an association or partnership of independent laborers for collective work and the execution of some specific job at their joint expense and with reciprocal bond. The artél, as a legal entity, owned the tools and implements required for the performance of the contracted work. Its profits were equally divided among the members of the artél.

Avséenko, Vasíly Grigórievich (1842–1913), mediocre novelist. He made his debut with the novel *The Storm* (1865). His best known belletristic work is *The Milky Way* (1875–1876). He was a regular contributor to Katkóv's *The Russian Messenger* (q.v.).

[B]

Bathóry (or Bathóri), Stephen, King of Poland and Lithuania (1576–1586), an able strategist; during the reign of Czar Iván Vasílievich, the Terrible (q.v.) he recaptured from the Russians a number of cities along the Russian-Lithuanian border, including Pólotzk and Velíkie Lukí; he besieged Pskov but was unable to capture it. In 1582, a ten-year truce between Bathóry and the Russian Czar was signed; under the terms of that treaty Russia lost Pólotzk and the Baltic coast.

Batýi, the Tartar Khan, at the head of a 300,000 Mongol army invaded Russia in 1237. Discord reigned among the Russian dukes, and the Tartars defeated them one by one despite their heroic resistance. In 1240 Batýi captured Kiev, thus completing his conquest of Russia, which lay devastated and helpless. This was the beginning of the Mongol yoke which lasted for almost two and a half centuries, till 1480.

Béltov, the hero of Hertzen's novel *Who Is to Blame?* typifying one of the progressive but "superfluous" men of the Forties who have lost all connection with their native soil. Turgénev's *Rúdin* is another specimen of the same pattern.

The Berlin Conference of 1878 under the presidency of the German Chancellor Prince Bismarck was convened as a result of the Russo-Turkish war and Russia's victory over Turkey, which terminated in the treaty of San Stefano (February 19, 1878), by virtue of which Turkey recognized the independence of Serbia, Montenegro and Rumania, and agreed to form an autonomous Bulgarian dukedom. Under the terms of that treaty, Russia received Bessarabia, a strip of land in Asia Minor (in Armenia) with the port of Batúm and the fortress Kars, while Turkey undertook to pay Russia an indemnity of 300,000,000 rubles. England and Austria at once started intriguing against Russia, insisting that the San Stefano treaty be revised. To this Russia reluctantly agreed, and, under the terms of the Berlin Conference, Bulgaria was divided into two parts—the Bulgarian dukedom, subordinate to Turkey, and Eastern Rumelia, which, though subordinate to the Sultan, was made autonomous and placed under the supervision of a Christian Governor-General. Bosnia and Herzegovina were placed under Austrian rule.

Bétzky, Iván Ivánovich (1704–1795), noted Russian statesman, educator and humanitarian during the reign of Catherine the Great. He was the natural son of Prince I. U. Troubetzkoý. On the initiative of Bétzky model Foundling Institutions were founded in Moscow (1763) and in St. Petersburg (1767). He was one of Catherine's principal collaborators in the field of public education.

Bielínsky, Vissarión Grigórievich (1810–1848), famous Russian critic of humble origin. A convinced Westerner, Bielínsky nevertheless "guessed" the universality and at the same time the national character of Púshkin's genius. He acclaimed Gógol in 1835 and enthusiastically greeted both the poetry and the prose of Lérmontov. His lengthy critique *Literary Reveries: An Elegy in Prose* (1834) is a masterful review of Russian literature from its beginnings in the XVIIIth Century to the early Thirties of the XIXth Century. During the period from 1843 to 1846 he wrote eleven essays on Púshkin. His was a brilliant pen, inspiring if not always convincing. Because of the lack of systematic education, his philosophical conceptions were contradictory and confusing. Even so, his captivating sincerity, genuine enthusiasm and passion for truth make him an outstanding figure in the history of Russian literary thought. Bielínsky was a realist, but his realism was colored with Hegelian idealism. He exercised an immense influence upon his contemporaries; his fiery but always didactic and partisan articles contributed much toward the emancipation of Russian public opinion, thus paving the way for the enactment of the great reforms in the Sixties.

Boborýkin Piótr Dmitrievich (1836–1921), noted Russian novelist; his best known works are: *China-Town* (1882) and *Vasíly Tiórkin* (1892).

Bolkónsky, Prince, one of the leading characters in Count Leo Tolstoý's (1828–1910) epic novel *War and Peace* (1868), the Russian Iliad.

Bolsháia Morskáia—one of the most fashionable streets in St. Petersburg.

Borís Godunóv (1825) by Púshkin, a tragedy which he dedicated to N. M. Karamzín, and in which, according to his own admission, he followed Shakespeare's pattern "in his free and broad treatment of the characters, in the extraordinary moulding of the types, and in his simplicity." *Borís Godunóv* is an unsurpassed piece of Russian drama which inspired M. P. Mussórgsky (1839–1881) to compose his ingenious opera bearing the same title (1872–1874).

Bótkin, Sergeí Petróvich (1832–1889), famous Russian clinician, professor at the Military Medical Academy in St. Petersburg.

Bulgárin, Faddeí Venedíktovich (1789–1859), of Polish descent, editor of the magazine *The Northern Bee* and an alleged agent of the Russian secret police, author of the once popular *Iván Víjigin;* ardent antagonist of Púshkin, who immortalized his name by several mordant and witty epigrams.

Burénin, Víktor Petróvich (1841–1926), noted Russian critic in *The New Times* and playwright. His pen was full of wit and sometimes full of venom.

[C]

The Captain's Daughter — Púshkin's major work in prose (1833–1836).

Cassation Departments, Criminal and Civil, of the Ruling Senate, in the system of the Russian reformed courts (November 20, 1864) were the courts of last appeal.

Cathedral Folks (1872) one of the best novels of N. S. Leskóv (q. v.). There is an excellent English translation of this work made by Isabel Hapgood.

Catherine the Great, Czarina (1762–1796), was not only familiar with the works of the French encyclopedists but corresponded with some of them, viz., with Voltaire (1694–1778), Diderot (1713–1784) and Dalembert (1713–1783). It was under their influence that the Empress wrote her famous *Nakáz* (Instruction) to the Committee of deputies elected by the people to frame a new Code of Laws (1767).

The Caucasian Captive (1820–1821), an early romantic poem by Púshkin; it was written at the time when Púshkin was still under the influence of Byron.

Cherniáiev, Mikhaíl Grigórievich (1828–1898), Russian soldier; he participated in the Crimean war (1854–1855), in the expedition against Tashkent (in Central Asia), which he captured on June 15, 1865. In 1875, having resigned from Russian

military service, he proceeded to Serbia. In 1876 he assumed command over the Serbian army. In 1882 he was appointed Governor-General of Turkestan, and in 1884 he was made a member of the War Council. Cherniáiev was an ardent Slavophile.

Chernyshévsky, Nikolaí Gavrílovich (1828–1889), noted Russian radical critic, economist of the Marxian orientation, revolutionist, author of the novel *What Is to be Done?* (1862) and editor of the radical monthly *Contemporary* (*Sovreménnik*). In 1855–1856, he wrote his valuable *Essays on the Gógol Period of Russian Literature*. Despite the didactic and utilitarian tendencies of his criticism, he recognized the genius of Púshkin. Karl Marx called Chernyshévsky *"der grosse Russiche Gelehrte und Kritiker"* ("the great Russian scientist and critic"). For his revolutionary activities he was arrested, tried and sentenced to seven years' hard labor and twenty years' exile. However, in 1883, he was permitted to take up residence in Ástrakhan, on the Caspian Sea, and thereafter in his native town Sarátov.

Childhood, Boyhood and Youth, Count Leo Tolstoý's autobiographical story, was written in 1852–1856.

Communal landownership among the peasants in pre-revolutionary Russia meant common ownership of the arable land and meadows by all the peasants of a given village. The commune, or *óbshchina,* composed of all such peasants, assigned the particular tracts of land for cultivation to the individual landlords who were tenants of the land the title to which was vested in the commune. At the same time the commune as an entity was responsible for the payment of taxes whether in the form of monetary levies or prestations in kind. The individual landlords of the commune had no right to dispose of, or to acquire title to, the land parcels assigned to them without the consent of the peasants' assembly, or *mir*, which was the executive organ of the *óbshchina*. The land occupied by the houses of the peasants, the houses themselves and other household structures (barns, stables, etc.), as well as the land used for the kitchen garden, were the exclusive property of the individual landlords. Every year, or once every three years, or from time to time, as need arose, the *mir* revised the status of the arable land within its jurisdiction, and at such times redistribution (*peredél*) of the arable areas took place; in this way periodical adjustments in the utilization of the communal land were effected. In Russian economic literature the question of the *óbshchina*, its advantages and disadvantages, its legal nature, its social effects and its influence upon agricultural techniques, was one of the most controversial. The Slavophiles were staunch supporters of this form of peasant landownership, whereas the Westerners, on the whole, were strongly in favor of its total abolition.

Crime and Punishment, one of the best known novels by Dostoiévsky (1866).

[D]

Dahl, Vladímir Ivánovich (1801–1872), famous Russian lexicographer who single-handed accomplished the stupendous task of compiling *The Interpretative Dictionary of the Living Great Russian Language* (completed in 1859), which still remains the main source for the study of the immensely rich, lexically complex and colorful Russian language. To the compilation of the *Dictionary* Dahl devoted forty-seven years. He also collected some 37,000 Russian proverbs and sayings. This compilation is also still unsurpassed. Dahl is the author (under the penname "The Cossack Lugánsky") of many novels, tales and short stories, of which the best known are: *Midshipman Potzelúiev, The Convict (Vagnák), New Pictures of Russian Life, Sailors' Leisure Hours,* and *The Tale about the Jew and the Gypsy.* Dahl was a friend of Púshkin, and he was present at the last moments of the poet, mortally wounded in a duel. (Púshkin died at 2:45 P.M., January 29, 1837.)

Danilévsky, Nikolaí Yákovlevich (1822–1895), Russian publicist, philosopher and naturalist; theoretician of the Slavophile doctrine, the author of a historico-philosophical treatise *Russia and Europe* (1871); noted anti-Darwinian. His treatise *Darwinism* appeared in 1885.

Davýdov, Denis Vasílievich (1784–1839), a noted poet, horseman and partisan in the war against Napoleon in 1812. In 1836, Púshkin sent him a copy of *The History of the Puga-*

chióv Rebellion with an autograph in which there are these lines:

A rider of the tame Pegasus
I wore of the antique Parnassus
The long outmoded poet's suit.
But even in this hard pursuit
Thou, wonder rider,—told in brief—
Thou wast my dad and honored chief.

(Boris Brasol's version)

Of course, Davydov never was Púshkin's "honored chief" in the realm of poetry, but his verses replete with hilarity and sincere humor were—and still are—very much in vogue. Count Leo Tolstoý, in his *War and Peace* (1868), portrayed Davýdov in the character of Vasíly Denísov.

Decembrists — participants in the revolutionary uprising which took place in St. Petersburg, on December 14, 1825, following the death of Emperor Alexander I on November 19, 1825, and the abdication of his elder brother Konstantin Pávlovich, who was then residing in Warsaw. Briefly, the story of the Decembrist revolt is as follows: On January 14, 1822, Grand Duke Konstantin in a letter addressed to Emperor Alexander I advised the latter of his desire to renounce the Throne. On February 2, 1822, Alexander I, in writing, acceded to his brother's determination to cede his sovereign rights, and on August 16, 1823, the Emperor issued a manifesto to this effect, naming his brother Grand Duke Nikolaí Pávlovich, next in the order of succession, heir to the Imperial Throne. This manifesto, however, was not promulgated; instead, four copies of it, in sealed envelopes, were delivered for safekeeping to the Moscow Cathedral of the Assumption, the Imperial (State) Council, the Ruling Senate and the Holy Synod, with the proviso that, immediately after the Emperor's passing, the seals should be broken and this act should be duly promulgated by the Senate. When the news of Alexander's death in Taganrog on the Azov Sea (South Russia) was received in St. Petersburg, and before the manifesto of August 16, 1823 had been promulgated, Grand Duke Nikolaí Pávlovich, who had no knowledge of its contents, took an oath of allegiance to his brother Konstantín, and his example was followed by the regiments of the Imperial Guard. Meanwhile Grand Duke Konstantín officially confirmed his determination not to ascend the throne, following which Grand Duke Nikolaí gave his consent to ascend the throne. Taking advantage of the confusion which arose in consequence of these events, a group of Russian officers of the Guard, most of whom were masons, refused to take the oath of allegiance to Emperor Nicholas I and swayed the men of their regiments to follow their example. The political aims of the revolutionists were divided: some of them sought to establish a constitutional monarchy; while others advocated a republican form of government. On the other hand, the mutinous soldiers had no political program whatsoever and merely obeyed the orders of their superiors. On December 14, 1825, the armed rebels assembled at the Senate Square. The Emperor ordered the loyal contingents of the Imperial Guard to line up in front of the Winter Palace; gradually they encircled the insurgents. Count Mikhaíl Andréevich Milorádovich, the Governor-General of St. Petersburg (the hero of 1812) sought to persuade them to disband; the soldiers were ready to return to their barracks but a pistol shot from the ranks of the rebels killed the Count on the spot. Not before artillery went into action did the mob disperse and was order restored. A committee to investigate the Decembrist movement was appointed by the Emperor. One hundred and twenty-one men were arrested and tried. Five men were sentenced to death, while the rest were exiled to Siberia.

Derjávin, Gavriíl Románovich. *See God.*

Derjimórda — a police "peace guardian" in Dmukhanóvsky's "enlightened" administration. "You just tell Derjimórda he should keep his fists under control; as a matter of routine he deals blows to both innocent and guilty." (*Revizor*, Act I, 5.)

Dmukhanóvsky, the corrupt bailiff, a character in Gógol's *Revizor.*

Dobroliúbov, Nikolaí Alexándrovich (1836–1861), noted Russian radical critic, a nihilist. Among his "æsthetical" slogans we read: "Not the execution but the purpose—this is what is important in art," or "the merit of literary productions is determined by what and how they propagandize," etc. His best known critical essays are: *The Dark Kingdom* (1859), an evaluation of Ostrovsky's *Thunderstorm*, *What is Oblómovschina* (1859)

on Goncharóv's *Oblómov* (q.v.), and *When Will the Real Day Come?* (1860) — an interpretation of Turgénev's (q.v.) novel *On the Eve.* Dobroliúbov died of consumption at the age of twenty-five.

The Domestic Records (*Otéchestvennia Zapíski*), a monthly founded in St. Petersburg in 1820 by P. P. Svinjín. In the Forties the magazine, which became the mouthpiece of the liberal Westerners, with Bielínsky (q. v.) as the most eloquent exponent of their philosophy, for many years exercised a potent influence upon the educated strata. Lérmontov's (q.v.) youthful poems and lyrical pieces posthumously appeared in *The Domestic Records.* In the Seventies the magazine was jointly edited by M. E. Saltykóv ("Schedrin") (q.v.) and N. A. Nekrásov (q.v.). During that decade on the pages of that periodical there appeared many noted literary works, such as P. D. Boborýkin's (q.v.) novel *Solid Virtues* (1870), V. S. Gárshin's (1855–1888) story *Four Days* (1877), Dostoiévsky's novel *The Raw Youth* (1875), a number of comedies by A. N. Ostróvsky (q.v.), etc. It was also in the Seventies that N. K. Mikhailóvsky (1842–1904), who in some quarters was regarded as the theoretician of the Socialist-Revolutionary Party, came out with a flood of radical articles, essays, feuilletons, etc., which strongly appealed to the underdeveloped minds of the college youths, but which, on the whole, conformed to the provisions of the Saltykóv "By-laws of the Skin Removers," viz., "without neglecting a single contemporary question one should deliberate upon every one of them in a manner which would lead to nothing." Darwin was Mikhailóvsky's principal target. In 1884, by order of the government, the publication of *The Domestic Records* was stopped.

Draper, John William (1811–1882), noted American physicist, physiologist and chemist of English birth (born at St. Helens, near Liverpool) the author of a once widely read book *History of the Intellectual Development of Europe* (1862), which has been translated into many languages. This treatise exercised a marked influence upon the European intelligentsia of the Sixties and Seventies. Draper wrote many valuable papers on radiant energy and an admirable *Textbook of Chemistry* (1846).

[E]

The Epoch, a short-lived magazine founded by M. M. Dostoiévsky (1820–1864), F. M. Dostoiévsky's brother, in the year of his death. The magazine ended its existence in February, 1865.

Evenings on the Farm near Dikánka (1831–1832) by N. V. Gógol. In these stories full of hilarity and humor Gógol ingeniously depicted the life in his native romantic Little Russia. Dikánka is a village in the province of Poltáva.

[F]

Fathers and Sons, one of Turgénev's best known novels. Among the characters in that novel Bazárov is an immortal prototype of the Russian nihilists.

Feast during the Plague (1830)–a miniature tragedy by Púshkin.

Fet, Afanási Afanásievich (1820–1892), natural son of Shenshín, a wealthy landowner in the province of Oriól, one of the gods of the Russian Parnassus. In his delicate, lacelike, melodious pieces Russian lyrical poetry reached its summit. The radical critics of the Fifties and Sixties, according to whose motto "Boots are more important than Shakespeare," bitterly denounced Fet's poetry, "where music and moonlight and feeling–are one." They hated his æsthetic leanings; they would not forgive him such pieces as this verbless lyrical gem:

Murmurs. Breezes. Trills and singing
Of the nightingale.
Silver touches. Gentle swinging
O'er the drowsy vale.
Lights and shadows. Strange sensations.
Visions full of grace,
And the magic of mutations
In that lovely face.
Clouds in purple. Amber blushes
'Cross the misty lawn.
Tears and kisses. Sudden flushes,
And the dawn! The dawn!
                    (Boris Brasol's version)

Fet was also a noted translator; among his best known versions are: Goethe's *Faust* and *Hermann und Dorothea,* Schopenhauer's *The World as Will and Idea* (1819) and *Fourfold Root of the Principle of Sufficient Reason* (1813) and Horace's

Odes, Satires and Epistles (1856–1883).

[G]

Gavroche, in Victor's Hugo's novel *Les Misérables* (1862), typifying the Parisian *gamin de rue*.

Geók Tepé—a former fortress of the Turkomans in Central Asia. In December, 1880, General Skóbelev at the head of 6,000 Russian troops attacked the fortress and carried it by storm although the defenders numbered 25,000.

God—one of the best known odes by Gavriíl Románovich Derjávin (1743–1816), which has been translated into virtually every language, including the Japanese. Derjávin was of Tartar descent. A poet of genuine but unruly talent, he was undeniably the most gifted and colorful representative of Russian literature of the XVIIIth Century. He became a sworn bard of Empress Catherine II (1762–1796) and of her brilliant age. Púshkin in his *Eugene Onégin* (Chapter VIII), referring to his own Muse, made the following allusion:

The world upon her smiled a greeting,
I soared upon my first success,
And old Derjávin, now retreating
Graveward, remarked us—stayed to
    bless.

(Oliver Elton's version)

Derjávin was a member of the Russian Imperial Academy, and during the reign of Emperor Alexander I (1801–1825) for a brief period was Minister of Justice.

Gógol, Nicholas V. (March 20, 1809–February 21, 1852) : Nicholas V. Gógol was born in the province of Poltáva, Little Russia, of noble parentage. In 1821, he matriculated in the Néjin High School. In 1825, Gógol's father died. In 1828, Gógol graduated at the High School and undertook his first journey to St. Petersburg. In 1831, he started teaching in a woman's college in St. Petersburg; there, he established close contacts with the leading Russian literary circles. During that year he published the First Part of *Evenings on the Farm near Dikánka*. The Second Part of the same Collection appeared in 1832. In 1834, Gógol was appointed Assistant Professor of World History at the St. Petersburg Imperial University. During that same year he completed his two comedies, *The Revizor* and *The Wedding*. In 1835, he started writing *Dead Souls*. On April 19, 1836, *The Revizor* was given for the first time on the Imperial dramatic stage at St. Petersburg. On January 29, 1837, Púshkin (q.v.) died, an event which proved the greatest misfortune in Gógol's life. From 1837 to 1839, Gógol spent most of his time in Rome. In 1840, he completed two comedies: *The Litigation* and *The Servants' Room*. During the same year, he finished a romantic novel, *Tarás Búlba*, and also *The Cloak*, one of his best short stories. In 1842, the First Part of *Dead Souls* was printed. In 1845, Gógol burned the manuscript of the Second Part of *Dead Souls*. In 1846, the *Selected Portions from the Correspondence with Friends* were printed in St. Petersburg. Early in 1848, Gógol undertook a pilgrimage to the Holy Land, and on May 16 of the same year he returned to Russia. On February 11, 1852, he again burned another version of the Second Part of *Dead Souls,* together with most of his other manuscripts. Gógol died in Moscow.

Goncharóv. *See Oblomov.*

Gostíny Dvor, in St. Petersburg, a huge block occupied by a large number of stores, facing on one side the Névsky Prospéct next to the Municipal Building (Duma).

Gradóvsky, Alexánder Dmítrievich (1841–1889), professor of government law at the Imperial St. Petersburg University. His treatises *Principles of Russian Government Law* (1875) and *Government Law of the Principal European States* (1886) in many respects may still be considered classics. Gradóvsky was a convinced Westerner.

Granóvsky, Timoféi Nikoláievich (1813–1855), noted Russian historian, a sworn liberal, a humanist of the finest pattern, and a convinced Westerner; professor of universal history at the Moscow University. He was an outstanding orator, and his public lectures (1843–1846) marked an epoch in the history of the Russian progressive intelligentsia.

Griboiédov. *See Woe from Wit.*

Grigóriev, Apollón Alexándrovich (1822–1864), after Bielínsky (q.v.) the most distinguished Russian critic,

exponent of "organic" criticism which maintains that every æsthetical phenomenon is an organic product of the whole historical process. He gave a masterful critical evaluation of Púshkin, Gógol and Ostróvsky (q.v.). In 1859 he expounded the basic tenets of his organic critique in a series of articles dealing with Turgénev's (q. v.) *Gentlefolks' Nest (The Russian Word,* 1859. Nos. 4, 5, 6, and 8).

Grigoróvich, Dmítri Vasílievich (1822–1899), a noted Russian novelist. His novels *The Village* (1847) and *Anton—The Poor Wretch* (1847), in which peasant life is depicted with false sentimentalism, on political rather than on literary grounds, were enthusiastically acclaimed by Bielínsky (q.v.). His other novels *The By-Roads* and *The Fishermen* (1852) suffer from the same defect. However, his *Literary Reminiscences* are a mine of information on the history of both Russian literature and the Russian theatre.

Grushnítzky, in *A Hero of Our Days,* by Lérmontov, is a vain young man, a braggart, and something of a coward.

Gué, N. N. (1831–1894), noted Russian painter. He is best known for his pictures *Peter I and Alexis, What Is Truth?* and *Púshkin in Mikháilovskoie* (Púshkin's estate in the province of Pskov).

The Gypsies (1824), a poem by Púshkin; it belongs to the Byronic period of his creative work. Dostoiévsky dwells on it in some detail in his Púshkin speech.

[H]

A Hero of Our Days (1839–1840) by Lérmontov is a masterpiece of Russian prose.

Hertzen, Alexánder Ivánovich, pen name Iskander (1812–1870), well-known Russian publicist and political emigrant, sometimes called the "Russian Voltaire." While attending the Moscow University, he joined a "circle" of which Bielínsky (q.v.) and N. P. Ogarióv (1813–1877), later a noted poet, were the moving spirits; their gospel at the time was socialism. Hertzen was exiled to the city of Viátka in Northern Russian, but he was soon permitted to settle in either capital. In 1847, he voluntarily left Russia after having written several novels, including *The Legend* and *Who Is to Blame?* In Western Europe he embraced extreme revolutionary doctrines. However, he became disillusioned in the revolution of 1848, and proclaimed that "the West is decaying" and also that "Europe is not asleep—she is dying." In July, 1857, he began to publish in London a revolutionary periodical, *The Bell* (*Kólokol*), which gained extraordinary popularity all over Russia. Emperor Alexander II was among its regular readers. In 1863, the Polish landed aristocracy, inspired by the Polish emigrants and the French radicals, organized a rebellion against the Russian rule. Hertzen, in his *Bell*, came out in support of the Polish uprising. This was the end of his popularity in Russia. He was the author of two remarkable books, *From the Other Shore* (1847–1859), which is a series of letters expounding the socialistic doctrine, and the fascinating *Memories and Thoughts* (1852–1855).

[I]

"I have experienced this feeling myself when . . . I unintentionally endorsed for publication a news item which should not have been printed without the express permission of the Minister of the Imperial Court." (Page 213.) Dostoiévsky refers to an article in *The Citizen*, of which he was then editor (1873), entitled *Kirghiz Deputies in St. Petersburg.* In that article the words of Emperor Alexander II addressed to Sultan Mahomet, the spokesman of the Kirghiz delegation, were quoted. Dostoiévsky was tried and sentenced to two days in a house of detention and twenty-five rubles' fine.

"I have seen a five-year-old boy . . ." (Page 229.) Dostoiévsky recalled the words of his little son Fédia who in December, 1875, was taken ill with scarlet fever.

"I will tell you a little anecdote . . ." (Page 235.) Dostoiévsky refers to a conversation which actually took place between him and his six-year-old daughter Lília.

"If seated in a row—Our skill we'll surely show." These two lines are from the fable *A Quartet* by Iván Andréevich Krylóv (1768–1844), one of the world's greatest fabulists, whose fame is equal to that of Æsop (560 B.C.) and La Fontaine (1621–1695); characterizing Krylóv's genius, the eminent English critic Maurice Baring said that he "has the talisman which defies criticism, baffles analysis, and defeats time: namely, charm." Krylóv was assistant to the Librarian of the Imperial Public Library in St. Petersburg.

Ilovaísky, Dmítri Ivánovich (1832–1920), Russian historian; the author of many textbooks on history for high schools. Author of *The History of the Riazán Dukedom* (1859) and *Inquiry into the Beginnings of Russia* (1876).

Ilyá Múrometz. *See* Múrometz, Ilyá.

Iván III (1462–1505), Grand Duke of Moscow. In 1480, his refusal to pay the customary contribution to the Tartar khans marked the end of the Mongol domination over Russia (1240–1480). In 1472, Ivan III married the Greek Empress Sophie Paleológ. In consequence of this event closer ties were established between the two Orthodox countries—Russia and Greece.

Iván Vasílievich, Czar, the Terrible (1530–1584). He was only three years old when his father Czar Vasíly III died (1533). Because of Ivan's minority, his mother Czarina Eléna assumed the regency. She died in 1538, whereupon the administration of the state fell into the hands of the Boyard Duma (Council). Countless intrigues ensued, many villainies were perpetrated by the rival boyard parties; oppression and persecution became general; the people suffered injustice of every kind. The young Czarévich, an extraordinarily gifted,

well-educated and observing boy, could not help viewing these abuses with deep concern. In 1547, he ascended the Moscow Throne, and the first years of his reign were marked by a series of wise and just administrative acts designed to alleviate the lot of the common people and to curb widespread injustice. In 1550 an important Code of Laws (*Sudébnik*) was enacted; it introduced the principle of self-government. On the initiative of the Czar the first printing office was established in Moscow (1563). In 1552, the Russian army headed by the Czar captured Kazán, the stronghold and capital of the Tartar Kazán Czardom, and in 1556, the Tartar capital, Astrakhan, on the Caspian Sea was annexed to the Russian state. These two victories put an end to Mongol aspirations as far as Russia was concerned. The Czar became a great hero in the opinion of the people, especially because it was also during his reign that Siberia became part of the Russian Czardom (1584). However, the last years of his reign were obscured with cruel persecution and wholesale executions of the boyards, whom he suspected—not without reason—of disloyalty.

[J]

Jukóvsky, Vasíly Andréevich (1783–1852), famous Russian romantic poet; brilliant translator of Johann Uhland (1787–1862), Schiller (1759–1805) and Goethe (1749–1832). Among his best original poems the following should be mentioned: *Svetlána* (1811), *The Bard in the Camp of Russian Warriors* (1812), *The*

Bard in the Kremlin (1814), *The Sleeping Czarévna* (1831). Púshkin thus characterized Jukóvsky's poetry:

His verses' captivating fascination
Through centuries will stand the jeal-
.ous test:
Youth, hearing them, will sigh for
fame's elation,
And silent Grief in them will find its
rest,
And mirthful Joy, will pause in meditation.

(Brasol's version)

Emperor Nicholas I (1825–1855) appointed Jukóvsky tutor to his eldest
son Grand Duke Alexander, the future Czar-Liberator, Alexander II
(1855–1881).

[K]

Kaidánov, Iván Kuzmích (1782–
1843), Russian historian, professor
of history at the Imperial Lyceum.

Karamzín, Nikolaí Mikháilovich
(1766–1826), famous Russian historian, the author of *The History of
the Russian State* (1816–1824). This
monumental work (11 volumes) became possible of achievement due
to the fact that Emperor Alexander
I had granted him a liberal subsidy
out of his own funds. (See Imperial
Ukaz of October 31, 1803.) Karamzín's *History* proved a great success
and is considered a classic. According
to Púshkin, Karamzín "revealed to
the Russians their own history." Karamzín was also the author of sentimental stories *Poor Liza* (1792) and
Natalia, the Boyard's Daughter
(1792). His *Letters of a Russian*

Traveller (1791) reveal "a fresh, human observation and a tender feeling for men and nature" (Laurie
Magnus, *A Dictionary of European
Literature*, p. 267, London, 1927).

Katkóv. See *Moscow Gazette.*

Kazán, Capture of. See Iván Vasílievich.

Khlestakóv, Iván Alexándrovich, the
"hero" of Gógol's play, *Revizor,*
is a petty young member of the administrative flock serving in one of
the countless St. Petersburg chanceries. As the curtain rises (Act
II) we see him stranded in a third-
rate hotel in Dmukhanóvsky's town.
The queer behavior of Khlestakóv:
the mysterious purpose that brought
him to a town which no one would
have reason to visit anyway, and
more convincing still, the fact that
he is stubbornly declining to settle
for his room and board,—all these
combined are irrefutable proof, to
the provincial officialdom, that Khlestakóv is no other than the much-
dreaded government inspector in disguise whose forthcoming arrival has
been revealed in a private letter
intercepted by the local postmaster.
Once arrived at this conclusion, the
city fathers hasten to pay Khlestakóv formal visits. He quickly sizes
up the situation and cleverly begins
to insinuate that he is the inspector
after all. Among the ensuing "comedy
of errors" Khlestakóv, the immortal
liar, with an air of virginal innocence,
confesses to his duped visitors that
he is short of funds, and they cheer-
fully leave with him their little cash
souvenirs in the hope that their of-

ficial sins will be overlooked. Dmu-khanóvsky invites Khlestakóff to stay as a guest at his house, where the young impostor promptly tries to make love, first to Miss Dmukhanóv-sky, and then to her virtuous mother. The latter, though quite pleased with his attentions, modestly reminds him: "But may I remark that, in a way, I am . . . married," to which Khles-takóff unhesitatingly remarks: "That's nothing. For love there's no distinc-tion. . . ." At last, however, he pro-poses to the sweet miss. Of course, this "honor" is gladly accepted by proud papa and mama Dmukhanóv-sky. At this juncture Khlestakóff departs from the Godforsaken town —ostensibly to pay a flying visit to his "rich uncle." He promises to be back in a day or two, and then the wedding is going to be celebrated. No sooner has Khlestakóff departed than his fraud is revealed by post-master Shpékin. He intercepts a let-ter which the "revisor" mails to a friend in St. Petersburg. In this epistle, candidly and with biting sar-casm, he recounts his provincial ad-venture. As the curtain is about to fall the arrival of the real revisor is announced—much to the horror of Dmukhanóvsky and his enlightened colleagues.

Khomiakóv, Aleksei Stepánovich (1804–1860), noted Russian historian, the author of *Notes on World His-tory* (1838 ff. Completed by the end of the Forties); theologian; critic; one of the foremost Slavophiles.

Kífa Mókievich, a queer fellow, a character in Gógol's (q.v.) novel *Dead Souls*. Speaking of him A. V. Drujínin, a noted Russian critic (1824–1864) remarked: "Our deep thinker Bouikovídov, at times, re-minded one of Kífa Mókievich. Now and then such thoughts and infer-ences invaded his brain that there was nothing the listener could do but throw up his arms and start howling in a most unbecoming voice." (*New Notes of a Journalist.*) Gógol himself said: "Kífa Mókievich is a chap of stubborn disposition."

Kífa Mókievschina is a state or dis-position akin to the character and proclivities of Kífa Mókievich (q.v.).

Koltzóv, Aleksei Vasílievich (1809–1842), noted Russian poet of humble descent. His father, a Vorónej com-moner, traded in cattle, timber and grain. Koltzóv's *Songs,* of which the first eighteen were published in 1835 by N. V. Stankévich (1809–1840), a young Russian amateur philosopher, are dedicated to the life and labors of the common people — peasants, wagoners, tradesmen. The steppe was his element. Koltzóv was an ardent admirer of Púshkin and a friend of Bielínsky. One of Koltzóv's best poems *The Forest* (1837) was dedi-cated to the memory of Púshkin.

Kopeíkin, Captain, in Gogol's *Dead Souls* a legendary brigand, a half-pay officer who, although he had lost one arm and one leg, had placed himself at the head of a band of robbers in the forests of the Ryazán province. The story of Captain Kopeíkin told by the Postmaster, forms part of Chapter X, Part I, of Gogol's novel.

Koróbochka, in Gógol's *Dead Souls*— an ignorant woman, a landowner from whom Tchítchikov (q.v.) purchases a few "dead souls."

Kostomárov, Nikolaí Ivánovich (1817–1885), noted Russian historian; professor of Russian history at the Universities of Kiev and St. Petersburg.

Kovalévsky, Egór Petróvich (1809–1868), noted Russian traveller and belles-lettrist.

Kraiévsky, Andreí Alexándrovich (1810–1889), editor of *The Voice* (q.v.), and *The Domestic Records* (q.v.).

Krestóvsky, Vsévolod Vladímirovich (1840–1895), Russian novelist, author of a once popular novel *The Petersburg Dens* (1863).

Krylóv, Iván Andréevich. See "If seated in a row."

Kuíndji, Arkhíp Ivánovich (1842–1910), brilliant Russian painter, a maestro of "lyrical" landscape, in which the moon and sun light effects are treated with ingenious insight.

Kuzmá Prutkóv is a nom de plume which was adopted by three poets: Count Alexei Konstantínovich Tolstóy (1817–1875), Alexeí Mikháilovich Jemchújnikov (1821–1908), and his brother Vladímir Mikháilovich Jemchújnikov (1830–1884). Kuzmá Prutkóv is a self-satisfied ass—much like Henri Monnier's (1805–1877) famous Prudhomme, who utters with an air of profound wisdom all sorts of nonsense and travesties: ("One cannot embrace the unembraceable"; "When thou throwest pebbles into the water look at the circles on its surface produced thereby, otherwise thy occupation will be useless"; "Deprive a man of society, and he will remain in solitude," etc.). Some of these "aphorisms" are full of irresistible humor, and even in our day enjoy real popularity. Of course, the poets attached no significance to these burlesque productions, which appeared from time to time in the monthly magazine *The Contemporary* in the section called "Literary Hotchpotch."

[L]

"Lame coopers who continue to construct the moon on Gorókhovaia Street." This is an allusion to Gógol's (q.v.) story *Memoirs of a Lunatic*. The "hero" of the story is Póprischin, a petty government functionary who imagines that he is Ferdinand VII, King of Spain. Under the date "February the Thirtieth" he records among other things the following: "But the moon is usually constructed in Hamburg, and it is very poorly constructed. I wonder why England fails to take notice of this. *The moon is constructed by a lame cooper, and one can see that the fool has no conception of what the moon is.*" Gorókhovaia Street was one of the principal thoroughfares in St. Petersburg. Dostoiévsky's reference to this street is incorrect. In Gógol's story Gorókhovaia Street is mentioned in connection with a barber who, according to Póprischin, in company with a midwife, seeks to spread Mohammedanism all over the world.

Lavrétzky, the hero of Turgénev's (q.v.) novel *Gentlefolk's Nest.*

Ledochówski, Count Mieczíslaw (1822–1902), Polish Jesuit, a favorite of Pope Pius IX. In 1875, he was appointed Cardinal. In 1874, he was sentenced by a German court to two years' imprisonment for anti-German propaganda. In 1876, he proceeded to Rome, where he became the leader of the anti-German party. In 1885, he was appointed to the important office of Segretario dei Brevi.

Lérmontov. *See "The Tale" about Kaláshnikov.*

Leskóv, Nikolaí Semiónovich (1831–1895), noted Russian novelist, the author of *Cathedral Folks* (1872), *The Enchanted Pilgrim, The Flea, The Devil's Dolls, The Ensealed Angel* (1873), etc. His style is rich and colorful with outstanding lexical qualities which were acknowledged by Dahl (q.v.), the famous Russian lexicographer. Leskóv's best stories and novels deal with the delineation of the customs and mode of living of the clergy, schismatics and Old-Believers.

The Liberator-Emperor: Alexander II (1855–1881). He is called "the Liberator" because by the stroke of his pen he liberated 22,000,000 Russian peasants (see Manifesto). Despite a series of far-reaching liberal reforms, the revolutionists, who, in 1879, organized under the name "Will of the People" (*Naródnaia Vólia*),

with headquarters in London, made a series of daring attempts upon the life of the Czar, and on March 1, 1881, he was killed by a bomb in St. Petersburg.

Liebig, Baron Justus von (1803–1872), noted German chemist.

Liprándi, Iván Ivánovich (1790–1880), Major-General, Russian historian. He helped to uncover the revolutionary activities of Petrashévsky (q.v.).

Liteínaia Street, later Liteíni Prospect—one of the principal streets in St. Petersburg.

Lithuanian Castle, an obsolete penitentiary in St. Petersburg. It was demolished during the early days of the 1917 revolution.

Lomonósov, Mikhaíl Vasílievich (1711–1765), famous Russian grammarian, chemist, physicist and poet. Brückner, the noted German historian of Russian literature, in his *Geschichte der Russischen Literatur,* p. 81, thus defined Lomonósov's scientific status: "metallurgist, geologist, chemist, electrician, astronomer, politico-economist, statistician, geographer, historian, philologist, critic, poet." Lomonósov was the son of a well-to-do peasant in the province of Archangel, who was engaged in fishery in the White Sea. At the age of nineteen, Mikhaíl Lomonósov left his parents' house and proceeded on foot to Moscow (some 800 miles) in order to educate himself. There he matriculated in the Slavic-Greek-Latin Academy; subsequently the government sent him to Freiburg, Germany, for the study of mining. Upon his return to Russia, he began to distinguish himself by his scientific discoveries in the fields of chemistry, physics and metallurgy; his thermology antedated by several decades the work of the Western European physicists, and in chemistry he was the precursor of Lavoisier (1743–1794). J. J. Shouválov, one of the most enlightened and influential statesmen during the reign of Empress Elizavéta Petróvna (1741–1761), the daughter of Peter the Great, gave full encouragement to Lomonósov, who soon became the leading spirit in the work of the Imperial Academy of Sciences. In 1755, he completed his *Russian Grammar*, which laid the foundation of the Russian literary and living language as distinguished from the ancient Church-Slavonic tongue. Lomonósov was elected honorary member of the Académie Française, the Stockholm and Bologna Academies of Science. The all-embracing genius of Lomonósov makes him one of the most impressive figures in the history of modern science. A comprehensive record of Lomonósov's work and achievements appears in *The Russian Biographical Dictionary*, vol. X, pp. 593–628.

[M]

Magnítzky, Mikhaíl Leóntievich (1778–1855) one of the most hideous court intriguers during the reign of Emperor Alexander I (1801–1825), a close friend and collaborator of M. M. Speránsky (1772–1839), an avowed liberal and mason, the author of the Institution of Ministries (1802) and of the State (Imperial) Council. At the same time Magnítzky posed as a devoted admirer of the ultra-conservative General Count A. A. Arakchéev (1769–1834). On March 17, 1812, Speránsky and Magnítzky were arrested on charges of conspiracy to undermine the monarchy and of conducting secret negotiations with Napoleon, who was just then busily preparing his invasion of Russia. Both men were exiled. However, in 1816, not only were they permitted to return to the capital but Speránsky was appointed Governor of the Pénza province and Magnítzky — Vice-Governor of the Vorónej province. Subsequently he was placed in charge of the Kazán district of public education.

Makóvsky, Vladímir Egórovich (1846–1920), a noted Russian genre painter. Among his best canvases are *The Failure of a Bank, The Optimist and the Pessimist* and *The Comforter*.

Manifesto of February 19, 1861. Emperor Alexander II (1855–1881) issued the famous Manifesto liberating 22,000,000 Russian peasants with land. This historical document ended with the words: "Cross thyself, Orthodox people, and invoke with us God's blessing upon thy free labor, the pledge of thy domestic happiness and public welfare." Serfdom was thus peacefully abolished, and the peasants became owners of 318,257,527 acres of arable land. This great reform was carried out on the initiative of the Czar himself. In this difficult work he was assisted by a group of enlightened and patriotic men, among whom Úrij Samárin, N. A. Miliútin, Prince V. A. Cherkássky, Grand Duke Konstantín Nikoláievich and J. I. Rostóvtzev deserve particular mention.

Manílov, in Gogol's *Dead Souls*, a character typifying an idle, incurable dreamer.

Márko-Vovchók, pen name of María Alexándrovna Márkovich (1834–1907), a mediocre woman novelist of liberal views; she wrote both in Russian and in the Little Russian, or Ukranian, dialect. Turgénev translated into Russian her *Ukranian Popular Stories* (1859).

Matéjko, Jan Alojzyn (1838–1893), famous Polish historical and portrait painter.

The Memoirs of a Lunatic by Gógol —a fantastic diary of a lunatic; it is included in Gógol's *Arabesques* (1835).

Mendeléev, Dmítri Ivánovich (1834–1907), famous Russian chemist, creator of the Periodic Table.

Meschérsky, Prince Vladímir Petróvich (1839–1914), editor of the conservative weekly magazine *The Citizen (Grajdanín)*, which was founded in St. Petersburg in 1872. Dostoiévsky and several prominent Russian novelists, as well as the outstanding poets of the Seventies and Eighties, including Count Alexis Tolstóy, A. N. Maikov, F. J. Tútchev and A. N. Apoúkhtin, were regular contributors to *The Citizen*. Meschérsky's

novel *One of Our Bismarcks*, depicting the Russian *beau monde*, deserves mention. Meschérsky is also the author of *My Reminiscences*, 1897–1912 (3 volumes).

The Messenger of Europe—an influential liberal monthly magazine, founded by N. M. Karamzín (q.v.) in 1802. In 1830, the periodical was discontinued. Its publication was resumed in 1866. Goncharóv's (q.v.) novel *The Abyss* was printed in *The Messenger of Europe*.

"Metal" and "fiend," literally "Metal and Sulphur" (*"metall i júpel"*). (Page 1044.) The word *jupel* in Russian means "burning sulphur"; in an allegoric sense it means a scarecrow, a monster bugbear or something of this kind. Some ignorant Moscow merchant wives in Ostróvsky's (q.v.) comedies were afraid of the word "metal"; others would be scared by the word "júpel." Thus one of these "heroines" says: "Truly, I am so very timid. . . . Whenever I hear the word '*júpel*' pronounced, my hands and feet begin to tremble." (*Difficult Days*, II, 2.)

Mikhailóvsky, N. K. *See The Domestic Records.*

Mir. See Communal landownership.

Molchálin, one of the characters in Griboiédov's comedy *Woe from Wit* (q.v.). Molchálin is the incarnation of triviality, subservience, "moderation and punctuality," a "yes-man" in a most despicable sense.

The Moscow Gazette, a conservative

daily, subsidized by the government. In 1851 Mikhaíl Nikíforovich Katkóv (1818–1887), one of Russia's most brilliant publicists, was made editor of that newspaper. In 1855, he founded the influential monthly magazine *The Russian Messenger* (*Rússki Véstnik*). Katkóv started his literary career as a liberal Anglophile but subsequently became one of the pillars of Russian Toryism. His philosophical conceptions were largely derived from Friedrich Schelling (1775–1854).

Múrometz, Ilyá (from the town Múrom of the Níjni-Nóvgorod province), most beloved legendary hero of the epoch of St. Vladimir, Grand Duke of Kiev (980–1015) under whom Russia embraced Christianity (988). In Russian folk-lore Ilyá Murómetz symbolizes not only gallantry and elemental "earth" force but equally the common Christian Russian people. His many exploits are directed against the pagan nomadic tribes, which were a real menace to the safety of the then young Russian state.

[N]

Necháiev case.—In 1869, Sergeí Gennádievich Necháiev, the son of a butler and a former school teacher, organized in Moscow a secret society under the name "People's Revenge" for the purpose of forcibly overthrowing the government and assassinating Emperor Alexander II (1855–1881). In one of his leaflets, Necháiev proclaimed that he would subject the Czar "to a cruel, solemn execution in the presence of the liberated plebeians and on the ruins of the state." Necháiev was an anarchist of the Bakúnin school (M. A. Bakúnin — 1814–1876); his cherished aim was to precipitate, first in Russia and thereafter in Europe, political and social chaos. He demanded from his associates blind obedience, and every member of the group was obligated to spy upon the others. The activities of this organization came to an abrupt end, owing to the fact that on November 21, 1869, in Moscow, the body of a certain Ivánov, a student of the local Agricultural Academy, was discovered in a lonely spot. It was soon found out that the murder had been committed by Alexis Kuznetzóv with the assistance of other accomplices. Kuznetzóv made a full confession and stated that he had murdered Ivánov at the instigation of Necháiev who suspected Ivánov of disloyalty to the organization. Kuznetzóv was tried by a jury, convicted and sentenced to ten years of hard labor. Necháiev managed to escape abroad. Dostoiévsky ingeniously depicted this case in his prophetic novel *The Possessed* (1871).

Nekrásov, Nikolai Alekséevich (1821–1877). The poem *Vlas* was written in 1854. In his tendentious poetry he expressed the sentiments of a "repenting nobleman." His magnum opus is the long poem *Who Lives Well in Russia* (1873). Among the other best remembered poems the following may be cited: *The Song to Eriómushka* (1858), *The Hawkers* (1861), *Frost—The Red Nose* (1863), *The Bear Hunt* (1867) and *The Russian Women* (1871–1872), dedicated to Princess Troubetzkáya and Princess Volkónskaya, who voluntarily followed their husbands, convicted of participating in the Decembrist revolt (q.v.) into exile.

Névsky Prospéct—the principal street in St. Petersburg.

The New Times, an influential Russian daily, with Slavophile and nationalistic leanings. In 1876 A. S. Suvórin became its editor.

Níkon, Patriarch of Russia (1605–1681), son of a peasant. At twelve he fled from his home and as a lay-brother entered the Saint Makáry Monastery on the Volga. Subsequently his relatives succeeded in persuading him to leave the monastery and to return to civilian life. He married and became a village priest. He had children, but they died. Thereupon he persuaded his wife to take the veil and at the same time he entered the Ezérsky Monastery near the river Onéga, where he soon became prior. In connection with some needs of his friars he proceeded to Moscow, and there he was introduced to Czar Alexeí Mikháilovich (q.v.). Níkon's religious zeal, keen mind, great learning and exemplary life produced a strong impression upon the Czar, and a close friendship developed between the two men. Owing to the Czar's influence Níkon was appointed Metropolitan of Nóvgorod. Following the death of Patriarch Joseph, Níkon was elected Patriarch of Russia (July 25, 1652), and the title of "Great Sovereign" was conferred upon him. His influ-

ence upon the affairs of state became so strong that he virtually became co-ruler with the Czar, and when, in 1654, during the Russo-Polish war, the Czar left Moscow to join the army, the administration of the state was entrusted to Níkon. Gradually Níkon grew arrogant and haughty, especially in his daily relations with the boyards. Upon the Czar's return to Moscow (1657), friction developed between him and the Patriarch which finally led to an open break. In 1658, Níkon renounced the title of Patriarch and retired to the Resurrection Monastery near Moscow. There he lived eight years in voluntary exile; but in 1666, the All-Russian Sobor unanimously condemned Níkon, officially deprived him of the title of Patriarch and exiled him to a remote monastery on the White Sea. There he remained fifteen years, and only in 1681, he received permission to return to Moscow. On his way to the capital he died. Níkon's patriarchate was marked with the beginning of the great schism in the Russian Orthodox church as a result of the revision and correction of the old prayer books.

The Nose—a fantastic story by Gógol which is included in his *Arabesques* (1835).

[O]

Oblómov, the famous novel (1858) by Iván Alexándrovich Goncharóv (1812–1891) is one of the finest specimens of Russian realistic fiction. Not only is Oblómov himself, the "hero" of the story, the incarnation of mental apathy, lack of initiative, repugnance against action of any kind, but he embodies the fundamental traits of a typically Russian disease which was widespread among the upper classes in the Thirties, Forties and Fifties, and which became known as *Oblómovschina* or *Oblómovism* — pathological laziness, despite natural kindness and intellectual acumen. This was the direct outgrowth of serfdom, where the master had at his disposal "three hundred Zakhárs" (Zakhár — Oblómov's manservant, or better—"man nurse") to comply with his slightest whim. Goncharóv, one of the outstanding Russian novelists, was also the author of *An Ordinary Story* (1847), *The Abyss* (1868), *Frigate Pallas* (1856) and *Million Torments* (1871), a brilliant critical evaluation of Griboyédov's immortal comedy *Woe from Wit* (q.v.).

Óbshchina. See Communal landownership.

Œil-de-bœuf in architecture—a circular or oval window generally used in the XVIIth and XVIIIth Centuries.

Old-Believers, Russian dissenters, who bitterly opposed the Church reform undertaken by Patriarch Níkon (1653–1657). Among other measures, the Patriarch decreed that the sign of the cross be performed with three fingers joined together, symbolizing the Holy Trinity, and not with two fingers, as hitherto, which was regarded as an indication of the dual nature of Christ—the divine and the human. In 1654, a Church Sobor, or Conference, convened by the Patri-

arch, adopted a resolution by virtue of which it was decided to carry out an extensive revision of the prayer books, which, in fact, were replete with all sorts of errors; these were due to the negligence of the copyists as well as to the conflicting texts from which copies were executed. On the other hand, the Patriarch prohibited the use and worship of "Latin" icons, *i.e.*, those painted by Western artists. These and similar decrees caused much resentment on the part of those Orthodox Russians who adhered to the old church traditions. The persecution of the Old-Believers was brought to an end by the Imperial manifesto of April 17, 1905, which granted the Russian people absolute freedom of worship and religion. In particular, the Old-Believers received permission to erect their churches, while the Old-Believers' priests were exempted from serving in the armed forces of Russia.

Ostróvsky, Alexánder Nikoláievich (1823–1886), the foremost Russian dramatist. For over half a century the Russian repertoire was wholly dependent upon his comedies and dramas, among which the following are the more popular: *The Poor Fiancée* (1852), *Poverty Is No Crime* (1854), *The Thunder-storm* (1859), *The Forest* (1871), *Wolves and Sheep* (1875) and *Guilty without Guilt* (1884). All these are genre plays depicting the customs and ways of living of the Russian middle class, particularly those of the provincial and Moscow merchants. In 1879, Ostrovsky wrote his delightful and justly famous *Snow Maiden* (*Snegúrochka*)

(1873)—"a Spring fairy tale in four acts and a prologue," to which N. A. Rímsky-Kórsakov (1844–1908) composed his immortal opera bearing the same name (1880–1881). Ostróvsky firmly established the realistic tradition in Russian drama.

[P]

Pechórin, the principal character in Lérmontov's *A Hero of Our Days,* is one of those "superfluous men" whose prototype was portrayed by Púshkin in his Eugene Onegin (1823–1831). See Dostoievsky's analysis of this type in his famous Púshkin speech (*Diary,* 1880).

Peredél. See Communal landowner-ship.

Peróv, V. G. (1834–1882), a noted Russian painter. His is one of the best portraits of Dostoiévsky. Peróv's art is didactic, with a satirical flavor. His pictures *The Fowler* (1870), *The Fisherman* (1871) and *The Hunters* are masterpieces of Russian genre painting.

Petrashévsky, Mikhail Vasílievich (1819–1867), a Russian government official in the Ministry of Foreign Affairs. In the Forties his house in St. Petersburg became a center for Friday evening discussions of political subjects. Most of the young men of the Petrashévsky circle (Petrashévtzi) were idealists naïvely believing in the blessings of the socialistic dogma, followers of François Fourier's (1772–1837) doctrine, as expounded in his work *Théorie de l'Unité Universelle* (1822) and of Claude Henri de Saint-Simon (1760–1825), a forerunner of revolutionary socialists of subsequent patterns. The Petrashévtzi were planning to equip a clandestine printing office. On April 24, 1849, Petrashévsky's house was raided by the police, and twenty-one members of his group were arrested and condemned to be shot. Among these was Dostoiévsky. At the last moment their sentences were commuted to various terms of imprisonment and exile.

"Petropávlooka" is a colloquial name for the fortress of Sts. Peter and Paul in St. Petersburg on the Neva, which was built by order of Peter the Great following the foundation of the new capital on May 16, 1703.

"Piccola Bestia." The tarantula incident recorded on Page 427 ff. occurred in Florence, in 1869.

Písemsky, Alekseí Feofiláktovich (1820–1881), noted Russian novelist of the realistic school. A man of unquestionable talent, Písemsky gave in his works *The Muff* (1850), *A Thousand Souls* (1858), *The Agitated Sea* (1863), *The Bourgeois* (1877) and *The Masons* (1880) a vivid picture of Russian life in the Forties and during the transition period preceding and immediately following the liberation of the Russian peasants. Radical critics vehemently attacked him for *The Agitated Sea* in which he portrayed (Part IV of the novel) Russian nihilists residing abroad and the disintegration of rural life in Russia as a result of the peasants' reform. His *Bitter Fate* (1860) is a powerful realistic drama, a worthy precursor of Count Leo Tolstoy's *The Power of Darkness* (1886).

Pogódin, Mikhaíl Petróvich (1800–1875), son of a peasant. Noted publicist and historian; appointed professor of Russian history at the Imperial Moscow University. In 1841, he founded in Moscow a conservative monthly magazine, *Moskvitiánin,* with a marked Slavophile tendency; this magazine was continued till 1855. Pogódin's principal works are: *On the Origin of Russia* (1824); *Historico-Critical Sketches* (1846) and *Ancient Russia prior to the Mongol Yoke* (1872).

Polish insurrection (1863–1864). France, Austria and England sent threatening notes to the Russian government demanding all sorts of concessions to the Poles. These demands were emphatically rejected. Poland was then divided into ten provinces which became an integral part of the Russian Empire.

Polónsky, Yákov Petróvich (1820–1898), one of Russia's greatest lyric poets. The metrical and lexical qualities of his verses are superb. Turgénev (q.v.) and Gógol praised highly his noble poetic talent with its humanistic leanings and romantic moods. In his Caucasian poems he painted magnificent pictures of the majestic scenery. *Grasshopper — The Musician* (1863) is among his best poems.

Póprischin — the "titular counsellor Póprischin" in Gógol's *Memoirs of a Lunatic,* who imagines himself Ferdinand VII, King of Spain.

Potúgin, one of the characters in Turgénev's (q.v.) novel *Smoke* (1867). He is a sworn Westerner.

Powder Plant—some six miles from St. Petersburg.

Prutkóv. *See* Kuzmá Prutkóv.

Pugachióv (Pugachëv), Emelián Ivánovich (1743?–1775), a Don Cossack and impostor, who, having assumed the title of Emperor Peter III (1761–1762), organized in 1773 a rebellion against the government of Catherine II (1762–1796) and the landowners. The ranks of the rebels were recruited from among peasants, Don and Yaitzk Cossacks, ex-convicts, fugitives from justice, the Kalmucks and Kirghizes. The revolt, which first broke out in the province of Orenburg, promptly spread south, north and west along the Volga and Ural rivers, as well as toward the Caspian Sea. Wherever the rebels succeeded in capturing a town or "fortress," they subjected the landowners, government officials and loyal officers and soldiers to wholesale extermination. Pugachióv's bands captured a number of important cities (Ufá, Samára, Sarátov, Pénza, Kazán, etc.). Only in September, 1774, the government troops succeeded in capturing Pugachióv, who, under the personal supervision of Field Marshal Suvórov (q.v.) was brought to Moscow in chains. On January 10, 1775, Pugachióv and his associates were executed in Moscow. After that the revolt was soon liquidated and the devastated towns, hamlets and estates gradually restored. Púshkin depicted the Pugachióv rebellion in his novel *The Captain's Daughter*, and he also wrote *The History of Pugachióv's Rebellion*.

Pugachióv's Rebellion, The History of (1833), by Púshkin. By order of Emperor Nicholas I (1825–1855), Púshkin was given access to the secret archives and reports of the civil and military authorities concerning Pugachióv and the spread of the revolt organized and headed by him. In addition to the official material, Púshkin examined a large number of private letters dating back to the Seventies of the XVIIIth Century, unofficial records of the revolt, etc. To make the publication of *The History* possible, the Emperor granted Púshkin a loan of 20,000 rubles ($10,-000). See Púshkin's *Diary*, under March 6, 1834.

Púshkin, Alexander S. (May 26, 1799–January 29, 1837), was born in Moscow. In October, 1811, he entered the Imperial Lyceum at Czárskoye Seló, then the summer residence of Emperor Alexander I. Púshkin's first poems, light and imitative, date back to the early part of 1812. In 1817, he graduated at the Lyceum and proceeded to St. Petersburg, where he joined the literary association, "Arzamás," of which Karamzín (q.v.), and Joukóvsky (q.v.), the former a noted historian, the latter a gifted romantic poet, were the leading members. During this early period, Púshkin wrote a long series of lyrical pieces, love stanzas, elegies and idylls which, though fully expressive of his youthful sentiments, revealed remarkable poetic power. In 1820, he wrote his first long poem, *Ruslán and Ludmíla*. Early in that year, in consequence of his mischievous epigrams, having invoked upon himself the displeasure of the Government, Púshkin was ordered to leave St. Petersburg for Ekaterinosláv on a government mission. There he fell ill, and he received permission to proceed for a cure to the Caucasus. It was while there that he began studying Byron. Having spent several months in the Caucasus, he proceeded to the Crimea, and thence to Kishinév in Bessarabia. Impressed by the Southern scenery, and under the influence of Byron, Púshkin wrote three poems: *The Caucasian Captive* (1821), *The Bakhchissaraí Fountain* (1823) and *The Gypsies* (1824). In 1824, Púshkin left Kishinév for Odessa, where, again, he got himself into trouble. Accused of bad behavior and of having uttered atheistic opinions, he was ordered to leave for Mikháilovskoie, his own estate in the Province of Pskov. Púshkin remained in this exile approximately two years; he lived there all alone with no one but Arína Rodiónovna, his old peasant nurse, to brighten his seclusion. The enforced sojourn in Mikháilovskoie proved beneficial to the poet's mental growth. There he conceived and completed his tragedy *Borís Godunóv* (1825), which was written under the marked influence of Shakespeare. During the same period he wrote the major part of *Eugene Onégin*, his *magnum opus*. In September, 1826, Púshkin received permission to leave Mikháilovskoie, and he proceeded to Moscow, where he was given an audience by Emperor Nicholas I. The two subsequent years Púshkin spent partly in Moscow and partly in St. Petersburg. In 1828, he completed *Poltáva*, a long poem dedicated to the memory of Peter the Great and the well known battle of Poltáva (1709), where the Russians defeated the invading army of Charles XII, King of Sweden. In 1829, Púshkin proposed to Natalie Goncharóva, a recognized beauty of the early Thirties, and on February 18, 1831, he married her in Moscow. In the autumn of 1830, he spent several weeks in Bóldino, another estate of his, in the Province of Níjni-Nóvgorod. There, within the brief period of four or five weeks, he wrote four miniature tragedies: *The Miser Knight; The Feast During the Plague; Don Juan;* and *Mozart and Salieri.* Each one of these tragedies is an unsurpassed masterpiece. In addition, he conceived and completed *The Little House in Kolómna,* a long poem in octaves. Beginning with the same year, Púshkin turned his attention to prose. In 1833, he completed his last big poetic work *The Bronze Horseman*—perhaps the most remarkable of his major poems —again portraying Peter the Great. The best of his works in prose are *The Bielkin Tales* (1830), *Doubróvsky* (1833), *The Queen of Spades* (1833), *History of Pougachióv's Rebellion* (1833) and *The Captain's Daughter* (1836). Insulted by the attentions which Baron Haeckern-Dantes, a young Guard officer, was paying to Natalie Púshkin, the poet, on January 27, 1837, fought a duel with his rival, and was fatally wounded by him. Púshkin died in St. Petersburg on January 29, 1837.

Pýpin, Alexánder Nikoláievich (1833–1904), noted Russian historian, publicist and historian of literature. In 1898, he was elected to the Imperial Academy of Sciences. His principal works are: *Russian Masonry in the XVIIIth and First Quarter of the XIXth Century* (in book form first published in 1916), *History of Russian Literature,* 4 volumes (1898–1899), *History of Russian Ethnography,* 4 volumes (1890–1892), *Bielínsky: His Life and Correspondence* (1876). Editor of the literary works of Empress Catherine II.

[Q]

The Queen of Spades, a novel by Púshkin (1833) to which P. I. Tchaikovsky (1840–1893) wrote his opera bearing the same title.

[R]

Rastrelli, Bartolomeo Francesco (1700–1771), famous Italian-Russian architect. He came to Russia from Italy at the age of sixteen and settled in St. Petersburg. The following are his best known buildings: the Winter Palace in St. Petersburg (1732–1736), the Great Palace at Czárskoe Seló (1750), the Smólni Monastery in St. Petersburg (1748), the St. Andrew Cathedral in Kiev (1747–1767), the palace of Count Stróganov in St. Petersburg, and the palace in Peterhof.

A Raw Youth, a novel by Dostoiévsky (1875).

Rectilinear: Dostoiévsky uses this word in the sense of a single-track mind devoid of flexibility.

Redemption sums, or redemption payments, or redemption loans, were payments which were made by the Russian Government to the landowners for their land allotted to the liberated peasants (February 19, 1861). These payments were supposed to have been repaid by the peasants to the Treasury in annual installments over a period of forty-nine years. However, a considerable portion of this indebtedness eventually was cancelled, and the peasants became owners of the lands tilled by them, acquiring full title thereto. Redemption payments, or loans, were made in the form of interest-bearing securities guaranteed by the State. In this connection it may be of interest to note that on February 19, 1861, i.e., two years before the abolition of slavery in the United States, over 20,000,000 Russian peasants were liberated from bondage by Emperor Alexander II. The Imperial manifesto liberating the peasants was accompanied by an act granting them roughly 318,257,527 acres of land suitable for tilling. On the average every one of the 8,450,782 peasant farms contained 37.18 acres. By January 1, 1917, that is, prior to the revolution, the peasants in European Russia owned about 50 per cent of the entire available acreage.

Redstock, Lord Grenville, an Oxford graduate. He served in the British Army, reaching the rank of Colonel. Ever since his Oxford days he was interested in missionary work. He came to St. Petersburg in the Seventies of the XIXth Century as a self-appointed missionary. He preached the doctrine that faith — and faith alone—in Jesus Christ is necessary for the salvation of the soul. Good deeds, according to him, serve merely as an obstacle to salvation. The Church, as an ecclesiastical institution, must be abolished; sacraments are worthless and sin is of no consequence so long as faith prevails. For a while Lord Redstock's doctrine was in vogue among the fashionable sets of St. Petersburg society. Among the most ardent disciples of Lord Redstock was Colonel Vasíly Alexándrovich Páshkov, a man of great wealth. For the propagation of the tenets of Redstockism he established in 1876 in St. Petersburg a Society for the Encouragement of Religious and Ethical Reading. He was the founder of a spiritual sect known as *Páshkovschina.*

The Reformer—Dostoiévsky refers to Peter the Great.

Repetílov, in Griboyédov's comedy *Woe from Wit* (q.v.), is a tireless causeur and a pathological liar.

Répin, Ilyá Efínovich (1844–1918), famous Russian painter of Cossack descent. His *Haulers, John the Terrible and His Son John,* and especially *The Cossacks' Reply to Sultan Machmond IV* are universally admired. In 1894, he was appointed professor of historical painting at the Imperial Academy of Arts in St. Petersburg.

Rúdin (1856), one of Turgénev's (q. v.) best-known novels. Rúdin's place is in the long gallery of the so-called "superfluous men" portrayed in Russian belles-lettres.

"A Russian Lady, Countess K." (Page 375.) Countess Kúshelev-Bezboródko.

The Russian Messenger, founded by Katkóv, was one of the most influential and widely read monthly magazines. Among its contributors were the Slavophiles S. T., K. S. and I S. Aksákov (q.v.); the Westerners I. S. Turgénev (q.v.), A. N. Pýpin (q.v.) and Boris Chichérin; the gifted poet Y. P. Polónsky (q.v.), the famous novelist Goncharóv (q. v.) and many other noted authors.

The Russian Women (1871–1872), one of the best-known poems by N. A. Nekrasov (q.v.).

[S]

Saltykóv, Mikháil Evgráfovich (1826–1889) (pen name—Schedrin), of noble descent, Russia's outstanding satirist; he was nicknamed by the rightists "the Russian Vice-Robespierre," as an allusion to the fact that this radical thinker held the office of vice-governor of the province of Riazán (1858) and later of the province of Tver (1860). In 1862, he resigned temporarily from government service, and became editor of the radical monthly *Contemporary* (*Sovreménnik*) in place of Chernyshévsky (q.v.), who had been arrested for revolutionary activities. Shortly thereafter, however, he was appointed president of the Pénza Court of Exchequer. At the age of forty-four, he tendered his resignation, and from that time on he gave all his time to literary pursuits. It is noteworthy that Saltykóv's satire mercilessly and mordantly chastised not only the Russian bureaucracy but likewise the loose-mouthed liberalism of the Sixties and Seventies, the bushy-haired nihilists and the radical intelligentsia. His ironical allusions to Chernyshévsky's novel *What Is to Be Done?* caused great indignation in the leftist camp. His best-known works are: *Provincial Sketches* (1856–1857), *Pompadours and Pompadouresses* (1863–1873), *Well-Intentioned Speeches* (1872–1876), *Messrs. Golovlyóvi* (1872–1876), *In the Realm of Moderation and Accuracy* (1874–1877), *Tales* (1880–1885) and *Bygone Days in Poshehónie* (1887–1889).

Samárin, Úry Fiódorovich (1819–1876), one of the outstanding Slavophiles and principal supporters of the liberation of the Russian peasants. Samárin was also a noted theologian.

"Save the Kings."—On February 4, 1799, Emperor Paul I (1796–1801) sent for Fieldmarshal Survórov, who was then living in exile on his estate, and ordered him to proceed to Italy to check the victorious offensive of the French revolutionary armies in Lombardy. On that occasion Paul bestowed upon the old Fieldmarshal the Grand Cross of the Order of Saint John of Jerusalem. Suvórov knelt before the Emperor and exclaimed: "God save the Sovereign!" to which

Paul said: "It is for you to save the Sovereigns!"

Schedrin. *See* Saltykóv.

Sebastopol Stories (1855) by Count Leo Tolstoý (1828–1910) are a record of his personal observations and experiences during the siege of Sebastopol (1854–1855). As a Russian army officer Tolstoý took part in the heroic defense of that fortress.

Senkóvsky, Ósip Ivánovich (1800–1858) (pen name "Baron Brambeus"), editor of the St. Petersburg magazine *Library for Reading;* professor of Oriental languages (Persian, Arabian, Tartar); translator of the novels: *The Bedouin, The Knight of the Cream-Coloured Steed* (from the Serbian language); *The Village Belle* (from the Tartar), etc.

Sennáia—a square and a slum precinct in St. Petersburg.

Sérgij of Rádonej, Saint (1314?–1392), of noble descent, founder of the famous Holy Trinity Monastery near Moscow, of which, in 1354, he became prior. This monastery acquired an important significance in Russian history, especially during the Troubled Epoch (q.v.) in Russia's struggle against the impostors and the Poles. Saint Sérgij was not only an exemplary Christian confessor of faith, but likewise a man of great political wisdom and executive ability. He became a close friend of the Moscow Metropolitan Saint Alexis, who, on many occasions, entrusted to Sérgij the difficult mission of bringing about peace between the contending dukes of the various Rus-

sian provinces. In 1380, the Moscow Grand Duke Dmítri Joánnovich proceeded to the Holy Trinity Monastery in order to consult Saint Sergij on the question whether Russia should openly challenge the Tartar rule. Saint Sérgij bestowed his blessing upon the Grand Duke and foretold his victory in the field. On September 8, 1380, the Grand Duke defeated Khan Mamái in the Kulikóv battle on the Don. This brilliant victory exercised a profound political and moral influence upon the destinies of the Russian state: (1) it raised in the minds of the people the prestige of Moscow as the rallying center of the struggle against the Tartars; (2) it proved to the nation the falsity of the legend of the Tartars' invincibility, and (3) it created in the minds of the people the conviction that the Moscow Grand Duke was the logical defender of the Russian state as a whole and *ipso facto* the political symbol of its unity (the idea of the Czar).

Skabichévsky, Alexánder Mikháilovich (1838–1910), mediocre radical critic, author of *The History of Russian Censorship* (1890), *The History of Russian Literature,* etc.

Skóbelev, Mikhaíl Dmítrievich (1843–1882), Russian general. In 1868 he was sent to Turkestan and with a brief interval remained in Central Asia till 1877. In 1874, he distinguished himself in the expedition to Khíva. For extraordinary bravery he was promoted to the rank of major-general and appointed Governor of Fergana. He took an active and prominent part in the Russo-Turkish war of 1877–1878; more particularly he distinguished himself during the siege and capture of Plevna. On September 3, 1877, he captured the Turkish stronghold Lovtcha. In January, 1878, he crossed the Balkans in a severe snowstorm, defeating the Turks at Senóva near Shípka. Because he always wore a white uniform and rode a white horse, he was called "the White General." Skóbelev was an ardent Panslavist. On July 7, 1882, he died of a heart attack in Moscow.

Skvozník-Dmukhanóvsky, Antón Antónovich, a hard, utterly dishonest bailiff who in touching union with a score of equally unscrupulous state functionaries, autocratically rules over a small and God-forsaken Russian provincial town in N. V. Gógol's (1809–1852) five-act comedy *The Revizor* (1834), which made his name immortal. (See Khlestakóv.)

Sobakévich—in Gógol's *Dead Souls*— a vulgar, gluttonous, massive landowner ("not finely tailored but solidly seamed") who sells his "dead souls" to Tchítchikov.

Solianoí Gorodók—in St. Petersburg, an agricultural museum and lecture hall.

Solovétzky Monastery on an island in the White Sea. It was founded by Saint Savváty and the monk Herman in 1436. Under the Soviet regime this famous monastery serves as a huge concentration camp, in which tens of thousands of prisoners are subjected to slave labor.

"Some eighteen months ago . . ." (Page 547.) The jurist mentioned by Dostoiévsky was the famous Russian criminalist, Anatóly Fiódorovich Kóni (1844– ?), member of the Imperial Academy of Sciences, and one of Russia's outstanding orators.

Songs of the Western Slavs (1833) by Púshkin. Their origin and literary significance is explained by Dostoiévsky.

Spasóvich, V. D. (1829–1906), of Polish descent, brilliant Russian jurist criminalist, advocate and literary critic. His essays *Púshkin and Mickiewicz before the Monument to Peter the Great, Lérmontov's Byronism* (1887), *Schiller's Friendship with Goethe* (1894) and *Púshkin in Modern Polish Literature and Criticism* (1891) are important contributions to the critical evaluation of the respective poets. In 1863, he published a *Textbook of Criminal Law*, which even in our day retains a certain interest.

The Sportsman's Sketches (1847–1851)—a collection of short stories by Turgénev.

Stundism (from the German word *Stunde* — hour), a religious sect which was founded in Germany in the latter part of the XVIIth Century by Jacob Spener (died in 1705). Early in the Seventies of the XIXth Century a German pastor by the name of Bonnenkempfer started preaching Stundism among the Little Russian peasants in the Khárkov province. Stundists reject the dogmas of the Russian Orthodox Church, sacraments, priesthood, etc., as well as civil authority of every kind. They confine themselves to the reading of the Scriptures and the singing of hymns. In several Southern provinces of Russia Stundist propaganda met with considerable success. Among the most noted Russian followers of Stundism Iván Riaboshápka, Gerásim Balabán and the brothers Tzibúlsky may be mentioned. Stundism was interdicted and prosecuted in Russia until 1905 when by virtue of an Imperial Manifesto full religious freedom was proclaimed.

Susánin, Ivan, a Russian national hero, who early in 1613 saved the life of the newly elected sixteen-year-old Czar Mikhaíl Fiódorovich Románoff. Polish armed bands which then invaded Russia were determined to assassinate the young Czar, who was residing at the time on one of his estates near Kostromá on the Vólga. The Poles lost their way in the virgin woods in that district. They ordered a peasant, by the name Susánin, to guide them to the Czar's residence. Susánin at once sent a secret messenger to warn the Czar of the impending peril, and meanwhile promised the Poles to show them the way to the Czar's palace. Acting as their guide, he deliberately led them astray into impassable forests. When, at length, the Poles found out that they had been double-crossed by Susánin, they killed him. Nevertheless the Czar was saved, and on March 14, 1613, he ascended the Russian throne. This episode inspired M. I. Glínka (1804–1857), the famous Russian composer, to compose his classic

opera *A Life for the Czar*, the performance of which was prohibited by the Soviet government. However, in 1942, because of the war, its performance was renewed for a while under the name *Iván Susánin*. At present it is again ostracized from the Russian operatic repertoire.

Suvórin, Alexeí Sergéevich (1834–1912), noted publicist, critic, playwright and conservative editor of the influential St. Petersburg daily *The New Times*. His best known dramatic piece is *Tatiána Répina* (1889). Suvórin was the owner of the Little Theatre in St. Petersburg.

Suvórov, Prince Alexánder Vasílievich (1730–1800), Russian fieldmarshal, undeniably the most brilliant Russian strategist and soldier. Among his principal victories the following may be mentioned: (1) the defeat of the Lithuanian Hetman Count Ogínski near Stolóvice, September 12, 1771; (2) the defeat of the Turks at Turtukaí May 10, 1773; (3) the defeat of the Turks near Kírburn, October 1, 1787; (4) the defeat of the Turks at Rímnik, September 11, 1789; (5) the siege and storming of the Turkish fortress Izmaíl, December 11, 1790; (6) capture of Warsaw, November 4–9, 1794; (7) the defeat of the French army at Trebbia in Italy, June 7–8, 1799; (8) the defeat of the French army under General Joubert at Novi, August 4, 1799; (9) the storming of the Devil's Bridge and the defeat of the French army in Switzerland, September 14, 1799. Suvórov has often been compared with Napoleon. However, Survórov, during his long military career, never suffered a defeat.

[T]

"The Tale" about *Kaláshnikov*, as Dostoiévsky erroneously calls it, is an ingenious epic poem by Mikhaíl Úrievich Lérmontov (1814–1841), after Púshkin the greatest Russian poet, known as the Russian Byron. The correct title of the poem is *The Song about Czar Iván Vasílevich, the Young Body-Guard and the Bold Merchant Kaláshnikov* (1837). Lérmontov wrote this ingenious *Song* when he had barely reached the age of twenty-three. His two greatest poems are *Mtzíri* (a Circassian convent novice) and *The Demon* (1829–1839). Both are dedicated to the Caucasus. His shorter lyrical pieces: *The Angel, The Nymph, Borodinó, Three Palm-Trees, The Prophet, The Twig of Palestine, The Gifts of Térek, The Dispute, First of January, The Death of a Poet* (dedicated to the death of Púshkin); *The Poet* and *The Dagger* are among the most precious gems in world poetry. Púshkin and Byron were the two formative influences in the development of his poetic genius. Like Púshkin, Lérmontov was killed in a duel.

The Tale about the She-Bear (1830) by Púshkin is an unfinished piece; it is a popular story of a she-bear who on a lovely spring morning, at dawn, was killed by a peasant with a hunting-pole; of the boundless grief of her husband, the dark-brown bear and the forest animals (the wolf, the beaver, the fox, the squirrel, the hedgehog, the hare, etc.) who express to him their sympathy because of the irreparable loss he has suffered.

Tatárinova, Ekaterína Filíppovna (1783–1856), was the daughter of Ekaterína Fiódorovna Booxhoevden, née baroness von Maltiz; the latter was a nurse of Grand Duchess Mary, the eldest daughter of Grand Duke Alexander (later Emperor Alexander I, 1801–1825), who died in infancy (1800). The nurse was given an apartment in the Mikháilovsky Castle in St. Petersburg (Emperor Paul's I palace). After the assassination of Paul (March 11, 1801) Ekaterína Fiódorovna was permitted to retain her rooms in the Castle. Her daughter Ekaterína Filíppovna married Iván Mikháilovich Tatárinov, an officer in the 3rd Infantry regiment of the Imperial Guard who was gravely wounded in the battle of Borodinó (August 26, 1812). After his death, Tatárinova, in 1815, came to live with her mother, and from that time on she began to devote herself to the practices of pietism. In 1817, she declared herself a prophetess. Her apartment in the Mikháilovsky Castle became a meeting place of castrates, convulsionists, mystics and all sorts of sectarians. Prince A. N. Golítzin, the then Minister of Ecclesiastic Affairs, took an interest in her, and it was through his influence that Alexander I accorded her an interview. However, in 1821, she was ordered to vacate her apartment, and all official support of her activities came to an end.

Tatiána, the heroine of Púshkin's

magnum opus Eugene Onégin (1823–1831). A brilliant evaluation of her character was given by Dostoiévsky in his famous Púshkin address in Moscow on June 8, 1880, the full text of which appears in *Writer's Diary* for that year.

Tchítchikov — the "hero" of Gógol's famous novel *Dead Souls* (1842), which is his *magnum opus*. Tchítchikov has often been compared with Khlestakóv (q.v.), although, in more than one respect, they are antipodes: Khlestakóv is slim and light as down, outspoken and eloquent; Tchítchikov is ponderous and fat as a Thanksgiving turkey, taciturn and reserved —a convinced positivist; Khlestakóv is a tireless *causeur,* and his world outlook is that of a loose-minded whig; Tchítchikov is a steadfast builder, a narrow-minded Tory, a slow thinker of the fundamentalist breed. Even so, Tchítchikov is but the prolongation of Khlestakóv, both having one common root, one underlying cause of their coexistence, which is elemental mediocrity. Khlestakóv survives in history as an immortal impostor, Tchítchikov as an un-rivalled schemer and money-getter.

"The suicide was a young girl . . ." (Page 469.) Dostoiévsky refers to the eldest daughter of A. I. Hertzen (q. v.) Elizabeth, who committed suicide by taking poison in November, 1875.

Theodosius Pechérsky, Russian Saint, was born in Kursk in the first half of the XIth Century. At the age of twelve he left his parents' home and proceeded to Kiev, where not long before that Saint Antony had founded the famous Kiev-Pechérsky Monastery (1051). When Antony retired from the Monastery to live in solitary seclusion, Theodosius was made prior. He introduced among the monks rigid discipline and himself strictly adhered to the principle of asceticism. He was the author of two ecclesiastical instructions to the people, ten instructions to the Kiev-Pechérsk friars and two epistles to the Kiev Grand Duke Iziasláv (1054).

Thersites, in Homer's *Iliad,* the ugliest, most scurrilous officer in the Greek army which besieged Troy. He always reviled Achilles, who finally slew him. Hence, an impudent railer at powers that be.

Thon, Konstantín Andréevich (1794–1881), noted Russian architect. He executed the plans and sketches for the famous church of Christ the Savior in Moscow (1835), which was demolished by the Soviet government in 1931, as well as of the Big Palace in the Moscow Kremlin (1837).

Tiápkin–Liápkin in Gogol's *Revizor,* the judge, one of the city's important stars in the constellation of the corrupt city officials. He, like the other officials, leaves a little "cash souvenir" with Khlestakóv, the imaginary "revizor."

Tikhon Zadónsky (1724–1783), Russian Saint, of humble descent. He spent his childhood and youth in abject misery. He attended the Nóvgorod Seminary in which he later became instructor. From 1763 to 1767 he was the ruling bishop in the Vorónej diocese. From that year until his death he lived in retirement in the Zadónsky Monastery devoting all his time to prayer, charity and the practice of Christian virtues. He wrote several remarkable books, among which *On True Christianity, Christian Instruction* and *The Rules of Monastic Life* deserve particular mention.

Tódleben, or Tótleben, Count Eduárd Ivánovich (1818–1884), brilliant Russian military engineer; he constructed the fortifications of Sebastopol (1854), and in 1877, the siege of the Turkish stronghold Plevna was conducted under his supervision. Plevna was captured by the Russians on November 28, 1877.

Tortzóv, Lubím, one of the principal characters in Ostróvsky's (q.v.) comedy *Poverty Is No Crime;* he is a déclassé, a drunkard, but a kind-hearted man with noble impulses.

The Troubled Epoch in Russia (1598–1613). Following the death of Czar Fiódor Ioánnovich (1584–1598), the son of Czar Iván the Terrible (q. v.) the Zemsky Sobor elected Borís Godunóv (q.v.), a favorite of Czar Ivan, and the late Czar Fiódor's brother-in-law, to the throne of Russia. But it was persistently rumored that Godunóv had been instrumental in the assassination, in May, 1591, of the young Czarévich Dmítry, Iván's youngest son and Czar Fiódor's only brother. Besides, Godunóv was of humble Tartar descent, and therefore quite unpopular among the ancient Russian boyard families. Godunóv was an enlightened ruler, and

his early legislation proves that he was an able statesman. However, suspicious of boyard intrigues, he began to persecute the nobles and thus aroused among them great indignation. In 1601 Russia began to suffer from a dreadful famine which was followed by an equally devastating plague. Popular discontent grew to a high pitch. Hunger-stricken peasants and all sorts of rebellious elements began to plunder the boyards' estates. Highway robberies spread all over Russia. In the presence of these political and social conditions, it was comparatively easy for an impostor to challenge the authority of Borís Godunóv. Such an impostor appeared in the person of a young man (exact date of birth is unknown) Grigóry Otrépiev who is supposed to have been the son of a government official. In the latter part of the XVIth Century he settled in Moscow, where he took religious orders, and shortly thereafter he began to spread the rumor that he was Czarévich Dmítry, miraculously saved from the hands of Godunóv's assassins. Realizing the danger of such propaganda, the Czar ordered Otrépiev to be seized. But he managed to escape, fled across the Lithuanian border and proceeded to Poland, where he enlisted in the service of a Polish magnate Wisznewézki. He convinced the latter as well as the Sandomir Waýwode Mnískzek that he was the son of Czar Iván the Terrible. Having embraced Roman Catholicism, Otrépiev, with the aid of the Jesuits, succeeded in securing formal recognition by King Sigismund of Poland of his status as lawful pretender to the Russian throne. Some 1500 Polish adventurers joined his ranks. He crossed the Russian border and the Cossacks and robbers' bands gave him active support. In April, 1605, Godunóv died, and in June of the same year, Dmítry the Impostor triumphantly entered Moscow at the head of his rebel army. He ascended the Throne, but his avowed pro-Polish sympathies and the fact that he had married Marína Mníszek, a Roman Catholic, caused widespread discontent. Taking advantage of this situation, Prince Vasíli Shuísky organized an uprising in Moscow, during which Dmítry was assassinated by the mob. From that time on, one impostor after another contested the Russian Throne. The Poles invaded Russia and captured Moscow. For six years, anarchy reigned throughout Russia. However, at the eleventh hour the spirit of patriotism prompted the Russians to rally around Prince Dmítry Mikháilovich Pojársky, who had formed a volunteer army. In August, 1612, Pojársky defeated the Polish Hetman Hodkiéwicz and liberated Moscow. In October of the same year, the remnants of the Poles, who were besieged in the Moscow Kremlin, were compelled to surrender, following which, on February 21, 1613, Mikháil Fiódorovich Románov was unanimously elected Czar of Russia. This put an end to anarchy. A monument to Prince Pojársky and the Níjni-Nóvgorod merchant Kozmá Mínin, who by his ardent patriotism helped to finance the volunteer army, was erected in the Moscow Kremlin.

Turgénev, Iván Sergéevich (1818–1883), one of the most famous Russian novelists and a noted dramatist. His works *The Sportsman's Sketches* (1847–1851), *Rúdin* (1856), *Gentlefolks' Nest* (1859), *On the Eve* (1860), *Fathers and Sons* (1862), *Smoke* (1867) and his shorter stories *The First Love, Asya* (1858), *The Torrents of Spring* (1871), *The Song of Triumphant Love* (1881), *Hamlet of the Schigróv County, Poems in Prose* (1882), have won for Turgénev universal fame. His works have been translated into all European languages. Maurice Baring has justly called Turgénev "the prose Virgil of Russian literature"; the brilliant French art critic Hippolyte Taine (1823–1893) considered Turgénev one of the greatest artists since Sophocles. Gustave Flaubert (1821–1880) and George Sand were among his enthusiastic admirers. In fact, his prose is matchless; it flows like the gentle murmurs of a tide; its elegance, rhythmical properties and crystal purity are inimitable. Turgénev was a convinced Westerner, a humanist in the best sense, and a liberal. In spite of this, time and again he was attacked by the Russian radical critics. Among his dramatic works *The Provincial Lady* and *A Month in the Country* are genuine masterpieces.

Tútchev, Fiódor Ivánovic (1803–1873), one of Russia's foremost lyrical poets—the four lines addressed to Russia, quoted on Page 425, are taken from a short poem of his. The first sixteen of his poems were published in 1836 by Púshkin in *The Contemporary*, which he then edited.

[U]

Úri Miloslávsky—a once popular historical novel (1829) by Mikhail Ivánovich Zagóskin (1789–1852). His other novels *Róslavlev or The Russians in 1812* (1831), *Askold's Tomb* (1833), *The Tempter* (1838), etc., replete with melodramatic effects, have met with but little success and are now forgotten.

[V]

Vasíly Shibánov, a poem by Count Alexeí Tolstoý (1817–1875), a brilliant Russian poet, playwright, the author of the famous historical trilogy: *The Death of Iván the Terrible* (1866), *Czar Fiódor Ioánnovich* (1868) and *Czar Borís* (1870); novelist, the author of *The Silver Prince* (1861), in which he gave a vivid picture of the epoch of Czar Iván the Terrible.

Viardot, Louis (1800–1883), co-founder with George Sand (1804–1876) of the *Revue Indépendante* (1841), husband of the famous French operatic mezzo-soprano (1821–1910) for whom I. S. Turgénev (q.v.) felt an ardent affection.

Víborgskaia Storoná — a borough in St. Petersburg.

Vlas. See Nekrásov.

The Voice (Gólos), a liberal daily founded in St. Petersburg in 1868 by A. N. Kraiévsky (q.v.).

[W]

"Whether 'tis beast that roars in gloomy woods" is the first line in Púshkin's poem *Echo* (1831), an adaptation from Thomas Moore's (1780–1852) *Echoes* with its first stanza:

How sweet the answer Echo makes
To Music at night,
When, roused by lute or horn, she wakes,
And far away o'er lawns and lakes
Goes answering light!

"The window to Europe." In the Introduction to Púshkin's great poem *The Bronze Horseman* (1833), Peter the Great is pictured standing on the desolate bank of the Neva and meditating about founding St. Petersburg, the new capital of Russia, on the shores of that river flowing into the Finnish Gulf. Says Peter:

Hence 'gainst the Swede we are to labor,
Here shall a mighty city rise
To the distress of our proud neighbor;
By nature we are destined here
To cut a window through to Europe . . .

       (Boris Brasol's version)

Woe from Wit (1824)—the immortal four-act comedy by Alesánder Sergéevich Griboiédov (1795–1829) with its ingenious epigraph:

Thus naughty Fate has ruled forever:
That fools for happiness be fit,
But they who happen to be clever
Should always suffer *woe from wit*.
       (Boris Brasol's version)

Tchátzky is the hero of the play. Eloquently, with idealistic zeal, he denounces the antiquated Moscow

beau monde of his days. His is a
progressive world outlook. At the
same time he ridicules foolish apish-
ness of Western customs and he bids:

Oh, let's adopt from those Chinese
Their prudent nescience of strangers.

Bielinsky (q.v.) belittled the literary
significance of *Woe from Wit*. Púshkin, however, in his letter to A. A.
Bestújev (January, 1825), predicted
that Griboiédov's ingenious verses
would become an integral part of
the living Russian language. Griboiédov was Russia's special envoy in
Persia. Some Armenians persecuted
by the Shah appealed to Griboiédov
for protection. He sent a sharp note
to the Persian government, but on
January 30, 1829, at Teheran, the
fanatical infuriated Persian mob
broke into the Russian embassy.
Griboiédov, with his sword in hand,
met the rioters in the vestibule and
gallantly defended himself until, overpowered, he fell and was assassinated.
His mutilated body was brought to
Tiflís and buried on Saint David's
mountain.

[Y]

Yat. In the pre-revolutionary Russian
alphabet, "yat" stood for a "soft
sound" of "e." The difference is closely
represented by the sound of yea in
the name Yeats compared with the
sound ye in the English word yet.
In the Russian alphabet there are
letters for the familiar European
vowel sounds A, E, I, O, U, and
also letters representing what in Russian are called the "soft sounds" of
those vowels and in English are most
closely represented by prefixing the
consonant Y to the respective vowel
sounds. In the new spelling introduced by the Soviet decree of December 23, 1917, the letter "yat"
was altogether eliminated. As a result
many linguistic nuances and finesses
can no longer be expressed.

[Z]

Zamoskvoréchie, a borough in Moscow on the right bank of the Moscow
river, residence of the old-fashioned
Moscow merchants.

INDEX TO THE DIARY